CW01654283

THE OXFORD HANDB(

ENGLISH LAW AND LITERATURE, 1500–1700

This *Handbook* triangulates the disciplines of history, legal history, and literature to produce a new, interdisciplinary framework for the study of early modern England. Scholars of early modern English literature and history have increasingly found that an understanding of how people in the past thought about and used the law is key to understanding early modern familial and social relations as well as important aspects of the political revolution and the emergence of capitalism. Judicial or forensic rhetoric has been shown to foster new habits of literary composition (poetry and drama) and new processes of fact-finding and evidence evaluation. In addition, the post-Reformation jurisdictional dominance of the common law produced new ways of drawing the boundaries between private conscience and public accountability.

Accordingly, historians, critics, and legal historians come together in this Handbook to develop accounts of the past that are attentive to the legally purposeful or fictional shaping of events in the historical archive. They also contribute to a transformation of our understanding of the place of forensic modes of inquiry in the creation of imaginative fiction and drama. Chapters in the Handbook approach, from a diversity of perspectives, topics including forensic rhetoric, humanist and legal education, Inns of Court revels, drama, poetry, emblem books, marriage and divorce, witchcraft, contract, property, imagination, oaths, evidence, community, local government, legal reform, libel, censorship, authorship, torture, slavery, liberty, due process, the nation state, colonialism, and empire.

Lorna Hutson is Merton Professor of English Literature at the University of Oxford. Educated in San Francisco, Edinburgh, and Oxford, she has taught at the Universities of St Andrews, UC Berkeley, Hull, and Queen Mary, London. She has served as Head of English at St Andrews (2008–11) and has held fellowships from the Folger, the Huntington, the Guggenheim, and the Leverhulme Trust.

Contributors

Alastair Bellany, Christopher Brooks, Martin Butler, Alan Cromartie, Frances E. Dolan, Martin Dzelzainis, Kathy Eden, Peter Goodrich, Paul D. Halliday, Edward Holberton, Robert A. Houston, Daniel J. Hulsebosch, Lorna Hutson, David Ibbetson, Norma Landau, James McBain, Margaret McGlynn, Bernadette Meyler, Mary Nyquist, Joshua Phillips, Paul Raffield, Joad Raymond, Jason P. Rosenblatt, Carolyn Sale, Ethan H. Shagan, Barbara J. Shapiro, James Sharpe, Quentin Skinner, Nigel Smith, Virginia Lee Strain, Tim Stretton, Henry S. Turner, Elliott Visconsi, Christopher N. Warren, Ian Williams, Luke Wilson, Jessica Winston, Andrew Zurcher

THE OXFORD HANDBOOK OF

ENGLISH LAW AND LITERATURE, 1500–1700

Edited by

LORNA HUTSON

OXFORD
UNIVERSITY PRESS

OXFORD
UNIVERSITY PRESS

Great Clarendon Street, Oxford, OX2 6DP,
United Kingdom

Oxford University Press is a department of the University of Oxford.
It furthers the University's objective of excellence in research, scholarship,
and education by publishing worldwide. Oxford is a registered trade mark of
Oxford University Press in the UK and in certain other countries

First published 2017
First published in paperback 2020

Published in the United States of America by Oxford University Press
198 Madison Avenue, New York, NY 10016, United States of America

British Library Cataloguing in Publication Data
Data available

Library of Congress Cataloging in Publication Data
Data available

ISBN 978-0-19-966088-9 (Hbk.)
ISBN 978-0-19-885735-8 (Pbk.)

Acknowledgements

I owe an enormous amount to Bradin Cormack, without whom this project could not have been conceived or brought to life. Most of the chapters in this Handbook first took shape as papers presented at one or the other of twinned conferences, 'The English Legal Imaginary, 1500–1700 I' and 'The English Legal Imaginary, 1500-1700 II' at the Universities of Princeton and St Andrews in April and May 2015. Bradin organized the first of these and co-hosted the second. At both he exhibited the fastidious creativity of thought well known to readers of his published work, thereby stimulating and enabling the interdisciplinary conversations that would come to fruition in this book.

I would also like to thank Jacqueline Norton, of Oxford University Press, for adventurously commissioning this Handbook, and for her support and the interest she has taken throughout. I am pleased, too, to have a chance to thank the Departments of English and History at Princeton University and the Department of English and the Centre for Mediaeval and Early Modern Law and Literature (CMEMLL) at the University of St Andrews for supporting the conferences. Debates, conversations, collaborations, and friendships there begun have continued as conferences papers developed into the chapters of this book. They will, I am confident, continue beyond the book's emergence into print. I am grateful to Rachel Holmes for her impeccable organization of the St Andrews conference, and for setting up and maintaining the blog through which work was shared at an early stage. Above all, however, I am grateful to all the contributors to this Handbook. Their engagement, creativity, and generosity during the conferences and their subsequent patience and helpfulness during the editing process have made the whole project a pleasure.

Among more particular debts, I owe thanks to Sharyn Brooks and to Michael Lobban. The historian Christopher Brooks (1948–2014) did more than anyone to enable us to see how crucial to the social and political history of early modern England were England's distinctive legal institutions and procedures. Chris's sudden death in 2014 bereaved the scholarly community at large, not least that part of it represented by this book. I am therefore very grateful to Sharyn, Chris's widow, and to Michael, his former colleague and friend, for locating the script of a lecture Chris gave in 2013 to the Centre for Mediaeval and Early Modern Law and Literature, which had been intended as a chapter for this book. Thanks are due also to my colleagues Jaqueline Rose and Rab Houston for helping reconstruct Chris's footnotes, as well as to Ian Williams and Tim Stretton for answering queries.

In all that I have said, the Centre for Mediaeval and Early Modern Law and Literature at St Andrews has featured prominently. This leads me to the thanks due to my colleague and co-director of CMEMLL, John Hudson, whose expertise in English legal history goes hand in hand with an inspiring openness to what literary texts have to say about the law. From John and from other CMEMLL historians of mediaeval Europe and late antiquity—notably Gadi Algazi, Caroline Humfress, William Miller, and Steve White—I have learned a great deal. I owe most, however, to John, who has been a support throughout the Handbook's gestation and who kindly read the introduction. I am also very grateful to Mary Nyquist, who likewise advised on the introduction. To all my postgraduate students at St Andrews, and to the Honours students in the years from 2006–2014 who took the course 'Law and Literature in Early Modern Europe' I would like to acknowledge thanks for their enthusiasm and pleasure.

I have other personal debts to record as well: to Stephen Orgel, for a kind and timely intervention, to my friend, Vicky Kahn, for her sage advice, and to my partner, Linda Hardy, who, in the time-honoured tradition of these kinds of acknowledgements, has to suffer being thanked for patience and long-suffering while I worked on the book. But Linda knows that my thanks go deeper than that.

LH

Contents

PART V LEGAL AND LITERARY IMAGINING

PART VI LIBEL, PUBLICATION, AND THE PRESS

PART VII LIBERTIES, SLAVERIES, AND ENGLISH LAW

PART VIII THE EXTRA-ENGLISH LEGAL WORLD: BETWEEN COLONY, NATION, AND EMPIRE

List of Figures

Abbreviations and Conventions

Essential bibliographies are given at the end of each chapter. Footnotes contain full bibliographic references to enable readers to locate works consulted for that chapter that are not in the chapter's bibliography.

Historians, literary critics, and legal historians follow different practices when it comes to modernizing or not modernizing the spelling and orthography of quotations from primary sources. As this is an interdisciplinary collection, we have not imposed a uniform practice of modernization or old-spelling/orthography in quotations from primary sources and readers will find variation across chapters in this respect. When no other edition is specified in a chapter's endnotes, quotations from Shakespeare given in the text are taken from William Shakespeare, *The Complete Works*, 2nd edn, ed. Stanley Wells, Gary Taylor, John Jowett, and William Montgomery (Oxford: Clarendon Press, 2005). The following abbreviations may be found in chapter endnotes and bibliographies:

AJLH	*American Journal of Legal History*
APC	*Acts of the Privy Council*
ASD	*Opera omnia Desiderii Erasmi Roterodami* (Amsterdam: North-Holland Publishing Company, 1969–)
BIHR	*Bulletin of the Institute of Historical Research*
CJ	*Journal of the House of Commons* (London: HMSO, 1802)
CLJ	*Cambridge Law Journal*
CPW	*Complete Prose Works of John Milton*, Don M. Wolfe, gen. ed., 8 vols (New Haven and London, 1953–1982)
CSLL	*Cardozo Studies in Law and Literature*
CSPD	*Calendar of State Papers, Domestic Series*
CWBJ	*The Cambridge Edition of the Works of Ben Jonson*, D. Bevington, M. Butler, and I. Donaldson, gen. eds, 5 vols (Cambridge: Cambridge University Press, 2012)
CWE	*Complete Works of Erasmus* (Toronto: University of Toronto Press, 1974–)
Co. Rep.	*Coke's Reports* (Coke's King's Bench Reports, originally published in 13 vols from 1600–1659. They form part of the *English Reports*, Vol. 76–7, 1572–1616).
EcHR	*Economic History Review*
EEBO	*Early English Books Online*

EHR	*English Historical Review*
ELH	*English Literary History*
ELR	*English Literary Renaissance*
ER	English Reports (Collection of 265 Law Reports from 1220 to 1867).
HJ	*Historical Journal*
HLR	*Harvard Law Review*
HLQ	*Huntington Library Quarterly*
HPT	*History of Political Thought*
HWJ	*History Workshop Journal*
ICW	*The Intellectual and Cultural World of the Early Modern Inns of Court*, ed. J. E. Archer, E. Goldring, and S. Knight (Manchester: Manchester University Press, 2011)
JBS	*Journal of British Studies*
JHI	*Journal of the History of Ideas*
JLH	*Journal of Legal History*
JR	*Juridical Review*
LHR	*Law and History Review*
LL	*Law and Literature*
LQR	*Law Quarterly Review*
N&Q	*Notes and Queries*
OBO	The Proceedings of the Old Bailey (accessed via <http://www.oldbaileyonline.org/>)
ODNB	Oxford Dictionary of National Biography (on-line version)
OHLE	*Oxford History of the Laws of England*, Sir John Baker, gen. ed. (Oxford: Oxford University Press, 2003–)
OJLS	*Oxford Journal of Legal Studies*
PMLA	*Publications of the Modern Language Association*
P&P	Past and Present
PQ	*Philological Quarterly*
PS	*Politics and Society*
REED	*Records of Early English Drama: The Inns of Court*, ed. Alan H. Nelson and John R. Elliott, Jr, 3 vols (Cambridge: D. S. Brewer, 2010)
RES	*Review of English Studies*
RD	*Renaissance Drama*
RQ	*Renaissance Quarterly*

SC	*The Seventeenth Century*
SCJ	*The Sixteenth Century Journal*
SEL	*Studies in English Literature, 1500–1900*
SP	*Studies in Philology*
SP	State Papers
SR	*Statutes of the Realm*
SQ	*Shakespeare Quarterly*
ShS	*Shakespeare Survey*
SS	Selden Society
STC	Short Title Catalogue
TLN	Through Line Numbers
TNA	The National Archives (UK)
TRHS	*Transactions of the Royal Historical Society*
UTLJ	*University of Toronto Law Journal*
YJLH	*Yale Journal of Law and Humanities*
YLJ	*Yale Law Journal*

Notes on Contributors

Alastair Bellany is Professor of History at Rutgers University. He is the author of *The Politics of Court Scandal in Early Modern England: News Culture and the Overbury Affair, 1603–1660* (2002); the co-author (with Thomas Cogswell) of *The Murder of King James I* (2015); and the co-editor (with Andrew McRae) of *Early Stuart Libels: An Edition of Poetry from Manuscript Sources* (2005).

Christopher Brooks was Professor of History at Durham University from 1980 to 2014. His books *Pettyfoggers and Vipers of the Commonwealth: The 'Lower Branch' of the Legal Profession in Early Modern England* (1986) and *Lawyers, Litigation and English Society since 1450* (1998) helped to revolutionize the study of legal history by resetting the focus on access to justice and court usage by ordinary people. His substantial monograph, *Law, Politics and Society in Early Modern England* (2009) used legal thought and practice as a way of re-interpreting social and political relationships in the period from the accession of the Tudors to the outbreak of the English Civil Wars in 1642. At the time of his death of a heart attack in 2014, Chris Brooks was working on a major study of the English law 1625 to 1688 for the *Oxford History of the Laws of England*.

Martin Butler is Professor of English Renaissance Drama at the University of Leeds. He is the author of *Theatre and Crisis 1632–1642* (1984) and *The Stuart Court Masque and Political Culture* (2008), and, with David Bevington and Ian Donaldson, is General Editor of *The Cambridge Edition of the Works of Ben Jonson* (7 vols, 2012).

Alan Cromartie is Professor of the History of Political Thought at the University of Reading. His publications on the history of English political thought and the history of ideas more generally include *Sir Matthew Hale: Law, Religion, and Natural Philosophy* (1995) and *The Constitutionalist Revolution: An Essay on the History of England* (2006), and *Liberal Wars: Anglo-American Strategy, Ideology and Practice* (2015). He has also edited Thomas Hobbes, *A Dialogue between a Philosopher and a Student, of the Common Laws of England* for the Clarendon Edition of the Works of Thomas Hobbes.

Frances E. Dolan is Distinguished Professor of English at UC, Davis. She is the author of five books, most recently *True Relations: Reading, Literature, and Evidence in Seventeenth-Century England* (2013), which won the John Ben Snow prize from the North American Conference on British Studies. Other books include *Twelfth Night: Language and Writing* (2014); *Marriage and Violence: The Early Modern Legacy* (2008); *Whores of Babylon: Catholicism, Gender, and Seventeenth-Century Print Culture*

(1999; 2005); and *Dangerous Familiars: Representations of Domestic Crime in England, 1550–1700* (1994).

Martin Dzelzainis is Professor of Renaissance Literature and Thought at the University of Leicester. He is currently editing the Histories for *The Complete Works of John Milton*; Andrew Marvell's verse and prose for the Oxford Twenty-First-Century Authors series; and (with Edward Holberton) *The Oxford Handbook of Andrew Marvell* (all for Oxford University Press). He is also General Editor, with Paul Seaward, of the Oxford edition of *The Works of Edward Hyde, Earl of Clarendon.*

Kathy Eden is Chavkin Family Professor of English and Professor of Classics at Columbia University. Her books include *Poetic and Legal Fiction in the Aristotelian Tradition* (1986); *Hermeneutics and the Rhetorical Tradition: Chapters in the Ancient Legacy and Its Humanist Reception* (1997); *Friends Hold All Things in Common: Tradition, Intellectual Property and the 'Adages' of Erasmus* (2001); and *The Renaissance Rediscovery of Intimacy* (2012).

Peter Goodrich is a Professor of Law and Director of the Program in Law and Humanities, Cardozo School of Law, New York. His previous books include *Reading the Law* (1986); *Legal Discourse* (1982); *Oedipus Lex* (1996); and more recently *Laws of Love* (2006); and, with Christian Delage, *The Scene of Mass Crime: History, Film and International Tribunals* (2012).

Paul D. Halliday is Julian Bishko Professor of History and Professor of Law at the University of Virginia. He is the author of *Habeas corpus: From England to Empire* (2010), among other works.

Edward Holberton is a lecturer in the Department of English at the University of Bristol. He is the author of *Poetry and the Cromwellian Protectorate: Culture, Politics and Institutions* (2009). With Martin Dzelzainis he is currently editing *The Oxford Handbook of Andrew Marvell*, and his research includes work on the relationship between Marvell and the diplomatic sphere, and a monograph project on literature, empire, and the Atlantic world during the period 1630–1740.

Robert A. Houston was born in Hamilton, Scotland, lived in India and Ghana and was educated at the Edinburgh Academy and St Andrews University before spending six years at Cambridge University as a research student (Peterhouse) and research fellow (Clare College). He has worked at the University of St Andrews since 1983 and is Professor of Early Modern History, specializing in British social history. He is a fellow of both the Royal Historical Society and the Royal Society of Edinburgh (Scotland's national academy), and a Member of the Academia Europaea. He is married to a university manager and lives in Edinburgh.

Daniel J. Hulsebosch (PhD, JD) is a legal and constitutional historian whose scholarship ranges from the early modern British Empire to the nineteenth-century United States and explores the relationships between migration, transnational sources of law, and the development of legal institutions and doctrines. His first book, *Constituting Empire: New York and the Transformation of Constitutionalism in the Atlantic World, 1664–1830* (2005), examined the intersection of constitutionalism and imperial expansion. He is now co-authoring a book entitled, *'A Civilized Nation': The International Dimensions of American Constitution-Making, 1774–1816*, which explores the intersection between the law of nations and American constitutionalism in the founding era.

Lorna Hutson is Merton Professor of English Literature at the University of Oxford. She has taught at the Universities of St Andrews, UC Berkeley, Hull, and Queen Mary, London. With Victoria Kahn she edited *Rhetoric and Law in Early Modern Europe* (2001); and with Erica Sheen *Literature, Politics and Law in Renaissance England* (2005). Her books include *The Invention of Suspicion: Law and Mimesis in Shakespeare and Renaissance Drama* (2007); and *Circumstantial Shakespeare* (2015).

David Ibbetson has been Regius Professor of Civil Law at the University of Cambridge since 2000, having formerly taught at the University of Oxford, and is currently President of Clare Hall. His research interest is broadly in the history of law, with a particular focus on England in the early modern period.

Norma Landau is Professor of History at UC, Davis. Her publications include *The Justices of the Peace 1679–1760* (1984); *Law, Crime, and English Society, 1660–1815* (2002); 'Indictment for Fun and Profit: A Prosecutor's Reward at Eighteenth-Century Quarter Sessions', *Law and History Review* (1999); 'Who Was Subjected to the Laws of Settlement?', *Agricultural History Review* (1995); and 'The Context of the Laws of Settlement', *Continuity and Change* (1992).

James McBain is an SNF researcher at the University of Fribourg, Switzerland, and a Research Associate of St Catherine's College, Oxford, contributing to the Early Drama at Oxford project (<http://edox.org.uk>), which he co-founded. He has published widely on late medieval and early modern drama and is the co-editor, with Elisabeth Dutton, of *Drama and Pedagogy* (2015).

Margaret McGlynn is Associate Professor of History at Western University in Ontario. Her research interests focus on common lawyers' understanding of the ways in which medieval ideas and structures could be made to work in the sixteenth century, often starting with the ways in which they taught the law. She has recently published *The Rights and Liberties of the English Church: Readings from the Pre-Reformation Inns of Court* with the Selden Society and is currently completing a project on the common law development of sanctuary and benefit of clergy under the early Tudors.

Bernadette Meyler is the Carl and Sheila Spaeth Professor of Law at Stanford University, where she teaches and writes on constitutional law and law and the humanities, focusing in particular on seventeenth- and eighteenth-century English and American common law and constitutionalism. Prior to arriving at Stanford, she served as a Professor of Law and English at Cornell University and the inaugural Mellon/LAPA Fellow in Law and the Humanities at Princeton University. She received her JD from Stanford and a PhD in English from UC, Irvine.

Mary Nyquist is Professor at the University of Toronto, where she teaches in the Centre for Comparative Literature, the Department of English, and the Literature and Critical Theory Program. Her research involves close textual analysis and centres on intersections among early modern or enlightenment literature, Euro-colonialism, law, and political philosophy. Awarded the Milton Society's title of 'Honored Scholar' in 2011 (an achievement award not confined to Milton studies), she recently co-edited with Feisal Mohamed *Milton and Questions of History: Essays by Canadians Past and Present* (2012), which won the Irene Samuel prize; and published *Arbitrary Rule: Slavery, Tyranny, and the Power of Life and Death* (2013).

Joshua Phillips is Associate Professor and Chair of the English Department at the University of Memphis. He is the author of *English Fictions of Communal Identity, 1485–1603* and has published articles on Spenser, Shakespeare, More, Montaigne, and on early modern culture and literature. He is currently at work on a book about monasticism and literature in post-Reformation England.

Paul Raffield is Professor of Law at the University of Warwick. He has published extensively in the fields of Law and Literature and Legal History. He is the author of *Shakespeare's Imaginary Constitution: Late Elizabethan Politics and the Theatre of Law* (2010); and *Images and Cultures of Law in Early Modern England: Justice and Political Power, 1558–1660* (2004). His next monograph, *The Art of Law in Shakespeare*, will be published by Hart/Bloomsbury in 2017. He is co-editor of *Law and Humanities* and a member of the Italian Cultural Association for the Study of Law and Literature.

Joad Raymond is Professor of Renaissance Studies at Queen Mary University of London. He has written and edited books about Milton, pamphlet culture, and the history of news. He is presently editing Milton's Latin defences for Oxford University Press's in-progress *Complete Works of John Milton*, and writing a history of news communication in early modern Europe for Penguin Books.

Jason P. Rosenblatt, Emeritus Professor of English at Georgetown University, is the author of *Renaissance England's Chief Rabbi: John Selden* (2006); *Torah and Law in 'Paradise Lost'* (1994); co-editor of a book on biblical narrative, *'Not in Heaven'* (1991); and editor of *Milton's Selected Poetry and Prose* (2010). He is at present co-editing Selden's *Table Talk* and working on a book on Selden and Milton, about scholarly and poetic genius.

Carolyn Sale is Associate Professor in the Department of English and Film Studies at the University of Alberta. Her work on early modern women writers and the law includes 'The "Roman Hand": Women, Writing and the Law in the *Att.-Gen. v. Chatterton* and the Letters of the Lady Arbella Stuart', *ELH*, 70 (2003); and chapters in *The History of British Women's Writing*, Vol. 2: *1500–1610* (2010) and in *Shakespeare* *and Judgment*, ed. Kevin Curran (2016). She is completing the book manuscript 'The Literary Commons: The Law and the Writer in Early Modern England, 1528–1628'.

Ethan H. Shagan is Professor of History at UC, Berkeley. He is the author of *Popular Politics and the English Reformation* (2003); *The Rule of Moderation: Violence, Religion and the Politics of Restraint in Early Modern England* (2011); and *A History of Modern Belief*, which is forthcoming from Princeton University Press.

Barbara J. Shapiro is Professor of Rhetoric, emerita and Professor in the Graduate School at UC, Berkeley. Her publications include *Probability and Certainty in Seventeenth Century England* (1983); *' Beyond Reasonable Doubt' and 'Probable Cause': Historical Perspectives on the Anglo-American Law of Evidence* (1991); *A Culture of Fact: England, 1500–1720* (2000); and *Political Communication and Political Culture in England, 1558–1688* (2012). Recent articles deal with oaths in early modern English legal settings and the eighteenth-century contribution to the legal doctrine of beyond reasonable doubt. She is currently doing research and writing on law reform in England 1500–1740.

James Sharpe took his BA and DPhil in Modern History at Oxford. He is a Professor at the University of York and has published extensively on the history of crime in the early modern period. He has also researched and published extensively on early modern English witchcraft, and is the author of *Early Modern England: A Social History 1550–1760* (2nd edn, 1997). More recently he is working on the history of violence, and has published *A Fiery and Furious People: A History of Violence in England* (2016).

Quentin Skinner is the Barber Beaumont Professor of the Humanities at Queen Mary University of London. Among his books are *The Foundations of Modern Political Thought* (1978); *Reason and Rhetoric in the Philosophy of Hobbes* (1996); *Liberty Before Liberalism* (1998); *Machiavelli* (2000); *Hobbes and Republican Liberty* (2008); *Forensic Shakespeare* (2014); and a three-volume collection of essays, *Visions of Politics* (2002).

Nigel Smith is William and Annie S. Paton Foundation Professor of Ancient and Modern Literature at Princeton University. His major works are *Andrew Marvell: The Chameleon* (2010); *Is Milton better than Shakespeare?* (2008); the Longman Annotated English Poets edition of *Andrew Marvell's Poems* (2003; rev. 2007); *Literature and Revolution in England, 1640–1660* (1994); and *Perfection Proclaimed: Language and Literature in English Radical Religion 1640–1660* (1989). He has also edited the *Journal of George Fox* (1998); and the Ranter pamphlets (1983; rev. 2014); and co-edited with Sara S. Poor, *Mysticism and Reform 1400–1750* (2015); and with Nicholas McDowell, the *Oxford Handbook to Milton* (2009).

Virginia Lee Strain is Assistant Professor of English at Loyola University of Chicago. Her publications include 'The Ensnared Subject and the General Pardon Statute in Late Elizabethan Literature', in *Taking Exception to the Law: Materializing Injustice in Early Modern English Literature*, ed. Don Beecher et al. (2011); and '*The Winter's Tale* and the

Oracle of the *Law*', *ELH* (2011). Her book, *Perfecting the Law: Legal Reform and Literature in Shakespeare's England*, is forthcoming from Edinburgh University Press.

Tim Stretton completed law and history degrees at the University of Adelaide and is currently Professor of History at Saint Mary's University in Halifax, Nova Scotia. He is the author of *Women Waging Law in Elizabethan England* (1998); the editor of a Camden Series volume, *Marital Litigation in the Court of Requests, 1542–1642* (2008); and co-editor with Krista Kesselring of *Married Women and the Law: Coverture in England and the Common Law World* (2013). His other publications include essays on masculinity, debt litigation, and Shakespeare's *The Merchant of Venice*.

Henry S. Turner is Professor of English at Rutgers University, where he specializes in Renaissance drama, the history of science, and intellectual history more generally. He is the author of *The English Renaissance Stage: Geometry, Poetics, and the Practical Spatial Arts, 1580–1630* (2006); *Shakespeare's Double Helix* (2008); and *The Corporate Commonwealth: Pluralism and Political Fictions in England, 1516–1651* (2016). He is the editor of *The Culture of Capital: Property, Cities, and Knowledge in Early Modern England* (2002); and *Early Modern Theatricality* (2012). He is currently working on several projects: on corporations in contemporary American culture, on Renaissance theories of fiction and art, and on Ben Jonson.

Elliott Visconsi is Associate Professor of English, Concurrent Associate Professor of Law and Chief Academic Digital Officer in the Provost's Office at the University of Notre Dame. He works broadly on early modern English and American literature, law, and political thought as well as a range of topics related to the First Amendment and freedom of speech in the digital age. He leads Notre Dame's digital strategy and is the co-founder of Luminary Digital Media, publisher of teaching and learning software with special emphasis on Shakespeare. His first book *Lines of Equity: Fiction and the Origins of Law in Restoration England* was published in 2008; articles have appeared in venues such as *Representations, Raritan, ELH*, and *Law & Literature*.

Christopher N. Warren is an Associate Professor of English at Carnegie Mellon University in Pittsburgh. His book *Literature and the Law of Nations, 1580–1680* was published in 2015. Warren is co-founder of the digital humanities project *Six Degrees of Francis Bacon*, and his work has appeared in *English Literary Renaissance, The Seventeenth Century, Digital Humanities Quarterly, Humanity*, and the *European Journal of International Law*. He has held visiting fellowships at Keble College, Oxford, the University of Chicago, and NUI Galway's Moore Institute, and he directs the Pittsburgh Consortium for Medieval and Renaissance Studies.

Ian Williams is a Lecturer in the Faculty of Laws, University College, London and has been a College Lecturer at Christ's College, Cambridge, and a Francis Bacon fellow at the Huntington Library. He was awarded the David Yale prize by the Selden Society in 2013.

Luke Wilson is Associate Professor of English at Ohio State University where he specializes in Renaissance literature, particularly in relation to legal history. His book,

Theaters of Intention: Drama and the Law in Early Modern England (2000), explores the sometimes obscure and often crazy relation between legal documents and the drama of the period. Since *Theaters of Intention*, he has published on a variety of topics in early modern literature and law: insurance law and theatrical risk; *Macbeth* and anti-natalism; manslaughter, 'tool abuse', and literary premeditation; and the changing logic of monetary compensation for bodily injuries from the Anglo-Saxon period to the early eighteenth century.

Jessica Winston is Professor of English at Idaho State University. Her research focuses on early modern literature and drama, especially the literary culture of the Inns of Court. She is coeditor of *Elizabethan Seneca: Three Tragedies* (2012) and author of *Lawyers at Play: Literature, Law, and Politics at the Early Modern Inns of Court, 1558–1581* (2016).

Andrew Zurcher is Fellow and Director of Studies in English at Queens' College, Cambridge. A longstanding interest in the influence of legal language and practice on the works of early modern English poets and dramatists, including Spenser, Donne, Shakespeare, Middleton, and Milton, culminated in the monographs *Spenser's Legal Language* (2007) and *Shakespeare and Law* (2010). In addition to several ongoing editorial projects, his current work focuses on the ways in which early modern legal and literary writers imagined, negotiated, and represented the relation between persons and material things.

INTRODUCTION

Law, Literature, and History

LORNA HUTSON

A Handbook of What?

Why have a 'handbook' on the subject of English law and literature in the period 1500–1700? The metaphor of the 'handbook' (after the Latin, *liber manualis*), which originally meant a small, portable book, to be kept on a desk or 'at hand' for information on a particular topic, is already fast becoming obsolete. (That old office staple, the 'Staff Handbook' now tends to be downloadable.) Rarely will future Oxford Handbooks be manually and conceptually grasped as wholes, rarely will their contents' pages be thumbed and their organization visible by a flick through the thickness of the leaves. Instead they will be part of a vast online database, individual chapters modularized, turned up by readers' electronic searches using keywords across a range of digital 'books'. Not that the *Oxford Handbook of Law and Literature 1500–1700* could have any claim to be a portable compendium or practical manual. Nevertheless, its very non-compendiousness is an argument for the value of its being contemplated as a holistic object, its chapters considered in relation to one another. It is precisely because a handbook of 'law and literature' offers not coverage of a pre-existing field or topic within a single discipline, but the vague conjunction of two very different disciplines, that it needs to be introductorily *taken in hand*, as it were, to discover what it is. The status and meaning of 'and'—this extremely permissive conjunction—has been debated, contested, and reconstituted with every book or article that has undertaken to treat law and literature since the term came to describe a legal studies 'movement' in the 1970s.[1] Yet, as Bernadette Meyler has neatly pointed out, the problem may be less to

[1] See, for example, Richard A. Posner, *Law and Literature*, 3rd edn (Cambridge, MA: Harvard University Press, 2009; the 1st edn, 1988, was subtitled '*A Misunderstood Relation*'); *Law and Literature*, ed. Michael Freeman and Andrew D. E. Lewis, *Current Legal Issues* series (Oxford: Oxford University

do with defining the nature of the conjunction than with the assumption of the dyad. Law and literature, Meyler argues, is properly not a liaison, friendship, or marriage, but a love-triangle or *ménage a trois*. As the period designation (1500–1700) of this book's title makes clear, there are not two disciplines cohabiting here, but three: they are law, literature, and *history*.[2]

The explicit naming of the third discipline has a clarifying effect when it comes to appreciating the interdisciplinary makeup of this Handbook, and the dialogues that emerge from its chapters. Literature is the Handbook's lead discipline. Of its thirty-eight contributors, twenty are from Literature, eleven from History, and seven from Law. Nevertheless, a striking feature of the twinned conferences held at Princeton and at St Andrews in April and May 2015 at which drafts of most of these chapters were presented was the sense of cross-disciplinary intelligibility, the eagerness and excitement with which questions and debate moved back and forth among speakers in legal history, literature, and history. Scholars in all three disciplines seemed to be working towards a holistic goal such as that defined by the late Christopher Brooks in his most recent book, where he said he sought to 're-integrate the history of law, legal institutions and the legal professions with the general political and social history' and—I would add—the *literature* of sixteenth- and seventeenth-century England.[3] The point here is not that the contributors to this Handbook experienced an interdisciplinary longing for the 'vanishing real' of the kind made fun of by Julie Stone Peters, but that the different disciplinary frameworks from which our questions arose were no longer an obstacle to our shared sense of having a stake in the emerging debates.[4] No one doubts the importance of developments in early modern England for the social, political, and colonial and economic history of western democracy, for the Anglo-American legal and constitutional traditions, and for Anglophone literature. But sometimes it is easier to see the way towards understanding the consequentiality of these developments in an interdisciplinary framework. This is the opportunity that I hope our exchanges between law, literature, and history afford. Yet how did the different disciplines arrive at this point? What shifts in thinking in legal, literary, and historical approaches to early modern England have made a Handbook like this one possible?

While books and studies illuminating the legal terminology of early modern literary texts have been around for a long time, the identifying of 'Law and Literature' as an interdisciplinary critical movement is usually traced back to the 1970s and 1980s and

Press, 1999); *Teaching Law and Literature*, ed. Austin Sarat, Cathrine O. Frank, and Matthew Anderson (New York: Modern Language Association of America, 2011).

2 Bernadette Meyler, 'Law, Literature and History: The Love Triangle', *UC Irvine Law Review*, 5 (2015): 364–91. Subha Mukherji also looks at law and literature in historical context in, 'Understood Relations: Law and Literature in Early Modern Studies', *Literature Compass*, 6.3 (2009): 706–25.

3 Christopher Brooks, *Law, Politics and Society in Early Modern England* (Cambridge: Cambridge University Press, 2008), 1.

4 Julie Stone Peters, 'Law, Literature and the Vanishing Real: On the Future of an Interdisciplinary Illusion', *PMLA*, 120.2 (2005): 442–53.

linked notably to the studies of James Boyd White, Richard Weisberg, Robin West, and Ian Ward.[5] Cogent critiques of the weaker aspects of this enterprise were launched by Jane Baron, who argued against the movement's conventional caricature of dry, rule-bound law, supplemented by literature's emotional nuance, and by Julie Stone Peters, who diagnosed the yearnings that drove the pursuit of a legally engaged literary criticism.[6] But these objections to a trans-historical interdisciplinary illusion should not apply to the rich three-way conversations between literature, history, and law that have been emerging, for the last twenty years, as each of the disciplines in the triad has refined and rethought the texts, archives, and institutions of early modern England as its object of study. Using very broad brush strokes and laying no claim to comprehensiveness, the next section will outline a selection of these interactions, starting with the literary-history encounter known as 'New Historicism' before turning to the history-law encounter referred to as the 'Law and Society' movement and then to some newly emerging rapprochements between legal history, intellectual history, and the study of rhetoric and poetics.

Early Modern Convergences: 'New Historicism', 'Law and Society', 'Rhetoric and Law'

In US literary departments in the 1980s, the old division between the literary text and its historical 'background' was rejected for a dynamic, chiastic understanding of the historical narrative as textually fabricated, and the literary text as a cultural event. Foundational articles appeared, analysing historical source texts alongside literary texts as discourses that were similarly engaged in shaping modes of political subjection or in producing representations in which subversive voices were ultimately contained and made serviceable to power.[7] Although the proponents of this criticism—known as New Historicists—were evidently, therefore, interested in questions of sovereignty and power, particularly as manifest in Ernst Kantorowicz's account of the sixteenth-century legal fiction of 'The King's Two Bodies', they focused

[5] James Boyd White, *The Legal Imagination* (Chicago: Chicago University Press, 1985); Richard Weisberg, *Poethics: And Other Strategies of Law and Literature* (New York: Columbia University Press, 1992); Ian Ward, *Law and Literature: Possibilities and Perspectives* (Cambridge: Cambridge University Press, 1995).

[6] Peters, 'The Vanishing Real'; Jane B. Baron, 'Law, Literature and the Problems of Interdisciplinarity', *YLJ*, 108.5 (1999): 1059–85.

[7] See, for example, Stephen Greenblatt, 'Invisible Bullets', in *Shakespearean Negotiations* (Oxford: Clarendon Press, 1984), 21–93; Louis Montrose, 'The Elizabethan Subject and the Spenserian Text', in *Literary Theory/Renaissance Texts*, ed. Patricia Parker and David Quint (Baltimore: Johns Hopkins, 1986), 303–40.

less on the legal dimensions of sovereignty or on the legal enforcement of power, than on sovereign power's theatrical deployment in royal spectacle and on the commercial stage. Influenced by Foucault's provocative genealogies of sexuality, of madness, and of punishment, New Historicists were suspicious of the old Whig history of evolving legal-constitutional forms: power was not to be conceived in terms of the prohibitive 'Law-as-Sovereign', but in terms of its productivity, its capacity to deploy techniques of all kinds, including those of representation, to produce the subject, the state, and the figurations of sovereignty itself.[8]

As New Historicism brought the excitement of higher stakes to the study of early modern literary texts, a number of historians responded to Foucault's innovative methodologies and were in conversation with literary critics over histories of the body, subjectivity, and the state.[9] But at another disciplinary intersection, historians on both sides of the Atlantic were affected by a new kind of history of law. The disciplinary trajectory of legal history in the twentieth century may be roughly divided, as Michael Lobban explains, between the 'internal' (lawyers focusing on the history of doctrines) and the 'external' (historians looking at the impact of legal agencies on particular societies).[10] While both strands look back to the pioneering work of F. W. Maitland, the 'internal' strand was revolutionized and taken forward by the work of S. F. C. Milsom and then by John Baker, both of whom opened up, for those in other disciplines, the prospect of understanding more about society in the past through the contemplation of changes and developments in specific legal doctrines, institutions, and modes of instruction, as well as in underlying legal ideas and forms of practice (such as trial).[11] The other, 'external' strand, as Lobban shows, manifested itself, in the US, in the 'Law and Society' movement, a movement energized and shaped by the innovative work of James Willard Hurst, who led the way in focused and local studies of the interactions of law and specific industries.[12] Hurst's work encouraged a turn in the work of historians with legal training or legal interests towards the interaction of law and society. As David Rabban

[8] Michel Foucault, *The History of Sexuality*, trans. Robert Hurley (Harmondsworth: Penguin, 1976), 1.94–7; see also Ernst Kantorowicz, *The King's Two Bodies: A Study in Political Theology* (Princeton: Princeton University Press, 1959). Foucault's genealogy of the modern state by way of its changing penal styles is explicitly conceived as homage to Kantorowicz's tracing of the state's emergence through the 'surplus power' of the king's doubled body. See *Discipline and Punish: The Birth of the Prison*, trans. Alan Sheridan (Harmondsworth: Penguin, 1977), 29.

[9] The University of California at Berkeley fostered such conversations through the journal *Representations*.

[10] Michael Lobban, 'The Varieties of Legal History', *Clio@Themis*, 5 (2012): 1–29. See also David Ibbetson, 'What Is Legal History a History of?', in *Law and History* (*Current Legal Issues* 6), ed. A. Lewis and M. Lobban (Oxford University Press, 2004), 33–40.

[11] S. F. C. Milsom, *Historical Foundations of the English Common Law* (London: Butterworths, 1969); J. H. Baker, *Introduction to English Legal History*, 2nd edn (London: Butterworths, 1979). On Maitland's influence on legal history, see John Hudson, *F. W. Maitland and the Englishness of English Law* (London: SS, 2007).

[12] James Willard Hurst, *Law and Economic Growth: The Legal History of the Lumber Industry in Wisconsin, 1836–1915* (Cambridge, MA: Belknap Press of Harvard University Press, 1964).

has shown, the 'Law and Society' movement also looks back to the innovative 'sociological jurisprudence' of Roscoe Pound (1870–1964).[13]

Historians of early modern England had already by the 1980s begun, for various reasons, to take a greater interest in the complex details of multiple jurisdictions and participatory legal procedures. Both historians of Tudor and Stuart government and those interested in understanding the lives of humbler or overlooked members of society were decisively affected by a new 'law and society' turn which took the form of detailed work on popular legalism and on levels of litigation. Christopher Brooks's magisterial study of the chronology of the increase in civil litigation, analysing the records of the courts of King's Bench and Common Pleas in the years 1560–1640, revealed the extent to which, in Brooks's own words, 'law-mindedness came imperceptibly to colour social relationships and ideals'.[14] A greater familiarity with the diversity of jurisdictions and their interrelations and with legal culture and procedure became essential to the understanding of social and cultural change. Part of what was being uncovered was a critique of the top-down models of early modern politics and government that had failed to recognize widespread popular participation in processes of community regulation and governance.[15] Cynthia Herrup's careful reconstruction of the processes that led to criminal indictments revealed the extent of lay initiative and participation in the criminal justice system. In the same year, 1987, Martin Ingram rewrote older histories of a decline in ecclesiastical jurisdiction, revealing, rather, a cooperation between officers of the church courts and Justices of the Peace, and throwing light, through the records of disputed 'tokens' of matrimonial promises, on countless scenes of ambiguous matrimonial contracting in the period's drama. Building on Christopher Brooks's work, Craig Muldrew used evidence for unprecedented levels of litigation to look at the cultural, interpersonal, and emotional aspects of capitalistic expansion across thousands of witnessed, recorded credit transactions.[16]

As social historians took a greater interest in legal procedures, institutions, and forms their work became more hermeneutically attentive. In allowing for what Natalie

[13] David Rabban, *Law's History: American Legal Thought and the Transatlantic Turn to History* (Cambridge: Cambridge University Press, 2013), 423–71.

[14] See Christopher Brooks, 'A Law-Abiding and Litigious Society', in *The Oxford Illustration History of Tudor and Stuart Britain*, ed. John Morrill (Oxford: Oxford University Press, 1996), 143. See also Brooks, *Pettyfoggers and Vipers of the Commonwealth: The 'Lower Branch' of the Legal Profession in Early Modern England* (Cambridge: Cambridge University Press, 1986).

[15] For pioneering work on crime in the context of community governance, see J. A. Sharpe, 'Crime and Delinquency in an Essex Parish', in *Crime in England 1550–1800*, ed. J. S. Cockburn (London: Methuen, 1977); and Sharpe, 'Enforcing the Law in the Seventeenth-Century English Village', in *Crime and the Law: The Social History of Crime in Western Europe since 1500*, ed. V. A. C. Gatrell, Bruce Lenman, and Geoffrey Parker (London: Europa Publications, 1980).

[16] See Cynthia Herrup, *The Common Peace: Participation and the Criminal Law in Early Modern England* (Cambridge: Cambridge University Press, 1987); Martin Ingram, *Church Courts, Sex and Marriage in England, 1570–1640* (Cambridge: Cambridge University Press, 1987); Craig Muldrew, *The Economy of Obligation: The Culture of Credit and Social Relations in Early Modern England* (London: Macmillan, 1998).

Davis, in her pathbreaking work on early modern France, called 'fiction in the archives', social historians became more and more aware of the legally purposeful shaping of genres, the strategic uses of narrative, the decorum of gender, and effects of status on vocabulary and credibility.[17] Tim Stretton analysed a specifically female culture of litigation in the Court of Requests. Laura Gowing's *Domestic Dangers* used ecclesiastical court depositions to reveal the extreme limitations on women's agency within semiotic structures that positioned them both as repositories of a household's sexual honour and as witnesses of least authority and credit. Malcolm Gaskill urged us to read the providential elements of both printed murder pamphlets and manuscript informations to Justices of the Peace not as signs of early modern people's superstitious beliefs, but as part of a complex mix of strategically deployed evidentiary practices.[18] At the same time, work on litigation and legal procedure led to a shift in the conception of what constituted political consciousness and state formation. Drawing on Christopher Brooks's figures on the increase in civil litigation, along with studies of criminal procedure and parish governance, historians such as Steve Hindle and Michael Braddick have rethought the processes of state formation, revealing the widespread participation of agents at all social levels.[19]

The legal turn taken by the social and political history of early modern England has given texture and detail to a literary criticism increasingly interested in the hermeneutic complexity of social processes. Subha Mukherji's *Law and Representation in Early Modern Drama* (2006) thus drew on cases of courtship resembling those so ably discussed by social historians. But Mukherji also used literary critical skills to probe the contradictions of a canon law that strove to reconcile the law's intention (that is, the Church's presumption in favour of matrimony) with the contested evidence (rings, tokens, letters) signifying the intentions of contracting parties.[20] Yet it would be wrong to suggest that the change exemplified by work like Mukherji's was merely incremental: that literary critics have merely become more aware of the legal complexity of the social processes depicted in the drama. On the contrary, the legal turn has enabled a shift in the analysis of the politics of early modern literary production (a significant critique of New Historicism) and a transformation of our understanding of the place of forensic modes of inquiry in the creation of imaginative fiction, imagined dramatic worlds.

17 Natalie Zemon Davis, *Fiction in the Archives: Pardon Tales and their Tellers in Early Modern France* (Stanford: Stanford University Press, 1987).

18 Malcolm Gaskill, *Crimes and Mentalities in Early Modern England* (Cambridge: Cambridge University Press, 2000).

19 Tim Stretton, *Women Waging Law in Early Modern England* (Cambridge: Cambridge University Press, 1998); Laura Gowing, *Domestic Dangers: Women, Words and Sex in Early Modern London* (Oxford: Clarendon Press, 1994); Steve Hindle, *The State and Social Change in Early Modern England, c.1550–1640* (London: Macmillan, 2000); Michael Braddick, *State Formation in Early Modern England* (Cambridge, 2000).

20 Subha Mukherji, *Law and Representation in Early Modern Drama* (Cambridge: Cambridge University Press, 2006); see also B. J. and Mary Sokol, *Shakespeare, Law and Marriage* (Cambridge: Cambridge University Press, 2003) and *Shakespeare's Legal Language* (London: Continuum, 2004).

New Historicist analyses were wonderfully demystifying of early modern English culture's investments in bodily or theatrical figurations of the monarch's sovereignty. Nevertheless, their tendency to see legal authority as a mere ruse or performance had an oddly re-mystifying effect, as if all that could be said about early modern literature was that it produced subjection to charismatic, monarchically embodied political sovereignty. From the turn of the millennium, however, literary critical work has increasingly turned to explore literary uses of legal language and legal institutions as a way of registering, among other things, a more diversely creative literary consciousness of the polity and political agency.[21] Writers of the period, major and minor (including, for example, Thomas More, George Gascoigne, Isabella Whitney, Thomas Kyd, Edmund Spenser, William Shakespeare, Ben Jonson, John Donne, John Webster, Thomas Middleton, Philip Massinger, and John Milton) were, as these and later studies show, aware of and creatively engaged with the technicalities of legal language and procedure.

Thus, for example, Luke Wilson's *Theaters of Intention* (2001) turned away from the then fashionable theoretical questions of subjection and sovereignty to explore literary and legal constructions of intention and agency. Whether dealing with the emergence of *assumpsit* in contract law, or with distinctions between manslaughter and murder, Wilson's work laid bare the inherently retrospective, fictional nature of intention and the different ways in which Shakespeare's *Hamlet* and Jonson's *Bartholomew Fair* both brilliantly depend on this idea.[22] Bradin Cormack similarly reoriented critical attention from questions of 'sovereignty' and 'power' *tout court*, to 'a power to do justice', that is, to sovereignty considered as 'jurisdiction'. Rather than giving us a deconstructive exposure of the performative origins of 'the force of law', Cormack analyzed its quasi-improvisatory emergence as an effect of administration, and at points of jurisdictional conflict. Cormack's analysis helps us see how creative opportunities open out, in both law and literature, at power's jurisdictional limits. He offers us new ways of reading, for example, early modern English literary engagements with maritime limits, and with the colonial uses of common law in Ireland.[23] Likewise, Andrew Zurcher's analysis of legal vocabulary in Spenser and Shakespeare is revealing about the political imaginations of these poets. Commenting, for example, on Shakespeare's substitution of a legal for a

[21] See, for example, Constance Jordan, *Shakespeare's Monarchies: Ruler and Subject in the Romances* (Ithaca: Cornell University Press, 1997); Elizabeth Hanson, *Discovering the Subject in Renaissance England* (Cambridge: Cambridge University Press, 1998); Karen Cunningham, *Imaginary Betrayals: Subjectivity and the Discourses of Treason in Early Modern Literature* (Philadelphia: University of Pennsylvania Press, 2002); Dennis D. Kezar, ed., *Solon and Thespis: Law and Theater in the English Renaissance* (Notre Dame: University of Notre Dame Press, 2007); Karen Cunningham and Constance Jordan, eds., *The Law in Shakespeare* (Basingstoke: Palgrave Macmillan, 2007); Erica Sheen, *Shakespeare and the Institution of Theatre* (Palgrave Macmillan, 2009); Donald Beecher et al., eds., *Taking Exception to the Law* (Toronto: University of Toronto Press, 2015); Gregory Kneidel, *John Donne and Early Modern Legal Culture* (Pittsburgh: Dusquene University Press, 2015).

[22] Luke Wilson, *Theaters of Intention: Drama and Law in Early Modern England* (Stanford: Stanford University Press, 2000).

[23] Bradin Cormack, *A Power to Do Justice: Jurisdiction, English Literature and the Rise of the Common Law, 1509–1625* (Chicago: Chicago University Press, 2007).

courtly vocabulary in sonnets, Zurcher writes 'love exists not between ruler and subject, but between persons'.[24]

In addition to legally inflected literary critical work such as Wilson's, Cormack's, and Zurcher's, richer analyses of the legal engagements of early modern literature have been made possible by analyses of the structural similarities between law and rhetoric. In an earlier phase, during the 1950s and 1960s, attempts to explore the convergence of rhetoric and law in sixteenth-century England had seemed to lead to a dead end. Promising studies by R. S. Schoeck (1953, 1983) and D. S. Bland (1967) did not lead to the expected further burst of productive work either on humanism's influence on law, or law's on drama.[25] Revisiting his 1953 article in 1983, Schoeck concluded gloomily that '[t]he whole question of rhetoric's influence on legal oratory does not seem to have excited the interest of legal historians'.[26] Latterly, however, foundational studies by Kathy Eden in literature and by Barbara Shapiro in history have revealed close connections between classical forensic rhetoric, humanist poetics and hermeneutics, and English legal and scientific developments in concepts of proof and evidence. Eden showed that the presentation of proof was fundamental to both legal procedure and tragic action, and that particularly important in Aristotelian poetics was the development of 'entechnic' or artificial proofs which use rhetorical art to reconstruct, through other 'circumstances' (time, place, manner, etc.) the probable motives or intention behind an action, deed, or 'fact' (*factum*). Shapiro has, also since the 1980s, examined the influence of the topics of artificial and inartificial proof on the development of Anglo-American concepts of evidence and 'fact' in legal and scientific culture.[27] Shapiro showed how Cicero's and Quintilian's discussions of artificial proof and of the topics or places ('accidents' or 'circumstances') from which proofs might be drawn came to shape the formal examination procedure of Justices of Peace, who were required to make inquiries into matters of suspicion.[28]

Eden's and Shapiro's work appeared together for the first time in an innovative collection entitled *Rhetoric and Law in Early Modern Europe* (2001) edited by Victoria Kahn

[24] Andrew Zurcher, *Shakespeare and Law* (London: Methuen, 2010), 63. See also Zurcher, *Spenser's Legal Language: Law and Poetry in Early Modern England* (Cambridge: Boydell and Brewer, 2007).

[25] Richard Schoeck, 'Rhetoric and Law in Sixteenth Century England', *SP*, 50.2 (1953): 110–27; Schoeck, 'Lawyers and Rhetoric in Sixteenth Century England' in *Renaissance Eloquence: Studies in the Theory and Practice of Renaissance Rhetoric*, ed. J. J. Murphy (Berkeley: University of California Press, 1983), 274–91; D. S. Bland, 'Rhetoric and the Law Student in Sixteenth Century England', *SP*, 53 (1967): 498–508; see further Lorna Hutson, 'Rhetoric and Early Modern Law', in *The Oxford Handbook of Rhetorical Studies*, ed. Michael MacDonald (http://www.oxfordhandbooks.com/view/10.1093/oxfordhb/9780199731596.001.0001/oxfordhb-9780199731596-e-033).

[26] Schoeck, 'Lawyers', 275.

[27] Kathy Eden, *Poetic and Legal Fiction in the Aristotelian Tradition* (Princeton: Princeton University Press, 1986); Barbara Shapiro, *'Beyond Reasonable Doubt' and 'Probable Cause': Historical Perspectives on the Anglo American Law of Evidence* (Berkeley: University of California Press, 1991); *A Culture of Fact: England 1550–1700* (Ithaca: Cornell University Press, 2000).

[28] See John H. Langbein, *Prosecuting Crime in the Renaissance: England, Germany, France* (Cambridge, MA: Harvard University Press, 1974).

and Lorna Hutson.[29] The political implications of shifting from New Historicism's concerns with questions of sovereignty and power to more legally and rhetorically inflected versions of such questions became apparent with Kahn's subsequent publications such as *Wayward Contracts* (2004), 'Political Theology and Fiction in *The King's Two Bodies*' (2009), and *The Future of Illusion* (2015).[30] Kahn's work offers new models of thinking of the relation of legal and poetic fictions, and of the relationship of person and office in the political sphere. In *Wayward Contracts*, she revealed analogies between the artifice of the political contract and the artifice of the literary text's contract with the reader. In her article on Kantorowicz, Kahn dismantled the prevalent New Historical reading of *The King's Two Bodies* as a narrative of the transfer of the aura of sacred authority from religion to the 'political body' of the monarch. Such readings, Kahn showed, confused Carl Schmitt's concept of the 'juristic person' as a vicarious, embodied representative of Christ, with Kantorowicz's contrasting interest in the juristic person as a corporation, that is, as a poetic *legal fiction* enabling the imagining of a polity separate from the embodied ruler. In *The Future of Illusion* Kahn again links law and fiction by arguing that to name the early modern problem of legitimizing political authority as the problem of 'political theology' misses the third term—*poiesis*, or poetic making—which is central to early modern meditations on the artful construction of political order. Kahn's emphasis on the power of legal/poetic fictions is a feature her work shares with new work on early modern colonialism, international law, and transatlantic slavery. Mary Nyquist analyses the conceptual dependence of English political liberty on the discursive racialization of liberty's antithesis, slavery, showing, for example, how the covert presence of the Roman law of war slavery crucially informs Hobbes's fiction of the state of nature.[31]

Moving away from political thought and back to literary criticism, more detailed analyses of the structural affinities between Roman forensic rhetoric and the evidential procedures of English common law have appeared in recent years, as have critiques. For Lorna Hutson, it is not so much a question of whether English judicial procedure

[29] Victoria Kahn and Lorna Hutson, eds., *Rhetoric and Law in Early Modern Europe* (New Haven: Yale University Press, 2001).

[30] Victoria Kahn, *Wayward Contracts: The Crisis of Political Obligation in England, 1640–1674* (Princeton: Princeton University Press, 2004); Kahn, 'Political Theology and Fiction in *The King's Two Bodies*', *Representations*, 106 (2009): 77–101; Kahn, *The Future of Illusion: Political Theology and Early Modern Texts* (Chicago: Chicago University Press, 2014). For other reassessments of Kantorowicz's work, see David Norbrook, 'The Emperor's New Body? *Richard II*, Ernst Kantorowicz and the Politics of Shakespeare Criticism', *Textual Practice*, 10 (1996): 329–57; Lorna Hutson, 'Not the King's Two Bodies: Reading the "Body Politic" in Shakespeare's *Henry IV*, parts I and II', in *Rhetoric and Law in Early Modern Europe*, 166–98; and Hutson, 'Imagining Justice: Kantorowicz and Shakespeare', *Representations*, 106 (2009): 118–42.

[31] Mary Nyquist, *Arbitrary Rule: Slavery, Tyranny and the Power of Life and Death* (Chicago: University of Chicago Press, 2013); see also Christopher N. Warren, *Literature and the Law of Nations, 1580–1680* (Oxford: Oxford University Press, 2015). On the colonial and imperial uses of English common law, see Hans S. Pawlisch, *Sir John Davies and the Conquest of Ireland: A Study in Legal Imperialism* (Cambridge: Cambridge University Press, 1985).

or the rules of Roman forensic rhetoric are accurately represented onstage by writers like William Shakespeare or Ben Jonson but rather that the techniques that enable us to *imagine* offstage fictional worlds and characters' interior lives (the techniques, in other words, that distinguish Shakespearean drama from the morality play) are derived from the same artificial proofs and topics of circumstance that were being widely adapted to the uses of English participatory justice.[32] Holger Schott Syme, on the other hand, has pointed out that for all the recent critical insistence on the dramatists' intimate knowledge of law, not a single surviving play written between the opening of the first commercial theatres in 1570 and their closure in 1642 depicts the English form of trial—trial by jury.[33] Quentin Skinner suggests that Shakespeare's legal knowledge has often been exaggerated and that more important is Shakespeare's engagement, in certain plays, with the rules of classical forensic rhetoric.[34] It is possible to show, however, that throughout the participatory system of English justice, as through the dialogue of English drama, runs a vocabulary of supposing, conjecturing, and inferring from circumstances and probabilities that shows the influence of judicial rhetoric, particularly in its concern with the discovery of arguments of artificial proof. This vocabulary links the work of participatory legal inquiry and conjecture to the work of the dramatic imagination.

The foregoing account of developments leading to the composition of this Oxford Handbook has been necessarily partial, focusing primarily on debates in literary criticism with occasional forays into social history and very little discussion either of advances in the 'internal' study of legal history (the study of doctrine) or in the 'external' explorations of critical legal studies. Yet the work of A. W. Brian Simpson, John Baker, R. H. Helmholz, and David Ibbetson has been foundational for the literary critical appreciation of sixteenth-century developments in land law, contract, *assumpsit*, and defamation at both canon and common law, as well as in a host of other areas.[35] On the Inns of Court as professional and educational institutions, the work of Wilfrid Prest, John Baker, and Margaret McGlynn has been transformative, while our understanding of the role of the Inns as sites of poetry, revelry, and political engagement has been much enriched by Alan Nelson and John Elliott's edition of the Inns volumes of the *Records of Early English Drama*, and by Paul Raffield's and Jessica Winston's work

[32] Lorna Hutson, *The Invention of Suspicion: Law and Mimesis in Shakespeare and Renaissance Drama* (Oxford: Clarendon Press, 2007); Hutson, *Circumstantial Shakespeare* (Oxford: Oxford University Press, 2015).

[33] Holger Schott Syme, '(Mis)representing Justice on the Early Modern Stage', *Studies in Philology*, 109 (2012): 63–85; see also Syme, *Theatre and Testimony in Shakespeare's England: A Culture of Mediation* (Cambridge: Cambridge University Press, 2014).

[34] Quentin Skinner, *Forensic Shakespeare* (Oxford: Clarendon Press, 2014), 7–8.

[35] A. W. Brian Simpson, *An Introduction to the History of the Land Law* (Oxford: Oxford University Press, 1961); Simpson, *A History of the Common Law of Contract: The Rise of Assumpsit* (Oxford: Clarendon Press, 1975); J. H. Baker, ed., *The Reports of Sir John Spelman*, 2 vols (London: SS, 1977); Baker, *OHLE: VI*; R. H. Helmholz, *Roman Canon Law in Reformation England* (Cambridge: Cambridge University Press, 1990); Helmholz, *OHLE: I*; David Ibbetson, *A Historical Introduction to the Law of Obligations* (New York: Oxford University Press, 1999).

on the cultural activities of the lawyers.[36] Peter Goodrich's innovative deconstructive and psychoanalytic approaches to legal language and common law hegemony have stimulated a new awareness of the disavowed affective and aesthetic dimensions of legal culture, and the psychic costs of dispensing with jurisdictional plurality.[37] With respect to the history of political thought, Christopher Brooks's call for a reintegration of political and legal history has been brilliantly answered by Alan Cromartie's *The Constitutionalist Revolution*, which, in tracing the increasingly expansive sense of what the common law was capable of handling within its ordinary power, helps explain how political opinion on the royal prerogative began to polarize. ('If ordinary royal power was legal, then occasional irregular proceedings must be expressions of non-legal power: of what was increasingly frequently referred to as royal *absolute* prerogative'.)[38] Further attention to these areas will be given in the following section, which introduces the chapters of the Handbook itself.

Handling the Handbook: A Reader's Guide

The Handbook's sections divide the contents thematically, with a mix of chapters by historians, literary critics, and legal historians in each section. Across the chapter contents as a whole analyses of canonical and lesser-known literary and dramatic works are integrated into accounts of major shifts in legal thought and practice, alluding to the period's greatest legal authors as well as to the collective common learning of the profession. Each section juxtaposes chapters that discuss closely related material from different disciplinary perspectives in the hope that this will prove illuminating and stimulating. For example, the first two sections, 'Textual and Interpretative Culture' and 'Literature and the Legal Profession 1500–1700', provide the reader with an opportunity to test against state-of-the-art scholarly analyses of the evidence some of the generalized claims commonly made about the importance of the Inns of Court to the politics and literary culture of early modern England. The following short narrative accounts of each section offer the reader a preliminary map of the book.

36 See Wilfrid Prest, *The Rise of the Barristers: A Social History of the English Bar, 1590–1640* (Oxford: Clarendon Press, 1986); J. H. Baker, *The Third University of England: The Inns of Court and the Common Law Tradition* (London: SS, 1990); Margaret McGlynn, *The Royal Prerogative and the Learning of the Inns of Court* (Cambridge: Cambridge University Press, 2003); *REED*; Paul Raffield, *Images and Cultures of Law in Early Modern England: Justice and Political Power, 1558–1660* (Cambridge: Cambridge University Press, 2004); *ICW*; Jessica Winston, *Lawyers at Play: Literature, Law and Politics at the Early Modern Inns of Court, 1558–1581* (Oxford: Oxford University Press, 2016).

37 See, for example, Peter Goodrich, *Languages of Law: From Logics of Memory to Nomadic Masks* (London: Weidenfeld and Nicholson, 1990).

38 Alan Cromartie, *The Constitutionalist Revolution: An Essay on the History of England, 1450–1642* (Cambridge: Cambridge University Press, 2006), 94.

Textual and Interpretative Culture

What emerges in Part I, 'Textual and Interpretative Culture', is the sharp contrast between, on the one hand, humanist pedagogy's broad dissemination of methods of literary composition based in Roman forensic rhetoric and, on the other hand, the closed learning exercises and controlled manuscript circulation of legal learning at the Inns themselves. Kathy Eden shows how forensic modes of inquiry, which proceed from the identification of the legal issue to the invention of proofs, structure even such non-legal intimate or imaginative compositions as familiar letters and plays. Her opening chapter thus helps to explain how, in Quentin Skinner's final chapter of the section, Shakespeare could presume a general awareness of the points of forensic rhetoric that underlie the crucial turn of Shylock's case in *The Merchant of Venice*. In between these chapters, Margaret McGlynn describes the lawyers' 'common learning' as emerging from their processes of working through and familiarizing themselves with messy, unstandardized manuscript compilations of readings on statutes and cases, while Ian Williams stresses the closed circulation of such personal manuscript compilations not only within the Inns, but very often within the fraternity of a single Inn. The idea that legal learning circulated widely outside the Inns is, then, probably a misconception and one that literary critics may need to be more cautious about. For James McBain, it is also a misconception to think that the literary activity of the Inns of Court was necessarily an offshoot of legal learning and pedagogical practice. McBain suggests rather that men were increasingly coming to the Inns from university, whence came the learning in those rhetorical and dialectical modes of invention that, as Eden shows, gave a forensic cast to drama, poetry, and literary composition in general.

Literature and the Legal Profession 1500–1700

As Part I challenges commonplaces about the cross fertilization of legal and literary learning in the Inns, so Part II revises accounts of the lawyers' professional identity and the politics of their poetry, revels, and masques from 1500–1700. This section includes a lecture given by the late Christopher Brooks whose death has been a great loss to scholarship in this field. In general, Brooks's figures on the enormous increase in litigation and the growth of the legal profession provide the section's statistical base. From Brooks's figures, Jessica Winston argues that the legal profession grew newly visible, drawing the usual kinds of anti-lawyer satire, but she also notes that, more unusually, these early modern English lawyers composed satirical epigrams against themselves. Examining the epigrams of Sir John Davies (1569–1626) who became Attorney General for Ireland, Winston teases out how Davies's satirical language actually contributes to the fashioning of a self-conscious professional identity. From the wit of epigram (which Ben Jonson said should always leave something unexpressed, to be 'understood'),[39] Peter Goodrich

[39] *CWBJ*, 5.378 (intriguingly, Jonson was here referring rather disparagingly to Sir John Davies!).

examines an analogously occluded legal genre, the emblem. In woodcuts, Goodrich argues, emblems present an enigma, a mystery hidden in full view, a witty transmission of legal learning, even a covert means by which the Latin culture of law infiltrated the insular learning of the common lawyers. Paul Raffield then considers the revels of the Inns of Court as conscious claims to the kind of communal political semi-autonomy described by Patrick Collinson in his now famous accounts of Elizabethan England as a 'monarchical republic'. Martin Butler qualifies Raffield's account, showing how, even as early as the 1590s, masque texts exhibit the contradictions of self-promotion and submission inherent in the position of a political elite with respect to the monarch. Butler argues, moreover, that the presence of Francis Bacon behind so many masques of the early seventeenth century qualifies any thesis of their consistent constitutional oppositionality. The section concludes with the provocative speculations of Christopher Brooks in a lecture given to the St Andrews Centre for Mediaeval and Early Modern Law and Literature in 2013. Brooks framed his talk with reflections on the difference between Shakespeare's sensuous and witty engagements with common law language in the 1590s and the self-serving aridity of common law language as depicted in William Wycherly's *The Plain Dealer* (1676) nearly a hundred years later. He then ranged with bold erudition over the causes and effects of the decline of the Inns as a site of legal education, political engagement, and legal and literary cross-fertilization at the end of the seventeenth century.

Administering the Law

Anti-lawyer satire may be a commonplace of western European literature, but the drama of early modern England is distinctive for its astonishing range of depictions, by no means always satirical, of lower officers of the law and of ordinary people's recourse to law as a form of social agency or constitutional imagining. Thus, for example, Shakespeare's *Taming of the Shrew* opens with an alehouse keeper threatening a drunk and disorderly Christopher Sly with the 'headborough' (Induction, 11). The first half of the Queen's Men's *Famous Victories* (1598) presents England's participatory justice system—hue and cry, watch, constables—trying to deal with the criminality of none other than England's Crown Prince, Henry. In Jonson's *Every Man in his Humour* (1601, 1615), a water bearer absurdly asks a Justice of Peace (Justice Clement) to bind a cowardly braggart to keep the peace, while Jonson's Caroline play, *A Tale of a Tub* (1633) registers, in its sympathy for the predicament of Toby Turf, High Constable of Kentish Town, the political pressures increasingly put on local officers by Charles I's personal rule. The chapters in Part III survey the historiography of local government, examine the evidential procedures of the criminal trial, and consider how English history plays invested in monarchical charisma simultaneously elicit the audience's desire for a vision of legal and administrative reform. First, James Sharpe explores the history of crime as an aspect of the history of local community, emphasizing the high levels of participation in parish government and countering the deplorable 'Dogberry effect' that led historians to underestimate the important contribution of constables and churchwardens. Then Norma Landau challenges a historiography that has presented the Justices of Peace as an unchanging institution. She shows how the identification of justices with local gentry emerged in the seventeenth century; their powers, judicial and administrative, first markedly increased and then decreased as much; over the same period, moreover, their qualification for local government ceased to depend on the loyalty of their armed tenants and consisted, rather, in the independence guaranteed by a landed income. Beginning with the assertion that trials are '*imaginative* reconstructions of past occurrences', Barbara Shapiro's chapter links us back to Part I in considering the rhetorical origins of modern credibility standards in early modern attitudes to conflicts of oaths in trial procedure and testimony. Virginia Strain's chapter finally challenges the New Historicist sense that Shakespeare's *Henry IV* plays present law and government as merely the cynical ruses of the elite, showing rather how carefully *Henry IV* part 2 works to delineate the reformed relation between legal authority and the monarch's person.

Temporal and Spiritual, Law and Conscience

One great event lying behind the increase of litigation in sixteenth-century England was, of course, the Reformation. This was also the watershed event behind the emergence of the common law's jurisdictional hegemony, but here what is at stake is not a territorial conflict of jurisdiction, but the whole question of the law's relation to conscience, the question of how to reconcile a justice based on the limits of what man can know with a justice that would try to adjudicate according to conscience, with all the risks of arbitrariness involved. All the chapters in Part IV engage with the extent to which spiritual life eludes jurisdiction, or to which religious life, as Joshua Phillips puts it, is beyond the secular law. Phillips looks at the way three plays depicting the reign of King John—by John Bale, George Peele, and Shakespeare—all variously register the jurisdictional threat posed to the polity by monastic immunity. Next, Alan Cromartie re-examines the intellectual history of common law equity. He traces the Christian identification of the Greek concept of *epieikeia* first with a divine master law and, subsequently, with a discretionary power reserved for the monarch. Christopher St German's influential theorization, he argues, 'tended to sever equity from kingship', and led eventually, via Plowden, to Edward Hake's identification of equity with the common law's capacity to develop by generating exceptions. Ethan Shagan's chapter on Richard Hooker and Jason Rosenblatt and Elliott Visconsi's chapters on John Selden describe learned attempts to carve out a space of inner liberty of conscience by describing all law, however touching on religious concerns, as civil in its institution. Rosenblatt recreates the drama of Selden's philological victory over the Presbyterians over the meaning of the Hebrew word for 'excommunication' or expulsion from the synagogue. He notes Selden's insistence that a man's fitness or not to receive the sacrament could not be the subject of judicial knowledge. Concurring, Elliott Visconsi's chapter further observes that, for all his anti-clericalism, Selden does not object to an established Church, seeing it as a kind of national legal tradition, that is, as 'an emanation of the dynamic religion and political traditions, customs, and social norms of a specific people'. Ethan Shagan notes that Hooker's *Laws of Ecclesiastical Polity* ingeniously offers 'a theological argument for why theology doesn't matter in the creation and enforcement of ecclesiastical law'. Unlike Visconsi, however, Shagan isolates the problem with trying to identify the Anglican Church as a specific kind of English legal tradition. The Anglican Church, he says, 'had legal jurisdiction over precisely the sphere of private, ethical, spiritual, and conscientious matters that *in some sense* transcended the remit of law itself'. However Hooker and Selden might try to limit the Church's regulatory power to matters external, the question of in what sense its jurisdiction touched on private, ethical, spiritual, and conscientious matters remained one which, as Shagan says, 'required theological answers'.

Legal and Literary Imagining

'Legal and Literary Imagining', the title of Part V, should evidently not be taken to define other sections as unconcerned with the relations of law and literature. Yet this section is more centrally focused than others on the question of how contemporary legal developments are registered in works of the imagination. Here we may be surprised to find Luke Wilson cautioning against the contemporary tendency to regard the literary text as a 'highly sensitive seismograph registering every cultural signal that crossed its path'. Demonstrating the extremely wobbly grasp of contract law exhibited by such a successful theatrical entrepreneur as Philip Henslowe, Wilson goes on to propose that contract should be understood, in literary terms, less as a local move in legal thinking and more as an element, like riddle or prophecy, that structures literary genre. The historian Tim Stretton, conversely, illuminates the genre known to literary critics as 'City Comedy' by pointing to transformative developments in economic relations and marriage practice. The customary right of dower was gradually, in this period, replaced by a negotiable contractual interest known as jointure; at the same time bonds increasingly came to be used to set down marital conditions and commitments. These major changes represented increased opportunities for those with wit to exploit them, and fewer protections for those without: a 'collective loss of contractual innocence', as Stretton calls it, offering a wonderfully illuminating survey of such legal instruments in the plots of Jacobean city comedy. The Inns men whose literary activities were discussed in Part II appear at the margins of Carolyn Sale's chapter. The female poet, Isabella Whitney, knew writers in the Inns and consciously invoked humanist ideas of *imitatio* and communal literary property in versifying, in her own *Swete Nosgay* (1573), the philosophical 'flowers' of Hugh Platt of Lincoln's Inn. Sale offers an innovative reading of Whitney's lively poetic will and testament to London in the context of the changes wrought by the Statute of Wills (1540) which worked, she argues, to reify abstract notions of ownership. Frances Dolan interrogates the commonplace identification of the witch as old and unmarried, the very antithesis of the perfect wife. She detects, in guides to marriage as well as in witchcraft cases, a language that evokes fears of the inaccessibility and dangerous efficacy of wifely wishes and desires. Henry Turner's chapter concludes Part V with an analysis of the fiction of the corporation as a legal person. Although Kantorowicz's analysis of this fiction as the king's 'body politic' has been much drawn upon in literary criticism, Turner's chapter is the first to explore in detail the intricate interdependences of its poetic and legal developments from Spenser and Shakespeare to Coke and Bacon.

Libel, Publication, and the Press

Literature and law are inevitably drawn together in the history of libel and censorship: one of the functions of the author, after all, is to be legally liable for publicly disseminated words. The mocking rhymes that James Sharpe discussed in the context of community regulation here reemerge as material coming before the Star Chamber in the early seventeenth century. Part VI looks at legal-literary connections in two ways. It considers how a heterogeneously derived set of legal actions and regulatory practices has been construed in interpreting the politics of censorship and prosecutions for libel pre-1640s and it examines how print and drama themselves exploited the ideological and emotional potential of the common law's identification of torture as extra-legal and tyrannical. David Ibbetson asks whether, as some literary critics have claimed, Roman law lies behind the English law of libel as formulated in Coke's report on the case of Lewis Pickering's libel on Archbishop Whitgift, known as *De libellis famosis*. Ibbetson first contextualizes the case within a history of common and canon law defamation and a history of the Star Chamber, before turning to Coke's authorial voice (discernible in the deletions and insertion in the manuscript). He concludes that nothing, in fact, hinged on Coke's distinction between the slander of a private person and that of a magistrate, and finds that the report's Roman colouring is superficial. Joad Raymond takes up the revisionists' case against an older Whig history of seventeenth-century censorship as the draconian, systematic control of public speech. Raymond argues while the Whig history has been rightly discredited, 'unsystematic' does not mean 'non-existent' and the argument that some licensing procedures were commercial does not mean that they were not available to the authorities for ideological use. Likewise, the lack of evidence for a ban on printed domestic news does not mean that the non-existence of such news shows there was no demand for it. Censorship, he concludes, is not a single system, but a spectrum of practices. Martin Dzelzainis offers an account of the complex ideological and professional implication of various agents—journeymen printers, stationers and authors—in the imposition of the Printing Act of 1662. Focusing on the coerced surveillance work of the dissenter, George Larkin, Dzelzainis amply illustrates the hazards of the journeyman printer's position with respect to the investigative procedures entailed by the Act. Finally, Alistair Bellany turns from libel as legally prosecuted to libel as exploitative of an emerging ideology of English common law liberty. Bellany investigates a crux in the legal history of English torture: the question of whether or not the use of torture was debated in the case of John Felton, the assassin of the Duke of Buckingham, in 1628. Bellany's focus is the burgeoning news culture, apparent in manuscript and print newsletters and 'libels', in which the martyrological drama of Felton's readiness to be tortured positioned the regime as tyrannous, polarizing political feeling.

Liberties, Slaveries, and English Law

Part VII concerns the emergence of the ideology of the English common law as superior to other laws and as the protector of English liberties, an ideology traceable back at least as far as John Fortescue's *De laudibus legum Anglie* (*c*.1470). Bellany's chapter in Part VI concludes with a reading of Philip Massinger's *The Roman Actor* (1626), thus forging a link with the opening chapter of Part VII, in which Bernadette Meyler poses the question of how Massinger's 1623 tragedy, *The Bondman*, a play about a slave rebellion, managed to appeal across the spectrum of seventeenth-century political opinion, from royalists to republicans. Meyler's answer involves an analysis of the politics of Senecan stoicism and its appropriation as a discourse in which a 'due course of law' incorporating equity offers a new vision of the state. The emergence of 'due process' as a legal ideal, indeed, as a national birthright is Paul Halliday's subject. Around the turn of the seventeenth century, Halliday explains, the language of birthright associated with the story Jacob and Esau migrated from theological to legal discourse. From its implication in a parable about salvation, the idea of birthright became the expression of a lay longing for greater specificity about the legal protections and procedural rights that English subjects could expect. In conclusion Halliday pays tribute to the power of this imagining, this transformation of a biblical story into the vision of a legal world. In the following chapter, Nigel Smith illustrates the kind of power to which Halliday refers in a discussion of John Lilburne's development of the rhetoric of the freeborn Englishman. As Smith argues, Lilburne offered an unprecedented account of the common law, and particularly of chapter 29 of Magna Carta, as a guarantor of liberties not of 'the subject' but of '*English*men'. Mary Nyquist traces the semantic incoherence of the term 'slave' and its cognates in the literature of the period, revealing the work of racialization performed both by semantic slippage and by its appearance, in some cases, in the more or less covert context of the Roman law of war slavery. Nyquist concludes by revealing the deployment of war slavery doctrine in the famously long and intricate denouement of Shakespeare's *Cymbeline*. In terms which recall Bernadette Meyler's opening discussion of the ideological stakes of representations of clemency and pardoning, Nyquist shows how Shakespeare's staging of the Britons' voluntary submission to Rome produces a vision of Britain as the tributary nation which (unlike colonial Ireland) will preserve its sovereignty and become imperial.

The Extra-English Legal World: Between Nation, Colony, and Empire

Chapters throughout the Handbook have cumulatively built up a picture of the period 1500–1700 as one which sees the emergence of an established Church 'like a legal tradition' and the emergence of an identification of Englishness with liberties protected by legal 'due process'. How does the emergence of this powerfully nationalistic common law ideology relate to what Dan Hulsebosch in Part VIII calls 'the extra-English legal world'? How does it relate to the uses of common law in England's colonization of Ireland and America, to the question of England's title to Scotland, to different Scottish legal traditions, to the rise of international law, and to the legal rights of emigrants to the American colonies? Like Nyquist's chapter in Part VII, all the chapters in Part VIII explore literary dimensions of these questions, ranging over epic and lyric poetry, history plays and heroic drama, and the language of charters. Andrew Zurcher takes up the topic of the common law's conceptualization of intention in sixteenth-century case thinking about homicide, equity, and contract. He argues that in all these areas the common law was endowing objects with intention much as poets use the figure of 'hypallage' to transfer intention and passion from a human agent to an object (i.e. 'angry blade'). Zurcher shows how both Spenser's epic poetry in *The Faerie Queene* and his colonial programme of Irish reform employ hypallage as a key figure. Acknowledging the value of legal-literary scholarship in the study of early modern England, Rab Houston surveys the potential for a similar approach to Scots poetry and legal institutions. His chapter reveals rich yet unexplored connections between early Scots literature and law: William Dunbar, Gavin Douglas, Robert Henryson, Alexander Montgomerie, and William Drummon of Hawthorndon all had legal connections and made use of legal terminology and trial scenes in their verse. Though the Scottish legal infrastructure differed from that of England, Houston makes a strong case for exploring the specificity of its early modern legal-literary relations.

Lorna Hutson and Christopher Warren take up, in different ways, the engagement of Shakespeare's *Henry V* with questions of justice and sovereignty. Hutson looks at Shakespeare's careful revision of key sources from the 1540s English invasion of Scotland that situate Henry V's invasion of France within a history of England's claim to overlordship over Scotland. She argues that Shakespeare makes brilliant use of forensic rhetoric to shift legal questions of national sovereignty into apparently universal questions of inwardness, so that we ask not, 'is this cause just?', but 'what is Henry thinking?' The result reimagines a tripartite war of English, Scots, and French as a vision of the plucky English against the might of 'overseas', thus covertly asserting English sovereignty over Scotland. Christopher Warren, by contrast, looks to *Henry V* to consider the history-versus-law question of whether it is by definition anachronistic to judge the past. He proposes Shakespeare knew Alberico Gentili's *De armis Romanis* (1599), which debates the justice of the Roman empire. Arguing for this as the source of Fluellen's 'disciplines of the Roman wars', Warren concludes that Shakespeare's play subjects Henry's expansionist wars to this emergent international legal scrutiny.

Edward Holberton and Dan Hulsebosch move the Handbook's concerns towards America and to legal and literary debates on the basis of England's imperium and with the rights, liberties, and privileges of emigrant colonists. Holberton's chapter demonstrates how Dryden's heroic drama explicitly contrasts English imperial claims with those of Spanish papal dominion and goes on to explore the tonal difficulties of Dryden's *Conquest of Granada* (1670) in terms of Dryden's sceptical interest in the new contractual theories of sovereignty which theoretically base political allegiance in volatile passions and interests. Hulsebosch examines the productive ambiguities of the formulae of 'liberties', 'privileges', and 'immunities' that, deriving largely from medieval and Tudor migrations to France and Ireland, were nevertheless repurposed and redeployed in the context of colonial emigration to America. Eschewing both the instrumentalist approaches which discount the legal formulae as cynical cover stories for self-interest, and the formalist approaches which take the formulae at the letter, Hulsebosch develops a functionalist approach, categorizing claims for liberties, privileges, and immunities according to a creative taxonomy of legal functions—doors, windows, floors, ceilings, and mirrors—that describe the emerging legal architecture of empire.

PART I

TEXTUAL AND INTERPRETATIVE CULTURE

CHAPTER 1

FORENSIC RHETORIC AND HUMANIST EDUCATION

KATHY EDEN

Two prominent voices in the chorus for 'humanizing' education in early sixteenth century England, Erasmus of Rotterdam and Thomas Elyot, remind their early modern readers of the deep ties between the literary studies that form the foundation of this education and the law. In his influential *The Book Named the Governor* (1531), Elyot, whose education included Oxford and the Middle Temple, traces back to ancient rhetoric 'the pleading used in Court and Chancery called moots'—the foundational exercise of legal training rooted in fictional cases still used in English and American law schools today; for the law student, like the ancient orator, must know how to identify the controversy in question, invent, arrange, and memorize his arguments, narrate events, prove his points, and refute his opponent, the very skills covered in the rhetorical manuals of Cicero and Quintilian.[1] On the other hand, Elyot bemoans the premature professionalization of the English lawyer, whose specialized education in the Inns of Court as early as age fourteen or fifteen stunts his intellectual and moral development, thereby depriving him and his country of the statesmanly wisdom that comes from a fuller exposure (through at least his twenty-first birthday) to the so-called 'circle of doctrine', an educational curriculum grounded in Erasmian *bonae literae*.[2]

As chief spokesman for this curriculum, the Dutch humanist himself, unlike Elyot, owes *his* perspective on education exclusively to the schools, including the grammar school and the university.[3] Inexperienced in the legal training undertaken by men like Elyot and his own best friend Thomas More, Erasmus nevertheless, like Elyot, records

[1] Sir Thomas Elyot, *The Book Named the Governor*, ed. S. E. Lehmberg (London: Dent, 1907; rpt New York: Dutton, 1962), 53–4.

[2] Elyot, *The Governor*, 46. On Elyot's 'circle of doctrine' as a translation of Quintilian's *orbs doctrinae*, a translation in turn of the Greek ἐνκύκλιος παιδεία, see Quintilian 1.10.1.

[3] On Erasmus' education, see Cornelis Augustijn, *Erasmus: His Life, Works, and Influence*, trans. J. C. Grayson (Toronto: University of Toronto Press, 1991), 21–9.

a dim view of its effects on the minds of the young. As part of this record, his satirical *Ciceronianus* (1528) blames More's limited literary output on his parents' decision to have their young son study English law, the most unliterary—even illiterate (*quibus nihil illiteratius*)—of studies.[4] But Erasmus' disdain for legal training should not obscure the profound impact of legal principles and practices on his wildly popular textbooks. Setting the course for English literary education for generations, these textbooks openly acknowledge their debt not only, like Elyot's mooting, to ancient rhetoric but to forensic rhetoric, the rhetoric of the law courts. What follows is a closer look at this debt of early modern English literary studies to legal rhetoric—a debt that not only looks back to curricular reforms elsewhere but that leaves a lasting mark on the building blocks and basic exercises of this reformed humanist curriculum.

Well underway by the time the *Ciceronianus* and *The Book Named the Governor* are being written, the 'humanizing' of education in England begins in the fifteenth century. At Oxford in particular, Englishmen are not only bringing the 'new learning' back from their Italian travels but welcoming their new-found Italian friends into their own academic circles. As one recent scholar of the period has persuasively demonstrated, these Italian humanists, many of them lawyers, are the product of a culture deeply entrenched in legal and rhetorical thinking.[5] Some of these early Italian visitors to England actually play a role in recovering the lost texts—like Cicero's *De oratore* and Quintilian's *Institutio oratoria*—that underwrite the revised university curriculum; others are reading and lecturing on these same texts, eventually at the behest of university authorities.[6]

Curricular reform in the grammar school, on the other hand, takes its direction from one English educator in particular who similarly finds inspiration in travelling abroad. In 1497 John Colet, another of Erasmus' friends, returns from Italy with big plans that will in time involve the Dutch humanist in revitalizing the teaching of the trivium to young boys. At Colet's request, Erasmus agrees not only to collaborate with William Lily on revamping an introduction to Latin grammar but also to revise his teaching notes on rhetoric into a textbook for St Paul's.[7] This revision, which becomes the bestselling *De copia verborum et rerum*, counts as essential reading for schoolmasters,

[4] Erasmus, *Ciceronianus* in *CWE*, 28, 423; in Latin, ASD, I–2, 678.

[5] Ronald G. Witt, *The Two Latin Cultures and the Foundation of Renaissance Humanism in Medieval Italy* (Cambridge: Cambridge University Press, 2012), 229–67. See also John Monfasani, 'Humanism and Rhetoric' in *Renaissance Humanism: Foundations, Forms, and Legacy*, ed. Albert Rabil, Jr, 3 vols (Philadelphia: University of Pennsylvania Press, 1988), 3.171–235.

[6] On the Italian influences on English humanism, including the visits of Poggio Bracciolini, who discovers the complete *Institutio oratoria* in 1416, and Gerardo Landriani, who discovers a complete *De oratore* along with the *Orator* and the *Brutus* in 1421, see Roberto Weiss, *Humanism in England during the Fifteenth Century*, 3rd edn (Oxford: Blackwell, 1967). See also Benjamin G. Kohl, 'Humanism and Education', in *Renaissance Humanism*, ed. Rabil, 3.5–22.

[7] On St Paul's, see T. W. Baldwin, *William Shakspere's Small Latine and Lesse Greeke*, 2 vols (Urbana: University of Illinois Press, 1944), 1.118–33, esp. 130, which maintains that 'the texts which Erasmus wrote for Paul's and elsewhere became almost universally the grammar school texts of England'. See also Joan Simon, *Education and Society in Tudor England* (Cambridge: Cambridge University Press, 1966), 73–80.

grammar-schoolers, and university students alike; and unlike most of its medieval predecessors, it folds preliminary training in logic into a broader rhetorical programme. In the English grammar school as in the university, in other words, rhetoric reclaims the status it enjoyed in antiquity as the master language art.

Fundamental to this art despite its development over time is its origin in legal dispute. In the oldest full-fledged history of this development, Cicero insists—on Aristotle's authority—that the Sicilians Corax and Tisias first formulated their rhetorical precepts as aids to citizens staking legal claims to private property (*Brutus* 46).[8] Aristotle himself confirms this origin with his complaint that rhetoricians of his own day continue to attend almost exclusively to forensic strategies (*Rhetoric* 1.1.10). And Quintilian offers further confirmation, despite his disdain (like Aristotle's) for those who restrict their treatment to forensic oratory (*Institutio oratoria* 3.1.1), by dividing the art of rhetoric into what pertains to the law courts and what does not (3.4.6) and by locating the original oratorical occasion, contrary to common wisdom, in the accusation rather than the defence (3.2.2). The very architecture of the ancient rhetorical manuals most widely used and highly regarded in early modernity, the pseudo-Ciceronian *Ad Herennium*, Cicero's *De inventione*, and Quintilian's own *Institutio oratoria*, reflects this historical reconstruction; for all of them give forensic oratory pride of place not only by treating it before deliberative and epideictic oratory but by devoting many (many) more pages to its treatment.[9] These same favourite manuals also make no effort to conceal the fact that the building blocks of invention, the part of the rhetorical art devoted to discovering available arguments, are designed initially to meet the demands of the law court.

Chief among these building blocks is the *causa*, the *cause* or *case*. All the manuals agree that there are three of them, the so-called *tria genera causarum*: forensic, deliberative, and epideictic. The term *causa* or *cause*, in other words, applies to any speech dealing with a set of particulars, whether it takes place at an assembly, a festival, or a trial (*De inv.* 1.6.8). On the other hand, the term *causa* never loses its legal pedigree, either in Latin or in English. Cicero cannot help reminding his readers that his own Greek authority, Hermagoras, considers legal oratory the genus and deliberative and epideictic oratory mere species (*De inv.* 1.9.12).

About a century and a half later, Quintilian laments the confusion regarding this term *causa*, inherited from the Greek term *aitia* (3.11.6), insofar as it can refer either

[8] On the rediscovery of Cicero's *Brutus* and its impact on early modern literary history, see Martin McLaughlin, 'Humanist Concepts of Renaissance and Middle Ages in the Tre- and Quattrocentro', *Renaissance Studies*, 2 (1988), 131–2; and Kathy Eden, 'Cicero *Redivivus* and the Historicizing of Renaissance Style' in *Inventing a Path: Studies in Medieval Rhetoric in Honour of Mary Carruthers*, ed. Laura Iseppi De Filippis (Turnhout: Brepols, 2012), 143–69.

[9] In the *Ad Herennium*, for instance, most of Book 1 and all of Book 2 address the forensic oration, while deliberative and epideictic oratory are covered in the beginning of Book 3 (3.2.2–3.8.15). Similarly, in the *De inventione*, Cicero addresses forensic oratory at 2.4.14–2.51.154, for a total of 130 paragraphs, in contrast to deliberative and epideictic, covered at 2.51.155–2.59.178, for a total of twenty-two paragraphs. On the impact of these manuals, with their forensic orientation, on Shakespeare's dramaturgy, see Quentin Skinner, *Forensic Shakespeare* (Oxford: Oxford University Press, 2014).

to the kind of case or to the motive for the act the case adjudicates. His illustration of this confusion, focusing on two famous cases alleging murder (Clytemnestra's killing of Agamemnon and Orestes' killing of Clytemnestra), sets in high relief the term's ineradicable forensic underpinnings. About a millennium and a half after Quintilian, Thomas Wilson, well educated in *bonae literae* as well as civil law and writing his *Art of Rhetoric* (1553) for other Englishmen wanting an education in oratory, echoes Cicero and Quintilian in pointing out that all orators handle *causes*. In doing so, however, Wilson highlights the legal dimension of this handling when he describes it as 'one affirming for his part and the other denying as fast again for his part'.[10] For it is the forensic occasion that makes a regular practice of meeting affirmations with denials. Both the affirmer and the denier, moreover, must first agree upon and then address in their arguments the key point of contention, the so-called *status* of the case.

Although he prefers to translate Latin *status* (and the Ciceronian *constitutio*) as *issue* rather than *state* (or *constitution)*, Wilson describes for his sixteenth-century English readers the fundamentally Hermagorean—which is to say, legal—*status* system endorsed by the combined authority of the *Ad Herennium, De inventione*, and *Institutio oratoria*. 'A state, therefore, in matters of judgment', Wilson explains,[11]

> is that thing which doth arise upon the first demand and denial made betwixt men, whereof the one part is the accuser, and the other part the person or persons accused. It is called a state because we do stand and rest upon some one point, the which must wholly and only be proved of the one side and denied of the other. I cannot better term it in English than by the name of an issue...

Further in keeping with his ancient authorities, Wilson enumerates three kinds of issue, each addressing a different question: the conjectural *status* asks 'whether the thing be or no' (Lat. *sitne?*); the legal or definitional asks 'what it is' (Lat. *quid sit?*); and the juridical or qualitative asks 'what manner of thing it is' (Lat. *quale sit?*).[12] Only a foolish orator, ancient and early modern rhetoricians agree, would begin to assemble his arguments before establishing the *status* of his *cause*. And these same rhetoricians insist that this fundamentally forensic strategy pertains to deliberative and epideictic oratory as well (*De inventione* 2.4.12–13; *Institutio oratoria* 3.6.1, 3.6.80–1). In the *De copia*, Erasmus even recommends it for his schoolboys since they too can benefit from 'the precepts of the rhetoricians concerning the main types of issue (*de causarum capitibus*), which Quintilian calls *status*, the Greeks στάσεις'.[13] Like their oratorically inclined elders, Erasmus insists,

[10] Thomas Wilson, *The Art of Rhetoric*, ed. Peter E. Medine (University Park: Penn State University Press, 1994), 46.

[11] Wilson, *Art of Rhetoric*, 122–3.

[12] Wilson, *Art of Rhetoric*, 123. See also *Ad Herennium* 1.10.18; *De inventione* 1.8.10–1.9.12; Quintilian 3.6.5 and 3.6.45–6. On the qualitative status and its impact on literature, see Wesley Trimpi, *Muses of One Mind: The Literary Analysis of Experience and Its Continuity* (Princeton: Princeton University Press, 1983), 243–361.

[13] Erasmus, *De copia*, *CWE*, 24, 605; ASD, I–6, 228 l. 796. On the status system, see Otto Alvin Loeb Dieter, 'Stasis', *Speech Monographs*, 17, no. 4 (1950), 345–69; Michael Sloan, 'Aristotle's *Nicomachean Ethics*

these youngsters must grasp the main point or issue to be argued before they begin not only to write or speak but even to consider inventing their arguments or proofs.

Schoolboys must also understand that proofs come in two kinds: those that require invention, which Quintilian and others call *artificiales* (Gr. *entechnoi*) in that they are products of the art, and those called *inartificiales* (Gr. *atechnoi*) because they are supplied by the case itself (*Institutio oratoria* 5.1.1–2). Among the *inartificial proofs*, according to Erasmus and others, are legal judgements, hearsay evidence, evidence extracted under torture, written evidence, oaths, and witnesses.[14] Not surprisingly, Erasmus' authority Quintilian introduces both kinds of proof in the context of forensic oratory in the fifth book of his twelve-book manual on educating the orator. Given the distance between the schoolroom and the courtroom, these inartificial proofs might seem to have little bearing on the composition exercises of the grammar school (see below, pp. 30–2). Invented or artificial proofs, on the other hand, are exactly what the schoolmaster must teach his young student to construct; and the *circumstances*, Erasmus leaves no doubt, are fundamental to this construction.

Once students have determined the status or issue informing their composition, in other words, they must turn their attention to its *circumstances*. These are key to finding (or 'inventing') compelling proofs or arguments.[15] Once again Erasmus' authority is Quintilian, who introduces the *circumstantiae* (Gr. *peristaseis*), like the inartificial proofs, as part of his treatment of forensic oratory, at once associating them with what is peculiar or *propria* to an individual case, in contrast to what applies commonly (*communia*) to all or most cases, and recommending them as the source of the strongest proofs.[16] Confirming both Quintilian's authority and the singular importance of the circumstances to rhetorical training, Wilson offers his English readers the following mnemonic in verse:[17]

> Who, what, and where, by what help, and by whose
> Why, how and when, do many things disclose.

as the Original Locus for the *Septem Circumstantiae*', *Classical Quarterly*, 105 (2010), 236–51. On the widespread use of Erasmus' *De copia* in English schools, see Baldwin, *Shakspere's Small Latine*, 2.179–96; Peter Mack, *A History of Renaissance Rhetoric, 1380–1620* (Oxford: Oxford University Press, 2011), 80–8.

[14] *CWE*, 24, 605; ASD, I–6, 230 ll. 806–9. See also *Ad Herennium* 2.6.9 and Quintilian 5.1.1–5.1.3; R. W. Serjeantson, 'Testimony: The Artless Proof', in *Renaissance Figures of Speech*, ed. Sylvia Adamson, Gavin Alexander, and Katrin Ettenhuber (Cambridge: Cambridge University Press, 2007), 181–94. For Aristotle on the two kinds of proof, see Kathy Eden, *Poetic and Legal Fiction in the Aristotelian Tradition* (Princeton: Princeton University Press, 1986; rpt Princeton Legacy Library, 2014), 12–24.

[15] *De copia*, *CWE*, 24, 604–5; ASD, I–6, 230 ll. 811–14.

[16] Quintilian 5.10.103–4. See also *De copia*, *CWE*, 24, 591–2; ASD, I–6, 218 ll. 514–28. On Veltkirchius's discussion of Erasmus' treatment of the circumstances in his widely used school commentary on *De copia*, see Baldwin, *Shakspere's Small Latine*, 2.316–18; and see D. W. Robertson, Jr, 'A Note on the Classical Origin of "Circumstances" in the Medieval Confessional', *SP*, 43 (1946), 6–14. For the impact of the circumstances on the literary production of the period, and especially on early modern English drama, see Lorna Hutson, *Circumstantial Shakespeare* (Oxford: Oxford University Press, 2015).

[17] Wilson, *Art of Rhetoric*, 60; on Quintilian's authority, see 62.

Immediately preceding this verse is a corresponding list that preserves even more clearly the legal dimension of circumstantiality:[18]

1. Who did the deed
2. What was done
3. Where it was done
4. What help had he to it
5. Wherefore he did it
6. How he did it
7. At what time he did it

Both list and verse, it is worth noting, are part of Wilson's treatment of epideictic (or demonstrative) oratory, which he, unlike his ancient predecessors but like many other early modern rhetoricians, discusses before deliberative and forensic, presumably in order of increasing complexity. For Wilson, in other words, the circumstances, despite their legal origin, are no less fundamental to a speech *praising* King David than to one *accusing* his enemy Goliath.[19] Wilson then ends an analysis of his own exemplary epideictic oration with the telling remark that 'by circumstances of things, a right worthy cause may be plentifully enlarged'.[20]

This 'plentiful enlargement' gets to the very heart of Erasmus' instruction to young schoolboys in the *De copia*, where the circumstances enable a number of strategies for enlarging or enriching student compositions, including comparison and description. Following Quintilian, Erasmus considers Cicero at once the grand master of the comparison richly circumstanced and the source of the theory behind the practice. Whereas Cicero briefly treats the comparison or *collatio* as a kind of similitude (*similitudo*) in a section of the *De inventione* on proof (1.49), Quintilian expands this treatment to include the fictitious supposition or, as the Greeks call it, the hypothetical (*kath'hypothesin*). Quintilian defines this hypothetical as 'putting forward something which, if true, would either destroy the point raised or strengthen it; and secondly, making the subject of the inquiry appear parallel to our fiction'.[21] Concerned that beginning students might not grasp from this definition the power of fiction to decide legal cases, the Roman schoolmaster provides a number of examples from the forum, relying mostly on Cicero's orations.

Looking out for his own young readers but less overt in linking the *comparison* to the law court, Erasmus aligns the Ciceronian *collatio* with the *parabola* (or *parable*), aligned in turn with the fictional narration (*ficta narratio*), defined, echoing Quintilian,

[18] Wilson, *Art of Rhetoric*, 60.

[19] Wilson, *Art of Rhetoric*, 60–5.

[20] Wilson, *Art of Rhetoric*, 65.

[21] Quintilian, *The Orator's Education*, trans. Donald A. Russell, 5 vols (Cambridge, MA: Harvard University Press, 2001), 5.10.96. On the role of fiction in literature and law, see Eden, *Poetic and Legal Fiction*.

as an *exemplum* introduced 'as if [it] were true because [it] will help us to get our point across'.[22] As an illustration of the hypothetical, however, Erasmus turns not to Cicero but to Plato, whose parable of the cave goes a long way in clinching Socrates' case for the reality of the noumenal world and against the reliability of sensory experience.[23] In *The Art of Rhetoric*, Wilson strongly endorses these 'feigned narrations' that 'help well to set forward a cause', offering More's hypothetical Utopia as a prime example.[24] Philip Sidney seconds this endorsement in his *Apology for Poetry*, which makes its case by highlighting the points of contact between the lawyer's legal fiction and the poet's 'imaginative ground-plot'.[25] Even if early modern grammar school students and their elders in university were unprepared to appreciate this deeper bond between literature and the law, their humanist education prepared them to develop this appreciation later in life and maybe even, like More and Sidney, to capitalize on it in their own imaginative fictions.

Whereas Cicero ranks first in the *De copia* as a maker of comparisons, fictional or otherwise, the consummate describer is Homer, who sets the scene with such *evidentia* or vividness (Gr. *enargeia*) that readers can easily imagine themselves as eye-witnesses.[26] For his treatment of this method of enrichment, Erasmus combines two discussions in Quintilian: one from Book 4, where *evidentia* features as a quality of the forensic narration; the other from Book 8, where it forms part of an inventory of stylistic tropes and figures.[27] In both sections, Quintilian stresses the orator's obligation to show rather than tell by bringing the events he narrates or the scenes he describes before the eyes (*ante oculos, in rem praesentem*) of the judge. Passing along the Roman schoolmaster's advice to his own young readers, Erasmus emphasizes in turn the role of the *circumstances* in creating this effect. 'I think I should remind you', he writes, 'that descriptions of this sort consist mainly in the exposition of circumstantial details (*circunstantiarum explicatione*), especially those which make the incident particularly vivid (*praesertim quae rem oculis maxime subiiciunt*), and give the narrative distinctiveness.'[28] Regarding the blind bard's unparalleled skill in creating this *evidential* effect, Erasmus then asks, 'Is there anything [Homer] does not display vividly before our eyes (*non exponit oculis*) by putting in the appropriate circumstantial detail (*aptis circunstantiis*), which, even if it sometimes seems insignificant, yet somehow or other presents the thing marvelously to

[22] *De copia*, *CWE*, 24, 634; ASD, I-6, 256 ll. 476–8.

[23] *CWE*, 24, 634–5; ASD, I-6, 256 ll. 476–258 ll. 493.

[24] Wilson, *Art of Rhetoric*, 222.

[25] Philip Sidney, *An Apology for Poetry*, ed. Geoffrey Shepherd (London: Thomas Nelson and Sons, 1965), 124. Like Wilson, Sidney cites the *Utopia* as a prime example (108). See also Eden, *Poetic and Legal Fiction*, 3–6 and 157–75.

[26] *De copia*, *CWE*, 24, 577–80; ASD, I-6, 202 l. 160–204 l. 242. On *evidentia*, including its association with the law court, see Eden, *Poetic and Legal Fiction*, 71–4 and 87–92.

[27] *Evidentia* is not the only stylistic figure with ties to the law court. On *martyria* or *testatio* in Henry Peacham's *The Garden of Eloquence*, see Serjeantson, 'Testimony', 188. On the relation between style and the law, and especially property law, see Kathy Eden, *The Renaissance Rediscovery of Intimacy* (Chicago: University of Chicago Press, 2012).

[28] *De copia*, *CWE*, 24, 579; ASD, I-6, 204 ll. 215–17.

our eyes' (*in modum rem oculis subiiciunt*)?[29] Even when seemingly far afield of forensic concerns, rhetorical circumstantiality, characteristic of the best poetry as well as the best oratory, retains its deep connection to legal evidence.

But the *circumstantiae* are fundamental not only to the task of the young writer or speaker. Young readers need them too, as the forward-looking schoolmaster Philoponus in John Brinsley's early seventeenth-century dialogue about the English grammar school, *Ludus Literarius* (1612), insists. Like Wilson, Brinsley's Philoponus offers an easily remembered verse—*Quis, cui, causa, locus, quo tempore, prima sequela*—which he mercifully follows with an explanation in English:[30]

> That is, who speaks in that place, what he speaks, to whom he speaks, upon what occasion he speaks, or to what end, where he spake, at what time it was, what went before in the sentences next [*sic*], what followeth next after. This verse I would have every such scholar to have readily; and always to think of it in his construing.

Although Brinsley, like Wilson, lists seven circumstances, the two lists do not completely overlap as Brinsley accommodates the rhetorical goal of persuasion to the hermeneutic goal of understanding, especially textual understanding. Despite the discrepancy, however, Brinsley's accommodation is rooted in ancient—especially forensic—rhetoric, which, as we have seen, takes written documents, including laws and testamentary evidence, into account among its inartificial proofs.

The ancient rhetorical manuals so fundamental to humanist education, in other words, address the rules for interpreting as well as composing discourse. In *De inventione*, for instance, Cicero provides guidelines for interpreting various kinds of writing, including laws, wills, and witness testimony, depending on whether their meaning is unclear as a result of the ambiguity of key words, some internal contradiction, or the underlying discrepancy between what the *scriptor*—who could be a legislator, a testator, or a witness—wrote and what he meant (1.13.17–18, 2.40.116–17).[31] Among the strategies for resolving these controversies, Cicero recommends examining what precedes the controversial passage or passages in the text and what comes after—Brinsley's *prima* and *sequela*: 'what went before' and 'what followeth next after'. Illustrating this recommendation with a legal case between a mother and son over disputed property, Cicero concludes:[32]

> from what precedes or follows in the document (*ex superiore et ex inferiore scriptura*) the doubtful point becomes plain. Therefore, if words are to be considered separately

[29] *De copia*, *CWE*, 24, 580; ASD, I–6, 204 ll. 238–40.

[30] John Brinsley, *Ludus Literarius: or, The Grammar Schoole* (Menston, England: The Scholar Press Limited, 1968), 123 (spelling modernized).

[31] See also Quintilian 7.6.1–7.9.15; Kathy Eden, *Hermeneutics and the Rhetorical Tradition: Chapters in the Ancient Legacy and Its Humanist Reception* (New Haven: Yale University Press, 1997), 7–19, 70–8.

[32] *De inventione*, trans. H. M. Hubbell (Cambridge, MA: Harvard University Press, 1949; rpt 1976), 2.40.117.

> by themselves, every word, or at least many words, would seem ambiguous; but it is not right to regard as ambiguous what becomes plain on consideration of the whole context (*ex omni considerata scriptura*).

Whereas the preeminent Roman orator (who also happens to be a lawyer) takes the law court with its presentation of evidence as the principal site of interpretive disputes regarding texts, his Elizabethan counterparts comfortably adapt the rhetorical rules of legal *interpretatio scripti* to a very different kind of *scriptura*.[33]

In *The Art of Rhetoric*, for instance, Wilson both rehearses the three Ciceronian legal strategies for resolving textual controversy and extends these strategies to reading the Bible, and especially the New Testament. Unlike Cicero, however, Wilson does not in good lawyerly fashion offer arguments on both sides of the question, that is *for* and *against* a strictly literal, in contrast to a spiritual (or equitable), interpretation of Scripture. On the contrary, he insists that a reading of Christ's laws would be absurd if 'taken according as they are spoken'.[34] On the other hand, Wilson, like Brinsley, follows Cicero's advice when faced with the task of 'prov[ing] that the will of the lawmaker is none other than I have said' by using 'the testimonies of other places in the Scripture, and compar[ing] them with these sentences, and so judg[ing] by just examination and diligent search the true meaning of the lawmaker'.[35] In keeping with this appropriation of legal to biblical hermeneutics, moreover, Wilson lays bare the link between the legal or definitional status and the hermeneutic portion of rhetorical practice when he labels this section 'The Interpretation of a Law, Otherwise Called the Legal State', followed by a discussion of 'Definition: What It Is'.[36] Like the early modern English orator-in-training, the reader-in-training must learn to assess what is controversial in the texts he reads and wield arguments or proofs to resolve these controversies.

As an accomplished civilian and a devout Christian, Wilson predictably focuses his reading skills on legal documents and holy writ; but as a young schoolboy, he, like other grammar-schoolers, would have honed these same skills on the comedies of Terence and the letters of Cicero. In the *De ratione studii* (1512), an instructor's manual often printed with *De copia*, Erasmus encourages teachers to train their students to read these dramatic and epistolary *argumenta* in light of their circumstances: not only when and where who said (or wrote) what to whom, but why and how it was said (or written)—a reading exercise designed to culminate in a goal the classroom shares with the courtroom: *iudicium* or judgement.[37] These same youngsters should also be taught to rely

[33] Eden, *Hermeneutics and the Rhetorical Tradition*, 41–78.

[34] Wilson, *Art of Rhetoric*, 129.

[35] Wilson, *Art of Rhetoric*, 130. See also Eden, *Hermeneutics and the Rhetorical Tradition*, 79–104.

[36] Wilson, *Art of Rhetoric*, 128. See *De inventione*, 2.51.53–4 and Quintilian 3.6.45–6.

[37] *De ratione studii*, *CWE*, 24, 687; ASD, I–2, 143 ll. 1–2, and *CWE*, 24, 689; ASD, I–2, 144 ll. 17–18. On *judgement* or *iudicium* (Gr. *krisis*) as the last of the four activities in reading literature or *enarratio poetarum*, see Quintilian 1.4.3 and Eden, *Hermeneutics and the Rhetorical Tradition*, 20–40.

on the 'places' or *loci*; for 'by the places and circumstances', Wilson insists, 'great matter might be made'.[38]

Taking into account their notorious complexity and near-inaccessibility to even the most ambitious advanced students, Erasmus folds these 'places of argument' or topics into the latter half of his *De copia*, conceding that '[a]nyone training with a view to acquiring eloquence will have to look at all the possible topics in turn'—a concession he follows with a promise: the student who practices using definitions, etymologies, genera, species, properties, differentiating characteristics, subdivisions, classifications, similarities, dissimilarities, contraries, contradictions, consequences, causes, results, comparisons, and the rest will find that these topics become second nature over time.[39]

Other early modern educators turn their attention more single-mindedly to these topics, taking Cicero's *Topica* as their authority. Among them is Erasmus' protégé Philip Melanchthon, the so-called *praeceptor Germaniae*, whose edition of this challenging Ciceronian treatise becomes a staple of the English grammar schools, substituting in some classrooms for not only the second book of the *Ad Herennium* but the second book of the *De copia*.[40] Even the older student undertaking to master English Common Law is advised to study this difficult ancient textbook. In *The Lawyer's Logike* (1588), Abraham Fraunce, educated first at Cambridge and then at the Inns of Court, touts its importance and accounts for its forensic orientation:[41]

> Tully, at the earnest request of Trebatius, a towardly lawyer of Rome, hath eloquently put down the first part of logike in his Topikes, to the precepts whereof he applieth law-like examples, for the better instruction of Trebatius and helpe of other Lawyers.

Written by a lawyer for a lawyer, Cicero's *Topica*, influential at every stage of education, virtually assures that both the early modern theory and practice of rhetorical composition will retain a forensic orientation.

Like his *De inventione*, in fact, Cicero's *Topica* enforces a fundamental split with obvious links to the law court between intrinsic and extrinsic arguments (*Topica* 8, 24, 95–6)—what Quintilian, following Aristotle's terminology, calls artificial and inartificial proofs. Testimony (*testimonium*), the evidence of a *testis* or legal witness, is the chief source of an argument from an extrinsic topic (*Topica* 72–3), while *definition* (Lat. *definitio*) and

[38] Wilson, *Art of Rhetoric*, 155.

[39] *CWE*, 24, 606; ASD, I–6, 230 ll. 823–9. Given Erasmus' advice here and his treatment of the topics elsewhere, Mack has, I think, underestimated their impact when he states in *Elizabethan Rhetoric* (Cambridge: Cambridge University Press, 2002), 40, that 'None of the textbooks in common use discussed what the Romans considered the more important elements of rhetorical invention: the theory of status, the general topics, and the special topics of judicial rhetoric.' Part and parcel of the complexity of the topics, as Erasmus notes, is the lack of agreement among the experts, including Aristotle, Cicero, Quintilian, and Boethius, on their number, order, and names.

[40] On the use of Cicero's *Topica* in the schools and Melanchthon's popular edition of it, see Baldwin, *Shakspere's Small Latine*, 2.13, 20–1, 31, and 108–37. For Mack's disagreement on the central role of Cicero's *Topica*, see *Elizabethan Rhetoric*, 46.

[41] Abraham Fraunce, *The Lawyers Logike* (Menston, England: Scolar Press, 1969), Preface.

division (Lat. *enumeratio, partitio, divisio*) are the two most widely used intrinsic topics.[42] 'Such is the excellency of distribution and definition', Fraunce asserts, 'that almost they alone do suffice for the absolute putting downe of an art.'[43] Easily elided with the definitional or legal status of the rhetorical manuals, topical definition answers the question *quid sit*: what is it? (*Topica* 26). And it does so, Cicero explains (*Topica* 28–9), by continuing to aggregate or enumerate the elements of the thing being defined until it moves beyond what is *common* to what is *proper*. 'When you have taken all the qualities which the thing you wish to define has in common (*communia*) with other things', Cicero explains, 'you should pursue the analysis until you produce its own distinctive quality (*proprium*) which can be transferred to no other thing.'[44] What belongs to some one thing (or some one person) and not to anything (or anyone) else, then, is its (or his) *property* both in logic and in law. Or, as Quintilian puts it, 'what is common to something else will cease to be a Property' (*quid autem commune cum alio est, desinet esse proprium*).[45] Topical definition, in other words, has deep roots in legal thinking, and especially in thinking about property law, where the basic divisions are between property that is private (*proprium*) and property that is common (*commune*), on the one hand, and between what is my private property (*proprium*) and what belongs to someone else (*alienum*), on the other.

This overlap between legal and logical thinking, reflected in Latin's various uses of *proprietas*, looks at least as far back as Aristotle, who borrows the legal language of accusation for his innovative formulation of the ten *categories* (one of which is property).[46] In *The Lawyer's Logike*, Fraunce's astute etymologies draw attention to Aristotle's borrowing. The Greek word *katēgoria*, Fraunce explains, is:[47]

> borrowed from the place of judgment, and applied to philosophical concepts. Κατεγορεῖσθαι signifieth to say, or affirme one thing of an other, as in accusations it is usually seen, and in arguments easily perceived: where one thing added to an other, is affirmed of the same, or else denied.

Like legal accusations or *katēgoriai*, logical *categories* call forth affirmations and denials, the regular practice of the law courts as 'places of judgement'. And Fraunce's etymology

42 On *testimony*, see also Fraunce, *Lawyers Logike*, 65. For Quintilian on *definition*, see 5.10.54–5. On the difference between *division* and *partition*, see Cicero, *Topica* 30.

43 Fraunce, *Lawyers Logike*, 57.

44 Cicero, *Topica*, trans. H. M. Hubbell (Cambridge, MA: Harvard University Press, 1949; rpt 1976), 29. See also Cicero, *Partitiones oratoriae* 12.41; Quintilian 5.10.58–60; and Fraunce, *Lawyers Logike*, 60.

45 Quintilian 7.3.24.

46 On the legal origins of linguistic *proprietas* or *propriety*, see Quintilian 8.2.1–11; and Eden, *Renaissance Rediscovery of Intimacy*, 44–8. In *Ludus Literarius* (109), Brinsley reminds us of the frequently overlooked distinction between *propriety* and *decorum* when he identifies the 'natural signification' of a word with its 'propriety' and 'word for word' translation as 'in good propriety'.

47 Fraunce, *Lawyers Logike*, 11. On Aristotle's borrowing from the specialized language of law in formulating other fields like psychology, see Eden, *Poetic and Legal Fiction*, 78–84. For Aristotle's acknowledgment that such borrowings, in the form of metaphorical usage, are necessary because of the insufficient supply of words, see *Rhetoric* 3.10.1–4.

of *definition* reveals a similarly legal pedigree. After defining *definition*, following Cicero and Quintilian, in terms of the fundamental division in property law between what is *common* and what is *proper*, Fraunce once again looks back behind the Latin to the Greek origin of the word:[48]

> A definition is called of the Grecians, ὅρος, ὁρισμός, ὁριστικὸς λόγος. Which is a translated word from boundes and limits of grounde. For as they hedge in and include the ground: so doth a definition limite and circumscribe, or, as it were binde in the nature of that which is defined.

Like *katēgoria*, in other words, *horos* has both a legal and a corresponding logical function in marking off or delimiting ground, a double function which the Latin term *definitio*—with its attention to *finis* as 'boundary' or 'limit'—reflects.

As taught in the most 'humanized' English grammar schools and universities of the sixteenth century, the building blocks of rhetorical invention, including *status*, the *circumstances*, the strategies for textual interpretation, and some of the most important *topics*, originally take shape in response to forensic demands. So does the structure of the oration as the most complex of the basic exercises, even though this structure develops to meet the requirements of the assembly and the festival as well as the law court. In keeping with this development, only the legal speech is likely to have all five parts regularly acknowledged by the rhetorical manuals (introduction, narration, confirmation, refutation, conclusion). Indeed, three of these five parts—narration, confirmation, and refutation—are identified primarily if not exclusively with forensic oratory, the context in which most of the ancient manuals discuss these parts in detail (Quintilian 3.9.1–5). For the deliberative speech often dispenses with a narration and even with an introduction, while the demonstrative (or epideictic) tends to lack a refutation and sometimes even a confirmation. In forensic oratory, on the other hand, confirmation and refutation do more than constitute the core of the case. They occasion victory or defeat (*Ad Her.* 1.10.18).

Accordingly, Cicero's *De inventione*, written in two books, devotes nearly the whole of the second book to these two key parts. The best narrations, moreover, are designed to anticipate the confirmations that follow them. In the *Institutio oratoria*, Quintilian compares these anticipations in the narrative to seeds and offers advice on how to sow them:[49]

> It will be useful also to sow some seeds (*semina*) of the Proofs, but in such a way that we never forget that this is still the Narrative (*narrationem*), and not the Proof (*probationem*). ... We can in fact give a taste in the Narrative of everything that we shall be treating in the Proof: person, motive, place, time, means, opportunity. ... The best

[48] Fraunce, *Lawyers Logike*, 63. On the *common* and *proper* elements of definition, see *Lawyers Logike*, 60.

[49] Quintilian 4.2.54–7. See also 4.2.79.

> preparatory remarks will be those which go unnoticed; thus Cicero very advantageously anticipates everything that shows that it was Clodius who lay in wait for Milo, and not Milo for Clodius.

To plant in the narration what Quintilian elsewhere calls *suspicions* (Lat. *suspiciones*), he here recommends a subtle use of the circumstances. His model for this narrative strategy is Cicero, and especially Cicero's narration in *Pro Milone*, which brilliantly sets the stage for his confirmation of his client Milo's innocence of the charge of premeditated murder.[50]

In *The Arte or Crafte of Rhethoryke* (1532), based on Melanchthon's *Elementorum rhetorices* (1531) and written by its own account for 'suche youthe as resorteth to your gramer schole', Leonard Cox, schoolmaster at Reading, recommends sending young students to the *Pro Milone* to learn how to use status, circumstances, places or topics, and the different parts of a speech.[51] Regarding one of these parts, Cox registers agreement with Quintilian. In the narration, which deliberative orations rarely include, Cox instructs, 'the accuser must craftily entermengle many suspicions which shall seem to make his matter provable'.[52] Also like Quintilian (4.2.63–4), Cox identifies this strategy with the *evidentia* of the narration—an identification that his countryman Wilson reinforces with yet another quality rooted in the law court.[53] For the narration, Wilson insists, must be no less a '*manifest* pointing of the matter' than 'an *evident* setting-forth of all things that belong unto the same' (italics mine).[54] The paradigm for such narrative vividness or *evidentia*, as we have seen, is the palpable presence of physical evidence—the bloody knife or, better still, the perpetrator caught in the act with his hand on the murder weapon.

While the most advanced grammar school students might on occasion try these strategies in their declamations, using the Ciceronian oration as a model, most of their literary efforts would go to writing themes, which Brinsley and others consider more appropriate to this pre-university stage of education.[55] Like the oration on which it is modelled, the declamation openly acknowledges its roots in the forum. Quintilian calls it 'practice in forensic pleading'—*forensum actionum meditatio*.[56] The theme, in contrast, seems more at home in the classroom, where schoolmasters set topics of varying complexity on a variety of subjects for students to handle in their compositions. At their

50 On the narrative strategy of planting *suspicion* and its role in education, see Lorna Hutson, *The Invention of Suspicion: Law and Mimesis in Shakespeare and Renaissance Drama* (Oxford: Oxford University Press, 2007), 104–45.

51 Leonard Cox, *The Arte or Crafte of Rhethoryke*, ed. Frederic Ives Carpenter (Chicago: The University of Chicago Press, 1899), 41, 78–80, 63, 44–5, 48, 72–3, 76–9.

52 Cox, *Arte or Crafte of Rhethoryke*, 68, 72.

53 Cox, *Arte or Crafte of Rhethoryke*, 73.

54 Wilson, *Art of Rhetoric*, 50. On the legal origin of *manifestum*, see OLD s.v. and Plautus, *Menaechmi* 594 and *Asinus* 569.

55 Brinsley, *Ludus Literarius*, 184–5, 189.

56 Quintilian 4.2.29. On declamation, see Stanley F. Bonner, *Roman Declamation in the Late Republic and Early Empire* (Liverpool: Liverpool University Press, 1949). For its role in grammar school education, see Baldwin, *Shakspere's Small Latine*, 2.355–79.

most complex, these themes could and did approach the declamatory exercise, with its five-part structure designed for accusation and defence. But forward-looking pedagogues like Brinsley's Philoponus insist that students need simpler, more age-appropriate writing assignments—the kind supplied by Aphthonius' so-called *Progymnasmata*, a collection of fourteen composition exercises ordered according to difficulty and accompanied by illustrative examples. Written in the late fourth century by a little-known teacher of rhetoric in Antioch, this sixteenth-century bestseller in the Latin translation of Rudolf Agricola and Giovanni Maria Cataneo with commentary by Reinhard Lorich ensures that even the lower forms of the early modern grammar school maintain close ties to the courtroom.[57]

Starting with the simplest discursive form of the fable, illustrated by the familiar tale of the ant and the grasshopper, Aphthonius' textbook graduates to more complex exercises that late antique as well as sixteenth-century commentators openly identify with forensic oratory. Among these more advanced exercises are the refutation (Gr. *anaskeuē*) and the confirmation (Gr. *kataskeuē*), numbering the fifth and sixth of the fourteen. Like the Roman manuals, Aphthonius considers these exercises key to rhetorical success.[58] So does Richard Rainolde, who in *The Foundacion of Rhetorike* (1563), a vernacular adaptation of Agricola's translation, repeats Aphthonius' affirming view of the refutation (here *confutation*), buttressed by the authority of Cicero:[59]

> This exercise of Rhetorike doth contain in it all strength of arte, as who would say, all partes of Rhetorike may copiously be handled in this parte, called confutation, so ample a matter Tully doth note this part to be.

And like Aphthonius, Rainolde grants equal status to the confirmation.[60]

Also forensic in orientation are the commonplace (Gr. *koinos logos*; Lat. *locus communis*), seventh in the line-up, and the introduction of a law (Gr. *nomou eisphora*; Lat. *legislatio*), the last of the fourteen. Rainolde's brief explanation for this last exercise, which he calls 'Legislation', leaves no doubt about its forensic pedigree. For in undertaking an 'oracion either in the defence of a Lawe, or againste a Lawe', the grammar school student who has advanced through the textbook is encouraged to hone the very skill fundamental to pleading in court: arguing on both sides of the question.[61] Like Aphthonius, Rainolde illustrates this practice with Solon's law regarding adultery. But the training that culminates in legal pleading is not the student's first encounter with these skills. In taking on

[57] On Aphthonius' influence, especially in the translation by Agricola, on the composition of themes, see Brinsley, *Ludus Literarius*, 182–4; Baldwin, *Shakspere's Small Latine*, 2,288–354; and Mack, *Elizabethan Rhetoric*, 27–9.

[58] Aphthonius, *Progymnasmata: Greek Textbooks of Prose Composition and Rhetoric*, trans. George A. Kennedy (Atlanta: Society of Biblical Literature, 2003), 101, 104; *Rhetores Graeci*, ed. Leonard Spengel, 3 vols (Leipsig: Tuebner, 1854), 2.28, ll. 3–4; 30, ll. 24–5. On the legal elements of the theme, including its attention to confirming and refuting, see Brinsley, *Ludus Literarius*, 179–81.

[59] Richard Rainolde, *The Foundacion of Rhetorike* (Menston, England: The Scolar Press, 1972), xxiiij^{v}.

[60] Rainolde, *Foundacion of Rhetorike*, xxviiij^{v}.

[61] Rainolde, *Foundacion of Rhetorike*, lix^{r}.

the *commonplace* earlier in his schooling, he has already cut his teeth on arguing *for* and *against*—that is, *for* virtue and *against* vice. As part of his argument, he has also learned to take the vicious intention of the accused—the tyrant, for instance—into account. Aphthonius tellingly compares the commonplace to 'a second speech (for the prosecution) and an epilogue (in a trial)'.[62] Rainolde reinforces this legal dimension by repeating the comparison, recommending the commonplace to both accuser and defender, and briefly returning to it later in the textbook with the following definition: 'But a Common place, is a certain exaggeration of a matter, induced against any person, convicted of any crime, or worthy defence.'[63] Like refutation and confirmation, then, the commonplace sets the grammar school theme in a decidedly forensic direction.

So, somewhat more indirectly, does the second exercise, the *narrative* (Gr. *diēgēma*), even though early modern commentators, most likely taking their cue from Aphthonius himself, associate narration with deliberative rather than forensic oratory.[64] For narrative (or narration), both in these rhetorical manuals and in the *Progymnasmata*, is closely linked to the circumstances—a link that Rainolde's adaptation, again following Agricola's Latin translation, strengthens in a number of ways: by promptly listing in the section on narrative six of these circumstances (who, what, where, when, how, and why); by indicating, in added marginal notes, the presence of the circumstances in the narrations added for illustration; and by featuring the circumstances later in the manual as the key to this second exercise. 'And also in every narracion', Rainolde concludes, 'the cause, the place, the person, the time, the fact, the manner how, are therein lively described'.[65] Either directly or indirectly, then, the Aphthonian theme, arguably the cornerstone of the writing component of grammar school education, prepares the student for declamatory practice (and in some cases for the law courts themselves) by incorporating forensically oriented structures and strategies into its graduated sequence of exercises.

But some of these same building blocks figure even earlier in the curriculum with the most basic exercise, the reading and writing of letters. In *De conscribendis epistolis* (1522), the most widely used letter-writing manual in the English grammar schools, Erasmus not only recommends Cicero's letters above all others, but he highlights the relation between forensic rhetoric and this most elementary discursive form.[66] To anyone naïve enough to wonder what letters have in common with law courts—*quid epistolae cum tribunalibus?*—Erasmus responds that letter-writers often find themselves accusing either their addressees or some other acquaintance or defending themselves.[67] Like orations, in fact, letters come in three kinds: persuasive, demonstrative or encomiastic, and judicial. In addition to accusation and defence, the judicial kind includes complaint, protest, justification, reproach, threat, invective, and entreaty (*querela, expostulatio, expurgatio,*

62 *Progymnasmata*, trans. Kennedy, 105; *Rhetores Graeci*, ed. Spengel, 2.32, ll. 24–5.

63 Rainolde, *Foundacion of Rhetorike*, xxxiij^{r}, liiij^{r}.

64 See Baldwin, *Shakspere's Small Latine*, 2.288–9.

65 Rainolde, *Foundacion of Rhetorike*, xij^{r}, xiij^{r-v}, lj^{v}.

66 On the role of Erasmus' textbook in the exercise of letter-writing in the English grammar school, see Baldwin, *Shakspere's Small Latine*, 2.239–87; and Mack, *Elizabethan Rhetoric*, 24–6.

67 Erasmus, *De conscribendis epistolis*, *CWE*, 25, 210; ASD, I–2, 520 ll. 10–13.

exprobatio, comminatio, invectiva, deprecatio)—forms that figure prominently in the literary production of Renaissance humanists.[68]

But it would be a mistake to think that only the judicial kind of letter relies on forensic rhetoric. The other kinds do as well, and not least of all insofar as they appropriate the oration's five-part structure. So Erasmus echoes Quintilian's advice on the forensic oration when he recommends for the persuasive letter a brief *exordium* or introduction followed by a narration that 'scatters the seeds, as it were' of the proofs before refuting any objections and then concluding.[69] Focusing in on the epistolary introduction, Erasmus similarly upholds a forensic paradigm. 'A proper beginning is determined according to precisely those principles which writers on rhetoric have handed down concerning the judicial class', he explains, 'but these teachings, which they correctly applied to speeches in the courtroom (*ad forenses causas*), should be modified to suit the peculiar characteristics of a letter' (*ad proprietatem epistolarem*).[70] Sometimes these modifications reflect the letter's greater flexibility. Whereas the legal oration is severely limited in its use of the indirect introduction or 'insinuation' (Lat. *insinuatio*), for instance, the letter may use it more freely. At other times, the forensic oration enjoys greater freedom than the letter because the orator, unlike the letter-writer, can alter his course in response to his audience's reactions.[71]

Although students early in their compositional training are unlikely to appreciate these refinements (any more than they would the workings of a legal fiction), Erasmus encourages their teachers not only to ease them into the finer points as they advance but to supply them with the *circumstantiae* that provide narrative detail and the *loci* or topics that furnish proofs.[72] Eventually, Erasmus assumes here as in *De copia*, the student will acquire his own supply. Accordingly, Erasmus returns throughout his manual on letter-writing to these two inventional building blocks, the circumstances and the topics, tying them closely to the theory of *status*.[73] He also reminds the young student and his teacher that a conjectural question (*status coniecturalis*) requires an approach different from a legal question (*constitutio negocialis*), recommending Cicero's letters as an especially rich source of the former.[74] Like the orator, in other words, the young letter-writer must sooner or later master the *status* as the starting point of his epistolary compositions. In light of this reliance on status, as well as on confirmations and refutations (*causae statum et confirmationes confutationesque*), Erasmus concludes that 'the same technique (*artificio*) is used in a letter as in a speech'.[75] The speech he has in mind, it should now be clear, is one delivered in a court of law.

68 *CWE*, 25, 71; ASD, I–2, 310 l. 13–311 l. 8. On the fourth or extraordinary kind that includes the familiar letter, see *CWE*, 25, 225; ASD, I–2, 541 ll. 11–26.

69 *CWE*, 25, 108; ASD, I–2, 366 ll. 3–14.

70 *CWE*, 25, 76; ASD, I–2, 319 ll. 11–13.

71 *CWE*, 25, 75–6; ASD, I–2, 318 l. 22–319 l. 10 and *CWE*, 25, 74–5; ASD, I–2, 317 l. 16–318 l. 6.

72 *CWE*, 25, 24–7; ASD, I–2, 231 l. 6–236 l. 13.

73 *CWE*, 25, 110; ASD, I–2, 370 ll. 7–12 and *CWE*, 25, 118–28; ASD, I–2, 383 l. 17–399 l. 8.

74 *CWE*, 25, 118; ASD, I–2, 382 ll. 18–23 and *CWE*, 25, 149; ASD, I–2, 434 ll. 7–11.

75 *CWE*, 25, 207; ASD, I–2, 516 ll. 11–15.

In *The Schoolmaster* (1570), Roger Ascham, teacher at Cambridge and tutor to the young Queen Elizabeth, justifies his attention to the details of early education with the reflection that 'we remember nothing so well when we be old as those things which we learned when we were young....'[76] Among the lessons learned by early modern English schoolboys, as we have seen, are ways of reading and writing with deep roots in forensic rhetoric. These roots, as we have also seen, reach back to an ancient rhetorical art shaped by the requirements of the law courts. The early modern classroom, in other words, retains from its direct and indirect reliance on a number of favourite ancient rhetorical manuals deep traces of the Roman forum; and these traces leave their mark in turn on not only the advanced student reading Cicero's *Pro Milone* and writing his own orations but the beginning grammer-schooler struggling to construe the plays of Terence while composing Ciceronian-style letters and Aphthonian-style themes. Fully in keeping with Ascham's reflection on the staying power of our earliest lessons, these forensic elements deeply embedded in humanist education also leave their mark, as subsequent chapters will show, on many of early modern England's literary masterworks.

Bibliography

Baldwin, T. W. *William Shakspere's Small Latine and Lesse Greeke*, 2 vols (Urbana: University of Illinois Press, 1944).

Eden, Kathy. *Poetic and Legal Fiction in the Aristotelian Tradition* (Princeton: Princeton University Press, 1986; rpt Princeton Legacy Library, 2014).

Eden, Kathy. *Hermeneutics and the Rhetorical Tradition: Chapters in the Ancient Legacy and Its Humanist Reception* (New Haven: Yale University Press, 1997).

Hutson, Lorna. *The Invention of Suspicion: Law and Mimesis in Shakespeare and Renaissance Drama* (Oxford: Oxford University Press, 2007).

Hutson, Lorna. *Circumstantial Shakespeare* (Oxford: Oxford University Press, 2015).

Kohl, Benjamin G. 'Humanism and Education', in *Renaissance Humanism: Foundations, Forms, and Legacy*, ed. Albert Rabil, Jr (Philadelphia: University of Pennsylvania Press, 1988), 3.5–22.

Mack, Peter. *Elizabethan Rhetoric* (Cambridge: Cambridge University Press, 2002).

Mack, Peter. *A History of Renaissance Rhetoric, 1380–1620* (Oxford: Oxford University Press, 2011).

Monfasani, John. 'Humanism and Rhetoric', in *Renaissance Humanism: Foundations, Forms, and Legacy*, ed. Albert Rabil, Jr (Philadelphia: University of Pennsylvania Press, 1988), 3.171–235.

Serjeantson, R. W. 'Testimony: The Artless Proof', in *Renaissance Figures of Speech*, ed. Sylvia Adamson, Gavin Alexander, and Katrin Ettenhuber (Cambridge: Cambridge University Press, 2007), 181–94.

Simon, Joan. *Education and Society in Tudor England* (Cambridge: Cambridge University Press, 1966).

[76] Roger Ascham, *The Schoolmaster*, ed. Lawrence V. Ryan (Charlottesville: University of Virginia Press, 1967), 34.

Skinner, Quentin. *Forensic Shakespeare* (Oxford: Oxford University Press, 2014).
Weiss, Roberto. *Humanism in England during the Fifteenth Century*, 3rd edn (Oxford: Oxford University Press, 1967).
Witt, Ronald G. *The Two Latin Cultures and the Foundation of Renaissance Humanism in Medieval Italy* (Cambridge: Cambridge University Press, 2012).

CHAPTER 2

IDIOSYNCRATIC BOOKS AND COMMON LEARNING

Readings on Statutes at the Inns of Court

MARGARET MCGLYNN

READINGS on statutes are both events and texts. The event is fairly straightforward. Though the evidence is scarce, we can be confident that readings had emerged as part of the educational programme of the Inns of Court by the early fifteenth century at the latest. The readers were usually men who had held the status of utter barrister within the Inn for a decade or more and who were also successful practising lawyers. Readings were held at each Inn twice a year, in the Lent and Autumn vacations, with the Lent vacation usually going to the senior or double reader.[1] They were the high point of the educational cycle, particularly the Lent reading, and were regularly attended by judges and serjeants who might return to their old Inns for the occasion, as well as by the students who were required to be there.

As the name suggests, each reader chose a statute on which to base his exposition of the law, and until the early sixteenth century the statute was almost always an ancient one, usually from the reign of Edward I or earlier.[2] The reader moved through the text clause by clause explaining the logic of the law and demonstrating its operation. The

[1] This sequence was sometimes interrupted by a call of serjeants, for the serjeants-elect were expected to deliver a third reading in their home Inn as part of their elevation to the coif. Serjeants' readings were usually gala affairs.

[2] Late fifteenth-century readers, usually serjeants, began to introduce statutes to the cycle, but they were often old statutes, such as *Prerogativa Regis*, chosen by both Robert Constable and Thomas Frowyk in 1495. With the exception of Gregory Adgore of the Inner Temple, who read on 1 Ric. III *c.* 1 in 1489/90, there is no evidence of a reading on a 'new' statute in the Inns until 1518, though the practice became increasingly common in the 1520s. See J. H. Baker, *Readers and Readings in the Inns of Court and Chancery* (London: SS, 2000), 31, 69, 78, 117, 119, 153. There are many gaps in our knowledge of the topics tackled by the readers in this period, but the vast majority of the surviving reading material deals with the 'old' statutes.

requirement that the readers base their discussion on a statute meant that a reading could wander over a fairly broad and not-entirely-predictable swathe of the law, though over time some standard topics tended to become associated with particular statutes. As well as lecturing, the reader presented cases that demonstrated the law in action, and members of the audience, from junior barristers to serjeants and judges, argued his cases, with the clear intention that the readings be an interactive learning experience. The whole exercise was designed to test the knowledge, ingenuity, and logic of both reader and audience.[3]

Later in the sixteenth century and into the early seventeenth century, the value of the readings seems to have declined, and contemporaries complained about them as a fairly sterile display of obscure learning, rather than a useful educational exercise. For this reason my discussion will focus on the century after 1470, when the process seems to have been well-developed, when substantial numbers of texts survive, and when readings still seem to have been an important method for developing the law, as well as for educating students. This period also saw print revolutionize both education and the transmission of texts, and the readings were not immune to these changes, though they demonstrate how older forms of teaching and learning persisted and functioned alongside the new.

Though gaps remain in our knowledge of the readings as event, they pale beside the gaps in our knowledge of the readings as texts. The surviving reading manuscripts have not been widely studied, and it is not hard to understand why. They are in Law French, paleographically challenging, technical, and in note form. In most manuscripts the notes appear as a continuous block of text, with no paragraphs or headings to mark a change of direction. As far as we know, none of the surviving notes belong to the readers before the late sixteenth century.[4] Most of the surviving manuscripts are student notes, often both anonymous and undated. Some don't even indicate what statute they are a reading on. For most historians, the first impulse would be to try to date these readings and if possible find their readers, and indeed John Baker has done phenomenal work along those lines.[5] But while he has made enormous strides in the process of figuring out who the readers were, and when and where they read, it has proved significantly more challenging to associate readers with the anonymous reading texts, and equally difficult to date the undated. The reason is quite simple: many of the surviving texts, certainly through the mid-sixteenth century, are compilations, gathered over years and in some cases over generations. The three manuscript images presented here (Figs 2.1, 2.2, and 2.3,) show how this process might work. In University College Oxford MS 163 there is unfilled space left for later notes at the bottom of the lecture on *c.* 2 of Westminster I.[6] In Cambridge

[3] W. P. Baildon and J. D. Walker, *The Records of the Honorable Society of Lincoln's Inn*, Vol. 1: *1422–1586* (London: Lincoln's Inn, 1897), 161; Edward Waterhous, *Fortescutus Illustratus* (London: Thomas Roycroft, 1663), 544–5; J. H. Baker, *OHLE*, 6.445–72.

[4] Eight manuscripts are clearly autograph, mostly from the seventeenth century.

[5] Baker, *Readers and Readings*.

[6] Reproduced by kind permission of The Master and Fellows of University College, Oxford. The page shown is fol. 78[v].

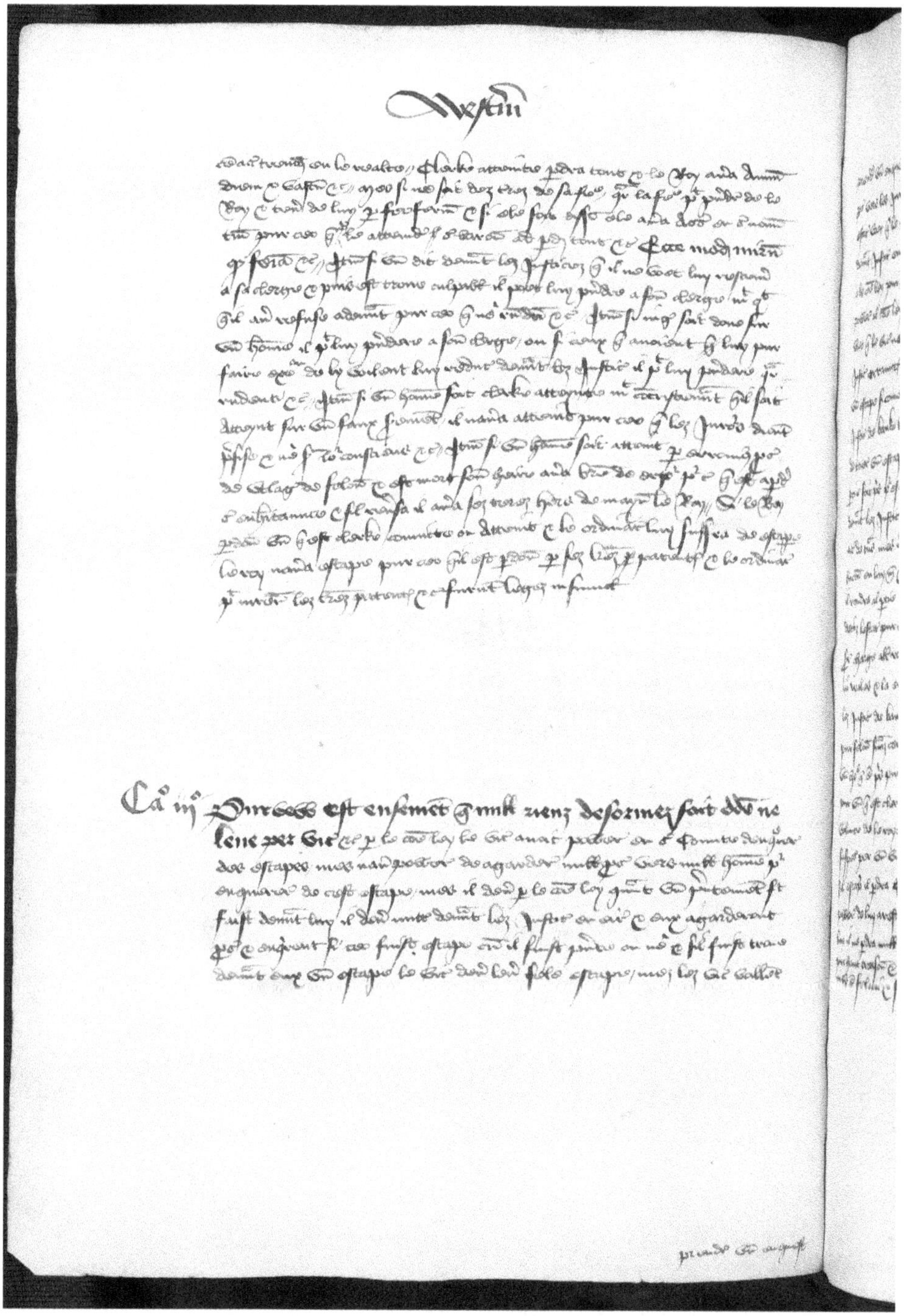

FIG. 2.1 University College Oxford MS 163, fol. 78^{v}, showing a reading on *c.* 2 of Westminster II. Reproduced by kind permission of The Master and Fellows of University College, Oxford.

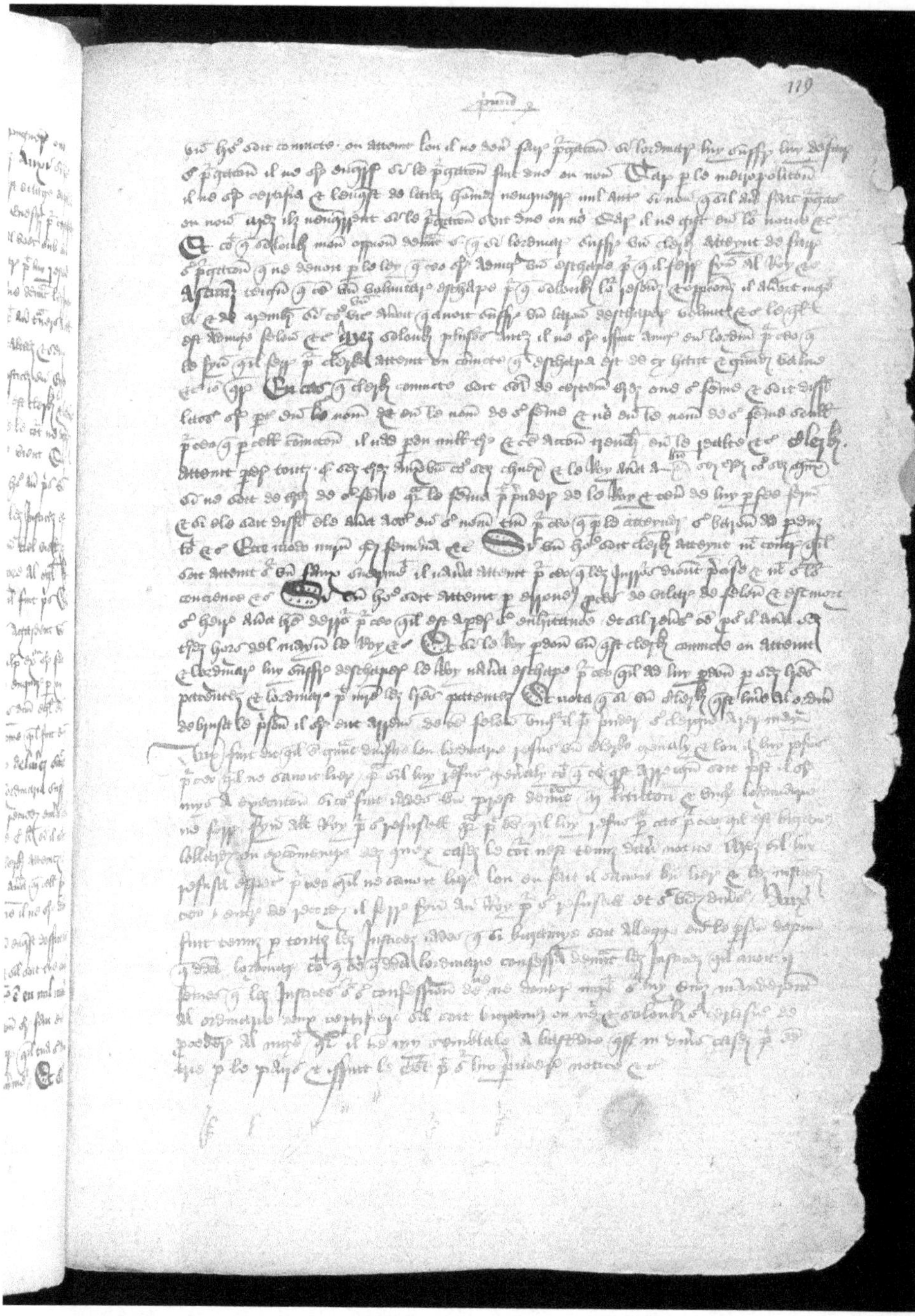

FIG. 2.2 Cambridge University Library MS Ee.5.22, fol. 119. Reproduced by kind permission of the Syndics of Cambridge University Library.

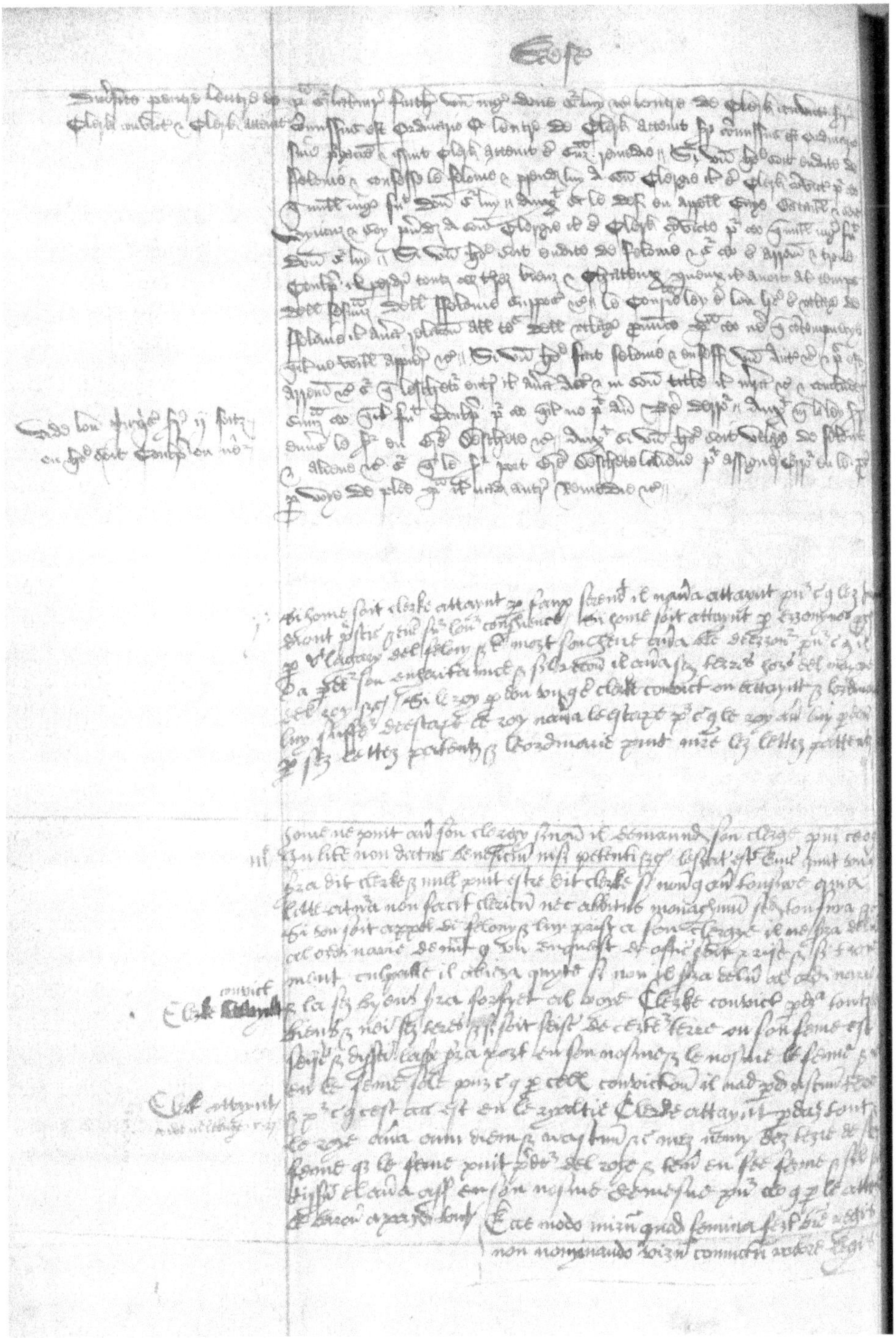

FIG. 2.3 Newcastle Manuscript, fol. 92v. Reproduced by kind permission of Northwestern University Law Library.

University Library MS Ee.5.22 notes have been added at the end of the lecture in the same hand.[7] Finally, in the Newcastle Manuscript notes have been added in a later hand, perhaps at different times.[8] When a reading manuscript like the CUL manuscript or the Newcastle Manuscript was copied, the scribe generally incorporated the notes into the body of his text, with little concern for whether the material flowed together, and with no attempt to provide a bridge or an explanation. He might later add his own notes in the blank spaces he had left as he copied, and the cycle might then be repeated with another scribe. Recognizing the ways in which these manuscripts were compiled helps us to deal with the complications of their contents. In this example, the Oxford manuscript dates from about 1430 and some of its text appears in the Cambridge manuscript, the core of which was probably written down in the 1460s, supplemented in the 1470s and then copied by this scribe, who later added more of his own notes.[9] The notes in the Newcastle Manuscript are drawn from a reading that appears in both the Oxford and the CUL manuscripts. In the Newcastle Manuscript the process of addition by other hands is clear; in the Cambridge manuscript we can see later additions by the same hand, but not the layers that came before this scribe; the Oxford manuscript looks like a single text, though, like the other two, it was most likely the product of different students gathering information at different times. This process of compilation, which is apparent in some manuscripts, most likely lies behind the apparently tidy text in many more, and explains many of their internal inconsistencies: though all of the content on the page probably originated with a man standing in the hall of an Inn of Court, it did not all originate with the same man in the same year (though there is a reasonable chance that it may have originated in the same hall, since collections seem to have circulated more often within the particular Inns than between them).[10]

The second problem we face with identification is that even when we have a named text, the relationship between the name and the text may still be problematic. Take for example the reading of Thomas Kebell on Westminster 1 cc. 1–2. This reading was delivered in the Inner Temple, most likely in the early 1470s, and it survives in BL MS Hargrave 87.[11] It covers the standard material lawyers discussed under these chapters of the statute: extortions against religious houses and benefit of clergy. This reading survived in another manuscript at the Inner Temple until World War II, and Bertha Putnam described it as a source for Thomas Marowe's 1503 reading in her edition of that text. The content she describes, however, bears very little resemblance to the Hargrave manuscript, as she says Kebell took 'as his main subject the question as to who were responsible for enforcing the statutes on the peace' as well as discussing 'surety of peace, riot,

[7] Reproduced by kind permission of the Syndics of Cambridge University Library. The page shown is fol. 119.

[8] Reproduced by kind permission of Northwestern University Law Library. The page shown is fol. 92^{v}.

[9] See Margaret McGlynn, ed., *The Rights and Liberties of the English Church: Readings from the pre-Reformation Inns of Court* (London: SS, 2015), 1–5; 32–51.

[10] See also Ian Williams's chapter in this volume.

[11] McGlynn, ed., *The Rights and Liberties of the English Church*, 21–31.

rout and assembly, escapes, and gaoler by inheritance'.[12] None of these questions appear in the Hargrave version. Without the manuscript to examine we can only speculate, but it does seem as if at least two versions of Kebell's reading circulated under his name, one on extortions against religious houses and benefit of clergy and one on the Justices of the Peace. Though both originated from the same lecture series, they led quite separate lives, and this reminds us that the many anonymous readings might also be connected in ways that are not easily visible. Furthermore, it raises questions about the value of attaching a name to a reading. Kebell was a successful lawyer: he was a justice of the peace, an assize justice, and a serjeant at law, though he never became a judge at Westminster. Ives associates him with the educational processes at his Inn, pointing to 'his major role in the training of an influential generation of lawyers'.[13] But the fact that his name was attached to two quite distinct parts of his reading suggests that it added no authority or context to the reading as a whole: a student might be interested in knowing what Kebell thought about JPs or benefit of clergy, but doesn't seem to have been concerned with what Kebell thought about Westminster I cc. 1–2, even though the notes were originally taken, and were later transcribed, in the context of a reading on that statute.

Looking more closely at this example, it quickly becomes clear that the student may in fact have come away with a fairly limited sense of what Kebell thought. The text in Hargrave 87 is typical in its approach to learning the law: across four folios (eleven printed pages) it refers directly to five statutes and indirectly to two cases, mentioning 'opinion in past times' and a stance which has been 'held lately'.[14] The authority of statute is clear, but reported cases hold the weight only of opinion—and anonymous corporate opinion at that—while the bulk of the text is supported by no external authority whatsoever, only by the inherent logic of its presentation. This text is clearer and more organized than many of the others on the same subject, and it is possible that Kebell's name and his reputation may have helped to preserve some of the integrity of his work as a compiler and presenter, but there is certainly no authorial voice here, and this is typical of the reading manuscripts. In many cases where a name remains attached to a reading the lawyer cannot be certainly identified, and reading texts cannot be identified for many of the most eminent of Tudor lawyers, who must have completed the ritual. It seems to be largely a result of accident when a name remains attached to a text: perhaps the student was present at the reading, knew the reader, or was a particularly fastidious scribe. For the most part, the students were far more interested in accumulating content than identifying the conduit: as Baker notes, Littleton's reference to a reading 'is not to a specific performance, but to a repeated assertion. The constant repetition of a point, without challenge, made it common learning'.[15] These manuscripts are the physical manifestation of those repeated assertions.

12 Bertha Putnam, *Early Treatises on the Practice of the Justices of the Peace in the Fifteenth and Sixteenth Centuries* (Oxford: Clarendon Press, 1924 rpt New York: Octagon Books, 1974), 184–5.

13 E. W. Ives, *The Common Lawyers of Pre-Reformation England* (Cambridge: Cambridge University Press, 1983), 58.

14 McGlynn, ed., *The Rights and Liberties of the English Church*, 25, 31.

15 J. H. Baker, *The Law's Two Bodies* (Oxford: Oxford University Press, 2001), 79.

If the identity and authority of the reader counted for little among Tudor law students, and the texts represent a conscious accumulation of knowledge and argument over years, the questions we can ask of them shift. If we can't attach firm dates and authors, it becomes harder to use the reading manuscripts as evidence of what the law was, or was understood to be, at any given time. Instead we need to think more about how this format was useful to students of the law and think more about how reading manuscripts were constructed, circulated, and used. When we discuss the manuscript readings, we most often refer to them as lecture notes, so the first obvious question is, when and how did these notes get written down? Did students actually take notes during the reading, or were they written down in recollection? There is no direct evidence from the Inns, and the two likeliest contemporary models were sermons and university lectures. Much of the surviving evidence on these is either from the medieval period or from the very late sixteenth and seventeenth centuries, so it is not an entirely safe guide to practice in between, but it gives some sense of the likely context.

Sermon notes circulated widely in the Middle Ages, and there appears to have been a system for collecting them, known as *reportatio*. Ann Blair explains that 'Reportators did not try to record the full text of a sermon; they identified the gist of the argument and its divisions, leaving quotations, exempla and explanations to be filled in later ... Different *reportationes* of the same sermon therefore often highlight different aspects of the sermon.'[16] Blair notes that the techniques of *reportatio* developed for sermons could transfer readily to the university classroom, and presumably to the Inns.[17] This would explain why very different versions of Kebell's reading circulated. It also receives some support from a famous observation of Sir John Fortescue, a rare source of information on legal education in the late fifteenth century. Fortescue explains why the Inns of Court were much better suited to teaching law than the universities, commenting that 'Reportantur eciam ea que in curiis regis placitantur, disputantur, et iudicantur, ac in libros ad futurorum erudicionem rediguntur in sermone semper Gallico', translated by Chrimes as 'Again, what is pleaded, disputed, and decided in the royal courts is reported and put

[16] Ann Blair, 'Student Manuscripts and the Textbook', in *Scholarly Knowledge: Textbooks in Early Modern Europe*, ed. E. Campi (Geneva: Droz, 2008), 43.

[17] Cf. Harold Love, *Scribal Publication in Seventeenth-Century England* (Oxford: Clarendon Press, 1993), 222. Blair notes that in universities the lecturers might prepare their own version of their lecture notes, which circulated together with student notes. This was most common in the theology faculty, where faulty notes might have the gravest consequences, 'Student Manuscripts', 44. William Gouge expressed a similar concern when faulty notes from his sermons circulated in the 1630s, presumably for similar reasons; see Frances Dolan, *True Relations: Reading, Literature, and Evidence in Seventeenth-Century England* (Philadelphia: University of Pennsylvania Press, 2014), 190, though Coke made a similar complaint about his speech to the Norwich assizes in the preface to the *Seventh Reports* (I am grateful to Ian Williams for this reference). See also John Craig, 'Sermon Reception', in *The Oxford Handbook of the Early Modern Sermon*, ed. P. McCullough, H. Adlington, and E. Rhatigan (Oxford: Oxford University Press, 2011), 190; and Christopher Burlinson, 'The Use and re-Use of Early-Seventeenth-Century Student Notebooks: Inside and Outside the University', in *Material Readings of Early Modern Culture: Texts and Social Practices, 1580–1730*, ed. J. Daybell and P. Hinds (New York: Palgrave Macmillan, 2010), 234–5.

into book form, for future reference, always in the French speech'.[18] It seems likely that Fortescue's 'reportantur' evokes the *reportationes* of medieval sermons: though the environment of church or court was different from the readings, it would not be surprising if the process were the same, with students working to jot down a core of useful, interesting, or surprising arguments, with the expectation that they would elaborate with examples or queries later as they reflected on what they had heard.[19]

Evidence from later in the sixteenth century similarly conflated sermons and lectures. Richard Holdsworth, master of Emmanuel College, 'counseled students to remember something at least ... in every dispute, Lecture, Sermon, Speech, or Discourse, which you shall heare & when you come to your studie write them downe ...'[20] Similarly, Bacon's editor suggests that he 'was in the habit of sitting down, from time to time, reviewing in memory the book he had last read, and jotting down those passages which, for some reason or other, he wished to fix in his mind'.[21] Note-taking could thus be the product of listening or of reading, and while we might imagine that notes of things heard would be rougher and less polished than notes of things read, this is not necessarily true—taking notes from a written text in the manner suggested above is not the same as copying. In both cases note-taking serves primarily as a memory exercise, a way of more firmly committing information to memory and/or integrating it with the reader's previous knowledge. The notes are the product of the learning exercise, but not necessarily its purpose. Their primary function was to develop memory, though they might also serve as a back-up if memory failed.[22]

Large numbers of manuscript readings survive, though they are generally not considered as a coherent body of material. Baker has catalogued 388 manuscripts containing lectures, readers' cases, or entire readings. About 260 manuscripts contain material from the sixteenth century or earlier.[23] These volumes vary a great deal in their make-up, however. Some are volumes that only contain readings, while others are mixed: many are collections of reports with a reading or two included, some are miscellaneous volumes with a number of different types of material including readings, and some seem to be topically oriented, most notably the volumes on forest law, which often include a reading on the charter of the forest along with instructions for holding courts and/or other records, statutes, and treatises concerning the forest. These numbers represent manuscript survival,

[18] Sir John Fortescue, *De Laudibus legum Angliae*, ed. and trans. S. B. Chrimes (Cambridge: Cambridge University Press, 1949), 114.

[19] But cf. R. H. Helmholz, 'University Education and English Ecclesiastical Lawyers 1400–1650', *Ecclesiastical Law Journal*, 13 (2011): 135–6.

[20] Quoted in Richard Yeo, 'Notebooks as Memory Aids: Precepts and Practices in Early Modern England', *Memory Studies*, 1 (2008): 124.

[21] Yeo, 'Notebooks as Memory Aids', 122.

[22] Yeo sets writing and remembering as opposites ('Notebooks as Memory Aids', 118–19) but it seems more common in the period to assume that one aided the other; see Blair, 'Student Manuscripts and the Textbook', 64.

[23] These numbers are rough because of the wide variation in the styles of manuscripts, the difficulties of dating them, and the chronological range of material in some volumes. There are about 114 manuscripts with reading material dating from 1600 to 1650 and about 14 after 1650.

so we have to be cautious in extrapolating from them, but the table below suggests that while the number of volumes containing material from readings increased across the period, possibly as a result of the growth in the population of lawyers, the number of volumes containing *only* readings fell as a proportion of the whole.

	15th century	1500–1550	1550–1600
Manuscripts with reading material	34	86	140
Manuscripts with **only** readings	17 (50%)	35 (40%)	24 (17%)
Reading-only manuscripts containing multiple readings	13 (38%)	12 (14%)	10 (7%)

Since reading notes did not usually stand alone, and indeed seem to have become more integrated with the collection of other kinds of legal texts across the sixteenth century, what other books would law students have had access to in the fifteenth and sixteenth centuries? Somewhat counter-intuitively, educational institutions in the fifteenth century generally did not have extensive libraries. There are references to a library at Lincoln's Inn in 1475, Gray's Inn in 1488, and the Inner Temple in 1506, but though members of the Inns seem to have bequeathed books fairly regularly, the books seem to have disappeared from the libraries with equal regularity, even when they were 'made faste'.[24] Baker concludes that 'the principal means of access to law books before 1640, despite their high cost, was through private ownership'.[25]

Though the institutional libraries may have been skimpy, the corporate library made up of the individual collections of the men living within the buildings is likely to have been rather more substantial. It is clear that the books that lawyers owned circulated within their Inns (and occasionally beyond), both as loans and by purchase or bequest.[26] Inventories show the kinds of collections we might expect: statutes, yearbooks, and abridgements. But the majority of the books in these collections were manuscript rather than print, and while the term 'abridgement' might lead us to assume a copy of Statham or Fitzherbert, we are just as likely to be talking about manuscripts, as in Sir Peter Arderne's library, which had 'my owne grete compiled booke of lawe covered with reed leddir and a horn upon itt' and 'a boke of law of parchmyn compiled and bokeled' or William Calow's library, which held 'ii books of abriggements, oon of myne owen

24 J. H. Baker 'Common Lawyers and the Inns of Court', in *Cambridge History of Libraries in Britain and Ireland* (Cambridge: Cambridge University Press, 2006), 1.458; cf. Scott Mandelbrote 'The Library of Peterhouse, Cambridge and the Problem of the Spatial Arrangement of Knowledge during the Sixteenth and Seventeenth Centuries', in *Museum, Bibliothek, Stadtraum: Räumliche Wissensordnungen 1600–1900*, ed. Robert Felfe and Kirsten Wagner (Münster: Lit, 2010), 24; Love, *Scribal Publication*, 221.

25 Baker 'Common Lawyers and the Inns of Court', 460.

26 J. H. Baker, 'The Books of the Common Law', in *The Cambridge History of the Book in Britain*, ed. Lotte Hellinga and J. B. Trapp (Cambridge: Cambridge University Press, 2013), 3.414; Baker, 'Common Lawyers and the Inns of Court', 449; cf. Love, *Scribal Publication*.

labour and thither of Lincolnesin labour'.[27] These wills suggest that lawyers expected both to compile their own legal collections and to have access to the corporate compilations of their Inns. And while Calow's reference to abridgements suggests reported cases, Arderne's more generic 'boke of law' likely reflects the common combinations of cases, treatises, and readings.

This highly personal approach to law books fits with what we know about the contemporary market. Law printing emerged with William de Machlinia (*fl.* 1482–1490) and Richard Pynson (*c.*1449–1529/30), but Baker suggests that the market was unstable.[28] The early printers focused on texts that were likely to appeal to the broadest market. Yearbooks had long been the key texts of the common law, preserving the various ways in which the lawyers had argued the law in the past, but Baker argues that the early printers focused on unusual yearbooks, texts that the lawyers were less likely to have copied for themselves. Port, Spelman, and Yorke's books stand as examples of the kinds of notes that the lawyers were taking for themselves, and remind us of the dangers of assuming that the yearbooks are a reliable index to the law.[29] But even with these volumes in hand, we need to be aware that many more cases, from both the Inns and Westminster, were heard, noted, and pondered, even if those notes were not of the same quality as Port's or Spelman's and even if they have not survived. Printed yearbooks were finding and filling a gap in the market, not replacing manuscript texts. Abridgements were a novelty of the fifteenth century, a digest of case law re-arranged by themes, in alphabetical order, rather than presented chronologically. They were well-suited to print, and Fitzherbert's *Graunde Abridgement*, printed in 1514–1517, was particularly influential: Baker suggests that it 'perhaps unwittingly encouraged the profession to see rummaging through case-law as the essence of legal scholarship'.[30] Nonetheless many lawyers also continued to make up their own abridgements to supplement the printed versions. The early Tudor printers never printed readings, probably because the market was too splintered: most lawyers would be interested in buying a yearbook or abridgement, but how many would want a reading on *c.* 13 of Westminster 2?[31] Over the first half of the sixteenth century the lawyer's library must have come to hold a combination of print and manuscript which grew and shifted as he progressed in the profession. Perhaps he started with a handful of manuscript yearbooks inherited from a family member, copied more from those circulating in the Inn and bought one or two in print to fill some gaps, compiled his own notebook, picked up a manuscript statute book, and finally invested in a copy of Fitzherbert. Print and manuscript would sit

27 Baker, 'Books of the Common Law', 416; Baker, 'Common Lawyers and the Inns of Court', 451. Arderne died in 1467, Calow in 1506.

28 Baker, 'Books of the Common Law', 425–8.

29 J. H. Baker, ed., *The Notebook of Sir John Port* (London: SS, 1986); J. H. Baker, ed., *The Reports of Sir John Spelman*, 2 vols (London: SS, 1977, 1978); J. H. Baker, ed., *Reports of Cases from the Time of King Henry VIII* (London: SS, 2003), 1.89–245.

30 Baker, *The Law's Two Bodies*, 83–4.

31 Baker, 'Books of the Common Law', 418–19. Harvard faced similar issues in this period; cf. Blair, 'Student Manuscripts and the Textbook', 58.

side-by-side on his shelf, with all the implications that held for the accumulation and transmission of knowledge.

Edmund Plowden's *Commentaries* are probably as good an example of this transitional process as we could ask for. Plowden entered the Middle Temple around 1539 after spending three years at Cambridge, and claims that he made two resolutions as he began his legal education: 'the first was to be present at, and to give diligent attention to, the debate of questions of law, particularly by those who were men of note and credit for their learning. The second, to commit to writing the things I heard, and the judgment on them, which seemed to me much better than relying on slippery memory, which often deceives her master'.[32] He planned to carry out these resolutions by attending moots and readings as well as the common law courts and chancery. In some ways Plowden is quite traditional: his plan to attend and learn from the debates and then to write them down was much as Fortescue had described. But Plowden also emphasizes two novelties. The first is to note particularly the arguments of those men who had the greatest reputation for learning: while it is clear that Plowden is not giving greater credence to men solely because of their status as judges—indeed since he is referring to moots and readings as well as the courts, it is entirely possible that he's talking about the views of men like Kebell—he is moving away from reliance on common learning towards the weight of individual opinion. The second is to focus on the judgement and to have an accurate record of that, rather than relying on 'slippery memory'.

While the genesis of Plowden's collection reflects both old and new approaches to learning the law, its journey into print is also presented ambivalently. Plowden says that his collection was intended only for his own instruction, but that the manuscript circulated, as such manuscripts had for generations, and that those who read it asked him to put it in print—a very new option. He claims that he resisted such pressure, for two reasons. In the first instance, he does not think that his own personal version of the debates should carry the same weight as the communal authority of the yearbooks, despite the fact that by 1571 he was very clearly a man 'of note and credit for [his] learning'.[33] This can be dismissed as a simple modesty topos, but it still suggests something of a struggle over the relationship between common learning and individual insight. Plowden's second reason for resisting publication is that his report is not verbatim, but summary. He argues that he is 'a man … of small memory to retain things uttered', which suggests that despite his modern desire to achieve a greater level of accuracy in reporting, he was still listening, remembering, and then writing in the traditional way.

Plowden's reluctance to commit his work to print was apparently overcome when he realized that his friends' clerks had copied his manuscript and had done so imperfectly. While their activity reflects traditional practices, Plowden's concern that the manuscripts in circulation were not an accurate representation either of his labour or of the law was new, as was his concern that such manuscripts might negatively affect his reputation as a man of learning. This sense of his work as a fixed volume was perhaps

[32] *Les Comentaries, ou les Reportes de Edmunde Plowden* … (London: 1571), prologue. STC 1182:02.
[33] Plowden's account of the yearbooks is clearly apocryphal.

the most novel element of Plowden's prologue. We have seen that the manuscript tradition in the Inns was fluid, with students drawing from work in circulation as they built their own collections, but Plowden strikes a different tone. The *Commentaries* is distinguished by his decision only to include cases that went to judgement, though he notes that along the way he had taken notes on some other cases, which he had passed on to others. Plowden warns that the reader should not accept these as his, but only those contained within his *Commentaries*. This desire to exercise close control over the logic and content of the volume is distinctly different from the earlier development of common learning, but very much more in line with the idea of individual authority as manifested in a volume with a unique author. While we know that students continued to gather their own volumes in the traditional way for many decades, Plowden set new priorities, evident in his discussion of his book's title. A relative innovation, the title both conveyed something of the author's intent, and was required because otherwise 'the student who cites any case out of this book could not let others know where the case may be found'. Though Plowden gathered his material in the traditional way, his concept of the structure and use of his book was firmly grounded in the new realities of print.

A similar transition is apparent in the ways in which lawyers accessed the material they were gathering. Humanists demonstrated a great deal of interest in how to take, organize, and retrieve notes as they developed commonplace books intended to make a store-house of knowledge easily accessible. While there is little direct evidence of this kind of discussion in the legal community before the end of the century, the number of students in the Inns who had attended university for some time, like Plowden, grew through this period, and it is likely that they had been exposed to this discussion.[34] Commonplace books were not a new concept in the sixteenth century, but the growing volume of information available meant that there was a special urgency to the discussion of how to manage the flow.[35] The two fundamental models of collection were chronological (e.g. yearbooks), which was fairly straightforward, and thematic (e.g. abridgements), which was rather more complex. Yeo argues that 'although individuals collected commonplaces in personal notebooks, it was assumed that these could be shared and read with profit by others because there was a broad consensus on the topics under which material might be gathered, absorbed and later exploited', and though he's not referring specifically to legal books, the same argument can obviously be applied.[36] This process of organization was both an individual one and a corporate one: although particular lawyers might organize their books differently, over the course of time some

[34] Rosemary O'Day, 'Universities and Professions in the Early Modern Period' in *Beyond the Lecture Hall: Universities and Community Engagement from the Middle Ages to the Present Day*, ed. P. Cunningham, S. M. Oosthuizen, and R. K. Taylor (Cambridge: University of Cambridge, Faculty of Education and Institute of Continuing Education, 2009), 95.

[35] See Ann Blair, 'Reading Strategies for Coping with Information Overload ca. 1550–1700', *JHI*, 64 (2003): 11–28.

[36] Yeo, 'Notebooks as Memory Aids', 123.

standard formats would emerge to serve a common need. In abridgements, for example, the headings chosen and their organization varied from lawyer to lawyer, but a standard set of topics emerged fairly quickly once that model developed. These structures provided a cultural means of accessing material, a set of assumptions about what was important to gather and how it should be best placed for easy retrieval.

The challenge with this idea is that while it applies nicely to the abridgements, it has no relevance for the reading manuscripts, which could also be considered as a form of commonplace, arranged thematically by statute. Within an individual reading the most common means of providing direction is the practice of highlighting words or phrases within the text, either by bolding or underlining, and the most common elements to be picked out are the text of the statute under consideration and the names of the speakers. Highlighting the statutory text serves not only to highlight the centrality of the statute to the learning exercise, but to practically mark transitions in the discussion, since the readers commonly start each section with 'The words of the statute are:....' Highlighting the names of the speakers serves a similar function: as in the yearbooks, marking the speaker also marks the beginning of a new element in the discussion, though many readings do not have any named speakers. Some readings have marginal notes, but they tend to be slender, and vary tremendously from text to text. Many are a simple 'nota' or 'query', though some serve as subject headings to the material under discussion. Some provide cross-references within the volume or summarize an argument, though these are rare. They don't seem calculated to provide access to information in the way we would expect of a finding aid, though they do perhaps direct the reader once he is already engaged with the text.

There is even less help when it comes to navigating entire manuscripts, whether they contain only readings or the characteristic mixture of texts. For example, BL MS Harley 1691 is a mixed manuscript, containing reports of cases from Edward IV to Henry VIII along with cases from readings, cases from known casebooks, such as John Carryll's, and readings. As with many of these manuscripts, it is in a variety of hands and a variety of layouts and has clearly come into being when shorter collections were bound together. The only way to know what's in this manuscript is to look through it. The case notes often follow the same model as the yearbooks, with marginal notes indicating that the entry deals with trespass, debt, etc., but the story is quite different when we turn to the reading texts. William Symonds' reading, for example, is simply broken into lectures and has only one marginal note that says 'this case was argued'. Hall's reading gives a little more guidance: along with the heading that opens the reading there are some brief marginal notes, and both the names of the speakers and the shift from one chapter of the statute to the next are highlighted, though that doesn't provide much guidance to the contents of the reading. The closest thing that Harley 1691 has to a table of contents is on the last page of the volume: a list of the readings it contains, in reverse order, without folio numbers.[37]

In contrast, BL MS Hargrave 87 is a large volume composed entirely of readings, which has a recognizable table of contents at the front of the volume with the names

[37] BL MS Harley 1691 fols 134–9; fols 171–86^{v}; fol. 210^{v}.

of readers, statutes, and folio numbers. The table of contents is all in the same hand, though obviously written at different times, suggesting that it reflects the construction of the volume.[38] The first section is fairly clear: the main hand in the collection wrote out some Inner Temple material from the 1490s with occasional comments from previous decades, along with a series of readings from 1499 to 1507, probably copying an earlier volume in circulation in the Inn. He added to this a pair of readings, quite possibly the pair from 1519, in a very different hand. The second section, again in the main hand, is a reading on Magna Carta *c.* 1, along with White's reading from 1531 and Marowe's 1503 reading on Westminster 1 *c.* 1, suggesting that the owner was both adding contemporary material and going back and filling in gaps from the earlier period. Around the same time he also bought or was given a series of earlier readings in a variety of hands, including one from outside the Inn. He wrote out one more reading, Massey's of 1520, and then acquired another anonymous reading in a hand of the same period. For the final section of the volume the compiler added two texts in fifteenth-century hands, and then readings from 1526 in the same hand as the anonymous reading following Massey's. What did he end up with?

Looking at the named readers, we can see the compiler gathered three generations of learning: John Green, Thomas Pygott, William Grevill, Thomas Marow, William Rudhall, and John Port from 1499 to 1507; Baldwin Malet, Francis Mountford, and Ralph Massey from 1519 to 1520; and William Conyngsby, Thomas Audley, and Henry White from 1526 and 1531. He did have some historical depth beyond this: he had the agglomeration of early learning in the first few texts, a copy of Kebell's reading as a pre-cursor to Marow's, and Port's reading was attributed to Thomas Frowyk (who actually read in 1495). And he had one view from outside the Inner Temple, Wadham's reading of 1505, in which there are explicit comparisons to Mountford's reading earlier in the volume.

What did he have in terms of content? There is a fair amount of repetition in the volume: *de donis* appears more than once, as does the assize of novel disseisin, damages to widows on a writ of dower, justices of the peace, and sheriffs imprisoning for felony without inquest. Many other topics appear only once, such as writs of right of advowson, quo warranto, distraint, and limitations of prescription. The volume is by no means a comprehensive introduction to the common law, but it is a fairly functional guide to a number of useful and important elements of it, with some topics covered from a variety of periods and perspectives and others dealt with only once. The combination of copying and purchasing may suggest a combination of direction and serendipity in the collection of the material, but that is often how collectors—and students—end up with what they have.

The work done on readings to date has focused on particular topics or periods, but has not yet considered how the original owners of these books would have used them. Working through this volume as a whole raises many questions that could only be answered by a proper edition—is the main hand that of the compiler or of a scribe he

[38] BL MS Hargrave 87, fol. 2.

employed?[39] If it was a scribe, what does this tell us about the value of copying notes? How much cross-referencing is there between the readings in the collection, and what does that tell us about its use? How would an owner manage the volume of material in this collection? The table of contents suggests one approach to both keeping track of and accessing the information in the volume, but even a quick glance through the manuscript makes it clear that the table of contents is not terribly accurate, which raises yet more questions.

Though yearbooks and abridgements demonstrate that the lawyers knew how to organize material both chronologically and thematically, there was little or no attempt to do this with reading manuscripts. There are four possible explanations for this (at least): as we have seen, the notes taken of readings were by-products of the learning process, and it could be argued that having served their purpose in developing memory, they were redundant—there was no need to index or organize them, because they would never be consulted again. This isn't a terribly convincing explanation though, since it is clear that these books held value for their owners—Arderne's and Calow's wills, for example, describe their notebooks as being written on parchment rather than paper, carefully bound in leather, and buckled, and they were individually bequeathed rather than lumped into a job lot of books. It could be argued that the notebooks served a totemic purpose for these men, that they sat on a shelf as evidence and reminder of their education, as a sign of status rather than as working books, and in some cases this was probably true. But there is also clear evidence that these books circulated and were copied, which brings us to the third explanation, that it was assumed that they would be read through rather than dipped into, presumably because their value lay in working out arguments rather than in furnishing individual points. Thinking through the logic of a particular part of the law was important both for students building their sense of the common learning and for practising lawyers refreshing their understanding. A scribe might choose to note down only a chunk of what he heard or read, but it would be a chunk that made sense either by itself, or in the context of the book into which it was being copied—at least in the scribe's mind. Finally, it is entirely possible that the idiosyncrasies of these volumes, which make them confusing to us, may have reduced the need for finding aids. The process of compiling a volume was iterative—every time a student added notes or new cases, he had to skim through the volume in order to find the best spot in which to add the new material. As his volume grew, so too did his familiarity with its outlines and structure, simply through repetition. While a yearbook or an abridgement simply contained too many individual pieces of information ever to be fully absorbed, a collection of readings held fewer, larger chunks, arranged in a way chosen by the owner, whether through his note-taking, his copying, or even his binding. His knowledge of them was likely to be intimate. Roger North, a later witness, comments that his brother 'used

[39] See Ian Williams's chapter in this volume, which suggests that manuscripts may have been copied by lawyers' clerks; see Plowden above. It is not clear whether the clerks were copying as part of their own education, or as part of their employment, or both.

to say, the looking over the Commonplace Book on any Occasion, gave him a sort of Survey of what he had read about Matters not then inquisited, which refreshed them somewhat in his Memory'.[40]

It is clear that through this period lawyers shared, copied, and combined manuscripts in such a way that each volume was unique. Even when the same text appears in multiple manuscripts it is rarely copied exactly, and each manuscript combines a variety of different texts. Each lawyer created his own 'boke of law' which reflected his education, needs, and interests, whether it was a volume of Lincoln's Inn's labour representing the accretion and agglomeration of wisdom within an Inn over time, or a book of his own labour representing his own passage through cases pleaded, argued, and judged, whether live in the king's courts, didactically through learning exercises, or in reflection on the volumes compiled by his predecessors. To modern eyes this approach to education seems idiosyncratic at best, incoherent at worst. How would a system that was largely student-directed, with no obvious curriculum, train effective lawyers? The obvious answer is that the system was focused on developing habits of mind rather than imparting a set body of information, and the readings played an important role in developing those habits, as well as in developing the law. This approach has frustrated many scholars. Ross, for example, complains that 'lacking a standardized corpus of texts free of the variations and silent redactions of manuscript transmission, and lacking a doctrine of binding precedent that made previous cases more than an index to past conventions, lawyers were effectively thrown back on this common learning for want of anything better'.[41] Besides being profoundly anachronistic, this complaint assumes that a standardized corpus of texts and a doctrine of binding precedent were automatically better than the common learning of the earlier period. It seems clear, however, that not all contemporary lawyers agreed. In the seventeenth century the Inner Temple, for example, required that at moots 'en arguing, les barristers ne doint cite les livers per nosme, 1 H. 7 etc., mes doint dirre "en un ancient liver"', though the benchers might cite more precisely.[42] Presumably they wanted the students to be able to understand and use the arguments from their reports, rather than simply relying on the authority of the citation. Similarly, William Fulbecke opposed reducing the unwieldy mass of case law, arguing that 'the cases are many in number, which must be read, remembred, and applied, which cannot be compassed but by extreame diligence. And whereas some pretending a lumpish idleness, would have the Lawe measured with narrowe limits, and woulde have the multitude of volumes, cases, rules, and diversities abridged and made lesse, surely they give large testimonie of their great desire of ease'.[43] From the multiple voices of individual lawyers sparring across the centuries, Fulbecke

[40] Roger North, *The Life of the Right Honorable Francis North …* (London: 1742), 17.

[41] Richard J. Ross, 'The Memorial Culture of Early Modern English Lawyers: Memory as Keyword, Shelter and Identity, 1560–1640', *YJLH*, 10 (1998): 267–8.

[42] J. H. Baker, ed., *Readings and Moots at the Inns of Court* (London: SS, 1990), 2.cxciii. Baker calls this 'pedagogic perversity' in 'Books of the Common Law', 413.

[43] William Fulbecke, *A Direction or Preparatiue to the Study of the Lawe* (London: 1600) STC/510:02 fol. 13^{v}.

expected students to produce, if not harmony, then perhaps a productive polyphony. Rather than looking for a clear and certain corpus, he saw a positive value in learning the law by working through its past practice in all its messiness, acquiring a sense for its logic and the gist of its principles, committing as much as possible of that mass to memory, and applying it as circumstances dictated.

There is no question that Plowden points out the direction in which legal authority would develop, but a perusal of reading manuscripts alongside EEBO reminds us again that the period of transition between manuscript and print was long and complex, and that the transition between the habits of learning, arguing, and citing that went along with those formats was equally complex. Anthony Grafton and Lisa Jardine argue that the humanist model of education 'displaced a system far better adapted to many of the traditional intellectual and practical needs of European society' replacing it with one that 'offered everyone a model of true culture as something given, absolute, to be mastered, not questioned—and thus fostered in all its initiates a properly docile attitude towards authority'.[44] Those comments could be applied to the model of legal education as it shifted in the late sixteenth and early seventeenth century, but the arguments of men like Fulbecke, and the survival of readings, and reading manuscripts, suggest that a substantial proportion of the legal profession continued to value their messy, idiosyncratic books and their common learning, even as they consulted and cited the new authorities.

Tudor readings, as they survive, are very much the products of the initiated. There is nothing of Littleton's lucid clarity about them, a clarity which suggests that English law, in its essence, might be understood by any literate citizen. The readings reflect—and sometimes seem to revel in—the complexity of the law as it was practised, and the necessity for any practising lawyer to master that complexity of both detail and principle if he were to survive and thrive. The readings also reflect the complexity of the interconnections between print and manuscript, created as they were by men increasingly comfortable with the structures and the logic of print, who nonetheless continued to find that the creation and circulation of manuscripts best served their educational needs. At first glance they seem to be the very opposite of an educational tool, designed to repel anyone who is not already familiar with their norms and assumptions. But for those initiated into those norms and assumptions they embody the evolution of common learning over generations and continue to fulfil their note-takers' intentions of making the intricacies of the law available to later generations.[45]

Bibliography

Baildon W. P. and J. D. Walker. *The Records of the Honorable Society of Lincoln's Inn*, Vol. 1: *1422–1586* (London: 1897).

[44] *From Humanism to the Humanities* (Cambridge, MA: Harvard University Press, 1986), xii, xiv.

[45] This research was supported by the Social Sciences and Humanities Research Council of Canada.

Baker, J. H. 'The Books of the Common Law', in *The Cambridge History of the Book in Britain*, ed. Lotte Hellinga and J. B. Trapp (Cambridge: Cambridge University Press, 2013), 3.411–32.

Baker, J. H. 'Common Lawyers and the Inns of Court', in *Cambridge History of Libraries in Britain and Ireland*, Vol. 1: *to 1640*, ed. Elisabeth Leedham-Green and Teresa Webber (Cambridge: Cambridge University Press, 2006), 448–60.

Baker, J. H. *The Oxford History of the Laws of England*, Vol. 6: *1485–1558* (Oxford: Oxford University Press, 2003).

Baker, J. H. *The Law's Two Bodies* (Oxford: Oxford University Press, 2001).

Baker, J. H., ed. *Readers and Readings in the Inns of Court and Chancery* (London: Selden Society, 2000).

Baker, J. H., ed. *Readings and Moots at the Inns of Court*, Vol. 2 (London: Selden Society, 1990).

Blair, Ann. 'Note Taking as an Art of Transmission', *Critical History*, 31 (2004), 85–107.

Blair, Ann. 'Student Manuscripts and the Textbook', in *Scholarly Knowledge: Textbooks in Early Modern Europe*, ed. E. Campi (Geneva: Droz, 2008), 39–73.

Burlinson, Christopher. 'The Use and Re-Use of Early-Seventeenth-Century Student Notebooks: Inside and Outside the University', in *Material Readings of Early Modern Culture: Texts and Social Practices, 1580–1730*, ed. James Daybell and Peter Hinds (Basingstoke and New York: Palgrave Macmillan, 2010), 229–45.

Craig, John. 'Sermon Reception', in *The Oxford Handbook of the Early Modern Sermon*, ed. Peter McCullough, Hugh Adlington, and Emma Rhatigan (Oxford: Oxford University Press, 2011), 178–97.

Dolan, Frances. *True Relations: Reading, Literature, and Evidence in Seventeenth-Century England* (Philadelphia: University of Pennsylvania Press, 2013).

Fortescue, Sir John. *De Laudibus Legum Angliae*, ed. and trans. S. B. Chrimes (Cambridge: Cambridge University Press, 1949).

Fulbecke, William. *A Direction or Preparatiue to the Study of the Lawe* (London: 1600).

Grafton, Anthony and Lisa Jardine. *From Humanism to the Humanities* (Cambridge, MA: Harvard University Press, 1986).

Helmholz, R. H. 'University Education and English Ecclesiastical Lawyers 1400–1650', *Ecclesiastical Law Journal*, 13 (2011), 132–45.

Ives, E. W. *The Common Lawyers of Pre-Reformation England* (Cambridge: Cambridge University Press, 1983).

Mandelbrote, Scott. 'The Library of Peterhouse, Cambridge, and the Problem of the Spatial Arrangement of Knowledge during the Sixteenth and Seventeenth Centuries', in *Museum, Bibliothek, Stadtraum. Räumliche Wissensordnungen 1600–1900*, ed. R. Felfe and K. Wagner (Berlin: Lit Verlag, 2010), 23–76.

North, Roger. *The Life of the Right Honorable Francis North* (London: 1742).

O'Day, Rosemary. 'Universities and Professions in the Early Modern Period', in *Beyond the Lecture Hall: Universities and Community Engagement from the Middle Ages to the Present Day*, ed. Peter Cunningham, Susan M. Oosthuizen, and Richard Kenneth Taylor (Cambridge: University of Cambridge Faculty of Education and Institute of Continuing Education, 2009), 79–102.

Plowden, Edmund. *Les comentaries, ou les reportes de Edmunde Plowden* (London: 1571).

Putnam, Bertha. *Early Treatises on the Practice of the Justices of the Peace in the Fifteenth and Sixteenth Centuries* (Oxford: Clarendon Press, 1924; New York: Octagon Books, 1974).

Ross, Richard J. 'The Commoning of the Common Law: The Renaissance Debate over Printing English Law, 1520–1640', *University of Pennsylvania Law Review*, 146.2 (1998), 323–461.

Ross, Richard J. 'The Memorial Culture of Early Modern English Lawyers: Memory as Keyword, Shelter, and Identity, 1560–1640', *Yale Journal of Law and the Humanities*, 10 (1998), 229–326.

Waterhous, Edward. *Fortescutus illustratus* (London: 1663).

Yeo, Richard. 'Notebooks as Memory Aids: Precepts and Practices in Early Modern England', *Memory Studies*, 1 (2008), 115–36.

CHAPTER 3

COMMON LAW SCHOLARSHIP AND THE WRITTEN WORD

IAN WILLIAMS

THE sixteenth and seventeenth centuries have been identified as the period in which the common law changed from a system of predominantly oral learning to one based primarily on texts.[1] By the 1570s lawyers consciously address texts to 'readers' and refer to their work as 'treatises', a type of written scholarship.[2] Early modern legal historians have tended to focus on printed and manuscript texts, especially law reports, but oral readings continued in the Inns of Court until 1642.[3] Even in the 1630s a judge could identify an argument made in court as originating in the Inns.[4] To overlook the continued oral scholarship of the Inns and focus solely on printed and manuscript texts is to misunderstand the early modern common law. However, lawyers clearly did regard texts as extremely important, with legal argument focusing increasingly on printed cases and occasional consideration of the relationship between printed and manuscript texts.[5] This chapter investigates the interactions and relationships between the continuing tradition of oral scholarship in the Inns of Court and the increased use of texts to circulate legal ideas up to around 1640. It raises questions about how legal scholarship circulated amongst the legal profession and the extent of such circulation, as well as the sources which common lawyers used in their scholarship.

[1] J. H. Baker, 'English Law Books and Legal Publishing', in *The Cambridge History of the Book in Britain*, Vol. 4: *1557–1695*, ed. John Barnard and D. F. McKenzie (Cambridge: Cambridge University Press, 2002), 474–5.

[2] For 'readers', see BL MS Add. 26047, fols 4, 5, and 12. For 'treatises', see London Metropolitan Archive MS COL/CS/01/011, fol. 83^v and BL MS Harley 5220, fol. 4^v.

[3] John H. Baker, *Readers and Readings in the Inns of Court and Chancery* (London: SS, 2000), 7. For more on the readings, see McGlynn's chapter in this Handbook.

[4] *Dawles v Baldwin* (1631) Cambridge University Library MS Gg.2.19, fol. 210.

[5] Ian Williams, '"He Creditted More the Printed Booke": Common Lawyers' Receptivity to Print, *c*.1550–1640', *LHR* 28 (2010), 39–70, doi: 10.1017/S0738248009990034.

Oral and Written Scholarship and Their Interaction

The relationship between oral readings, manuscript, and print is complex. Two Elizabethan students did not distinguish between law reports they found in printed volumes and cases discussed at readings in the Inns, freely mixing the two sources in collections of maxims produced in the 1580s, as did Thomas Gibbon in his notebook from early in the reign of Charles I.[6] While readings themselves were rarely printed (although sometimes in some sense published in manuscript), the boundaries between oral and written scholarship were porous. Material from readings was reused in written scholarship, and an author's writings might be the basis for a reading.

For example, the prefaces to the first and third volumes of Edward Coke's *Reports* were taken, in part, from the speeches which preceded Coke's readings in Lyon's Inn and the Inner Temple.[7] William Prynne's 1662 reading on the Petition of Right repeated points which Prynne had previously made in print, sometimes in very similar language. For example, in his reading, Prynne observes that Coke 'grossly asserts' that the *Modus tenendi Parliamentum* is a pre-Conquest text, an error Prynne described as a 'gross confident mistake' in print in 1657.[8] Sometimes the relationship between readings and written scholarship is more opaque. William Fleetwood's reading included discussion of the laws of the forest;[9] he also collected and wrote a large volume of material on the topic, some of which is addressed to 'readers' rather than an oral audience, but there is insufficient evidence to understand how these various works interacted.[10] Sometimes an originally oral reading influenced manuscript scholarship, which itself affected a printed work. For example, Marowe's reading on Justices of the Peace influenced Fleetwood's discussion of the topic in manuscript. Both Fleetwood and Marowe influenced Lambarde's printed *Eirenarcha*.[11]

The contemporary, sometimes inadequate, state of written literature occasionally acted as a spur for readings at the Inns on particular topics. Edward Littleton delivered a reading in the Inner Temple on a statute concerning merchants, explaining that his choice was due to the number of cases which arose in relation to the topic. He observed that nevertheless there was 'no mention of [this] learning in the printed books of the

[6] BL MS Hargrave 207, fols 63, 64^{v}, 66^{v}, 71^{v}, 76, and 77; BL MS Hargrave 318, fols 26, 27, 45^{v}, 50^{v}, and 95^{v}; BL MS Harley 980, fols 5^{v}, 81, 86.

[7] Ian Williams, 'The Tudor Genesis of Edward Coke's Immemorial Common Law', *SCJ*, 43 (2012): 107–10.

[8] BL MS Hargrave 98, fol. 53^{v} and William Prynne, 'The Preface to the Reader' in *An Exact Abridgement of the Records in the Tower of London*, ed. William Prynne (London: William Leake, 1657), sig. A6–A6^{v}.

[9] London Metropolitan Archive MS CLC/270/MS00086, fol. 159^{v}.

[10] London Metropolitan Archive MS CLC/270/MS00086 and BL MS Add. 26047, fols 4 and 12.

[11] J. D. Alsop, 'William Fleetwood and Elizabethan Historical Scholarship', *SCJ*, 25 (1994): 162, doi:10.2307/2542557.

common law'.[12] Prynne did not address some topics in his reading precisely because he had already written about them, presumably to an adequate standard.[13] A similar justification can be seen for written scholarship. William Lambarde wrote that his *Eirenarcha*, a printed manual for Justices of the Peace, was written because of the inadequacy of existing works.[14] Unusually, William Fleetwood justified some of his written work on the forest laws on the basis that he was addressing different issues to those covered in George Treherne's 1520 reading, which circulated widely in manuscript.[15]

The relationship between readings is more complex. Consultation of previous readings, so far as possible, may have been standard preparation for a reader's own work. Henry Sherfield lent his reading to Richard Townsend, observing that 'he doth intend to reade on the same Lawes'.[16] However, the reasons for such consultation varied. Mere repetition of earlier readings was not typical from the Elizabethan period onwards, seemingly in contrast to the situation in the fifteenth century, when Littleton could write that he had 'often heard' a point in a reading on the Statute of Westminster II.[17] Mirow's study of readings on the Statute of Wills reveals that only one unusual reading, Hugh Hare's from 1592, features direct 'borrowing of material, citations, and legal thought' from an earlier reading.[18] Instead, readers used prior readings for assistance in their own efforts. In 1640, Edward Bagshaw referred to the lack of 'help of other mens labours' in preparing his reading 'as not knoweing that it was ever read on before'.[19] Citation of readings was also rare. While Bagshaw openly referred to John Dodderidge's reading delivered at New Inn in 1592–1594 he may have acknowledged Dodderidge's influence both because Dodderidge's reading had already been printed (as the *Compleat Parson* in 1630) and to demonstrate his own labour. Bagshaw expressly cited from a manuscript copy of the reading, 'the printed copy being very erronious & false'.[20]

A marked departure from the earlier tradition in readings was that some readers consulted prior work to ensure originality. When John Bankes delivered his reading in Gray's Inn in 1631, he acknowledged that there had been recent readings on the same statute and that he had seen some of the material from those readings. Bankes said that 'I would not treate of that which they have delivered'.[21] Such originality may have had a pedagogical purpose given that readings did circulate. When the readings

[12] BL MS Hargrave 372, fol. 54.

[13] BL MS Hargrave 98, fol. 33.

[14] William Lambarde, *Eirenarcha: or of The Office of Justices of Peace* (London: R. Newbery and H. Bynneman, 1581), sig. A2.

[15] BL MS Add. 26047, fol. 4v. For Trehearne's reading, see Baker, *Readers and Readings*, 117.

[16] Hampshire Record Office: Jervoise of Herriard Collection: MS 44M69/L25/6/1, entry for 2 July 1631.

[17] Thomas Littleton, *Les Tenures des monsieur Littleton* (London: Richard Tottel, 1581), fol. 112v (s.481).

[18] Matthew Mirow, 'The Ascent of the Readings: Some Evidence from Readings on Wills', in *Learning the Law: Teaching the Transmission of English Law 1150–1900*, ed. Jonathan Bush and Alain Wijffels (London: Hambledon Press, 1999), 244; M. C. Mirow, 'Bastardy and the Statute of Wills: Interpreting a Sixteenth-Century with Cases and Readings', *Mississippi Law Journal*, 69 (2000): 366–7.

[19] BL MS Stowe 424, fol. 3v.

[20] BL MS Stowe 424, fol. 8.

[21] BL MS Harley 5141, fol. 83.

in Lincoln's Inn on the Statute of Wills, delivered by John Briscoe in 1623 and Henry Sherfield in 1624, are combined 'these two readings provide a comprehensive treatment of the statute', suggesting a deliberate strategy of originality by the two readers.[22] By ascertaining what previous readers had covered, a reader could fill gaps, just as readings and written scholarship were intended to fill gaps in the printed and manuscript sources. In this respect oral, manuscript, and printed scholarship were motivated by similar concerns.

The oral scholarship of the readings may have inspired other examples of common law scholarship in the early modern period. William Staunford's book on the prerogative took the 'statute' *Praerogativa Regis* as its base, like the readings on that text which began in the late fifteenth century.[23] Edward Coke's *Second Institutes* was a collection of glosses on statutes, largely replicating the coverage which may have formed a cycle of readings in the fifteenth century.[24]

A less obvious example is the glosses and commentaries on Littleton's *Tenures* which first appear in the Elizabethan period. There are sufficient surviving copies to suggest that these works, or perhaps the production of them, were an important part of legal studies in early modern England and may have constituted a distinct genre of legal literature. In addition to his well-known printed *Commentary on Littleton*, Coke glossed his own copy of *Littleton* extensively.[25] William Fleetwood produced a 'Tractatus' on the first chapter of *Littleton*,[26] while Edward Littleton wrote 'notes of coment upon the first two bookes of Littleton' which he thought worthy of printing.[27] A civilian gloss on *Littleton* seems to have circulated in the early seventeenth century.[28] A further anonymous commentary on the *Tenures* from around the 1620s was printed in the nineteenth century.[29] Fleetwood's text is particularly revealing, as it is followed by a 'Lecture' on *Littleton* also attributed to Fleetwood. Readings on chapters of *Littleton* could be delivered in the Inns of Chancery, and presumably Fleetwood's lecture was one of these.[30] The relationship between the written glosses and commentaries, and the Inns of Chancery readings, is unclear. Fleetwood's 'Tractatus' could not have been delivered orally as it survives, given the presence of two diagrams. It may

22 Mirow, 'Ascent of the Readings', 232–3.

23 William Staunford, *An Exposicion of the Kinges Prerogative* (London: Richard Tottel, 1567). For the readings on *Praerogativa Regis*, see Margaret McGlynn, *The Royal Prerogative and the Learning of the Inns of Court* (Cambridge: Cambridge University Press, 2003).

24 Edward Coke, *The Second Part of the Institutes of the Lawes of England* (London: M. Flesher and R. Young, 1642). On the cycle of readings, see Baker, *Readers and Readings*, 3.

25 John H. Baker, 'Coke's Notebooks and the Sources of His Reports', *Cambridge Law Journal*, 30 (1972): 61–2, doi: 10.1017/S0008197300008692.

26 BL MS Harley 5225, fols 11–16.

27 John H. Baker, 'The Newe Littleton', *CLJ*, 33 (1974): 147, doi: 10.1017/S0008197300091339.

28 John H. Baker, 'Roman Law at the Third University of England', *Current Legal Problems*, 55 (2002): 141–2, doi: 10.1093/clp/55.1.123.

29 Henry Cary, ed., *A Commentary on the Tenures of Littleton; Written Prior to the Publication of Coke upon Littleton* (London: Saunders and Benning, 1829), from BL MS Harley 1621.

30 BL MS Harley 5225, fol. 16^{v}; Baker, *Readers and Readings*, 189.

be that the Elizabethan and later works on *Littleton* are a form of literature filling the gap as fewer lawyers attended Inns of Chancery before the Inns of Court. This may be too neat; readings on *Littleton* must have been a late fifteenth-century, or later, development, too recent to have inspired imitation.[31] Instead, the glosses and commentaries may simply reflect the importance of *Littleton* to early modern lawyers. There is certainly evidence that reading *Littleton* was the first stage in a legal education in the seventeenth century.[32]

Other written scholarship is not obviously associated with existing legal education or the Inns. Such works often had an explicitly practical focus, such as manuals for Justices of the Peace or guides to writing legal instruments. The purpose behind some other written scholarship is less clear, but patronage and relations with prominent individuals were clearly relevant to some productions. Some legal writing, as well as non-legal writing by lawyers, was probably an attempt to acquire patronage, although such patronage has not yet been investigated as a topic.[33] Henry Finch's *Nomotexnia* was almost certainly a successful attempt to rejuvenate a lawyer's career, at least in its later drafts and printed form.[34] Similarly, Robert Snagg sent a copy of his reading about Chancery's place in the English legal system to the Lord Keeper, Christopher Hatton.[35] Sometimes, such texts were not unsolicited gifts but requested by an interested party. For example, James Morice sent an edited version of his reading on the prerogative to William Cecil in 1578, 'for that your Honour required a sight of my travaile concerning the kings Prerogatives'.[36] Cecil's request also served as a justification for both alteration of the reading from an oral exercise to a text and the reworking of the content of the original reading. A patron might, on occasion, be an important element in the final work, something which is evident in Thomas Egerton's role as a lawyer who acted as a patron for legal works. Ferdinando Pulton's work editing statutes was impossible without Egerton's

[31] Although in 1626 Lincoln's Inn could describe such readings as authorized by 'ancient lawes and customes' (W. P. Baildon, ed., *The Records of the Honorable Society of Lincoln's Inn: The Black Books* (London: H. S. Cartwright, 1898), 2.265.

[32] James O. Halliwell (ed.), *The Autobiography and Correspondence of Sir Simonds D'Ewes* (London: Richard Bentley, 1845), 1.178–9.

[33] For non-legal writing by lawyers, see, e.g., BL MS Sloan 1065, 'An Abstract of Boterus Della Ragione di Stato' by the lawyer Richard Etherington to Chief Justice Henry Hobart for 'your speciall undeserved favour allready received by mee' (fol. 2^{v}). My thanks to Richard Serjeantson for drawing this to my attention. The importance of a lawyer's relationship with long-standing clients, as well as the role of patronage in securing advancement, can be seen in the careers of Edward Coke and John Davies. See Allen D. Boyer, *Sir Edward Coke and the Elizabethan Age* (Stanford: Stanford University Press, 2003), 37–9, 42–4, 216–17, and 246–9; and Hans S. Pawlisch, *Sir John Davies and the Conquest of Ireland: A Study in Legal Imperialism* (Cambridge: Cambridge University Press, 1985), 17–25. More generally, see Louis A. Knafla, 'The "Country" Chancellor: The Patronage of Sir Thomas Egerton Baron Ellesmere', in *Patronage in Late Renaissance England*, ed. French R. Fogle and Louis A. Knafla (Los Angeles: William Andrews Clark Memorial Library, 1983), 66.

[34] Wilfrid Prest, 'The Dialectical Origins of Finch's *Law*', *CLJ*, 36 (1977): 344–5, doi: 10.1017/S0008197300009245X.

[35] Robert Snagg, *The Antiquity and Original of the Court of Chancery* (London: Henry Seile, 1654), 1.

[36] BL MS Egerton 3376, fol. 2.

intervention,[37] but more significantly Egerton may have amended a draft version of the dedicatory preface to Davies's Irish *Reports*.[38]

On occasion, legal works could be specifically commissioned. Edward Coke wrote two works at the request of others. The *Little Treatise of Baile and Mainprize*, printed in 1635, also circulated in manuscript.[39] The surviving manuscripts refer to the text as having been '[w]ritten att the Request of Sir William Haydon'. Coke is also reported as having written 'A Discourse touchinge the unlawfulnes of private Combates' in 1609, 'at the, request of the Lord, Henry Howard, Earle of Northampton'.[40] Both of these texts may have been related to patronage: William Haydon was a prominent figure and landowner in Norfolk, an area from which Coke derived much of his legal practice;[41] Coke also had a long relationship with the Howard family in legal matters,[42] although it is less clear if this persisted after Coke's appointment to the Bench.

A particular individual of interest for questions of patronage is Thomas Sackville, whose career spans literature, law, and politics. Coke's manuscript circulation of his report of *Shelley's Case*, together with a dedicatory letter, may have been an attempt to gain patronage from Sackville, who had several connections with the Inner Temple, Coke's own Inn.[43] While Coke's manuscript may have been unsolicited, there is evidence that Sackville, like Cecil, encouraged legal scholarship. While Cecil asked for a copy of a reading which had already been delivered, Sackville seems to have approached John Dodderidge, whose outline of a never-completed treatise on the prerogative was written in response to 'your Lordshipps commaundement … To write in the Mayntenaunce of the Auncient Praerogatives Royall of her Maiestie drawne out of the Lawes Constitutions and Recordes of the Realme', something Dodderidge described as an 'imposed charge'.[44] An interesting example of Sackville's intervention in the world of legal writing is John Kitchin's *Le Court Leete*, first printed in 1580. The third printing, in 1585, begins with a dedication to Thomas Sackville in which Kitchin writes that Sackville had valued his earlier work and required him 'moreover to write'.[45] Obediently, Kitchin substantially expanded his earlier work.

[37] Virgil B. Heltzel, 'Ferdinando Pulton, Elizabethan Legal Editor', *HLQ*, 11 (1947): 77–9, doi: 10.2307/3816033.

[38] Henry E. Huntington Library Ellesmere MS 2622. The alterations to this draft were included in the 'Preface Dedicatory' to John Davies, *Le Primer Reports des Cases et Matters en Ley resolves et adiudges en les Courts del Roy en Ireland* (Dublin: John Franckton, 1615). The alterations are in a hand which could be Egerton's, but this is not certain.

[39] Edward Coke, *A Little Treatise of Baile and Mainprize* (London: William Cooke, 1635); BL MS Harley 444, fols 185–202; BL MS Stowe 145, fols 80–98^{v}.

[40] Bodleian MS Tanner 85, fols 29^{v}–41^{v}, printed in John Gutch, *Collectanea Curiosa; or Miscellaneous Tracts Relating to the History and Antiquities of England and Ireland* (Oxford: Clarendon Press, 1781), 1.9–12.

[41] Boyer, *Sir Edward Coke*, 40–4.

[42] Boyer, *Sir Edward Coke*, 37–9.

[43] David A. Smith, 'Was There a Rule in *Shelley's Case*?' *JLH*, 30 (2009): 62, doi: 10.1080/01440360902765449.

[44] BL MS Harley 5220, fols 2 and 4.

[45] John Kitchin, *Le court leete, et court baron* (London: Richard Tottell, 1585), sig. A2.

The Circulation of Legal Scholarship

Non-lawyers may have known little of legal developments not covered in print. The Elizabethan author of a history of the law of England clearly did not know about the preceding half century of defamation jurisdiction in the common law courts, something which was not covered in printed sources.[46] Printed legal scholarship was available to the wider public, although the extent to which non-lawyers acquired such books has not yet been investigated in detail.[47] The focus of this section is on the circulation of legal scholarship within the legal profession, particularly the bar. As printed works were available both new and second hand, the particular concern is access to oral and manuscript legal scholarship.

The circulation of oral scholarship seems relatively simple: each of the Inns was a closed society during readings with only members and specially invited guests present. Good evidence of this can be found in two collections of legal maxims from the 1580s. As the readings are spread over a period of around five years in each volume, the collections were probably compiled by students. In each collection there are references to cases put at readings. In one manuscript all of the readings are from Lincoln's Inn;[48] in the other all but one of the readings are from the Middle Temple.[49] Such isolation presumably explains the surviving collections of readings, often in close temporal proximity, from single Inns.[50] Some collections of readings are more diverse, and can be seen as later compilations, such as one containing material from readings in Gray's Inn, the Inner Temple, Lincoln's Inn, and Lyon's Inn between the late fifteenth century and 1580.[51] Some of these collections clearly circulated and were copied, such as two identical manuscripts of readings from the 1560s in Gray's Inn and the Inner Temple.[52]

While the readings themselves were closed, material from readings could circulate in manuscript.[53] The originally oral readings became valuable texts. Henry Sherfield

46 BL MS Harley 4317, fols 11^{v}–12. The author only refers to *Scandalum Magnatum*, criminal regulation by JPs and proceedings in the church courts as remedies for defamation. The author refers to Elizabeth as the current monarch on fol. 1.

47 A useful starting point will be Richard J. Ross, 'The Commoning of the Common Law: The Renaissance Debate over the Printing of English Law', *University of Pennsylvania Law Review*, 146 (1998): 323–461, doi: 10.2307/3312623.

48 BL MS Hargrave 207, fols 63, 64^{v}, 66^{v}, 71^{v}, 76, and 77.

49 BL MS Hargrave 318, fols 26–7, 50^{v}, 95^{v}. Edward Heron's 1587 reading in Lincoln's Inn is mentioned on fol. 45^{v}. It is possible that knowledge of this reading was acquired through a text, but a report of a single case may also have been communicated orally through a personal connection.

50 e.g. BL MS Harley 1631 which features notes from readings in Gray's Inn from 1595–1599.

51 BL MS Harley 3209, see Baker, *Readers and Readings*, 286–7.

52 BL MS Lansd. 1134 and Cambridge University Library MS Ff.5.17. See J. H. Baker, *A Catalogue of English Legal Manuscripts in Cambridge University Library* (Woodbridge: Boydell Press, 1996), xxxiv and 251.

53 Why readings were not printed until 1630 (Dodderidge's *Compleat Parson* is the first) is unknown.

recorded loans of his manuscripts, including readings, in his financial records.[54] Whether manuscripts of readings were available commercially is unclear and evidence is extremely limited. There is plenty of evidence of law reports being circulated and reproduced scribally, but much less evidence for readings.[55] In the one detailed study of the output of a Caroline scribe, Peter Beal's 'Feathery Scribe', there is a considerable body of legal work, including a collection of material on Chancery totalling over one thousand pages.[56] Clearly legal material was produced by scribes as part of a commercial enterprise. However, no material from the Inns of Court has been identified as written by the Feathery Scribe. This could simply be an accident of survival, but the Feathery Scribe's legal output does not include any more technical works, including any law-French material.

One possible explanation is that scribal work for lawyers was carried out by specialist scribes; this may explain the seemingly high price per page paid by Lincoln's Inn for a manuscript work.[57] An alternative, perhaps related, explanation is suggested by William Fleetwood's presentation copy of legal material related to London. Fleetwood's volume was prepared by his own clerk.[58] In the preface to Plowden's *Commentaries*, Plowden refers to the manuscript reports which he lent to friends being obtained by their clerks, showing that lawyers' private clerks were involved in the circulation of manuscript material.[59] If lawyers' own servants undertook copying for their masters, more technical material may not have left the households of lawyers and so not circulated scribally.

Nevertheless, it has been suggested that despite the vagaries of manuscript circulation, some early modern readings were intended primarily as treatises, meant to circulate as texts, rather than as oral scholarship which came to be written down.[60] Certainly some readings survive in sufficient numbers and detail to suggest that this did occur. Some readers may have released their texts to circulate through scribal publication. James Whitelocke's lengthy reading on benefices was probably deliberately circulated and many copies survive.[61] However, there are only a handful of readings of which sufficient copies survive to suggest widespread circulation. For many other readings, the evidence suggests something considerably more limited.[62]

One of the readings which Mirow suggests should be considered as a treatise is Henry Sherfield's 1624 reading in Lincoln's Inn on the Statute of Wills and its explanation.

54 Hampshire Record Office: Jervoise of Herriard Collection: 44 M69/L25/1–6, unpaginated. The references to some of these loans in Baker, *Readers and Readings*, 236 are incorrect following recataloguing.

55 Baker, *A Catalogue of English Legal Manuscripts*, xlii–xliii.

56 Peter Beal, *In Praise of Scribes* (Oxford: Clarendon Press, 1998), 96 (referring to Harvard Law School MS 1034) and 211–68.

57 Beal, *In Praise of Scribes*, 69–72, n. 12. Lincoln's Inn paid 7½*d.* per page. The other evidence collected by Beal for scribal costs suggests prices of 1*d.*–5*d.* per page were more common.

58 London Metropolitan Archive MS COL/CS/01/011, insert after front cover.

59 Edmund Plowden, *Les Comentaries, ou les Reportes* (London: Richard Tottel, 1571), sig. ¶3.

60 Mirow, 'Ascent of the Readings', 238.

61 Baker, *Readers and Readings*, 235.

62 Baker, *A Catalogue of English Legal Manuscripts*, xxxiv.

Several copies of the reading survive and there is some evidence from Sherfield himself about how the text circulated. Sherfield's four books of his reading remained in his possession, but he lent them to four other lawyers in the decade after the reading was delivered. In July 1631 Richard Townsend borrowed the books as he was about to read on the same statute. The books were also lent to Oliver St John and William Prynne.[63] A Mr Romsey of Gray's Inn borrowed Sherfield's text of his recapitulation of the reading.[64] Such direct borrowing from the author raises questions about the utility of written readings as treatises. Several years after the reading was delivered, even a relatively experienced practitioner such as Richard Townsend seems to have had to approach the original reader for access to the text, rather than obtaining it from a colleague or in the marketplace. Half of the borrowers of Sherfield's reading were, like Sherfield, members of Lincoln's Inn, perhaps revealing that manuscript circulation, even of treatise-like readings, was to some extent limited by the divisions between the Inns, an issue also identified in relation to earlier readings by McGlynn in this handbook.[65]

It is notable, for example, that Sherfield seems not to have trusted Townsend with Sherfield's own notes on his reading. While Sherfield recorded loans in his account book, in the case of Townsend he also noted the presence of two witnesses to the handing over of the manuscript, one of whom, Sherfield's brother, frequently acted as a witness to his financial transactions. Furthermore, Sherfield specified that the books of the reading were 'to be kept safely for his use and to be delivered backe to me safe as they are without defasing'.[66] These explicit conditions suggest that Sherfield was uncomfortable with the loan to Townsend and needed to clarify the limits of acceptable use. Unlike Sherfield and most of the other borrowers of his notes, Townsend was not a member of Lincoln's Inn. This might explain Sherfield's concern: Townsend was a relative stranger.

Such a limitation on circulation, and concern about relative strangers, may have been a shared norm. When Matthew Hale left his writings to Lincoln's Inn, he expressly limited their use to members of the Inn.[67] Hale explained '[t]hey are a treasure not fit for

[63] Hampshire Record Office: Jervoise of Herriard Collection: 44M69/L25/6/1, entry for 2 July 1631; 44M69/L25/3, entry for 23 June 1627; 44M69/L25/5/1, entry for 14 November 1633.

[64] Hampshire Record Office: Jervoise of Herriard Collection: 44M69/L25/5/1, entry for 14 November 1633. I have not found any 'Romsey' admitted to Gray's Inn in this period (Joseph Foster, ed., *The Register of Admissions to Gray's Inn 1521–1889* (London: Hansard, 1889)). The recapitulation of Sherfield's reading is BL MS Hargrave 402, fols 34–59.

[65] Sherfield recorded eleven loans of manuscript material, five of which were of Court of Wards material to the father and son members of the Inner Temple, Nicholas and Hugh Cholmely. Sherfield does not record any other loans of his collections concerning the Court of Wards. Of the remaining six loans, four were to members of Lincoln's Inn. Two were of Sherfield's reading, another was of Robert Constable's 1489 reading, also in Lincoln's Inn (Hampshire Record Office: Jervoise of Herriard Collection: 44M69/L25/1, rear flyleaf, loan to William Noy in 1609). The final loan was of antiquarian material (Hampshire Record Office: Jervoise of Herriard Collection: 44M69/L25/3, entry for 17 February 1626, loan to William Hakewill). The two remaining loans were those of Sherfield's reading to Townsend and Romsey.

[66] Hampshire Record Office: Jervoise of Herriard Collection: 44M69/L25/6/1, entry for 2 July 1631.

[67] Joseph Hunter, ed., *A Catalogue of the Manuscripts in the Library of the Honourable Society of Lincoln's Inn* (London: Eyre and Spottiswoode, 1838): vii.

every man's view, nor is every man capable of making use of them'. While this might explain Hale's ban on the printing of his writings, it does not explain their restriction to members of Lincoln's Inn. Presumably members of other Inns would also have been 'capable of making use of them' and so Hale must have had another reason for limiting availability to members of a single Inn. Another explanation for circulation focused on individual Inns may be practicality, in that it may have been easier to make contact with, and recover materials from, members of a lawyer's own Inn. Certainly Sherfield recorded that he received his reading back from Oliver St John at another Lincoln's Inn reading, an event which all lawyers in the Inn were expected to attend.[68]

Hale's will also demonstrates that even posthumous circulation of manuscript material might be limited. While death deprived a lawyer of physical control over his manuscripts, testamentary instructions might continue to limit circulation, at least in the short term. James Dyer left all of his manuscripts and other law books to his nephews. As relatives often attended the same Inn, such gifts to family members may also have acted to limit the circulation of material outside particular Inns of Court. It was only after much persuasion that a restricted selection of Dyer's manuscript case reports was printed and two more decades before the manuscript was obtained by Edward Coke.[69]

When it did occur, textual circulation of scholarship could be incomplete and unreliable. Borrowing seems to have depended largely upon personal connections, and such connections might not suffice to obtain desired texts. When describing the preparations for his 1631 reading, John Bankes acknowledged that he had seen 'conceipts' from readings delivered in different Inns in 1628 and 1629 on the same statute.[70] As Mirow explains, conceits were 'short points of law extracted by note takers from the readings'.[71] Bankes, in other words, did not have access to the full text of earlier readings, nor seemingly, the readers' own material. Also in 1631, Hugh Cholmely of the Inner Temple lent Henry Sherfield of Lincoln's Inn 'a little book of some notes' of a reading.[72] Sherfield did not receive the full text of the reading, but only some notes, which may well have been from an audience member, rather than the reader's own. The material was based upon the oral presentation, mediated via the listener's understanding. As a result, the knowledge of unheard readings which circulated in manuscript risked incompleteness and inaccuracy. Such limitations may explain why, in 1573, Wray J. could only refer to what 'he had heard ... the opinion of the Middle Temple' to be, and why early modern judges could identify particular views of the law as attributable to individual Inns.[73]

[68] Hampshire Record Office: Jervoise of Herriard Collection: 44M69/L25/3, entry for 23 June 1627.

[69] John H. Baker, *Reports from the Lost Notebooks of Sir James Dyer* (London: SS, 1993), xxxv–xxxviii.

[70] BL MS Harley 5141, fol. 83.

[71] Mirow, 'Ascent of the Readings', 245.

[72] Hampshire Record Office: Jervoise of Herriard Collection: 44M69/L25/5/1, entry for 26 February 1631.

[73] John Baker, *Baker and Milsom Sources of English Legal History: Private Law to 1750*, 2nd edn (Oxford: Oxford University Press, 2010), 145; *Dawles v Baldwin* (1631) Cambridge University Library MS Gg.2.19, fol. 210 (view of the Inner Temple).

Sources for Common Law Scholarship

The circulation of material and ideas is one approach to the relationship between speech, manuscript, and print in legal scholarship. Another is to consider the range of sources upon which that scholarship was based. Early modern legal scholarship was increasingly based on reading texts. Coke informed students that when attending readings they would hear cases and could then 'finde out *and reade* the case so vouched' [emphasis added], clearly assuming the cases were based upon those available as texts.[74] As preparation for his reading, Robert Snagg wrote that he had 'looked into' previous readings, just as John Bankes said he had 'seene' material from prior readings on the same topic.[75] Unlike the fifteenth-century lawyer Littleton, early modern lawyers did not refer to what they had 'heard' at readings.[76]

Legal scholarship, particularly in the Inns of Court, was not based solely on printed texts. As Baker observes, even in the Inns of Chancery, 'the students were told of earlier inns of court readings, of cases depending in the courts, and of other unpublished authorities of various kinds'.[77] Such scholarship was also not grounded simply on a combination of print and manuscript. Information about cases pending in the courts, for example, does not seem to have circulated in textual form. Such use of non-textual material was not unique; several readers made use of their personal knowledge and experience, whether as practitioners or legislators, to inform their readings.

Personal experience could provide more than just knowledge of sources. John Bankes justified his choice of statute on the basis that he had been a Member of Parliament when it was enacted and 'therefore have some Advantage to knowe the meaninge of it'.[78] Francis Phillips explained that he had chosen his statute to enable him to consider the customs of London, his practice having 'given me occasion to looke further into the customs of that citty then most others of my profession'.[79] Such personal experience was not always acknowledged. Robert Snagg's 1581 reading on Chancery included discussion about whether a peer could be arrested for contempt of the Chancery, or if the privilege of peers from arrest protected him.[80] Nowhere in the reading as it survives is it mentioned that precisely this question arose in the early 1570s.[81] Snagg's knowledge of the

[74] Edward Coke, *The First Part of the Institutes of the Lawes of England. Or, A Commentarie Upon Littleton* (London: John More, 1628), fol. 70.

[75] Snagg, *The Antiquity and Original*, 2; BL MS Harley 5141, fol. 83.

[76] Littleton, *Les Tenures*, fol. 112^{v} (s. 481).

[77] John H. Baker, 'The Inns of Court and Legal Doctrine', in *The Common Law Tradition: Lawyers, Books and the Law*, ed. John H. Baker (London: Hambledon Press, 2000), 47.

[78] BL MS Harley 5141, fol. 83.

[79] BL MS Hargrave 267, fol. 3.

[80] Snagg, *The Original and Antiquity*, 80–3.

[81] On the case, see M. A. R. Graves, 'Freedom of Peers from Arrest: The Case of Henry Second Lord Cromwell, 1571–1572', *AJLH*, 21 (1977): 1–14, doi: 10.2307/844922.

case probably came not from text, but his own personal experience; Snagg was an MP in 1571–1572, just as the issue was discussed and decided in the House of Lords.[82]

New materials were quickly adopted in legal scholarship, whether decisions of the courts or contemporary scholarship. Edward Coke's *Commentarie on Littleton* was printed in 1628 and was cited in two readings in 1631 and another in 1632.[83] William Lambarde's *Archeion* incorporated material from Bodin's *République*, first printed in 1576, in a draft section completed in 1579.[84] New cases were similarly introduced into readings quickly. Mirow has shown that *Butler and Baker's Case*, printed in Coke's *Third Reports* in 1602 was discussed in Augustine Nicholls' reading of the same year,[85] and that other readers used cases found in printed volumes within a few years of printing.[86]

Manuscript or unwritten material seems a little more problematic. Hugh Hare's 1592 reading on the Statute of Wills did not discuss the 1591 decision in the then-unprinted *Butler and Baker's Case*, despite its obvious relevance.[87] However, this is exceptional. Readers on the Statute of Wills did generally make use of unprinted material, especially to consider recent cases.[88] The same concern with recent scholarship can be seen in John Bankes's description of the preparations for his 1631 reading, where he acknowledged that he had seen material from readings delivered in different Inns in 1628 and 1629 on the same statute.[89]

Both personal experience and texts were not used uncritically in readings, which were consequently more than an opportunity to expound the law. In Snagg's discussion of contempt of Chancery it was not mentioned that Snagg's conclusion was contrary to that reached by the House of Lords.[90] The disagreement was consequently not overt, but does demonstrate that readings in the Inns could be a means of (implicitly) censuring decisions as bad law. Similarly, views expressed in texts could be rejected. In his reading on the prerogative, James Morice observed that in Brooke's *Graunde Abridgement*, Brooke described a case as holding that judges could not be required to

[82] P. W. Hasler, ed., *The History of Parliament: The House of Commons, 1558–1603* (London: Boydell and Brewer, 1981), 3.408–9.

[83] Richard Townsend (Cambridge University Library MS Dd.5.51, fol. 22^{v}); John Wilde (Cambridge University Library MS Dd.5.8, fol. v); Edward Littleton (BL MS Hargrave 372, fol. 54). The first reference to the *Commentarie on Littleton* I have found in a reported case is earlier: *Pope v Tinker* (1629) Cambridge University Library MS Gg.2.19, fols 49–50.

[84] Ian Williams, 'Developing a Prerogative Theory for the Chancery: The French Connection', in *Law and Authority in British Legal History, 1200–1900*, ed. Mark Godfrey (Cambridge: Cambridge University Press, 2016), 43–6.

[85] *Butler and Baker's Case* (1591) 3 Co. Rep. 25; Mirow, 'Ascent of the Readings', 252.

[86] Mirow, 'Ascent of the Readings', 242–4.

[87] Mirow, 'Ascent of the Readings', 247.

[88] Mirow, 'Ascent of the Readings', 242–7.

[89] BL MS Harley 5141, fol. 83.

[90] In 1572 the House of Lords held that Henry, second Lord Cromwell, could not be arrested for contempt of Chancery (see Graves, 'Freedom of Peers from Arrest'). Snagg seems to have considered that arrest of peers for contempt of the Chancery should be possible, although the report is qualified, referring to the matter as a 'great case' on which he would not decide the law (Snagg, *The Original and Antiquity*, 80–4).

provide advice to the king concerning cases in which the king was a party.[91] Morice rejected this conclusion, 'since it is not small part of the Justices allegiance expressed in their oath faithfully and lawfully to Councell and advise the king in his affaires'. However, Morice went further, stating that '[i]f his Maiestie therefore demand the opinion of his Justices ... if they conceale or deny to declare the same the king hath iust cause to displace them and according to the law to correct and punish them'.[92] Morice's view, in his reading, would seem not only to reject Brooke's interpretation of the case, but also the underlying premise of the case itself, in which Henry VII accepted the judges' refusal to advise him.[93] The same critical approach can also be seen in written scholarship. William Fleetwood even applied it to George Treherne's widely circulated reading on the law of the forest, describing Treherne as incorrect when records were to the contrary.[94]

One feature of the texts discussed so far is their relative insularity. Not the geographic parochialism for which Pocock criticized the common lawyers and which has long been exploded, but a disciplinary narrowness.[95] Early modern common law scholarship relied heavily upon legal sources. Even Bodin's *République*, now usually regarded as a work of political thought, was categorized by John Dodderidge as a work by a French lawyer.[96] There are of course exceptions. Henry Finch's *Nomotexnia* began with a selection of maxims taken from other disciplines, such as theology, grammar, and logic, although these maxims were immediately linked with legal sources to demonstrate their relevance.[97]

Where appropriate, non-legal material could be used in legal scholarship. When considering questions about the meaning of Latin words, or etymology, use of classical sources was entirely appropriate. William Fleetwood's argument that the Star Chamber, *camera stellata*, was 'soe called of the Serpent Stellio ... For the forme of the said serpent was in Colour blewe, al to be speckle with spots shyneinge in the night bright like unto Starres' echoes Ovid's *Metamorphoses*, a widely known text in Elizabethan England.[98] The argument may have seemed particular apposite as Ovid's description occurs in the context of a punishment, just as the Star Chamber operated as a criminal court.

Other use of non-legal sources was rare and tended to occupy a very particular place in both the physical arrangement of law books and legal scholarship. While many lawyers do not seem to have incorporated non-legal material into their notes, a printed

91 Presumably citing Robert Brooke, *La graunde abridgement* (London: Richard Tottel, 1573): tit. Judgement, pl. 157.

92 BL MS Egerton 3376, fol. 36v.

93 (1486) YB Trin. 1 Hen VII, fol. 25a, pl. 1 at fol. 26a.

94 BL MS Add. 26047, fols 7–7v.

95 On geographical insularity, see Christopher Brooks and Kevin Sharpe, 'Debate: History, English Law and the Renaissance', *P&P*, 72 (1976): 137–8, http://www.jstor.org/stable/650331.

96 BL MS Harley 5220, fol. 6.

97 Henry Finch, *Nomotexnia, cestascavoir un description del common leys dangleterre solonque les rules del art* (London: Societie of Stationers, 1613), fols 3–15.

98 Folger Shakespeare Library V.b.303, fol. 26; Ovid, *Metamorphoses* (London: William Heinemann, 1916), 271 (5.446–5.461).

edition of Littleton's *Tenures* owned by Thomas Egerton features manuscript annotations from Aristotle and Cyprian on the rear flyleaves.[99] One of Egerton's commonplace books includes material from Plato, Aristotle, Cyprian, Aquinas, and Joachim Hopper on the inner flyleaves.[100] A similar arrangement can be seen in Edward Coke's commonplace book, which was preceded by a selection of material under the heading 'de legibus', drawn from Cicero, Isidore, Thomas More's *Utopia*, and St German's *Doctor and Student*.[101] Similarly, a collection of material related to London, written by William Fleetwood, includes a selection of more jurisprudential topics such as 'De Aequitate' and 'De Judice', but only at the very rear of the volume.[102] Fleetwood's collection included references to Aristotle's *Politics* and *Ethics*, *Bracton*, Justinian's *Institutes*, Fortescue's *De laudibus legum Angliae*, Aulus Gellius, and Augustine's *City of God* (although this final work was only cited from an intermediate source). Most of these texts would have been just as familiar to educated non-lawyers as to common lawyers; they were part of wider intellectual culture. For none of these three lawyers, some of the most successful of Elizabethan and Jacobean England, does such non-legal material appear in the body of the notebooks themselves. The substance of the law was determined by legal sources, not philosophy or theology. Even John Dodderidge's commonplace book, which incorporates a wider range of material, falls into this model, incorporating material from the civil law, but no non-legal sources.[103]

This physical locating of non-legal material outside the main body of doctrine is reflected in the way non-legal sources were typically used in legal scholarship, namely as introductory or prefatory material. We do not, for example, see common lawyers using poets as an authoritative source of law, unlike in the civilian tradition. While Grotius could cite Ovid's *Metamorphoses* as one of the authorities demonstrating that the waters of a river were *res communis*, when Matthew Hale discussed the law in relation to rivers, his sources were limited to legal texts, despite Hale's own knowledge of Grotius's work.[104]

This does not mean the non-legal sources were unimportant; their physical and intellectual location meant that they literally framed doctrinal material and placed the common law within a wider intellectual and cultural heritage. They shaped the theory of, and ideas about, law for common lawyers and could equally have done so for non-lawyers. Such references were rarely fully developed theories. Instead, the various texts form a collection of assumptions and uncontested commonplaces about law which seem to

[99] Thomas Littleton, *Les Tenures*, Henry E. Huntington Library RB 62239.

[100] Henry E. Huntington Library Ellesmere MS 496, fols 2^v–3^v.

[101] BL MS Harley 6687, fol. 7.

[102] BL MS Add. 26047, fols 113–20.

[103] BL MS Hargrave 407.

[104] Govaert C. J. J. van den Bergh, 'Auctoritas Poetarum in Court: A Footnote to the History of *Institutes* 3.23.2 and *Digest* 1.8.6.5 and 7', in *Fundamina: A Journal of Legal History: Essays in Honor of Eric Pool*, ed. Rena van den Bergh (Pretoria: South African Society of Legal Historians, 2005), 346; Matthew Hale, 'A Treatise in Three Parts', in *A Collection of Tracts Relative to the Law of England*, ed. Francis Hargrave (London: E. Brooke, 1787), 5–10. On Hale's knowledge of Grotius' *De iure belli ac pacis*, where Ovid is cited, see Alan Cromartie, *Sir Matthew Hale 1609–1676: Law, Religion and Natural Philosophy* (Cambridge: Cambridge University Press, 1995), 46.

have been widely shared amongst the legal profession. Cicero's *De legibus*, for example, was a common point of reference throughout the period.[105] Occasional glimpses also suggest that non-legal sources shaped the form of legal scholarship by providing a guide to method. When reading in New Inn, Dodderidge referred to Cicero's *De officis* to justify commencing the reading with a definition of the subject matter.[106]

When non-legal sources are cited in substantive, not prefatory, discussions, this is probably a hint that legal sources were lacking on the point in question. John Dodderidge admitted as much when explaining why his proposed treatise on the prerogative would make use of more than legal texts:

> for that their ar no more Prerogatives Royall medled with all by the said Lawes but sutche onlye as tyme gave occation to debate and call into question whiche althoughe they be manye yeat in deede ar they but somme fewe of a greater nommber yt shall be requisite in this Treatise somme tyme in yeildinge of Reasons and for more varietye to have recourse to the fountaynes themselves I meane the fountaynes of Divinitie Philosophie The Lawes of Nations and Recordes oute of which all lawes but espetially the lawes of this Realme ar evidentlye deduced.[107]

Dodderidge highlights his proposed use of non-legal materials and justifies this on the basis of the inadequacy of legal material. Generalizing from Dodderidge's admission seems plausible. For example, when Edward Coke explained the illegality at common law of monopolies or brothels, he did so on the basis of the law of God drawn from Scripture, followed by other non-legal material.[108] The typical references in the rest of the *Institutes* to cases or statutes are notable only for their absence.

Concluding Remarks

This chapter has highlighted the continuing role of oral scholarship in the legal profession. Lawyers made use of, and sought out, material from readings and incorporated such material into their notebooks and their own readings. Both oral and written legal scholarship also made extensive use of texts, rapidly adopting new sources, not entirely uncritically. Despite the important role of texts, the inadequacy of existing writings was described as justification for both oral and written scholarship, while the traditional forms of oral scholarship in the Inns also inspired printed and manuscript texts.

105 BL MS Harley 4990, fol. 146v (an anonymous reading probably from the 1530s); Finch, *Nomotexnia*, fol. 3; BL MS Add. 25251, fol. 33 (John Briscoe's reading in 1623).

106 BL MS Harley 5053, fol. 1.

107 BL MS Harley 5220, fol. 4v.

108 Edward Coke, *The Third Part of the Institutes of the Laws of England* (London: M. Flesher, 1644), 181 and 205.

Scholarship was also produced which was never intended for oral dissemination. Reasons such as patronage can be identified as at least one cause of some such works, and the chapter has also noted the role of individuals in soliciting such texts from lawyers, although more work remains to be done on both of these topics, both of which might draw fruitfully on scholarship outside traditional legal history.

The circulation of ideas from readings amongst the legal profession was increasingly a textual activity although such circulation was uneven and unreliable. There is stronger evidence of the circulation of both oral and written scholarship within individual Inns than between them. By the seventeenth century it was no longer possible to refer to a text as 'of Lincolnesin labour', as Thomas Frowyk described a manuscript abridgement in his will, but we might legitimately consider whether it is more appropriate to refer to scholarship in an Inn of Court, rather than the learning of the Inns of Court.[109] These limitations should not be taken too far. Even if a particular piece of scholarship cannot be assumed to represent 'the law', it serves, like a dissenting judgement, to show what was thinkable.[110]

In some respects, lawyers were also relatively isolated from other groups in early modern England. Common law scholarship relied heavily upon purely legal sources. Reference to non-legal material was admitted to be a sign of inadequacy in the legal texts. However, for certain important topics, especially more theoretical issues, lawyers were happy to make use of a wider range of textual sources, typically those with general currency in early modern England. While the Inns of Court might have been relatively separate from each other, and doctrinal legal scholarship from other disciplines, broad ideas of the role of law, equity, and justice were shared amongst lawyers and non-lawyers alike.

Bibliography

Alsop, J. D. 'William Fleetwood and Elizabethan Historical Scholarship', *Sixteenth Century Journal*, 25 (1994): 155–76.

Baildon, W. P., ed. *The Records of the Honorable Society of Lincoln's Inn: The Black Books*, Vol. 2 (London: 1898).

Baker, J. H. *A Catalogue of English Legal Manuscripts in Cambridge University Library* (Woodbridge: Boydell Press, 1996).

Baker, J. H. 'Coke's Notebooks and the Sources of His Reports', *Cambridge Law Journal*, 30 (1972): 59–86.

Baker, J. H. 'English Law Books and Legal Publishing', in *The Cambridge History of the Book in Britain*, Vol. 4: *1557–1695*, ed. John Barnard and D. F. McKenzie (Cambridge: Cambridge University Press, 2002), 474–503.

[109] John H. Baker, 'The Books of the Common Law', in *The Cambridge History of the Book in Britain*, Vol. 3: *1400–1557*, ed. Lotte Hellinga and J. B. Trapp (Cambridge: Cambridge University Press, 1999), 416 n. 38.

[110] Charles Donahue, Jr, '"The Hypostasis of a Prophecy": Legal Realism and Legal History' in *Law and Legal Process: Substantive Law and Procedure in English Legal History*, ed. Matthew Dyson and David Ibbetson (Cambridge: Cambridge University Press, 2013), 6.

Baker, J. H. 'Roman Law at the Third University of England', *Current Legal Problems*, 55 (2002): 123–50.
Baker, J. H. 'The Books of the Common Law', in *The Cambridge History of the Book in Britain*, Vol. 3: *1400–1557*, ed. Lotte Hellinga and J. B. Trapp (Cambridge: Cambridge University Press, 1999), 411–32.
Baker, J. H. 'The Inns of Court and Legal Doctrine', in *The Common Law Tradition: Lawyers, Books and the Law*, ed. J. H. Baker (London: Hambledon Press, 2000), 37–51.
Baker, J. H. 'The Newe Littleton', *Cambridge Law Journal*, 33 (1974): 145–55.
Baker, J. H. *Readers and Readings in the Inns of Court and Chancery* (London: Selden Society, 2000).
Baker, J. H. *Reports from the Lost Notebooks of Sir James Dyer* (London: Selden Society, 1993).
Baker, J. H. *Baker and Milsom Sources of English Legal History: Private Law to 1750*, 2nd edn (Oxford: Oxford University Press, 2010).
Beal, Peter. *In Praise of Scribes* (Oxford: Clarendon Press, 1998).
Boyer, Allen D. *Sir Edward Coke and the Elizabethan Age* (Stanford: Stanford University Press, 2003).
British Library Additional MS 25251, fols 26–52, 'John Briscoe's Reading on Wills' (1623).
British Library Additional MS 26047, 'William Fleetwood on the Forest Laws'.
British Library Egerton MS 3376, 'James Morice's Reading (1578)'.
British Library Hargrave MS 98, fols 31–55, 'William Prynne's Reading (1662)'.
British Library Hargrave MS 207, 'Readings and Moots Associated with Lincoln's Inn in the 1580s'.
British Library Hargrave MS 267, 'Francis Phillips' Reading (1661)'.
British Library Hargrave MS 318, 'Elizabethan Collection of Legal Maxims'.
British Library Hargrave MS 372, 'Readings from the Inner Temple (1631–1635)'.
British Library Hargrave MS 402, fols 34–59, 'Henry Sherfield's Reading (1624)'.
British Library Hargrave MS 407, 'John Dodderidge's Commonplace Book'.
British Library Harley MS 444, fols 185–202, 'Edward Coke's *Little Treatise of Baile and Mainprize*'.
British Library Harley MS 980, 'Thomas Gibbon's Commonplace Book, Reign of Charles I'.
British Library Harley MS 1631, fols 310–22, 'Readings from Gray's Inn in the 1590s'.
British Library Harley MS 3209, fols 9–36, 'Collection of Readings, Various Inns, Sixteenth Century'.
British Library Harley MS 4317, 'Origin of the Laws of England, Elizabethan'.
British Library Harley MS 4990, fols 146–71, 'Anonymous Reading, *c*.1530s'.
British Library Harley MS 5053, 'John Dodderidge's Reading (1593–1594)'.
British Library Harley MS 5141, fols 83–110, 'John Bankes' Reading (1631)'.
British Library Harley MS 5220, 'John Dodderidge's Proposed Treatise on the Royal Prerogative'.
British Library Harley MS 5225, '"*Tractatus*" and "Lecture" on *Littleton* by William Fleetwood'.
British Library Harley MS 6687, 'Edward Coke's Notebooks'.
British Library Lansdowne MS 1134, 'Readings from Gray's Inn and the Temples (1551–1565)'.
British Library Sloane MS 1065, 'Richard Etherington's "An Abstract of Boterus *Della ragion di stato*"'.
British Library Stowe MS 145, fols 80–98v, 'Edward Coke's *Little Treatise of Baile and Mainprize*'.
British Library Stowe MS 424, fols 3–36v, 'Edward Bagshaw's Reading (1640)'.
Brooke, Robert. *La graunde abridgement* (London: 1573).

Brooks, Christopher W. and Kevin Sharpe. 'Debate: History, English Law, and the Renaissance', *Past and Present*, 72 (1976): 133–42.

Cambridge University Library MS Dd.5.8, 'John Wilde's Reading (1631)'.

Cambridge University Library MS Dd.5.51, fols 22–30v, 'Richard Townsend's Reading (1631)'.

Cambridge University Library MS Ff.5.17, 'Readings from Gray's Inn and the Temple (1562–1565)'.

Cambridge University Library MS Gg.2.19, 'Law Reports from the Reign of Charles I'.

Cary, Henry, ed. *A Commentary on the Tenures of Littleton; Written Prior to the Publication of Coke upon Littleton* (London: 1829).

Coke, Sir Edward. *A Little Treatise of Baile and Mainprize* (London: 1635).

Coke, Sir Edward. *Quinta par relationum* (London: 1605).

Coke, Sir Edward. *The First Part of the Institutes of the Lawes of England* (London: 1628).

Coke, Sir Edward. *The Second Part of the Institutes of the Lawes of England* (London: 1642).

Coke, Sir Edward. *The Third Part of the Institutes of the Lawes of England* (London: 1644).

Cromartie, Alan. *Sir Matthew Hale 1609–1676: Law, Religion, and Natural Philosophy* (Cambridge: Cambridge University Press, 1995).

Davies, Sir John. *Le primer reports des cases et matters en ley resolves et adiudges en les courts del roy en Ireland* (Dublin: 1615).

Donahue, Charles. '"The hypostasis of a prophecy": Legal Realism and Legal History', in *Law and Legal Process: Substantive Law and Procedure in English Legal History*, ed. Matthew Dyson and David Ibbetson (Cambridge: Cambridge University Press, 2013), 1–16.

Finch, Henry. *Nomotexnia, cestascavoir un description del common leys dangleterre solonque les rules del art* (London: 1613).

Folger Shakespeare Library MS V.b.303, 'William Fleetwood on the Star Chamber'.

Foster, Joseph, ed. *The Register of Admissions to Gray's Inn 1521–1889* (London: 1889).

Graves, M. A. R. 'Freedom of Peers from Arrest: The Case of Henry Second Lord Cromwell, 1571–1572', *American Journal of Legal History*, 21 (1977): 1–14.

Gutch, John. *Collectanea Curiosa; or Miscellaneous Tracts Relating to the History and Antiquities of England and Ireland*, Vol. 1 (Oxford: 1781).

Hale, Sir Matthew. 'A Treatise in Three Parts', in *A Collection of Tracts Relative to the Law of England*, ed. Francis Hargrave (London: 1787), 1–248.

Halliwell, James O., ed. *The Autobiography and Correspondence of Sir Simonds D'Ewes*, Vol. 1 (London: 1845).

Hampshire Record Office MS 44 M69/L25/1-6, 'Account Books of Henry Sherfield from the Reign of Charles I'.

Hasler, P. W., ed. *The History of Parliament: The House of Commons, 1558–1603*, Vol. 3 (London: Boydell and Brewer, 1981).

Heltzel, Virgil B. 'Ferdinando Pulton, Elizabethan Legal Editor', *Huntington Library Quarterly*, 11 (1947): 77–9.

Henry E. Huntington Library Ellesmere MS 496, 'Thomas Egerton's Commonplace Book'.

Henry E. Huntington Library Ellesmere MS 2622, 'Draft of the Preface to John Davies's Irish Reports'.

Hunter, Joseph, ed. *A Catalogue of the Manuscripts in the Library of the Honourable Society of Lincoln's Inn* (London: 1838).

Kitchin, John. *Le court leete, et court baron* (London: 1585).

Knafla, Louis A. 'The "Country" Chancellor: The Patronage of Sir Thomas Egerton Baron Ellesmere', in *Patronage in Late Renaissance England*, ed. French R. Fogle and Louis A. Knafla (Los Angeles: William Andrews Clark Memorial Library, 1983).

Littleton, Thomas. *Les Tenures des Monsieur Littleton* (London: 1581).
London Metropolitan Archives MS COL/CS/01/011, 'The *Liber Fleetwood*'.
London Metropolitan Archives MS CLC/270/MS00086, 'William Fleetwood on the Forest Laws'.
McGlynn, Margaret. *The Royal Prerogative and the Learning of the Inns of Court* (Cambridge: Cambridge University Press, 2003).
Mirow, M. C., 'Bastardy and the Statute of Wills: Interpreting a Sixteenth-Century with Cases and Readings', *Mississippi Law Journal*, 69 (2000): 345–71.
Mirow, Matthew. 'The Ascent of the Readings: Some Evidence from Readings on Wills', in *Learning the Law: Teaching the Transmission of English Law 1150–1900*, ed. Jonathan Bush and Alain Wijffels (London: Hambledon Press, 1999), 227–54.
Ovid, *Metamorphoses* (London: William Heinemann, 1916).
Pawlisch, Hans S. *Sir John Davies and the Conquest of Ireland: A Study in Legal Imperialism* (Cambridge: Cambridge University Press, 1985).
Plowden, Edmund. *Les comentaries, ou les reportes* (London: 1571).
Prest, Wilfrid, 'The Dialectical Origins of Finch's *Law*', *Cambridge Law Journal*, 36 (1977): 326–52.
Ross, Richard J. 'The Commoning of the Common Law: The Renaissance Debate over the Printing of English Law', *University of Pennsylvania Law Review*, 146 (1998): 323–461.
Smith, David A. 'Was There a Rule in *Shelley's Case*?' *Journal of Legal History*, 30 (2009): 53–70.
Snagg, Robert. *The Antiquity and Original of the Court of Chancery* (London: 1654).
Staunford, William. *An Exposicion of the Kinges Prerogative* (London: 1567).
van den Bergh, Govaert C. J. J. 'Auctoritas Poetarum in Court: A Footnote to the History of *Institutes* 3.23.2 and *Digest* 1.8.6.5 and 7', in *Fundamina: A Journal of Legal History: Essays in Honor of Eric Pool*, ed. Rena van den Bergh (Pretoria: South African Society of Legal Historians, 2005), 326–46.
Williams, Ian. '"He Creditted More the Printed Booke": Common Lawyers' Receptivity to Print, *c.*1550–1640', *Law and History Review*, 28 (2010): 39–70.
Williams, Ian. 'The Tudor Genesis of Edward Coke's Immemorial Common Law', *Sixteenth Century Journal*, 43 (2012): 103–23.

CHAPTER 4

'ATTENTIVE MINDES AND SERIOUS WITS'

Legal Training and Early Drama

JAMES MCBAIN

In an important recent essay on classical rhetoric and early modern law, Lorna Hutson makes a compelling case for the need to appreciate the influence of topical invention upon early modern legal practice.[1] With evidence drawn from both legal reasoning (Coke's report on *Calvin's Case*) and textbooks (for example, Michael Dalton's *Countrey Justice* or Richard Bernard's *Guide to Grand Jury Men*), the way in which a synthesis of rhetoric and dialectic was taught, particularly at the universities, is shown to have considerable influence on the development of legal practice. This ground-breaking argument is particularly significant because it represents a pertinent challenge to a sense of isolationism espoused by many leading legal historians, who have sought to maintain a view of the law in the period as being distinct from, and effectively untouched by, humanistic studies outside the walls of the Inns of Court. Sir John Baker, for example, is very careful to differentiate the many 'rationalist' developments he traces in legal thinking from 'humanist scholarship in a narrow, technical sense',[2] a position which is endorsed by David Ibbetson in his consideration of Gabriel Harvey's legal scholarship.[3] Baker might well be right to draw attention to 'a deep conservative element in the common law which often conspires to deny or conceal any sense of movement',[4] but such a barrier should invite closer scrutiny rather than represent a foregone conclusion.

[1] Lorna Hutson, 'Rhetoric and Early Modern Law', in *The Oxford Handbook of Rhetorical Studies*, ed. Michael MacDonald (Online publication date: January 2015); <http://www.oxfordhandbooks.com/view/10.1093/oxfordhb/9780199731596.001.0001/oxfordhb-9780199731596-e-033> accessed 30 January 2016.

[2] Sir John Baker, *OHLE*, 6.17.

[3] David Ibbetson, 'Humanism and Law in Renaissance England: The Annotations of Gabriel Harvey', in *Reassessing Legal Humanism and its Claims:* Petere Fontes?, ed. Paul J. du Plessis and John W. Cairns (Edinburgh: Edinburgh University Press, 2015), 282–95.

[4] Baker, *OHLE*, 6.17.

As Hutson's essay demonstrates, humanism is likely to have been more profoundly embedded than previous studies have allowed and a broader understanding of how we approach education and training represents an excellent revelatory approach. Thus, whilst Baker focuses on the apparent impossibility of ascertaining 'how many common lawyers read Arts at University',[5] simultaneously acknowledging and dismissing the relevance of humanistic developments that occurred within Arts courses, Hutson instead provides a rigorous account of the particular influence of Coke's education at Trinity College, Cambridge, to support her case. Similar contextual support could incidentally be provided for Dalton, who also spent time at Trinity, and for Richard Bernard, who proceeded to MA status at Christ's College, Cambridge, prior to any interest in the law.

The focus of this essay is the relationship of legal training and indigenous drama at the Elizabethan Inns, rather than upon developments within primary law as such, and so my consideration of rhetoric is as a means of accounting for literary composition. But my argument aims similarly to challenge a sense of isolation. Humanistic studies were not explicitly fostered by Inns curricula; indeed, as I argue, much that we know about early modern legal education comes from reports written in the hope of reforms that would have brought it into line with pedagogical practice elsewhere. Nevertheless, figures such as Coke and Dalton would clearly have understood and assimilated their legal training in relation to previous study at university and it is remarkable that so many of the writers with whom I am concerned here shared at least a propaedeutic humanistic grounding before they arrived at the Inns—in fact most of them received far in excess of that. My particular contention is that Innsmen used their literary ability to distinguish themselves from their peers, but my wider purpose is to argue that the more we can interrogate the relationships between the Inns and elsewhere, the better our understanding of the Inns themselves will be.

In what follows, I draw upon a particular example, *The Misfortunes of Arthur* (1588), to consider how both literary and legal work are represented within the text. Rather than provide a sustained reading of the play itself, however, I aim to use it to address more fundamental issues of legal and wider humanist training. In turn, I hope that this approach will enable readers to understand the extent to which dramatic writing at the Inns and elsewhere should be seen to be linked. It is entirely understandable that scholars, particularly those from outside of the field of legal history, should assume that law students would have received extensive rhetorical training to support mooting and the wider need to present arguments effectively. In fact, there is no evidence that such training was formally provided, other than through demonstration, and contemporaneous accounts seem to indicate that it was not available. It has also been argued that a number of vernacular 'arts of rhetoric' produced in the period would have been aimed at a legal market, but the evidence for specific address towards law students is generally unconvincing.[6] Indeed, rather than offering precise and practical rhetorical

[5] Baker, *OHLE*, 6.16.

[6] See, for example, Paul Raffield, *Images and Cultures of Law in Early Modern England* (Cambridge: Cambridge University Press, 2004), 22.

guidance for law students, many of these guidebooks instead seem to serve primarily to demonstrate their authors' superior learning. If scholarship concerning the generally limited educational experience, and lack of formal rhetorical training, of the majority of Innsmen is correct, then it follows that many of those who composed drama there were unrepresentative; they might be seen as members of a cultural elite within their institutions, almost always the products of previous education that was far broader and more formally rhetorical than the legal learning exercises shared with their peers. Recognition of this fact is important because, in the establishment of the field of 'law and literature', the focus in many instances of discussions of literary works associated with the Inns of Court has been an emphasis on the legal context alone, often at the detriment of equally significant associations and links. This essay seeks to redirect that critical impetus.

The Misfortunes of Arthur serves well as a *terminus ad quem* for the coverage of this essay since, as Alan Nelson observes, from the date of its performance onwards, 'the Inns of Court tended to concentrate on revels and masques rather than on plays' and whilst 'plays continued to be performed ... [they were performed] by professional companies rather than gentlemen members'.[7] Although the *Records of Early English Drama* volumes for the Inns trace the existence of dramatic activity from 1412 to 1413, with the exception of the scant detail of Sergeant Roo's ill-fated 'Lord Governance and Lady Public Weal' of 1526–1527, we are unable to positively identify a particular play before *Gorboduc*, performed as part of the Inner Temple's Christmas Revels of 1561–1562. In fact, in terms of individual plays, we have texts of only five that were written and performed by Innsmen themselves within this period: in addition to *Gorboduc*, *Supposes*, and *The Misfortunes of Arthur*, we have *Jocasta* and *Gismond of Salerne*.[8] We can sensibly sub-divide further; whilst all of these plays were initially performed as part of Revels festivities, three of them (*Gorboduc*, *Gismond*, and *Misfortunes*) were also subsequently reprised for a royal audience. Innsmen enjoyed a propinquity to power, both in a geographical sense and also in terms of the numerous connections and friendships fostered by institutional kinship, and the opportunities that Inns playwrights had to play before the Queen have so far dominated critical responses, with the result that attempts to consider these plays as serious literary compositions in their own right, rather than as straightforward, if contentious, tools of political persuasion, are remarkably rare. These plays certainly do offer potential counsel, but they function through a wider cultural allusiveness and intertextuality too: *Gorboduc*'s Eubulus, for example, the King's secretary whose name is almost always glossed simply as 'wise counsellor', would surely bring his namesake from *Acolastus* to the minds of an informed original audience; *Gismond of Salerne* frequently invokes Dolce's *Didone* to figure the Queen, over a decade before William Gager's more celebrated *Dido*

[7] Alan H. Nelson, 'Emulating Royalty: Cambridge, Oxford, and the Inns of Court', *Shakespeare Studies*, 37 (2009): 67–76, 67. On masques, see Martin Butler's chapter in this volume.

[8] *REED*, 2.757–61.

play; and whilst Marie Axton primarily locates *The Misfortunes of Arthur* within her wider account of political engagement, she is careful to argue simultaneously that we should consider its authors alongside John Lyly, a self-consciously literary writer whose *Gallathea* and *Endymion* were performed as part of the same court season.[9]

When members of Gray's Inn presented *The Misfortunes of Arthur*, on 28 February 1588, it was altered for its royal audience with the addition of a new introduction, written by Nicholas Trotte. Whilst the new section superficially praises the Queen, as we might expect, it is simultaneously, and conspicuously, rather more concerned with writing and with the playwrights themselves. Thus the introduction begins with the arrival on stage of Three Muses, who lead a group of five gentlemen students as captives. One of the Muses opens by declaring how the students have been taken so that they could be made to provide entertainment for Elizabeth, adding that they had to be captured, rather than persuaded, because of their misguided loyalty to their legal work. We are told in no uncertain terms that law and poetry are seen as oppositional by legal authority, interestingly figured in Astrea:

> [Astrea] takes up flowring wits,
> Whom first she schooleth to forget and scorne
> The noble skills of language and of Arts,
> The wisedome, which discourse of stories teach,
> The ornaments which various knowledge yeelds;
> But Poesie she hath in most disdaine,
> And Marshals it next Follyes scorned place.[10]

We are then told what replaces 'these noble skills':

> Then, when she hath these worthy Prints defac'd
> Out of the mindes that can endure her hand,
> What doth she then supplie in steede of these?
> Forsooth some olde reports of altered lawes,
> Clamors of Courts, and cavils upon words,
> Grounds without ground, supported by conceit,
> And reasons of more subtiltie than sense,
> What shall I say of Moote points straunge, and doubts
> Still argued but never yet agreed? (19–27)

And finally, there is condemnation of the linguistic failings of legal work, designed to further force a wedge between law and eloquence:

[9] Marie Axton, *The Queen's Two Bodies: Drama and the Elizabethan Succession* (London: Royal Historical Society, 1977), ch. 5, 61–72.

[10] *The Misfortunes of Arthur*, in *Early English Classical Tragedies*, ed. John W. Cunliffe (Oxford: Clarendon Press, 1912), ll. 12–18. Subsequent references appear within the text.

And shee [Astrea], that doth deride the Poets lawe,
Because he must his words in order place,
Forgets her formes of pleading more precise,
More bound to words then is the Poets lore:
And for these fine conceits she fitly chose,
A tongue that Barbarisme it selfe doth use. (28–33)

This is obviously rather parodic of legal work, but nevertheless it is a useful articulation of familiar complaints. One of the Gentleman Students is then allowed to reply and his argument is both powerful and precise. Far from it being the case that they were captured unawares, the student instead states that they knew that they would be called upon to perform for the Queen and that they therefore willingly submit to her jurisdiction, whilst initially maintaining no sense of duty to the Muses at all. Indeed, the men claim to have denied the Muses' call before. The question of dutiful loyalty is then considered in relation to Astrea, once again, with the student carefully seeming to acknowledge the initial rejection of both poetry and significantly also of wider eloquence:

No eloquence, disguising reasons shape,
Nor Poetrie, each vaine affections nurce,
No various historie that doth leade the minde
Abroad to auncient tales from instant use,
Nor these, nor other moe, too long to note,
Can winne *Astreas* servants to remove
Their service, once devote to better things. (68–74)

The student then provides an alternative account of exactly what legal training entails and why it should be valued so highly:

They with attentive mindes and serious wits,
Revolve records of deepe Judiciall Acts,
They waigh with steaddy and indifferent hand
Each word of lawe, each circumstance of right,
They hold the grounds which time & use hath sooth'd. (75–9)

And legal method and language are defended:

One doubt in mootes by argument encreas'd
Cleares many doubts, experience doth object.
The language she first chose, and still retaines,
Exhibites naked truth in aptest termes. (83–6)

Significantly, the Gentleman Student then returns to the issue of poetry and, with a register befitting themes of conquest within the play ahead, argues that actually the relationship of poetry and legal training is not quite as simplistic as the debate so far would have one believe:

> Yet never did we banish nor reject
> Those ornaments of knowledge nor of toungs.
> *That* slander envious ignorance did raise.
> With Muses still we entercourse allowe,
> T'enrich our state with all there forreine fraight. (92–6)

Within fewer than a hundred lines, Trotte is able effectively to introduce the play ahead, which combines Gaufridian and Senecan material to chart the destruction of the line of Pendragon through misguided conquest and incestuous civil war. But its political themes of duty and allegiance are secondary here to a primary consideration of eloquence and poetry, and their relationship with the law. We are presented with two competing accounts of legal work—either it engenders corrupt and self-indulgent sophistry, or it is an illuminating, lucid, and profoundly just occupation—but neither description seems particularly convincing as a basis for literary composition. How then do we get from these accounts to an explanation of how this play, and indeed any of the other lawyers' plays, could be composed?

To address this question is to confront one of the central paradoxes posed by the early modern Inns. On the one hand, the routine of readings and moots, a repetitive engagement with practice and observation, was highly specific and technical. Lawyers would certainly have needed to be able to argue flexibly and to produce arguments on either sides of cases, but material to be discovered was limited in range—vocational common learning rather than the wider rhetorical strategies and commonplaces that we have recently come to see as the skeleton upon which so much early modern drama was constructed.[11] On the other hand, scholars have fairly observed that the Inns were also places where communities of men took opportunities for both intellectual and literary engagement. As Sarah Knight observes, 'the Inns provided a suitable transitional space for many students to exercise their creativity, whether as poets, dramatists, or actors'.[12] But whilst we know that legal and literary work did coalesce, we should ask whether the Inns, and particularly their learning, were merely contexts or more positively pretexts for drama? The most reliable answer might well be the former, a response to be found in the irony that the best accounts that we have of early modern legal training come from within calls for educational reform. From Sir John Baker's pioneering anatomy of early modern law onwards, descriptions of learning exercises have often either cited or paraphrased a report on the Inns drawn up for Henry VIII

11 For the best accounts, see: Joel Altman, *The Tudor Play of Mind: Rhetorical Inquiry and the Development of Elizabethan Drama* (Berkeley: University of California Press, 1978); and Lorna Hutson, *The Invention of Suspicion: Law and Mimesis in Shakespeare and Renaissance Drama* (Oxford: Oxford University Press, 2007).

12 Sarah Knight, 'Literature and Drama at the Early Modern Inns of Court', in *ICW*, 218.

by Nicholas Bacon, Robert Cary, and Thomas Denton, for example, in which the current *status quo* is first described, before the authors provide proposals for alternative arrangements.[13] The initial report refers briefly to literary culture during the festive Revels, 'In this Christmas time, they have all manner of pastimes, as singing and dancing, and in some of the houses ordinarily they have some Interlude or tragedy played by the gentlemen of the same house, the ground, the matter wherof, is devised by some of the gentlemen of the house.'[14] But it is striking that whilst the Inn's Hall provides a space for performance, there is no explicit link made between the quotidian business of learning that would usually occupy it and the skills required to 'devise' a play. Indeed, the report criticizes current practice for denying students access to a wider range of intellectual engagement, 'how many good and gentle wits within this your grace's realm have perished[?]', the authors ask.[15]

By contrast, the report's proposal for a new 'house of students' argues for a broad humanist curriculum, in which languages, rhetoric, and classical literature would be paramount in order to support eloquence alongside law. Moots would be conducted in pure Latin and pure French, and, after two years, when linguistic competence was sufficient, declamations would be introduced during vacations. In fact, Nicholas Bacon was involved in two reports on education during his career and on both occasions argued for a combination of legal and humanist study, alongside physical exercise, to produce accomplished and useful young men. In the 1561 *Articles devised for the bringing up in vertue and lerninge of the Queenes Majesties wardes*, he suggested the provision of a new educational institution specifically for wards, which would have provided a more rigorous and demanding training than at the Inns.[16] The school would employ five schoolmasters to deliver a curriculum combining law, classics, modern languages, music, and sport. Bacon suggests daily lectures in law, each prefaced by an examination to test the knowledge gained from the previous reading. And, since the Latin master would have most time with the students, eloquence would be supported throughout.

With such emphasis on the introduction of humanist oratory in both of these reports, we should perhaps conclude that eloquence was currently inadequately fostered at the Inns. It has been suggested that Revels playing was one of the ways in which eloquence was learned, that 'the staging of drama was an effective educational device, employed by the Inns to instil the skills of oratory and performance that were central to the work of the successful common lawyer'.[17] But this seems extravagantly optimistic. Wider revels performances might well have involved large numbers of the Innsmen

[13] J. H. Baker, *The Reports of Sir John Spelman, vol. II, SS*, 94 (1977), 131.

[14] C. H. Williams, ed., *English Historical Documents, 1485–1558* (London: Eyre and Spottiswoode, 1967), 563–73, 567.

[15] *English Historical Documents*, 564.

[16] The report is printed in Robert W. Wienpahl, *Music at the Inns of Court* (Ann Arbor: California State University, 1979), 25–8.

[17] Raffield, *Images and Cultures of Law*, 26–7.

as participants, but the composition and performance of plays clearly limited the vast majority of students to the role of audience members. Sir John Baker estimates that around ten thousand young men were admitted to either Inns of Court or Chancery between 1450 and 1550 and there is no reason to think that a lower figure would stand for the following century.[18] By contrast, and even accounting for the loss of a majority of evidence, it is striking that the editors of the *REED* volumes identify just thirty-eight of those men up to 1642 who can positively be identified as playwrights, with a further dozen who contributed speeches or devised short masques to be played between acts of larger plays.[19]

Eloquence is clearly also seen as the key issue at stake in the introduction to *The Misfortunes of Arthur*; the lawyers stand accused of using barbarous language and rejecting the noble rhetorical skills that Arts would teach. The gentleman student states in response that 'Astreas servants' convey their 'naked truths in aptest terms', but certainly reject eloquence if that equates to a distortion of reason. Within the reality of how the Inns actually functioned, there is no evidence that classical rhetoric was ever formally taught, albeit some contemporaneous accounts can be reasonably misconstrued.[20] One of the most frequently cited texts concerning early modern legal training and its rhetorical basis is a passage from Sir Thomas Elyot's *The Book Named The Governor* (1531), in which the author apparently praises the practice of mooting:

> It is to be remembered that in the learning of the laws of this realm, there is at this day an exercise wherein is a manner, a shadow, or figure of the ancient rhetoric. I mean the pleading used in Court and Chancery called moots ... The case being known, they which be appointed to moot do examine the case, and investigate what they therein can espy, which may make a contention, whereof may rise a question to be argued, and that of Tully is called *constitutio*, and of Quintilian *status causae* ... Moreover there seemeth to be in the said pleadings certain parts of an oration, that is to say for *narrations*, *partitions*, *confirmations*, and *confutations*, named of some *reprehensions*, they have *declarations*, *bars*, *replications*, and *rejoinders*, only they lack the pleasant form of beginning, called in Latin *exordium*; they that have studied rhetoric shall perceive what I mean.[21]

It is important to understand how this section fits within the wider text, however, which was primarily written to propose a reformed educational programme for those destined for roles in governance. Across the work, Elyot presents an ideal humanist regime and it is significant that the anticipated promise of his ideas develops from the new training being markedly different to that which has gone before: '*if* there might once happen

[18] Baker, *OHLE*, 6.446.

[19] *REED*, 1.813–15.

[20] See Lisa A. Perry, 'Legal Handbooks as Rhetoric Books for Common Lawyers in Early Modern England', in *Learning the Law: Teaching and the Transmission of English Law 1150–1900*, ed. Jonathan A. Bush and Alain Wijffels (London: Hambledon, 1999), 273–85.

[21] Sir Thomas Elyot, *The Book Named The Governor*, ed. S. E. Lehmberg (London: Dent, 1962), 53–4.

some man, having an excellent wit, to be brought up in such form as I have hitherto written [i.e. 'exactly or deeply learned in the art of an orator, *and* also in the laws of this realm'] ... undoubtedly it should not be impossible for him to bring the pleading and reasoning of the law to the ancient form of noble orators'.[22] In a similarly worded passage elsewhere, we read that children are currently committed to the law at such an early stage that other studies are denied: 'I think verily that if children were brought up as I have written, and continually were retained in the right study ... until they passed the age of twenty-one years, and then set to the laws of this realm ... undoubtedly they should become men of so excellent wisdom.'[23] For Elyot, that is, students should spend their formative years acquiring linguistic facility and literary experience to appreciate classical eloquence properly before they then begin to apply their learning. Indeed, at the beginning of the section in which the apparent comparison of classical oratory and mooting appears, Elyot states quite clearly that the 'reverend study [of law]' is [currently] 'void of all eloquence'.[24] The 'shadowy' comparison of rhetoric and contemporaneous mooting might thereby be seen as an idealized account, an example by which a central element of contemporaneous legal training is validated by its possible proximity to a classical standard of oratory to which it, along with the remainder of the curriculum, should be raised. The final confirmation that this is the genuine sense of the passage arrives at the end of the quotation above—who, we might ask, are included among 'they that have studied rhetoric'? For the rest of the book to make sense, it is surely axiomatic that the majority of men whose education has come from the Inns alone are not among that cohort. Rather than demonstrating rhetorical facility, Elyot's text should instead be understood as pointing to a lack of rhetorical training at the Inns, which consequently raises a challenge to the likelihood of an unreformed curriculum of learning exercises being able to support and sustain literary composition.

Implicitly accepting such a vacuum of formal rhetorical training, both literary and legal scholars have argued for the influence of vernacular rhetorical manuals, such as those written by Leonard Cox and Thomas Wilson, at the Inns instead.[25] By this model, we have a reliance on rhetorical learning through practice and observation, in addition to any rhetorical knowledge that had previously been learnt elsewhere. Simultaneously we have an image of lawyers needing to learn through vernacular paraphrase, presumably without the linguistic capacity to approach classical sources themselves. It is worth pausing briefly over this point to consider the implications of a need for vernacular cradles for rhetorical learning. It is certainly true on the one hand that Gabriel Harvey wrote a marginal note in his Quintilian to state that Wilson's *Art of Rhetoric* was 'the daily bread of our common pleaders and discoursers',[26] and that he owned and annotated a number of Wilson's works. But as Catherine Nicholson observes, Harvey was 'no

22 Elyot, *Governor*, 54 (italics mine).
23 Elyot, *Governor*, 52.
24 Elyot, *Governor*, 51.
25 Raffield, *Images and Cultures*, 21.
26 Virginia F. Stern, 'The Bibliotheca of Gabriel Harvey', *RQ*, 25 (1972): 1–62, 48.

proletarian in matters of eloquence' and whilst it might well be the case that the average common pleader relied upon the vernacular Wilson, the marginal note should probably not be seen as an unqualified compliment either way; the very fact that Harvey, who was interested in civil law throughout his academic career and subsequently practised at Doctors Commons, writes the note in his Latin Quintilian is suggestive of an assertion of difference.[27] A reliance on Cox's *Art of Rhetoric* would be even more condemnatory of standards at the Inns. The author, who was probably master of Reading School at the time of writing, goes out of his way to stress its elementary nature throughout.[28]

With a much better provenance than the texts of either Cox or Wilson, in terms of both an Inns of Court origin and its intended audience, John Hoskyns' *Direccions for Speech and Style* is a rhetorical guide that was apparently written for a young law student at the Middle Temple, to which Hoskyns was himself admitted in 1593. We might see the occasion for such a text as, once again, pointing to a lack of formal rhetorical education and the text is potentially useful in detailing how a lawyer might use rhetorical knowledge to his advantage. In a section dealing with direct address, for example, he writes:

> *APOSTROPHE* is a turning of your speech to some new person, as to the people when your speech before was to the judge, to the defendant, to the adversary, to the witnesses, as:
>
> And herein you witnesses are to consult with your own consciences and to enter into true examination of your memory. Did you mark his looks? Did you note his speeches? Did you truly observe the particular proceedings of the action?[29]

The advice immediately following relates to Prosopopoeia and Hoskyns writes:

> But to animate and give life is *PROSOPOPOEIA*, as, to make dead men speak; as
>
> If your forefathers were now alive and saw you defacing so goodly a principality by them established, would they not say thus?[30]

It is perhaps worth immediately muddying the waters again, however. Hoskyns' own eloquence can be accounted for by his pre-legal studies; he had been at both Westminster and Winchester, before continuing to MA level at New College, Oxford. Indeed, he seems to have turned to law only after having been expelled from both his fellowship and the University for writing 'bitterly satirical' attacks.[31] And whilst some of the examples

[27] Catherine Nicholson, 'Englishing Eloquence: Sixteenth Century Arts of Rhetoric and Poetics', in *The Oxford Handbook of English Prose, 1500–1640*, ed. Andrew Hadfield (Oxford: Oxford University Press, 2013), 9–26, 25.

[28] Leonard Cox, *The Art or Crafte of Rhetoryke* (London: 1532).

[29] John Hoskyns, *Direccions for Speech and Style*, in *The Life, Letters, and Writings of John Hoskyns, 1566–1638*, ed. Louise Brown Osborn (New Haven: Yale University Press, 1937), 162.

[30] Hoskyns, *Direccions*, 163.

[31] Wilfrid Prest, 'Hoskins, John', *ODNB*.

provided in his text pertain to law, the majority come from Sidney's *Arcadia*, as is the case with the prosopopoeiac godfathers here. Equally, although prosopopoeia might be useful, if it was new to the young student who received the text and the gift of the copy of Sidney, he had clearly missed out on many of the basics of rhetorical education that we know were central to the progressive but elementary learning exercises at grammar schools throughout the land. What seems at first to be simply a text for the mediation of rhetorical knowledge is simultaneously therefore a display of wider learning from elsewhere and a signal that the intended audience at an Inn of Court might well be lacking in relatively basic devices and figures of speech.

An alternative account of the distance between legal training and wider humanistic literary education is evident in that conspicuous references to classical authors within legal writing have been dismissed by Sir John Baker as 'really little more than a show of fashionable rhetoric', far from integral to the functioning of law.[32] If we move forward slightly beyond my historical cusp, there is a similar suggestion in William Fulbecke's *Direction or Preparative to the Study of Law* that rhetoric and classical knowledge should be seen as superfluous to the proper business of legal study:

> The writings of wise and grave common-weal men learned in the law are not to be censured by Grammarians, and Rhetoricians, who make a gallant gloss of *Clytemnestras mules*, Alexander's horse, and such frivilous vanities. For their study was far different, being for the general good and commodious government of the common-weal. And if any man reprove them for want of sharpness of invention, and fineness of wit, let him be well advised, and consider the substance of their works, and he shall find, that they carried *Mercury* in their brain, and not on their tongue, and that they wanted not wisdom, though they were defective in rhetoric.[33]

As well as perhaps helping, once again, to confirm a general lack of conventional eloquence among lawyers, and particularly those who had continued long enough to have published legal works, we might note that Fulbecke is also letting us know that he is seeking to distinguish himself from the 'everyman-lawyer' here. The reference to 'Clytemnestras mules' is from Cicero's description of a lavish performance, employing six hundred mules, to mark the opening of the Theatre of Pompey in 55 BC.[34] The reference to Alexander's horse might well refer to the work of the Italian scholar and antiquary, Onofrio Panvinio, and his suggested identification of the Quitinal 'Horse Tamers' statue with Alexander and Bucephalus.[35] So Fulbecke is writing here as a lawyer, a member of Gray's Inn, and stating that lawyers do not need to know these things … but by the way, he is an exception and he does know.

32 Baker, *OHLE*, 6.448.

33 William Fulbecke, *Direction or Preparative to the Study of Law* (London: 1600), 52;

34 Cicero, *Epistulae ad familiares*, 7.1.2, cited in *The Context of Ancient Drama*, Eric Csapo and William J. Slater (Ann Arbor: University of Michigan Press, 1994), 283.

35 Panvinio's identification is made in his *Reipublicae Romanae Commentariorum libri tres* (Venice: 1558). I am very grateful to the anonymous reviewer of my essay for this suggestion.

And he should know, because prior to legal training, he had spent seven years studying at Oxford.[36]

Fulbecke's intellectual journey from university to Inn is one shared by Sir Nicholas Bacon, who was ideally placed to suggest the educational reforms I detailed earlier. He attended the progressive school at Bury Abbey and then went to Corpus Christi, Cambridge. After graduation (and we know that he ranked highly among his cohort) and then time either at an Inn of Chancery or abroad, he was admitted to Gray's Inn and quickly rose through the ranks, both through his own talents, but also quite probably through networks of friends, colleagues, and relations.[37] Amongst many accomplishments, Bacon was a celebrated orator; it is he who is famously memorialized by Puttenham, who 'once found him sitting in his gallery alone with the works of Quintilian before him', even if Puttenham's other mention of him is rendered slightly curious by the evidence of this source.[38] Puttenham has at this point been arguing for decorum, the need to fit style to circumstance, and writes:

> Wherein I report me to them that knew Sir Nicholas Bacon … or the now Lord Treasurer [William Cecil] and have been conversant with their speeches made in the Parliament house and Star Chamber. From whose lips I have seen to proceed more grave and natural eloquence than from all the orators of Oxford or Cambridge; but all is as it is handled, and maketh no matter whether the same eloquence be natural to them or artificial (though I think rather natural), yet they were known to be learned and not unskilful of the art when they were younger men.[39]

Bacon's eloquence is clearly deemed to be exceptional—there would be no point in Puttenham referring to it otherwise, just as Ben Jonson will later identify Bacon's eloquence as 'singular and almost alone at the beginning of Queen Elizabeth's times'.[40] For Puttenham, this is all the more remarkable for the fact that Bacon is a lawyer and politician in London, rather than an Oxbridge orator, as if eloquence, however admirable, is somehow out of place at the Inns. Like Bacon, Cecil was Cambridge educated, however, as indeed was Puttenham, prior to his admission to the Middle Temple.

To draw attention to a small number of lawyers who were exceptionally eloquent might seem anachronistically selective but it is, in fact, ironically to recognize an element of differentiation that was seen as desirable within the Henrician proposal for reform. To date, critical focus has justly been directed towards the call for the formal inclusion of these intellectual elements that were not currently provided by the Inns—the fact, for example, that the report argues that a regular part of the curriculum should be for 'one of the excellent knowledge in the Latin and Greek tongue to read some orator

[36] D. R. Woolf, 'Fulbecke, William', *ODNB*.

[37] Robert Tittler, 'Bacon, Sir Nicholas', *ODNB*.

[38] George Puttenham, *The Arte of English Poesie* (1589), in *English Renaissance Literary Criticism*, ed. Brian Vickers (Oxford: Clarendon Press, 1999), 223.

[39] Puttenham, *Arte*, 222.

[40] Jonson, 'Discoveries', *CWBJ*, 7.530, ll. 649–50.

or book of rhetoric, or else some other author which treateth of the government of a common-wealth', a clear yoking together of eloquence and political substance with an enforcement of classical rhetorical sources.[41] It should be seen as equally significant however that the report fundamentally also calls for a two-tiered system. Whilst all students would be raised to a much more respectable level of humanist knowledge and facility than the current provision, there would be an elite body of 'King's Scholars' at the new institution who would enjoy particular privileges. They would be selected at the outset as being different; whilst ordinary students could be admitted at 20 years of age, the 'Company' as the scholars might be known, would have to be 22. Only these scholars could become the equivalent of Readers and, perhaps most significantly of all, the two best scholars would be assigned a significant literary function. At times of war, whilst all students could potentially employ their martial and leadership skills, the chosen two scholars would also be charged with writing reports to record any useful details, with those reports being kept at the 'house' for future reference. It is a very interesting method of epistemological accretion that seems very enlightened, anticipating the collection of 'histories' at the Royal Society by more than a century. And at all times, in fact, one of the functions of the chosen two would be to write histories. They would be given unique access to history in the making, so to speak; were someone to be arraigned on a charge of treason, the scholars would have access to the interrogation so that they could write from the most informed perspective.

In the absence of detail, one imagines that literary and rhetorical skill would be critical in the process of selection and, indeed, the report envisages that the histories reported would be evidential in a rhetorical as well as a straightforwardly factual sense:

> Forasmuch as it seemeth no wise convenient, that neither the politic government of this imperial realm, and the noble acts of the governors of the same, which are undoubtedly worthy of eternal memory and fame; neither on the other side the detestable and devilish acts attempted against the common-wealth ... and the due and just punishment for the same sustained, should in any wise either by negligence or lack of knowledge be drowned in forgetfulness or buried in ignorance, but that they should be rather chronicled and remain in histories for ever, whereby our posterity seeing (as it were before their eyes) ... should better provide for the security of this realm: we therefore most humbly desire [the appointment of] two of his greatest students to put forth in writing the history and chronicle of this realm.[42]

There are clearly significant connections being made here between effective historical writing, that which causes posterity to see it 'as it were before their eyes', a political function, and both a legal and broader humanist education, all of which together would certainly allow for literary composition. But it is important to immediately remind ourselves that this represents a proposed ideal, rather than the reality of actual legal

[41] *English Historical Documents*, 571.
[42] *English Historical Documents*, 572–3.

training. The fact that 'King's Scholars' were never appointed as a literary elite within legal institutions, however, does not mean that individuals could not effectively impersonate these roles. Indeed, literary historians have often sought to emphasize the legal context of prominent writers with Inns associations without perhaps investigating their educational backgrounds sufficiently closely. If we consider the authors of the Senecan translations that are often seen as Inns works, for example, it is difficult to argue for legal training playing any part in their composition. Jasper Heywood spent over a decade at Oxford, becoming a fellow of All Souls when he had to leave Merton, and only subsequently joined Gray's Inn once he finally had to leave Oxford for non-conformity.[43] Alexander Neville was at St John's College, Cambridge, prior to joining an Inn, if indeed he ever did.[44] Although he does not appear on any register of admission, he is among the clique who challenged George Gascoigne (who had probably been at Trinity College, Cambridge, prior to Gray's Inn) to a poetic contest as a rite of admission to the group, an explicit formation of an exclusive literary network within one of the Inns, rather than a number of poets who just happened to have their work supported by the Inns' wider culture.[45] The alternative possibility, that he was not a member of Gray's Inn and that the poetic clique therefore had bounds beyond it, would be even more interesting. John Studley was BA, MA, and fellow of Trinity, Cambridge. He might have later become a member of Barnards Inn subsequent to his academic career but that would obviously also post-date his translations.[46] And Thomas Nuce was a student and then fellow at Pembroke, Cambridge, with no evidence of legal training at all.[47] As well as translating the spurious *Octavia*, Nuce provided defensive commendatory verses to Studley's translation of *Agammemnon*, a text that, as with his *Medea*, was sold as emanating from Trinity College, Cambridge. I make the point because, whilst we often look for Inns connections for these plays, such as a probable dedicatory poem by Thomas Blundeville, it is important that we also maintain a focus on the text as primarily a Cambridge production.[48] And finally Thomas Newton, who provided the tenth translation to his assembled volume of Senecan tragedies, was educated at both Oxford and Cambridge and had no training at the Inns.[49]

This is not to say that legal elements and associations with these works, such as a dedication from someone we know to have been writing at the Inns, are not important. But it is vital not to privilege a particular way of balancing influences in seeking to understand networks of literary production properly. And writers at the Inns might well have been more significantly in dialogue with fellow writers at the universities than with their fellow Innsmen. Sarah Knight's point that 'even more than at contemporary universities, a

[43] Dennis Flynn, 'Heywood, Jasper', *ODNB*.

[44] Elisabeth Leedham-Green, 'Neville, Alexander', *ODNB*.

[45] See George Gascoigne, *A Hundreth Sundrie Flowres*, ed. G. W. PigmanIII (Oxford: Clarendon Press, 2000), 278 n. 61.

[46] T. P. J. Edlin, 'Studley, John', *ODNB*.

[47] Nick de Somogyi, 'Nuce, Thomas', *ODNB*.

[48] Jessica Winston, 'Seneca in Early Elizabethan England', *RQ*, 59 (2006): 29–58, 32.

[49] Gordon Braden, 'Newton, Thomas', *ODNB*.

two-way traffic of authorship and influence ran between the Inns and the public theatres'[50] might well be true for the late Elizabethan and Jacobean periods, but prior to the establishment of professional playhouses, the flow of ideas between the Universities and Inns was equally significant and should invite more sustained research.

To return to *The Misfortunes of Arthur*, informed by background information about literary writing among an elite at the Inns, is to see a continuation of the theme. We know relatively little about Nicholas Trotte; only his name is given on the Gray's Inn register of admissions in 1573, but we know that he became an MP and that his financial generosity was repeatedly exploited by Francis Bacon, who was also involved in *Misfortunes of Arthur* with a part in providing the dumb shows.[51] More importantly however, we know that Trotte, like Bacon, had been at Cambridge prior to joining Gray's Inn. Thomas Hughes, the main author of the play, had both studied and been a fellow at Queen's College, Cambridge, prior to joining Gray's Inn,[52] incidentally the same college at which Christopher Yelverton, who assisted Bacon with the dumb shows, had also spent two years.[53] William Fulbecke, as I detailed above, who provided two alternative scenes for the Royal performance, spent seven years at Oxford prior to Gray's Inn. Finally John Lancaster, who 'directed these proceedings', had been at Queen's College, Oxford, prior to legal training.[54] It is worth pausing again to put some of these background details into some perspective and to see how exceptional writers who were at the Inns might have been. In *The Professions in Early Modern England*, Rosemary O'Day calculated that in 1561, significant for Heywood's *Thyestes* and *Gorboduc*, only 13 per cent of Innsmen had previously been to one of the universities and so the concentration among our men is exceptional. In 1581, the figure had risen to 42 per cent, but we can see that the degree of educational experience involved in *The Misfortunes of Arthur* is still remarkable.[55] As I mentioned in relation to the proposal for the new 'house of learning', alongside a broad humanist curriculum, a fundamental feature of reform was to be a company of peculiarly able literary scholars who would in turn have been particularly useful to the commonweal. I have also suggested that a great majority of writers connected with work associated with the Inns were actually part of a minority—even at the end of the period—in having a broad university education prior to any legal training—a rhetorical training that would have helped some towards literary composition. In both instances therefore, in the proposal of an ideal that never came to fruition and the reality as far as records can document, we can see networks within networks, communities within communities, as being vital

50 Knight, 'Literature and Drama', 218.

51 'Trotte, Nicholas', in *The House of Commons 1558–1603*, ed. P. W. Hasler, 3 vols (London: HMSO, 1981), 3.591–2.

52 P. J. Finkelpearl, 'Hughes, Thomas', *ODNB*.

53 David Ibbetson, 'Yelverton, Christopher', *ODNB*.

54 'Labdon-Ledsam', in *Alumni Oxonienses*, 868–92 <http://www.british-history.ac.uk/alumni-oxon/1500-1714/pp868-892> [accessed 28 June 2015].

55 Rosemary O'Day, *The Professions in Early Modern England, 1450–1800* (Harlow: Longman, 2000), 129.

to an exploration of the relationship of legal training and early drama. And that seems to be something that Trotte's introduction gives us too. To return closely to the text is to notice that the gentleman student carefully distinguishes '*they*'—the bulk of the law students with their admirable dedication to their vocation from '*we*'—those exceptional few who have not rejected wider intellectual engagement.

Within Trotte's introduction, we clearly have an emphasis on the lawyers' capability as masters of legal reasoning, a group uniquely capable of using evidence from textual records and then providing impartial counsel. But importantly, that is not the same thing as being able to produce a text that 'makes dead men speak' or brings history 'as it were before [men's] eyes', which is a much rarer thing. Gray's Inn, as a whole, might share in the glory of having entertained the Queen, but it is the few who have used their literary talents to articulate their dedication and put themselves forward for future service who see themselves as most worthy of regard. Although equated at first, we ultimately therefore have a significant and self-imposed distance between those with merely 'attentive minds' and those with the ability to properly use their 'serious wits'. And whilst the writers, with the exception of Francis Bacon, might not have gone on to illustrious legal careers, their learning should serve, as with the examples of Coke and Dalton, to emphasize links between institutions of learning and the likely migration of humanist knowledge.[56]

Bibliography

Archer, Jayne Elisabeth, Elizabeth Goldring, and Sarah Knight, ed. *The Intellectual and Cultural World of the Early Modern Inns of Court* (Manchester: Manchester University Press, 2011).

Axton, Marie. *The Queen's Two Bodies: Drama and the Elizabethan Succession* (London: Royal Historical Society, 1977).

Baker, J. H. *The Oxford History of the Laws of England*, Vol. 6: *1485–1558* (Oxford: Oxford University Press, 2003).

Baker, J. H., ed. *The Reports of Sir John Spelman*, Vol. 2 (London: SS, 1977).

Csapo, Eric and William J. Slater. *The Context of Ancient Drama* (Ann Arbor: University of Michigan Press, 1994).

Cunliffe, John W., ed. *Early English Classical Tragedies* (Oxford: Clarendon Press, 1912).

Elliott, John R. et al., eds. *Records of Early English Drama: Oxford*, 2 vols (Toronto: University of Toronto Press, 2004).

Elyot, Sir Thomas. *The Book Named the Governor*, ed. S. E. Lehmberg (London: Dent, 1962).

Fulbecke, William. *Direction or Preparative to the Study of Law* (London: 1600).

Gascoigne, George. *A Hundreth Sundrie Flowres*, ed. G. W. PigmanIII (Oxford: Clarendon Press, 2000).

Hasler, P. W., ed. *The House of Commons 1558–1603*, 3 vols (London: HMSO, 1981).

Horner, Olga. '"Fulgens and Lucres": An Historical Perspective', *Medieval English Theatre*, 15 (1993): 49–86.

[56] I would like to record my gratitude to a former student, Wilkie Hollens, whose work on Inns plays challenged my own thinking and ultimately led to this essay.

Hoskyns, John. '*Direccions for Speech and Style*', in *The Life, Letters, and Writings of John Hoskyns, 1566–1638*, ed. Louise Brown Osborn (New Haven: Yale University Press, 1937), 103–66.
Hutson, Lorna. *The Invention of Suspicion: Law and Mimesis in Shakespeare and Renaissance Drama* (Oxford: Oxford University Press, 2007).
McBain, James. '"By Example and Gode Reason": Reconsidering Commonplaces and the Law in "Fulgens and Lucres"', *Medieval English Theatre*, 28 (2006): 3–28.
Medwall, Henry. *The Plays of Henry Medwall*, ed. Alan H. Nelson (Cambridge: D. S. Brewer, 1980).
Nelson, Alan H. 'Emulating Royalty: Cambridge, Oxford, and the Inns of Court', *Shakespeare Studies*, 37 (2009), 67–76.
Nelson, Alan H. and John R. Elliott, eds. *Records of Early English Drama: Inns of Court*, 3 vols (Cambridge: D. S. Brewer, 2010).
Nicholson, Catherine. 'Englishing Eloquence: Sixteenth Century Arts of Rhetoric and Poetics', in *The Oxford Handbook of English Prose, 1500–1640*, ed. Andrew Hadfield (Oxford: Oxford University Press, 2013), 9–26.
O'Day, Rosemary, *The Professions in Early Modern England, 1450–1800* (Harlow: Longman, 2000).
Oxford Dictionary of National Biography (Oxford: Oxford University Press, 2004).
Perry, Lisa A. 'Legal Handbooks as Rhetoric Books for Common Lawyers in Early Modern England', in *Learning the Law: Teaching and the Transmission of English Law 1150–1900*, ed. Jonathan A. Bush and Alain Wijffels (London: Hambledon, 1999), 273–85.
Raffield, Paul, *Images and Cultures of Law in Early Modern England* (Cambridge: Cambridge University Press, 2004).
Stern, Virginia F. 'The *Bibliotheca* of Gabriel Harvey', *Renaissance Quarterly*, 25 (1972): 1–62.
Vickers, Brian, ed. *English Renaissance Literary Criticism* (Oxford: Clarendon Press, 1999).
Walker, Greg, ed. *Medieval Drama: An Anthology* (Oxford: Blackwell, 2000).
Wienpahl, Robert W. *Music at the Inns of Court during the Reigns of Elizabeth, James, and Charles* (Northridge: University Microfilms International for California State University, 1979).
Williams, C. H., ed. *English Historical Documents, 1485–1558* (London: Eyre and Spottiswoode, 1967).
Winston, Jessica. '"A Mirror for Magistrates" and Public Political Discourse in Early Elizabethan England', *Studies in Philology*, 101 (2004): 381–400.
Winston, Jessica, 'Seneca in Early Elizabethan England', *Renaissance Quarterly*, 59 (2006): 29–58.

CHAPTER 5

WHY SHYLOCKE LOSES HIS CASE

Judicial Rhetoric in The Merchant of Venice

QUENTIN SKINNER

I

My aim is to explore a new approach to a familiar set of questions about the trial scene in Act IV of *The Merchant of Venice*.[1] What are the intellectual materials out of which the scene is constructed? Can we hope to identify the sources of Shakespeare's technical vocabulary and legal arguments?[2] Until recently, two related answers dominated the critical literature. The trial scene, it was claimed, 'symbolises the confrontation of Judaism and Christianity as theological systems' and 'develops the sharpest opposition of Old Law and New in terms of their respective theological principles, Justice and Mercy'.[3] Among the many critics who adopted this perspective, some in turn took the

[1] This chapter reconsiders and develops the discussion in Quentin Skinner, *Forensic Shakespeare* (Oxford: Oxford University Press, 2014), 142–8, 210–17, 220–5. For reading and commenting on this new version I am particularly indebted to Kathy Eden, Susan James, Claire Landis, Rhodri Lewis, Richard Strier, and the editor of the present volume.

[2] For a recent restatement of the significance of these questions see Andrew Zurcher, *Shakespeare and Law* (London: The University of Chicago Press, 2010), 270.

[3] For the pioneering discussion (here quoted) see Barbara K. Lewalski, 'Biblical Allusion and Allegory in "The Merchant of Venice" ', *SQ*, 13 (1962): 331, 338. But for a similar reading see also C. L. Barber, *Shakespeare's Festive Comedy: A Study of Dramatic Form and Its Relation to Social Custom*, new edn, with foreword by Stephen Greenblatt (Princeton: Princeton University Press, 2012), 212. For similar claims, see Lawrence Danson, *The Harmonies of The Merchant of Venice* (New Haven: Yale University Press, 1978), 70; John S. Colley, 'Launcelot, Jacob and Esau: Old and New Law in *The Merchant of Venice*', *Yearbook of English Studies*, 10 (1980): 184; Barbara Tovey, 'The Golden Casket: An Interpretation of *The Merchant of Venice*', in *Shakespeare as Political Thinker*, ed. John Alvis and Thomas G. West (Durham: Carolina Academic Press, 1981), 229; Michael J. Willson, 'A View of Justice in Shakespeare's *The Merchant of Venice* and *Measure for Measure*', *Notre Dame Law Review*, 70 (1995): 713; Daniela Carpi,

main allegorical contrast to be between Shylocke and Anthonio,[4] with Anthonio standing for charity and love by contrast with Shylocke's demand for strict justice.[5] But most critics preferred to see in Portia the emblematic figure who calls for 'the reconciliation of Justice and Mercy'[6] and represents the view that 'the New Law takes precedence over the Old'.[7]

A second and more specific argument was frequently allied with this approach. The trial was also taken to reflect the belief, increasingly widespread in Elizabethan England, that the most effective means of arriving at merciful rather than unduly rigorous verdicts was to apply the principles of equitable jurisdiction in place of the stricter demand for justice embodied in common law.[8] Seen from this angle, the trial came to be viewed as a dramatization of 'the conflict between the two systems of law',[9] with Portia 'adopting precisely the attitude of the Court of Chancery of the period'.[10]

These arguments undoubtedly capture something of importance about the structure of the scene. As a number of critics have recently pointed out, however, they both appear to run into difficulties. One problem arises in connection with the alleged symbolic contrast between Shylocke and Anthonio. If the former is a representative of the Old Law, he must be presumed to have some acquaintance with the relevant books of the Old Testament. But these contain repeated calls for justice to be tempered with mercy, and in the book of Micah we are even rhetorically asked 'what doth the Lord require of thee, but to do justly, and to love mercy, and to walk humbly with thy God?'[11] A further

'Law, Discretion, Equity in *The Merchant of Venice* and *Measure for Measure*', *Cardozo Law Review*, 26 (2005): 2322; Heather Hirschfield, '"We All Expect a Gentle Answer, Jew": *The Merchant of Venice* and the Psychotheology of Conversion', *ELH*, 73 (2006): 61; John Flood, '"It Droppeth as the Gentle Rain": Isaiah 45:8 and *The Merchant of Venice* IV.1.181', *N&Q*, 253 (2008): 177; and for further references see B. J. Sokol and Mary Sokol, 'Shakespeare and the English Equity Jurisdiction: *The Merchant of Venice* and the two texts of *King Lear*', *RES*, 50 (1999): 417–39.

4 Lewalski, 'Biblical Allusion', 331; Colley, 'Launcelot, Jacob and Esau' 184; Tovey, 'The Golden Casket', 232; Flood, '"It Droppeth as the Gentle Rain"', 177.

5 Tovey, 'The Golden Casket', 232; Flood, '"It Droppeth as the Gentle Rain"', 177; Carpi, 'Law, Discretion, Equity', 2322.

6 Willson, 'A View of Justice', 711; Danson, *Harmonies*, 63; John Cunningham and Stephen Slimp, 'The Less into the Greater: Emblem, Analogue, and Deification in *The Merchant of Venice*', in *The Merchant of Venice: New Critical Essays*, ed. John W. Mahon and Ellen Macleod Mahon (2002), 244; Penny Gay, *The Cambridge Introduction to Shakespeare's Comedies* (Cambridge: Cambridge University Press, 2008), 55.

7 Colley, 'Launcelot, Jacob and Esau', 185.

8 The pioneering article is Maxine MacKay '*The Merchant of Venice*: A Reflection of the Early Conflict between Courts of Law and Courts of Equity', *SQ*, 15 (1964): 371–5. See also George W. Keeton, *Shakespeare's Legal and Political Background* (London: Pitman, 1967), 144–5; W. Nicholas Knight, 'Equity, *The Merchant of Venice*, and William Lambarde', *ShS*, 27 (1974): 93–104; Danson, *Harmonies*, 83–6; M. M. Mahood, 'Introduction to *The Merchant of Venice*', in *The New Cambridge Shakespeare* (Cambridge: Cambridge University Press, 2003), 17; Peter G. Platt, *Shakespeare and the Culture of Paradox* (Farnham: Ashgate, 2009), 112–15.

9 Carpi, 'Law, Discretion, Equity', 2320.

10 Keeton, *Legal and Political Background*, 145.

11 See Micah, 6: 8, as noted in Jay L. Halio, 'Portia: Shakespeare's Matlock?', *Cardozo Studies in Law and Literature*, 5 (1993): 60. See also Martin D. Yaffe, *Shylock and the Jewish Question* (Baltimore: The John Hopkins University Press, 1997), 159–60; Sokol and Sokol, 'English Equity Jurisdiction', 422; Roger

difficulty is that it is hard to see in Anthonio a proponent of love and charity by contrast with Shylocke. Just as Shylocke expresses hatred for Anthonio,[12] so Anthonio compares Shylocke with the devil and warns him that he will continue to spurn and spit on him (TLN, 414, 485, 1.3.91 and 445–6, 485, 1.3.122–3). Both characters lead sober lives, but both are troubled by violent feelings of loathing and perhaps self-loathing too.[13]

It is likewise difficult to see in Portia a figure devoted to the furtherance of equity in its legal meaning, or even in its broader sense as a principle of impartiality. Her famous paean to the quality of mercy can hardly be construed as an appeal to equitable jurisdiction in place of strict justice. She calls for mercy, not equity, a concept to which she makes no reference.[14] But mercy is not the same as equity, even if the aim of applying equitable jurisdiction is generally to bring about a more merciful result.[15] Portia is not in any case in a position to ask for equity to be applied, if only because everyone in court accepts the legality of Shylocke's bond.[16] She is left appealing not from one jurisdiction to another, but rather to a higher realm above the reach of law.[17]

Once Shylocke rejects her appeal, moreover, Portia abandons any concern for compassion and love. It is she who most explicitly invokes the Old Law when she tells Shylocke that, 'as thou urgest justice, be assurd/Thou shalt have justice more then thou desirst' (TLN, 2122–3, p. 503, 4.1.311–12). Nor is her conduct of the trial equitable in the more general sense. She arrives as an imposter in borrowed robes, fraudulently allowing the duke of Venice to believe that she is a Doctor of Laws from Rome (TLN, 1961 and 1974, p. 501, 4.1.152 and 164). She fails to inform the duke of several disabling objections to her taking part in the trial, including the fact that she is sheltering Shylocke's daughter, that Shylocke's loan to Anthonio was taken out in favour of her husband, and that

Stritmatter, '"Old" and "New" Law in *The Merchant of Venice:* A Note on the Source of Shylock's Morality in Deuteronomy 15', *N&Q*, 245 (2000): 71.

12 William Shakespeare, *The Merchant of Venice*, in *The Complete Works: Original-Spelling Edition*, ed. Stanley Wells and Gary Taylor (Oxford: Clarendon Press, 1986), TLN, 357, p. 484 (1.3.34) and 1868, p. 500 (4.1.60). Further references to this edition will appear in the text.

13 On their similarities, see Thomas Moisan, '"Which Is the Merchant Here? And Which the Jew?": Subversion and Recuperation in *The Merchant of Venice*', in *Shakespeare Reproduced: The Text in History and Ideology*, ed. Jean E. Howard and Marion F. O'Connor (London: Methuen, 1987), 105; John Lyon, *The Merchant of Venice* (London: Prentice Hall, 1988), 109; Daniel J. Kornstein, *Kill All the Lawyers? Shakespeare's Legal Appeal* (Princeton: Princeton University Press, 1994), 64; Kiernan Ryan, *Shakespeare's Comedies* (Basingstoke: Palgrave Macmillan, 2009), 116–18.

14 As noted in Thomas C. Billelo, 'Accomplished with What She Lacks: Law, Equity, and Portia's Con', in *The Law in Shakespeare*, ed. Constance Jordan and Karen Cunningham (Basingstoke: Palgrave Macmillan, 2007), 112; Gary Watt, *Equity Stirring: The Story of Justice Beyond Law* (Oxford: Hart Publishing, 2009), 217.

15 See E. F. J. Tucker, 'The Letter of the Law in "The Merchant of Venice"', *ShS*, 29 (1976): 93–101; Joan O. Holmer, *The Merchant of Venice: Choice, Hazard and Consequence* (Basingstoke: Palgrave Macmillan, 1995), 212–13; Sokol and Sokol, 'English Equity Jurisdiction', 426; Billelo, 'Accomplished with What She Lacks', 114.

16 As noted in Billelo, 'Accomplished with What She Lacks', 109–26.

17 See Sokol and Sokol, 'English Equity Jurisdiction', 426; Richard Posner, *Law and Literature*, 3rd edn (Cambridge: Harvard University Press, 2009), 148–9.

any payment made in lieu of the bond will need to be drawn from her own resources. When she proceeds to conduct the trial she acts both as prosecutor and judge, and she concludes by demanding a criminal conviction in a civil suit.[18]

The problem with these objections, however, is that if we accept them—as I think we must—we need to find some new answers to the questions I posed at the outset. Some commentators have responded by wondering if this remains a worthwhile task to undertake. The trial presents a spectacle of such shocking racial hatred and violence that it might seem best forgotten. This reaction cannot fail to command respect, but I shall assume in what follows that, in spite of its deeply painful character, the scene remains worth trying to understand, and I shall offer an account of it that enables us, I believe, to solve the puzzles I have raised.

II

My basic suggestion is that we ought not to attempt to relate the trial directly to the legal ideas or practices of late Elizabethan England. We ought instead to focus on Shakespeare's reliance on the advice contained in a number of classical manuals of judicial rhetoric about how to conduct a persuasive case in court. In particular, I shall argue, we need to concentrate on the precepts to be found in Cicero's *De inventione*, in the anonymous *Rhetorica ad Herennium*, and in Quintilian's *Institutio oratoria*. Shakespeare was closely acquainted with all these texts,[19] but I shall mainly take my quotations from Cicero's *De inventione*, since several references in *The Merchant of Venice* suggest that this was the handbook at the front of Shakespeare's mind while writing the trial scene. It is true that he transposes Cicero's straightforward taxonomies into a highly complex and ambiguous register. I shall argue, however, that the resulting scene is underpinned by a strong organizing structure, and that this is largely supplied by the principles of judicial rhetoric.

If we turn to Cicero's *De inventione*, we find that he begins by listing the three forms of rhetorical utterance and the five elements in a judicial speech, after which he turns to examine what he describes as the *constitutio* of a legal cause.[20] Needing a translation of this term in his *Arte of Rhetorique* in 1553, Thomas Wilson rendered it as 'issue',[21] a decision quickly endorsed by English legal as well as rhetorical writers.[22]

[18] Owen Hood Phillips, *Shakespeare and the Lawyers* (London: Routledge, 1972) notes numerous objections raised by lawyers to the conduct of the trial; Posner, *Law and Literature*, 142–9 reviews what he describes as its legal absurdities.

[19] For evidence see Skinner, *Forensic Shakespeare*, 9n.

[20] Marcus Tullius Cicero, *De inventione*, ed. and trans. H. M. Hubbell (London: William Heinemann Ltd, 1949), 1.8.10, 20.

[21] Thomas Wilson, *The Arte of Rhetorique* (London: 1553), sig. M, 4^{v}.

[22] Among legal writers, see, for example, Thomas Smith, *De republica Anglorum* [1583], ed. Mary Dewar (Cambridge: Cambridge University Press, 1982), 96.

To ask about the *constitutio* of a legal cause was thus taken to be equivalent to enquiring into the specific question at issue that needs to be answered in court. As Cicero summarizes, 'the *constitutio* is the name we give to the *quaestio* out of which the *causa* is born'.[23] Given that there will always be two sides to any such question, we can also say that we are speaking of the specific *controversia* or dispute that needs to be resolved.[24] To speak of a judicial *causa*, the *Rhetorica ad Herennium* agrees, is thus to refer 'to some controversy that has arisen' between two declared adversaries.[25]

During the trial scene in *The Merchant of Venice*, all parties reveal a precise knowledge of this legal vocabulary. The scene begins with the duke addressing Anthonio the merchant:

DUKE. What, is *Anthonio* heere?
ANTHONIO. Ready, so please your grace.
DUKE. I am sorry for thee, thou art come to aunswere
A stonie adversarie,

TLN, 1810–12, p. 499 (4.1.1–4)

As the duke is obliged to admit, Anthonio is confronting an adversary who has raised a legal question, and Anthonio must now attempt to answer it.

Formally opening the proceedings, the duke observes that the question arises from the fact that Shylocke 'now exacts the penalty' of his bond with Anthonio, which is 'a pound of this poore Merchants flesh' (TLN, 1830–1, p. 500, 4.1.22–3).[26] The duke subsequently announces that he has appointed Bellario, a learned doctor from Padua, to determine the case. But Bellario explains in a letter that he is sick, and has sent a young doctor from Rome named Balthazer (Portia in disguise) to act in his place. Meanwhile, Bellario adds, he has 'acquainted him with the cause in controversie between the Jew and Anthonio the Merchant' (TLN, 1962–3, p. 501, 4.1.153–4). Portia now enters, and the duke greets her in similarly correct judicial style:

Are you acquainted with the difference
That holds the present question in the Court.

TLN, 1977–8, p. 501 (4.1.167–8)

As we have seen, to ask about a *quaestio* before a court is to enquire into the *constitutio* of the cause. Portia duly responds by assuring the duke that 'I am enformed throughly of the cause' (TLN, 1979, p. 501, 4.1.169). She is ready for the trial to begin.

23 Cicero, *De inventione*, 1.8.10, 20: 'quaestionem ex qua causa nascitur constitutionem appellamus'.

24 Cicero, *De inventione*, 1.8.10, 20.

25 *Rhetorica ad Herennium*, ed. and trans. Harry Caplan (London: 1954), 1.2.2, 4: 'Iudiciale est quod positum est in controversia.'

26 Anthonio has entered into what was known as a penal bond with conditional defeasance, a type of agreement still enforceable in Shakespeare's time. See Posner, *Law and Literature*, 143.

If we return to Cicero's analysis of the specific questions liable to arise at this juncture, we find that (after some prevarication) he isolates three main possibilities. The *quaestio* may prove to be about a matter of fact; that is, about whether or not some particular action or event took place. When this is the issue to be decided, we are said to be dealing with a *constitutio coniecturalis*, and here the correct procedure is to put forward a conjecture about what may have happened and set about testing it.[27]

A second possibility is that, as Cicero and the *Rhetorica ad Herennium* agree, the problem may arise *in scripto*.[28] The controversy, in other words, may be about the meaning of a text. When this is the question at issue, we are said to be dealing with a *constitutio negotialis*, or what the *Rhetorica ad Herennium* prefers to call a *constitutio legitima*.[29] Both writers warn that these causes give rise to a number of distinctive hermeneutic difficulties. Some will be about matters of detail such as ambiguities and the definition of terms, but two more general problems will also need to be addressed, and both writers begin by singling them out.

First you will need to decide whether to focus on the *verba ipsa* of the text at issue, or whether to ask for the *sententia scriptoris* to be investigated.[30] You must decide, that is, whether to call on those judging your case 'to pay attention to nothing except what exactly is written',[31] or else to concentrate on 'the intention of your adversaries'.[32] Second, you must take care to ensure that your plea is not challenged or nullified by the existence of a *lex contraria*, a contrary law.[33] The problem here arises 'when one law permits or orders something to be done, while another forbids it'.[34] This kind of contradiction can all too readily undermine your case, because it may be open to your adversary to argue that the law supporting his side 'is concerned with matters of greater importance', and is therefore the one that ought to be upheld by the court.[35]

The third and final possibility is that you may be involved in a *constitutio iuridicalis* or 'juridical' cause, in which the question at issue is whether some particular action has or has not been performed *recte* and *iure*.[36] To recover how these terms were understood in Shakespeare's time, we need to turn for a moment to the Latin–English dictionaries of the period.[37] They agree that, when we speak of having acted *recte*, we are claiming to have behaved rightfully as opposed to wrongfully, and hence without

[27] Cicero, *De inventione*, 1.8.10, 20; cf. *Rhetorica ad Herennium*, 1.9.18, 34.

[28] Cicero, *De inventione*, 1.8.17, 34; *Rhetorica ad Herennium*, 1.9 19, 34.

[29] Cicero, *De inventione*, 1.11.14, 30; *Rhetorica ad Herennium*, 1.11.19, 34.

[30] Cicero, *De inventione*, 1.8.17, 34 and 2.42.121–2, 290; *Rhetorica ad Herennium*, 1.11.19, 34.

[31] Cicero, *De inventione*, 2.43.125, 292: 'nihil eos qui iudicent nisi id quod scriptum spectare oportere'.

[32] Cicero, *De inventione*, 2.43.125, 292 on the 'intentio adversarium', and 2.47.138, 306 on speaking 'contra scriptum'.

[33] Cicero, *De inventione*, 2.49.144, 312; cf. *Rhetorica ad Herennium*, 1.11.20, 36.

[34] *Rhetorica ad Herennium*, 1.11.20, 36: 'cum alia lex iubet aut permittit, alia vetat quippiam fieri'.

[35] See Cicero, *De inventione*, 2.49.145, 312, on which of the contrary laws 'ad maiores ... pertineat.'

[36] On acting *recte*, see Cicero, *De inventione*, 1.11.14, 30 and 2.23.69, 232; *Rhetorica ad Herennium*, 1.14.24, 44. On acting *iure*, see Cicero, *De inventione*, 1.11.15, 30; *Rhetorica ad Herennium*, 1.14.24, 42.

[37] On these works, see DeWitt T. Starnes *Renaissance Dictionaries: English–Latin and Latin–English* (Austin: University of Texas Press, 1954), 48–67, 85–110, 114–46.

blame.[38] They likewise agree that, when we speak of acting *iure*, we are either laying claim to something that is ours 'of good ryght', or else to something allowed to us by 'Lawe, right [and] good dealing' in civil affairs.[39]

Reflecting on such juridical causes, Cicero distinguishes two different possibilities. You may be able to claim that your case is *absoluta*, by which he means that 'the question as to what is *ius* and contrary to *ius* will be contained in your plea itself', as will 'the question of what is *rectus* and what is not *rectus*'.[40] You will be able to affirm, in other words, that the plea you are laying before the court is wholly in accordance with justice and right. The alternative is that your case may be *adsumptiva*, by which Cicero means that you may be obliged to admit that you acted in such a manner that 'it is not possible to offer any firm response' to your adversary in court.[41] If you find yourself in this predicament, your only recourse will be to produce a *confessio*, that is, an admission of your adversary's case combined with a plea for mercy or a request to be pardoned.[42] This type of plea can in turn take one of two forms. You may be able to attempt a *purgatio*, an excuse based on admitting the facts while denying responsibility. But you may find that you can only submit a *deprecatio*, admitting that you acted *cum consulto*, with full intention and foresight, while nevertheless asking to be acquitted.[43]

Cicero warns that it is extremely rare for such cases to succeed. But when he turns at the end of Book I of *De inventione* to discuss the most persuasive means of rounding off a speech, he nonetheless offers some advice about how to win forgiveness from a court. You need to present what he calls a *conquestio*, 'a type of oration specifically designed to capture the pity of your hearers' and thus to induce a merciful response.[44] As to how this can be done, he places his entire faith in the use of *loci communes*, resonant and widely accepted maxims that you can hope to apply to your case. He ends by listing a number of specific *loci* that can be deployed in the hope of arousing compassion, ending with the suggestion that we should speak 'in such a way as to show that our own soul is filled with mercy towards others', and that we hope for mercy ourselves.[45]

As soon as Shylocke is summoned into court, he makes it clear that he considers his cause to be a *constitutio iuridicalis*, and at the same time *absoluta* in character. As we have seen, to assert that your cause is absolute is in part to claim that you have acted *recte*, without doing any wrong, and are thus free of blame. This is precisely the contention with which Shylocke answers the duke's outraged question: 'How shalt thou hope

[38] Thomas Elyot, *Bibliotheca Eliotae … by Thomas Cooper the Third Tyme Corrected* (London: 1559), sig. 3P, 2^{v} and 3^{r}; Thomas Cooper, *Thesaurus Linguae Romanae & Britannicae* (London: 1565), sig. 5O, 3^{v}; Thomas Thomas, *Dictionarium tertio … emendatum* (Cambridge, 1592), sig. 2S, 1^{v}.

[39] Elyot, *Bibliotheca*, sig. 2R, 8^{v}; Cooper, *Thesaurus*, sig. 3Y, 2^{v}; Thomas, *Dictionarium*, sig. 2D, 1^{v}.

[40] See Cicero, *De inventione*, 1.11.15, 30: 'Absoluta est quae ipsa in se continet iuris et iniuria quaestionem.' Cf. Cicero, *De inventione*, 2.23.69, 232: 'Absoluta est quae ipsa in se … recti et non recti quaestionem continet.'

[41] Cicero, *De inventione*, 1.11.15, 30: 'assumptiva [est] quae ipsa ex se nihil dat firmi ad recusationem'.

[42] Cicero, *De inventione*, 1.11.15, 30.

[43] Cicero, *De inventione*, 1.11.15, 30; cf. *Rhetorica ad Herennium*, 1.14.24, 42–6.

[44] Cicero, *De inventione*, 1.55.106, 156: 'Conquestio est oratio auditorum misericordiam captans.'

[45] Cicero, *De inventione*, 1.56.109, 160: 'animum nostrum in alios misericordem esse ostendimus'.

for mercy rendring none?' Shylocke responds: 'What judgment shall I dread doing no wrong?' (TLN, 1896–7, p. 500, 4.1.88–9). You must also seek to establish that your cause is just, and thus that you are simply laying claim to what is yours by right. This is how Shylocke opens his case, alluding to the traditional definition of justice as *ius suum tribuere*, the act of rendering to each his due:

> I have possest your grace of what I purpose,
> And by our holy Sabaoth I have sworne
> To have the due and forfet of my bond,
>
> TLN, 1843–5, p. 500 (4.1.35–7)

Shylock reiterates his claim when putting his final request to the duke:

> The pound of flesh which I demaund of him
> Is deerely bought, tis mine and I will have it:
> If you deny me, fie upon your Law,
> There is no force in the decrees of Venice:
> I stand for judgement, aunswer, shall I have it?
>
> TLN, 1907–11, p. 500 (4.1.99–103)

With this demand for *ius* in the sense of right and good dealing, Shylocke brings the statement of his plea to a close.

III

After anatomizing the different *genera* of *constitutiones*, Cicero devotes the rest of Book 1 of his *De inventione* to his other major concern, the correct way of organizing the components of a judicial speech.[46] Before turning to this analysis, however, he pauses to consider the moral standing of the various types of cause that typically come before the courts. If you are planning to enter a plea, he cautions, 'it is essential to think beforehand about the type of cause in which you are involved', and here again he lays out three main possibilities.[47]

If you are fortunate, you may be engaged in a *causa honesta*. An 'honest' cause 'is one that can be expected immediately to win goodwill in the mind of your audience without your even having to make a speech about it'.[48] The reason for this favourable reaction, the *Rhetorica ad Herennium* explains, is that 'you will be defending something that seems to everyone worthy of defending, or attacking something that seems to everyone deserving

[46] The transition occurs at Cicero, *De inventione*, 1.14.19, 38.

[47] Cicero, *De inventione*, 1.15.20. 40: 'necesse est genus suae causae diligenter ante cognoscere'.

[48] Cicero, *De inventione*, 1.15.20. 40: 'Honestum causae genus est cui statim sine oratione nostra favet auditoris animus.'

of attack'.[49] A second and associated possibility is that your cause may be partly honest and partly *turpis* in character. If we return to the Latin–English dictionaries, we find that *turpis* was held to mean 'foule: filthie: Dishonest: unhonorable'.[50] Cicero duly warns that any cause liable to this kind of assessment 'will give rise to some offence'.[51]

While the *causa honesta* and the *causa turpis* are taken to be the principal types of plea,[52] Cicero and Quintilian both consider the further possibility that your cause may be *admirabilis*.[53] According to the Latin–English dictionaries of the time, to say of an utterance that it is *admirabilis* is to regard it as 'mervaylous, to be wondred at', and hence as 'strange'.[54] To speak of a strange cause is thus to refer to a plea that will seem to most people an astonishing one to put forward in court.

No one ever suggests that Shylocke's cause is inherently *turpis* or foul, and thus can simply be denounced and dismissed. Even Anthonio concedes that Shylocke's plea is valid, and thus that 'no lawfull meanes can carry me/Out of his envies reach' (TLN, 1817, 499, 4.1.9–10). The duke, however, is far from willing to conclude that Shylocke's cause must therefore be regarded as *honesta* or honest.[55] On the contrary, he excoriates Shylocke in his opening address for his unnatural cruelty, condemns him for his malice and urges him to withdraw his plea (TLN, 1826–34, p. 500, 4.1.18–26). How then should Shylocke's cause be classified? With her opening words to Shylocke, Portia gives the answer:

PORTIA. Is your name *Shylocke*?
SHYLOCKE. *Shylocke* is my name.
PORTIA. Of a strange nature is the sute you follow,

TLN, 1982–3, p. 501 (4.1.172–3)

According to Portia, Shylocke's cause can only be classified as a *causa admirabilis*, a strange suit.[56]

Shylocke's case may be strange, but there is nothing illegal about it, as Portia is at once obliged to admit:

PORTIA. Of a strange nature is the sute you follow,
Yet in such rule, that the Venetian law
Cannot impugne you as you doe proceed.

[49] *Rhetorica ad Herennium*, 1.3.5, 10: 'cum aut id defendimus quod ab omnibus defendendum videtur, aut oppugnabimus quod ad omnibus videtur oppugnari debere'.

[50] Cooper, *Thesaurus*, sig. 6K, 5^{v}, repeated in Thomas, *Dictionarium*, sig. 3C, 5^{v}.

[51] Cicero, *De inventione*, 1.15.20, 40: 'et benivolentiam pariat et offensionem'.

[52] For example, *Rhetorica ad Herennium*, 1.3.5, 10.

[53] They also consider further *genera*, while agreeing that they are of little significance. See Cicero, *De inventione*, 1.15.20, 40; Quintilian, *Institutio oratorio*, ed. and trans. Donald A. Russell, Vol. 2 (London: 2001), 4.1.41, 198.

[54] Elyot, *Bibliotheca*, sig. B, 6^{r}; Cooper, *Thesaurus*, sig. D, 1^{r}; Thomas, *Dictionarium*, sig. B, 4^{r}.

[55] *Rhetorica ad Herennium*, 1.3.5, 10: 'cum aut id defendimus quod ab omnibus defendendum videtur'.

[56] But for different readings, see Graham Holderness, *The Merchant of Venice* (Harmondsworth: Penguin Books, 1993), 46; Kornstein, *Kill All the Lawyers?*, 67.

(*To Anthonio*) You stand within his danger, doe you not?
ANTHONIO. I, so he sayes.
PORTIA. Doe you confesse the bond?
ANTHONIO. I doe.

TLN, 1983–8, p. 501 (4.1.173–8)

Portia acknowledges that Shylocke's cause is juridicial: the facts about the bond are not in dispute; the only question is what law and justice prescribe. She also accepts that Shylocke's plea is absolute: he is simply claiming a right, and cannot be legally impugned. Given that this is so, the only plea she can enter on Anthonio's behalf must be correspondingly assumptive. She can do no more, that is, than enter a *confessio* in his name. Nor can she hope to do so in the form of a *purgatio*, admitting that Anthonio signed his agreement while denying that he did so *cum consulto*. As Anthonio has just acknowledged, he freely consented to the terms of Shylocke's bond. Portia is thus left with no option but to offer a *deprecatio*—a straightforward plea for mercy—and she wastes no time in making this move:

PORTIA. Doe you confesse the bond?
ANTHONIO. I doe.
PORTIA. Then must the Jew be mercifull.

TLN, 1987–8, p. 501 (4.1.77–8)

As Portia recognizes, Anthonio is in the desperate position of a defendant who lacks a legal case.

Faced with the insistence that he must be merciful, Shylocke retorts 'On what compulsion must I, tell me that' (TLN, 1989, p. 501, 4.1.179). Without further preamble, Portia responds by delivering her celebrated speech on the quality of mercy as a heavenly gift. Critics have sometimes described the sudden introduction of this intensely sententious oration as a magnificent irrelevance.[57] But Portia is reacting in exactly the manner recommended by the classical theorists of judicial rhetoric. As we have seen, they advise that, if you have no option but to issue a *deprecatio*, you must ground it as much as possible on familiar and resonant *loci communes*, concentrating on such topics as the value of mercy and the infirmity of mankind, and culminating in the affirmation that your own heart is filled with compassion towards others.[58]

Portia begins by telling Shylocke that, in asking what should compel him to be merciful, he has misapprehended the nature of the virtue:

The qualitie of mercie is not straind,
It droppeth as the gentle raine from heaven
Upon the place beneath:

TLN, 1990–2, p. 501 (4.1.180–2)

[57] See, for example, Danson, *Harmonies*, 63, who also quotes D. J. Palmer describing the speech as 'a piece of superfluous rhetoric'.

[58] Cicero, *De inventione*, 1.56.109, 160.

Because mercy stands in contrast with the demands of law, it can only be exercised without straining or constraint, and we should therefore think of it as similar to other gifts of God. Here Shakespeare alludes to a prayer found in several of the collections of meditations popular in Elizabethan England. They counsel that, in times of 'raging tempests, and unseasonable weather' we should appeal to God 'of thy mercie' to 'convert the thunder into gentle raine'.[59] Shakespeare transforms the prayer into an image likening mercy itself to gentle rain dropping from heaven upon the place beneath.

Next Portia offers Shylock a number of reasons for exhibiting mercy towards Anthonio instead of calling for strict justice. One consideration frequently emphasized by Tudor writers of commonplace books was that, as John Larke puts it in his *Boke of wisdome* of 1575, 'he which shall have mercy of another, he shall fynde mercy for him selfe'.[60] Thomas Cogan in *The Well of Wisedome* of 1577 agrees that 'he that is mercifull doth himselfe a benefite'.[61] Portia begins by speaking of mercy in the same terms:

> it is twise blest,
> It blesseth him that gives, and him that takes,
>
> TLN, 1992–3, p. 501 (4.1.182–3)

She then proceeds to invoke a further set of popular maxims and principles. Seneca in his *De clementia* had assured Nero that 'the man who holds a place closest to the gods is the one who is kind and generous',[62] a sentiment given wide currency after Domenicus Mirabellius included it in his book of *sententiae* in the form of the claim that 'nothing is more befitting than mercy in a prince'.[63] Robert Hitchcock in his translation of Francisco Sansovino, which he published as *The Quintesence of wit* in 1590, similarly describes 'using of clemencie' as 'a thing proper and perticular to great

[59] See, for example, Johann Habermann, *The Enimie of Securitie or A Dailie Exercise of Godly Meditations Drawne out of the Pure Fountaines of the Holie Scriptures*, trans. Thomas Rogers (London: 1579), 326, 331. The passage is repeated word for word in Thomas Bentley, *The Monument of Matrones Conteining Seven Severall Lamps of Virginitie, or Distinct Treatises* (London: 1582), 479. For a later example see [John Bodenham], *Bel-vedére Or The Garden of the Muses* (London: 1600), 2. I have not seen any edition of the play in which Shakespeare's allusion has been recognized.

[60] John Larke, *The Boke of Wisdome* (London: 1575), sig. J, 8^r.

[61] Thomas Cogan, *The Well of Wisedome, Conteining Chiefe and Chosen Sayinges … Bestowed in Usuall Common Places in Order of A.B.C.* (London: 1577), 67. Cf. Proverbs 11:17: 'The merciful man doeth good to his own soul.'

[62] Seneca, 'De clementia', in *Moral Essays*, Vol. 1, trans. and ed. John W. Basore (London: 1928), 1.19.9, 414: 'proximum illis [deis] locum tenet is, qui … beneficus ac largus [est]'.

[63] Domenicus Mirabellius with Bartholomaeus Amantius and Franciscus Tortius. *Polyanthea. hoc est Opus … sententiarum* (Lyon, 1600), 164, col. 2, citing Seneca, 'De clementia': 'Nullum magis decet clementia, quam principem.' Mirabellius's work was first published in 1503 and thereafter frequently reprinted. On Mirabellius, see Ann Moss, *Printed Commonplace-Books and the Structuring of Renaissance Thought* (Oxford: Oxford University Press, 1996), 206–7; Skinner, *Forensic Shakespeare*, 296.

and woorthy minds',[64] while Octavianus Mirandula goes further in his collection of *loci communes* when he adds, quoting Claudian, that 'mercy alone makes us equal to the gods'.[65] Portia draws heavily on this received wisdom in developing her case:[66]

> Tis mightiest in the mightiest, it becomes
> The throned Monarch better then his crowne....
> It is an attribute to God himself;
> And earthly power doth then show likest gods
> When mercie seasons justice:
>
> TLN, 1994–5, 2001–3, pp. 501–2 (4.1.184–5, 191–3)

With these familiar sentiments Portia rounds off her paean to mercy as a godlike quality.

Portia's *laudatio* is by no means at an end, however, for she concludes by adding a specifically Christian argument no less frequently encountered in Elizabethan compilations of *loci communes*. If we call for justice instead of mercy, the argument runs, we can never hope to be saved. Cogan speaks of him 'that sheweth no mercy' and asks 'how dare he aske forgivenes of his sinnes';[67] Larke reminds us that 'Our Lord Jhesu sayth, pardon other gladly, if thou wilt have pardon';[68] and John Marbeck in his *Booke Of Notes and Common places* of 1581 adds that 'There shall be no judgment without mercie, for because ther can no man living, be found cleane'.[69] Portia ends by echoing these warnings:

> Though justice be thy plea, consider this,
> That, in the course of justice, none of us
> Should see salvation: we doe pray for mercy,
> And that same prayer, doth teach us all to render
> The deedes of mercie.
>
> TLN, 2004–8, p. 502 (4.1.194–8)

[64] Robert Hitchcock, *The Quintesence of Wit … Wherin Is Set Foorth Sundrye Excellent and Wise Sentences* (London: 1590), fol. 40^{v}.

[65] Octavianus Mirandula, *Illustrium poetarum flores … in locos communes digesti* (London: 1598), 174: 'sola deos aequat clementia nobis'. While 1598 was the date of the first London printing, Mirandula's text had been circulating widely since its first publication in 1507. See Moss, *Printed Commonplace-Books*, 95, 189; Skinner, *Forensic Shakespeare*, 296–7.

[66] It is usually said that Portia is drawing directly from the Bible. See, for example, Richard Noble, *Shakespeare's Biblical Knowledge and Use of the Book of Common Prayer* (London: 1935), 167; Stritmatter, '"Old" and "New" Law', 70–2; John Flood, '"It Droppeth as the Gentle Rain"', 176–7. I am arguing that, by the time Shakespeare was writing, the 'wisdom' books of the Old Testament had been so extensively mined in collections of commonplaces that many of their maxims had passed into general currency. On this point see Mahood, *The Merchant of Venice* (2003), 199–200.

[67] Cogan, *Well of Wisedome*, 67, referring to Ecclesiasticus 28:4.

[68] Larke, *Boke of Wisdome*, sig. J, 8^{r}.

[69] John Marbeck, *A Booke Of Notes and Common Places* (London: 1581), 783: *sub* 'Originall sinne'. Marbeck refers us to Basil's commentary on Psalm 32. For the entry on 'Mercie', see Marbeck, *A Booke Of Notes*, 709.

Finally she acknowledges that she is offering nothing more than a *deprecatio*, and admits that the only reason why she has spoken at such length is 'To mittigate the justice of thy plea' (TLN, 2009, p. 502, 4.1.199).

Portia's speech offers a magnificent example of Shakespeare's capacity (much celebrated by T. S. Eliot) to conjure great poetry out of conventional materials, but it is perhaps not surprising that it makes no impression on Shylocke, especially as Portia's commonplaces are entirely classical and Christian in provenance. This is no doubt what Shakespeare's original audience would have expected, but it is not clear why such exhortations should carry any weight with someone not of the Christian faith. Revealing at once that he remains unmoved, Shylocke simply reverts to his earlier insistence that he is asking for nothing more than his legal rights:

> My deeds upon my head, I crave the law,
> The penalty and forfaite of my bond.
>
> TLN, 2012–13, p. 502 (4.1.202–3)

With this final rejection of mercy in favour of law the trial appears to be at an end. Portia accepts the justice of Shylocke's plea, 'Which if thou follow, this strict Court of Venice/Must needes give sentence gainst the Merchant there' (TLN, 2010–11, p. 502, 4.1.200–1). Bassanio calls on her to wrest the law in Anthonio's favour, but she explains that 'It must not be, there is no power in Venice/Can altar a decree established' (TLN, 2024–5, p. 502, 4.1.214–15). Shylocke reacts with a cry of congratulation: 'A Daniell come to judgement: yea a Daniell' (TLN, 2029, p. 502, 4.1.219). As far as he is concerned, the claim that his plea is absolute has finally been vindicated.

IV

Turning to Portia at what he takes to be his moment of triumph, Shylocke exclaims 'O wise young Judge how I doe honour thee' (TLN, 2030, p. 502, 4.1.220). With her next words, however, Portia suddenly opens up a new vista—possibly reminding us (some critics have suggested) that *porta* in Latin means a door.[70] She now asks Shylocke 'I pray you let me looke upon the bond' (TLN, 2031, p. 502, 4.1.22). Portia is giving notice that the question at issue in Shylocke's case is not exclusively *iuridicalis*, a matter of determining whether his plea is in line with law and right; it is also *negotialis*, a matter of how to interpret a specific written document, in this case the text of Shylocke's bond.

[70] As noted in Grace Tiffany, 'Names in *The Merchant of Venice*', in *The Merchant of Venice: New Critical Essays*, ed. John W. Mahon and Ellen Macleod Mahon (2002), 360.

It is true that this does not at first appear to make any difference. As soon as Portia studies the contract, she exclaims:

> Why this bond is forfait
> And lawfully by this the Jew may claime
> A pound of flesh, to be by him cut off
> Neerest the Merchants hart:
>
> TLN, 2036–9, p. 502 (4.1.226–9)

She therefore makes one final appeal: 'be mercifull/Take thrice thy money, bid me teare the bond' (TLN, 2039–40, p. 502, 4.1.229–30). But Shylocke responds by calling for judgement, and Anthonio now echoes his request. Portia accordingly replies by delivering her verdict:

> Why than thus it is
> You must prepare your bosome for his knife.
>
> TLN, 2050–1, p. 502 (4.1.240–1)

Shylocke cannot resist another triumphant cry: 'O noble Judge, o excellent young man' (TLN, 2052, p. 502, 4.1.242).

By this time, however, many members of Shakespeare's original audience would undoubtedly have been shaking their heads. To anyone schooled in the classical *ars rhetorica*, Shylocke's exclamation would have sounded unguardedly premature. He appears oblivious of the fact that, if the question now before the court arises out of a *constitutio negotialis*, and is thus about how the text of his bond should be interpreted, he will need to move with great circumspection as he negotiates the two hermeneutic questions that cannot fail to arise.

As we have seen, the first of these is whether he should take his stand exclusively on the *verba ipsa*, 'the very words' of his bond, or whether he should make some appeal to the *sententia scriptoris*, the intentions and purposes underlying the text. Portia is always careful to maintain a balance between these two approaches. When she initially concedes the lawfulness of Shylocke's bond, she does so in part because the precise wording requires it, but also because the intention underlying the relevant law makes it applicable to the case in hand:

> For the intent and purpose of the law
> Hath full relation to the penaltie,
> Which heere appeareth due upon the bond.
>
> TLN, 2053–5, p. 502 (4.1.243–5)

By contrast, Shylocke always insists on the exact wording of his agreement and nothing more. 'I stay here on my Bond' (TLN, 2048, p. 502, 4.1.238). When Portia pronounces that this allows him to cut a pound of flesh 'Neerest the Merchants hart' (TLN, 2039, p. 502, 4.1.229), he relishes the exactitude of her phrasing, even quoting Cicero's formula about 'the very words':

> I, his breast,
> So sayes the bond, doth it not noble Judge?
> Neerest his hart, those are the very words.
>
> TLN, 2058–60, p. 502 (4.1.248–50)

When Portia calls for a surgeon to stand by, Shylocke again insists on the exact wording of his agreement. His reason for ignoring her request is that no such requirement appears in the text: 'I cannot finde it, tis not in the bond' (TLN, 2068, p. 502, 4.1.258).

Shylocke next discovers, however, that he has made a disastrous choice (TLN, 2104, p. 502, 4.1.294). Portia responds by reiterating her verdict, presenting it in two parts. First she allows Shylocke his pound of flesh:

> The Court awards it, and the law doth give it. . . .
> And you must cut this flesh from off his breast,
> The law alowes it, and the court awards it.
>
> TLN, 2105–6, 2108–9, p. 503 (4.1.295–6, 298–9)

Shylocke turns at once to Anthonio: 'come prepare' (TLN, 2110, p. 503, 4.1.300). But Portia interrupts him to deliver the second part of her verdict:

> Tarry a little, there is some thing else,
> This bond doth give thee heere no jote of blood,
> The words expresly are a pound of flesh:
>
> TLN, 2111–13, p. 503 (4.1.301–3)

Shylocke has asked for nothing but the words of his bond to be considered, and what they expressly state is that he is allowed flesh but nothing more.

The disastrousness of Shylocke's choice is suddenly revealed. If he had followed Portia's lead and asked in addition for the *sententia scriptoris* to be assessed, he would have been able to save himself. Cicero explains that, if you insist on addressing the underlying purpose of any legal arrangement, you can always argue that 'something which seems inherently obvious does not need to be expressly stated'.[71] Shylocke could have claimed that, since it is inherently obvious that no one can cut off a pound of flesh without spilling blood, his bond must be understood to permit him blood as well as

[71] Cicero, *De inventione*, 2.47.139, 306: 'eum quae perspicua videret esse non ascripsisse'.

flesh, because it would otherwise be impossible for him to have any flesh at all.[72] As it is, however, he is left facing the dilemma that the words of his bond allow him flesh but no blood.

The overwhelming majority of critics have taken this to be the crux of the case. They begin by quoting the line 'This bond doth give thee heere no jote of blood.'[73] They then declare—in a much favoured metaphor—that this is the moment at which the tables are turned.[74] The reason is said to be that Shylocke 'cannot have the flesh' after all; it has been 'made impossible' for his bond to be executed, so that the penalty becomes 'unenforceable' and 'cannot be exacted'.[75] Portia is thus able to win by nothing more than a verbal quibble and a trick.[76]

It is arguable, however, that to treat this moment as pivotal is to overlook the most essential element in the construction of Portia's case. To appreciate this further element, we need to remember that there are two questions we must be sure to consider before bringing forward a *constitutio negotialis*. As I have been noting, the first is whether we ought to ask for the *sententia scriptoris* to be considered. If Shylocke had followed this option he would undoubtedly have been able to answer Portia's initial objection that his bond allows him flesh but no blood. But he would still have been left confronting the second question: is it possible that there may be a *lex contraria* that challenges the legal standing of the bond as a whole? It is evident from Shylocke's way of presenting his

[72] As noted in Kornstein, *Kill All the Lawyers?*, 70; Posner, *Law and Literature*, 144.

[73] Keeton, *Legal and Political Background*, 144; Danson, *Harmonies*, 119; Alice N. Benston, 'Portia, the Law, and the Tripartite Structure of *The Merchant of Venice*', in *The Merchant of Venice: Critical Essays*, ed. Thomas Wheeler (New York: Garland Publishing, Inc., 1991), 174; Halio, 'Portia: Shakespeare's Matlock?', 61; Kenneth Gross, *Shylock is Shakespeare* (Chicago: The University of Chicago Press, 2006), 100; Janet Adelman, *Blood Relations: Christian and Jew in 'The Merchant of Venice'* (Chicago: University Chicago Press, 2008), 125; Ryan, *Shakespeare's Comedies*, 119; Watt, *Equity Stirring*, 216; John Drakakis, 'Introduction' to *The Merchant of Venice* (The Arden Shakespeare), (London: Bloomsbury Publishing, 2010), 103; David Margolies, *Shakespeare's Irrational Endings: The Problem Plays* (Basingstoke: Palgrave Macmillan, 2012), 101.

[74] See Benston, 'Tripartite Structure', 174; Halio, 'Portia: Shakespeare's Matlock?', 62; M. M. Mahood, *Merchant of Venice*, 16, 22; Ryan, *Shakespeare's Comedies*, 119; Barber, *Shakespeare's Festive Comedy*, 210; Margolies, *Shakespeare's Irrational Endings*, 101. Richard Strier, 'Shakespeare and Legal Systems: The Better the Worse (but Not Vice Versa)', in *Shakespeare and the Law: A Conversation among Disciplines and Professions*, ed. Bradin Cormack, Martha C. Nussbaum, and Richard Strier (Chicago: The University of Chicago Press, 2013), 191 prefers to say that 'the "no jot of blood" proviso brings the proceedings to a halt'.

[75] For these claims see, respectively, John Russell Brown, ed. 'Critical Introduction' to *The Merchant of Venice* (London: Methuen, 1955), lii; and Grace Tiffany, 'Law and Self-Interest in *The Merchant of Venice*', in *William Shakespeare's The Merchant of Venice*, new edn, ed. Harold Bloom (New York: Infobase Publishing, 2010), 180; Gross, *Shylock is Shakespeare*, 100; Billelo, 'Accomplished with What She Lacks', 109; Zurcher, *Shakespeare and Law*, 274.

[76] On Portia's quibbling, see Russell Brown, 'Introduction', *Merchant*, xlix; Keeton, *Legal and Political Background* 140; Margolies, *Shakespeare's Irrational Endings*, 101. On her alleged trick, see Colley, 'Launcelot, Jacob and Esau', 185; A. G. Harmon, *Eternal Bonds, True Contracts: Law and Nature in Shakespeare's Problem Plays* (Albany: State University of New York Press, 2004), 103; Watt, *Equity Stirring*, 214; Margolies, *Shakespeare's Irrational Endings*, 103.

case—as Portia has clearly noticed—that this is not a question he has asked himself. But as she next goes on to point out, there is in fact a relevant *lex contraria*:

> Take then thy bond, take thou thy pound of flesh,
> But in the cutting it, if thou doost shed
> One drop of Christian blood, thy lands and goods
> Are by the lawes of Venice confiscate
> Unto the state of Venice.
>
> TLN, 2114–18, p. 503 (4.1.304–8)

Shylocke is stunned. 'Is that the law?' (TLN, 2120, p. 503, 4.1.310). It seems extraordinary that he should not have known about a piece of legislation expressly designed to protect Christian citizens against violence, especially from aliens like himself.[77] But Portia is able to assure him that there is indeed such a law, and that 'Thy selfe shalt see the Act' in which it is promulgated (TLN, 2121, p. 503, 4.1.310).[78]

Cicero had particularly admonished plaintiffs to ensure that their cause is not subject to being overturned by a contrary law that can be shown 'to deal with more important matters', since 'this is the law that will be taken to have the greater claim to be upheld'.[79] It is Shylocke's failure to heed this advice that enables Portia to triumph over him. As she admits throughout the trial, the law in Venice extends to the protection of aliens, so that Shylocke has private rights that the court must respect.[80] But such rights are subject to public law, and thus to the provisions of such Acts as the one designed to protect Christian citizens from harm. It is true that, in a commercial city such as Venice, it might not seem obvious that the provision of such protection is more important than the upholding of freedom of contract.[81] But no one questions Portia's crucial contention that, if Shylocke insists on his contract, the penalty annexed to violating the contrary law will come into effect.

It is not correct, therefore, to say that Portia's verdict renders Shylocke's bond impossible to execute.[82] He can still insist on the terms of his bond, and Portia urges him to do so. 'Take then thy bond, take thou thy pound of flesh' (TLN, 2114, p. 503, 4.1.304). If he

[77] As noted in Posner, *Law and Literature*, 145; Anthony Julius, *Trials of the Diaspora: A History of Anti-Semitism in England* (Oxford: Oxford University Press, 2010), 192. On aliens (including Jews) in Shakespeare's London, see James Shapiro, *Shakespeare and the Jews* (New York: Columbia University Press, 1996), 187–9. Emma Smith, 'Was Shylock Jewish?', *SQ*, 62 (2013): 188–219, stresses that Shylocke's alien status is what is chiefly significant.

[78] Inge Leimberg, *'What May Words Say ... ?' A Reading of 'The Merchant of Venice'* (Lanham: Fairleigh Dickinson University Press, 2011), 93 mentions contrary laws, but the only commentary I have seen in which their importance is discussed is Jane Donawerth, *Shakespeare and the Sixteenth-Century Study of Language* (Chicago: University of Illinois Press, 1984), 208–9.

[79] See Cicero, *De inventione*, 2.48.145, 312 on the need to consider 'utra lex ad maiores ... pertineat', since 'ea maxime conservanda putetur'. See also Quintilian, *Institutio oratorio*, 7.7.7–8, 3.274.

[80] As noted in Ian Ward, *Shakespeare and the Legal Imagination* (London: Butterworths, 1999), 132.

[81] For an exploration of this problem, see Strier, 'Shakespeare and Legal Systems', 190–2.

[82] As noted in Holmer, *Choice, Hazard and Consequence*, 199, 207.

does so, however, he will be obliged to pay the penalty for infringing the relevant contrary law, and will forfeit his entire estate. The reason why this moment marks the true turning-point in the trial is that Portia has correctly guessed that, as soon as Shylocke is made aware of the penalty, he will find it too severe to contemplate. His bond is not unenforceable, but the effect of the contrary law is to make him decide not to enforce it.

It is now Shylocke's turn to ask for mercy, and when Portia rejects his plea he has no alternative but to give up:

> SHYLOCKE. Shall I not have barely my principall?
> PORTIA. Thou shalt have nothing but the forfeiture
> To be so taken at thy perrill Jew.
> SHYLOCKE. Why then the devill give him good of it:
> Ile stay no longer question.
>
> TLN, 2148–52, p. 503 (4.1.338–42)

The question to which Shylocke here refers, the *quaestio* he had brought before the court, was whether he should be permitted to impose the terms of his penal bond. With his own decision not to impose it, there is nothing left for him to say, as he acknowledges when he declares that 'Ile stay no longer question.' The hypocritical Christians have many additional humiliations to heap upon him before he is permitted to leave the court, but this is the moment at which he is forced to recognize that he has lost his case.

Bibliography

Adelman, Janet. *Blood Relations: Christian and Jew in The Merchant of Venice* (Chicago: University of Chicago Press, 2008).

Arber, Edward. *A Transcript of the Registers of the Company of Stationers of London; 1554–1640 A.D.* (London: 1875–1894).

Barber, C. L. *Shakespeare's Festive Comedy: A Study of Dramatic Form and Its Relation to Social Custom* (Princeton: Princeton University Press, 2012).

Benston, Alice N. 'Portia, the Law, and the Tripartite Structure of "The Merchant of Venice"', in *The Merchant of Venice: Critical Essays*, ed. Thomas Wheeler (New York: Garland Publishing, Inc, 1991), 163–94.

Bentley, Thomas. *The Monument of Matrones Conteining Seven Severall Lamps of Virginitie, or Distinct Treatises* (London: 1582).

Billelo, Thomas C. 'Accomplished with What She Lacks: Law, Equity, and Portia's Con', in *The Law in Shakespeare*, ed. Constance Jordan and Karen Cunningham (Basingstoke: Palgrave Macmillan, 2007), 109–26.

[Bodenham, John]. *Bel-vedére Or The Garden of the Muses* (London: 1600).

Brown, John Russell, 'Critical Introduction', in William Shakespeare, *The Merchant of Venice*, ed. John Russell Brown (London: Methuen, 1955), xxxvii–lviii.

Carpi, Daniela. 'Law, Discretion, Equity in "The Merchant of Venice" and "Measure for Measure"', *Cardozo Law Review*, 26 (2005): 2317–29.

Cicero, Marcus Tullius. *Rhetorica ad Herennium*, ed. and trans. Harry Caplan (Cambridge, MA and London: Harvard University Press, 1954).

Cicero, Marcus Tullius. *Rhetoricorum ad c. herennium libri quattuor. M. T. Ciceronis De inventione libri duo* (London: 1579).
Cicero, Marcus Tullius. *De inventione*, ed. and trans. H. M. Hubbell (London: William Heinemann Ltd, 1949).
Cogan, Thomas. *The Well of Wisedome, Conteining Chiefe and Chosen Sayinges ... Bestowed in Usuall Common Places in Order of A.B.C.* (London: 1577).
Colley, John S. 'Launcelot, Jacob, and Esau: Old and New Law in "The Merchant of Venice"', *Yearbook of English Studies*, 10 (1980): 181–9.
Cooper, Thomas. *Thesaurus linguae romanae & britannicae* (London: 1565).
Cunningham, John and Stephen Slimp. 'The Less into the Greater: Emblem, Analogue, and Deification in "The Merchant of Venice"', in *The Merchant of Venice: New Critical Essays*, ed. John W. Mahon and Ellen Macleod Mahon (London: Routledge, 2002), 225–82.
Danson, Lawrence. *The Harmonies of 'The Merchant of Venice'* (New Haven: Yale University Press, 1978).
Donawerth, Jane. *Shakespeare and the Sixteenth-Century Study of Language* (Chicago: University of Illinois Press, 1984).
Drakakis, John. 'Introduction', in William Shakespeare, *The Merchant of Venice*, ed. John Drakakis (London: Bloomsbury Publishing, 2010), 1–159.
Elyot, Thomas. *Bibliotheca Eliotae ... by Thomas Cooper the Third Tyme Corrected* (London: 1559).
Flood, John. '"It Droppeth as the Gentle Rain": Isaiah 45:8 and "The Merchant of Venice" IV.1.181.' *N&Q*, 253 (2008): 176–7.
Gay, Penny. *The Cambridge Introduction to Shakespeare's Comedies* (Cambridge: Cambridge University Press, 2008).
Gross, Kenneth. *Shylock is Shakespeare* (Chicago: University of Chicago Press, 2006).
Habermann, Johann. *The Enimie of Securitie or a Dailie Exercise of Godly Meditations Drawne Out of the Pure Fountaines of the Holie Scriptures*, trans. Thomas Rogers (London: 1579).
Halio, Jay L. 'Portia: Shakespeare's Matlock?', *Cardozo Studies in Law and Literature*, 5 (1993): 57–64.
Harmon, A. G. *Eternal Bonds, True Contracts: Law and Nature in Shakespeare's Problem Plays* (Albany: State University of New York Press, 2004).
Hirschfield, Heather. '"We All Expect a Gentle Answer, Jew": "The Merchant of Venice" and the Psychotheology of Conversion', *English Literary History*, 73 (2006): 61–81.
Hitchcock, Robert. *The Quintesence of Wit [...] Wherin Is Set Foorth Sundrye Excellent and Wise Sentences* (London: 1590).
Holderness, Graham. *The Merchant of Venice* (Harmondsworth: Penguin Books, 1993).
Holmer, Joan O. *The Merchant of Venice: Choice, Hazard and Consequence* (Basingstoke: Palgrave Macmillan, 1995).
Hood Phillips. Owen. *Shakespeare and the Lawyers* (London: Routledge, 1972).
Julius, Anthony. *Trials of the Diaspora: A History of Anti-Semitism in England* (Oxford: Oxford University Press, 2010).
Keeton, George W. *Shakespeare's Legal and Political Background* (London: Pitman, 1967).
Knight, W. Nicholas. 'Equity, "The Merchant of Venice", and William Lambarde', *Shakespeare Survey*, 27 (1974): 93–104.
Kornstein, Daniel J. *Kill All the Lawyers? Shakespeare's Legal Appeal* (Princeton: Princeton University Press, 1994).
Larke, John. *The Boke of Wisdome* (London: 1575).

Leimberg, Inge. '*What May Words Say …?' A Reading of 'The Merchant of Venice'* (Lanham: Fairleigh Dickinson University Press, 2011).
Lewalski, Barbara K. 'Biblical Allusion and Allegory in "The Merchant of Venice"', *Shakespeare Quarterly*, 13 (1962): 327–43.
Lyon, John. *The Merchant of Venice* (London: Prentice Hall, 1988).
MacKay, Maxine. '"The Merchant of Venice": A Reflection of the Early Conflict Between Courts of Law and Courts of Equity', *Shakespeare Quarterly*, 15 (1964): 371–5.
Margolies, David. *Shakespeare's Irrational Endings: The Problem Plays* (Basingstoke: Palgrave Macmillan, 2012).
Merbecke, John. *A Booke Of Notes and Common Places* (London: 1581).
Mirabellius, Domenicus, Bartholomaeus Amantius, and Franciscus Tortius. *Polyanthea. hoc est opus* […] *sententiarum* (Lyon: 1600).
Mirandula, Octavianus. *Illustrium poetarum flores* […] *in locos communes digesti* (London: 1598).
Moisan, Thomas. '"Which Is the Merchant Here? And Which the Jew?": Subversion and Recuperation in "The Merchant of Venice"', in *Shakespeare Reproduced: The Text in History and Ideology*, ed. Jean E. Howard and Marion F. O'Connor (London: Methuen, 1987), 188–206.
Moss, Ann. *Printed Commonplace-Books and the Structuring of Renaissance Thought* (Oxford: Oxford University Press, 1996).
Noble, Richard. *Shakespeare's Biblical Knowledge and Use of the Book of Common Prayer* (London: Society for Promoting Christian Knowledge, 1935).
Platt, Peter G. *Shakespeare and the Culture of Paradox* (Farnham: Ashgate, 2009).
Posner, Richard. *Law and Literature*, 3rd edn (Cambridge, MA: Harvard University Press, 2009).
Quintilian. *Institutio oratoria*, ed. and trans. Donald A. Russell, 5 vols (Cambridge, MA and London: Harvard University Press, 2001).
Ryan, Kiernan. *Shakespeare's Comedies* (Basingstoke: Palgrave Macmillan, 2009).
Seneca. 'De clementia', in *Moral Essays*, Vol. 1, ed. and trans. John W. Basore (Cambridge, MA and London: Harvard University Press, 1928), 356–446.
Shakespeare, William. *The Complete Works: Original-Spelling Edition*, ed. Stanley Wells and Gary Taylor (Oxford: Clarendon Press, 1986).
Shakespeare, William. *The Merchant of Venice*, ed. M. M. Mahood (Cambridge: Cambridge University Press, 2003).
Shapiro, James. *Shakespeare and the Jews* (New York: Columbia University Press, 1996).
Skinner, Quentin. *Forensic Shakespeare* (Oxford: Oxford University Press, 2014).
Smith, Emma. 'Was Shylock Jewish?', *Shakespeare Quarterly*, 62 (2013): 188–219.
Smith, Thomas. *De republica anglorum: A Discourse on the Commonwealth of England* [1583], ed. Mary Dewar (Cambridge: Cambridge University Press, 1982).
Sokol, B. J. and Mary Sokol. 'Shakespeare and the English Equity Jurisdiction: "The Merchant of Venice" and the Two Texts of "King Lear"', *The Review of English Studies*, 50 (1999): 417–39.
Starnes, DeWitt T. *Renaissance Dictionaries: English–Latin and Latin–English* (Austin: University of Texas Press, 1954).
Strier, Richard. 'Shakespeare and Legal Systems: The Better the Worse (but Not Vice Versa)', in *Shakespeare and the Law: A Conversation Among Disciplines and Professions*, ed. Bradin Cormack, Martha C. Nussbaum, and Richard Strier (Chicago: Univerity of Chicago Press, 2013), 174–200.

Stritmatter, Roger. '"Old" and "New" Law in "The Merchant of Venice": A Note on the Source of Shylock's Morality in Deuteronomy 15', *N&Q*, 245 (2000): 70–2.
Thomas, Thomas. *Dictionarium tertio* [...] *emendatum* (Cambridge: 1592).
Tiffany, Grace. 'Names in "The Merchant of Venice"', in *"The Merchant of Venice": New Critical Essays*, ed. John W. Mahon and Ellen Macleod Mahon (London: Routledge, 2002), 353–67.
Tiffany, Grace. 'Law and Self-Interest in "The Merchant of Venice"', in *William Shakespeare's The Merchant of Venice*, ed. Harold Bloom (New York: Infobase Publishing, 2010), 173–85.
Tovey, Barbara. 'The Golden Casket: An Interpretation of "The Merchant of Venice"', in *Shakespeare as Political Thinker*, ed. John Alvis and Thomas G. West (Durham: Carolina Academic Press, 1981), 215–37.
Tucker, E. F. J. 'The Letter of the Law in "The Merchant of Venice"', *Shakespeare Survey*, 29 (1976): 93–101.
Veron, John. *A Dictionary in Latine and English* [...] *Newly Corrected and Enlarged* [...] *By R*[alph] *W*[addington] (London: 1575).
Ward, Ian. *Shakespeare and the Legal Imagination* (London: Butterworths, 1999).
Watt, Gary. *Equity Stirring: The Story of Justice Beyond Law* (Oxford: Hart Publishing, 2009).
Wilson, Thomas. *The Arte of Rhetorique, for the Use of All Suche as Are Studious of Eloquence* (London: 1553).
Willson, Michael J. 'A View of Justice in Shakespeare's "The Merchant of Venice" and "Measure for Measure"', *Notre Dame Law Review*, 70 (1995): 695–726.
Yaffe, Martin D. *Shylock and the Jewish Question* (Baltimore: John Hopkins University Press, 1997).
Zurcher, Andrew. *Shakespeare and Law* (Chicago and London: University of Chicago Press, 2010).

PART II

LITERATURE AND THE LEGAL PROFESSION 1500–1700

CHAPTER 6

LEGAL SATIRE AND THE LEGAL PROFESSION IN THE 1590S

John Davies's Epigrammes *and Professional Decorum*

JESSICA WINSTON

How should lawyers conduct themselves both on and off the job? Complaints about lawyers go back to ancient times, but in England in the 1590s fervent expressions of contempt for legal practitioners circulated persistently, especially in poems and plays. During the sixteenth century, the English common law legal profession expanded rapidly even as it centralized to London, and the suddenly new and visible professional group drew criticism for its unprofessional behaviour, criticism that extended beyond legal practice to personal attributes: lawyers were avaricious, selfish, duplicitous, wanton, and (not the least) dull. Authors of the period, including many who were members of the English legal societies, the Inns of Court, registered and played up this suspicion of the profession.[1] Writing in 1588, the same year he was called to the bar of Gray's Inn, Abraham Fraunce criticized common lawyers as 'upstart *rabulae forenses*' (courthouse pettifoggers), calling them 'seditious cavillers', who 'under a pretence of law become altogether lawless to the continual molestation of ignorant men, and the general overcharging of the country'.[2]

This chapter argues that, in the face of dramatic changes in the legal profession, such views of lawyers are an attempt to shape the limits of professional decorum and

[1] Paul Raffield, for example, argues that satirical dramatic representations of lawyers in the seventeenth century criticized a legal system that lacked moral authority and served individual profit, rather than society. See 'A Discredited Priesthood: The Failings of Common Lawyers and their Representation in Seventeenth Century Satirical Drama', *LL*, 17 (2006): 365–95.

[2] Abraham Fraunce, *The Lawiers Logike* (London: William How for Thomas Gubbin and T. Newman, 1588), sig. 4^{r}.

behaviour. Members of the public and, equally strikingly, those inside the profession employed literary production to effect this shaping by advancing negative examples. John Davies (1569–1626), a one-time member of the Middle Temple (adm. 1587) and barrister, offers a signal instance. Like other authors associated with the Inns, in his *Epigrammes* (written *c.*1592–1595; published *c.*1598–1599), Davies presents satirical portraits of lawyers, Inns-of-Court men, and their social milieu, and his negative caricatures participate in the censure of legal professionals of the time. Yet, Davies's is also a compelling case because, unlike his contemporaries, he wrote in a more proactive way, going beyond negative exempla to construct, in the speaker of the *Epigrammes*, a positive *ethos* for legal men, based on the one-time dominant, but by the later sixteenth century seemingly outmoded model of the gentleman lawyer.

In developing these points, this chapter has two aims: One involves an important and understudied aspect of the relationship between the legal and literary cultures of the Inns of Court. I suggest that the literary culture of the Inns was energized by and responded to major transformations in the size and structure of the legal profession.[3] Early modernists have tended to argue that the literary culture of the Inns was the result of location and institutional culture—the fact that the societies brought together generally educated men in a lively urban environment, and required little, if any, actually studying.[4] In this view, literary production was a leisure activity, pursued by young men with time on their hands. While literary production was a recreational activity, I aim to show that in the 1590s legal satire was engaged with the law, for it expressed and responded to very particular historical concerns among the public and also among legal men about the legal profession's lack of a respectable public and professional *ethos*. A second aim concerns Davies's *Epigrammes*. Critics tend to view this as verse similar to and continuous with the larger field of epigrammatic and satirical writings of the time. This chapter reads the *Epigrammes* anew, arguing that this satirical verse works as response to the larger dynamics of the legal profession, yet even as Davies participates in a general fashion for legal satire, his *Epigrammes* functions in a distinctive way by offering a constructive image of professional conduct.

The Legal Profession in the 1590s

During the sixteenth century, the legal profession developed into a large, visible, and London-centred professional group.[5] Driving this shift was the sudden and sharp rise in

[3] For a development of this point relative to the 1560s, see Jessica Winston, *Lawyers at Play: Literature, Law, and Politics at the Early Modern Inns of Court, 1558–1581* (Oxford: Oxford University Press, 2016).

[4] For one clear articulation of this thesis, see Wifrid Prest, *Rise of the Barristers: A Social History of the English Bar, 1590–1640*, Oxford Studies in Social History (Oxford: Oxford University Press, 1991), 193.

[5] On the early modern legal profession as profession, see Edward Gieskes, *Representing the Professions: Administration, Law, and Theater in Early Modern England* (Newark: University of Delaware Press, 2006), 114–61.

litigation, especially in the Central Courts, beginning in the 1550s and peaking around 1640.[6] The dynamics of this shift are complicated. Contemporaries explained it in terms of the faults in society or humankind.[7] Sir John Davies attributed the rise in legal actions to the problems of plenty:

> [T]he commodities of the earth being more improved, there is more wealth, and consequently there are more contracts real and personal than there were in former ages. Besides there is more luxury and excess in the world, which breedeth unthrifts, bankrupts, and bed debtors, more covetousness, and more malice, which begetteth force and fraud, oppression and extortion, breach of the peace, and breach of trust. Out of these fountains innumerable suits do spring, which make the courts of justice to swell.[8]

Giving this social picture a more neutral formulation, modern historians posit that the rise in litigation likely arose out of structural transformations in the English economy: increased land transfers after the dissolution of the monasteries, a rise in mercantilism and overseas trade, and a growing capitalist system of exchange. Wilfrid Prest explains the relationship between social change and law: 'Virtually every major political, economic, and social development in Tudor and early Stuart England helped to create more work for common lawyers in general, and barristers in particular.'[9] Thus the pattern of litigation in England supports the 'curvilinear thesis', whereby 'periods of rapid social change produce a great deal of litigation as the law is adapted to new economic and social relationships'.[10] Indeed, on a per capita basis, the period from 1560 to 1640 may have been more litigious than any other in English history.[11]

To litigate, you need a lawyer. But as legal actions increased, the number of lawyers did not keep pace. As early as 1558, when Elizabeth came to the throne, at every level, lawyers were 'thin on the ground'.[12] Despite the classic argument that by the early seventeenth century the oversupply of men aiming for the learned professions was producing an era of 'alienated intellectuals', Prest has documented that the legal profession was 'undermanned rather than overcrowded'.[13] The absence of seasoned barristers created a genuine need for lawyers to do everyday legal work.[14]

6 Christopher Brooks, *Lawyers, Litigation and English Society since 1450* (London: Hambledon Press, 1998), 61.

7 Brooks, *Lawyers*, 13.

8 John Davies, *Le primer report des cases & matters en ley resolues & adjudges en les courts del Roy en Ireland* (Dublin: John Franckton, 1615), *6^{r}; see also Brooks, *Lawyers*, 14.

9 Prest, *Rise*, 49.

10 Brooks, *Lawyers*, 91.

11 Brooks, *Lawyers*, 12.

12 Christopher Brooks, *Law, Politics, and Society in Early Modern England* (Cambridge University Press, 2008), 61.

13 Mark Curtis, 'The Alienated Intellectuals of Early Stuart England', *P&P*, 23 (1962): 25–43; Prest, *Rise*, 78.

14 Lewis Abbott, 'Public Office and Private Profit: The Legal Establishment in the Reign of Mary Tudor', in *The Mid-Tudor Polity, c.1540–1560*, ed. by Robert Tittler and Jennifer Loach (Totowa: Rowman and Littlefield, 1980), 137–58 (156).

Over time, the Inns of Court expanded to meet this need, although it took time. Admissions to the Inns, while varying from year to year, did not rise sharply until the 1580s,[15] which kept the number of lawyers relatively static, as a consequence of the seven years of study usually required to become a barrister.[16] At the same time, the Inns did not have space to house a large influx of new members: as it was they alarmed Elizabeth's government by admitting more members than they could house.[17] Beginning in the 1560s, the Inns embarked on massive building works, such as the magnificent Middle Temple Hall (built 1562–1572). This was a testament to the increased confidence of the profession at the time, but also just to the need for more space. Although individuals self-financed new chambers,[18] it was decades before the Inns and the legal profession expanded enough to begin meet the country's litigation needs. In the period before the Civil War, although individual barristers must always have been unemployed or under-employed, the supply of lawyers never surpassed demand.

Alongside the increase in litigation and, eventually, in the number of lawyers, there were other, related shifts in legal culture—especially the rise and centralization of the common law. Through the sixteenth century, English legal life involved multiple kinds of law and multiple jurisdictions in London and the provinces.[19] During the first half of the sixteenth century, legal business was divided equally between London and other locales. Thereafter, legal work increasingly centralized to the capital, as more and more business flowed to the central common law courts.[20] The number of cases in late stages at the King's Bench and Common Pleas rose from 2,100 in 1490 to 29,000 in 1640.[21] Corresponding to this shift, as the legal profession grew, it developed new internal hierarchies, gradually dividing into an 'upper' branch of barristers, those who had advanced to the bar of an Inn of Court and who could plead cases in London's central courts, and the 'lower' branch of solicitors or attorneys, trained at the Inns of Chancery.[22] A significant consequence of these changes was that by the early 1590s lawyers had become a sizeable and visible professional group in London; and the public took notice. In

[15] For instance, in the period from 1560 to 1578, total admissions for all four Inns ranged from 61 to 166 per year; but in the period from 1579 to 1603, they ranged from 129 to 247. Louis A. Knafla, 'The Matriculation Revolution and Education at the Inns of Court in Renaissance England', in *Tudor Men and Institutions: Studies in English Law and Government*, ed. by Arthur J. Slavin (Baton Rouge: Louisiana State University Press, 1972), 232–64 (260).

[16] Prest, *Rise*, 73.

[17] Wilfrid Prest, *Inns of Court under Elizabeth I and the Early Stuarts, 1590–1640* (Totowa: Rowman and Littlefield, 1972), 18.

[18] Prest, *Inns*, 18–19.

[19] Christopher Brooks, *Pettyfoggers and Vipers of the Commonwealth: The 'Lower Branch' of the Legal Profession in Early Modern England* (Cambridge: Cambridge University Press, 1986), 96; also Gieskes, *Representing the Professions*, 117.

[20] Brooks, *Pettyfoggers*, 96.

[21] While numerous factors underlie this shift, one important one is the movement in population itself from the provinces to London. See Brooks, *Pettyfoggers*, 100–1; also Gieskes, *Representing the Professions*, 133.

[22] Prest, *Rise*, and Brooks, *Pettyfoggers*, together provide an overview of this development.

Shakespeare's 2 *Henry VI*, when one of Jack Cade's rebel confederates wants to 'kill all the lawyers', he mouths a commonplace gripe about lawyers, but he also comments on a new, late sixteenth-century reality—in London, there was growing hostility toward lawyers as a newly noticeable social and professional group.[23]

Attitudes toward Lawyers

As the number of lawyers increased, so did public suspicion and aversion.[24] Wilfrid Prest observes of the correlation that 'hostility towards common lawyers seems to have burgeoned precisely as the profession grew in size and social prominence during the sixteenth century'.[25] Early modern poetry and drama registers these public misgivings, portraying legal men as dull, graceless, greedy, unlettered spendthrifts, duplicitous practitioners who use their esoteric legal learning for their own gain, rather than for the good of their clients.[26] It is worth pointing that while such representations focus on men involved in the common law, they do not distinguish in meaningful ways among types of legal men, whether 'upper branch' barristers, 'lower branch' solicitors or attorneys, or those whose legal backgrounds are not at all clear, such as Tangle in Middleton's *The Phoenix* or Throat in *Ram Alley*, wrangling 'pseudo-attorneys', 'hangers-on of the law who populated the fringes of legal London'.[27] In late sixteenth- and early seventeenth-century literature, 'lawyer' generally means anyone who accepts money to facilitate a layperson's encounter with the law.[28]

Anti-lawyer stereotypes appear in casual jabs at legal men, as when Faustus says of law, 'his study fits a mercenary drudge,/Who aims at nothing but external trash'; or, in *Romeo and Juliet* (*c*.1595), when we learn that Queen Mab 'gallops o'er a lawyer's lip,/And then he dreams of smelling out a suit'.[29] In his epigram 'On Cheverel, the Lawyer' (pub. 1616; the name means soft, kid-leather), Ben Jonson links the lawyer's love of money to his pliability and duplicitousness: 'on both sides he takes fees,/And pleaseth both'.[30] Similar ideas appear in more extended portrayals, for instance in Jonson's *Volpone* (perf.

23 2 *Henry VI*, 4.2.70.

24 Brooks, *Lawyers*, 22.

25 Prest, *Rise*, 287.

26 Prest, *Rise*, 289. 'Unlettered' here means not learned in the classics and liberal arts.

27 Gieskes, *Representing the Professions*, 114; Subha Mukherji, 'Middleton and the Law', in *Thomas Middleton in Context*, ed. Suzanne Gossett (Cambridge: Cambridge University Press, 2011), 106–14 (110).

28 This definition fits with the broadest, and oldest, definition of 'lawyer, n.' in *OED Online*: 'One versed in the law; a member of the legal profession, one whose business it is to conduct suits in the courts, or to advise clients, in the widest sense embracing every branch of the profession [...]'. Web. 29 May 2015.

29 Christopher Marlowe, *Dr Faustus*, in *The Complete Plays*, ed. F. Romany and R. Lindsey (London: Penguin, 2003), 1.1.34; *Romeo and Juliet*, 1.4.77–8.

30 *Ben Jonson: A Critical Edition of the Major Works*, ed. Ian Donaldson (Oxford: Oxford University Press, 1985), 234. In Shakespeare, 'Cheveril' describes a pliant wit or conscience (*Romeo and Juliet*, 2.3.72;

1606), where one character describes the lawyer Voltore (i.e. vulture) and 'men of [his] large profession':

> That, with most quick agility, could turn,
> And re-turn, make knots, and undo them;
> Give forked counsel; take provoking gold
> On either hand, and put it up.[31]

In John Day's *Law-trickes* (1608), lawyers are vultures, 'land monsters', 'whose vulture avarice / Devours living men'; and in Lording Barry's *Ram Alley* (1611), the legal man is also associated with insatiable hunger for money: the lawyer Throat 'swallowed' the inheritance of one character 'at one gob' (i.e. in one mouthful).[32] E. F. J. Tucker has catalogued negative portrayals of lawyers in a book whose title, *Intruder into Eden*, captures another main idea. English land was an Eden until devoured by those double-dealing sowers of dissension—the lawyers.[33] As a character in Robert Greene's *James the Fourth* (1598) says to a lawyer: 'Our state was first, before you grew so great, / A lantern to the world for unity.'[34]

Although litigation was both necessary and common, and many individual lawyers were respected, lawyers were thought not respectable for a number of reasons. If lawyers helped Englishmen and women to manage social and business relationships, the suspicion was also that lawyers encouraged the lawsuits from which they profited.[35] One sixteenth-century play asks of lawyers: 'Are you not those that should maintain the peace, / Yet are the only patrons of our strife?'[36] Another early seventeenth-century author reinforces the idea, looking back to Plato for authority, 'Plato made it a great sign of an intemperate and corrupt commonwealth where lawyers and physicians did abound.'[37]

Twelfth Night, 3.1.11; *All is True* [*Henry VIII*], 2.3.32). Jonson brings these associations together, making the lawyer's malleable wit an extension of his flexible professional morals.

31 *Volpone*, in *Ben Jonson*, ed. by Ian Donaldson, 1.3.53; 55–9. Although Voltore is a civilian, Gieskes observes that the play 'speak[s] to English ideas, English fears, and English law' (*Representing the Professions*, 144). But see also Lisa Klotz, 'Ben Jonson's Legal Imagination in Volpone', *SEL*, 51.2 (spring, 2011): 385–408.

32 John Day, *Law-Tricks, or Who Would Have Thought It* (London: Richard More, 1608), sig. B1^{v}; Robert Duncan Fraser, 'Ram Alley, Or Merry Tricks (Lording Barry, 1611): A Critical Edition', unpublished doctoral thesis, University of Sussex, 2013, 1.1.33.

33 E. F. J. Tucker, *Intruder into Eden: Representations of the Common Lawyer in English Literature, 1350–1750* (Columbia: Camden House, 1984).

34 Robert Greene, *The Scottish Historie of Iames the Fourth* (London: Thomas Creede, 1598), sig. I2^{v}. While set in Scotland, the lines here about 'our state', meaning something like 'our natural condition', are a general comment about moral corruption, with the 'lawyer' representing a type, not a Scottish lawyer or an English one. See Robert Greene, *James the Fourth*, ed. by Norman Sanders, *The Revels Plays* (London: Methuen, 1970), xli and xlvii.

35 Brooks, *Lawyers*, 23–4.

36 Greene, *Scottish Historie*, sig. I2^{r}.

37 Robert Burton, *Anatomy of Melancholy* (London: John Lichfield and James Short for Henry Cripps, 1621), sig. Ee1^{r}.

Prest proposes that lawyers were scapegoats for failings of society, and perhaps helped to divert hostility away from the ruling elite.[38] Certainly, practising lawyers had the potential to develop very lucrative careers, ones that could vault those of relatively modest social origins into new social strata, with a predictable social response. In 1553, Thomas Wilson explained that the law was easy money: 'The lawyer never dieth a beggar' and 'surely for the getting of money, a little [i.e. effort] will do as much good oftentimes as a great deal. There is not a word in the law, but it is a grote in the lawyer's purse.'[39] Such lucrative possibilities excited charges of money-grubbing and social climbing. But the same portraits that reflect a hatred of lawyers show the significance of law and lawyers for early modern daily life: a vexation with the behaviour, values, and dispositions of members of this sizable and important professional group with whom, however, a large percentage of the population had to interact.[40]

Legal Habitus

The concerns expressed in these representations did not lie with the public alone, but reflected, and perhaps even gave rise to, attitudes within the legal profession, an internal frustration with a lack of a respectable, professional *ethos*. Professions have their own patterns, habits, and practices, their own learned, yet engrained 'deep structures of behaviour', what Pierre Bourdieu calls a 'habitus'.[41] In the sixteenth century, the habitus of the legal profession was in flux. Edward Gieskes has argued that in the early sixteenth century, the size and the communal nature of training in the Inns helped to create lawyers who acted like lawyers 'without the need for explicit standards of regulation'.[42] In other words, the group sustained its own habitus, its own 'internal protocols and assumptions, characteristic behaviours, and self-sustaining values'.[43] As groups expand, they become more diversified, in terms of the attitudes and interests and values of those who are part of it. And this was true of the early modern English legal profession, which as it expanded also diversified, most significantly in social background, as entrants to the Inns of Court came from a broader range of backgrounds. As noted earlier, the profession gradually separated, also, into two branches, the 'upper branch' of

38 Prest, *Rise*, 287.

39 Thomas Wilson, *The Arte of Rhetorique* (London: Richard Grafton, [1553]), sig. E4^{v}; F1^{r}.

40 Brooks, *Lawyers*, 73.

41 Pierre Bourdieu, 'The Force of Law: Toward a Sociology of the Juridical Field', intr. and trans. Richard Terdiman, *Hastings Law Journal*, 38 (1987): 805–53 (807). See also Pierre Bourdieu, *In Other Words: Essays Towards a Reflexive Sociology*, trans. Matthew Adamson (Stanford: Stanford University Press, 1990), esp. 9–10; and *The Logic of Practice*, trans. Richard Nice (Stanford: Stanford University Press, 1990), esp. 54. For Bourdieu, the notion of 'habitus' is applicable to groups beyond the professions.

42 Gieskes, *Representing the Professions*, 126.

43 Terdiman's introduction, in Bourdieu, 'The Force of Law', 806.

barristers trained at the Inns of Court, and a 'lower branch' of more practically oriented solicitors trained at the subordinate Inns of Chancery.[44] Such changes challenged the possibility of shared dispositions, and also demanded that each branch of the legal profession, 'upper' and 'lower', develop its own distinct behaviours, its own habitus. One idea expressed in the period was that the Inns of Court were losing their identity by letting in the riff raff.[45] But as the legal profession developed a two-tiered structure, it also became more difficult to create a shared set of dispositions and behaviours even among the social ranks traditionally admitted to Inns, what John Ferne in the *Blazon of Gentry* (1586) describes as 'gentlemen of blood and coat-armour', as opposed to the 'brood' of yeomen and merchants.[46]

These internal struggles for professional self-definition illuminate the negative depictions of lawyers issuing from the pens of Innsmen and the larger network of their friends and associates. In his second satire, John Donne (adm LI 1592) has Coscus hurl 'His title of barrister, on every wench, / And wooes in language of the pleas and Bench'. He also aims only for self-advancement as one of the 'men which choose / Law practice for mere gain'.[47] Thomas Overbury (adm MT 1597) complains of one 'mere common lawyer' that 'indeed he is all for money'.[48] John Marston (adm MT 1592) satirizes lawyers in *Histrio-Mastix*, which may have been written for the Middle Temple revels of 1597–1598.[49] In the play, the allegorical character Pride calls lawyers 'concord's enemies'; he then encourages the lawyers (whose names 'Fourcher' and 'Voucher' are common law legal terms), to 'use your wisdom to enrich yourselves', ignoring law and justice:

> Make deep success high steward of your store.
> Enlarge your mighty spirits, strive to exceed,
> In buildings, riot, garment's gallantry.[50]

Histrio-mastix details the decline of an ideal, peaceful society through greed, pride, and envy. The play targets women, merchants, and professional actors, but it presents

[44] Brooks, *Pettyfoggers*; and Christopher Brooks, ed., *Admissions Record of Barnard's Inn, 1620–1869* (London: SS, 1995), 20.

[45] See, for instance, John Ferne, *The Blazon of Gentrie* (London: John Windet for Andrew Maunsell, 1586), sigs G6^{v}–G7^{r}.

[46] Ferne, *The Blazon of Gentrie*, G6^{v}–G7^{r}.

[47] Donne, 'Satyre 2', in *Complete English Poems*, ed. C. A. Patrides, Everyman's Library edn (New York: Knopf, 1991), ll. 47–8; 63–4.

[48] Thomas Overbury, *A Wife Now the Widovv ... Whereunto are Added Many Witty Characters [...]* (London: T. C[reede] for Lawrence Lisle, 1614), sig. F2^{v}. See also Prest, *Rise*, 289.

[49] On this play's relation to the Middle Temple revels, 1598–1599, see Philip Finkelpearl, *John Marston of the Middle Temple: An Elizabethan Dramatist in His Social Setting* (Cambridge: Harvard University Press, 1969), 119–24. The lawyers' names are drawn from common law legal terms: 'Fourcher' is a legal move in which defendants delay an action by appearing alternately in a law suit instead of together; 'Voucher' is the summoning a person to court to authorize the title to property; *OED Online* (28 February 2014).

[50] John Marston, *Histrio-Mastix; or, The Player Whipt* (London: [George Eld] for Th: Thorp, 1610), sig. D1^{r}.

lawyers as especially susceptible to vice, both cause and index of societal decline. In responding to public vexation at lawyers' practice, these representations begin to assert, also, through negative examples, at least the limits of legal habitus—what lies outside of acceptable public and internal-professional norms.

As these portraits indicate, the vices of lawyers are often are described as personal failings: lawyers are greedy, seeking to 'enrich' themselves and to display this wealth ostentatiously in their residences and attire, and through their leisure pursuits. The interrelation of the professional and the personal underlies the persistent association of lawyers and prostitutes. In *Ram Alley*, one young man complains of 'two suckers' (i.e. parasites) who have taken all of his money, 'a lawyer and a whore'.[51] Donne makes the comparison explicit: lawyers are 'worse than imbrotheled strumpets prostitute'.[52] A related idea is that lawyers, who ought to prize law and justice, are instead part and product of the marketplace. Thus in *Skialetheia* (1598), Everard Guilpin (adm GI 1591) criticizes the lawyer, who is both 'a merchant, and a gentleman / That is scarce honest, live he how he can'.[53]

This line of censure extended to include those being trained in the law. Although critics have read portraits of junior members of the Inns as evidence of the historical social milieu of the legal societies,[54] we should understand them too as continuous with the satire directed against their seniors, in part because the criticisms are similar, focusing on spendthrift, market-driven men preoccupied with external show and personal enjoyment. The wastrel Inns-of-Court man emerges as a literary type in *Alarum against Usurers* (1584), written by Thomas Lodge of Lincoln's Inn and dedicated to members of all four Inns. It describes the career of a junior member, who for want of a suit of clothes, falls into the grip of a usurer, and ends in the employ of the usurer himself. Such criticism was a constant refrain, occurring in a similar form three decades later, for example, in Overbury's *Characters* (1615), which describes a 'fantastic' Innsman ('fantastic' in the sense of given to showy dress), who worries about worldly things—his dress and revenues: 'His very essence he placeth in his outside, and his chiefest prayer is that his revenues may hold out for taffety cloaks in the summer and velvet in the winter. ... To his acquaintance he offers two quarts of wine for one he gives.'[55]

Like the majority of members of the Inns, writers like Donne, Marston, and Overbury did not pursue legal careers, and some of their negative portrayals of legal men might well register a lack of interest in the law or even sympathy with the wider public's hostility toward lawyers. As James Sanderson suggests, however, such satire was also fashionable, in-group behaviour: 'Satire and sardonic comment probably appeared to the young wits of the Inns of Court as modish ways of gaining attention and of demonstrating their keen perceptions of the foibles of others and their superiority to such

51 Fraser, ed., *Ram Alley*, 1.1.54; 57.

52 Donne, 'Satyre 2', l. 64.

53 Guilpin, *Skialetheia. Or, A Shadowe of Truth, in Certaine Epigrams and Satyres* (London: I[ames] R[oberts] for Nicholas Ling, 1598), sig. B2^{r}.

54 See Finkelpearl, *John Marston*, 11–15.

55 Overbury, *New and Choise Characters* (London: Thomas Creede for Laurence Lisle, 1615), sig. 6^{v}.

out-of-date sentiments as romantic love and its lyric celebration in undiscriminating, sugared styles.'[56] Even as satire created connection within the Inns, it highlighted real conflicts that riddled the Inns' social world.[57] Michele O'Callaghan argues that such verse stems from a tradition of verbal flyting, and represents the Inns as a 'conflicted, fraught social space'.[58] Lynne Magnusson observes that scoffing was an important feature of in-group communication, and 'Inns of Court men took pastime, delight and hurt in shaming performances.' In this way ritualized scoffing helped to equip and train one for life at the Inns.[59]

In the 1590s, this fashion of verbal flyting and ritualized linguistic shaming was relatively new. In the 1560s, the literary and social environment of the Inns was very different. For one, although there were numerous writers at or associated with the law and legal profession—namely Barnabe Googe (1540–1594; adm. Staple Inn, *c*.1560), George Turberville (George Turberville (1540?–1610?; Inn not known) and George Gascoigne (1523?–1577; adm. GI 1555)—these writers did not routinely jibe at fellow Innsmen or lawyers, although Gascoigne offers a mild satire of the civil lawyer Cleander in *Supposes* (1566).

By the 1590s, what had changed? The growth of the legal profession, already alluded to, is certainly a factor, and particularly the rapid expansion of the barristers as a professional group. With the diversification of the Inns' student body in terms of total numbers and social backgrounds, the legal societies were indeed an increasingly 'fraught social space', and the legal profession a group that could increasingly ask what an Innsman should be, or by extension what a lawyer should be. As the legal profession broadened, Innsmen and legal practitioners renegotiated professional habitus.[60] Moreover, this negotiation was all the more fraught for competing with a dominant and negative public vision of the tastes, dispositions, and behaviours of lawyers. These circumstances raised questions: what exactly was an 'Inns of Court' man? How should he behave? what exactly was a lawyer, and how should he behave? O'Callaghan aptly comments on 1590s Inns-of-Court verse that the negative portraits were 'intended to provide ridicule, thus clarifying the proper personage of the gentleman lawyer through his anti-type—the gallant'.[61]

[56] James Sanderson, *Sir John Davies* (Boston: Twayne, 1975), 39.

[57] For more on these conflicts, their literary expression and political dimensions, see Martin Butler's chapter in this volume.

[58] Michele O'Callaghan, *The English Wits: Literature and Sociability in Early Modern London* (Cambridge: Cambridge University Press, 2007), 31.

[59] Lynne Magnusson, 'Scoff Power in *Love's Labour's Lost* and the Inns of Court: Language in Context', *ShS*, 57 (2004): 196–208 (207).

[60] Gieskes (*Representing the Professions*, 121–38) suggests that the negotiation of professional habitus stems from the rise of law as a profession from its history in the early sixteenth century, where the profession was more like a guild. J. H. Baker, however, demonstrates that it is possible to describe the legal profession, as a profession, prior to the middle of the sixteenth century. See *The Legal Profession and the Common Law: Historical Essays* (London: Hambledon, 1986), especially, 'The English Legal Profession, 1450–1550', 75–98.

[61] O'Callaghan, *English Wits*, 27.

The Gentleman Lawyer in John Davies's *Epigrammes*

In the middle of the sixteenth century, the gentleman lawyer was the main model for legal professionals in England.[62] The model goes back to Cicero, but it took influential shape in England in Thomas Elyot's *Boke Named the Governour* (1531), which emphasizes that leaders should be educated in liberal studies as well as law and use their whole learning to serve the commonweal.[63] Building on this model, in his *Accidens of Armorie* (1562), Gerard Legh describes the Inner Temple as a place where men 'use all other exercises of body and mind [...] to adorn by speaking, countenance, gesture, and use of apparel the person of a gentleman'. Gentlemen come to the Inns to 'learn to rule, and obey by law, to yield their fleece to their prince and commonweal'.[64] While this image continued to circulate through the later parts of the sixteenth century, by the 1590s the gentleman lawyer seemed a waning ideal from a bygone era, far less relevant than the image of the venal, two-faced, grasping dullard represented in contemporary literature and drama.

When John Davies sought to bring back 'proper personage of the gentleman lawyer', he did so not only through negative but also positive examples of what an Inns lawyer should be. In one of his 'Trencher poems' (*c.*1602–1605), he explicitly conveyed his ideal:

> My practice is the law; my robe, my tongue, my pen
> Wealth and opinion gain, and make me judge of men.
> The known dishonest cause I never did defend,
> Nor spun out suits at length, but wished and sought an end,
> Nor counsel did bewray, nor of both parties take,
> Nor ever took I fee for which I never spake.[65]

Davies's lawyer uses his position (his robe) and his learning and rhetorical skills (his tongue and pen) to earn status and reputation (wealth and opinion). Unlike the lawyers in the works of Davies's contemporaries, however, he earns his reputation through right-dealing: he defends honest causes, tries to limit the length of lawsuits, keeps counsel, works only for one party in a case, and he does the work he's been paid to do. This is the

62 The other model is the lawyer as oracle, a sacerdotal priest who divines the truth of the unwritten law and pronounces it for others. For instance, in 1559, William Bavand, a member of the Middle Temple, wrote that the 'lawyer's house [...] is as it were the oracle of the whole city', in reference to Cicero's *De oratore* 1.200. Bavand, *A Woorke of Ioannes Ferrarius Montanus, Touching the Good Ordering of a Common Weale* (London: John Kingston for John Wight, 1559), sig. R1^{v}. On the concept of the 'legal oracle' in early modern law and literature, see Virginia Lee Strain, '*The Winter's Tale* and the Oracle of the Law', *ELH*, 78 (2011): 557–84.

63 Elyot, *Boke Named the Gouernour* (London: Thomas Berthelet, 1531), fol. 55^{r}, 59^{v}. See also the discussion of Elyot's view on the role of lawyers in the commonweal in Brooks, *Lawyers*, 205.

64 *REED*, 2.267.

65 Robert Kreuger, ed. *Poems of Sir John Davies* (Oxford: Oxford University Press, 1975), 225–6.

model that Davies advanced also in his *Epigrammes*, which aims to represent a positive model of the gentleman lawyer—for himself and the profession.

Before exploring Davies's project further, it is important to note that Davies's representations of lawyers and law students parallel other satirical writings at the Inns, such as those by Marston. In one epigram Davies describes the mendacious Crassus, who 'tells lies so rife' simply *because* 'He is a lawyer'.[66] Davies also offers this well-known portrait of Publius, who 'oft leaves his books' to visit the 'dogs and bears' in Southwark:

> Publius, student at the common law,
> Oft leaves his books and for his recreation
> To parish garden doth himself withdraw
> Where he is ravished with such delectation
> As down amongst the dogs and bears he goes
> Where whiles he skipping cries, 'To head! To head!'
> His satin doublet and his velvet hose,
> Are all with spittle from above bespread.
> Then is he like his father's country hall,
> Stinking with dogs and muted all with hawks
> And rightly too on him this filth doth fall,
> Which for such filthy sports his books forsake,
> Leaving old Plowden, Dyer, and Brooke alone,
> To see old Harry Hunks and Sakerson.[67]

Publius is the son of a country gentleman, who fails to fully inhabit his class position when he departs from the Inns, crossing into different precincts to pursue carnal delights. His departure alters his appearance as his doublet and hose become covered with dirt and spit. Yet this cosmetic alteration suggests concerns that are more specific to legal culture, namely that Publius's identity as a law student is not stable; he is truly himself in the filth of Southwark. The portrait bears the hallmarks of urban and possibly class snobbery, ridiculing those with *declassé* 'country' tastes, who are presumably used to the stink of dogs and hawks, and who thus naturally delight in these 'filthy sports'. Yet the sense of degeneration blends urban snobbery with another idea, the difficulty of maintaining the *habitus* of the Innsman over and against the *habitus* of one's familial and geographic origins. As in other writers of the time, here readers are warned by negative example: Publius shouldn't have forsaken his books.

Against such negative models, Davies develops a positive ideal of the gentleman lawyer in the figure of the speaker of the *Epigrammes*. Across the series, Davies's 'In Gallum' is the epigram where this legal persona appears most explicitly:

> Gallus hath bin this Sommer in Friesland,
> And now returned he speaks such warlike words

66 'In Crassum. 37', in Krueger, ed., *Poems*, 145.
67 'In Publium. 43', in Kreuger, ed., *Poems*, 148.

As if I could their English understand,
I feare me they would cut my Throat like swords.
He talks of counterscarfes and casemates,
Of parapets, curteynes and Pallizadois,
Of flankers, Ravelings, gabions he prates,
And of false brayes, and sallies and scaladose:
But to requite such gulling termes as these,
With words of my profession I replie:
I tel of foorching, vouchers, counterpleas,
Of Withernams, essoynes, and champartie.
So neyther of us understanding eyther,
We part as wise as when we came together.[68]

Here, the speaker meets a pretentious amateur soldier who parrots the military jargon he learned after a summer in the Low Countries: 'He talks of counterscarfes and casemates, / Of parapets, curteynes, and pallizadois' (5–6). In a jocular effort to defend himself against Gallus's would-be machismo, the speaker responds with a list of 'words of [his] profession', the specialized vocabulary of the common law: 'I tel of foorching, vouchers, counterpleas, / Of withernams, essoynes, and champartie' (11–12).[69] The passage is not exactly satirical. Where in Marston's *Histrio-mastix*, the terms 'fourcher' and 'voucher' occurred as satirical signifiers, here Davies deploys them as markers of a professional domain, a part of the speaker's identification of himself as someone in the legal 'profession', with the prolonged training and formal qualification for a career.[70] In this way, Davies satirizes a would-be soldier through the eyes of a professional common law lawyer. This legal perspective is not isolated to the poem, since the lawyer is the speaker of the *Epigrammes* as a whole. Although he elsewhere never identifies himself as clearly with the law, the persona is always the same: a first-person speaker with a consistent affect and tone, who is never aligned with another occupational category. The lawyer is literally the central voice of the *Epigrammes*, too, appearing halfway through the series, at number twenty-four in a sequence of forty-eight.

This legal persona is a fictionalized version of Davies, although not so simply as one might initially think. Davies composed epigrams between 1592 and 1595, when he was a

68 'In Gallum. 24', in Kreuger, ed. *Poems*, 139. While I have modernized spelling throughout, I have kept original spelling here, since the modernized terms throw off the verse's tight rhyme and metre.

69 In Martial's epigrams, a 'gallus' is a castrated priest of Cybele (3.24, 3.81, 7.95), and in 3.81, he is a priest who, although he should properly engage in fellatio with other men, instead has oral sex with women—that is, someone who is no longer a man, but who pretends to be one. The name Gallus, however, appears in numerous epigrams (1.108, 2.47, 2.56, 3.27, 3.92, 4.16, 10.56, 10.82) which don't carry these particular associations (e.g. in Book 10, Gallus is an overbearing master). Nevertheless, referring back to a 'gallus', Davies's use of the name 'Gallus' might imply pretense and put-on, perhaps compensatory, machismo.

70 'Profession, n.', definitions II.a, b, and c, in *OED Online*; web. 20 May 2015.

junior member of the Middle Temple. While the Inns were law schools, they also functioned as something like 'finishing schools',[71] places where sons of the aristocracy and the gentry, who did not intend a common law career, came to acquire some legal knowledge and to develop the sophisticated urbanity and social network that would help them to prosper at court and in other exclusive social and political circles.[72] Davies's epigrams grow out of and reflect this milieu, satirizing a range of types who frequented the Inns—practising lawyers, as well as the braggarts and wastrels who, like Publius, occupied themselves with playgoing, whoring, bear-baiting, and fashion. Since Davies himself was training to be a lawyer in the busy social world of the Inns, why wouldn't his speaker reflect his own position and milieu?

By the time the *Epigrammes* were published (*c.*1598–1599), however, Davies did not have a profession, legal or otherwise. Although he was called to the bar on 4 July 1595, he was disbarred in the winter of 1597–1598. That season he participated in the Middle Temple revels, where he found himself repeatedly ridiculed by his one-time friend Richard Martin and other Templars, who among other things posted libels 'against him in all the famous places of the city, as Queenhithe, Newgate, the Stocks, Pillory, Pissing Conduit'.[73] A short while later, on 9 February, Davies infamously marched into a quiet dinner in the Middle Temple Hall, struck Martin on the head with a bastinado, ran to the bottom of the hall, grabbed his servant's sword, shook it over his head, then scurried down to the water steps to escape in a boat.[74] Davies was immediately expelled from the Middle Temple and briefly imprisoned. He moved to Oxford and worked for several years to restore his fortunes, most immediately to regain admission to the Temple.[75] He wrote to powerful men, asking for their help, and he wrote speeches, entertainments, and verse to win favour.[76] In 1599, he published the flattering *Hymnes of Astraea in Acrosticke Verse* for Elizabeth and *Nosce Teipsum,* which has long been read as 'the fruit of his humiliation and repentance', the grave, philosophical verse of a remorseful man in the midst of 'self-scrutiny and penitence'.[77] About this time too, in 1598–1599, Davies adapted his epigrams for publication, adding two new poems to verses already

[71] Although anachronistic, the phrase is useful and appears frequently in studies of the Inns, for example in the title of J. H. Baker's 'The Third University, 1450–1550: Law School or Finishing School?', in *Intellectual and Cultural World of the Early Modern Inns of Court*, ed. Jayne Elisabeth Archer, Elizabeth Goldring, and Sarah Knight (Manchester: Manchester University Press, 2011), 8–31 (8).

[72] Finkelpearl, *John Marston*, 3–80; Prest, *Inns*, 21–3; 153–4.

[73] Benjamin Rudyerd, *Prince D'Amour, or Prince of Love* (London: William Leake, 1660), 80.

[74] For another interpretation of this incident, see Martin Butler's chapter in this volume.

[75] STC dates the publication to 1599, although others have suggested dates as early as 1596. On the dating of the volume, see Susanna Hop, '"What Fame is This?": John Davies's *Epigrammes* in Late Elizabethan London', *Renaissance Journal*, 2.3 (2005): 29–42.

[76] Kreuger, ed., *Poems*, xxxvi.

[77] Quoted in G. A. Wilkes, 'The Poetry of John Davies', *HLQ*, 25 (1962): 283–98 (291, 292), who argues that *Nosce Teipsum* was written in the early 1590s, and should be understood as a collection of Renaissance commonplaces that offered 'a way to respectability that Davies would be unwilling to refuse' (192–3).

in circulation to create a group that read newly like a discrete set.[78] The timing suggests that the published *Epigrammes* were also part of Davies's project of professional and social rehabilitation. If the legal man of the *Epigrammes* was initially a mouthpiece for Davies, after the incident in the Middle Temple Hall, this speaker was a palimpsest and projection, both a residue of Davies's past and a proleptic claim to his future.[79] Who was the would-be now?

Earlier in his career, Davies had earned some fame for his verse, with one contemporary titling him 'our English Martial'.[80] Indeed, his epigrams appear to have sparked a vogue for the form that lasted from 1590 to 1630. Lawrence Manley ties the sudden and sustained popularity of epigrams to the unprecedented expansion of London: the epigram is a quintessentially urban and urbane form, characterized by profusion and brevity, as the poems compress descriptions of places and persons into concise verse. In late sixteenth- and early seventeenth-century London, the epigram provided a form to respond to and resist urban expansion by condensing, and hence seeking to fix, the evolving spaces and proliferating groups in the metropole. The form aims to 'put everything neatly in its place'.[81] While Davies's *Epigrammes* clearly participate in this larger trend, they are shaped most profoundly by the particular urban transformation charted above, which was directly related to Davies's specific training and career goals: the changing size and status of the legal profession, particularly the barristers, in late sixteenth-century London. Although Davies does satirize lawyers, Inns-of-Court men, and the amusements of London at the time—taverns, brothels, and the public theatre—he does more than catalogue the excesses of his immediate social milieu. In his speaker, Davies constructs a model of lawyerly decorum. As Davies's editor, Robert Kreuger, observes, the speaker of the *Epigrammes* is a man 'whose reason so thoroughly controls his will, his affections, his body, and the world around him that he presents to the world an unflawed surface, invulnerable and impassible'. [82] In other words, the speaker is controlled, dispassionate, and disengaged from the world and marketplace, in the way a lawyer might be, though not the negatively imagined lawyer of contemporary satire.

Read in this way, Davies's *Epigrammes* appear less as a formative instance of an emerging popular genre than as a distinctive work that seeks to shape the profession by commenting on the behaviour of the social world from which the profession emerged. In

[78] The final two poems are newly composed, since they do not appear in any of the extant manuscripts. These final epigrams mirror the initial two, so that epigram 1 'Ad Musam' is matched by the new epigram 48, 'Ad Musam', and epigram 2 'Of a Gull' is matched with the new epigram 47, 'Meditations of a Gull'. For this argument, see Hop, 'What Fame is This?'.

[79] In addition, the epigrams bear the imprint 'Middleborough', which could be a Dutch province, but most critics agree that the imprint is false. 'Middleborough' could allude to 'Middle Borough', i.e. the region of the Middle Temple, thus also casting Davies back into this space. For this suggestion, see also Hop, 'What Fame is This?'.

[80] Everard Guilpin, *Skialetheia*, epig. 20 (sig. A6^{r}). Kreuger records other contemporary references to Davies's reputation for epigrams (xxxvi–xxxvii).

[81] Lawrence Manley, *Literature and Culture in Early Modern London* (Cambridge: Cambridge University Press, 1995), 409–30 (quotation appears on 422).

[82] Kreuger, ed., *Poems*, lx.

this way, Davies's epigrams differ from others of the time. In general, English epigrams are a genre associated with bodily tastes—the bitter flavours of salt, gall, and vinegar, especially—and with bodily harm—venomous spit, biting, and piercing.[83] They also act as prosthetic extensions. In the words of William Kerwin, they are a 'moral lash' or 'weapon directed by one body against another';[84] to borrow a turn of phrase from Davies's contemporary, Everard Guilpin, epigrams 'heal with lashing'.[85] Thus, even as epigrams aim to fix the urban world physically and morally, they blur physical and moral boundaries. Here again Davies's *Epigrammes* are different. They certainly offer up moral judgement (Crassus shouldn't lie; Publius really ought to read his law books), but the speaker does not lash out; he maintains his distance from and indifference to his subjects: in the meeting with Gallus, the speaker walks away. With his legally impassive speaker, Davies reforms through example—that is, he shapes for the growing legal profession an ideal set of dispositions, perceptions, habits, attitudes, and behaviours, the habitus for the emerging professional field.[86] Davies's own reform thus also encapsulates a larger shift, with his personal and professional transformation playing out within and also offering a model for the ethos of the legal field as a whole.

To see how this works more fully, we should turn back to 'In Gallum'. At first, the epigram seems a straightforward criticism of affectation: Gallus, a mere tourist, pretends to be a soldier when he is not. Yet the poem concerns pretence less than professional decorum, and it develops this point by contrasting the amateur soldier with the professional lawyer. Unlike the soldier, the lawyer has the education and expertise to legitimately speak legalese. And he deploys his legal word-horde not to out-Gallus Gallus, but to get out of a conversation with him, when he realizes that Gallus is only pretentious babble. The speaker returns with his own esoteric speech, yet his response does not suggest that experience, 'profession', alone authorizes the ostentatious display of professional knowledge.

The epigram develops this point by contrasting the speaker's interchange with Gallus with another conversation—that with the poem's reader. In addressing the reader, the speaker goes outside of law, to the liberal discourse of poetry, thus displaying his ability to communicate in multiple registers, modifying his style, vocabulary, and tone. More precisely, he turns to the sonnet, but rather than use the sonnet to display his worship of an unattainable lady, he turns it to demonstrate his desire for social connection. While distancing himself from Gallus, the narrator elicits the reader's sympathy. Perhaps because the epigram criticizes overt, posturing displays of esoteric knowledge, the speaker does not draw attention to the craft underlying his verse. While the epigram

[83] Alistair Fowler, 'The Formation of Genres in the Renaissance and After', *New Literary History*, 34 (2003): 185–200 (191–4). In an early epigram, Everard Guilpin tells his reader that he will 'only spit [his] venom, and away' ('To the Reader. 2', *Skialetheia*, sig. A3^{v}).

[84] William Kerwin, 'Epigrammatic Commotions', in *Shakespearean Sensations: Experiencing Literature in Early Modern England*, ed. Katherine A. Craik and Tanya Pollard (Cambridge: Cambridge University Press, 2013), 157–72 (163).

[85] Guilpin, *Skialetheia*, sig. C1^{v}.

[86] For a discussion of early modern legal habitus, see Gieskes, *Representing the Professions*, 125–7, 160.

is certainly a poem—a sonnet even—with a regular metre, compressed form, and inventive and difficult rhymes ('pallizadois' and 'scaladose'!), the verse does not call attention to the poem as poem (in the vein of the first sonnet of Sidney's *Astrophil and Stella* or George Herbert's 'Jordan (1)'). Moreover, the narrator also elicits sympathy by meeting Gallus verbal barrage with reserve: while Gallus has four lines, with eleven military terms, the speaker has two with only six legal terms, even as he more than requites Gallus on the obscurity front. While one might have a general sense of Gallus's 'warlike' terms, such as 'parapets' and 'flankers', it is nearly impossible without legal training, or at least a legal dictionary, to know what 'withernam' or 'champartie' mean. In this poem, it is the affected dilettante who ostentatiously displays what he knows, or thinks he knows. The professional lawyer keeps his emotions and his learning under wraps.

At the same time, the speaker upholds the law as an alternative to violence. Gallus seems a little unhinged: after a single summer abroad, he comes back chattering 'warlike words'. Yet Gallus's prattle has an aggressive, threatening edge. As the narrator says, 'I feare me [the words] would cut my Throat like swords.' The narrator then neutralizes this violent potential by recourse to the terms of law. While his words are more esoteric than Gallus's, they are different in that they are dull—to a layperson, could the term 'withernam' ever be exciting? In essence, the speaker turns common law and lawyerly obscuring into a virtue, using legal dullness to disarm the verbally, potentially physically, menacing Gallus. In this way, the epigram also reinforces the value of law as central to a stable society. Christopher Brooks has explained that in the sixteenth century, 'law had a moral purpose' and 'it constituted the means by which the kingdom, or political society, and the community became one and the same thing'—a shared value, a common wealth.[87] In the early part of the century, the legal printer John Rastell expressed this view when he wrote that 'a good reasonable common law maketh a good common peace and a common wealth among a great commonality of people'.[88] In 1559, the Lord Keeper, Sir Nicholas Bacon asserted that the law is foundational to peace and prosperity, claiming that 'by the law (you know) every man enjoyeth the fruits, pleasures, and commodities of his goods, lands, liberty, and life'.[89] By referring to common law terms, terms that help to protect land and property, the speaker attempts to convey that Gallus's aggression threatens life and prosperity, but the law protects these things (at least as the narrator presents himself as using it).[90] Early modern representations of law often upheld the law, while denigrating its representatives.[91] The legal persona of this epigram

[87] Brooks, *Law, Politics*, 25–6.

[88] John Rastell, *Exposiciones T[er]mino[rum] Legu[m] Anglo[rum]* (London: [John Rastell], [*c.*1525]), sig. A1r. On the centrality of law in the commonwealth, see John Baker on 'Individualism and the "Common Weal"' in *OHLE*, 6.30–4.

[89] 'Speeches of Sir Nicholas Bacon', Folger MS V.a.143, fol. 18.

[90] The idea that law protects land and prosperity is relative: Whose prosperity? Later in his life, John Davies contributed to the conquest of Ireland by promoting judge-made law over native Irish customs of landholding and inheritance. See Hans S. Pawlisch, *John Davies and the Conquest of Ireland: A Study in Legal Imperialism* (Cambridge: Cambridge University Press, 1985).

[91] Gieskes, *Representing the Professions*, 117–18.

is equal to the law, however; he is the idealized gentleman lawyer who uses his liberal and legal knowledge for societally beneficial ends—to maintain the peace and prosperity of the commonweal.

It is important, then, to note that the epigram does not seek to reform Gallus, to lash him, to teach him a lesson. The two depart with 'neither of us understanding either' and 'as wise as when we came together'. In the end, the speaker presents himself as truly wise, while Gallus continues to be merely a 'gull' or fool. Yet one reason that the epigram does not reform Gallus is that Gallus is not an object of reform. Rather, the epigram's purpose is to hold up the *speaker* as a model of behaviour, and in its construction of the legal professional 'In Gallum' thus highlights an important aspect of John Davies's *Epigrammes* as a whole: the poems function to delimit professional decorum—that is, to demonstrate how lawyers in general should comport themselves, not just as lawyers, but as members of the public sphere. Davies's epigrams do not simply criticize lawyers and Innsmen for unprofessional behaviour, but seek to manifest the ethos of the gentleman lawyer. To be sure, the *Epigrammes* participate in the vehement satirical treatment of lawyers and Innsmen in the period. Yet even as these satirical treatments iterate public hostilities, they manifest a larger effort—from within and outwith the profession—to develop and promulgate a model for lawyers, whether through negative or positive example.

Did Davies achieve his aim? In 1602, he was reinstated to the Middle Temple, and he went on to a successful career, eventually becoming the Attorney General for Ireland, and in that sense the poetic project of 1598–1599 must have helped to put him on this upward path. The *Epigrammes*, however, had no chance to reform the profession. Shortly after publication, they suffered a dire fate—being publicly burnt following the passage of the Bishops' Ban of 1599. The ban explicitly names the *Epigrammes* along with other satires of the period by Joseph Hall, John Marston, and Everard Guilpin. Critics have argued variously that Davies's *Epigrammes* were singled out because they were published with Marlowe's translations of Ovid's randy poetry and Marlowe was the problem; or because they, like other satires of the period, threatened ideological norms.[92] Yet unlike those other 'Tamburlaines of vice' in the period,[93] such as Marston or Guilpin, Davies's *Epigrammes* were not scurrilous or morally offensive or openly aggressive (although they of course could have been defamatory in their initial context). Another possibility is that the *Epigrammes* suffered Davies's own story. After all, only shortly before publishing the *Epigrammes*, Davies had cudgelled another man in public. He was one of—if not arguably the most—aggressive, flyting, potentially subversive satyrs of the Inns. Perhaps in 1599, as for many critics still today, it was difficult to see such a legally transgressive, violent man as an exemplar of personal constancy and control or legal professionalism.

[92] See for example, Ian Frederick Moulton, '"Printed Abroad and Uncastrated": Marlowe's *Elegies* with Davies's *Epigrams*', in *Marlowe, History, and Sexuality: New Critical Essays on Christopher Marlowe*, ed. Paul Whitfield White (New York: AMS Press, 1988), 77–90; and William R. Jones, 'The Bishops' Ban of 1599 and the Ideology of English Satire', *Literature Compass*, 7.5 (2010): 332–46.

[93] The original phrase is 'Tamburlain of vice', in Guilpin, *Skialetheia*, sig. C1^{v}.

Even though he wrote dispassionately and carried a crisp wit, to many his pen looked—and continues to look—like a bastinado.[94]

Bibliography

Abbott, Lewis. 'Public Office and Private Profit: The Legal Establishment in the Reign of Mary Tudor', in *The Mid-Tudor Polity, c.1540–1560*, ed. Robert Tittler and Jennifer Loach (Totowa: Rowman and Littlefield, 1980), 137–58.

Baker, J. H. *Oxford History of the Laws of England*, Vol. 6: *1483–1558* (Oxford: Oxford University Press, 2003).

Baker, J. H. 'The Third University, 1450–1550: Law School or Finishing School?', in *Intellectual and Cultural World of the Early Modern Inns of Court*, ed. Jayne Elisabeth Archer, Elizabeth Goldring, and Sarah Knight (Manchester: Manchester University Press, 2011), 8–31.

Bavand, William. *A Woorke of Ioannes Ferrarius Montanus, Touching the Good Ordering of a Common Weale* (London: 1559).

Bourdieu, Pierre. 'The Force of Law: Toward a Sociology of the Juridical Field', ed. and trans. Richard Terdiman, *Hastings Law Journal*, 38 (1987): 805–53.

Bourdieu, Pierre. *The Logic of Practice*, trans. Richard Nice (Stanford: Stanford University Press, 1990).

Bourdieu, Pierre. *In Other Words: Essays Towards a Reflexive Sociology*, trans. Matthew Adamson (Stanford: Stanford University Press, 1990).

Brooks, Christopher W., ed. *Admissions Record of Barnard's Inn, 1620–1869* (London: SS, 1995).

Brooks, Christopher W. *Law, Politics, and Society in Early Modern England* (Cambridge: Cambridge University Press, 2008).

Brooks, Christopher W. *Lawyers, Litigation and English Society since 1450* (London: Hambledon Press, 1998).

Brooks, Christopher W. *Pettyfoggers and Vipers of the Commonwealth: The 'Lower Branch' of the Legal Profession in Early Modern England* (Cambridge: Cambridge University Press, 1986).

Burton, Robert. *Anatomy of Melancholy* (London: 1621).

Curtis, Mark. 'The Alienated Intellectuals of Early Stuart England', *Past and Present*, 23 (1962): 25–43.

Davies, Sir John. *Le primer report des cases & matters en ley resolues & adjudges en les courts del roy en Ireland* (Dublin: 1615).

Davies, Sir John. *Poems of Sir John Davies*, ed. Robert Kreuger and Ruby Nemser (Oxford: Oxford University Press, 1975).

Day, John. *Law-Tricks, or Who Wovld Have Thought It* (London: 1608).

Donne, John, *Complete English Poems*, ed. C. A. Patrides (New York: Knopf, 1991).

Elyot, Thomas. *Boke Named the Gouernour* (London: 1531).

Ferne, John. *The Blazon of Gentrie* (London: 1586).

Finkelpearl, Philip J. *John Marston of the Middle Temple: An Elizabethan Dramatist in His Social Setting* (Cambridge, MA: Harvard University Press, 1969).

[94] Segments of this chapter were prepared for the 'Matter of Wit' seminar at the Shakespeare Association of America (Vancouver, Canada, 2015), and the English Legal Imaginary, Part II (University of St. Andrews, 2015). Participants in those meetings provided valuable questions and comments, as did Edward Gieskes and William Kerwin, who separately provided feedback on a full draft.

Folger Shakespeare Library MS V.a.143.
Fowler, Alistair. 'The Formation of Genres in the Renaissance and After', *New Literary History*, 34 (2003): 185–200.
Fraser, Robert Duncan. '*Ram Alley, Or Merry Tricks* (Lording Barry, 1611): A Critical Edition' (PhD Thesis: University of Sussex, 2013).
Gieskes, Edward. *Representing the Professions: Administration, Law, and Theater in Early Modern England* (Newark: University of Delware Press, 2006).
Greene, Robert. *The Scottish Historie of Iames the Fourth* (London: 1598).
Guilpin, Everard. *Skialetheia. Or, A Shadowe of Truth, in Certaine Epigrams and Satyres* (London: 1598).
Hop, Susanna. '"What Fame is This?" John Davies's *Epigrammes* in Late Elizabethan London', *Renaissance Journal*, 2.3 (2005): 29–42.
Jones, William R. 'The Bishops' Ban of 1599 and the Ideology of English Satire', *Literature Compass*, 7.5 (2010): 332–46.
Jonson, Ben. *Ben Jonson: A Critical Edition of the Major Works*, ed. Ian Donaldson (Oxford: Oxford University Press, 1985).
Kerwin, William. 'Epigrammatic Commotions', in *Shakespearean Sensations: Experiencing Literature in Early Modern England*, ed. Katherine A. Craik and Tanya Pollard (Cambridge: Cambridge University Press, 2013), 157–72.
Knafla, Louis A. 'The Matriculation Revolution and Education at the Inns of Court in Renaissance England', in *Tudor Men and Institutions: Studies in English Law and Government*, ed. Arthur J. Slavin (Baton Rouge: Louisiana State University Press, 1972), 232–64.
Magnusson, Lynne. 'Scoff Power in "Love's Labour's Lost" and the Inns of Court: Language in Context', *Shakespeare Survey*, 57 (2004): 196–208.
Manley, Lawrence. *Literature and Culture in Early Modern London* (Cambridge: Cambridge University Press, 1995).
Marlowe, Christopher. *The Complete Plays*, ed. F. Romany and R. Lindsey (London: Penguin, 2003).
Marston, John. *Histrio-Mastix; or, The Player Whipt* (London: 1610).
Moulton, Ian Frederick. '"Printed Abroad and Uncastrated": Marlowe's "Elegies" with Davies' "Epigrams"', in *Marlowe, History, and Sexuality: New Critical Essays on Christopher Marlowe*, ed. Paul Whitfield White (New York: AMS Press, 1988), 77–90.
Mukherji, Subha. 'Middleton and the Law', in *Thomas Middleton in Context*, ed. Suzanne Gossett (Cambridge: Cambridge University Press, 2011), 106–14.
Nelson, Alan H. and John R. Elliott, Jr. *Records of Early English Drama: Inns of Court*, 3 vols (Cambridge: D. S. Brewer, 2010).
O'Callaghan, Michelle. *The English Wits: Literature and Sociability in Early Modern London* (Cambridge: Cambridge University Press, 2007).
Overbury, Thomas. *New and Choise Characters* (London: 1615).
Overbury, Thomas. *A Wife Now the Widovv* [...] *Whereunto Are Added Many Witty Characters* [...] (London: 1614).
Oxford Dictionary of National Biography (Oxford: Oxford University Press, 2004).
Oxford English Dictionary, 2nd edn (Oxford: Oxford University Press, 1989).
Prest, Wilfrid. *Inns of Court Under Elizabeth I and the Early Stuarts, 1590–1640* (Totowa: Rowman and Littlefield, 1972).
Prest, Wilfrid. *Rise of the Barristers: A Social History of the English Bar, 1590–1640* (Oxford: Oxford University Press, 1991).

Rastell, John. *Exposiciones t[er]mino[rum] legu[m] anglo[rum]* (London: [*c*.1525]).
Rudyerd, Benjamin. *Prince D'Amour, or Prince of Love* (London: 1660).
Sanderson, James. *Sir John Davies* (Boston: Twayne, 1975).
Shakespeare, William. *The Oxford Shakespeare: The Complete Works*, ed. Stanley Wells, Gary Taylor, et al., 2nd edn (Oxford: Oxford University Press, 1986, 2005).
Strain, Virginia Lee. '"The Winter's Tale" and the Oracle of the Law', *English Literary History*, 78 (2011): 557–84.
Tucker, E. F. J. *Intruder into Eden: Representations of the Common Lawyer in English Literature, 1350–1750* (Columbia, SC: Camden House, 1984).
Wilkes, G. A. 'The Poetry of John Davies', *Huntington Library Quarterly*, 25 (1962): 283–98.
Wilson, Thomas. *The Arte of Rhetorique* (London: [1553]).

CHAPTER 7

THE EMBLEM BOOK AND COMMON LAW

PETER GOODRICH

My topic is that of clandestine histories and specifically the unwritten narrative of the legal emblem in the fashioning of early modern common law. There is no better starting point than the expansive second edition, the first and much smaller volume having appeared in 1614, of John Selden's *Titles of Honor*. In the dedicatory epistle addressed to 'my most beloved Friend, *Edward Heyward* of Cardeston in Norfolk', itself a species of insertion for protection of the work, Selden proffers an impassioned defence of learning.[1] His adversary is 'the common enemy Ignorance, or that which is next to it, some fragment of Knowledge supported only with an illiberal exercise of depraved Reason'. In a curious wording, Selden then remarks upon the need to protect 'the front of any piece of good Learning raised out of Liberall disquisition'. The front, meaning the form and frame, the figure of knowledge, is the object of custody, and by proximate association it is the face, the *frons* and *frontis*, that needs integument and covering. There follows, and this is my point, an *argumentum ad camelum*, a story of common law and covering, of leaden-footed custom and the jewels, the *emblemata* of civil law.

The exemplary anecdote is taken from Lucian and relates that an Ægyptian King, eager to entertain his people, 'shewd them a blacke Camel, shining with most rich trappings and such jewels as were not beneath the value of some great Princes possessions'. The populace responded in dilatory fashion to the unusual colour of the camel, instead of 'being taken with the Rare Noveltie and the precious Glorie that accompanied it'. The jewels in the coat or covering of the camel were the true wealth and knowledge and Selden immediately remarks, 'I will take leave to say it' that his work is done 'out of rich and most select Stores and Cabinets of Civill Learning.' The jewels are islands of knowledge, disciplines from an archipelago of learning in which all islands are visible from

[1] John Selden, *Titles of Honor* (London: Stansby, 1631), n.p. The 1st edn is John Selden, *Titles of Honor* (London: Stansby, 1614).

the shores of other isles, and thus cry out for travel, for passage between disciplines, 'Mutuall Commerce', as opposed to remaining within the 'narrow captivitie of some Profession that they are fettered in'.

The camel, for Selden, is common law, slow-footed custom in the hieroglyphic dictionary, over which has been thrown the much greater glory and covering of the bejewelled coat.[2] The jewels are *emblemata*, insertions into the solemn tradition, the 'beaten rhode' of the *mos britannicus* and they provide a translation of the *pegmata*, of the shelves, devices, scaffolds, and theatrical machinery by which terms the civilian lawyers variously understood the legal emblem. For the ever-inventive Selden, the legal emblem is an *exemplum*, a store and cabinet of civilian learning. It comes in the coat of common law and is worth much more in juristic coinage than the slow-witted local custom and the particularities of parochial tradition. It is for this reason that the author translates and augments the Latin treatise of Pancirolus, *notitia utraque dignitatum*, the devices and notes of both offices. In a Latin work on the law of images Selden thus appropriately commends the Roman law upon which his treatise is founded.[3]

My argument is that Selden's book is exemplary, his theory of emblems as cabinets of civilian learning which are transmitted without being noticed by the local populace, hidden in plain sight, augurs a theory of the hidden history of law's visibility. The legal emblem was a visual representation, a pictorial depiction of Latin norms, of civilian maxims and rules that were thus covertly but paradoxically visibly transported into common law. The legal emblem book, and derivative depictions in legal texts, such as *Titles of Honor*, as also in Bosewell's *Works of Armorie*, Legh's *Accedens of Armory*, in Dugdale's *Origines juridiciales*, or indeed in Coke's *Institutes*, proffer and provide the most direct transmission of civilian norms, of maxims, mottos, and principles drawn from Roman law into the text and particularly the unwritten tradition, the custom of common law. The etymology of cabinet can help elucidate the point. The emblem as a cabinet, a storehouse of knowledge of the universal law, has its roots, according to Varro, in *cavus*, meaning a niche, an alcove, a hollowed-out space which, as with a *pegma*, a term brilliantly dissected by our leading contemporary authority, Dr Hayaert, is a site where a statue, an image, an effigy or mask can be located and displayed.[4] More than that, *cavus aedium*, references the interior of the household, an inner court, a private space which is subject less to law than to the governance of practice, the disposition of the administration, a question of the political theology of *oikonomia*, namely what Selden references, in the first edition of *Titles of Honor*, as *œconomic* rule: 'Communitie

[2] On the significations of the camel, see Orus Apollo de Ægypte, *Des Significations des notes hieroglyphiques des Ægyptiens* (Paris: Kerver, 1543), n.p. where the hieroglyph of the camel is said to represent a heavy and slow-footed person. Paolo Giovio, *Dialogo dell'imprese militari et amorose* (Lyons: Roviglio, 1559) at 53 reproduces a devise image of a camel putting its foot in water, with the motto 'il me plaict la trouble'.

[3] Guido Pancirolus, *Notitia utraque dignitatum* (Lyons: Gabiano, 1608 edn). On the imagistic sources of the work, see Selden, *Titles of Honor* (1631) ch 1.

[4] Valérie Hayaert, *'Mens emblematica' et humanisme juridique: Le cas du 'Pegma cum narrationibus philosophicis' de Pierre Coustau (1555)* (Geneva: Droz, 2008).

of life, and Civill Societie, beginning first in particular families, under Oeconomique rule (representing what is now a common-welth). . . .'[5]

Jurisdictions of the Image

My starting point is a critical and sophisticated version of the argument that the emblem is an outmoded, irrelevant, and aesthetically poor form of figurative depiction. It has thus been argued recently and fluently by Anselm Haverkamp that the emblem tradition is best understood as a species of *confessio infirmitatis*.[6] His inspiration is Quintilian and a divagation in the *Institutio oratoria* where the forensically inspired rhetorician adopts the scholastic position that *exempla* from other disciplines or from matters otherwise impertinent to the case being argued are illicit and inappropriate insertions, *emblematis exornarentur*, flung into the pleading.[7] These ornamental intrusions, even if most beautiful in form, are dismissed as *supervacua*, entirely empty. They are extreme (*summam*) confessions of weakness, mere images, signs of excess and feeble thought and thus *emblemata* become in one subsequent history figures of dubiety and distraction. Most famously, the lawyer François Hotman dubs textual interpolations in the *Corpus iuris civilis, emblemata Triboniani*, the fingerprints of improper emendations, the barbarisms of the compiler of that sketchy collection.[8]

I hesitate to heckle Haverkamp, who is concerned primarily with the form of the emblematic picture, the woodcut, which he derives from painted altar panels and that he consigns to the domain of illustration, to an epistemology of stating the obvious, namely the divine provenance of law. This he argues becomes otiose with the emergence of a modern public sphere dependent not upon divinity but upon the populace and opinion, as also upon *scriptura* and not *pictura*. The modern economy of writing and image operates under novel 'visibility conditions' within which the emblem is an outmoded, rigid, and ineffective form of visual depiction. This argument has sound art historical grounds and an apparent plausibility. It is also a most useful starting point for considering, as is my plan, a broader meaning, and a more juristic history of the emblematic image as the archetypal *aenigma iuris*, which I will address primarily in its state of exception, which is to say in its use in the *mos britannicus*, the Anglican common law.

Quintilian's designation of the emblem as an expression of forensic weakness betrays an unease with the insertion of figures and specifically with digression and excess in the

[5] Selden, *Titles of Honor* (1614 edn) at 2.

[6] Anselm Haverkamp, '*Confessio infirmitatis*, or, A Productive Digression: iconic difference taken apart and put to good use in legal affairs', in *Genealogies of Legal Vision*, ed. P. Goodrich and V. Hayaert (London: Routledge, 2015), 104–6.

[7] Quintilian, *Institutio oratoria* (Cambridge: Harvard University Press, 1920), 2.4.27.

[8] See Hayaert, *Mens emblematica*, 143–7. For François Hotman's views of the compilers of the *Corpus*, see *Anti-Tribonian ou discours d'un grand et renomme Iurisconsulte de nostre temps sur l'estude des loix* (Paris: Perrier, 1569).

construction of legal arguments. The context for this investment in and opposition to inapposite borrowings from other *loci* is properly rhetorical and it is in relation to an expanded sense of rhetoric that the place of the visual, of oratorical *enargeia*, of what will become the *emblemata*, the emblematic juridical depiction of institutions, places, norms and their infraction, is best addressed and apprehended. What is at issue is in the first instance the insertion of the *mise en scène*, the staging of the jurisdiction, the context, in the argument itself. Structure becomes momentarily visible and two crucial features of the early history of the emblematical are immediately apparent. First, the emblematic is linked to excess, to a theatrical and properly histrionic staging of exemplary instances. Thus, and Barbara Nagel has touched upon this, the other crucial reference to the emblematical should be to a sense that we find in Suetonius' history of Tiberius.[9] The *emblemata* are here theatrical and exemplary *tableaux vivants*, vivid enactments of scenes of excess or of ideals, of corruption or virtue, from which subjects should learn and to which, where appropriate, subjects should aspire. More than that, the *emblemata* are excessive in a dual sense of being too much, —in the case of Tiberius they were generally pornographic *exempla*, —and in the sense of being enigmatic, which is to say plural and often paradoxical in their intimations.

The *emblemata* may in Quintilian appear to be, as Haverkamp argues, inappropriate commonplaces, *loci* and arguments drawn from extraneous disciplines, but the better descriptor of these intrinsically theatrical interventions, of what would later be expressly termed *pegmata*, in Latin, cabinets in English, would be a category of *locus plenus* that relates less to the topics of argument than to rhetorical *actiones*, to the all-important art of delivery. The emblem announces, screens, and demonstrates jurisdiction because, for lawyers, the opening moment of the juridical theatre, as for instance of the *in vivo* trial, is that of establishing the space of legality, the community of amity, and the ethical order within which these *dramatis personae* and their performances become the animation of law. Take a very simple example, the opening illustrated letter from the C of 'Communitie' in the first chapter of the first edition of *Titles of Honor*. Two figures encroach the C. The one on the left, *sinistra*, has a slightly darkened aura and is seemingly repelled by the perilunar letter. The cape is flowing and the left hand is raised in the figure of a serpent's head raised slightly above the poorly portrayed *caput lupinum* that appears to cover this outlaw's head. To the right a cherubic, shield-bearing figure, with a less threatening, outstretched floral-shaped open right hand is entering the yawning embrace of the C. To this, we need to add the key feature at the heart of the depiction, which is a blank escutcheon, a shield with no coat armour, devise, or other impress. It awaits the mark of honour and the inscription of law. It is *tabula rasa*, an empty space, and a window into which community and norm will be engraved.

The blank shield, the empty and not yet inscribed space at the heart of this devise is suggestive of a frontispiece, the opening of a work, a window onto the 'communitie' of

[9] Barbara Nagel, 'The Tyrant as Artist: Legal Fiction and Sexual Violence under Tiberius', *Law and Literature*, 25 (2013): 286. Piyel Haldar, 'A Gesture', *Law and Humanities*, 8 (2014): 304 also picks up on this sense of figurative depiction, verbal or pictorial, of exemplary scenes.

which the first word speaks. Here jurisdiction is signalled as the power to decide, the authority to inscribe the escutcheon and notate the order of honour and the marks of dignity. Rhetorical delivery requires staging and this is especially true of legal actions, be they oral or scriptural. The emblematic is thus the opening of action, the founding and unfolding of the dissemination of legality. The picture is the subtle and frequently overlooked annunciation of juridical appearance, the taken for granted moment of citation to the authoritative collection of laws, the scripture of the *Corpus iuris*, or to the ceremonial and sartorially complex enactments of legal dominion. The emblem is to be understood best as bound to legal practice, to pleadings as actions, and thus to the appearance in discourse of the practices, the customs and uses, the *exempla* and cases, that law and common law in particular is developed to both stage and dissimulate. The emblem is a performance of the *involucrum*, an integument, it enfolds and hides multiple senses, different levels as well as distinctive objects of reference and recollection. It is, to take up Haverkamp's theme again, both foreign and familiar, an alien intrusion and a well-known commonplace or storehouse, a cabinet of what are discreetly termed maxims and other *regulae iuris* that are presented as being indigenous to the *mos britannicus*, but that are, as their very language clearly indicates, of civilian provenance in what was always at some level 'our' Rome.[10] It is to the recollection and reconstruction of the place of images in the theatre of law, and specifically the role of emblematic depiction prior to and incorporated into the textual tradition of the books of law, that I will address my argument as a mild corrective and amicable expansion of Haverkamp's cautels.

Liber pauperum

The starting point for any account of the legal emblem within the common law tradition has to be the continental and thoroughly civilian provenance of this idiosyncratic form. The *emblemata* have an older root in the classical *notitia dignitatum* and in the heraldic tradition of *symbola heroica, impresa* (*notitia*) and devices in particular that the Inns of Court had begun to systematize in the mid-sixteenth century, but the specific tradition of juridically authored emblem books can be treated as a relatively autonomous, continentally inspired phenomenon. The emblem books had their links to the tradition of legal signs, concerned primarily with heraldic and vexillological codes, first treated in a semi-systematic way by Bartolus in his *Tractatus de insigniis*.[11] The emblem book, with its woodcut images, a generality of normative topics and the addition of explanatory

[10] On the maxim *Roma communis nostra patria est*, and on the related bifurcation, *dua sunt genera Romanorum*, see Pierre Legendre, *L'Autre Bible de l'occident: le monument romano-canonique* (Paris: Fayard, 2009); and Legendre, *L'Empire de la vérité: Introduction aux espaces dogmatiques industriels* (Paris: Fayard, 2001).

[11] Bartolus de Saxoferrato, *Tractatus de insigniis* [c.1250] is available in E. J. Jones, *Medieval Heraldry* (Cardiff: Lewis, 1943), and in a dual language text in *A Grammar of Signs*, ed. O. Cavalla et al. (Berkeley: University of California Press, 1994).

vernacular verses marked a novel departure both aesthetically and theoretically. What is most important from the perspective of common lawyers is simply that these are civilian law books, the *Corpus iuris* to be sure, as Hayaert has evidenced, in her treatment of emblems in the Senneton and other editions, but also the much more variegated texts of juridical theology that we associate with a plethora of lawyers writing in the genre that Alciato inaugurated.

The emblem books that became popular in England and which we associate, *inter alia*, with the lawyers Geffrey Whitney, Abraham Fraunce, George Wither, as also though more diversely with Palmer, Paradin, and Combe, and with the numerous translations of legal emblem books, ironically form the most direct and explicit reception of Roman law within the early modern common law tradition.[12] Here, unquestionably, in the didactic, moralizing mode of *emblemata*, civilian learning and Roman legal forms, meaning the institutional structure of persons, things and actions are incorporated into the antique and unsurpassed body of Anglican law. The *mos britannicus*, and I am here expanding and digressing upon the work of Susan Byrne on the *mos hispannicus*, is most distinctively exposed as a combination of classical mythology, patristic theology, literary and legal adages, maxims and rules that in translation come to represent that peculiar mixture, that disciplinary and methodological *concordia discors* that is the *mos britannicus*, the Anglican Roman law.[13]

The emblem book was a mode of reception of Roman law by the back door in a legal culture that after the Act of Supremacy and the distinct establishment of a Church of England was politically pitched against the continental and civilian legal traditions. The endless glosses and other tinctures of Normanism were the object of ridicule and so integument, opacity, the covering of pictures was a subtle and lateral way of introducing classical and civilian images into common law thought while, in more formal terms, it constituted an occluded transmission of the Roman *ius imaginum* into what were expressly designated the houses of honour, the Inns of Court which according to Legh in his *Accedens of Armory* reflected the heavenly hierarchy and the nine orders of angels.[14] Anglican juridical-theology thus relayed a visual *corpus* of emblematic norms and other dispositive institutions and rules that had their provenance and gained their initial formulation in the Roman law tradition of the continent. This was a humanistic forensic exercise, which brought with it not only the *triplex ordo* of the emblem but also the Trinitarian form of Roman legal structures.

The emblem book played the more or less visible role of transmitting the Latin culture of law to an insular jurisdiction and it did so in a way that could generally be overlooked in both senses of the term. This can be formulated somewhat more precisely by borrowing again from Haverkamp and adverting to the aesthetic form of the *emblema*. The

[12] On the English sources of *emblemata*, see Peter Goodrich, *Legal Emblems and the Art of Law: Obiter Depicta as the Vision of Governance* (Cambridge: Cambridge Univerisity Press, 2014).

[13] Susan Byrne, *Law and History in Cervantes' 'Don Quixote'* (Toronto: University of Toronto Press, 2012).

[14] Gerard Legh, *The Accedens of Armory* (London: Totell, 1572), fol. 135.

emblem book was a picture book, it was what in that period was called *liber pauperum, Book of the Poor* or by direct association, of the illiterate. Where the *liber pauperum* was in theological jargon a book for those that could not read—*pro lectione pictura est*, the picture takes the place of knowing how to read—it has a rather more specific history and meaning in common law. The *Liber pauperum* was a mid-twelfth-century student legal text written by the Lombardian lawyer Vacarius as an educational tool for those who could not obtain, could not study, or could not afford the complete text of the inordinately lengthy *Corpus iuris civilis* itself.[15] The *Liber pauperum* is a compilation of key passages from the *Code* and the *Digest* arranged for students in such a way as to provide easy and cheap access to the method and the practical substance of the universal law.

The aims of the *Liber* are set out in the prologue where Vacarius specifies a double purpose and a dual law. The first law is natural reason and is embedded in our being, *lex cognationis*, and then there is a second law, a revealed law, which for Vacarius, although this is not without contention, is the law of the Gospels, *lex caritatis*. The study and observance of both laws is to be encouraged and the prologue makes clear that 'knowledge of the good and the just' is what is necessary for all citizens.[16] This parallels the opening of the *Digest* (1.1.1) and the book that follows on from this preliminary statement of purpose collects and collates brief passages of the law for the benefit not only of those who wanted to practise as canon lawyers in England, but also for those *qui legibus istis non utuntur*, meaning simply all those who planned to train and practise in the Anglican common law and therefore needed to know but were not going to directly use the universal jurisprudence, the *leges legum*, that underpinned the local and still plural jurisdictions of *mos britannicus*.[17] The *Liber pauperum* thus had a trans-jurisdictional scope and proffered, as Stein has shown, *generalia* that might be useful in interpreting canon, civil, and common law.[18]

From the point of view of juridical theology, that of the two laws, and of the triplex order of the *mos britannicus*, the *exemplum* of the *liber pauperum* provides a most intriguing and telling introduction to the prehistory and the form that the *emblemata iuris* will later take. What matters for my purposes, for the tracing of the advent and significance of images within the *mos britannicus*, is that the *Liber pauperum* is a reception of Roman law in common law and however much the so-called *pauperistae* were from time to time attacked and ridiculed, the first connotation of *Liber pauperum* is of a law book, an introductory and didactic text of legal adages, maxims, *exempla*, and rules of method. This can be seen in simple form in the representation of law and lawmaking, cases and statutes, in an image of the insignia of 'illustrious magistrates (*quaestoris*)' from Pancirolus (Fig. 7.1). The portrait on the draped table shows the image of the

[15] F. de Zulueta, ed., *The 'Liber Pauperum' of Vacarius* (London: SS, 1927); and for extended commentary on Vacarius and his work, see Jason Taliadoros, *Law and Theology in Twelfth-Century England: The Works of Master Vacarius (c.1115/20–c.1200)* (Turnhout: Brepols, 2006).

[16] *Liber pauperum*, (Prologus) I—*utriusque legis viam duce domino perficere cupiens, quo facile omnes ad boni et equi scientiam provocarem.*

[17] *Liber pauperum* at 2.

[18] Peter Stein, *The Teaching of Roman Law in England around 1200* (London: SS, 1990).

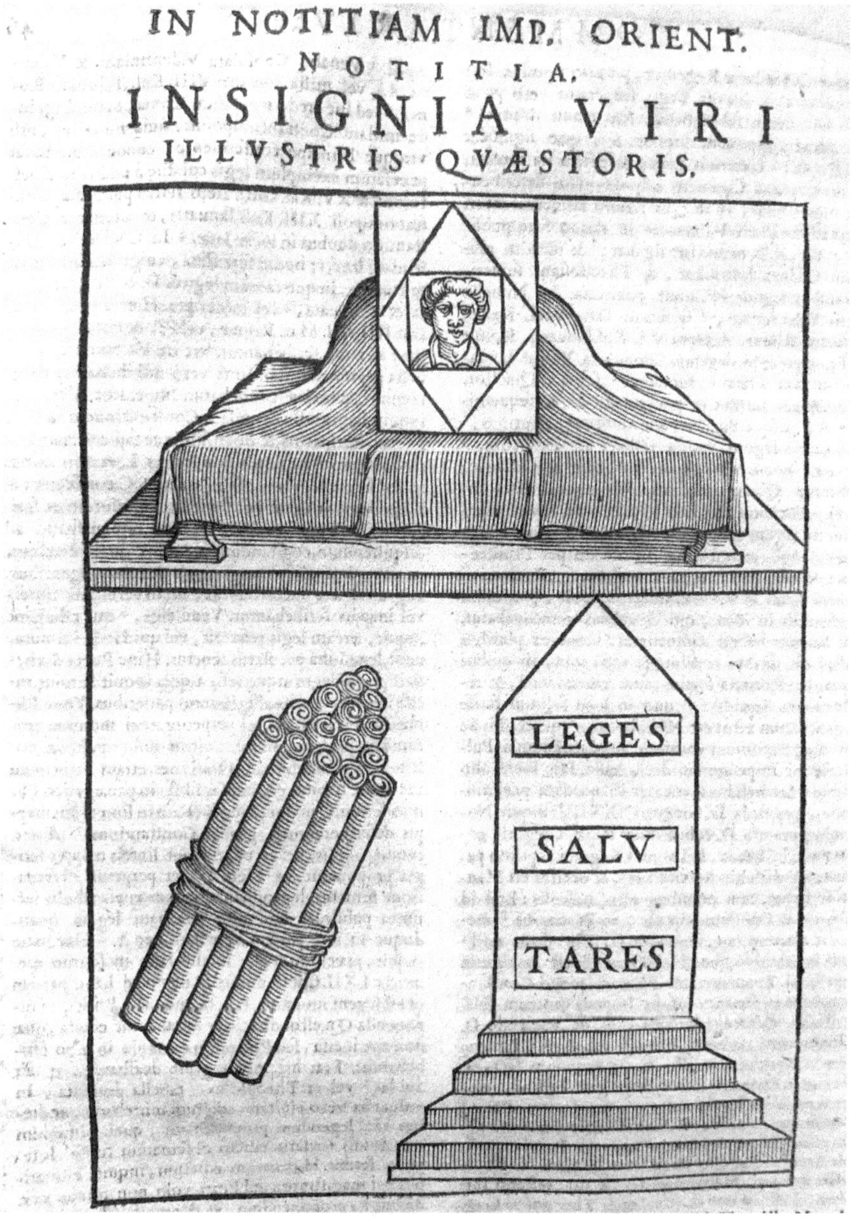

FIG. 7.1 Guido Pancirolus, 'Illustris Quaestoris', *Notitia utraque dignitatum* (Lugudini: Gabiano, 1608) fol. 46^{v}. Reproduced by kind permission of Peter Goodrich.

sender of the laws, the vicarious of the divinity, and in this case the emperor of the orient. The authorizing image of the sovereign sits above the scrolls, the medium of making law, and the table of statutes, the 'salutary laws' that will remedy the traumas and conflicts of the polity. Magistrate and law are here visible and yet occluded in that the codicil that sends the written authorization is closed, here not even in the form of a clasped book, lacking all depth, and the scrolls and the table of laws are equally simply surfaces, closed books, whose face is to be sufficient precedence and evidence of legitimacy. Here, according to the commentary 'all the laws, edicts, and sanctions promulgated by the Prince are to be stored'.[19] After which comes a listing of the various offices of the magistrates, their places, offices and duties.

The image introduces the jurisdiction of those delegates of the sovereign who administer the city and the dominions of empire and the purpose of the depiction is the generic one of indicating the commission, the vicarious status of the holder of such office. In further images, the precise *insiginia*, medallions, and devises of office are depicted and maps are provided of the various places and distributions of administrative power. From here it is a short step to the more figurative representations of office and accompanying scriptural grants of commission that we find in Selden's later work (Fig. 7.2). Here, in a more emblematic but also theatrical depiction we see a baron spiritual and temporal clasping his letters patent in his right hand, walking, and looking west—to England, to the occident—with his dual *personae* and two laws depicted in the two different ruffs

FIG. 7.2 John Selden, *Titles of Honor* (London: Stansby, 1631). Reproduced by kind permission of Peter Goodrich.

[19] Pancirolus, *Notitia*, 46^{v} col. 1.

and in the fur and sartorial luxury of the right side, compared to the austere and blank cloak draped over the left. Authority is depicted, as Selden puts it, as priority and legitimacy, as precedence based upon authoritative grant, usually beginning '*de gratia nostra*', by our grace, and offering *ad apparentiam*, for sensible apprehension, the image of proper place and portent.

The simple point is that the earlier *Liber pauperum* in its double form, and most significantly here as introductory administrative and legal text, can help us understand the status of the *emblemata iuris* when these later books continue the work of the *notitia dignitatum* in keeping the spirit and principles, the visible *generalia* of Roman law alive in a fiercely nationalistic and rather confused Anglican jurisdiction. By the mid-sixteenth century, *liber pauperum* now meant picture book, a text for the illiterate, which means not so much that these were immediately for non-lawyers and non-clerics, but that they provided a visiocratic code, a series of dramatic enactments that form a visual template for political and *oeconomic* disposition. The emblems staged exemplary scenes and provided the template for the hierarchy of citizens first and most significantly in their *oikonomic* capacity, as social beings subject more to governance of the law of laws, to images, than to any positive, municipal black letter legal promulgations. It is no accident that the Vacarian *Liber pauperum* early on expends time on the relation of law to equity, on the abrogation of unjust legal rules by custom or by humane and equitable interpretation. It also talks somewhat controversially but indicatively of the connection between *affectio* and *traditio*, a good enough metaphor for the marriage of the subject to the community, which is the sole *topos* and purpose of law to preserve. There is a pre-law, an as yet unformed but sensible jurisdiction, nature, or reason that is amenable to an interdisciplinary conjunction and dissemination in emblematic forms. It is these founding scenes, these moments of annunciation of jurisdiction, of places and roles, public and private, that the picture books relay in their role as *liber pauperum* and carry forward *in parte infidelium*, in this ostensibly hostile Anglican sphere of *translatio imperii*.

Aenigmata iuris

The importance of the play upon, and the ambiguity of, the term *liber pauperum* as law book and book of images lies in the second crucial aspect of the *emblema juris* which is its classically juristic role in the art of dissimulation. The maxim *qui nescit regnare nescit dissimulare*, common to both the *mos italicus* and the *mos britannicus* is indicative of an art of law that could never directly represent either its sources or its confusion of disciplines, the *auctoritates philosophorum et poetarum* that have to be dressed in Latin and laconically embedded in the manner of maxims or, as I am arguing here, as images, meaning both persons and pictures.[20] Thus the signs of office had to be inscribed visibly,

[20] Thus St German, *Doctor and Student* [1523] (London: SS, 1974) at 57–9 stating that 'maxims have always been taken for law in this realm. … For every one of those maxims is sufficient authority for

worn and performed according to a prior and precedent order of legitimate inscription and sacred authorization. Pancirolus provides the most extensive tableaux of such notations in his depictions of the authorized administrative and *œconomic* places, properly termed dispositions. Thus *Divina providentia* provides the explicit order and manner of authority (Fig. 7.3). The two angels hold aloft the portrait of the emperor and below there are four further authorizing portraits, representing military and legal authority, virtue and happiness being their interior mirrors. The array of books, codes, and codicils between the portraits marks and imagines the emperor's grant of authority, each time in a thick book, a *codex*, inscribed with an acronym beginning *Foelix liber*, felicitous book. Acronym and encryption are the very reason why law needs art, philosophy and poetics, pictures and verse, because it cannot state directly what it intends in relation to 'divine providence, his foresight and legacy for the future'. Law cannot regulate unknown circumstances, nor can it be present, as text or practice, in the quotidian circulations of a far-flung polity, its alcoves and the other opaque interiors of its *œconomic* inhabitation. Like the sovereign, law is generally not there, it governs but does not rule. What happens, the impress of role and office, starts in the interior, on the right side of the image, in the domestic *œconomy*, in the ethical space of the imaginary, with all its rules of place and manners of behaving, of role and function.

To the extent that what is most important to the *magister scriniorum* and to the office of *memoriæ epistolarum et libellorum*, to cite another portrayal of the insignia, is the internalization and enactment of the order and norms of precedence, their quotidian and *œconomic* practice, it is not law but interior template and ontology of disposition, of custom and precedence that is to be inculcated. It does not matter if the subject knows, it matters that the subject does, and the more that the practice and incorporation can be unthinking, automatic, internally inscribed through pattern and repetition, the better that the justice that precedes and subtends law will operate (Fig. 7.4). Following directly after the insignia of the illustrious masters of the private affairs of divine houses—*rerum privatarum domus divinae*—the visual annotations of domestic disposition are portrayed with peculiar expansiveness.[21] The picture shows two *codicilli* on draped tables. Each *codex* faces the other in that the books have their clasped pages turned towards their complements and have portraits to indicate the importance of this legitimation and governance. On the right, staring out toward the viewer, the image is of the authorization of the domestic equerries and shows, contained in an unbroken circle, two angels holding aloft the conjoint effigies of the domestic couple. Beneath the spouses, here visibly joining affection and tradition, *affectio et traditio*, is a circle of hearts and a wedding band. These are signs of the *lex amatoria* and of a justice, an affection that exceeds and in Pauline doctrine fulfills the law.

himself'. The exemplary though largely unfinished work on maxims is Francis Bacon, *A Collection of Some Principall Rules and Maximes of the Common Lawes of England, with Their Latitude and Extent* (London: More, 1630).

[21] Panicrolus, *Notitia*, at fol. 56ʳ.

FIG. 7.3 Pancirolus, 'Divina providentia', *Notitia utraque dignitatum*.

FIG. 7.4 Pancirolus, 'Notitia comes domesticorum', *Notitia utraque dignitatum.*

The officers and attendants of the household, knights and footmen belong to an ethical order and internal economy—at root *oikonomia*—that offers the authorized disposition of places and roles. These are spelled out, the various and detailed enumerations of attendants for kitchen, laundry, supplies, bedchambers to stables and gardens. These are the places in the court of the nobility, but the ontology of such images and tabulations is exemplary and to be mimicked. This can be seen on the right side of the *notitia comes domesticorum*, where the masculine side of the household looks to the left and offers six unbroken circles at the heart of which is the sun. The halcyon centre marks the paradoxical coincidence of the distant exterior planet and the heart of the interior, *intima* and *extima* conjoined. Taken further, the sun denotes divinity, that crescendo of light that both reveals and hides the blinding force of the divine. The circle depicts eternity and marriage, around which angels hold up a tablet with the portrait of a human head signifying the ruler of the household whom the footmen are to maintain. Around the tablet is another circle with small stones or tablets (*tesserulis*) jutting interstitially while the orb itself *in toto* expressly marks the protection of the household and the benevolent oversight of *Dei providentia* who watches and guards the two principals of the household.[22]

If we consider the advent of images, of woodcut depictions in juridical texts, they are liminal devices that represent in an easily accessible form the presence of authority.[23] They are, as discussed, initially signs of sovereignty and office, military and administrative investitures, which were generally derived from the *imagines* in the *notitia dignitatum* and further heraldic works, to represent a 'droict des gens' or *ius gentium* that ironically, in the case of common law, has an appeal far beyond the limits of municipal government. These *symbola heroica* can provide an important clue to the visual *exempla* that the *emblemata iuris* transmit. They have a dual status as being both enigmatic and emblematic. Start with the enigmatic function. As with any ensign of authority, and particularly and expressly with the *aenigmata iuris* coined by the Spanish grammarian and lawyer Antonio Nebrija in his work of that title, published in 1506, there is a significant degree of learning, of specialized erudition that accompanies the depiction of authority, in its full genealogical sense, which inevitably traces it to hierarchy and eventually via the *vicarius Dei*, to God.[24] Those who rule do so by specialized means, by virtue of their knowledge of the *arcana imperii*, the hieroglyphics of power, and that message requires the expression of an absent and invisible source in a temporal and visible, though elliptical and properly speaking involuted, form.

The *aenigmata iuris* are specifically signs of obscure or difficult knowledges. Where Pancirolus inserted *emblemata*, images of the prince on statues as the sign of authority both present and absent in the public sphere, and as *stellae* in his text, these are within a tradition of *imagines* that identify and sanctify public spaces but also carry with them the juristic sense of the image as *veritas falsa*. The pictorial depiction is by the early sixteenth century expressly an *aenigma*, and it is this sense of irresolvable plurality of meanings that Nebrija takes up and in his turn offers a more complicated definition. The *aenigmata iuris* are legal terms of art that have become obscure by virtue of their excision and compilation in fragmentary form in the *Corpus iuris*. The legitimacy of these fragments depends upon tracing them back to their forgotten roots in classical sources, in mythological, literary, and poetic texts. The enigma is a reference to a forgotten source and so Nebrija, in the prologue to his *Aenigmata*, published as an appendix to the 1612 edition under the title *Accursii somnium*, distinguishes between the prophetic and the juristic meaning of enigmas. 'It is one thing', he remarks, 'to be a prophet but it is quite another to be an interpreter. The former declares their mind without thinking (*illic*

22 Pancirolus, *Notitia*, 58^{v} col. 1.

23 As, for example, in Pancirolus, *Notitia*, at 17^{v}.

24 Antonio de Nebrija, *Vocabularium utriusque iuris* (Venice: Zalterium, 1612); which edition is bound together with *Lexicon iuris civilis*, and the wonderful introduction to the first edition of the *Aenigmata iuris* (1506), 'De Glauco et Diomede, Accursii somnium'.

spiritus neutra praedicit), the latter requires erudition and the copiousness of words so as to explain and interpret.'[25] Accursius thus, in failing to refer to the Greek sources of the Homeric reference in the preface to the *Digest*, to an exchange between Glaucus and Diomedes, ends up with a prophetic and not a legal interpretation, one which Nebrija rather endearingly terms *sensus legis ridiculus*.[26]

The legally ridiculous, the textual fantasy of the dreaming Accursius, may be philologically execrable but it can also be of great importance in juridical theology. The *aenigmata* may be juridical hieroglyphs, cloaked in the 'dark vesture of emblems' that Philipot later refers to as their Greek origins but that simply evidences an esoteric and foreign substrate to the juristic text.[27] It legitimates by providing an invisible, which is to say enigmatic, source. When this source is depicted visually, as in Coustau's *Pegma* of 1555, when it becomes an emblem, the enigmatic and the emblematic are joined in the *muta eloquentia* of an image of two soldiers exchanging suits of armour but saying nothing, indeed there is a cloud between them, thus constituting an invisible as well as a visible exchange, both *aenigma* and *emblema* at one and the same time (Fig. 7.5). The emblem deserves brief description, although the philological details can be dispensed with insofar as Hayaert has detailed them at length and with great finesse already.[28]

Start with the context from which the depiction is drawn. There is a reference in the second preface to the *Digest* in which Justinian states that here 'an exchange of laws has been devised, even such as in Homer, that father of all virtue, Glaucus and Diomedes made between themselves when they exchanged dissimilar things; Gold for bronze, the worth of a hundred oxen for nine'.[29] The literary figure, a poetic reference to Song 6 of the *Iliad*, is extracted from the text and depicted as a visual figure. The letters become figures, the metaphors pictures, with all of the play and polysemy that this implies. Note then that the figure extracted is in content of heraldic and military import. War precedes and limits law and if we are to understand the morphology of the legal, the agonistic and antinomic context of the juridical needs to be recollected. The preface to the *Pandects*, the collection of all the laws, represents itself emblematically as an exchange, a change in the sense of disguise, and also as an agreement that, at the price specified, augurs peace and law, books and not swords. Behind agreement lies force, and this is most evident in the woodcut picture that shows military leaders, clad in armour, bearing swords, wearing extravagantly plumed helmets, exchanging breast plates, with a military encampment in the background. Next the classical reference should be noted. The reference to Homer is to the authority of the poet, to a literary emblem in the legal presentation and

[25] Nebrija, *Vocabularium*, at 390^{v}.

[26] Nebrija, *Vocabularium*, at 393^{v}.

[27] Thomas Philipot, *A Brief Historical Discourse of the Original and Growth of Heraldry, Demonstrating upon what Rational Foundations, that Noble and Heroick Science is Established* (London: Holt, 1672) at 1.

[28] Hayaert, *Mens emblematica*, 210–32.

[29] *Digest* (ed. Watson) at liv.

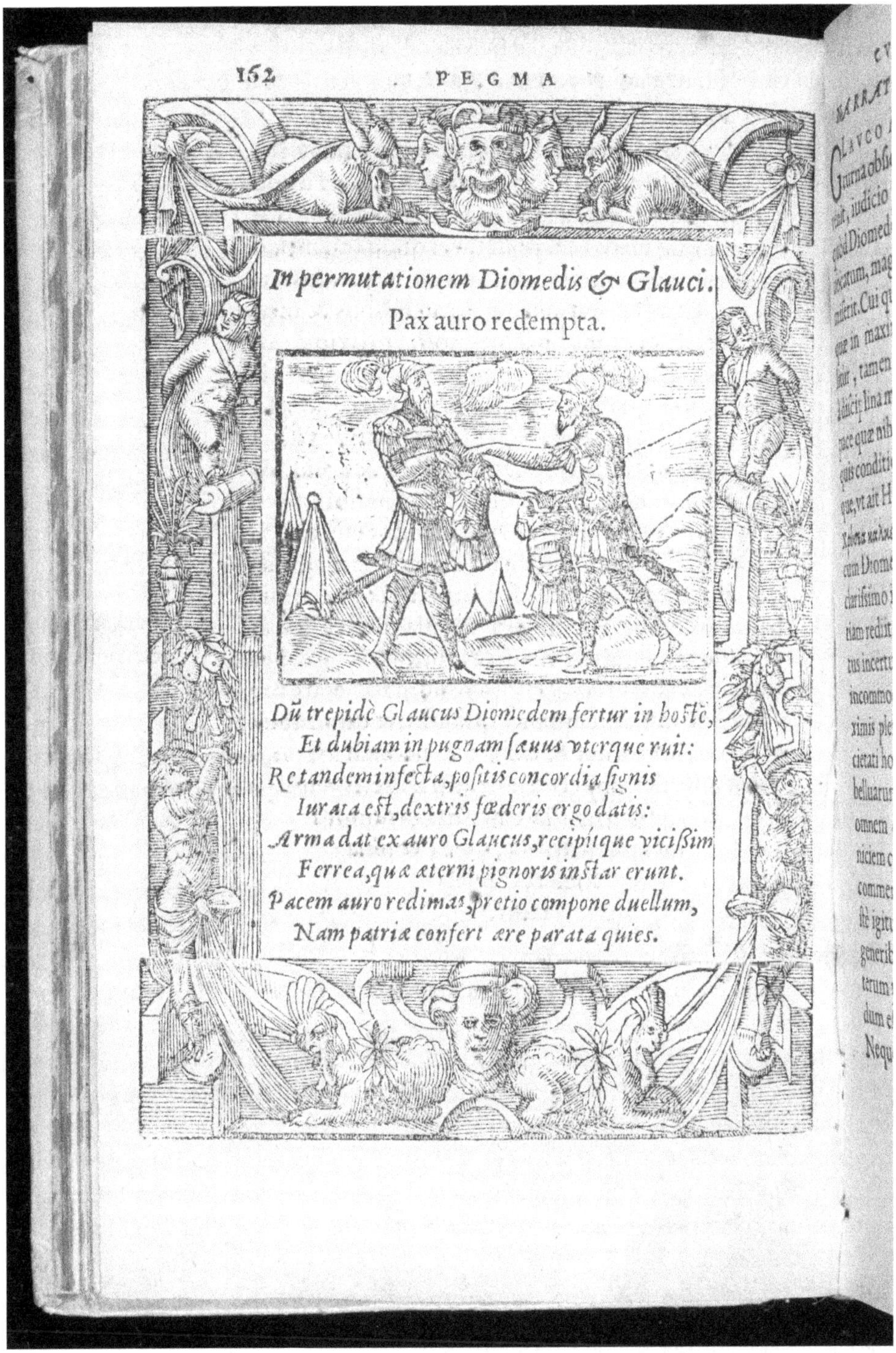
162 PEGMA

In permutationem Diomedis & Glauci.

Pax auro redempta.

Dũ trepidè Glaucus Diomedem fertur in hostē,
Et dubiam in pugnam sæuus vterque ruit:
Re tandem infecta, positis concordia signis
Iurata est, dextris fœderis ergo datis:
Arma dat ex auro Glaucus, recipitque vicißim
Ferrea, quæ æterni pignoris instar erunt.
Pacem auro redimas, pretio compone duellum,
Nam patriæ confert ære parata quies.

FIG. 7.5 Pierre Coustau, 'In permutationem Diomedis & Glauci', *Pegma cum narrationibus philosophicis* (Lyon: Bonhomme, 1555). Reproduced by kind permission of the Rare Book Collection, Lillian Goldman Law Library, Yale Law School.

as with all figures it brings a degree of malleability, an element of expansiveness and of enigma, of opportunity and potential freeplay.[30]

The enigma of the image lies both in the classical reference to Greek poetry, and to a lengthy tradition of interpreting the exchange and its context, as well as in the opacity of the image. Reading beyond the lines that the compiler Tribonian reproduces in the *Digest*, the exchange is in fact treated as a sign of cowardice, and the gods drive Glaucus mad. The glossator Accursius, like Tribonian, fails to understand the two-edged character of the reference and it is the later humanists who have to restore the full meaning, first Nebrija, and then, in our emblem, Coustau. Even here there is a complication in the sense that the picture cannot show, cannot demonstrate, the uneven quality of the exchange, and it is the text that has to make the point, even while claiming that the resultant agreement is an even one. Gold is a small price for peace, in Coustau's version. It is indeed generally as a template of agreement that the reference and the depiction are taken to relay. The depiction is taken up in the English emblem books as the sign of concord between military leaders, the mark of treaties as contracts as also of the classical in the modern. It is that play of image and reference that I wish to emphasize. The picture says both more and less than the text, it is a plurality, a view that begins to gain expression in Nebrija, for whom, and here I am eliciting a theory from the dictionary itself, the image belongs to a double order and bears a double meaning, *duplicem sententiam*, in the medieval theological treatises which gain expression in the dictionary's distinction between *iconomus* and *œconomus*. The term *iconomus* is defined within the lexicon as the imagery manipulated by and used in the governance of the ecclesiastical polity. The lexicon then defines *œconomus* as belonging also to the genre of the image and treats it as being a subset of the *iconomus*. Disposition is conceived as a spiritual affair, an ordering of the imaginary which is a matter of *regimen animarum*, to use the Augustinian phrase, and then of an imperial and familial *œconomus* which is more briefly defined as the law (*curatorem*) of the household, of Aristotle's '*œconomica*'.[31]

The *aenigma* in the emblem belongs to the *iconomus*, to the hierographic aspect of the image, to the invisible and unsaid which in Pauline theology is expressed in the concept of occlusion: *nunc videmus per speculum in ænigmate*. If we move to the other key text on the enigma, the magnificent François Menestrier's *Philosophie des images enigmatiques* published in 1694, very late in the era of the *mens emblematica*, a synoptic and theoretical work of great systematic and imaginative value, we find in the opening pages of the book that the *aenigmata*, enigmatic images, are distinguished from *emblemata* by virtue of their obscurity compared to emblems which are moralizing, didactic, explained, and accessible. Later however Menestrier expressly includes under enigmatic images, immediately after the notations of cabalists, the insertions (literally the incantations) of jurisconsults, and makes reference to the *Digest*.[32] If we turn to Menestrier's

[30] On the enigmatic in law, see Goodrich, 'Legal Enigmas: Antonio de Nebrija, *The Da Vinci Code*, and the Emendation of Law' 30:1 *OJLS*, 71 (2010).

[31] Nebrija, *Vocabularium*, 151^{r}. *iconomus dicitur ille, cui ecclesiastica res gubernanda mandatur*, with a reference to the Code *Imperatorum, de iuram*.

[32] Menestrier, *La philosophie des images enigmatiques* (Paris: Baritel, 1694) at 159.

earlier treatise *La philosophie des images*, the double face of the image is schematically presented in a chart of 'hierographie' in which the sacral image—the iconomic—is split between the hieroglyphic, which is the picture (*id est picturam*), and the symbol which is scriptural (*id est scripturam*).[33] He continues to argue that the picture (*figure*) in the devise is hieroglyphic and the words are symbols. The same is true of emblems which also bear a double meaning, *ancipitia vocabula*, and are Janus-faced.

The image represents a double law, and it is precisely in this emblematic transmission of the Janus of common law, the doubling of legality as both Roman *and* Anglican, as hieroglyphic *and* municipal, as just *and* as rigorous, as particular *and* general that the simultaneously dissimulative and similitudinous visual *exempla* play their crucial role. Borrowing again from Menestrier who is endlessly suggestive, the enigma may be understood by those who know the referents of the *prosopopeia* that are figured in the depictions but the function of the enigmatic image is more generally and simply defined *ut delectet et approbetur* meaning that by virtue of the very plurality of their significations they are capable of pleasing and affirming a multitude of different apprehensions while always reserving a singular and ultimate referent.[34] What then do these Janus-faced images, the *facies altera* of common law, evidence of the use of emblems? The answer is that they belong simultaneously and seductively to the imperial *artes arcanae et abstrusae* and to a law that is *purum putum*, simple and clear. The enigmatic image is not simply plural but is also a call of faith, a glimpse of the unseen and unsayable, a mystic figure of an imaginary congregation.

If we move to the common lawyers, the law is supported, as Coke put it by the hieroglyph of the crown, by the *flores quae faciunt coronam*, which is to say maxims and principles, and in the earlier idiom of St German, the true law is by nature implanted in the reason of men and specifically in their reflection of the image of God (*ad ymaginem dei creatam*). German goes on to cite the Psalms: 'The light of thy countenance is inscribed upon us, that is to say the light of truth, for the light of God's countenance is truth.'[35] The referent of this curious legal genealogy is that of the crescendo of optical metaphors that Agamben nicely delineates as the vanishing point of the divinity.[36] The closer the brighter and so also the less visible. The greater the light, the less that is seen. At the same time, and this is the truly enigmatic aspect of the enigma, there is a transformation, a visual pleasure, an ease of access and 'contentment of sight' that this is law that is emblematized and that it has both a presence and a mystery, a meaning that is evident only to those learned in the profession and true to the hidden cause: 'It is particularly in the Enigmas that one tastes this double pleasure, that of apprehending something that one does not know; and that of admiring the skill, spirit and artifice of those who made the Enigma, who enveloped it so well, and who, despite the veils, the shadows and affectations can see and find in them their meaning.'[37] The *aenigmata iuris* are custodial

[33] Menestrier, *La philosophie des images* (Paris: Caille, 1682) 72–3.
[34] Menestrier, *Images enigmatiques*, at 109.
[35] St German, *Doctor and Student*, at 12–14.
[36] Agamben, *Kingdom and Glory*, at 203.
[37] Menestrier, *Images enigmatiques*, at 108.

visual forms, indicators of law, dispositions of place and personality but ultimately and benevolently, for the populace, for the *œconomic* and its governance the ultimate and singular, because monotheistic meaning resides only in the hands of those who understand the enigma that is buried in each *emblem*. This observation can propel us to a final set of considerations and a theory of the legal emblem as precisely the artistic in the juridical, the figuration within law of what law cannot say.

Emblema omnes tangit

Chasseneuz's *Catalogus gloriae mundi*, first published in 1529, adumbrates and orders the hierarchies of acclamation and glorification after early on remarking that honour touches all.[38] The emblem, I will now suggest, effects a similar purpose in law, that of providing in visual form a depiction of the symbolic order that forms the imaginary background, in Selden's argot the backface of common law. It may help to recapitulate a little before moving forward. The emblem book is a progeny, I have suggested, of the *Liber pauperum*. It smuggles Roman law, civilian *exempla*, and banned foreign texts into the *mos britannicus*, the fiercely nationalist Anglican law. The *mos britannicus* is in that sense distinguished by the extravagance of its dissimulations, the covert character of its undisclosed philosophical, literary, and poetic *exempla*. The emblem book had the peculiar importance in England not only of smuggling in a contraband law, but also in a very deliberate sense enacting through the publication of these picture books the very transmission that these *emblemata* enacted. It was not only that this importation of *muta eloquentia*, of the most visible form of rhetorical *actio*, offered instruction in foreign methods but it was in simple publication and dissemination the incorporation and promulgation of the action that emblems advocate.

What I am seeking to suggest is that the *emblemata iuris* introduced into the prelegal domain of the common law, into the realm of what Sir John Doderidge calls the 'conversations of men', the domain of custom and use, immemorial patterns and itinerant practices, and in the most direct manner possible, which is to say not very direct at all, the Roman structure of the social, the trinity that 'Gaius noster' formulated, of persons, things, and actions. As Selden has it on the title page of the first edition of his *Mare clausum, non solus*, this English law is not a singular but rather a several enterprise, a part of a larger juristic tradition and whole. He emphasizes the point with a further maxim, *iuxta exemplar* (*Romanorum*), a quite express citation to the Roman sources and inheritance of a 'commune ley' that is in its structural form the British *ius commune*. The common lawyers benefited from a covert but manifestly visible, juridical imaginary of inherited and imported symbols. A code of iconomic figures that could, as Pancirolus well argues, indicate the presence of an absent sovereign, the inhabitation of a realty and reality of things owned and occupied, and finally a legally sanctioned order of actions, which is to say offices, roles, and rules of life. The emblem,

[38] Barthèlemy Chasseneuz, *Catologus gloriae mundi* (Venice: Valgrisii, 1576).

in touching all, in forming the rule book of visible symbols, the figures of lawful living, expresses the conjunction that Agamben has recently elaborated of life and rule, *forma vitae* and *regula iuris*, which the *legis actio* collapses in the phrase *actus vitamque ac regulam*.[39]

Legal emblems manifest structure, and specifically the Trinitarian juristic structure of sovereignty, the order of persons, the *ius imaginum* as the English translate the Gaian *ius personarum*, which, recollect, even for Gaius was to be seen. Thus, in the *Institutes*, we read: *et prius videamus de personis*, namely we first see persons. I have suggested that the legal emblem tradition made this visible order, the hierography of the juridico-political, momentarily quite manifest in the arcane and lucifugous space of a textually obsessed law. More than that, the emblem declares what the common lawyers term an unwritten and 'undeclared' law.[40] The *ius non scriptum* is *ius quaesita alteri*, law inscribed outwith the text by way of *muta eloquentia*, in images and in extra-legal, which is to say non-documentary, but homonymous deeds.

Unlike the altar panel which invites the subject to prayer, to abscond from the world, to divest materiality and deed in favour of investment in the evanescent and invisible, the emblem proffers a more complicated relation to action. The third division of the law is precisely that of making actions visible, where, in the language that Gaius established, the person is made to do something or more literally—*dare facere praestare oportere*.[41] I will leave it to some other occasion to reassemble the exact workings of legal actions, or in common law the infinite particularities of pleadings, and rather offer a more general conclusion to my original question, that of why the emblem book was invented and promulgated by lawyers and what the images of law that it circulated portend and in their residual and more populist visiocratic forms still convey. My answer, cognate and complicit with this occasion, is that it helped to reintroduce and establish the *universalia* of the civil law, the *mores* that subtend and exceed the law and form the structure of the social as such, into the *mos britannicus*. The emblem book thus enacted, through the universal idiom of images, the international roots and commonalities of common law. Lest the English common lawyers forgot or in a moment of extreme exceptionalism attempted to exclude the basic structures of occidental action, the amity of words and images, of speech and persons, face and deed, the emblem book subtly divided the sensible and ensured the persistence of humanism within what was at the time a distinctively unlearned tradition of common law.

[39] Agamben, *The Highest Poverty: Monastic Rules and Form-of-Life* (2013) at 70.

[40] Peter Stein, *Regulae iuris*, 3–9.

[41] Gaius, *Institutes*, 4.2. (232/233—'he ought to convey, do, or answer for something').

Bibliography

Agamben, Giorgio. *The Highest Poverty: Monastic Rules and Form-of-Life* (Stanford: Stanford University Press, 2013).

Bacon, Francis. *The Elements of the Common Lawes of England* [...] *a Collection of Some Principall Rules and Maximes of the Common Law, with Their Latitude and Extent* (London: 1630).

Byrne, Susan. *Law and History in Cervantes' 'Don Quixote'* (Toronto: University of Toronto Press, 2012).

Chasseneuz, Barthèlemy. *Catologus gloriae mundi* (Venice: Valgrissi, 1576).

German, Christopher St. *Doctor and Student* [1523] (London: Selden Society, 1974).

Giovio, Paolo. *Dialogo dell'imprese militari et amorose* (Lyon: Roviglio, 1559).

Goodrich, Peter. *Legal Emblems and the Art of Law: Obiter Depicta as the Vision of Governance* (Cambridge: Cambridge University Press, 2014).

Haldar, Piyel. 'A Gesture: A Review of Peter Goodrich, *Legal Emblems and the Art of Law: Obiter Depicta as the Vision of Governance*', *Law and Humanities*, 8.2 (2014), 304–18.

Haverkamp, Anselm. '*Confessio Infirmitatis*, or, a Productive Digression: Iconic Difference Taken Apart and Put to Good Use in Legal Affairs', in *Genealogies of Legal Vision*, ed. P. Goodrich and Valérie Hayaert (London: Routledge, 2015), 104–17.

Hayaert, Valérie. *Mens emblematica' et humanism juridique: Le cas du 'Pegma cum narrationibus philosophicis' de Pierre Coustau (1555)* (Geneva: Droz, 2008).

Hotman, François. *Anti-Tribonian ou discours d'un grand et renomme iurisconsulte de nostre temps sur l'estude des loix* (Paris: Perrier, 1569).

Legh, Gerard. *The Accedens of Armory* (London: Totell, 1572).

Legendre, Pierre. *L'empire de la vérité: Introduction aux espaces dogmatiques industriels* (Paris: Fayard, 2001).

Legendre, Pierre. *L'autre bible de l'occident: le monument romano-canonique* (Paris: Fayard, 2009).

Ménestrier, Claude-François. *La philosophie des images* (Paris: Caille, 1682).

Ménestrier, Claude-François. *La philosophie des images enigmatiques* (Paris: Caille, 1694).

Nagel, Barbara. 'The Tyrant as Artist: Legal Fiction and Sexual Violence under Tiberius', *Law and Literature*, 25.2 (2013), 286–310.

Nebrija, Antonio de. *Vocabularium utriusque iuris* (Venice: Zalterium,1612).

Pancirolus, Guido. *Notitia utraque dignitatum* (Lyon: Gabiano, 1608).

Philipot, Thomas. *A Brief Historical Discourse of the Original and Growth of Heraldry, Demonstrating upon what Rational Foundations, that Noble and Heroick Science is Established* (London: Tyler and Holt, 1672).

Quintilian. *Institutio oratoria*, ed. and trans. H. E. Butler (Cambridge, MA: Harvard University Press, 1920).

Selden, John. *Titles of Honor* (London: Corles, 1631).

Stein, Peter. *The Teaching of Roman Law in England around 1200* (London: Selden Society, 1990).

Taliadoros, Jason. *Law and Theology in Twelfth-Century England: The Works of Master Vacarius (c.1115/20–c.1200)* (Turnhout: Brepols, 2006).

Vacarius, *The Liber Pauperum of Vacarius*, ed. F. de Zulueta (London: Selden Society, 1927).

CHAPTER 8

THE MONARCHICAL REPUBLIC, CONSTITUTIONALITY, AND THE LEGAL PROFESSION

PAUL RAFFIELD

Introduction

> First the Musicke of Violenze began to play, during which came in upon the stage sixe wilde men clothed in leaves. Of whom the first bare in his necke a fagot of small stickes, which they all both severally and together assayed with all their strengthes to breake, but it could not be broken by them. At the length one of them plucked out one of the stickes and brake it: And the rest plucking out all the other stickes one after an other did easely breake them, the same being severed: which being conioyned they had before attempted in vaine. After they had this done, they departed the stage, and the Musicke ceased. Hereby was signified, that a state knit in unitie doth continue strong against all force. But being divided, is easely destroyed. As befell upon Duke Gorboduc dividing his land to his two sonnes which he before held in Monarchie.[1]

This was the dumb-show that preceded Act One of *The Tragedy of Ferrex and Porrex*, better known as *Gorboduc*, written by two student members of the Inner Temple, Thomas Norton and Thomas Sackville, and performed during the Inner Temple revels of Christmas 1561–1562 in the presence of Sir Robert Dudley. Shortly afterwards, on 18 January 1562, the play was performed by the same actors (all members of the Inner

[1] Thomas Norton and Thomas Sackville, *The Tragidie of Ferrex and Porrex* (London: Iohn Daye, 1570), sig. A.iii^{r}.

Temple) before the queen, in the Palace of Whitehall. The 'fagot of small stickes' to which the above stage direction refers was a replica of the Roman *fasces lictoriae* ('bundle of the lictors'). Used as a sign of office by subordinate government officials known as lictors, the *fasces* is more generally recognized as a symbol of the Roman Republic, representing the political ideal of strength through unity. The use of republican imagery by Norton and Sackville is peculiar, given that the polity depicted in the play is predicated upon a monarchical model (Gorboduc is described in the *dramatis personae* as 'King of great Brittaine').

It is the purpose of this essay to address the above peculiarity in the context of the Elizabethan monarchical republic, as reflected in the cultural, social, and juridical practices of the English legal profession, and manifested especially in the mimetic rites of the Inns of Court. Of particular relevance to my analysis is the description by Gerard Legh of his visit to the Inner Temple (included in *The Accedens of Armory*, published in 1562) during the revels at which *Gorboduc* was originally performed, locating the play in the institutional landscape of the legal community at the Inns of Court. In a broader theoretical context, I consider the republican themes addressed by *Gorboduc* in relation to contemporaneous political literature (notably Sir Thomas Smith's *De republica Anglorum*) and with reference to a prototypical work of early modern English constitutional theory, *De laudibus legum Angliae*, written by the late fifteenth-century Lancastrian Chief Justice, Sir John Fortescue. Finally, I analyse the play in the context of Renaissance theories surrounding the art of poetic drama, with especial reference to the ideal articulated by Sir Philip Sidney in *The Defence of Poesie*, that poetry performed a crucial political and moral role (in conformity with the didactic purpose of its ancient Greek progenitor), which was to teach as well as to delight.[2]

The Republic of the Inner Temple, 1561–1562

Patrick Collinson employed the term 'monarchical republic' to encapsulate the idea of the 'traditions of localised self-government' in early modern England and the centrality of these traditions to the quotidian governance of the Elizabethan state.[3] At the outset, it is important to emphasize that in Tudor England the word 'republic' was not antithetical to the institution of monarchy; rather, *res publica* referred to the common-weal or state,

[2] Alasdair Macintyre argues convincingly that 'In all those cultures, Greek, medieval or Renaissance, where moral thinking and action is structured according to some version of the scheme that I have called classical, the chief means of moral education is the telling of stories': Alasdair Macintyre, *After Virtue: A Study in Moral Theory* (London: Duckworth, 1981), 114.

[3] Patrick Collinson, 'The Monarchical Republic of Queen Elizabeth I', in *Elizabethans* (London: Hambledon and London, 2003), 31–58, 33. See also, John F. McDiarmid, ed., *The Monarchical Republic of Early Modern England: Essays in Response to Patrick Collinson* (Aldershot: Ashgate, 2007).

literally the 'public thing'. It was this definition that the lawyer and diplomat Sir Thomas Smith contemplated when in 1565 he wrote *De republica Anglorum*, published in 1583. For Smith, belief in the English Republic was totally compatible with the proposition that 'the kingdome of Englande is farre more absolute than either the dukedom of Venice is, or the kingdome of the Lacedemonians was'.[4] Nor was Smith foreseeing the seventeenth-century constitutional and political conflict between Crown and Parliament when he stated that 'The most high and absolute power of the realme of Englande, is in the Parliament.' The absolute power to which Smith here refers is simply the sovereign power to make laws, 'whereupon justlie no man can complain, but must accommodate himself to finde it good and obey it'.[5] In other words, as Mary Dewar notes, the stark assertion by Smith of the absolute power of Parliament is concerned not with the relationship between Crown and Parliament, but rather with 'the relationship between government and the governed'.[6] The English *res publica* or 'Common Wealth', which Smith envisaged, had a king at its head but its body was made up 'of a multitude of free men collected together and united by common accord and covenauntes among themselves'.[7] For all its intimations of the absolute power of king and Parliament, the English commonwealth described by Smith is predicated upon an Aristotelian model, in which the bond of friendship, or alternatively what may be termed civic association, forms the basis of the ideal polis.[8]

The Inner Temple revels of 1561–1562, at which *Gorboduc* was first performed, were attended on 27 December by the herald and scholar Gerard Legh. His description of these festive rites and the concomitant observations which he made, regarding the communitarian ethos of the Inner Temple, form the distinctive conclusion to his book on heraldic emblems, entitled *The Accedens of Armory*. For Legh, honourable members of the Inner Temple were the embodiment of classical virtues, while the Inn itself was a manifestation of the utopian state, whose citizens lived and learnt together in relationships of total concord.[9] Symbolism drawn from the classical world is a salient feature of Legh's account of the revels, in which Sir Robert Dudley played the part of Palaphilos, Constable-Marshall to the goddess Pallas Athena. According to Legh, he met Palaphilos in Temple Church, whereupon the Constable-Marshall 'courtcouslie saluted me saying, for that I was a straunger, and seming by my demeanour a lover of honour I was

[4] Sir Thomas Smith, *De republica Anglorum*, ed. Mary Dewar (Cambridge: Cambridge University Press, 1982), 85. On the functions of the Elizabethan Parliament, see Geoffrey R. Elton, 'Parliament in the Sixteenth Century: Functions and Fortunes', *HJ*, 22 (1979): 255–78; also, Geoffrey R. Elton, *The Parliament of England, 1559–1581* (Cambridge: Cambridge University Press, 1986).

[5] Smith, *De republica*, 78.

[6] Smith, *De republica*, Introduction, 4.

[7] Smith, *De republica*, 57.

[8] Aristotle, *The Nicomachean Ethics*, trans. J. A. K. Thomson (London: Penguin, 2004), 200–1, 8.1, 1155a1–32. Burrow observes of *De republica Anglorum* that its author (despite his claims to the contrary) presents 'a single, Aristotelian model of what a commonwealth suited to the English temperament should be': Colin Burrow, 'Reading Tudor Writing Politically: The Case of *2 Henry IV*', *The Yearbook of English Studies*, 38 (2008): 234–50, 240.

[9] Legh's visit to the Inner Temple is discussed in Peter Goodrich, 'Eating Law: Commons, Common Land, Common Law', *JLH*, 12 (1991): 246–67.

his geste of right'.[10] The Inner Temple was honouring Dudley at the revels for his 'earnest intercession to the Queen', regarding a dispute with the Middle Temple over ownership of one of the Inns of Chancery, Lyon's Inn. Sir William Dugdale records that the Middle Temple had lost valuable land when Somerset House was built and consequently had 'endeavoured to take away Lyons Inne' from the Inner Temple. Dudley's intervention was instrumental in ensuring that Lyon's Inn maintained its affiliation to the Inner Temple. The 'magnificent Christmas' of 1561 (as described by Dugdale)[11] was of unprecedented extravagance, in celebration of the above outcome.

The dispute between the Middle Temple and the Inner Temple is relevant to the argument that the Inns of Court were constituted as discrete, microcosmic republics: they were (and they remain) self-regulating, autonomous institutions, outside the jurisdiction of the Cities of London and Westminster. Collinson has argued that in political terms, early modern England functioned within a monarchical framework as 'a series of overlapping, superimposed communities which were also semi-autonomous, self-governing political cultures'.[12] The Inns of Court may collectively be described as one such political culture, a feature that distinguished them from all others being their extraordinary level of independence from interference by external agents (most notable in this context was the Crown)[13] and the absorption of their members by the royal court. Elevation from the Inns of Court to the royal court was an obvious route to political advancement, and the revels provided a useful forum at which potential 'favourites' might readily be identified.[14] This pragmatic approach to royal patronage was explicitly acknowledged in the Introduction to a dramatic work entitled *The Misfortunes of Arthur* (a dramatization of the mythography surrounding the life and death of King Arthur, written by Thomas Hughes et al.), which was performed for Elizabeth I by members of Gray's Inn on 28 February 1588. The entertainment started with five student members of Gray's Inn being presented to the queen. They were captives of three Muses, who offered them as a gift to Her Majesty, with the following explanation:[15]

A dame there is whom men Astrea terme,
She that pronounceth oracles of lawes,

[10] Gerard Legh, *The Accedens of Armory* (London: Richard Tottel, 1576), sig. 120r.

[11] Sir William Dugdale, *Origines Juridiciales or Historical Memorials of the English Laws* (London: F. and T. Warren, 1666), 150.

[12] Patrick Collinson, '*De republica Anglorum*: Or, History with the Politics Put Back', in *Elizabethans*, 1–29, 16.

[13] An example of such independence was the exemption of the Inns of Court from compliance with Tudor sumptuary laws; see Paul Raffield, *Images and Cultures of Law in Early Modern England: Justice and Political Power, 1558–1660* (Cambridge: Cambridge University Press, 2004), 157–82.

[14] At the Inner Temple revels of 1561–1562, Christopher Hatton, a law student noted for his dancing skills, officiated as 'Master of the Game'; as Dugdale notes in parentheses, 'He was afterwards Lord Chancellour of England' (this despite his lack of experience in the legal profession): *Origines Juridiciales*, 150. On the 'Favourite' in Elizabethan and Jacobean England, see J. H. Elliott and L. W. B. Brockliss, eds., *The World of the Favourite* (New Haven: Yale University Press, 1999).

[15] Nicholas Trotte, 'The Introduction', in *Certaine Devises and shewes presented to her Maiestie by the Gentlemen of Grayes-Inne at her Highnesse Court in Greenwich*, ed. Thomas Hughes et al. (London: Robert Robinson, 1587).

Who to prepare fit servants for her traine,
As by commission, takes up flowring wits.

In Book I of Ovid's *Metamorphoses*, Astraea, Goddess of Justice, fled from mankind's wickedness during the Iron Age, ascended to the heavens, and became the constellation Virgo. As counsellors, the captive law students would of course serve the Goddess of Justice, but the classical symbolism extended beyond a simple representation of the relationship between lawyers and justice. In the iconography that surrounded Elizabeth I, the Virgin Queen of England was strongly associated with Astraea.[16] The implication is clear: Astraea/Elizabeth takes up the 'flowring wits' / law students, preparing them for a life of service to 'her traine': the student counsellors are to become counsellors to the queen. The relevance of the poetic muse to juridical procedure is a theme to which I shall return.

As Wilfrid R. Prest has noted, barristers of the early modern period went by the term 'counsellor', a title they shared with advisers to the monarch. Prest makes the reasonable observation that the shared title may not have been entirely coincidental, given the expectation that common lawyers would be involved in all aspects of public life.[17] It seems that Sir Thomas Elyot envisaged such duality of meaning when, in *The Book Named the Governor*, he asserted that the study of law equipped men with 'so excellent wisedom that throughout all the worlde shulde be founden in no comune weale more noble counsaylours'.[18] Godfrey Goodman, Bishop of Gloucester between 1624 and 1655, was exaggerating, but arguably only slightly, when he stated that lawyers 'became more absolute governors than any legal prince in Christendom'. In the next sentence, he extended the analogy between the power of the legal profession and the absolute rule of princes: 'So that to be a lawyer, which I did conceive to be ministerial, was indeed to be a governor of one's country.' He lists some of the various aspects of national governance in which lawyers played a central and indispensable part. This included fulfilling roles as recorders, town clerks, Justices of the Peace, trustees ('a feoffee in trust'), and executors.[19] Goodman was of course writing from the perspective of a seventeenth-century prelate; but his depiction of lawyers as pivotal and pervasive figures in the governance of the nation was not inaccurate, nor would it have been in Elizabethan England. The infiltration of the legal profession into all areas of public life was facilitated by the statutory recognition of the Bar in 1531, as an independent body of practitioners whose members

[16] 'All duty to gods and to men lay vanquished; and Justice the Maiden was last of the heavenly throng to abandon the blood-drenched earth', Ovid, *Metamorphoses*, trans. David Raeburn (London: Penguin, 2004), 12, 1.148–50. Bate notes that 'Queen Elizabeth was mythologized as the returned Astraea of Virgil's fourth eclogue', William Shakespeare, *Titus Andronicus*, ed. Jonathan Bate (London: Arden Shakespeare, 1995), Introduction, 28. See also, Frances A. Yates, *Astraea: The Imperial Theme in the Sixteenth Century* (London: Routledge and Kegan Paul, 1975), 75–80.

[17] Wilfrid R. Prest, *The Rise of the Barristers: A Social History of the English Bar, 1590–1640* (Oxford: Clarendon Press, 1991), 236.

[18] Sir Thomas Elyot, *The Boke Named the Governour* (London: T. Bertheleti, 1531), sig. 55^{r}.

[19] Godfrey Goodman, *The Court of King James the First*, ed. J. S. Brewer, 2 vols (London: Richard Bentley, 1839), 1.294. Goodman wrote this work in response to Sir Anthony Weldon's *The Court and Character of James I* (published in 1652), but it remained unpublished until the 1839 edition, cited above.

were qualified for public office (the Statute of Sewers, *23 H. 8. cap. 5*), thus enabling the institutional expansion of the legal profession throughout the remainder of the sixteenth century. Colin Burrow convincingly argues that early modern England was effectively governed through an interconnected web of '"networks and affinities", "juridical structures", and "projects"';[20] a model of governance to which Goodman coincidentally alluded, and to which may be added the observation that common lawyers were identifiable in every area of these networks, affinities, and projects. Through their presence and influence at the royal court, they were demonstrably at the centre of the web; but lawyers also expected their brethren to be integral to the governance of the common-weal at all levels: nationally, regionally, and locally.[21]

The foundational skills that enabled lawyers to fulfil their roles as magistrates of the common-weal were of course acquired at the Inns of Court;[22] and (as Legh reflected on his visit to the Inner Temple) the young members of the Inn 'repaire thither to learne to rule'. But the primary motivation for many of these men was not the acquisition of technical, juridical, and forensic skills: these were merely the instruments that facilitated election to the magistracy of England. Indeed, in the thirty pages of *The Accedens of Armory* that constitute Legh's description of his visit, there is no reference to the pedagogical role of the Inn; its author concentrates instead on the themes of communality and amity, all against a backdrop of antiquity in which characters from classical mythography meld into the imagistic realm of the Inner Temple (the utopian nature of which is lent emphasis by Legh's description of the Inn as an 'Iland'). The Inner Temple as described by Legh is a *locus amoenus*, an idyllic 'province ... not great in quantite, but auncient in trewe nobilitie',[23] and immune to the jurisdiction of municipal law that pertains beyond its walls and gates. As with other sixteenth-century texts of a broadly republican (although not anti-monarchical) nature, the human body serves as a symbol of the state (in this instance the symbolic state or empire of law); each organ, tendon, and member working interdependently for the good of the whole:[24]

> That he of you, and you of him, being severall members, maye create and conioyne, one unseperable body, as the whole maye supporte the partes, eche parte serving his place to upholde the whole. For things devided, carye their onelye strength, which being together, double their enduring.

[20] Burrow, 'Reading Tudor Writing Politically', 235.

[21] Prest notes a decision in 1596 of the Benchers of Gray's Inn not to elect a member of the Inn to the Bench, on the grounds that he was unfit 'to be employed at such services of the commonwealth as are expected to be performed by men of such place': quoted in Prest, *Rise of the Barristers*, 236.

[22] On the educational exercises undertaken by law students in the early modern period, see Raffield, *Images and Cultures*, 9–42.

[23] Legh, *Accedens*, sig. 119^{v}.

[24] Legh, *Accedens*, sig. 126^{r}. Included in this genre of 'republican' literature is *The Boke Named the Governour*, at the start of which Elyot states that 'A publike weal is a body lyvyng, compacte or made of sondry astates and degrees of men', sig. 1^{r}.

The image of the 'one unseperable body' recalls the Roman *fasces*, the bundle of sticks deployed in the dumb show before Act One of *Gorboduc*: 'a state knit in unitie doth continue strong against all force. But being divided, is easely destroyed'. Whilst not intrinsically critical of the institution of monarchy per se, there is strong emphasis throughout *The Accedens of Armory* on the virtues of 'politique government', or *ius politicum*; which is to say, government with the assent of the populace.[25] In the canon of sixteenth-century humanist and neo-classical literature, republican sentiments such as those expressed by Legh (and earlier, by Elyot) were incompatible with the Imperium of the monarch. This was an issue of especial importance following the Act of Supremacy 1534 (*26 H.8. cap. 1*), which had the effect of arrogating to the Crown the necessary jurisdictional authority with which to enforce the Imperium.

Legh argued that it was through the communality of the Inn that 'amitie is obtained & continued', and that by being 'norished together in one place', honourable members might develop 'such unitie of minds and manners, as lightly never after is severid, then whiche is nothinge more profitable to the comon weale'.[26] The tone of the above passage is Aristotelian, implying the existence of an active citizenry, motivated in the best interests of the commonwealth. The reference to 'amitie' may be interpreted not only in the context of relations between members of the Inn, but also with regard to the profit that such amity might bring the 'comon weale' of the nation. The ancient political arrangement of *amici principis* (friends or counsellors to the ruler) was indissolubly linked by humanist writers of the sixteenth century to the principle of limited monarchy.[27] Elyot, for example, wrote of the 'mooste pernicious danger', which is faced by those rulers who 'refuse counsaile, or prohibite libertie of speche'. He cited the instance of Plutarch, King of Lacedaemonia, who, when asked how a realm should 'be best and mooste surely kepte', replied: ' "If (saide he) the prince give to his frendes libertie to speake to hym things that be iuste, & neglecteth not the wronges that his subiecte sustaineth.' "[28]

De Laudibus Legum Angliae: In Praise of English Law?

The original formulation of the political relationship between king and mediating friend or counsellor is *The Politics* of Aristotle, in Book 3 of which (as John Guy notes) the

[25] Collinson argues that monarchy should support 'a mixed polity partaking of elements both royal and political, which is to say, popular and representative', Collinson, '*De republica Anglorum*', 16.

[26] Legh, *Accedens*, sig. 119^{v}.

[27] With reference to Elizabeth I, Guy argues that 'friends' of the monarch were also her 'colleagues', who 'support, but also limit, her power', John Guy, 'Tudor Monarchy and its Critiques' in John Guy ed., *The Tudor Monarchy* (London: Arnold, 1997), 78–109, 81.

[28] Elyot, *Boke*, sig. 119^{v}.

friends of the monarch perform the function of subverting 'the legitimacy of monarchy based solely on the sovereign's will'.[29] In the late fifteenth century, the role of counsellor in expounding the political and societal benefits of limited monarchy to a future king was notably represented in *De laudibus legum Angliae*, written by Sir John Fortescue (Lord Chief Justice in the reign of Henry VI), *c.*1470. The relationship of *amicitia*, in which freedom of speech was a *sine qua non* for the relationship between prince and learned counsellor, is a defining feature of *De laudibus*, where the rhetorical device of the dialogue between the Lord Chancellor and Edward, Prince of Wales (both of whom were exiled in France during the Wars of the Roses) serves to humanize the role of *amicus principis*, in the form of the fictionalized version of himself which Fortescue presents to the reader.[30] To some extent, Fortescue's *De laudibus* (and his later work, *De dominio regali et politico*, published in 1715 as *Difference Between an Absolute and Limited Monarchy*, and in 1885 under the title *The Governance of England*) performed the function of a template or prototype for the numerous treatises of the sixteenth century on the generic subject of kingship.[31] *De laudibus* is distinguished from these by its exclusive and particular concern with English kingship and the relationship therein between Crown and common law. A principal theme of this work was the constitutional settlement and especially the role of common law in restricting the power of the monarch (in the early seventeenth century, principles of law as propounded in *De laudibus* were cited as a form of precedent by Sir Edward Coke throughout *The Reports*, in order to imply the constitutional hegemony of common law; for example, in his report of *Postnati. Calvin's Case*, Coke cites Fortescue in support of his thesis that 'the law of nature is part of the law of England').[32] The nature of English government is accordingly 'not only Regal,

[29] Guy, 'Tudor Monarchy', 81. 'Monarchical rulers ... appoint large numbers of men to be their eyes and ears, hands and feet; for such men as are friendly to themselves and to their rule, they make sharers in it', Aristotle, *The Politics*, trans. T. A. Sinclair (London: Penguin, 1992), 228, 3.16, 1287b25.

[30] Fortescue described himself in *De laudibus* as '*Cancellarius Angliae*', although Selden states that: 'It seems, being with Henry VI. driven into Scotland, he was made his Chancellor, the Memory whereof (as it could hardly be otherwise) wants in the Patent Rolls', Sir John Fortescue, *De laudibus legum Angliae*, ed. John Selden (London: R. Gosling, 1737), Preface, i. For a recent discussion of *De laudibus*, see Paul Raffield, *Shakespeare's Imaginary Constitution: Late Elizabethan Politics and the Theatre of Law* (Oxford: Hart Publishing, 2010), 159–73.

[31] See for example, Machiavelli's *The Prince*; Bodin's *Les six livres de la république*; James I's *The Trew Law of Free Monarchies*.

[32] *Postnati. Calvin's Case*, Part 7 (1608) of *The Reports of Sir Edward Coke, Knt. In English*, ed. George Wilson, 7 vols (London: Rivington, 1777), 4.1a, 12b. In addition to Elyot's *Book Named the Governor* and Smith's *De republica Anglorum*, included in the sixteenth-century juristic sub-genre of constitutional and political theory is Christopher St German's *Doctor and Student*, published in two parts between 1528 and 1530. Like *De laudibus*, it employs the dialogue form. Any attempt at law-making which contravened the law of reason was, according to St German, 'void and against justice': Christopher St German, *Dialogues Between a Doctor of Divinity and a Student in the Laws of England*, ed. William Muchall (Cincinnati: Robert Clarke, 1874), 5. On St German and the constitutional sovereignty of the common law, see Alistair Fox and John Guy, *Reassessing the Henrician Age: Humanism, Politics and Reform, 1500–1550* (Oxford: Blackwell, 1986), 100; see also John Guy, *Christopher St German on Chancery and Statute* (London: SS, 1985).

but Political' (*dominium politicum et regale*).[33] The apparent parity between 'regal' and 'political' establishes Fortescue's work as a Bractonian interpretation of limited monarchy: '*Ipse autem rex non debet esse sub homine sed sub deo et sub lege, quia lex facit regem*' ('The king must not be under man but under God and under the law, because law makes the king.')[34] The word 'political' is used by Fortescue to imply not only the consent of Parliament, but also the guidance and wise counsel of the judiciary, who perform a rabbinical or didactic role, as '*Sacerdotes*, (Priests): The Import of the Latin Word (*Sacerdos*) being one who gives or teaches Holy Things.'[35]

The enduring title *De laudibus legum Angliae* was given to Fortescue's work by John Selden, who edited the 1616 edition. It is at least arguable that Selden intended the title to be less a triumphal statement in praise of the superiority of English law over rival jurisdictions, than a topical allusion to the capacity of English law to constrain the absolutist tendencies of James I.[36] Prior to this edition, the first English translation of Fortescue's work was Robert Mulcaster's, published in 1567 under the title *A Learned Commendation of the Politique Lawes of England*.[37] The year of publication (less than ten years after the accession of Elizabeth I) is relevant to the thesis that in the monarchical republic of Elizabethan England, moves were afoot to redress the imbalance of power, initiated by the adherence of Henry VIII (following the 1534 Act of Supremacy) to an anti-Bractonian political philosophy that rendered the king 'under God but not the law, because the king makes the law'.[38] In Henrician England, to use the language of Fortescue, '*dominium regale*' had prospered at the expense of '*dominium politicum*'.

The theme of counselling is established in the Introduction to *De laudibus*, in which Fortescue informs the reader that the young Prince Edward 'applied himself wholly

[33] Fortescue, *De laudibus*, 16; Sir John Fortescue, 'The Governance of England', in *On the Laws and Governance of England*, ed. Shelley Lockwood (Cambridge: Cambridge University Press, 1997), 83–123, 83.

[34] Henry de Bracton, *De legibus et consuetudinibus Angliae* (*c*.1235), trans. Samuel E. Thorne, 4 vols (Cambridge, MA: Belknap Press, 1968–1977), 2.33. Noting the similarity between Fortescue and Bracton, Cromartie remarks that 'What readers found in Fortescue, however, was unimpeachable authority—the word of a Chief Justice—for a range of near-republican opinions', Alan Cromartie, *The Constitutionalist Revolution: An Essay on the History of England, 1450–1642* (Cambridge: Cambridge University Press, 2006), 21.

[35] Fortescue, *De laudibus*, 4–5. Cromartie notes that although Parliament made the laws, its intention was interpreted through the 'judge's conception of what was beneficial for the nation': Alan Cromartie, 'The Constitutionalist Revolution: The Transformation of Political Culture in Early Stuart England', *P&P*, 163 (1999): 76–120, 98.

[36] For example, see the assertion of James I that 'the King is above the law': 'The Trew Law of Free Monarchies', in *King James VI and I: Political Writings*, ed. Johann P. Sommerville (Cambridge: Cambridge University Press, 1994), 75. Barnes argues that, during the reign of James I, *De laudibus* 'seemed a prescription against the infection of tyranny': Thomas G. Barnes, 'John Fortescue', in *Shaping the Common Law: From Glanvill to Hale, 1188–1688*, ed. Allen D. Boyer (Stanford: Stanford University Press, 2008), 46–60, 47. See Glenn Burgess, *Absolute Monarchy and the Stuart Constitution* (New Haven: Yale University Press, 1996).

[37] Barnes notes that in 1513, John Rastell 'had referred descriptively to Fortescue's work as "de laudibus legum Anglie" ': Barnes, 'John Fortescue', 243, n. 2.

[38] Quoted in Guy, 'Tudor Monarchy', 84.

to Martial Exercises'. Occasionally the prince would 'attack and assault the Young Gentlemen his Attendants', for which abuse of his majestic status the Lord Chancellor 'accosts the Prince', gently chiding or rebuking him.[39] Instead of explicitly reprimanding the prince for his despotic conduct, the Lord Chancellor persuades him that, while he is 'right glad' to see him practise the skills of warfare, Prince Edward is destined to be a king rather than a soldier, and that therefore 'I could wish to see You Zealously affected towards the Study of the Laws'.[40] In his depiction of the relationship between the Lord Chancellor and the prince, Fortescue was presenting two archetypes: the wise and benevolent patriarch and the impressionable, impetuous prince (a relationship which Shakespeare was to dramatize to extraordinary effect in *The Second Part of King Henry Fourth*, in the scenes between the Lord Chief Justice and Prince Henry).[41] No such archetypal relationship attended the three successors (four, if the nine-day 'reign' of Lady Jane Grey is included) to Henry VIII, thus complicating the nature of the bond between monarch and counsellor. Edward VI ascended the throne in his minority, rendering it the least problematic of the post-Henrician, Tudor successions: precedent existed for the creation of a council of regency, which would govern until the king achieved his majority. Regarding the accessions of Mary I and Elizabeth I, the issue of gender politics and especially the status of an unmarried queen regnant was thrust to the forefront (to Mary may be attributed the additional factor of her extreme devotion to the Papacy). For the purposes of this essay, I must confine myself to discussion of Elizabeth I, although it is worth noting the particular circumstances surrounding the succession of her two immediate predecessors, as a cumulative effect of these was the consequent discussion both in royal court and Inns of Court circles as to the nature of kingship itself.[42] Such was the case with the Inner Temple revels of 1561–1562, as witnessed in the subject matter of *Gorboduc*.

In 1558, prior to the death of Mary I, John Knox had written and published *The First Blast of the Trumpet Against the Monstrous Regiment of Women*. Described as 'the classic of misogyny', Knox railed therein against the perceived idolatry of rule by a woman: [43]

> And no lesse monstrous is the bodie of that comonwelth, where a woman beareth empire. For ether doth it lack a laufull heade (as in very dede it doth) or els there is an idol exalted in place of the true head.

[39] Fortescue, *De laudibus*, Introduction, lxiv.

[40] Fortescue, *De laudibus*, 1.

[41] See Raffield, *Shakespeare's Imaginary Constitution*, 173–81.

[42] McLaren notes that the notion of the 'citizen' was developed along political and spiritual lines in the reign of Edward VI, 'allowing for the infusion of adult male "virtue" into the body politic during the reign of a minor king'. She further notes that during the reign of Elizabeth I, 'citizens' were interpreted as men, actively involved 'in the service of the monarchy, to protect and defend the common weal in the absence of a (godly) king': Anne McLaren, 'Reading Sir Thomas Smith's *De republica Anglorum* As Protestant Apologetic', *HJ*, 42 (1999): 911–39, 912.

[43] John Knox, *The First Blast of the Trumpet Against the Monstrous regiment of Women* (Geneva: J. Poullain and A. Rebul, 1558), sig. D3^{v}. On Knox and the accession of Elizabeth I, see Alice Hunt, *The*

John Aylmer (who, following his exile in Switzerland, returned to England immediately after the accession of Elizabeth I) responded to the misogynist rant of Knox in *An Harborowe for faithful Subiectes*, in which he robustly defended the principle of female succession to the Crown and strongly rebutted the arguments of Knox. It is noteworthy of *An Harborowe* that Aylmer defended female monarchy not solely on the grounds of the right of the regnant queen to succeed, but rather because 'it is not she that ruleth but the lawes, the executors whereof be her iudges, appointed bi her, her iustices of peace and such other officers'.[44] The constitutional settlement described by Aylmer is a mixed polity, along the lines envisaged by Fortescue. Aylmer termed these constituent parts 'Monarchie', 'Oligarchie' (the nobility), and 'Democratie' (the gentry): 'wherein ech one of these have or shoulde have like authoritie'.[45] Of far greater resonance than the triangular demarcation of power, as sketched by Aylmer above, is his statement that the realm is governed not by the queen, but by the laws, which are administered by the judiciary and other officers of the legal system.[46] Writing in 1559, Aylmer foresaw what would become a characteristic feature of Elizabethan rule: the capacity of the queen's Privy Council to 'contemplate the world and its affairs with some independent detachment', engaging from time to time in what Collinson called 'headless, conciliar government'.[47]

The perils of headless government are writ large in the plot of Norton and Sackville's *Gorboduc*, in which the king:

> divided his realme in his life time to his sonnes, Ferrex and Porrex. The sonnes fell to discention. The yonger killed the elder. The mother that more dearely loved the elder, for revenge killed the yonger. The people moved with the crueltie of the fact, rose in rebellion and slew both father and mother. ... And afterwardes for want of issue of the prince whereby the succession of the crowne became uncertaine, they fell to civil warre.[48]

Norton and Sackville subverted and dramatized the themes of the ideal *res publica*, which Legh addressed in allusive terms in *The Accedens of Armory*. The authors inverted Legh's utopian vision of the idyllic common-weal, offering instead a dystopian

Drama of Coronation: Medieval Ceremony in Early Modern England (Cambridge: Cambridge University Press, 2008), 147–50; also, Guy, 'Tudor Monarchy', 93–4.

44 John Aylmer, *An Harborowe for Faithfull and Trewe Subiectes, against the late blowne Blaste, concerninge the Government of Wemen* (Strasborowe, 1559), sig. H.3^{v}.

45 Aylmer, *An Harborowe*, sig. H.3^{r}.

46 Concerning the reference by Aylmer to Justices of the Peace, it is worth noting the observation of Gleason that 'The justices of the peace symbolize the polity of England', John Howes Gleason, *The Justices of the Peace in England, 1558–1640: A Later Eirenarcha* (Oxford: Clarendon, 1969), 1; see also, the expansive but accurate claim made for JPs by Trevelyan, that they were 'of the utmost significance for the future of our constitution and our law': George Macaulay Trevelyan, *English Social History: A Survey of Six Centuries from Chaucer to Queen Victoria* (London: Longman's, Green, and Co., 1942), 171.

47 Collinson, 'Monarchical Republic', 42.

48 Norton and Sackville, 'The Argument of the Tragedie', in *Ferrex and Porrex*, sig. A.i^{v}.

representation of a headless and fractured state. The play is noteworthy not only in an historical and literary sense, as the first five-act Senecan tragedy to be written in blank verse and performed on the English stage (as well as being a source for Shakespeare's *Titus Andronicus* and *King Lear*); but also, for the audacity of its authors in devising a plot in which the royal succession provided the narrative thrust of the play.[49] In *The Accedens of Armory*, Legh does not refer directly to the performance of *Gorboduc* at the Inner Temple revels of 1561–1562; but he makes a guarded reference to the Tudor royal succession at the start of his account, which testifies to his awareness of the problem, even only three years into the reign of Elizabeth I:[50]

> our most dread soveraigne, the Queenes maiestie that now is, of whome I pray God, if it be his will, to send some fruite, as well to the comfort of her maiestie, as to the greate ioye of all her subiectes, & stable suertie of this realme.

In *Gorboduc*, advice over the succession is offered to the king from a variety of sources: three of the principal roles are described in the *dramatis personae* as counsellors to King Gorboduc and his sons Ferrex and Porrex. These are Arostus, Dordan, and Philander (a fourth character, Eubulus, although described as a secretary to the king, acts *ex officio* as *amicus principis*). The advice to Gorboduc not to divide the realm between his sons was ignored, to devastating effect. Dordan prophetically foresaw the dreadful consequences to the realm: 'I feare the fatall time now draweth on, / When civil hate shall end the noble line / Of famous Brute and of his royal seede.'[51] Insofar as Brutus was the archetype and originary of unitary English kingship, the audience would immediately have associated this reference with Elizabeth I and the Tudor dynasty. So long as a successor to the unmarried, Virgin Queen remained unknown or unnamed, the possibility on her death of descent into civil war was a prescient fear: the precedent lay in the internecine fight for dynastic supremacy between the Houses of York and Lancaster, enacted less than a hundred years before the first performance of *Gorboduc*. That a primary purpose of *Gorboduc* was to address through historical or mythical allusion the issue of the royal succession may be inferred from a report of the performance before the queen at Whitehall, on 18 January 1562, in which the author referred to speculation concerning the possible marriage of Elizabeth to either Robert Dudley or King Eric XIV of Sweden:[52]

[49] In his analysis of *Gorboduc*, Graves argues that 'The political purpose of the drama is confirmed, not only by the occasion and venues of its only two English performances, but also by its theme and content': Michael A. R. Graves, *Thomas Norton: The Parliament Man* (Oxford: Blackwell, 1994), 92. For the argument that *Gorboduc* 'was probably a source for *Titus Andronicus*', see Dympna Callaghan and Chris R. Kyle, 'The Wilde Side of Justice in Early Modern England and *Titus Andronicus*', in *The Law in Shakespeare*, ed. Constance Jordan and Karen Cunningham (Basingstoke: Palgrave Macmillan, 2007), 38–57, 41.

[50] Legh, *Accedens*, sig. 118^{r}.

[51] Norton and Sackville, *Ferrex and Porrex*, sig. D.i^{v}.

[52] BL Add. MS 48023, fol. 359^{v}, quoted *REED*, 2.684. The report is in a collection of the papers of Robert Beale. The 'shadowes' refers to the dumb-shows which preceded each act of the play. See also Henry James and Greg Walker, 'The Politics of *Gorboduc*', *EHR*, 110 (1995): 109–21.

> The shadowes were declared by the Chor[us]. Firste to signyfie unytie, the 2. [second] howe that men refused the certen and toocke the uncerten, wherby was ment that yt was better for the Quene to marye with the L[ord] R[obert] knowen then with the K[ing] of Sweden.

Poet-Lawmakers of the Renaissance

In *The Defence of Poesie* (published in 1595, but written *c.*1583), Sir Philip Sidney expressed great admiration for *Gorboduc*, especially its 'stately speeches, and well sounding Phrases'. He appreciated also the 'notable moralitie' of the play, 'which it doth most delightfully teach; and so obtayne the very end of Poesie'. Sidney thus acknowledged the didactic purpose of poetry, as he did the political function of tragedy, when he asserted that the tragic form 'maketh Kinges feare to be Tyrants'. Sidney was emphatic that poetry was a form of mimesis, representation, or imitation (a definition which he derived from *The Poetics* of Aristotle): 'a speaking picture: with this end, to teach and delight'.[53] In a similar work, by Sidney's near contemporary George Puttenham (a nephew of Sir Thomas Elyot), entitled *The arte of English poesie*, the author reminded the reader of the foundations of western law in the mythography of ancient Greece; the strong implication being that law was originally recorded neither as imperial proclamation nor as statute, but rather as a work of art. Puttenham related the myth of Orpheus, who tamed wild beasts through the medium of harmonious sound, which emanated from his lyre. Thus was recorded through metaphor the civilizing moment when law was introduced into society.[54] Much as Fortescue attributed a sacerdotal role to lawyers, giving or teaching 'Holy Things'; so Puttenham described the ancient poets as 'the first Priests and ministers of the holy misteries'. It was this 'holiness of life' (combined with their gravity, wisdom, and worldly experience) which qualified poets to become:

> the first lawmakers to the people, and the first polititiens, devising all expedient meanes for th'establishment of Common wealth, to hold and containe the people in order and duety by force and vertue of good and wholesome laws, made for the preservation of the publique peace and tranquillitie.[55]

53 Sir Philip Sidney, *The Defence of Poesie* (London: W. Ponsonby, 1595), sigs I.4^{v}, F.3^{v}, C.2^{v}. In the opening few lines of *The Poetics*, Aristotle states that epic poetry, tragedy, comedy, dithyrambic poetry, and music 'are all (taken together) imitations', Aristotle, *The Poetics*, trans. Malcolm Heath (London: Penguin, 1996), 3, 1447a.

54 See Horace, *Ars Poetica*, on the myths of Orpheus and Amphion: 'Poets the first Instructers of Mankind, / Brought all things to their proper, native Use; / Some they appropriated to the Gods, / And some to publick, some to private ends: Promiscuous love by marriage was restrain'd / Cities were built, and usefull Laws were made', *Horace's Art of Poetry Made English by the Right Honourable the Earl of Roscommon* (London: H. Herringman, 1680), 23.

55 George Puttenham, *The Arte of English Poesie* (London: R. Field, 1589), 4, 5.

In the early nineteenth century, the poet Shelley made an identical observation to that made by Puttenham: it was the participation of poets in the eternal and the infinite, together with their understanding and expression of humanity, that qualified them to be 'the institutors of laws, and the founders of civil society'.[56] At the end of the twentieth century, Martha Nussbaum made the same claim: with reference to Walt Whitman's 'By Blue Ontario's Shore', Nussbaum cited the 'poet-judge' as the embodiment of equitable justice.[57] This 'equable man' was the personification of natural equity (or *epieikeia*) in law.[58]

Returning to Sidney's definition of poetry as a 'speaking picture', he was alluding to the capacity of this particular aesthetic form to act upon the visual imagination through the use of metaphor. As S. K. Heninger has noted regarding *The Defence of Poesie*, Sidney anticipated by nearly four hundred years the questions asked by Wittgenstein, regarding the correlation between the word and the pictorial image: 'What really comes before our mind when we *understand* a word?—Isn't it something like a picture? Can't it *be* a picture?'[59] In the mimetic realm of the Inns of Court revels, the speaking picture manifested itself through the medium of poetic drama, written by members of the Inns, as in the case of *Gorboduc*.[60] Norton and Sackville were not unique among their fellow lawyers in attempting to master the poetic craft. I refer above to *Certaine Devises and shewes presented to her Maiestie by the Gentlemen of Grayes-Inne at her Highnesse Court in Greenwich*, which was a collaborative effort between junior and senior members of Gray's Inn. These included Francis Bacon, Francis Flower, William Fulbecke, Thomas Hughes, John Lancaster, Nicholas Trotte, Christopher Yelverton; and a member simply entitled 'Maister Penroodocke', who (with Francis Flower and John Lancaster) 'directed these proceedings at Court'.[61] The Introduction that precedes *The Misfortunes of Arthur* (the principal entertainment in *Certaine Devises and shewes*) articulated concern expressed by some Elizabethan lawyers over the use and purpose of legal language. The three Muses who processed before the queen with their five captive law students

[56] Percy Bysshe Shelley, *A Defence of Poetry* in *Sidney, An Apology For Poetry; Shelley, A Defence of Poetry*, ed. H. A. Needham (London: Ginn and Co., 1931), 65–109, 71.

[57] Martha Nussbaum, *Poetic Justice: the Literary Imagination and Public Life* (Boston, MA: Beacon Press, 1995), 80.

[58] 'Of these States the poet is the equable man': Walt Whitman, 'By Blue Ontario's Shore', in Walt Whitman, *Leaves of Grass*, ed. Jerome Loving (Oxford: Oxford University Press, 2009), 269.

[59] Ludwig Wittgenstein, *Philosophical Investigations*, trans. G. E. M. Anscombe (Oxford: Blackwell, 1953), 54; S. K. Heninger, Jr, *Sidney and Spenser: The Poet as Maker* (University Park: Pennsylvania State University Press, 1989), 224.

[60] The building of the London playhouses from the late 1560s onwards facilitated the emergence of playwriting as a profession. In the reign of James I, elaborate dramatic masques were written by professional dramatists for performance by Inns of Court members at the royal palaces. See for example, Francis Beaumont, *The Masque of the Inner Temple and Gray's Inn, Presented Before His Maiestie in the Banquetting House at White-hall* (1612); George Chapman, *The Memorable Maske of the Two Honorable Houses or Inns of Court; the Middle Temple, and Lyncolns Inne* (1613); Thomas Middleton, *The Inner-Temple Masque or Masque of Heroes* (1619). The above masques are discussed in Raffield, *Images and Cultures*, 124–56.

[61] Hughes et al., *Certaine Devises*, sig. G.2^{r}.

complained that lawyers held poetry 'in most disdaine'; that although lawyers were 'More bound to words then is the poets lore', they spoke in 'A tongue that barbarisme it selfe doth use': the hybridized language of the English law courts, law-French.[62] The Introduction or Prologue to *The Misfortunes of Arthur* was of course part of the entertainment, one of the 'Certaine Devises' presented to the queen, which makes it even more surprising that the occasion should have been used by its lawyer-poet authors as a forum for self-scrutiny and self-criticism. One of the captive law students responded defensively to the Muse, arguing: 'Yet never did we banish nor reject / Those ornaments of knowledge', and that 'With Muses still we intercourse allowe, / T'enrich our state with all their forreine fraight.' The same student suggested even that the practice by lawyers of the poetic craft had not been confined to this one auspicious occasion: 'Not now the first time as your selves best knowe, / Ye Muses sought our services to commaund.'[63] If, as Nussbaum claims, 'only poets are fully equipped to embody norms of judgment'; and further, that the work of poets represents 'equitable judgment[s]',[64] then the importance of poetry, or rather the importance of its ethical and didactic context to the lawyer, becomes self evident.

In 1588, the same year in which *Certaine Devises and shewes* was performed at Greenwich, *The Lawiers Logike*, by Abraham Fraunce, was published. In it, Fraunce (poet, scholar, member of Gray's Inn, and protégé of Sir Philip Sidney) criticized legal education at the Inns of Court for its intrinsic lack of ethical, logical, and structural foundation. The inevitable consequence of such an education, he argued, was to produce legal technocrats (described pejoratively by Fraunce as 'upstart *Rabulae Forenses*'), rather than juristic scholars. In a peculiar echo of the criticism levelled at lawyers by the Muse in *Certaine Devises and shewes*, Fraunce lambasted a legal system the spoken language of which was a bastardized form of Norman French (or 'Hotchpot French', as he termed it): 'having in seaven years space met with six French words, home they ryde lyke brave Magnificoes, and dashe their poore neighboures children quyte out of countenance, with Villen in gros, Villen regardant, and Tenant per le curtesie'.[65] Returning briefly and finally to the Inner Temple revels of 1561–1562 and the fantastical description of these by Legh in *The Accedens of Armory*, the allusions therein to the poetic muse and the centrality of poetry to the institutional life of the Inn are striking. They suggest that the characterization by Fraunce of Elizabethan legal education as 'hard, harsh, unpleasant, unsavoury, rude and barbarous' was neither fair nor entirely accurate.[66] Apart from

62 Hughes et al., *Certaine Devises*, Introduction. On law-French, see J. H. Baker, 'The Three Languages of Common Law', *McGill Law Journal*, 43 (1998): 5–24; also, J. H. Baker, *Manual of Law-French* (Amersham: Avebury, 1979).

63 Hughes et al., *Certaine Devises*, Introduction.

64 Nussbaum, *Poetic Justice*, 80, 81.

65 Abraham Fraunce, *The Lawiers Logike, exemplifying the præcepts of Logike by the practise of the common Lawe* (London: T. Gubbin and T. Newman, 1588), sig. 4^{r-v}. On Fraunce and the 'failure' of common law, see Peter Goodrich, *Languages of Law: From Logics of Memory to Nomadic Masks* (London: Weidenfeld and Nicolson, 1990), 15–52.

66 Fraunce, *Lawiers Logike*, sig. 2^{v}.

celebrating the part played by Dudley in ensuring that the Inner Temple retained its affiliation with Lyon's Inn, it appears that these revels served to solemnize the inauguration of Pegasus as the newly adopted emblem of the Inner Temple; replacing the original emblem of two Knights Templar, sitting astride a warhorse.[67] Legh narrates the myth of Pegasus, emphasizing the correlation between the legendary winged horse and the poetic muse: Pegasus struck the peak of Mount Helicon with its hoof, thereby uncovering the waters of the Hippocrene, the source of poetic inspiration. Relating the myth to the Inner Temple and its lawyer-poets, Legh states that the inspirational waters burst their banks, reaching distant countries, and washing over foreign 'Temples, dedicate to Godes, as places meete for Pallas Muses, to inhabite and make there pastance'.[68]

It is noteworthy in relation to discussion of both an aesthetics of Elizabethan legal language and the poetic imagination of common lawyers, that on 29 November 1561, less than one month before Legh visited the Inner Temple, the Chief Justice of the Common Pleas (Sir James Dyer) and six of his judicial brethren, 'by the queen's command assembled at Serjeant's Inn in Fleet-Street, to confer together in order to understand the law in a certain case'.[69] The case in question was the *Case of the Dutchy of Lancaster*, and the salient issue of law was whether the Crown was bound by the terms of a lease made by Edward VI during his minority. The decision of the court that the queen could not avoid the terms of the lease made by her half-brother, 'by reason of his nonage', was based upon the metaphysical phenomenon of the king's two bodies: 'what the king does in his body politic cannot be invalidated or frustrated by any disability in his natural body.'[70] Much has been written about this case since Ernst H. Kantorowicz wrote his magisterial work on the subject of medieval political theology, *The King's Two Bodies*;[71] but commentators tend to overlook the fact that Dyer and his fellow judges employed the visual imagery of the two conjoined bodies as a means of representing the principle that, like her subjects, the queen was accountable to law, as interpreted by her judges. In *Willion v Berkley*, heard in Trinity term 1561, only a few months before the *Case of the Dutchy of Lancaster*, the argument that the body natural of the king was subsumed by the body politic was rejected by a majority of the judges; Anthony Brown, J. stating that 'the person of the

[67] Pearce accredits Legh with the adoption by the Inner Temple of the heraldic device of Pegasus: Robert A. Pearce, *A Guide to the Inns of Court and Chancery* (London: Butterworths, 1885), 219–20. On the iconography of the Inner Temple, see Sir George Buc, *The Third Universitie of England. Or A Treatise of the Foundations of All the Colledges, Auncient Schooles of Priviledge, and of Houses of Learning, and Liberall Arts, within and above the Most Famous Cittie of London.* (London: Thomas Adams, 1615), 971–3.

[68] Legh, *Accedens*, sig. 118^{v}.

[69] *Case of the Dutchy of Lancaster, The Commentaries or Reports of Edmund Plowden*, 2 vols (Dublin: H. Watts, 1792), 1.212.

[70] Plowden, *Case of the Dutchy of Lancaster*, 1.213.

[71] Ernst H. Kantorowicz, *The King's Two Bodies: A Study in Medieval Political Theology* (New Jersey: Princeton University Press, 1957); for recent discussions of Kantorowicz, see Lorna Hutson, 'Not the King's Two Bodies: Reading the "Body Politic" in Shakespeare's *Henry IV, Parts 1 and 2*', in *Rhetoric and Law in Early Modern Europe*, ed. Victoria Kahn and Lorna Hutson (New Haven: Yale University Press, 2001), 166–98; Raffield, *Shakespeare's Imaginary Constitution*, 88–101.

king shall not rule the estate in the land, but the estate in the land shall rule the person of the king'.[72] These and other cases heard during the 1560s illustrate the manner in which the poetic imagination of the judiciary was directed towards representing the constitutional theory of limited monarchy. In the Elizabethan monarchical republic, the Crown was subject to law, the purpose of which was 'to relieve the people from trouble, and to take away mischief from them'.[73]

Bibliography

Barnes, Thomas Garden. 'John Fortescue', in *Shaping the Common Law: From Glanvill to Hale, 1188–1688*, ed. Allen D. Boyer (Stanford: Stanford University Press, 2008), 46–60.

Buc, Sir George. *The Third Universitie of England. Or a Treatise of the Foundations of all the Colledges, Auncient Schooles of Priviledge, and of Houses of Learning, and Liberall Arts, within and above the Most Famous Cittie of London* (London: 1615).

Collinson, Patrick. 'The Monarchical Republic of Queen Elizabeth I', in *Elizabethans*, ed. Patrick Collinson (London: Hambledon and London, 2003), 31–58.

Cromartie, Alan. *The Constitutionalist Revolution: An Essay on the History of England, 1450 1642* (Cambridge: Cambridge University Press, 2006).

Fortescue, Sir John. *De laudibus legum angliae*, ed. John Selden (London: 1737).

Fortescue, Sir John. 'The Governance of England', in *On the Laws and Governance of England*, ed. Shelley Lockwood (Cambridge: Cambridge University Press, 1997), 83–123.

Goodrich, Peter. 'Eating Law: Commons, Common Land, Common Law', *The Journal of Legal History*, 12 (1991): 246–67.

Graves, Michael A. R. *Thomas Norton: The Parliament Man* (Oxford: Blackwell, 1994).

James, Henry and Greg Walker. 'The Politics of "Gorboduc"', *English Historical Review*, 110 (1995): 109–21.

Kantorowicz, Ernst H. *The King's Two Bodies: A Study in Medieval Political Theology* (Princeton: Princeton University Press, 1957).

Legh, Gerard. *The Accedens of Armory* (London: 1576).

McDiarmid, John F., ed. *The Monarchical Republic of Early Modern England: Essays in Response to Patrick Collinson* (Aldershot: Ashgate, 2007).

Norton, Thomas and Thomas Sackville. *The Tragidie of Ferrex and Porrex* (London: 1570).

Puttenham, George. *The Arte of English Poesie* (London: 1589).

Raffield, Paul. *Images and Cultures of Law in Early Modern England: Justice and Political Power, 1558–1660* (Cambridge: Cambridge University Press, 2004).

Raffield, Paul. *Shakespeare's Imaginary Constitution: Late Elizabethan Politics and the Theatre of Law* (Oxford: Hart Publishing, 2010).

Sidney, Sir Philip. *The Defence of Poesie* (London: 1595).

Smith, Sir Thomas. *De republica anglorum: A Discourse on the Commonwealth of England* [1583] ed. Mary Dewar (Cambridge: Cambridge University Press, 1982).

72 Plowden, *Willion v Berkley, Commentaries*, 1.245.

73 Plowden, *Hill v Grange, Commentaries*, 1.178, *per* Broke, C. J.

CHAPTER 9

THE LEGAL MASQUE

Humanity and Liberty at the Inns of Court

MARTIN BUTLER

Masques and the Ideology of the Law

The winter of 1622/3 saw two conflicting pieces of Christmas festivity in London. On 19 January the court witnessed Ben Jonson's masque *Time Vindicated to Himself and to His Honours*, a show that was in essence a defence of censorship. King James was in the middle of a crisis: he was being urged to intervene in the European war in support of his daughter Princess Elizabeth and her husband, the Palatine Prince, who had been expelled from their hereditary lands in Germany by their Habsburg enemies in what was the beginning of the Thirty Years' War. But James was reluctant to row back on his diplomacy, which had centred on détente with Spain, or to involve himself in a conflict that was likely to be expensive and unpredictable. He also did not take kindly to being told what policies to follow. The preceding year had seen a tide of newsbooks, sermons, satires, and gossip urging him to change course, and he took action against this by issuing directions to preachers, limiting the topics for their sermons, and publishing proclamations against 'the excess of lavish and licentious speech in matters of state'.[1] In *Time Vindicated*, Jonson dramatized the conflict between stable, peace-loving kingship and its opponents. The antimasquers were a rabble of citizens, individually named Eyes, Ears, and Nose, and collectively labelled The Curious, who stirred up trouble by talking freely about public affairs. 'The Time's now come about', they boast, 'And promiseth all liberty. / We shall do what we list, / Talk what we list, / And censure whom we list and how we list.' Together they plan to do 'Something that is unlawful, / Ay, or unreasonable, / Or impossible. / Let't be uncivil enough, you hit us right.'[2] Eventually The Curious were

[1] *Stuart Royal Proclamations: James I*, ed. J. F. Larkin and P. L. Hughes (Oxford: Oxford University Press, 1973), 495–6, 519–21.

[2] *CWBJ*, 5.622, 628. For discussion, see M. Butler, *The Stuart Court Masque and Political Culture* (Cambridge: Cambridge University Press, 2006), 262–4.

expelled from the masque, but the only protection from their impertinence was James's prudence in limiting free speech. The masque presented a choice between a world given over to mindless disruption, and one where the king guaranteed the authority of law by policing what men could think and speak.

Only a few days earlier, though, two of the Inns of Court had hosted some very different festivals, as reported by the letter-writers Joseph Mede and John Chamberlain. That Christmas the Middle Templars elected a lord of misrule, and he held a feast for his followers. In the course of this the Christmas lord began 'a health to the distressed Lady Elizabeth, and having drunk, kissed his sword, and laying his hand upon it, took an oath to live and die in her service', a ceremony that was then repeated around the room. When this display of loyalty to the Protestant cause came to the ears of the real king, he was said to be 'highly displeased'.[3] Meanwhile, at midnight on Twelfth Night, the gentlemen of Lincoln's Inn concluded their own Christmas revelry by firing off some ordnance they had borrowed from the Tower of London. This woke the king at Whitehall, who took it for an insurrection and cried out 'Treason, treason!' The court was raised, and the Earl of Arundel ran into the royal bedchamber with his sword drawn to protect the king's person.[4] These pieces of unruly behaviour by lawyers, one a political demonstration, the other a case of innocent high spirits, document the climate of paranoia which Jonson's masque was seeking to damp down, but they also point to the potentially contradictory valences of revelry within Whitehall and without. To be sure, the characters in Jonson's antimasque were vulgar citizens, and their low status does not really correspond to that of the gentlemen enjoying their pleasures in the Inns of Court. After all, Jonson had many friends in these societies. Nonetheless, the masque's anxiety about liberty, its representation of the problems posed by an emerging public sphere, and its focus on the borderline where satire turns into subversion all point to the very different functions which, in these two spaces, could be played by festivity, and masquing in particular. When in 1616 Jonson dedicated his comedy *Every Man Out of His Humour* to the Inns of Court, he called them 'the noblest nurseries of humanity and liberty in the kingdom'.[5] By his terms 'humanity' and 'liberty', he was probably alluding to the boisterous and ritualized cultural play staged by the lawyers every Christmas; yet in 1623 it was precisely the freedom of these times of privilege which had come to seem problematic.

In the festival texts which Jonson prepared to celebrate the new king's accession in 1604, he emphasized that James needed to rule with respect for law. In the pageants publicly presented to James as he arrived at Westminster, Jonson highlighted the significance of Westminster Hall as:

> the judging chair
> To this thy special kingdom; whose so fair
> And wholesome laws in every court shall strive

[3] *REED*, 2.697 [all quotations modernized]. This volume is a nearly complete anthology of all records and texts relating to Inns of Court revels.

[4] *REED*, 2.697–8.

[5] *CWBJ*, 1.427.

By equity and their first innocence to thrive.
The base and guilty bribes of guiltier men
Shall be thrown back, and Justice look as when
She loved the earth, and feared not to be sold
For that which worketh all things to it, gold.[6]

This expectation that James would reform the administration of law and be a fountainhead of equity was given a constitutional twist in the *Panegyre* offered by Jonson to James the next day, to mark the occasion of his first meeting with Parliament. This poem imagines James processing from Whitehall to Westminster and being secretly tutored in legal expertise by Themis (the ancient goddess of right, and mother of Dike, goddess of justice):

She then remembered to his thought the place
Where he was going, and the upward race
Of kings preceding him in that high court;
Their laws, their ends, the men she did report …
She showed him who made wise, who honest acts;
Who both, who neither; all the cunning tracts
And thriving statutes she could promptly note;
The bloody, base and barbarous she did quote;
Where laws were made to serve the tyran' will;
Where sleeping they could save, and waking kill[.][7]

The new king's duty to law is staged in the secret conversation that he has with Themis. As Themis makes clear, not all laws are good, and a wise ruler will pursue some diligently and allow others quietly to lapse. Nonetheless, the crucial point is that James is a constitutional monarch, whose authority is enshrined in his Parliament's acts and statutes.

In the context of most court festivity, however, this was not a theme that received much air time. On the contrary, in the masques performed at Whitehall every Christmas, the king's power was typically represented as exceptional and beyond restraint. In the masques' fables, the monarch calmed storms, defeated monsters, or brought about a premature spring by his simple presence. Generally court masques proclaimed kingly power as miraculous and, for the sake of their fictions, capable of suspending the rules of everyday. So, for example, in *The Masque of Blackness*, danced in 1605 to celebrate the Union of the kingdoms, it is the king's unique double body, simultaneously King of England and King of Scotland, that brings into being the miracle of British identity. Lawyers and constitutional experts in Parliament had worried about the proposed Union's legal implications—as Sir Edwin Sandys put it in the debates on the new name, 'By what laws shall this "Britain" be governed?'[8]—but *The Masque of*

[6] *CWBJ*, 2.460.

[7] *CWBJ*, 2.479.

[8] *Journal of the House of Commons*, 1.187.

Blackness represented that constitutional shift as already accomplished in the marvellous person of the king. Similarly, in 1612, in the wake of a fractious assembly in which James failed to get the financial settlement he wanted, and in which lawyers like Richard Martin and John Hoskyns led the attack on his power to levy impositions, Jonson found himself, in the masque *Love Restored*, writing in praise of unparliamentary taxation. In this show, the money god Plutus turns up at Whitehall and complains about the court's wastefulness, but he is re-educated by Cupid, god of Love, who urges subjects to give generously to the king's needs. In an overt allusion to the device of using benevolences or 'forced loans' to raise money, Plutus is told that James will 'never crave / His aids, but force him as a slave'.[9] Of course, the implication of these masques is always that James has internalized the principles of law and can be trusted to rule himself, or can at least be made to respect them. Restrictions on free speech are defensible in *Time Vindicated* because the king understands what the masque calls the 'difference 'twixt liberty and licence'.[10] Nonetheless, on festival occasions, the limits and meanings of liberty were always implicitly in contention.

The Symbolic Functions of Inns of Court Revelry

In masques and revelry generated from within the Inns of Court, the perspective was rather different, for entertainments mounted by the lawyers happened in a more open-ended context, where legal themes could be foregrounded, highlighted, and debated. They acted as vehicles for promoting respect towards the prestige of the legal profession, as well as for voicing the ideology and values to which, as a group, the lawyers were attached. How far these revels amounted to an effective counterweight to the principles asserted in festivities emanating from Whitehall is an interesting question. In a recent book, Paul Raffield has argued that Inns of Court festivity was openly confrontational, and functioned as the public centrepiece of an emerging legal counter-culture focused on the societies. He suggests that Inns of Court masques created 'a pictorial vision of the commonwealth as envisaged by the practitioners of common law', representing 'the intellectual and moral primacy of common law' as 'sacred and incontrovertible', and offering a symbolism which consciously asserted 'the claim of common lawyers to represent, interpret and uphold the Ancient Constitution'.[11] But it seems doubtful that the lawyers' revels were ever as programmatic as this implies. For all that these festivities tended to follow similar patterns, their structure and ideology were often muddled and

9 *CWBJ*, 4.210; Butler, *The Stuart Court Masque*, 205–7.

10 *CWBJ*, 5.627.

11 P. Raffield, *Images and Cultures of Law in Early Modern England* (Cambridge: Cambridge University Press, 2004), 144, 156.

incoherent, and the affirmation of law was by no means their sole or primary purpose. Raffield's interpretation also assumes a straightforward opposition between Whitehall and the Inns of Court, and gives little weight to the social and cultural interplay between the two spaces. It might be truer to see festive culture as permitting an ongoing dialogue between the crown and the legal community, which enabled the lawyers to develop their professional relationship with Whitehall while establishing their own distinctive socio-cultural identity and, in some cases, seizing opportunities for personal advancement.

First, it is necessary to distinguish between two different kinds of festivity. On the one hand there were the regular celebrations that were held by the students at Christmas under the leadership of seasonally elected lords of misrule, some but not all of which led to full-blown masques. These were the events in which would-be lawyers mimicked forms of political authority by setting up their own pretend courts, appointing officers, counsellors, heralds and champions, and holding parliaments, trials, diplomatic missions, revels, dances, and occasionally acts of warfare in an extended game that satirized but also rehearsed the realities of political life. These festivals were both ambiguous parody of and homage to the responsibilities which some of the participants aspired to assume for real. As a 1540 report by Nicholas Bacon and others put it, the students' mock-courts imitated such rules 'as are exercised in the King's highness' house, and other noble men, and this is done only to the intent that they should in time come to know how to use themselves'[12]—that is, playful imitation functioned as practice for their later careers. Gerard Legh similarly wrote in 1561 that members of the Inns of Court 'repair thither to learn to rule, and obey by law, to yield their fleece to their prince and commonweal', and also to 'use all other exercises of body and soul whereunto nature most aptly serveth, to adorn by speaking, countenance, gesture and use of apparel, the person of a gentleman'.[13] The internalization of social skills through game-playing went hand in hand with acquiring the professional abilities of a lawyer.

Such lively festivals created scope for controversy, and typically the conflicts they provoked were either internal, directed at the Benchers, the senior members who governed the Inns in times outside Christmas, or civic, directed against the representatives of London power, the mayor and corporation, who were caught up in the rowdiness when the revellers' activities spilled out into the streets. The Inns' parliament books are full of Benchers' complaints about seasonal 'disorder and excess' and directives trying to limit its impact, particularly the disruption caused when Christmas princes attempted to extract money and homage from reluctant students by beating down their chamber doors.[14] In 1591 Richard Martin and eight other Middle Templars were fined £20 and put out of commons for making 'outcries in the night', taking money 'of diverse gentlemen of this house in name of the lord of misrule his rent', and using 'reproachful and

[12] *REED*, 1.62. Report by Nicholas Bacon, Thomas Denton, and Robert Cary, printed in Edward Waterhouse, *Fortescutus Illustratus* (1663), 546.

[13] Gerard Legh, *The Accidens of Armoury*, 1561; quoted in *REED*, 2.367.

[14] From many instances, see *REED*, 1.109, 218. Raffield incorrectly assumes that all members of the Inns took part in the revels. The Benchers participated in what were termed the 'old measures', the

contemptuous words' to the Benchers. There were 'throngs and tumults' at Gray's Inn in 1594, and 'disorder and scurrility' at the Inner Temple in 1611. In 1614, four Middle Templars were fined for nocturnal riots, 'striking up of drums and blaring of horns, as well within the house as in the streets'. Christmas kings also liked to adopt provocative names, such as Jack Straw or the King of Cockneys, which signalled their disregard for authority, so much so that in 1519 the Benchers of Lincoln's Inn suppressed Jack Straw's adherents and banned further use of the name.[15]

As for civic skirmishes, it was a joke maintained throughout the revels that Christmas princes pretended suzerainty over the local manors, demanding homage from 'Bartholomeus de Bloomsbury', 'Hieronymus Paludensis de Knightsbridge', 'Lucy Negro Abbess [i.e. brothel-keeper] de Clerkenwell', and the like,[16] and offering their followers protection against 'the savage and barbarous incursions of the vulturine ballives and treacherous ambushments of the harpeian catchpoles' (i.e. sheriffs and sergeants).[17] However, actual forays beyond the walls could run into trouble. Several London mayors were admitted to membership of the Inns under the sponsorship of Christmas lords, but a lord of misrule might find himself languishing in jail for offences on the streets—as in 1628, when the Inner Temple Christmas prince had to apologize for breaking into city houses while pretending to levy rents. Confronted by the mayor, he had tried to pull rank by claiming his jurisdiction was superior, but found himself committed to the Counter. As Joseph Mede sardonically commented, 'the interview of princes is never without danger of some ill accident'.[18]

The other distinctive festivities were the grand ceremonial masques which were occasionally taken to court, some—like *Proteus and the Adamantine Rock*, the culminating event in the 1594–1595 Gray's Inn season—devised when the student revelry was particularly elaborate, but more commonly arranged as special one-offs by the whole fellowship, and funded by a general tax on all members. These occasions received the greatest publicity and left behind some remarkable texts, especially in the years after 1603. They were, though, comparatively infrequent, since they required the cooperation of the entire Inn or collaboration between Inns, and so were difficult to mount, and because they were costly, and so were only staged when there was an incentive for an eye-catching public statement. The most famous such shows were the two mounted for Princess Elizabeth's wedding in 1613 (*The Memorable Masque*, otherwise known as *The Masque of the Middle Temple and Lincoln's Inn*, and *The Masque of the Inner Temple and Gray's Inn*) and *The Triumph of Peace* staged in 1634 as a collaborative effort between all

ceremonial dances traditionally associated with Christmas (which may have been little more than walking around the hall), but the Christmas sports were largely the initiative of the students.

15 *REED*, 1.47, 118–19, 145, 177; 2.396–7.

16 These are titles from the 1594–1595 *Gesta Grayorum*; a similar list can be found for the 1617–1618 Gray's Inn revels (*REED*, 2.488–9, 493–6).

17 *REED*, 2.489.

18 *REED*, 2.699.

four societies to apologize for the offence given by the publication of *Histriomastix*, written by one of their number, William Prynne.

Each of these celebrations was staggeringly expensive—the Middle Temple budgeted £850 for its share of *The Memorable Masque*—and left behind a trail of debt in the account books. In 1613 Gray's Inn was threatening members with loss of chambers if they didn't cough up their euphemistically named 'voluntary contributions', and Lincoln's Inn was still chasing unpaid bills a year later.[19] Unsurprisingly, when in 1614 it was hinted at court that the lawyers should offer some masque in honour of the wedding of the king's favourite, the Earl of Somerset, the societies declined, explaining that 'their expenses [had] been already extraordinary in shows, which they performed with greater affection than they can afford'.[20] *The Triumph of Peace* was even more expensive, and cost more than the two earlier shows put together; in some Inns the masque money was still being pursued five years later.[21] The great advantage of having a Christmas prince was that he often paid for his own revels: the Inner Templars acknowledged in 1640 that their prince usually kept 'a good table at his own proper charge for the honour of the house in the entertainment of strangers, whereby the charge of the house is much lessened'.[22] The Cornish gentleman Richard Vivian, who was Middle Temple Prince in 1636, staged a masque for Henrietta Maria and her German nephews, Princes Charles Louis and Rupert, as part of his festivities. For this he paid £3,000, which was half the inheritance he had just received on his father's death. Vivian's show earned him a knighthood, but as Sir John Finet commented, *Vix Priamus tanti*.[23]

The symbolic function of the student revels was partly celebration of the legal profession but, more broadly, the creation of a space in which a newly emerging elite urban society could establish and explore its cultural identity. For the students, the revels were a holiday from otherwise dry studies. So in *The Masque of Mountebanks* (Gray's Inn, 1617–1618) the fiction is that the performers are knights who have been imprisoned by the enchanter Obscurity in his study, but are released to enjoy delights due to youth. With similar irony, Francis Beaumont's parody 'Grammar Lecture' (written for the Inner Temple *c.*1605) divides its audience into 'revellers' and 'plodders'. Notwithstanding the emphasis on liberty, the revels texts often have a student-focused obsession with their studies, constantly intruding heavy-handed in-jokes and legal humour. At its best, the humour on display must have demanded an answering quickness of mind from its hearers—as with John Hoskyns's 'Fustian answer made to a tuftaffata speech' spoken in

19 *REED*, 1.173–4, 183.

20 Letter of Samuel Calvert, 14 December 1613; quoted in *A Book of Masques in Honour of Allardyce Nicoll*, ed. T. J. B. Spencer and S. W. Wells (Cambridge: Cambridge University Press, 1967), 153.

21 The total bill was £5013, divided equally between the four Inns, though Bulstrode Whitelocke asserted that the public display added £10,000, since the suits worn by the hundred gentlemen walking in the procession through the streets each cost £100. See T. Orbison, 'The Middle Temple documents relating to James Shirley's *The Triumph of Peace*', *Malone Society Collections*, 12 (1983): 40–2.

22 *REED*, 1.358.

23 'Priam [and all of Troy] was not worth such a price': Ovid, *Heroides*, 1.4 (*REED*, 1.343). Finet was Master of Ceremonies at Whitehall.

Le Prince D'Amour (the Middle Temple Christmas revels of 1597–1598), which became famous for its witty inversion of all the standard tropes of rhetoric. At its worst—as in the elephantine legal jokes of *Gesta Grayorum* (the Gray's Inn season of 1594–1595), the deliberately tedious address to the jury in *Le Prince D'Amour*, and the resoundingly unfunny paradoxes devised for the Gray's Inn revels of 1617–1618—the texts assume an audience which took pleasure in poking fun at drily technical jargon or arcane points of legal practice. This aspect of the festivity has not travelled well historically.

Moving beyond the law, the revels texts also celebrated the aspiration of their performers and the challenging metropolitan landscape in which they found themselves.[24] In the two sets of spectacular festivals staged in the 1590s, *Gesta Grayorum* and *Le Prince D'Amour*, the performances acted as points of intersection between different modes of discourse and social behaviour. With their mock-courts, retinues of officials, and parody orders of knighthood—all with elaborately proclaimed codes of behaviour and fines for transgression—and with their orations, dances, debates, fictional quests, and fake trials, these intricate sequences of shows positioned their participants in a border zone where legal learning crossed over with the constantly shifting conduct of modern manners. They brought together the chivalric ethos of an aristocratic honour community, the neoplatonic cult of the sovereign, the professional expertise of the lawyer's craft, satire on the educational grind, and an obsession with fashions, consumerism, and etiquette which testified to how far the termers' horizons extended beyond law-books. Parody of legal and political forms was entangled with rules about fashions, the use of tobacco, love-locks, and toothpicks, about oaths, gambling, and debts, and especially about women—the best way to court them, satisfy them sexually, and avoid the dangers of cosmetics, over-commitment, and the clap. A deep vein of misogyny ran through these revels, articulating, with often coarsely scatological vulgarity, the termers' sexual and social anxieties. The implied target of their satire was the incompetent gentleman, who was dogged by money problems, did not know how to dress or conduct himself, and above all was inadequate in bed, either trapped by ugly women or unable to acquire a mistress.

So too the ceremonial mode was frequently aggressive, marking out symbolic boundaries by staging the participants' self-display and competitiveness. Often this was merely playful, as when a sorcerer was put on trial in *Gesta Grayorum* for supposedly disrupting the games on their most public night. Sometimes, though, the violence was serious, as when John Davies scandalized onlookers by physically assaulting the Prince D'Amour, Richard Martin, a misdemeanour which led to his expulsion from the Middle Temple. Davies had sought to promote himself in the revels by arrogantly adopting the festive pseudonym Erophilus (= the lover of desire), a title used by the Earl of Essex in the 1595 Accession Day show *Love and Self-Love*, but was unkindly nicknamed Stradilax (= straddle-arse, a vulgar allusion to his way of walking) by the other revellers. Davies's fatal

[24] For an excellent discussion, see Michelle O'Callaghan, *The English Wits: Literature and Sociability in Early Modern England* (Cambridge: Cambridge University Press, 2007), 10–34.

response to his chaffing shows how the symbolic conflicts in these rough games acted out tensions and humiliations which could have painfully personal consequences.[25]

At their most elaborate, the revels percolated into the ceremonial life of the Elizabethan court, the pretended authority of the Christmas prince existing in a rich relationship of challenge and compliment with that of the real sovereign, especially when his rule impinged on her own ceremonial. A special frisson was felt in *Gesta Grayorum* when the prince and his retinue attended a banquet given by the Lord Mayor, 'the streets being thronged and filled with people to see the gentlemen as they passed by, who thought there had been some great prince, in very deed, passing through the city'; and again at the prince's return from a voyage to 'Muscovy', when he was greeted by cannon shot from the Tower at the queen's command.[26] This frisson was especially crucial to *Le Prince D'Amour*, in which the proclamation of the prince's authority, pronounced at the outset by his chivalric champion, was answered by a second champion speaking for the Lady of the Fortunate Island, who objected that his title was usurped:

> I tell thee, sir knight, that the truly regal title of Prince d'Amours, wherewith thou gildest thy tyrannical lord, is the essential cognizance of my dread sovereign. She it is who, though the beams of her majesty infuse awe and reverence, yet tempers the dazzling rays thereof with the gracious aspect of bounty. Other princes accounting regal power chiefly to consist in the enlarging of their territories; [but] she, by uniting men's hearts unto her, hath made herself a mind-subduing conqueror.[27]

This collision over jurisdiction in the first day's speeches was left unresolved, and implicitly powered the dynamic of the succeeding events. It foregrounded the underlying structural frame at work in the entire revels, the tension between the young lawyers' unruly aspiration and the sovereign's benevolent rule.

The same dynamic is at work in *Gesta Grayorum*, in the masque which, at the end of the festivities, the revellers took to court. The fiction of *Proteus and the Adamantine Rock* was that the Christmas prince and his followers had been captured by Proteus, the god of mutability and the changeable mundane world. Their prison was a magically magnetic stone, the very lodestone which drags iron towards the polestar, but they were liberated from it by the queen's superior gravitational pull. The masque informs Proteus that, since Elizabeth is safely installed in men's hearts, her erotic magnetism defeats any power which would seduce them from her:

> What can your iron do without arms of men?
> And arms of men from hearts of men do move …
> Lo, Proteus, then, the attractive rock of hearts …

25 On Sir John Davies, see also Chapter 6 in this volume.

26 *REED*, 2.413–14, 424.

27 *REED*, 2.442.

Your rock claims kindred of the polar star,
Because it draws the needle to the north,
Yet even that star gives place to Cynthia's rays[.]

This fiction dramatizes the tensions immanent in royal service, staging the lawyers' contradictory drives towards self-promotion and submission, projected in the opposing powers of Proteus and Elizabeth. The lawyers' futures depend on the queen's patronage, and while they find their vocation in offering her love and service, it requires them to forfeit their liberty on a higher plane. 'Yield victory, and liberty, and thanks', the masque tells Proteus; 'Shadows before the shining sun do vanish ... / And counsellors of false principality / Do fade in presence of true majesty.'[28] The speeches for this show were written by Francis Davison, whose father was Essex's unsuccessful candidate for the secretaryship of state. Other speeches performed earlier in the revels were by Francis Bacon, who was Essex's similarly unsuccessful candidate for the post of Attorney General. The involvement of these two aspiring gentlemen suggests how the masque and revels alike were enmeshed in desires and frustrations which shaped the lives of the whole Elizabethan political class.[29]

The Baconian Masque

After these ambitious festivals, it would be fifteen years before the Inns of Court attempted anything so eye-catching again. What transformed the situation was the vogue for masquing at Stuart Whitehall, where grand Christmas festivity was pursued more vigorously than under Elizabeth, and masques acquired a high profile as mirrors of crown policy. The decade of the 1610s, especially the years between the Palatine marriage in 1613 and the outbreak of European warfare in 1619, was the heyday of masquing by the termers. Unlike the politically divided 1600s and 1620s, the 1610s were a time of relative constitutional consensus, a circumstance which encouraged a greater degree of communication between festivities at Whitehall and the Inns of Court. Six Inns of Court masques survive from this period, four of which were danced at court, as was at least one other show for which no text survives.[30] The vulgarity of the termers' humour went down well at James's Whitehall—the court was reported as enjoying the 'witty ribaldry'

[28] *REED*, 2.432–4.

[29] This point is made by Richard McCoy, 'Lords of Liberty: Francis Davison and the Cult of Elizabeth', in *The Reign of Elizabeth I: Court and Culture in the Last Decade*, ed. J. A. Guy (Cambridge: Cambridge University Press, 1995), 212–28. See also McCoy's 'Law Sports and the Night of Errors: Shakespeare and the Inns of Court', and Bradin Cormack's 'Locating *The Comedy of Errors*: Revels Jurisdiction at the Inns of Court', both *ICW*, 286–301 and 264–85; and D. Lanier, 'Stigmatical in the Making: The Material Character of *The Comedy of Errors*', *ELR*, 23 (1993): 81–112.

[30] The lost text was a Middle Temple masque presented to the Earl of Buckingham in 1617; perhaps this was just a dance. Additionally, members of all four Inns tilted at Prince Charles's investiture, 1616.

in *The Masque of Mountebanks* (its misogynistic jokes, in other words)[31]—but the lawyers also used these occasions to promote their professional status and cement political contacts at court. Although the decade saw ideological conflicts starting to emerge out of questions of law, notably Sir Edward Coke's questioning of the jurisdiction of ecclesiastical and prerogative courts, by and large the lawyers' masques set out to ameliorate disagreements which might otherwise undermine their reciprocal understanding with the Crown.

These masques typically presented the lawyers in heroic and reforming roles: in Francis Bacon's phrase, as lions under the throne. In *The Masque of the Inner Temple and Gray's Inn* (1613), the setting was the ancient Olympic Games, and the masquers adopted the personae of chivalric knights, brandishing swords which alluded both to their martial spirit and their commitment to justice. Rather more pointed was *The Memorable Masque* (1613), which staged the coalescence of law and commerce in service to the Crown. For this, the lawyers processed to Whitehall dressed as Virginian princes, come to celebrate the Palatine wedding but also bringing the hoped-for New World wealth from city to court. The fable showed Eunomia (Law) and Plutus (Riches) joining together in alliance, implying that this economic bounty, when it came, would need sensible stewardship. In the antimasque, Capriccio, a shallow 'man of wit', was mocked, but the Virginian princes were led to the Temple of Honour by Eunomia, who, being the personification of Law, was Honour's guardian and priest. As the masque's argument put it, 'none should dare access to Honour but by Virtue, of which Law, being the rule, must needs be the chief'.[32] The moving spirit behind this resonant fable was Sir Edward Phelips, who was a director of the Virginia Company as well as Master of the Rolls.[33] Less ambitious but significantly more meritocratic was the *Masque of Heroes*, danced by the Inner Templars in 1619 but not repeated at court. In this charming small-scale show, prefaced by comic speeches about the onset of the new year, the performers were introduced as modern versions of the Nine Worthies, 'lamps of honour' and 'sons of brightness', who had been raised to the heavens in reward for their virtue.[34] This assertion that the masquers' worth was innate carried its own ideological point, for these legal heroes did not need the monarch's approval for their validation. Perhaps this corresponded to the more radical climate of the Inner Temple, for this was where Sir Edward Coke had his chambers.

Paul Raffield suggests that all the masques from this decade should be read as texts challenging the Crown, symbolic assertions of the authority of Common Law as promoted by Coke.[35] However, the name that continually recurs around them is Sir Francis Bacon. It was Bacon who was 'the chief contriver' of the *Masque of the Inner Temple and Gray's Inn*, who arranged for the masquers to travel to Whitehall by barges along

31 *REED*, 2.696 (letter to Dudley Carleton by Nathaniel Brent).

32 *REED*, 2.510. The motto *Sic virtus honorem* also appears in *Gesta Grayorum* (*REED*, 2.387).

33 This point is strongly made by O'Callaghan, *The English Wits*, 16.

34 *REED*, 2.590.

35 Raffield, *Images and Cultures of Law*, 135, 153–4.

the Thames, and who pleaded with the king for a second chance when audience overcrowding caused the planned performance to be cancelled.[36] It was Bacon who provided £2,000 for *The Masque of Flowers*, danced by the Grayans in honour of Somerset's wedding, and whom the masque's printed text calls 'the principal ... person' behind the show, who had 'graced in general all the societies of the Inns of Court in continuing them still as third persons with the nobility and court in doing the king honour'.[37] And it was Bacon who was the principal guest at the Gray's Inn performance of *The Masque of Mountebanks* and whose brother-in-law, Sir John Pakington, was one of the visiting spectators admitted to the society by the Christmas prince, along with the businessman Sir Arthur Ingram and the king's cousin Lord Aubigny.[38] At this time, Bacon was at the height of his career, the preeminent lawyer and perhaps the most influential man in the kingdom after the royal favourites Somerset and Buckingham. He was appointed Attorney General in 1613, Lord Keeper in 1617, and Lord Chancellor in 1618; when James was absent in Edinburgh in 1617, it was Bacon who held the fort in the Privy Council. These masques projected the respect the law could boast under someone who had parlayed his legal expertise into a role at the heart of the Jacobean state. While spectators would have understood them as showcases for the profession, they would probably have read their informing principles as closer to the Baconian model of princely governance than to Coke's Common Law ethos. The masques did not contest royal supremacy but emphasized the need to preserve a two-way relationship between law and prerogative, and promote the king's ultimate responsibility as the earthly embodiment of divine justice.

The interweaving of law and politics in these occasions can be gauged by focusing on two masques associated with the great favourite, Somerset: *The Masque of Flowers* and *The Golden Age Restored* (the latter not an Inns of Court show, but a masque with legal themes danced at Whitehall after Somerset's fall from power). Bacon funded *The Masque of Flowers* because Somerset's wedding was an opportunity to acknowledge his obligations in the wake of his promotion to Attorney General. The Solicitor General, Sir Henry Yelverton—a lawyer almost as wealthy as Bacon—offered to contribute £500, but Bacon rebuffed him because (said John Chamberlain) he needed to assume 'the whole charge with the honour. Marry, his obligations are such as well to his majesty as to the great lord [Somerset] and to the whole house of Howards [the bride's family, Earls of Suffolk] as he can admit no partners'.[39] Unsurprisingly, the masque's fiction eschewed legal motifs, concentrating instead on the king's power to promote deserving subjects. The symbolism turned on horticulture, depicting the court as a garden in which flowers were transformed into men by the warm royal sun—an obvious metaphor for the king's freedom to promote whichever friends he wanted to honour with his bounty. The antimasques were playful, depicting a merry war between devotees of tobacco and wine

36 *REED*, 2.688–9; Spencer and Wells, *A Book of Masques*, 129.

37 *REED*, 2.537.

38 *REED*, 1.201.

39 *REED*, 2.692.

concerning which was superior: this entertainment did not feature virtuous 'worthies' and 'Arthur's knights', but offered 'roaring boys' whose dances would 'chase away ill sprites'.[40] Into this carefree paradise, the Gray's Inn masquers were introduced as choice plants flourishing in the garden, a testimony to the well-run state over which James presided:[41]

> All things return with time,
> But seldom do they higher climb;
> Yet virtue sovereign
> Mends all things, as they come again.
> This isle was Britain in times past,
> But then was Britain rude and waste;
> But now is Britain fit to be
> A seat for a fifth monarchy.

Bacon had been closely associated with the reinvention of Britain under its Scottish ruler. His masque offered a characteristic vision of constitutional progress, a state advancing steadily out of barbarity and into decent modern civility.

But ironically this 'fifth monarchy' did not last, since scarcely a year after *The Masque of Flowers* was performed Somerset fell from grace, fatally tainted by his wife's involvement in Sir Thomas Overbury's murder, and outmanoeuvred by his new rival, Buckingham, in the struggle for the royal affections. Soon Somerset would find himself facing charges of murder and treason, a process culminating in the reign's most sensational state trial—the Crown's case against him being led by Edward Coke and Somerset's former client Francis Bacon. Whitehall's celebration of this astonishing turnaround was *The Golden Age Restored*, a masque which represented the court as miraculously saved from catastrophe by Pallas, goddess of divine wisdom, and led into a new age of justice by the goddess Astraea. Astraea, said the masque, had fled the earth with the last golden age, but now that treason and corruption were purged she would return, bringing back justice free from favouritism or money, 'And in the midst of so much gold, / Unbought with grace or fear unsold, / The law to mortals give.' This fiction boldly transformed the sordid events around Somerset into a fable of judicial renewal in which sovereignty and law were represented as at last going hand in hand. The Iron Age was chased away, and replaced by aristocratic masquers 'that justice dare defend, and will the age sustain'.[42] Whether this mythologizing of Somerset's trial was convincing is a moot point—after all, these masquers were not principled spokesmen for justice but members of the faction who stood to benefit from the favourite's fall—but it demonstrates how much the Jacobean court wanted to claim for itself constitutional as well as political legitimacy.

40 *REED*, 2.543. Raffield (146) asserts that the dispute between wine and tobacco allegorizes a conflict between Common Law and Civil Law, but his case is not persuasive.

41 *REED*, 2.547.

42 *CWBJ*, 4.460–1, 457.

Even if Astraea's return was embarrassingly belated, never (claimed the masque) had royal justice so much deserved celebration as at this moment.

Legal Festivity and the Caroline State

In the 1620s, after Coke and Bacon both fell from power, and as England was gripped by the European war and the constitutional debates which unfolded from it, so the numbers of masques taken to Whitehall by lawyers dwindled almost to nothing.[43] This was a sign of the strains created between Stuart government and the legal community by the decade's divisive politics, prominent amongst which were the controversies over freedom of speech mentioned at the beginning of this essay. But it also reflected the attrition of the previously vibrant festival culture hosted by the Inns. Although the societies' lords of misrule or masters of the revels are intermittently recorded in their account books down to 1641, at all four Inns the Benchers sought to rein in Christmas misbehaviour, restricting access, shortening the period of revelry, and variously objecting to tobacco, the drinking of healths, and the presence of female spectators.[44] Few of these later lords of misrule set up court with the splendour seen in the 1590s. Instead, Christmas revelling seems to have become more charged with respect for discipline and good manners.

The changing culture is evident in the festivities held at the Middle Temple in 1628–1629, under Bulstrode Whitelocke as Christmas prince. Whitelocke describes in his autobiography how he presided over a group of twenty supporters, whose ceremonies and dancing were so publicly esteemed that they were visited by 'much company of gentlemen and ladies, and some of them of great quality', and invited to dance at court and in private houses. Whitelocke is, though, concerned to emphasize the politeness and good order of their proceedings. When quarrels broke out, he claims, he stepped in to prevent them becoming violent, and although his followers used the Devil tavern on Fleet Street as their rehearsal space—where the 'Sons of Ben' held court, just outside the Temple—they avoided any lapse into insobriety:[45]

> When they met at the tavern their business was to practise their dancing, and to exercise both their wits and bodies, and not to cloud their reason or parts with excess or debauchery, but to improve their judgments and knowledge by good discourse and conversation, and sometimes by putting of [law] cases; and they did appear together

[43] A Middle Temple masque was presented at court in 1621, though this may have been little more than a sequence of dances. See *REED*, 1.208, and, for the probable cost, see the lawsuit cited by Mary Sullivan, *Court Masques of James I* (New York, 1913), 173–4. Sullivan also records (172–3) that suits and vizards were rented for an Inner Temple masque at Christmas 1627/8, though there is no clear evidence of court performance.

[44] See, for example, the Inner Temple orders of 1628–1629: *REED*, 1.220.

[45] *REED*, 2.223–4.

> much more like to grave ancients in a council chamber than to young revellers in an house of drinking.

Whitelocke—who in the 1650s became Cromwell's ambassador to Sweden and sat on the republican Council of State—ascribes to his revels a sobriety which was a long way from the riotously transgressive misbehaviour associated with the previous generation's festivity. His account points to new codes of conduct becoming ingrained in Caroline London, and to expectations about genteel civility and self-control which were working to damp down the robustly disruptive humour that had previously been so prominent.[46]

The consequences are apparent in the rule of the one Caroline Christmas prince who did achieve some fame, Richard Vivian of the Middle Temple. Vivian reigned during the winter season 1635–1636, when the young exiled Palatine princes were residing at their uncle's court, and invited them to the Middle Temple with their aunt, Henrietta Maria. His revels were coloured by the youthfully militaristic politics for which the termers were always enthusiastic. His councillors debated thinly veiled political topics concerning elective monarchy and princes who had lost their inheritance, and his masque, *The Triumphs of the Prince D'Amour*, presented his followers in the role of heroic knights, eager for battle overseas. Without exception, masques at Whitehall always emphasized the value of peace, but Vivian's show, with its emphasis on the termers' devotion to Mars and its expectation of irresistible conquests on the foreign battlefield—so different from the praise of naval strength which was the furthest in this direction that royal masques ever went—was the one festival text from the whole period to voice a whole-hearted enthusiasm for war. But though the termers' political passions were predictable, gallant support for the Palatine cause being a constant in much of their festivity, on this occasion the etiquette seems to have been relatively restrained. The masque avoids vulgarity, confining its humour to mockery of swaggering cavaliers 'of the cheaper quality, such as are said to roar, not fight',[47] and the termers' military fervour is legitimated by their expressions of amorous devotion to the queen. Their fervent embrace of military preparedness sits in somewhat uncomfortable tension with their need to display their qualifications as loyal and well-mannered gentlemen.

The single most famous Inns of Court event before the Civil War was *The Triumph of Peace*, a masque offered to the court by all four societies in 1634 and preceded by a grand procession through the streets which proclaimed the lawyers' wealth and importance. Ostensibly designed as an apology for the insult given to the queen by William Prynne, a member of Lincoln's Inn, the lawyers took the opportunity of public dialogue with the Crown to present a conspectus of the relationship between government and law. At this time, for the sake of raising cash without recalling Parliament, Charles was straining his prerogative powers to their limits. In a process that would eventually culminate in the legal case over Ship Money, he was extending the Crown's feudal powers, such

[46] An early precursor of this development is the masque *Ulysses and Circe*, danced at the Inner Temple in 1615, which politely eschews vulgarity, even in the antimasque.

[47] *REED*, 2.615. For full discussion, see Butler, *Stuart Court Masque*, 321–6.

as distraint of knighthood and the forest laws, exploiting his economic rights for fiscal purposes, such as the ability to grant monopolies for inventions or fine breaches of proclamations, and conducting an administrative drive which required judges and magistrates to tighten up social discipline by implementing the full force of his proclamations. The committee charged with preparing the masque was no mere collection of termers, but included senior representatives of the Inns, and men with track records both as Charles's supporters and critics: such as the jurist and parliamentarian John Selden, the Attorney General Willliam Noy, Sir John Finch (in 1628–1629 the conspicuously loyal Speaker of the House of Commons), Sir Edward Herbert (who in 1626 had managed Buckingham's impeachment), and Edward Hyde (who later led the parliamentary attack on Ship Money). Unsurprisingly, the argument devised by this group of constitutional experts concerned the duties and obligations of law.

The Triumph of Peace presented images of a state suffering from too much law and too little. Staged inside a proscenium decorated with figures of Minos and Numa, mythical law-giving kings, its antimasques satirized monopolies granted for ludicrous inventions and drew attention to social disorders arising in times of peace, such as vagrancy, prostitution, and unlicensed taverns. The masquers themselves were introduced as the children of Irene (Peace), Eunomia (Law), and Dike (Justice). In the dialogue between these symbolic figures, Peace complained to Law of the dangers of unregulation, that she was 'lost with them / That know not how to order me'. Together, they expounded the way that Justice depended on Peace and Law combining in harmony:[48]

IRENE. Thou dost beautify increase,
And chain security with peace.
EUNOMIA. Irene fair, and first divine,
All my blessings spring from thine.
IRENE. I am but wild without thee, thou abhorrest
What is rude, or apt to wound,
Canst throw proud trees to the ground,
And make a temple of a forest.
EUNOMIA. No more, no more, but join
Thy voice and lute with mine.
BOTH. The world shall give prerogative to neither,
We cannot flourish but together.

Their dialogue affirms that only through her embrace of Law could Peace ensure that Justice would descend. The masque was complimentary to the aspirations of Caroline kingship but equally emphatic about respect for law, properly understood and interpreted, being enshrined at the heart of government. Strikingly, the language of this exchange, with its emphasis on 'security' and 'prerogative', underlines the constitutional

[48] Spencer and Wells, *A Book of Masques*, 296–7.

implications of the rule of law, that law guarantees royal privileges but also protects fundamental rights and liberties for the subject. As the Chorus summed it up:

> Irene enters like a perfumed spring,
> Eunomia ripens everything,
> And in the golden harvest leaves
> To every sickle his own sheaves.

Leaving to every sickle his own sheaves was a neat formula for lawyers professionally concerned about safeguarding property rights, protecting the sanctity of mine and thine, and maintaining the separation between the king's power and the freedoms of the subject.

The Triumph of Peace exemplifies the opportunities and limitations of the lawyers' masquing culture at this moment of political uncertainty. Charles was pleased by the show, and ordered it to be repeated a few days later. Probably he took it as a compliment to the legality of his government, an articulation of the values he admired and the policies he thought he was already pursuing. He was, after all, in many respects an excessively legalistic monarch, who liked to test the validity of his policies by consulting with his judges and by defending his actions in high profile trials, such as the Ship Money case. At the same time, though, Charles's legalism took inadequate account of differences over the interpretation of law, and of the political cost of merely technical correctness in legal application. The masque's language and imagery served the lawyers' purposes by emphasizing their crucial place in the Caroline state, and the need to preserve the unity between the king and his judges. On the other hand, it articulated these concerns in a language of compliment and consensus which ran the risk of eliding areas of ideological disagreement that would later turn out to be crucial, particularly the difference between the king's perception of his legal obligations and that of the legal community at large. *The Triumph of Peace* was a triumph for the Inns of Court, and made the case for the interdependence of government and law, but it was the last time the lawyers attempted to talk back to Charles in his own symbolic language. Future legal critiques of the Caroline state would take other forms than masques.

Bibliography

Bentley, Gerald Eades, ed. *A Book of Masques: In Honour of Allardyce Nicoll* (Cambridge: Cambridge University Press, 1967).

Butler, Martin. *The Stuart Court Masque and Political Culture* (Cambridge: Cambridge University Press, 2006).

Cormack, Bradin. 'Locating "The Comedy of Errors": Revels Jurisdiction at the Inns of Court', in *The Intellectual and Cultural World of the Early Modern Inns of Court*, ed. Jayne Archer, Elizabeth Goldring, and Sarah Knight (Manchester: Manchester University Press, 2011), 264–85.

Jonson, Ben. *The Cambridge Edition of the Works of Ben Jonson*, ed. David Bevington, Martin Butler, and Ian Donaldson, 5 vols (Cambridge: Cambridge University Press, 2012).

Lanier, Douglas. 'Stigmatical in the Making: The Material Character of "The Comedy of Errors"', *English Literary Renaissance*, 23 (1993): 81–112.

Larkin, J. F. and P. L. Hughes, ed. *Stuart Royal Proclamations*, Vol. 1: *Royal Proclamations of King James I, 1603–1625* (Oxford: Oxford University Press, 1973).

McCoy, Richard. 'Law Sports and the Night of Errors: Shakespeare and the Inns of Court', in *The Intellectual and Cultural World of the Early Modern Inns of Court*, ed. Jayne Archer, Elizabeth Goldring, and Sarah Knight (Manchester: Manchester University Press, 2011), 286–301.

McCoy, Richard. 'Lords of Liberty: Francis Davison and the Cult of Elizabeth', in *The Reign of Elizabeth I: Court and Culture in the Last Decade*, ed. J. A. Guy (Cambridge: Cambridge University Press, 1995), 212–28.

Nelson, Alan H. and John R. Elliott, Jr, ed. *Records of Early English Drama: The Inns of Court*, 3 vols (Cambridge: D. S. Brewer, 2010).

O'Callaghan, Michelle. *The English Wits: Literature and Sociability in Early Modern England* (Cambridge: Cambridge University Press, 2007).

Orbison, Tucker et al., eds. 'The Middle Temple Documents Relating to James Shirley's "The Triumph of Peace"', *Malone Society Collections*, 12 (1983).

Raffield, Paul. *Images and Cultures of Law in Early Modern England* (Cambridge: Cambridge University Press, 2004).

Sullivan, Mary. *Court Masques of James I* (New York: G. P. Putnam, 1913).

CHAPTER 10

PARADISE LOST?

Law, Literature, and History in Restoration England

CHRISTOPHER BROOKS

I

THE title and content of this lecture carry a lot of baggage for me.[1] If it were not for a beguiling invitation from Lorna Hutson to visit the University of St Andrews and the Centre for Medieval and Early Modern Law and Literature, I doubt I would be writing it at all. As a legal historian I am aware of the really significant amounts of work that has been done in the rediscovered field of law and literature. Most of the conversations I had last academic year about early modern English law were with literary scholars. While I'm delighted about this, I don't feel qualified to write or say anything in particular about a defined topic in the law and literature field. Although I am an early modern

[1] This is the text of the Annual Lecture for the Centre for Medieval and Early Modern Law and Literature, delivered by the late Professor Christopher Brooks at the University of St Andrews 9 October 2013. The editor is indebted to Michael Lobban, Chris Brooks's former colleague at Durham and now at the London School of Economics, for kindly providing two (incomplete) texts of the lecture from Chris Brooks's notes, one 'Paradise Lost Law and Lit lecture' (text A) and one 'Paradise Lost version as delivered' (text B). Thanks to Jacqueline Rose and Rab Houston of the University of St Andrews for their generous and painstaking detective work in reconstructing Chris's endnotes. Thanks are also due to Michael Lobban for providing the images of Huntington MS HM46323, to Chris's widow, Sharyn Brooks, and to Ian Williams and Tim Stretton for help with queries. Authorial endnotes are unmarked; endnotes reconstructed or added by Jacqueline Rose are prefixed [JR], those by Rab Houston are prefixed [RH], those by Ian Williams [IW], and those by Lorna Hutson [LH]. The text published here largely follows text A. Lacunae in text A will be supplemented by material from text B (which contains both a typescript and handwritten insertions) in square brackets. Readers should bear in mind that the text still bears the marks of informal, oral delivery; had Chris lived he would have revised and annotated it for the Handbook. For all its informality, it represents the profoundly original and stimulating new directions Chris Brooks's work was taking in the last years of life, when he was engaged in research for the *Oxford History of the Laws of England, 1625–1689*.

historian in no small part because of a very early attraction to the profane poetry of Dr John Donne, I don't feel that I can take the time necessary to steep myself adequately in the literature of the period. You could say I've taken the pledge to stick largely with the nuts and bolts of the legal and social life. Yet, I'd have to admit that this has not always been the case. I began my undergraduate studies in the USA by reading English, and in my early work on the legal profession, going back to the 1970s, I made some forays into literature, in particular city drama, to see whether there was support there of what I found in other kinds of source.

I take it that this is a vice of the general historian, as opposed to the legal scholar, or the scholar of literature, and while I'm sure you'll be able to point out the pitfalls, this is the path I want to pursue in this lecture. The first part of it consists of observations arising from comparisons between my vision of legal culture between roughly 1550 and 1640 and my (very selective) understanding of the language and literature. For me a particularly important question in connection with this is whether or not both the great excrescence of legal culture in this period, and the extensive crossover with literature, were in some respects unique (the paradise in my title). The principal reason for this is that in my current work as a legal historian, I am finding that in the Civil War years, and those after the Restoration of 1660, the relationship between law and social and political life was changing. I'll try to explain this in the second part of the lecture, and will conclude by considering how far a resort to literature might help me to define my understanding more clearly, and asking for any help you can give me.

II

For a long time now my view of the particular significance of the late sixteenth and early seventeenth centuries in the very long history of English law has been based on some crude statistical findings I put together back in the 1970s about the amount of litigation in the courts at the time, as well as the number of practising lawyers in England's two-tier legal system. As time has passed, various kinds of studies have largely confirmed the statistical outline, though, as sometimes happens, the interpretative consequences across various fields of literary and historical studies have had a somewhat uneven impact. But in order to give an over-view as succinct as possible, I would put it something like this. From the early sixteenth century onwards a combination of technical procedural innovations, combined with political changes and the first real pulse of demographic growth in England since the mid-fourteenth-century Black Death, created by the end of the reign of Elizabeth in 1603 a very distinctive institutional and cultural bloom for English law. Nearly all courts, from the secular to the ecclesiastical, from the central to the local, were bursting with business, evidently more per head of population than there was before or has been ever since. The numbers of qualified lawyers increased many fold. The Inns of Court and Inns of Chancery in London, the places where they trained, and where they stayed during termly visits to London from the provinces, achieved institutional and architectural high water marks best illustrated by the building of new chambers to accommodate new members and new Halls for the communal commensality that was such an important part of their social life as well as spaces for the oral learning exercises, including moots and lectures, that formed a key element in legal education.[2]

As further research has developed these insights, evidence of the pervasive influence of law in all aspects of early modern life has only increased. The importance of great test cases such as those involving Impositions in the first decades of the seventeenth century, or the case of Ship Money in the 1630s, seems to be associated with what some of us feel it might be helpful to describe as a 'juristic or juridical state', and something like a law relating to the liberty of the subject/citizen was also being developed.[3] Much of what we now know about social and economic life comes from the exploitation of court records. Law seems to be a key to understanding economic relationships in both a rural and an urban setting (including customary tenures and obligations) as well as those between individual and local communities.[4] Going further, I would even say that the laws of England between 1350 and 1640 had been generated largely from the interaction of judges, juries, litigants, and lawyers, and therefore in a very real sense belonged to the community as a whole. Statute passed by Parliament had long been recognized by lawyers as essential to their understanding of how the system worked, and in this sense I don't think any contemporary would recognize as true Conrad Russell's dictum that Parliament was an event rather than an institution.[5] Contemporary lawyers were also acutely aware of the difference between common law and statute law, yet the most remarkable feature of the system was that an effective consensus accepted that judges appointed by the Crown would with a reasonable degree of impartiality act as the keepers of a body of law that was made incrementally on a case-by-case basis, recorded in law reports of the arguments made in court, and taught at the Inns of Court through the oral learning exercises and lectures (readings on statutes) given in them. [Common learning (written as well as oral) was a system of unwritten law.][6]

[2] C. W. Brooks, *Lawyers, Litigation and English Society* (London: Hambledon Press, 1998), esp. chs 2–4. Customary tenants as against their landlords, and the rights of the subject as against the king, had become a predominant metaphor in national political life: 'a people whose property could be taken from them at the will of the monarch were slaves, not subjects ... they were serfs or villeins, rather than free tenants whose rights to property were protected by law.' See C. W. Brooks, *Law, Politics and Society in Early Modern England* (Cambridge: Cambridge University Press, 2008), 190.

[3] [RH] See C. Muldrew, 'From a "Light Cloak" to the "Iron Cage": An Essay on Historical Changes in the Relationship between Community and Individualism', in *Communities in Early Modern England*, ed. A. Shepard and P. Withington (Manchester: Manchester University Press, 2000), 161–6.

[4] Brooks, *Law, Politics and Society*, chs 8, 9, 11, 13.

[5] [JR] C. Russell, *Parliaments and English Politics, 1621–1629* (Oxford: Oxford University Press, 1979), 3: 'even in a period of frequent Parliaments such as the 1620s, a Parliament was an event and not an institution.'

[6] Taken as a whole the evidence of legal change over the one hundred years prior to the civil war would seem to point to a society that used legal institutions on a level not matched before, or, indeed, afterwards, and a body of law that had responded to social and economic change to the extent that it could be claimed the laws of England helped to make the liberty of the subject under the law a social

Given views such as these, it should come as no surprise that my reaction to the recrudescence of the interest in law and literature is basically, hooray, this is grist for my mill. Work, both already published, or ongoing, is asking interesting questions about literature stretching, as far as I'm aware, from the late fifteenth century [through the mid-seventeenth. There is so much to talk about that I am going to talk very little about it except to say that I've recently been glad to read unpublished work that, inter alia, probes some of Shakespeare's ruminations about the nature of polity and its governance, explores contemporary understanding of the relationship between inebriation and personal responsibility, and investigates how political prisoners and political imprisonment came to figure in the literature. Though I sometimes find myself irritated by a kind of template argument which seems to suggest that poets and dramatists reached the places the lawyers did not in terms of their understanding of law, I put this down to the failure of legal historians to fully adumbrate a world of legal learning and manuscript writing that was far deeper, more polyvalent, than is commonly appreciated, or can be found in existing writing. Much of the literary scholarship on legal history is exemplary.

At the same time, however, thinking about law and literature has also led me to think why this is a subject which seems particularly, or even uniquely, appropriate to the late sixteenth and seventeenth centuries, and here I'll only offer two points which I hope might generate some discussion after the lecture. First, I'd suggest that the growing memberships of the Inns of Court and Chancery were active participants in the social and political life of London and Westminster, both the city and the seat of government, and London, including the Inns, was also the centre of literary life. I appreciate that this is a statement so vague that the best way to make it carry some meaning is to pause for a couple of minutes to look at a manuscript I have come across fairly recently at the Huntington Library containing juvenile poems to parents by one of the Calverley family in Yorkshire, and poems by John Donne, Henry Wotton, and Francis Davison as well as political poems; all surrounded by a law dictionary (See Figures 10.1, 10.2, and 10.3,).[7]

There is a lot of work to be done before this manuscript can be properly understood, but one of the underlying characteristics seems to be that it is all about the meaning and use of words, and the idea of words or word fields is one that is becoming increasingly intriguing to me. One manifestation of this is the feeling I get when reading depositions in law cases that I am hearing accounts of all kinds of functions and malfunctions in society that are little different from those found in city drama, in the works of Webster or Middleton.[8] Law clerks spent hours and scribbled millions of words recording these episodes, and some legal pleadings, most notably bills in the Court of Chancery, written

value. According to the common lawyers themselves, if England had ever been a feudal society, it had evolved over the fifteenth and sixteenth centuries into one of landholdings of various different sizes, and according to a bewildering array of tenures, but where no man, however lowly, had to do homage to another just because he paid rent to him. The rise of the yeomanry and the urban middling sort are at least as important a feature of social, economic, and legal life as the rise of the gentry.

7 Huntington MS HM 46323.

8 [LH] See Tim Stretton's chapter in this volume.

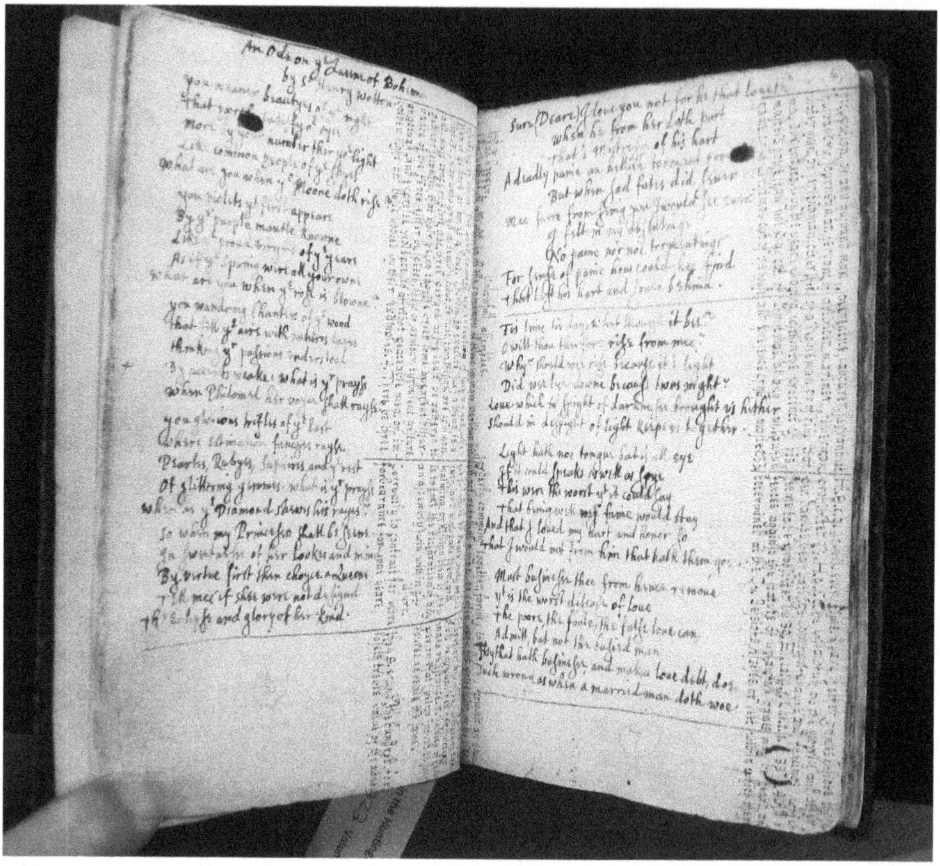

FIG. 10.1 Huntington MS 4623, fols 32ᵛ–33ʳ, showing poems by Sir Henry Wotton, 'An Ode on ye Queene of Bohemia', Francis Davison, 'Sure, (Deare) I loue you not, for he that loueth', and John Donne, 'Tis time, [t]is day, what though it bee?' Running vertically along the margins in an italic hand are copious notes on English laws, here pertaining to unlawful games. Reproduced by kind permission of the Huntington Library.

by barristers, were attempts to sum up the entire story, whilst casting it in a form that would meet the requirements of the court.

At the same time, on the literary side, I've also been struck by the potential significance of the widespread use of legal language, particularly by Shakespeare, something that has of course long been of interest to scholars of law and literature. In the second edition of his book, *The Law in Shakespeare*, which was published in 1884, Cushman K. Davis had little doubt that there was more systematic use of legal language in Shakespeare than in any other non-legal English writer.[9] Furthermore, while Davis thought that Shakespeare often seemed to have a quite competent legal knowledge of what some of his examples illustrate, what delights and really fascinates me is that Shakespeare developed legal

9 Cushman K. Davis, *The Law in Shakespeare* (Washington: Washington Law Book Co., 1883).

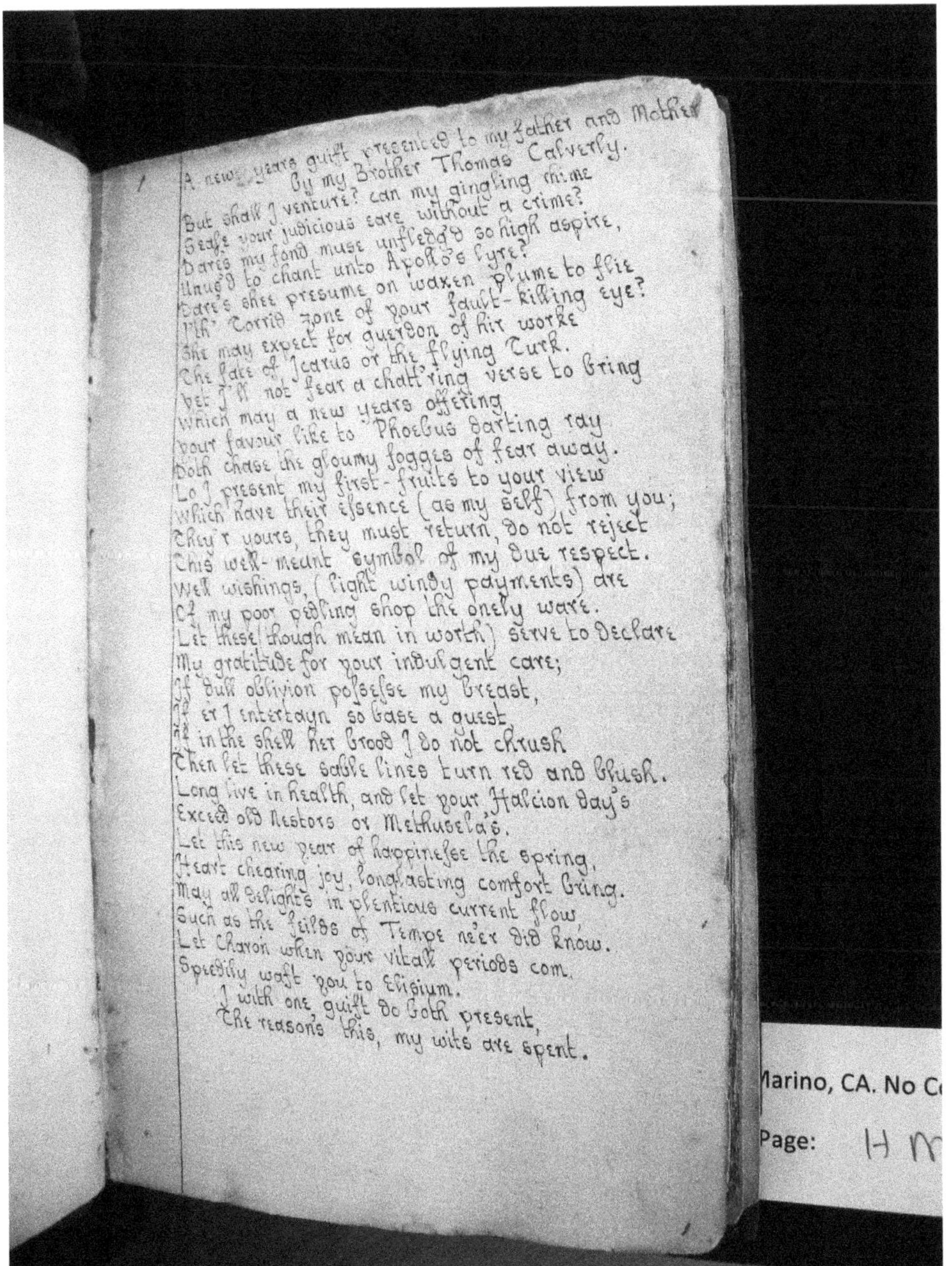

FIG. 10.2 Huntington MS 4623, showing poem, 'a new years gift presented to my father and mother by my brother Thomas Calverly'. Reproduced by kind permission of the Huntington Library.

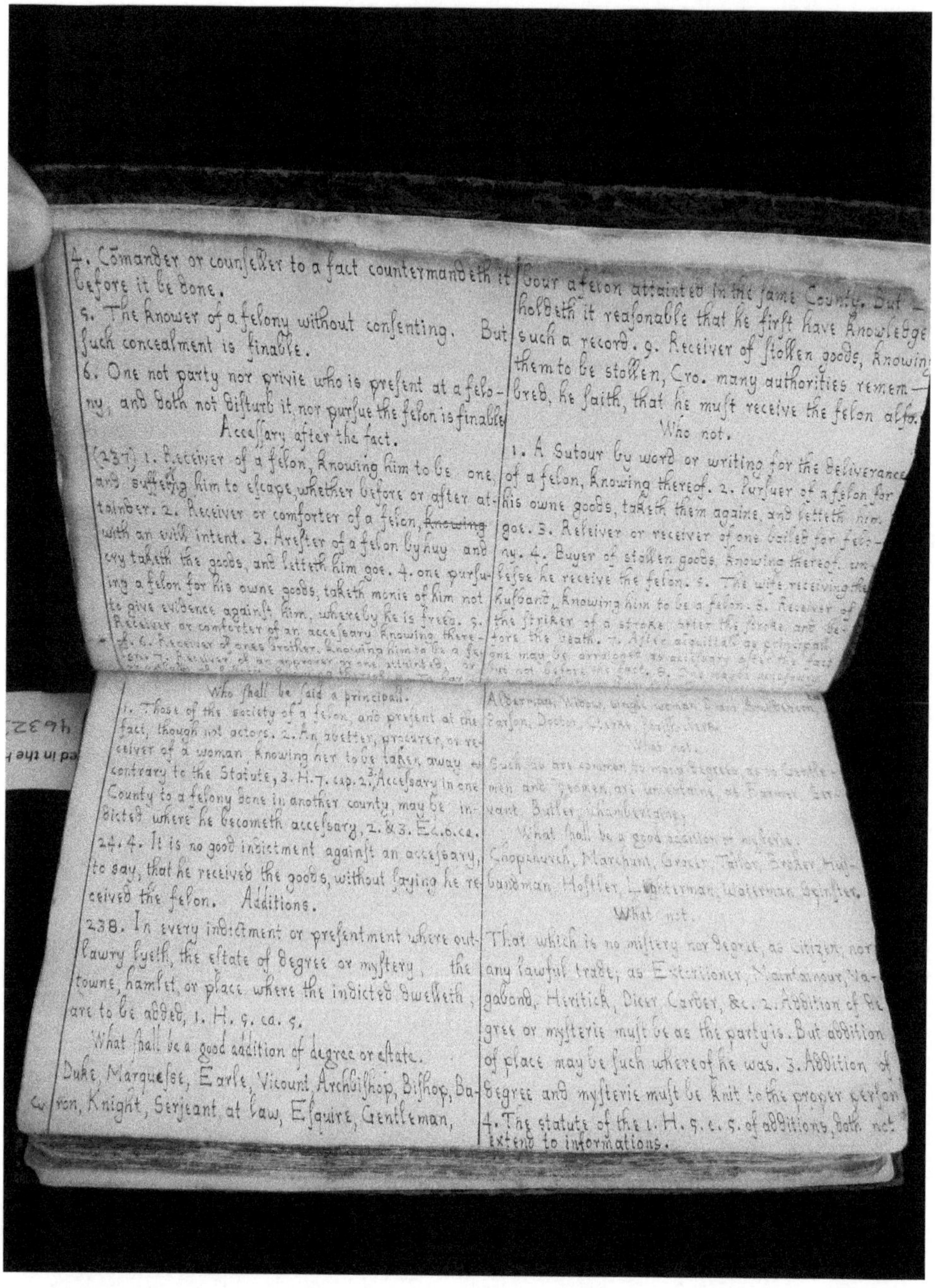

FIG. 10.3 Huntington MS 4623, showing notes on English laws, here pertaining to felony, and to definitions of principal and accessory, and the making of indictments. Reproduced by kind permission of the Huntington Library.

metaphors in a way which no mere lawyer could imagine, and Davis is good at describing how this worked. For instance, in a scene from *Love's Labour's Lost*, Boyet, wishing for a kiss, prays for a grant of pasture on the lips of one of the Princess's ladies in waiting. This leads Shakespeare to think of the law of common of pasture, and the lady replies that her lips are 'no common'. This suggests the distinction between tenancy in common and tenancy in severalty, so she adds 'though several they be' (3.1.223):

CATHERINE. You sheep and I pasture—shall that finish the jest?
BOYET. So you grant pasture for me.
CATHERINE. Not so, gentle beast
My lips are no common, though several they be.
(*LLL*, 3.1.221–3)

This and similar uses of legal language in Shakespeare give me goose bumps. Reading this particular passage in Southern California, it seemed to work not just because it was an unexpectedly brilliant application of the dry language of customary land law to an intimate act, but because part of its sensuousness lay in the fact that it evoked, for contemporaries, the actual English landscape and resonances of the social relations which surrounded it. Nevertheless, you also want to ask why someone would choose to use language in this way. One answer may simply be of course that the process of writing for the stage, which included making manuscript copies, led dramatists like Shakespeare to come into contact with legal terminology. Or is it, more grandly, that the phenonomenon that I observe as the boom in early modern litigation resulted in the permeation of law into so many aspects of life that it significantly expanded the capacity of the English language to describe social, political, and romantic relationships?].[10]

III

This is all well and good, but while I expect many of you will want to question me about it, the problem that has been vexing me, and which I want to concentrate on in the second part of the lecture, arises directly from the fact that I have been concentrating my work over the past few years into the period of the Civil Wars of the 1640s, the political mutations of the 1650s, and the restoration of the Stuart monarchy in 1660 and, finally, its downfall in 1688. Furthermore, it is now generally accepted that nearly all of the quantitative dimensions of the legal culture I have been describing changed dramatically during the course of the 1690s and the early years of the eighteenth century. Litigation declined, the size of the bar shrunk, and the Inns of Court in London nearly went bankrupt.

One of my biggest problems with the period from 1640 to 1689 is that it has been both relatively neglected and over-determined in what is often dated historiography. While

[10] The omission of this whole passage from text A suggests that Chris Brooks intended to rewrite this part of the lecture before publication.

no Marxist interpretation has made anything like a running, we now know much more about early modern social structure and the role of law in it than was the case back in the 1970s, which was the last time anyone showed much interest.[11] For this reason, I have found it useful to think in terms of revolution, military dictatorship, and counter revolution, if these are terms associated with unusually severe social, political, and religious discontinuities, or bouleversements, not unlike, say, what we sometimes describe as the recent 'Egyptian revolution'.[12]

But, on the face of it, and as has often been argued, the Civil War epoch could well be described as one of little lasting change despite events such as the execution of Charles Stuart, and the creation of a republic whose legal writs replaced the king's peace with that of the public, and which ran in the name of the keepers of the liberties of the people of England.[13] In the end it is hard to see that the very long-term relationship between London and the legal profession could have worked any way but to the advantage of Parliament, and those members of the legal profession who supported it. When Charles attempted to establish the courts (which were after all his courts) in Oxford, the two Houses responded to a request that they should send him centuries of legal records by declaring all of the king's judges dead and appointing new ones.[14] By 1646, the dockets of the major courts at Westminster were filling up rapidly. From this point onwards, furthermore, everything suggests that rates of litigation, or levels of court usage, were equal to if not higher than historic peaks in the early seventeenth century. There was a lot of work for lawyers.

The age produced the greatest legal publicist in English history, Serjeant William Sheppard, who received an annual stipend for acting as Cromwell's chief law reformer. There were many notable jurists, including Sir Matthew Hale, Heneage Finch, lord keeper Nottingham, and of course the scholar John Selden, as well as politicos such as Oliver St John and the prodigiously long-lived Sir John Maynard, both of whom built new houses in the latest styles within what we would today call the greater London area. Edward Hyde, the Earl of Clarendon, thought that common lawyers had engineered the downfall of the Church of England in the early 1640s,[15] and there appear to me to have

[11] [RH] Here Chris Brooks may have been thinking of G. R. Elton, 'The Rule of Law in Sixteenth-Century England', in *Tudor Men and Institutions: Studies in English Law and Government*, ed. A. J. Slavin (Baton Rouge: Louisiana State University Press, 1972), 265–94. Douglas Hay, Peter Linebaugh, John G. Rule, E. P. Thompson, and Carl Winslow, 'Preface', in *Albion's Fatal Tree: Crime and Society in Eighteenth-Century England* (Harmondsworth: Pantheon, 1975). E. P. Thompson, *Whigs and Hunters: The Origin of the Black Act* (Harmondsworth: Pantheon, 1975), 258–69. Thompson, and later Brooks, distanced themselves from Christopher Hill, who consistently regarded the law as a crude instrument of oppression and exploitation. C. Hill, *Liberty against the Law: Some Seventeenth-Century Controversies* (London: Penguin, 1996), 338.

[12] [LH] A reference to the so-called 'Arab Spring', the revolutions and protests that began in Tunisia and spread through the countries of the Arab League in 2010–2012.

[13] [JR] *Acts and Ordinances of the Interregnum, 1642–60*, ed. C. H. Firth and R. S. Rait (London: Wyman and Sons, 1911), 1.1262, 2.6. See S. Kelsey, *Inventing a Republic: The Political Culture of the English Commonwealth, 1649–1653* (Manchester: Manchester University Press, 1997), 93.

[14] [JR] *Journals of the House of Commons*, 3.356 (1 January 1644); see also 3.358–60 (6 January 1644).

[15] [JR] Edward Hyde, Earl of Clarendon, *The History of the Rebellion and Civil Wars in England*, ed. W. D. Macray, 6 vols (Oxford: Oxford University Press, 1888), 1.404.

been a fair number of individuals who may well have thought that they were the architects, or at least facilitators, of the Restoration of the Stuart monarchy as well. Despite a significant body of pamphlet literature that called for reforming the law, and the support law reform received from Oliver Cromwell, and in fits and starts, the Rump Parliament, there were a very small number of significant changes that saw out the Restoration.[16] The translation of legal proceedings and technical legal writings from Latin and French into English was reversed by statute with the return of the king. It is true that the abolition of feudal tenures (or those pertaining to large land-holders) was also significant in the way both the greater aristocracy and gentry managed their patrimonies, but all of the old courts, King's Bench, Common Pleas, Chancery, along with their large staffs of fee-taking clerks and under-clerks continued to fill every corner of the legal district of Holborn, both inside and outside the legal Inns.

Yet completely pursuant to the English legal tradition these continuities in institutions, or forms, masked what appear to me to have been some fundamental transformations. First, while lawyers did well, the Inns of Court and Inns of Chancery as educational institutions suffered severe damage. Taking for example Lincoln's Inn, whose membership included William Prynne, Oliver St John, Sir John Glynne, Matthew Hale, and others, there is a complete gap in the record, between August 1642 and 1644.[17] What seems to have happened is that everybody went back home, or to the wars; except of course those like St John or Bulstrode Whitelocke, a long-serving Chancery judge who found that being part of the parliamentary war effort made them full-time Londoners. They wanted to have their families with them and the families appear fairly often, at least in the early 1640s, to have shared digs with each other that were outside the precincts of the Inns. Bulstrode Whitelocke, who chronicled his meals faithfully, sometimes ate at the Middle Temple, not in the Hall (I think), but usually he dined privately with family, friends, or professional colleagues.[18] As Parliament began to get the upper hand in the war, orders were issued, in 1644, to seize the chambers of those who adhered to the enemy. By 1646, lawyers must have been beginning to come back in significant numbers, although the situation changed yet again after Pride's Purge in December 1648. Some

[16] [RH] See D. Veall, *The Popular Movement for Law Reform, 1640–1660* (Oxford: Oxford University Press, 1970). Also N. L. Matthews, *William Sheppard, Cromwell's Law Reformer* (Cambridge: Cambridge University Press, 1984); A. Likhovski, 'Protestantism and the Rationalization of English Law: A Variation on a Theme by Weber', *Law & Society Review*, 33 (1999), 365–91.

[17] [IW] Sir John Glynne (1603–1666) was admitted to Lincoln's Inn in 1621, bar 1628, and bench 1641: see the *ODNB* entry by Keith Lindley and also J. H. Baker, *Readers and Readings in the Inns of Court and Chancery* (London: SS, 2000) 223. [LH] Oliver St John (*c.*1598–1673) and William Prynne (1600–1669) are perhaps better known as having studied together at Lincoln's Inn, St John being called to the bar in 1626 and Prynne in 1628. See the *ODNB* entries by W. Palmer and W. Lamont respectively. For Sir Matthew Hale (1609–1676) as a member of Lincoln's Inn, see Alan Cromartie's *ODNB* entry and Ian Williams's chapter in this volume.

[18] [JR] *The Diary of Bulstrode Whitelocke, 1605–1675*, ed. R. Spalding (Oxford: Oxford University Press for the British Academy, 1990), 214 and 680 for meals in the Temple Hall, the latter in 1663; *passim* for other meals.

retreated either to the country or to Europe at this time, but by 1652, there was evidently a shortage of chambers at Lincoln's Inn.

Nevertheless the traditional communal life of the Inns proved difficult to resurrect. Members in the late forties and fifties did not want to pay for commons [residence and meals], and no one was willing to stay on for learning exercises that traditionally took place during the vacations in the legal terms. Prompted by the high court judges, the governing bodies of the Inns finally made a serious attempt to re-introduce the learning exercises in 1651, but these came to nothing, evidently because there was little enthusiasm amongst the busy middle-ranking lawyers to give them or potential students to listen to them. Tellingly, the governors of Lincoln's Inn appear to have been successful in securing funding for Archbishop James Ussher's Sunday lectures, but they missed an opportunity to use the bequest of the library of John Selden as the foundation for a resource that could have been used by students of all of the Inns because of lack of funding.

This was the beginning of the end for what Sir John Baker has described as the greatest law school the world has ever known.[19] Legal lectures of the kind that form such a significant body of source material for me for the period before 1640 just do not exist for another two hundred years, when the perpetually vexed problem of English legal education began to be addressed again. There is not enough evidence to support a conspiracy theory, but it is worth comparing one of the last readings given before the outbreak of war with one of the first ones made afterwards. On the eve of the Bishops Wars against Scottish Covenanters, a barrister called Edward Bagshaw planned a series of readings that recapitulated nearly all of the by then familiar arguments about the relationship between the common law and the clergy. In an unprecedented measure, Archbishop Laud convinced the king to suppress the lectures and threatened Bagshaw with prosecution by High Commission. Bagshaw rode out of London towards Northampton accompanied by forty members of the legal Inns. He was subsequently elected a member of Parliament for the London borough of Southwark, who later asked him to present the Root and Branch petition to the House of Commons, and he was one of the principal architects of the exclusion of bishops from the House of Lords.[20] By comparison, when the solicitor general, Sir Heneage Finch, gave a lecture on the royal prerogative at the Inner Temple in August 1661, Charles II, the Duke of York, and various other dignitaries arrived on a barge and were treated to a lavish dinner, with music, that was served by no less than fifty junior members of the Inn. But, so far as is known, only one manuscript copy of Finch's lecture actually survives.[21]

[19] [LH] J. H. Baker, 'The Third University of England: The Inns of Court and the Common Law Tradition' (London: SS, 1990).

[20] Described in Brooks, *Law, Politics and Society*, 218–20; also Jacqueline Rose, *Godly Kingship in Restoration England: The Politics of the Royal Supremacy, 1660–1688* (Cambridge: Cambridge University Press, 2011), 70–3.

[21] [JR] Harvard Law School, MS 5125, fols 1–55. Baker, *Readers and Readings*, 101, 497; W. Dugdale, *Origines iuridicales* (1666), 157.

While the atrophy of the learning exercises at the Inns has long been recognized, most interpretations tend to gloss over it, usually with the explanation that after 1660 the greater availability of printed law books made up for the collapse of the out-dated oral learning exercises, but this, I think, is implausible and ignores some of the more significant consequences. First of all, printed law books did not emerge in impressive quantity or quality in the Restoration era. The published reports are in general so wanting in authority that legal scholars normally feel they have to go to the old-fashioned manuscript collections for accurate accounts of the arguments made in court.[22] Furthermore, many of the more general and descriptive works such as, for instance, the manuals for JPs, in fact had their origins in readings at the Inns of Court, and if there were no readings there was no incentive for successful practising lawyers to go into print with new works of this kind.

At the same time, the collapse of the learning exercises was accompanied by the atrophy of the collective life of the Inns as homosocial spaces with a collective identity that they had been in the pre-Civil War days based broadly on the Ciceronian ideal of the role of law and lawyers in both the state and civil society. In addition the learning exercises, some of which, like modern university lectures, were better than others, were part of a largely oral world where legal and constitutional ideas were vented and argued about, not just in London, but in towns and villages as well, in conjunction with the speeches lawyers (or country squires with some legal learning) made in the localities, on the election of mayors, or at meetings of quarter sessions or assize. From the outbreak of the Civil War onwards, we can only imagine what such arguments might have looked like because the sociability that had been at their core broke down. It cannot be right to ignore the potential significance of the fact that in an age when parliamentary ordinances (or statutes) achieved their supremacy, there were no more lectures on statutes. During significant changes in the form of government of the polity, the collective voices of the legal profession were not heard as loudly as they had been in, say, the reign of Queen Elizabeth. More concretely, this removal of a space where English legal thought could be redigested and developed was particularly unfortunate at a time when some serious legal and political questions were being asked, and I want to dwell for a couple of minutes on two of them. The first is the question of contracts and obligations; and the second is that having to do with the use of civil power to coerce religious observance.

In talking about obligations, I'm glad to be able to refer to Victoria Kahn's learned and aptly titled book *Wayward Contracts*.[23] Concentrating on the writings of Milton, Hobbes, and Margaret Cavendish, she probes the multitude of questions that were thrown up in an age when the acute problem of why anyone should maintain their loyalty to a political regime was regularly discussed in terms of a contract, the conditions under which it was made, as well as those in which might permit one or another

[22] [RH] On the vitality of manuscript culture, notably among lawyers, see Harold Love, *Scribal Publication in Seventeenth-Century England* (Oxford: Oxford University Press, 1993).

[23] Victoria Kahn, *Wayward Contracts: The Crisis of Political Obligation in England, 1640–1674* (Princeton: Princeton University Press, 2004).

of the parties to break it. Furthermore, as Kahn also points out, the writers she discusses resorted to modes of political thought that aimed either for abstract mathematical reasoning along the lines of Hobbes, as well as the development of arguments from either divine law or natural law, as in the case of Milton. While I could quibble about bits and pieces of the argument, on the whole I think Kahn is right. Yet, while I would maintain that it is significant that Milton and John Locke were the sons of a London notary, and a west-country solicitor respectively, the thought of lawyers does not figure much in the argument. One reason for this is that there is not much evidence of extensive legal thought about the subject in this way, and this in itself is significant. Pre-1640s legal thought in fact contained many of the ingredients in the arguments. A view that civil society was created by some form of mutual consent in order to escape a potentially Hobbesian state of nature where there would be a war of all against all, was part of school-boy reading of Cicero. The notion of self interest in the form of a need to protect land and goods as well as wives and children was widely touted in legal discourse as a reason for actively participating in civil society. Furthermore, obligations in the form of contractual obligations to do or not do something were the bread and butter of the legal system, where the penal bond with conditional defeasance was the standard legal instrument. Based on the idea that a failure to perform would result in the implementation of a previously agreed penalty (normally monetary, but of course explored to the hilt in *The Merchant of Venice*) the bond could be cruel but it also reflected a high degree of human agency in the making and in taking responsibility for its consequences. The bond had also for centuries replaced any moral or religious obligation to pay the debt (or relieve it) with the coercion of a monetary penalty. At the same time the notion of equity, which might take some account of the circumstances, or deceit or fraud by one of the parties, was a known part of that aspect of legal thought associated with the Court of Chancery, and both during the pre-Civil War period and during the 1640s and 1650s the jurisdiction of the Court of Chancery was the one most subject to calls for reform both inside and outside of the legal profession.

It is striking that no specifically legal argument developing these lines of thought emerged during the so-called Engagement controversy, which arose in the wake of the execution of the king and the establishment of the Republic.[24] Thanks, however, to a manuscript treatise on the nature of laws that was written by Hale, probably in the early 1660s, we know what such an argument written in the natural law idiom of Hobbes and Milton looked like.[25] Following the lead of his mentor, John Selden, who developed his own views about natural law theory in *Mare clausum*, a work that adopted the language

[24] [JR] On this, see Q. Skinner, 'Conquest and Consent: Thomas Hobbes and the Engagement Controversy', in *The Interregnum: The Quest for Settlement, 1646–60*, ed. G. E. Aylmer (London: Macmillan, 1972); G. Burgess, 'Usurpation, Obligation and Obedience in the Thought of the Engagement Controversy', *HJ*, 29 (1986), 515–26; E. Vallance, 'Oaths, Casuistry, and Equivocation: Anglican Responses to the Engagement Controversy', *HJ*, 44 (2001), 59–77.

[25] [LH] MS Hargrave 13, 'Treatise on the Law of Nature Attributed to Sir Matthew Hale', Lincoln's Inn Library.

of the Dutch thinker Hugo Grotius in order to argue against him over English maritime jurisdiction, Hale developed his thoughts in this work on the basis of a single God-given natural law: that we should keep our promises, without any qualification at all.

As Richard Tuck has observed, the logic of the views advanced by Hale and Selden look like forming the basis for a theory of political obligation even stricter than that of Hobbes.[26] Yet, the fact is that Hale's work was never published and there is no evidence that it was widely known. There had never been anything quite like it before, and I think it is fair to say that there never was anything quite like it afterwards. There were many possible reasons for this, but I'd argue that the principal one was that the only thing the lawyers could offer during the crisis that really mattered to people was some kind of certainty about the laws they lived under and which they looked to still to defend their persons and property. When this was the primary issue, exploring the reasons why people might legitimately break their contracts, or change the laws under which they lived did not seem a particularly wise thing to do. Furthermore, one of the principal complaints of common lawyers before the civil wars had been that Churchmen like Laud interfered in secular affairs in ways that violated the nature of the vocation, and which depended upon scriptural authority and older clerical writings to assert the opinions that they claimed were based on notions of divine law. [Selden once quipped that the problem with bringing religious thought into the equation was that a contract made between two men over some business deal might be brought into question by one of the parties who would begin to cite scripture about why he should be able to get out of it.] Indeed, such was Hale's scepticism about abstract theories that he comprehensively endorsed the rather introverted, or closed, tradition of common law thought typified by Coke in a short manuscript treatise that he wrote in response to an attack on the common law by Thomas Hobbes. '[I]f the most refined Braine under heaven would go about to enquire by speculation, or by reading Plato or Aristotle, or by considering the laws of the Jews or other nations to find out how lands descend in England ... he would lose his labour ...' because those laws were simply positive laws made either through customary judgements in court, or as a result of explicit parliamentary statute.[27]

At the same time, after the Restoration, Hale, like Sir Francis North, was acutely aware that fraud, particularly in connection with the conveyancing of land was endemic, and though they attempted to do something about it in the form of a statute of frauds, and less successfully, the creation of registries of deeds, deception and fraud clearly stand out as features of nearly every aspect of Restoration culture, including the politics and the literature.[28] In the purely legal sources this seems to emerge most clearly in connection

[26] [JR] R. Tuck, *Natural Rights Theories: Their Origin and Development* (Cambridge: Cambridge University Press, 1979), 100.

[27] [JR] 'Reflections on Mr Hobbes his *Dialogue*', printed in W. S. Holdsworth, *A History of English Law*, 15 vols (London: Methuen, 1962–1965), 5.500–13, at 505. Discussed in A. Cromartie, *Sir Matthew Hale, 1609–1676: Law, Religion, and Natural Philosophy* (Cambridge: Cambridge University Press, 1995), 98–103.

[28] [JR] 'Mr Vaughan' was given leave to bring in a bill presenting frauds in making conveyances on 31 March 1664; it was first read on 6 April and for a second time, and was committed, on 18 April. On the

with the greatly expanding use of mortgages, from the Interregnum onwards, to raise money and the growing involvement of land in the market for credit, phenomena which were also associated with the simultaneous development in both London and the provinces of something like deposit banking and enormous real estate business such as that managed by the sometime Lord Mayor of London, Sir Robert Clayton.

According to a surprising statement in the commonplace book of the lawyer and politician Sir Henry Powle, a lack of transparency about what people were really worth and owed lay at the heart of all English business transactions, including those of merchants as well as the gentry.[29] And in a remarkable speech he gave in Parliament against a measure for introducing the registration of titles to land, Heneage Finch, a future Lord Chancellor, went so far as to remind MPs that the ability to keep their titles secret was a safeguard against confiscations by the Crown that might take place in times of political or religious controversy. Given views such as these and the well-known licentiousness of Restoration court life, it seems right to wonder whether there was a more general, and socially respectable, culture of anti-nominianism, or disregard for law that marked a real cultural shift from before the Civil War years. As Steven Zwicker has shown, during the 1650s Isaac Walton used Georgic conventions in *The Complete Angler* to advocate a retreat from commerce, litigation, and all of the kinds of contestation that had resulted from years of civil turmoil.[30] In a similar vein, I recall being struck some years ago by the debauched (drunken) alienation that is reflected in the royalist poetry of the same years. During the Interregnum, the abolition of the ecclesiastical courts, the jurisdictions that had previously been charged with maintaining moral law and what contemporaries called sexual continence, took place with remarkably little sign that anyone was really sorry to see them go. Although they were resurrected after 1660, political doubts about their legitimacy, and permanency, appear to have made it difficult to recover whatever role they had previously played in maintaining a common sense of moral standards.[31] Furthermore, although I admit the links are somewhat speculative, this line of thought also brings me to one of the most interesting, and understudied, literary genres of the period (though I use the term with due caution), the murder pamphlet. Though accounts of notorious murders, often within a domestic setting, existed before the civil wars, there seems to me little doubt that they had become a pretty profitable

last occasion it was accompanied by a bill for registering conveyances of sales and mortgages. *Journals of the House of Commons*, 8.540, 544, 545. See also the section on masquerading and illusions in J. Spurr, *England in the 1670s: 'This Masquerading Age'* (Oxford: Blackwell, 2000), 110–16. [RH] P. Zagorin, *Ways of Lying: Dissimulation, Persecution and Conformity in Early Modern Europe* (Cambridge, MA: Harvard University Press, 1990).

29 [LH] Sir Henry Powle comments that registers of men's debts, mortgages, and securities were likely to produce great inconveniences to men's credit by 'laying open their debts to the view of all ye world', which will 'make people afraid to trust', Beniecke MS 75, fol. 130.

30 [JR] S. N. Zwicker, *Lines of Authority: Politics and English Literary Culture, 1649–1689* (Ithaca: Cornell University Press, 1993), 69–70.

31 [JR] On the Restoration ecclesiastical courts, see D. A. Spaeth, *The Church in an Age of Danger: Parsons and Parishioners, 1660–1740* (Cambridge: Cambridge University Press, 2000); [RH] R.

line of publishing during the second half of the century, and I think that someone with a strong stomach could make an interesting study of them.[32] Often based on reports of trials in London and at assizes around the country, these sometimes appear to reflect concerns that a failure of social, religious, and legal institutions to instil proper standards of behaviour had led eventually to terrible results. But just as often what strikes me is a depiction of people who inexplicably or suddenly lost control of themselves, either out of some form of uncontrolled passion, or simply because their moral hard-wiring had somehow gone terribly wrong. Maybe it is best to see these as early examples of the kind of melodrama that is still evidently enjoyed by millions today in the form of TV crime shows, but maybe they should also be examined for what they might tell us about changing sensibilities about the capacity of social organization in the form of law to bridle disturbed human passion and emotion, a particular sinister side of the same disturbed consciences that pursued litigation, engaged in fraud, or led people to endanger their souls by following heterodox religious beliefs.

Having arrived at this gloomy point, however, I want to introduce a few words of qualification; I've come to give an account of law and lawyers, not to bury them. It could, for a start, be argued that the professional defence and insistence on adherence to what lawyers called the fundamental laws of the land meant that the changes in government and authority during the Interregnum, including what the rest of Europe considered a military dictatorship,[33] continued with relatively little fundamental change to social and economic relationships. At the same time, Interregnum judges seem to have been willing to follow public opinion in giving greater say to juries in determining questions about whether there were extenuating circumstances that might need to be taken into account about the performance of the terms of a contract or customary rights to land. They also helped to expand the concept of property in English land law by accepting the right of land-holders of all kinds, including so-called customary tenants, to pass on their holdings through inheritance, or to alienate or sell it as they thought best suited their interests. Sir Matthew Hale, the leading judge of the Restoration period up to his death in 1674, was an extremely accomplished and thoughtful man even though his principal legal writings, which were extensive, were not published until after his death.[34] If there

B. Outhwaite, *The Rise and Fall of the English Ecclesiastical Courts, 1500–1860* (Cambridge: Cambridge University Press, 2006).

[32] [JR] There are some: L. Robson, 'No Nine Days Wonder: Embedded Protestant Narratives in Early Modern Prose Murder Pamphlets', PhD thesis (Warwick, 2003); P. Marshall, 'Piety and Poisoning in Restoration Plymouth', in *Elite and Popular Religion*, ed. K. Cooper and J. Gregory, *Studies in Church History*, 42 (Boydell, 2006); J. Sharpe, '"Last Dying Speeches": Religion, Ideology and Public Execution in Early Modern England', *P&P*, 107 (1985), 144–67; P. Lake, 'Deeds against Nature: Cheap Print, Protestantism and Murder in Early Seventeenth-Century England', in *Culture and Politics in Early Stuart England*, K. Sharpe and P. Lake (London, 1994); P. Lake, 'Popular Form, Puritan Content? Two Puritan Appropriations of the Murder Pamphlet in Mid-Seventeenth-Century London', in *Religion, Culture and Society in Early Modern Britain*, ed. A. Fletcher and P. Roberts (Cambridge: Cambridge University Press, 1994).

[33] [JR] See A. Woolrych, 'The Cromwellian Protectorate: A Military Dictatorship?', *History*, 75 (1990), 207–31.

[34] See the *ODNB* entry by Alan Cromartie.

had not been a Popish Plot or a Glorious Revolution, we might pay more attention to the role of the judicial bench in presiding over the Court that was established in the wake of the Great Fire of 1666, and which was charged with the extremely onerous task of resolving the complex claims between landlords and tenants that arose in connection with the rebuilding of London in the aftermath. The city of London thought so much of it that it expressed its gratitude by commissioning portraits of all of the judges who had participated.

Yet the problem is, of course, that the Popish Plot and the Glorious Revolution did occur, and they had been preceded since 1640 by decades of confessional controversy and political factionalism so intense that it led to the emergence of the first distinct political parties, the Whigs and the Tories. Sometimes described as a period that saw the 'triumph of the lawyers',[35] I want to suggest instead that these controversies proved particularly toxic to the traditional judge-made law of the pre-1640 era.

As Jacqueline Rose has shown recently, the legal and constitutional questions associated with what Sir John Neale called the 'nationalization' of the English Church were diabolically complex and have a history that goes back to Henry VIII's break from Rome in the 1530s.[36] All I need to say here is that the municipal law of England and the common lawyers and judges had been frequently been involved. Having experienced the episcopate of Laud, lawyer MPs led the campaign against the right of bishops to sit in the House of Lords, and some of the long-lived of them such as Sir Harbottle Grimston and Sir John Maynard remained hostile to the temporal pretensions of the episcopal hierarchy of the established Church right up till the 1680s. At the same time, as the 1640s progressed, influential figures such as John Selden were adamantly opposed to the establishment of Presbyterianism along the Scottish model because they thought that it might result in a theocracy.[37] Selden and others were particularly concerned with how far temporal powers, including the secular legal consequence of excommunication, should be put in the hands of any Church whatever its constitution and whether it was established by statute law or not. But their hostility to the idea that scriptural interpretation should be a justification for human action and their hard wired anti-clericalism inclined them to favour some kind of control over the clergy, if not necessarily the laity. Selden was probably content with the situation after 1649, when the abrogation of the law requiring attendance at church on a Sunday co-existed with a form of established Church, combined with 'tryers and ejectors' in the provinces who were left to determine the suitability of ministers. In the desperate days of the autumn of 1659 Selden's protegé, and loyal Cromwellian, Bulstrode Whitelocke presided over a meeting of the Council of State which declared that religious belief should be one of the things that was beyond the law-making reach of the secular state.[38] Less than a year later, when the restoration of

[35] [JR] M. Landon, *The Triumph of the Lawyers: Their Role in English Politics, 1678–1689* (Tuscaloosa: University of Alabama Press, 1970).

[36] Rose, *Godly Kingship*.

[37] See Jason Rosenblatt's chapter in this volume.

[38] [LH] Possibly in BL Add. MS 37343, which Brooks elsewhere describes as including material published in Whitelock's *Memoirs of the Civil Wars*, as well as unpublished material on the relation between Church and State. See also Whitelock, *Diary*, 535–6.

the monarchy was inevitable, Matthew Hale mulled over the options of congregationalism, presbyterianism, and episcopacy, and opted rather reluctantly for episcopacy.

In Hale's opinion, although bishops could be as troublesome as presbyters, they were at least under the control of the state (Crown), and in any case the common law had shown that it could keep their excesses in bounds through ancient temporal remedies such as writs of *habeas corpus* and prohibitions.[39] What Hale evidently did not clearly foresee was that the Restoration church settlement created a relatively narrow Church of England that excluded Presbyterians as well as other, more radical groups such as Quakers, and that this settlement would come during the course of the 1660s by penal legislation passed by Parliament, which made proof of religious conformity a necessary qualification for holding public office, and which prosecuted meeting of conventicles or the presence of non-conformist ministers within five miles of towns enforced by severe penalties such as imprisonment and periods of transportation to the colonies. And, of course, to make things even more complicated, both Charles II and James II, no doubt inspired largely, though not exclusively, by a desire to relieve the pressure on Catholics attempted to use prerogative measures, known as declarations of indulgence in order to relieve the repression directed against them.

Restoration politics revolved thereafter around the enforcement of the penal legislation (including the Test Act of 1673) and sympathy for the position of Protestant non-conformists. Quakers drew increasingly systematically on the advice of lawyers to try and evade the worst consequence of the so-called Clarendon Code.[40] Ironically, Bulstrode Whitelocke, the loyal parliamentarian and Cromwellian, was asked by Charles II to write the legal brief in support of a licensed toleration that was proposed in his first declaration of indulgence. His second declaration, issued in 1672, was more fully detailed in terms of its specific operation and seems to reflect some of the legal learning that was being rehearsed in a case known as *Thomas v Sorrell* that was running at just about the same time.[41] In this case which was in fact about the granting of licenses to member of the Vintners Company, Sir John Vaughan, yet another friend of Selden (like Hale he was the executor of Selden's will) ruled in such a way as to argue that the king, as head of the Church, could offer licensed toleration so long as it could not be shown to cause harm to any other of his subjects. This was in its way a classic and somewhat elegant solution to the problem. Yet the declarations were of course vehemently opposed in Parliament as illegal extensions of the royal prerogative, and this was an argument which most common lawyers found it very hard to counter. Whitelocke acknowledged in his brief that penalties against non-conformists and Catholics that were introduced by parliament could only be relieved by parliamentary legislation, a point that was explicitly made by Hale in his own (very poorly reported) judgement in the case of *Thomas v Sorrell*.[42]

[39] [JR] M. Hale, *Historia placitorum coronae*, 2 vols (1736), 2.329–30; Rose, *Godly Kingship*, 116–20.

[40] C. Horle, *The Quakers and the English Legal System, 1660–1688* (Philadelphia: University of Pennsylvania Press, 1988).

[41] [JR] Rose, *Godly Kingship*, 91–2, 169–71.

[42] [JR] Cromartie, *Hale*, 127–31; but cf. Rose, *Godly Kingship*, 171, who reads Whitlocke to say that only parliament could remove the king's power to dispense. See BL Add. MS 21099, fol. 196^{r-v} and *The King's Right of Indulgence in Spiritual Matters ... Asserted* (1688), 54.

As the political controversy continued to broil over these issues as the reign of Charles entered the period of the Exclusion Crisis and the Popish Plot, and then of the even more tempestuous reign of James II, the problem for the lawyers was that there were in effect quite persuasive legal arguments on either side of the question.[43] Moreover, until the time of James II, the judges were given only limited scope to declare on them one way or another (remember *Thomas v Sorrell* was known as the Case of Wine), and it's striking to me that they in fact managed to bring very little that was new to the table in terms of the arguments they made. Whitelocke, for instance, openly acknowledged that much of the material in his brief had been collected by him before the civil wars, a fact that is verified by his surviving papers.[44] Most damaging of all, of course, the monarchs eventually found that they could attempt to solve the impasse by sacking judges and then replacing them on a scale that was unprecedented in English history. By the middle of the 1670s newly appointed judges openly acknowledged their partisanship, and during the reign of James II, the process had become so politicized that every single member of the judicial bench was sacked in the wake of his downfall in 1689.

It is hard to see how the integrity of the old judge-made system of common law could survive intact after being on the one hand overwhelmed by political factionalism, and on the other firmly put in its place by the fully developed advent of the supremacy of parliamentary statute. Susan Owen has suggested that many of the issues involved in the conflicts of the ecclesiastical polity in the Restoration period were rehearsed in the highly politicized, and quite extensive corpus of historical and political drama of the period, and it may be that it is worth going back to some of these works to look more carefully about how the notion of the rule of law was characterized.[45] But what she does tell us is that Whig lawyers on the whole were the sticklers for the strict letter of the law, whilst Tories stressed their greater willingness towards leniency and hence toleration. Lawyers were also subjected to a particularly vicious forms of satire which included labelling them as incompetent, self-interested cuckolds. I was delighted, for instance, to discover John Crowne's caricature of the aged Sir John Maynard as a dotty fee-taker with slurred speech so severe that it is hard to understand exactly what he was supposed to be saying, perhaps because Crowne wanted to characterize him as having nothing important to say.[46] Yet Maynard was a pretty remarkable political survivor who had suffered imprisonment during the civil wars for speaking out against the Army, and who was one of those lawyers whom the Presbyterian memorialist Roger Morrice labelled as having long been a friend of the non-conformists.[47]

[43] [JR] Rose, *Godly Kingship*, ch. 6.

[44] [JR] R. Spalding, *The Improbable Puritan: The Life of Bulstrode Whitelocke, 1605–1675* (1975), 279 n. 40; BL Add. MS 21099.

[45] [LH] Susan Owen, *Restoration Theatre and Crisis* (Oxford: Clarendon Press, 1996).

[46] [LH] In John Crowne's play, *The City Politiques* (1683). See Owen, *Restoration Theatre*, 99.

[47] [JR] M. Goldie, *Roger Morrice and the Puritan Whigs* (Woodbridge: Boydell, 2007), esp. 185–90. Morrice was Maynard's chaplain.

What this suggests to me is that characterizations of law in Restoration drama probably need to be approached with considerable caution, a point I'd like to develop just a little further by reference to one of William Wycherley's plays, *The Plain Dealer* (1677). [Although I discovered this work largely by accident, it is perfect for my purposes. Wycherly, like several other dramatists of his time, was known to reside in the Inns of Court. The leading male in the play, the self-proclaimed Plain Dealer, is a sea-captain on leave after an unsuccessful engagement with the Dutch, but, although he sometimes talks the language of honesty, he engages in ploys and deceptions to win his mistress, Olivia, a married woman who is herself hardly straightforward or of the highest moral standards. The supporting characters all have ends they are trying by various means to pursue, including Lady Blackacre, a litigious widow, who is keen to prevent her son from gaining control of his inheritance and her jointure, even if that means maintaining that he is not the legitimate heir of her husband by declaring him a bastard. There are lots of references to law, and one of the central scenes takes place in Westminster Hall, where Lady Blackacre has come to follow her litigation. Most of the wit in the play is at the expense of lawyers. The satire is wicked, if not all that penetrating. I admit to having some difficulty understanding exactly why audiences evidently found it entertaining, and even hilarious, perhaps a problem I would have shared with a legal old-timer like Sir John Maynard. Far from springing wonderful and unexpected metaphors out of dry legal language, the law, even from the perspective of Westminster Hall, seems to have little purchase on any kind of reality. Whereas pre-Civil War comedies frequently satirized procedural complexities and the clerical world that was responsible for them, *The Plain Dealer* points its barbs at the more learned barristers and Inns of Court men. Vacation times at the Inns of Court are dominated by revels and gambling rather than law lectures and legal learning. The numerous lawyers Lady Blackacre employs are only interested in their fees, and some of the best lines in the play are in her characterizations of what lawyers say in court. Council in Chancery merely tell stories; those in the Common Pleas say the same things over and over again, whilst those in the King's Bench involve harsh, prolix, and incomprehensible exchanges.

Although it undoubtedly has to be taken with a grain of satirical salt, it should be easy enough to see from the picture I have tried to draw of the legal history of the period that Wycherly's characterization of English law and lawyers must have had some purchase, and that it could only increase as the politicization of the bench and bar increased during the late 1670s and 1680s. Maybe it even reflects the early stages of that disconnection between law and society manifested in the decline of litigation and the contraction in the legal life of both metropolitan and provincial England. Yet rather than looking at changes in law as a reason for this, maybe I should look at changes in the character of society, and for better or worse I'm inspired to this point by Lady Blackacre, a character who is not crucial to the plot of *The Plain Dealer*, but who seems central to the play. Although she takes the litigious widow to new heights in making herself her own lawyer, the character type was already familiar from Elizabethan times (as for instance Tim Stretton shows), and Wilfred Prest some years ago in fact found traces of a so-called female solicitor who acted for clients in the late 1690s and early 1700s.[48] Blackacre is over the top but I like her. In the 1630s, after all, a relatively unknown barrister published a book called *The Lawes Resolution of Women's Rights* and I have argued elsewhere that the legal concept of coverture, which subsumed a married woman's rights into those of her husband, in fact made women more rather than less aware of theirs. Yet if I like her, I suppose I also have to assume that most of Wycherly's audience found her absurdly overbearing and very funny. And if I accept this as the perspective of the audience, do I also assume that they were laughing at the only character in the play who seems to have a clue about how law affected social relationships? She describes matrimony as a prison and at one point refers to the role of *habeas corpus* in moving women from one prison to another, a prescient observation that points to the use of the famous writ in the later eighteenth century by married women who were escaping the confinement by their husbands either in their homes or in insane asylums. In describing marriage as worse than excommunication, she seems to be aware of the central jurisprudential problem of the age, why the coercive power of the state should be used to penalize people who made choices, and entered into obligations, either on the grounds of conscience or because of the uncontrolled power of their passions.]

Bibiliography

Brooks, C. W. *Lawyers, Litigation and English Society* (London: Hambledon Press, 1998).

Brooks, C. W. *Law, Politics and Society in Early Modern England* (Cambridge: Cambridge University Press, 2008).

Horle, C. *The Quakers and the English Legal System, 1660–1688* (Philadelphia: University of Pennsylvania Press, 1988). Huntington MS HM 46323.

Kahn, Victoria. *Wayward Contracts: The Crisis of Political Obligation in England, 1640–1674* (Princeton: Princeton University Press, 2004).

Landon, M. *The Triumph of the Lawyers: Their Role in English Politics, 1678–1689* (Tuscaloosa: University of Alabama Press, 1970).

Owen, Susan. *Restoration Theatre and Crisis* (Oxford: Clarendon Press, 1996).

Rose, Jaqueline. *Godly Kingship in Restoration England: The Politics of Royal Supremacy, 1660–1688* (Cambridge: Cambridge University Press, 2011).

Spalding, R., ed. *The Diary of Bulstrode Whitelock, 1605–1675* (Oxford: Oxford University Press for the British Academy, 1990).

Tuck, Richard. *Natural Rights Theories: Their Origin and Development* (Cambridge: Cambridge University Press, 1979).

[48] [LH] See Tim Stretton, *Women Waging Law in Elizabethan England* (Cambridge: Cambridge University Press, 1998), 43–69; Wilfrid Prest, '"One Hawkins, A Female Sollicitor": Women Lawyers in Augustan England', *HLQ*, 57 (1994): 353–8.

PART III

ADMINISTERING THE LAW

CHAPTER 11

LAW ENFORCEMENT AND THE LOCAL COMMUNITY

JAMES SHARPE

THE study of communities, and the experience of the men and women who lived in them, has been a persistent theme in the social history of early modern England over the last four decades. This focus has generated a number of excellent studies, albeit with differing emphases and differing conclusions as to what exactly that experience entailed.[1] This interest in early modern communities has intersected with research on the history of crime in the early modern period. Scholars rapidly became aware that local crime control practices added a distinctive dimension to their subject, that community values might be influential in defining wrong-doers and deciding what should be done about them, that there were courts other than the assizes and quarter sessions, and that there was a need to research more deeply into those local office holders, notably parish constables, whose input into the law and order system was increasingly recognized as vital.[2] It became apparent that the community might have ideas about law enforcement

[1] The more important examples of this genre include: David G. Hey, *An English Rural Community: Myddle under the Tudors and Stuarts* (Leicester: Leicester University Press, 1974); Margaret Spufford, *Contrasting Communities: English Villagers in the Sixteenth and Seventeenth Centuries* (Cambridge: Cambridge University Press, 1974); Keith Wrightson and David Levine, *Poverty and Piety in an English Village: Terling 1525–1700*, 2nd edn (Oxford: Oxford University Press, 1995); Marjorie Keniston McIntosh, *A Community Transformed: The Manor and Liberty of Havering, 1500–1620* (Cambridge: Cambridge University Press, 1991); and a welcome example of a study of an urban community, David Underdown, *Fire from Heaven: The Life of an English Town in the Seventeenth Century* (London: Harper Collins, 1992). Mention should also be made of an important pioneering work, W. G. Hoskins, *The Midland Peasant: The Economic and Social History of a Leicestershire Village* (London: Macmillan, 1957).

[2] For two pioneering essays, see J. A. Sharpe, 'Crime and Delinquency in an Essex Parish', in *Crime in England 1550–1800*, ed. J. S. Cockburn (London: Methuen, 1977); and J. A. Sharpe, 'Enforcing the Law in the Seventeenth-Century English Village', in *Crime and the Law: The Social History of Crime in Western Europe since 1500*, ed. V. A. C. Gatrell, Bruce Lenman, and Geoffrey Parker (London: Europa Publications, 1980).

different from those of central government, and that there were two, or possibly more, concepts of order operating in the period.[3] Thus the study of law enforcement and crime control in early modern England had to encompass not only the national developments involving parliamentary legislation and the processes of state formation and not only the role of county elites as demonstrated by the activities of Justices of the Peace, but also embrace what has been described as the 'Politics of the Parish'.[4]

Unfortunately, reaching a precise definition of 'community' remains difficult. Alan Macfarlane, indeed, has noted a 1970s study which considered ninety-four different definitions of the concept, none of which proved totally satisfactory.[5] Perhaps the best way forward here would be to see 'community' operating in two dimensions. First, as a geographical area to which people feel an affinity. Thus people might feel themselves members of a village, urban, or county community, and derive at least part of their identity from that.[6] Second, there is the notion that 'community' implies a set of shared values, an idea best illustrated in early modern England by the notion of neighbourliness.[7] Historians of early modern English society are agreed, however, that the old sociological notion of the pre-industrial or 'traditional' world being characterized by tightly knit, immobile communities awaiting the transition to 'modernity' is a myth.[8] There were immense regional variations, but even relatively remote villages experienced some turnover of population: the early modern English village or small town might have been a 'face-to-face' society, but the faces were constantly changing. And historians would also agree that communities in the early modern period, both urban and rural, were being subjected to pressures from outside which challenged, changed, and possibly destroyed established notions of community: the gradual population increase of between *c.*1530 and *c.*1640, which had dire implications for grain prices and real wages, and which in many villages sharpened social stratification; the steady growth of capitalism, which likewise challenged existing social and moral structures, and also integrated even remote parishes and small towns into a national economic system; the deeper penetration of Protestant religious values into both urban and rural communities, challenging not only Catholicism but also traditional religious practices and attitudes; and the processes of state formation, again something which integrated even remote villages into

3 Keith Wrightson, 'Two Concepts of Order: Justices, Constables and Jurymen in Seventeenth-Century England', in *An Ungovernable People: The English and Their Law in the Seventeenth and Eighteenth Centuries*, ed. John Brewer and John Styles (London: Hutchinson, 1980).

4 Keith Wrightson, 'The Politics of the Parish in Early Modern England', in *The Experience of Authority in Early Modern England*, ed. Paul Griffiths, Adam Fox, and Steve Hindle (London: Macmillan, 1996).

5 Alan Macfarlane, in collaboration with Sarah Harrison and Charles Jardine, *Reconstructing Historical Communities* (Cambridge: Cambridge University Press, 1977), 2.

6 One very relevant consideration should be noted: many essential categories of administrative record are grouped on a parochial, manorial, borough, or county basis, so there is the constant risk of our notions of geographically based community being skewed by the record-keeping practices of contemporary administrators.

7 Wrightson, 'Politics of the Parish in Early Modern England'.

8 A point stressed by Macfarlane, *Reconstructing Historical Communities*, 1–2.

a national system, and which, even if only partially, extended the reach of Westminster into local society.[9]

In this essay my main focus will be on the period *c.*1530–1640, one which is seen as being characterized by the processes alluded to above. We need to consider, however, how these processes differed from what had gone before. As I pointed out in 1982, much of the early work on crime and the community in early modern England, my own included, failed to pay sufficient attention to work on crime and control on the medieval manor.[10] In the century before the coming of the Black Death in 1348 England experienced a population growth on a par to that experienced *c.*1530–1630, with the population of England at the beginning of the fourteenth century at least equalling that of the mid-seventeenth. The pressures thus created led manorial jurors, generally drawn from the upper reaches of village society, to attempt to control delinquent poorer villagers along lines that have been delineated for the early modern period. Thus on the Ramsey Abbey estates in the fourteenth century, 'the criminal justice system and the social system of the villages were bound closely together', so that 'manipulation of judicial system through jury service gave the village oligarchs … a powerful weapon for dominating their villages'.[11] Jurors serving on royal juries in fifteenth-century Gloucestershire, like parish officers around 1600, were drawn into the agenda of the state, and became 'willy-nilly, members of the expanding universe of consensual politics'.[12] Despite these earlier parallels, the interlocking processes of state formation, the development of capitalism and the progress of the Reformation combined to create a situation in the late Elizabethan and early Stuart periods which represented a marked change from what had gone before. Certainly Marjorie Keniston McIntosh, in an important study of late medieval social discipline, recognizes a quantum change towards the end of the sixteenth century.[13]

The overall changes at play can usefully be illustrated by adapting comments on the nature of economic change over this period by Joan Thirsk:

> When one has grasped the full diversity of England as a whole, then much of the dynamism in the kingdom's economic and social development in the sixteenth and seventeenth centuries may be seen to have come from localised changes, setting up a chain of reactions and interactions between neighbouring, varied, but closely-interdependent, regions and communities. Each and all of them became increasingly

[9] These processes are delineated brilliantly in Wrightson and Levine, *Poverty and Piety*.

[10] J. A. Sharpe, 'The History of Crime in Late Medieval and Early Modern England: A Review of the Field', *Social History*, 7 (1982): 187–203.

[11] Barbara Hanawalt, *Crime and Conflict in English Communities 1300–1348* (Cambridge, MA: Harvard University Press, 1979), 32, 52; see also J. A. Raftis, 'The Concentration of Responsibility in Five Villages', *Medieval Studies*, 28 (1966): 92–118; and Anne DeWindt, 'Peasant Power Structures in King's Ripton', *Medieval Studies*, 38 (1976): 236–67.

[12] R. B. Goheen, 'Peasant Politics? Village Community and the Crown in Fifteenth-Century England', *American Historical Review*, 96 (1991): 42–62; the quotation is at 50.

[13] Marjorie Keniston McIntosh, *Controlling Misbehaviour in England, 1370–1600* (Cambridge: Cambridge University Press, 1998), 210.

> reliant on the others, as first one and then another was more insistently, and then permanently, drawn into the mainstream of commercial marketing.[14]

Few would disagree with this model of the development of marketing and capitalism in early modern England. But this idea of partial, local, piecemeal, yet interconnected development furnishes an equally fruitful means of approaching the broader cultural and social shifts referred to in the previous paragraph. The two crucial elements extending their reach and their influence were Protestantism and central authority. Gradually, the inhabitants of England's nine thousand or so parishes became exposed to the new forms of religion prescribed in the 1559 religious settlement and preached by the university-educated clergy who came to minister to them. Some parishioners at least welcomed the new teaching and the new type of minister, internalized the values which were preached, and applied them to their own lives and to those of their co-parishioners. Likewise, the authority of the state became ever more intrusive. Writers of manuals for Justices of the Peace might complain about the increase in the workload for these officials which Elizabethan and early Stuart legislation created, but parochial officials, above all parish constables, were likewise having their duties increased, and likewise being subjected increasingly to the demands of central government and were possibly becoming more aligned with its values.

At the basis of our story, therefore, there lies the interplay between central authority and local communities over law enforcement, social discipline, and the maintenance of order more generally. What needs to be stressed is that there is considerable evidence that awareness of, use of, and possibly respect for the law had penetrated fairly deeply into English society.[15] People broke the law, and such records as survive from the assizes and similar courts indicate high levels of indictment for felony, and high levels of execution, in the period *c.*1580–1640.[16] Conversely, from the late Middle Ages it is obvious that people were accustomed to using the law for dispute resolution, frequenting a wide range of courts to do so. Although our focus in this essay is on controlling local crime and misbehaviour, the courts of the period also offered the settlement (and, indeed, pursuit) of civil differences between neighbours. For those who could afford to litigate in them, there were the courts of common law and equity at Westminster. More locally, suits between parties could be pursued at the manorial court, through the ecclesiastical cause at the church courts, on a writ of *nisi prius* at the assizes, at hundred courts, and at borough courts. Most Englishmen (and possibly women) of moderate property would have been involved in civil litigation at some time, and for some of them litigating was a familiar experience.[17] Involvement with the law might also come through jury service, through being a witness in a court case, or through participation in local office holding.

[14] Joan Thirsk, *The Rural Economy of England: Collected Essays* (London: Hambledon Press, 1984), ix–x.

[15] See J. A. Sharpe, 'The People and the Law', in *Popular Culture in Seventeenth-Century England*, ed. Barry Reay (London: Routledge, 1988).

[16] J. A. Sharpe, *Crime in Early Modern England 1550–1750*, 2nd edn (London: Longman, 1998), 81–90.

[17] High levels of involvement in litigation are demonstrated by Craig Muldrew's estimate, based on massive research on local court archives, that in the 1580s taking all England's courts together some 1,102,367 lawsuits a year, or rather more than one per household, would be initiated nationally: *The*

As an extreme illustration of this last point, the Manchester manorial leet meeting of 5 October 1620 listed seventeen jurors, then named 102 men appointed to various offices, from the Boroughreeve and the catchpole and the two constables to officers for supervising marketing, 'scavingers' charged with maintaining the cleanliness of various streets, and officers to ensure that the 'mastive dogs & bitches & greate mungrell currs' owned by Mancunians should be kept chained and muzzled and not allowed to roam the streets.[18] These jurors and officers constituted a fair proportion of the adult male population of a town which numbered around three thousand inhabitants, indicating both the dimensions of control which a well-governed small town might aspire to, and the willingness of its inhabitants to participate in that process of control.

Dispute settlement in a spectrum of tribunals ranging from the manorial court to those at Westminster had clearly habituated people to using the law. There were also a number of courts through which they could attempt to deal with the criminal or disorderly, whether neighbours or interlopers into the community. The assizes dealt with serious crime, felony, but presentment of lesser offences could take place there. The quarter sessions were, by about 1600, largely dealing with non-capital offences, and were also the forum at which large numbers of administrative and nuisance offences were presented. Where they still existed, manorial courts might witness the presentment of local nuisance offenders, among them scolds and hedgebreakers, and might also try cases of assault. From about 1580, after a post-Reformation slump, the ecclesiastical courts tried religious nonconformists and the sexually immoral, as well as a broader range of nuisance offenders, in increasing numbers.[19] The use of the term 'nuisance offender', which will recur regularly in this essay, reminds us of a basic fact. On the level of the early modern parish or small town community, the law would frequently be invoked not so much in reaction to a specific offence, but rather as a means of restraining, correcting, or punishing broader, and sometimes multifaceted, forms of misbehaviour. At issue was a concern over social regulation, over personal behaviour, and with forms of what were to be considered undesirable conduct, such as drunkenness, sexual misconduct, gambling, living idly, and disruption through verbal and physical violence. There was a clear concept of what proper neighbourly behaviour was, and much of the business coming through the local courts stemmed from breaches of this.

In such a situation much depended on the quality of parochial officers. Godfrey Goodman, vicar of Stapleford Abbots in Essex between 1606 and 1620, had clear ideas on this subject:

> Here in the country with us, if a man's stock of a few beasts be his own, and that he lives out of debt, and paies his rent duly and quarterly, we hold him a very rich and

Economy of Obligation: The Culture of Credit and Social Relations in Early Modern England (London: Macmillan, 1998), 236.

18 *The Court Leet Records of the Manor of Manchester*, ed. J. P. Earwaker, 12 vols (Manchester: Henry Blackcock, 1884–1890), 3.26–9.

19 These tribunals are discussed in Sharpe, *Crime in Early Modern England*, ch. 2, 'Courts, Officers and Documents'.

> sufficient man; one that is able to doe the King and country good services; we make him a constable, a sidesman, a head-borough, and at length a church-warden; we raise him by degrees, we prolong his ambitious hopes, and at last we heape all our honours upon him. Here is the great governor amongst us.[20]

Such studies as have been so far undertaken confirm this impression that local office holders—constables, churchwardens, and following the Poor Law Acts of 1598 and 1601 overseers of the poor—were drawn from the petty gentry, the yeomanry, and the richer artisans and tradesmen. In some villages the same men would serve in these roles, probably more than once, forming a 'loose oligarchy' which in effect ran their respective parishes. To these office holders might be added, on locations where manorial court were still active, manorial jurors. Thus investigation into the village background of witchcraft accusations in North Moreton, on the Oxfordshire/Berkshire border, reveals that manorial jurors in the late Elizabethan and Jacobean periods were drawn from the main farming families in the parish, families which also supplied constables and churchwardens.[21] These local notables were exactly the sort of 'able and sufficient men' from whom it was felt local office holders should be drawn. Obviously the men holding these offices were not invariably of irreproachable character, but, insofar as information is available, they were generally men likely to be thought well of by their neighbours: the type of personality traits seen as desirable among such officers is suggested by Edward Riches of Langford in Essex, reported for 'drinking himself drunk to the end that it might be a reasonable excuse for him not to be churchwarden'.[22] And despite the obvious burdens that a year as constable or churchwarden might incur, a fair number of eligible men seemed happy to take these offices on. A clue for one possible motivation is provided by William Parker of Myddle in Shropshire, who bribed the brother of the village's rector to ensure that he would be chosen as churchwarden because 'he affected to be counted somebody' in the parish.[23]

Earlier understanding of parish constables was badly skewed by the availability of a familiar literary stereotype of inefficient and comic parish officers in the shape of Dogberry and Verges.[24] Research into the early modern parish constable, however, suggests a more complex and more positive situation. If nothing else, the sheer variety of tasks which constables were expected to perform indicates a faith among contemporaries in the effectiveness of the office. The expense accounts of the constables of

[20] Quoted in C. Bridenbaugh, *Vexed and Troubled Englishmen 1590–1642* (Oxford: Clarendon Press, 1968), 242.

[21] James Sharpe, *The Bewitching of Anne Gunter: A Horrible and True Story of Football, Witchcraft, Murder and the King of England* (London: Profile Books, 1999), 27–8.

[22] F. G. Emmison, *Elizabethan Life: Morals and the Church Courts* (Chelmsford: Essex County Council, 1973), 233; Riche claimed that 'he is lame and cannot come and travail about the office', and offered 13s 6d to the use of the poor to be excused.

[23] Richard Gough, *The History of Myddle*, ed. David G. Hey (Harmondsworth: Penguin Books, 1981), 239.

[24] E.g. the comments of A. L. Rowse, *The England of Elizabeth: The Structure of Society* (London: Macmillan, 1950), 356.

Manchester, to take a very full example, illustrate the point. In the accounting year 1612–1613, for instance, we find the constables claiming money for disbursements made to two 'Grecians' (presumably scholars of some sort, but in any case recognized as legitimate travellers), repairing the bars in the window of the town dungeon, conveying men suspected of felony to the county gaol at Lancaster, paying a drummer to attend a militia muster, conveying a cripple by cart to Chetham, whipping a Nottinghamshire man and 'his supposed wyffe' as vagrants, whipping another man at the direction of a local justice for 'filchinge', and for whipping four individuals for fornication.[25] Research by Joan R. Kent has provided a much deeper understanding of the early modern English constable. As she confirms, the parish constable system did not constitute anything like a modern professional police force. But, arguably, it met the expectations of the day, and the men filling to office, in large measure, discharged their duties as diligently as they could, despite being in a situation where they were constantly subject to the rival demands of central government or of county Justices of the Peace, and those of their neighbours. They were also characteristically drawn from the 'better sort' of villager, in both economic and behavioural terms, and were increasingly literate.[26] Perhaps the most telling comment on contemporary expectations about parish constables comes from somebody rather further up the governmental hierarchy, Oliver Cromwell when Lord Protector. On 13 April 1657 Cromwell, addressing a committee from Parliament, searched for an appropriate analogy to explain why he had not accepted the crown:

> So far as I can, I am ready to serve you not as a king, but as a constable ... for truly I have, as before God, often thought that I could not tell what my business was, nor what I was in the place I stood in, save comparing myself to a good constable set to keep the peace of the parish.

One suspects that the image which Cromwell was attempting to evoke among his listeners was of something rather more substantial than Dogberry.[27]

If the duties of constables were expanding, so too were those of churchwardens. The office of churchwarden was initially an essentially parochial one: they were appointed by their neighbours to look after the possessions of their local parish churches, an increasingly important matter in the later Middle Ages when in many parishes, parishioners seem to have made a heavy material and emotional investment in their local church. But over the sixteenth and early seventeenth centuries these parochial officers became increasingly involved in ecclesiastical discipline. The churchwardens' first

[25] *The Constables' Accounts of the Manor of Manchester from the Year 1612 to the Year 1647, and from the Year 1743 to the Year 1778*, ed. J. P. Earwaker (Manchester, 1891), 1.5–7.

[26] Joan R. Kent, *The English Village Constable 1580–1642: A Social and Administrative Study* (Oxford: Clarendon Press, 1986).

[27] W. C. Abbott, ed., *The Writings and Speeches of Oliver Cromwell* (Cambridge, MA: Harvard University Press, 1947), 4.407.

civil duties seem to have dated from Henry VIII's reign, when they were given responsibility for helping to provide arms for soldiers and help for injured veterans. Their role really expanded after the Reformation, when central authority needed to ensure conformity to religious changes. In 1552 the first statute was passed requiring everybody to attend church on Sunday, and after the reversals of Mary's reign Protestantism returned again with the 1559 Act of Settlement which, *inter alia*, tasked the churchwardens with collecting the fines due from those who did not attend church, and disburse the funds thus collected for the benefit of the poor of the parish. This legislation initiated a sort of local administrative 'mission creep', through which the churchwardens found themselves responsible not just for collecting fines from those failing to attend church, but also for detecting and presenting them to the ecclesiastical courts, along with fornicators, adulterers, people drinking in the alehouse during time of divine service, people who worked on the Sabbath, and a broad range of local nuisance offenders who had disquieted their fellow parishioners, or had at least disquieted the more respectable among them. These and other responsibilities were enshrined in the visitation articles issued on a regular basis to churchwardens by bishops and archdeacons, and the official expectations about the contribution of the churchwardens to the maintenance of parochial religious conformity and morality were embedded in the canons of 1604. Thus the churchwarden, perhaps even more than the constable, demonstrates how local officers were sucked into the machinery of the early modern English state.[28]

Constables, churchwardens, overseers of the poor and manorial jurors were all drawn from the 'better sort' of the village, rarely gentry, but from the yeomen and more substantial husbandmen and artisans who formed the social centre of gravity of most rural communities. These men must have felt themselves increasingly distanced from the growing mass of poor which the broader socio-economic changes of the period created. An easily accessible and much reprinted body of 'rogue literature' has long made the historian and the literary scholar familiar with the vagrant threat of the period, although archival work has much modified the received wisdom which this literature created. Examining a broader range of sources reveals that as well as the vagrant threat, contemporaries were concerned about the potentially disorderly resident poor, those 'lewd and idle' people who were increasingly seen as troublesome by social commentators, legislators, and the more respectable elements in the community. In 1601 Parliament passed an Act 'To avoid and prevent diverse misdemeanours in lewd and idle persons'. The preamble of this Act provides an interesting insight into one set of activities which the well affected of the parish were clearly finding irritating and also of the type of people felt to be involved in them:

[28] I have based this account largely on Eric Carlson, 'The Origins, Functions and Status of the Office of Churchwarden, with Special Reference to the Diocese of Ely', in *The World of Rural Dissenters, 1520–1725*, ed. Margaret Spufford (Cambridge: Cambridge University Press, 1995); see also J. S. Craig, 'Co-operation and Initiative: Elizabethan Churchwardens and the Parish Accounts of Mildenhall', *Social History*, 18 (1993): 357–80.

> Unlawful cutting or taking away of corn and grain growing, robbing of orchards and gardens, digging up or taking away fruit-trees, breaking of hedges, pales or other fences, cutting or spoiling of woods or under-woods standing and growing, and such like offences, are now more commonly committed by lewd and mean persons than in former times; and that the said offences are great causes of the maintaining of idleness, and the persons which commit the same, are not for the most part able, nor have wherewith to make recompense or satisfaction.[29]

It may be a little hyperbolic to talk of a 'criminalization of the poor' in this period, but in some localities, and in the social analyses of at least some contemporary observers, something very like this process was taking place.

Evidence of how concerns about control and the maintenance of order might become focused on a local level is provided by a remarkable document, the Swallowfield Articles of December 1596.[30] Swallowfield was a chapelry of Shinfield parish lying on the borders of Berkshire and Hampshire, and in the aftermath of the disastrous harvest of 1596, the third of a run of bad harvests, the settlement's 'chief inhabitants' were obviously anxious to achieve tighter control of their community. These articles may, indeed, have been symbolic of a transition in community government, away from the old-style manorial institutions towards the 'select vestries' or 'town meetings' which by the 1590s were beginning to demonstrate how, in many places, parish government was becoming concentrated in the hands of the richer inhabitants. The articles are redolent of traditionally minded upper villagers trying to get to grips with the effects of economic dislocation and, probably unconsciously, of the consequences of sharpened social stratification.[31] They began by noting that there were no Justices of the Peace resident in the area, and that the chief inhabitants had therefore put their articles together 'to the end that we may the better and more quietly lyve together in good love and amyte to the praise of God, and the better serving of her ma[jes]tie'. Many of the articles were indeed concerned with the desire to 'live quietly', but some were clearly adjusted to the concerns of the 1590s. Householders providing shelter for pregnant women whose offspring might prove to be a burden on the parish were singled out for special attention. Likewise, if a single woman gave birth, the village authorities, with the assistance of the justices if necessary, were to discover the identity of the father, and force him to pay maintenance. Poor people who might 'malepertlye compare w[i]th their betters & sett them at nought' were to be warned to behave better, and reported to the justices as 'comon disturbers of peace & quietnes' if they failed to do so. Parish officers were not to be censured for performing their offices, 'but shalbe used w[i]th all gentellnes both in word and deed'. 'Pilferers, backbyters [i.e. slanderers, malicious gossips], hedge breakers & myscheveous persons' were to be suppressed. Couples were not to be allowed to marry unless they

[29] Statute 43 Elizabeth I, cap. 7; the provisions of this statute suggest that its enforcement created yet more work for justices and constables.

[30] S. Hindle, 'Hierarchy and Community in the Elizabethan Parish: The Swallowfiled Articles of 1596', *HJ*, 42 (1999): 835–51.

[31] For the articles, see Hindle, 'Hierarchy and Community', 848–51.

had sufficient means to support themselves, and nobody was to keep 'inmates', poor lodgers who might become chargeable to the township, those frequenting alehouses on the Sabbath were to corrected, while drunkards were to be fined or, if poor, put in the stocks. And, to help maintain ideological control servants were to be sent to church on Sunday rather than sent out on business, so that they could hear 'that wiche shall ther be delyverd by the mynyster out of the word of God for their edifycation'. One is left wondering in how many other settlements of the period the 'chief inhabitants' envisaged imposing similar controls.

Among the more routine presentment of those failing to attend church or failing to pay church rates, or of fornicators and adulterers, the presentments at the ecclesiastical courts sometimes refer to general nuisance offenders whose conduct had caused disquiet in their communities. James Mills, of Duncton in Sussex, was presented in 1623 for talking and behaving badly in service time, and for verbal abuse and misbehaviour towards the minister. He was also presented 'for a common swearer and an ordinary drunkard', who had come to church on Whit Sunday drunk and had sworn 'most horribly' in the churchyard while communion was being administered. His behaviour, the presentment declared, was such that 'we cannot, no, not at service time, be quiet for him'.[32] Likewise John Titman, of Woodham Mortimer in Essex, was presented in 1592 for having two wives living, for not receiving communion the previous Easter, for not coming 'orderly' to church, and for being a brawler and 'skowlder' with his neighbours.[33] Female petty offenders were well represented by two women from Graffam, in Sussex, presented in 1621. Joan Harman was sexually immoral, a 'gadder up and downe', and was also a 'common carry tale' and a 'maker of lyes', and hence by implication a disrupter of her community. She had, moreover, entered marriage contracts with '2 or 3 knaves', but had married none of them. She was presented alongside Elizabeth Williams, who had wandered about the country with a 'debauched knave', claiming he was her husband, a claim she retracted after being excommunicated. She was, however, with child by him, but suffered a miscarriage after falling over a stile.[34] Another Sussex presentment, in this case involving Mary Robins of Shipley, carried a clear indication of community disapproval at immoral conduct. Robins had last Christmas been delivered of a bastard, fathered on her, she confessed, by John Hall. The presentment continued 'this woman is an impudent queane and hath had one bastard already, wherefore we desire of the court that some severe course may be taken with her, to make her an example unto others'.[35]

Where a manorial leet was active local nuisance offenders might be presented there. One such was Henry Abbott junior of Earls Colne in Essex, presented for a variety of offences at one sitting of the local leet. He drew blood of William Clark, and seriously damaged one of his fingers; he came out of his house into the street one night and abused

[32] *Churchwardens' Presentments (17th century) Part I, Archdeaconry of Chichester*, ed. H. Johnstone (Sussex Record Society, 49, 1947–1948), 71.

[33] Paul Hair, *Before the Bawdy Court* (London: Elek, 1972), 113

[34] *Churchwardens' Presentments (17th Century) Part I*, ed. Johnstone, 8.

[35] *Churchwardens' Presentments (17th Century) Part I*, ed. Johnstone, 68.

the parish watchmen; he himself refused to serve in the watch; he verbally abused many of his honest neighbours 'with very gross reproaches and words'; he habitually played at cards, dice, and tables and other unlawful games; and he was a sower of discord among his neighbours.[36] By the early seventeenth century, however, such offenders were increasingly likely to be dealt with by quarter sessions, for the problem they constituted could relatively easily be addressed by binding over, either to be of good behaviour, or to keep the peace. Accordingly, 'articles of complaint' against troublesome neighbours feature in quarter sessions records. One such troublesome neighbour was Robert Godfrey, an alehouse-keeper from Blackmore in Essex whose misbehaviour came to the attention of the Essex bench in 1621. He was a blasphemer, 'dycer', quarreller, and had broken the peace. He was suspected of felony, of receiving stolen goods, and of harbouring suspicious persons. He was an infrequent church attender, and was suspected of having fathered a bastard on his maidservant, his wife having been the first to level suspicions against him on that account. He kept a disorderly alehouse which the justices had three times, unsuccessfully, tried to suppress, he carried beer out to the ill-affected of the parish, and he had recently been found dead drunk by the constables after an alleged twenty-four hours of solid drinking.[37] Another example is provided by Henry Cartlage (or Cartledge) alias Webb of Bromsgrove in Worcestershire, whose neighbours requested to have bound over for good behaviour in 1617. Cartlage had already been bound over at the previous session, had verbally abused a woman involved in that process, had threatened to litigate at London against those who had given evidence, and had struck the dog of a man named Parr, declaring 'good behaviour or not if I may not strike the man I will strike the dog'. He had called Kenelm Grit a cuckold and his wife Alice a whore, and threatened to hang a pair of horns outside their house (he had, apparently, done so on a previous occasion). More generally, he was described as a man of evil behaviour, a common drunkard, a blasphemer, an abuser of his neighbours, about whom he made false reports, and a disturber of the peace. He was duly bound over.[38]

As well as the instigation of formal procedures against local deviants, there was a whole spectrum of informal sanctions which members of the community could invoke against petty offenders, or those who, although they had committed no criminal offences, had offended community norms.[39] Perhaps the most striking of these were English versions of the charivari, known variously as skimmingtons or ridings ('riding the stang' in the north). These varied in format, extent, and degree of elaboration, but generally shared a number of core elements. These manifestations of the desire of the community (or at least part of the community) to mock transgressions of locally

[36] Macfarlane, *Reconstructing Historical Communities*, 59; Macfarlane does not date this presentment, although it is probably from *c.*1600.

[37] Essex Record Office (hereafter ERO), Chelmsford, Q/SR 233/128.

[38] *Calendar of the Quarter Sessions Papers*, vol. 1: *1591–1643*, ed. J. Willis Bund (Worcestershire Record Society, 1900), 252.

[39] For an overview of these, see Martin Ingram, 'Ridings, Rough Music and Mocking Rhymes in Early Modern England' in *Popular Culture in Seventeenth-Century England*, ed. Reay.

approved norms were, in the late Tudor and early Stuart periods, apparently directed most frequently against men who were felt to be exercising insufficient husbandly control over their wives. Surrounded by a crowd beating on basins and using other means to create a cacophony known to historians as 'rough music', a number of men would support a pole on which two other men, one dressed as a woman, assumed the roles of the couple in question. This assembly would parade outside the house of the unfortunate victim of their mockery, and sometimes range more widely in the surrounding area.[40] Another fairly widespread manifestation of disapproval of misconduct, and especially sexual misconduct, was the mocking rhyme. An interesting demonstration of the spread of literacy, these would sometimes appear in several copies within a village or small town, and draw attention to the sexual activities of one or several of its members.[41] Such informal community sanctions were sometimes reflected in the official punishments meted out by local authorities. The punishment of sexual offenders, particularly brothel keepers, by borough courts frequently involved offenders being carted or otherwise paraded through the streets with basins being beaten around them, an officially sanctioned version of the charivari and rough music. A more vicious conflation of formal and informal shaming punishment occurred at Burton on Trent in 1618, when a couple who had been posing as brother and sister were found in bed together, and aroused communal ire against their immorality. Apparently under the direction of the local constable they were dragged from the house where they lodged, paraded through the streets, subjected to rough music and cries of 'a whore and a knave', put in the town stocks overnight, and then banished from the town.[42]

Against such instances of what Keith Thomas has termed 'the tyranny of local opinion' might be set numerous instances in which local authorities showed considerable flexibility in their treatment of wrong-doers.[43] Indeed, one of the determining characteristics of the local law enforcement system in this period was the way in which constables, churchwardens, and Justices of the Peace frequently exercised discretion in such matters. There is some evidence of local nuisance offenders being formally prosecuted after previous warnings. Daniel Finch of Great Burstead in Essex habitually came home drunk and abused his wife and children, but had been admonished a number of times by the parish constables and other 'honest neighbours' before he was presented to the quarter sessions.[44] Other, less desirable, factors might inhibit prosecution. In 1610 the incumbent of Sydenham in Oxfordshire described how his life was being made a misery by the disorderly behaviour of two brothers, Robert and John Sule, but that the churchwardens would not present them because they were loathe to offend Robert

[40] Martin Ingram, 'Ridings, Rough Music and the "Reform of Popular Culture" in Early Modern England', *P&P*, 105 (1984): 79–113.

[41] Adam Fox, 'Ballads, Libels and Popular Ridicule in Jacobean England', *P&P*, 145 (1994): 47–83.

[42] Joan R. Kent, '"Folk Justice" and Royal Justice in Early Seventeenth-Century England: A Charivari in the Midlands', *Midland History*, 8 (1983): 70–85.

[43] Keith Thomas, *Religion and the Decline of Magic: Studies in Popular Beliefs in Sixteenth- and Seventeenth-Century England* (London: Weidenfeld and Nicholson, 1971), 526.

[44] ERO, Q/SR 242/23.

Sule, who was Sydenham's miller and hence somebody whom it was best not to antagonize.[45] Parish officers might also put in a good word for those they were reporting to officialdom. Thus in another case from Sydenham the churchwardens, presenting William Heifeelde and Ellin Higges, 'the one a bachelor, the other a widdowe', for having conceived a child out of wedlock, pointed out that 'they are now lawfully married since Easter, ij poore folks, living ever since the former acte honestlye and orderly together, I praye you shew them what favoure possiblye yow maye'.[46] Sometimes, indeed, those troubled by petty criminals took matters into their own hands without invoking formal action. Richard Gough, in his account of Myddle in Shropshire, noted the fate of Reece Wenlocke, a member of one of the more troublesome families in the township. Wenlocke was known as an habitual hedgebreaker, taking wood from their hedges for firewood, and concerns grew over further depredations when news spread that he had made a new oven, since, 'according to the manner of such things, it was first to be burnt, to be made fit for use'. A servant lad decided to make appropriate precautions:

> As he walked by a hedge, which was neer Reece's house, he saw there a great dry stick of wood, and took it home with him, and bored a hole in the end of it with an augur, and put a quantity of gun powder in it, and a peg after it, and put it again into the hedge. And it happened that Reece Wenlocke, among other hedgewood, took this stick to burn in his oven, and when he cast it into the fire in the oven, it blew up the top of it, and set fire to the end of the house.[47]

One feels this would have given more satisfaction to the parishioners of Myddle than Reece being formally prosecuted.

Consideration of criminally inclined families returns us to the behavioural divergence between richer and poorer villages. Certainly, something like the divergence along these lines indicated by Keith Wrightson and David Levine for the village of Terling (known to social historians as the 'Terling Model') was experienced elsewhere, but other studies have not demonstrated it in quite such a clear-cut fashion. Martin Ingram, in a study of Keevil in Wiltshire, found similarities between that settlement and Terling in terms of demographic pressure and enhanced social stratification, but he found that that attempts at reforming popular culture and imposing godly discipline were much more fragmented and confused.[48] More pertinently, two studies of Essex parishes show a less certain pattern. At Earls Colne over the late sixteenth and early seventeenth century, a situation like that obtaining at Terling occurred, with the input of Puritanism and evidence of respectable behaviour among those chosen for parochial office, but the poor

[45] *The Churchwardens' Presentments in the Oxfordshire Peculiars of Dorchester, Thame and Banbury*, ed. S. A. Peyton (Oxfordshire Record Society, 10, 1928), 161.

[46] *Churchwardens' Presentments*, ed. Peyton, 163.

[47] Gough, *History of Myddle*, ed. Hey, 107–8.

[48] Martin Ingram, 'Religion, Communities and Moral Discipline in Late Sixteenth and Early Seventeenth-Century England: Case Studies', in *Religion and Society in Early Modern Europe 1500–1800*, ed. Kaspar von Greyerz (London: Allen and Unwin, 1984), 190.

were not disproportionately represented among offenders, with many people of property other than office holders being prosecuted for a range of offences.[49] At Kelvedon in Essex, examination of offenders in the period 1600–1640, taking in manorial and ecclesiastical courts along with quarter sessions and assizes, revealed that a large proportion of men of property were prosecuted for minor offences, and that among the parish's constables was the egregious offender John Ayly. The keeper of Kelvedon's 'Unicorn' inn, between 1613 and 1638 Ayly was presented before the archdeacon's court for failing to attend church, swearing, keeping ill rule in his house, or selling drink on the Sabbath (for which he was presented more or less annually in the 1620s), and for sexual immorality, involving a long-term liaison with a servant of his named Avis Shepheard, and a less lengthy involvement with the wife of John Francis. None of this prevented him from being appointed constable for Felix Hall manor in Kelvedon in 1631.[50] Moreover, doubts about the connection made between Puritanism and social control by Wrightson and Levine were raised by Margaret Spufford.[51]

Thus the 'Terling Model' established by Wrightson's and Levine's study may not be universally applicable in its fully developed form. Yet it remains clear that the developments the study alludes to—the growth of capitalism, sharper social stratification, the ever-extending reach of central authority, the impact of godliness—were gradually working their way into English communities and interacting with the long-standing desire for order, stability, and hierarchy within those communities. Consider an order against scolds made in 1620 by the manorial court jury at Manchester. 'Beinge fullye and at large informed by the testimonye of manye of their sufficient and well reputed neighboures' the jurors decided to take action against Isabel Rychardson and Alice Worthington alias Greenhalghe, two women who had been identified as scolds and disturbers of their neighbours. The jury presented them as common scolds, and:

> Doe earnestly intreate the Steward of this court to see them punished according to the lawe to the end that theire neighboures might lyve in peace and quiet the[y] beinge so notorious that all godlye and well disposed people doe wonder that the[y] have beene so longe spared lyvinge in a towne where theire ought to be better carriage & government which if theise and other abuses be not speedilye reformed wee maye looke and expecte that the greate steward of heaven and earth will revenge theise and other the lykke synnes which raigne amongst us which God in his mercye remove far from us.[52]

A number of pertinent themes run together in this presentment: the concerns of the 'better sort', of the 'sufficient and well reputed neighboures' who brought the two women

[49] Robert van Friedenburg, 'Reformation of Manners and the Social Composition of Offenders in an East Anglian Cloth Village: Earls Colne, Essex, 1531–1642', *JBS*, 29 (1990): 347–85.

[50] Sharpe, 'Crime and Delinquency in an Essex Parish'.

[51] Margaret Spufford, 'Puritanism and Social Control', in *Order and Disorder in Early Modern England*, ed. Anthony Fletcher and John Stevenson (Cambridge: Cambridge University Press, 1985).

[52] *Court Leet Records of the Manor of Manchester*, ed. Earwaker, 3.31.

to the manorial authorities' attention and the 'godlye and well disposed people' whose interests had to be protected; the sense of civic pride, that a place like Manchester should be well governed; and, finally, the expectation that if these two disorderly women were not disciplined, God, 'the greate steward of heaven and earth', would execute divine vengeance against the town.

The study of law, crime control, and the local community is therefore a complex one, involving a number of issues. In this brief overview it has been possible to do little more than flag up some of the main issues and indicate the direction of some of the existing work on the subject. What comes across most clearly is the breadth of relevant sources and the real potential for future research. However this research is prosecuted, and whatever its results, it will have at its centre the interplay between those national processes which we have noted and the lives of individuals as the communities in which they lived were affected and modified by these processes. At the end of a pioneering analysis of the background to prosecutions at quarter sessions, T. C. Curtis commented that:

> the dominant role of the law enforcement process in seventeenth-century Cheshire was not, therefore, simple confrontation between the offender and the impersonal might of the state. It was, rather, an intricate chorus of negotiation between all the parties and interests who felt they had a proper concern in the matter ... the law, and its precise letter, were not viewed in the depths of the country as they would have been in King's Bench or the Inns of Court. Not that the law was regarded as a simple matter, but that local men regarded it less as an unalterable score and more as a theme upon which they could improvise.[53]

I hope that this chapter has given at least an outline indication of the range of those improvisations, and of the contexts within which they were operating.

One final issue needs to be raised. The main concern in this essay is with *c.*1580–1640, currently regarded as the key period in which new relationships within the local community, and new relationships between local communities and central authority were formed. How the themes and processes with which we concerned ourselves worked themselves out in the post-Restoration period remains largely uncharted territory. There are a few leads. Levels of serious crime, and of execution for felony, dropped massively over the seventeenth century.[54] The current state of research (more work here is urgently needed) suggests that the business of the correction side of the ecclesiastical courts declined, and changed its nature as presentments of community nuisance offenders and the sexually incontinent declined in favour of the presentment of religious nonconformists.[55] The decline of witchcraft prosecutions, so firmly rooted in interpersonal disputes on a community level, is well known, and although quantifying this would be difficult,

[53] T. C. Curtis, 'Quarter Sessions Appearances and Their Background: A Seventeenth-Century Regional Study', in *Crime in England*, ed. Cockburn, 153–4.

[54] Sharpe, *Crime in Early Modern England*, 82–90.

[55] Fluctuations in church court business over the long term are discussed in R. B. Outhwaite, *The Rise and Fall of the English Ecclesiastical Courts, 1500–1860* (Cambridge: Cambridge University Press, 2006).

there is also a sense that prosecutions of another characteristic community offence, scolding, also fell in number. Local nuisance offenders were doubtless still there, but they did not seem to whip up the same intensity of feeling among the 'better sort' of their communities. When they did, it is possible that controlling them through the poor law, or through the summary action of Justices of the Peace, action of which few records survive before the eighteenth century, were seen as a more appropriate course than presenting them at the ecclesiastical or, where they existed, manorial courts. Studies of social tensions on a community level in the eighteenth century suggest a rather different set of variables than those at play in the late Elizabethan and early Stuart periods. Thus study of law enforcement at a community level provides considerable reinforcement to the impression that the years *c.*1580–1640 constituted a distinctive episode in English social history.

Bibliography

Bridenbaugh, C. *Vexed and Troubled Englishmen 1590–1642* (Oxford: Clarendon Press, 1968).

Bund, J. W. Willis, ed. *Calendar of the Quarter Sessions Papers*, Vol. 1: *1591–1643* (Worcester: Baylis, 1900).

Carlson, Eric. 'The Origins, Functions, and Status of the Office of Churchwarden, with Special Reference to the Diocese of Ely', in *The World of Rural Dissenters 1520–1725*, ed. Margaret Spufford (Cambridge: Cambridge University Press, 1995), 164–207.

Craig, J. S. 'Co-operation and Initiative: Elizabethan Churchwardens and the Parish Accounts of Mildenhall', *Social History*, 18 (1993): 357–80.

Cromwell, Oliver. *The Writings and Speeches of Oliver Cromwell*, ed. W. C. Abbott, 4 vols (Cambridge, MA: Harvard University Press, 1937–1947).

Curtis, T. C. 'Quarter Sessions Appearances and their Background: A Seventeenth-Century Regional Study', in *Crime in England 1550–1800*, ed. J. S. Cockburn (London: Methuen, 1977), 135–54.

de Windt, Anne. 'Peasant Power Structures in Kings Ripton', *Medieval Studies*, 38 (1976): 236–67.

Earwaker, J. P., ed. *The Constables' Accounts of the Manor of Manchester from the Year 1612 to the Year 1647, and from the Year 1743 to the Year 1778*, 3 vols (Manchester: 1891–1892).

Earwaker, J. P., ed. *The Court Leet Records of the Manor of Manchester*, ed. J. P. Earwaker, 12 vols (Manchester: 1884–1890).

Emmison. F. G. *Elizabethan Life: Morals and the Church Courts* (Chelmsford: Essex County Council, 1973).

Fox, Adam. 'Ballads, Libels and Popular Ridicule in Jacobean England', *Past and Present*, 105 (1984): 47–83.

Goheen, R. B. 'Peasant Politics? Village Community and the Crown in Fifteenth-Century England', *American Historical Review*, 96 (1991): 42–62.

Gough, Richard. *The History of Myddle*, ed. David G. Hey (Harmondsworth: Penguin, 1981).

Hair, Paul. *Before the Bawdy Court* (London: Eleck, 1972).

Hanawalt, Barbara. *Crime and Conflict in English Communities 1300–1348* (Cambridge, MA: Harvard University Press, 1979).

Hey, David G. *An English Rural Community: Myddle under the Tudors and Stuarts* (Leicester: Leicester University Press, 1974).

Hindle, Steve. 'Hierarchy and Community in the Elizabethan Parish: The Swallowfield Articles of 1596', *The Historical Journal*, 42 (1999): 835–51.

Hoskins, W. G. *The Midland Peasant: The Economic and Social History of a Leicestershire Village* (London: Macmillan, 1957).

Ingram, Martin. 'Religion, Communities and Moral Discipline in Late Sixteenth and Early Seventeenth-Century England', in *Religion and Society in Early Modern Europe*, ed. Kaspar von Greyerz (London: Allen and Unwin, 1984), 177–93.

Ingram, Martin. 'Ridings, Rough Music and the "Reform of Popular Culture" in Early Modern England', *Past and Present*, 105 (1984): 79–113.

Ingram, Martin. 'Ridings, Rough Music and Mocking Rhymes in Early Modern England', in *Popular Culture in Seventeenth-Century England*, ed. Barry Reay (London: Routledge, 1988), 166–97.

Johnstone, Hilda, ed. *Churchwardens' Presentments, 17th Century: Archdeaconry of Chichester*, Vol. 1 (Chichester: Sussex Record Society, 1948).

Kent, Joan R. '"Folk Justice" and Royal Justice in Early Seventeenth-Century England: A Charivari in the Midlands.' *Midland History*, 8 (1983): 70–85.

Kent, Joan R. *The English Village Constable 1580–1642: A Social and Administrative Study* (Oxford: Clarendon Press, 1986).

Macfarlane, Alan, Sarah Harrison, and Charles Jardine. *Reconstructing Historical Communities* (Cambridge: Cambridge University Press, 1977).

McIntosh, Marjorie Keniston. *A Community Transformed: The Manor and Liberty of Havering, 1500–1620* (Cambridge: Cambridge University Press, 1991).

McIntosh, Marjorie Keniston. *Controlling Misbehaviour in England 1370–1600* (Cambridge: Cambridge University Press, 1998).

Outhwaite, R. B. *The Rise and Fall of the English Ecclesiastical Courts 1500–1860* (Cambridge: Cambridge University Press, 2006).

Peyton, S. A., ed. *The Churchwardens' Presentments in the Oxfordshire Peculiars of Dorchester, Thame, and Banbury* (Dorchester: Oxfordshire Record Society, 1968).

Raftis, J. A. 'The Concentration of Responsibility in Five Villages', *Medieval Studies*, 28 (1966): 92–118.

Rowse, A. L. *The England of Elizabeth: The Structure of Society* (London: Macmillan, 1950).

Sharpe, J. A. 'Crime and Delinquency in an Essex Parish', in *Crime in England 1550–1800*, ed. J. S. Cockburn (London: Methuen, 1977), 90–109.

Sharpe, J. A. 'Enforcing the Law in the Seventeenth-Century English Village', in *Crime and the Law: The Social History of Crime in Western Europe Since 1500*, ed. V. A. C. Gatrell, Bruce Lenman, and Geoffrey Parker (London: Europa Publications, 1980), 97–119.

Sharpe, J. A. 'The History of Crime in Late Medieval and Early Modern England', *Social History*, 7 (1982): 187–203.

Sharpe, J. A. 'The People and the Law', in *Popular Culture in Seventeenth-Century England*, ed. Barry Reay (London: Routledge, 1988), 244–70.

Sharpe, J. A. *Crime in Early Modern England 1550–1750*, 2nd edn (London: Longman, 1998).

Sharpe, J. A. *The Bewitching of Anne Gunter: A Horrible and True Story of Football, Witchcraft, Murder, and the King of England* (London: Profile Books, 1999).

Spufford, Margaret. *Contrasting Communities: English Villagers in the Sixteenth and Seventeenth Centuries* (Cambridge: Cambridge University Press, 1974).

Spufford, Margaret. 'Puritanism and Social Control', in *Order and Disorder in Early Modern England*, ed. Anthony Fletcher and John Stevenson (Cambridge: Cambridge University Press, 1985), 41–57.

Thirsk, Joan. *The Rural Economy of England. Collected Essays* (London: Hambledon Press, 1984).

Thomas, Keith. *Religion and the Decline of Magic: Studies in Popular Beliefs in Sixteenth- and Seventeenth-Century England* (London: Weidenfeld and Nicolson, 1971).

Underdown, David. *Fire from Heaven: The Life of an English Town in the Seventeenth Century* (London: Harper Collins, 1992).

van Friedenburg, Robert. 'Reformation of Manners and the Social Composition of Offenders in an East Anglian Cloth Village: Earl's Colne, Essex, 1531–1642', *Journal of British Studies*, 29.4 (1990): 347–85.

Wrightson, Keith. 'Two Concepts of Order: Justices, Constables, and Jurymen in Seventeenth-Century England', in *An Ungovernable People: The English and Their Law in the Seventeenth and Eighteenth Centuries*, ed. John Brewer and John Styles (London: Hutchinson, 1980), 21–46.

Wrightson, Keith. 'The Politics of the Parish in Early Modern England', in *The Experience of Authority in Early Modern England*, ed. Paul Griffiths, Adam Fox, and Steve Hindle (London: Macmillan, 1996), 10–46.

Wrightson, Keith and David Levine. *Poverty and Piety in an English Village: Terling, 1525–1700*, 2nd edn (Oxford: Clarendon Press, 1995).

CHAPTER 12

THE CHANGING PERSONA OF THE JUSTICES AND THEIR QUARTER SESSIONS

NORMA LANDAU

THIS essay's title, 'The Changing Persona of the Justices and their Quarter Sessions', is at odds with the historiography of the Justices of the Peace. Historians have presented a portrait of the justices as unchanging: throughout the ages the justices embodied the English propensity for 'self-government at the king's command'.[1] From their emergence in the fourteenth century to their partial replacement by county councillors at the end of the nineteenth century, the justices—we have been told—were local gentry who volunteered to administer the local government of their county.[2] This essay challenges that depiction, and does so in two ways. First, it argues that until the later seventeenth century many justices were not local gentry, or, if they were local gentry, were not appointed as justices because they were local gentry. The essay suggests, instead, that the composition of the justices' bench reflected change both in the definition of England's upper social strata and in Westminster's reach. Second, the essay argues that, until the later seventeenth century, what the justices did is not accurately designated by the label 'local government'. The label assumes a differentiation of function between central and local government. This essay argues instead that such differentiation appeared in the early modern era, for the tale of the early modern justices is the local story of the emergence of the early modern state.

[1] Alfred B. White, *Self-Government at the King's Command: A Study in the Beginnings of English Democracy* (Minneapolis: University of Minnesota Press, 1933).

[2] Bertha H. Putnam, 'The Transformation of the Keepers of the Peace into the Justices of the Peace 1327–1380', *TRHS*, 4th ser., 12 (1929): 19, 26, 34; Esther Moir, *The Justices of the Peace* (Harmondsworth: Penguin, 1969), 16, 19–20; Simon Walker, 'Yorkshire Justices of the Peace, 1389–1413', *English Historical Review*, 108 (1993): 281, 281–2.

Justices held their office by virtue of appointment by the Lord Chancellor to a county's commission of the peace. That commission was collectively embodied in the justices' appearance at Quarter Sessions, the justices' court held quarterly in each county. During the early modern era, the commission's persona as embodied at Quarter Sessions became that which has dominated their historiography: the justices were provincials who did not consider their judicial service to be a means of obtaining Westminster's favour; instead, as independent gentry, they were the nearly autonomous rulers of their localities. Just as local government emerged in the early modern era, so too did a persona fit for local governors.

The Justices of the Peace

Two sites, each a base of power, shaped a county's commission of the peace: Westminster, the seat of government; and the county, where that government was exercised. Each of the four varieties of appointee to commissions of the peace—gentry, officers of the law courts, courtiers and members of departments of state at Westminster, and peers—embodied the power of one or both of Westminster and the county. Examination of the lists of those appointed as justices demonstrates that, over the course of the early modern era, the impact of Westminster's representation on the commission's persona markedly diminished, while that of the county's markedly increased.

One great dynamic shapes the changes in county commissions of the peace from their creation in the fourteenth century to the close of the early modern era: the inexorable expansion of the number of men on each commission. Fourteenth-century statute decreed that there be just eight justices on a commission. By 1621, there were roughly 2,000 non-clerics and non-peers on the commissions of England and Wales. By 1679, there were about 2,500 such justices, and by 1702, about 3,700.[3] From the reign of Henry VII, and perhaps earlier, almost all of the commissions' expansion was due to the appointment of more gentry and of those aspiring to gentry status.[4]

The gentry had not always been the overwhelming majority of the justices. Until the mid-fifteenth century, gentry might well be a minority.[5] Nor were the gentry who were

[3] 14 Ric. 2 *c.* 11. Christopher Haigh and Alison Wall, 'Clergy JPs in England and Wales, 1590–1640', *HJ*, 47 (2004): 233, 234–5; Norma Landau, *The Justices of the Peace, 1679–1760* (Berkeley: University of California Press, 1984), 74, 82. The count for 1702 excludes Lancashire.

[4] Margaret M. Condon, 'Ruling Elites in the Reign of Henry VII', in *Patronage, Pedigree and Power in Later Mediaeval England*, ed. Charles Ross (Gloucester: Sutton, 1979), 125; Peter Clark, *English Provincial Society from the Reformation to the Revolution: Religion, Politics and Society in Kent 1500–1640* (Hassocks: Harvester, 1977), 126–7; Susan M. Wright, *The Derbyshire Gentry in the Fifteenth Century*, *Derbyshire Record Society*, 8 (1983): 104–5, 108–9.

[5] Nigel Saul, *Knights and Esquires: The Gloucestershire Gentry in the Fourteenth Century* (Oxford: Clarendon Press, 1981), 132; J. R. Lander, *English Justices of the Peace 1461–1509* (Gloucester: Sutton, 1989), 59, 156; Walker, 'Yorkshire', 292, 302, 303, 305–6; Carol Arnold, 'The

justices necessarily the leading gentry of their county.[6] However, from the later fifteenth century on, it became increasingly likely that leading gentry would be their county's justices. It therefore might seem that the expansion of the commissions would in itself be sufficient explanation of the transformation of the justices' persona to that of the gentry. Such an interpretation would ignore alteration in definitions of England's upper social strata, which the conclusion of this section will explore; and also ignore the changing impact of other varieties of appointee on commissions of the peace, which is the subject of the following pages.

The gentry's base of power was the county. All other varieties of appointee had, at a minimum, some association with Westminster—with the monarch's court, departments of state, and courts of law. Obviously, a monarch would want to insure that justice be administered in his interest. So, when in the fourteenth century justices in their Quarter Sessions were given authority to try indictments for felony and misdemeanour, their rule was tempered by the proviso that at least one justice designated by Westminster as 'learned in the law'—justices henceforth to be known as members of the quorum—be among those presiding at such trials.[7] Those 'learned in the law' were men trained in the law—barristers practising in the central courts, and local men with legal knowledge who undertook legal and administrative tasks. Such men would be eager to obtain more rewarding employments, and so susceptible to Westminster's influence.[8] Foremost among those learned in the law were the judges; and so important did Westminster deem the judges to a county's commission of the peace that a new commission, naming the judges who would be presiding at the county's forthcoming Assizes as justices of the quorum, was issued for each county before the judges began riding each of their two yearly assize circuits.

Until well into the early modern era, Assizes (where the judges presided) and Quarter Sessions (where the justices presided) might be held as a conjoint sitting, and for good reason. Until 1537, Assizes had authority to try indictments, but not to take them. Quarter Sessions had such authority. Acting at Quarter Sessions, judges could take indictments; and so they did.[9] The judges' acquisition in 1537 of the power to take indictments under the commissions regularly issued for Assizes made it less essential that they be members of the commissions of the peace in the counties where

Commission of the Peace in the West Riding of Yorkshire, 1437–1509', in *Property and Politics: Essays in Later Medieval English History*, ed. Tony Pollard (Gloucester: Sutton, 1984), 118.

6 Lander, *English Justices*, 41, 159, 160; Saul, *Knights*, 134; Wright, *Derbyshire*, 104–5; Christine Carpenter, *Locality and Polity: A Study of Warwickshire Landed Society, 1401–1499* (Cambridge: Cambridge, 1992), 267.

7 Edward Powell, 'The Administration of Criminal Justice in Late Medieval England: Peace Sessions and Assizes', in *The Political Context of Law: Proceedings of the Seventh British Legal History Conference, Canterbury 1985*, ed. Richard Eales and David Sullivan (London: Hambledon, 1987), 51–6.

8 Anthony Musson and W. M. Ormrod, *The Evolution of English Justice: Law, Politics and Society in the Fourteenth Century* (Houndsmills, Basingstoke: Macmillan, 1999), 55–68; Lander, *English Justices*, 33–5; Walker, 'Yorkshire', 292, 305–6, 282–3.

9 Amanda Bevan, 'The Henrician Assizes and the Enforcement of the Reformation', in *Political Context*, ed. Eales and Sullivan, 61–76; Walker, 'Yorkshire', 290–1.

they held Assizes. So, it may be that their acquisition of this power marks the barely perceptible onset of attenuation of the judges' connection with the commission of the peace. Nonetheless, it was not until the later 1670s that the Crown Office, the office at Westminster responsible for inscribing commissions of the peace, became notably lax in insuring that the judges presiding at a county's Assizes were also members of its commission of the peace.[10]

It seems likely that Assizes's acquisition of the power to take indictments also diminished the influence of the quorum as a whole on the county's commission. Amanda Bevan suggests that Assizes's acquisition of this power stimulated the transfer of both indictment and trial of serious crimes from Quarter Sessions to Assizes, so rendering the presence of men representing the law and Westminster less essential to commissions of the peace.[11] Once a mark of legal knowledge or of remarkable association with Westminster, appointment to the quorum could now become merely a signal of local prestige. As a result, the proportion of justices on a county commission's quorum grew apace. By 1680, 86 per cent of the justices, and by 1714 all but a handful, were members of the quorum.[12] Created as Westminster's instrument for managing the justices, by the later seventeenth century—and probably by the later sixteenth century—the quorum was so altered that it could no longer serve Westminster's purpose.

Similarly, by the later seventeenth century the commission's persona no longer proclaimed Westminster's influence through appointees affiliated with the monarch's court or departments of state. This reduction of Westminster's imprint served to emphasize the role of both gentry and justices as representatives of their county. Nowhere is this transformation more apparent than in the appointment of members of the royal affinity as justices of the peace.[13]

Ever since the late fourteenth century, when Richard II invited 300 to 400 knights to assume unpaid part-time positions at court, monarchs had been reaching out to local notables, enrolling them in the ranks of their personal servants and followers, and appointing these members of their affinity to commissions of the peace—to the commissions of their county of residence, and sometimes to the commissions of other

[10] S. C. Ratcliff and H. C. Johnson, eds., *Warwick County Records*, Vol. 7: *Quarter Sessions Records, Easter, 1674 to Easter, 1682* (Warwick, 1946), xliv; H. C. Johnson, ed., *Warwick County Records*, Vol. 8: *Quarter Sessions Records, Trinity, 1682 to Epiphany, 1690* (Warwick, 1953), lviii.

[11] Bevan, 'Henrician Assizes', 305–6.

[12] These counts exclude the dignitaries at the beginning of each commission's list of justices; Landau, *Justices*, 84. For the quorum under the Tudors: Michael L. Zell, 'Early Tudor JPs at Work', *Archaeologia Cantiana*, 93 (1978 for 1977): 125, 140–3; Thomas G. Barnes and A. Hassell Smith, 'Justices of the Peace from 1588 to 1688—A Revised List of Sources', *BIHR*, 32 (1959): 221, 223.

[13] Chris Given-Wilson, *The Royal Household and the King's Affinity: Service, Politics and Finance in England 1360–1413* (New Haven: Yale, 1986), 203. Given-Wilson states that the term 'royal affinity' could designate all men attached to the monarch or to the monarch's departments of government. However, he also uses the term to distinguish unpaid, part-time courtiers from other associates of the monarch and the monarch's government.

counties as well.[14] Under Henry VII, and especially under Wolsey and Cromwell (Henry VIII's chief ministers), this programme for representing the monarch's will in the county's government intensified.[15] In contrast, under Henry VIII's Tudor heirs the royal affinity declined and then disappeared.[16] Although the royal affinity re-appeared under both the early and the later Stuarts, no historian has discovered a Stuart programme of appointing these men to commissions of the peace. The disappearance of the knight or esquire appointed to a county commission because he was a member of the royal affinity decreased the monarch's knowledge of government in the counties and attenuated the justices' performance as the monarch's vice-regents, while at the same time emphasizing the cogency of the gentry's claims to power founded on their influence in the locality.

Similarly, over the course of the early modern era the effect of the appointment of courtiers and office holders on the commissions' persona markedly diminished. As of the late fifteenth century, a significant number of justices were courtiers or office holders. From 1461 to 1509, 222 household officers, all gentry, were appointed to commissions of the peace. So were 190 other gentry who served in other departments of government.[17] Appointment of courtiers as justices, sometimes to the commissions of counties in which they did not reside, continued to the Civil War and indeed thereafter, although the number of these appointees diminished from the early seventeenth century, and historians have seldom noted courtiers appointed as justices after the Restoration.[18] On the other hand, as Westminster spawned departments of government and these departments regularly conducted business in a county, the monarch's government insured that the department be represented on that county's commission of the peace. So, for example, members of the

14 Given-Wilson, *Affinity*, 203–4, 226, 234, 250–1, 264; Walker, 'Yorkshire', 303; Craig A. Robertson, 'Local Government and the King's 'Affinity' in Fifteenth-Century Leicestershire and Warwickshire', *Transactions of the Leicestershire Archaelogical and Historical Society*, 52 (1978 for 1976–1977): 37, 37–45.

15 John Guy, 'Thomas Wolsey, Thomas Cromwell and the Reform of Henrician Government', in *The Reign of Henry VIII: Politics, Policy and Piety*, ed. Diarmaid MacCulloch (London: Macmillan, 1995), 53–6; David Starkey, 'The Age of the Household: Politics, Society and the Arts c.1350–c.1550', in *The Context of English Literature, The Later Middle Ages*, ed. Stephen Medcalf (London: Methuen, 1981), 263, 270–1; Lander, *English Justices*, 140, 143.

16 Alan Bryson, '"The speciall men in every shere". The Edwardian regime, 1547–1553' (PhD thesis, University of St Andrews, 2001), 228–230; William Baxter Robison, 'The Justices of the Peace of Surrey in National and County Politics, 1483–1570' (PhD dissertation, The Louisiana State University and Agricultural and Mechanical College, 1983), 149, 357–8; Felicity Heal and Clive Holmes, *The Gentry in England and Wales, 1500–1700* (London: Macmillan, 1994), 196–7; Pam Wright, 'A Change in Direction: The Ramifications of a Female Household, 1558–1603', in *The English Court from the Wars of the Roses to the Civil War*, ed. David Starkey et al. (London: Longman, 1987), 158; Neil Cuddy, 'The Revival of the Entourage: The Bedchamber of James I, 1603–1625', in *English Court*, ed. Starkey et al., 184; Neil Cuddy, 'Reinventing a Monarchy: The Changing Structure and Political Function of the Stuart Court, 1603–88', in *The Stuart Courts*, ed. Eveline Cruikshanks (Stroud: Sutton, 2000), 67–8, 73–4.

17 Lander, *English Justices*, 42. For such appointments in the late fourteenth century: Saul, *Knights*, 132; Walker, 'Yorkshire', 303.

18 Guy, 'Wolsey', 54; Clark, *Provincial Society*, 18–20; Michael Zell, 'Kent's Elizabethan JPs at Work', *Archaeologia Cantiana*, 119 (1999): 1, 6; J. H. Gleason, *The Justices of the Peace in England, 1558 to 1640* (Oxford: Clarendon, 1969), 49.

Navy Board appeared on the commissions of counties important to the Board's affairs.[19] Yet, even though some courtiers and office holders were members of county commissions under the later Stuarts, they made little impact on the commission's persona, and what impact they made was ever decreasing. How could it be otherwise when the number of such appointees diminished while the size of the county commissions soared?

There remains one further group of appointees who emblazoned Westminster's power on the commissions of the peace: the monarch's counsellors (from Henry VIII's reign, the monarch's privy counsellors). Just as the impact of Westminster's other representatives on the commissions' persona diminished by the later seventeenth century, so did that of the privy counsellors. However, while the decreased influence of Westminster's other representatives resulted from a reduction in the number of these appointees, the decline in privy counsellors' impact on the commissions' persona resulted from inflation in the number of men so appointed.

From at least the later fourteenth century, monarchs appointed their counsellors to commissions of the peace. On occasion, one or two counsellors might be appointed to every, or almost every commission. Under Elizabeth and the early Stuarts, two to four members of the privy council—always including the Lord Chancellor and the Lord Treasurer—appeared on every commission of the peace.[20] Throughout most of Charles II's reign, a larger number of privy counsellors—but less than half of the privy council—was appointed to the commission of every county.[21] Like his predecessors, Charles was simultaneously informing his subjects of the structure of power in his government and endowing a few selected ministers with power to act as a justice in every county in the land.

The message conveyed by the monarch's choice of privy counsellors as justices changed abruptly in 1680, after opponents of Charles's government gained places in his privy council, reconstructed the membership of all commissions of the peace, and placed all members of the privy council on every commission of the peace.[22] Clearly, the

[19] Lionel K. J. Glassey and Norma Landau, 'The Commission of the Peace in the Eighteenth Century: A New Source', *BIHR*, 45 (1972): 247, 264 n. 4.

[20] Gleason, *Justices, 1558 to 1640*, Appendices A–F; Lander, *English Justices*, 31; Condon, 'Ruling Elites', 121. Monarchs also appointed members of the Council of Wales and of the Council of the North to the commissions of counties subject to these Councils. The Council of Wales, and its successor, the Council of the Marches, wielded jurisdiction over Cheshire, Shropshire, Herefordshire, Worcestershire, and Gloucestershire, as well as Wales. Both Councils were abolished in 1641, and only the Council of the Marches, stripped of its criminal jurisdiction, was restored at the Restoration. It was abolished in 1689. James S. Cockburn, *A History of English Assizes, 1558–1714* (Cambridge: Cambridge, 1972), 36–9; Lander, *English Justices*, 15; Guy, 'Wolsey', 55 n. 79; Jennifer Carter, 'Law, Courts and Constitution', in *The Restored Monarchy 1660–1688*, ed. J. R. Jones (Totowa: Rowman and Littlefield, 1979), 85; 1 Wm. and Mar. *c.* 27. 16 Chas I *c.* 10.

[21] Eight privy councillors on Somerset's commission for 1674 and 1675 were also on Warwickshire's commission for 1675 and 1677, and on Kent's commission for 1679. (Somerset Record Office [hereafter R.O.], Q/JC76, 77. *Warwick County Records*, Vol. 7, xxviii, xxx–xxxv. TNA, Assi 35/120/5.)

[22] *Warwick County Records*, Vol. 7, xxiv–xxvii; S. N. Esquire, *A Catalogue of the Names of all His Majesties Justices of the Peace* (London: Davies, 1680), A2, 1. The entire privy council did not appear on Lancashire's commission until 1687: Lionel K. J. Glassey, *Politics and the Appointment of Justices of the Peace 1675–1720* (Oxford: Oxford University Press, 1979), 272.

privy council was informing the country about major change in the balance of power at Westminster. What was less clear and became increasingly unclear was the relation of the monarch's councillors to any county's commission of the peace. The number of privy counsellors was large and grew larger. As the Crown Office seems to have had difficulty insuring that the name of a privy counsellor be removed from a commission's list of privy counsellors when he was removed from the privy council, a commission might well list as privy counsellors men who were no longer privy counsellors. So, the number of men listed on a commission as privy counsellors swelled. In April 1679, just before all privy counsellors appeared in the commissions, there were eight privy counsellors on Kent's commission. As of April 1688, thirty-three men were identified as privy counsellors on Kent's commission; as of November 1694, forty-nine men; and in July, 1713, eighty-one men.[23] What had once been a clear statement of the location of power was now an interminable list of men who at some time had (and perhaps still had) some influence somewhere or other.

The decision to appoint all privy counsellors as justices of every county also diluted the ability of the fourth and last group of appointees to affect the persona of a county's commission simply by being listed as justices. That group was peers who had holdings or influence in a county. A county's peers had been appointed as its justices since the fourteenth century.[24] Before the later seventeenth century, the list of peers in a county's commission identified those wielding the most influence in the county, and indeed beyond. However, from 1680 on, if a peer had minor influence in a county and was also a privy counsellor, contemporaries could not determine whether his inclusion in that county's commission constituted recognition and so enhancement of his local power, or should instead be attributed to the commission's *pro forma* recitation of the names of all privy counsellors.[25]

Similarly, by the later seventeenth century, the list of peers at the head of a county's commission no longer signified the connection of all members of the commission to power beyond the county, including Westminster. Unlike the gentry, peers had holdings in more than one county; and, unlike the gentry, they had influence at Westminster. Nonetheless, despite disparities in their wealth and influence, peers and gentry had been considered members of the same social order. In the fourteenth century, when the commission of the peace was created, peers and gentry together constituted England's nobility. The peers were greater nobility, and the gentry lesser nobility.[26] However, by the late sixteenth century, even though the categorization of peers and gentry as members of one social order still shaped discourse, the conceptual dissociation of peers from

[23] TNA, Assi 35/120/5. Kent Archives Office [hereafter A.O.], Q/JC17, 24, 36.

[24] Lander, *English Justices*, 31–2, 109–10, 156; Walker, 'Yorkshire', 283–5; Virgoe, 'East Anglia', 78; Condon, 'Ruling Elites', 121, 125; Arnold, 'West Riding', 117–19.

[25] Historians also encounter this difficulty. From the 1680s until the 1730s, Westminster's lists of commissions of the peace usually did not note whether a privy councillor would be on a county's commission if he were not a privy councillor. On occasion, these records do not note any of the names of justices listed among a commission's dignitaries: Glassey and Landau, 'New Source', 249–50, 255. For the list of dignitaries, see text at nn. 27–31 below.

[26] K. B. McFarlane. *The Nobility of Later Medieval England* (Oxford: Clarendon, 1973), 142–3, 123–4.

gentry had already begun. Dissociation is evident in change in the rank and precedence accorded peers' sons, a change inscribed in the documents that were commissions of the peace.

Until the sixteenth century, peers' sons sported titles identical to those of substantial landowners who were not peers. Like the gentry, peers' sons were knights and esquires. There were no courtesy titles—that is, no titles indicating that a man's father was a peer and so distinguishing him from those who were neither peers nor peers' offspring. By the early seventeenth century, use of courtesy titles was well established.[27] The oldest son of a duke, a marquess, or an earl, as well as the younger son of a duke or a marquess, now appeared in a commission under a courtesy title, and so commingled with its list of peers. There remained as unacknowledged peers' offspring just those who would eventually acquire the honorific 'honourable'—the younger sons of earls and all sons of viscounts and barons. Many of these sons acquired their distinction from the ruck of justices in 1676, when their fathers, as members of the House of Lords, ordered that younger sons of earls and the oldest sons of viscounts and barons be listed before the judges,[28] so clearly incorporating these sons into what was becoming the commissions' introductory list of dignitaries.

Commissions of the peace had not originally opened with a list of dignitaries. Instead, they began with a recitation of the names of the justices listed in order of precedence as decreed by the Earl Marshal. In the mid-1670s, that list acquired a new structure. The name and office of either the attorney-general or the solicitor-general was interjected in the list;[29] and this interjection established a boundary within the commission's list. In 1680, that boundary was strengthened.[30] Now the names of both attorney- and solicitor-general appeared at the end of a list of officers of state and the monarch's household, peers, peers' sons, bishops, privy councillors, and judges—men of distinction possessed of power beyond the county and associated with Westminster. After the attorney- and solicitor-general came the other justices, just a miniscule proportion of whom held office at Westminster. The overwhelming majority of this list of non-dignitaries were county gentry or men aspiring to that status. By the late seventeenth century both contemporary analyses and the document appointing Justices of the Peace presented peers and gentry as two distinct and separate social orders.[31] By the late seventeenth century, but not before, the document listing the personnel of commissions of the peace could be

[27] Sir Anthony Wagner and G. D. Squibb, 'Precedence and Courtesy Titles', *Law Quarterly Review*, 89 (1973): 352, 356–8.

[28] G. D. Squibb, *Precedence in England and Wales* (Oxford: Clarendon, 1981), 33–4. Commissions of the peace issued in the reign of Charles II after 1676 listed the sons specified in the Lords' order before the judges, but commissions issued from 1689 placed these sons after the solicitor-general. These sons regained the precedence specified in the Lords' order *c.*1710 or 1711. I do not know when the younger sons of viscounts and barons were first placed in the commission's list of dignitaries.

[29] These officers were inserted at some time between January 1674 and July 1675: Somerset R.O., Q/JC76, 79; *Warwick County Records*, Vol. 7, xxxii; Kent A.O., Q/JC14. TNA, Assi 35/120/6, 35/121/3, 4.

[30] S.N., *Catalogue*, 1; Somerset R.O., Q/JC87; Kent A.O., Q/JC15.

[31] J. V. Beckett, *The Aristocracy in England 1660–1914* (Oxford: Blackwell, 1986), 19.

interpreted as beginning with a decorative list of dignitaries and then proceeding to the list of gentry who did the commission's work.

As the dignitaries' behaviour demonstrates, this interpretation has considerable validity. The essay's third section will show that, by the later seventeenth century, the commission's grandees were ceasing to attend Quarter Sessions and so participate in that court's embodiment of the commission of the peace. As the essay's second section will show, to at least some extent this decrease in the grandees' attendance at Quarter Sessions can be attributed to decline in its exercise of a range of powers.

Quarter Sessions

It is a commonplace of the historiography of early modern England that the powers of the justices of the peace increased greatly in the sixteenth and seventeenth centuries, and that the justices' Quarter Sessions was this new power incarnate.[32] In contrast, this section argues that during the early modern era the range of powers exercised by Quarter Sessions markedly increased, and then markedly decreased. In part because, unlike its early modern predecessors, the Quarter Sessions of the last Stuarts exercised a range of powers restricted to what might be termed 'local government', it was more autonomous than these predecessors. In part because Quarter Sessions under the last Stuarts conducted just 'local government', justices with power beyond the county were less interested in attending Quarter Sessions. As a result, by the close of the early modern era, the Justices of the Peace could be portrayed as county gentry—provincial, to be sure; but also rulers of the county.

Quarter Sessions exercised both judicial and administrative power. That, during the early modern era, its exercise of a range of powers first increased and then diminished is best illustrated by the history of one of the powers it wielded as a criminal court: the power to hang. The pattern here is stark. There is considerable doubt as to whether in the 1470s Quarter Sessions tried or executed felons with any frequency.[33] In contrast, Elizabethan Quarter Sessions clearly did both try and execute felons, and did so with considerable frequency.[34] By the 1590s, both Westminster and the judges were directing the justices to consign trial of difficult charges and very serious crime to the judges at Assizes. Although county Quarter Sessions still executed convicts, decline in its exercise of this power was now well underway, and in some counties may even have begun before

[32] Anthony Fletcher, *Reform in the Provinces: The Government of Stuart England* (New Haven: Yale, 1986), 87–8.

[33] Lander, *English Justices*, 166 n. 62.

[34] James S. Cockburn, *Calendar of Assize Records, Home Circuit Indictments, Elizabeth I and James I, Introduction* (London, HMSO, 1985), 22; Tony Hopkins, 'Quarter Sessions and the Justice of the Peace in Monmouthshire', *Monmouthshire Antiquary*, 29 (2013) 47, 49. I am grateful to Christabel Hutchings for sending me a copy of this article.

the 1590s.[35] By the late 1660s, Quarter Sessions was no longer a hanging court. The latest sentence of death pronounced at a county Quarter Sessions so far noted by historians is that delivered at Norfolk Sessions in 1665.[36] Well before the end of the seventeenth century, county Quarter Sessions had relinquished its most awe-inspiring punishment.

In yielding trial of capital crimes to the judges at Assizes, the justices restricted Quarter Sessions's exercise of its jurisdiction to minor charges of appropriation of property, violation of the common, disorderly behaviour such as riot and assault, failure to perform communal obligations such as repair of a highway, violation of laws regulating the local economy such as those regulating apprenticeship, and violation of the laws enforcing the Church of England's monopoly of religious practice.[37] By the late seventeenth century, the justices at Quarter Sessions were determining indictments important to the good order of local communities. However, aside from indictments for violation of the laws regulating religion, which rarely came before Quarter Sessions after 1689, later Stuart Quarter Sessions were not adjudicating problems preoccupying the nation's government at Westminster.

Like Quarter Sessions' judicial powers, its administrative powers and its use of those powers escalated during the sixteenth century—so much so that, as A. Hassell Smith has argued, by the end of the century Westminster was devising expedients to circumvent county Quarter Sessions.[38] In contrast, at the close of the Stuart era, county Quarter Sessions were no longer administering many matters vital to the realm's governance, matters that they had administered earlier under the Tudors or early Stuarts. As a result, in its administrative guise, as in its judicial guise, late seventeenth-century Quarter Sessions executed powers of local government while other bodies administered and adjudicated matters of national concern. A brief survey of three major matters subject to county Quarter Sessions—taxation, the militia, and transportation's

[35] Cockburn, *Assizes*, 89–96; Louis A. Knafla, *Kent at Law 1602*, Vol. 1: *The County Jurisdiction: Assizes and the Sessions of the Peace* (London: HMSO, 1994), xxix; Cynthia Herrup, *The Common Peace: Participation and The Criminal Law in Seventeenth-Century England* (Cambridge, 1987), 46, 49, 114; R. H. Silcock, 'County Government in Worcestershire, 1603–1660' (PhD thesis, University of London, 1974), 196; Thomas Garden Barnes, *Somerset 1625–1640* (Cambridge, MA: Harvard, 1961), 51–2; B. W. Quintrell, 'The Government of the County of Essex, 1603–1642' (London University PhD thesis, 1965), 73; Terry Hearing and Sarah Bridges, eds., *Dorset Quarter Sessions Order Book 1625–1638: A Calendar, Dorset Record Society*, 14 (Dorchester, 2006), showing orders for hanging in 1632, 1635, and 1636.

[36] Keith William Parry, 'Crime and Punishment in Early Modern England, with Special Reference to Seventeenth-Century Norfolk' (PhD thesis, University of East Anglia, 2003), 65 n. 156.

[37] W. LeHardy, ed., *Hertfordshire County Records*, Vol. 6 (Hertford, 1930), xxix; M. E. W. Maddison, 'The Justices of the Peace and the Administration of Local Government in the East and West Ridings of Yorkshire between 1680 and 1750' (PhD thesis, University of Leeds, 1986), 266–7; David Lemmings, *Law and Government in England during the Long Eighteenth Century* (Houndsmills: Palgrave Macmillan, 2011), 29; Landau, *Justices*, 242–3; Robert B. Shoemaker, *Prosecution and Punishment: Petty Crime and the Law in London and Rural Middlesex, c.1660–1725* (Cambridge: Cambridge University Press, 1991), 128, 130.

[38] A. Hassell Smith, *County and Court: Government and Politics in Norfolk, 1558–1603* (Oxford: Oxford, 1974). My argument here builds on chs 5, 6, 11, 12, 13.

infrastructure—reveals Quarter Sessions' rise under the Tudors and partial supersession by the end of Stuart rule.

Among their other duties, Tudor and early Stuart justices collected taxes for the monarch—subsidies, benevolences, forced loans, etc. The justices were a major component of Westminster's fiscal machine. By the later seventeenth century, they were a less important component of that machine—a disengagement of justices and Westminster emphasized by the story of purveyance. Purveyance was an impost levied for the monarch from Quarter Sessions. Each Quarter Sessions negotiated for its county about the purveyance to be inflicted upon it. In debating purveyance, and in representing the county's objections to purveyance to the privy council, county Quarter Sessions were adopting a role similar to that of France's provincial Estates.[39] Just as France's central government tried to manage the Estates, so too did the privy council try to manage Quarter Sessions. In 1592, the privy council demanded that each Quarter Sessions nominate just a few of its members, who would act for and bind the county.[40] Despite Westminster's ingenuity, such devices did not eliminate Quarter Sessions' protests about purveyance, or indeed other taxation.

From the late seventeenth century on, contention between Westminster and Quarter Sessions over taxation markedly abated, for the administrative structure of the realm's fiscal machine altered so as to diminish the justices' centrality to that machine. Purveyance illustrates that machine's operation. Purveyance disappeared at the Restoration, when the monarchy surrendered a number of dues in return for an excise tax. From the Restoration on, customs and excise together constituted most, and an increasingly larger portion, of Westminster's revenue.[41] Customs and excise were administered by Westminster's bureaucracy. From the Restoration on, responsibility for administering taxation manifested the stigmata of functional design: most of the taxation destined for the centre was collected by the centre.

Similar functional differentiation likewise diminished Quarter Sessions' powers over the militia. Under the early Tudors, all Justices of the Peace were members of the county commissions responsible for mustering the militia. As commissioners for the militia, the justices administered the militia. At Quarter Sessions, as Justices of the Peace, the justices administered the militia rates and otherwise assisted in activating the militia. In contrast, in the last two decades of the sixteenth century, Westminster created a new administrative structure for the militia, and that structure circumvented Quarter Sessions' control over the militia. From 1585, a Lord Lieutenant appointed as a permanent county officer headed each county's militia. He, in turn, was associated with a

[39] Smith, *County and Court*, 95, 115–16, 294–301, 303; Clark, *Provincial Society*, 146, 227; Michael J. Braddick, *The Nerves of State: Taxation and the Financing of the English State, 1588–1714* (Manchester: Manchester, 1996), 81–2.

[40] Smith, *County and Court*, 115–16. Similarly, in the 1630s the privy council allocated the collection of ship money to the sheriffs, so demeaning the justices' status: Clark, *Provincial Society*, 360.

[41] Braddick, *Nerves*, 10–11; John Brewer, *The Sinews of Power: War, Money and the English State, 1688–1789* (Cambridge, MA: Harvard, 1988), 96–8.

very small number of deputy lieutenants. Between them, Lord Lieutenant and deputy lieutenants made all the county's decisions about the militia, while the justices and their Quarter Sessions became mere handmaidens of the more august lieutenancy. Quarter Sessions was now required to levy militia rates which its members had not determined; and Quarter Sessions objected.[42]

Just as the Restoration had rendered Quarter Sessions' powers over purveyance irrelevant, so it voided Quarter Sessions' power as it related to the militia. The militia acts of 1662 and 1663 endowed the lieutenancy with statutory power sufficient to conduct the militia without reference to Quarter Sessions.[43] Nor was such dissociation the extent of the Restoration's re-organization of military might. It was at the Restoration that the English first endowed their monarch with a standing army. That endowment eventually had the effect of introducing a functional differentiation between Westminster's responsibility for troops to be deployed abroad, and the county's responsibility for its militia.

As with purveyance and the militia, so with transportation's infrastructure—with roads, bridges, and harbours: sixteenth-century empowerment of the justices and Quarter Sessions was followed first by circumvention of the justices and Quarter Sessions, and then in the later seventeenth century by differentiation of the justices' and Quarter Sessions' responsibilities from those created at Westminster's behest. In the mid-sixteenth century, Parliament empowered the justices by placing responsibility for maintenance of a highway on the parishes it traversed, and placing responsibility for supervision of that maintenance on the justices, who could command that a parish's inhabitants labour to repair the roads. By the later sixteenth century, the Crown was attempting to insure maintenance of highways, bridges, piers, and harbours it considered particularly important by granting patents for their construction or repair, authorizing the patentees to levy local rates for that repair, and at the same time converting the justices in Quarter Sessions into the patentees' agents for so mulcting the locality. As A. Hassell Smith has demonstrated, in Norfolk such patents and patentees stimulated contention among justices at Quarter Sessions (where justices duelled because of such a patent) and among justices riding to Quarter Sessions (where one justice ambushed another because of such a patent).[44]

As with purveyance and the militia, so with the patentee for transportation's infrastructure: in the later seventeenth century a new differentiation of responsibilities both reduced the bounds within which the justices exercised their powers, and increased their ability to administer the matters left under their control. On the one hand, in 1670, 1691, and 1702, Parliament passed statutes empowering Quarter Sessions to levy rates for maintenance of roads and bridges. No longer would it be necessary to secure a patent

[42] Smith, *County and Court*, 114, 124–31, 227.

[43] A. Hassell Smith, 'Militia Rates and Militia Statutes 1558–1663', in *The English Commonwealth 1547–1640*, ed. Peter Clark, Alan G. R. Smith, and Nicholas Tyacke (New York: Harper and Row, 1979), 109–10.

[44] Smith, *County and Court*, 97, 229–34, 303.

and its attendant patentee to raise money to repair these facilities.[45] On the other hand, Parliament also formulated a new version of the patentee for improvement of transportation's infrastructure. Under the later Stuarts, Parliament passed local statutes empowering specified bodies—for example a town corporation, or people listed by name in the local statute—to levy duties on those using new or improved facilities such as piers, harbours, and rivers, and to use such prospective duties as security when borrowing funds to make these innovations.[46] Such statutes had the effect of rendering the justices and Quarter Sessions responsible for maintaining the infrastructure of transportation customary to a county, while allocating responsibility for innovation to those prepared to assume its attendant obligations.

As the preceding tales of taxation, militia, and transportation's infrastructure suggest, change in the range of Quarter Sessions' exercise of its power provides the local chapter of the story of the rise of the early modern English state. When that state was being created, in the century and a half before the Civil War, Westminster reached out to the justices and Quarter Sessions, enlisting them to act as Westminster's agents in Westminster's concerns. So, debates roiling government at Westminster—debates about taxation, prerogative power, monopolies, etc.—also roiled Quarter Sessions—a court which became 'the parliament of the provincial community'.[47] Because they were so connected to and important to Westminster, the justices and Quarter Sessions were constantly subjected to Westminster's attention. The privy council sent them directives, prodding them to undertake a variety of tasks, and to report their progress in the execution of those tasks. So, too, in order to facilitate execution of those tasks, the privy council summoned justices before it; and justices manipulated the privy council's penchant for intervention so as to bring their opponents before the council board.[48] At Assizes, the judges likewise imposed themselves on the justices' administration of the county, in some instances acting as an extension of the privy council, and in others going beyond that remit to demand that the justices account to them for execution of their ordinary judicial and administrative duties.[49] Under Elizabeth and the early Stuarts, when the justices and their Quarter Sessions might be portrayed as at the

45 Sidney and Beatrice Webb, *English Local Government*, Vol. 5: *The Story of the King's Highway* (London: Longmans Green, 1913), 14–15, 19–23; 22 Ch. II *c.* 12 (1670); 3 Will. and Mary *c.* 12 (1691); 1 Ann *c.* 12 (1702).

46 For example: Bridlington Pier, 8 and 9 Will. III *c.* 29 (1696); Road Repair (Hertfordshire, Cambridgeshire, Huntingdonshire), 15 Ch. II *c.* 1 (1663); Rivers Wye and Lugg, 7 and 8 Will. III *c.* 14 (1695).

47 Clark, *Provincial Society*, 145–6. See also: Smith, *County and Court*, ch. 12 and 275–6; Heal and Holmes, *Gentry*, 207–8; Ann Hughes, *Politics, Society and Civil War in Warwickshire, 1620–1660* (Cambridge: Cambridge University Press, 1987), 51.

48 E.g. Smith, *County and Court*, Part III.

49 B. W. Quintrell, *Proceedings of the Lancashire Justices of the Peace at the Sheriff's Table during Assizes Week, 1578–1694*, *The Record Society of Lancashire and Cheshire*, 121 (1981), 12, 35, 43–4, 48, 171–7; Cockburn, *Assizes*, 7, 10, 153–4, 156–7, 173, 179.

height of their power, government at Westminster interpenetrated government of the county.

In contrast, by the close of the early modern era, when Westminster had differentiated its government from that of the counties, when Westminster had created governmental machinery dedicated solely to tasks deemed fundamental to the central government, the justices and their Quarter Sessions attracted less and less of Westminster's attention. The privy council became decreasingly interested in summoning justices before it. Indeed, so distanced did the central government become from county government that, unlike historians of earlier decades, historians of the last Stuarts' reigns cannot use Westminster's records to discover what the nation's justices were doing. Like the privy council, the judges at Assizes became less proactive as supervisors of county government. No longer did the judges monitor the justices; instead they waited until they tried a relevant case before pronouncing on matters in what was becoming the justices' domain.[50] The judges' decisions set the parameters within which the justices acted, with a great deal of autonomy, on matters within their domain. Increasingly, that domain consisted of matters that were not of immediate interest to Westminster. In other words, the justices and their Quarter Sessions' concerns were limited to what we now identify as 'local government'.

Compared to the matters perturbing the central government, those brought before Queen Anne's Quarter Sessions might seem trifling, so trifling that many analyses omit the justices, their Quarter Sessions, and local government from definitions of the state.[51] Nonetheless, Westminster's involvement in county government throughout most of the early modern era suggests that the governors of early modern England considered county government to be a matter of state. When the English state became differentiated, with some matters relegated to central government and others to local government, county government did not cease to be a part of the state. What did diminish was county government's activity in matters that might be labelled 'political', especially matters on which England's newly created parties had taken a stand. Quarter Sessions were parliaments no more. In part, because the last Stuarts' Quarter Sessions exercised power over a more limited range of matters than had its early modern predecessors, and in part because decisions on the matters consigned to the last Stuarts' Quarter Sessions were considered less vital to national life than were decisions at these Quarter Sessions' predecessors, the last Stuarts' justices were less likely to attend Quarter Sessions than their predecessors. Decline of desire to attend Quarter Sessions did not infect all types of justices to the same degree. Therefore, change in Quarter Sessions' exercise of its range of powers altered the persona of the justices at Quarter Sessions.

[50] Cockburn, *Assizes*, 185, 187; Quintrell, *Sheriff's Table*, 12, 35, 45, 48.

[51] Michael J. Braddick, *State Formation in Early Modern England c.1550–1700* (Cambridge: Cambridge University Press, 2000), 13–20 provides a theoretical justification for inclusion of local government in definitions of the state. That such justification is considered necessary reveals the extent to which discussions of the English state have omitted local government.

The Justices at Quarter Sessions

Although the conventional portrait of the justices assumes that the 'working commission'—the justices who acted in Quarter Sessions and out of Quarter Sessions—was the county gentry,[52] it was not until the close of the Stuart era that the gentry's persona became Quarter Sessions'. Least likely to attend late-Stuart Quarter Sessions were the justices whose power as individuals and whose aspirations extended far beyond the county. By the time the last Stuart died on the throne, such justices either never or hardly ever attended Quarter Sessions. That had not always been the case.

Before the late seventeenth century, justices immediately recognizable as agents of the monarch's law and government had enhanced the grandeur of Quarter Sessions' bench. From the later fourteenth century to the early seventeenth century, the monarch's judges regularly appeared at the Quarter Sessions of the counties in which they lived.[53] No historian has reported sighting a judge at a later Stuart Quarter Sessions. Similarly, while Yorkist and early Tudor courtiers and officers of the royal household occasionally appeared at Quarter Sessions,[54] there are no reports of such appearance by their later Stuart successors, i.e. members of departments of the central government appointed to a county's commission because the department conducted important business in the county.

However, it is not the presence or absence of judges, courtiers, or household officers at Quarter Sessions that has provided the foundation for portrayal of county government as forever the province of the gentry. What has been considered probative, perhaps because it seems noticeable, has been the absence from Quarter Sessions of peers and their sons; and because the overwhelming majority of privy counsellors were peers and their sons, the absence of privy counsellors. Portrayals of Quarter Sessions's bench as continuously populated just by gentry assume that peers and their sons were not present. These portrayals can make that assumption because the evidence on this point is unusually opaque.

For all of the mediaeval era, and most of the early modern era, the only fairly complete set of records of attendance at Quarter Sessions is the pipe rolls' list of payments to justices for attending Quarter Sessions. In 1390, Parliament decreed that such payments be made only to justices who held a rank lower than that of knight banneret. (The

52 e.g. Fletcher, *Reform*, 5.

53 Saul, *Knights*, 132; Lander, *English Justices*, 33–5, 63, 65, 67, 68, 70, 73; Bevan, 'Henrician Assizes', 66; Helen Margaret Speight, 'Local Government and Politics in Devon and Cornwall 1509–1549' (PhD thesis, University of Sussex, 1991), 134; Hopkins, 'Monmouthshire', 48; Smith, *County and Court*, 192; Jeffrey R. Hankins, 'Local Government and Society in Early Modern England: Hertfordshire and Essex, *c*.1590–1630' (PhD dissertation, Louisiana State University and Agricultural and Mechanical College, 2003), 115; Rong Xiang, 'The Staffordshire Justices and their Sessions 1603–1642' (PhD thesis, University of Birmingham, 1996), 203ff.

54 Lander, *English Justices*, 63, 64, 73, 112, 119–20; Condon, 'Ruling Elites', 125; Clark, *Provincial Society*, 18–20.

non-hereditary rank of knight banneret became virtually extinct in the sixteenth century.) All peers and their sons, except the younger sons of barons, were not outranked by the knight banneret.[55] Therefore, the best records of attendance at Quarter Sessions contain no trace of attendance by all peers and most of their sons.

There are other documents noting attendance at Quarter Sessions, but simple counts of the number of peers appearing in these documents are unlikely to yield an accurate account of their propensity to attend or change in that propensity, because both the survival rate of these documents, and the information they contain vary, and do so in a non-random fashion: the later the date of these documents, the greater the chance both that they survive and that they list Quarter Sessions' attendees. Because these documents have been subjected to nuanced analysis for only a few scattered periods, current historiography allows presentation of just a very rough outline of trends in peers' attendance at Quarter Sessions.

According to J. R. Lander, Quarter Sessions' attendance by peers and the monarch's counsellors in the later fifteenth century 'was more frequent than a long series of *ex cathedra* pronouncements on the matter allow'. Margaret Condon found that peers' attendance at Quarter Sessions increased in the second half of Henry VII's reign.[56] Studies of individual counties suggest that peers attended no less frequently in Elizabeth's reign, and that this level of attendance either continued or declined under the early Stuarts.[57] In contrast, David Heifetz presents evidence that, in the years immediately following the Restoration, peers and their sons attended the Quarter Sessions of at least some counties more frequently[58]—perhaps as a show of support for the restored regime. Within a decade or so, their attendance declined.[59] By the end of the seventeenth century, not only was the propensity of peers and their sons to attend Quarter Sessions less than it had been in Henry VII's reign, but the likelihood that any county Quarter Sessions could boast that a peer had graced its bench during the year was probably less than it had been in Henry VII's reign—and this despite a threefold increase in the number of peers from the early sixteenth century to the late seventeenth century. As a result, by the close of the

[55] Saul, *Knights*, 7; Squibb, *Precedence*, 98–100; 14 Ric. II c. 11.

[56] Lander, *English Justices*, 31, 59–60, 73; Condon, 'Ruling Elites', 121, 125; Zell, 'Early Tudor', 138.

[57] Smith, *County and Court*, 27; Quintrell, *Sheriff's Table*, 14, 37; David L. Heifetz, 'The Justices of the Peace in Hampshire, 1625 to 1675' (PhD dissertation, University of California at Irvine, 1978), 52–3; David C. Cox, 'Shropshire Justices of the Peace before the 18th Century', in *Cinderellas and Packhorses: A History of the Shropshire Magistracy*, ed. David J. Cox and Barry S. Godfrey (Little Logaston: 2005), 20; Hankins, 'Hertfordshire and Essex', 112–18; Xiang, 'Staffordshire', 203; Hearing and Bridges, *Dorset Order Book*, *passim*, showing attendance of Henry Hastings and Lord Digby.

[58] Heifetz, 'Hampshire', 53–4, 58.

[59] P. J. Norrey, 'The Relationship between Central and Local Government in Dorset, Somerset and Wiltshire, 1660–1688' (PhD thesis, University of Bristol, 1988), 217; S. A. Peyton, ed., *Minutes of Proceedings in Quarter Sessions held for ... Kesteven in the County of Lincoln, 1674–1695*, Vol. 2: *Lincoln Record Society*, 26 (1931 for 1929), *passim*; Peter Joseph Le Fevre, 'Justices and Administration: The Political Development of Sussex, 1660–1714' (PhD thesis, CNAA, Brighton Polytechnic, 1989), 133ff.; *Warwick County Records*, Vol. 8, li, liii; James M. Rosenheim, 'County Government and Elite Withdrawal in Norfolk, 1660–1720', in *The First Modern Society*, ed. A. L. Beier, David Cannadine, and James M. Rosenheim (Cambridge: Cambridge University Press, 1989), 114.

seventeenth century the gentry and those aspiring to gentry status virtually monopolized Quarter Sessions' bench, and so established its persona.

These later Stuart gentry, who determined the stereotype of the justices and their Quarter Sessions, represented concepts of county governors that, aside from their relative dissociation from Westminster's power and from noble grandeur, differed from that of their gentry predecessors as justices in at least two ways. First, these justices were more truly volunteers. Under the Tudors and early Stuarts, justices had been threatened with removal from the commission of the peace, and so with loss of the prestige intrinsic to appointment to the commission, if they did not assume the duties of their office.[60] By the early eighteenth century, such threats were not even a faded memory. Justices were not removed from the commission if they did not act as justices, and had not been so removed for decades. As one would therefore expect, a significantly larger proportion of later Stuart justices than of their early modern predecessors either never acted as justices or remained in the commission when they were too sick or old to act. So, justices who actually graced Quarter Sessions' bench now embodied the virtue of public service.

Second, in comparison to its predecessors, the later Stuart bench personified another characteristic now associated with virtuous public service: the capacity for independent judgement. By the later seventeenth century, it was thought that the gentry could make independent judgements because they had, in their lands, an independent source of income. In the fifteenth century, their lands provided a different foundation for the gentry's inclusion in the commission of the peace. In the fifteenth century, 'administrative power had to be backed up with ... readily available force', force 'that came in the first instance from' the justice's 'tenants'. Justices might well arrive at Tudor and even Jacobean Quarter Sessions supported by armed bands.[61] In that environment, there was little reason to appoint gentlemen with no qualification for office other than a landed estate if that estate was too small to support the requisite band of tenants. Under the later Stuarts, such gentlemen were Justices of the Peace, exerting the influence intrinsic to their office, ruling their neighbourhoods, and parading at Quarter Sessions not their intimacy with the greatest in the land, but instead their local self-government, albeit at the monarch's highly attenuated command.

Bibliography

Barnes, Thomas Garden. *Somerset 1625–1640* (Cambridge, MA: Harvard University Press, 1961).

Beckett, J. V. *The Aristocracy in England 1660–1914* (Oxford: Blackwell, 1986).

[60] Smith, *County and Court*, 34, 237; Zell, 'Early Tudor', 158; Barnes and Smith, 'List of Sources', 227; Haigh and Wall, 'Clergy JPs', 243; Diarmaid MacCulloch, *Suffolk and the Tudors: Politics and Religion in an English County 1500–1600* (Oxford: Oxford University Press, 1986), 338; Hughes, *Warwickshire*, 53; Fletcher, *Reform*, 9.

[61] Carpenter, *Locality and Polity*, 47–8; Lawrence Stone, *The Crisis of the Aristocracy 1558–1641* (Oxford: Clarendon, 1965), 238, 251; Heal and Holmes, *Gentry*, 176–7; Robison, 'Surrey', 134.

Bevan, Amanda. 'The Henrician Assizes and the Enforcement of the Reformation', in *The Political Context of Law: Proceedings of the Seventh British Legal History Conference, Canterbury 1985*, ed. Richard Eales and David Sullivan (London: Hambledon, 1987), 62–76.

Braddick, Michael J. *State Formation in Early Modern England c.1550–1700* (Cambridge: Cambridge University Press, 2000).

Clark, Peter. *English Provincial Society from the Reformation to the Revolution: Religion, Politics and Society in Kent 1500–1640* (Hassocks: Harvester, 1977).

Cockburn, James S. *A History of English Assizes, 1558–1714* (Cambridge: Cambridge University Press, 1972).

Fletcher, Anthony. *Reform in the Provinces: The Government of Stuart England* (New Haven: Yale University Press, 1986).

Glassey, Lionel K. J. *Politics and the Appointment of Justices of the Peace 1675–1720* (Oxford: Oxford University Press, 1979).

Guy, John. 'Thomas Wolsey, Thomas Cromwell, and the Reform of Henrician Government', in *The Reign of Henry VIII: Politics, Policy and Piety*, ed. Diarmaid MacCulloch (London: Macmillan, 1995), 35–57, 253–9.

Heal, Felicity and Clive Holmes. *The Gentry in England and Wales, 1500–1700* (London: Macmillan, 1994).

Herrup, Cynthia. *The Common Peace: Participation and the Criminal Law in Seventeenth-Century England* (Cambridge: Cambridge University Press, 1987).

Knafla, Louis A. *Kent at Law 1602*, Vol. 1: *The County Jurisdiction: Assizes and the Sessions of the Peace* (London: HMSO, 1994).

Landau, Norma. *The Justices of the Peace, 1679–1760* (Berkeley: University of California Press, 1984).

Lander, J. R. *English Justices of the Peace 1461–1509* (Gloucester: Sutton, 1989).

Powell, Edward. 'The Administration of Criminal Justice in Late Medieval England: Peace Sessions and Assizes', in *The Political Context of Law: Proceedings of the Seventh British Legal History Conference, Canterbury 1985*, ed. Richard Eales and David Sullivan (London: Hambledon, 1987), 49–59.

Quintrell, B. W. *Proceedings of the Lancashire Justices of the Peace at the Sheriff's Table during Assizes Week, 1578–1694* (Manchester: *Record Society of Lancashire and Cheshire*, 1981).

Saul, Nigel. *Knights and Esquires: The Gloucestershire Gentry in the Fourteenth Century* (Oxford: Clarendon Press, 1981).

Smith, A. Hassell. *County and Court: Government and Politics in Norfolk, 1558–1603* (Oxford: Oxford University Press, 1974).

Smith, A. Hassell. 'Militia Rates and Militia Statutes 1558–1663', in *The English Commonwealth 1547–1640*, ed. Peter Clark, Alan G. R. Smith, and Nicholas Tyacke (New York: Harper and Row, 1979), 93–110.

Walker, Simon. 'Yorkshire Justices of the Peace, 1389–1413', *English Historical Review*, 108 (1993): 281–313.

CHAPTER 13

LAW AND THE EVIDENTIARY ENVIRONMENT

BARBARA J. SHAPIRO

TRIALS are imaginative recreations of past occurrences.[1] To that end the legal community evolves a wide range of devices and thoughtways that are broadly labelled the law of evidence. Witnessing, credibility, testimony, doubt, suspicion, equivocation, conscience, fact, and oaths are frequent topics in law and literature studies. In one way or another, all of them raise questions of truth-telling, fact-finding, and epistemology. Legal historians have been slow to turn to these topics, perhaps because most legal scholars view the law of evidence as not having emerged until the late eighteenth century. An exception, legal scholar and evidence specialist William Twining, has for some time urged the legal community to look at the epistemological assumptions relating to the law of evidence.[2] This essay attempts to extend his call for a broader view of legal evidence. It pursues philosophical, scientific, and other approaches to evidence, in an attempt to illuminate the cross currents of the evidentiary environment of the common law courts of the early modern period. That environment included beliefs about oath-taking in and out of legal settings, the introduction of trial witnesses and the subsequent problems of assessing their credibility, the rhetorical origins of early modern credibility standards, the role of casuistry in developing notions of the 'satisfied conscience' and the concern with doubt, the role of character witnesses, circumstantial evidence and the evolving language of verdicts from 'satisfied conscience' to the familiar 'beyond reasonable doubt', as well as the early modern concerns with the importance of mercy. I begin with oaths because

[1] Portions of this essay have appeared in 'Oaths, Credibility and the Legal Process in Early Modern England', Part 1, *Law and Humanities*, 6.2 (2012): 145–78; Part 2, *Law and Humanities*, 7.1 (2013): 19–54.

[2] William Twining, *Theories of Evidence: Bentham and Wigmore* (Stanford: Stanford University Press, 1985); William Twining, 'Evidence as a Multi-Disciplinary Subject,' *Law, Probability, and Risk* 2 (2003): 91–107; William Twining, *Rethinking Evidence: Exploratory Essays*, 2nd edn (Cambridge: Cambridge University Press, 2006), 35. See also Roger Park and Michael Saks, 'Evidence Scholarship Reconsidered: Results of the Interdisciplinary Turn,' *Boston College Law Review*, 47 (2006): 949–1032.

oaths were a prominent feature of litigation before witnesses came to play a central role in common law jury trials.

Oaths

Oaths were a ubiquitous feature of early modern English political and legal life. There were assertory oaths, in which oath takers promised to tell the truth about some event that had taken place in the past, as well as promissory oaths in which they promised to fulfill the duties of a particular office or pledged loyalty to the state or monarch. There were also oaths of office ranging from the king's coronation oath to numerous oaths administered by justices of the peace to a host of minor officeholders. Justices presiding over quarter sessions also dealt with sworn witnesses and sworn jurors. Oaths were sworn by sureties for keeping the peace as well as by keepers of taverns and alehouses and many sellers of commodities. Some oaths were assiduously kept, but the experience of oaths casually taken and casually disregarded was pervasive. Though widely condemned, 'vile' or blasphemous swearing and casual swearing were a feature of English life that elicited periodic efforts at control and punishment. Oaths were both highly valued and often ignored or slighted in practice.

Although considerable scholarly attention has been given to loyalty oaths to the monarch and governing regimes, and more recently to oaths of office, less attention has been given to oaths in the early modern legal context.[3] We know relatively little about the extent to which oaths taken by witnesses, grand jurors and jurors were taken with the expectation of divine punishment for their violation. There was, indeed, great faith in the truth eliciting potential of oaths, and yet there were circumstances in which that faith must have been brought into doubt or completely abandoned as to a particular oath by a particular witness.[4]

[3] For loyalty oaths and oaths of office, see Conal Condren, *Argument and Authority in Early Modern England: The Presupposition of Oaths and Offices* (Cambridge: Cambridge University Press, 2006); D. M. Jones, *Conscience and Allegiance in Seventeenth Century England: The Political Significance of Oaths and Engagements* (Rochester: University of Rochester Press, 1999); John Spurr, 'Perjury, Profanity and Politics', *The Seventeenth Century*, 8.1 (1993), 29–50. See also John Kerrigan, 'Shakespeare, Oaths and Vows', *Proceedings of the British Academy*, 167 (2010), 61–89; Frances Shirley, *Swearing and Perjury in Shakespeare's Plays* (London: Allen and Unwin, 1979).

[4] George Fisher argues that the 'perceived divine power of the oath to compel truthful testimony' was central to early modern English evidence law. He believes that the legal system's dependence on the perceived credibility of oaths demanded that it avoids trial practices that might reveal conflicts between testimonies given under oath. While Fisher recognizes a 'great lurch forward' in 1696 when witnesses called by accused traitors were first permitted to testify under oath and 1702 when that right was extended to all witnesses, he nevertheless maintains that the legal system 'struggled' to protect juries from having to deal with competing oaths and credibility conflicts. See George Fisher, 'The Jury as Lie Detector', *YLJ*, 107.3 (1997): 580–3.

Legal writers have remarkably little to say about oaths, and some were quite cynical. In the early seventeenth century John Selden noted that 'Now Oathes are so frequent, they should be taken like pills swallow'd whole, if you chew them you find them bitter, if you think of what you sweare twill hardly goe down.'[5] Another commentator indicated that the world was divided between those who would swear to nothing and those who would swear to anything.[6] It was often proclaimed that loose and profane swearing undermined the sanctity of the oaths. If some oaths were becoming a matter of form instead of sincere religious commitment with serious spiritual consequences for violation, and if oath breaking was taken to be frequent, then oath-taking in the legal setting must be carefully examined.

Because legal writers, judges and other legal professionals rarely discussed oaths, apart from the oath *ex officio*, our understanding of oaths is derived largely from clerics preaching at the assizes. A typical example is that of John Tillotson for whom the oath was 'the surest ground of Judicial proceedings and the most firm and sacred bond that can be laid upon all that are concerned in the administration of public Justice' and the 'utmost credit that we can give to anything'.[7]

In order to fully understand the role of oath-taking in courts we must consider when and why oath-taking by witnesses was introduced, rationales for excluding defence witnesses in felony and treason cases from testifying under oath, and what actually occurred when conflicting sworn testimony by witnesses encountered the sworn duty of grand and petty jurors to find the truth.

Oath-Taking by Witnesses

Witnesses were not a feature of medieval jury trials and only became common in the common law courts during the sixteenth century.[8] It is unclear when or why they began to testify under oath or why defence witnesses in felony and treason cases were refused the oath, but it is likely that oaths began to be tendered when witnesses were first introduced. By the mid-sixteenth century witnesses were already compelled to appear. Passed in 1563 the first perjury statute suggests that the prospect of divine punishment was no longer considered sufficiently daunting to ensure the truth of sworn testimony.[9]

[5] John Selden, *Table Talk*, ed. Frederick Pollock (London: Quaritch, 1927), 87.

[6] Spurr, 'Perjury, Profanity', 33.

[7] John Tillotson, *The Lawfulness and Obligation of Oaths* (London, 1681), Dedication, 3–4. See also 7, 24, 28–9. For Robert Sanderson oaths were religious acts designed to show 'that a Thing doubtful, may by invoking the test of God, have the greatest certainty of which it is capable'. Robert Sanderson, *The Nature and Obligation of Oaths* (London: 1716), 3–4. (First given as a course of lectures in 1646.)

[8] Some witnesses have been detected as early as the fourteenth century and some appeared occasionally in the fifteenth century. See discussion in Daniel Klerman, 'Was the Jury Ever Self-Informing?' *Southern California Law Review*, 77 (2003): 123–50.

[9] 5 Elizabeth I *c.* 9. Suborning witnesses was also a great concern.

In civil cases jurors heard testimony given under oath by both plaintiff's and defendant's witnesses, and so heard conflicting sworn testimony and presumably chose which witnesses to credit, doubt, or reject. The same was true of misdemeanour proceedings. In Chancery, Star Chamber, and Admiralty there was also sworn testimony on both sides. Complaints about vexatious and malicious suits suggest that the English public was alert to the possibility of false accusations and false witnessing and familiar with conflicting testimony given under oath.

The rationale for denying the oath to defence witnesses in cases of felony and treason was not obvious, even to such highly esteemed lawyers as Sir Edward Coke who indicated that there was no legal authority for excluding sworn defence testimony. His *Institutes* proclaimed that there was not 'a scintilla juris' against it and that the denial could be traced to no statute, ancient author, case, or record.[10] Sir Matthew Hale too indicated that 'the reason' for refusing the oath to defence witnesses was 'not manifest'.[11] The most esteemed lawyers could not justify or explain the exclusion. Even the notorious Judge Jeffreys remarked that it was 'a hard case' that 'for a two-penny trespass' men were entitled to counsel and his 'witnesses on oath, but if he shall commit murder … nay, high treason … he shall neither have counsel, nor his witnesses examined on oath'.[12]

The only extended discussion occurred in 1607 when Parliament considered proposals for a Union between England and Scotland. Views varied greatly with some arguing that defence witnesses should not be permitted to testify at all. One speaker felt that if 'civil litigants may have sworn witnesses then those on trial for their lives certainly should'. According to another speaker credibility could best be determined by the jury, who were more familiar with the witnesses than the judges. Sir Anthony Cope argued that 'testimony is but to informe the Jury, who may believe as they see cause for if they find by circumstances that a bad fellow saith true they may believe them *et contra*'. Another commenting on the denial of the oath to the defence, suggested that after Elizabeth 'the courts grew so heartily ashamed of a doctrine so unreasonable and oppressive for the prisoner, the consequence of which still was, that the jury gave less credit to the prisoner's evidence'. Another, using language that would become familiar to readers of the *Institutes*, indicated that though defence witnesses in England were not heard under oath, it was 'not the Law of England … for there is no one book or case in all the Law to that effect'. Another, however, favoured retaining the current practice because 'men will be more prone to forswear themselves' in cases of life and therefore commit perjury, and another because criminals would prepare their witnesses in advance of the trial and have 'ready a strange Crew of damned witnesses'.[13] The final legislation affected only the border areas between England and Scotland. It provided that all witnesses

[10] Sir Edward Coke, *The Third Part of the Institutes of the Laws of England* (London: 1644), 79.

[11] Sir Matthew Hale, *The History of the Pleas of the Crown* (Philadelphia: 1847 [1736]), 283.

[12] Thomas Bayly Howell, ed., *A Complete Collection of State Trials*, 34 vols (London: 1809–1826), 10.147, 267.

[13] Robert Bowyer, *The Parliamentary Diary of Robert Bowyer, 1606–1607*, ed. David Harris Wilson (Minneapolis: University of Minnesota Press, 1931), 311, 318, 326, 329, 358–60.

would be sworn 'for the better discoverie of Truth and for the better informacion of the Conscience of the Jurie and Justice' and their 'credit' 'referred to the Jurors'. A royal proclamation of the same year, which dealt with the entire country, declared that jurors were not tied to the 'evidences and proofs produced' and were to discern the credit of witness testimony according to their 'consciences and understandings'.[14] When in 1610 a parliamentary subcommittee on grievances proposed that accused persons be permitted to testify under oath, the king was unwilling to accept the reform because he believed that men would perjure themselves for their friends.[15]

Interest in allowing defence witnesses to testify under oath revived in 1652–1653. A Leveller tract advocated that witnesses should be 'sworn on both sides in all trials'.[16] The Hale Commission, appointed by the Rump to reform the law, also recommended that defence witnesses be allowed to testify under oath.[17] Revolutionary-era legislation making adultery a felony and revision of courts martial procedure provided that defence witnesses be sworn.

Oaths and witness credibility became highly politicized during the Popish Plot treason trials and the subsequent trials of leading Whig figures when it was widely believed that the false testimony of prosecution witnesses resulted in wrongful convictions. Following the Revolution of 1688 several parliamentary bills included the right of defense witnesses to testify under oath. The legislation that finally emerged in 1696, however, granted that right only to cases of treason and it was not until 1702 that the right to testify under oath was extended to all witnesses.[18] While it is clear that oaths were a ubiquitous feature of political, economic, and legal life from the time witnesses were introduced into jury trials, there was never great confidence in the oath's efficacy to always produce truthful testimony. There was a general belief that sworn testimony offered a greater prospect of reliability than unsworn testimony and that juries were capable of evaluating the credit of testimony whether given under oath or not.

The Grand Jurors' Oath

Grand jurors too were under oath and, like jurors, were pledged to the truth. The promise was to tell or present the truth, the whole truth, and nothing but the truth. Since

14 James F. Larkin and Paul L. Hughes, eds, *Stuart Royal Proclamations*, (Oxford: Clarendon Press, 1973), 1.167–71.

15 Wallace Notestein, *The House of Commons, 1604–1610* (New Haven: Yale University Press, 1971), 354.

16 *The Fundamental Laws and Liberties of England* (London: 1653), 4; John Cooke, *The Vindication of the Law* (London: 1652), 22.

17 Mary Cotterell, 'Interregnum Law Reform: The Hale commission of 1652', *English Historical Review*, 83 (1968): 389.

18 Evidence writers Geoffrey Gilbert and John Morgan attributed the 1696 legislation to the incredibility of the king's witnesses who had been 'contradicted by men only of better credit upon their words'. See Geoffrey Gilbert, *The Law of Evidence* (London: Printed by Henry Lintot, 1756), 159; John Morgan, *Essays upon the Law of Evidence* (London: Printed for J. Johnson, 1789), 48–9.

grand jurors were advised to consider the credibility of prosecution witnesses from at least the early seventeenth century, their oaths encountered the oaths of prosecution witnesses. A tract dealing with cases of witchcraft, dedicated to Sir Edward Coke and the judiciary, indicated that witnesses testifying to supernatural acts were credible only if they were 'sufficient, able to judge, free from exception of malice, partialities, distractions, folly, and if ... there bee justly deemed no deception of sense, mistaking of reason or imagination'.[19] Another tract advised grand jurors not to passively accept testimony offered on oath—they must inquire diligently into 'the wisdom and discretion of the witnesses, whether they can discern well between reall and counterfeit acts' and distinguish the testimony of partisans, friends, and relations from 'indifferent relaters'. The 'fearful, superstitious ... children or old silly persons [were] not easily credited'.[20] Oaths might or might not be sufficient, standing alone, to support a *billa vera*. From at least the end of the sixteenth century charges to grand juries admonished them to heed their oaths.[21]

Controversy over the grand juror's oath emerged in the late seventeenth century. The position thought by Zachary Babington to have had the approval of 'all the learned Judges' was that, in spite of their oaths, grand jurors were failing to find indictments when they should have or were unjustifiably reducing felony charges to lesser offences. Babington argued that the word 'truth' in the grand jurors oath should be understood in a 'legal' rather than 'in a plain literal and Grammatical sense'. 'A Supposal is all that can be inferr'd from the Indictment.'[22] A quite different view was offered by Whigs who stressed the oath's obligation to 'diligently inquire'. Grand jurors must 'weigh the circumstances and the Witnesses, and search out the Truth'. Their oath required them to 'diligently Inquire into the Quality, Repute and Circumstances of what they [i.e. witnesses and accusers] deposed and whether they do not Swear out of Malice, Subornation, Self Interest, Combination or, some ill Design'.[23] This position was used to defend the

[19] John Cotta, *The Trial of Witchcraft* (London: 1616), 80–1.

[20] Richard Bernard, *Guide to Grand Jurors in Cases of Witchcraft* (London: 1627). John Langbein and J. S. Cockburn, however, suggest that grand juries had been reduced to a largely ceremonial function. See John H. Langbein, *Prosecuting Crime in the Renaissance* (Cambridge: Harvard University Press, 1974), 119–20, 127, 127n; J. S. Cockburn, *A History of English Assizes, 1558–1714* (Cambridge: Cambridge University Press, 1972), 73–9. Sir Thomas Browne noted credulity is 'an easie assent to what is obtruded, or a beleeving at first hear what is delivered by others. This is a weakeness of the understanding, without examination assenting unto things which from their nature and causes doe carry no perswasion; whereby men often swallow falsities for truths, dubiosities for certainties, feasibilities of possibilities, and things impossible as possibilities themselves'. *Pseudodoxia Epidemica*, in *The Prose of Sir Thomas Browne*, ed. Norman J. Endicott (New York: Anchor Books, 1967), 118.

[21] Conyers Read, ed., *William Lambarde and Local Government: His 'Ephemeris' and Twenty-Nine Charges to Juries and Commissions* (Ithaca: Cornell University Press, 1962), 75, 80, 88, 108, 112, 116, 122, 160. He also indicated that grand jurors were not to reject 'the oath of any man whom law holdeth for credible and which also giveth credit each man that hath not beforetime been lawfully discredited', 127.

[22] Zachary Babington, *Advice to Grand Jurors in Cases of Blood* (London: 1677), 4, 79, 115, 118, 119, 123–4, 125–6, 130.

[23] Henry Care, *English Liberties, or the Free-Born Subject's Inheritance* (London: 1682), 13–15, 216–17.

ignoramus verdict of the London grand jurors who had refused to indict Lord Shaftsbury for treason.

If grand jurors were obligated to believe what the witnesses swore but their own oaths required them to believe in their consciences that the accused was guilty before giving *billa vera*, a conflict of oaths would necessarily occur whenever a *billa vera* was not returned. Some commentators rejected the view of those like Babington who argued that the truth of a true bill should be understood as no more than a reasonable supposition supported by testimony assumed to be true, arguing that grand jurors had to be fully persuaded that the bill they swore was true.[24] *A Guide to English Juries* also rejected the view that 'that the Grand-Jury are not to be Judges of the Credibility of the Evidence' holding that it was unreasonable to indict or convict for a capital crime 'upon the Oath of a strange or bad Fellow's Evidence'. Grand jurors were 'as much on their Oath as any other Jury'. If sworn testimony alone were sufficient the grand jury would be 'only a piece of needless Formality'.[25] Some treated the grand jury oath to return true verdicts as a 'matter of form' while others insisted that the oath required full persuasion 'according the best of their Understandings'.[26]

THE OATH AND THE TRIAL JURY

Trial jurors were also under oath, swearing to 'true deliverance make ... according to your Evidence'.[27] There is no reason to believe that jurors were more or less likely to believe in divine punishment than other oath takers. If jurors faced conflicting sworn testimony in civil suits and misdemeanours even before the legislation of 1696 and 1702, they must have considered which witnesses under oath were and were not truthful or credible. While jurors may have viewed oaths in civil cases and misdemeanours somewhat differently than in felony or treason due to capital punishment for the convicted, there is little reason to believe that they automatically considered the oaths of prosecution witnesses to be of more consequence than their own.[28] Sir Thomas Smith insisted that judges were to remind jurors they must 'have an eye to your oaths, and to your dutie'.[29]

[24] Sir John Vaughan, *Ignoramus Vindicated* (London: 1681), 1–2. One grand juror in the Shaftsbury proceedings insisted, 'If we are not left to consider the Credibility of the Witnesses, we cannot satisfy our Conscience.' The judge indicated that they were not to consider the credit of the witnesses.

[25] *A Guide to English Juries: Setting Forth Their Antiquity, Power, and Duty* (London: 1725), 12. See also 37–9, 52–4.

[26] Richard Garnet, *A Guide to the Knowledge of the Rights and Principles of Englishmen* (London: Robert Gosling, 1771), 110, 169, 176, 177.

[27] *The Book of Oaths* (London: Robert Gosling, 1715) 113. Jurors and witnesses were often sworn in groups, a practice that may have reduced the awesomeness of the oath.

[28] Thomas More, 'Debellacyon of Salem and Bizance', in *The Complete Works of St Thomas More*, ed. John Guy et al. (New Haven, Yale University Press), 2.

[29] Sir Thomas Smith, *De republica Anglorum: A Discourse on the Commonwealth of England*, ed. Mary Dewar (Cambridge: Cambridge University Press, 1982), 114.

Jurors swore to base their verdicts on the basis of evidence, a term that referred to documents of differing evidentiary value and the direct testimony of witnesses. In civil cases the emphasis was on the former. In criminal cases witnesses were more important, but 'circumstances', later called circumstantial evidence, often played a role as well.

Central to our concern is how juries, and especially criminal juries, were instructed to deal with the testimony they heard. Did judges instruct them to believe that oath supported testimony was superior to that of non-oath supported defence witnesses and defendants? Were they asked to consider witness credibility? As early as the sixteenth century Christopher St German had suggested that juries were not bound to follow witnesses.[30] During his trial for treason Sir Thomas More attempted to undermine the credibility of Richard Rich pointing to his bad reputation, untrustworthiness, and dubious credibility. Early in the seventeenth century Lord Chancellor Bacon stated that the law of England left 'the discerning and credit of testimony wholly to the juries' consciences and understanding'.[31] In a Star Chamber prosecution, in a jury's verdict against 'pregnant evidence', jurors denied the charges, saying that they knew the 'Credibility and estimation' of the deponents and witnesses and asserted that they personally knew more 'in the matter than was given in evidence'. The chief Crown witness was known 'to be of light behavior and small credit', and they had acted 'according to their oaths, conscience and the truth of the matter'.[32] Here jurors gave priority to their own oath over the oaths of the prosecution witnesses they heard.

Sir Matthew Hale described the role of jurors in assessing witness credibility. Both parties have 'Liberty of excepting either to the Competence of the Evidence, or the Competency or Credit of Witnesses. … [The] very Manner of a Witnesses's delivering his Testimony will give a probable indication whether he speaks truly or falsely; and by this Means has the Opportunity to correct, amend or explain his Testimony upon further Questioning of him'. Jurors should consider the 'very Quality, carriage, Age, Condition, Education and Place of Commorance of Witnesses'. The jury's opportunity 'for confronting the adverse Witnesses' and 'observing the Contradiction of Witnesses sometimes of the same Side', also provided 'great Opportunities' to gain 'the true and clear Discovery of the Truth'. Jurors were entitled to 'give the more or less Credit to their Testimony' because they were judges of the fact and 'the Truth of Evidence'. 'If there be just cause to disbelieve what a Witness swears, they are not bound to give their verdict according to the Evidence or Testimony … and they may sometimes give Credit to one Witness, tho' oppos'd by more [than] one'. Jurors may 'pronounce a Verdict contrary

[30] Christopher St German, *A Dialogue betwixte two englyshemen, whereof one was called Salem, and the other Bizance* (London: 1533); see also Sir Thomas More, *The Debellacyon of Salem and Bizance*, in *The Complete Works of St Thomas More*, Vol. 10, ed. John Guy et al. (New Haven: Yale University Press, 1963), 361.

[31] Sir Francis Bacon, *The Works of Francis Bacon*, Vol. 1, ed. James Spedding, Robert Ellis, and Douglas Heath (London: Longman, 1857–1874), 276; Paul Hughes and James Larkin, *Tudor Royal Proclamations* (New Haven: Yale University Press, 1964), 1.167–71.

[32] Quoted in Thomas Andrew Green, *Verdict According to Conscience* (Chicago: University of Chicago Press, 1985) 142n.

to such Testimonies, the Truth whereof they have just Causes to suspect' because they 'know a Thing to be false that a Witness swore to be true, or may know a Witness to be incompetent or incredible'.[33] A long list of commentaters, legislation, judicial instruction, and authorities insist that jurors must assess the credibility of witness testimony.[34]

Credibility and English Culture

Credibility concerns were to be widely found outside the legal environment as well as within it. Thomas Hobbes, for example, indicated that the evaluation of testimony involved both 'the saying of the man' and 'his virtue'.[35] Historians often referred to witness credibility and expressed a preference for first-hand testimony.[36] One Restoration-era historian suggested that historians were, like witnesses and jurors, on oath to 'assert the verity of all matters of Fact' and tell 'the whole truth, and nothing but the truth'.[37]

Credibility has been discussed in a number of disciplinary contexts. Its role in the new empirical science of the seventeenth century has been emphasized by Steven Shapin and Simon Schaffer who have argued that gentlemanly status was the primary criterion for establishing truth and reliability.[38] I and others emphasize the role of skill, fidelity,

[33] Sir Matthew Hale, *The History of the Common Law of England*, ed. Charles M. Gray (Chicago: University of Chicago Press, 1971), 163–4.

[34] Treason legislation of 1661 required two lawful and credible witnesses. *Bushel's case* (1670) 124 E.R. 1006 made it clear that jurors might consider their own knowledge of defendant or prosecution witnesses because they sometimes knew 'that what is deposed in court, is absolutely false'; Howell, *State Trials*, 6.1009–10. The lack of credibility of witnesses in the Popish Plot trials exposed the danger of believing all testimony given under oath. A tract of 1680 by John Hawles emphasized that 'When any Matter is sworn ... whether it shall be believed or not, or whether it be true or false in point of fact, the Jurors are proper Judges.' They must consider whether witnesses may have been suborned or have 'any Malice or Sinister Design'. They must have a 'special regard to the Circumstances or Incoherences of their Tales, and endeavor by apt Questions to sift out the Truth or to discovery the Villany'. John Hawles, *The Englishman's Right* (London: 1732 [1680]), 48. See also *The Power and Privilege of Juries Asserted* (London: 1681), 5–7; A tract of 1682 indicated that in considering testimony 'Jurors are not to swallow it [testimony] without chewing of it, and examining the possibility of the whole, and the consistency of one part with another.' They should consider the motives, nature, and manner of the prosecution for malice or 'unusual and unbecoming rigour and violence in the pursuit'. [E. Bohun]; Robert Ferguson, *The Second Part of No Protestant Plot* (London: 1682), 20, 30–1. See also *A Guide to English Juries, Setting Forth their Antiquity, Power and Duty* (London: 1682); George Stanhope, *The Duty of Juries* (London: 1701), 13, 14. Many judges emphasized that 'if you are not satisfied that which the Witnesses have Sworn is true ... then you are to Acquit him'. *The Arraignment, Tryal and Condemnation of Sir John Friend* (London: 1696), 44. See also Kevin Crosby, 'Bushell's Case and the Juror's Soul', *JLH*, 33.3 (2012): 251–90.

[35] Thomas Hobbes, *Leviathan*, ed. Michael Oakshott (London: Penguin Books, 1985), 132.

[36] See Barbara J. Shapiro, *A Culture of Fact: England, 1550–1720* (Ithaca: Cornell University Press, 2000), 47–51.

[37] Thomas Gumble, *The Life of General Monck* (London: 1671), Preface.

[38] See Steven Shapin and Simon Schaffer, *Leviathan and the Air-Pump: Hobbes, Boyle, and the Experimental Life* (Princeton: Princeton University Press, 1989); Steven Shapin, *The Social History of Truth: Civility and Science in Seventeenth Century England* (Chicago: University of Chicago Press, 1994).

impartiality, and the number of observers as well as social status as criteria for establishing belief in natural phenomenon and experimental results.[39] Empirically oriented naturalists, following Bacon, emphasized the role of credibility and doubt in reporting natural phenomenon. Reliable reports depended on persons of credit, preferably many of them. Whether the witness was 'a vain-speaking and light person or sober and severe' would 'bear on the weight of the evidence'. These views, which echo legal language, were also expressed by Robert Boyle and Thomas Sprat, historian of and propagandist for the early Royal Society.[40]

Discussions of witness credibility were also to be found in Restoration-era religious writings providing rational proofs for belief in Christianity by showing that events recorded by the Apostles were credibly related. The writings of John Wilkins, John Tillotson, Gilbert Burnet, and Edward Stillingfleet were typical of the genre. Stillingfleet wrote that the 'greatest evidence which can be given to a matter of fact, is the attesting of it by those persons who were eyewitnesses of it'. If attested by 'a sufficient number of credible persons', it was unreasonable to distrust testimony. The Apostles were credible witnesses, having 'no motive to lie' and no 'mean or vulgar motives'. Their credibility was enhanced by 'the greatest constancy to themselves and uniformity with each other'.[41] In 1696 Steven Nye defended the testimony of the Apostles on similar grounds, saying that although there was no such thing as 'indubitable evidence', one 'cannot make any reasonable doubt of it' and 'ought to acquiesce fully and perfectly in it'.[42] This 'beyond reasonable doubt' language would later be adopted by the law.[43]

Restoration views about credible testimony were given philosophical form in Locke's *Essay on Humane Understanding*. Locke wrote 'one must take into account the number, integrity and skill of the witnesses and whether they had an interest in speaking contrary to the truth'. Also to be considered was the 'consistency of the parts, and circumstances of their relation'. Criteria for assessing the credibility of witnesses were also featured in the popular logic treatise of Isaac Watts and early treatises on the law of evidence. [44]

[39] See Barbara J. Shapiro, 'Gently Boyle', *Metascience*, 6 (1994): 1–23; Barbara J. Shapiro, 'Testimony in Seventeenth-Century English Natural Philosophy: Legal Origins and Early Development', *Studies in the History and Philosophy of Science*, 33.2 (2002): 243–63; Richard W. Serjeantson, 'Testimony and Proof in Early-Modern England', *Studies in the History and Philosophy of Science*, 30.2 (1999): 195–236.

[40] Bacon, *Works*, 4.26. See also 9.24–6, 28, 30–2, 252, 260–2; Robert Boyle, *The Christian Virtuoso* in *The Works of Robert Boyle* (London: 1772), 235; Thomas Sprat, *History of the Royal Society*, ed. Jackson Cope and H. W. Jones (St Louis: University of Washington in St Louis, 1958), 70, 85, 93, 99, 100.

[41] Edward Stillingfleet, *Origines Sacrae, or a Rational Account of the Christian Faith* (London: 1662), 260, 285–6, 287–8. See Barbara J. Shapiro, 'Religion and the Law: Evidence, Proof and "matter of fact", 1660–1700', in *Law, Crime and English Society 1660–1830*, ed. Norma Landau (Cambridge: Cambridge University Press, 2002), 185–208.

[42] Steven Nye, *A Discourse Concerning Natural and Revealed Religion* (Glasgow: 1696), 3, 53, 136, 144–5.

[43] See Barbara J. Shapiro, *'Beyond Reasonable Doubt' and 'Probable Cause': Historical Studies in the Anglo-American Law of Evidence* (Berkeley: University of California Press, 1991).

[44] John Locke, *An Essay Concerning Humane Understanding* (London, 1690; Isaac Watts, *Logick* (London: 1724), 284, 410–13, 463–4; According to Gilbert's treatise on evidence, if a case relied on a single witness, that witness must be of particularly high credit. If equal in number and credit, the

Classical Rhetoric as a Source of Credibility Standards

The degree to which testimony might be taken as truthful, was, as we have seen, employed in a variety of disciplines. The criteria for evaluating testimony were derived from the classical and Renaissance rhetorical traditions that formed the basis of humanistic culture. Those traditions, based on Aristotle, Cicero, and Quintilian, focused on probable rather than certain knowledge. They distinguished inartificial proofs, which included witnesses, tortures, and contract, from artificial ones, which were 'invented' by the orator.[45] According to Cicero arguments might be made from the causes of the action and from the character of the person involved. Cause dealt with premeditation and with impulses such as anger or grief. Power, wealth, and enmity might be invoked to show 'that no one else had a motive for committing the crime' or 'no one had so strong or sufficient a motive'. Inferences might be drawn from a person's gender, ancestors, kin, age, temperament, and physical constitution. Arguments based on a person's lifestyle, which was associated with education and home life, were useful in attack or defence. Arguments for credibility might also be developed from an individual's fortune, wealth, favour, fame, success, or failure. 'Habit' and 'interest' might be used in evaluating those testifying to past happenings. A defendant might be discredited by citing conviction or suspicions of previous criminal acts or anything that detracted from his honour and reputation. In defence the orator should invoke the likelihood of the defendant's innocence and his upright character.[46]

The categories and language of the classical rhetoricians were adopted and adapted in the canon, civil, and common law traditions to make credibility judgements and were familiar to educated English lawyers and non-lawyers. Erasmus' widely used textbook, *De copia*, included considerations of family, race, country, sex, age, physical appearance, inclinations, previous acts, and sayings in describing persons generally as well as for arriving at conclusions as to the 'confirmation and credibility' of their accounts.[47] Thomas Wilson's *Arte of Rhetoric* (1553) employed categories of parentage, sex, education, inclination, and nature in evaluating individuals. 'Circumstances' relating to where, when, and how the deed in question had been done as well as the individual's will

jury must consider their 'skill' which would 'appear from the Reasons and Accounts they give of their knowledge'. Credit would be judged from 'from his State and Dignity in the World' because 'Men of easy circumstances' were less likely to commit a perjury. Greater credit should also be given to men 'of good Manners and clear Conversation', *The Law of Evidence*, 1–2, 153, 155, 157–8.

45 See also the chapter by Kathy Eden in this volume.

46 Cicero, *De inventione*, 1.24–5, 27, 28; 2.5–8, 9–10, 11–12, 13, 14.

47 Erasmus, *On Copia of Words and Ideas* (1512), ed. D. King and H. D. Rix (Milwaukee: Marquette University Press, 1963), 57.

or power to do the act, his inclinations and occupation, and whether he was a haunter of alehouses were part of the rhetor's evaluative repertoire.[48]

This rhetorical terminology was adopted in the popular justicing manuals of William Lambarde, Richard Crompton, and Michael Dalton for use by Justices of the Peace in examining those accused of or having witnessed crimes. Criteria for crediting and discrediting testimony were well known, having been enshrined in the education system and disseminated in the justicing manuals.[49] Character witnesses frequently referred to similar criteria in testimony that might well determine trial outcomes. The reputations of the prosecutor, the defendant, and their witnesses might be introduced with the aim of enhancing or diminishing the credibility of testimony, as might be the accused's habits of life and trustworthiness. In one instance the accuser was said to be of 'very ill character', who might 'swear to anything'.[50]

Casuistry

The rhetorical tradition also contributed to reasoning about moral issues. Religious thought was permeated with questions of conscience and had, during the medieval and Renaissance period, developed a practice of casuistical thinking that in Protestant England focused on individual rational decision-making on moral issues. Using a form of probable reasoning, one could reach a 'satisfied' or 'sure' conscience and thus be able to act appropriately. The casuistical tradition distinguished between degrees of certainty that were associated with the sure conscience, the probable conscience, the doubting conscience, and the overly scrupulous conscience and was particularly concerned with the problem of doubt. Moral certainty was distinguished from mathematical certainty, a certainty that overcame any and all doubts. The concept of the 'satisfied conscience', that achieved 'moral certainty', the highest degree of certainty in moral and factual matters, would often appear in jury instructions to indicate how sure jurors must be in reaching their decisions. Over time the terminologies of 'satisfied conscience' and 'moral certainty' and later 'belief beyond reasonable doubt', all of which were found in casuistry, became enshrined in the language of the law. If one could believe accusatory testimony without encountering reasonable doubt, it was appropriate to convict. If doubt occurred and the doubt was not unreasonable or capricious, acquittal was the appropriate verdict.

Both the rhetorical and casuist traditions thus came to play a role in the evidentiary environment of the law, just as concepts such as 'matter of fact', a long-standing legal

[48] Sir Thomas Wilson, *Arte of Rhetorique*, ed. Thomas J. Derrick (New York: Garland, 1982), 184–8, 190–5, 234, 236.

[49] See Barbara J. Shapiro, 'Classical Rhetoric and the English Law of Evidence', in *Rhetoric and Law in Early Modern Europe*, ed. V. Kahn and L. Hutson (New Haven: Yale University Press, 2001).

[50] John M Beattie, *Crime and the Courts in England, 1660–1800* (Princeton: Princeton University Press, 1986), 440–2.

concept, would be borrowed and adapted by natural historians and natural philosophers. Borrowing of conceptual categories from discipline to discipline was common, and disciplines dealing with truths that were within the realm of probability rather than certainty employed a common language. This was particularly true for those concerned with the believability of accounts of 'matters of fact'.[51]

'Circumstances'

Theologians attempting to prove the existence of God often utilized inferences drawn from observation of His creation. In such matters Bishop Butler emphasized 'the importance of collateral things ... in the Evidence of Probability' and that 'the Weight of Circumstantial Evidence ... is often altogether as convincing, as That, which is the most express and direct'.[52] Conclusions or inferences drawn from experiments or other natural events were also made by seventeenth-century virtuosi. Presumptions and circumstances or 'circumstantial evidence', both of which had their origins in the classical rhetorical tradition, also played a role in the early modern English evidentiary environment.[53] Initially neither were treated as 'evidence', which was limited to documents and witnesses. Presumptions were developed by canon and then civil and common lawyers. 'Presumptions of law' were rules of the court such as that children were the legitimate offspring of the mother's husband. These were taken as true and were not rebuttable. Others were 'presumptions of fact', drawn from indirect proof or 'circumstances' and might be rebuttable. For instance flight generated a presumption but not proof of guilt. There was a commonly used scale of presumptions which ran from light to probable to violent, the last often being sufficient to convict. The most frequently mentioned violent presumption was one engendered by a man standing over a dead man, bloody sword in hand.

'Circumstances', and what from the mid-eighteenth century would come to be called 'circumstantial evidence', might be presented to juries. These were 'signs' that might point to or away from guilt. Possession of stolen goods was often, but not always, sufficient to convict for theft. In crimes unlikely to have been witnessed, such as witchcraft,

[51] See Shapiro, *Probability and Certainty in Seventeenth Century England*; Shapiro, *A Culture of Fact*.

[52] Joseph Butler, *The Analogy of Religion* (London: 1736), 272. Circumstances 'joined together' might provide 'the proper force of evidence', 356–7. From the mid-eighteenth century to the beginning of the nineteenth, belief that circumstantial evidence was preferable to direct evidence led to frequent utterance of the maxims, 'Circumstances can't lie' and 'facts can't lie'. See Alexander Welsh, *Strong Representations: Narrative and Circumstantial Evidence in England* (Baltimore: Johns Hopkins University Press, 1992).

[53] See Barbara J. Shapiro, 'Presumptions and Circumstantial Evidence in the Anglo-American Legal Tradition 1500–1800', in *The Law of Presumptions: Essays in Comparative Legal History*, ed. Richard H. Helmholz and W. David H. Sellar (Berlin: Duncker and Humblot, 2009), 153–88; David J. Seipp, 'Presumptions in Early English Common Law', in ibid., 117–37.

rape, poisoning, or fraud, indirect proof or 'circumstances' might lead to conviction. For much of the sixteenth and seventeenth centuries, direct or so-called 'positive' testimony of witnesses was preferred to 'circumstances'. The preference lasted until the mid-eighteenth century when some judges began to assert that 'circumstances' provided better proof because witnesses often lied. The practice of drawing conclusions from such non-testimonial sources became commonplace.

Competence and Credibility

Competent or legal witnesses were those whom the law allowed to testify. Spouses, children, those convicted of certain crimes, and the mentally incapacitated were excluded as were interested parties in civil cases. The testimony of legally competent accessories, who were frequently pardoned in exchange for testimony, was troublesome and their credibility often doubted. There was some discussion about whether juries were required to accept such testimony as truthful without corroboration. Hale emphasized the distinction between competency and credibility, emphasizing the latter. [54]

Multiple Witnesses

Although English legal authorities were unanimous in stating that the testimony of a single witness was sufficient to convict in most cases, they often indicated that two or more witnesses were preferable.[55] *A Guide to Juries* indicated two were preferable because one might 'invent or contrive any story for Malice or Envy'.[56] Two witnesses were required in cases of treason and perjury. At times one witness supported by 'circumstances' was sufficient.

Character Witnesses

Character witnesses were often employed as a means of shaping the jury's verdict. Such testimony might suggest that the defendant was not the sort of person who was likely to have committed the act in question or that the person prosecuting did or did not have a reputation for verity. Judges often encouraged defendants to bring character witnesses

[54] Hale, *History of the Common Law*, 163.

[55] Ecclesiastical and civil law courts required two witnesses. A two-witness requirement was favoured by those who wished to follow Scripture.

[56] *A Guide to Juries*, 40.

who might testify as to their habits of life and trustworthiness or to the accuser's 'very ill character'. Thomas Green's investigation of medieval trials, and both Cynthia Herrup's and John Beattie's studies of early modern trials, indicate that the character and reputation of the accused often played a role in jury verdicts and often resulted in acquittals.[57] Evidence, whether direct or circumstantial, and the number of witnesses and oaths were not the sole consideration in jury verdicts.

Oath Breaking and Perjury

Thus far we have looked at some of the evidentiary language used in the courts and elsewhere. Now we turn to the behaviour of juries and other members of the court. Some, and perhaps most, jurors appear to have taken their oaths to give a truthful verdict seriously, and some no doubt feared for their souls if they violated their oath. Jury perjury, however, was not new in the early modern era. A statute of 1331 referred to 'the great fearless and shameful perjury' which 'daily increases in the common jurors of the realm',[58] and one of 1433 again complained of the jury perjury that 'doth abound and increase daily'.[59]

We look at two possible indicators of how far jury oaths compelled jury findings. First, there were occasions on which the juror's oath was seen as particularly relevant because of what was thought to be inappropriate judicial behaviour. The second is the frequency with which jurors acquitted or found guilty of a lesser offence in spite of oath-supported testimony of guilt or jury belief in guilt. Judicial pressures on juries to convict were countered in John Hawles's often reprinted pamphlet that warned jurors that if they did not follow their 'own Judgment or Understanding, you have abused your oath'. They were not to follow the judge's direction if they had 'no just reasons for it' or if they had a 'contrary opinion'.[60] Another Restoration-era tract similarly asserted that if jurors followed judicial direction instead of deciding 'according to his own Conscience and best Understanding', they were acting 'falsely, contrary to their Oaths'.[61]

A high rate of acquittals was characteristic of both the medieval and early modern periods. During the medieval era only about 50 per cent of those tried for murder and 31 per cent of those tried for theft were convicted.[62] Acquittals were frequent even in the

[57] Cynthia B. Herrup, *The Common Peace: Participation and the Criminal Law in Seventeenth-Century England* (Cambridge: Cambridge University Press, 1987), 144–5; John M. Beattie, *Crime and the Courts in England 1660–1800* (Princeton: Princeton University Press, 1986), 440–2.

[58] 11 H 6. C. 4.

[59] 28 Edw 3, *c*. 12.

[60] John Hawles, *The Englishman's Right* (London: 1680), 26, 44, 45, 46. See also *Billa Vera, or the Arraignment of Ignoramus* (London: 1680), 17.

[61] *The Power and Privilege of Juries Asserted* (London: 1681), 4–5, 6.

[62] Barbara Hanawalt found a 12 per cent conviction rate for homicide and a 30 per cent conviction rate for theft; *Crime and Conflict in English Communities 1300–1348* (Cambridge, MA: Harvard University

face of substantial evidence. It appears that medieval jurors often gave mercy a higher priority than either their oath or the evidence. Jury oath violation thus appears to have been fairly common during the period in which oaths are thought to have been most powerful. Acquittal rates continued to remain high after the introduction of witnesses, and acquittals given against the evidence common. About 40 per cent of those indicted by grand juries were acquitted. There were frequent complaints that 'pious perjuries', by trial juries often led to acquittals against the weight of evidence in order to avoid the death penalty. Felony thefts were frequently knowingly reduced in value, so as to avoid capital punishment. Judges as well as jurors were complicitous in this falsification. Thus on some occasions neither jury oaths nor evidence appear to have been decisive.

The Judiciary

Given the absence of lawyers in criminal trials, judges were important in shaping trial outcomes. Their prestige meant that their words were taken seriously. They questioned and sometimes browbeat witnesses. The opportunity to comment on the evidence and to sum up the evidence just prior to the verdict meant that judicial interpretation of witness testimony would weigh heavily on the jurors. Jurors, who were far less educated than judges and were of lower social status, were unlikely to act at cross purposes to judges whom they knew to be highly experienced in the evaluation of evidence. Juries may have been judges of the fact, and judges of the law, but judges had a considerable opportunity to shape the jury's understanding of the evidence and thus often played a role in trial outcomes. Judges also frequently were in a position to modify the effect of a guilty verdict by a recommendation for pardon, a request that was usually honoured by the Crown.

Conclusion

This essay has suggested that early modern common law courts employed a number of epistemologically related concepts and practices, some of which worked in tandem with one another. Oaths were important but did not play the overwhelming role often attributed to them. Notions of witness credibility were widely known in many disciplinary areas and were sufficiently well known to insure that the truthfulness of sworn

Press, 1979), 59. R. B. Pugh found a 21 per cent rate for homicide and a 31 per cent rate for theft; 'Some Reflections of a Medieval Criminologist' *Proceedings of the British Academy*, 59 (1973), 6–7. Thomas Green found 2/3 to 3/4 of those tried for capital theft were acquitted. He concluded that medieval trials were 'as much as assessment of just deserts as it was the truth of the case at hand'; *Verdict According to Conscience*, 34, 60–6, 127.

testimony was not taken for granted. The language of legal proof was not so different from the language of other disciplines that focused on truth and fact-finding by means of observation and testimony. There was widespread belief that juries, though under oath, often produced verdicts that might be influenced by pressure of various kinds and were frequently willing to commit 'pious perjuries' letting mercy rather than truth guide their decisions. We have seen that the language of the law was not constant and that the language of 'satisfied conscience', or the 'satisfied understanding' would be eventually replaced by their cognate 'beyond reasonable doubt', a term encountered in religious and other writings before it entered the legal setting. We have seen that the language used for assessing credibility has a long history, a history that was indebted to classical rhetoric and was generally transmitted by early modern educational institutions. We noted that the epistemological environment was not a static one and that the evidentiary status of 'circumstances' changed over time. The legal epistemological environment was a complex one in which various institutions and concepts jostled with one another. Courts were a site where truth was the goal, but also a site in which jury verdicts might be tempered by mercy or the testimony of character witnesses. Some thought such verdicts were appropriate and just, others called them perjured. Oaths and credibility issues might be in conflict or at least in tension and so might truth and mercy.

The trial employed a series of sometimes contradictory devices to create as true a story as humanly possible of previous events, but sometimes, unhappy with the story, judges and/or jury chose to rather consciously rewrite it.

Bibliography

Anon. *Billa Vera, or the Arraignment of Ignoramus* (London: 1680).

Anon. *The Book of Oaths* (London: 1715).

Anon. *The Fundamental Lawes and Liberties of England* (London: 1653).

Anon. *The Power and Privilege of Juries Asserted* (London: 1681).

Babington, Zachary. *Advice to Grand Jurors in Cases of Blood* (London: 1677).

Bacon, Francis. *The Works of Francis Bacon*, Vol. 1, ed. James Spedding, Robert Ellis, and Douglas Heath (London: 1857–1874).

Beattie, John M. *Crime and the Courts in England, 1660–1800* (Princeton: Princeton University Press, 1986).

Bernard, Richard. *Guide to Grand Jurors in Cases of Witchcraft* (London: 1627).

Bowyer, Robert. *The Parliamentary Diary of Robert Bowyer, 1606–1607*, ed. David Harris Wilson (Minneapolis: University of Minnesota Press, 1931).

Boyle, Robert. 'The Christian Virtuoso', in *The Works of the Honorable Robert Boyle*, 6 vols (London: 1772).

Browne, Thomas. 'Pseudodoxia Epidemica', in *The Prose of Sir Thomas Browne*, ed. Norman J. Endicott (New York: Anchor Books, 1967).

Bushel's Case [1670] 124 E. R., 1006.

Butler, Joseph. *The Analogy of Religion* (London: 1736).

Care, Henry. *English Liberties, or the Free-Born Subject's Inheritance* (London: 1682).

Cicero, *De inventione*, trans. H. M. Hubbell (Cambridge, MA: Harvard University Press, 1949).

Cockburn, J. S. *A History of English Assizes, 1558–1714* (Cambridge: Cambridge University Press, 1972).
Coke, Sir Edward. *The Third Part of the Institutes of the Lawes of England* (London: 1644).
Condren, Conal. *Argument and Authority in Early Modern England: The Presupposition of Oaths and Offices* (Cambridge: Cambridge University Press, 2006).
Cooke, John. *The Vindication of the Law* (London: 1652).
Cotta, John. *The Trial of Witchcraft* (London: 1616).
Cotterell, Mary. 'Interregnum Law Reform: The Hale commission of 1652', *English Historical Review*, 83 (1968): 689–704.
Crosby, Kevin. 'Bushell's Case and the Juror's Soul', *Journal of Legal History*, 33.3 (2012): 251–90.
Erasmus, Desiderius. *On Copia of Words and Ideas* [1512], ed. D. King and H. D. Rix (Milwaukee: Marquette University Press, 1963).
Ferguson, Robert. *The Second Part of No Protestant Plot* (London: 1682).
Fisher, George. 'The Jury as Lie Detector', *The Yale Law Journal*, 107.3 (1997): 575–713.
Friend, Sir John. *The Arraignment, Tryal and Condemnation of Sir John Friend* (London: 1696).
Garnet, Richard. *A Guide to the Knowledge of the Rights and Principles of Englishmen* (London: 1771).
Gilbert, Geoffrey. *The Law of Evidence* (London: 1756).
Green, Thomas Andrew. *Verdict According to Conscience* (Chicago: University of Chicago Press, 1985).
Gumble, Thomas. *The Life of General Monck* (London: 1671).
Hale, Sir Matthew. *The History of the Common Law of England*, ed. Charles M. Gray (Chicago: University of Chicago Press, 1971).
Hale, Sir Matthew. *Historia placitorum coronae: The History of the Pleas of the Crown*, Vol. 2 (Philadelphia: 1847).
Hanawalt, Barbara. *Crime and Conflict in English Communities 1300–1348* (Cambridge, MA: Harvard University Press, 1979).
Hawles, John. *The Englishman's Right* (London: 1680).
Herrup, Cynthia B. *The Common Peace: Participation and the Criminal Law in Seventeenth-Century England* (Cambridge: Cambridge University Press, 1987).
Hobbes, Thomas. *Leviathan*, ed. Michael Oakshott (London: Penguin Books, 1985).
Howell, Thomas Bayly, ed. *A Complete Collection of State Trials*, 34 vols (London: 1809–1826).
Hughes, Paul and James Larkin. *Tudor Royal Proclamations*, Vol. 1 (New Haven: Yale University Press, 1964).
Jones, D. M. *Conscience and Allegiance in Seventeenth Century England: The Political Significance of Oaths and Engagements* (Rochester: University of Rochester Press, 1999).
Kerrigan, John. 'Shakespeare, Oaths and Vows', *Proceedings of the British Academy*, 167 (2010): 61–89.
Klerman, Daniel. 'Was the Jury Ever Self-Informing?', *Southern California Law Review*, 77 (2003): 123–50.
Langbein, John H. *Prosecuting Crime in the Renaissance* (Cambridge, MA: Harvard University Press, 1974).
Larkin, James F. and Paul L. Hughes, eds. *Stuart Royal Proclamations* (Oxford: Clarendon Press, 1973).
Locke, John. *An Essay Concerning Humane Understanding* (London: 1690).
More, Thomas. *The Debellacyon of Salem and Bizance*, in *The Complete Works of St Thomas More*, Vol. 10, ed. John Guy et al. (New Haven: Yale University Press, 1963).

Morgan, John. *Essays Upon the Law of Evidence* (London: 1789).
Notestein, Wallace. *The House of Commons, 1604–1610* (New Haven: Yale University Press, 1971).
Nye, Steven. *A Discourse Concerning Natural and Revealed Religion* (Glasgow: 1696).
Park, Roger and Michael Saks. 'Evidence Scholarship Reconsidered: Results of the Interdisciplinary Turn', *Boston College Law Review*, 47 (2006): 949–1032.
Person of Quality. *A Guide to English Juries: Setting Forth Their Antiquity, Power, and Duty* (London: 1725).
Pugh, R. B. 'Some Reflections of a Medieval Criminologist', *Proceedings of the British Academy*, 59 (1973).
Read, Conyers, ed. *William Lambarde and Local Government: His 'Ephemeris' and Twenty-Nine Charges to Juries and Commissions* (Ithaca: Cornell University Press, 1962).
Sanderson, Robert. *A Discourse Concerning the Nature and Obligation of Oaths* (London: 1716).
Seipp, David J. 'Presumptions in Early English Common Law', in *The Law of Presumptions: Essays in Comparative Legal History*, ed. R. H. Helmholz and W. D. H. Sellar (Berlin: Duncker and Humblot, 2009), 117–37.
Selden, John. *Table Talk*, ed. Frederick Pollock (London: Quaritch, 1927).
Serjeantson, Richard W. 'Testimony and Proof in Early-Modern England', *Studies in the History and Philosophy of Science*, 30.2 (1999): 195–236.
Shapin, Steven. *The Social History of Truth: Civility and Science in Seventeenth Century England* (Chicago: University of Chicago Press, 1994).
Shapin, Steven and Simon Schaffer. *Leviathan and the Air-Pump: Hobbes, Boyle, and the Experimental Life* (Princeton: Princeton University Press, 1989).
Shapiro, Barbara J. *'Beyond Reasonable Doubt' and 'Probable Cause': Historical Studies in the Anglo-American Law of Evidence* (Berkeley: University of California Press, 1991).
Shapiro, Barbara J. *A Culture of Fact: England, 1550–1720* (Ithaca: Cornell University Press, 2000).
Shapiro, Barbara J. 'Classical Rhetoric and the English Law of Evidence', in *Rhetoric and Law in Early Modern Europe*, ed. Victoria Kahn and Lorna Hutson (New Haven: Yale University Press, 2001), 54–72.
Shapiro, Barbara J. 'Gently Boyle', *Metascience*, 6 (1994): 1–23.
Shapiro, Barbara J. 'Oaths, Credibility and the Legal Process in Early Modern England. Part 1', *Law and Humanities*, 6.2 (2012): 145–78.
Shapiro, Barbara J. 'Oaths, Credibility and the Legal Process in Early Modern England', Part 2, *Law and Humanities*, 7.1 (2013): 19–54.
Shapiro, Barbara J. 'Presumptions and Circumstantial Evidence in the Anglo-American Legal Tradition 1500–1800', in *The Law of Presumptions: Essays in Comparative Legal History*, ed. R. H. Helmholz and W. David H. Sellar (Berlin: Duncker and Humblot, 2009), 153–88.
Shapiro, Barbara J. *Probability and Certainty in Seventeenth Century England: A Study of the Relationships Between Natural Science, Religion, History, Law, and Literature* (Princeton: Princeton University Press, 1983).
Shapiro, Barbara J. 'Religion and the Law: Evidence, Proof and "Matter of Fact", 1660–1700', in *Law, Crime and English Society 1660–1830*, ed. Norma Landau (Cambridge: Cambridge University Press, 2002), 185–208.
Shapiro, Barbara J. 'Testimony in Seventeenth-Century English Natural Philosophy: Legal Origins and Early Development', *Studies in the History and Philosophy of Science*, 33.2 (2002): 243–63.

Shirley, Frances. *Swearing and Perjury in Shakespeare's Plays* (London: Allen and Unwin, 1979).
Smith, Thomas. *De republica anglorum: A Discourse on the Commonwealth of England* [1583], ed. Mary Dewar (Cambridge: Cambridge University Press, 1982).
Sprat, Thomas. *History of the Royal Society*, ed. Jackson I. Cope and H. W. Jones (St Louis: Washington University Press, 1958).
Spurr, John. 'Perjury, Profanity and Politics', *The Seventeenth Century*, 8.1 (1993): 29–50.
St Germain, Christopher. *A Dialogue Betwixte Two Englyshemen, Whereof One Was Called Salem, and the Other Bizance* (London: 1533).
Stanhope, George. *The Duty of Juries* (London: 1701).
Stillingfleet, Edward. *Origines Sacrae, or a Rational Account of the Christian Faith* (London: 1662).
Tillotson, John. *The Lawfulness and Obligation of Oaths* (London: 1681).
Twining, William. 'Evidence as a Multi-Disciplinary Subject', *Law, Probability, and Risk*, 2 (2003): 91–107.
Twining, William. *Rethinking Evidence: Exploratory Essays*, 2nd edn (Cambridge: Cambridge University Press, 2006).
Twining, William. *Theories of Evidence: Bentham and Wigmore* (Stanford: Stanford University Press, 1985).
Vaughan, John. *Ignoramus Vindicated* (London: 1681).
Watts, Isaac, *Logick* (London: 1724).
Welsh, Alexander. *Strong Representations: Narrative and Circumstantial Evidence in England* (Baltimore: Johns Hopkins Press, 1992).
Wilson, Thomas. *Arte of Rhetorique* [1560], ed. Thomas J. Derrick (New York: Garland, 1982).

CHAPTER 14

LEGAL REFORM AND 2 *HENRY IV*

VIRGINIA LEE STRAIN

The Beginning of Kingdomes

... [A]lwayes the mightier, and more mischievous, did (as bulls in the *Heard*) gore and grieve the weaker and better sort. Then fled men (as *Cicero* conjectureth) to some one among them, excelling others in *Vertue*, and submitted themselves unto him, praying that hee would by *equity* save them from *injury*, and maintaine both the *mightiest* and the *meanest* in one indifferencie of *right* and *justice*. And truly, so long as they found this at hand, they tooke for *Law* whatsoever hee pronounced, and they obeyed (as an Oracle) whatsoever was commanded by him.

The Beginning of Lawes

But when as (at the length) hee also either did convert to his singular gaine, that Authority which was given unto him for the common benefit of others, or else dealt not a like measure unto all; but abandoning *Iustice*, made *Lust* his *Iudge*, and *Might* his *Minister*; then forthwith alteration of the former estate followed, and then were *lawes* and *rules* of *Iustice* devised, within the which ... the power of *Governors* should henceforth be bounded ...[1]

[1] William Lambarde, *Archeion; or, The High Courts of Justice in England*, ed. Charles H. McIlwain and Paul L. Ward (Cambridge: Harvard University Press, 1957), 10–11. On Lambarde's contribution to legal reform, see Wilfred Prest, 'Judicial Corruption in Early Modern England', *Past and Present*, 133 (1991): 67–95; and 'William Lambarde, Elizabethan Law Reform, and Early Stuart Politics', *JBS*, 34.4 (1995): 464–80.

In the opening section of the *Archeion, Or, A Discourse upon the High Courts of Justice in England*, William Lambarde provides an account of the mythical origins of society that draws a historical distinction between the political and the legal. While kingdoms were formed for the benefit of subjects, the object of the law is, first, the governors themselves, the regulation of whom underwrites justice and the common weal. The law is presented as formalizing in order to reform its own magistrates. A primary function of the justice system is to prevent the maintenance of the social order from transmogrifying into an offence like 'maintenance', through which the process of law is corrupted by the self-interested interference of men in authority.[2] The result is that the mythical origin of the law deconstructs into a practice for the preservation of the law that marks, at the same time, the state's progress. Legal reform structures change and continuity, giving both the law and the state their history and historicity.

This chapter takes as its focus legal reform's role as a mediator between magisterial corruption and state formation in legal-political writings and in Shakespeare's dramatization of a national past. I will flesh out the forms and discourses of legal reform in early modern English culture and in *2 Henry IV*, specifically. If reform appears largely as a deferred personal-political strategy that is initially introduced in the Crown Prince's famous first soliloquy in *Part One*, reform is an impersonal, external, diffuse, and legal principle in *Part Two*.[3] The question is not, as it has traditionally been posed, whether Prince Hal really reforms, but how each agent and group that is represented in this sequel constructs a durable or disastrous relationship, through reform, to the forces of state formation. Such a hermeneutic is invited by the structure of the sequel itself, in which Hal's delayed entrance and few scenes offer ample opportunities to explore the legal-political agendas and potential of others. In his pioneering essay, 'Invisible Bullets', Stephen Greenblatt conflates the motives of all the aristocratic agents in the play with self-interest: 'the whole state seems ... a conspiracy of the great to enrich and protect their interests under the name of commonwealth.'[4] This chapter argues, to the contrary, that Shakespeare presents various rationales and strategies for reform that demand our serious, rather than cynical, consideration. Most importantly, by reimagining the role of reform within the play, a new perspective emerges on the questions of character, law, politics, and history that come to a head in the young king's reconciliation scene with the Chief Justice.

[2] As Lambarde explains, maintenance occurs 'when one that hath none *interest* to a matter in question ... will doe any thing for the *one partie*, to the hinderance of the free course of *Iustice* against the *other*', typically through intimidation or bribery (98).

[3] The possibility of such a reading is hinted at by Jonathan Crewe: 'the repetition of the reform-attempt [across three plays] begins to call for its own accounting. Its apparent compulsiveness (or sociopolitical compulsoriness) implies that a good deal is invested in it, not just by Hal, but by those in the plays who expect it of him—and then also by Shakespeare ... perhaps by a political imperative of "reform" that Shakespeare receives and transmits' ('Reforming Prince Hal: The Sovereign Inheritor in 2 *Henry IV*', *RD*, n.s. 21 [1990]: 226).

[4] Stephen Greenblatt, 'Invisible Bullets', in *The Greenblatt Reader*, ed. Michael Payne (Malden: Blackwell Publishing, 2005), 146.

A Historical Refrain

A critical discourse has yet to fully coalesce around the topic of legal reform in early modern legal and cultural studies, yet reform is integral to an understanding of the law's social, political, and literary functions. The researcher faces a problem of scale: defined too broadly, legal reform becomes nearly synonymous with law and governance itself; defined too narrowly and the phenomenon of reform, including its cultural recurrence, is forgotten in evaluations of the success or failure of particular measures. The topic pivots ambivalently between theory and practice, as well. Sixteenth-century humanists applied their reformist zeal to the English law in treatises that 'aimed to reveal the paramount virtues of English law by removing its impurities, and to delineate its logical order by countering the obscure idiosyncrasies of English practice relative to its civilian counterpart on the Continent'.[5] These abstract, systemic, or comparative approaches to the law's improvement typically outlined too much or too little action for practitioners, yet their rhetoric did frequently inform reform activities.[6] In his classic study on *Ancient Law*, Henry Maine outlined three practices through which the 'law had been adapted to the needs of society ... legal fictions, equity and legislation'.[7] In response to the immense 'innovation and expansion' of the English legal system over the course of the sixteenth and seventeenth centuries, a much wider scope of activities was undertaken.[8] Nancy Matthews particularizes the extensive range of legal reform practices in the early modern period, and, in the process, defines the topics that such a field of study would need to address:

> Law reform, a term used widely in the seventeenth century, could be broadly defined as an effort to achieve a greater degree of justice, an exercise that might be accomplished through procedural reform or by altering the laws themselves. It could also mean the endeavor to gain a better understanding of legal principles or to publicize what was known of the settled law. More practically, it could involve an effort to facilitate a greater efficiency in the administration of justice ... [C]orruption and ignorance [were] problems which had long been recognized to be endemic in both law enforcement and in the administration of the courts. Proposals to exert effective controls over officials entrusted with responsibilities had been formulated by

[5] Bradin Cormack, *A Power to Do Justice: Jurisdiction, English Literature, and the Rise of Common Law* (Chicago: Chicago University Press, 2008), 194.

[6] See e.g. Abraham Fraunce, *The Lawiers Logike, exemplifying the praecepts of Logike by the Practise of the common Lawe* (London: 1588).

[7] A. K. R. Kiralfy, 'Law Reform by Legal Fictions, Equity and Legislation in English Legal History', *AJLH*, 10 (1966): 3.

[8] David Chan Smith's important new monograph charts the numerous changes that were collectively felt to be generating critical 'uncertainty' in the law by the end of the sixteenth century: *Sir Edward Coke and the Reformation of the Laws: Religion, Politics and Jurisprudence, 1578–1616* (Cambridge: Cambridge University Press, 2014).

> government administrators and members of parliament from Elizabeth's reign up to the time of the civil war ... From the 1590s through the 1630s privy councillors, judges and parliamentary committees all were raising questions about the state of the law and law enforcement ...[9]

Those questions were raised just as frequently in early modern literature, in which justices, lawyers, and subjects were regularly represented in attempts to exploit the law for gain and as hapless victims of the law or legal tricks. Literature's extensive representation and analysis of the daily experience of the law included 'the management of [the law's] failings', demonstrating that '[s]ubjects' and professionals' imperfect knowledge and execution of a variety of imperfect laws was a widespread source of anxiety'.[10]

The scope of this chapter is limited to the relationship between magistracy and reform. Like Lambarde, a number of legal and literary writers linked the administration of the law to the origins of order and disorder in the commonwealth. In an expression repeated throughout the period, Bracton succinctly explained that 'it is of little value that law exists in the state if there are none to administer it'.[11] William Baldwin's 'Epistle', in *A Myrroure For Magistrates*, sketches the relationship between magistrates and the commonwealth at greater length, but still in fairly conventional terms:

> there is nothing more necessary in a common weale, than that officers be diligent and trusty in their charges ... where offices are duly ministred, it can not be chosen, but the people are good, whereof must nedes folow a good common weale. For if the officers be good, the people can not be yll. Thus the goodnes or badnes of any realme lyeth in the goodnes or badnes of the rulers ... For in dede the welth and quiet of everye common weale, the disorder also and miseries of the same, cum specially through them.[12]

Yet, Lambarde warns, 'rare a thing it is, for great men arrayed with high Authoritie, to containe themselves within prefixed limits and pale of their power' (65). Sir Thomas Smith provides a nationalistic explanation for this phenomenon: inured to warfare, English 'Captaines and souldiers' fight amongst themselves and their neighbours in

[9] Nancy Matthews, *William Sheppard, Cromwell's Law Reformer* (Cambridge: Cambridge University Press, 1984), 1–2. On legal reform in the seventeenth century, see Anthony Fletcher, *Reform in the Provinces: The Government of Stuart England* (New Haven: Yale University Press, 1986); Barbara Shapiro's articles, 'Codification of the Laws in Seventeenth Century England', *Wisconsin Law Review*, 2 (1974): 428–65, 'Law Reform in Seventeenth Century England', *AJLH*, 19.4 (1975): 280–312, and 'Sir Francis Bacon and the Mid-Seventeenth Century Movement for Law Reform', *AJLH*, 24.4 (1980): 331–62; and Donald Veall, *The Popular Movement for Law Reform, 1640–1660* (Oxford: Clarendon Press, 1970).

[10] Virginia Lee Strain, 'Shakespeare's Living Law: Theatrical, Lyrical, and Legal Practice', *Literature Compass*, 12.6 (2015): 253.

[11] Henry de Bracton, *Bracton on the Laws and Customs of England*, trans. with revisions and notes by Samuel E. Thorne (Cambridge: Belknap Press of Harvard University Press, 1968–1977), 2.26.

[12] William Baldwin, 'Epistle', in *A Myrroure For Magistrates, Wherein May Be Seen by Example of Other, with Howe Greuous Plages Vices Are Punished: and Howe Frayle and Vnstable Worldly Prosperitie Is Founde, even of Those, whom Fortune Seemeth Most Highly to Fauour* (London: 1559), 2^{r-v}.

peacetime: 'insolent at home, and not easie to be governed by Lawe and politike order, men of power beginning many fraies, and the stronger by factions and parties offering too much injurie to the weaker, were occasions of making good Lawes.'[13] This passage comes from Smith's account of the origins of the Star Chamber, the court that developed a self-conscious concern with the execution of the law, and thus with the behaviour and character of the magisterial class. The Star Chamber itself became, in the early seventeenth century, associated with the arbitrary execution of political power. Before its relatively sudden decline and dissolution, however, legal authorities and writers upheld the court as the pinnacle of a structurally equitable justice system. Smith, Lambarde, Bacon, and Coke revered the Star Chamber for its control of the offences associated with the governing classes who were uncorrectable by lesser authorities or the lower ranks.[14]

The 'good lawes' to which Smith refers are the statutes that established the authority of Star Chamber. Lambarde quotes the statute from the third year of Henry VII's reign that outlines the court's Tudor jurisdiction. Within the preamble we find a catalogue of the most frequent infractions that threatened the just administration of the law:

> The King our Soveraigne Lord remembreth, how by unlawfull *Maintenances*, giving of *Liveries*, *Signes*, and *Tokens*, and by *Retainders*, by *Indentures*, *Promises*, and other *Writings*, or otherwise, *Embraceries* of his *Subjects*, untrue demeaning of *Sheriffes*, in making *Pannels*, and other untrue *Returnes*, by taking of *Money* by *Iuries*, by great *Riots*, and unlawfull *Assemblies*, the policie and good rule of the *Realme* is almost subdued; and for not punishing those inconveniences ... the *Law* of the *Land* in execution may take little effect, to the encrease of *Murthers*, *Robberies*, *Perjuries*, and unsuretie of all men living, and losses of their lands and goods, to the great displeasure of *Almightie God* (88–9)

Surveying a much wider collection of sources, Christopher Brooks finds that 'nearly all of those offences with which the fifteenth-century gentry is charged—maintenance, tampering with juries and the abuse of power to further private ends—were common enough in the sixteenth and seventeenth centuries ... Judging from the content of petitions to parliament and the preambles to statutes against retaining, rhetoric calling for the restraint of the over-mighty was part of public discourse' throughout the early modern period.[15]

As Olga Horner and James McBain's studies on the early Tudor interlude writer, Henry Medwall, illustrate, these offences provided a framework through which writers

[13] Thomas Smith, *De republica Anglorum*, ed. Mary Dewar (Cambridge: Cambridge University Press, 1982), 126.

[14] Edward Coke, *The Fourth Part of the Institutes of the Laws of England: Concerning The Jurisdiction of Courts* [London: 1648], 65, 66).

[15] Christopher W. Brooks, *Law, Politics and Society in Early Modern England* (Cambridge: Cambridge University Press, 2008), 281.

could analyse legal-political conditions in comparison with humanist values.[16] In the second part of *Fulgens and Lucrece*, 'the earliest surviving full-length secular play in English',[17] Lucrece's decision between two suitors is structured as a formal debate about the nature of true nobility, whether it is a function of blood or virtue. Medwall 'represents two opposing factions in the English ruling classes: Cornelius as a member of the land-owning, lawless nobility, and Gaius, a commoner, as the ideal officer of state upholding the lawful authority of Henry VII and his council'. Cornelius is charged with 'the uniquely English offences of maintenance and retaining, exclusively connected with the illegal arrogation of power by the English aristocracy'. The text is 'sharply topical, quoting the language of contemporary legislation to identify the issue of order versus rebellion' (Horner 51–2). Based on the evidence of early sixteenth-century proclamations and statutes, McBain concludes that 'maintenance, retaining, and embracery, understood as being connected, were considered together as far more sinister than mere individual crimes', and that 'Medwall similarly emphasizes the scope of the danger, since Cornelius' ignoble criminality is clearly seen to present a wider threat to the safe functioning of the "commonweal"' (18–19).

As a discourse, legal reform combined the nominal and verbal senses of 'refrain': within the legal-political and literary systems, reform was a repeating complaint that emphasized the public necessity of magisterial restraint. It asserted a structural link between the magistrate's relationship to the law and the development of the commonwealth. The rest of this chapter treats Shakespeare's extended analysis of legal reform within his dramatization of the political transition from Henry IV to Henry V. Between the aristocratic rebels, Falstaff and the Eastcheap revellers, and the corrupt country Justices of the Peace, most of the lesser and more egregious offences listed in the Star Chamber statute are represented or alluded to in *2 Henry IV*. This picture of general disorder, however, is complicated by the depiction of the rebels as sincere, would-be reformers of the commonwealth. In the next section, I argue that the relationship between legal reform and legitimate rule is first explored through the rebels' poetic characterization of their political project that aims 'to pluck a kingdom down / And set another up' (1.3.49–50). Through the negotiations that bring the rebellion to an end, however, Prince John institutes a categorical distinction between rebels and rightful magistrates. Because of his personal history and reputation, this distinction presents the greatest challenge to Hal's legitimacy as king. It is precisely the fusion of rebelliousness and rule that shapes Henry IV's nightmares and Falstaff's fantasies of Henry V's future reign. The heir apparent has significant parallels with the character type represented by

[16] Olga Horner, '*Fulgens and Lucres*: An Historical Perspective', *Medieval English Theatre*, 15 (1993): 49–86; James McBain, '"By Example and Gode Reason": Reconsidering Commonplaces and the Law in *Fulgens and Lucres*', *Medieval English Theatre*, 28 (2006): 3–28.

[17] Alan H. Nelson, 'Medwall, Henry (*b.* 1462, *d.* after 1501)', in *Oxford Dictionary of National Biography*, online edition, ed. Lawrence Goldman (Oxford: Oxford University Press, 2004), <http://www.oxforddnb.com/view/article/18504> (accessed 1 July 2015).

Medwall's Cornelius. Hal's legendary intrusion in a trial, in which he punches the Chief Justice for sentencing a follower for theft, is, in a way, simply another example of aristocratic maintenance that threatens the justice and order of the country. The key difference lies in the subsequent reformation of Henry V's relationship to the law. In the third section below, I investigate the new king's reconciliation with the Chief Justice, through which reform comes to structure the relationship between their offices and to generate a pattern for national progress.

'Success of Mischief'

While 'good laws' may have been the unintended consequence of the misconduct of great men, according to Lambarde and Smith, the Elizabethan *Homilie agaynst Disobedience and Wylful Rebellion* rehearses the way in which such offences could be driven mistakenly by, or disingenuously presented as, reform to governance. The homily contrasts the Queen's experienced counsellors, the proper reformers of the commonwealth, with degenerate rebels who illicitly attempt to appropriate authority from and over their betters:

> Now concerning pretences of any redresse of the commonwealth, made by rebelles, euery man that hath but halfe an eye, may see howe vayne they be, rebellion beyng ... the greatest ruine and destruction of all commonwealthes that may be possible. And who so loketh, on the one part, vppon the persons and gouernement of the Queenes moste honourable counsellers, by the experiment of so many yeres proued honourable to her Maiestie, and moste profitable and beneficial unto our countrey and countreymen, and on the other part, consydereth ... the rebelles them selues, the reformers, as they take vpon them, of the present gouernement, he shall find that the most rash and hare-brayned men, the most greatest vnthriftes ... and suche as for theftes, robberies, and murthers ... are alwayes most readie to moue rebellion, or to take part with rebels. And are not these meete men, trowe you, to restore the common wealth decayed, who haue so spoyled and consumed all theyr owne wealth and thrift?[18]

Based on the logic of the homily, Henry IV's fears, voiced in *Part One*, that the Crown Prince would take part in the Percys' rebellion, makes excellent sense. Through this lens, Hal and Falstaff's degeneracy seem to leave them particularly vulnerable, 'through vassal fear, / Base inclination, and the start of spleen, / To fight against [Henry IV] under Percy's pay'.[19] In this passage from the homily, those in power, the

[18] *An Homilie agaynst Disobedience and Wylful Rebellion* (London: 1570), G1^{v}–G2^{r}.

[19] William Shakespeare, *1 Henry IV*, in *The Complete Works*, ed. Stanley Wells and Gary Taylor (Oxford: Oxford University Press, 2005), 3.2.124–6. All subsequent citations of Shakespeare's works will be to this edition.

Queen's trusty counsellors, and the rebels are presented as mutually exclusive camps, yet Shakespeare's histories, and the chronicle histories upon which they are based, blur the distinction. If the sovereign's counsellors are the best positioned to reform the realm, this can only complicate our interpretation of the complaints of the aristocratic rebels in the second tetralogy, and it points the way to the potential acceptance of rebellious reform practices under certain conditions.

The argument of the homily was counterpointed by Foxe's *Acts and Monuments* and Holinshed's *Chronicles*. As Janelle Greenberg explains, these writers helped shape the narrative and ideology of the so-called ancient constitution by recounting the Norman Conquest and its aftermath in a way that justified rebellion when it championed English law in opposition to unjust rulers. According to Holinshed, 'on numerous occasions the English, refusing to bend to the Norman sword, launched "mutinies and rebellions for the retaining of St Edward's laws", later "called the common laws" ... And so it went with the Conqueror's successors, who, whenever "they sought to purchase the people's favor", promised "to abolish the laws ordained by their father, [and to] establish other more equal, and restore those which were used in S. Edward's days"'. Likewise, in the 1570 edition of *Acts and Monumentes*, which was sent to every cathedral church, Foxe included a section in which he presents William I as a perjurer who rescinded his coronation oath 'to set up good laws and customs, such as be wholesome and approved: such as be otherwise, to repeal them, and thrust them out of his kingdom'. Foxe, with Queen Mary in mind, transformed his medieval and Saxon source material 'into a convincing historical justification for resistance'.[20]

Greenberg's account of Holinshed and Foxe sheds light on the rebels' rationale in *1 Henry IV* and their repeated accusations of Henry IV as, specifically, an oath-breaker.[21] But the reform imperative distinguishes, more than it unites, the rebels of *Part One* and *Part Two*. As James Simpson writes, the fifteenth century 'began with the *coup d'etat* of Henry IV against Richard II in 1399, and was to witness a further five violent seizures of the crown ... Civil war is the leitmotif of fifteenth-century political history, and, unlike the civil war of the seventeenth century, the internal wars of the fifteenth arouse no philosophical passions for one side or another whatsoever. These are philosophically neutral wars, fought for power'.[22] A similar historical picture emerges in 3.1 of *1 Henry IV*, in which the rebel generals argue across a map about the division of England: the opportunity to make legitimate nationalistic claims is lost

[20] Janelle Greenberg, *The Radical Face of the Ancient Constitution* (Cambridge: Cambridge University Press, 2001), 99–100, 97, 95, 98. See also Alison Wall, *Power and Protest in England 1525–1640* (London: Hodder Arnold, 2000), 163–80.

[21] On the importance of oaths versus waste in the second tetralogy, see Andrew Zurcher, *Shakespeare and Law*, Arden Shakespeare (London: Methuen Drama, 2010), 103–52.

[22] James Simpson, *The Oxford English Literary History: Volume 2: 1350–1547: Reform and Cultural Revolution* (Oxford: Oxford University Press, 2004), 197–8.

as extremely idiosyncratic, self-interested personalities clash over the shape of brand new territories. In 2 *Henry IV*, however, there is no such fissure among the rebels over territory. The sequel is structured so as to distance the rebellion that ends at Gaultree from the one that ended at Shrewsbury. Instead of infighting, the Archbishop of York and the other leaders deliberate over their methods, using poetics to analyse the practical problem of *reconstructing* rather than *dividing* England. Pivotal to our understanding of the rebels' project is Bardolph's construction analogy that shifts the focus from the outcome of battle to the reforming process of rebellion.

Reflecting upon the missteps of their predecessors at Shrewsbury, Lord Bardolph depicts Hotspur's heroic dementia as a function of the extreme difference between the young knight's chivalric aspirations and his actual resources:

> [He] lined himself with hope,
> Eating the air on promise of supply,
> Flattering himself in project of a power
> Much smaller than the smallest of his thoughts:
> And so, with great imagination
> Proper to madmen, led his powers to death
> And winking leap'd into destruction. (1.3.27–33)

In contrast, Bardolph champions careful planning that hinges on the repeated cross-referencing of figures in the imagination with fact:

> When we mean to build,
> We first survey the plot, then draw the model;
> And when we see the figure of the house,
> Then must we rate the cost of the erection,
> Which if we find outweighs ability,
> What do we then but draw anew the model
> In fewer offices, or, at least, desist
> To build at all? Much more in this great work—
> Which is almost to pluck a kingdom down
> And set another up—should we survey
> The plot of situation and the model,
> Consent upon a sure foundation,
> Question surveyors, know our own estate,
> How able such a work to undergo,
> To weigh against his opposite; or else
> We fortify in paper and in figures,
> Using the names of men instead of men,
> Like one that draws the model of a house
> Beyond his power to build it, who, half-through,
> Gives o'er, and leaves his part-created cost
> A naked subject to the weeping clouds,
> And waste for churlish winter's tyranny. (1.3.41–62)

The rebel's construction analogy expresses the ideal of reform/rebellion as a process that moves forward through successive revisions that end in the material realization and durability of an intention. In a critique of the reputation of 'constructivism' in the social and natural sciences, Bruno Latour suggests that visiting actual construction sites provides 'an ideal vantage point to witness the connections between humans and non-humans … at the time of their most radical metamorphosis'. He explains that the view of a construction site 'provides a rare glimpse of what it is for a thing to emerge out of inexistence by adding to any existing entity its time dimension … And indeed, in all domains, to say that something is constructed has always been associated with an appreciation for its robustness, quality, style, durability, worth, etc.'[23] The building is a material expression of the temporal processes of planning, building, and inhabiting—linking past, present, and future. Construction confers on the bare materials and the human agents a historical narrative and identity.

While Bardolph's construction analogy is presented as a correction to Hotspur's methods, in the final analysis, it more vividly depicts ruins than success and implicates the inherent drawback of rebellion as a legal-political reform strategy. It is impossible not to imagine the real destruction of rebellion laying waste to the countryside when the house analogy is introduced for the second time as an unfinished structure, abandoned to the 'tyranny' of the elements. It is that inevitable destruction that the homily-writer imagines when he claims that rebellion is a remedy 'farre worse then anye other maladies and disorders that can be in the body of a common wealth' ($B1^v$):

> Surely that whiche they falsely cal Reformation, is in deede not only a defacyng or a deformation, but also an vtter destruction of al common wealth, as … doth right wel and to well appeare by theyr doyng in suche places of the countrey where rebels do route, where though they tary but a very litle while, they make such reformation, that they destroy all places, & undo al men where they come … ($G2^{r-v}$)

The image of a building that has been abandoned halfway through construction and the latent image of a building that has been wasted by war look the same. On the one hand, Bardolph poetically succeeds in demonstrating the necessity of first distinguishing between figure and fact before taking action. On the other hand, in the case of rebellion, the alignment of figure and fact, or the collapse of difference into sameness, does not result in state-building, in 'pluck[ing] a kingdom down / And set[ting] another up'. Instead of the historical progress promised by construction, a stasis emerges as material continuity is stripped of its significance. If the homily, Foxe, and Holinshed require us to recognize rebellion as a form of legal reform, the second tetralogy also requires us to recognize rebellion as a way of life, as a military-political practice of recurrent 'civil butchery' (*1 Henry IV*, 1.1.13). Through the construction analogy, Bardolph attempts—but fails—to present an alternative pattern to the unregenerative repetition of rebellion

[23] Bruno Latour, *Reassembling the Social: An Introduction to Actor-Network Theory* (Oxford: Oxford University Press, 2007), 88, 89.

that has stagnated the forces of state formation. As Bardolph's fellow rebel, Hastings, asserts at Gaultree,

> And though we here fall down,
> We have supplies to second our attempt.
> If they miscarry, theirs shall second them;
> And so success of mischief shall be born,
> And heir from heir shall hold his quarrel up
> Whiles England shall have generation. (4.1.270–5)

Rebellion, as a reform practice, offers the promise and power of iterability but not progress. Heirs succeed heirs, perpetuating the action of rebellion without ever achieving its objectives.

Instead of representing the 'success of mischief' through a battle scene that would put the rebels' preparations and Hastings' claims to the test, the inevitable confrontation between the Archbishop's and the king's forces takes the form of a parley through which political right is determined by rhetorical might. The king's general, Prince John of Lancaster, takes the upper hand through verbal craftiness in a scene that replaces the principle of mimesis that was championed by Bardolph with the performative power of rhetoric. In response to the above speech, John declares, 'You are too shallow, Hastings, much too shallow, / To sound the bottom of the after-times' (4.1.276–7). Subsequently, the prince upbraids the Archbishop of York for lacking the kind of insight that was championed in the construction analogy: 'Most shallowly did you these arms commence, / Fondly brought here, and foolishly sent hence' (4.2.344–5). The prince's choice of epithets associates the rebels with Shallow, the corrupt Justice of the Peace whose grasp of the past (his recollection of youthful days at an Inn of Chancery) and current administration of local justice are as loosely committed to fact as Hotspur's rages or Falstaff's lies. The comparison forged by John's word choice ultimately alerts us to the ethical and deliberative differences between the corrupt characters who populate Shallow's Gloucestershire orchard and the sincere and methodical rebels. The wide gap here between figure and fact thus does more to align John himself with the Gloucestershire set. Yet that same gap will present no obstacle to the performative force that John's rhetoric will exercise. This redescription of the rebels will become, over the course of the parley, part of material political reality.

In dubbing the Archbishop 'shallow', 'fond', and 'foolish', John's primary intention is to identify deliberative weakness with a weak political right. The prince thereby invites the audience's evaluation of his own judgement and right, which are established and linked in his royal commission. The commission outlining his authority as the king's representative is described in explicitly judicial terms, associating him with the more positive legal figure of the Chief Justice: he has the right 'To hear, and absolutely to determine, / Of what conditions [the rebels] shall stand upon' (4.1.164–5). Through this office, John wields an interpretative authority that does not reflect a preexisting truth so much as it decides what will be accepted as such. In this episode, the judicial power to originate performative interpretations is used to determine and to demonstrate legitimate political power. John lulls the rebels into a false sense of security by agreeing to the reforms outlined in their articles. The king's party then waits to see the rebel forces disband before arresting the leaders for treason.[24] The stunned Archbishop asks, 'Will you thus break your faith?' (4.1.337), but the prince is extremely careful not to present himself as an oath-breaker:

> I promis'd you redress of these same grievances
> Whereof you did complain; which, by mine honour,
> I will perform with a most Christian care.
> But, for you rebels, look to taste the due
> Meet for rebellion and such acts as yours. (4.1.339–43)

Through his strategically narrow or strict interpretation of the terms of their negotiations, John extricates the work of reform in the commonwealth from rebellion. He thereby establishes the distinction drawn in the homily between the sovereign's counsellors (the fit reformers) and rebels. As Westmoreland claims earlier in the same scene, 'There is no need of any such redress, / Or if there were, it not belongs to you' (4.1.95–6). The project of reforming the commonwealth, moreover, of redressing the rebels' grievances, is effectively begun with the removal of the country's illegitimate leaders.

Through the parley, political authority is legitimized by a judicial distinction between rebel and ruler and demonstrated through one kind of reform practice. The scene thus not only determines the rebels' fate, but it also establishes the terms of Prince Hal's own political transformation to king. Any kind of change on Hal's part, however, seems highly improbable.[25] The central proponents of this view within the play are Henry IV and Falstaff, whose predictions for the next reign are inspired by precedent. They both imagine Hal's imminent installation as a successful form of the 'success of mischief' in which the prince's rebelliousness is fused with rule, and the relationship between king and commonwealth is mediated by corruptive fellowship. Richard Strier observes that Henry IV imagines a future 'in which conviviality merges into serious criminality':[26] 'From every region, apes of idleness' will 'Revel the night, rob, murder, and commit / The oldest sins the newest kind of ways' (4.3.251–5). The

[24] John's legal casuistry usually elicits critical distaste. See Paul A. Jorgenson, 'The "Dastardly Treachery" of Prince John of Lancaster', *PMLA*, 76 (1961): 488–92.

[25] Lorna Hutson argues that the rhetorical construction of Hal's intentions over the course of the play prepare us to accept his reformation, while the earlier play, *The Famous Victories of Henry the Fifth*, relies on the logic of conversion: 'Not the King's Two Bodies: Reading the "Body Politic" in Shakespeare's *Henry IV, Parts 1* and *2*', in *Rhetoric and Law in Early Modern Europe*, ed. Victoria Kahn and Lorna Hutson (New Haven: Yale University Press, 2001), 166–89.

[26] Richard Strier, 'Shakespeare and Legal Systems: The Better the Worse (but Not Vice Versa)', in *Shakespeare and the Law: A Conversation among Disciplines and Professions*, ed. Bradin Cormack, Martha C. Nussbaum, and Richard Strier (Chicago: University of Chicago Press, 2013), 180.

same scenario greases Falstaff's imagination, who, upon hearing of Henry IV's death, proclaims, 'Let us take any man's horses—the laws of England are at my commandment. Blessed are they that have been my friends, and woe to my Lord Chief Justice' (5.3.134–7).

Instead of imagining, let alone proposing, any kind of limitation to the monarch's personal rule, Henry IV attempts to supplant one type of friend—Falstaff—with another. He instructs his son, Thomas of Clarence, who 'hast a better place in [Hal's] affection / Than all [his other] brothers', on how to become a royal favourite in the new court: the king's 'temper … must be well observed' (4.3.36). If Thomas can take advantage of the king's 'tear for pity', 'Chide him for faults' when 'his blood [is] inclined to mirth', and avoid him when incensed, then Thomas 'shalt prove a shelter to [his] friends, / A hoop of gold to bind [his] brothers in' (4.3.31–43). Henry IV depicts a reign reduced to the stereotypical tantrums of the over-mighty, void of any intentions or actions that might be driven by a sense of duty. This picture of the young king's personality and future proves quite shallow, however. In the first few moments of Henry V's reign, friendship is supplanted by the law and legal reform as the principal mediators of the sovereign's relationship to the commonwealth. While the court, not just Falstaff, anticipates that the Chief Justice will be stripped of his position, the new king instead stages a reconciliation with his legal minister. Together, they dialogically move the topic of character in the direction of the representational structure and responsibilities of office-holding that perpetuated early modern governance.

Offend and Obey and Again

As A. R. Humphreys explains, '[n]o previous treatment of Henry IV's reign or Henry V's accession gives the Lord Chief Justice the prominence he has in Shakespeare, where Hal's conduct with him is made a central element on which to display the conversion to kingliness …'[27] In the play's sources, the Chief Justice only enters the narrative when he has the prince imprisoned for threatening or striking (depending on the source) the judge while he is sentencing one of the prince's servants.[28] While Shakespeare increases the Chief Justice's role ('The early scenes when [the judge] embodies order against anarchy are purely Shakespeare's own'[29]), he follows Holinshed's example by presenting this key episode in the form of a recollection. According to the *Chronicles*, after his coronation, Henry V 'call[s] to mind how once to hie offense of the king his father, he had with his fist striken the cheefe iustice for sending one of his minions (vpon desert) to

[27] Humphreys, xxxix.

[28] Anon., *The Famovs Victories of Henry the Fifth* (London: 1598); Raphael Holinshed, *Holinshed's Chronicles of England, Scotland and Ireland*, Vol. 3, ed. Henry Ellis (London: 1808); Thomas Elyot, *The Boke Named the Gouernour* (London: 1531); John Stow, *The Annales of England* (London: 1592).

[29] Humphreys, xxxix.

prison, when the iustice stoutlie commanded himselfe also streict to ward, & he (then prince) obeied' (3:61). Shakespeare makes the surprising decision to report, when he could dramatize, the incident, foregoing the naturally compelling material of a trial scene and a fist fight.[30] By having Henry V and the Chief Justice retell and reimagine the incident in Act V, the playwright opts instead to draw attention to his characters' legal-political representation practices. The story of the prince's former trespass and correction becomes the instrument through which the relationship between king and judge, and, as a consequence, England's political future, are reformed.

In 5.2, Henry V first recalls the incident and frames it as an accusation against the Chief Justice, who had dared to have the Crown Prince arrested. The judge then mounts a self-defence that educates the new king in the nature of office-holding:

> I then did use the person of your father;
> The image of his power lay then in me;
> And in th'administration of his law,
> Whiles I was busy for the commonwealth,
> Your Highness pleased to forget my place,
> The majesty and power of law and justice,
> The image of the King whom I presented,
> And struck me in my very seat of judgment;
> Whereon, as an offender to your father,
> I gave bold way to my authority
> And did commit you. (5.2.73–82)

The Chief Justice is considered unique among Shakespeare's legal characters, because he is an unequivocally positive exponent of his profession.[31] Known only as 'Chief Justice', we are invited to equate his character with his title. He has perhaps been overlooked in criticism as simply an allegory of justice, but Paul W. Kahn's description of the sublimation of the individual as a key feature of the judicial persona encourages us to reconsider the Chief Justice's figurative value as a professional achievement that testifies to his skill and integrity.[32] Importantly, the judge's identification with his office, which guarantees his objective judgement, is achieved by preserving the structure of a representation. We are asked to see and hear the king in the person and voice of the Chief Justice, not simply because of the king's authorizing power, but because the king's actual absence is essential to seeing the Chief Justice as upholding an office, as precisely

[30] Shakespeare could have followed the example of *Famovs Victories*, and staged the thief's trial and the prince's punch and imprisonment ($B2^r$–$B4^r$). On the rhetorical effects of report, see Hutson, 'Not the King's Two Bodies', and *The Invention of Suspicion: Law and Mimesis in Shakespeare and Renaissance Drama* (Oxford: Oxford University Press, 2007), especially 217–35.

[31] Daniel Kornstein, *Kill All The Lawyers? Shakespeare's Legal Appeal* (Princeton: Princeton University Press, 1994), 135.

[32] Paul W. Kahn, *The Cultural Study of Law* (Chicago: University of Chicago Press, 1999), 79–81.

not speaking for himself. Thus the judge's identification with his office is enabled by the reassertion of the distinction between title and man that is collapsed in the thought of Henry IV and Falstaff when they imagine the future rule of Henry V. Nothing could seem more distant from the judge's impersonal embodiment of office than Hal's personal rebelliousness, yet it is this model of office-holding that the new king adopts over the course of this scene.

The Chief Justice goes on next to recast the past episode as a hypothetical case for Henry V's judgement. He asks the new king to imagine himself in the position of the father: 'Question your royal thoughts, make the case yours, / Be now the father, and propose a son ...' (5.2.82–3). Henry V takes the Chief Justice's hypothetical case and establishes it as an inevitability in the time to come. Instead of generating the same predictions of lawlessness that inspired the imaginations of Henry IV and Falstaff, however, the new king enlarges the scope of the precedent so that not only his transgression but his reform, too, will be repeated:

> You are right, Justice, and you weigh this well.
> Therefore still bear the balance and the sword;
> And I do wish your honours may increase
> Till you do live to see a son of mine
> Offend you and obey you, as I did.
> So shall I live to speak my father's words:
> 'Happy am I, that have a man so bold
> That dares do justice on my proper son;
> And not less happy, having such a son
> That would deliver up his greatness so
> Into the hands of Justice.' (5.2.101–11)

Henry V projects a future in which his son, by course, repeats the same offence only to be similarly humbled, and in which Henry V repeats his own father's past response apparently verbatim. A progressive temporality emerges that enshrines the reform of the monarch's relationship to law at the heart of dynastic and national progress. The improbability of Hal's reform is nullified by his reform's certain repetition in the future that retroactively necessitates his reform as a function of this larger pattern. The categorical distinction between rebel and ruler, instituted by John, is historicized by Henry in much the same way that the historical reform of injustice results in political progress in Lambarde's *Archeion*. The danger of rebelliousness, to Henry's legitimacy and to the commonwealth, dissolves as Henry inscribes it as his past and the past. Even when it is projected into the future and transferred to his hypothetical son, the past is represented in the instant of its reformation. The king is both redeemed and displaced from the centre of his own story, however, since his past is turned into an unfolding pattern by depersonalizing (through its future iterability by another) an episode that was integral to the prince's personal legend. His actions—and the responsibility for them—are abstracted from him as part of the staging of his maturation.

Like the Chief Justice's self-defence that emphasizes the king's absence to illuminate the representational structure of office-holding, Henry V will go on to use the rejection of Falstaff to publically guarantee the distinction between title and man that, in turn, excuses the young king's rejection of his best friend. In *The Garden of Eloquence*, Henry Peacham defines the figure of dicaeologia as 'a forme of speech by which the Orator either defendeth his cause by equitie, or excuseth it by necessitie', and offers the following example: 'I forsooke my friend, but the lawes compelled me: I kept friendship most faithfully, as long as the lawes permitted me.'[33] A similar (and to most, a lamentable) irreconcilability between friendship and law emerges in *2 Henry IV*. Henry's excuse for forsaking Falstaff is the king's obligation to uphold the law and to reform or remove the unjust legal-political associations at court and within the legal-political system.

The recalibrated relationship between sovereign and judge has further consequences for the metaphorical significance of the father–son relationship through which political legitimacy is represented and critiqued across the two-play sequence. Typically, the metaphor of father and son justified political relationships and hierarchies by naturalizing them. Paul Raffield reads the Chief Justice's relationship with Henry V through medieval and early modern legal authorities' appropriation of the metaphor: '[t]he symbol of fatherhood, of an imaginary father to whom all true subjects of law owe allegiance and from whom all law originates, is a metaphysical conceit to which judges and jurists of the early modern period made allusion'. He argues that the relationship between king and judge in Shakespeare's play recalls the Chancellor's paternal relationship with the Prince of Wales in John Fortescue's medieval treatise, *In Praise of the Laws of England*. The Chancellor (Fortescue) encourages the reform of the prince's conduct through the study of his nation's laws (hitherto he had focused on military exercises). Once the Prince of Wales 'has "transcribed the Law" into his "very habit and Disposition" he will "deservedly obtain the Character of a Just Prince"'.[34] On this reading, the Bractonian principle that a king must submit himself to the law, 'for there is no *rex* where will rules rather than *lex*' (2:33), is naturalized as filial duty and is actualized by Henry V's reformed behaviour at the end of *Part Two*.

Several factors, however, challenge the unidirectional trajectory of the reformation suggested by Raffield's reading of the law's metaphoric paternity. Most obviously, kings, no less than judges, represented themselves or were represented as the father to the nation. *Part One* and *Part Two*, moreover, are structured around the actual father–son relationship between Henry IV and Henry V that manages to reinforce the link between paternity and monarchy while weakening the force of the metaphor. As Meredith Evans points out, 'the patrilineal line of succession' from Henry IV to Henry V 'is vulnerably short and without a stable origin', so that to invoke it as a force of legitimacy would be rhetorically shortsighted.[35] And although the metaphor most commonly conveys the

[33] Henry Peacham, *The Garden of Eloquence* (London: 1593), 115–16.

[34] Paul Raffield, 'The Ancient Constitution, Common Law and the Idyll of Albion: Law and Lawyers in *Henry IV, Parts 1 and 2*', *Law and Literature*, 22.1 (2010): 38, 26.

[35] Meredith Evans, 'Rumor, the Breath of Kings, and the Body of Law in *2 Henry IV*', *SQ*, 60.1 (2009): 16.

sense of authorization-by-origin, 'father' loses precisely this force as more men embody the role or as origins multiply in the plays. The role of 'father' is played by Henry IV, Falstaff, Hal/Henry V himself, and finally the Chief Justice.[36]

In the final act of *Part Two* the reformed relationship between king and judge instrumentalizes the father–son metaphor's semantic or figurative irresolution. Both men are compared to father and son over the course of their dialogue; when they claim to represent the father, they assert their authority as office holders and over each other but in a momentary, contingent fashion. When the Chief Justice asks Henry to imagine himself as the late king, but in the future, he puts Henry in the position of playing his own father, just as the Chief Justice claims to do in his office as a judge. 'You shall be as a father to my youth, / My voice shall sound as you do prompt mine ear' the new king tells his newly re-commissioned judge and counsellor (5.2.117–18). Having just quoted his actual father, apparently word for word ('So shall I live to speak my father's words'), Henry V now claims he will also go on in the future to quote the father-like Chief Justice. Later, however, during the rejection of Falstaff, the king puts the Chief Justice in charge of supervising the knight's reform by calling upon the judge 'To see performed the tenor of my word' (5.5.69). 'And, as we hear you do reform yourselves', he tells Falstaff, 'We will according to your strengths and qualities, / Give you advancement' (5.5.66–8): the king will also act upon the judge's report or words. This shuttling of voices between bodies derails the quest for 'an ultimate source of legitimate authority' (Raffield 24) and instead structures a future-oriented relationship in which each office holder activates the obligation of the other to reform his own or another's relationship to the law.

'Father' loses its foundational sense and instead comes to function primarily as a logical 'relatiue', as defined by Thomas Wilson in *The Rule of Reason*: 'Relatiues are those, which are comprehended with other, or the which are named one with an other ... As when I say a father, I can not call him, except I vnderstand a sonne that he hath ... Therefore we may see, that Relatiues are referred euermore to an other, neither can they be taken absolutely, without hauing respect to some other worde.'[37] In Wilson's account of relatives, the word 'father' points to an association rather than an origin. Here, fathers and sons mutually constitute and distinguish one another. The result of this semantic shift in Shakespeare's text is the establishment of a relationship between monarch and law whose hierarchy is—unlike genealogical father–son pairs—responsive, reversible, but, importantly, not collapsible. The structure of relatives and of office-holding offer a blueprint for future legal-political relations that promise to purge the commonwealth of corruptive associations in the form of friendship and rebellion.

[36] Paul Raffield and Kenji Yoshino both point out that the Chief Justice emerges as one of the last in a series of father figures for Hal/Henry V; Kenji Yoshino, 'The Choice of the Four Fathers: Henry IV, Falstaff, the Lord Chief Justice, and the King of France in the Henriad', *YJLH*, 22.2 (2010): 417–37.

[37] Thomas Wilson, *The Rule of Reason, Contayning the Arte of Logike* (London: 1567), 12^{r}.

Conclusion: 'The Laws of This Realm Are the Best in Fact or Potentiality'

Legal and literary historians are most attracted to Fortescue's *In Praise of the Laws of England* for its contribution to the discourse on the ancient constitution. In the sixteenth and seventeenth centuries, the text was received by legal apologists as an authoritative source on the common law's historical origins. One passage in particular has been understood, then and now, as 'an attempt to play down all of the major constitutional upheavals of the realm … since its first institution by Brutus' band of Trojans':[38]

> the realm has been continuously ruled by the same customs as it is now, customs which, if they had not been the best, some of those kings would have changed for the sake of justice or by the impulse of caprice … [no other laws] are so rooted in antiquity. Hence there is no gainsaying nor legitimate doubt but that the customs of the English are not only good but the best. (26–7)

Despite these lofty claims, Shelley Lockwood argues that Fortescue was not attempting to present a historical argument. Instead, he was 'instilling faith in an idealised system of government, thereby highlighting the gap between ideal and actual in order to stimulate reform' (xxv). Fortescue's contribution to the reform discourse, however, is not exhausted by the distinction between the 'ideal and actual'. *In Praise of the Laws of England* repeatedly commends the English legal-political system for its structural accommodation of legal reform through the institution of Parliament:

> all other laws in use in the realm, if they are defective in any respect, can be amended in every parliament. So it can be rightly concluded that all the laws of this realm are the best in fact or potentiality, since they can easily be brought to it in fact and actual reality. And to do this as often as equity requires it, every king is bound by his oath solemnly taken at the time of his receiving the crown. (78)

The claim for the superiority of English law is rooted here in its capacity for improvement, and that superiority, in turn, is responsible for the legal system's continual adoption through the ages. Far from suppressing or ignoring historic change at law, Fortescue identifies it as distinctly English, a function of the government's characteristic 'mixte state'. Legal reform, on this account, generates and perpetuates England. The sovereign's legitimacy, moreover, is underwritten by his response to the difference between the 'fact' and 'potentiality' of the law, a claim reasonably supported by

[38] Shelley Lockwood, 'Introduction', in John Fortescue, *On the Laws and Governance of England*, ed. Shelley Lockwood (Cambridge: Cambridge University Press), xxxi.

the coronation oath that required monarchs not only to uphold but also to reform the law.

The debate on nobility that is staged in Medwall's *Fulgens and Lucrece* focuses squarely on the difference between the 'ideal and actual'. Lucrece (and, in effect, the audience) is asked to choose between the idealization of noble conduct, personified by Gaius, and the reality of the maintaining and retaining degenerate aristocrat, Cornelius. Shakespeare's history play, however, keeps pace with the more sophisticated reasoning of Fortescue's treatise by offering an extensive representation and analysis of legal reform as a central instrument of political progress. Throughout the play, relationships affecting the generation of political legitimacy and order—the relationship between fact and figure, rebel and rightful magistrate, king and judge, father and son, past and future—are reimagined through the discourse and strategies of reform. After Henry V's reconciliation with the Chief Justice, the play's meditation on legal reform is completed by the invocation of its most explicit institutional form. The king's intention to fulfil his royal duty is signalled by references to Parliament:

> Now call we our high court of parliament,
> And let us choose such limbs of noble counsel
> That the great body of our state may go
> In equal rank with the best-govern'd nation;
> That war, or peace, or both at once, may be
> As things acquainted and familiar to us;
> [*to* LORD CHIEF JUSTICE] In which you, father, shall have foremost hand.
> [*to all*] Our coronation done, we will accite,
> As I before remember'd, all our state ... (5.2.133–41)

Henry V fashions himself as a force for national reform and progress by calling Parliament into being and England's 'mixte state' into action, an act that operates reflexively as a sign of his own reform, or the reorientation of his relationship to office-holding, to the law, and to the commonwealth.

Bibliography

Anon. *An Homilie agaynst Disobedience and Wylful Rebellion* (London: 1570).

Anon. *The Famovs Victories of Henry the Fifth* (London: 1598).

Baldwin, William. 'The Epistle', in *A Myrrovre For Magistrates* (London: 1559), 2^{r}–3^{v}.

Bracton, Henry de. *Bracton on the Laws and Customs of England*, ed. and trans. Samuel E. Thorne, 4 vols (Cambridge, MA: Belknap Press, 1968–1977).

Brooks, Christopher W. *Law, Politics, and Society in Early Modern England* (Cambridge: Cambridge University Press, 2008).

Burrow, Colin. 'Reading Tudor Writing Politically: The Case of "2 Henry IV"', *The Yearbook of English Studies*, 38.1 (2008): 234–50.

Coke, Sir Edward. *The Fourth Part of the Institutes of the Lawes of England* (London: 1648).

Cormack, Bradin. *A Power to Do Justice: Jurisdiction, English Literature, and the Rise of Common Law, 1509–1625* (Chicago: University of Chicago Press, 2008).

Crewe, Jonathan. 'Reforming Prince Hal: The Sovereign Inheritor in "2 Henry IV"', *Renaissance Drama*, 21 (1990): 225–42.

Elyot, Thomas. *The Boke Named the Gouernour* (London: 1531).

Evans, Meredith. 'Rumour, the Breath of Kings, and the Body of Law in "2 Henry IV"', *Shakespeare Quarterly*, 60.1 (2009): 1–24.

Fletcher, Anthony. *Reform in the Provinces: The Government of Stuart England* (New Haven: Yale University Press, 1986).

Fortescue, Sir John. *On the Laws and Governance of England*, ed. Shelley Lockwood (Cambridge: Cambridge University Press, 1997).

Fraunce, Abraham. *The Lawiers Logike, Exemplifying the Praecepts of Logike by the Practise of the Common Lawe* (London: 1588).

Greenberg, Janelle Renfrow. *The Radical Face of the Ancient Constitution: St Edward's 'Laws' in Early Modern Political Thought* (Cambridge: Cambridge University Press, 2001).

Greenblatt, Stephen. 'Invisible Bullets', in *The Greenblatt Reader*, ed. Michael Payne (Malden: Blackwell Publishing, 2005), 121–60.

Holinshed, Raphael. *Holinshed's Chronicles of England, Scotland, and Ireland* [1587], ed. Henry Ellis, 6 vols (London: 1807–1808).

Horner, Olga. '"Fulgens and Lucres": An Historical Perspective', *Medieval English Theatre*, 15 (1993): 49–86.

Hutson, Lorna. 'Not the King's Two Bodies: Reading the "Body Politic" in Shakespeare's "Henry IV", Parts 1 and 2', in *Rhetoric and Law in Early Modern Europe*, ed. Victoria Kahn and Lorna Hutson (New Haven: Yale University Press, 2001), 166–89.

Jay, Martin. 'Historical Explanation and the Event: Reflections on the Limits of Contextualization', *New Literary History*, 42.4 (2011): 557–71.

Jorgenson, Paul A. 'The "Dastardly Treachery" of Prince John of Lancaster', *PMLA*, 76 (1961): 488–92.

Kahn, Paul W. *The Cultural Study of Law: Reconstructing Legal Scholarship* (Chicago: University of Chicago Press, 1999).

Kerrigan, John. '"Henry IV" and the Death of Old Double', *Essays in Criticism*, 40.1 (1990): 24–53.

Kiralfy, A. K. R. 'Law Reform by Legal Fictions, Equity and Legislation in English Legal History', *The American Journal of Legal History*, 10 (1966): 3–14.

Kornstein, Daniel. *Kill All the Lawyers? Shakespeare's Legal Appeal* (Princeton: Princeton University Press, 1994).

Lambarde, William. *Archeion; or, The High Courts of Justice in England*, ed. Charles H. McIlwain and Paul L. Ward (Cambridge, MA: Harvard University Press, 1957).

Latour, Bruno. *Reassembling the Social: An Introduction to Actor-Network Theory* (Oxford: Oxford University Press, 2007).

Maine, Henry Sumner. *Ancient Law: Its Connection with the Early History of Society, and Its Relation to Modern Ideas* (London: 1861).

Matthews, Nancy L. *William Sheppard, Cromwell's Law Reformer* (Cambridge: Cambridge University Press, 1984).

McBain, James. '"By Example and Gode Reason": Reconsidering Commonplaces and the Law in "Fulgens and Lucres"', *Medieval English Theatre*, 28 (2006): 3–28.

Nelson, Alan H. 'Medwall, Henry (*b.* 1462, *d.* after 1501)', in *Oxford Dictionary of National Biography*, online edn, ed. Lawrence Goldman (Oxford: Oxford University Press, 2004), <http://www.oxforddnb.com/view/article/18504> (accessed 1 July 2015).

Ponet, John. *Shorte Treatise of Politike Power, and of the True Obedience which Subiectes Owe to Kynges and Other Ciuile Gouernours, with an Exhortacion to All True Naturall English Men* (Strasbourg: 1556).

Prest, Wilfrid. 'Judicial Corruption in Early Modern England', *Past and Present*, 133 (1991): 67–95.

Prest, Wilfrid. 'William Lambarde, Elizabethan Law Reform, and Early Stuart Politics', *The Journal of British Studies*, 34.4 (1995): 464–80.

Raffield, Paul. 'The Ancient Constitution, Common Law, and the Idyll of Albion: Law and Lawyers in "Henry IV", Parts 1 and 2', *Law and Literature*, 22.1 (2010): 18–47.

Shakespeare, William. *King Henry IV, Part 2*, ed. A. R. Humphreys (Arden Shakespeare) (London: Methuen Drama, 1981).

Shapiro, Barbara. 'Codification of the Laws in Seventeenth-Century England', *Wisconsin Law Review*, 2 (1974): 428–65.

Shapiro, Barbara. 'Law Reform in Seventeenth-Century England', *The American Journal of Legal History*, 19.4 (1975): 280–312.

Shapiro, Barbara. 'Political Theology and the Courts: A Survey of Assize Sermons *c.*1600–1688', *Law and Humanities*, 2.1 (2008): 1–28.

Shapiro, Barbara. 'Sir Francis Bacon and the Mid-Seventeenth-Century Movement for Law Reform', *The American Journal of Legal History*, 24.4 (1980): 331–62.

Simpson, James. *The Oxford English Literary History*, Vol. 2: *1350–1547: Reform and Cultural Revolution* (Oxford: Oxford University Press, 2004).

Smith, David Chan. *Sir Edward Coke and the Reformation of the Laws: Religion, Politics and Jurisprudence, 1578–1616* (Cambridge: Cambridge University Press, 2014).

Smith, Sir Thomas. *De republica Anglorum: A Discourse on the Commonwealth of England* [1583] ed. Mary Dewar (Cambridge: Cambridge University Press, 1982).

Strain, Virginia Lee. 'Shakespeare's Living Law: Theatrical, Lyrical, and Legal Practice', *Literature Compass*, 12.6 (2015): 249–61.

Strain, Virginia Lee. 'The "Ensnared Subject" and the General Pardon Statute in Late Elizabethan Coterie Literature', in *Taking Exception to the Law: Materializing Injustice in Early Modern Literature*, ed. Don Beecher et al. (Toronto: University of Toronto Press, 2015), 100–19.

Strier, Richard. 'Shakespeare and Legal Systems: The Better the Worse (But Not Vice Versa)', in *Shakespeare and the Law: A Conversation Among Disciplines and Professions*, ed. Bradin Cormack, Martha C. Nussbaum, and Richard Strier (Chicago: University of Chicago Press, 2013), 174–200.

Veall, Donald. *The Popular Movement for Law Reform, 1640–1660* (Oxford: Clarendon Press, 1970).

Wall, Alison. *Power and Protest in England 1525–1640* (London: Arnold, 2000).

Wilson, Thomas. *The Rule of Reason, Contayning the Arte of Logike* (London: 1567).

Yoshino, Kenji. 'The Choice of the Four Fathers: Henry IV, Falstaff, the Lord Chief Justice, and the King of France in the Henriad', *Yale Journal of Law & the Humanities*, 22.2 (2010): 417–39.

Zurcher, Andrew. *Shakespeare and Law* (London: Methuen Drama, 2010).

PART IV

TEMPORAL AND SPIRITUAL, LAW AND CONSCIENCE

CHAPTER 15

IMMUNITIES AND MONASTICISM

Bale to Shakespeare

JOSHUA PHILLIPS

As a relatively new genre in sixteenth-century England, albeit one with a long genealogy, the history play served as a field of experimentation, cultivated by playwrights interested in revising the way that history and drama were understood.[1] In this chapter, I examine the construction of legal history in a series of sixteenth-century plays about King John of England (r. 1199–1216) that differently take up the legal shape of, and legal claims to, immunity and community, for which I consider the situation of the religious in Reformation England as a test case.[2] Here, I explore how plays written by John Bale, George Peele, and William Shakespeare used their representations of King John to attend, in a post-Reformation context, to the legal complexities of monasticism as a social practice.[3]

Before taking up these English history plays, however, I want to consider an essay by Montaigne, one of the sixteenth century's great theorists of personal and legal identity, as a prompt for thinking about the nature of community.[4] In *De L'Amitié*, Montaigne

[1] See Peter Happé, *English Drama before Shakespeare* (London: Longman, 1999), 220, 241–7.

[2] I derive much of my understanding of the terms immunity and community in this paper from the works of Roberto Esposito, especially his *Communitas: The Origin and Destiny of Community*, trans. Timothy Campbell (Stanford: Stanford University Press, 2010), and *Terms of the Political: Community, Immunity, Biopolitics*, trans. Rhiannon Noel Welch (New York: Fordham University Press, 2013).

[3] *John Bale's 'King Johan'*, ed., intro., and notes Barry B. Adams (San Marino: The Huntington Library, 1969); George Peele, *The Troublesome Reign of John, King of England*, ed. and intro. Charles R. Forker (Manchester: Manchester University Press, 2011); William Shakespeare, *King John* in *The Norton Shakespeare*, ed. Stephen Greenblatt et al. (New York: W. W. Norton and Co., 1997). Until relatively recently, the authorship of *The Troublesome Reign* and its relation to Shakespeare's play were unresolved questions. Brian Vickers, however, has now provided convincing answers to those questions, as summarized in the introduction to Forker's edition of *The Troublesome Reign*, 6–30.

[4] About Montaigne and law, see André Tournon, *Montaigne: la glose et l'essai* (Lyon: Presses Universitaires de Lyon, 1983); Ullrich Langer, 'Justice légale, diversité et changement des lois: de la

recounts a story, 'an ancient singular example', that he views as both unsettling and normative. The story concerns Eudamidas, a Corinthian, who, finding himself near death, makes his last will and testament, which names his closest friends Charixenus and Aretheus as beneficiaries. '*To* Aretheus', the will states:

> *I bequeath the keeping of my mother, and to maintaine her when she shall be old: To* Charixenus *the marrying of my daughter, and to give her as great a dowry as he may: and in case one of them shall chance to die before, I appoint the surviver to substitute his charge, and supply his place.*[5]

While outsiders mocked the will, the two friends were 'very well pleased, and received it with singular contentment'. Montaigne presents this story as paradigmatic, casually commenting that where it goes wrong is only in the number: true friendship is shared between two people, not three. Because Montaigne's story indirectly addresses issues that monasticism poses to law, I explore it here as exemplary, that is, as something that provides an ideal, a form, a constellation of ideas, but that is always necessarily different from what it exemplifies.[6] 'This example', as Florio's translation has it, 'is very ample'.[7] For my purposes, Montaigne's anecdote raises three issues: (1) the distinction made between two people and three; (2) the relation of possession and non-possession to community; and (3) the focus on legal instruments, specifically the will and the dowry.

It is possible, productive even, to see Montaigne's gloss on the story of Eudamidas as a purposeful misreading. As noted, Montaigne takes exception to the idea of 'the multitude of friends: For, this perfect amity I speake of, is indivisible .... Common friendship may bee divided .... but this amitie which possesseth the soule, and swaies it in all soveraigntie, it is impossible it should be double' (151). Curiously, Montaigne here uses his example as an exception to the very case he is attempting to build, making exemplary a story that contradicts what he wants to prove, that friendship involves only two and no more. What Montaigne refuses to acknowledge is that this story concerns not friendship so much as community, a fact alluded to in his reference to 'common friendship' and his

tradition aristotélicienne à Montaigne', *Bulletin de la Société des Amis de Montaigne*, 8.21–4 (2001): 223–32 (this entire volume is devoted to the topic of 'Montaigne: La Justice'). See also Katie Chenoweth, 'The Force of a Law: Derrida, Montaigne, and the Edict of Villers-Cotterêts (1539)', *The Comparatist*, 36.1 (2012): 67–85.

[5] *The Essayes of Montaigne: John Florio's Translation*, intro. J. I. M. Stewart (New York: The Modern Library, 1933), 151, italics in original.

[6] On the idea of the example see, Allen D. Boyer, 'Drama, Law, and Rhetoric in the Age of Coke and Shakespeare', in *The Law in Shakespeare*, ed. Constance Jordan and Karen Cunningham (Houndmills, Basingsroke: Palgrave Macmillan, 2010), 30–2. Boyer points out that 'To the student of rhetoric, *exempla* were cases, relevant and analogous instances. To the student of law, *exempla* were opinions entitled to respect' (30). And by the 1590s in England, 'The *exemplum* had become the case report, a set of facts to which interpretations could be applied. New cases were decided, and new law was made, as the lawyers clinched their arguments by applying newly coined maxims to the facts of a case—using *sententiae* to put an advocate's gloss on *exempla*' (31).

[7] 'Cet exemple est bien plein'. Note how Florio imitates the internal rhyme of the original (151).

use of the word 'soveraigntie'. Indeed, while, as Laurie Shannon has noted, 'sixteenth-century friendship does not bespeak larger social or national formations in microcosm', that is true only of friendships consisting of two.[8] With the addition of a third, one moves to 'common friendship', that is, community.

In early modern England, the common law helped define sovereignty and community through its interpretations, limitations, and regulations of property. But there is another way to understand community. As Roberto Esposito notes, 'Dictionaries ... tell us that the ancient and presumably originary meaning of *communis* had to be "he who shares an office [*carica*], a burden [*carico*], a task [*incarico*]"'. From here it emerges that '*communitas* is the totality of persons united not by a "property" but precisely by an obligation or a debt; not by an "addition" [*più*] but by a "subtraction" [*meno*]: by a lack, a limit that is configured as an onus'.[9]

Montaigne's exemplary story of Eudamidas's will reveals a similar argument. What Eudamidas leaves to his friends, and what makes their friendship exemplary, is not property but rather obligation or debt. Their microcommunity of three constitutes itself by the obligations to which the members are subject, such that the death of one merely increases the obligations of the others. For Esposito, this process 'expropriates them of their initial property ... of the most proper property, namely, their very subjectivity' (7). For Montaigne, it expands the self into a corporate 'friend'—a single soul in multiple bodies. For both, the formation of community sacrifices that which, if retained, keeps one individuated. Although Esposito does not mention the religious in his work (his interest lies in the modern rather than the early modern period), his reflections on community help us to take account of how early modern monasticism came into conflict with the law, since the very constitution of cenobitic religious orders was always at odds with legal practices and discourses designed around individuating property relations.

A final aspect of Montaigne's anecdote that bears mentioning concerns how the community in question, the friendship, is *institutionalized*, realized as an example at the moment it is registered in and ordered by a legal instrument: the will. The friendship that Montaigne describes was perfect before Eudamidas died. Like other friendships that Montaigne mentions in the essay, it followed its own logic, a logic above, heedless of, and free from legal prescription. What makes the story notable, though, is how Eudamidas uses the instruments of the law against itself to establish a fierce autonomy and a sense of community at odds with that proposed by the law itself. If the purpose of wills is, at least partly, to retain across generations rights in property, Eudamidas employs his will to unsettle individuated ownership. Where law tends to want to isolate responsibility, then, Eudamidas uses the legal instrument to disperse it. And so Montaigne's example serves to show how communal practices embedded in legal instruments can act as a threat and limit to the law.

[8] Laurie Shannon, *Sovereign Amity: Figures of Friendship in Shakespearean Contexts* (Chicago: Chicago University Press, 2002), 18.

[9] Esposito, *Communitas*, 6.

The Drama of Immunity

Is it striking that in the English drama of the late sixteenth century the religious—monks, friars, nuns—so frequently play a part, though they had ceased to exist in English social life half a century earlier? One can point to several reasons for their continued presence in the literary sphere. First, these figures belonged now to a rather rich literary lineage stretching from before Dante through Chaucer, including folktales, satires, and romances, a lineage in which they often functioned as stock characters, with full-blown associations. Second, writers continued to set their texts in the past when these figures would have had a place. Finally, these figures are often used to represent the threat posed to monarchical sovereignty by communal practices and formations. Monastic orders often presented themselves in their Rules as holy communities, withdrawn from the state or political realm in which they were situated and withdrawn from the world of property. As the *Rule of St Benedict* says, 'Suche stuff that he hath not yeven before to folke that ben poore or other wyse, openly shall he thenne yeve to the monestary / noo thyng reservyng unto hym-selfe; for after that tyme he may have noo propirte / not as moche as his owne body.'[10] Here we see the very expropriation of subjectivity which Esposito discusses. In becoming a part of the community, they give up that, which in much philosophical/political thought defines subjectivity: ownership of the self. Similarly, in the *Rule of Augustine*, the initiates read:

> 3. The main purpose for your having come together is to live harmoniously in your house, intent upon God, with one heart and one soul (Acts 4:32).
> 4. Therefore call nothing your own, but let everything be yours in common.[11]

In both these texts, the initiate's relation to property becomes a synecdoche for the order's relation to the state: renunciation of worldly life produces autonomy.

It is not surprising, then, that so much anti-monastic rhetoric focuses on the failure of such orders to maintain a proper separation from worldly life. Anti-fraternal satires present case after case of the avaricious monk, the gluttonous friar, the lecherous nun.[12] In early sixteenth-century England, the visitation records picked up and expanded this rhetoric, partly as a way to justify dissolving the religious houses. Richard Layton, one of Cromwell's examiners, writes that he is sending 'a book of Our Lady's miracles' (found in the library of Monk Farleigh, Wiltshire, a Cluniac cell of Lewes), which is 'well able to

[10] *Three Middle-English Versions of the Rule of St Benet*, ed. Ernst A. Kock (London: Kegan Paul, Trench, Trubner, and Co., Ltd, 1902), 136.

[11] *The Rule of Our Holy Father St Augustine, Bishop of Hippo: A Translation from the Latin*, trans. Robert P. Russell (Villanova: Province of St Thomas of Villanova 1976), http://www.augustinianmonks.com/welcome/ruleofstaugustine.html.

[12] See Penn Szittya, *The Antifraternal Tradition in Medieval Literature* (Princeton: Princeton University Press, 1986).

match the Canterbury Tales; such a book of dreams as you never saw'.[13] Another examiner, John Bartelot, describes how he 'found the prior of the Crossed Friars in London at that time being in bed with his whore, both naked' (44). The point here is not the veracity of the reports, but rather the conventional critique of the religious that the reports trade in. Whether voiced by Chaucer or sixteenth-century reformers, the claim is the same: the religious are bound to the things of this world.

From a legal standpoint, however, the real problem was never with monasticism's proximity to the world, but rather its distance. Erasmus, for one, 'believed it would be useful if monks were brought more completely under the authority of the bishops . . . . What such tighter episcopal supervision meant was the extension of episcopal oversight to houses legally exempt from such control'.[14] And Luther complained that 'Monks hold themselves in a class apart from all other Christians'.[15] Continuous with this accusation, the religious houses in early sixteenth-century England claimed a kind of exemption or immunity that was at odds with a legal system that was progressing steadily if inconsistently towards centralization, towards a single law for all. If, for a figure like Thomas More, that progress constituted, in Bradin Cormack's words, a 'jurisdictional disorder effected by the consolidation of royal power at the expense of the ecclesiastical jurisdiction', it would nevertheless shape the English political and social culture of Tudor England.[16] And, although the king's appropriation of all jurisdictional authority from the Pope certainly defines the English Reformation, the clash between the common law and canon law courts was much more muted than one would expect. In the sixteenth century, according to J. H. Baker, 'The English ecclesiastical courts, with their staple business of family and probate law, were generally distanced from the theological debates attending the Reformation and the rise of Protestantism, and generally escaped alteration' (131). Far more disruptive were the religious houses and their occupants. These created complications for English legal culture that early modern literary works, including the plays by Bale, Peele, and Shakespeare, tried to acknowledge and articulate.

Setting the Stage for Monasticism

Early modern narratives about King John powerfully reflect these jurisdictional conflicts of the sixteenth century, having at their disposal John's dispute with the Pope, which led to the king's excommunication, as well as the historical events surrounding

[13] G. H. Cook, *Letters to Cromwell and Others on the Suppression of the Monasteries* (London: John Baker Publishers, 1965), 38.

[14] G. W. Bernard, *The King's Reformation: Henry VIII and the Remaking of the English Church* (New Haven: Yale University Press, 2005), 228.

[15] 'The Judgment of Martin Luther on Monastic Vows' in *Luther's Works*, 44, ed. James Atkinson (Philadelphia: Fortress Press, 1966): 263.

[16] Bradin Cormack, *A Power to Do Justice: Jurisdiction, English Literature and the Rise of Common Law, 1509–1625* (Chicago: Chicago University Press, 2008), 91.

AD 1215. In that year King John signed Magna Carta, while in Rome the Fourth Lateran Council issued its momentous edicts. The former would be taken up in the later sixteenth and seventeenth centuries as a kind of founding document of English shared governance; the latter established transubstantiation as orthodoxy, limited the number of religious houses, asserted the primacy of the Pope, and clarified the procedure for dealing with accusations against ecclesiastics. At Runnymede and Rome, the seeds of jurisdictional conflict were sown, and dramatists in the sixteenth century fixed on these events as a way of making sense of their own legal and cultural situation.

Like all history plays, Bale's *King Johan*, Peele's *Troublesome Reign*, and Shakespeare's *King John* divide our temporal focus. We pay attention most directly to the moment the events represented in the plays take place: here the first fifteen years of the thirteenth century. But we also hear the hum of the time in which each play was written and staged. It is important to acknowledge at the outset, as most scholars now agree, that Peele and Shakespeare, writing in the 1590s, did not read or even have knowledge of Bale's earlier play from the mid-1530s.[17] My purpose in this chapter then is correspondingly to explore neither how Peele and Shakespeare adapted an earlier work, nor even how the playwrights differently handled discrete historical events. Rather, I treat the three texts as a series of historically situated symptomatic responses in English culture (and more broadly Western European culture) to a single cause. And the cause is monasticism.

Like other medieval and early modern writers, John Bale used King John's reign for a variety of polemical purposes.[18] Rooted in the tradition of the English allegorical drama, *King Johan*, Bale's strange morality/history hybrid, feels less like a plotted set of events and characters than a series of embodied contentions, of opposed, recognizable forces vivified. Yet the play is concerned not merely with timeless truths, but with political struggles in historical time. Specifically, it rehearses the quarrel in which King John tried to refuse Pope Innocent III's choice for Archbishop of Canterbury, Stephen Langton. Confronting personified abstractions who argue for Papal supremacy, King John valiantly but unsuccessfully tries to maintain his sovereignty against Rome. The play winds up looking forward to Imperial Majesty, a stand-in for Henry VIII and, in a later version, to Elizabeth, for its sense of resolution.

In *King Johan*, Bale sets in motion an extended deliberation on the source and role of the law. John's declaration at the beginning of the play that he is there 'To reforme the laws and sett men in good order, / That trew iustyce may be had in every bordere' (20–1) calls forth the character England, a 'poore wedowe' come to complain to the King of having been 'ungodly usyd' by the clergy, who have been abetted by:

[17] However, see James H. Morey, 'The Death of King John in Shakespeare and Bale', *SQ*, 45.3 (Autumn, 1994), 327–31, for an argument that 'the accounts of the death of John by Shakespeare and by Bale are significantly alike and … that the parallels between the deaths of John's monkish poisoner and Judas Iscariot must be considered when assessing the character of John at the end of Shakespeare's play' (327). Even Morey, however, stops short of claiming that Shakespeare based his play on Bale's.

[18] See Carole Levin, 'A Good Prince: King John and Early Tudor Propanda', *SCJ*, 11.4 (Winter, 1980), 23–32; and May Mattson, *Five Plays about King John* (Uppsala: Acta Universitatis Upsaliensis, 1977).

> Suche lubbers as hath dysgysed heads in [th]er hoodes,
> Whych in ydelnes do lyve by other menns goodes:
> Monkes, chanons and nones, in dyvers coloure and shappe,
> Bothe whyght, black and pyed. (1.36–9)

In this way, at the very beginning of his play, Bale links the necessity of legal reform to the presence of the religious; their existence in England undermines a juridically sound nation, an idea Bale emphasizes throughout the play. Part of the problem with the religious, Bale makes explicit, is their relation to ownership; living by 'by other menns goodes', they exist outside of a productive economy and thus become illegible to the legal economy.

If the main historical antagonists of *King Johan* are the Pope and his agents—including the religious—the main *allegorical* antagonist is Sedition (later identified with Stephen Langton). Through this character, Bale establishes the religious as fundamentally contrary to national sovereignty. Sedition claims that 'In every relygyon and munkysh secte I rayne' (1.187). Already threatened by those who purport to 'rayne,' the King expresses his interest, asking 'Yff thow be a cloysterer, tell of what order thow art' (1.193), but Sedition insists that he plays a part 'In every estate of [th]e clergye' (1.194), especially among the religious. Moreover, he claims 'this company hath provided for me mortmayne / For [th]at I myght ever among ther sort remayne' (1.205–6).[19] This claim is a conceptual crux for the play's legal argument. Mortmain, according to the *OED*, is 'The condition of lands or tenements held inalienably by an ecclesiastical or other corporation; lands or tenements so held'. Lord Coke commented that:

> the true cause of the name and the meaning thereof was taken from the effects … so as the lands were said to come to dead hands as to the lords for that by alienation in mortmaine they lost wholly their escheats, and in effect their knights-service for the defence of the realme, wards, marriages, reliefes and the like; and therefore was called a dead hand, for a dead hand yeeldeth no service.[20]

While eschewing property, the religious relied on various theoretical constructs structured for their use or enjoyment, rather than ownership, of property. This ambiguous relation to property was important to their own identity as a community; from the law's point of view it was a defining relation because it substantiated the claim to immunity. So, when Sedition avers that 'this company hath provided for me mortmayne', it is

[19] The *OED* does not list any English uses of the term as far back as 1215, the approximate date of the events represented in the play. The *OED* adds 'Alienations in mortmain, as being injurious to the rights of the crown and the mesne lords, were forbidden under English law by Act 7 Edw. I, st. 2 (see quot. 1279 in etymological note) and many subsequent Acts, known as the "Statutes of Mortmain". In practice, however, such grants continued after 1279, but now required prior royal licence.'

[20] A. H. Oosterhoff, 'The Law of Mortmain: An Historical and Comparative Review', *UTLJ*, 27.3 (Summer, 1977), 257–334, 259.

possible to hear the accusation being directed both at the audience ('this company')—as having provided to Sedition (and thus monasticism) a perpetual property in England and at the religious ('this company')—as having established sedition permanently in England. Since property held in mortmain could not be alienated and was not subject to traditional feudal dues, the religious were able through it to remain outside of the normal patterns of property law, this through a kind of immunizing loophole within the law itself. And so, Bale's play suggests that Papal jurisdictional claims undermine common law culture. Such interference produces, according to the play, unstable situations that will undermine English cohesion until resolved.

Legal Critique and Dramatic Convention

Throughout Bale's play, then, the religious are identified as sources of civil unrest, as elements that unsettle a legal apparatus trying to establish itself more securely. George Peele's *The Troublesome Reign of King John* similarly uses John's period of rule to explore, but now at more length, property, immunity, and the law. If Bale's play wants to engage with the relations of king and Pope, of the temporal and spiritual powers, as a way of typologizing Henry VIII and celebrating his fulfilment of John's work, Peele seems more interested in the law's internal relations, of how law relates to itself, and how it reproduces itself through practices such as inheritance. Peele's *Troublesome Reign*, which in contrast to Bale's play does not engage in allegorical representation, begins with a juxtaposition of two similar legal cases. First, the French king (on behalf of Prince Arthur) claims that King John is not the rightful possessor of the English throne since Arthur is John's deceased older brother's son. Then, John is asked to adjudicate a case in which a younger brother asserts that he, rather than his older brother, is the rightful heir of the family's property. The sheriff brings in the brothers—Philip (the elder) and Robert Falconbridge—describing how they:

> unnaturally falling at odds about their father's living, have broken your Highness' peace in seeking to right their own wrongs without course of law or order of justice, and unlawfully assembled themselves in mutinous manner, having committed a riot, appealing from trial in their county to your Highness. (1.77–83)

This passage thematizes one of the major issues of all the King John plays: people at all levels of the political spectrum seek 'to right their own wrongs without course of law'. Replete with legal terms—the father's 'living', the king's 'peace', unlawful assembly, mutiny, 'riot', appeal 'from trial in their county'—the sheriff's speech invites reflection on the language by which the law imagines and legitimates ownership. According to the play's most recent editor, 'Falconbridge's inheritance, being too problematic for local adjudication, has been referred to the highest court of appeal, the King himself.'[21] While George W. Keeton has described this scene as one that 'abounds with legal absurdities', it does reflect John's extensive involvement in legal cases.[22] J. H. Baker points out that John concerned himself more fully with the administration of justice in England than did his Plantagenet forebears, noting that he 'seems to have been chiefly responsible for encouraging such [legal] proceedings before himself. So far did this trend proceed that in 1209 the Bench at Westminster was completely discontinued'.[23] John's personal involvement in the law seems to have encouraged playwrights to turn to his reign as a site in which to explore the law.

In Peele's play, King John, at first, criticizes the younger brother, Robert Falconbridge, for daring to 'make a question in so plain a case' (1.114), but Robert turns that critique back on the King with the assertion that 'The proof [is] so plain, the argument so strong' (1.161). Here Peele sets in motion the key arguments of his play, that what looks like clear proof is liable to be met by an equally clear yet opposed legal proof; that there must be some mechanism by which to adjudicate those claims; and that this mechanism is sovereign power. The King announces, 'This is my doom, and this my doom shall stand / Irrevocable, as I am King of England' (1.213–14). The irony here is that, given the French king's claim, the audience does not truly know whether John is, in fact, the proper 'King of England'. Taken together, the scenes double down on the question of opposed viewpoints and judicial decision, since the legitimacy of the monarch's 'doom' itself must be in question, subject to challenge.

Robert Falconbridge disputes his older brother Philip's right as heir because, he claims, his older brother is 'base born and base begot—no Falconbridge'.[24] Although King John is skeptical, he decides to let Philip and his mother pronounce the 'doom', asking them who the father was. Philip finally admits that he is 'no Falconbridge', claiming 'I am King Richard's son' (l.282). Unlike in Shakespeare, where, as we shall see, it does not matter who the biological father is, here John tells Philip that this admission has lost him 'thy living and thy land' (l.288). Then, as if in compensation, John redubs him Richard Plantagenet and rewards him. The structure of the renunciation and recovery is suggestive. In choosing to 'let land and living go', in renouncing his right to lands and then accepting King Richard as his father, Philip Falconbridge gains a freedom that is akin to that of the monk who gives up his own property in exchange for the higher community that is the family of the king. In the first scene, Peele introduces inheritance

[21] *Troublesome*, n. 85 (120).

[22] George Keeton, *Shakespeare's Legal and Political Background* (New York: Barnes and Noble, 1967); quoted in ibid.

[23] J. H. Baker, *An Introduction to English Legal History* (London: Butterworths, 1979), 19. If John's actions here are characterized by a certain monarchical overreach, they do not appear to represent a dangerous incursion into, much less a neglect of, the legal system.

[24] Robert claims, correctly it turns out, that Philip is the son of Richard the Lion Heart. The ambiguity of the term 'base born' is highlighted here as Philip, though conceived out of wedlock, is the child of a king.

law as a paradigm of all law, as natural, evident, and self-regulating, the 'certain right of England's ancient law' (110). But when asked to do work, that law becomes elusive, self-contradictory, and subject to power, which allows Peele to show the law of inheritance, which fails to name or define Philip, ceding its authority and enfranchising him to choose his own jurisdiction.

Throughout the play, doubled claims of sovereignty have the tendency to produce a sense of immunity, since they reveal that one may be subject to neither. When an Austrian Duke refuses Philip the Bastard's challenge to a duel, King John admits his lack of sovereignty: 'we cannot force the duke to fight, / Being a subject unto neither realm' (1.5.38–9). Neither of France, nor of England, the Duke inhabits a liminal space of apparent autonomy, 'subject unto neither realm'. Later, Pandulph, the Pope's emissary, threatens that John will be excommunicated for refusing to accept Stephen Langton as Archbishop.[25] John replies, 'as I am king, so will I reign next under God, supreme head both over spiritual and temporal' (1.5.79–81). The adverbial phrase 'as I am king' recapitulates the basic question of whether John is in fact the rightful king. Moreover, it points to the problem posed by communities that locate their sovereignty differently: the monks, who, claimed as subjects by both the Pope and the king, think of themselves as 'subject unto neither realm', their allegiance being to their rule. This evasion of subjecthood can also be produced by the idea that conscience trumps the law. When, for example, Prince Arthur is imprisoned, he uses that argument to persuade the king's henchman not to murder him, that is, to disobey the king; although 'a subject dwelling in the land / Is tied to execute the King's command', Arthur says, 'Yet God commands, whose power reacheth further' (1.12.80–2). To ignore the King's command on the basis of conscience is to claim a freedom from all temporal jurisdiction.

King John seems to understand the threat that conscience represents, and he connects it explicitly to the immunity of monks. He decides to use them as a means to assert his worldly power, saying, 'where I of abbots, monks and friars / Have taken somewhat to maintain my wars, / Now will I take no more but all they have. / I'll rouse the lazy lubbers from their cells, / And in despite I'll send them to the Pope' (1.5.123–6). A few scenes later, having won the battle in France and taken Arthur prisoner, he returns to his purpose of divesting the monks of their holdings. He makes Philip his executor (in effect, his Thomas Cromwell), telling him to 'Ransack the abbeys, cloisters, priories. Convert their coin unto my soldiers' use. / And whatso'er he be within my land / That goes to Rome for justice and for law, / While he may have his right within the realm / Let him be judged a traitor to the state' (1.9.16–24). Anachronistically invoking the concept of *praemunire*, which would become so important during the Reformation, and ordering that the religious houses be ransacked, John asserts a total sovereignty over the Church and the

[25] In the context of this discussion, it is perhaps worth noting that while Pope Innocent III chose Stephan Langton as Archbishop, and the king wanted John de Gray, the monks 'were more than ever determined that one of their own number should fill the vacancy. They secretly held an election and chose their prior, Reginald'. W. L. Warren, *King John* (Berkeley: University of California Press, 1961), 161.

religious.[26] Philip is eager to do the plundering, musing, 'I long to be at home / To dive into the monks' and abbots' bags, / To make some sport among the smooth-skin nuns, / And keep some revel with the fausen friars' (9.42–4). In scene 13, Philip makes good on that promise as he arrives at a monastery and finds the expected lechery and treasure. This representation, borrowed from a long line of anti-fraternal satires, sees the monks not as defined by a threatening autonomy, but rather as minions of the Pope, corrupted by their access to financial and sexual favours. Peele's play thus cultivates the elements of a legal critique of sovereignty itself, only to preemptively dismantle that critique by reverting to a conventional representation of the religious. Moreover, in taxing the religious, King John can imagine that he has successfully asserted his sovereignty over them; the play, however, suggests otherwise.

Shakespeare and Sovereign Vows

Where Bale allegorizes the struggle for power between Pope and king, representing the religious as both cause and instrument of civil discord, Peele dramatizes contradictions within the law. He presents the religious as potentially autonomous but then undermines his critique by reverting to conventional stereotypes. Shakespeare, in contrast, sets up his play as a meditation on law itself, and specifically on immunity and the sovereign exception.[27] The beginning of Shakespeare's play inherits from Peele the juxtaposition of two cases, one in which King John's legal standing is challenged and one in which national law is revealed as synonymous with the will of the king (as long as he can enforce it). Like Peele's play, Shakespeare's *Life and Death of King John* opens first with France demanding the kingdom for Arthur, based on inheritance protocols, followed by the conflict of the Falconbridge brothers, the younger Robert claiming the right of inheritance over his elder brother, Philip. In both cases, the outcome rewards those whom the law—as the play understands it—should not support.

When King John asserts his right to the throne based on 'Our strong possession and our right for us', his mother and ally, Queen Eleanor, pointedly corrects him: 'Your strong possession / much more than your right / Or else it must go wrong with you and me' (1.1.39–42). Here the play asks the reader to acknowledge the lack of legitimacy in John's claim, while simultaneously reminding us that possession itself—no matter how acquired—functions as a form of legitimacy. In the second case, Robert Falconbridge

[26] The charge of praemunire, which was used to bring down Wolsey, made it an offence to 'prosecute in a foreign court a suit which was triable in an English jurisdiction, and in particular to turn from an English court to the Papal courts. Praemunire was first created by the Statutes of Provisors of 1351 and 1353', B. J. Sokol and Mary Sokol, *Shakespeare's Legal Language: A Dictionary* (London: Continuum, 2004), 277.

[27] See Ken Jackson, '"Is It God or the Sovereign Exception?": Giorgio Agamben's *Homo Sacer* and Shakespeare's *King John*', *Religion & Literature*, 38.3 (Autumn, 2006), 85–100.

asserts his inheritance rights based on the claim that his elder brother Philip is a bastard (fathered by King Richard with Lady Falconbridge rather than by her husband) and, further, that Sir Falconbridge 'upon his deathbed / ... by will bequeathed / His lands to me, and took it on his death / That this my mother's son was none of his' (1.1.109–11). As Sokol and Sokol note, 'King John replies correctly by reciting the common law rule that married women cannot bear bastards', even if the father's will names the younger brother heir. Before the 1540 Statute of Wills, 'a simple devise of lands by will was nearly impossible, while the customary rule of primogeniture prevented the disinheritance of an elder son of family lands'.[28] Shakespeare's scene contrasts with the analogous one in *The Troublesome Reign*, where John rules that Philip should lose his lands due to his illegitimacy. While Shakespeare presents a more accurate version of the law, his scene also emphasizes the force of legal fictions. The case in question turns on the fact that the law recognizes a concept of paternity starkly at odds with ordinary language usage. As if to highlight the artifice, the scene then undoes the legal judgement it has just staged. Despite the decision that awards Philip his father's estate, King John and his mother convince him to abjure his rights of inheritance in order to serve them.[29] Philip later recounts, 'I have disclaimed Sir Robert; and my land, / Legitimation, name, and all is gone' (1.1.247–8). In this statement, Philip asserts an autonomy—linked to a renunciation of 'legitimation'—that will haunt the play. And so, in the end, the illegitimate king remains on the throne, while the younger brother inherits his father's estate. The result is a sociopolitical world defined by the sovereign exception, in which the rule of law seems defined by caprice. In Ken Jackson's view, 'Shakespeare comes very close to casting the whole question of sovereign legitimacy as a matter of pure and simple violence or force'.[30]

Like Bale and Peele, Shakespeare invokes the religious as an important part of King John's story. Within the first fifty lines of his play, he declares that 'our abbeys and priories shall pay / This expeditious charge' of going to France to defend his right to the throne (1.1.48–9). In all three plays, then, the religious are made to occupy a position of burden and exemption: in Bale, they exist outside the community because they fail to pay their debts to it, while in Peele and Shakespeare, they are identified as those who will be made to bear the burden precisely because of their attempts to live beyond the law.

If the idea of living beyond the law collapses for all three writers into the idea of lawlessness, the reasons and expressions differ. Bale associates the religious with the Pope and thus asserts that they necessarily lack all legal standing. Peele sees them as purveyors of sexual and financial misdeeds. For Shakespeare, the lawlessness relates to a single

[28] Sokol and Sokol, *Shakespeare's Legal Language*, 28.

[29] Among the scholars who have recentlty discussed inheritance in Shakespeare's *King John* are Thomas Anderson, '"Legitimation, Name, and All Is Gone": Bastardy and Bureaucracy in Shakespeare's *King John*', *Journal for Early Modern Cultural Studies*, 4.2 (Fall–Winter, 2004), 35–61; and James P. Saeger, 'Illegitimate Subjects: Performing Bastardy in *King John*', *The Journal of English and Germanic Philology*, 100.1 (January, 2001), 1–21.

[30] 'Is It God or the Sovereign Exception?', 86.

incident, found also in his two predecessors. The identification of the religious with lawlessness in this context stems from the English *Brut Chronicle*, which reported that King John, after a long dispute with the Pope, was poisoned by a monk.[31] Bale elaborates on the scene. In his play, the Archbishop and the Cardinal plot against King John, while a figure called Dissimulation harvests the poison of a toad. Absolving the monk who will deliver the poison, the Archbishop tells him that his soul will be sung to paradise: five brothers, he says, 'wyll daylye praye for the sowle of father Symon, / A Cisteane monke which poysened kynge Iohn' (2047). Here, Bale invokes a whole set of conventional criticisms of monks: that they are involved with esoteric, even demonic, knowledge; that they are secretive, political, and ruthless; that they are central to the practice of indulgences, purgatory, and intercessory prayer; and that, in contrast to their claims to poverty, they are avaricious, stealing from, rather than helping, the 'nedye'.

Peele too makes much of the conflict. He has the soon-to-be killer, Monk Thomas soliloquize, 'Is this the king that never loved a friar / Is this the man that doth condemn the Pope / … / Is this the king that aims at abbeys' lands?' (2.6.84–8). The revelation of the poisoning and the death scene provide the dramatic climax to Peele's play. Realizing what has happened, the King cries out, 'The monk! The devil! The poison 'gins to rage. / It will depose myself, a king, from reign' (2.8.46–7). Like Bale, Peele equates the religious with the Pope and the devil; both writers suggest that the problem posed by monasticism is primarily one of jurisdictional politics. After the king's death, Philip (the Bastard) explains, 'This is the fruit of popery when true kings / Are slain and shouldered out by monks and friars' (2.8.114–15). The effect, as we have seen, is that at the end of *The Troublesome Reign*, Peele withdraws from the complexity at which his text had hinted to present a more straightforward tension between two forces: the Catholic Church (including the religious) and the English sovereign. John's son, Prince (now King) Henry, thus begins his own reign with the words: 'Sweet Uncle, if thou love thy sovereign, / Let not a stone of Swinstead Abbey stand, / But pull the house about the friars' ears' (2.9.16–162). Staged as a rehearsal and justification of the Dissolution, this scene acknowledges the threat that monasticism poses to English sovereignty and law but retreats from identifying that threat as anything other than contested jurisdiction.

Shakespeare, however, is interested less in jurisdictional conflict than in immunity and exception. He is rather more terse about John's death, building up complexity by paring away explanation. In his play, one character simply relates that, 'The King, I fear, is poisoned by a monk … A monk, I tell you, a resolved villain' (5.6.24–30). Whereas Bale and Peele have their characters carefully explain why the Church still wants King John dead and how the monk will murder him, Shakespeare offers his playgoers a resounding silence. The monk never even makes an appearance onstage and, as Forker points out, we are left to puzzle out why he murdered the king.[32] Indeed, by the end of Shakespeare's play the king has reconciled with, or rather submitted to, the Pope. Thus, if we believe

[31] Adams, introduction to *John Bale's 'King Johan'*, 33.

[32] *Troublesome*, 283, n. 66.

the monk to be merely an instrument of the Pope, there is little reason for him to kill the king. Framed this way, the killing represents not the clash of jurisdictional power so much as the frightening autonomy of the religious; they function not as a weapon of the Pope but rather as figures devoted to a form of life, subject to no law as such.

All three histories explore the problem of divided loyalties for the law, but Shakespeare's play finds something even more worrisome: the monk whose loyalties are not divided, but totally withdrawn. Although the word monasticism is derived from the Greek *monos*, 'alone', cenobitic—rather than eremitic—monasticism had by the Renaissance become the dominant monastic form, providing a powerful example of what a community could be.[33] As we have seen, though, a community—as Esposito defines it—is not a kind of corporate existence or organic entity, not a *res publica*, but rather a kind of lack or debt, that to which one has an obligation. What degrades community, according to Esposito, is dispensation from obligation. Seen in this light, monasticism's legal aporia stems from the fact that it depends essentially on an immunity from the community of the polis, or the kingdom, or, as we shall see, even the Church.[34] Theodore de Beza, the Protestant disciple of Calvin, who had great influence in England, makes such an accusation against monks, claiming that:

> they deny that they bée subiectes to the Bishop within their Di|ocesse, ... if they alleadge their Priueledge of exemption, let them shewe that the holye ghost doth euer deny or gainsay himself.[35]

Here Beza, like many other Reformers, honed in on the religious' immunity, their 'Priviledge of exemption', as an unjustifiablly disruptive social force. Indeed, as mentioned before, even Erasmus 'believed it would be useful if monks were brought more

[33] As G. W. Bernard notes, in *The King's Reformation: Henry VIII and the Remaking of the English Church* (New Haven: Yale University Press, 2005), 'In May 1529 Wolsey was granted executive powers to proceed, converting abbacies into bishoprics and uniting monasteries unable to support twelve members.... In justification, it was maintained that religion could not be properly observed except in communities with sufficient monks or nuns. Individuals scattered in small monasteries brought nothing but discredit on religion' (231).

[34] Many of the criticisms of the Jesuits, even from other Catholics, aim at the immunities that the order claims, immunities that unsettle jurisdictions and undo community. Antoine Arnauld (1560–1619) in *The arrainment of the whole society of Iesuits in France*, 1594, for example, claims that:

> This new felowship, ... endowed with so many and sundrie priuileges, licences and freedomes, ... it bringeth in ... an vtter ouerthrow of monasticall life & tending rather to the pulling downe then to the building vp of the Christian faith. (24)

The problem, as Arnaud sees it, is that the Jesuits do not distinguish themselves from secular priests ('carying no difference') in appearance or duties as monks do ('in shaving of their crownes', etc.), and yet they are endowed 'with so many and sundrie priuileges, licences and freedomes' that mark them out *ex communitatem*. It is the same accusation that Protestant reformers make against monks. They don't want to bear the burden (the '*munus*') that delineates the community, but they want privileges that only the community can grant, privileges related to the proper workings of the community.

[35] *A briefe and piththie summe of the Christian faith*, 180.

completely under the authority of the bishops ... [with] the extension of episcopal oversight to houses legally exempt from such control' (228). Both to Protestant Reformers and Catholics, monastic exemptions or immunity presented itself as a problem.

Giorgio Agamben has recently analysed how monastic immunity develops logically, almost inevitably, from within the intellectual framework of monasticism.[36] Agamben describes how the monastic rule differs from the prescription, the regulation, the law, since 'A norm that does not refer to single acts and events, but to the entire existence of an individual, to his *forma vivendi*', is no longer recognizable as law (26). Moreover, this kind of norm has a specific genealogy: 'The blossoming of monastic rules beginning from the fifth century ... which tends toward an undecidability of *regula* and *vita*, constitutes, according to [St] Thomas, a phenomenon that is substantially alien to the Roman juridical tradition and to law *tout court*' (29). In other words, monasticism is organized not by a finite set of prescriptions, but rather as a holistic way of living that distances it from externally imposed prescriptions. Embodying a monastic rule, the religious assert an immunity from the law.[37]

An earlier scene in Shakespeare's play remarkably encapsulates the problems of immunity and the law. In Act 2, King John and King Philip both arrive at the French town of Angers, the former to claim it for himself, the latter to claim it for Arthur, whom he declares the rightful King of England. King Philip's language is instructive, entreating the citizens 'To pay that duty which you truly owe / To him that owes [owns] it' (2.1.247–8). For Shakespeare, here, clearly influenced by feudal theory, a community is constituted by the 'duty' that one 'owes' to it. The sense of obligation that defines community and subjecthood can be heard especially clearly in the polysemy of the word 'owe', which simultaneously means 'to be indebted to' and 'to own'. Those two concepts are inextricably linked as part of a relationship of mutual obligation. To refuse that duty is to claim an immunity, which is precisely what the citizens of Angers do. They adamantly refuse to choose a side, replying rather 'In brief, we are the King of England's subjects. / For him and in his right we hold this town'. Assured of himself, King John states, 'Acknowledge then the King, and let me in'. But the Citizen replies, 'That can we not; but he that proves the king, / To him will we prove loyal; till that time / Have we rammed up our gates against the world' (2.1.270–2). At this moment, the citizen occupies what I have been arguing is the subject position of monasticism, embodying its

[36] Giorgio Agamben, *The Highest Poverty: Monastic Rules and Form-of-Life* tr. Adam Kotsko (Stanford: Stanford University Press, 2013).

[37] The clearest place to consider that source for immunity is, perhaps, in the fourteenth-century quarrel between Pope John XXII and the Franciscans over the issue of property. Although articulated in the fourteenth century, this debate underlies the entire history of cenobitic monasticism, from its earliest stages through the sixteenth century, since 'the contemplative orders regarded landownership as necessary for their independence and autonomy from the secular power'. What the religious required, ultimately, was a way to exercise dominion without owning anything. Only such an arrangement could guarantee the autonomy they needed, but it then expressed itself externally as a kind of a threat to the sovereign. Richard Tuck, *Natural Rights Theories: Their Origin And Development* (Cambridge: Cambridge University Press, 1987), 20.

threat to the legal order: recognizing no king, no earthly ruler but the True King, they remain loyal only to a form-of-life, their gates rammed up in the interim against the world. And it is precisely this claimed exemption from obligation to any identifiable legal authority that puts the citizens of Angers in Shakespeare at risk of destruction, as it would put the monasteries themselves in the path of destruction in the 1530s, when Bale was writing his play.

Shakespeare continues his exploration of religious immunity by turning to the illocutionary act that transforms a subject into a member of an order. Agamben points out that 'The problem of the relationship between the rules and the law is complicated by the fact that beginning at a certain point the profession of the monastic life was associated with the pledge of a vow. The vow is an institution that, like the oath, most likely belongs to that more archaic sphere in which it is impossible to distinguish between law and religion' (37). Such vows are central to much of the plot of all three King John plays.

In Bale, when King John asks Nobility and Clergy why they hew to the Pope rather than to the king, Nobility replies, 'For I toke an othe to defend [th]e chyrche ever more' (1474). Clergy adds 'I am proffessyd to the ryghtes eccleysastycall' (1476). The King criticizes these reasons: 'Yowr othe is growndyd, fyrst, uppon folyshenes, / And yowr professyon uppon moche pevyshenes' (1484–5). For Bale, much is at stake in the swearing of oaths and vows. Indeed, he titled his massive partisan history of the religious *The actes or vnchast examples of the Englysh votaryes,* as if the very act of vowing oneself to something were a soul-threatening proposition. And for Bale and many of the reformers, that is exactly the case. Cornelius Martin, for example, explains, in his *Principles Concerning Vowes*:

> A Vow is a promise of things lawfull, and possible, made vnto God, with aduised deliberation, and to a godlie end; wherby a man bindeth himselfe to the performance of some thing.
>
> But we are to take heede, that wee vowe nothing that is vnlawfull; . . . . For it is vnlawefull to promise, or to offer any thing vnto God, that displeaseth him: Next, wee are to bee carefull, that our vowes be not of light, and jesting matters: third|ly, that they be not of thinges that are impossible for vs to performe.[38]

And Thomas Becon says even more simply, 'Whatsoeuer is not of fayth, is sinne, sayth the Apostle. But these monasticall vowes are not of fayth (for they haue no grounde in the worde of God) therfore are they sinne.'[39] The question of the vow, and of the oath, was central to sixteenth-century society.[40] And the Reformers attended to all the particularities of the vow as a way of showing that the very act by which one joined a religious order

[38] Théodore de Bèze, *Propositions and principles of diuinitie propounded and disputed in the vniuersitie of Geneua* (Edinburgh: Waldegrave, 1591).

[39] Thomas Becon, *The reliques of Rome contayning all such matters of religion* (London, 1563).

[40] See, for example, John Michael Gray, *Oaths and the English Reformation* (Cambridge: Cambridge University Press, 2013).

was in itself hateful to God. Martin Luther wrote an entire tract on the subject, arguing that 'the monastic vow is in itself a most dangerous thing because it is without the authority and example of Scripture.'[41]

While Shakespeare does not explicitly address the vows of the religious in his play, he does stage the problems at the heart of religious vows. In Act III of *The Life and Death*, just as the French King Philip concludes a marriage settlement with King John, Cardinal Pandolf enters accusing John of heresy. King Philip does not want to side against John, because, he says, they are now 'coupled and linked together / With all religious strength of sacred vows' (3.1.228–9). He asks whether he shall 'unswear faith sworn' (3.1.245). But the Cardinal replies, 'O, let thy vow / First made to heaven, first be to heaven performed' (3.1.265–6), since what 'thou swor'st is sworn against thyself / And may not be performed by thyself' (3.1.194–5), and since:

> It is religion that doth make vows kept,
> But thou hast sworn against religion:
> By what thou swear'st, against the thing thou swear'st;
> And mak'st an oath the surety for thy troth:
> Against an oath the truth; thou art unsure
> To swear: swear'st only not to be forsworn—
> Else what a mockery should it be to swear? (3.1.279–86)

The Cardinal's cynicism about vows and his essential point that vows taken to unholy ends are no true vows were familiar points made by mid-century Reformers, including Bale, against the religious. The Cardinal's words underline those moments when two (or more) seemingly legitimate duties come into conflict, with few means of distinguishing which presents the best case. Even more threatening, perhaps, is the Cardinal's initial claim that 'It is religion that doth make vows kept, / But thou hast sworn against religion'. The implication here is that the only vows that truly bind are religious vows; political vows or oaths, he seems to imply, that challenge established religion (read: Roman Catholicism) hold no power. For an audience attuned to the significance of political oaths, the Cardinal's language may have produced a shudder of recognition. Underlining the inefficacy, indeed the emptiness of political oaths compared to religious vows, Shakespeare's play ends with two opposed scenes of vows being played out. King John achieves 'victory' over the French by vowing himself to the Pope (which he earlier swore he would not do) and through the English lords' withdrawal from an oath to the French Dauphin. Finally, the play ends with the monk's poisoning of King John, suggesting that the monk's vow overreached any supposed obligations to king or Pope. In returning to oaths and vows throughout the play, Shakespeare highlights the illocutionary act that creates the religious as followers of a form-of-life that exists always beyond the reach of the law.

[41] 'The Judgment of Martin Luther on Monastic Vows', trans. James Atkinson, in *Luther's Works*, 44, ed. James Atkinson (Philadelphia: Fortress Press, 1966), 252.

This chapter has argued that the plays of Bale, Peele, and Shakespeare construct various versions of a legal history concerned with the problem monasticism posed for English legal culture. Both Bale's and Peele's plays provide a legal rationale for the dissolution of the monasteries. Depicting the religious as foreign agents devoted to undermining the king, Bale's *King Johan* drives toward the conclusion that a sovereign must eliminate all rival claimants, that such an act is the foundation of any effective law-bound community. Peele introduces mitigating factors, showing that the law is always in an unstable relationship with itself, that legal justifications for inheriting an estate, for example, may not apply to inheriting a crown. But in both of these plays, the religious are ultimately presented as figures in a simple legal equation; as representatives of the Pope and Church law, the religious infringe the rights of the sovereign. Shakespeare focuses much more forcefully on the artifice of sovereignty. Here, the strongest legal maxim is a tautology and an illocutionary act. And for Shakespeare, the religious do not threaten the law by positing another law, but by withdrawing from it, by claiming an exemption that is, by definition, uncontrollable. Where Bale and Peele see in the story of King John an auspicious precursor to the dissolution of the monasteries, Shakespeare points to a graver outcome: the mutual threat that religious communities and the law pose to one another.

Bibliography

Agamben, Giorgio. *The Highest Poverty: Monastic Rules and Form-of-Life*, trans. Adam Kotsko (Stanford: Stanford University Press, 2013).

Anderson, Thomas. '"Legitimation, Name, and All Is Gone": Bastardy and Bureaucracy in Shakespeare's *King John*', *Journal for Early Modern Cultural Studies*, 4.2 (Fall/Winter, 2004): 35–61.

Baker, J. H. *An Introduction to English Legal History* (London: Butterworths, 1979).

Bale, John. *John Bale's 'King Johan'*, ed. Barry B. Adams (San Marino: The Huntington Library, 1969).

Bernard, G. W. *The King's Reformation: Henry VIII and the Remaking of the English Church* (New Haven and London: Yale University Press, 2005).

Cook, G. H. *Letters to Cromwell and Others on the Suppression of the Monasteries* (London: John Baker Publishers, 1965).

Cormack, Bradin. *A Power to Do Justice: Jurisdiction, English Literature, and the Rise of Common Law, 1509–1625* (Chicago: University of Chicago Press, 2008).

Esposito, Roberto. *Communitas: The Origin and Destiny of Community* (Stanford: Stanford University Press, 2010).

Gray, John Michael. *Oaths and the English Reformation* (Cambridge: Cambridge University Press, 2013).

Jackson, Ken. '"Is It God or the Sovereign Exception?" Giorgio Agamben's *Homo Sacer* and Shakespeare's *King John*', *Religion & Literature*, 38.3 (Autumn, 2006): 85–100.

Jordan, Constance and Karen Cunningham, ed. *The Law in Shakespeare* (Basingstoke: Palgrave Macmillan, 2010).

Kaartinen, Marjo. *Religious Life and English Culture in the Reformation* (Basingstoke: Palgrave Macmillan, 2002).
Keeton, George W. *Shakespeare's Legal and Political Background* (New York: Barnes and Noble, 1967).
Levin, Carole. 'A Good Prince: King John and Early Tudor Propanda', *The Sixteenth Century Journal*, 11.4 (Winter, 1980): 23–32.
Mattson, May, ed. *Five Plays about King John* (Uppsala: Acta Universitatis Upsaliensis, 1977).
Montaigne, Michel de. *The Essayes of Montaigne: John Florio's Translation*, ed. J. I. M. Stewart (New York: The Modern Library, 1933).
Peele, George. *The Troublesome Reign of John, King of England*, ed. Charles R. Forker (Manchester: Manchester University Press, 2011).
Saeger, James P. 'Illegitimate Subjects: Performing Bastardy in *King John*', *The Journal of English and Germanic Philology*, 100.1 (January, 2001): 1–21.
Shakespeare, William. 'King John', in *The Norton Shakespeare*, 2nd edn, ed. Stephen Greenblatt, et al. (New York: W. W. Norton and Company, 1997), 492–549.
Sokol, B. J. and Mary Sokol. *Shakespeare's Legal Language: A Dictionary* (London: Continuum, 2004).
Szittya, Penn. *The Antifraternal Tradition in Medieval Literature* (Princeton: Princeton University Press, 1986).
Tuck, Richard. *Natural Rights Theories: Their Origin and Development* (Cambridge: Cambridge University Press, 1987).
Warren, W. L. *King John* (Berkeley: University of California Press, 1961).

CHAPTER 16

EPIEIKEIA AND CONSCIENCE

ALAN CROMARTIE

HUMAN social interaction has a complexity exceeding the predictive powers of human legislators; in consequence, rule-based procedures that offer no scope for discretion from time to time give rise to some injustice. If those charged with operating such procedures prefer upholding rules to setting right perceived unfairness, they are likely to face threats of interference. In the early modern period, this simple social logic was thought to find expression in the intermittent tension between the common law judges and the Lord Chancellor. In theory and sometimes in practice, the Chancellor was the monarch's most important minister; his institution, Chancery, was the secretariat that served the courts by issuing their writs. It was natural that litigants should look to him to act outside the usual legal framework, and natural, if he agreed that there might have been unfairness, that he should draw the matter to his own consideration by granting a request for an injunction.

There were, of course, competing understandings of this practice. Sir Thomas More allegedly told his judicial critics that the need for his injunctions was the direct result of their timidity or negligence:

> If the judges of every court—unto whom the reformation of the rigour of the law, by reason of their office, most especially appertained—would upon reasonable considerations by their own discretion, as they were as he thought in conscience bound, mitigate and reform the rigour of the law themselves, there should from thenceforth by him no more injunctions be granted.[1]

On More's view, the authority of 'conscience' required the use of 'discretion' to mitigate 'rigour'. But there were plainly other ways to characterize the problem, including ones contrasting the security offered by rules with the increased uncertainty caused by relaxing them. Participants in this debate inevitably made choices reflecting and encouraging quite different ideas of what the law was and why it should be valued.

[1] *Two Tudor lives*, ed. R. S. Sylvester and D. P. Harding (New Haven: Yale University Press, 1962), 221–2.

This essay has little to add to more technical treatments of the actual relations between English jurisdictions. Its focus is on a considered attempt to *theorize* those relations, that is, to make sense of what happened in court in terms that had been borrowed from non-professionals. The common lawyer Christopher St German's Latin-language *Dialogus de legum Angliae fundamentis et de conscientia* (1528), later revised and amplified in English as *A Dyaloge bytwyxt a Doctoure of Dyvynitie and a Student in the Laws of Englande: of the groundes of the sayd Lawes and of Conscience* (1531),[2] was in this sense a theorization; as its title indicated, it offered an account of 'laws' and 'conscience' with reference to ideas supplied by the Doctor of Divinity—a theologian—that played no necessary part in the day-to-day professional life of lawyers.

One such idea was the concept of *epieikeia* as Aristotle had expounded it, especially in the brief but famous passage of *The Ethics* in which it is described as 'a rectification of legal justice'.[3] All Aristotle's Latin-speaking readers could see that this '*epieikeia*' meant something overlapping with the Latin '*aequitas*' (and therefore with its Anglicized derivative 'equity'). But Aristotle's understanding of a puzzling term had elements that *aequitas* did not completely capture, which was doubtless why the commentary tradition so often preferred sometimes bizarre transliterations to the most natural single-word translation. As we shall see, St German made interpretative choices that tended to diminish the uncertainties of meaning, but did not utterly eliminate them. With the help of ideas that had become connected with *epieikeia*, he showed how the Chancellor's 'conscience' could be rescued from the charge of being a licence for subjectivism, and how its equitable operations could be assimilated into the common law. But his writings were themselves creatively ambiguous, leaving open possibilities that others could exploit, especially about the role that was or might be played by appealing to a lawmaker's 'intention'. In making the Aristotelian term a part of the common law's language, he facilitated novel ways of thinking, with consequences extending beyond his professional world for the ways in which that law could be imagined. The best way of explaining what he did and why it mattered is to describe the interpretative opportunities that the Greek word's long history had made available.

The Idea of *Epieikeia*

The adjective *epieikês*, found in the *Iliad*, originally meant something like 'seemly' or 'fitting'. Like many Greek appraisive terms, it had social connotations; the quality referred to by the noun *epieikeia* was one that was appropriate to a high-status person: the man

[2] For the complex bibliographical history of the Latin and successive English versions, including the English-language *Second Dialogue* (1530), see *St German's Doctor and Student*, ed. T. F. T. Plucknett and J. L. Barton, SS, 91 (1974), lxix–lxxvi.

[3] Aristotle, *The Nicomachean Ethics*, ed. and trans. H. Rackham (London: Loeb Classical Library, 1934), 314. All classical texts are cited from the Loeb Classical Library editions. I have freely amended translations.

who could be trusted to do the decent thing. In classical times, to lay claim to *epieikeia* was to assert a visible respectability; it was possible to argue, for example, that 'the strongest proof of my *epieikeia* is that those of the younger men who spend their time in playing dice or drinking or such dissipations are as you will observe against me',[4] or that 'it may be taken as a sign of my *epieikeia* that you can easily exact a legal penalty from others, but find no ground of censure in me'.[5] A French scholar has suggested that the term's social bearing is captured by the phrase 'les gens comme il faut'.[6]

The route by which this general term of moral approbation came to refer particularly to 'equitable' behaviour appears to have been its link with the high-status attributes of clemency, restraint, and moderation. There was, at all events, an expectation that *epieikeia* was likely to be in tension with strict 'justice'. In consequence, *epieikeia* had its critics. According to Thucydides, the demagogic Cleon deplored the influence of 'the three things most prejudicial to rulership: pity and pleasure in words and *epieikeia*'.[7] At the more aristocratic end of the Greek political spectrum, Plato's late work *The Laws* pronounced that 'the *epieikês* and lenient, wherever employed, is an infringement of the perfect and exact against right justice';[8] as the laws were a way of projecting the legislator's wisdom into a future from which he was absent, *epieikeia* was at best a regrettable dilution of philosophic rule.

Plato's pupil Aristotle's *The Art of Rhetoric* reveals that he was right to be suspicious. Aristotle introduces *epieikeia* in the part of this treatise discussing appeals to 'the laws'; it is a moral value that a speaker can invoke to neutralize the fact that 'the laws' are against him. In such a situation, *epieikeia* presupposes that a particular written law is in some respect deficient. Sometimes the alleged deficiency results from a simple mistake (a failure to foresee the readily foreseeable). At other times, though, it reflects the nature of human affairs: the legislator was obliged to speak in general terms, but was aware that there would be as yet unknown occasions on which the rule allowed of an exception. There might, for instance, be a law that punished the use of iron as a weapon. Such a law could hardly offer an exhaustive catalogue of iron objects that it might refer to. In consequence, a man wearing a ring who struck a blow would be a criminal 'according to the written law, but according to the truth he does not offend against justice, and this is what is *epieikês*'.[9]

It was clear, though, that *epieikeia* was more than an excuse for failing to apply the law as written. The *Art of Rhetoric* noted that the term could be used to describe a fairly wide range of behaviour patterns:

> It is *epieikês* to pardon human weaknesses, and to look, not to the law, but the legislator; and not the words but to the intention of the legislator; not to the action itself but

[4] *Lysias*, ed. and trans. W. R. M. Lamb (London: Loeb Classical Library, 1930), 380.

[5] *Demosthenes against Meidias, Androtion, Aristocrates, Timocrates, Aristogeiton*, ed. and trans. J. H. Vince London: Loeb Classical Library, 1935), 140.

[6] Jacqueline Romilly, *La douceur dans la pensée Grecque* (Paris: Les belles lettres, 1979), 61.

[7] *Thucydides*, 4 vols (London: Loeb Classical Library, 1919), ed. and trans. C. F. Smith, 3.66.

[8] Plato, Laws, ed. and trans. R. G. Bury. (London: Loeb Classical Library, 1926), 414.

[9] Aristotle, *The Art of Rhetoric*, ed. and trans. J. H. Freese (London: Loeb Classical Library, 1926), 146.

> to the precedent state of mind; not to the part but to the whole; not to what a man is now, but to what he has been, always, or generally; to remember good rather than ill treatment, and benefits received rather than those conferred; to bear injury with patience; to be willing that a judicial sentence be nominal rather than real; to prefer arbitration to litigation, for the arbitrator looks to what is *epieikês*; the judge to law.[10]

In ordinary usage, then, the word *epieikês* frequently meant little more than 'decent'. But the reception of the term by Aristotle's medieval and early modern interpreters was shaped by the more specialized discussion in *The Ethics*.

Here Aristotle focused upon the problem posed by *epieikeia*'s relationship with 'justice', noting that *epieikês* was sometimes interchangeable with general terms meaning 'good', but that 'it seems strange that what is *epieikês* should be praiseworthy if it is contrary to what is just'.[11] The solution to the puzzle was that 'the *epieikês* is just, but not according to law, but a rectification of legal justice'; the need for this rectification did not, however, arise from a shortcoming in the legislator, but from the recalcitrant nature of his materials: 'in matters then in which it is necessary to speak generally, but it is not possible to do so correctly, the law takes into consideration the majority of cases, although it is not unaware of the error this involves'.[12] In such a situation, it was right to fix the problem by saying what 'the legislator himself would say if he were there, and would have legislated if he had known';[13] so far from being a menace to the legislator's rule, *epieikeia* was a means to realize what he wanted. A celebrated simile explained the basic point:

> This is the reason too why not all things are in accordance with law, because it is impossible to make a law about some things, so that an ad hoc decree (*psêphisma*) is necessary. For the rule of the indefinite is itself indefinite, like the Lesbian builder's lead rule. For it adapts to the shape of the stone and is not rigid, and the *psêphisma* adapts to practical affairs.[14]

Aristotle's claim is simple: human political affairs are recalcitrant to rules and occasional ad hoc adjustments are therefore necessary. But the notion of adjusting the letter of the law so as to achieve the result that the lawgiver would have wanted was to encourage a misunderstanding. It has been easy to assume that Aristotle's purpose was to set out a method of interpreting the law: a way of generating determinate replies to questions thrown up by law's application. On this view, the Lesbian rule is a kind of formula that yields, as it were, a single curve that is a guide to action. But a moment's thought reveals that this cannot be quite right. If 'what the legislator would have said' is what

[10] Aristotle, *Art of Rhetoric*, 146–8.
[11] Aristotle, *Ethics*, 314.
[12] Aristotle, *Ethics*, 314.
[13] Aristotle, *Ethics*, 316.
[14] Aristotle, *Ethics*, 316.

the historical Solon or Lycurgus would have said, the judge becomes the servant of the historian; but if it is what a reasonable man would have said, the thought-experiment is completely needless. The intellectual work is manifestly being done by our conception of the reasonable.

In any case, the elaborate discussion in *The Ethics* concludes by saying that 'it is clear who the *epieikês* is: the man who by choice and habit does such things, and does not stand upon his rights unduly, but tends to take less than his share even if he has law to help him.'[15] The interpretative problem is not difficult to state: if *epieikeia* is just the technique that constructs or imputes an intention, then it is hard to see why those who master this technique should have a bias towards leniency.[16] Yet it is clear the decent thing is also the merciful thing; the idea of *epieikeia* seems inextricably linked to that of clemency and moderation. Of course, the problem vanishes if it is realized that *epieikeia* refers to a broad family of virtues that may—but need not—find their most appropriate expression in a concern for legislative intention; the difficulty has arisen only for later readers with a more narrowly juristic mindset. Such readers were, however, to be a powerful force in shaping the term's subsequent reception.

Medieval Reception and Interpretation

Needless to say, St German, a professional common lawyer, interpreted *epieikeia* as a lawyerly technique; he took it for granted the notion referred to a *method* that yielded, and was meant to yield, determinate conclusions that could in practice guide judicial action. The tradition to which he belonged went back to Aquinas (1224–1274), who not only assumed that what he called '*epikeia*' was what 'among us is called *aequitas*', but chose to interpret *aequitas* in quite a narrow fashion.[17] During the middle decades of the thirteenth century, *aequitas* could refer to the important principle demanding that similar cases be similarly treated (the sense that is found in the common law treatise 'Bracton').[18] It could also refer to *aequitas canonica*, the virtue that supposedly pervaded canon law, influentially defined by his contemporary Hostiensis as 'justice tempered by the sweetness of mercy'.[19] Aquinas himself was aware of the fact that the 'term *epieikeia* is applied in Greek by a similitude to all kinds of moderation'.[20] He also acknowledged that 'punishments are not intended by the legislator for their own sake but as a kind of

[15] Aristotle, *Ethics*, 316.

[16] For interesting discussion of this asymmetry, see Martha Nussbaum, 'Equity and Mercy', *Philosophy and Public Affairs*, 22 (1993): 83–125.

[17] Aquinas, *Summa theologiae*, II–IIae, 120, art. 1.

[18] Bracton, *De legibus et consuetudinibus Angliae*, ed. S. E. Thorne (3 vols), 2.25.

[19] John Guy, *Christopher St German on Chancery and Statute* (London: SS, supp. ser. 6, 1985), 72.

[20] Aquinas, *Summa theologiae*, Iia–IIae q. 120, art. 2.

medicine for offences'. It followed, he thought, that 'the *epiiches* does not appoint more punishment than is necessary to restrain sins' (a view, it will be noted, that supplies no explanation of Aristotle's bias towards mercy).[21] But he showed no real interest in any of these senses. When he linked *epieikeia* with the Latin *aequitas*, he took it that this 'equity' referred to natural law, in other words that the term referred to a kind of master-law that had the power of trumping merely positive legislation. The bridge to this position was the concept of intention.

Aquinas's best-known single illustration of his view involved a city that was under siege:

> Suppose that in a besieged city a law should be established that the gates of the city are to be kept closed. This is good for the collective safety (*communis salus*) for the most part; but if it were to happen that the enemy were to pursue certain citizens by whom the city is preserved, it would be disastrous for the city if the gates were not opened to them: and so in such a situation the gates ought to be opened, contrary to the words of the law, in order that the collective welfare (*communis utilitas*) should be protected, which the lawgiver intended (*intendit*).[22]

Here the lawgiver's intention is presumed to have been guided by the 'collective welfare' (*communis utilitas*). Elsewhere, a little more space is left for a concern for 'justice' that may be rather broader in conception:

> to obey the law in some cases is against the equity of justice (*aequalitas iustitiae*) and against the common good (*bonum commune*), which the law intended (*intendit*). Thus a law has decreed that deposits should be returned, because it is for the most part just to give back an item that is left upon deposit, but it may happen sometimes to be harmful, as for instance if a madman deposited his sword and then demanded its return while he was in a state of mania or someone were to demand something deposited back in order to fight against his country. In these and similar circumstances, it would be bad to follow the established law, but it is good to ignore the words of the law and follow what the logic of justice (*iustitiae ratio*) and the collective welfare demand. This is the object of *epikeia* which among us is called *aequitas*.[23]

It is clear, though, that the general thrust of this interpretation is an outgrowth of a broader political theory that stresses the controlling idea of common good as the criterion of legitimacy. In consequence, *epieikeia* became 'political'; its use became an attribute of those who were entrusted with the highest forms of power. This was a new departure. As we have seen, the Aristotelian analysis was mainly concerned with the puzzle of its relationship with 'justice'; the problem belonged to the theory of the virtues that was the subject matter of *The Ethics*. No doubt because he saw it as an individual

[21] Aquinas, *Sententia libri ethicorum*, book V, lectio xvi, n. 12.
[22] *Summa theologiae*, I–IIae, q. 96, art. 6.
[23] *Summa theologiae*, II–IIae, q. 120, art. 1.

virtue that might on occasion be exercised in purely private dealings, Aristotle did not connect it with his undoubted emphasis upon the common good. The term is not found in a passage within *The Politics* on which it was sometimes subsequently projected: the famous discussion of whether it is better to be ruled by 'the best man' or 'the best laws'.[24] Aquinas, by contrast, saw his *epikeia* as part of the arrangements that secured the common good; it followed that he emphasized that those who served the common weal by making positive law should also (except in emergencies) be those who modified that legislation.[25] Given the general character of his philosophy, this public political virtue had to be found a place within what Aquinas believed was a law-governed universe. In his capacity as an exegete, in his late commentary on *The Ethics*, he noted that:

> In Greek *epiiches* is understood as what is appropriate (*conveniens*) or fitting (*decens*); it is derived from *epi* meaning above and *ikos* meaning 'obedient' because through *epiichia* someone is obedient in a more excellent way when he follows the *intentio* of a legislator when the words jar with it.[26]

A slightly different version of the besieged-city example (in which a group of foreigners defends the citizens by breaking a law preventing them climbing the walls) is used to illustrate the point that 'it would be against natural law that a punishment should reward benefactors. And thus it is fitting in this instance that the naturally just should direct the legally just'.[27]

For present purposes, this view had two important features. On the one hand, its appeal to natural law (a rule) unwittingly abandoned the doubts about all rules that had in fact been central to Aristotle's thought; Thomistic *epieikeia* was not so much the virtue that copes with the failure of rules as the technique of letting certain rules be trumped by others. On the other, its restriction of the use of *epieikeia* to those entrusted with political power facilitated its identification with qualities traditionally expected of a ruler, especially the kingly attribute of clemency. Both features can also be found in the thought of St German's favourite author, the versatile conciliarist Jean Gerson (1363–1429). In Gerson's view, all valid laws are accompanied by 'exceptions' derived from higher laws of God or nature, and 'there is no need for that exception to be continually subjoined to law, but an express statement of the same is not required'.[28] The effect of such exceptions was broadly understood. As a conciliarist propagandist, Gerson called for General Councils to have recourse to '*epikeia* or sound equity (*bona aequitas*), which interprets the letter of positive laws according to the *intentio* of the legislators rooted (*radicata*) in the eternal and immutable rules of divine law'. Such rules included a long

[24] Aristotle, *The Politics*, ed. and trans. H. Rackham (London: Loeb Classical Library, 1944), 254–70.

[25] *Summa theologiae*, I–IIae, q. 96, art. 6.

[26] Aquinas, *Sententia libri Ethicorum*, book V, lectio xvi, n. 1.

[27] Aquinas, *Sententia libri Ethicorum*, book V, lectio xvi, n. 9.

[28] Jean Gerson, *Oeuvres complètes*, ed. P. Glorieux, 10 vols (Paris: Desclée, 1960), 3.83; cf. St German, *Doctor and Student*, 97. St German's borrowings from Gerson are traced in Zofia Rueger, 'Gerson's

list of principles appropriate to an imperfect world, including the permissive tags that 'necessity has no law', that 'it is permitted to meet force with force', and even that 'a common error makes law'; the idea of an intention 'rooted' in the law of nature turned out to be remarkably permissive.[29]

In the same passage, he went on to stress that mathematical certainty was not to be expected in such matters; the exponent of *epikeia* was licensed to consider 'all particular circumstances of the sort that the legislator could not foresee or express' with an eye to the outcome if the law were literally observed. When the result would be a breach of divine or eternal laws 'contrary to what ought to be the *intentio* of the legislator', he should pronounce that 'the written law should be thus or thus applied, or abandoned', in accordance with the Aristotelian image of 'a Lesbian rule that was leaden, not iron, that is, flexible and not immutable'.[30] Elsewhere, the idea of 'exceptions' attached to every law shaded into a more general appeal to the law's spirit: a monastic superior invoking *epikeia* could be seen as being 'as it were a living law tempering dead laws' (*tanquam lex viva moderatrix legum mortuarum*).[31]

St German's best-known English predecessor was led, for his own reasons, in a similar direction. In his famous panegyric of the English common law, *De laudibus legum Angliae*, Sir John Fortescue (1394–1479) had praised the laws of England for forcing English monarchs to rule 'politically' (in consultation with, and therefore subject to the consent of, an assembly of their subjects). The explanation was historical; it had been the *intentio* of the people in creating this distinctive form of kingship that it should be no threat to their private property.[32] In his less famous, more elaborate treatise *De natura legis naturae*, he noted that there were occasions when the king should act alone:

> You, O king who rules politically, rule also your kingdom regally when the situation demands it, for not all circumstances can be covered by the statutes and customs of your realm, so the remaining circumstances are left to your will; at your will too you always control all criminal matters and you temper and remit all penalties while you can do this without hurt to your subjects and offence to the laws and customs of your realm. *Epikaia* too is left to your wisdom in case the rigour of the words of the law confounding its intention (*mens*) should harm the common good (*commune bonum*). For the man who repels a sudden enemy attack by climbing the walls without permission is not judged to have offended against a law prohibiting climbing the walls of the city, for then observation of that law would have swallowed it up with its authors.[33]

Concept of Equity and Christopher St German', *History of Political Thought* 3 (1982): 1–30; and Guy, *St German on Chancery*, 72–3.

[29] Gerson, *Oeuvres*, 6.143–4.

[30] Gerson, *Oeuvres*, 6.144.

[31] Gerson, *Oeuvres*, 2.238.

[32] Sir John Fortescue, *De laudibus legum Angliae* (Cambridge: Cambridge University Press, 1942), 32–4.

[33] Fortescue, *Works*, 1.85.

There is clearly a large debt here to Aquinas (Fortescue's preferred version of the now-standard besieged-city example suggests that he had studied the commentary on *The Ethics* as well as the discussions in the *Summa*). But there are also several interesting differences. Though Fortescue treats what he calls 'absolute power' (*potestas absoluta*) as a requirement of the law of nature, he sees that power as an instrument for the fulfilment of the law of *England*. Thus the king:

> is considered to have absolute power (*potestas absoluta*) not however in order that he might do away with (*solvere*) a complete (*perfecta*) law, but so that by reason of the law of nature, which is natural *aequitas*, he might himself better fulfil the law of his kingdom. For the written law was as it were dead under a covering of words.[34]

The necessity, on occasion, of this *potestas absoluta* explains why the king can be said to be '*lex viva*' and also why 'it is rightly said by the Philosopher that a kingdom is better ruled by the best king than the best law'.[35]

It is not clear if St German had ever seen a copy of Fortescue's *De natura legis naturae*. But whether or not he had done so, the comparison is instructive. Fortescue's great achievement had been to forge a link between the idea of common good and the idea of the sanctity of private property as realized in a positive law system. St German referred to *De laudibus* with approval,[36] and made, it can be argued, quite a similar connection between *aequitas/epikeia* and the content of the law. But implicit in his theory was a new development discouraging the use of such politically charged phrases as *potestas absoluta* and *lex viva*. At the heart of his theorization was a new attitude that tended to sever equity from kingship.

St German's Theory

St German's core conviction was carefully set out in the 'Prologue' to his earliest publication: he aimed to state 'the principles or grounds of the laws of England and how conscience ought to be formed in many cases in accordance with the same principles and grounds'. In particular, he was insistent that 'human law rightly constituted' determines 'possession of lands and ownership of things. And what is possessed by the precepts of laws of this kind is justly possessed, but what is held against them is unjustly held'.[37] In other words, it was for common lawyers (as opposed to canon lawyers or anybody else) to determine the formalities deciding who owned what. This conviction was set in the context of a broadly Thomist view (put into the mouth of the 'Doctor') that 'the law of man the which sometime is called the law positive is derived (*deducta*) by reason as a

34 Fortescue, *Works*, 1.85–6.
35 Fortescue, *Works*, 1.86.
36 St German, *Doctor and Student*, 282.
37 St German, *Doctor and Student*, 2–4.

thing which is necessarily and probably following of the law of reason and of the law of God'. The deduction should be 'probable' in the sense that it appears 'to many and specially to wise men to be true'; the law should moreover be 'just' with respect to its 'end' (the common good), its 'author' (a man with appropriate authority), and its 'form' (the appropriate distribution of its burdens).[38] In practice, human rulers possessed a wide discretion, especially in determining the nature of the sanctions by which the laws derived from God and nature should be enforced on fallen human beings.

At the heart of St German's new framework for understanding law was a transformed perception of the relationship between the common law and courts of 'conscience'. On what appears to have been the standard view, the Chancellor's equitable interventions were something that was utterly distinct in character from ordinary common law procedures: he did not claim to settle or to transfer legal rights; he 'rectified the conscience of the party', that is, he coerced litigants (outside the legal process) in such a way as to produce appropriate results. St German himself insisted that the Chancellor's *subpoena* 'shall never be directed to the judge but to the party plaintiff or to his attorney'.[39] Strictly speaking, there was thus no interference with anything decided by the ordinary judges; in S. F. C. Milsom's striking and helpful metaphor, 'the two systems moved on different planes and could not collide'.[40] There were thus at least two senses in which the 'English' side of the court of Chancery could be considered as a 'court of conscience': it was informed and motivated by the Chancellor's 'conscience': and its object of attention was the 'conscience' of the party, which it 'rectified'—that is, 'set straight'—when moral decision-making had for some reason somehow gone awry. Both senses suggested obvious and important criticisms. If one focused on the Chancellor's own conscience, then one could see that conscience, untrammelled by the law, as nothing but an arbitrary opinion. If one focused on his object of attention—the conscience of the party—then he could be presented as intruding in a sphere that was in fact the business of confessors.[41]

St German's theorization offered an understanding that escaped these criticisms without, however, endorsing implausibly high claims for the superior wisdom of established principles. On the one hand, he avoided the conventional idea that the power of the judges was merely 'ordinary', but that the Chancellor's was 'absolute' (an idea with the political implication that the monarchical power of which the Chancellor was a vessel was also absolute in character).[42] On the other, he avoided an over-reaction. His works repeatedly refer to a current of opinion defending the remarkably immoderate position that 'all the law of the realm is the law of reason'; the threat of an authority that seemed entirely

[38] St German, *Doctor and Student*, 27. In passages translated by St German, I follow St German's version.

[39] St German, *Doctor and Student*, 105.

[40] S. F. C. Milsom, *Historical Foundations of the English Common Law*, 2nd edn (Cambridge: Cambridge University Press, 1981), 93.

[41] Guy, *St German on Chancery*, 79–80, 88.

[42] *Diversite de courtz* (London: 1523), sig. A6^{v}.

lawless encouraged extreme statements of the adequacy of law.[43] Such statements were encouraged by the common lawyers' habit of identifying 'reason' with highly specific outcomes of legal *reasoning*. As St German's 'Student' explained, 'it is not used among them that be learned in the laws of England to reason what thing is commanded or prohibit in the law of nature'; instead, they pronounced that 'reason will that such a thing be done'.[44] This 'reason' included what the Student called 'the law of reason secondary particular', which was 'that law that is derived upon divers customs general and particular and of divers maxims and statutes ordained in this realm'.[45] St German rejected the idea that 'reason' in this broad sense was in no way arbitrary: the fact that the law's 'maxims' could be altered by a statute was after all enough to show they were not natural.[46] The law consisted both of universal principles and other, local rules of merely human origin.

St German thus accepted that generally good laws from time to time conflicted with higher principles. He also accepted that such situations would necessarily involve a certain role for 'conscience'. But he found a way to minimize the threat that conscience posed. In his hands, conscience ceased to be a specialized and private kind of knowledge or motivation, becoming instead an *event* that necessarily involved the simple application of a pre-existing rule.[47] As he realized, he was singling out one aspect of a concept that was inherently ambiguous:

> First, conscience says and means knowledge per se and in this sense conscience is a natural act that is not just cognitive but also motive: it also inclines the soul to pursue good and fly evil … But secondly—also more properly—conscience (*conscientia*) says and means knowledge (*scientia*) with (*cum*) another thing, that is to say with some particular act. And then it means a certain acceptance or acceptation on the part of reason whereby it accepts or rejects some particular thing and thus conscience properly speaking is nothing other than a kind of application or ordering of knowledge to some particular act and then it is more of an act than a disposition or power.[48]

So far from being a rule-free threat to a knowable rule-governed order, conscience was thus dependent on pre-existing rules of which it was an *act* of application.

These rules might be the laws of God or nature, but they might equally be positive laws laid down by the customs and statutes of the community. All such laws were binding in conscience unless and until they conflicted with a higher-order law, in which case it might be appropriate for the Chancellor to step in. To take the stock example, a buyer

[43] St German, *Doctor and Student*, 37, 75. For an eloquent statement of this extreme position, see the manuscript 'The Replication of a Serjeant at the Laws of England' printed in Guy, *St German on Chancery*, 99–105, esp. 102–3.

[44] St German, *Doctor and Student*, 31–3.

[45] St German, *Doctor and Student*, 35.

[46] St German, *Doctor and Student*, 56.

[47] The scholastic source is probably Aquinas. For details, see Timothy C. Potts, *Conscience in Medieval Philosophy* (Cambridge: Cambridge University Press, 1980), 50–4.

[48] St German, *Doctor and Student*, 86–8.

who loses his receipt (or fails to obtain one) had no judicial protection against being made to pay twice. St German stressed that it was *not* a legal principle that this unfortunate person 'ought of right' to pay again 'for that law were both against reason and conscience'. There was, however, a procedural rule 'that the defendant shall not plead that he oweth not the money ne can in no wise discharge himself in that action' unless he supplied a receipt 'or some other writing sufficient in the law'. This was a quite defensible provision 'to avoid a great inconvenience that else might happen to come to many people that is to say that every man by a nude parole and by a bare averment should avoid an obligation'.[49] It was nonetheless the case that the careless or unfortunate litigant 'may be holpen by a *subpoena*, and so he may in many other cases where conscience serveth for him'.[50] But the equity involved was less an outside intervention than something that grew out of the existing legal system: it was itself an action that was based upon a rule that common law (in a large sense) allowed for.

Given this expectation, it was not at all surprising that St German's views drew heavily on Gerson; the Gersonian idea of a tacit exception explained why an appropriate rule could always be located. His initial introduction of the idea of 'equity' was actually a list of semi-proverbial commonplaces that he had taken over without acknowledgement from his conciliarist predecessor:

> Equity is a rightwiseness that considereth all the particular circumstances of the deed the which also is tempered with the sweetness of mercy. And such an equity must alway be observed in every law of man and in every general rule therof and that knew he well that said thus. Laws covet to be ruled by equity. And the wise man saith: be not over much rightwise for the extreme rightwiseness is extreme wrong.[51]

In general, however, his borrowings were less uncritical. Their tendency was to obscure the side of Gerson's thinking that treated *epikeia* as being flexible. Where Gerson had been happy to endorse 'interpretation', St German thought 'interpretation' illegitimate, preferring the more modest 'exposition'.[52] Gerson spoke favourably of 'dispensation';[53] St German avoided the concept. Gerson approved the maxim *communis error facit ius*; St German was at best doubtful of its soundness.[54] In consequence, he focused on the seminal idea that:

> It is also called by some men *epicaia*. The which is no other thing but an exception of the laws of God or of the law of reason from the general rules of the law of man: when

[49] St German, *Doctor and Student*, 77.

[50] St German, *Doctor and Student*, 79.

[51] St German, *Doctor and Student*, 95–7; cf. Gerson, *Oeuvres*, 9.95–6. St German's only addition to this passage is the equally Gersonian assertion 'And such an equity ... rule thereof'. For details of Gerson's own sources, see Rueger, 'Concept of Equity', 16.

[52] St German, *Doctor and Student*, 166.

[53] Gerson, *Oeuvres*, 9.99.

[54] Gerson, *Oeuvres*, 6.144 cited at St German, *Doctor and Student*, 162.

> they by reason of their generality would in any particular case judge against the law of God or the law of reason.[55]

'Exceptions' had their place in situations in which the 'general rules of the law of man' collided with—and were trumped by—a higher-order law. But the force of the exception derived from the intent that was presumed to underpin all valid human law: 'if any law were made by man without any such exception expressed or implied it were manifestly unreasonable and were not to be suffered for such cases might come that he that would observe that law should break both the law of God and the law of reason'.[56] St German's first example discussed the situation of someone who had made a vow never to eat 'white meat and after it happeneth to him to come there where he can get none other meat'. Such a case was 'excepted secretly from his general avow by this equity or epikay'[57] His second example was a variant of the familiar story of the city under siege:

> if a law were made in a city that no man under the pain of death should open the gates of the city before the sun rising, yet if the citizens before that hour fleeing from their enemies come to the gates of the city and one for the saving of the citizens openeth the gates ... he offendeth not the law. For that case is excepted from the said general law by equity ... and so it appeareth that equity rather followeth the intent of the law than the words of the law.[58]

On the view that St German derived from his theory of conscience, such 'equities' involved the application of a rule that trumps or qualifies another rule. Such rules could be developed within the common law; there were, for instance, rules that made allowances for infants.[59] For the most part, though, the problems that arose from the law's rigour were dealt with by the Chancellor through *subpoenas*. Though these were interventions from outside the usual courts, they nonetheless formed part of a unified system; it was after all professional lawyers who requested them, so much so that 'daily bills be made by men learned in the law of the realm to have *subpoenas* ... And the law will in many cases that there shall be such remedy in the Chancery'. But for the fact that such events gave rise to no common law record, 'it had not been much inconvenient to have assigned such remedy in the Chancery upon such equities for the seventh ground of the law of England'.[60]

This 'seventh ground' was not in fact particularly permissive. A law that barred the Chancellor from all kinds of intervention would be a law against the law of nature; in other words, it would fail to be a law at all. But St German defended the well-known Lancastrian statute (4 Henry IV *c.* 22) forbidding him from issuing an injunction after

55 St German, *Doctor and Student*, 97; cf. Gerson, *Oeuvres*, 3.83.
56 St German, *Doctor and Student*, 97.
57 St German, *Doctor and Student*, 97.
58 St German, *Doctor and Student*, 97–9.
59 St German, *Doctor and Student*, 103.
60 St German, *Doctor and Student*, 105.

judgement, on the grounds that the alternative was that 'the plaintiffs or demandants should seldom come to the effect of their suit ne the law should never have end'.[61] For similar reasons, the Chancellor could not issue a *subpoena* if somebody had been 'estopped' from a well-founded claim by a previous non-fraudulent but contradictory statement that he or she had ignorantly placed upon the record. Nor could he help a widow who truthfully maintained that her husband had coerced her into levying a fine that had the effect of extinguishing a valid interest. The reason for this toughness in undoubtedly hard cases was the danger that 'releases and other writings should be of small effect and upon every light surmise all writings might come in trial'.[62] Because the rationale applied to any jurisdiction, it bound the Chancellor as much as any other judge.

Conclusion

To read St German as this essay has done is to read him as a thinker making choices. In the long perspective offered by the development of the meaning of the term *epieikeia*, the most striking single feature of those choices is the extreme rule-mindedness of his presuppositions. Where Aristotle had seen *epieikeia* as the means by which one copes with the shortcomings of all rules, St German saw it as a mechanism that used one rule to qualify another. Unlike Gerson and Fortescue, he seems to have had no interest in *revivifying* law by bringing in an extra-legal agent. The notion as he understood it involved him in locating a higher principle to qualify the effects of a statute or maxim. Such principles—the laws of God and nature—were not of course human creations. But the decision whether to enforce them by coercion involved the *same kind* of thought process as the judges might perform: an attempt at a deduction whose premises included both natural principles and facts about the existing legal system.

From a legal historian's standpoint, this was a step towards a long-term future in which 'equity' turned into a second kind of 'law' as cumbersome and rule-bound as the original. But it also had two subtle and non-technical results, both of them ultimately traceable to the availability, within St German's thinking, of an appeal to legislative intention. The first was a marked narrowing of the idea of equity (as the professional lawyer understood it) so as to exclude the authentically Aristotelian view that it involved a certain bias towards clemency. The later Tudor writers who took most from *Doctor and Student* both noticeably discouraged such suggestions. In 1597, Samuel West insisted on 'a difference between equity and clemency, for equity is always most firmly knit to the will of the law, which way so ever it bends, whether to clemency or to severity'.[63] In about 1600, Edward Hake took the same view in his unprinted work *Epieikeia*. Hake was happy to identify *epieikeia* with 'mercy' but was equally sure that mercy could involve severity:

[61] St German, *Doctor and Student*, 107.
[62] St German, *Doctor and Student*, 289.
[63] William West, *Of Symboleography*, the second part (1597), 'Of the Chancerie', sig. a4.

> Notwithstanding that by the same *epieikeia* the letter of the law is otherwhiles [sometimes] sharpened or quickened by exposition to the punishing of some particular offences (which likewise is done by *epieikeia*), yet thereby the law ceaseth not to be righteous, nor the *epieikeia* thereof doth thereby change his course or nature. For who knoweth not that there is *misericordia puniens* [a mercy that punishes] as well as *misericordia parcens* [a mercy that spares].[64]

A second, related, consequence was even more far-reaching. In assimilating the use of *epieikeia* to ordinary common law judicial reasoning, St German promoted a fusion between law and history. He would himself have been surprised at this development. Although he made use of historical reconstruction to show how particular common law rules could have rational beginnings (a rule that had no such beginning was not a law at all),[65] the reasoning that he expected of the Chancellor involved no detailed knowledge of England's legal past. He did, however, note that even within the common law 'a man may be excepted from ... the rigour of a statute by the law of reason and sometime by the intent of the makers of the statute'.[66] In other words, he thought that *epikeia* included the procedures by which the common law recovered the 'intent' behind a statute. In the later sixteenth century, those procedures increasingly demanded intellectual operations that were historical in character: they interpreted the statutes by reference to the 'mischief' that they had remedied, quite often in the light of a further theory about the common law's priorities. To understand a statute was to have grasped the problem to which the enactment in question was a rational response.

The great Elizabethan law reporter Edmund Plowden (1518–1585), who documented statements of this dominant approach,[67] defended judgements modifying the letter of the law as expressions of 'equity which some call *epichaia* which often puts an exception to the generality of the text for reasonable cause'.[68] Unlike St German, he believed that *epichaia* was 'no part of the law, but a moral virtue that reforms the law'. But this idea (which he derived from commentaries on Aristotle's *Ethics*)[69] was inconsistent with the implications of his metaphors, which speak of the flesh and the spirit, the shell and the kernel, the letter and the 'internal sense' of statutes; the way in which he characterized the hermeneutic task appeared to exclude the idea of *external* correction.[70] Moreover, his historical understanding of the statutes involved him in relating their particular provisions to preferences allegedly embedded in the system. Hake understood this problem,

64 Edward Hake, *Epieikeia: A Dialogue on Equity in Three Parts*, ed. D. E. C. Yale (New Haven: Yale University Press, 1953), 104.

65 St German, *Doctor and Student*, 286.

66 St German, *Doctor and Student*, 103.

67 See the interesting discussion by Georg Behrens, 'Equity in the Commentaries of Edmund Plowden', *JLH*, 20 (1999): esp. 32–46.

68 Plowden, *Commentaries*, 465b, translated from *Cy ensuont certeyne cases reportes per Edmunde Plowden* (London: 1579).

69 Plowden, *Commentaries*, 466b.

70 Plowden, *Commentaries*, 465a

and criticized Plowden for treating *epieikeia* as 'no part of the law'.[71] For Hake, *epieikeia* pervaded common law and was indeed the motor of its development. Here the appeal to history fused with Gerson's principle that every law contains its own 'exceptions'. Reason confronted by experience had a tendency to generate corrections to the system that over time would harden into maxims:

> these and all other the like exceptions which in the beginning were *tacitae* and hidden (as to the visible aspect of the law) are now become expressed even as the laws themselves are so as a man may say of them that they are themselves become grounds or maxims.[72]

In consequence, it was not too much to say that 'the common law of England would ... seem to be a law consisting for the most part of equity'.[73]

Hake's brilliant manuscript treatise had little 'influence' because, to the best of our knowledge, it found few if any readers. But it documents the existence of an intellectual link that would in time give rise to some political implications. His explicit correction of Plowden involved a *de-personalization* of the activities that were involved in equitable justice. The equity he asserted was 'the equity of the law and not of the judge'.[74] In consequence, the preferences of real historical actors—whether parliamentary lawmakers or judges—could be effaced by charitable presumptions arising from perception of the law's priorities. Much of what could be mistaken for 'discretion' involved 'divers things which the common law itself is said to favour, as life, liberty, a woman's dower, infancy, coverture, privilege of arts and sciences, plaintiffs in every action *prima facie* and sundry other things'.[75] Thus the idea of *epikeia* as St German understood it—the use of rules to modify each other—facilitated the collapse of 'historical' intentions back into impersonal statements of the 'reason' of the law. We have here a part of the background to Sir Edward Coke's assertion that 'the laws have been by the wisdom of the most excellent men, in many successions of ages, by long and continual experience (the trial of light and truth) fined and refined, which no one man (being of so short a time) ... could ever have effected or attained unto'.[76] The imaginative force of this conception of the law implied, of course, a vision of the country's institutions as drawing their authority from an accumulation of lessons of professional experience. But it also, in the long term, implied a politics that treated all forms of discretion as illegitimate and that required, in turn, a fundamental reassessment of the traditional picture of the role of monarchy.

[71] Hake, *Epieikeia*, 9.
[72] Hake, *Epieikeia*, 50.
[73] Hake, *Epieikeia*, 55.
[74] Hake, *Epieikeia*, 13.
[75] Hake, *Epieikeia*, 115.
[76] Coke, *Seventh Reports*, Calvin's case, 3b.

Bibliography

Primary

Aquinas, Thomas. <http://corpusthomisticum.org>.
Aristotle. *Art of Rhetoric*, ed. and trans. J. H. Freese (London: Loeb Classical Library, 1926).
Aristotle. *Nicomachean Ethics*, ed. and trans. H. Rackham (London: Loeb Classical Library, 1934).
Aristotle. *Politics*, ed. and trans. H. Rackham (London: Loeb Classical Library, 1944).
Behrens, G. 'Equity in Commentaries of Edmund Plowden', *The Journal of Legal History*, 20.3 (1999): 25–50.
Fortescue, Sir John. *Sir John Fortescue, Knt, His Life, Works and Family History*, 2 vols, ed. Thomas Fortescue, Lord Clermont (London: 1869).
Gerson, Jean. *Oeuvres complètes*, ed. P. Glorieux, 10 vols (Paris: Desclée, 1960).
Hake, Edward. *Epieikeia: A Dialogue on Equity in Three Parts*, ed. D. E. C. Yale (New Haven: Yale University Press, 1953).
Klinck, Dennis R. *Conscience, Equity and the Court of Chancery in Early Modern England* (Farnham: Ashgate, 2010).
Milsom, S. F. C. *Historical Foundations of the English Common Law*, 2nd edn (Cambridge: Cambridge University Press, 1982).
Nussbaum, Martha. 'Equity and Mercy', *Philosophy and Public Affairs*, 22.2 (Spring, 1993): 83–125.
Plowden, Edmund. *Cy ensuont certeyne cases reportes per Edmunde Plowden* (London: 1579).
Rueger, Z. S. 'Gerson's Concept of Equity and Christopher St German', *History of Political Thought*, 3.1 (1982): 1–30.
St German, Christopher. *Christopher St German on Chancery and Statute* (London: SS, 1985).
St German, Christopher. *St German's Doctor and Student*, ed. T. F. T. Plucknett and J. L. Barton (London: SS, 1974).

CHAPTER 17

THE ECCLESIASTICAL POLITY

ETHAN H. SHAGAN

I

RICHARD Hooker's *Of the Lawes of Ecclesiastical Politie*, conceived and written in the 1590s but published sporadically between 1593 and 1662, is among the most cited and least read works in the canon. Any modern scholar of law and literature would list it among the ten most important works on law produced in Renaissance England—many would rank it the most important of all—generally without having more than a vague idea of what it actually says. If they have read it at all, they have likely read the brief sections reproduced in the excellent little volume edited by Arthur S. McGrade for the Cambridge Texts in the History of Political Thought series, excerpts chosen to reflect modern preoccupations with abstract legal and constitutional theory rather than the Reformation debates which motivate and structure the original work.[1]

This chapter will not offer a thorough analysis of Hooker's *Lawes*; I have analysed the text and its interventions elsewhere, as have many other, more learned scholars.[2] Instead, this chapter is about the long-term problem in the English Reformation—the problem of ecclesiastical polity, and its awkward relationship to legislation, enforcement, and

[1] Arthur S. McGrade, ed., *Hooker: Of the Laws of Ecclesiastical Polity* (Cambridge: Cambridge University Press, 1989).

[2] See e.g. Ethan Shagan, *The Rule of Moderation: Violence, Religion and the Politics of Restraint in Early Modern England* (Cambridge: Cambridge University Press, 2011), 111–48; Torrance Kirby, ed., *A Companion to Richard Hooker* (Leiden: Brill, 2008); Torrance Kirby, ed., *Richard Hooker and the English Reformation* (Dordrecht: Kluwer, 2003); Torrance Kirby, *Richard Hooker, Reformer and Platonist* (Aldershot: Ashgate, 2005); Torrance Kirby, *Richard Hooker's Doctrine of the Royal Supremacy* (Leiden: Brill, 1990); A. J. Joyce, *Richard Hooker and Anglican Moral Theology* (Oxford: Oxford University Press, 2012); Arthur McGrade, ed., *Richard Hooker and the Construction of the Christian Community* (Tempe: MRTS, 1997); Philip Secor, *Richard Hooker and the Via Media* (Bloomington: AuthorHouse, 2006); W. Speed Hill, ed., *Studies in Richard Hooker: Essays Preliminary to an Edition of his Works* (Cleveland: Press of Case Western Reserve University, 1972).

jurisprudence—that produced what we must acknowledge is a truly bizarre and anomalous result: early modern England's most transcendently important work on law was actually a book about the Church.

This problem, and Hooker's relationship to it, are well worth the effort to understand. Readers of early modern English literature occasionally come up against explicit references to ecclesiastical law, as in Ben Jonson's *Epicene, or The Silent Woman*, where Clerimont recalls meeting Corpus, the fat author of the *Juris canonici* (2.3.67–75).[3] But in countless other literary texts, whether readers know it or not, the heart of the matter is the problem of ecclesiastical polity: the capacity of public law to regulate private lives, from sexuality to conscience. After all, the ecclesiastical polity is, on the most abstract level, the space where religion acts as a form of worldly governance; this space encompasses not only the regulation of formal worship, but also takes cognizance of oaths and debts, marriage and sexuality, blasphemy and indecency, and much more besides. This is the very stuff of narrative, and it is no exaggeration to say that most of the plots of Renaissance imaginative literature take place in the ecclesiastical polity as much or more than in the civil polity. Understanding what made the laws of the ecclesiastical polity so confused and contested can thus enormously aid our understanding of that literature.

So what was the problem? According to the statutory framework by which England separated from Rome, ecclesiastical law should have been a simple matter.[4] The Crown acquired legal jurisdiction over the Church, after which the mediaeval church courts simply became royal courts, another of the myriad jurisdictions, like the High Court of Admiralty or the Court of Exchequer Chamber, through which the Tudors maintained justice. But the idea that the Church was just another legal jurisdiction was never more than fantasy; the Church was also the bride of Christ, with the keys to the kingdom of heaven. So when the church courts sat in judgement, did their judges act as royal officers maintaining order, or as God's ministers curing souls? Was the law they enforced the law of England, or was it the law of God? How much leeway did human magistrates or ministers have to make ecclesiastical law, and who had authority over it? Moreover, once the royal government won jurisdiction over the Church, ecclesiastical law in the new church-state was never limited to the increasingly obsolete but oddly persistent jurisdiction of the ecclesiastical courts. Parliament and the Crown quickly joined the business of making ecclesiastical law, now enforceable in ostensibly civil courts and indistinguishable from other laws that regulated the lives of English subjects.

[3] *CWBJ*, 3.416.

[4] On English ecclesiastical law, see e.g. Richard Helmholz, *OHLE: I*; Gerald Bray, ed., *Tudor Church Reform: The Henrician Canons of 1535 and the Reformatio Legum Ecclesiasticarum* (Woodbridge: Boydell Press, 2000); R. B. Outhwaite, *The Rise and Fall of the English Ecclesiastical Courts, 1500–1860* (Cambridge: Cambridge University Press, 2006); Ralph Houlbrooke, *Church Courts and the People during the English Reformation, 1520–1570* (Oxford: Oxford University Press, 1979); Martin Ingram, *Church Courts, Sex, and Marriage in England, 1570–1640* (Cambridge: Cambridge University Press, 1987). On the modern situation, see Norman Doe, *The Legal Framework of the Church of England: A Critical Study in a Comparative Context* (Oxford: Oxford University Press, 1996).

These anomalies and ambiguities were magnified by England's chaotic Reformation, which obstinately refused to adjudicate pesky theological difficulties. I will argue here that the same religious fudges and compromises which partially protected England from the confessionalizing impulses of early modern Europe also undermined the coherence of the ecclesiastical polity, leaving questions of ecclesiastical law dangerously unresolved. This was the problem that Richard Hooker and others tried to solve, offering constitutional models to structure the adjudication of disputes over ethics and conscience in the English church-state. Yet because all of these models would have required theological consensus in order to produce legal consistency, none of them proved capable of bringing coherence to ecclesiastical law. Their failure reverberated deep into the modern era, haunting and sometimes threatening England's precocious state rationality. Ecclesiastical law was, I will argue, the stubborn remainder in the English Reformation, the term in England's religio-political equation that refused to reduce or balance out.

II

To begin, I want to offer a few examples of the inadequacy of the English Reformation to create coherent ecclesiastical law. This inadequacy can be revealed by burrowing down into any of dozens of seemingly small issues on which the needs of the Church of England to remain flexible in its theology clashed with the needs of the same Church to be clear in its laws.

Take, for instance, a particularly nasty tempest, not in a teapot but instead perhaps on a tea tray: the controversy over wafer cakes in Queen Elizabeth's reign. The Catholic Eucharist had traditionally used special bread known in England as wafer cakes or singing cakes. By contrast, the 1559 *Book of Common Prayer*—every word of which acquired statutory authority in the 1559 Act of Uniformity—stated that 'to take away the superstition which any person hath or might have in the bread and wine, it shall suffice that the bread be such as is usual to be eaten at the table with other meats, but the best and purest wheat bread that conveniently may be gotten'.[5] Now, of course, there was already a problem built into the novelty of a prayer book, written in the idiom of religious devotion, acquiring statutory authority: in what sense could phrases like 'it shall suffice' and 'conveniently may be gotten' produce legally binding requirements, or in what sense were they intrinsically advisory rather than enforceable? But nonetheless, given the widespread assumption among magistrates at the time that the rubrics of the prayer book were indeed requirements, the issue should have been simple: ordinary wheat bread, rather than special bread, should be used in communion. However, there remained a

[5] Christopher Haigh, '"A Matter of Much Contention in the Realm": Parish Controversies over Communion Bread in Post-Reformation England', *History*, 88.291 (July, 2003): 393–404, 394.

loophole. The same Act of Uniformity also stated that, in case of any irreverence or contempt of the ceremonies of the Church, the Queen had the authority to 'ordain and publish such further ceremonies or rites, as may be most for the advancement of God's glory, the edifying of his Church, and the due reverence of Christ's holy mysteries and sacraments'.[6] And the Queen, always nervous about innovations that stank of Geneva, wasted no time in doing so: the 1559 Royal Injunctions included an order that 'for the more reverence to be given to these holy mysteries', instead of plain bread, sacramental bread should be 'bigger in compass and thickness, as the usual bread and wafer heretofore named singing cakes'.[7] Yet despite this injunction, which apparently required a return to something like the old practice, the provision in the new prayer book was never revised or repealed.

So what was the legal status of communion bread? To Archbishop Matthew Parker, writing to Sir William Cecil, the answer was clear: 'They that like not the injunctions force much the statute in the book. I tell them they do evil to make odious comparison betwixt statute and injunction, and yet I say and hold, that the injunction hath authority by proviso of the statute.'[8] In other words, Parliament had made the Queen supreme governor of the Church of England, so she had statutory authority to make ecclesiastical law overruling statute. This (logically somewhat flawed) argument was to become standard fare among those who favoured strong royal authority over the Church, for instance in defences of the Court of High Commission, a new ecclesiastical court that had neither theological basis nor constitutional authority except that the Queen had convened it.[9] And yet on the issue of wafer cakes, Parker lost, and lost badly, not because of any formal adjudication or change in government policy, but because of the progress of the Reformation. Throughout the 1560s, as Christopher Haigh has shown, ecclesiastical courts followed the Queen's injunction and prosecuted more radical Protestant ministers and parishioners for refusing to use old-style wafer cakes. But so many Protestants—and not just Puritans like the authors of the 1572 *Admonition to Parliament*—could see that even the *Book of Common Prayer* regarded wafer cakes as superstitious, that attempts at legal enforcement of the Elizabethan injunction broke apart upon the shoals of theology. By the late 1570s, without one jot of law having changed, ecclesiastical courts had flipped on their heads and instead were now following the prayer book to prosecute conservative ministers and parishioners for using the old wafer cakes. The ecclesiastical polity, then, was not simply the government acting in the spiritual realm; it could also be imagined as the unfolding of the Reformation according God's design, and the content of ecclesiastical law thus always depended

[6] *SR*, 1 Elizabeth *c*. 2.

[7] Haigh, '"A Matter of Much Contention"', 394.

[8] Quoted in Thomas Lathbury, *A History of the Book of Common Prayer and Other Books of Authority*, 3rd edn (Oxford: Messrs Parker, 1875), 107–8.

[9] See Ethan Shagan, 'The English Inquisition: Constitutional Conflict and Ecclesiastical Law in the 1590s', *The Historical Journal*, 47.3 (September, 2004): 541–65; Roland Usher, *The Rise and Fall of the High Commission* (Oxford: The Lawbook Exchange, Ltd, 1913).

to at least some degree on what that design was taken to be. Theology mattered in the enforcement of law, because the law itself was in some sense an act of exegesis, a reflection of changing and contested religious norms.

For another example, take the controversy over baptism by midwives. In the Middle Ages, women attendants had often performed *in extremis* baptisms of infants who seemed likely to die in childbirth, in order to promote them out of limbo into paradise. The 1559 *Book of Common Prayer*, following custom, included a special liturgy 'Of them that be baptized in private houses in time of necessity'.[10] While it stated that private baptism should only be performed when absolutely necessary, 'the child so baptized is lawfully and sufficiently baptized and ought not to be baptized again in the church', even if she or he unexpectedly survived. Protestant opinion in Europe was divided on this issue: Lutherans tended to appreciate lay baptism as a logical extension of the priesthood of all believers, while the Reformed tended to disapprove of lay baptism as assigning superstitious significance to the outward ceremony, as if God had not already decided whether the souls of infants were saved. As Reformed opinion spread in England, a 1576 convocation actually voted to interpret the rubric in the prayer book—very loosely—as having meant only that ordained ministers could baptize in private houses, rather than that midwives could do so. But the Queen refused to give her assent to this radical interpretation, and midwife baptism remained common.

And there the issue stood until the accession of James VI and I, who was astounded that the Church he inherited allowed such a superstitious practice. At the 1604 Hampton Court Conference, King James declared that he 'utterly disliked' lay baptism and, according to the quasi-official account of the conference by William Barlow, James 'grew somewhat earnest against the baptizing by women and laics'.[11] Another, unofficial manuscript account gives a more explicit description of the king's earnestness. James reportedly said, 'He had as leave his child were baptized by an ape as by a woman.' When told by a conservative cleric that if he banned baptisms by women 'all antiquity would be overthrown', James responded, as a good Protestant, that 'as well might they, by color of antiquity, bring in prayer for the dead'. When the Bishop of Peterborough then offered an ancient example of baptisms *in extremis* performed with sand instead of water, the king answered in his inimitable style, 'A turd for the argument, he might as well have pissed on them, for that had been more liker to water than sand.' After two hours of further debate, 'it was concluded that none should baptize but ministers, and that if the fathers did require it in time of danger of death, the ministers should come to their homes and baptize their children'.[12] The prayer book itself was thus revised so that the offending section became entitled 'Of them that are to be baptized in private houses in

[10] Brian Cummings, *The Book of Common Prayer: The Texts of 1549, 1559, and 1662* (Oxford: Oxford University Press, 2011), 146–7.

[11] William Barlow, *The Summe and Substance of the Conference, which, it Pleased his Excellent Majestie to Have* (London: V. S. for Mathew Law, 1605), sig. B4^{v}.

[12] BL Harleian MS 828, fols 32–8. This manuscript was first discovered by Roland Usher and printed in *The Reconstruction of the English Church*, 2 vols (New York: D. Appleton, 1910), 2.342–3.

time of necessitie *by the Minister of the Parish, or any other lawfull Minister, that can be procured.*'[13]

However, the 1604 Jacobean prayer book, unlike the 1559 Elizabethan prayer book, never acquired statutory authority. And even if it had, it merely omitted lay baptism rather than banning it outright, because banning it might have implied that people previously baptized by midwives needed to be rebaptized, an innovation which was anathema to the whole Christian tradition and smacked of Anabaptist heresy. So, while lay baptism was irregular, it was nonetheless valid, and there was simply no way to make it illegal without opening up a huge theological can of worms. Thus, the prayer book remained, rather awkwardly, a description of best practices rather than a legally binding framework—even after 1662, when a new version of the prayer book omitting lay baptism *did* acquire statutory authority.

A third and more obviously consequential issue was the legal status of Roman Catholics. Simply put: was it illegal to be a Roman Catholic in post-Reformation England? Well, yes and no. In theory, the law prosecuted crimes but did not make windows into men's souls. But if the law did not penetrate the soul, neither did the soul wholly contain Roman Catholicism: like all religions, and more than some, Catholicism was also a series of practices and institutions. During Queen Elizabeth's reign, recusancy laws required attendance at Church of England worship under pain of rapidly escalating fines. Attendance at unauthorized worship was also banned, as was administering Catholic sacraments, as was harbouring a Catholic priest, as was merely being a Catholic priest.[14] This last led to an oft-cited but perhaps apocryphal example of Jesuit casuistry: when asked by the inquisitor 'Are you a priest?' the priest was supposed to answer 'No, I am not a priest' but then silently in his mind reserve the rest of the sentence, 'of Apollo'. In sum, then, English law circumscribed certain Catholic activities deemed seditious or dangerous to the state, but seemed to avoid any robust legal prohibition of Catholicism itself.

But did it really? Catholics worked tirelessly to expose the absurdity of this legal regime. In his famous 'brag', for instance, the missionary priest Edmund Campion stated that he was strictly forbidden by the Jesuit order from meddling in any matters of state, and that he was a wholly loyal Englishman who would never commit any crime against his sovereign; his job was simply to fulfil his canonical office by reconverting England

[13] See e.g. Church of England, *Book of Common Prayer* (London: Robert Barker, 1604), sig. R3v.

[14] On the legal impediments to Catholicism, see e.g. Stefania Tutino, *Law and Conscience: Catholicism in Early Modern England, 1570–1625* (Aldershot: Ashgate, 2007); Michael Questier, 'Conformity, Catholicism and the Law,' in *Conformity and Orthodoxy in the English Church, c.1560–1660*, ed. Peter Lake and Michael Questier (Woodbridge: Boydell Press, 2000); Peter Lake and Michael Questier, *The Trials of Margaret Clitherow: Persecution, Martyrdom and the Politics of Sanctity in Elizabethan England* (London: Bloomsbury, 2011); Alexandra Walsham, *Catholic Reformation in Protestant Britain* (Farnham: Ashgate, 2014); Thomas McCoog, *The Society of Jesus in Ireland, Scotland, and England, 1541–1588: 'Our Way of Proceeding?'* (Leiden: Brill, 1996); J. C. H. Aveling, *Catholic Recusancy in the City of York, 1558–1791* (London: Catholic Record Society Publications, 1970).

to Catholicism, and he more or less dared the regime to arrest him for it.[15] When they called his bluff and sent Campion to the gallows in December 1581, he refused to admit any crimes against the state and wished the Queen a long and prosperous reign. According to Thomas Alfield's account of Campion's execution, when asked his opinion of the papal bull excommunicating Queen Elizabeth, Campion refused to answer. But when asked 'whether he renounced the pope', he replied that 'he was a Catholic'. To this, one of his interrogators replied, 'In your Catholicism … all treason is contained.'[16] This answer, in its magnificent clarity, was the centrepiece of Alfield's account, because it so pitilessly undermined the regime's claim that merely being Catholic did not violate the laws of the ecclesiastical polity.

And on this issue, Puritans and Jesuits ironically agreed. For Puritans, ecclesiastical law was not simply the whim of Parliament but the unfolding of the Reformation, and at the end of the day there could be no room for Antichrist in a properly functioning ecclesiastical polity. The great Puritan leader Thomas Cartwright, for instance—who had been Lady Margaret's Professor of Divinity at Cambridge before being stripped of his office by John Whitgift—argued that Catholics ought to be excommunicated from the Church rather than coerced into it, after which the state was bound to enforce the Old Testament judicial penalty for idolatry, which was death. Once papists were purged from the Church, in Cartwright's view they became solely the responsibility of the civil magistrate—although whether he imagined civil magistrates as officers in an ecclesiastical polity, or whether he thought the excommunicate had been removed altogether to the civil polity, is not entirely clear. Regardless, the magistrate ought to force excommunicated papists to attend sermons so that they might be converted. They were to be regularly 'examined how they profit', and 'if they profit not, to punish them. And, as their contempt groweth, so to increase the punishment, until such times as they declare manifest tokens of unrepententness; and then, as rotten members that do not only no good nor service in the body, but also corrupt and infect others, cut them off'.[17] Cartwright was not arguing here that ecclesiastical law ought to be changed to authorize these procedures; he was rather arguing that the procedures of ecclesiastical law were eternally established in Scripture and hence England, as a godly Protestant polity, already had such laws.

I could offer many more examples, large and small. In sum, I want to suggest that the incoherence of ecclesiastical law went far beyond the sense in which every system of jurisprudence inevitably fails in its loftiest aspirations. In this case, a series of theological issues would need to have been resolved in order to produce consensus about what the ecclesiastical polity was and what its laws were for. And since those very issues had

[15] See Peter Lake and Michael Questier, 'Puritans, Papists, and the "Public Sphere" in Early Modern England: The Edmund Campion Affair in Context', *Journal of Modern History*, 72.3 (2000): 587–627.

[16] Thomas Alfield, *A True Reporte of the Death & Martyrdome of M. Campion Jesuite and Preiste* (London: R. Rowlands or Verstegan, 1582), sig. C2r.

[17] John Ayre, ed., *The Works of John Whitgift*, 3 vols (Cambridge: Cambridge University Press, 1851–1853), 1.386.

intentionally been elided rather than confronted in the English Reformation, the most basic issues of ecclesiastical law remained frighteningly inchoate.

III

The work of Richard Hooker can usefully be imagined as a response to this demonstrable disorder. Hooker wrote at a moment in the late 1580s and 1590s when these various conflicts were at their height, and a wide array of theological and ecclesiological factions were interpreting law according to their very different views of ecclesiastical polity. Puritans, who regarded the ceremonialism of the *Book of Common Prayer* as rank popery and a stumbling block to evangelical conversion, argued that their Christian liberty freed them from any ecclesiastical laws that violated their consciences. In practice, this meant that Puritan ministers refused to follow rubrics of the prayer book they found offensive, like wearing the required vestments or asking questions to infants during baptism, and many Church of England officials were hard-pressed to explain why they should prosecute these conscientious Protestants when so many unreconstructed Catholics were running around the country unmolested. At the same time, Roman Catholics claimed that they could be loyal English subjects without being subjects of the ecclesiastical polity at all; they argued that there was no intrinsic connection between religious affiliation and civic identity, hence England's ecclesiastical laws were binding only upon those who acknowledged the monarch as supreme governor of the Church. Presbyterians—at this point a subset of Puritans who regarded the government of the Church of England as unscriptural and hence unlawful—claimed that the English church courts had no jurisdiction at all because they lacked biblically mandated discipline. In essence, Presbyterians regarded ecclesiastical law as a higher law, discoverable in Scripture and universally binding upon Christians. Hence human governments had virtually no discretion, they merely enforced (or failed to enforce) the law as godly ministers defined it. By the later 1580s, there were also more radical views appearing in embryo, denying that the ecclesiastical polity was any larger than the individual congregation, which was, on religious matters, acknowledged by Scripture as a commonwealth entire unto itself.

Hooker's masterpiece *Of the Lawes of Ecclesiasticall Politie* was an attempt to bulldoze through this morass and explain why ecclesiastical law was not an unfolding of the Reformation, and did not require conscientious doctrinal assent, but was simply a matter of obedience to properly constituted authority. The heart of Hooker's argument was that the views of his Puritan opponents—that 'nothing ought to be established in the Church which is not commanded in the word of God', and that non-scriptural ecclesiastical laws were not binding if they violated the conscience—were categorically wrong, misunderstanding both the nature of ecclesiastical law and the nature of Christian liberty. Puritans, Hooker alleged, treated the Gospel as if it were an Old Testament law book, instituting fixed rules that allowed no deviation, but it was not so. 'Are we bound while the world standeth to put nothing in practice but only that which was at the very first?' Hooker asked with mock incredulity.[18] No indeed, for 'the Gospel, by not making many things unclean as the Law did, hath sanctified those things generally to all, which particularly each man unto himself must sanctify by a reverend and holy use'.[19] Most things, that is, are not forbidden to Christians, nor are they required; instead God left them indifferent, to be used or not used as is most expedient.

For Hooker, however, the spiritual indifference of so much outward behaviour was not an invitation to individual liberty, but rather an invitation *to make good laws*. As he put it,

> Those things which the law of God leaveth arbitrary and at liberty are all subject unto the positive laws of men, which laws for the common benefit abridge particular men's liberty in such things, as far as the rules of equity will suffer. This we must either maintain or else overturn the world and make every man his own commander.[20]

This last line is particularly important: the Puritans claimed immunity from ecclesiastical laws which violated their consciences, but Hooker argued that this was as much as to suggest that 'every man is left to the freedom of his own mind' whether to follow the law, which essentially rendered it no law at all. The Puritan argument, he claimed with some hyperbole, 'shaketh universally the very fabric of government, tendeth to anarchy and mere confusion, dissolveth families, dissipateth colleges, corporations, armies, overthroweth kingdoms, churches, and whatsoever is now through the providence of God by authority and power upheld'.[21] God's purpose in leaving so many things indifferent was not to loose mere anarchy upon the world, but to 'make that provision by laws which is most convenient and fit'.[22]

This was the core of Richard Hooker's case in the central books of the *Lawes*: that there could be no such thing as conscience against a well-founded law, because obedience in outward and indifferent matters was principally due not to the abstract religious principles behind the law, but to the law itself. But in subsequent centuries, what became much more famous about Hooker's *Lawes* was not this authoritarian framework, but the political theory that he used to explain exactly how ecclesiastical laws could be well-founded in the first place. That is, for Hooker, the ecclesiastical polity was not somehow separated from or in tension with the civil polity, but rather they were precisely coterminous, the same body politic performing two different functions. In a famous passage, he argued

[18] Richard Hooker, *The Folger Library Edition of the Works of Richard Hooker*, 7 vols, ed. W. Speed Hill (Cambridge, MA: Harvard University Press, 1977–1998), 2.75 (5.20.4). Hereafter cited as WRH.

[19] WRH, 1.151 (2.3.1).

[20] WRH, 2.374–5 (5.71.4). On Hooker's views of what exactly 'equity' will suffer, see Ethan Shagan, 'Religious Nonconformity and the Quality of Mercy: *The Merchant of Venice* in Reformation Context', *The Oxford Handbook of the Age of Shakespeare*, ed. R. Malcolm Smuts (Oxford: Oxford University Press, 2016).

[21] WRH, 1.237–8 (3.9.3).

[22] WRH, 1.236 (3.9.1).

that there are many different polities among men, and 'Church' is simply a title rightfully given to any polity that has true religion. Thus, just as a triangle remains the same shape regardless of which of its sides functioned as the base, so the civil and ecclesiastical polities are the same body when it performs different functions:

> We hold that, seeing there is not any man of the Church of England but the same man is also a member of the commonwealth, nor any man a member of the commonwealth which is not also of the Church of England; therefore, as in a figure triangular the base doth differ from the sides thereof, and yet one and the selfsame line is both a base and also a side (a side simply; a base if it chance to be the bottom and underlie the rest), so, albeit properties and actions of one kind do cause the name of a commonwealth, qualities and functions of another sort the name of a Church to be given unto a multitude, yet one and the selfsame multitude may in such sort be both.[23]

It thus made perfect sense that, since the English state made its laws through the Crown in Parliament, so, too, ecclesiastical laws should be made by the Crown in Parliament—the civil and ecclesiastical polities were, after all, two different faces of the same commonwealth. Likewise, just as the Queen had power to appoint civil judges to rule in her name, so she had power to appoint ecclesiastical judges to rule in her name. And just as civil laws changed over time, binding the consciences of the subjects who consented to those laws in Parliament, so ecclesiastical laws might change over time and be equally binding. From the point of view of political theory—and this is the part that modern readers tend to know about—Hooker's key point was that the English did not make their laws arbitrarily but by consent: every English subject consented to parliamentary statutes through their representatives, and having had a voice in the making of law, they could not justly condemn a law they did not like just because they found themselves in the minority. Indeed, the whole point of law was that it served the public good by restraining individual private goods, a process which would be impossible if those who disagreed with the law were exempted from its provisions. Hooker wrote, 'Jurisdiction is a yoke which law hath imposed on the necks of men, in such sort that they must endure it for the good of others, how contrary soever it be to their own particular appetites and inclinations.'[24] Or, as he put it elsewhere, 'In things indifferent, what the whole Church doth think convenient for the whole, the same if any part do willfully violate, it may be reformed and inrailed again by that general authority whereunto each particular is subject.'[25] Thus, no claim of individual conscience could free subjects from obedience to ecclesiastical laws, any more than from obedience to laws against theft or murder.

The beauty of this system was that it was a theological argument for why theology does not matter to the creation and enforcement of ecclesiastical law. This was ostensibly a version of the ecclesiastical polity that anyone could get behind, regardless of their

[23] WRH, 3.319 (8.1.2).
[24] WRH, 2.283 (5.62.16).
[25] WRH, 1.332 (4.13.7).

confessional affiliation, because rather than bowing to religion, law neatly sidestepped religion. The ecclesiastical polity could, if it wished, ban wafer cakes or allow them, ban lay baptism or allow it, ban Roman Catholicism or allow it, and everyone had to go along because the law itself was an act of sovereignty over matters indifferent rather than an act of religious interpretation.

Now, of course, Hooker's *was* a theological argument, regardless of its elaborate claims not to be. Buried between its bookends of abstract theoretical speculation about sovereignty and jurisdiction in Books 1 and 8, Books 2 through 7 contained well over a thousand pages of intense religious polemic, backed by countless controversial scriptural and patristic citations, effectively accusing the Puritans of Anabaptism for daring to assert what had previously been more or less assumed by everyone: that ecclesiastical law was not quite at the discretion of magistrates like other laws, but was a unique species with unique religious requirements. But nonetheless, Hooker's ostensible refusal to accept the legal arbitration of the Spirit is what made his *Lawes* so attractive to those who saw the English Reformation as essentially national and communal rather than confessional, who valued piety above orthodoxy, and who came to regard enthusiasm rather than popery as the greatest threat to the Church of England.

Now, of course, Hooker's system was prescriptive rather than descriptive: alternative Presbyterian and Independent visions also had their innings, and large minorities always rejected Hooker's view that Christians could outsource their consciences to parliamentary representatives. The English Church never really became a Hookerian Church, however much he was lionized. But nonetheless, there was something sublime about Hooker's view that the state's cognizance of religion was no more or less shaped by divine law, and no more or less binding upon Christian subjects, that its cognizance of contracts or torts. Hooker is thus in some sense a hero of liberal modernity and the victory of rationalist constitutionalism; he tamed the English Reformation and made it safe for the nineteenth century.

IV

Except that he didn't. Because just as Hooker was starting to get really popular as a political theorist nearly a century after his death, his vision of the ecclesiastical polity suddenly became obsolete. That is, Hooker's whole edifice was built upon the proposition that there is '[not] any man a member of the commonwealth which is not also of the Church of England,' and after 1689, this dramatically ceased to be the case: tens of thousands of dissenting English subjects were no longer members of the Church of England at all.

And yet, in a crowning act of incoherence, the 1689 Toleration Act did not dismantle the ecclesiastical polity when it authorized religious pluralism; instead, it left dissenters still members of that polity despite not being members of the Church of England. The stated intent of the 1689 Act was to free Protestant dissenters from civil penalties for their nonconformity. Thus it voided only those laws and canons (or sections of laws and canons) that punished subjects for their mere dissent; it did not void laws that placed positive requirements upon subjects and regulated their lives. So, despite not being members of the same Church, because they remained members of the same ecclesiastical polity, Anglicans and dissenters retained all of their canonical obligations to one another, as codified in an enormous legal tradition that had been created in the utterly different conditions of religious monopoly and legal uniformity.

I want to briefly describe one example of this persistence of the Old Regime, relating to an issue we have already discussed: the problem of lay baptism.[26] In September 1839, a girl named Elizabeth Cliff was born in the village of Gedney, Lincolnshire, daughter to Thomas Cliff, blacksmith, and his wife Sarah Cliff, both Wesleyan Methodists. On 1 October, the parents brought Elizabeth Cliff to be baptized by the Methodist Reverend Elisha Balley, according to the Methodist rite. Less than three months later, the infant Elizabeth Cliff died, cause unspecified, a victim of one of the thousand natural shocks that flesh was heir to in the nineteenth century. On 16 December, the distraught father came to the vicar of the parish, Thomas Sweet Escott, and requested that he bury his daughter in the churchyard and perform the burial service over her. Escott refused. The following morning, the Methodist Reverend Robert Bond again begged Escott to bury the baby, and again Escott refused. As one of the lawyers prosecuting Escott would later describe this failure to meet his professional and ethical obligations, 'It would have been more consistent with the defendant's calling if he had erred, in this matter, on the side of humanity' (59). Instead, Elizabeth was buried in the churchyard of Gedney by her parents, without the services of the parish minister.

As a result, the Methodist Frederick Mastin, a prominent Lincolnshire farmer and patron to the Cliff family, initiated a prosecution (technically he 'promoted the office of the judge', a way for plaintiffs to initiate essentially criminal proceedings) against the priest Thomas Escott in the Court of Arches. The precise accusation was that he had violated Canon 68 of the canons published in 1604, entitled 'Ministers not to refuse to christen or bury'. The canon read:

> No minister shall refuse or delay to christen any child according to the form of the *Book of Common Prayer* that is brought to the church to him upon Sundays or holy days to be christened, or to bury any corpse that is brought to the church or churchyard, convenient warning being given him thereof before, in such manner and form as is prescribed in the said *Book of Common Prayer*; and if he shall refuse to christen

[26] The principal documentation for the case is in W. C. Curteis, ed., *A Full Report of the Case of Mastin v. Escott* (London: Crofts and Blenkarn, 1841); and George Brodrick and William Fremantle, eds., *A Collection of the Judgments of the Judicial Committee of the Privy Council in Ecclesiastical Cases Relating to Doctrine and Discipline* (London: John Murray, 1865). Page numbers in parentheses are references to W. C. Curteis, ed., *A Full Report of the Case of Mastin v. Escott*. I am writing about this subject at much greater length elsewhere, in an article co-authored with my colleague Thomas Laqueur; the material here is based upon my own research, but I want to thank Professor Laqueur for invaluable discussions of it with me.

> the one, or bury the other (except the party deceased were denounced excommunicated *majori excommunicatione* for some grievous and notorious crime, and no man able to testify of his repentance) he shall be suspended by the bishop of the diocese from his ministry by the space of three months. (1)

Since the infant Elizabeth Cliff had not been excommunicated for any grievous and notorious crime, the only remaining legitimate grounds of refusal to bury her would have come from the rubric for burial in the *Book of Common Prayer*, which in 1662 had legally created two new exceptions: ministers were forbidden to bury suicides and those who died 'unbaptized' (5).

Of course, 'unbaptized' was the key term here, a word open to diverse theological interpretations. Over the course of several days, the prosecution argued that little Elizabeth's baptism had been a lawful baptism, even though she was not baptized by an ordained minister, because a Methodist was, at law, simply one class of layperson, and in the seventeenth century it had been established in English law that a lay baptism was irregular but not invalid. They also pointed out one amusing *reductio ad absurdum* of any argument that a lay baptism was invalid: the eighteenth-century Archbishop of Canterbury Thomas Secker had himself been baptized by a nonconformist minster without episcopal ordination, i.e. a layman, hence by Escott's logic he should not have received Christian burial, nor should any of the infants whom he baptized, including King George III (76).

Not so, said Escott's defence:

> The question here is not whether these persons are or are not members of the Church of Christ, but whether they are members of our own Church—of the Church of England as by law established in this country. If not, what right can the fact of their being members of the Church of Christ give them to have the burial service of the Church of England read over their remains? (140)

Escott's attorneys claimed that the relevant canons and statutes had been written at a time when there was only one legally recognized Church, hence in the canon law of burial, 'in sense, any person not in communion with the Church of England is unbaptized' (122). Or elsewhere: '[Methodists] are no longer members of the Church of England; whether they are members of the universal Church of Christ is not the question for discussion' (152). In the opinion of Escott and his defence team, a logical consequence of the Toleration Act and the advent of religious pluralism in England was that 'they who baptize in these cases should be responsible for the burial of infants who die in their own persuasion' (109).

In short, the heart of the matter was a battle for the Church of England to retain meaningful boundaries and identity in the anomalous and untenable condition where that Church remained a branch of the state which owed services to all subjects, despite the fact that many subjects were no longer members of the Church of England at all. If according to English law Wesleyans could not be excluded from the solemn rites of the Church of England despite their manifest schism, then according to Escott's lawyers 'every person in the country must be within the pale of the Church; and the Church of England will be placed in a situation in which it has never yet been attempted to place any Church in any age or in any other country' (167). On the one hand English law gave every person the right to choose their own religion, but on the other hand English law gave every person a right to the services and ministry of the Church of England; this was an intolerable contradiction that had to be corrected, and the centrepiece of Escott's defense was therefore that it violated his conscience to perform his holy office for a schismatic.

But the judge in the case, Sir Herbert Jenner, found for the prosecution, as did the Judicial Committee of the Privy Council when the case was appealed, arguing that nonconformists did indeed have a right to the services of the Anglican ministry and to burial in the public property of the churchyard. According to Jenner, a victory for Escott would 'almost amount to a declaration that in the eyes of the law the great body of dissenters ... are not to be considered Christians' (227). Once the controversy was reduced to the legal validity of lay baptism, in other words, it was an open and shut case. But of course, it was no such thing, because it also reduced the Anglican clergy to the status of mere civil servants. Escott's conviction thus became a *cause célèbre* for conservatives in the Church of England, who were just beginning to see that Establishment came with burdens as well as benefits. Now, in a wonderful irony, instead of Puritans arguing for nonconformity, it was High Church Anglicans like Thomas Escott who argued that they should not be forced to obey the laws of England against their conscience, because ecclesiastical law was not just a matter of statute but rather the unfolding of the Reformation.

V

So to return to the question with which we began: why is it that perhaps the most important book on law written in early modern England was actually a book about the Church? The answer is not that the Church was at the cutting edge of legal modernity, as fans of Richard Hooker have so often claimed, but rather just the opposite: the hopelessly convoluted and contradictory *ancien régime* of the English Church was so great a threat to England's legal rationalization and centralization that even the brilliant Richard Hooker proved powerless to stop it.

I have argued here that the heart of the problem, and the reason it could not be resolved, was that the ecclesiastical polity faced a fundamental dilemma: it had legal jurisdiction over precisely the sphere of private, ethical, spiritual, and conscientious matters that *in some sense* transcended the remit of law itself. The question of *in what sense*—when was ecclesiastical law a matter of legislators and courts, and when was it a matter of conscience and exegesis? Could magistrates make ecclesiastical law at will, or were they bound to spiritual norms?—inevitably required theological answers, and England remained theologically fragmented from the birth of the ecclesiastical polity under Henry VIII all the way through its painfully slow demise in the three centuries after 1689.

Scholars of law and literature need to understand this problem because it is at least implicitly invoked in the countless literary and dramatic crises that ensue when public authority tries to press private conscience into conformity. English Protestant ministers seem to have stopped publishing explicitly religious plays after Nathaniel Woode's *The Conflict of Conscience* was published in 1581, but English Protestant playwrights never stopped worrying about the state's capacity to bind the consciences of its subjects.[27] In *Measure for Measure*, the 'precise' Angelo decides that the people of Vienna have too much sexual freedom, even while he coerces Isabella into sex; an Athenian law in *A Midsummer Night's Dream* allows Hermia to be put to death if she will not marry the suitor chosen by her father. In Marlowe's *The Jew of Malta*, the Christian governor of Malta plunders Jewish estates unless they convert, to which the Jew Barabas responds, 'Is theft the ground of your religion?' (1.2.99).[28] The interpretation of these scenes, whether tragic or comic, might be transformed if it were recognized that in early modern English minds the state that is enforcing these consciences is not the civil polity but an ecclesiastical polity whose contours, jurisdiction, and coercive authority were all deeply ambiguous and disputed. When, in these and other literary texts, is ecclesiastical law properly made and enforced by magistrates, and when are magistrates limited in their legislation and prosecution by scriptural warrant and the unfolding of the Reformation? This is not the place to try to provide an answer, but this essay has suggested that these and countless other Renaissance literary texts begged the question.

Bibliography

Bray, Gerald, ed. *Tudor Church Reform: The Henrician Canons of 1535 and the Reformatio Legum Ecclesiasticarum* (Woodbridge: Boydell Press, 2000).

Haigh, Christopher. '"A Matter of Much Contention in the Realm": Parish Controversies over Communion Bread in Post-Reformation England', *History*, 88.291 (July, 2003): 393–404.

Helmholz, R. H. *Roman Canon Law in Reformation England* (Cambridge: Cambridge University Press, 1990).

Helmholz, R. H. *The Oxford History of the Laws of England*, Vol. 1: *The Canon Law and Ecclesiastical Jurisdiction from 597 to the 1640s* (Oxford: Oxford University Press, 2004).

[27] Erin Kelly, 'Conflict of Conscience and Sixteenth-Century Religious Drama', in *ELR*, 44.3 (Autumn, 2014): 388–419.

[28] Christopher Marlowe, *The Jew of Malta*, ed. T. N. R. Rogers (New York: Dover, 2003). On *Measure for Measure*, issues of ecclesiastical polity have indeed received significant consideration. See e.g. Sarah Beckwith, 'Medieval Penance, Reformation Repentance and *Measure for Measure*', in *Reading the Medieval in Early Modern England* (Cambridge: Cambridge University Press, 2007), 193–204; Peter Lake, *Antichrist's Lewd Hat: Protestants, Papists, and Players in Post-Reformation England* (New Haven: Yale University Press, 2002), ch. 15; Debora Shuger, *Political Theologies in Shakespeare's England: the Sacred and the State in 'Measure for Measure'* (New York: Palgrave, 2001).

Hill, W. Speed, ed. *Studies in Richard Hooker: Essays Preliminary to an Edition of his Works* (Cleveland: Press of Case Western Reserve University, 1972).

Houlbrooke, Ralph. *Church Courts and the People during the English Reformation, 1520–1570* (Oxford: Oxford University Press, 1979).

Ingram, Martin. *Church Courts, Sex, and Marriage in England, 1570–1640* (Cambridge: Cambridge University Press, 1987).

Joyce, A. J. *Richard Hooker and Anglican Moral Theology* (Oxford: Oxford University Press, 2012).

Kirby, Torrance. *Richard Hooker's Doctrine of the Royal Supremacy* (Leiden: Brill, 1990).

Kirby, Torrance. *Richard Hooker, Reformer and Platonist* (Aldershot: Ashgate, 2005).

Kirby, Torrance, ed. *A Companion to Richard Hooker* (Leiden: Brill, 2008).

Lake, Peter and Michael Questier. 'Puritans, Papists, and the "Public Sphere" in Early Modern England: The Edmund Campion Affair in Context', *Journal of Modern History*, 72.3 (2000), 587–627.

Lake, Peter and Michael Questier. *The Trials of Margaret Clitherow: Persecution, Martyrdom, and the Politics of Sanctity in Elizabethan England* (London: Bloomsbury, 2011).

McGrade, Arthur, ed. *Richard Hooker and the Construction of the Christian Community* (Tempe: MRTS, 1997).

Outhwaite, R. B. *The Rise and Fall of the English Ecclesiastical Courts, 1500–1860* (Cambridge: Cambridge University Press, 2006).

Questier, Michael. 'Conformity, Catholicism, and the Law', in *Conformity and Orthodoxy in the English Church, c.1560–1660*, ed. Peter Lake and Michael Questier (Woodbridge: Boydell Press, 2000), 237–61.

Secor, Philip. *Richard Hooker and the Via Media* (Bloomington: AuthorHouse, 2006).

Shagan, Ethan. 'The English Inquisition: Constitutional Conflict and Ecclesiastical Law in the 1590s', *The Historical Journal*, 47.3 (September, 2004): 541–65.

Shagan, Ethan. *The Rule of Moderation: Violence, Religion, and the Politics of Restraint in Early Modern England* (Cambridge: Cambridge University Press, 2011).

Tutino, Stefania. *Law and Conscience: Catholicism in Early Modern England, 1570–1625* (Aldershot: Ashgate, 2007).

CHAPTER 18

MAKING LAW AND RECORDING IT

John Selden on Excommunication

JASON P. ROSENBLATT

THE life and work of John Selden (1584–1654), acknowledged by his contemporaries and by posterity to be the most learned person of seventeenth-century England, fall within the compass of this volume, combining literary wit and philology with juridical thinking. Philology is not a value-free discipline, and Selden applied a historico-philological approach to ancient texts in order to assert the authority of civil institutions and to defend against the ecclesiastical abuse of power.

In mid-1640s England, the flashpoint in the struggle between state and church—Parliament and the Presbyterians—was excommunication, and no one fought harder against its control by the church than Selden. He opposed the Presbyterians' many attempts in the Westminster Assembly of Divines to exclude, even for unenumerated sins, anyone it identified as scandalous or ignorant from the sacrament of the Lord's Supper. As a corollary, and respecting decorum to a remarkable degree, he defended parliamentary rule in a number of venues, always adjusting his arguments to his audience: on the floor of the Westminster Assembly; in the House of Commons, where he was one of the few survivors to continue in the Long Parliament his opposition to the king that began in the 1620s; at table while living in a ménage à trois with the Earl and Countess of Kent, where his transcribed conversation found its way into the literary canon as *Table Talk*; in the massive three volumes of *De synedriis*, his study of the Great Synedrion as a continuous civil rather than ecclesiastical institution from the time of Moses until the destruction of the second temple; and, less successfully, in his study at Whitefriars. It was there that poet and MP Edmund Waller confessed, at his arraignment by the Commons for treason in 1643, that he imparted to Selden and two fellow MPs, Bulstrode Whitelocke and William Pierrepont, the plot that he had contrived 'to surprize the City *Militia*, and some Members of Parliament, and to let in the King's forces … [and] to dissolve the Parliament'. Selden and his company 'did so inveigh against any such thing, *as treachery and baseness, and that which might be the occasion of shedding much blood, That* (he said) *he durst not for the awe and respect he had for* Selden ... *communicate any of the particulars ... but was almost disheartened himself to proceed in it*'.[1]

Johann Sommerville, noting the permanent reversal of 'the clericalism of the Laudian regime', goes so far as to say that 'arguably, if there was a revolution in the mid seventeenth century, it was Erastian and not puritan in nature'.[2] And, as Robert Baillie, one of the Scots commissioners of the Westminster Assembly, in exasperated defeat, described Selden, 'This man is the head of the Erastians.'[3] The abundant evidence of Selden's important struggles against ecclesiastical abuse in the matter of excommunication contrasts with the meagre evidence, if any, of John Milton's engagement with this issue. The famous last line of the poet's attack on the Westminster Assembly in his sonnet with a tail, *On the New Forcers of Conscience*, 'New Presbyter is but old Priest writ large', might be the most apt summary of Selden's massive *De synedriis*, but there is no sign that Milton ever read that work. Certainly he never explicitly attacks excommunication. In both his *Doctrine and Discipline of Divorce* and the *Areopagitica* he praises both Selden and his recondite study of the rabbinic Noachide laws, *De jure naturali & gentium, iuxta disciplinam Ebraeorum* ['On Natural Law and the Law of Nations according to the Teaching of the Jews']. That work hardly seems as relevant to his own political and religious interests. His sonnet attacks plurality and the grouping of English churches in classes, but neither of these would seem to matter as much to Milton as the unrestrained power of church elders to unify the church by coercing conformity and purging uncomplying members at will.

In 1646, when he wrote the sonnet, Milton would surely have sympathized with the pro-Army, anti-Scots, and pro-Erastian Independent members of the Assembly, who tended toward toleration on issues of religious heterodoxy. The desire to excommunicate virtually at will was inextricable from opposition to toleration. The Presbyterian *Letter of the Ministers of the City of London Presented ... to the Reverend Assembly of Divines ... against Toleration* (1 January 1646) makes this explicit. And in the same month, Jeremiah Whitacre preached a sermon to a combined gathering of the Lords, Commons, and Members of the Assembly, emphasizing church unity and opposing toleration. The sermon concluded with a warning against schism and a defense of church hierarchy, 'that the whole body might be fitly joined together'.[4] How different from Milton's great defence of schisms and sectaries in the *Areopagitica*, where the perfection

[1] Bulstrode Whitelocke, *Memorials of the English Affairs* [from the reign of Charles I to the Restoration of Charles II] (London: 1682), 66.

[2] Johann P. Sommerville, 'Hobbes, Selden, Erastianism, and the History of the Jews', in *Hobbes and History*, ed. G. A. J. Rogers and Tom Sorell (London and New York: Routledge, 2000), 163.

[3] Robert Baillie, *The Letters and Journals of Robert Baillie*, ed. David Laing, 3 vols (Edinburgh: 1841–1842), 2.265.

[4] Quoted in George Yule, *Puritans in Politics: The Religious Legislation of the Long Parliament 1640–1647* (Appleford: Sutton Courtenay Press, 1981), 169. See also the argument for religious conformity, citing verses from the building of Solomon's temple, in Thomas Hill, *The Good Old Way, God's Way* (24 April 1644), 39.

of 'The Temple of the Lord ... consists in this, that out of many moderat varieties and brotherly dissimilitudes that are not vastly disproportionall arises the goodly and the gracefull symmetry that commends the whole pile and structure.'[5] And yet nothing more can be managed than a tentative eking out of a few Miltonic lines possibly alluding to excommunication.

The attention paid to Selden in relation to Milton in this essay will parallel not only their respective investments in the topic of excommunication but also their presence in English political life in the 1640s. One example of that difference is particularly striking. In a famous passage in *The Reason of Church Government*, Milton explains that he was forced to abandon his plans to become a minister, 'Church-outed by the Prelats':

> perceaving what tyranny had invaded the Church, that he who would take Orders must subscribe slave, and take an oath withall, which unlesse he took with a conscience that would retch, he must strait perjure, or split his faith, I thought it better to preferre a blamelesse silence before the sacred office of speaking bought, and begun with servitude and forswearing. (*YP*, 1.823)

As the Yale editor points out, by the time Milton was thirty, 'all hope of church reformation under Laudian primacy had ended' (822 n. 160), and the oath that repulsed Milton is the obnoxious 'Et Cetera' oath, part of the Canons imposed by William Laud in 1640. The oath was ridiculed because aspiring clergymen would be required to swear not to alter institutions that it does not even specify. The formula includes the statement, 'nor will I ever give my consent to alter the government of this Church by archbishops, bishops, deans, and archdeacons, &c.'[6]

In November 1640, the same month as the opening of the Long Parliament and three months before he would be imprisoned in the Tower, William Laud wrote to Selden offering to annul the canons for church government containing the hated oath in exchange for escaping a criminal charge. He begins: 'I understand that the bysynes about the late Cannons will be handled againe in your House to Morrow.' He notes that the Commons has laid aside the matter of ship money—a tax unfairly levied by Charles I during peacetime and extended even to inland counties—'as a thinge yt will dye of it selfe, & I am glad it will have so quiett a death. Maye not these unfortunat Cannons be sufferd to dye as quietlye ... ?'[7]

During Laud's subsequent trial on the charge of treason, Selden obliged him by supplying at his request the transcript from a Patent Roll of Edward III for use in his defence.[8] It did not help. But Selden was able to honour a more modest request. On 8

5 John Milton, *Areopagitica* (1644), in *Complete Prose Works of John Milton*, gen. ed. Don M. Wolfe, 8 vols (New Haven: Yale University Press, 1953–1972), 2.555. This Yale edition of Milton's prose will be abbreviated as *YP*.

6 The text of the oath appears in Samuel Rawson Gardiner, *History of England 1603–1642*, 10 vols (London: 1891), 9.146.

7 Laud to Selden, Lambeth, 29 November 1640. BL MS Selden supra 108 fol. 137.

8 G. J. Toomer, *John Selden: A Life in Scholarship*, 2 vols (Oxford: Oxford University Press, 2009), 2.564–5 n. 10. This magnificent work is an indispensable guide to Selden's intellectual life.

November 1645, he was one of four members of the House appointed to draw up an ordinance concurring with the decision of the House of Lords to accept the petition of the Archbishop of Canterbury concerning the manner of his execution two days hence, on 10 January: 'That it might be done by taking off his Head only.' This session ended with a reading of the ordinance, which states, in part:

> Whereas *Wm*. Archbishop of *Canterbury* stands adjudged attainted of High Treason by Ordinance of both Houses of Parliamment; and is thereby to suffer the Pains of Death, as a Person attainted of High Treason should or ought to do; It is now *Ordained* by the Lords and Commons assembled in Parliament, That as touching his corporal Punishment, the Head only of the said Archbishop shall be cut off at the *Tower Hill*, at the accustomed Place there used for such Purpose: And that afterwards, his Head and Body shall be delivered unto his Servants, or some of them, to be by their Care buried.[9]

Once prelacy was abolished, it was not easy to find a replacement. Selden was the most influential representative of the House of Commons to the Westminster Assembly of Divines, but the twenty members of the Commons were outnumbered by the 149 divines. (These proportions varied during the ten years that the Assembly met, from 1643–1653.) His signature appears first among the MPs in the summoning ordinance (May 1643) that created the Assembly 'to be consulted with by the Parliament' for reforming the doctrine and discipline of the English church. On opening day, 19 July 1643, jealously guarding parliamentary privilege, Selden, along with William Pierrepont, another MP, thwarted the Assembly's plan to begin its deliberations by calling a fast that would provide an opportunity to address the nation's most serious problems. By insisting that the ordinance had assigned the Assembly only the limited role of petitioner, Selden wanted to discourage anyone in this still nascent body from ever imagining that control over ecclesiology could be wrested from Parliament. This would be his primary mission in the Assembly. Chad Van Dixhoorn has pointed out the privileges that his learning and prestige had earned him: 'Selden was the only MP whose writings and speeches were quoted in the Assembly, and who held the floor with speeches as long as the theologians.' And he enjoyed the distinction of being referred to by everyone in the Assembly—even by his Presbyterian adversaries—not as 'the previous speaker' but as the 'learned gentleman'.[10] Despite this deference, however, many of Selden's most learned arguments fell on deaf ears. His immense

[9] *CJ*, 4.13–14. This dispassionate record is especially chilling at a time when ISIS sends out videos of its beheadings. But criminals could be hanged, disemboweled, emasculated, and quartered. As Hilary Mantel reminds us in her Thomas Cromwell trilogy, beheadings were reserved for the elite.

[10] The information in this paragraph comes from the Introduction by Chad Van Dixhoorn to his immensely valuable edition of *The Minutes and Papers of the Westminster Assembly 1643–1652*, 5 vols (Oxford: Oxford University Press, 2012), 1.2, 15–17, and 165–9 (the summoning ordinance). Future references to the volume and page number of *Assembly* are to this edition.

knowledge of classical and rabbinic sources sometimes worked against him, provoking some of the ministers, for whom only New Testament verses were authoritative. Selden would have to rely on Parliament to accomplish what he could not in the Assembly.

By 'petitioner,' he must have intended the posture of a humble supplicant, but the Assembly interpreted it instead as license to inundate Parliament with petitions. These always observed the formality of humility, sometimes even redundantly, as in their '*humble petition in pursuance of their humble advice formerly delivered into the House concerning persons not to be admitted to the Sacrament*'.[11] There would be many such petitions, and excommunication would take up a tremendous amount of the Assembly's time.[12] The Assembly would become increasingly strident in its demand for unlimited jurisdiction over determining scandalous and ignorant persons in the face of the Commons' increasingly less patient demands for a defined list. An unremarkable petition, repeating earlier requests that such persons be barred from the Lord's Table, sent on 5 March 1645, unintentionally drove the first wedge between the Lords and the Commons, satisfying the former but not the latter. From that point on—and despite its employment of 'humble' three times in a single sentence (*Assembly*, 5.176–7)—the Assembly ended its assigned advisory role to the Commons and began an adversarial one. The petition of 7 August 1645 concluded with a threat:

> Should things be so ordered (which God forbid) that any wicked & scandalous persons might without controll thrust themselves upon this Sacrament; wee do evidently foresee, that not only wee but many of our godly Brethren must be put upon this hard choice, either to forsake our Stations in the Ministry, which would be to us one of the greatest Afflictions, or else to partake in other men's sinnes, & thereby incurre the danger of their plagues. (*Assembly*, 5.234–5)

This was of course a struggle for jurisdictional power between the Assembly and Parliament, with the former either grudgingly complying or else ignoring the latter's persistent requests for specificity in identifying the scandalous and ignorant. Baillie succinctly expressed the Presbyterians' frustrated desire: 'We required to have power to exclude all scandalous as well as some, ... [but] the general they would not grant.'[13]

Finally, on 16 March 1646, Parliament issued an ordinance granting its own provincial commissions rather than the general assembly of the church the power to try

[11] (1 August 1645). William A. Shaw, *A History of the English Church during the Civil Wars and under the Commonwealth 1640–1660*, 2 vols (London: Longmans, 1900), 1.267.

[12] For example, sessions 303–311 (*Assembly*, 3.391–427), 349–52 (3.490–6), 354–76 (3.499–528), and 387–400 (3.550–9). For the full text of petitions claiming the authority specifically to excommunicate—excluding those addressing the right to censure and those asserting divine right in general—see *Assembly*, 5.176–7, 183–5, 188–92, 200–2, 210–18, 231, 257–8, and 299–302.

[13] Baillie, *Letters*, 2.307.

unenumerated scandals in every shire, thus making them the final court of appeal.[14] The Assembly's reply flirted with sedition:

> there is still a great defect in the Enumeration of scandalous sinnes; very many scandalous sinnes … being still omitted: And that the Provision of Commissioners … appeares to our Consciences to be so contrary to that way of Government which Christ hath appointed in his church … that wee dare not practise according to the Provision ….[15]

That the right to exclude belongs to the 'several Elderships … wee must, as formerly we have done, say expressely, It belongs unto them by Divine Right, & by the Will and appointment of Jesus Christ' (*Assembly*, 5.302). The House responded on 30 April 1646 by censuring the Assembly, charging it with breach of privilege, and suggesting that individual members might be subject to prosecution (*Assembly*, 4.82–97; *CJ*, 4.514–21).[16]

The Assembly's exorbitant and importuning requests for the power to excommunicate by divine right give specificity to the analogy in Selden's *Table Talk* of a bride on her wedding night whose impatience is unseemly:

> If this excommunication were quite taken away, the presbyters would be quiet; 'tis that they have a mind to, 'tis that they would fain be at. Like the wench that was to be married; she asked her mother when 'twas done, if she should go to bed presently? No, says her mother, you must dine first; And then to bed mother? No, you must dance after dinner; And then to bed mother? No, you must go to supper; And then to bed mother? & c.[17]

Selden at table can freely express his otherwise suppressed contempt of the Presbyterian members of the Assembly. The libidinous bride becomes an adulterous wife:

> The clergy would have us believe them against our own reason; as the woman would have had her husband against his own eyes when he took her with another man,

14 *An Ordinance of the Lords and Commons Assembled in Parliament for Keeping of Scandalous Persons from the Sacrament of the Lords Supper … and Supplying of Defects in Former Ordinances and Directions of Parliament Concerning Church-Government* (16 March 1646).

15 *Assembly*, 5.301–2, with MS underlining possibly in the hand of a parliamentary reader.

16 Sir John Evelyn began the session with a display of mordant wit: 'The House of Commons having not long since received a paper which bore the title of a petition, they did observe many things in it hardly consistent with the nature of that title …. The House of Commons is very sensible of the faithfull & usefull indeavours of your selves, & though they had not been soe often remembered of it, they would not have forgotten it.' But he reminds the Assembly of the 'great deale of trouble' that the petition has cost the House, 'which did find things in it that did strike at the foundation & rootes of the priviledges of parliament. Had this come from any but from this place or from any assembled …' The gap in the manuscript produces an effect of anacoluthon (4.85).

17 'Excommunication', in *The Table Talk of John Selden*, ed. Samuel Harvey Reynolds (Oxford: Clarendon, 1892), 67–8.

> which she stoutly denied: What! will you believe your own eyes before your own sweet wife?[18]

Coincidentally, Van Dixhoorn, editor of the Assembly minutes and a Presbyterian minister, also uses a marriage analogy, but from the other side of the aisle: 'The Commons ... acted not unlike a disgruntled spouse unwilling to understand his or her partner, arguing that the petition was unclear, and asking what "ignorant" and "scandalous" meant.'[19] One can understand the Assembly's frustration: the petition that means the most to them is frustratingly deferred by unsympathetic Mother Parliament. The House of Lords supports it; the divines assembled at Sion College present it; it is read by the Commons more than once; and then Parliament appoints a committee.

The Assembly's discomfiture may owe something to Parliament's many requests for specificity, which would be consistent with Selden's strategy: what exactly must one know in order not to be ignorant? What sins exactly are scandalous? He had earlier defeated the Assembly on the question of heresy in the same way:

> Give me leave to tell you what was the end of the House: not only to make some law & declaration against the opinions, but to proceed against the persons . . . . You do not give them hint enough how to proceed . . . . Unlesse you doe let the House of Commons know that ther be of those things that are direct Herisyes, then they cannot know how to proceed against them that have already disturbed you. (22 September 1643, *Assembly*, 2.145)

Predictably, the Assembly declined his request to provide specific examples of heresy. Selden was a deep-rooted Erastian, asserting the human rather than divine origin of excommunication and rejecting absolutely any clerical claims to civil jurisdiction. His hand is evident in the Commons' famous nine queries required of the Assembly specifically in reaction to the breach of privilege.[20] Although Selden handled contracts and conveyances and stayed out of the courtroom, he knew the litigator's first rule: never ask a question to which you don't already know the answer. Seven of the nine questions ask for scriptural proof that the Presbyterian clergy has *jure divino* powers. The sixth can stand in for all of them:

> Whether by the Word of God, the power of Judging and Declaring what are such Notorious and Scandalous Offences, for which persons guilty thereof are to be kept from the Sacrament of the Lord's Supper, and of conventing before them, trying,

[18] 'Clergy', *Table Talk*, 43. Many comedians have riffed on the punchline, most notably Richard Pryor. Amazon even sells a Pryor T-shirt emblazoned with a colloquial adaptation of the line: <http://www.youtube.com/watch?v=4zOA7SbNDQ>.

[19] Van Dixhoorn, *Introduction*, *Assembly*, 1.31.

[20] Toomer, *Selden*, 2.574 n. 77; see also Reynolds, *Table Talk*, 209: 'Selden, who had had a hand in framing these queries, was well aware that search as they would, they would never find answers to them in the text of Scripture.'

> and actual suspending from the Sacrament of the Lord's Supper such Offenders accordingly, is either in the Congregational Eldership, or Presbytery, or in any other Eldership, Congregation, or persons; and whether such powers are in them only, or in any of them, and in which of them, *Jure divino*, and by the will and appointment of Jesus Christ.[21]

The Commons committee that drafted the queries knew that it would be impossible for the Assembly to answer them affirmatively, and as if to underscore the point it required all signatories who might do so to 'set down their positive Opinions, with the expresse Texts of Scripture upon which their Opinions are grounded'. By asking for time when it knew it had been defeated, the Assembly became the object of yet another demeaning characterization in *Table Talk*: the deadbeat who cannot pay his share of the bar bill:

> When the queries were sent to the Assembly concerning the *jus divinum* of presbytery, their asking time to answer them, was a satire upon themselves. For if it were to be seen in the text, they might quickly turn to the place and show us it. Their delaying to answer makes us think there's no such thing there. They do just as you have seen a fellow do at a tavern reckoning, when he should come to pay his share; he puts his hands into his pockets, and keeps a grabling and a fumbling and shaking, at last tells you he has left his money at home; when all the company knew at first he had no money there; for every man can quickly find his own money.[22]

Unlike *Table Talk*, Selden's speeches in the Assembly are riddled with lacunae, but his stupendous work of scholarship, *De synedriis*, fills in all of the gaps to overflowing. Often an entire chapter provides the context for an otherwise lost spoken sentence transcribed as an incoherent fragment. Selden's penchant for digressions that sometimes become excurses is well known; those excurses can even become monographs, such as the 145-page treatise on the sabbath included in *De jure naturali et gentium*, even though it is not one of the seven rabbinic Noachide precepts that constitute the book's topic. The most extreme example occurs in Book 1 of the three-volume *De synedriis* (1650, 1653, 1655), which intends to be a history of one of those precepts: דינים *dinim* (L., *de judiciis*), the requirement that every society establish 'courts or a judicial system, including those obligations which we usually call "civil" '.[23] The bulk of the book consists of a 300-page treatise on excommunication, denying Presbyterian claims of divine right and ecclesiastical control.[24] It is even more learned than his early, great, and never superseded parallel

[21] *Assembly*, 1.215; and printed in *Questions Propounded to the Assembly of Divines by the House of Commons, April ult. 1646 Touching the Point of Jus Divinum in the Matter of Church-Government* (1646), 3–8.

[22] 'Presbytery', in *Table Talk*, 156–7.

[23] John Selden, *De iure naturali & gentium, iuxta disciplinam Ebraeorum* (1640), sig. A4r: 'de Judiciis seu Regimine Forensi atque Obedienta quam Civilem vocitamus.'

[24] *De synedriis*, in *Joannis Seldeni iurisconsulti opera omnia*, ed. David Wilkins, 3 vols in 6 parts (London: 1726) 1.cols 761–1891. All book, chapter, and page numbers refer to this edition, abbreviated as *Syned.* Chapters 7–13 (cols 826–1083) are explicitly devoted to the topic, but Selden returns to it

work, *The Historie of Tithes* (1618), which also refuted clerical *jure divino* arguments. In *De synedriis*, he notes the similarity: 'the debate over this issue has certainly had a history very like the argument about, say, the law of tithes, in which a number of scholars have likewise argued fiercely that the clergy deserves its tithes because of a divine command that predated the giving of the Law at Sinai and then reappeared in Christianity.' He appeals to 'fair and open-minded' readers to weigh the claims and counter-claims.[25] The latter work did not get him into trouble as the first one did, even though it is far more explicitly polemical.

Gillespie vs. Selden

The 'great debate'[26] on excommunication in the Assembly, on 20–21 February 1644, pitted Selden, aged 59, against the Presbyterian George Gillespie, one of the Scottish commissioners, who was only 31 and who would die aged 35. Gillespie spoke more than 150 times in the Assembly, but only this exchange was selected for the nineteenth-century hagiographic introduction to his papers, 'as at once the most striking and the best authenticated'. The scene is set: the Jerusalem Chamber of Westminster Abbey, so crowded for this great event that Gillespie, unrecognized, is turned away. 'Can ye not admit a *pinning*?' he asks, a mere pin inserted in the interstices of the great wall of learned divines. Neither Charles Herle nor Stephen Marshall, gifted Presbyterian orators, is equal to the task of answering Selden's 'long and elaborate speech … with [its] great display of minute rabbinical lore'. One of Gillespie's Scottish brethren turns to him in this emergency: 'Rise, George, rise up, man, and defend the right of the Lord Jesus Christ to govern, by his own laws, the church which he hath purchased with his blood.' Thus urged, Gillespie rises, with no notes except for a scribbled '*Da lucem Domine*', Lord give light, and so utterly refutes the astonished Selden that he confesses, 'in a tone of bitter mortification, "That young man, by this single speech, has swept away the learning and labour of ten years of my life"'. And those who had obstructed Gillespie's entry into the hall are heard to say, 'It was well that we admitted the *pinning*, otherwise the building would have fallen.'[27]

frequently in subsequent chapters. Heartfelt thanks to Michael Wyetzner, who sent me his important translation in progress of Selden's major rabbinical works, upon which I rely heavily.

[25] *Syned.* 1.10.1074. Selden dismisses this five-hundred-page work of immense learning in a parenthesis: '(I once published in English a little work [*opusculum*, a trifle] on this subject, which earned me a great deal of hostility from certain presumptuous and bad-tempered individuals.)'

[26] Toomer, *Selden*, 2.573. Many of Selden's contemporaries agreed that both in the Assembly and in Parliament excommunication was 'the great business of the Church' (Whitelocke, *Memorials*, 163, on Selden's speech in Parliament). See also Yule, *Puritans in Politics*, 151, quoting Sir Henry Vane: 'there is no greater power in this Kingdom' than that of excommunication. Walter Yonge, BM Add. MSS 18780, fol. 114.

[27] W. M. Hetherington, *Memoir of the Rev. George Gillespie*, in *Assembly of Divines: Notes of Debates and Proceedings of the Assembly … By George Gillespie*, ed. David Meek (Edinburgh: 1846), xxii–xxiii.

Nothing about this account is true. Gillespie took extensive notes, which misleadingly indicate that he spoke immediately after Selden, although he did not speak until the next day.[28] The minutes reveal disappointingly that there was no debate, because the speakers proceeded from antithetical first principles. Selden based his historico-philological secular argument on religious texts—the Bible and the Talmud—to prove that excommunication is a civil institution of human origin and therefore under parliamentary jurisdiction. Gillespie employed typology to emphasize the spiritual nature of excommunication as a divine institution entrusted to the clergy.[29] In general, Gillespie in the Assembly either misunderstood Selden's arguments or peremptorily rejected them as irrelevant. And in his published scholarship, he deliberately distorted them into compliance with his own absolutely antithetical arguments. In an earlier face-to-face exchange on the floor of the Assembly, Gillespie cited Selden's own scholarship against him:

> GILLESPIE: The learned gentellman in his 4 *lib.* doth expound the putting out of the synagogue not meant soe much of the place or assembly as a seperation from the people & church itselfe....
>
> SELDEN: For that cited by me in my booke. That will not prove a distinction of church & state. The businesse of excommunication exercised with jurisdiction never spoken of in scripture in the Jewes state for matters ecclesiasticall. & it did never otherwise.
>
> GILLESPIE'S RESPONSE TO THE CORRECTION: Nothing yet brought to make us change our opinion of a distinction. (12 December 1643, *Assembly*, 2.443)

Gillespie, referring to 4.9 of *De iure naturali et gentium* (1640), either mistakenly or with effrontery reaches a conclusion directly opposed to the one in the chapter. Its headnote reads: 'An aside about the Gospel term *aposynagōgi*; that is, *those who were put outside the synagogue*.'[30] Insisting that meaning depends on context, Selden, in the chapter in question, acknowledges that sometimes the Gospel uses *synagogue* to mean a place of worship, but with regard to excommunication it means the larger community. He regards it as a Greek translation of the Hebrew bible's עדה *edah* ['congregation, company assembled together by appointment'][31] and קהל *qehal* ['assembly, convocation, congregation'][32] He quotes the commentary on Matthew 6 of 'an exceptional scholar' [Erasmus]: '"Synagogue" refers to the small assemblies that would take place on streets, in the markets, or in public places.'[33] An excommunicate, while deprived of social contacts, is not excluded from sacred rites. As he states in the same headnote,

[28] *Assembly*, 1.26 n. 28; see also Toomer, *Selden*, 2.573 n. 72.

[29] *Assembly*, 2.520–2, for Selden; 525–7, for Gillespie.

[30] *De iure*, 4.9.518.

[31] *A Hebrew and English Lexicon of the Old Testament ... based on Gesenius*, ed. Francis Brown, S. R. Driver, and Charles A. Briggs (Oxford: Clarendon, 1907; rpt 1968).

[32] *Hebrew and English Lexicon*. Selden translates the word as *gathering of the people*, or *the entire people*, or *all the congregation* ['*populi conventum* seu *totem populum* seu *Ecclesiam universalem*'], *De iure*, 4.9.522.

[33] *De iure*, 4.9.522: '*Synagoga*, inquit, *significat conventicula quae fieri solent in plateis ac foro seu triviis*.'

'Excommunicates were allowed to enter the Temple' ['Excommunicato Templum ingredi fas'] (4.9.518). Moreover, Selden is very clear about the fact that 'excommunication took the form of a verdict or declaration by the court' (518). He makes the point with perfect clarity in *Table Talk*: 'There's no such thing as spiritual jurisdiction; all is civil.'[34]

Selden courteously corrects the misreading of his chapter, and Gillespie, ignoring the correction, returns to an earlier exchange. He remains unconvinced by Selden's evidence, massively supported in his scholarship, that there was no distinction in the Jewish state between civil and ecclesiastical jurisdiction: 'State & church are synonims with relation to them .... No court of Jurisdiction that did necessarily consist of priests & Levites only, or lay men only' (*Assembly*, 2.442).

In his vehemently anti-Erastian monograph *Aarons Rod Blossoming* (1646),[35] Gillespie consistently and deliberately misrepresents Selden's position on topics that they had debated two and three years earlier. He also wilfully misreads *De iure naturali*, exploiting Selden's scholarly prestige and turning the chief Erastian opponent into a Presbyterian ally on matters of ecclesiology. The scope of Gillespie's mischief in distorting Selden's arguments is almost infinite. In a single sentence, he repeats, deliberately this time, his earlier misreading of Selden as part of a vicious attack on William Prynne, admittedly an unpleasant person who opposed toleration, but who, surprisingly, was allied with Selden in opposing ecclesiastical control of excommunication. In *De iure* (4.9.523), Selden cited Ezra 10:8 as the earliest text confirming his view that 'to be *aposynagōgos*' is to be removed only from social contact but not from holy places. He also cited 'the learned Louis Capel ... in his collection of passages from the gospel of John' to make the same point. Gillespie, who reads *synagogue* only as a place of worship, perverts Selden's argument in order to attack Prynne, who shares Selden's position:

> Finally M. *Selden de Jure nat. & Gentium. lib. 4. cap. 9.* p. 523. agreeth with *Lud. Capellus* that the separation from the Congregation *Ezra* 10.8 ... *is the very same with casting out of the Synagogue*, which confuteth further that which M. *Prynne* holds.[36]

Selden must also have felt betrayed to discover, at the head of a chapter, a statement that expressed perfectly his own point of view, only to see it rejected and his prestige exploited to support a view that he abhorred:

> It hath been affirmed by some who pretend to more skill in Jewish antiquities than others, that though the Jewes had an excommunication which did exclude a man from civill fellowship ... yet no man was ... excommunicated ... from the Temple, Sacrifices, and holy assemblies. To these I shall in the first place oppose the judgement of others who have taken very much pains in searching the Jewish antiquities,

[34] 'Jurisdiction', *Table Talk*, 88.

[35] George Gillespie, *Aarons Rod Blossoming, or, The Divine Ordinance of Church-Government Vindicated, so as the Present Erastian Controversie Concerning the Distinction of Civill and Ecclesiasticall Government, Excommunication, and Suspension, is Fully Debated and Discussed* (1646).

[36] Gillespie, *Aarons Rod*, 70.

> and are much esteemed for their skill therein . . . . Mr. *Selden* extendeth the Jewish Excommunication so farre, as to comprehend an exclusion from fellowship in prayer and holy assemblies.[37]

Gillespie also cites 'Master *Selden*' on the differences in severity among three forms of excommunication in the Talmud. But Selden, who understands that two of those forms are mere synonyms of one another, respectfully rejects the view of Johannes Buxtorf that the ban called *shammatha* is more severe than the other two: 'with all due respect to that great scholar, I think it is a fact that we can find nothing like this claim in rabbinic literature'.[38]

And indeed, Selden's wide and deep knowledge of the Talmud, which always reports opposing arguments, must have been a factor in his decision always to give a fair hearing ('ut rite perpendantur introspicimus')[39] to positions that he ultimately rejects. Gillespie exploits this generosity by quoting Selden as if he approved those positions. He notes that both Grotius and Selden cite the same passage in Tertullian regarding the condition of anathema, which would bar someone from praying with others. But this is clearly not Selden's own position, as Gillespie knows very well. This does not prevent him from accusing Prynne of committing the sin that is all his own:

> I cannot but take notice that Master *Prynne* doth very much mistake and misrepresent Mr. *Selden*, as if he held the Jewish excommunication to have been no more but a shutting out from civill company or fellowship, whereas he clearly holds *lib. 4. de jure nat. & Gent. cap. 9. p. 522.* that he who was excommunicated by the Jewish *cherem*, was put away and cast off from fellowship in prayer, and from all religious fellowship.[40]

Selden was no saint, but his scholarly integrity and courtesy were exceptional and far exceeded those of his religious opponent. Gillespie called Erastus 'that pestilence that walketh in darknesse through London and Westminster'.[41] Thomas Coleman, a minister and member of the Assembly, so well versed in rabbinic scholarship that he was sometimes called Rabbi Coleman, was working on a translation of Erastus into English when, as Gillespie describes it, 'it pleased God to visit him with sicknesse', and soon after, 'The Lord was pleased to remove him by death, before he could do what he intended in this, and other particulars.'[42] Although Selden, in *De synedriis*, has no love for the Presbyterians, he attacks none of them personally. Surely his long monograph on excommunication is driven by his negative experience in the Assembly six years

37 Gillespie, *Aarons Rod*, 38.

38 Gillespie, *Aarons Rod*, 45; Selden, *De iure*, 4.9.520.

39 Selden, *Syned.* 1.10.1028.

40 Gillespie, *Aarons Rod*, 45.

41 Gillespie, *Nihil respondes: Or, a Discovery of the Extream Unsatisfactorinesse of Master Colemans Peece, Published Last Weeke under the Title of A Brotherly Examination—Re-examined* (1645), 31.

42 Gillespie, *Aarons Rod*, 168.

earlier. And yet remarkably, among the hundreds of documents he quotes to support his views—some from his collection of rare and even unique old manuscripts—he quotes from none of the far more accessible records of the Assembly. In fact, he dismisses that entire experience in a one-sentence parenthesis:

> (It does not matter that a number of persons with a smattering of knowledge may have explained this issue differently in their English writings about the judicial authority over sacred rites which they feel should be granted them by divine law.)[43]

Except for Coleman, whom Selden praises for his learning and honourable service (*Syned.* 1.13.1076), Gillespie and his fellow Scottish commissioner, the brutal Samuel Rutherford,[44] are the only two members of the Assembly to be mentioned in *De synedriis*. Selden has read *Aarons Rod*, with its perversion of his scholarship and its sanctimonious passage on his comrade in arms Coleman, but it appears only in two footnotes, and without censure: in a list of the many scholars who assert that Judas did not participate in the sacrament, alongside Musculus, Zanchius, and Beza, where he is one of 'a number of English writers who in recent years have fought some very fierce battles over this issue';[45] and, alongside Rutherford, as an English supporter of Beza's attempted refutation of Erastus,[46] although he adds that plentiful additional examples could be cited that forcefully drive their argument home. Unless one has read their books on excommunication, Selden's reader has no way of knowing that they are the 'Englishmen with a smattering of knowledge' he has in mind.

SELDEN'S BOLD READINGS OF SCRIPTURE

Unless the excitement of the 'great debate' occurs in the gaps and ellipses of the Assembly minutes, a lacunose text, the crowd would have been disappointed. But the clarification and extensive scholarly elaboration in Selden's magisterial scholarship of remarks in the Assembly reveal much about his cast of mind. One example must suffice, selected because without the background of that scholarship it would be opaque. Here in its entirety is his discussion of Acts 15:28–9:

43 *Syned.* 1.7.875: '(utcunque a sciolis aliquot, in scriptis suis de jurisdictione sibi circa sacra ex jure divino asserenda Anglicanis, aliorsum trahatur)'.

44 See Samuel Rutherford, *The Divine Right of Church Government and Excommunication* (1646). This chief theorist of the militant wing of the Scottish Covenanters begins his dedicatory epistle to the Earl of Loveden, Chancellor of Scotland, with the prayer that 'Jesus Christ the wonderful, the Counsellor, the mighty God ... dye his Garments in the blood of his *Enemies*' (sig. A2^r).

45 *Syned.* 1.8.913: 'praeter Anglicanos aliquot scriptores, qui enixissime nuper hac de re contenderunt' ['Georg. Gillespius in *Virga Aaronis*, lib. 3. cap. 8, &c.'].

46 *Syned.* 1.10.1021: 'Georg. Gillespius in *Aaronis Virga* Anglice, & Samuel. Rutterfordius, lib. *De iure divino regiminis ecclesiasticae Anglice* item. Londini 1646.'

> In the first sinod, 15 Act. . . . I thinke the very particulars are ther & here determined. The Commons doe comprehend the *necessaria* imposed. The common bookes have but that. But in good editions, that compendium of keeping the morall law *quod tibi fieri non vis*. . . . *In Complutensis*, in the King of Spaines bible, in. . . . (*Assembly*, 2.145)

Here it breaks off. The standard reading of these New Testament verses has the letter written by the council held in Jerusalem in the early days of the church laying no greater burden on gentile converts to Christianity than to do 'these necessary things': to abstain from offerings to idols, from blood, from what has been strangled, and from fornication. But in *De iure naturali* (7.12.838–40), Selden points out that the Complutensian polyglot bible printed in Alcala de Henares, the Antwerp Polyglot, Irenaeus, and Cyprian, as well as the Ethiopic translation add to the council's letter, 'and whatever you do not want done to yourselves, do not do to others'.[47] He calls it 'this famous principle of equity, which is also the essential foundation of human society'.[48] He adds that this principle appears in the preface to the law code of King Alfred of England, and he quotes it in Old English and in Jewish sources, including Tobit (4:16ñ) and Philo. The Latin fragment in the Assembly minutes is taken from the biography of Severus Alexander attributed to Aelius Lampridius:

> He was fond of a saying which he had heard from some Jews or Christians and remembered ever since, and which he would have a herald read out whenever he wanted to chastise someone 'What you do not wish to be done to you, do not do to another.' ['QUOD TIBI NON VIS ALTERI NE FECERIS.'] He loved that idea so much that he had it inscribed on the wall of his palace and on public buildings.[49]

Selden is familiar with Greek, Latin, Syriac, Arabic, and Ethiopic manuscripts, as well as 'a very old [Greek] manuscript [the Codex Alexandrinus] which arrived from the East not long ago ... housed in the library of the royal palace of St. James', with the variant reading 'to do what is necessary' instead of 'to do these necessary things' (7.12.840).

Selden's access to variant readings of many biblical texts must feed the natural skepticism that he reveals throughout *Table Talk*, although it coexists with faith in the authority of the ancients. In *De iure*, relying mostly on rabbinic texts, he justifies augmenting the biblical account of Cain and Abel in Genesis 4:8, which he translates literally from the Hebrew, following those manuscripts that split the verse into two lines to emphasize, as he points out, 'an empty space in the middle':

> And Cain said to his brother Abel
>
> And when they were in the field Cain rose up against his brother Abel, and killed him.[50]

[47] *De iure*, 7.12.839. The addition reads: '& quaecunque non vultis fieri vobis, aliis ne faciatis'.

[48] *De iure*, 7.12.838: 'celeberrima hac aequitatis regula atque ingenti humanae societatis firmamento'.

[49] *De iure*, 7.12.839.

[50] *De iure*, 7.4.803: 'ויאמר קין אל הבל אחיו

What did Cain say? Selden quotes from his copy of ס' אמרי שפר (*Verba elegantiae*), by Naphtali b. Joseph Ashkenazi (Venice, 1601), which states that twenty-eight verses are missing from the text. Several editions of the Pentateuch, including one printed in Constantinople (1551) and 'the very ancient Jerusalem Targum', which includes an argument between the brothers preceding the murder, declare the existence of narrative augmentation. Moreover, texts ranging from the Aramaic translation of Scripture to the Koran (5:27–32) posit a fatal disagreement between the brothers regarding 'the judgments and punishments associated with God and the world to come' (7.4.803–4). Selden also quotes a passage adapted from the midrash *Genesis Rabbah*. It is interesting to consider that Milton, who read and praised *De iure naturali et gentium*, might have been especially interested in this discussion. After all, he created his own midrash on Genesis in *Paradise Lost*, and Matthew Poole, author of *Synopsis criticorum*, characterizes Milton as 'a late ingenious and learned Writer', whose augmentation of Scripture through dialogue reasonably explains 'How the Serpent could speak, and what the Woman conceived of his speech, and why she was not affrighted, but continued the discourse with it.'[51]

Selden's exhaustive digression in *De synedriis* (2.4.1247–53) on the only biblical verse that explicitly mentions the three persons of the Trinity (1 John 5:7) concludes that it must have been interpolated no earlier than the fourth century.[52] The many bibles surveyed (in Greek, Syriac, Arabic, Latin, Danish, German, and English) include the priceless fifth-century Codex Alexandrinus, presented by the Patriarch of Constantinople to Charles I. (Selden had access to the royal library, which boasted the Codex as its most valuable possession, through his friendship with the royal librarian, Patrick Young, and with his devoted follower Whitelocke, who was put in charge of its collection of the late king's rare books and medals.) As if Selden's dizzying arabesques of anti-Trinitarian speculation were not enough, he also provides a comprehensive fair hearing for the opposite view, beginning with St Jerome in his prologue to the canonical letters ('assuming of course that he really was the author' [1249]), who considers translations to be corrupt if they *omit* the explicit affirmation of the Trinity.

Selden's intellectual boldness also prompts him to quote without condemnation previously unknown extracts of anti-Christian polemic, in the original Arabic, from his own manuscripts. He calls al-Sheikh Ali Abd al-Karim, known as al-Jīlī, 'an exceptional Muslim theologian and philosopher' ['theologum & philosophum in Mahumedanis eximium'], who asserts that the Mother, that is, the Virgin Mary, is the third person of the Trinity, a view also expressed in the Koran (Sura 5:116).[53] He devotes four large folio columns in *De synedriis* (1.12.1047–50) to excerpts from his unique manuscript (Bodl. Lib.

ויהי בהיותם בשדה ויקם קין אל הבל אחיו ויהרגו
Et dixit Cain ad Abelem fratrem suum
Et cum essent in agro, surrexit Cain adversus suum fratrem Abel & interfecit eum.'

[51] Matthew Poole, *Annotations Upon the Holy Bible* (1683; 3rd edn, London: 1696), sig. B3^r.

[52] See Toomer, *Selden*, 2.731.

[53] *Syned.* 2.4.1243.

Arch. Selden B.8) of an anti-Christian polemical treatise sent by Ahmad b. Abdallah, 'a truly learned man' ('viro sane doctissimo'), to Maurice Prince of Orange in 1612. Ahmad attacks what he sees as the illogic of the Trinity, 'because what is one is not three, and what is three is not one', as well as the Christian error of 'mak[ing] of mere attributes persons or substances'.[54]

Ahmad also distinguishes between Christian and Muslim views of confession and penance. He derides the former, which gives the power of absolution to a priest, who knows nothing of the heart of the sinner, for that is known only to God. Selden clearly concurs with his reasoning, 'however morally impure [his religion may be] otherwise' ['utcunque alias impurissima'], which accords with his own view in *Table Talk*:

> No man living can tell whether I am fit to receive the sacrament; for though I were fit the day before, when he examined me, at least appeared so to him, yet how can he tell what sin I have committed that night, or the next morning, or what impious atheistical thoughts I may have about me, when I am approaching the very table?[55]

He makes the same point on the floor of the House of Commons in September 1645, when, as Whitelocke reports, 'The House fell into the debate of the great business of the Church, the points of *Excommunication*, and *Suspension* from the Sacrament':

> *Selden* declared his Opinion … *That under the Law, every sinner was* eo nomine [by that name], *to come to offer, as he was a sinner*. … *No man is kept from the Sacrament,* eo nomine, *because he is guilty of any sin, by the Constitution of the reformed Churches, or because he hath not made satisfaction. Every man is a sinner, the difference is only, the one is private, and the other a sinner in publick. The one is as much against God, as the other.*[56]

Milton On Excommunication

Turning from Selden on excommunication to Milton means changing from certainty to tentative speculation. In either the latter half of 1646, the same year that both Gillespie and Rutherford published their books on excommunication, or early in 1647, the Trinity Manuscript places 'On the New Forcers of Conscience', which names Rutherford as one of them, immediately after the sonnet 'A book was writ of late', which names Gillespie as 'Galasp', to rhyme with 'gasp'. It is at least worth noting that neither of them attacked Milton's divorce tracts, so they may simply represent an Assembly whose 'intents were

54 *Syned*. 2.4.1244.
55 'Sacrament', *Table Talk*, 170.
56 Whitelocke, *Memorials*, 163.

cleere to be no other then to have set up a spiritual tyrannie by a secular power to the advancing of thir owne authoritie above the magistrate'.[57] Milton's position on excommunication in the 1640s can be inferred only indirectly, from his respectful disagreement with David Paraeus, who had invoked Matthew 18:17 to insist that 'strangers to the spirit of Christ', imitating the hardheartedness of the Jews, be 'exclude[d] from the company of the faithful ... in accordance with the precept Let him be to thee as a heathen'.[58] Milton replies:

> I am not willing to discover the forgettings of reverend men, yet here I must. What article or clause of the whole new Cov'nant can Paraeus bring to exasperat the judicial Law, upon any infirmity under the Gospel? ... the Gospel hath not the least influence upon judicial Courts, much lesse to make them sharper, and more heavy.[59]

But even in this instance Milton explicitly cites only fines and imprisonment as the two civil penalties Paraeus would impose on those who divorce.

One can only suggest that excommunication might squeeze in alongside plurality, church hierarchy, and a new liturgy as abuses attempted by the Assembly, whose venality and power-grabbing he condemns in 'On the New Forcers of Conscience':

> Dare ye for this adjure the civil sword
> To force our consciences that Christ set free,
>
> Men whose life, learning, faith, and pure intent
> Would have been held in high esteem with Paul
> Must now be named and printed heretics
> By shallow Edwards and Scotch what-d'ye-call.
> But we do hope to find out all your tricks,
> Your plots and packings worse than those of Trent,
> That so the Parliament
> May with their wholesome and preventive shears
> Clip your phylacteries, though balk your ears. (5–6, 9–17)

Knowing of the Assembly's insistence that it can brand as scandalous anyone it wishes, perhaps Milton is remembering that 'shallow Edwards' in his *Gangraena*, 'dared to call him, a person of pure life, learning, faith, and ... intent, a heretic, because of his views on divorce'.[60] 'Scotch what-d'ye call' refers almost certainly to Gillespie, whose name is spelled ten different ways by the scribe of the Assembly in its minutes,[61] and not, despite

57 Milton, specifically attacking the Assembly, in *History of Britain, YP*, 5:466.
58 David Paraeus, *Operum theologicorum* (Frankfurt: 1628), 3.488.
59 Milton, *The Doctrine and Discipline of Divorce, YP*, 2.352.
60 See Thomas Edwards, *Gangraena* (1646), 34, which includes Milton's doctrine of divorce in its long list of heresies; he summarizes Milton's treatise in *The Second Part of Gangraena* (1646), 10–11.
61 *Assembly*, 1.20.

the consensus of editors otherwise, to Robert Baillie, whose name is easy to pronounce. And one might go so far as to speculate that the famous deletion from line 17 of the original '*Cropp ye as close as marginall P*[rynne']*s eares*' might owe something to the fact that Prynne, who had attacked as heretical Milton's *Doctrine and Discipline of Divorce*,[62] nevertheless vigorously opposed ecclesiastical control of excommunication. In fact, he was the object of the most vicious attacks by Gillespie and Rutherford.

One of Selden's incidental comments in *De synedriis*, on Matthew 16:19, a central text on excommunication, should remind us of why we might have expected Milton to speak out more unequivocally on the subject. Rejecting the Presbyterian argument that the keys of the kingdom given to Peter refer to the power of excommunication, he points out that keys are for keeping insiders in and outsiders out but not for driving out those who are inside. For that the metaphor of pitchfork or whip ('furca aut flagellum') would make sense. 'But laws', he adds, 'are not to be derived from metaphor' ('ex metaphoris ejusmodi jura … elicere … periculosa', 1.9.924).[63] Even so, the law of excommunication in Selden's legal imaginary is connected with exile. And while drawing distinctions between them, he nevertheless gives a fair hearing to theologians who saw the expulsion from paradise of our first parents and the barring of Satan and his angels from 'the communion of paradise, that is, of the saints', as excommunication.[64] And in addition to an extensive discussion of the Hebrew Bible's word חרם, which means both *sacred* and *doomed to destruction*, Selden quotes extensively from ancient texts to demonstrate how 'the more serious of the interdictions inflicted by both the Greeks and the Romans were often combined with … *threats* and *curses* or *anathemata*, which devoted criminals to the gods below, called for their destruction and complete misfortune, and made them sacred.'[65] Milton is well aware of this interdiction, as when God pronounces humankind 'to destruction sacred and devote' (*Paradise Lost*, 3.208), and when Adam first breaks his inward silence to lament that Eve is 'now to death devote' (9.901).

In 1646, the deep implications of the most pressing question of church discipline had not taken hold of the great poet of exile. Selden's vast learning helped him to take the imaginative leap that the poet could or would not. The young man who signed his name 'John Milton, Englishman' would eventually become the disillusioned older man, exiled in Restoration London, who would write, 'One's country is where it is well with one.'[66] In time, the power of his longing for a place to call home would require the scope of an epic.

[62] William Prynne, *Twelve Considerable Serious Questions, Touching Church Government* (c.16 September 1644), 7. Milton challenged Prynne to prove his charge that the treatise advocated '*divorce at pleasure*'. He asked that Prynne not reply with his typical 'old and stale suppositions' in 'the gout and dropsy of a big margent, litter'd and overlaid with crude and huddl'd quotations'. (*Colasterion*, *YP*, 2.723–4).

[63] Selden, *Syned.* 1.9.924–5.

[64] Selden, *Syned.* 1.11.1022–3.

[65] Selden, *Syned.* 1.10.1002: 'Interdictionum autem harum eis quae graviores essent tum apud Graecos tum Romanos conjungi saepius solebant ἀραί, seu *dirae* ac *maledictiones*, seu anathemata, quibus diis inferis & in perniciem sui summumque infortunium devovebantur & sacri fiebant facinorosi.'

[66] Milton, *Familiar Letters, The Works of John Milton*, ed. Frank Allen Patterson et al. (New York: Columbia University Press, 1931–1938), 12.115.

Bibliography

Baillie, Robert. *The Letters and Journals of Robert Baillie*, ed. David Laing, 3 vols (Edinburgh: 1841–1842).

Brown, Francis, S. R. Driver, and Charles A. Briggs, ed. *A Hebrew and English Lexicon of the Old Testament* [...] *Based on Gesenius* (Oxford: Clarendon Press, 1907; rpt 1968).

Gardiner, Samuel Rawson. *History of England from the Accession of James to the Outbreak of the Civil War 1603–1642*, 10 vols (London: Longmans, Green, and Company, 1883–1908).

Gillespie, George. *Aarons Rod Blossoming, or, the Divine Ordinance of Church-Government Vindicated, so as the Present Erastian Controversie Concerning the Distinction of Civill and Ecclesiasticall Government, Excommunication, and Suspension, Is Fully Debated and Discussed* (London: 1646).

Hetherington, W. M. 'Memoir of the Rev George Gillespie', in George Gillespie, Notes of Debates and Proceedings of the Assembly of Divines and Other Commissioners at Westminster, February 1644 to January 1645, 2 vols, ed. David Meek (Edinburgh: 1846), 1.xx–xxxiii.

House of Commons. *Journal of the House of Commons* (London: 1802).

House of Commons. *March 1646: An Ordinance of the Lords and Commons Assembled in Parliament for Keeping of Scandalous Persons from the Sacrament of the Lords Supper [...] and Supplying of Defects in Former Ordinances and Directions of Parliament Concerning Church-Government* (London: 1646).

House of Commons. *Questions Propounded to the Assembly of Divines by the House of Commons, April ult.1646: Touching the Point of Jus Divinum in the Matter of Church-Government* (London: 1646).

Milton, John. *Complete Prose Works of John Milton*, ed. Don M. Wolfe, 8 vols (New Haven: Yale University Press, 1953–1972).

Milton. John. *The Works of John Milton*, ed. Frank Allen Patterson et al., 18 vols (New York: Columbia University Press, 1931–1938).

Poole, Matthew. *Annotations upon the Holy Bible*, 3rd edn (London: 1696).

Rutherford, Samuel. *The Divine Right of Church Government and Excommunication* (London: 1646).

Selden, John. *De jure naturali & gentium, juxta disciplinam ebraeorum* (London: 1640).

Selden, John. *Joannis Seldeni jurisconsulti opera omnia*, ed. David Wilkins, 3 vols (London: 1726).

Selden, John. *The Table Talk of John Selden*, ed. Samuel Harvey Reynolds (Oxford: 1892).

Shaw, William A. *A History of the English Church during the Civil Wars and Under the Commonwealth 1640–1660*, 2 vols (London: Longmans, 1900).

Sommerville, Johann P. 'Hobbes, Selden, Erastianism, and the History of the Jews', in *Hobbes and History*, ed. G. A. J. Rogers and Tom Sorell (London and New York: Routledge, 2000), 160–88.

Toomer, G. J. *John Selden: A Life in Scholarship*, 2 vols (Oxford: Oxford University Press, 2009).

Westminster Assembly. *The Minutes and Papers of the Westminster Assembly 1643–1652*, ed. Chad Van Dixhoorn, 5 vols (Oxford: Oxford University Press, 2012).

Whitlocke, Bulstrode. *Memorials of the English Affairs [...] from the Beginning of the Reign of King Charles the First, to King Charles II His Happy Restauration* (London: 1682).

Yule, George. *Puritans in Politics: The Religious Legislation of the Long Parliament 1640–1647* (Abingdon: Sutton Courtenay Press, 1981).

CHAPTER 19

SELDENISM

ELLIOTT VISCONSI

LATE in November 1654, John Selden, the glory of the English nation and the dictator of all English learning, lay in his elegant home at Whitefriars near to death. The great scholar—author of major works of political theory: *Mare clausum* (1632); *De jure naturali et gentium* (1640); English legal and ecclesiastical history: *Janus Anglorum* (1611), *History of Tithes* (1616), *Titles of Honor* (1614), *Dissertatio ad Fletam* (1633); and studies of the ancient Syrian religion and the ancient Jewish commonwealth: *De diis Syriis* (1617), *Uxor Hebraica* (1646), *De synedriis* (1650–1655)—had navigated the political turbulence of his last decade with remarkable agility. Behind him were the numerous achievements of a stunning scholarly career and the approbation of a measured and generous political life, and the manner of his leave-taking was to become a question of significant public curiosity. In those days, Selden's personal religious beliefs were of special concern to his diverse admirers, given that he was widely perceived to share Hobbes' Erastian rejection of any political model in which the 'ghostly authority' of the church was a rival to the supremacy of the civil sovereign.[1]

[1] As he outlines in *Leviathan*, for Hobbes, the church might very well be a garden walled off from the world or it might be administered by a Pope or committee of presbyters, but in no case did religious belief authorize resistance to the duly constituted sovereign. The plain effect of such confusion was 'civil war and dissolution' of the commonwealth:

> temporal and spiritual government are but two words brought into the world to make men see double and mistake their lawful sovereign. There is … no other government in this life, neither of state nor religion, but temporal; … and that governor must be one, or else there must needs follow faction and civil war in the commonwealth; between the Church and the State; between spiritualists and temporalists; between the sword of justice and the shield of faith; and (which is more) in every Christian man's own breast, between the Christian and the man.

Leviathan was meant to be a theoretical bomb thrown against priestcraft rather than at religion or Christianity, and while Hobbes was widely accused of materialist atheism (and all sorts of other wicked positions), his stated aim was not to institute a radically secular commonwealth. Hobbes's chief goal was to describe a political architecture through which civil peace and social tranquility might be achieved, and while the church had an ethical, pastoral, and persuasive role to play in the work of political

Although he counted many churchmen among his close friends (including Archbishop Ussher, who preached his funeral sermon), Selden was a persistent and committed adversary of the arrogant and often zealous abuse of historical and philological materials by an overreaching clergy and other equally mendacious political actors. Selden had been a thorn in the side of the cozy clerical establishment for most of his career, at least since he ran afoul of the church hierarchy by publishing his *History of Tithes* in 1616, a searching historical critique of clerical privilege and misguided scriptural interpretation that unleashed the 'fiercest storm' of hostile resistance that might be imagined. In his Galileo moment, the young Selden was called before the High Commission and forced to renounce the *History of Tithes* in the following manner:

> I most humbly acknowledge my error which I have committed, in publishing the History of Tithes, and especially, in that I have at all, by shewing any Interpretation of holy Scriptures, by medling with Counsels, Fathers, or Canons, or by whatsoever occurres in it, offered any just occasion of Argument, against any right of maintenance of *Iure Divino*, of the Ministers of the Gospel; beseeching your Lordships to receive this ingenuous, and humble acknowledgment, together with the unfeigned protestation of my grief, for that through it I have so incurred both his Majesties and your Lordships displeasure, conceived against me in behalf of the Church of England.[2]

This humiliation was a blow Selden would not soon forget. As Anthony à Wood tells it, 'this usage sunk so deep into his stomach, that he did never after affect the bishops and clergy, or cordially approve their calling, 'tho many ways were tried to gain his to the church's interest'.[3] Twenty years on, when Selden was seated in the Long Parliament and included in the Westminster Assembly of Divines, he would continue his struggle to use historical and philological scholarship as a corrective against unwarranted clerical authority. In the Long Parliament and in the Westminster Assembly of Divines, Selden argued fiercely in debate against the excommunicating power—especially as vested in presbyters—and in favour of both limited Catholic toleration and an Erastian theory of church and state, in which the church was necessarily subordinated to the civil sovereign in order to preserve political stability, social cohesion, and pastoral efficacy.[4]

education, for Hobbes as for Selden it was essential that the commonwealth not be divided against itself; Thomas Hobbes, *Leviathan*, ed. Edwin Curley (Indianapolis: Hackett, 1994).

2 David Lloyd, *Memoires of the Lives, Actions, Sufferings and Deaths of those Personages, that Suffered by Death, Sequestration, Decimation: Or Otherwise for the Protestant Religion and the Great Principle Thereof, Allegiance to Their Soveraigne, in Our Late Intestine Wars from the Year 1637 to 1660: With the Life and Martyrdom of King Charles I* (London: 1668), 518–21.

3 Anthony à Wood, *Athenae Oxoniensis*, Vol. 3, ed. Philip Bliss, 369. Throughout this chapter I am especially indebted to the appropriately monumental and excellent scholarly biography of Selden: G. J. Toomer, *John Selden: A Life in Scholarship*, 2 vols (Oxford: Oxford University Press, 2009).

4 John Rushworth, *Historical Collections of Private Passages of State* (London: 1708), 5.573; 'Mr Selden's Speech Touching Excommunication and Suspension From the Sacrament.'

One of the most widely reported anecdotes of Selden's political career describes well his hostility to the current mode of amateurish historical wish-fulfilment that he found so appalling. In 1645, Selden had been a lay participant in the Westminster Assembly, where he rebuked the unprofessional enthusiasm or outright incapacity of many clergymen by bludgeoning them with philology. In the debates of that body tasked with settling the new direction of the English church, 'Mr. *Selden* spake admirably, and confuted divers of them in their own Learning. And sometimes when they had cited a Text of Scripture to prove their Assertion, he would tell them, *Perhaps in vour little Pocket Bibles with gilt Leaves* (which they would often pull out and read) *the Translation may be thus, but the* Greek *or the* Hebrew, *signifies thus and thus;* and so would totally silence them.'[5]

So too in Selden's scholarly works and private writings do we encounter at once his endorsement of serious (sceptical) philosophical inquiry into religion and his open hostility to manipulative priestcraft. In *De successionibus in bona defuncti* (1631), for instance, Selden outlines his enduring opposition between scholarship and enthusiasm:

> Those Christians that renounced the church of Rome on account of many ordinances and opinions which to them appeared contrary to divine authority, did not choose to form ... their own [church] without a prudent selection from the ancient historians of that church, from annals, fathers, councils, canons, received opinions, judicial determinations, and the like: and they who forwardly reject such a selection, rashly explaining the Holy Scriptures by the sole efforts of their own understanding, are found occasionally to disturb the peace of Christendom by ridiculous and impious innovations.

Serious, principled religious reform flows through tradition, the thickly textured body of intellectual resources through which ecclesiastical doctrine and discipline has been transmitted and transformed. The resemblance to English law here implied is no accident: for Selden, ecclesiology, scriptural interpretation, and common law were dynamic, living traditions best conserved by a class of learned professional interpreters but normally threatened by enthusiasts, zealots, and ambitious amateurs.

In a 1646 letter to the Hebraist Francis Tayler, Selden would outline the political urgency of their shared endeavors in promulgating a serious account of the norms, customs and texts of ancient Judaism:

> Without [Talmudic] doctrine, the triumphs celebrated by the pretentious and otherwise learned ignorance of many are either ridiculous or dangerous ... these, through utter lack of knowledge of the origins and primal sources of things and practices which are found in the Bible, boldly manufacture dreams for themselves, but dreams which are to their own advantage among men, and cunningly impose these as burdens on others. That is how the Papists often behave; so too do others, who, if anyone opposes them, immediately put forward the 'new lights' which have as it were risen in

[5] Bulstrode Whitelock, *Memorials of English Affairs*, Vol. 1. (Oxford: Oxford University Press, 1853), 208–9.

> the heavens for them. [It is essential to be guided by a true perception of rabbinical] doctrine, whence the whole of Christianity arose; without it, we are often deceived in our judgments of sacred matters, and deceive [others] by guesswork and propagating the monstrous offspring of whatever ingenuity [we possess].[6]

The pattern here on display describes aptly Selden's aims; by deploying the telescope of philology, responsible contemporary political and religious actors could pierce the veil of enthusiasm and obfuscation as they constructed a new English model of the proper relations between church and state in a moment of revolutionary promise. In Selden's view, religious scholarship (annals, decisions, tracts, midrash, canons, histories) was not mere antiquarianism, but rather was a necessary professional corrective to the hot-blooded enthusiasm or outright deception—those boldly manufactured dreams and those monstrous offspring of human ambition—foisted upon the English public by ambitious and charismatic prophets new inspired.

Despite his scholarly and forensic efforts, Selden seems to have been a half-hearted politician and an indifferent barrister; in his epitaph, he describes himself as unsuited for the bustle of courts.[7] In 1642, for instance, Selden may have spurned the office of Chancellor as an unwelcome imposition upon his ease. According to the Earl of Clarendon, it was understood that Selden 'would absolutely refuse the place, if it were offer'd him. He was in years, and of a tender constitution; he had for many years enjoyed his ease, which he loved; was rich; and would not have made a journey to York, or have lain out of his own bed, for any Preferment, which he had never affected'.[8] Although he had served in public offices with distinction (if not to the delight of his clerical adversaries), Selden's preference for a life of ease was plainly apparent to contemporary observers.

Selden died on 30 November 1654. What happened in those last weeks and days was to become a matter of some dispute after Selden's magnificent funeral, over which the great scholar's close friend Archbishop Ussher presided. Since Selden was broadly understood to be a fellow traveller with Hobbes in framing an Erastian church–state solution and in opposing zealotry and priestcraft, his many admirers were concerned to defend his posthumous reputation from a too-close affiliation with the notorious Hobbes, while his adversaries saw in his end an opportunity to rehabilitate the great scholar and attach his prestige to the cause of the established church. The contest over Selden began properly after the Restoration, when the Church of England was re-established and a new generation of divines and royalist historians began to flex their muscles again. David Lloyd, for instance, included Selden in his arch-royalist 1668 *Memoires of the Lives of Eminent Personages*, but described the illustrious scholar with grudging admiration and pious scolding both, a pattern that would become customary. Lloyd's Selden is admirable for his capacious learning, largeness of soul, and diligent work-rate, even if he is no

[6] The letter from Selden to Tayler is printed in full by Toomer, 2.845–7.

[7] Selden's autobiographical epitaph likewise is printed in Toomer's appendix: 2.828–9.

[8] The autobiographical *Life of Edward, Earl of Clarendon* (London: 1761), 1.24–5.

friend of the clergy. Lloyd reports on Selden's rebuke of the pocket-Bible divines, but the royalist historian spends most of his time in reporting Selden's humiliating retraction of the *History of Tithes* and his subsequent attachment to Archbishop Laud.[9]

John Aubrey, one of the century's most prolific collectors of biographical material, provides one of the most lastingly influential pictures of Selden as scholar and voluptuary but no politician. Arriving at the Inner Temple to pursue a legal career, young Selden:

> was quickly taken notice of for his learning, and was solicitor and steward to the Earl of Kent, whose countess being an ingenious woman and loving men, would let him lie with her. After the Earl's death he married her. He did lie with Mrs Williamson (one of my lady's women) a lusty bouncing woman, who robbed him on his death-bed. I remember in 1646 or 1647 they did also talk of my lady's she-blackamoor ... He was one of the assembly of divines, and Whitlock, in his memoirs, says he was wont to mock the assembly men about their little gilt Bibles, and would baffle them sadly: said he 'I do consider the original.' ... He never owned the marriage with the Countess of Kent till after her death, upon some law account. He never kept any servant in his own service, but my lady's were all at his command; he lived with her in White Friars, which was ... a noble dwelling. He kept a plentiful table, and was never without learned company.
>
> ...
>
> When he was near death, the minister (Mr Johnson) was coming to him to absolve him: Mr Hobbes happened then to be there: said he, 'What, will you that have written like a man, now die like a woman?' So the minister was not let in.
>
> ...
>
> Mr Selden had got more by his prick than he had done by his practice. He was no eminent practiser at bar; not but that he was or might have been able enough; but after he had got a sweet ease he chiefly addicted himself to his more ingenious studies and records. I have heard some divines say (I know not if maliciously) that 'twas true he was a man of great reading, but gave not his own sentiment.[10]

Aubrey hands down a Selden closely attached to ease and to Hobbes—the illustrious Selden enjoys his mistresses and a life of comfort, scoffing at the consolations of religion as he nears his end. This picture of Selden as a Hobbesian libertine and unrepentant sceptic was at the core of a struggle to control his memory, a contest largely fought between churchmen rather than jurists and legal historians.

A sympathetic advocate for the learned Selden was the nonconformist minister Richard Baxter, one of the most influential and prolific writers in the cause of toleration that the seventeenth century would know. Baxter was troubled by the reports of Selden's end, and so he went right to the source—Sir Matthew Hale, the great jurist, legal historian, sometime Lord Chief Justice, and one of Selden's four executors. Like Selden,

9 David Lloyd, *Memoires*, 519–21.

10 John Aubrey, *Brief Lives*, ed. Richard Barber (Rochester: Boydell and Brewer, 1982), 283–4.

Hale was widely admired for his scholarship, moderation, professional competence, and commitment to reconciliation. As Baxter writes, L. C. J. Hale

> was a great Lamenter of the Extremities of the Times; and the violence and foolishness of the predominant Clergy, and a great desirer of such abatements as might restore us all to serviceableness and Unity. . . . He often offered to the Lord Chancellor to resign [. . .], when he was blamed for doing that which he supposed was Justice. He had been the Learned *Selden*'s intimate friend, and one of his Executors: And because the *Hobbians* and other Infidels would have persuaded the World that *Selden* was of their mind; I desired him to tell me truth therein: And he assured me that *Selden* was an earnest Professor of the Christian Faith, and so angry an Adversary to *Hobbs* that he hath rated him out of the Room.[11]

This account of Selden is consistent with Hale's reconciliatory character—Hale was himself a tireless voice opposing religious extremism, rampant partisanship, and naïve scripturalism. Here we see Hale recasting Selden in his own image. Hale was like Selden a scholar of real excellence committed to sceptical inquiry into English legal history, political philosophy, and the anthropology of religion.[12] Hale was an earnest professor of Christianity (far more openly pious than Selden and far more opposed to Hobbes) and a broadly admired jurist. Combating the popular perception of Selden's infidelism, Hale imputes to Selden a generalized faith in Christianity rather than any sort of concrete confessional identity; in so doing, he resists the tendency towards sentimental memorialization so common to the age and allows Selden to retain his philosophical principles.

But the record of Selden's last moments was not always so generous or reconciliatory. There are several manuscript accounts of Selden's death that cast the great scholar in a less principled light. In one anonymous account, for instance, the sceptical Selden loses his nerve as death approaches:

> I have not many particulars of Mr. Selden's sickness, onely when he seemed near his end and believed it then he began to think [speak ?] of religion and another world, and gave a strickt charge that neyther Rosingham nor Hobbs (his constant guests formerly) should be admitted unto him. A little before he dyed he assayed him to kneel in his bed to receave the Communion . . . my Lord Primate, he that preacht his funerall sermon . . . he did it (?) with admirable devotion; and he sayd also that he was a great honor to Xtian religion; that whereas most men take it by course and custome and . . . [that he looked?] upon it by choyce as indubitably the . . . . Beste . . . [calumniating] all others. The Primate sayd though about 45 yeares ago he had . . . elements of the Eastern tongues from him, yet in most of them he came to be soe much before him as he was before the other when he came first to be instructed by him . . . . The last I hear is that all his imperfect and unprinted papers and notes he caused to be

[11] Gilbert Burnet, *The Life and Death of Sir Matthew Hale, kt* (London: 1682), 199–200.

[12] Elliott Visconsi, 'The Invention of Criminal Blasphemy: Rex v. Taylor, 1676', *Representations*, 103 (Summer, 2008): 30–52.

> brought out before him while he lay upon his deathbed, and saw them burned before his eyes.[13]

The picture here of Selden is mixed; the illustrious scholar turns to the consolations and rituals of Christianity only as death threatens, and perhaps most strikingly for a scholar of his calibre, is reported to have ordered from his deathbed 'all his imperfect and unprinted papers and notes [to be] burned before his eyes'. The telegraphic endorsement of Christianity in the middle section of this fragment testifies to Selden's bona fides, but this account is far from a celebratory memorial; here Selden seems conventionally desperate, the sceptic quailing as his principles are put to the test. This fragment shares much with an early eighteenth-century account of Selden's end:

> Mr. Selden upon his deathbed disclaimed all Hobbisme and the like wicked and Atheisticall opinions, commanded that neither Mr. Hobbs nor Capt. Rossingham should be admitted to him, confessed his sins, and desired absolution, which was given him by Archbp. Usher; but amongst other things he much deplored the loss of his time in studying of things more curious than usefull, and wished that he [had] rather executed the office of a justice of peace than spent his time in that which the world calls learning.[14]

The tone has changed by this point: Selden is now a hypocrite or an apostate to his infidelism, and once again we see a clerical reporter's now open and plainly fabricated hostility to the useless curiosities of 'what the world calls learning'.

Finally in 1728, when the churchman David Wilkins wrote his Latin 'Vita Joannis Seldeni' to accompany his massive three-volume edition of Selden's works, he reiterated approvingly a 1670 account of extremely dubious quality, in which Selden once again is seen to regret the unconsoling vanity of his scholarly endeavours and find comfort in the promises of Scripture: 'he could not recollect any passage out of infinite books and manuscripts he was master of, wherein he could rest his soul, save out of the holy scriptures, wherein the most remarkable passage that lay most upon his spirit was Titus 2, 11–14'.[15] In those verses, among other counsels Paul reminds Titus that the salvific grace of God has appeared to all men, teaching us to deny ungodliness and wordly lusts so that we might live righteously in this fallen world. If anything, these scriptural *dicta* are a tacit

[13] Macray, *Annals of the Bodleian Library*, 2nd edn (Oxford: Oxford University Press, 1893) 110–12.

[14] MS Rawlinson; Macray, *Annals*, 110.

[15] Wilkins, 'Vita Joannis Seldeni,' in *Opera omnia*, Vol. 1 (1728). Toomer dismisses this as an 'apologia in ridiculous form'; see *Selden: A Life in Scholarship*, 2.790. In the King James Bible Titus II, 11–14 reads as follows:

> 11. For the grace of God that bringeth saluatio, hath appeared to all men; 12. Teaching vs that denying vngodlinesse and worldly lusts we should liue soberly, righteously and godly in this present world; 13. Looking for that blessed hope, and the glorious appearing of the great God, and our Sauiour Iesus Christ; 14. Who gaue himselfe for vs, that he might redeeme vs from all iniquitie, and purifie vnto himselfe a peculiar people, zealous of good workes.

rebuke to Selden, who cultivated a life of scholarly ease and physical comfort (including, if Aubrey is to be credited, the comforts of the flesh). By the 1720s, Wilkins has handed down a rehabilitated Selden, a pious scholar whose undisputed learning can be admired free from the taint of infidelism thanks to his belated recognition of the merits of Christianity; Wilkins offers us a narrative of repentance and devotional reclamation akin to other popular narratives of moral rehabilitation such as Defoe's *Roxana* (1726); it is no small irony that Wilkins' *Life* displays just the sort of interested historical projection that Selden opposed so ardently. Unlike Hobbes, the 'monster of Malmesbury', Selden has been reclaimed for the Church of England—taking communion, finding consolation only in Scripture, repenting of his sceptical and unproductive scholarship.

But as much as Selden promoted the cause of scholarship and performed his role as learned scourge of many bumbling divines, he had been strikingly silent upon the question of the instruction and cultivation of the general public. Even an influential tract such as *Mare clausum* was not calculated to find a truly broad audience, and certainly his densely written and philologically uncompromising Latin works of religious anthropology (*De diis Syriis, Uxor Hebraica, De synedriis*) were pitched purely to a scholarly community. And indeed, although he was intermittently interested in poetry as a genre for the conservation of national cultural traditions, unlike contemporaries such as Davenant, Milton, Marvell, and even Hobbes, Selden seems never to have tried his hand at serious literature (tragedy, epic, heroic poetry, translation of classical epic), the age's preferred medium for cultivating the ethical and political judgement of the English public.[16] Selden never wrote his crossover book; he made little effort to wrestle his erudition into the service of systematic and broadly accessible legal, religious, and political commentary. That work, as Jason Rosenblatt has documented in his study of Selden's scholarly afterlife, was left for others.[17]

In the months following the revolution of 1688, publishers brought forth a raft of hitherto seditious or politically inflammatory writings now thought safe for printing, the most famous example of which is Locke's *Two Treatises of Government*.[18] Among this corpus was a slim volume assembled by Rev. Richard Milward at some point before his death late in 1679. This widely popular collection was the conduit of Selden's public reputation; its full title is *Table-Talk: Being the Discourses of John Selden Esq; or His Sence of Various Matters of Weight and High Consequence Relating Especially to Religion and State*

[16] Some of the general treatments of this topic include: Nigel Smith, *Literature and Revolution in England 1640–1660* (New Haven; Yale University Press, 1994); Sharon Achinstein, *Literature and Dissent in Milton's England* (Cambridge: Cambridge University Press, 2003); Steven N. Zwicker, *Lines of Authority: Politics and English Literary Culture 1649–1689* (Ithaca: Cornell University Press, 1996); and Elliott Visconsi, *Lines of Equity: Literature and the Origins of Law in Later Stuart England* (Ithaca: Cornell University Press, 2008).

[17] Jason Rosenblatt, *Renaissance England's Chief Rabbi: John Selden* (New York: Oxford University Press, 2006). See also Toomer, 2.824–7.

[18] Steven Pincus, *1688: The First Modern Revolution* (New Haven: Yale University Press, 2009). See also Richard Ashcraft, *Revolutionary Politics and Locke's Two Treatises* (Princeton: Princeton University Press, 1986).

(London: E. Smith, 1689).[19] Milward had been Selden's friend and his proto-Boswell, and he seems to have collected the apothegms, sayings, and unguarded opinions emitted by the scholarly 'Glory of the Nation' during the twenty years of their friendship. As he writes in the epistle dedicatory addressed to Selden's executors,

> I am confident any thing of his would find acceptance with you, and truly the sense and notion here is wholly his, and most of the words. I had the opportunity to hear his Discourse twenty years together, and least of all Excellent things that usually fell from him might be lost, some of them from time to time I faithfully committed to writing, where here digested into this Method, I humbly present to your hands: you will quickly perceive them to be his by the familiar illustrations wherewith they are set off, and in which way you know he was so happy, that (with a marvelous delight to those that heard him) he would presently *convey the highest points of Religion, and the most important Affairs of State to an ordinary apprehension.* (16, my emphasis)

Here Milward makes plain his ambitions—he hopes to fill the gap Selden left vacant, communicating the illustrious scholar's excellent opinions on church and state clearly to an 'ordinary apprehension'. Milward appeals to Selden's executors to test the collection against their own experience, authenticating both the intellectual content and the portrait of Selden's life assembled in the *Table-Talk*. Although the *Table-Talk* is often dismissed by Selden scholars as a trifling work of limited value and dubious authenticity, I propose that Milward's collection is meant to function as a work of popular constitutional commentary specific to the toleration debates of the late 1660s and early 1670s, the decade when Milward likely assembled the *Table-Talk* before his death in 1680.

Milward collects Selden into an oracle of 'church and state', presenting him as an accessible anthropologist of religion whose own belief is beside the point, who has the tools with which to describe proper legal and ecclesiological reforms to English constitution in a moment when that constitution is hotly and violently contested. Milward's Selden is part of a generational intellectual struggle against naïve scriptural fundamentalism, priestcraft, enthusiasm, and the tyranny over conscience—a language and style of argument I call 'English civil religion'; The *Table-Talk* is part of a comprehensive public rethinking of the constitutional posture of established religion in the years between 1660 and 1689.

Table-Talk as Constitutional Commentary

The *Table-Talk* is a breezy read, and it makes a winning contrast to Selden's crabbed Latinity. Part of the stated aim of the collection is to provide intimate access to the

[19] Rev. Richard Milward, ed., *Table-Talk: Being the Discourses of John Selden* (London: 1689). All future references will be noted parenthetically in the text.

everyday Selden, to make his insights vivid and persuasive for a common audience, but Milward refrains from including the sort of salacious gossip commonly attached to the illustrious scholar. Milward fails to provide a brief biography of his subject, choosing instead to let Selden's wit and intelligence stand for the man himself; perhaps befitting a scholar of his accomplishment, Selden's ideas and his creative wit are asked to serve in the office of biography. Milward's method is simple and his editorial hand is light—he organizes his materials alphabetically and gives entries the space they seem to merit. In some cases, a Selden quip about imprisonment or things indifferent merits a sentence or two, while crucial topics such as conscience, monarchy, or Scripture can stretch to several pages. In a wink to his reputation, Milward's Selden more than once defends pleasure and ease: while ascetic self-denial is the fashion of the times, for Selden such a posture is 'the greatest accusation that can be upon the maker of all good things. If they be not to be us'd, why did God make them?' (44).

But the main aim of the *Table-Talk* is to transform and methodize Selden's legal and religious scholarship into an accessible work of lay constitutional commentary on the proper relations between church and state. As Reid Barbour has suggested, the *Table-Talk* is too often understood as an uncomplicated work of Hobbesian secularism, and the sceptical Selden's anthropology of religion is imagined as derisive of clerical authority and Christian belief equally.[20] But the text itself offers us another position, one less corrosive than skeptical, less secular than functionalist, not hostile to religious belief or institution but critical of priestcraft. The *Table-Talk* promotes a vision of church and state—an English constitutional settlement in which the supremacy of the civil sovereign is necessary in order to protect individual religious belief and the shared social norms of the community equally. In this account, religious traditions and individual conscience are especially to be defended by conservatorial lay professionals, scholars like Selden who are best equipped to puncture the impositions of a self-aggrandizing clergy and the wild enthusiasm of anti-intellectual zealots. In *Table-Talk* the main nodes of argument touching the church–state question (scattered throughout they text as they may be) are as follows: individual conscience, temporal supremacy, and priestcraft.

Selden's personal motto was 'liberty above all things', and like his later admirers such as Milton and Locke, he saw liberty of conscience as a perpetually imperiled dignitary right. For Selden, liberty of conscience is indelibly vested in the self-actuating individual who must nonetheless rely upon the guidance of intellectual traditions and collective social norms. Religious belief is for Selden fully a matter of individual volition—'howsoever glorious the church is, everyone chooses out of it his religion, by which he governs himself, and lets the rest alone' (39). He has little time for the various tests and doctrinal impositions that seek to carve windows into men's souls. The sincerity of a prayer, the fitness of a believer for the sacrament, the thinking of heresy are all for Selden inward transactions between the believer and God, and as such are properly of no concern to clerical or temporal interlopers. 'No man', he writes, 'can tell whether or not I am fit to

[20] Reid Barbour, *John Selden: Measures of the Holy Commonwealth* (Toronto: University of Toronto Press, 2003), 9–21.

receive the Sacrament: for though I were fit the day before, when he examined me … yet how can he tell what sin I have committed that night, or what … impious Atheisticall thoughts I may have about me, when I am approaching to the very table?' (105–6). As touching heresy, 'tis a vain thing to talk of a heretick, for a man for his heart can think no otherwise that he does think' (80). Even idolatry, the third rail of seventeenth-century Protestantism, is for Selden to be negotiated between the individual and God, since any external show of devotion (true or false) may be feigned or performed insincerely: 'Idolatry is in a man's *thought*, not in the opinion of another. Put case I bow to the Altar, why am I guilty of Idolatry? Because a stander-by thinks so? I am sure I do not believe the Altar to be God, and the God I worship may be bow'd to in all places and at all times' (54, my emphasis).

But howsoever much Selden hopes to carve out a domain of inner liberty, he recognizes that the claims of conscience are all too often used for lawlessness, mischief or sedition: 'pretending religion and the Law of God, is to set all things loose: When a Man has no mind to do something he ought to do by his Contract with Man, then he gets a Text, and Interprets it as he pleases, and so thinks to get loose' (104). Conscience so practiced is for Selden a concrete threat to the general rule of secular law, rather than a challenge to any specific legal prohibition. 'Suppose', Selden remarks, 'an Anabaptist comes and takes my horse, I sue him, he tells me he did according to his conscience, his conscience tells him all things are common among the Saints, what's mine is his, therefore you do ill to make such a law, if any man takes another's horse he shall be hanged. What can I say to this man?' (39). What indeed does Selden say to such claims? He appeals repeatedly to the rule of law as a secular contract between men, which he describes affirmingly as both the emanation of tradition and an expression of durable social norms and practices (40–1).

Law is embedded in and springs forth from social life; for Selden, law is a functional contract and an expression of sovereign will (in the prince or the community) but it does not require a transcendental truth claim. Law can be a *nomos* without a narrative. To support such a claim, Selden cites anti-witchcraft laws approvingly:

> The Law against Witches does not prove there be any; but it punishes the malice of those people that use such means, to take away mens Lives. If one should profess that by turning his Hat thrice and crying Buz he could take away a man's life (though in truth he could do no such thing) yet this were a just Law made by the State, that whosoever should turn his Hat thrice and cry Buz; with an intention to take away a mans life, shall be put to death. (117)

This is a vaguely embarrassing example of unvarnished sovereign authority, but it is consistent with Selden's positions: he acknowledges that witchcraft is a social phenomenon rather than a supernatural one but is untroubled by the capital sanction visited upon the malicious troublemakers who seek to create fear and turbulence. The anti-witchcraft law is an unusually vivid example of Selden's vision of secular law as a fungible contract; so too are marriages and kings' expressions of a secular will to contract. While each may be outfitted with transcendental claims, those truth claims are unverifiable ornament: 'marriage is nothing but a Civil Contract' (69) and a 'king is a thing men have made for their own sake, for quietness' sake' (60).

But for Selden religion is not merely another civil contract dressed up by grace and revelation; it is essential to individual ethics and collective cohesion both, for in his account, civil society is debased without religion:

> They that cry down moral-honesty, cry down that which is a great part of Religion, my Duty towards God, and my Duty towards man. What care I to see a man run after a sermon if he couzen and cheat as soon as he comes home. On the other side Morality must not be without Religion, for if so, it may change, as I see convenience. Religion must govern it. He that has not Religion to govern his Morality is not a dram better than my Mastiff-Dogg; so long as you stroke him and please him, and do not pinch him, he will play with you as finely as may be, he is a very good moral-Mastiff, but if you hurt him, he will fly in your Face and tear out your Throat. (76)

Religion, in this account, helps to fix and enforce moral norms; it is a functional or instrumental good that inhibits personal hedonism and other forms of antisocial conduct. Selden's moral-mastiff is a caricature of Hobbesian self-interest, but the core claim here is that religion is an essential adhesive for a stable civil society because it imposes limits upon human appetites. As in his discussion of oaths, Selden finds religion *qua* religion to be socially and politically essential but here he offers no doctrinal or confessional credo, no insistence upon the specific truths of Christianity or indeed even of Protestantism.

Selden, tutored by his legal research and especially by his studies of religion in antiquity, understood that religious division was inevitable since there was no worldly technique through which the true faith might be identified. Milward provides an especially generous account of Selden's remarks on religion, which he seems to have seen as one of *Table-Talk*'s most crucial entries. Religious difference is inevitable at the individual and collective level both. According to Selden each believer, whatsoever their confessional position, assembles his or her religion as an act of idiosyncratic will: 'religion is like fashion, one man wears his doublet slashed, another lac'd, another plain; but every Man has a Doublet: so every man has his Religion. We differ about the trimming . . . . Men say they are of the same Religion for quietness sake; but if the matter were well examin'd, you would scarce find Three any where of the same Religion in all points' (102). The conflict is even more durable at the level of the state: 'disputes in religion will never be ended', Selden comments, 'because there wants a measure by which the business would be decided' (103–4).[21]

[21] The search for such a measure is at the heart of Selden's scholarly enterprise, according to Barbour, 11–14.

Reconciliation is a distant hope, but since for Selden the 'difference is eternal', the only plausible remedy for endless ideological strife is the imposition of temporal supremacy. The sovereign is to be, in this model, the arbiter and referee between parties rather than the 'king of souls' imposing godly belief into the inner experience of the subject. Selden puts the question, for instance, of 'whether the Church or Scripture [is the best] Judge of religion? Answer: in truth neither but the State' (102). The temporal sovereign, that king made for quietness sake, allows religion to flourish and so too 'it may be cast out, when the state pleases' (30). Selden plays upon this Erastian string throughout the *Table-Talk*; 'there's no such thing as spiritual jurisdiction, all is civil, the Churches the same with the Lord Mayors ... If the Clergy say the church ought to be govern'd thus, and thus, by the word of God, that is Doctrine all, that is not Discipline' (59). Moreover, according to Selden, 'Christ himself was a great observer of the Civil power, and did many things only justifiable, because the State requir'd it' (88). Selden insists that the clergy stick to their domain—the spiritual—where they are free to develop and promulgate whatever doctrine they so choose as they pursue their pastoral mission. However, in the matter of discipline, that imposition of religious authority into political and social life, Selden is far more sceptical; as we have seen above, he cultivates a 'liberty interest' in individual religious conscience and resists the close alliance between the temporal and spiritual domain.

In large part guided by his studies of English legal history and of the ancient Jewish commonwealth, Selden admits to the impossibility of achieving a true separation between church and state, but insists nonetheless on disentangling these domains as thoroughly as possible. Selden's studies have taught him that it is inevitable that clergy will intervene in temporal affairs (25) and indeed that it is 'a foolish thing to say ministers must not meddle with Secular Matters, because his own profession will take up the whole man' (74). Since the clerical office is pastoral rather political, Selden exhorts the clergy to 'seriously attend to [their] calling' (74) and refrain from political bustling in the world. The major check that requires clerics to stay in their lanes is the reiteration of temporal supremacy, the Erastian stance that since churches are invited into kingdoms, so too they 'may be cast out, when the State pleases' (30). Bishops are, moreover, entirely 'unfit to Govern because of their Learning; they are bred up in another Law, they run to the Text for something done amongst the Jews that nothing concerns England' (26).

But howsoever much Selden insists upon temporal supremacy, he makes no objection to an established Church, and indeed remarks that episcopacy is the form of church government most suited to the English mixed constitution (28). Moreover, howsoever much he supports individual scholarly inquiry and devotional searching, Selden insists that divines adhere to the practices of an established Church:

> A minister should preach according to the Articles of Religion Established in the Church where he is. To be a Civil Lawyer let a man read Justinian, and the Body of the Law, to conform his brain that way, but when he comes to practice, he must make use of it so far as it concerns the Law received in his own Country. To be a

> Physician let a man read Gallen and Hypocrates; but when he practices, he must apply his Medicines according to the temper of those Mens bodies with whom he lives.... So to be a Divine, let him read the whole Body of Divinity, the Fathers and the Schoolmen, but when he comes to practice, he must use it and apply it according to those Grounds and Articles of Religion that are establish'd in the Church, and this with sence. (72–3)

The brief here is plain; like a legal tradition, an established Church is an emanation of the dynamic religion and political traditions, customs, and social norms of a specific people or nation. Selden's establishment here enjoys no specific truth-claim and is largely a functional remedy for a collective need for religious guidance; it is significant precisely because it expresses the durable (if not fixed) religious norms of the people. For instance, Selden remarks without protest, in France Protestants 'have no bishops... because they live in a Catholic country, and they will not have Catholic Bishops; therefore they must govern themselves as well as they may' (29). This is an assimilationist paradigm rather than a proto-liberal one; for Selden, establishments confer symbolic prestige and describe the shared religious norms and historical self-understanding of a national community, contributing functionally to social cohesion by erecting and maintaining a visible tradition in the face of rampant enthusiasm.

In defense of tradition *qua* tradition, Selden inveighs repeatedly against 'preaching by the spirit' (92), against what he perceives to be irrational, anti-intellectual, and demotic enthusiasm: 'preaching by the spirit ... is most esteemed by the common people, because they cannot abide Art or Learning, which they have not been bred up in' (92). Such religious fervour is irregulable and antisocial; unchecked by the counsel of tradition or the guidance of the learned professionals, enthusiasm of this vulgar style spurns the shared religious norms of the nation and in so doing tears at the social fabric. Selden famously laments the injunction 'scrutamini scripturas', two words that have 'undone the world, because Christ spake it to his disciples, therefore we must all, Men, Women, Children, read and interpret the Scripture' (20), particularly because such a charge has telescoped into a brief for amateurish, uncounselled reading—a pattern that fuels the private spirit. In his argument against enthusiasm and scriptural fundamentalism, the philologist Selden is eager to remind his audience that the Bible is a contingent product of a long tradition of human interpretive and scholarly labour; while it does possess a truth-claim, Scripture is communicated through fallible human actors. It is a bracing riposte to contemporary scriptural literalists to assert that 'although we call the Scripture the Word of God (as it is) yet it was writ by a man, a mercenary man, whose copy either might be false or he might make it false' (21–2). To illustrate further the contingent assemblage and transmission of the scriptural text, Selden describes the translation of the King James Bible: he provides an affirmative portrait of a serious scholarly enterprise in which the collaborative interpretive labour and judgement of the illustrious but fallible translators hands down Scripture.

But as supportive of establishments and other functional expressions of shared religious norms as he may be, Selden reserves his most vigorous scorn for priestly fraud—a concept that was in the seventeenth century often styled 'priestcraft'.[22] For Selden, manipulative priests are predators, 'grievous wolves' worthy of only contempt. A corrupt clergy pollutes the tradition it purports to conserve, it aggravates fear and dissension to serve its ends, and it intrudes in the political sphere at the expense of its pastoral function.[23]

Having been cudgelled by the clerical hierarchy for his *History of Tithes* and likewise having denounced in parliamentary debate the excommunicating power as an invented bid for political power (a point reiterated in the *Table Talk*), the fact that Selden would rebuke clerical overreaching into the temporal domain is no surprise. He unfolds a catalogue of clerical impositions into the machinery and language of government, including the ridiculous but persistent claim that Bishops are *jure divino* beyond the scope of English law (28) and the naked solicitation of power and preferment. The corrupt clergy, Selden remarks, 'would have us believe them against our own reason' (36) and 'will make right Sheep of us' (90), but they are most fixated upon soliciting the favour of the prince: 'the Clergy tell the prince they have Physick good for his Soul and good for the Souls of his People, upon that he admits them; but when he [inevitably] finds by Experience they both trouble him and his People, he will have no more to do with them' (36). Moreover, that same priestly malefactor arrogates to himself dominion undeserved over individual political obligation: 'a Clergy Man goes not a dram further than thus, you ought to obey your prince in general ... [but] how to obey him you must be inform'd by those whose profession it is to tell you' (36).

The common people are especially vulnerable to priestcraft, for they lack the scholarly resources and/or political shrewdness to see through religious manipulation. Selden suggests that 'the English priests would do that in English which the Romish would do in Latin, keep the people in ignorance' (91). The sceptical Selden more aggressively rejects the sacralization of clerics, seeing priesthood as a guild office rather than a sanctification of an ordinary man:

> a priest has no such thing as an indelible Character, what difference do you find betwixt him and another man after Ordination? Only he is made a Priest ... by Designation: as a Lawyer is call'd to the Bar, then made a Serjeant; all men that would get power over others, make themselves as unlike them as they can, upon the same ground the Priests made themselves unlike the Laity. (72)

Equipped with this aura of sacral mystery, a malevolent clergy is free to commit bad-faith fraud upon the untutored people. As an example Selden looks to exorcism:

> casting out Devils is meer Juggling, they never cast out any but what they first cast in. They do it where for Reverence no man shall dare to Examine it, they do it in a

22 Mark Goldie, 'Priestcraft and the Birth of Whiggism', in *Political Discourse in Early Modern Britain*, ed. N. Phillipson and Q. Skinner (Cambridge: Cambridge University Press, 1993).

23 The phrase 'grievous wolves' is Milton's famous rebuke of priestly frauds of just this sort. See John Milton, *Paradise Lost*, ed. David Kastan (Indianapolis: Hackett, 2008), 12.508–37.

> Corner, in a Mortice-Hole, not in the Marketplace. They do nothing but what may be done by Art, they make the Devil fly out of the window in the likeness of a Bat, or a Rat ... [but] why not in some shape we Paint him in, with Claws and Horns. By this trick they gain much, gain upon Mens fancies, and so are reverenc'd ... and certainly if the Priest deliver me from him that is my most deadly Enemy, I have all the Reason in the World to Reverence him. (43)

This is venomous priestcraft, a naked exploitation of the desire for spiritual consolation designed only to bolster the authority and esteem of the exorcist. It is a remarkable irony that Selden likewise objected to deathbed conversions as an unusually venal abuse of office: 'for a priest to turn a man when he lies a-dying, is just like one that hath a long time solicited a woman, and cannot obtain his end; at length makes her drunk, and so lies with her' (99).

As with all of the antisocial impositions upon individual and collective religious practice Selden despises, there are two remedies for such naked badness; the rule of secular law and the guidance of a tradition rooted in the shared religious norms, customs, and practices of the community. In each case, it falls to responsible lay professionals (scholars and jurists especially) to conserve and transmit these traditions to posterity—Selden possesses an archetypal 'common-law mind', after all.

In the pages above, I have tried to provide a coherent account of the constitutional argument in the *Table-Talk* and have suggested that such an argument (whatsoever the degree of Milward's authenticity) ought to be understood not as a sub-scholarly curiosity or as pulp secularism, but rather as a document reflective of the flourishing language of an English civil religion that emerges in the 1660s and 1670s as the work of a heterogeneous group of intellectuals. Whether or not the *Table-Talk* is an authentic reflection of Selden's actual sentiments is beside the point; Milward's Selden practices a sceptical anthropology of church and state that sees religion as functionally and ethically necessary for a thriving state. Religious institutions and Scripture itself are contingent, flawed, and rooted in the messiness of human life; individual belief is ad hoc and fully privatized. Political sociability takes the place of an insistence upon doctrinal correctness and the therapeutic reform of the soul. Tradition (like the English common law) is a living conversation, an emanation of the dynamic social norms and historical self-understanding of the English people to be conserved especially by principled lay professionals such as Hale and especially Selden. This language of English civil religion—assimilationist rather than liberal, inconsistently tolerant rather than fully pluralist, establishmentarian and traditional—was far more durable and influential than Selden and his peers might have imagined.

Bibliography

à Wood, Anthony. *Athenae Oxoniensis*, Vol. 3, ed. Philip Bliss (London: 1815).

Achinstein, Sharon. *Literature and Dissent in Milton's England* (Cambridge: Cambridge University Press, 2003)

Ashcraft, Richard. *Revolutionary Politics and Locke's Two Treatises* (Princeton: Princeton University Press, 1986).

Aubrey, John. *Brief Lives*, ed. Richard Barber (Rochester: Boydell and Brewer, 1982).

Barbour, Reid. *John Selden: Measures of the Holy Commonwealth* (Toronto: University of Toronto Press, 2003).

Burnet, Gilbert. *The Life and Death of Sir Matthew Hale, kt* (London: 1682).

Champion, Justin. 'Some Forms of Religious Liberty: Political Thinking, Ecclesiology, and Freedom in Early Modern England', in *Religious Toleration in the Atlantic World: Early Modern and Contemporary*, ed. Eliane Glaser (Basingstoke: Palgrave Macmillan, 2014), 41–72.

Charter of Rhode Island and Providence Plantation, June 15, 1663. The Avalon Project at Yale Law School: <http://avalon.law.yale.edu/17th_century/ri04.asp>.

Goldie, Mark. 'The Civil Religion of James Harrington,' in *The Languages of Political Theory in Early Modern Europe*, ed. Anthony Pagden (Cambridge: Cambridge University Press, 1987), 197–224.

Goldie, Mark. 'Priestcraft and the Birth of Whiggism', in *Political Discourse in Early Modern Britain*, ed. N. Phillipson and Q. Skinner (Cambridge: Cambridge University Press, 1993), 209–31.

Hobbes, Thomas. *Leviathan*, ed. Edwin Curley (Indianapolis: Hackett, 1994).

Hoxby, Blair. *Mammon's Music: Literature and Economics in the Age of Milton* (New Haven: Yale University Press, 2004).

Journal of the House of Commons, Vol. 8: *1660–1667*, (London: His Majesty's Stationery Office, 1802).

Lloyd, David. *Memoires of the Lives, Actions, Sufferings and Deaths of Those Personages, That Suffered by Death, Sequestration, Decimation: Or Otherwise for the Protestant Religion and the Great Principle Thereof, Allegiance to Their Soveraigne, in Our Late Intestine Wars from the Year 1637 to 1660: With the Life and Martyrdom of King Charles I* (London: 1668).

Macray, W. D. *Annals of the Bodleian Library*, 2nd edn (Oxford: Oxford University Press, 1893).

Milward, Rev. Richard, ed. *Table-Talk: Being the Discourses of John Selden* (London: 1689).

Pincus, Steven. *1688: The First Modern Revolution* (New Haven: Yale University Press, 2009).

Post, Robert. 'Cultural Hetereogeneity and the Law: Blasphemy, Pornography, and the First Amendment', 76 *California Law Review*, 197 (1988): 297–335.

Rosenblatt, Jason. *Renaissance England's Chief Rabbi: John Selden* (New York: Oxford University Press, 2006).

Rushworth, John. *Historical Collections of Private Passages of State*, Vol. 5 (London: 1708).

Smith, Nigel. *Literature and Revolution in England 1640–1660* (New Haven; Yale University Press, 1994).

Spurr, John. *The Restoration Church of England* (New Haven: Yale University Press, 1991).

The Life of Edward, Earl of Clarendon, Vol. 1 (London: 1761).

Toomer, G. J. *John Selden: A Life in Scholarship*, 2 vols (Oxford: Oxford University Press, 2009).

Two Speeches of George, Earl of Bristol, With Some Observations of Them (London: 1674).

Visconsi, Elliott. 'King Philip's War and the Edges of Civil Religion in 1670s London', in *Religion, Culture, and the National Community in the 1670s*, ed. Tom Corns and Tony Claydon (Cardiff: University of Wales Press, December 2010), 148–68.

Visconsi, Elliott. 'The Invention of Criminal Blasphemy: *Rex v. Taylor*, 1676', *Representations*, 103 (Summer, 2008).

Visconsi, Elliott. *Lines of Equity: Literature and the Origins of Law in Later Stuart England* (Ithaca: Cornell University Press, 2008).
Whitelock, Bulstrode. *Memorials of English Affairs*, Vol. 1 (London: 1682).
Wilkins, David. 'Vita Joannis Seldeni', in *Opera omnia*, Vol. 1 (London: 1728).
Williams, Roger. *The Complete Writings of Roger Williams*, Vol. 3: *The Bloudy Tenent of Persecution For Cause of Conscience*, intro. Edwin Gaustad (Eugene: Wipf and Stock, 2007).
Zwicker, Steven N. *Lines of Authority: Politics and English Literary Culture 1649–1689* (Ithaca: Cornell University Press, 1996).

PART V

LEGAL AND LITERARY IMAGINING

CHAPTER 20

CONTRACT

LUKE WILSON

It has been the assumption of the best work on early modern literature and contract law over the past decade or so that (good) literary texts are supremely responsive to the conceptual complexities that it is the business of legal history to trace out. The contemporary tendency is to place a premium on readings that demonstrate intimate and deep links between literature and contiguous discourses and institutions, on the assumption that the literary text emerged out of a saturated cultural matrix and registered, in theory, like a highly sensitive seismograph, every cultural signal that crossed its path. But we are perhaps too ready to imagine literary texts as so acutely sensitive not only to the technicalities of legal practice and theory but to all the shifting currents of interest and anxiety that, flowing from legal questions, is supposed to permeate the discursive fabric of the culture. To say so is not to impugn the very fine recent critical work in the field, the strength of which resides precisely in its insistence on getting specific, and on saving specificity from the defects of an older literary-legal antiquarianism, but simply to acknowledge that there may be a limit to legal resonances that literary texts are capable of registering, and to make sure to take in the range of what it's possible to say about contract in relation to literature. Contract, as a feature of literary texts, engages not only with contemporaneous developments in contract law, but also with deep structural features of contract relatively impervious to circumstances of the immediate moment. Making good on this as a general claim about the literature of the period is not the purpose of this essay, which, instead, first suggests through a single example how close the law of contract in fact was to the institution of the theatre, and then considers a few aspects of how contract functions *as a literary device* in the drama, again through just a few examples.

Late in the sixteenth century, the theatrical entrepreneur Philip Henslowe made note of a loan to the itinerant actor Martin Slather:

> [lent vnto marter slather the 22 of June 1596 the some of viij li of good & lafulle mony of Ingland to be payd the same daye moneth folowinge or els to forfete for not paying

of the same xvj^{li} where vpon he hath bownd hime selfe by tackynge of a j d vpon & a sumsett wittnes to this edward alleyn & his wife][1]

This is just one of the hundreds of contractual transactions Henslowe recorded in the memorandum book that has come to be known as his *Diary*: mostly loans and sales to companies, playwrights, and players, but also several agreements with players to play for a particular company, and so on. Such agreements must have been virtually ubiquitous in the theatre business, and are likely to be typical of an 'economy of obligation' that depended on complex interpersonal webs of credit and trust.[2] But in the context of Henslowe's accounts this agreement with Slather is unusual, too. Eight pounds was a large sum relative to the amount of most of Henslowe's loans, but most of these loans, and even some for larger amounts, are significantly less elaborate; in most cases amounts are loaned out for specified purposes but without conditions of repayment or other legal niceties. In contrast, the agreement with Slather contains, in small compass, elements of the most important functional and conceptual aspects of contract law circa 1596. Henslowe's description indicates that he thought of the loan itself as having the form of a conditional (or penal) bond, a loan of money to Slather at no cost provided repayment occurs before a fixed date, and so called because if it does not, Slather will be liable for a penalty of double the amount of the original loan. This was, and had been since the mid-fourteenth century, the most common way in which loans of money, and agreements to perform in exchange for money or other services, were secured. Conditional bonds were litigated under the action of debt, and when in the beginning of the fourteenth century it was established that to succeed in the alternative action of covenant a sealed deed was required, covenant fell out of use, the conditional bond became the preferred instrument, and debt on a conditional bond became the preferred action.[3] It is also, of course, the form of the 'bond' by which Shylock loans money to Antonio. Without calling it a conditional bond, Henslowe's description seems careful to mention all the formal requirements of such a bond, including a

[1] *Henslowe's Diary*, ed. R. A. Foakes, 2nd edn (Cambridge: Cambridge University Press, 2002), 49 (fol. 22). The square brackets are editorial, indicating that the entry has been crossed out in the manuscript, presumably to mark the cancellation of the debt.

[2] See Craig Muldrew, *The Economy of Obligation: The Culture of Credit and Social Relations in Early Modern England* (New York: St Martins, 1998) *passim*.

[3] D. J. Ibbetson, *A Historical Introduction to the Law of Obligations* (Oxford: Oxford University Press, 2006), 28–33, 92–3; J. H. Baker, *An Introduction to English Legal History*, 4th edn (London: Butterworths, 2002), 318–26; A. W. B. Simpson, *A History of the Common Law of Contract: The Rise of the Action of Assumpsit* (Oxford: Clarendon Press, 1975), 90–122. Baker notes that conditional bonds 'remained in widespread use until Victorian times' (325), despite an inclination in Chancery from the late fifteenth century onwards to relieve penal conditions that amounted to more than the plaintiff's actual losses, a policy adopted by the common law courts themselves by the late seventeenth century. Simpson (*History*, 118–22) attributes the long slow decline of the penal bond to the emergence of the modern distinction between a penalty and actual liquidated damages, only the latter of which is recoverable. For the enormous popularity of the conditional bond as a financial instrument see Muldrew, *Economy*, 109–11.

date certain for repayment, and the condition that double the amount would be payable upon forfeiture.[4]

Apparently to secure this bond, which in legal terms would have been considered secure in itself, Henslowe invokes the idea of an *assumpsit*—a way of referring to a verbal promise that, as we will see, represents the tip of the iceberg of a very large amount of law—and also seems to gesture, in mention of the 'tackynge of a j d', toward consideration, an idea that had come to occupy a central place in contract law in connection with the emerging law of assumpsit. The history of the action on the case for assumpsit is the central feature of the story told by legal historians about the rise of modern contract doctrine, and for that reason has also figured prominently in accounts of the relation between literature and contract produced by literary scholars.[5] Assumpsit evolved as an alternative means of redress in cases of disputes over informal agreements.

Of the actions theoretically available to try contract disputes at common law—covenant, detinue, debt, and action on the case for assumpsit—the latter had in the course of the sixteenth century emerged as the one best suited to resolving disputes concerning informal agreements and also (as it turned out) to supplying the foundation for a general theory of contract. Since the 1340s, covenant had been disabled as a general contractual remedy by the introduction of a requirement that the action could only be brought where the agreement was contained in a sealed document.[6] Detinue, in which the plaintiff argued that the defendant withheld something to which the plaintiff had a contractual or proprietary claim, alleged a 'contractually neutral withholding of possession' and applied normally only to chattels.[7] Debt was a far more flexible remedy, and it was over debt that assumpsit 'triumphed' in Slade's Case (1596–1602). The ruling in that

[4] A condition calling for a forfeiture twice the amount of the loan was usual, but not invariable. And not all conditional bonds were for money loans, so that one might agree to build a house for another by a certain date and if not to pay him a fixed amount, typically something in excess of the latter's actual consequential losses. This was preferred (by creditors, at least), because rather than suing for unspecified damages to be awarded by a jury, the creditor could sue for the stipulated amount under debt. See Ibbetson, *Historical*, 29.

[5] For the legal scholarship on assumpsit, see Simpson, *History*; Ibbetson, *Historical*, 126–51 and passim; Baker, 330–45 and *passim*; David Ibbetson, 'Assumpsit and Debt in the Early Sixteenth Century: The Origins of the Indebitatus Count', *CLJ*, 41 (1982): 142–61; David Harris Sacks, 'The Promise and the Contract in Early Modern England: Slade's Case in Perspective', in *Rhetoric and Law in Early Modern Europe*, ed. Victoria Kahn and Lorna Hutson (New Haven: Yale University Press, 2001), 28–53. Attempts to make use of this scholarship in the context of law and literature include Don E. Wayne, 'Drama and Society in the Age of Jonson: An Alternative View', *Renaissance Drama*, 13 (1982): 103–29; Charles Spinosa, 'Shylock and Debt and Contract in *The Merchant of Venice*', *CSLL*, 5.1 (Spring, 1993): 65–85, revised and expanded as 'The Transformation of Intentionality Debt and Contract in *The Merchant of Venice*', *ELR*, 24 (1994): 370–409; Luke Wilson, 'Ben Jonson and the Law of Contract', *CSLL*, 5.2 (1993): 281–306; Wilson, *Theaters of Intention: Drama and the Law in Early Modern England* (Stanford: Stanford University Press, 2000), 70–86; Andrew Zurcher, 'Consideration, Contract and the End of *The Comedy of Errors*', in *Shakespeare and the Law*, ed. Paul Raffield and Gary Watt (Oxford: Hart, 2008), 19–37.

[6] Ibbetson, *Historical*, 28.

[7] Baker, *Introduction*, 392.

case resolved a jurisdictional dispute between the court of Common Pleas and the court of King's Bench over the provision of remedies for breach of contract. Where Common Pleas had required that such suits be tried under debt, which was one of the traditional forms of action in the ancient register of writs, King's Bench had gotten into the habit of permitting the same causes of action to be tried as actions on the case. Such actions had originated as remedies for causes of action falling under none of the writs in the register, but their use had been gradually generalized to cover categories of action in such a way as to complement, or in some cases overlap with, the traditional actions. In the case of contract, King's Bench permitted actions on the case for assumpsit, which conceptualized the contract as having originated in, or as having subsequently produced, a promise or undertaking to perform. In the action of debt, it was understood that where one party had not performed, a relationship of debt obtained; assumpsit instead rested on the idea that a promise had been made. Where that promise was made subsequently (a situation in a form of assumpsit called *indebitatus assumpsit* ('being indebted, he promised ...'), it was easy enough to see it as founding a separate cause of action. But where there was no claim that an explicit, separable promise had occurred, the question arose whether the contract itself could be taken as implying a promise on which an assumpsit might rest. Slade's Case, in the end, held that it could; in Coke's famous words, 'every contract executory imports in itself an assumpsit'—so that King's Bench might, without contradiction, try contract disputes as if they involved promises to perform, as actions on the case for assumpsit.[8]

Henslowe's mention of Slather's 'tackynge of a j d vpon & a sumsett' (that is, accepting payment of a penny when he gives his promise to repay the loan), clearly responds to the rule that a bare promise was not enforceable without some consideration why it should be. This often took the form of some payment accepted by the promisor, though it might take other forms as well.[9] Since Golding's Case (1586), it had effectively become a rule that every action on the case for assumpsit must aver three things: promise, breach of promise, and consideration.[10] Since the law did not require and was not interested in

[8] 4 Co. Rep. 94b in *ER*, vol. 76, 1077; the full report runs 1072–9. Coke's became the dominant account of the case, but eleven other manuscript reports were produced; see J. H. Baker, 'New Light on *Slade's Case*', *CLJ*, 29 (1971): 51–67. The manuscript reports are transcribed in J. H. Baker and S. F. C. Milsom, *Sources in English Legal History: Private Law to 1750* (London: Butterworths, 1986), 420–41. The legal scholarship on Slade's Case is extensive. See especially David Ibbetson, 'Sixteenth Century Contract Law: *Slade's Case* in Context', *OJLS*, 4 (1984): 295–317; Baker, *Introduction*, 344–9; H. K. Lücke, 'Slade's Case and the Origin of the Common Counts', *LQR*, 81 (July, 1965): 422–45 (pt 1), 81 (October, 1965): 539–61 (pt 2), 82 (January, 1966): 81–96; A. W. B. Simpson, 'The Place of Slade's Case in the History of Contract', *LQR*, 74 (1958): 381–96.

[9] Baker shows how by the 1580s consideration had effectively merged the principle of *quid pro quo*, with its emphasis on reciprocality, with the Canon law notion of *causa* as a more capacious motivation for entering into an agreement; Baker, *Introduction*, 339–41. J. H. Baker, 'Origins of the 'Doctrine' of Consideration, 1535–1585', in *On the Laws and Customs of England: Essays in Honor of Samuel E. Thorne*, ed. Morris S. Arnold, Thomas A. Green, Sally A. Scully, and Stephen D. White (Chapel Hill: University of North Carolina Press, 1981), 341; and David Ibbetson, 'Assumpsit and Debt in the Early Sixteenth Century: The Origins of the Indebitatus Count', *CLJ*, 41 (1982): esp. 154–5.

[10] Simpson, *History*, 406.

seeking out the precise language in which a promise had been made provided that it was averred that a promise *had* been made, consideration became necessary as a visible confirmation of a promise that itself need not actually have occurred.[11]

Henslowe thus had reason to associate assumpsit and consideration. At the time he wrote, John Slade had already brought his bill against Humphrey Morley, and the first ruling in Slade's Case, at the Exeter assizes, was to come within the year, on 8 March 1596 (i.e. 1597), though the final ruling was not to come until 1602.[12] Henslowe would presumably have known nothing of this. He was, however, clearly aware that the two notions ought to come together, and why. And yet there is something strange about Henslowe's usage, beginning with his use of 'assumpsit' as a substantive. The word had its origin in a Latin phrase that began appearing in legal pleadings as early as 1361.[13] In these early actions on the case for misfeasance, it appears as a verb indicating an undertaking or taking in hand that is ambiguously an attempt, a taking into one's possession, and a promise to accomplish something.[14] As actions on the case for assumpsit came to be used in lieu of debt around the beginning of the sixteenth century, it was usually claimed that the defendant *assumpsit et fideliter promisit*—assumed and faithfully promised—to the plaintiff to perform some action. The transformation of the Latin verb into an English substantive began in case reports and by the 1580s the word had made its way into English vernacular works.[15]

But exactly what did Henslowe think he was doing in using the word and more broadly in recording the loan to Slather in the way he did? This is a question that has engaged readers of the *Diary* at least since E. K. Chambers wondered whether these memoranda 'constitute the formal instruments under which the agreements were effected, or are merely notes for [Henslowe's] information'.[16] I suggest that, certainly in the case of the many small loans Henslowe made, and probably in the case of loans like this one, no such 'formal instruments' existed, and that, for Henslowe, his memorandum book *was* his documentation, even though, as Neil Carson surmises, these notes, 'in the form in which they exist (neither signed nor sealed)', would have had little legal force.[17]

11 Simpson, *History*, 407.

12 Baker and Milsom, *Sources*, 420.

13 Baker, *Introduction*, 330 n. 6.

14 See Wilson, *Theaters*, 188–9. Baker (*Introduction*, 330 n. 6) notes that in the Humber Ferry Case (1348)—the first known case in which a breach of covenant was tried as trespass—the term used in the report is *emprist*, the French equivalent of *assumpsit*.

15 William Warner's *Albion's England* (1586) may represent the first vernacular use of 'assumpsit' in the loose but legally inflected sense of a promise or agreement (12; sig. B2^{v}). It appears again in Greene's *Never Too Late* (1590), and again in Lodge's *The Devil Conjured* (1596). Thereafter the word appears fairly commonly in vernacular publications, and is mentioned in at least four plays before the closing of the theatres: Chapman's *Sir Giles Goosecap* (1606), Jonson's *Alchemist* (1611), Fields' *Amends for Ladies* (1618), and Brome's *The Sparagus Garden* (1640).

16 E. K. Chambers, *The Elizabethan Stage*, 4 vols (Oxford: Oxford University Press, 1923), 2.154. For more on this question see Wilson, *Theaters*, 99–104.

17 Neil Carson, *A Companion to Henslowe's Diary* (Cambridge: Cambridge University Press, 1988), 33. A cluster of somewhat similar memoranda later in the *Diary* (Foakes, 238–42; fols 233, 232^{v}, 232, 231, 230^{v}) document Henslowe's agreements with several players (ten in all) to play with him at the Rose

In any case, since an 'assumpsit' *was* a verbal promise, and the action on the case upon an assumpsit evolved to handle cases where there was no written record, memorializing that promise in writing is an at least mildly paradoxical act, but one characteristic of the vernacular adaptation of the Latin verb as an English substantive, an act which exemplifies the familiar process by which the law retroactively shapes behaviour. To call a promise an 'assumpsit' is (or must initially have been) to imagine it as already translated into a legal case, already in controversy, the promise already suspected of having been broken.[18] Harder to explain is what Henslowe might have been thinking in juxtaposing a conditional bond and an assumpsit. As we have seen, these are two distinct legal ideas that do the same thing only at the most general level of supplying a legal framework for the enforcement of certain kinds of bargains. How they do this could not be more different; but if you have a conditional bond, you would not normally have any need for an assumpsit, and vice versa. Henslowe *may* be thinking in a vague way of the legal situation involved in the species of action called *indebitatus assumpsit* (from the expression used in the declaration: 'being indebted, [the defendant] promised ...'), where the use of action on the case for a debt was rationalized by the suggestion that an existing indebtedness could be consideration for a subsequent promise.[19] But if this is so, Henslowe was confused, since the establishment of the indebitatus count in the 1540s had depended on overcoming the doctrine prohibiting two separate forms of action (here, debt and assumpsit) to lie on one cause by pointing out that debt, which provided for the recovery only of the initial amount in question, could not adequately compensate any additional damages the plaintiff might have sustained; assumpsit, as a tortious action in which damages were set by a jury, could. But the conditional bond that Henslowe seems to imagine as secured by the (nominally) subsequent assumpsit carried its own, very stiff, provision for damages in the condition. In short, it's hard to see how positing an assumpsit on top of a conditional bond makes legal sense.

The question of how Henslowe thought about these transactions, what he thought he was doing in recording them as he did, shows that the question What is a contract? is more complicated than it may appear. One the one hand, in the common law, a contract could designate something that did not materially exist, and the existence of which even as a historically locatable agreement or 'meeting of the minds' was not at all settled. Even in the case of covenant, which required a sealed deed, it was never in doubt that the deed was not itself the covenant but only evidence that there was a covenant. In the case of the conditional bond, in contrast, the bond was dispositive rather than evidentiary: it *was* the obligation, and common lawyers were not inclined to look behind the bond in

for a period of time, usually two or three years, or else to forfeit amounts of sometimes 100 marks and sometimes 40 pounds. In each case Henslowe uses the word 'assumpsit', though he appears by turns to think that assumpsit and consideration are the same thing (using the expression '& a sumsett of ij d'), and that they are simply connected (e.g. 'Receued of me iij d vpon & A sumsette'), as he does in the agreement with Slather.

[18] I return below to the idea of what Andrew Zurcher calls 'legal pessimism'; 'Consideration'.

[19] See Ibbetson, 'Assumpsit and Debt', 149–51; Baker, *Introduction*, 343–4.

search of how or why it had come into being; they did not in general admit that the bond reflected any social facts beyond a current relation of obligation, and oral testimony as to such facts was not allowed as a response to debt on a bond.[20] In Henslowe's case, it is unclear whether any conditional bond existed. For him, it is the assumpsit, and no bond, that binds Slather to the terms of the penal condition ('whereupon he hath bownd hime selfe by tackynge of a j d . . .'). If this helps make sense of his combination of the two forms (no actual bond, hence the need for an assumpsit), it also turns on its head the very premise of the conditional bond that it nevertheless invokes.

The point is not that Henslowe did not understand the law, but rather that it functioned for him in a sphere of practice mostly outside the actual courts of law.[21] The kind of sense his legal references make is dependent on the context in which they appear. This usage is unorthodox, and it reflects a highly practical, intuitive, improvisatory, one might say tactical engagement with the law. This is law as it functions outside of legal institutions themselves. I began with the passage from Henslowe in order to show, first of all, in a direct, material way, what is of course not to be doubted, that the theatre business *was* a business, was permeated with contractual imaginings beyond what would have obtained in the social milieus supporting other forms of literary production. Explication of the passage has also shown that Henslowe's usages stand astride, but do not dip much into, a vast depth of legal history and practice. I want finally to suggest that the model for how Henslowe's use of the terms and conceptual structures of contract law on the production side of the theatrical business is both bound to the law and free to deform it, works as well for the often far more complex engagements with contract we encounter in the end product of the theatre industry, the texts of plays themselves.

Contract talk may be described as what Bakhtin calls a primary speech genre, one of a virtually infinite repertoire of relatively stable types of utterances—rejoinders in dialogue, military orders, kinds of business documents, everyday narration, and so on—while the context in which such contract talk appears corresponds to what he calls 'secondary (complex) speech genres' (like literary texts), which are composed of multiple primary speech genres.[22] It is important for the generic identity of contract to preserve its origin in actual forms of discourse; but I am less interested in contract as expressed in embedded speech acts, specific strings of words, though these are to be met with in Renaissance drama from time to time, the best known example being the contractual Induction to Jonson's *Bartholomew Fair*, than in the underlying contractual

[20] Simpson, *History*, 95–8. Tim Stretton notes however that precisely this reluctance led the Chancery to offer remedies that did what the common law courts refused to do, by looking behind the bond; see 'Conditional Promises and Legal Instruments in *The Merchant of Venice*', in *Taking Exception to the Law: Materializing Injustice in Early Modern English Literature*, ed. Donald Beecher, Travis DeCook, Andrew Wallace, and Grant Williams (Toronto; University of Toronto Press, 2015), 71–99.

[21] For the argument that Henslowe's text needs to be understood in relation to the genre to which it properly belongs, which she identifies as that of the memorandum book, see S. P. Cerasano, 'Henslowe's "Curious" Diary", *Medieval and Renaissance Drama in England*, 17 (2005): 72–85.

[22] 'The Problem of Speech Genres', in M. M. Bakhtin, *Speech Genres and Other Late Essays*, trans. Vern W. McGee (Austin: University of Texas Press, 1986), 62.

forms, which can be described by way of Alastair Fowler's distinction between kind and mode, the latter arising as the selective, adjectival extension of a parent kind, an extension that retains only some of its parent's identifying features. Contract is in this sense a *modal* element in literary works that owe their overall structure to some (other) kind.[23] In early modern English dramatic texts, contract is typically both a local and a pervasive structural element.

If contract is properly understood as both a primary kind and a modal extension of that kind, genre itself has important resemblances to contract, and is frequently described as contractual. The most commonly cited authority for this view is Fredric Jameson: 'Genres are essentially literary *institutions*, or social contracts between a writer and a specific public, whose function is to specify the proper use of a particular cultural artifact.'[24] Contract becomes in this reading a metaphor for genre itself, so that it is the genre of genre, or, more precisely, the modal presence not simply of the kind from which it derives but of genre itself. To describe genre as a contract is to suggest that genre is a set of conventions understood as held commonly by the author of a work and the readers/spectators of that work, *as if* these have been agreed contractually between them, and, more importantly, that genre is fundamentally *temporal* in structure, both in the sense that it structures interpretive *expectations* and in the sense that a prominent feature of generic differentiation involves outcomes or endings. A contractual understanding of genre emphasizes the anticipatory structure of the experience of genre, the way in which assumptions about genre and expectations of outcomes are reciprocally produced in the experience of reading a playtext or watching a performance.

All genres imply outcomes, and contract may appear in any genre. But contract is especially a feature of early modern comedy as opposed to other dramatic kinds, and comedy perhaps has a special relation to the question of endings. This is so first of all because, as Lynda Boose remarks, the sense of obligation to gratify audience expectations, to supply what you will, as you like it, all the more heightened in an increasingly commercialized theatrical milieu, seems to find expression in the almost invariable tendency of even satirical comedies to conclude, contractually, in marriage, so that plot structure and circumstances of production mutually reinforce one another.[25] But this may be a special case of a more general association between comedy and contract.

[23] Alastair Fowler, *Kinds of Literature: An Introduction to the Theory of Genres and Modes* (Cambridge: Cambridge University Press, 1982), 106–11. Contractual elements in literary works cannot be called simple *motifs* because, in both Bakhtin's terms and Fowler's, they derive from an antecedent kind or genre.

[24] Fredric Jameson, *The Political Unconscious: Narrative as a Socially Symbolic Act* (Ithaca: Cornell University Press, 1981), 106. See also Heather Dubrow, *Genre* (London: Methuen, 1982), 37; John Frow, *Genre* (London: Routledge, 2006), 52, 104, 116; David Fishelov, *Metaphors of Genre: The Role of Analogies in Genre Theory* (University Park: Pennsylvania State University Press, 1993), 85–7. The most thoroughgoing account of genre as a form of contract is to be found in Victoria Kahn, *Wayward Contracts: The Crisis of Political Obligation in England, 1640–1674* (Princeton: Princeton University Press, 2004), 15–20, 290 n. 40, and *passim*.

[25] Lynda E. Boose, 'The Comic Contract and Portia's Golden Ring', *ShS*, 20 (1988): 241–54.

Castelvetro comments that when tragic agents 'suffer an injury they neither seek redress from magistrates, nor possess their souls with patience, but settle their own accounts', while comic agents 'are in the habit of obeying the magistrates, of conforming to the laws, of submitting to injuries and losses, and of seeking redress for the loss ... from authorities and ordinances'.[26] As Oliver Arnold puts it, 'comic agents are defined precisely by their subjection to the law and by their dependence on higher powers—be they juridical institutions or benevolent fairies—to provide felicitous endings to their troubles'.[27] The law involved in comedy is not always contract law, of course; but, as Aristotle notes, contract is not merely a branch of law among many:

> We may argue that a contract is a law, though of a special and limited kind; and that, while contracts do not of course make the law binding, the law does make any lawful contract binding, and that the law itself as a whole is a sort of contract, so that any one who disregards or repudiates any contract is repudiating the law itself.[28]

This means that contract stands in relation to law, as it does in relation to genre, as both instance and essence.

Contract is thus in a unique position, both generally and, I would argue, in the drama of Shakespeare. But if it is to be understood not only as a more or less sensitive register of the relatively local moves of legal thinking and practice but also as responsive to deeper and slower-moving influences, its relation to comparably distinguishable generic elements in the plays themselves needs to be made clear. I single out two: riddle and prophecy. These are related to contract as indicated schematically in Figure 20.1, where each of the three shares with one of the other two certain features that the third lacks. Thus while the riddle (absolutely) and the prophecy (typically) share a reliance on obscurity, contract, at least when it is not framed to deceive, aims to make all its conditions and consequences clear. Prophecy and contract are fundamentally future-oriented, though where contract is commissive, prophecy is merely assertive; and in prophecy the future is normally both more remote and of universal rather than individual significance. Both contrast with the riddle, the answer to which does not depend on eventualities, even if its answer may only become clear later on; if you don't get it, you nevertheless could have. Contract and riddle, finally, resemble one another, and differ from prophecy, in being structured as a conversation. Riddles typically take the form of a description of the object whose identity is in question, and in the Anglo-Saxon tradition often end with a challenge ('Say who I am'). Riddles are always at least implicitly interrogative, and assume an interlocutor, though the ideal riddle is one that that interlocutor cannot

[26] *Poetica d'Aristotele Vulgarizzata et Sposta* (1529), quoted in Oliver Arnold, 'The King of Comedy: The Role of the Ruler and the Rule of Law in Shakespeare's Comedies', *Genre*, 31 (1998): 3.

[27] Arnold, 'King of Comedy', 3.

[28] Aristotle, *Rhetoric* 1.15 (1376b5–11), trans. W. Rhys Roberts, in *The Basic Works of Aristotle*, ed. Richard McKeon (New York: Random House, 1941), 1377.

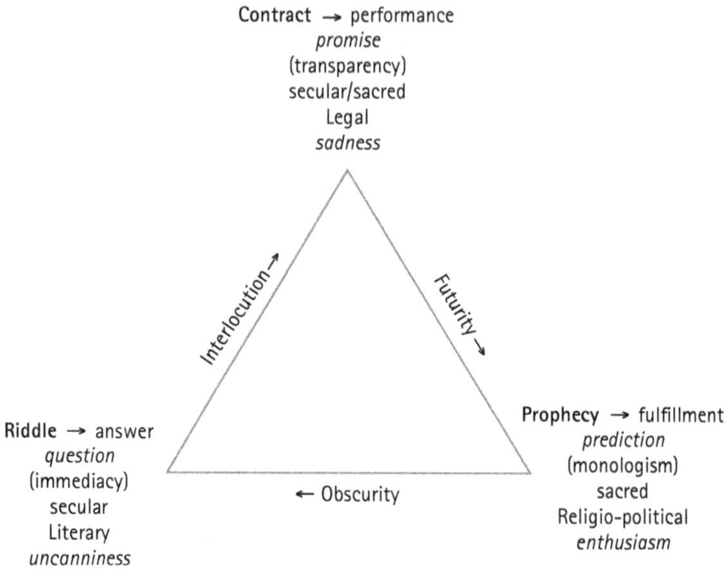

FIG. 20.1 Contract, Riddle, Prophecy.

solve.[29] In the contract as a written form, interlocution may consist in no more than the parties' signatures or marks; but at least to the extent that it is understood as bilateral, it too is implicitly interlocutory.

Prophecy leans away from riddle and toward contract in answering rather than asking a question, and in encouraging revelation rather than failure to recognize, at least for those who have eyes to see and ears to hear, in contrast to the riddle, which relies on *not* being solved. Obscurity is important to the genre of prophecy even though not invariably present in it. But although it may be understood, that understanding cannot be confirmed outside of future events, whereas the answer to a riddle is typically something that's right in front of you, a *thing* you encounter in everyday life, one you could have recognized from its description.[30]

[29] On the formal dialogism of the riddle as 'a stylised contest between questioner and respondent, waged as a struggle for possession of a secret or hidden knowledge', see Frow, *Genre*, 36; and especially Patricia Dailey, 'Riddles, Wonder and Responsiveness in Anglo-Saxon Literature', in *The Cambridge History of Early Medieval English Literature*, ed. Clare A. Lees (Cambridge: Cambridge University Press, 2013), 451–72.

[30] On the materiality and familiarity of the objects that are the answers to Anglo-Saxon riddles, see Daniel Tiffany, 'Lyric Substance: On Riddles, Materialism, and Poetic Obscurity', *Critical Inquiry*, 28 (2001): 72–98. Riddle answers are also immanent to the riddle itself in the sense that the words of the riddle and word(s) of the answer point to the same referent; see Frow, *Genre*, 34. In terms of its 'disposition', riddle is thus self-contained, in contrast to contract and prophecy, where the supplemental component is fundamentally extrinsic to the speech act of the form itself.

Finally, each genre stands as the central figure of a broad institutional category. Prophecy is fundamental to Scripture and indeed to any teleological religious discourse, and, while prophecy in early modern England functioned as a popularly accessible alternative to scriptural knowledge, even where prophecy was purely political or even personal it depended for its authority on its assumed supernatural character.[31] As we have seen, for Aristotle the contract is both enforced by law and a law of a kind itself; because early modern English contract was intimately associated with, if distinct from, the promise as an originally theological construct, and because it appears in both commercial and marital contexts, it can be described as both secular and sacred. And the riddle, as if in default of legal and religious authority, is central to the literary, the secular, and to common, lived experience: particularly and perhaps uniquely in the English literary tradition, the Anglo-Saxon riddle is recognized as the 'earliest secular poetry in English'.[32]

As the triangulation of the three forms in Figure 20.1 suggests, each is susceptible to merging and mixing with the other two; in Shakespeare, especially, the distinctions tend to cross into ambiguity. Riddle and prophecy have an ancient connection in the oracular mode of classical literature; the riddling nature of both political and religious prophecies in the early modern period is well documented, and we need look no further than *Macbeth* to see it in Shakespeare.[33] But riddle and prophecy both can take on a contractual tincture in incorporating an element of contingency, the riddle when it is embedded in a secondary genre as a 'neck riddle' in either of two varieties: in order to avoid death or gain something one seeks, one must either answer a riddle or pose a riddle that cannot be answered. In such cases, the riddle forms part of a conditional structure: if you can answer, I will do/not do this; or, if I cannot answer, I will do/not do this. Such conditional promises are effectively contractual once they are acted upon or 'undertaken'. Prophecy may be said to be the opposite of contract in the sense that it presents itself as dealing in inevitabilities where contract is essentially about contingencies.[34] It is not

31 To identify the source of the authority of prophecy with religion *tout court* is to oversimplify, especially because of the centrality of the Galfridian strain of political prophecy to forms of early modern English prophecy. See Keith Thomas, *Religion and the Decline of Magic: Studies in Popular Beliefs in Sixteenth and Seventeenth Century England* (New York: Oxford University Press, 1971), 389–432. Even so, prophecy is associated with the sacred in a way that contract and riddle are not.

32 Tiffany, 'Lyric Substance', 72, relying on W. P. Ker's work on the literariness of the early English riddle. See also Andrew Walsh, *Roots of Lyric: Primitive Poetry and Modern Poetics* (Princeton: Princeton University Press, 1978), 25–46. For Anglo-Saxon riddles, see *The Exeter Book Riddles*, trans. Kevin Crossley-Holland (New York: Penguin, 1979).

33 On the obscurity of early modern prophecy, see Thomas, *Religion*, 128–46, 389–408. Tom Mould describes the generational transformation of prophecy into riddle in 'Prophetic Riddling: A Dialogue of Genres in Choctaw Performance', *Journal of American Folklore*, 115 (457/8): 395–421. See also Avraham Oz, *The Yoke of Love: Prophetic Riddles in 'The Merchant of Venice'* (Newark: University of Delaware Press, 1995).

34 Linguistically, promises and predictions are not so distinct; it is common to express promises as predictions, as when we say 'It'll get done' and mean that we are promising to do it. On the question of why we tend to understand assertions ('I will do it') about future actions as specifically commissive ('I promise to do it'), see Mikhail Kissine, 'From Predictions to Promises: How to Derive Deontic Commitment', *Pragmatics and Cognition*, 16 (2008): 471–91.

unusual, however, for prophecy to take on an attenuated contingency, as in the subgenre of prophecy that takes the form *When x happens, then so too will y*. A good example is the parody of a pseudo-Chaucerian prophecy, possibly derived from Puttenham, spoken by the Fool in Folio *King Lear*.[35]

Where *If ... then* in the case of the embedded riddle implies a true contingency, *When ... then* in prophecy is conditional in hardly more than the neutral sense of predicting that two occurrences will happen together or the one following the other, one perhaps as a sign of the other but without any necessary causal or, a fortiori, volitional component. But the ambiguity of 'then' is one of the elements that make the interrelation of these forms, again especially in Shakespeare, so suggestive, as for example in Bertram's letter to Helen in *All's Well*: 'When thou canst get the ring upon my finger, which never shall come off, and show me a child begotten of thy body that I am father to, then call me husband; but in such a then I write a never' (3.2.55–8). Bertram's feeble gestures here in the direction of the opacity of the riddle in its oppositional form (getting the ring that cannot be gotten, getting the child when I won't go to bed with you) don't make things any better, but his real mistake is to combine the offer of a contingent promise to perform with the presumptuous certainty of prophecy; Helena, of course replaces his *when ... ~~then~~ never* with her own *when ... ~~never~~ then*.[36] One way to describe the uncomfortable feeling we get from *All's Well* is as a function of this unhappy combination of contractual and prophetic genres. The contractual dimension of Bertram's 'offer' supplies a taste of the comic ideology of consensual engagement, while a prophetic tonality underlies what amounts to a unilateral threat on Bertram's part, which Helena is able to convert into the bilateral, contractual form Bertram has supplied under negation, to produce an agreement Bertram never meant to undertake. This instance is of course just one of many interrelated contractual relationships in *All's Well*, all of which participate in elements of riddle and prophecy. But it suggests that the mixing of the three forms in question signals a generic instability, as in *All's Well* the prominence of both riddle and prophecy is perhaps a measure of the extent to which the play strains comic expectations.

A similar argument might be made about the neck riddle that opens *Pericles*, that in mingling contract and riddle it announces the generic indeterminacy of what is to follow. And one need hardly look further than *The Merchant of Venice* for evidence that these three forms are for Shakespeare closely linked in a way that seems to signal an unstable mixing of genres. Some of the implications are obvious. It's easy to see how the casket test, for example, is a form of neck riddle but by the same token has a contractual dimension, with 'choosing' aligned closely with a contractual 'undertaking', a taking in hand or promising. And you might say that Portia reads the bond as one might read a

[35] *King Lear*, F 3.2.79–94; George Puttenham, *The Art of English Poesy*, ed. Frank Whigham and Wayne A. Rebhorn (Ithaca: Cornell University Press, 2007), 309. Its derivation from Puttenham does not explain the Fool's attribution of it to Merlin. See Terence Hawkes, 'The Fool's "Prophecy" in *King Lear*', *N&Q*, n.s., 7 (1960): 331–2.

[36] On oppositional and non-oppositional riddles, see Robert A. Georges and Alan Dundes, 'Toward a Structural Definition of the Riddle', *Journal of American Folklore*, 76 (1963): 111–18.

riddle (what is it that is flesh but no blood and weighs not a scruple more or less than a pound?); and the substantial thingness of the stipulated penalty may also owe something to the materiality and immediacy of the answer to the riddle.

And again, the question of agency in relation to prophecy that is explored in *Macbeth* might be described as a generic confusion in which contractual thinking finds its way into the anti-volitional, anti-contingent atmosphere of prophecy, producing on Macbeth's part a mistaken, essentially contractual, kind of *If ... then* way of thinking; *What must I perform to make this happen?*, Macbeth in effect asks, as if misreading riddle and prophecy as pseudo-contractual forms. Conversely, the generic instability of *Doctor Faustus*—its apparent commitment to farce and pathos almost simultaneously—stems first and foremost from its incorporation of the genre of contract, which cannot be wholly dissociated from comic entailments, as if, in this, the play is a tragicomedy of a special kind.[37]

Figure 20.1 places contract in opposition to the axis of obscurity, and I suggested that contract has no place for obscurity; but of course contracts can be obscure in all sorts of ways, as the history of contract law itself makes clear. It would be useful to consider in detail the various kinds of infelicity that beset contract, including breach, fraud, mistake, and frustration; but at any rate it should be clear that an entirely felicitous contract is unlikely to be of much literary (or for that matter legal) interest.[38] By way of concluding, I will briefly consider another infelicitous contract in Shakespeare that has attracted recent critical attention: the business of the chain in *The Comedy of Errors*. Andrew Zurcher ingeniously reads this dispute as figuring the concern that allowing actions on the case for assumpsit where debt was available violated the double remedy doctrine, which held that one cause could not give rise to two actions.[39] Antipholus of Ephesus has promised to pay Angelo for the chain, but has not received consideration; Antipholus of Syracuse has received consideration (the chain), but has made no promise. Thus Angelo should have an action of debt against Antipholus of Ephesus and an action of assumpsit against Antipholus of Syracuse, so that 'What Shakespeare has effectively allegorized in the brothers was one of the chief points of contention during Slade's Case.'[40] The fit is indeed striking, and against the objection that Slade's Case was not initiated until 1596, and the play had been performed by 1594, it is important to note that these issues were of long standing, and did not crop up suddenly when Slade's Case came along. Zurcher

[37] Although contract, as we have seen, has a very strong association with comic form, it would be wrong to associate riddle and prophecy, with, respectively, tragedy and romance (or tragicomedy), in quite the same way, though it may be that specific admixtures are more characteristic of one genre than another.

[38] Disputes as to breach are of course the basis of most cases involving contract. The doctrines of mistake (where the making of the contract was in some way faulty, short of overt fraud) and frustration (where circumstances change after the making of the contract so as to make it impossible to perform) did not emerge until the nineteenth century. On mistake, see Catherine MacMillan, *Mistakes in Contract Law* (Oxford: Hart, 2010); on frustration, see Ibbetson, *Historical*, 224, 258.

[39] On the double remedy doctrine, see Baker, *Introduction*, 342–5.

[40] Zurcher, 'Consideration', 30.

also links the series of errors attaching to this contract with a new pessimism about 'the knowability of the human subject' that accompanied or perhaps determined assumpsit's treatment of consideration *as* promise.[41] Zurcher argues that the pervasive pessimism of characters in *The Comedy of Errors* represents a specifically *legal* pessimism tied to the shift from the contractual action of debt to the tortious action on the case for assumpsit, where the remedy was damages rather than payment of the actual amount in dispute, with the implication that all assumpsits assume a failure of performance. This explanation, suggestive as it is, may be too specific. After all, as we have seen, the alternative and predominant form of contract, as expressed in the conditional bond, was designed so as to make default on the debt the only structurally anticipated outcome, resulting in, as Tim Stretton puts it, 'hundreds of thousands of Elizabethans making promises to each other that they did not envisage keeping'.[42] It may be that the pessimism Zurcher identifies in the play—in Egeon, in Adriana—stems from less specific and more durable aspects of both comedy and contract than he allows. After all, Antonio in *The Merchant of Venice* suffers from an almost identical fatalism, one that seems to anticipate, and also grows in consequence of, his bond.[43] Dissatisfaction of one kind or another is almost obligatory at the commencement of a comedy, and while Antonio's and Egeon's fatalism may be distinguished from (for example) Orlando's determination to thrive at the opening of *As You Like It*, it is not entirely separable either. I would suggest that this fatalism is properly a structural feature of contractually inflected comedy generally, and also that it represents a partial and finally inadequate response to the situations of uncertainty that it is the business of comedy to generate and (more or less) resolve.

If it is possible, as Figure 20.1 suggests, to associate each of the three forms represented there with a particular affect, the riddle and the contract stand in a special relation to one another. The riddle is paired with the uncanny in the sense that it involves familiarity exposed in strangeness, and strangeness in the familiar (as epitomized in the close relation between the riddle and incest, as in *Pericles*, or, in the *Exeter Book* riddles, the genitals; and also more generally the unrecognizability of familiar things). Contract, in contrast, carries an almost opposite affective charge, that of a sort of weary uncertainty that may be described as sadness, pessimism, or fatalism: one is both uncertain as to the cause of one's weariness and weary of the uncertainty itself: 'It wearies me, you say it wearies you' (1.1.2), remarks Antonio. This is, somewhat surprisingly, the affective register of Shakespearean comedy's commitment both to satisfactory performance and to the infelicities of contract this may involve.[44] As Heather Dubrow puts it, in the matter of the contract of genre, 'codes may be violated ... and contracts broken', and it is through

[41] Zurcher 'Consideration', 31.

[42] Stretton, 'Conditional Promises', 78.

[43] See Luke Wilson, 'Drama and Marine Insurance in Shakespeare's London', *The Law in Shakespeare*, ed. Constance Jordan and Karen Cunningham (New York: Palgrave Macmillan, 2007), 127–42.

[44] It is attributable to *Doctor Faustus*'s intimacy with the comic that Faustus's fatalism has so strong a resemblance to Antonio's and Egeon's. He too sees ends in beginnings and seeks to 'make an end immediately'; *Doctor Faustus*, ed. Roma Gill, rev. edn (London: Methuen, 2008), 5.72. Faustus's sadness, that is, his pessimism, is in this sense distinct from his spiritual despair.

such violations—the disappointment of generic expectations—that both generic conventions and their limitations come to be performed in the experience of the reader or playgoer.[45] At the same time, precisely *fidelity* to the contract, the scrupulous fulfilment of its conditions, can have a similar effect, as in Shakespeare's insistence on concluding his comedies with marriages that strain credibility.[46]

The 'legal pessimism' of contract, as Zurcher observes, is very much a form of complacency, of self-reassurance: things are bad, true, but it doesn't really matter. This affective combination is at the heart, I think, of what contract does, on a very wide scale of cultural and historical generality, well beyond the margins of the technical dimensions of the English law of contract, in *Dr Faustus*, easily, but, far more remotely, in the legend of the cheirograph (contract) of Adam, which essentially supplements the fall from grace as a result of Satan's deceit and the sins of the protoplasts with an explanation of the postlapsarian human condition as the result of a contract executed by Adam *by mistake*, and involving no sin, no disobedience to God.[47] Error is thus domesticated and secularized as mistake, and the result is the sadness of the subject of contract.

I began by suggesting that the richly specific and more or less local scholarly work in law and Shakespeare reaches its theoretical limit at the point at which the literary becomes infinitely responsive to legal context; this response, whether it is resistive, amplificatory, parodic, demystifying, or supplemental, amounts to an allegorical representation of legal issues. I stress that this is a theoretical limit that is not reached in the fine, historically and critically nuanced work of the past decade or so. It remains possible, however, to question some of these readings on the grounds of over-specificity of explanatory frameworks. Charles Spinosa's emphasis on Slade's Case perhaps too readily merges complicated and nominally narrow legal issues into a narrative of epochal cultural and conceptual change.[48] Andrew Zurcher perhaps is too specific in attributing the pervasive pessimism of characters in *The Comedy of Errors* to a specifically *legal* pessimism tied to the shift from the contractual action of debt to the tortious action on the case for assumpsit. And I myself perhaps unnecessarily reify the distinction between the atemporality of debt and the temporal protraction of assumpsit as in effect allegorized in theatre's characteristic preoccupation with duration.[49] Clearly, however, the way forward involves literary scholars continuing to refine their understanding of the history of the law, both in its details and as a narrative open to evidence from a range of disciplinary perspectives and committed to registering broad patterns of change and continuity. Attention must also be paid, I've argued, to continuities in literary form that, while undoubtedly linked to legal history, demand also to be taken on their own terms and in their own idiom. In the argument I've outlined here, contract as it appears in literary

[45] Dubrow, *Genre*, 37.

[46] Boose, 'Comic Contract', 242.

[47] See Michael E. Stone, *Adam's Contract with Satan: The Legend of the Cheirograph of Adam* (Bloomington: Indiana University Press, 2002), esp. 116.

[48] Spinosa, 'Transformation'.

[49] Wilson, *Theaters*, 78–82.

contexts is in principle always a mixed form, always to some degree exhibits affinities with other distinguishable literary forms, and particularly with riddle and prophecy, which in turn themselves will typically bear traces of the contractual.

Bibliography

Arnold, Oliver. 'The King of Comedy: The Role of the Ruler and the Rule of Law in Shakespeare's Comedies', *Genre*, 31 (1998): 1–31.

Baker, J. H. 'Origins of the "Doctrine" of Consideration, 1535–1585', in *On the Laws and Customs of England: Essays in Honor of Samuel E. Thorne*, ed. Morris S. Arnold, Thomas A. Green, Sally A. Scully, and Stephen D. White (Chapel Hill: University of North Carolina Press, 1981), 336–58.

Baker, J. H. 'New Light on *Slade's Case*', *Cambridge Law Journal*, 29 (1971): 51–67.

Baker, J. H. and S. F. C. Milsom. *Sources in English Legal History: Private Law to 1750* (London: Butterworths, 1986), 420–41.

Boose, Lynda E. 'The Comic Contract and Portia's Golden Ring', *Shakespeare Studies*, 20 (1988): 241–54.

Ibbetson, David. 'Assumpsit and Debt in the Early Sixteenth Century: The Origins of the Indebitatus Count', *Cambridge Law Journal*, 41 (1982): 142–61.

Ibbetson, David. *A Historical Introduction to the Law of Obligations* (Oxford: Oxford University Press, 2006).

Ibbetson, David. 'Sixteenth Century Contract Law: *Slade's Case* in Context', *Oxford Journal of Legal Studies*, 4 (1984): 295–317.

Kahn, Victoria. *Wayward Contracts: The Crisis of Political Obligation in England, 1640–1674* (Princeton: Princeton University Press, 2004).

Lücke, H. K. 'Slade's Case and the Origin of the Common Counts', *Law Quarterly Review*, 81 (July, 1965): 422–45 (pt 1), 81 (October, 1965), 539–61 (pt 2), 82 (January, 1966), 81–96.

MacMillan, Catherine. *Mistakes in Contract Law* (Oxford: Hart Publishing, 2010).

Sacks, David Harris. 'The Promise and the Contract in Early Modern England: Slade's Case in Perspective', in *Rhetoric and Law in Early Modern Europe*, ed. Victoria Kahn and Lorna Hutson (New Haven: Yale University Press, 2001), 28–53.

Simpson, A. W. B. *A History of the Common Law of Contract: The Rise of the Action of Assumpsit* (Oxford: Clarendon Press, 1975).

Simpson, A. W. B. 'The Place of Slade's Case in the History of Contract', *Law Quarterly Review*, 74 (1958): 381–96.

Spinosa, Charles. 'Shylock and Debt and Contract in "The Merchant of Venice"'. *Cardozo Studies in Law and Literature*, 5.1 (Spring, 1993): 65–85.

Spinosa, Charles. 'The Transformation of Intentionality Debt and Contract in "The Merchant of Venice"'. *English Literary Renaissance*, 24 (1994): 370–409.

Stretton, Tim. 'Conditional Promises and Legal Instruments in *The Merchant of Venice*', in *Taking Exception to the Law: Materializing Injustice in Early Modern English Literature*, ed. Donald Beecher, Travis DeCook, Andrew Wallace, and Grant Williams (Toronto: University of Toronto Press, 2015), 71–99.

Wayne, Don E. 'Drama and Society in the Age of Jonson: An Alternative View', *Renaissance Drama*, 13 (1982): 103–29.

Wilson, Luke. 'Ben Jonson and the Law of Contract', *Cardozo Studies in Law and Literature*, 5.2 (1993): 281–306.

Wilson, Luke. 'Drama and Marine Insurance in Shakespeare's London', in *The Law in Shakespeare*, ed. Constance Jordan and Karen Cunningham (New York: Palgrave Macmillan, 2007), 127–42.

Wilson, Luke. *Theaters of Intention: Drama and the Law in Early Modern England* (Stanford: Stanford University Press, 2000).

Zurcher, Andrew. 'Consideration, Contract and the End of *The Comedy of Errors*', in *Shakespeare and the Law*, ed. Paul Raffield and Gary Watt (Oxford: Hart Publishing, 2008), 19–37.

CHAPTER 21

CONTRACT AND CONJUGALITY IN EARLY MODERN ENGLAND

TIM STRETTON

THE character Portia in *The Merchant of Venice* is famous for her legal dexterity in denying Shylock his 'pound of flesh', and for navigating the terms of her father's will to marry Bassanio. A less remarked upon achievement is her securing of an unusual measure of autonomy and economic independence in marriage. By tricking Bassanio into giving away a ring that represents her property and his fidelity, and then having him vow never again to be untrue, she schools him in his duties as a husband. Under the common law principle of 'coverture' all of her property (including her ring) in England would fall under his control, but she can be argued to equivocate when she continues to refer to her house as her own and reflects to Bassanio that she is 'though yours, not yours' (3.2.20). In short she negotiates not only her marriage but also the foundations of her married life, as if negotiating the terms of a contract.[1] This embryonic contractual thinking, in a play full of bonds and bands and other legal instruments, marks an evolution in thinking about both contract and conjugality that would come to fuller fruition in the seventeenth century. Attitudes to contract in its broad sense—legally enforceable agreements between parties—were changing, in a society that was becoming more legally minded and commercial. So too were the conditions of many marriages, thanks to developments in marriage contracts, marriage settlements, and marital separations, and women's growing involvement in and familiarity with legal instruments, investments, and litigation. This essay argues that the prominence of marriage plots, marriage contracts, and legal trickery in English Renaissance drama resulted in part from a tension between these new developments in economic relations and marriage practice and the resilience of what might be termed the ideology of marriage.

[1] Natasha Korda, '"Dame Usury" Gender, Credit, and (Ac)counting in the Sonnets and The Merchant of Venice', *SQ*, 60 (2009): 129–53; Subha Mukherji, *Law and Representation in Early Modern Drama* (Cambridge: Cambridge University Press, 2006): 37–41.

A number of critics have detected in Jacobean drama a cultural shift away from a traditional vision of society formed of reciprocal obligations between (and within) the social ranks of a status hierarchy, towards a more self-interested notion of social obligations based on contractual thinking.[2] City comedies burst at the seams with greedy characters set upon social climbing and economic advancement, inspiring satire and attracting scorn both within and outside their plays. The character Quomodo, in Thomas Middleton's *Michaelmas Term* (1604), personifies this new way of thinking and behaving, as he and his associates employ intricate legal devices and threats of litigation to trick the naive country gentleman Easy out of his lands: where Shylock manipulates a legal instrument to seek revenge, Quomodo simply wants to get rich quick.[3] Similarly, Ben Jonson's *The Alchemist* (1610) explores the alchemical ability of new money to dissolve the supports of the traditional social and political order, and his *Bartholomew Fair* (1614) famously begins with the playwright sending a bookholder and scrivener on stage to make a contract with the audience.

Again and again in these plays that depict financial motives for relationships, marriages take centre stage, encouraging audiences to celebrate honest and honourable matches and recoil at the raw self interest of characters motivated 'by money, not love' or 'by force, not faith, / by appointment, not affection' who join together in the knot of matrimony 'doone with / greatest arte and least trueth, with best collours and worst / conceits' (Lyly, *Gallathea* 4.2.44–5; 52–4).[4] Scholars continue to debate the meaning and satirical intent of these obviously exaggerated treatments of commodification.[5] However, most now accept that their inspiration is to be found in the growth of an increasingly market-based economy, characterized by a dramatic expansion in transactions involving credit, in which fluid capital and the pursuit of commercial gain began to challenge the previously unquestioned dominance of landed wealth.[6]

Marriage Settlements and Separate Estates

Contractual thinking about marriage was obviously not new in the decades either side of 1600, but for centuries negotiations over marriage had concentrated on two specific

[2] Luke Wilson, 'Ben Jonson and the Law of Contract', *CSLL*, 5.2 (1993): 281–3; *Theaters of Intention* (Stanford, 2000); Don E. Wayne, 'Drama and Society in the Age of Jonson: An Alternative View', *RD*, n.s., 13 (1982): 103–29.

[3] Dave Postles, *Microcynicon: Aspects of Early-Modern England* (Loughborough, 2014), 36.

[4] *The Complete Works of John Lyly*, ed. R. Warwick Bond, 3 vols (Oxford: The Clarendon Press, 1902, reissued 1967), 2.429–72.

[5] See, for example, Mukherji, *Law and Representation*; Theodore B. Leinwand, *Theatre, Finance and Society in Early Modern England* (Cambridge: Cambridge University Press, 1999).

[6] Craig Muldrew, *The Economy of Obligation: The Culture of Credit and Social Relations in Early Modern England* (Houndsmills, Basingstoke: Palgrave, 1998); Postles, *Microcynicon*, 35–49.

moments in a union's lifecycle: its making—the contracting of marriage and the pooling of resources in a husband's hands; and its aftermath—the provision of resources for the surviving spouse. Little legal attention was paid to the period in between, when the common law rules of coverture dictated that any estates in land a wife possessed fell under her husband's control and all other property became his outright.[7] This began to change in the sixteenth century with the utilization of equitable devices such as uses and trusts, first to keep specified property out of husbands' hands and then to give wives a measure of autonomy during marriage, through such means as providing income for their sole use or reserving to them the ability to write a will of their separate property or to raise dowries or portions for children from a previous marriage.[8] John Fletcher makes fun of the intricacy of conditions in such documents in *The Tamer Tamed* (*c*.1609), where Maria's efforts to 'turn' Pettruccio and 'bend him as I list' (1.2.173) include a written set of demands for him that specify:

> liberty and clothes,
> When and in what way she will, continual monies,
> Company, and all the house at her dispose.
> No tongue to say 'Why is this?', or 'Whither will it?'
> New coaches and some buildings she appoints here
> Hangings, and hunting horses, and for plate
> And jewels for private use, I take it,
> Two thousand pounds in present. Then for music,
> And women to read French.[9] (2.5.137–44)

These settlements and devices are well known, although recent scholarship is emphasizing their significance, with Natasha Korda suggesting that they altered existing conceptions of the conjugal debt spouses owed each other, and Allison Tait arguing that they would go on to spell '[t]he beginning of the end of coverture'.[10] Few scholars, however, have pondered the origins of these innovations.

Two developments are significant here. The first, which was all but complete by the sixteenth century, was the steady displacement of dower, a widow's right to a life interest in a third of her husband's real estate, by jointure, either a specified estate in land or, more commonly, a secured fixed income akin to a pension. Dower focused on the extent of a husband's property at his death and applied almost automatically,

[7] Amy Louise Erickson, *Women and Property in Early Modern England* (London: Routledge, 1993), 99–101; B. J. Sokol and Mary Sokol, *Shakespeare, Law, and Marriage* (Cambridge: Cambridge University Press, 2003), 117–32.

[8] Maria L. Cioni, 'The Elizabethan Chancery and Women's Rights', in *Tudor Rule and Revolution: Essays for G. R. Elton from His American Friends*, ed. DelLoyd J. Guth and John W. McKenna (Cambridge: Cambridge University Press, 1982), 159–82; Erickson, *Women and Property*, 104–7.

[9] John Fletcher, *The Tamer Tamed*, ed. Lucy Munro (London: Methuen Drama, 2010).

[10] Korda, 'Dame Usury'; Allison Tait, 'The Beginning of the End of Coverture: A Reappraisal of the Married Woman's Separate Estate', *Yale Journal of Law and Feminism*, 26 (2014).

while jointure focused on the value of a wife's dowry, 'the portion / and sinew of her fortune' (Shakespeare, *Measure for Measure*, 3.1.222–3) and had to be arranged. There were practical reasons for this change, most notably because dower did not apply to lands held in uses (the forerunners of trusts), but the conceptual realignment it initiated was significant.[11] In short, dower was a customary right and jointure a contractual interest. Instead of a widow benefiting under dower from a share of the marital estate she had helped to create and support, she received income calculated as a proportion her initial contribution to the marriage.[12] The terms of some jointures arranged for dowries or portions to be paid in instalments or else indicated the amount of money that would be returned to a wife's family—i.e. refunded—if she were to die within the first months or years after marriage.[13] These monetary calculations of a wife's value and what she deserved in widowhood occurred at the making of marriage, not its conclusion (say, in the terms of a will), as illustrated by the scene in *The Taming of the Shrew* when Petruchio learns of the extent of Katherine's portion from Baptista and responds:

> And for that dowry I'll assure her of
> Her widowhood, be it that she survive me,
> In all my lands and leases whatsoever.
> Let specialties be therefore drawn between us,
> That covenants may be kept on either hand. (2.1.123–7)

The negotiating of further rights in a marriage settlement was a natural extension of this process. The incentive to evade or modify the unique English rules of coverture and rights to dower led significant numbers of men and women (and their families) to negotiate legally binding marriage settlements. As Calantha muses to Nearchus in John Ford's *The Broken Heart* (1625–32),

> Were I presently
> To choose you for my lord, I'll open freely
> What articles I would propose to treat on
> Before our marriage.[14] (5.3.38–41)

Amy Erickson goes so far as to suggest that the widespread familiarity with legal instruments and their enforcement prompted by this increasingly heavy reliance

[11] Erickson, *Women and Property*.

[12] Initially joint estates in lands that passed to the survivor, jointures increasingly took the form of annuities.

[13] The lines from *Measure for Measure*, quoted above, come from a scene recounting how Angelo reneged on his contracted marriage to Mariana when he learned of the loss of her dowry (3.1.210–25).

[14] John Ford, *The Broken Heart*, ed. Donald K. Anderson, Jr (Lincoln: University of Nebraska Press, 1968).

on settlements, which were largely unnecessary within the property regimes of other European jurisdictions, may have played a part in the early emergence in England of a recognizably capitalist economy.[15]

Marital Separations

The second development that almost certainly influenced the rise of conditions attaching to marital settlements was (paradoxically enough) changes to marital separations. The English church famously forbade divorce permitting remarriage, except by a full annulment declaring that the marriage had never been valid. Nevertheless, in cases of proven adultery or marital cruelty it permitted judicial separations 'from bed and board' and separation orders often stipulated the maintenance or alimony a husband would pay his estranged wife. The penalty for non-payment was excommunication, but as the power of this threat diminished, church officials increasingly utilized conditional bonds with money penalties for non-payment that could be recovered at common law.[16] As an example of the church's difficulty with enforcement, in the 1570s George Puttenham was so lax in observing the terms of a separation order concerning his estranged wife Dame Elizabeth Windsor that the Privy Council had to intervene. Councillors demanded that he comply with the Court of Arches' original terms concerning Dame Elizabeth, namely:

1. She shall be sojourned in the house of the Lord Delaware, with her diet paid, with two women and necessary attendants, viz four men, two of them grooms;
2. three suits of apparell of silks yearly and one of velvet every second year, with all other necessary furnitures decent for her;
3. Her coach furnished for her and £20 yearly for her extraordinary expenses.[17]

These were just the sort of terms that began to appear in women's marriage settlements, in particular those of experienced widows who, like Elizabeth Windsor, had reason to crave legal and economic security, and which from at least the 1590s Chancery showed itself willing to enforce.[18] Around the time that Fletcher satirized extravagant terms and conditions in *The Tamer Tamed*, Jonson parodied them through inversion in *Epicene: or The Silent Woman* (1609), where Mrs Otter asks her husband:

> Is this according to the instrument, when I married you? … Who allows you your horsemeat and man's meat? Your three suits of apparel a year? Your four pair of

[15] Amy Louise Erickson, 'Coverture and Capitalism', *History Workshop Journal*, 59 (2005): 1–16.

[16] For an example of the ineffectiveness of excommunication, see Jessica L. Malay, *The Case of Mistress Mary Hampson: Her Story of Marital Abuse and Defiance in Seventeenth-Century England* (Stanford University Press, 2014).

[17] Council Register 13 July 1579, *APC*, n.s., vol. 11, 1578–80, 188–9; *CSPD* I 1547–80 (1856), 626.

[18] Cioni, 'The Elizabethan Chancery', 161–2.

> stockings, one silk, three worsted? Your clean linen, your bands, and cuffs when I can get you to wear 'em?[19] (3.1.24, 29–32)

An escalating reliance on common law bonds and deeds to enforce the terms of separations provided a model for couples who began to employ deeds or bonds to engineer mutually agreed private separations that bypassed the church courts altogether. In the mid-1560s, for example, when Thomas Bennett of All Cannings in Wiltshire left his wife, the couple drew up 'certain covenants touching the separation'.[20] In the following decades a growing number of couples put their hands or seals to private agreements to live apart, make maintenance payments, and not to bring or sponsor suits in ecclesiastical courts (for restitution of conjugal rights, separation or alimony), in equity courts (for alimony) or at common law (for debt or restitution of conjugal rights by means of a writ of habeas corpus). Such agreements flouted ecclesiastical law and led to a chorus of complaints from figures of authority in church and state.[21] They were also extremely difficult to enforce, yet appear to have given a measure of security to the few couples separating by mutual private agreement in defiance of church rules: only if they were discovered or if a party came to object to the arrangement would the matter be tested in court.

A small but growing number of individuals, then, negotiated exceptions to the two main certainties of marriage; that it was for life and that a husband controlled all of the marital resources. Some couples even found ways to circumvent the church's prohibition against remarriage before 'death us departe'.[22] The problem of collusive annulments, for example, led the authors of the ecclesiastical canons of 1604 to ban annulments based solely on the uncorroborated testimony of the interested parties. The same canons also demanded that in cases of separation for adultery, the innocent and the guilty party enter into conditional bonds promising not to contract marriage while their estranged spouse remained alive, on pain of a money penalty.[23] These attempts to clamp down on couples who sought greater control over their marital affairs can also be read as evidence of the fragility of existing ecclesiastical authority and procedures. So too might the passing of the Bigamy Act the previous year, that transformed bigamy from a sin into a felony attracting the death penalty.[24] Another spur for these developments was real (and feigned) confusion among ordinary English men and women about what did and did not constitute a divorce and the legality of remarrying after a separation.[25] When

19 *CWBJ*, 3.432.

20 Martin Ingram, *Church Courts, Sex and Marriage in England, 1570–1640* (Cambridge: Cambridge University Press, 1987), 149.

21 Tim Stretton, 'Marriage, Separation and the Common Law in England, 1540–1660', in *The Family in Early Modern England*, ed. Helen Berry and Elizabeth Foyster (Cambridge: Cambridge University Press, 2007).

22 'The Forme of Solemnization of Matrimonie', *Book of Common Prayer* (1549).

23 *Constitutions and Canons Ecclesiastical* (1604), nos. 105, 107.

24 1 Jac *c*. 11. Scholars of ecclesiastical courts disagree. See Ingram, *Church Courts*; R. H. Helmholz, *OHLE* 1.

25 Ingram, *Church Courts*, 179; Stretton, 'Marriage, Separation and the Common Law'.

authorities prosecuted Hercules Fuljambe in Star Chamber for his marriage to a third wife, while his two former wives were still living, he robustly defended his behaviour by alleging that church divines had assured him that it was legal to remarry after a separation on the grounds of adultery.[26] John Day may have been playing upon this more worldly or secular attitude to divorce when he had his character Lurdo in *Law Tricks* gloat about ending his marriage to the Countess, explaining how

> two sufficient men
> Swore her a harlot, and the partiall Bench
> Inspir[ed] by my good Angels (Angels wings
> Sweepe a cleare passage to the feat of Kings)
> Seald our divorce.[27] (1.1.46–50)

In England at this time an angel was a coin worth ten shillings, and if there is any ambiguity in the double meaning, Day puts it to rest when Lurdo confirms that 'not without some counsel of the lawe ... I purchac'd a divorce' (1.1.240–2).

Marriage Contracts

A similar shift away from church courts towards common law and equity courts, and the employment of written instruments to constitute private agreements, can be detected in relation to marriage contracts. A couple's verbal agreement to marry using the present tense constituted the marriage contract that made a union binding, or as the Dutchess explains in Webster's *The Duchess of Malfi* (1612–1613), 'I have heard lawyers say a contract in a chamber, / *Per verba de presenti*, is absolute marriage' (1.1.467–8). (Pre-contracts, by contrast, used language in the future tense indicating an intention to marry.)[28] Litigation over marriage contracts had been a mainstay of the church courts for centuries, however cases over disputed contracts became 'very rare indeed' after 1600, at the very time they became an increasingly common device in drama.[29]

Church court actions over contracts centred on the validity of a marriage (or in the case of pre-contracts, of competing marriages). They fell from favour as a result of a growing acceptance of the need for church-sanctioned public marriage ceremonies, and also because more and more couples chose to set down their agreements in bonds and

[26] Lewis Dibdin and Charles E. H. Chadwyck Healey, *English Church Law and Divorce* (London: 1912), 58.

[27] John Day, *Law Tricks* (Oxford: Malone Society Reprints, 1950).

[28] John Webster, *The Duchess of Malfi*, ed. Brian Gibbons, 4th edn, New Mermaids Series, (London: A & C Black, 2001).

[29] Helmholz, *OHLE*, 1.521–64; Ingram, *Church Courts*, 171–6; Ralph Houlbrooke, 'The Making of Marriage in Mid-Tudor England: Evidence From the Records of Matrimonial Contract Litigation', *Journal of Family History*, 10 (1985): 339, 351. See, for example, Shakespeare's *Measure for Measure* and

other legal instruments that were actionable in common law and equity courts. These newer 'contracts' recorded commitments to marry in writing and could be used to guarantee the payment of promised portions or the creation of agreed jointures. They focused less on the validity of marriages and more on the financial consequences of marrying or failing to fulfil a promise to marry. Legal actions at common law concerning marriage, which were on the rise, sought not the confirmation of marriages, but money damages for breech of promise.[30]

The nature of common law instruments lent themselves to sharp or unconscionable uses that were of a different type than cases the church usually adjudicated. Reynolde Boothe, for example, entered a bond with a penalty of £200 with the condition that he would marry Anne Blackthorne by May of 1587 or pay her £100. He assumed that default could only arise if he failed to marry or pay Anne, and expressed astonishment when Anne put the bond in suit at common law to claim the penalty 'uppon *her* refusal to marye' him.[31]

Some cases that remained in the church courts in the later sixteenth century and afterwards also involved attempts to manipulate the law of marriage for personal gain, echoed in the mock depictions of church court proceedings over pre-contract in Middleton and Dekker's *The Roaring Girl* (1611). These concentrate on the extortion of money through misuses of law, summed up in Master Gallipot's warning:

> Be wise, sir, let not you and I be tossed
> On lawyers' pens; they have sharp nibs and draw
> Men's very heart-blood from them.[32] (3.2.215–17)

Other individuals pleaded pre-contracts from many years in the past to escape the confines of later church-solemnized marriages, but ecclesiastical authorities proved less and less willing to condone this form of constructive divorce.[33] Such attempts to manipulate ecclesiastical process to advantage bring to mind Touchstone's preference in *As You Like It* (*c.*1599) to be married by Sir Oliver Martext rather than by a priest in a church,

> for he is not like to
> marry me well, and not being well married, it will be
> a good excuse for me hereafter to leave my wife. (3.3.82–4)

As You Like It; Middleton and Dekker, *The Roaring Girl*; Webster, *The Duchess of Malfi*; Thomas Dekker, *Match Me in London*; John Ford, *Broken Heart*.

30 Christopher Brooks, *Law, Politics and Society in Early Modern England* (Cambridge: Cambridge University Press, 2010), 381–2.

31 *Boothe v. Blackborne*, TNA, C2 ELIZ B13/52, mm. 1, 3 (emphasis added). Anne disputed this version of events.

32 Thomas Middleton and Thomas Dekker, *The Roaring Girl*, ed. Andor Gomme (London: Ernest Benn Limited, 1976).

33 Frederik Pedersen, *Marriage Disputes in Medieval England* (2000), 59–84; Ingram, *Church Courts*, 176; Helmholz, *OHLE*, 1.527–9.

Legal Instruments

A common feature of the developments examined here is an increasing reliance on bonds and other legal instruments. The rapid expansion of marketing in the mid-sixteenth century, fuelled by sustained population growth and an expanding reliance on credit, produced a vibrant but volatile economy in which defaults on loans became common, leading many to seek the security of formal signed and sealed written instruments. Bonds brought a measure of certainty to transactions, by providing legally actionable evidence of agreements backed by severe penalties for non-performance (usually 100 per cent of the value of the debt or transaction). English men and women employed conditional bonds for a bewildering array of purposes, from securing loans and purchases to the policing of trustees and executors and the enforcement of legal, ecclesiastical and governmental orders, and their ubiquity in the later sixteenth and seventeenth centuries is almost impossible to exaggerate.[34] However, bonds produced their own problems, especially as they were largely non-transferable, and disputes over defaults on bonds often ended in the courts.

Private litigation during this period reached staggering proportions, with perhaps a million or more cases a year being fought in England and Wales during a period when the population was only just reaching, and then slowly passing, four million.[35] The vast majority of these legal actions involved debt, and while oral agreements drove litigation in local courts, in the central Westminster courts of Common Pleas and King's Bench lawsuits over bonds predominated, their levels increasing by almost 800 per cent between 1560 and 1640.[36] Sealed bonds appeared to be taking over, and as the sixteenth century gave way to the seventeenth more legal instruments were in existence than ever before and more individuals were 'putting bonds in suit' at common law to claim penalties for default, helping to create a culture of law and litigiousness that left its stamp on countless plays and literary works.

A significant number of the targets of common law actions on bonds brought counter suits complaining of unfairness in the prerogative or equity courts of Chancery, Requests, Star Chamber, and the Equity Side of Exchequer. Most baulked at having to pay penalties out of all proportion with their original debts or agreements or with the actual losses bondholders had sustained. Under common law rules, holders of uncancelled bonds could claim penalties even if the debt had been repaid in full, on the basis that the person making payment had neglected to cancel the bond, or in cases where most but not all of the amount owing had been satisfied. In the minds of

[34] Postles, *Microcynicon*, 35–49; David Hawkes, *The Culture of Usury in Renaissance England* (New York and Houndsmills, Basingstoke: Palgrave Macmillan, 2010); C. W. Brooks, *Pettyfoggers and Vipers of the Commonwealth: The 'Lower Branch' of the Legal Profession in Early Modern England* (Cambridge: Cambridge University Press, 1986).

[35] Muldrew, *Economy of Obligation*, 236.

[36] Brooks, *Pettyfoggers*, 68.

common law authorities, to do otherwise would be to defeat the very purpose for which parties created written instruments under seal. Yet the results could prove extremely inequitable, given the scale of penalties and the short duration of loan periods (typically three months), leading to parties having to pay amounts equivalent to 300, 400, or even as much as 800 per cent annual interest. It is little wonder that Shylock's focus in *The Merchant of Venice* (*c.*1598) is not on interest rates—he charges no interest on Antonio's loan—but on forfeitures.[37]

The prerogative or equity courts provided remedies to aggrieved debtors and bond defaulters in some, but not all, of these instances, and vocal criticism of harsh bond actions remained common. In light of record levels of litigation it seems likely that concerns about commodification and unscrupulous behaviour found in drama and in the literature of complaint resulted not just from the growing tentacles and practices of an increasingly mercantile economy, but also from the unprecedented growth of legal instruments and their misuse; from the 'Law Tricks' of Day's title. The language of bonds, conditions, sureties, defaults, and forfeitures abounds in Elizabethan and Jacobean poetry, prose, and drama, and it is surely no coincidence that *Michaelmas Term* (1604), identified above as one of the first Jacobean plays to exhibit a more cynical vision of human relations and the routes to personal advancement, is set in a world of law courts and the immoral use of legal instruments. The strictness of common law procedures over bonds and the automatic application of penalties, which could ensnare the unwary as well as hold defaulters to account, inspired growing cynicism in many quarters about the impersonality of law and economic relations. As the character Old Carter reflects in Rowley, Dekker, and Ford's *The Witch of Edmonton* (1621), when he refuses to give security for a marriage portion, 'Bonds and bills are but / tarriers to catch fools and keep lazy knaves busy' (1.2.15–16).[38]

Disquiet over the inflexibility of bonds, and the incommensurability of losses suffered and penalties claimed, helped to prompt the growth of alternative instruments, such as promissory notes, and of alternative legal actions, such as assumpsit.[39] However, bonds remained popular for centuries and all of the available forms of agreements and associated legal processes fostered a reliance on contractual thinking in the general sense I have been using—legally enforceable agreements between parties.[40] It is interesting

[37] See Tim Stretton, 'Conditional Promises and Legal Instruments in *The Merchant of Venice*' in *Taking Exception to the Law: Materializing Injustice in Early Modern English Literature*, ed. Donald Beecher et al. (Toronto: University of Toronto Press, 2015), 71–99.

[38] William Rowley, Thomas Dekker, and John Ford, *The Witch of Edmonton*, ed. Peter Corbin and Douglas Sedge (Manchester and New York: Manchester University Press, 1999).

[39] Actions of *assumpsit* concentrated on what parties to an agreement had actually promised (*assumpsit* means undertaken) or could be implied to have promised. This focus on the intentions of the negotiating parties was a key step in the development of modern contract law and influenced dramatists as well as legal commentators in the early seventeenth century.

[40] Barbara Kreps, 'Playing the Law for Lawyers: Witnessing, Evidence and the Law of Contract in *The Comedy of Errors*', *ShS*, 63 (2010): 262–71; David Harris Sacks, 'Slade's Case in Perspective', in *Rhetoric and Law in Early Modern Europe*, ed. Victoria Kahn and Lorna Hudson (Yale University Press: New Haven, 2001); David Ibbetson, 'Sixteenth Century Contract Law: *Slade's Case* in Context', *OJLS*, 4 (1984): 295–317.

to note that in *Bartholomew Fair* Jonson never refers to the comic 'contract' with the audience that opens the play as a contract. Instead the text refers to 'Articles of agreement, indented' (i.e. an indenture) by which 'It is covenanted and agreed' and 'the author promiseth' various things, in witness whereof it had been 'preposterously put to your seals already'. The penalty for failing to observe the conditions is to be left to 'the mercy of the author, as a forfeiture to the stage' (Induction, 55; 60; 115; 109–10).[41] As Luke Wilson has pointed out, the spirit of Jonson's speech reflects the emerging view of contractual relations based around reciprocal promises and the intentions of the contracting parties associated with the legal action of *assumpsit*, with audience members allowed to judge the play only in proportion to the price of their tickets, but he couched it in the deeply familiar language of indentures and conditional bonds.[42]

In what might be characterized as a collective loss of contractual innocence, growing numbers of English men and women became accustomed to the primacy of the letter, rather than the spirit, of written agreements. Thanks to the particularly inflexible nature of conditional bonds, they were learning to beware of written conditions and fine print on parchment and paper, as the certainty of writing under seal supplanted or acted to erode the values of a traditional world built around face-to-face relations (although it is important to remember that the number of oral agreements marked with rituals such as handshakes, the drinking of alcohol, and the exchange of tokens was also increasing dramatically at this time).[43] In Jonson's *Epicene*, when the character Morose is 'tendered ... a writing to sign' he shows himself resistant to the sharp legal practices coming to characterize this increasingly contractual world, answering: 'Here, I deliver it thee as my deed. If there be a word in it lacking or writ with false orthography, I protest before—I will not take the advantage' (5.4.163–4). The irony here is that it is Morose's enemies who 'take the advantage', tricking him into signing away a third of his estate of 1500 a year for life.

Women and Contractual Agreements

Women, whether single, married or widowed, were deeply enmeshed in this new world of legal instruments. Ongoing research is revealing the extent of women's participation in credit networks, particularly as moneylenders, and their reliance on deeds, indentures, and bonds that specified dates of repayments, conditions, and penalties for default.[44]

[41] *CWBJ*, 4.281–2.

[42] As the character Ursula proclaims later in the play, 'Drink your draught of Indenture, / your sup of Covenant' (2.4.41).

[43] Muldrew, *Economy of Obligation*, 37–94.

[44] Judith Spicksley, 'Usury Legislation, Cash, and Credit: The Development of the Female Investor in the Late Tudor and Stuart Periods', *EcHR*, 61 (2008): 277–301; Judith Spicksley, '"Fly with a Duck in Thy Mouth": Single Women as Sources of Credit in Seventeenth-Century England', *Social History*, 32.2 (May,

Amy Froide argues that women were 'in the vanguard' of the employment of written credit instruments because of the particular difficulties they could face in enforcing agreements, especially in light of the transformation or suspension of their independent legal status that marriage could bring.[45] Their participation in credit networks increased the need for negotiating settlements if they married or remarried, to protect their capital and perhaps to carve out the ability to continue to control their investments. The volatility of a market centred more and more on money and credit rather than on estates in land provided further incentives, as prospective wives had reason to shield assets not only from their husbands, but also from their husbands' creditors.

The ability of these changing economic conditions to influence marriage negotiations can be observed in the life of the Elizabethan silk woman Alice Barnham. Building on her expertise in the traditional world of silk, Alice amassed considerable wealth through her participation in the new economy, both in partnership with her husband and then as a widow, by lending money and using imported silk as collateral for loans apparently designed to skirt prohibitions in the Statute of Usury. During her widowhood she considered the offers of marriage of Sir Thomas Ramsay, a wealthy former Lord Mayor of London. However, in discussions surrounding her marriage settlement, Sir Thomas asked her to call in a lease that attracted rents below the market rate, suggesting that the couple could use the house as a summer retreat. Alice recovered the leased property in Sir Thomas's presence and he 'named a speedy date' for the consummation of their marriage, whereupon Alice stopped him in his tracks. She is reported to have told him:

> be not so hasty, except it be to appoint your wedding day with some other wife, for on me I assure you you must not reckon. For I shall never think myself happily bestowed upon a husband that setteth so small a value on me as you have done in making this little improvement of my jointure (for that I know was indeed your aim) a necessary condition of your match with me.

As she further explained to Sir Thomas, his nature was 'so set upon covetousness as would have given me but small comfort in you'.[46] Covetous husbands can be found in

2007): 187–207; Korda, 'Gender, Credit and (Ac)counting', 138; Amy Froide, *Never Married: Singlewomen in Early Modern England* (Oxford: Oxford University Press, 2007), 128–41; Mary Prior, 'Wives and Wills 1558–1700', in *English Rural Society, 1500–1800: Essays in Honor of Joan Thirsk*, ed. John Chartres and David Hey (Cambridge: Cambridge University Press, 1990); and see Barbara J. Todd, 'Fiscal Citizens: Female Investors in Public Finance before the South Sea Bubble', in *Challenging Orthodoxies: The Social and Cultural Worlds of Early Modern Women*, ed. Sigrun Haude and Melinda S. Zook (Burlington: Ashgate, 2014); Margaret Hunt, *The Middling Sort: Commerce, Gender and the Family in England 1680–1780* (Berkeley and Los Angeles: University of California Press, 1996); Craig Muldrew, '"A Mutual Assent of her Mind"? Women, Debt, Litigation, and Contract in Early Modern England', *HWJ*, 55 (2003): 47–71.

45 Froide, *Never Married*, 134–5.

46 L. C. Orlin, ed., 'The Character of Sir Martin Barnham, Knight', in *Renaissance Historicisms*, ed. James Dutcher and Anne Lake Prescott (Newark: University of Delaware Press, 2008), 259–90, lines 166–95.

every age, but an increasing reliance on liquid forms of capital to pay debts and to fund investments and speculative ventures, sharpened the scrutiny many individuals paid to prospective wives' (and husbands') portfolios of wealth, providing ample raw materials for playwrights' and writers' explorations of motivations for marriage.

Women and Litigation

Female characters feature prominently in legally themed plays, for in dramatic terms their indeterminate status and position as outsiders provided a useful medium for critiquing laws, legal behaviour, and systems of justice.[47] Yet, the appearance of women in legal settings would not have surprised contemporary audiences. Coinciding with women's increased participation in credit networks and business ventures, and the growth in the use of legal instruments, was a rise in the number of female plaintiffs and defendants engaged in litigation. Tens of thousands of women a year participated in lawsuits, many involving bonds. As well as being the victims of the harsh enforcement of bond penalties, women were also the initiators of actions to claim penalties. Women predominated as executors and administrators of deceased men's and women's estates, shouldering the duties of administration in 70 per cent of cases, and were active in suing on bonds the deceased had held, a number of which (their opponents alleged) involved debts or agreements that had been long since settled.[48] Furthermore, it was not just unmarried women and widows who went to law. In virtually all of the central common law, prerogative, and ecclesiastical courts, the single largest category of female litigant by marital status was married women.[49] In some instances legal conventions demanded that a husband include his wife's name 'for conformity' when bringing suit to claim or defend estates or interests, including bonds, that he held 'in right of his wife', but many wives joined their husbands in cases where their participation was not required. This occurred for practical reasons—to ensure any remedy, settlement, or damages would apply in the event that a husband died—but also because of the integral part many women played in the marital economy.[50]

In an even greater blow to the presumptions of coverture, a small but highly significant minority of married women brought or defended lawsuits against their husbands in prerogative or equity courts, including Chancery, the Court of Requests, Star Chamber, the Durham Chancery, and the Equity Side of Exchequer as well as in courts

[47] Mukherji, *Law and Representation*, 206.

[48] Amy Louise Erickson, 'An Introduction to Probate Accounts', in *The Records of the Nation*, ed. Geoffrey Martin and Peter Spufford (Woodbridge, Suffolk: The Boydell Press, 1990), 273–86; Tim Stretton, *Women Waging Law in Elizabethan England* (Cambridge: Cambridge University Press, 1998).

[49] The majority of wives were named alongside their husbands, but some brought or answered actions alone, especially in the church courts; Laura Gowing, *Domestic Dangers: Women, Words and Sex in Early Modern London* (Oxford: Oxford University Press, 1996).

[50] Stretton, *Women Waging Law*, 129–42.

with mixed jurisdictions such as the Chancellor's court in Cambridge. In publicly challenging their husbands, fiercely asserting their rights, defending their assets and wages, claiming alimony, and attempting to ensure their personal safety, these women expanded the repertoire of the autonomy available to married women in situations where a key rationale of coverture—that it bolstered the bond of marriage—became difficult to sustain.[51]

Taken together, developments in all these areas confirm that a growing number of women, including married women, were investing money, securing assets through innovations in the creation and enforcement of marriage settlements and other equitable devices, and going to law to protect or defend their interests. Thomas Middleton did not have to look far for inspiration when he had Valeria in *The Widow* (1615–1617) utilize an equitable device to protect her property, as it closely resembles the one his own widowed mother, Anne Middleton, employed.[52] More and more women on stage and in life were thinking and acting contractually and braving this new culture of fine print, lawyers, and frequent recourse to law. Not everyone approved of these exercises of independence, with some observers sharing the sentiment of the character Moll in Middleton and Dekker's *The Roaring Girl* (1611), who reminds the audience, that:

> if every woman would deal with their suitor so honestly,
> poor younger brothers would not be so often gulled with old
> cozening widows, that turn o'er all their wealth in trust to
> some kinsman, and make the poor gentleman work hard for
> a pension. (2.2.58–62)

Enforced Marriages

The increasing incidence of women exercising some contractual freedom and a greater degree of choice in their marriages and property arrangements (especially in second or subsequent marriages) brought to the fore questions of consent, free will, and legal capacity that, as Frank Whigham observes, recur frequently in the drama and literature of the age.[53] Thomas Dekker, for example, has his character Cordolente in *Match Me in London* (1631) lament the injustice of the arranged marriage of Tormeilla with the powerful lines: 'She lov'd him not; was she contracted to him? / Can he lay claime to her by

[51] Cioni, 'Elizabethan Chancery', 161–2; Stretton, *Women Waging Law*, 143–54.

[52] Subha Mukherji, 'Middleton and the Law', in *Thomas Middleton in Context*, ed. Suzanne Gossett (Cambridge: Cambridge University Press, 2011), 108.

[53] Frank Whigham, *Seizures of the Will in Early Modern English Drama* (Cambridge: Cambridge University Press, 1996).

Law?' (2.1.64–5).[54] Arranged marriages proceeded on the assumption that familial duty outweighed personal freedom. Forced or fraudulent marriages gave thought to neither, and writers were quick to include them in literary and dramatic works to highlight consent through its absence. It is here that authors contrived manipulations of an ecclesiastical law that required only an exchange of promises in the present tense or a marriage licence to trap the unwilling or the unwary into binding marriage contracts for life, such as the stolen and altered marriage licence Quarlous uses to marry Purecraft in Jonson's *Bartholomew Fair*. As already noted, actual cases of this sort were becoming uncommon in the church courts, but criminal prosecutions in the Middlesex Sessions and then Star Chamber of a particularly outrageous fraudulent marriage inspired Dekker, Rowley, Ford, and Webster to write the (now lost) play *Keep the Widow Waking*. In July of 1624 Tobias Audley, a lowly tobacco seller, conspired with accomplices to ply Anne Elsdon or Ellesden, a widow well over twice his age, with copious quantities of strong alcohol over a period of three days. Having obtained a marriage licence permitting marriage without the customary reading of banns in church on three separate occasions, and with the assistance of a disreputable clergyman who had been promised a share of Anne's £6,000 fortune, Tobias 'married' Anne when she was so incapacitated by drink that she was unable to speak. He then proceeded to make off with as much of her money, plate, jewellry, and conditional bonds as he could carry, claiming everything as her husband until his ruse was exposed and he was arrested and died in prison awaiting trial.[55]

Further up the social scale, crown sales of wardships included the right to arrange a ward's marriage for profit, ignoring family interests and gaining a ward's consent by threatening their disinheritance. As Justice Overdo's ward Grace explains in *Bartholomew Fair*, 'he bought me sir; and now he will marry me to his wife's brother, this wise gentleman you see, or else I must pay value o' my land' (3.5.230–2). These lucrative sales based on an anachronistic feudal precedent provoked outrage from affected elites under Queen Elizabeth. These complaints grew in intensity as sales expanded in volume and value under James I and Charles I, reaching a crescendo in the turbulent 1640s.[56] A key concern with this practice, as George Wilkin's, *The Miseries of Enforced Marriage* (1607) makes clear, was that it not only undermined patriarchal power within families, but it also placed male wards in a position of powerlessness similar to daughters.[57] The contrast between the compromised autonomy of women like Anne Elsdon and the small but growing numbers of male and female wards whose marriages were being sold to the highest bidder, on the one hand, and the increasing autonomy some women were

[54] *The Dramatic Works of Thomas Dekker*, ed. Fredson Bowers, 4 vols (Cambridge: Cambridge University Press, 1953–1961), 3.251–363.

[55] C. J. Sisson, *Lost Plays of Shakespeare's Age* (New York: Humanities Press, 1970), 80–94; Mukherji, *Law and Representation*, 186–92.

[56] Joel Hurstfield, *The Queen's Wards: Wardship and Marriage under Elizabeth I*, 2nd edn (London: Frank Cass, 1973); H. E. Bell, *An Introduction to the History and Records of the Court of Wards and Liveries* (Cambridge: Cambridge University Press, 1953).

[57] Whigham, *Seizures of the Will*, 125–6; David Atkinson, 'Marriage Under Compulsion in English Renaissance Drama', *English Studies*, 67.6 (1986): 483–504.

negotiating for themselves, on the other, helped to give the subject of marital consent a powerful resonance within wider society.[58]

The Politics of Marriage

Practices that undermined the rules of coverture, by allowing women with access to legal resources to evade some of their effects, helped to put marriage in the spotlight, encouraging the testing of longstanding assumptions about the authority of husbands and the balance of power and property within unions. Meanwhile, enforced marriages of various kinds underlined the vital need for consent in the making of marriage. Recognizing the extent to which thinking about marriage was in flux in early modern England helps explain the malleability of its employment as a metaphor for the relationship between governor and governed, seen most starkly in its employment by supporters of both sides in the Civil Wars.[59] The political theory of Thomas Hobbes and John Locke focuses intently on the nature of the conjugal bond, and they and other theorists wrote as if they were invoking a largely fixed and universally accepted relationship against which to measure, critique, or endorse the hotly contested institution of monarchy. In fact, both sides of their analogy were unstable, with the dominion of husbands made less certain by the ability of wives to negotiate separate estates and assert separate rights.

In considering the relationship between the marriage contract and the social contract it is useful to consider the origin and changing uses of the word 'contract' itself. Prior to the late sixteenth century the language of contract was most frequently employed not in relation to law or commerce but to marriage, referring to the various kinds of marriage contracts or agreements to marry discussed above. In Shakespeare's plays, for example, the word contract and its variants appear thirty times (leaving aside those that mean 'to shrink') of which twenty-seven relate to marriage and three to treaties contracting peace between kingdoms. None refers unequivocally to a commercial agreement between individuals.[60] The legal sense of the word existed, but it was employed far less often than the words covenant and bargain, and most references to written contractual agreements identified them by the instruments that recorded or embodied them: indenture, articles of agreement, deeds, bills, bonds, bands, statutes staple, and so on. According to the *Oxford English Dictionary*, the first use of contract to refer to 'a writing in which the terms of a bargain are included' dates from 1611.[61] The strong popular association

[58] Sokol and Sokol, *Shakespeare, Law, and Marriage*, 42–55; Whigham, *Seizures of the Will.*

[59] Victoria Kahn, *Wayward Contracts: The Crisis of Political Obligation in England, 1640–1674* (Princeton: Princeton University Press, 2004); Su Fang Ng, *Literature and the Politics of the Family in Seventeenth-Century England* (Cambridge: Cambridge University Press, 2007).

[60] *Concordance of Shakespeare's Complete Works*: <http://www.opensourceshakespeare.org/concordance/>.

[61] *Oxford English Dictionary*, s.v.

of the word contract with marriage, and with the reciprocal nature of marital obligations and their endurance over time, raises intriguing questions about the evolution of its legal meaning and the possible influence of this meaning on the naming of The Great Contract of 1610 as well as what became known as the Social Contract. Both of these ongoing agreements based on reciprocal obligations and mutual consent differed from simple covenants, and their names add weight to the importance of the linkages between contract and conjugality. Peter Goodrich is one of the rare scholars to emphasize the extent to which the term contract 'was often synonymous with marriage', and he argues that 'it was from the law of spousals that many of the doctrines of modern contract law were first taken' including 'rules relating to capacity, to duress, to consideration, to offer and acceptance in *praesentia* and *absentia*, to present and future intent, and to the plea of non est factum'. [62] Conjugality was present at the birth of contract, something that attempts to distinguish 'domestic' from 'public' spheres serve to obscure.

The Historiography of Marriage

The indeterminacy of the meaning and practice of marriage in early modern England enhanced its appeal to dramatists and their audiences, and helps us to understand why, for example, critics can continue to find in the actions and speeches of Petruccio and Katherine in Shakespeare's *The Taming of the Shrew* (1590–1592) evidence for a bewildering array of positive and negative interpretations, not just of the play itself, but also of the conditions of couples' lives outside the playhouse. Similar differences of opinion and approach have divided historians. Scholars used to place the institution of marriage at the heart of bold models of social change that posited, in various formulations, a move from sacrament to contract, from status to contract, and the rise of companionate marriages and affective individualism.[63] Resistance to these overarching narratives has produced an equally strong emphasis on the continuity of early modern marital values and the complexity of practices and motivations.[64] The identification of increasingly contractual approaches to the making, managing, enduring, and breaking of marriages has the potential once again to place the focus on change. The challenges to the

[62] Peter Goodrich, *Oedipus Lex: Psychoanalysis, History, Law* (Berkeley: University of California Press, 1995), 205. See also 'The Posthumous Life of the Postal Rule: Requium and Revival of *Adams v. Lindsell*', in *Feminist Perspectives in Contract Law*, ed. Linda Mulcahy and Sally Wheeler (London: Glasshouse Press, 2005); Peter Goodrich, 'Gender and Contracts', in *Feminist Perspectives on the Foundational Subjects of Law*, ed. A. Bottomley (London: Cavendish, 1996).

[63] Lawrence Stone, *The Family Sex and Marriage in England 1500–1800* (New York: Harper and Row, 1977); Henry Sumner Maine, *Ancient Law* (London: 1861); John Witte, *From Sacrament to Contract: Marriage, Religion, and Law in the Western Tradition* (Westminster: John Knox Press, 1997).

[64] Ralph Houlbrooke, *The English Family 1450–1700* (London: Longman, 1984); Alan Macfarlane, *Marriage and Love in England 1300–1840* (Oxford: Basil Blackwell, 1986).

authority of ecclesiastical justice and the emergence of private separations set down in deeds or bonds, for example, provide evidence that certain onlookers were coming to view marriage as less sacramental and more contractual, even though the institution of marriage itself held firm. The prescriptive ideals of marriage, as depicted in sermons and conduct literature providing advice on marriage, proved much more resistant to these influences, changing little between the 1560s and 1650s. The sheer volume of prescriptive advice on the themes of familial duty, wifely subordination, and the obligations of husbands may suggest that authors had cause to remind their readers of familiar values, because those values were under assault. However the advice itself remained constant. Marriage remained an essential element in family strategies, with love a desirable but not an essential element within unions. The fixation in drama on marriages for love, set against marriages for money, reflected changing economic realities more than a dramatic reevaluation of the importance of personal affection: the contrast between romantic love and pure avarice was starker in a money economy buoyed by colossal levels of debt and credit. It is worth observing, however, the number of plays in which marriages for love end in unexpected riches for the couple. Many of the most prized marriages in Renaissance drama combine love *and* money.

Limits on Contractual Freedom

In observing and highlighting the new opportunities available to women to flex against the restraints of marriage, it is important to remember that the restraints themselves persisted and perhaps even intensified. As Craig Muldrew points out, 'when patriarchal political authority came under question during the civil war and commonwealth, so too did the peculiar question of independent wives' contractual responsibility, and this meant that coverture came under legal and philosophical scrutiny by the end of the seventeenth century'.[65] The common law always considered contracts between husband and wife void and therefore unenforcable, because married women were *sub potestate viri* (subject to the power of their husbands) and therefore lacked the ability freely to consent to a legal agreement. In the later seventeenth century common law justices hardened their attitude to married women's autonomy still further. *Manby v Scott* (1659), one of the most significant and scrutinized legal decisions of the later seventeenth century, confirmed that a husband and wife could not modify the terms of their marriage by contract, for it would be 'against nature as well as God'. The majority decision went so far as to reflect that if a wife who lived apart from her husband without his consent were to face death by starvation, because she could not get anyone to sell her food on credit, she had only herself to blame and the law would provide her no remedy.[66] Even in the

[65] Muldrew, 'A Mutual Assent of her Mind', 49.

[66] *Manby v. Scott*, 83 *ER*, 781, 783, 902, 980, 995, 1008, 1035, 1042–3, 1065.

Court of Chancery, which was expanding the equitable relief it offered to women during marriage, procedural changes restricted married women's freedoms in other ways. In the sixteenth century wives brought suits in Chancery against their husbands alone and in their own names, but from the late 1620s onwards wives could not sue alone and had to enlist the assistance of a *prochaine amy*—a next friend—to bring actions on their behalf, just as children did.[67] At the very time that opportunities for certain women were increasing, the ideology of marriage and the principle and ethos of coverture were becoming more restrictive, as an increasingly contractual view of marriage and human relations favoured individuals with knowledge and resources, but worked against those who lacked either or both. From the later seventeenth century onwards the growing complexity and cost of legal instruments and of lawsuits put legal advice and litigation concerning marriage settlements out of the reach of increasing numbers of couples, which only exacerbated this growing divide. However, over the longer term this gulf between legal 'haves' and 'have nots' became so stark that lawmakers could no longer ignore it, and it was a driving factor behind eventual legal reform.[68]

Acknowledgements

I would like to offer thanks to Katherine Crooks for her insights and assistance, and to Krista Kesselring, Cynthia Neville, Christy Luckyj, and Peter Goodrich for their references and suggestions.

Bibliography

Atkinson, David. 'Marriage Under Compulsion in English Renaissance Drama', *English Studies*, 67.6 (1986): 483–504.

Bell, H. E. *An Introduction to the History and Records of the Court of Wards and Liveries* (Cambridge: Cambridge University Press, 1953).

Brooks, Christopher W. *Law, Politics and Society in Early Modern England* (Cambridge: Cambridge University Press, 2010).

Brooks, Christopher W. *Pettyfoggers and Vipers of the Commonwealth: The 'Lower Branch' of the Legal Profession in Early Modern England* (Cambridge: Cambridge University Press, 1986).

Calendar of State Papers Domestic, Vol. 1: *1547–80*, ed., Robert Lemon (London: 1856).

Church of England. *Book of Common Prayer* (London: 1549).

Church of England. *Constitutions and Canons Ecclesiasticall* (London: 1604).

Cioni, Maria L. 'The Elizabethan Chancery and Women's Rights', in *Tudor Rule and Revolution: Essays for G. R. Elton from His American Friends*, ed. Delloyd J. Guth and John W. McKenna (Cambridge: Cambridge University Press, 1982), 159–82.

Day, John. *Law Tricks* (Oxford: Malone Society Reprints, 1950).

Dekker, Thomas. *The Dramatic Works of Thomas Dekker*, ed. Fredson Bowers, 4 vols (Cambridge: Cambridge University Press, 1953–1961).

[67] E.g. TNA PRO C6/375/21 *William Blake & Anne Bliss wife of William Bliss v William Bliss.*

[68] Tait, 'Beginning of the End of Coverture'.

Dibdin, Lewis and Charles E. H. Chadwyck Healey, *English Church Law and Divorce* (London: 1912).
Erickson, Amy Louise. 'Coverture and Capitalism', *History Workshop Journal*, 59 (2005): 1–16.
Erickson, Amy Louise. 'An Introduction to Probate Accounts', in *The Records of the Nation*, ed. Geoffrey Martin and Peter Spufford (Woodbridge: The Boydell Press, 1990), 273–86.
Erickson, Amy Louise. *Women and Property in Early Modern England* (London: Routledge, 1993).
Fletcher, John. *The Tamer Tamed*, ed. Lucy Munro (London: Methuen Drama, 2010).
Ford, John. *The Broken Heart*, ed. Donald K. Anderson, Jr (Lincoln: University of Nebraska Press, 1968).
Froide, Amy. *Never Married: Singlewomen in Early Modern England* (Oxford: Oxford University Press, 2007), 128–41.
Goodrich, Peter. *Oedipus Lex: Psychoanalysis, History, Law* (Berkeley: University of California Press, 1995).
Gowing, Laura. *Domestic Dangers: Women, Words, and Sex in Early Modern London* (Oxford: Oxford University Press, 1996).
Hawkes, David. *The Culture of Usury in Renaissance England* (New York and Basingstoke: Palgrave Macmillan, 2010).
Helmholz, R. H. *The Oxford History of the Laws of England*, Vol. 1: *The Canon Law and Ecclesiastical Jurisdiction from 597 to the 1640s* (Oxford University Press: Oxford, 2004).
Houlbrooke, Ralph. *The English Family 1450–1700* (London: Longman, 1984).
Hurstfield, Joel. *The Queen's Wards: Wardship and Marriage under Elizabeth I*, 2nd edn (London: Frank Cass, 1973).
Ingram, Martin. *Church Courts, Sex, and Marriage in England, 1570–1640* (Cambridge: Cambridge University Press, 1987).
Jonson, Ben. *Bartholomew Fair*, ed. Edward B. Partridge (Lincoln: University of Nebraska Press, 1964).
Jonson, Ben. *The Cambridge Edition of the Works of Ben Jonson*, ed. David Bevington, Martin Butler, and Ian Donaldson (Cambridge and New York: Cambridge University Press, 2012).
Johnson, Eric M., ed. 'Concordance of Shakespeare's Complete Works', in *Open Source Shakespeare: An Experiment in Literary Technology* (Fairfax: George Mason University, 2003–2016), <http://www.opensourceshakespeare.org/concordance/>.
Kahn, Victoria. *Wayward Contracts: The Crisis of Political Obligation in England, 1640–1674* (Princeton: Princeton University Press, 2004).
Korda, Natasha. '"Dame Usury": Gender, Credit, and (Ac)counting in the *Sonnets* and *The Merchant of Venice*', *Shakespeare Quarterly*, 60 (2009): 129–53.
Middleton, Thomas and Thomas Dekker. *The Roaring Girl*, ed. Andor Gomme (London: Ernest Benn Limited, 1976).
Leinwand, Theodore B. *Theatre, Finance, and Society in Early Modern England* (Cambridge: Cambridge University Press, 1999).
Lyly, John. *The Complete Works of John Lyly*, ed. R. Warwick Bond (Oxford: Clarendon Press, 1967).
Macfarlane, Alan. *Marriage and Love in England 1300–1840* (Oxford: Basil Blackwell, 1986).
Maine, Henry Sumner. *Ancient Law* (London: 1861).
Manby v. Scott (1661–1663) 83 ER 781, 783, 902, 980, 995, 1008, 1035, 1042–3, 1065.
Mukherji, Subha. *Law and Representation in Early Modern Drama* (Cambridge: Cambridge University Press, 2006), 37–41.

Mukherji, Subha. 'Middleton and the Law', in *Thomas Middleton in Context*, ed. Suzanne Gossett (Cambridge: Cambridge University Press, 2011).

Muldrew, Craig. '"A Mutual Assent of Her Mind"? Women, Debt, Litigation, and Contract in Early Modern England', *History Workshop Journal*, 55 (2003): 47–71.

Muldrew, Craig. *The Economy of Obligation: The Culture of Credit and Social Relations in Early Modern England* (Basingstoke: Palgrave, 1998).

Orlin, L. C., ed. 'The Character of Sir Martin Barnham, Knight', in *Renaissance Historicisms: Essays in Honour of Arthur F. Kinney*, ed. James Dutcher and Anne Lake Prescott (Newark: University of Delaware Press, 2008), 259–90.

Oxford English Dictionary, 2nd edn (Oxford: Oxford University Press, 1989).

Postles, Dave. *Microcynicon: Aspects of Early-Modern England* (Loughborough: Dave Postles, 2014).

Prior, Mary. 'Wives and Wills 1558–1700', in *English Rural Society, 1500–1800: Essays in Honor of Joan Thirsk*, ed. John Chartres and David Hey (Cambridge: Cambridge University Press, 1990).

Privy Council. *Acts of the Privy Council*, Vol. 11: *1578–80*.

Rowley, William, Thomas Dekker, and John Ford. *The Witch of Edmonton*, ed. Peter Corbin and Douglas Sedge (Manchester and New York: Manchester University Press, 1999).

Sisson, C. J. *Lost Plays of Shakespeare's Age* (New York: Humanities Press, 1970).

Sokol, B. J. and Mary Sokol. *Shakespeare, Law, and Marriage* (Cambridge: Cambridge University Press, 2003).

Spicksley, Judith. 'Usury Legislation, Cash, and Credit: The Development of the Female Investor in the Late Tudor and Stuart Periods', *Economic History Review*, 61 (2008): 277–301.

Stone, Lawrence. *The Family, Sex, and Marriage in England 1500–1800* (New York: Harper and Row, 1977).

Stretton, Tim. 'Conditional Promises and Legal Instruments in *The Merchant of Venice*', in *Taking Exception to the Law: Materializing Injustice in Early Modern English Literature*, ed. Donald Beecher et al. (Toronto: University of Toronto Press, 2015), 71–99.

Stretton, Tim. 'Marriage, Separation, and the Common Law in England, 1540–1660', in *The Family in Early Modern England*, ed. Helen Berry and Elizabeth Foyster (Cambridge: Cambridge University Press, 2007), 18–39.

Stretton, Tim. *Women Waging Law in Elizabethan England* (Cambridge: Cambridge University Press, 1998).

Tait, Allison. 'The Beginning of the End of Coverture: A Reappraisal of the Married Woman's Separate Estate', *Yale Journal of Law and Feminism*, 26.2 (2014): 1–51.

Todd, Barbara J. 'Fiscal Citizens: Female Investors in Public Finance before the South Sea Bubble', in *Challenging Orthodoxies: The Social and Cultural Worlds of Early Modern Women*, ed. Sigrun Haude and Melinda S. Zook (Burlington: Ashgate, 2014), 53–76.

Webster, John. *The Duchess of Malfi*, ed. Brian Gibbons, 4th edn (London: A & C Black, 2001).

Whigham, Frank. *Seizures of the Will in Early Modern English Drama* (Cambridge: Cambridge University Press, 1996).

Wilson, Luke. 'Ben Jonson and the Law of Contract', *CSLL*, 5.2 (1993): 81–306.

Wilson, Luke. *Theaters of Intention: Drama and the Law in Early Modern England* (Stanford: Stanford University Press, 2000).

Witte, John. *From Sacrament to Contract: Marriage, Religion, and Law in the Western Tradition* (Louisville: Westminster John Knox Press, 1997).

CHAPTER 22

THE LITERARY THING

The Imaginary Holding of Isabella Whitney's 'Wyll' to London (1573)

CAROLYN SALE

Introduction

In 1573, the poet Isabella Whitney published what is believed to have been her second book, *A Sweet Nosgay or Pleasant Posye Contayning a Hundred and Ten Phylosphicall Flowers*. Part of the output of the adventurous printer Richard Jones, the *Nosgay* survives in a single copy in the British Library.[1] Often characterized as a verse miscellany, the *Nosgay* in fact has three well-structured sections. The first includes a hundred and ten 'phylosophicall flowers' or *sententiae* that Whitney translated into a stanza each from a book published the year before by a student of Lincoln's Inn, Hugh Plat. The second section involves several 'familier Epistles and friendly Letters' to or from her sisters, her brothers, her male cousins, and at least one other male friend. And the third section presents a mock or fictional 'Wyll' entitled 'The maner of her Wyll, & what she left to London: and to all those in it: at her departing.'[2] Though the *Nosgay* suggests that the book is intended to 'recreate [the] mynde' (Evii^{r}) of a particular readership, that of the young men at the Inns of Court and Chancery, this chapter pursues the question of what the *Nosgay*'s final poem offers by way of recreation to the legal imaginations of all prospective readers.

Surviving wills from early 1570s London tend to assert that the testator is at the time of writing 'whole in mind', confident that his or her soul will find its final place with God,

[1] Richard Jones (fl. 1564–1613), *ODNB*.

[2] Isabella Whitney, *A Sweet Nosgay, or Pleasant Posye: Contayning a Hundred and Ten Phylosphicall Flowers* (London: Richard Jones, 1573), sig. Eiii^{r}. All further references to the *Nosgay* will be furnished directly in the text.

and most concerned to have his or her body buried in the parish church. Where the will disposes of anything other than the testator's person, the dispositions are of chattels, not land, the great majority of testators not having land to dispose of, and the chattels most often cited are articles of clothing, kitchen implements, bedding, and other furniture. Clearly there is some discursive latitude within the genre, and the fact that one's will would have to be read at more than one scene, including in the probate court, for it to be proved and executed, gives their writers some opportunity for a last word (if only to arrange for another last word from a priest at the scene of their burial). But a will's institutional task made any such opportunity limited; a will had its brief discursive life at the scene at which it was written, and the scenes at which it was proven and executed, and it then disappeared into institutional archives. Whitney's literary will both playfully acknowledges and breaks from these constraints, both by presenting itself as the testament of a sole testator who has in fact nothing to give and offering itself to readers as an artefact in print.

The sardonic opening informs readers that Whitney (or her poetic persona) is 'Whole in body, and in minde, / but very weake in Purse', and writing her wyll 'for fear it wyll be wurse' (Eiii^{r}). Whitney's adherence to form is meant (as she notes) to make it possible for her readers to bear 'witness' that she has 'a steadfast brayne' even as her break with form enables her to let others 'know' a 'wyllynge minde' that could not find its life in any will to be proven in a probate court. And while Whitney puts into verse precisely the elements that are the key features of ordinary wills of the period by disposing of her own soul and body, the first 'To God the Father and the Son', the latter 'to the Graue', we hear that she has imagined that her place in the meantime will be the living grave of debtor's prison:

> What makes you standers by to smile,
> and laugh so in your sleeue:
> I thinke it is, because that I
> to Ludgate nothing geue.
> I am not now in case to lye,
> here is no place of iest:
> I dyd reserue, that for my selfe,
> yf I my health possest.
> When dayes of paiment did approch,
> I thither ment to flee.
> To shroude my selfe amongst the rest,
> That chuse to dye in debt:
> Rather then any Creditor,
> Should money from them get. (Evi^{r})

The 'iest' of the *Wyll* has its limits, Whitney suggests, in the material conditions to which it responds, which are not the poet's alone, but general. London has certainly let her down: 'Thou neuer yet, woldst credit geue / to boord me for a yeare: / or with Apparell me releue / except thou payed weare' (Eii^{v}), she complains. But the city lets down all to whom it fails to give productive place, or one or another 'yeldynge year' (Cvi^{r}). Nothing, so the fiction goes, can be done about her own situation, but something can be done about those whom she must leave behind as her friends hustle her away from London. The *Wyll* thus bequeaths its various legacies with careful attention to ensure not only that London's people 'in goodly store' (Eiii^{v}) are all 'fed and clad' (Eiiii^{v}) and but that anything she fails directly to provide will be supplied by a boy 'by the Stoks' who 'will aske you what you lack' (Eiiii^{r}). Her dispositions include her own book, left at her printer's for others 'to bye' so he may 'haue somewhat to his share' (Evi^{v}) and Whitney satirically presents herself as compelled to provide all of London's judicial machinery, including a nag on Holborn Hill who will help break the neck of the condemned or gallop from the preace' (Evi^{r}). After final lines of complaint, these more to her friends than to London, Whitney presents the solitariness of the scene of writing at her residence in Abchurch Lane on the 'xx. of October . . . ./ . . . ANNO DOMINI: A Thousand: v. hundred seventy three' (Eviii^{r}), where she has only 'Paper, Pen and Standish' by as witnesses.

Scholarly approaches since Betty Travitsky's foundational article in *English Literary Renaissance* in 1980, which made the 'Wyll', published with Travitsky's glosses, newly accessible to a generation of scholars, have tended to cohere around the idea of the *Wyll* as a print commodity in which Whitney, 'an angry, economically disenfranchised actor', 'inserts herself into a legal and economic sphere in which, as a young, unmarried woman, she has no standing' in order to establish her 'individual agency' as 'professional writer' and 'create a myth of ownership to which she asks her readers to bear witness'.[3] For Jill Ingram, the 'whole point' of the poem is 'assertive self-interest', and the social change desired that of a 'workable capitalist society'.[4] Rarely has any literary text been, as Crystal Bartolovich suggested in 2009, so 'persistently misrecognized'.[5] 'We are inclined', Margaret de Grazia has noted, 'to look back to the [early modern period] for signs of an emergent modernity', and 'ways in which women, despite the law's curtailments, began to exercise [a] self-determining agency [that] follow[s] the progressive trajectory towards possessive individualism'. 'It is as if', she writes, 'we want all roads to lead to private property'. But, as she reminds readers, '[t]he distinguishing feature of land in England was that it was in theory *owned* by the monarch and only *held*—by descent, transfer, or purchase, by his subjects', with these land-holding arrangements including 'a number of rights . . . held in common' such as pasturage or turbary ('digging

[3] Laurie Ellinghausen, 'Literary Property and the Single Woman in Isabella Whitney's *Sweet Nosgay*', *SEL*, 45.1 (2005): 1–22; Wendy Wall, *The Imprint of Gender: Authorship and Publication in the English Renaissance* (Ithaca: Cornell University Press), 300. Lorna Hutson, *The Usurer's Daughter: Male Friendship and Fictions of Women in Sixteenth-Century England* (London: Routledge, 1994), reads the 'Wyll' in the context of the whole *Nosegay*, as a mock-testament, and sees Whitney as witty and ironic.

[4] Jill Ingram, 'Response to Julie Crawford', *Early Modern Culture: The Electronic Seminar* 5 (2006) <http://emc.eserver.org/1-5/ingram_response.html>, paragraphs 14 and 28).

[5] Crystal Bartolovich, '"Optimism of the Will": Isabella Whitney and Utopia', *Journal of Medieval and Early Modern Studies*, 39.2 (2009): 407–32, 411.

for metals or peat').[6] This chapter is concerned with the 'Wyll's' relationship to these facts of early modern English culture.

The chapter grants Bartolovich's assertion that the 'Wyll' 'denounces the role of inheritance in perpetuating economic inequality from the past into the future' as it pursues 'a properly common London'.[7] It seeks, however, to be more precise about the ways in which London, in Whitney's poetic 'vision', 'becomes the collective possession of "all"' with all of its goods to be 'universally shared'.[8] To do that, it sets the 'Wyll' in relation to legal materials produced at the Inns of Court that suggest the early modern thinking about property to which the 'Wyll' is a response. The chapter is particularly interested in the 'Wyll' as a response to the cultural effects of the Statute of Wills (1540). Whitney's generation was the first to grow up in a culture whose ideas of property were altered by that statute, which broke with the rules of primogeniture to allow those who held rights in land to dispose of them by a last will and testament in writing. As the work of the legal historians S. F. C. Milsom and David Seipp suggests, one of the consequences of the statute was to affirm and reify abstract notions of ownership that had been emerging across the late fifteenth and early sixteenth centuries. I turn to legal materials that capture for us changing thinking about property after the statute so that we may set the 'Wyll' in relation to an emergent culture of ownership and an existing but diminishing culture of holding things in common.

There is no question that the *Nosgay* is an engagement with literary culture at the Inns. The philosophical 'flowers' of its first part are, as noted above, lifted from a book published the year before by Hugh Plat, a student at Lincoln's Inn. The *Nosgay* is dedicated to another student at the Inns, George Mainwaring. Whitney's brother, Geoffrey, one of her correspondents in the book's second section, is believed to have been at either Thavies' Inn or Furnivall's.[9] And the other young men to whom Whitney writes, though their identity is obscured by reference to them only by initials, may all have been at one or another Inn. As J. H. Baker notes 'a considerable part of the gentry of the England went through the system', England's 'third university', 'if only for a brief spell of residence'.[10] The *Nosgay* may, moreover, have a literary debt not only to Plat's *Floures*, but the far more well-known verse miscellany published by another student at the Inns, George Gascoigne, *Hundredth Sundrie Flowers* (1573), which includes its own fictional testament, that of Dan Bartholomew, who declares his continuing love for his beloved even as he dies. In the intriguing figurative topography that she lays out in her dedicatory epistle to the reader, that topography in which she steals from Plat's 'garden' after

6 Margreta De Grazia, (1994), 'Afterword', in *Women, Property, and the Letters of the Law in Early Modern England*, ed. Nancy Wright, A. R. Buck, and Margaret Ferguson (Toronto: University of Toronto Press, 1994), 301.

7 Bartolovich, 'Optimism', 408–9.

8 Bartolovich, 'Optimism', 418, 421.

9 Geoffrey Whitney (1548?–1600/1), *ODNB*.

10 J. H. Baker, 'The Third University 1450–1550', in *The Intellectual and Cultural World of the Early Modern Inns of Court*, ed. Jayne Elisabeth Archer et al. (Manchester University Press: Manchester and New York), 10.

journeys through 'VIRGILL, OVID, MANTUAN' that have 'brusyed' her 'brayne' (Av^{v}), Whitney depicts herself as thrust out of a certain 'lane' by a male friend as terrain noxious to her health.[11] Whitney's trope suggests that the *Nosgay's* literary activities, which end with the 'Wyll', are an incursion not only into a literary domain that another would fence off (Plat claims to have created a 'thornie hedge' and 'a gate both great and strong' to keep 'craftie theeues' out of the 'grounde' of his text),[12] but also an incursion into the legal domain. The 'Wyll's' fictive address is to 'London'. but its substantive address is to institutional legal cultures from which Whitney, as a woman, was excluded.[13]

Whitney has no real property and apparently no chattels to bequeath. She is thus in the terms of the statute that played such a shaping role in early modern English culture, the Statute of Wills, an impossible testator. She does, however, have the ability to make playful use of the legal from the domain of the literary. With her appropriation of Plat's 'flowers', the *Nosgay* asserts a relationship with the literary as material that the book refuses to let be enclosed, and with its literary appropriation of the legal genre of the will, a genre that very few sixteenth-century Englishmen and even fewer women made use of,[14] it asserts a relationship with the law as primary force for organizing material relations. In both cases, Whitney is doing the same work: representatively making use of discursive material to model dispositions—to the literary in the first case, and to the legal in the second—to be taken up by the reader, who is cast as both beneficiary and executor of the 'Wyll' along with all others comprehended within its ostensible beneficiary and executor, 'London'. Chastised by more than one of her male correspondents for her complaints about her material circumstances, Whitney promises 'quietness', but then 'she fayneth as she would die' in order to make her WYLL and Testament' (Eii^{r}). The 'Wyll' thus reads as a retort to those who would thrust any form of 'quietness' upon her. But the retort is also to a legality that has placed her in unsustainable circumstances, a legality that she challenges with a discursive act that would bind others together, at least in imagination, in a kind of property holding predicated upon, but perhaps more radical than, the humanist philosophy most famously articulated in Erasmus's first adage: 'Al things with friends in com[m]on are / at least it should be so / That pleasures might imparted bee / so likewise grief, or woe' (Bviii^{r}).[15] A literary experiment in humble materials, the 'Wyll' makes use of a resource that cannot be enclosed to offer its rejoinder to

[11] See Peter Goodrich, *Oedipus Lex: Psychoanalysis, History, Law* (Berkeley, Los Angeles, and London: University California Press, 1995), 2–4, for the perceived unhealthiness of legal study in the period and the edict that law students were 'to accompany with women rarely' (3).

[12] Hugh Plat, Hugh (1581), *The Floures of Philosophie with the Pleasures of Poetrie Annexed* (London: 1581), sig. Mvi^{r}.

[13] See Sale, 'The Courts', in *The History of British Women's Writing*, Vol. 2: *1500–1610*, ed. Caroline Bicks and Jennifer Summit (Houndsmills: Palgrave Macmillan), 199–224.

[14] Lloyd Davis, 'Women's Wills in Early Modern England', in *Women, Property, and the Letters of the Law in Early Modern England*, ed. Nancy Wright, A. R. Buck, and Margaret Ferguson (Toronto: University of Toronto Press, 1994), 219–36, 223.

[15] On the political philosophy of Erasmus's *Adages*, see Kathy Eden, *Friends Hold All Things in Common: Tradition, Intellectual Property, and the Adages of Erasmus* (New Haven and London: Yale Univerity Press, 2001).

a legal system that establishes and protects not only relations to land but a privileged relationship to the making, practice, and adjudication of law;[16] and what it asserts, contra the legality that obtains, is not the possibilities of absolute possession of any thing, but rather conceptions of occupation and use—conceptions by which the 'Wyll' would cultivate the discursive capacities of all.

Dyer's Reading (1552) on the Statute of Wills (1540)

The Statute of Wills was a response to the difficulties occasioned by the Statute of Uses (1536), designed to restrain 'fraudulent feoffementes fynes recov[er]yes and other assurances craftely made' by which the king was deprived of his feudal incidents in the form of one-third of the value of any land held by knight's service when it changed hands at the possessor's death. The fraud or 'covin' principally came in the form of a legal device whereby a person was 'seized' to the 'use' of another.[17] Under the feudal system of 'seisin', in which '[t]o be seized denoted a condition rather than an event', feudal lords put their tenants 'in' to a holding, or made 'seisin' to them, to give them tenurial place and rights of use in a certain holding of land. One could inherit 'a right against the lord to be seized, to be made tenant of that tenement', but 'not a direct property interest in the land', all real property in the feudal system being held, as noted above, by the king.[18] The 'use', which enabled a feoffor to pass to another a holding in land under the fiction that the beneficiary or feoffee merely held the land for the feoffor (the *cesty qui use*), effectively let the feoffor give to another lands that would remain in the feoffee's hands at the time of his death.[19] The Statute of Uses aimed to guarantee that no land held by knight's service could remain in a feoffee's hands without the king receiving his due by abolishing the device, which, strictly speaking, had never been allowed by the common law.[20] The statute had barely passed, however, when lawyers went to work to imagine how they might on behalf of their clients circumvent it.[21] Out of fear that lawyer's imaginations might

[16] David Ibbeston, 'Common Lawyers and the Law before the Civil War', *Oxford Journal of Legal Studies*, 8.1 (1988): 142–53, 143, 146.

[17] *Statutes of the Realm* (2007), Vol. 3: *1509–1545*, online, TannerRitchie Publishing in collaboration with the Library and Information Services of the University of St Andrews, 539; J. H. Baker, *OHLE*, 6.1483–1558 (Oxford: Oxford University Press 2003) 654–7.

[18] S. F. C. Milsom, *The Legal Framework of English Feudalism* (Cambridge: Cambridge University Press, 1976), 41; David Graeber suggests a derivation of the 'real' in 'real property' not from the Latin *res* but from the Spanish (and law French) 'real' for 'royal', *The Utopia of Rules* (Brooklyn and London: Melville House, 2015), 86.

[19] J. M. W. Bean (1968), *The Decline of English Feudalism: 1215–1540* (New York: Manchester University Press, 1968), 136.

[20] Baker, *OHLE*, 6.671.

[21] Baker, *OHLE*, 6.680–1.

continue to find ways to 'subvert' the common law, Henry VIII changed the common law to allow testamentary devising of land.[22] As of 1540, a testator might will away his or her land 'at his will and pleasure' in any form s/he chose as long as land to which feudal incidents were attached delivered to the king his third.

In a 1552 Reading on the Statute at the Middle Temple by James Dyer (subsequently judge and then justice of the Common Pleas) we see the ordinary effect of the Statute on thinking about land-holding and property in mid-sixteenth-century England. In its sixth 'division', entitled 'Who shall be said to have a sole estate in Fee-simple so that he may devise it, and who not', Dyer's Reading presents two hypothetical cases that involve a pair of sisters. The more complex of these reads as follows:

> Feme Tenant in general Taile hath issue a daughter, and her Husband dyeth, she taketh a second Husband, and hath issue another daughter, the Husband and Wife by fine discontinue, and take back an Estate special Taile and die, the younger daughter enters to the use of her self and her sister, she enters with her, and occupieth in Common, the younger daughter shall be sole seised of the one moity in taile, and of the other moity in Fee. *Quaerae.*[23]

The query presumably relates to the circumstance that is unusual here, that in which 'use' of property imagined to be an occupation in common becomes, for the younger sister, a situation in which she is 'sole seised' of both of the moieties, which have descended to her by different means. It might also relate to the means by which the sisters aimed to occupy the property in common. Neither of these elements features in a subsequent fictional case a mere three items along in Dyer's list for which there is no 'quaerae':

> A feme Inheretrix hath issue a daughter, her husband dyeth, she taketh a second husband, and hath issue another daughter, the husband and wife exchange the land of the wife for other land in Fee, and after the wife dyeth, and the husband dyeth, the daughters enter into the land taken in exchange, the younger shall be sole seised.[24]

What is clear: both of Dyer's hypothetical cases support the rule that an individual must be sole seized in order to exercise the power to devise under the Statute whether the holding is in fee simple, fee simple in coparcenery, or 'in comen in fee simple'.[25] In the first instance, the one that generates the 'quaerae', the rule is secured despite the fact that one fictional sister wished to occupy in common with another. One sister's seeming right to dispose of the property at her 'will and pleasure', then, comes at a cost—the cost of another arrangement, the 'common' occupation, or the means by which the other sister was also benefiting from the property in question. Both the 'division' and Dyer's

[22] *Statutes* (1509–1545) 540. For the use's imputed 'subv[er]cion of the auncyent common Lawes of this Realme', see Baker, *OHLE*, 6.667.

[23] *Three Learned Readings Upon Three Very Usefull Statutes* (London: 1648), sig. C3v.

[24] *Learned Readings*, sig. C3v.

[25] *Statutes* (1509–1545), 902.

fictional case exemplify the common law's interest in finding the person to define as sole possessor even where the persons themselves might wish to hold the property in question in common.

Real *devising* or invention would shatter these limitations. The emphasis of Dyer's Reading is, however, entirely consistent with the view offered by David Seipp on the emergence of the sole proprietor in sixteenth-century England. As Seipp has argued, 'writings of sixteenth-century lawyers on property in land and ownership of land' 'invoke a stark mental image of one solitary person alone in complete and exclusive possession of one tract of land',[26] a situation intensified when the Statute of Wills eradicated compulsory primogeniture to make it possible for someone without customary ties to the land to inherit it by testamentary devise. Ownership of land could thus become abstract possession in a new way, with consequences for how everyone thought about both land-as-property and property more generally. 'As land become more "property-like"', Seipp writes, 'the newly named "owner" acquired more freedom to alienate, to extract value in new ways, and to exclude others, while the long-recognized rights of others over the same land were diminished.'[27] Legal thought in the period pursued an 'internal compulsion toward increasing simplification',[28] and the simplification furthered by the statute is that of the 'sole seized' or the solitary 'owner'. As Henry Sherfield notes in an early seventeenth-century reading on wills, the Statute in effect made a 'lord' out of anyone who had rights in use of any holding in land, no matter how humble the holding.[29] The Statute could not, however, make a 'lord' out of anyone who held no land at all.

A testator 'all sole alone' (Avii^r^) who has in fact no real property to bequeath, Whitney takes a circumstance that is impossible in the law's terms—as Plowden demands in a 1566 treatise, 'to what end should law give power to them to make testaments that can have no goods to their own uses to bestow?'[30]—in order to flout the premises of a system freshly affirmed by the Statute, the common law of property in land as a system of parcellation and subinfeudation presided over by the feudal sovereign that privileges an 'owner' who is sole seized over those attempting to imagine some other relationship to property, some other kind of holding. Imagining herself as a person who holds no land or chattels but is nevertheless capable of bequeathing *something*, Whitney makes the 'Wyll' a means of disavowing an interest in the law's forms of property, especially as strongly ramified, after the Statute of Wills, in the figure of the sole proprietor, in favour of a holding in which everyone has their 'share' without being 'seized' of any 'real' property at all. On the one hand, the 'Wyll's' imagination seems to hearken back to earlier historical conceptions; on the other, it would seem to anticipate that which does not yet

[26] David Seipp (1994), 'The Concept of Property in the Early Common Law', *Law and History Review*, 12.1 (1994): 29–91, 87.

[27] Seipp, 'Property', 89.

[28] Seipp, 'Property', 91.

[29] Henry Sherfield, 'Reading on Wills', BL MS Hargrave 402 (1623), fol. 53^v^.

[30] Edmund Plowden, BL MS Harley 849 (1566), fol. 6^r^.

exist. *Paramour v Yardley*, heard in 1579, shows us precisely the kind of historical thinking within which the Statute of Wills was in tension.

Paramour v Yardley

The case is reported by Edmund Plowden in his *Commentaries*. Published in two volumes in 1571 and 1579 respectively, the *Commentaries* is the fruit of Plowden's work preparing, for his own learning, accounts of cases that he heard in the king's central courts in the 1560s and 1570s. This material then became highly valuable instructional material for students at the Inns of Court. Plowden's attempt to capture the legal arguments in full makes the *Commentaries* an important source of legal thinking in the period. In the case of *Paramour v Yardley*, in which an historic case from the reign of Henry VI is cited at some length, we have direct evidence of the kind of thinking about property that the Statute of Wills displaces.

Paramour v Yardley involves an action of trespass of Richard Paramour against Raphael Yardley and George Smart, servants of Thomas Robinson, from whom Paramour claims to hold a lease. The controversy centres on whether Thomas's mother, Grace Robinson, had been free to grant her sister, Wilgfort Tanfield, a lease of one of the properties received from her husband under his will, which gave Grace 'the Occupation and Profits' of all Robinson's 'Lands and Leases' until their son Thomas came of age 'to the Intent that she, with the Profits of his Lands and Leases, might educate his Issues'.[31] This 'Intent' fits neatly within the purview of the Statute of Wills, which claims that its objective is to ensure that all of the king's 'obedient and loving Subjectes [might] use or exercise themselfis according to their estatis degrees faculties and qualities', and more particularly be able to 'keepe and maynteigne their hospitalities and families', including providing for the 'good educations and bringing up of their lawfull generacions'.[32] Much of the legal debate turns on whether Grace held the property as executor or legatee, with the Court endorsing the latter proposition—partly, so the argument goes, because it is better for her to have the property to her own use rather than to the use of the testator. This proposition did not, however, fully decide the legal questions, for the question remained of what it was that Grace held: 'For it was said on behalf of the Defendants that the Devise to the wife of the Occupation and Profits of the Land was not a Devise of the land itself but of a Profit or Interests to be taken out of the land.'[33]

The Serjeant arguing the case for Paramour invokes a case from 37 Henry 6 to deny that any distinction can be made between 'possession and estate of the land itself' and any 'Profit a prendre' out of the land. (If she were to take 'profits', Grace would be free

[31] Edmund Plowden, *The Commentaries, or Reports of Edmund Plowden* (London: 1761), 542.

[32] *Statutes* (1509–1545), 744.

[33] Plowden, *Commentaries*, 541.

to take and dispose of the lease to her sister.) The historic case is invoked to exemplify a rule—'in some Things the Occupation, Profit or Use is a distinct Thing from the Property'[34]—that is subsequently argued does *not* apply to Grace's holding. In land, so the argument goes, occupation, profit, or use cannot be separated from possession, 'for there he who has the Occupation and Use of it has the Property of it for the Time'.[35] The logic is quite clearly that of the Statute of Uses—s/he who has the use must be understood to have the possession. There was therefore no 'distinct profit' that Grace could bestow upon another, especially given that the profits of the lands and leases could not be used for any other intent than that specified in Robinson's will. That the alternate conception must be acknowledged shows us, however, that there were competing paradigms for how Grace Robinson's relationship to the land might be construed, and that one of these privileges an historic conception of 'occupation and use' associated with chattels over absolute possession. There is some irony to the historic logic being denied application to land, given that Seipp finds that in general notions of property in land were being directly informed by property logic that applied to chattels.[36] But the irony perhaps shows us the difference that the Statutes of Uses and Wills had made, especially as the former lashes 'use' to 'possession'.

Paramour v Yardley involved a 'Book called the *Grail*' devised by Testator A to be enjoyed first by legatee B and then legatee C, with A's executors responsible for ensuring that after C's death the book should be given 'to the Use of a Church'.[37] Before B died, however, he handed the book over to the church wardens, who brought an action of trespass against C for removing it from the church. The action was upheld by the court. There was no talk, however, of A's intention as testator being defeated. A's intention as testator could, it seems, only be properly exercised in relation to the book as property, not the book as a thing that might be 'occupied'. The logic of the occupation and use of the Book of the Grail is that of the feudal system, in which all land, is strictly speaking, being merely used by those who hold it while the property itself lies with another, the king. The Serjeant arguing the case for Paramour exploits the difference that the Statutes of Uses and Wills had made to argue that the logic no longer applies to land.

The jurisprudence of the case affirms a preference not only for a stable sense of absolute possession that temporary 'Occupation' may not disrupt, but also for land as a kind of property less available to any flexible or innovative sense of holding than a book. This may explain, at least in part, why Whitney's 'Wyll' involves no disposition of land, and focuses instead on the disposition of things in 'Streets, full fraught therewith' so that no one 'neede not farre to seeke' (Eiii[v]). Not only does Whitney's 'London' have everything it needs for all its people, everything is available to everybody:

34 Plowden, *Commentaries*, 542.
35 Plowden, *Commentaries*, 543.
36 Seipp, 'Property', 90.
37 Plowden, *Commentaries*, 542.

In many places, Shops are full,
I left you nothing scant.
Yf they that keepe what I you leaue,
aske Mony: when they sell it:
At Mint, there is such store, it is
unpossible to tell it. (Ev^{r})

There are at least two consequences to the 'Wyll's' fantasy that its distribution of London's goods to all is made possible by an endless supply of money at the Mint. These consequences suggest the 'Wyll's' interest in the very concepts that the Serjeant in *Paramour v Yardley* acknowledged only to deny their applicability to land.

In its infinite availability, money works against its function as the triangulator creating and promulgating exchange value. Exchange remains, but with the triangulator deprived of its ability to produce surpluses from its act of abstracting value. Money thus cannot enable sophisticated forms of accumulation, and cannot work with an increased market for land in transferring wealth away from those working the land or producing commodities of various kinds to a landed few in a system of subinfeudation that vests land-holdings in some while leaving others entirely without. The unlimited 'store' at the Mint in the first instance funds possession: everyone may have everything they need, for the coin of the realm goes to supplying their needs and wants. But as a substitute for that from which value derives in the feudal system, land, the endless supply of money at the Mint is the sign of another system of value toppling a system that assigns only limited rights of use to some in favour of a culture in which one occupies and uses rather than owns.

The 'Wyll' is not disposing of properties to be owned, or properties to be subject to the exclusive dominion of any sole proprietor. It is disposing of properties to be occupied—to be enjoyed and put to use. This enjoyment and use are, moreover, to occur within a larger dynamic, one whereby the circulation of London's goods not only meets the needs of those who in any way 'lack', but where no 'Occupation' is exclusive. This is not to say that things do not get used up, and the use of any given thing, especially where it is a consumable, may not seem, as Locke will later argue, to constitute exclusive possession, but rather that the earlier 'flowers' set the reader up to read the dispositions from a moral perspective in which it is understood that any such possession is in fact discouraged. As flower 6 declares, 'For to abound in euery thing, / and not their vse to know: / It is a pinching penury: / wherefore, thy goods, bestow' (Bii^{r}).

Taken seriously, the morality espoused by flower 6 is one that requires a disavowal of any interest in absolute possession. One possesses, by its logic, in order to 'use'; and where one has access to an abundance of things—more than what one might oneself use—one's things should be bestowed upon others. One's acts of use, moreover, if they were to be consistent with the political philosophy of the 'flowers' and Whitney's use of materials found in Plat's 'garden', would themselves not be use for oneself, but use that permits participation in a culture of sharing. Proper 'use' within this alternate legality would be achieved, ultimately, only where one leaves what one has occupied and used fully open to the occupation and use of others. There is no decisive, static possession.

The occupation and use of London by London that the 'Wyll' advances has a debt not only to historic conceptions of occupation associated with chattels, as *Paramour v Yardley* suggests, but historic conceptions of use, especially the Roman conception of the 'usufruct' as received into English law in a 'momentary contact' between the two in the thirteenth century, when the corporation of London bestowed properties in London upon the Franciscan monks for their 'beneficial occupation'.[38] It is an irony of English legal history that this 'beneficial occupation', which bestows 'the right to the temporary enjoyment of the thing, as distinct from the ownership of it',[39] 'without right to change the character of the property',[40] enabled the development of the kind of 'use' that the Statute of Uses would declare, in 1536, defrauded the king. One kind of 'use', explicitly set apart from notions of ownership, paved the way for the rise of another that bolstered an abstract ownership slowly untethered from the constraints of the 'real' as constituted by land-holdings from the king. We cannot say if any particular 'use' was designed as a rejection of feudal principles or the common law of property as a set of rules derived from them, but it is clear that the concatenation of uses (which were so widespread, Baker notes, that the late fifteenth-century lawyer Frowyk claimed that 'the greater part of the land of England was in feoffments upon trust')[41] did not alter land-holdings in England to make them in any sense more 'common'.

Whitney's invention differs from the legal inventiveness that produced and reified the 'use' in its connection back to notions of beneficial occupation, especially for a community. The political point of the 'Wyll', however, is that Whitney has not in fact had beneficial occupation and use of London's materials or materiality, and in this she is representative of all those who lack the 'credit' for any such use. Use is what she models when she helps herself to Plat's 'flowers'; use is what she would bequeath. But this 'use' is not merely 'usufructuary', for it depends vitally, in clear contradistinction to the legal conception of the 'usufruct', on alteration. One uses what comes to one's hands in order to shape it in some new way and pass it on, and one's labour, while it is to be 'respected' (Aiiii^{v}), is not to lead to proprietary claims. Whitney is not Locke's 'sister'.[42] In Whitney's vision, one does not labour to possess; one labours in order to contribute to and benefit from a culture in which everyone 'participates' their goods to others.

This philosophy finds exemplary expression in Whitney's claim to 'London' that 'If any other thing be lackt / in thee, I wysh them looke / For there it is: I little brought / but no thing from thee tooke' (Ev^{r}). She came with little, but made what she could, and when she leaves London she leaves behind her the books she has published even as she herself takes nothing from it as her own. Creditless, she made less than she might have, for she

[38] Frederick Pollock and Frederic William Maitland, *The History of English Law* (London: Cambridge University Press, 1968), 238; but see also Bean, *Decline*, 128–9.

[39] Bean, *Decline*, 127.

[40] David Walker, *The Oxford Companion to Law* (Oxford: Clarendon Press, 1980), 1268.

[41] Baker, *History*, 654.

[42] Bartolovich, 'Optimism', 410.

had no *place* from which to make, the system not providing, nor any individual wishing for her, as Robert Curtis did for his son in his 1573 will, an 'occupacion'.[43] She made, however, what she could by occupying and using materials that Erasmus asserted ought to be regarded as 'common property'.[44] Holding to the logic that property ought to be held in common for the use of all, the 'Wyll' implicitly devises nothing more than the 'Occupation' of any thing.

Whitney's use of Plat's literary materials is thus always caught up with the legal, and not merely in the strict sense about which she presents herself as worrying, with her concern that Plat will 'fume' to see his flowers 'borne aboute' (Cv^v) by her and (in a private property vanguard) take legal action against her. It is legal in that her beneficial occupation of the literary domain, which she insists needs no authorization, involves the use of the literary for the imagining of the possibilities of an alternative legality that would ensure precisely what the common law as feudal system does not, productive place for all. All that is in London figuratively passes through the hands of the 'Wyll's' 'Aucthour' (like the water in the poor man's hands that is a gift to Darius in the dedicatory letter to Mainwaring) so that the literary thing may serve as the means of disavowing an interest in the common law's forms of property in favour of the possibilities of an unusual form of holding—something other than 'occupation' of anything solely for one's own pleasure, something other than a 'use' that secures the dominion of an 'owner', and something more, still, than the kind of beneficial occupation and use in which one leaves what one has occupied and used unaltered. The vision is not about having 'the practical benefits of ownership' while still being able to 'say that [one] owned nothing'.[45] The vision, rather, is of London as a dynamic scene of stuffs in circulation, or goods on the go, in which nothing settles into absolute possession or any exclusive occupation. As the final intransitive verb of flower 6 suggests, one holds and uses in order to *bestow* in activity that does not take any particular person as its object.

Whitney has no heirs; she has, instead, those to whom she would bequeath responsibility, with ultimate responsibility residing with London as corporation:

> Reioyce in God that I am gon,
> out of this vale so vile.
> And that of ech thing, left such store,
> as may your wants exile.
> I make thee sole executor, because
> I lou'de thee best.
> And thee I put in trust, to geue
> the goodes vnto the rest. (Evii^V)

[43] Robert Curtis, London Metropolitan Archives Manuscript DL/C/B/005/MS09172/008B (1573), fol. 29^r.

[44] *CWE: Adages 1i1 to 1v100*, 16.

[45] Pollock and Maitland, *History of English Law*, 138.

The conveyance to the imaginary corporate person serves not only as the means of subverting the logic whereby the power of devising is seized only by and for the sole seized, but also for underscoring that all holding is temporary: one holds in order to give 'goodes' to others, and receives because one gives. The 'Wyll's' drama of occupation and use is that of a self-contained, self-sustaining system of production and use in which all *participate* and from which no 'third' may be siphoned off.

The Literary Thing

The *Nosgay* counters a legality and legal practices that would oppose a culture of holding all things in common, I have been arguing, in two ways: by exemplifying use of material held in common in the 'flowers', and by tying that use, in the 'Wyll', to the imagining of relations to property that break with a culture of ownership inculcated by the feudal system and then further secured by the right to dispose of land by testament under the Statute of Wills. The *Nosgay* opposes such a culture in the first instance by making no bid on the part of its author for place, profit, or personal advancement of any kind. (All Whitney asks, she claims more than once, is for the book to 'speede'.) It opposes it in the second by exemplifying the creative dimension of use. One uses to invent, and one's invention is then made a gift, a gift to cultivate friendship not simply between author and dedicatee, but author and all those whom the text addresses: every reader, and every reader joined with others as the potential executors of its imaginary holding, which binds all together in a corporation responsible for 'exiling' all of its members' 'wants'.

This is more radical than the proposition that friends hold all things in common. Friendship can accomplish much, as we see in a codicil to the will of Alice Rydgley, widow, in which she declares that Anne and Margery Wakeman shall not have a lease left to them in her will, 'Nor yet shall … haue possesse or enioye any other legacye or bequest therein', unless they:

> shall and will givyethe p[er]mytte & suffer Elizabeth Patye wydowe [her] poore woman, to haue holde & enioye the little housse y^{t} she nowe dwelleth in for & duringe ye tearme of her naturall lyffe wthout theyr or any of theyr lett troble or evyction.[46]

Rydgeley's will could take action for Patye. It could not, however, address the general problem that Whitney's 'Wyll' takes up as she, having lost her service to a 'vertuous Ladye' (Cvi^{v}), 'falls' to writing, at first to put into verse roughly one in six of Plat's 'flowers', next, to represent her attempts to bind friends to her through discursive acts, and then, to write the 'Wyll'. A fiction not capable of achieving anything in relation to any land-holding anywhere, the 'Wyll' is paradoxically productive, and productive in ways

[46] Alice Rydgeley, London Metropolitan Archives manuscript DL/C/B/005/MS09172/007C (1571) fol. 109^{r}.

that exceed what the law can imagine or execute, especially as an entity managed by those specially furnished to act in relation to it because of their possession of property in land. The 'literary' always has the capacity to imagine that which does not exist, and in the case of the 'Wyll' it imagines property relations that comprehensively take care of all rather than selectively care for kin or friend.

The capacity on display is the capacity for the possibility of legal invention from outside legal institutions. Rather than permitting notions of discrete singular holdings of land in a system underwritten by the great singular proprietor of the sovereign to govern the legal imaginations of readers, the 'Wyll' opens up another idea of social organization and the possibility of another kind of sovereignty than that which takes form and in through feudal holdings of land. It does this in part by bringing into view persons that have no direct influence over law, even as it conspicuously does not distinguish individuals or differentiate between them, to locate in everyday scenes and acts of production the possibility of another legal system, one that would privilege and protect these persons in their material needs and their acts of making, the prevailing land-holding system being in no sense a system of or for the 'commons'.[47] There is, after all, no guarantee in the early modern English common law that the king's 'thirds' need to be expended in any other way than the king chooses—no need, that is, for the king's thirds to support the *fiscal*, especially in the form of the intellectual capacities of the realm's members. Plowden asserts that the King has his 'capacity to the use of his corporation and not otherwise',[48] a view entirely consistent with medieval conceptions of the fiscal sovereign, especially as elaborated by Ernst Kantorowicz in his 1957 book *The King's Two Bodies*, which lashes fiscal sovereignty to the sovereign's responsibilities in regard to the *fisc* conceived as *res quasi sacrae* and *res publica*, or the public things that take the king as their (sacred) symbolic figure.[49] In its most radical formulation, fiscal sovereignty finds in the king (especially as the civilian theorist Baldus would have it) the figure of the realm as corporate public intellection.[50] Significant jurisprudence in England in the period makes of the king something else entirely—the king may be 'the most excellent thing' but nothing requires him to nurture the capacities of all to contribute to *res publica*[51]—and the statutory development of 1540, which affirmed a new kind of property, property in land, by finding the 'means to do', as Milsom notes, 'what the feudal structure had precluded, namely dispose of land by will', bolstered one form of sovereignty over another. The 'Wyll' works to another end. It encourages reader-executors to find in its poetic spectacle of London's productive power their own creative potential as potential

[47] Henry VIII was firm on this point when responding to objections to the Statute of Uses; see Baker, *OHLE*, 6.679.

[48] Plowden, BL MS Harley 849, fol. 6^r.

[49] Kantorowicz takes other writings of Plowden as his starting-point. As Parmiter *Edmund Plowden: An Elizabethan Recusant Lawyer* (Southampton: Catholic Record Society, 1987) notes, Kantorowicz 'does not mention the *Treatise* which was apparently unknown to him', 91 n. 28.

[50] Ernst Kantorowicz, 'Mysteries of State An Absolutist Concept and Its Late Medieval Origins', *Harvard Theological Review*, 48.1 (1955): 65–91, 89–90.

[51] Sale, 'The Courts', 137–57.

that might and should be expressed, as it is in the students at the Inns of Court 'full of Actiuyitie' (Evii^{r}), in relation to the making and adjudication of law.

What the 'Wyll' properly wills, then, in its imaginative subsumption of the legal by the literary, is activity. It would facilitate a particular kind of making—the making of social forms, that activity in relation to which all law-making, the primary creative activity by which social relations are shaped, plays a privileged role. In this context, the literary act of 'willing' is an exemplary seizing of discursive potential by and on the part of those who possess no land which would open up the making of law by all. The 'Wyll' breaks with an idea of social organization centred on feudal holdings of land (that system that gives a few a privileged relationship to law) in favour of a corporate holding, fiscal in Baldus's sense, that supports the discursive activity of all, without any distinction between 'estatis degrees faculties [or] qualities'. And what it appeals to is the capacity of reader-executors to make law, in the first instance, by taking seriously the imaginative act of the 'Wyll' as an act that, put to various kinds of use, might inaugurate a new legality as something to be produced and cultivated by members of the corporation of the realm through acts of discursive exchange and collective willing rather than dictated by a form of sovereignty reified in a system of 'seisin'.

The imagined holding is certainly, as Crystal Bartolovich has argued, utopic.[52] There is no real property here to pass, by the invention, to anyone. The point is that the imaginary is set against the 'real', and Whitney's writing hand—'I / ... / did write this Wyll with my owne hand / and it to London gaue' (Eviii^{v})—is metonymic: it is the hand of the unpropertied symbolically turning back upon the system that would make the power to will under the Statute of Wills the power of a few to make it instead a capacity to be exercised by anyone at all.[53] This capacity must then achieve its effects as a matter of concatenation with the wills of others, for as John Briscoe notes in his Reading on Wills in 1624, only the 'vndoubted vniversall will of [a] people' has any genuine authority as law.[54]

To possess Whitney's book in 1573, as an artefact that still needed to be purchased with actual coin of the realm, would have been a paradoxical experience, one that affirmed the relative privilege of the owner even as the owner-reader had the opportunity to experience another idea of the book, that of its potentially illimitable occupation and use in a 'London' in which everyone has the same opportunity to 'occupy' any given thing, and thus the same opportunity to make from it—a London, in short, which everyone is treated as a friend entitled to the same rights of use in things held in common as anyone else. But while the 'literary thing' may be, as Pierre Macherey has suggested, endlessly generative—'Not only is the literary thing produced, but we must also say that it produces, that it is productive, that is, that it has a fecundity proper to it that it is ultimately inexhaustible' (30)—its productivity depends, like the productivity

52 Bartolovich, 'Optimism', 412, 426.

53 For related thinking in contemporary political philosophy, see Jacques Rancière, *Hatred of Democracy*, trans. Steve Corcoran (London: Verso Books, 2006).

54 John Briscoe, BL Add. MS 25251 (1624), fol. 33^{v}.

of any other thing, on its availability to use. Whitney's trope for the book's effects, a common one—the book's leaves give off a scent that the reader may breathe in to experience the book's moral virtues—is one way of imagining the book as having the capacity to be used without ever being used up, its 'scent' signifying immaterial effects or 'benefits' that do not affect or in any way diminish the materiality of the text.[55] The text may be given while always itself remaining the same, though the copies in which it is dispersed about are, as Whitney notes, subject to possible destruction. But more importantly, the trope imagines the literary thing's capacity to possess everyone without itself being the exclusive possession of anyone.

The *Nosgay* thus imagines its own taking-up and use in terms that defy the ideas of ownership so strongly ramified by the Statutes of Uses and Wills, with the former transmuting use into possession and the latter favouring the proprietary holdings of the 'sole' over any holding in common. This thing that is given, this literary thing which can be used without being used up, is testament to the possibility of illimitable possession—not of the literary, but by it. From outside legal authority and the institutions that promulgate it comes an act—an extended poetic instance of literary devising—that appeals to the eradication of any law or use of any law that would militate against *it* as the means of achieving radical alteration of a system that serves the poet and others ill. The 'Wyll' is a celebration of the literary as the epitome of discursivity that cannot be enclosed and which may, as a public act of imagination, do legal work—in the case of Whitney's 'Wyll', the legal work of imagining another order of occupation, use, and possession than that presided over by the feudal sovereign.

In the 'Wyll', in short, the kind of author who would arise in relation to the existing ideas of property (Plat) through an act that reiterates its logic (Plat would turn *use* of literary material into proprietary possession) is trumped by the author who uses the idea of devising with genuine wit to will relations to law that would leave none in Whitney's place, as the 'aucthour' feigning her death in order to give to others what she did not have, the opportunities to 'fall' at will, to any kind of discursive making, whether the making of literature or the making of law. In its bare survival, the book is testament to losses from both the literary and the legal that we cannot measure. We certainly do not have the 'dayntier thing' (Av^{r}) or 'longer worke' (Bi^{v}) that Whitney and one of her male correspondents promise from her. But thanks to the *Nosgay's* sole surviving copy, the 'Wyll' comes forward in time in search of the 'donees' in which it might vest as a text that may now, where liberated from 'paywalls', be 'dispersed about' in innumerable digital leaves to the prospective executors who might bring its law into being. That law would wrest the 'common' from the 'sole' in favour of a legality of 'occupation' and 'use' rather than one supporting absolute 'possession', and wrest it through the literary thing that defies, as exemplary fact, any singular 'occupation'.

55 On this point, see also Hutson, *Usurer's Daughter*, 126.

Bibliography

Baker, J. H. *The Oxford History of the Laws of England*, Vol. 6: *1483–1558* (Oxford: Oxford University Press, 2003).

Baker, J. H. 'The Third University 1450–1550', in *The Intellectual and Cultural World of the Early Modern Inns of Court*, ed. Jayne Elisabeth Archer, Elizabeth Goldring, and Sarah Knight (Manchester and New York: Manchester University Press, 2011), 8–24.

Baker, J. H., ed. *Readers and Readings in the Inns of Court and Chancery* (London: SS, 2000).

Bartolovich, Crystal. '"Optimism of the Will": Isabella Whitney and Utopia', *Journal of Medieval and Early Modern Studies*, 39.2 (2009): 407–32.

Bean, J. M. W. *The Decline of English Feudalism: 1215–1540* (New York: Manchester University Press, 1968).

Brace, Patricia. 'Isabella Whitney, *A Sweet Nosegay*', in *A Companion to Early Modern Women's Writing*, ed. Anita Pacheco (Oxford: Blackwell, 2002), 97–109.

British Library Add. MS 25251, John Briscoe 'Reading on Wills' (1624).

British Library MS Harley 849, Edmund Plowden, 'Treatise on the Succession' (1566).

Clarke, Danielle, ed. *Isabella Whitney, Mary Sidney, and Aemilia Lanyer: Renaissance Women Poets* (London: Penguin Books, 2000).

Crawford, Julie. 'Women (Authors) on Top', *Early Modern Culture: The Electronic Seminar* 5 (2006).

Davis, Lloyd. 'Women's Wills in Early Modern England', in *Women, Property, and the Letters of the Law in Early Modern England*, ed. Nancy Wright, A. R. Buck, and Margaret Ferguson (Toronto: University of Toronto Press. 1994), 219–36.

de Grazia, Margreta. 'Afterword', in *Women, Property, and the Letters of the Law in Early Modern England*, ed. Nancy Wright, A. R. Buck, and Margaret Ferguson (Toronto: University of Toronto Press, 1994), 296–304.

Dyer, Sir James. *Three Learned Readings Made Upon Three Very Usefull Statutes* (London: 1648).

Eden, Kathy. *Friends Hold All Things in Common: Tradition, Intellectual Property, and the Adages of Erasmus* (New Haven and London: Yale Univerity Press, 2001).

Ellinghausen, Laurie. 'Literary Property and the Single Woman in Isabella Whitney's *Sweet Nosgay*', *Studies in English Literature*, 45.1 (2005): 1–22.

Erasmus, Desiderius. *Collected Works of Erasmus: Adages 1i1 to 1v100*, ed. and trans. Margaret Mann Phillips (Toronto: University of Toronto Press, 1982).

Gascoigne, George. *A Hundreth Sundrie Flowres Bounde Up in One Small Poesie Gathered Partely (by Translation) in the Fyne Outlandish Gardins of Euripides, Ovid, Petrarke, Ariosto, and Others* (London: 1573).

Goodrich, Peter. *Oedipus Lex: Psychoanalysis, History, Law* (Berkeley: University California Press, 1995).

Graeber, David. *The Utopia of Rules* (Brooklyn and London: Melville House, 2015).

Great Britain. *Statutes of the Realm*, Vol. 3: *1509–1545* (Burlington: TannerRitchie Publishing in collaboration with the Library and Information Services of the University of St Andrews, 2007).

Holdsworth, W. S. 'The Genesis of the Statute of Uses', *English Historical Review*, 325 (1967): 673–97.

Hutson, Lorna. *The Usurer's Daughter: Male Friendship and Fictions of Women in Sixteenth-Century England* (London and New York: Routledge, 1997).

Ibbeston, David. 'Common Lawyers and the Law before the Civil War', *Oxford Journal of Legal Studies*, 8.1 (1988): 142–53.
Ingram, Jill. 'A Case for Credit: Isabella Whitney's "Wyll and Testament" and the Mock Testament Tradition', *Early Modern Culture: The Electronic Seminar* 5 (2006).
Ingram, Jill. 'Response to Julie Crawford', *Early Modern Culture: The Electronic Seminar* 5 (2006).
Kantorowicz, Ernst H. 'Mysteries of State an Absolutist Concept and Its Late Medieval Origins', *Harvard Theological Review*, 48.1 (1955): 65–91.
London Metropolitan Archives MS DL/C/B/005/MS09172/008B, Robert Curtis' Will (1573).
London Metropolitan Archives MS DL/C/B/005/MS09172/007C, Alice Rydgeley's Will (1571).
Macherey, Pierre. 'The Literary Thing', *Diacritics*, 37.7 (2007): 21–30.
Milsom, S. F. C. *The Legal Framework of English Feudalism* (Cambridge: Cambridge University Press, 1976).
Milsom, S. F. C. *A Natural History of the Common Law* (New York: Columbia University Press, 2003).
Mirow, M. C. 'Readings on Wills in the Inns of Court, 1552–1631' (PhD Thesis: Univerisity of Cambridge, 1993).
Oxford Dictionary of National Biography (Oxford: Oxford University Press, 2004).
Parmiter, Geoffrey. *Edmund Plowden: An Elizabethan Recusant Lawyer* (Southampton: Catholic Record Society, 1987).
Plat, Hugh. *The Floures of Philosophie with the Pleasures of Poetrie Annexed* (London: 1581).
Plowden, Edmund. *The Commentaries, or Reports of Edmund Plowden* (London: 1761).
Pollock, Frederick and Frederic William Maitland. *The History of English Law* (London and New York: Cambridge University Press, 1968).
Rancière, Jaques. *Hatred of Democracy* (London: Verso Books, 2006).
Sale, Carolyn. 'The Courts', in *The History of British Women's Writing*, Vol. 2: *1500–1610*, ed. Caroline Bicks and Jennifer Summit (Basingstoke and New York: Palgrave Macmillan, 2010), 199–224.
Sale, Carolyn. '"The King Is a Thing": The King's Prerogative and the Treasure of the Realm in Plowden's Report of the Case of Mines and Shakespeare's *Hamlet*', in *Shakespeare and the Law*, ed. Paul Raffield and Gary Watt (Oxford: Hart Publishing, 2008), 137–57.
Seipp, David. 'The Concept of Property in the Early Common Law', *Law and History Review*, 12.1 (1994): 29–91.
Sherfield, Henry. 'Reading on Wills' (1623). British Library MS Hargrave 402.
Travitsky, Betty. 'The "Wyll and Testament" of Isabella Whitney', *English Literary Renaissance*, 10.4 (1980): 76–94.
Walker, David. *The Oxford Companion to Law* (Oxford: The Clarendon Press, 1980).
Wall, Wendy. *The Imprint of Gender: Authorship and Publication in the English Renaissance* (Ithaca: Cornell University Press, 1993).
Whitney, Isabella. *A Sweet Nosgay, or Pleasant Posye: Contayning a Hundred and Ten Phylosphicall Flowers* (London: 1573).

CHAPTER 23

WITCH WIVES

FRANCES E. DOLAN

THE stereotypical witch was socially marginal: poor, old, sometimes deformed, contentious, and unmarried. Early modern commentators as well as modern historians concur on this. Addressing the fact that the majority of the accused were not only women, but 'a very limited sample of their sex', historian James Sharpe, for instance, points out that the accused were often 'widows or women otherwise living outside the conventional hierarchies of family or household'; and so 'outside normal patterns of control'.[1] Many historians of witchcraft have contrasted witch and wife, not only assuming that most accused women were unmarried but placing them at opposite ends of a gendered moral continuum. For example, Stuart Clark has convincingly argued that conceptualizations of witchcraft were organized around contrariety and inversion so that 'witches were women-on-top *par* excellence'. Louise Jackson avers that 'the witch was the stereotypical opposite of the good wife'.[2] In contrast, I am interested in wife and witch as more alike than different. At one level the difference between the two legal categories is clear. The wife is defined by her relation to her husband and her duties, the witch by her relation to Satan and her crimes. But in other ways it is less clear. That uncertainty compounds as we will see when the witch and wife come together in the same person.

While many were vulnerable to accusation in part because they were not married, some of the accused were wives. Recent work on male witches suggests that accused men were sometimes vulnerable to accusation because of their relationship to their wives.[3]

[1] James Sharpe, *Instruments of Darkness: Witchcraft in Early Modern England* (Philadelphia: University of Pennsylvania Press, 1997), 172. See also James Sharpe, *The Bewitching of Anne Gunter* (New York: Routledge, 2000), 67–8; and Keith Thomas, *Religion and the Decline of Magic* (New York: Scribner's, 1971), 562, 568, and passim.

[2] Stuart Clark, *Thinking with Demons: The Idea of Witchcraft in Early Modern Europe* (Oxford: Oxford University Press, 1997), 132; Louise Jackson, 'Witches, Wives and Mothers: Witchcraft Persecution and Women's Confessions in Seventeenth-Century England', *Women's History Review*, 4.1 (1995): 63–83, esp. 72.

[3] Malcolm Gaskill, 'The Devil in the Shape of a Man: Witchcraft, Conflict and Belief in Jacobean England', *Historical Research*, 71 (1998): 142–71; see also Deborah Willis, 'The Witch-Family in

The habitual naming of married suspects as 'so and so's wife' is a reminder that, when a married woman was accused of witchcraft, her husband was always under scrutiny as well even if he did not end up being prosecuted himself. My goal here is not to demonstrate that there were married witches (there were) or to make qualitative or quantative arguments about their significance relative to other witches. I am interested, instead, in how the witch wife, standing at one of the many crossroads of law and literature, condenses and expresses concerns about what all wives want and what kinds of bargains wives would make if they could. In the witch wife, we can see the embodiment of wishes that can change the world, of fantasies that materialize. Lurking behind the extraordinary stories of demon lovers and efficacious maleficia lie very ordinary concerns about the inscrutable yet industrious interiority of women, especially wives.

Before turning to works explicitly about witchcraft, I want to consider how concern with wives' opaque interiority, mal-efficient wishes, and ability to conjure possibility informs advice on marriage. Many writers of marital advice counsel husbands not to domineer over their wives or hold them in subjection through fear or force but rather to recruit their wives' good will. While such advice has often been read as evidence of reciprocity and companionship in early modern marriage or of the rising prestige of romantic love, I want to emphasize its instrumentality. Harnessing one's wife's regard is strategic. Even as they advise husbands not to provoke fear in their wives, conduct books themselves assume or instil a particular kind of fear in husbands—fear of what their wives might be thinking. In a passage from John Dod and Robert Cleaver's conduct book, *A Godly Forme of Houshold Government* (a passage to which, I confess, I have often returned), they argue that:

> the husband that is not beloved of his wife, holdeth his goods in danger, his house in suspition, his credit in ballance, and also sometimes his life in perill: because it is easie to beleeve that shee desireth not long life unto her husband, with whom she passeth a time so tedious and irksome.[4]

A husband can only sleep soundly if he has done all he could to prevent his wife from despising him in her heart or plotting his demise. As part of his argument against marriage, Roland du Jardin warns his male readers that 'the first night that thy wife shall enter into thy marriage bed, she will beginne to hope for thy death'.[5] In a text with a rather different purpose, William Gouge's hefty and earnest *Of Domesticall Duties*, Gouge makes explicit the possibility that wishes lead to or become deeds. He argues that one effect of adultery is that 'By it husbands and wives are stirred up to wish, and long after one anothers death: and not only inwardly in heart to wish it, but outwardly also

Elizabethan and Jacobean Print Culture', *Journal of Early Modern Cultural Studies*, 13.1 (Winter, 2013): 4–31.

4 John Dod and Robert Cleaver, *A Godly Forme of Houshold Government* (London: 1630), sigs K2^{v}, L3.

5 Roland du Jardin, *A Discourse of the Married and Single Life. Wherein, By Discovering the Misery of the One, is Plainely Declared the Felicity of the Other* (London: 1621), sigs H8–H8^{v}.

in deed to practise it'. Gouge warns that, even when wishes do not become practices, wishes mire one in a kind of devil's bargain by stirring up God's mischievous side. Gouge warns those who wish their spouse dead that:

> sometimes according to their wish [God] taketh away good husbands and wives from those that are evill: and when they are gone he maketh their losse to be so sensibly felt, as those ungodly wishers doe, (as we speake) in every veine of their heart repent them of their rash wishes. Yea, to aggravate their wretchednesse the more, he giveth them such crabbed and perverse husbands and wives in the roome and stead of those good ones (for seldome comes a better) as they are forced in many deepe sighs and groanes to wish (but all in vaine) their former wives and husbands alive againe, and so to verifie the proverbe, *A good thing is not so well discerned by enjoying, as by wanting it.*[6]

Variants of the word 'wish' appear four times in this passage. Wish operates as verb and noun; Gouge characterizes the spouses he conjures as 'ungodly wishers' who end up wishing (but in vain) that they had not rashly wished in the first place. Wishing one's dead spouse alive again is as big a problem as wishing one's living spouse dead. Gouge advises widows and widowers that they must not remarry unless they can transfer their affection to a new spouse and refrain from talking about and idealizing the dead. To do so, he suggests, is a kind of necromancy.

> But as the vertue of a person deceased may not be buried with the dead corps: so neither may the person be kept above ground with the memorie of his or her vertue: which after a sort is done, when love of the partie deceased either taketh away, or extenuateth the love of the living. This is to give dominion to the dead over the living: which is more then the law enjoyneth (Q2).

In these passages, Gouge suggests that both husbands and wives might wish themselves into the dangerous territory of the occult and that their wishes might be effective and thereby exceed the law, scriptural and common.

Ungodly wishing lies at the centre of witchcraft statutes as well. Neither capturing nor shaping belief in any simple way, witchcraft statutes set forth a powerful story with life and death consequences, one that changed over time. Luke Wilson makes a cautious but provocative suggestion about the 1604 statute that has not yet been taken up by historians of witchcraft or of women. Distinguishing itself from earlier statutes, this one emphasized demonic compacts, prohibiting any person or persons to 'use practise or exercise any invocation or conjuration of any evil and wicked spirit, or … consult, convenant with, entertain, employ, feed, or reward any evil and wicked spirit to or for any intent or purpose'. It also criminalizes the 'intent' to provoke unlawful love, damage property, or cause bodily injury or death 'although the same be not effected and

[6] William Gouge, *Of Domesticall Duties* (London: 1622), sigs P6^{v}, Q7–Q7^{v}.

done'.[7] Historians have argued that it did so in response to continental witchlore, with its emphasis on diabolical compacts, as well as the desire for material evidence that, Keith Thomas argues, subtended the obsession with a devil's compact in the seventeenth century.[8] Wilson argues that the statute might also bear a relationship to 'the emergence of contract in the first few years of the seventeenth century as a topic of particular legal and popular interest'.[9] Wilson suggests that in witchcraft statutes 'the common-law identification of conjuration with compulsion represses a contrary contractual etymology' that assigns agency to witch and devil alike.[10] This 'latent contractualism' emerges in explicit terms in the 1604 statute, which casts witches as 'doing business with demons, entering into bilateral exchange relationships with them'. Wilson concludes that while 'these alterations had little practical impact on witchcraft prosecutions themselves, or on popular mythology, they nevertheless significantly reconceptualized the legal situation of the witch'. Perhaps they also registered an ongoing reconceptualization of the wife's situation. According to Wilson, 'The abrupt statutory contractualization of the (usually female) witch's relation with the devil in 1604 served contradictory functions, at once inculpating her as full partner in a voluntary transaction and allowing her an executive authority not elsewhere readily available to her' as well as defining her by her competence more than her gender.[11] Assigning women agency only so as to incriminate them is a familiar move. But positioning the witch as the devil's partner makes witchcraft prosecutions and the stories they churn up a kind of testing ground for the idea of marriage as a contract, an idea that, arguably, is not yet fully realized.[12] Building on Wilson's suggestion, I here focus on how representations of witchcraft posit the witch wife as a wisher, a willer, a pledger, and a plotter, thereby exploring new possibilities for and old fears about what women want and what they will do to get it.

[7] 1 Jac. I, c. 12 (1604), *Statutes of the Realm*, vol. 4, pt 2, 1028. This statute remained on the books until 1736.

[8] Thomas, *Religion and the Decline of Magic*, 442–4, 575. Thomas argues that 'stricter standards of proof, based primarily upon evidence of compact' followed the 1604 statute. 'What they now wanted was sworn evidence that the witch kept a familiar or bore the devil's mark on her person; most decisive of all, they hoped for her free confession that she had entered into a pact with Satan' (575). Paradoxically, these stricter standards of proof led to a higher acquittal rate.

[9] Luke Wilson, *Theaters of Intention: Drama and the Law in Early Modern England* (Stanford: Stanford University Press, 2000), 185.

[10] Wilson, *Theaters of Intention*, 189–90.

[11] Wilson, *Theaters of Intention*, 186, 193.

[12] In *Wayward Contracts: The Crisis of Political Obligation in England, 1640–1674* (Princeton: Princeton University Press, 2004), Victoria Kahn shows that it was possible to imagine marriage as a contract in the early modern period, although not really one between equals (171–95). On how the social order depends on women's wills and willing submission, see Kathryn Schwarz, *What You Will: Gender, Contract, and Shakespearean Social Space* (Philadelphia: University of Pennsylvania Press, 2011). See also Craig Muldrew, '"A Mutual Assent of Her Mind"? Women, Debt, Litigation and Contract in Early Modern England', *HWJ*, 55 (2003): 47–71. Many feminists challenge the assumption that viewing marriage as a contract necessarily entails viewing spouses as equal parties to that contract. See, for example, Wendy Brown, *States of Injury: Power and Freedom in Late Modernity* (Princeton University Press, 1995), 135–65.

I rely on the numerous pamphlet accounts of witchcraft that both literary critics and historians interested in witchcraft must share as their primary body of evidence.[13] These pamphlets usefully blur the distinction between law and literature since we can only seldom reach outside or prior to them for other records of a given case. Although they are often the fullest accounts of legal proceedings available to us, they yet commit themselves to emphases, erasures, and reorganizations driven by the imperative to tell an engaging story (more than recount a sequence of events or explain legal procedures with strict accuracy). My interest here is in how such stories, played out on page and on stage, explored the problem of the wife's imagination and volition, among the many other things that they accomplished.

'Whatsoever She Wished Came to Pass': The Witch's Ill Wish

One might expect to find witch and wife conjoined in the wife who uses witchcraft to gain the upperhand over her husband or just to get rid of him. Given that witchcraft registered as felony when it resulted in murder, one might expect an overlap between witchcraft and that other gendered subset of murder, petty treason, or the killing of one's husband (or master).[14] Some students of witchcraft have assumed such a connection. Alan R. Young, for instance, claims that 'The supposed betwitching of a husband is not uncommon, though there are no actual court indictments for this offence in the Elizabethan period.'[15] Without indictments, what would be the evidence that this charge was 'not uncommon'? In 1566, what has been called the first witchcraft pamphlet recounts that one Mother Waterhouse 'confessed, that because she lyved somwhat unquietly with her husbande she caused sathan to kyll him, and he did so about ix yeres past, syth which tyme she hath lyved a widow'.[16] Eighty years later, another pamphlet claims of Mother Lakeland that 'Her husband she bewitched (as she confessed) whereby

[13] Frances E. Dolan, *True Relations: Reading, Literature, and Evidence in Seventeenth-Century England* (Philadelphia: University of Pennsylvania Press, 2013), 52–86. See also Anna Bayman, '"Large Hands, Wide Eares, and Piercing Sights": The "Discoveries" of the Elizabethan and Jacobean Witch Pamphlets', *Literature and History*, 16.1 (2007): 26–45; Marion Gibson, *Reading Witchcraft: Stories of Early English Witches* (London: Routledge, 1999).

[14] On petty treason, see Frances E. Dolan, *Marriage and Violence: The Early Modern Legacy* (Philadelphia: University of Pennsylvania Press, 2008), 67–96; and 'Tracking the Petty Traitor across Genres', *Ballads and Broadsides in Britain, 1500–1800*, ed. Patricia Fumerton and Anita Guerrini (Burlington: Ashgate Press, 2010), 149–71.

[15] Alan R. Young. 'Elizabeth Lowys: Witch and Social Victim, 1564', *History Today*, 22 (December, 1972): 879–85, esp. 879.

[16] *The Examination and Confession of certaine Wytches at Chensforde in the Countie of Essex* (1566), sigs Bi^{v}–Bii^{r}. Gibson includes this text and identifies it as the first in *Early Modern Witches: Witchcraft Cases in Contemporary Writing* (London: Routledge, 2000), 10–24.

he lay in great misery for a time, and at last dyed.' She was 'burned to death, because she was the death of her husband, as she confessed.'[17] In other words, while those convicted of witchcraft in England were hanged, rather than burned as is commonly thought, Mother Lakeland in this instance received a petty traitor's sentence of burning at the stake.[18] Her status as wife trumped her status as witch, determining her punishment. Spectacular and gruesome, that punishment, which links the petty traitor to the heretic, suggests that domestic treason is an even more heinous offense than witchcraft.

Witchfinders Matthew Hopkins and John Stearne cast one of the many women against whom they built cases as a petty traitor. Two seasoned witnesses accused Susanna Stegold in Hintlesham of practising her powers or 'trying her skill' on a pig and then graduating from that to killing her husband. John Easte testified:

> her husband beinge a bad husband she wished he might depart from her meaneinge as she said that he shold die and presently after he died mad.... but beinge asked whither she bewitched him to dead or noe, and said she wished ill wishes to him and what so ever she wished came to pas.[19]

While Easte's statement does not tell us anything reliable about what Stegold said or felt or believed she had done, it tells an arresting story about the terrifying power that might be assigned to a wife's ill wish by Hopkins and Stearne's efficient machine for generating prosecutions. If the wish is something any wife might be feared to harbour, it's the witch's power that turns the wish into a weapon. In Easte's account, Stegold wished her greedy pig might never eat again and it died; she wished her husband might depart from her and he went—first mad and then to the grave. While some sceptics, beginning with Scot, took the witch's belief in the effectiveness of her wishes as evidence, in itself, of her delusion, the prospect of the effective ill wish animated the statute's emphasis on intentions as well as many popular accounts of trials.[20]

Like the witchfinders Hopkins and Stearne, and their dependable repeat witnesses, scholars are particularly apt to conjure up the unexpressed motives and desires of wives

[17] *The Lawes against WITCHES, and CONJURATION ... Also, the Confession of Mother Lakeland* (London: 1645), 7–8.

[18] Malcolm Gaskill points out that, although 'almost every witch convicted in England since 1563 had been hanged', even contemporaries 'muddled' witches' executions with the burning of heretics—and petty traitors—so that the burning of witches quickly hardened into 'indelible myth', persisting to this day; Malcolm Gaskill, *Witchfinders: A Seventeenth-Century Tragedy* (Cambridge: Harvard University Press, 2005), 173–4. Gaskill also offers a detailed discussion of Mother Lakeland's case, 174–9.

[19] C. L'Estrange Ewen, *Witch Hunting and Witch Trials: The Indictments for Witchcraft from the Records of 1373 Assizes Held for the Home Circuit, 1559–1736* (London: K. Paul, 1929), 298. Both Richard Glanfield and John Easte testified as to what Stegold had told them. Gaskill identifies Glanfield as a 'watcher' who 'testified against all the Hintlesham witches and participated in the interrogations at Chattisham' (Gaskill, *Witchfinders*, 102). Easte testified against another accused witch in Hintlesham, Susan Marchant.

[20] Reginald Scot, *The Discoverie of Witchcraft* (London: 1584), Book I, iii. Thomas cites the 1667 case of Ursula Clarke who claimed that 'she had never wished nor cursed anything in her life but it came to pass' (Thomas, *Religion*, 523).

and witches. In her widely cited study of witches' confessions, Louise Jackson takes Easte's second-hand statement as granting access not only to what Stegold said but also to the experiences and feelings that might have motivated her. Jackson speculates that 'she may well have been beaten or ill-treated'. For Jackson, Susanna's 'confession' and apparent belief in the devil seem 'to have been a way of coping with guilt or hiding the emotional trauma'.[21] Of the accused witch Anne Bodenham, to whom I will return below, Diane Purkiss goes so far as to claim that she 'got some pleasure and satisfaction from her self-fashioning as witch even if it also killed her'.[22] Jackson and Purkiss, like many others, describe the accused's confessions as both unreliable and irresistible, evidence of their interrogators' desires as much as the accused's own, yet, at the same time, the only evidence we have of subjectivities that should not be reduced to delusion, deceit, or victimization. At a moment of extreme powerlessness, the accused might have threatened or dreamed that their wishes had the power to make mischief in the world. But we can't know. To join the project of conjuring up the accused's feelings is to join Hopkins and Stearne, elaborating on inculpatory stories about what wives wish and why.

The Witch's Will

In some accounts of married women accused of witchcraft, the husband's appearances indicate both uncertainty surrounding a witch wife's autonomy and the contested nature of a husband's authority once his wife has fallen under suspicion. *The Most Strange and Admirable Discoverie of the Three Witches of Warboys Arraigned, Convicted and Executed at the Last Assises at Huntington* (London: 1593), for example, presents a complicated picture of a husband attempting to stand between his wife, Alice or Mother Samuel, and those busily attempting to entrap her into confession. This case preceded the 1604 witchcraft statute, although Mother Samuel supposedly confessed that she had 'forsaken my maker, and given my soule to the divel' and, according to Marion Gibson, came 'as close as any English account of this period to a confession of sex with the devil'.[23] Focusing on a suspect who is both defiant and bewildered, the pamphlet combines a narrative of a wife's disorderliness (from her family's point of view) with a narrative of a witch's problematic recalcitrance (from her accusers' point of view). From both perspectives, the text presents the accused's attempts to strike her own bargains and please her various constituencies as a problem. The Warboys case centres on the alleged possession of five young girls in the Throckmorton family (and various maidservants as well). According to this detailed pamphlet, the Throckmorton family employed various tactics to demonstrate that Mother Samuel was responsible for the possessions and to secure a confession from

[21] Jackson, 'Witches, Wives and Mothers', 73, 74.

[22] Diane Purkiss, *The Witch in History: Early Modern and Twentieth-Century Representations* (London: Routledge, 1996), 145, 170.

[23] Gibson, *Reading Witchcraft*, 125, refering to sigs $O2^v$–O^v.

her. First Henry Pickering, the possessed girls' uncle and 'then a scholar of Cambridge', tried to separate her from her husband, lying in wait for her with several of his friends. When they saw her leave her house, 'they determined rather to follow her whither she went than stay her return, because her husband was a froward man and would not suffer her to talk with any if he might know it' (255).[24] When the amateur investigators managed to waylay her, she got away by claiming fear of her husband: 'In the end she would needs be gone, saying that her husband would beat her for her long tarrying' (255).

Master Throckmorton, the girls' father, next contrived to get John Samuel to let him have Alice stay in his house because only her presence alleviated the children's symptoms: 'he offered very largely for it; which was to allow him (if it came to ten pounds in the year) for the board and wages of the best servant in Huntingdonshire to do his business, if he would, in her stead'. In other words, Throckmorton offered to pay for a kind of substitute wife for John Samuel; he also attempted to appease Samuel's sense of responsibility for his wife by claiming that, although he proposed to take her away, he would not treat her ill. When John Samuel refused, Throckmorton arrived with all his afflicted daughters and threatened to billet them on the Samuels (although he did propose to provide for their necessities). Samuel, in response, put out the fire and threatened to starve the girls. But by night-time, Throckmorton wore Samuel down and he agreed to allow his wife to stay with the Throckmortons. According to the pamphlet, John Samuel almost outwitted Throckmorton by getting his wife out of town before she could be moved to the Throckmorton house, but then she returned and confessed the scheme, at which point 'he utterly forswore the matter, and presently fell upon his wife and beat her very sore with a cudgel—many being present—before she could be rescued by them' (263). Several times, Alice confesses and then recants that confession, usually when she has gotten away from the Throckmortons and spent time with her husband and daughter. Perhaps this is why the writer feels compelled to counter the rumour that 'this Mother Samuel now in question was an old simple woman, and that one might make her by fair words confess what they would'. Finally, advised that she has confessed once again, John Samuel would have struck her 'had not others stood betwixt them' (279). This remarkably detailed account lays out the story as one in which John and his daughter Agnes Samuel interfere in the process of discovering witchcraft and securing a confession. References to their violence serve to incriminate them as disorderly and to position Alice as both the chief witch and a pathetic or sympathetic figure. But the way the story is told also suggests that once the Throckmortons fasten upon Alice, she is no longer a wife, or at least, their claims on her overrule her husband's.

Mother Samuel's expressed concern that her husband will beat her if she does not return home and then witnesses' accounts that he did beat her 'very sore' reinforce the association between wife and witch, reminding us that Alice Samuel is married by making her husband the villain of the piece. Yet the pamphlet also suggests that once

[24] An excerpted version of this pamphlet can be found in *Witchcraft in England, 1558–1618*, ed. Barbara Rosen (Amherst: University of Massachusetts Press, 1991), 239–97. Page numbers in the text are from Rosen's edition. On this pamphlet, see Gibson, *Reading Witchcraft*, 104–9, 120–6.

suspicion attaches to Alice, she is no longer exactly 'Samuel's wife'. According to this account, John Samuel was an abusive husband. But his eruptions of violence all occur when he tries to assert his own prerogative against incursions by higher-status men and to prevent his wife from incriminating herself, him, and their daughter. Throughout, the account suggests that John Samuel and his daughter Agnes try to control Alice and to defy the Throckmortons. The possessed girls lecture Alice on her 'naughty manner of living' and 'her lewd bringing up of her daughter, in suffering her to be her dame, both in controlling of her and beating of her' (269, G3^{v}). But, of course, it is these young girls who control her and her fate. As Marion Gibson argues, the pamphlet writer's 'unusual interest in the marital discord of the Samuels ... and what goes on inside their house in private ... highlights' the parallels between the two disordered families, the Throckmortons and the Samuels.[25] Rather than disorderliness leading to the suspicion or accusation of witchcraft, here the suspicion produced or exacerbated conflict between Alice Samuel and her husband and daughter and pulled her out of the marital household. She was certainly an irrepressible speaker, both depended upon to confess and chided for being loud and for not allowing anyone else to talk. She insisted that she 'must have her will'. But even if she defied authority in some ways, she bowed to it in others. The statuses of wife and witch both subordinate Alice, subjecting her to various forms of abuse, and provoking her resistance. But these statuses also conflict as the contests over where Alice Samuel is and whose she is attest. John Samuel counters the Throckmorton's assertion that she is their witch with his own insistence, however violent, that she is his wife, and a bad one. His failure to keep her in his house or under his control ultimately proved fatal to the whole family, all three of whom were executed.[26] On the pressing question of who or what Alice Samuel is, John remains if anything less certain than her accusers, at least according to their account. He simply could not predict or control his wife.

That fatal failure suggests the appeal of occult access to information about one's spouse. For example, John Lambe, the Duke of Buckingham's notorious physician/advisor, whose murder by a mob presaged the Duke's similar fate, offered his clients such access.[27] *A Briefe Description of the Notorious Life of John Lambe* describes him as turning from physic to:

> other mysteries, as telling of Fortunes, helping of diverse to lost goods, shew-to young people the faces of their Husbands or Wives, that should be, in a Christall

[25] Gibson, *Reading Witchcraft*, 106.

[26] In the end the whole family was executed and their goods went to Sir Henry Cromwell, husband of Lady Cromwell, whom Alice was accused of bewitching to death (Rosen, 297 n. 59; Gaskill, *Witchfinders*, 204). In other pamphlets, too, accused womens' husbands try to protect or defend their wives. A case appended to Thomas Potts' lengthy discussion of *The Wonderfull Discovery of Witches in Lancashire* (1612) censures Jennet Preston's husband for claiming she was innocent and had been 'maliciously prosecuted' (sig. X4^{v}).

[27] On this fascinating case, see Frances E. Dolan, 'Reading, Writing, and Other Crimes', in *Feminist Readings of Early Modern Culture: Emerging Subjects*, ed. Valerie Traub, M. Lindsay Kaplan, and Dympna Callaghan (Cambridge: Cambridge University Press, 1996), 142–67; Purkiss, *Witch in History*, 147–53; and Malcolm Gaskill, 'Witchcraft, Politics, and Memory in Seventeenth-Century England', *HJ*, 50.2 (2007): 289–308.

> glasse: revealing to wives the escapes and faults of their Husbands, and to husbands of their wives. By which meanes, whether truly or falsely told, he wrought so much upon their credulity, that many mischiefs and divisions were wrought betweene marryed people.[28]

In this account, while young people long to discover their future spouses' identities, once married they are just as interested in the mystery of what their spouses are up to. The motive that drives customers to the cunningman shifts from faces to 'escapes and faults', from appearances to the unseen. Either way, marriage looms large among the mysteries Lambe helps customers navigate. The pamphlet suggests that it does not matter whether the intelligence he offered was 'truly or falsely told'. In either case, access to 'escapes and faults' works 'mischiefs and divisions' between married people. The idea of the conjurer or cunningman as a guide to predicting and then tracking one's spouse pops up in other kinds of texts as well. In Jonson's *Epicene*, for example, Truewit warns Morose off marriage by advising that whoever he marries, she will go 'in disguise to that conjurer and this cunning woman, where the first question is, how soon you shall die? Next, if her present servant love her?' (2.2.93–5). Whether instructing or delighting, securing death or provoking laughter, whether in pamphlets proclaiming their fidelity to legal process or in comedies, early modern texts register the suspicion that what your spouse really wants to know is how soon you will die. As Young Chartley remarks ruefully in Heywood's *Wise Woman of Hodgdon*, without access to divorce, 'this "Till death us do part" is tedious' (3.2.288).[29] One needs at least an enchanted glass to envision an end if not magical means of hurrying it on.

Another witch wife, Anne Bodenham, often called Doctor Lambe's student, had her own conjuring glass. According to the fullest account of her case, Edmond Bower's *Doctor Lamb Revived*, those who ultimately accused her first came to her door with inquiries into lost objects, not-yet-found loves, and the occult actions and motives of family members. But Bodenham's crystal ball does not make her own interiority any less troublesome than Alice Samuel's. Bodenham's husband makes three appearances in this pamphlet. First, Bodenham expresses her regret at finding herself accused of witchcraft in terms of its effect on her husband: 'twill break my Husbands heart, he grieves to see me in these Irons: I did once live in good fashion, and did not lie as now I doe' (E3^{v}).[30] Her husband's grief and her own dismay merge into one. Next, she evades Bower's demand for a book that will document contracts with the devil with signatures in blood—a fantasy of incontrovertible evidence of demonic pacts—by claiming that she hid it from her husband (E1^{v}). After she's convicted, her husband makes his

[28] *A Briefe Description of the Notorious Life of John Lambe, otherwise called Doctor Lambe* (Amsterdam: 1628), 2.

[29] *CWBJ*, 3.414. Thomas Heywood, *Wise Woman of Hogsdon* in *Thomas Heywood*, ed. A. Wilson Verity (New York: Scribner's, 1890).

[30] Edmond Bower, *Doctor Lamb Revived, or, Witchcraft Condemn'd in Anne Bodenham, A Servant of His* (London: 1653). See also James Bower, cleric, *Doctor Lamb's Darling: Or, Strange and Terrible News from Salisbury* (1653), which Gaskill describes as 'a derivative, more sensationalist account' ('Witchcraft, Politics', 292).

third appearance in Bower's text. This time it is Bower who brings him up as a check on Bodenham's will.

> And she said, she had made her Will, and given Legacies to many of her friends. But I told her, her Husband might choose whether he would let them have them: she replyed, If he doe not, the Devill shall never let him be quiet. (F1^{v})

This passage is often read as evidence of the gendered disorder witchcraft unleashed. Malcolm Gaskill, for instance, argues that Bodenham's reply to Bower 'was a challenge to male supremacy bordering on treason'.[31] I once wrote that 'Having denied throughout any alliance with the devil, Bodenham invokes him at last to help her outwit the legal and social restrictions on a married woman's autonomy; she acts like a witch when reminded that she is a wife.'[32] Here, I want to emphasize that Bower insists on Bodenham's contracts—with her customers, with the devil, with those she recruits into witchcraft, and with her husband—even as he chides her for presuming to make a will and to dictate conditions to her husband.

The Demon Husband

Witchfinders Hopkins and Stearne seem especially interested in one perspective on the witch wife: her imagined desire for a demon husband. According to Stearne, the Devil preys on the vulnerable, such as the bereaved and impoverished, who 'would have their wants satisfied and their desires fulfilled, be it by what means it possible can be'.[33] But what were their wants and desires? Many students of witchcraft, understandably, emphasize sexual fantasy and guilt.[34] The details of congress with the devil have been much discussed—the devil is like a man but not exactly; he is consistent but cold. While the (often second-hand) confessions Stearne and Hopkins extract describe sex with demons, the witnesses, usually not the accused themselves, never claim that what the witches sought was sex. Instead, they claim that they sought 'an Husband, who should maintaine her ever after'.[35] As Keith Thomas points out, 'what is pathetic about most of these temptations is that the bait was so small'.[36] Stearne's account of Thomazine

31 Gaskill, 'Witchcraft, Politics', 305.

32 Dolan, 'Reading, Writing', 156.

33 John Stearne, *A Confirmation and Discovery of Witch-Craft* (London: 1648), sig. B2^{r}.

34 Walter Stephens, *Demon Lovers: Witchcraft, Sex, and the Crisis of Belief* (Chicago: University of Chicago Press, 2002); Lyndal Roper, *Witchcraze: Terror and Fantasy in Baroque Germany* (New Haven and London: Yale University Press, 2004), 82–103.

35 *A True and Exact Relation of the Severall Informations, Examinations, and Confessions of the Late Witches, Arraigned and Executed in the County of Essex* (London: 1645), sigs A3–A3^{v}. On Clarke, see Gaskill, *Witchfinders*, 48–54. On the relation of Hopkins and Stearne to changing standards of evidence, see Gaskill, 'Witchcraft and Evidence in Early Modern England', *P&P* 198 (February, 2008): 33–70.

36 Thomas, *Religion*, 520.

Ratcliffe casts the demon as a substitute husband, who appeared to her shortly after her husband's death, 'in the shape of her husband', speaking 'in the voyvce of her husband' and 'told her, he would be a loving husband to her, if she would consent to him, which she said, she did, and then he told her, he would revenge her of all her enemies, and that she should never misse any thing, in which she said, she found him a lyer'.[37] Do these fantasies of what a widow might want from a new husband, demon or man, warn that the demon husband won't follow through? Or is this a reflection on the job description of husband embedded in the inculpatory fantasy of what witch wives want but don't get?

Hopkins testifies that Rebecca Weste told him that the Devil married her by taking her by the hand, leading her about her chamber, and promising 'to be her loving husband till death, and so avenge her of her enemies'. She, in turn, 'promised him to be his obedient wife till death, and to deny God and Christ Jesus', and then sent him to kill her enemy's son, 'which he did within one fortnight; and that after that shee tooke him for her God, and thought he could doe as God'.[38] Conflating husband, devil, and God, lackey and idol, Hopkins's account of this demon marriage stresses Weste's role in taking the devil's hand—that is, agreeing to marry him—as much as her responsibility for murder.

Hopkins and Stearne collect many similar testimonies, arguing that the stories resemble one another because they are true. For many students of witchcraft, the confessions capture some truth not only about the interrogators' fantasies but about those of the accused. As Gaskill, for instance, writes:

> Sometimes there was a sexual edge to the questions posed by the witchfinders, but the stories they took away amounted to more than the fulfilment of their own repressed fantasies. In the confessions of these women could be heard the lament of age for vanished youth, yearning for intimacy and kindness, indulgence in heart-fluttering seduction and abandon.[39]

Perhaps. But the testimonies Hopkins and Stearne generate focus not on romance as much as on sustenance, protection, and revenge. Whoever might be the source of the fantasies they record, those fantasies focus not on demon lovers but on demon husbands, not on seduction but on bargains, quasi-marital exchanges in which women offer sex in exchange for protection and are disappointed.

The Witch Wife on Stage

I want to conclude by drawing attention to two plays that focus explicitly on the husband's perception of his wife as a witch. In one case, Jonson's *The Devil Is an Ass*, the

[37] Thomazine's midnight negotiations with her apparent husband survive to us in two statements from other people, John Stearne and Abigail Briggs. See Stearne, *A Confirmation*, sig. D2^{v}; Ewen, 300.

[38] *A True and Exact Relation ... Essex*, sigs B3^{v}–B4^{r}. On Weste, see also Stearne, *Confirmation*, sig. F2^{v}.

[39] Gaskill, *Witchfinders*, 113.

husband, Fitzdottrel, falsely accuses his wife of bewitching him in a gambit to eliminate her (and thereby wrest control of their property back from her). In another, Heywood and Brome's *The Late Lancashire Witches*, the husband, Master Generous, resists the evidence that his wife of many years is a witch. Mistress Fitzdottrel is falsely accused. Mistress Generous, the play suggests, is actually a witch. But both plays create more room for scepticism about witchcraft charges than one generally finds in pamphlet accounts. Furthermore, the two plays, performed twenty years apart, present mirror views of the disturbing overlap of wife and witch.

In Jonson's *The Devil Is an Ass* (1616), Fitzdottrel pretends to be bewitched by his wife as the final skirmish in a years' long conflict regarding control of their property. According to Mrs Fitzdottrell, marriage has compromised her control of her fortune; she cannot stop her husband from squandering it on clothes and speculation. 'The wealthy portion that I bought him, spent; / And through my friends' neglect no jointure made me' (4.6.22–3).[40] Ultimately, however, she gains the upper hand through a complicated series of manoeuvres by which Fitzdottrel, through a 'deed of feoffment' (which is explained further at 4.6.43–6), confers control of his property on Manly, while Wittipol claims he will keep the deed 'for your wife's good, / Who will know better how to use it' (4.7.68–9). Fitzdottrel could not have conferred his property directly on his wife in this way. The 'Conglutination of persons' in marriage, *The Lawes Resolutions of Women's Rights* explains, 'forbiddeth all manner of feoffing or giving by the one unto the other, for a man cannot give any thing to himselfe'.[41] So the plot depends on the logic of coverture to outwit coverture.[42] Fitzdottrel fears he has become: 'my wife's ward; / Likely to lose my land, ha' my throat cut— / All by her practice!' (4.7.78–80). As so often, the husband imagines that the wife's empowerment will slide into murder. To be her ward is to be marked for death. To reverse the situation, Merecraft advises him to feign demonic possession, basing his performance on those described in pamphlets about notorious cases. Everill quickly leaps from witchcraft to the claim that she 'practised with those two [Manly and Wittipol] as sorcerers' and gave him 'potions, by which means you were / Not *compos mentis* when you made your feoffment' (5.3.10–12). The play depends upon an audience's knowledge of the legal status of a wife with regard to deeds of feoffment and jointures and of what can pass as proof in possession cases. Merecraft proposes witchcraft as a cover story, a way of redressing Fitzdottrel's disenfranchisement that occludes his own foolishness (acknowledging that he was *non compos mentis*) and makes the conspiracy he suspects—'A plot o'your wife's to get your land'—into a felony for which she might hang (5.3.1–16). And it almost works because it is so plausible,[43] not because Fitzdotterel knows how to perform demonic possession but because the idea of a plotting witch wife

40 *CWBJ*, 4.583. Further references to this edition in the text.

41 T. E., *The Lawes Resolutions of Womens Rights: OR, The Lawes Provision for Woemen* (London: 1632), sig. I4^{v}.

42 On coverture, see also Tim Stretton's chapter in this volume.

43 Lorna Hutson, '"I Will Conclude / Out of the Circumstances": Proof and Probability in *The Devil is an Ass*', *Les Usages de la preuve d'Henri Estienne à Jérémy Bentham*, ed. N. Vienne-Guerrin and J. P. Schandeler (Paris: Hermann, 2014), 119–36, esp. 135.

is so conventional. Sir Paul Eitherside, a 'lawyer and Justice' thinks 'The proofs are pregnant' (5.8.77). Mrs Fitzdottrel is left with nothing to say through this denouement. Her last words in the play are 'Fie, Master Fitzdottrell! / What do you mean to counterfeit thus?' (5.8.47–8).[44] Rather abruptly, Fitzdottrel abandons the counterfeiting, although he insists that Manly and Wittipol 'are cozeners still, / And ha' my land, as plotters with my wife— / Who, though she be not a witch, is worse: a whore!' (5.8.148–50). Manly defends her, telling Sir Paul that Fitzdottrel has imposed a 'misconstruction' on his wife (and deceived Sir Paul as well) and that their own machinations sought only to succour Mrs Fitzdottrel, 'who hath an equal right', presumably with her husband (159–65). While Mrs Fitzdottrel risked conviction for witchcraft, the plot of *The Devil Is an Ass* rewards her with greater control over her property, even with the rather remarkable claim to an 'equal right' in it. Yet she achieves this control not because she schemed, as her husband suspected, but because she refused to betray her husband sexually and appealed to her would-be seducer (Wittipol) to help her as a friend. Having survived her association with the witch and the whore, the wife remains a contracter who has achieved her will, even if through others' machinations.

The tone of *The Late Lancashire Witches* (1634) is much less clear, in part because the play was based on an actual case. The accused had been convicted in Lancashire but when suspicion fell on their chief accuser, a boy, they were called up to London so the case could be reviewed. They were in jail awaiting the final verdict while the play was on the stage. The play thus defers judgement, even as it stages their antics as 'mirth' or 'sport'.[45] Mrs Generous is a long-married woman who turns to witchcraft as a way of slipping the traces of marital constraint and disporting herself with her gossips. After a night observing the 'gentle fashion' of sleeping apart in the summer, her husband, Master Generous, makes his customary early morning visit and finds that his wife has 'slept not in my house tonight' (4.1.1560).[46] He ruminates on their long history, his reluctance to succumb to distrust now 'in her age', and his worry that she has entered into a 'contract', not with Satan but with his groom (4.1.1561–4). Generous soon learns that witchcraft rather than adultery has drawn his wife from their bed. 'Thunderstruck' by her confession that she is a witch, he first asks her: 'Hast thou made any contract with that fiend, / The enemy of mankind?' (4.2.1694–5). She admits that she has. Lamenting that it would have been better had they burned together at the stake 'Then such a compact ever had bin made', he presses 'how farre doth that contract stretch?' (1706). She answers

> What interest in this Soule, my selfe coo'd claime
> I freely gave him, but his part that made it
> I still reserve, not being mine to give. (1707–9)

[44] On learning to counterfeit possession from books, see, among others, Sharpe, *Bewitching of Anne Gunter*, 8.

[45] For a summary of criticism on and debate about the play, see Dolan, *True Relations*, 79–84.

[46] Citations are to the Brome online octavo edition, edited by Helen Ostovich, <http://www.hrionline.ac.uk/brome/viewOriginal.jsp?play=LW&type=TEXT>. Subsequent parenthetical citations refer to this edition.

Although she convinces him of her penitence and he forgives her, ultimately he decides that he cannot countenance a witch wife. The Soldier presents him with the paw he has cut off of a cat and it is Mrs Generous's hand, bearing her wedding band. When Arthur asks 'know you the hand?' Generous replies 'yes and too well can reade it' exploiting the familiar metonomy of hand/handwriting (5.2350). Her nephew Whetstone expresses his hope that she will remember him in her will (2374–5) and continues the punning: 'Hath my Aunt been playing at handee dandee, nay then, / if the game goe this way, I feare she'l have the worst hand on't' (5.2415–16). 'Is this the hand once plighted holy vowes, / And this the ring that bound them?' Generous asks (2343–4). It is. But Generous insists on matching it to his wife's stump nonetheless. Circulating as a prop on stage, the witch wife's severed hand draws attention to her status as an agent who makes and breaks contracts. As we have seen, witchfinders Hopkins and Stearne describe the devil's compact not only as a marriage but explicitly as a covenant in which the witch wife gives her hand to the devil. Squire Generous probes the overlap essential to the witch wife: the same hand that plighted her troth to her husband, plights it to the devil. The second contract trumps the first. As she says after claiming to disown witchcraft at her husband's behest, 'once and ever a witch'. Mistress Generous gave her hand to another and now it is gone—but it is also present as an object detached from her and standing in evidence against her.

How is Generous to solve the problem of the witch wife? Vowing never to see his wife again, Generous announces 'I must deliver you / Into the hand of Justice' (2425–6). The accused who were waiting in a London jail at the time the play was in performance were ultimately acquitted, although they do not seem to have been released. In the play's epilogue, the playwrights align themselves with Master Generous, declining to compete with the processes of justice, referring the outcome 'to time', and insisting that they only 'represent as much / As they [the witches] have done before law's hand did touch upon their guilt'. The epilogue suggests that what the accused have done—their crime—is not in dispute. The question is only their punishment. As a whole, the play suggests both a popular fascination with an ongoing case and a disregard for having its legal issues explored on the stage. Yet it departs from the interest in the minutiae of legal proceeding we find so often in the drama, despite or because of its intimate relationship to an ongoing investigation. Whereas *The Devil Is an Ass* contemplates malicious proceeding and falsified evidence, *The Late Lancashire Witches* does not, even though it was the scepticism at the heart of Jonson's play that brought the accused to London and made their story news.

In one play, an asinine husband turns to the law to eliminate his wife so that he can better exploit their property—but fails. In the other, a 'generous' husband depends on the law as the only way to get a witch wife off his hands—with uncertain results. In both plays, suspicion of witchcraft attaches to the troubling figure of the wife who is free to make bargains with the devil. Squires Fitzdotterel and Generous both imagine their wives contracting at odds with their marriage vows. But neither does. Mrs Fitzdotterel honours her vows. Even though *The Late Lancashire Witches* presents Mrs Generous as, indeed, a witch, she seeks sport with her fellows, not her husband's destruction. In the witch wife, whom scholars have largely ignored, we find a figure whose wilfulness is at once central to her alleged witchcraft, integral to her ability to function as a wife and a subject under the law, and distressingly inscrutable. The witch wife's will can make things happen. But one would need a crystal ball to understand what motivates her or any wife.

Bibliography

Anon. *A Briefe Description of the Notorious Life of John Lambe, Otherwise Called Doctor Lambe. Together with His Ignominious Death* (Amsterdam: 1628).

Anon. *A True and Exact Relation of the Severall Informations, Examinations, and Confessions of the Late Witches, Arraigned and Executed in the County of Essex* (London: 1645).

Anon. *The Examination and Confession of Certaine Wytches at Chensforde in the Countie of Essex* (London: 1566).

Anon. *The Lawes against Witches, and Conjuration* [...] *Also, the Confession of Mother Lakeland, Who Was Arraigned and Condemned for a Witch, in Ipswich in Suffolke* (London: 1645).

Bayman, Anna. '"Large Hands, Wide Eares, and Piercing Sights": The "Discoveries" of the Elizabethan and Jacobean Witch Pamphlets', *Literature and History*, 16.1 (2007): 26–45.

Bower, Edmond. *Doctor Lamb Revived, or, Witchcraft Condemn'd in Anne Bodenham, a Servant of His* (London: 1653).

Brown, Wendy. *States of Injury: Power and Freedom in Late Modernity* (Princeton: Princeton University Press, 1995).

Clark, Stuart. *Thinking with Demons: The Idea of Witchcraft in Early Modern Europe* (Oxford: Oxford University Press, 1997).

Dod, John and Robert Cleaver. *A Godly Forme of Houshold Government* (London: 1630).

Dolan, Frances E. 'Reading, Writing, and Other Crimes', in *Feminist Readings of Early Modern Culture: Emerging Subjects*, ed. Valerie Traub, M. Lindsay Kaplan, and Dympna Callaghan (Cambridge: Cambridge University Press, 1996), 142–67.

Dolan, Frances E. *Marriage and Violence: The Early Modern Legacy* (Philadelphia: University of Pennsylvania Press, 2008).

Dolan, Frances E. 'Tracking the Petty Traitor across Genres', in *Ballads and Broadsides in Britain, 1500–1800*, ed. Patricia Fumerton and Anita Guerrini (Burlington: Ashgate, 2010), 149–71.

Dolan, Frances E. *True Relations: Reading, Literature, and Evidence in Seventeenth-Century England* (Philadelphia: University of Pennsylvania Press, 2013).

du Jardin, Roland. *A Discourse of the Married and Single Life. Wherein, by Discovering the Misery of the One, is Plainely Declared the Felicity of the Other* (London: 1621).

Edgar, Thomas. *The Lawes Resolutions of Womens Rights: Or, the Lawes Provision for Woemen* (London: 1632).

Ewen, C. L'Estrange. *Witch Hunting and Witch Trials: The Indictments for Witchcraft from the Records of 1373 Assizes Held for the Home Circuit, 1559–1736* (London: K. Paul, 1929).

Gaskill, Malcolm. 'The Devil in the Shape of a Man: Witchcraft, Conflict and Belief in Jacobean England', *Historical Research*, 71 (1998): 142–71.

Gaskill, Malcolm. *Witchfinders: A Seventeenth-Century Tragedy* (Cambridge, MA: Harvard University Press, 2005).

Gaskill, Malcolm. 'Witchcraft, Politics, and Memory in Seventeenth-Century England', *The Historical Journal*, 50.2 (2007): 289–308.

Gaskill, Malcolm. 'Witchcraft and Evidence in Early Modern England', *Past and Present*, 198 (February, 2008): 33–70.

Gibson, Marion. *Reading Witchcraft: Stories of Early English Witches* (London: Routledge, 1999).

Gibson, Marion. *Early Modern Witches: Witchcraft Cases in Contemporary Writing* (London: Routledge, 2000).

Gouge, William. *Of Domesticall Duties* (London: 1622).

Hutson, Lorna. '"I Will Conclude / Out of the Circumstances": Proof and Probability in "The Devil Is an Ass"', in *Les Usages de la Preuve d'Henri Estienne à Jérémy Bentham*, ed. N. Vienne-Guerrin and J. P. Schandeler (Paris: Hermann, 2014), 119–36.

Jackson, Louise. 'Witches, Wives and Mothers: Witchcraft Persecution and Women's Confessions in Seventeenth-Century England', *Women's History Review*, 4.1 (1995): 63–83.

Kahn, Victoria. *Wayward Contracts: The Crisis of Political Obligation in England, 1640–1674* (Princeton: Princeton University Press, 2004).

Muldrew, Craig. '"A Mutual Assent of Her Mind"? Women, Debt, Litigation, and Contract in Early Modern England', *History Workshop Journal*, 55 (2003): 47–71.

Potts, Thomas. *The Wonderfull Discovery of Witches in Lancashire* (London: 1612).

Purkiss, Diane. *The Witch in History: Early Modern and Twentieth-Century Representations* (London: Routledge, 1996).

Roper, Lyndal. *Witchcraze: Terror and Fantasy in Baroque Germany* (New Haven and London: Yale University Press, 2004).

Rosen, Barbara, ed. *Witchcraft in England, 1558–1618* (Amherst: University of Massachusetts Press, 1991).

Schwarz, Kathryn. *What You Will: Gender, Contract, and Shakespearean Social Space* (Philadelphia: University of Pennsylvania Press, 2011).

Scot, Reginald. *The Discoverie of Witchcraft* (London: 1584).

Sharpe, J. A. *Instruments of Darkness: Witchcraft in Early Modern England* (Philadelphia: University of Pennsylvania Press, 1997).

Sharpe, J. A. *The Bewitching of Anne Gunter* (New York: Routledge, 2000).

Stearne, John. *A Confirmation and Discovery of Witch-Craft* (London: 1648).

Stephens, Walter. *Demon Lovers: Witchcraft, Sex, and the Crisis of Belief* (Chicago: University of Chicago Press, 2002).

Thomas, Keith. *Religion and the Decline of Magic* (New York: Scribner's, 1971).

Willis, Deborah. 'The Witch-Family in Elizabethan and Jacobean Print Culture', *Journal of Early Modern Cultural Studies*, 13.1 (Winter, 2013): 4–31.

Wilson, Luke. *Theaters of Intention: Drama and the Law in Early Modern England* (Stanford: Stanford University Press, 2000).

Wilson Verity, A., ed. *Thomas Heywood* (New York: 1890).

Young, Alan R. 'Elizabeth Lowys: Witch and Social Victim, 1564', *History Today*, 22 (December, 1972): 879–85.

CHAPTER 24

CORPORATE PERSONS, BETWEEN LAW AND LITERATURE

HENRY S. TURNER

> They say miracles are past, and we have our philosophical persons to make modern and familiar things supernatural and causeless.
>
> (*All's Well That Ends Well*)[1]

Artificial Persons

> Persons are either natural or artificial. The only natural persons are men. The only artificial persons are corporations. Corporations are either aggregate or sole. This, I take it, would be an orthodox beginning for a chapter on the English Law of Persons, and such it would have been at any time since the days of Sir Edward Coke.[2]

So began the legal historian Frederic William Maitland in 'The Corporation Sole', an essay published more than a century ago, in 1900. But Maitland's comment still stands as an epigraph for our own moment, when the rights and powers of corporations have become the subject of intense public debate and no small amount of individual consternation. Originating in Roman law, extending across the medieval period to Coke,

[1] William Shakespeare, *All's Well That Ends Well*, ed. Susan Snyder, Oxford Worlds Classics (Oxford: Oxford University Press, 1993/1998 rpt), 2.3.1–3.

[2] F. W. Maitland, 'The Corporation Sole', *The Collected Papers of Frederic William Maitland*, ed. H. A. L. Fisher, 3 vols (Cambridge: Cambridge University Press, 1911), 3.210–43, 210. The arguments that follow extend those of Henry S. Turner, *The Corporate Commonwealth: Pluralism and Political Fictions in England, 1516–1651* (Chicago: University of Chicago Press, 2016).

Hobbes, and Blackstone, and from there to the American nineteenth century and the more recent *Citizens United* and *Hobby Lobby* decisions by the US Supreme Court, the corporation has always been with us. And yet we no longer recognize how great a variety of corporate groups once existed and how widely significant they were to early modern political life. Joint-stock companies, the most controversial form of corporation today, emerged as distinctive institutions only as of the 1550s, and they existed alongside other corporations of very different types, each of which acted as a group person distinct from the members who made it up. The nature of this peculiar group identity was, then as now, the subject of subtle technical arguments and even of metaphysical speculation; it unfolded in the law courts, as we might expect, but it also found a distinctively literary expression, not least because the corporation implied formal and imaginative problems that literary writers, and especially dramatists, were especially well equipped to address.

There are good reasons to begin any biography of the corporate person where Maitland begins: with Coke. For Coke's arguments, notably in *Calvin's Case* (1608) and the case of *Sutton's Hospital* (1612), succinctly illustrate the ways in which English common law sought to define the limits and capacities of corporate entities, approaching them at once as quasi-mystical bodies with metaphysical properties and as purely artificial, legal institutions created to suit a variety of specific purposes. At the same time, the cases also point up the limits of a purely legal history of the corporation and direct us toward its distinctively literary dimension: to the ways in which the law uses mimetic and rhetorical effects to call corporate persons into existence; to notions of fiction that have long lain at the heart of legal discussions of corporate personhood; and finally to underlying philosophical questions concerning the nature of group persons, as well as to the limits of our own current approaches to thinking about corporations as examples of collective life, collective action, and collective purpose.

At issue in both *Calvin's Case* and *Sutton's Hospital* were the two major types of corporation known to Coke's period: the corporation sole, or that species of corporation that had only one member, and the corporation aggregate, or the corporation formed out of many different individuals who seek to pursue a collective project. The most important example of a corporation sole was the king, who could stand not as a mortal person but as an immortal corporation-of-one in the interest of undertaking legal actions pertaining to property and feudal obligation. Many readers will recognize the theory from the work of Ernst Kantorowicz, who drew his inspiration from the *Reports* of Edmund Plowden, the great sixteenth-century common lawyer.[3] Maitland, whose own detailed study of the corporation sole was influential on Kantorowicz's account, found the notion an absurdity that hardly resolved the legal problems for which it had supposedly been invented. Nevertheless, the theory featured prominently in the arguments made on both sides of *Calvin's Case*, which had been arranged to force a resolution to the question of whether, after the accession of the Scottish

[3] Ernst Kantorowicz, *The King's Two Bodies* (Princeton: Princeton University Press, 1957).

James VI to the English throne as James I, James's Scottish subjects were to be treated as aliens in English law. Coke himself quoted Plowden to argue that 'the King hath two capacities in him,'

> one a natural body, being descended of the blood royal of the Realm; and this body is of the creation of Almighty God, and is subject to death, infirmity, and such like; the other is a politic body or capacity, so called, because it is framed by the policy of man ... and in this capacity the King is esteemed to be immortal, invisible, not subject to death, infirmity, infancy, nonage, &c.[4]

In Coke's view the decisive aspect of the case lay not in the king's possession of an invisible, corporate body politic 'framed by the policy of man', as he put it, but rather in the unique status of the king's 'natural person', i.e. his genealogical position within a line of succession that endowed him with distinct 'capacities' and obligations. Since the corporate body politic ultimately depends on the *natural* 'person' and its unique endowments, only the king as a mortal man can unify the two Crowns together, even as the two bodies politic of England and Scotland as a whole remain distinct.

Both David Norbrook and Lorna Hutson have queried Kantorowicz's use of Plowden, arguing that the subsequent uptake of the notion of the king's two bodies by the first generation of New Historicists helped perpetuate a theory that emphasized mystified royal power and the singular person of the king, while overlooking the degree to which corporate arguments could also be used in the period to describe collective, public forms of political power—a notion of 'public weal' and 'commonweal' that was already central to sixteenth-century political thought and that would become only more prominent in the 1640s.[5] Here we encounter the corporation's other long-standing type: what Coke called the 'corporation aggregate of many', or that group formed in law in order to undertake an activity that is best pursued, or that might *only* be pursued, in a collective fashion. The sixteenth century was familiar with many such corporations aggregate, which ranged in size from the universal Church, extending across territories and indeed across time, to the angels in Heaven—who formed a spiritual corporation, according to Richard Hooker—to the kingdom, or the community of the realm, to Parliament, to English corporate towns, to the two universities of Oxford and Cambridge, to the new joint-stock companies devoted to trade and exploration, and down to individual parish churches, chantries, and hospitals.

The case of *Sutton's Hospital* (1612), indeed, the most important statement of English common law on corporations, concerned the foundation of a charitable hospital in the former London Charterhouse by Thomas Sutton, one of the richest

[4] *The Selected Writings and Speeches of Sir Edward Coke*, ed. Steve Sheppard, 3 vols (Indianapolis: Liberty Fund, 2003), 1.166–232, 189. All citations of Coke and Bacon are to this edition.

[5] Hutson, 'Not The King's Two Bodies: Reading the "Body Politic" in Shakespeare's *Henry IV*, Parts 1 and 2', in *Rhetoric and Law in Early Modern Europe*, ed. Victoria Kahn and Lorna Hutson (New Haven: Yale University Press, 2001), 166–98, 176; David Norbrook, 'The Emperor's New Body? *Richard II*, Ernst Kantorowicz, and the Politics of Shakespeare Criticism', *Textual Practice*, 10 (1996): 329–57.

citizens in England, a foundation that had been disputed by Simon Baxter, one of Sutton's heirs. Coke's report on the case provides an especially clear definition of corporate types:

> a Corporation aggregate of many is invisible, immortal, & resteth only in intendment and consideration of the Law ... They may not commit treason, nor be outlawed, nor excommunicate for they have no souls, neither can they appear in person, but by Attorney ... A Corporation aggregate of many cannot do fealty, for an invisible body cannot be in person, nor can swear ... it is not subject to imbecilities, or death of the natural body, and divers other cases. (371–2)

Bacon, who argued the opposing side and lost the case, sought to establish that Sutton's grant of corporation was invalid on the grounds that he had established the corporation *before* he had founded the actual hospital; the result, he argued, was a non-entity, a 'Mathematical or Utopical Hospital' (350), as he called it, that was nothing but a 'Cypher' (349) or empty placeholder. Rather than a substantial, actually existing thing with a legitimate building, endowment, and Board of Governors (who included, as it happened, Coke himself), in Bacon's view Sutton had created only an unreal, immaterial entity that lacked a proper place—it was *merely* fictional, like the imagined community that More's work had made famous. Coke, irritated by the analogy (and by Bacon himself), responded by invoking technical arguments drawn from scholastic natural philosophy, notably Aristotle's *De generatione et corruptione*, in order to establish that corporations, too, were as real as any natural thing. But he also countered with a technical definition of the corporation as a *legal* rather than a literary fiction: the corporation 'is invisible, immortal, & resteth only in intendment and consideration of the Law.'

Coke's formula was by no means original to him or to his period. But although the corporation aggregate had a clear precedent in Roman law, Roman jurists did not in fact recognize a modern notion of corporate 'personhood': they distinguished between particular, actual existing groups and their classification into abstract types; they assigned property and rights to groups as abstractions, but they did so without assigning personality or will to these abstractions or extending to them all the rights enjoyed by natural persons.[6] Throughout Roman law, the term *persona* should be understood in its broadest sense as *homo* or human being, the preexisting natural person to whom legal duties or rights can be attributed or denied, rather than as an artificial legal category; slaves, for instance, were recognized as 'persons' in the sense that they were natural men like

[6] P. W. Duff, *Personality in Roman Private Law* (Cambridge: Cambridge University Press, 1938), esp. 1–25, 48–50, 206–36; W. W. Buckland, *A Textbook of Roman Law: From Augustus to Justinian*, 3rd edn, rev. Peter Stein (Cambridge: Cambridge University Press, 1963/first pub. 1921), 173–7; Buckland and Arnold D. McNair, *The Roman Law and Common Law*, 2nd edn, rev. F. H. Lawson (Cambridge: Cambridge University Press, 1965/first pub. 1936), 54–6.

other men, even though they had no claim to the legal rights or remedies that freemen enjoyed (not least rights over their own bodies) and were, for that reason, also classified as things, or property.

A notion of corporate personhood as distinct from the natural persons who make it up clearly appears only as of the early thirteenth century; the legal historian J. P. Canning has even argued that medieval jurists *invented* the modern concept of the legal person as a formal abstraction when they began to apply it to corporations aggregate for the first time, and thus also to compare and contrast them explicitly with natural human beings.[7] Innocent IV (1195–1254), to whom a modern notion of corporate personhood is usually attributed, had declared that corporations were nothing but 'names of law and not of [natural] persons' (*nomina sunt iuris, et non personarum*) and that they were 'fictional' or 'feigned' persons: *collegiam in causa universitatis fingatur una persona*, as Innocent put it, using the etymological root of 'fiction' from *fingere*, 'to fashion' or 'to form', often in a plastic sense.[8] For Baldus de Ubaldis (*c.*1327–1400), the corporation was a mental abstraction that could be compared to the relation of form to matter, since the corporate body is 'perceived rather by the intellect than by the senses' (*que magis intellectu quam sensus percipitur*).[9]

As Canning has emphasized, the medieval jurist's notion of the corporation as 'fictional' or 'artificial' person was a practical designation that was entirely compatible with the corporation's actual existence and its collective action. In describing the corporate person as a 'fiction', the jurists emphasized its *artificial* and *conventional* quality rather than its *illusoriness*, and this is precisely the sense in which Coke, too, speaks of the corporation as a legal creature, in contrast to Bacon's more playful (and yet serious) invocation of Utopia.[10] In a sense, the question between the two rivals concerned what *kind* of fiction the corporation might be: was it as insubstantial as a signifier and frivolous as a thought-experiment, or was it a practical device endowed with all the force of law—as consequential, in some cases, as the will of an absolute monarch? The case of *Sutton's Hospital* had raised a set of philosophical questions that the law alone could not settle, which was why Coke found himself turning to Aristotle, 'Nature's Secretary', as he had called him in *Calvin's Case*. What was the nature of this personated abstraction: this *idea* created 'by the policy of man' that took the form of a *fictional person* but which was at the same time an *institution* and an associational *group* established for a collective purpose?

7 J. P. Canning, 'The Corporation in the Political Thought of the Italian Jurists of the Thirteenth and Fourteenth Centuries', *HPT*, 1 (1980): 9–32, 15.

8 I cite Innocent IV from Manuel J. Rodriguez, 'Innocent IV and the Element of Fiction in Juristic Personalities', *The Jurist*, 22 (1962): 287–318, 299 and 310, 307.

9 Cited by Canning, 'Corporation in the Thought of the Italian Jurists', 13–14.

10 Canning, 'The Corporation in the Political Thought of the Italian Jurists', 15–19; Rodriguez, 'Innocent IV and the Element of Fiction', 316–17.

Persona Ficta

In order to give this question further definition and texture—in order better to understand the ontology of the corporation, to risk a pretentious phrase—we must now leave the courtroom and turn to the poets. For despite its legal limitations, the notion of the corporation sole manifestly left its impression on poets and playwrights of the sixteenth and seventeenth centuries. Edmund Spenser would seem to have the theory directly in mind in his letter addressed to Sir Walter Ralegh that prefaces *The Faerie Queene*, where an analogy with the king's two bodies furnishes him with a famous theory of allegory. Spenser writes that:

> In that Faery Queene I meane glory in my generall intention, but in my particular I conceiue the most excellent and glorious person of our soueraine the Queene, and her kingdome in Faery land. And yet in some places els I do otherwise shadow her. For considering she beareth two persons, the one of a most royall Queene or Empresse, the other of a most vertuous and beautifull Lady, this latter part in some places I doe expresse in Belphoebe, fashioning her name according to your owne excellent conceipt of Cynthia (Phoebe and Cynthia being both names of Diana).[11]

Spenser has adapted a legal theory to a literary purpose, and the distinctiveness of his language of 'persons' can be gauged by comparing the quite different explanation of allegorical characterization by Torquato Tasso in his *Gerusalemme Liberata* (1575, pub. 1581), as rendered in Edward Fairfax's 1600 English translation:

> *Heroicall Poetrie* (as a liuing Creature, wherein two natures are conioined) is compounded of *Imitation* and *Allegorie*: with the one she allureth vnto her the mindes and eares of Men, and maruellously delighteth them; with the other, either in vertue or knowledge, she instructeth them. And as the heroically written *Imitation* of an *Other*, is nothing else, but the patterne and image of humane action: so the *Allegorie* of an Heroicall Poem is none other than the glasse and figure of Humane Life.[12]

Tasso's language of interior and exterior, mind and body, passion and actions positions his theory of allegory in a mimetic tradition that is more continuous with Sir Philip Sidney's *Defense of Poesy* (*c.*1580) than with Spenser's 'Letter', since it emphasizes a combination of sensuous apprehension and intellective understanding in the service of ethical instruction. Like Sidney, that is, Tasso describes an 'art' of poetic composition that draws its inspiration from an amalgam of neo-classical principles and a neo-Platonic, quasi-occult metaphysics of nature, and like Sidney he imagines his characters

[11] Edmund Spenser, 'Letter of the Authors ... To the Right Noble, and Valorous, Sir Walter Raleigh, Knight', *The Faerie Queene* (1590), ed. A. C. Hamilton (London: Longman, 1977).

[12] *Godfrey of Bulloigne, or The Recouerie of Ierusalem* (London, 1600), A2^{v}.

as heroic figures at home in the traditions of epic and romance, modelled on 'human action' and 'human life' in ways that are familiar, albeit distantly, from Aristotle's *Poetics*. Although Spenser, too, invokes the complement between a 'general' principle and a 'particular' example that was so central to Sidney's definition of the poetic intelligence, his explanation in the 'Letter' suddenly seems relatively bare by comparison to Tasso's showy neo-classicism: a simplified sketch of allegory in the mode of political theology, coloured with a flattering reference to the Ovidian themes and mythic characterization that marked the Ralegh circle and formed such an important strand in Elizabeth's iconography.

Spenser's 'Letter' thus also invites a comparison that Tasso's does not, however, for he seems to imagine his characters not simply as mythic icons but as species of corporate persons. What could this mean? In order to explore his analogy further, it will be helpful to distinguish several principles extending across legal and literary discourses alike; adapting conventional terminology for my purposes, I shall call them *personhood, personation, personification*, and *personality*:

> *Person, personhood*: the bare formal envelope to which we attribute identity, agency and capacity in law; by extension, the human being in general, although the philosophical interest and political importance of the 'person' as a legal category shows itself most saliently in the moment when it is attributed to non-human entities of various kinds (animals, plants, machines) or when it is deprived from human entities (such as slaves, or women—as in Maitland's causal usage at the opening of this essay, above);
>
> *Personation*: the mimetic representation of human beings and anything to which a quality of 'personhood' may be attributed, especially through figuration; a 'literary' term, therefore, one that is especially typical of the stage and necessary to the projection of what we recognize as dramatic character;
>
> *Personality*: psychological inwardness, motivation, temperament, and other associated qualities: the 'roundedness' that we associate with individual human beings but sometimes also animals and even non-animate objects. In literary terms, the notion of 'personality' pushes us beyond 'personation' and toward a concept of a recognizably lifelike fictional character, in poetry and on stage but especially in the novel;
>
> *Personification*: the mimetic representation of an abstract idea in figural form, especially through the donation of voice and 'face' to an idea; hence personification's frequent associations with apostrophe and prosopopoeia.
>
> When a *personation* or *personality* becomes exemplary in some way—the more its psychological or historical particularity is inflated by a general principle that applies across circumstances and occasions—the more it can be said to approach *personification*.[13]

[13] I draw on Elizabeth Fowler, *Literary Character: The Human Figure in Early English Writing* (Ithaca: Cornell University Press, 2003), esp. 16–17, 24–8; Barbara Johnson, 'Anthropomorphism in Lyric and Law', *YJLH*, 10 (1998): 549–74, and her 'Apostrophe, Animation, and Abortion', in *A World of Difference* (Baltimore: Johns Hopkins University Press, 1987), 184–222; Helen Cooper, 'The Afterlife of Personification', in *Medieval Shakespeare: Pasts and Presents*, ed. Ruth Morse, Helen Cooper, and Peter

Bearing these terms in mind, we may now return to Spenser's 'Letter' to find that it is, predictably enough, more complex than it first appears. Despite declaring that the Queen 'beareth two persons', the passage describes at least four: (1) the Faery Queen; (2) the 'person' of 'our soueraine the Queene'; (3) the 'Lady'; who is sometimes also figured as (4) 'Belphobe'. The conceptual relations among these persons quickly assume several dimensions: 'our souereine the Queene' sits at the centre of an overlapping, quasi-Trinitarian complex, since she is 'the Queene' in her particular capacity but 'the Faery Queene' in her general capacity, and also 'a most virtuous and beautifull Lady' who is sometimes 'shadowed' in other names Spenser does not specify in the Letter but whom readers will recognize in other characters, both good and bad (i.e. Una and Britomart but also Lucifera).

Nor is the ontological status of each figure as clear as we might wish: the Faerie Queene, for instance, is a type of fictional person, and other characters in the poem also refer to her as Gloriana. But the Faerie Queene never actually appears in the poem that bears her name; as a minimal sketch of a *personation*, Gloriana has already begun to swell into *personification* so as to reveal the idea of Glory, an idea that here assumes the form of a fictional figure but which is itself, strictly speaking, of a different philosophical order. This phasing into personification, as it were, in turn allows the idea of Glory to attach itself to the bare person of the Queene, whom Spenser would seem to align with the historical and natural person of Elizabeth (as the term 'particular' suggests) but who also carries the aura of the general idea, both political and ethical, that has been bound to the personification. *Both* the Queen and the Lady are figures who flicker between particular fictional specification and general conceptual essence, a hybrid state that Spenser captures well through the allusion to mythical figures such as Cynthia or Diana, who possess a similar mixed human and metaphysical quality.

In describing overtly fictional and allegorical characters such as Belphoebe or Gloriana as 'personations', I am using a term that Spenser himself uses in the dedication of his *Mother Hubberds Tale* (1591) to Anne Spenser (no relation), the Lady Compton, where he describes the delightful 'simplicity and meannesse' that he has 'personated' in the fable of the Fox and the Ape that Mother Hubberd tells the plague-stricken narrator.[14] Here 'personated' is also a native translation for the work's full title, *Prosopopoia, or Mother Hubberds Tale,* a rhetorical technique that Spenser has elevated into a minor lyric genre, using it to layer personation upon personation in the service of an extended political allegory. George Puttenham's *Art of English Poesie* similarly identifies '*prosopopeia*' with what he calls 'the Counterfeit Impersonation'; like Spenser, Puttenham associates both *prosopopoeia* and personation with fiction more generally and with allegory

Holland (Cambridge: Cambridge University Press, 2013), 98–116; and two essays by Andrew Escobedo, both of which have been especially influential on my thinking: 'Daemon Lovers: Will, Personification, and Character', *Spenser Studies*, 22 (2007): 203–25, and 'Allegorical Agency and the Sins of Angels', *ELH*, 75.4 (2008): 787–818.

[14] *The Yale Edition of the Shorter Poems of Edmund Spenser*, ed. William A. Oram et al. (New Haven: Yale University Press, 1989), 327–79, esp. 323–4, 334.

specifically (his example is the *Roman de la Rose*, as translated by Chaucer), especially in its capacity for ascribing human characteristics to non-human things in the service of ethical instruction.[15]

More commonly, however, the term 'personate' described a specifically theatrical mode of *mimesis*: 'to personate, to acte, to imitate any person, to acte or play a part in a play', as John Florio defined '*personáre*' in his Italian–English dictionary.[16] To 'personate' is to bring characters to life, as Thomas Heywood vividly explains in his *Apology for Actors* (1611):

> what English blood seeing the person of any bold English man presented and doth not hugge his fame, and hunnye at his valor, pursuing him in his enterprise with his best wishes, and as being wrapt in contemplation, offers to him in his hart all prosperous performance, as if the Personater were the man Personated, so bewitching a thing is liuely and well spirited action, that it hath power to new mold the harts of the spectators and fashion them to the shape of any noble and notable attempt. (B4^{r})

Shakespeare, too, makes regular use of the term 'personate' throughout his work, as when Maria declares in *Twelfth Night* that Malviolio 'shall find himself most feelingly personated' in the 'obscure epistles of love' that she has forged from Viola, which capture 'the colour of his beard, the shape of his leg, the manner of his gait, the expressure of his eye, forehead, and complexion' (2.3.149–53). Here the 'personation' is a crafted or counterfeit imitation of a specific individual, a usage that sometimes also acquires an overtly allegorical dimension, as when the sycophantic Poet of *Timon of Athens* offers a verse allegory to his would-be patron: 'One do I personate of Lord Timon's frame, / Whom Fortune with her ivory hand wafts to her; / Whose present grace to present slaves and servants / Translates his rivals' (1.1.70–3).

Elsewhere Shakespeare emphasizes the emblematic capacity of the 'personation', often to spectacular metatheatrical effect. In *A Midsummer Night's Dream*, when Quince proposes that 'one must come in with a bush of thorns and a lantern and say he comes to disfigure, or to present, the person of Moonshine' (3.1.54–6), Shakespeare has rejoined the act of emblematic personation to the 'person' thereby represented, only now this 'person' is a *personification* in the mode of *prosopopoeia*, an inhuman thing or idea given concrete form by means of the actor's art. The usage recalls the conventions of the medieval mysteries, presented by the guild ancestors of the rude mechanicals, in which characters and ideas might be represented by the *personnage*: a non-human figure made of various media—automata, statues, paintings, or tapestries—that was understood to be at once real *and* fictional, animate *and* inanimate, actor and character at the same time.[17]

[15] George Puttenham, *The Art of English Poesy*, ed. Frank Whigham and Wayne A. Rebhorn (Ithaca: Cornell University Press, 2007), 324.

[16] *Queen Anna's New World of Words* (1611), 371.

[17] Laura Weigert, 'Stages', in *Early Modern Theatricality*, ed. Henry S. Turner (Oxford: Oxford University Press, 2013), 24–46, esp. 38–42.

Even as Coke and Bacon were debating the technical definitions of corporations, in other words, literary writers were beginning to seize on the imaginative potential of personated abstractions and use them for diverse purposes. Spenser's *Faerie Queene* could reinforce a mystical ideology that associated political power tightly with the royal presence and the royal character, but it also began to trouble that ideology by acknowledging its blatant artifice; soon, of course, the poem leaves the orthodoxies of political legitimacy or ethical instruction behind to wander into a far more speculative territory populated by uneasy figures and scenes of astonishing intellectual complexity or affective intensity. For Spenser, too, as for Tasso or Puttenham, the language of 'persons' had also become a way of forging a distinctively literary critical idiom and thus of elevating the philosophical seriousness of poetry, carving out a discursive space for the art of the poet in a culture that often viewed it with skepticism or hostility and that still preferred its truths in scriptural form. Spenser has taken possession of the monarch's immortal body and thrown it forward into a radical poetic project: using fiction to invent a series of absolute ideas that are *metaphysical* but at the same time no longer fully *theological*, and to give these ideas artificial life in human form.

For Shakespeare, meanwhile, a corporate imaginary furnished a powerful way of exploring the capacities of theatre: the artifice of its representation, the satiric space it opened onto all manner of questions, its potential for unorthodox philosophical speculation and penetrating political commentary. For the early modern world was changing, and many of Shakespeare's tragedies take as their point of departure the political and ethical crises that ensue when corporate groups that had once provided a basis for a common constitutional order begin to disintegrate, whether under the pressures of succession disputes, civil war, sheer personal ambition, or larger tectonic tensions between republican and monarchical ideals of governance. *Coriolanus*, to take one of several examples, offers no closure to the political 'gap of both' that Coriolanus opens in his impassioned speech to the Senate: it imagines no mythic, Hobbesian contract, no Leviathan-like sovereign who could replace the king and forge a new corporate commonwealth. Urged by Volumnia to become an *actor* before the people—'frame / Thyself, forsooth, hereafter theirs, so far / As thou hast power and person' (3.2.84–6)—Coriolanus falters. 'Like a dull actor now', he confesses at the end of the play, 'I have forgot my part, and I am out / Even to a full disgrace' (5.3.40–2). Theatre holds up the mirror not to nature but to itself, only to discover that it has become inadequate to the task of filling the vacuum in political concepts that its own mimetic procedures have revealed.

Theatrical Persons

Maitland is not entirely correct, therefore, to say that 'the only artificial persons are corporations'. Hobbes's transformative insight was to find a way to join a notion of personhood derived from the theatre to a theory of corporations both aggregate and sole, and thereby to generate Leviathan, the person of the 'Commonwealth, or State'.[18] The sovereign's relationship to the State is 'representational' for Hobbes not only because the monarch acts as the delegate of the people but because he *personates*—the term is Hobbes's—an abstract and fictional entity that is distinct from people and sovereign alike and who unifies them into a body that they were not before. 'Whosoever beareth the person of the people, or is one of that assembly that bears it', Hobbes argues, 'beareth also his own natural person' (2.19.4); soon he states that the sovereign has 'two capacities, one natural and another politic (as a monarch hath the person not only of the commonwealth, but also of a man)' (2.23.2).[19]

For Hobbes the representational relationship is no longer mystical or metaphysical but technical and performative, in the strong philosophical sense as well as in a specifically theatrical way. For *persona* originally designated the role or artificial mask worn by the stage actor, as Hobbes observes: 'So that a *person* is the same that an *actor* is, both on the stage and in common conversation; and to *personate* is to *act*, or *represent*, himself or another; and he that acteth another is said to bear his person, or act in his name' (*Lev.* 1.16.3). In *De homine* (*c.*1630–1640, pub. 1658, 1668), Hobbes explicitly calls this act of impersonation 'fictional', devoting a chapter to what he now calls '*De homine fictitio, sive De persona*' and where he allows greater prominence to the play between *persona* as 'human being' and *persona* as 'character'.[20] Hobbes has substituted a purely formal and pragmatic concept for a long-standing theological idea of *persona* as a translation of the Greek *hypostasis* or 'substance', a translation that he objects to in the strongest possible terms because of the dubious metaphysics of essences that it implies.[21] 'In the kingdom of God there may be three persons independent, without breach of unity in God that reigneth', Hobbes concedes, 'but where men reign, that be subject to diversity of opinions, it cannot be so' (2.29.16).

But if Hobbes found a source for his new political theory of the State by conjoining the corporation aggregate to a theory of representation as theatrical impersonation, the imagination of playwrights, too, had been captured by the fact that the theatre companies were themselves among the most successful examples of the new joint-stock companies that were familiar to Hobbes (a shareholding member of both the Virginia

[18] Thomas Hobbes, *Leviathan*, ed. Edwin Curley (Indianapolis: Hackett Publishing Company, Inc., 1994), 'The Introduction', 3.

[19] On Hobbes's use of *persona*, see Paul Dumouchel, '"Persona": Reason and Representation in Hobbes's Political Philosophy', *SubStance*, 25.2 (1996): 68–80; David Runciman, *Pluralism and the Personality of the State* (Cambridge: Cambridge University Press, 1997), esp. 6–33 and 223–65; Runciman, 'Debate: What Kind of Person is Hobbes's State? A Reply to Skinner', *Journal of Political Philosophy*, 8 (2000): 268–78, responding to Quentin Skinner, 'From the State of Princes to the Person of the State', *Visions of Politics*, 3 vols (Cambridge: Cambridge University Press, 2002), 2.268–413, esp. 387–94 and 309–404.

[20] *De homine* 2.15.1, *Thomae Hobbes Malmesburiensis Opera Philosophica*, ed. Sir William Molesworth, 5 vols (London: John Bohn, 1839–1845), 2.130–2.

[21] *Lev.* 1.16.12; 2.29.16; 3.41.9; 3.42.3. On the theatrical origins of the term *persona* and its theological fortunes, see John Parker, 'Persona', in *Cultural Reformations: Medieval and Renaissance in Literary History*, ed. Brian Cummings and James Simpson (Oxford: Oxford University Press, 2010), 591–608.

and Bermuda Companies) and that have become so dominant in our own political culture. We could find a no more sophisticated or amusing study of theatre as a corporate commercial enterprise than Ben Jonson's *The Alchemist* (1610), which not only exposes alchemy, medicine, Puritanism, commonwealth industrial projects, and Hebrew scholarship as pretenders to moral authority but does so by explicitly playing on the corporatist language and organizational structure of the play companies themselves. Face, Subtle, and Doll compose a 'venture tripartite' in which the work is 'begun out of equality' and the members hold 'all things in common', an ironic echo of the Ciceronian phrase that Erasmus and More had made famous (1.1.134–5).[22] But despite Doll's exhortation to mend division, Face and Subtle squabble constantly over authority and the profits they imagine. Scenically the play is organized not around individual characters but rather a series of shifting group-formations of two, three, four or more persons; the art of Subtle, Face, and Doll lies in managing these many different part-forms, allocating roles to one another and to others and rushing to coordinate them into a seamless illusion. The art of the play company is the same, since, as Tiffany Stern and Simon Palfrey have demonstrated, what we today encounter as a fully realized 'play' was, theatrically considered, a much less stable assemblage of part-scripts and cues, each shuffled around and often revised independently of the others.[23]

The challenge for Jonson was to compose a 'poem', as he often called it, out of this assemblage of bodies, props, words, and ideas, a 'work' that could endure beyond the actors who first performed it and thus become a new kind of literary critical object. Much like Spenser, Tasso, or Puttenham, in other words, Jonson seeks a coherent *theory* of drama, and one suspects that he embraced the overtly emblematic and allegorical form of the masque so enthusiastically in part because of the theoretical opportunity it afforded him.[24] The prefatory comment to *The Masque of Queens* (1609), for instance, combines Horatian precepts with a quasi-Platonic critical idiom, anchoring dramatic form around an act of royal personation and informing Jonson's reader that '*it was ... my first and special regard, to see that the nobility of the Invention should be answerable to the dignity of their Persons*.'[25] The earlier *Hymenaei* (1606) had cast the exigencies of royal performance in the more pretentious mode of metaphysical speculation, in terms reminiscent of Tasso's allegory: 'It is a noble and just advantage that the things subjected to understanding have of those which are objected to sense', Jonson opines, 'So short-lived are the bodies of all things in comparison of their souls.'[26]

But Jonson's metaphysics tends to deflate fairly quickly once it leaves the printed page, and the irrefutable circumstantiality of stage performance continued both to aggravate his spleen and to inspire his considerable powers of invention. Perhaps because

[22] *CWBJ*, 3.570.

[23] Simon Palfrey and Tiffany Stern, *Shakespeare In Parts* (Oxford: Oxford University Press, 2007).

[24] See Henry S. Turner, *The English Renaissance Stage: Geometry, Poetics, and the Practical Spatial Arts, 1580–1630* (Oxford: Oxford University Press, 2006), esp. 244–61.

[25] *CWBJ*, 3.305.

[26] *CWBJ*, 2.667.

the group formed by the occasion of public performance was so temporary and also so fickle, Jonson found himself continually entangled in a contest over the terms by which his art might be judged. In the Induction to *Bartholomew Fair* (1614), a Book-holder and a Scrivener enter to present the audience with an indenture that makes explicit the commercial relationship that now governs the theatrical transaction. The author, they report, agrees to furnish the audience with a 'new sufficient play called *Barthol'mew Fair*' (Induction, 60–1), and the audience must agree in turn to remain in their places for two and half hours, to limit their judgements to the amount of money they have paid to gain entrance, and to remain consistent in that judgement: what they approve today, they must also approve tomorrow and the day after that. 'You were e'en as good to go to Virginia', the Stage-Keeper confides to the audience before the play, 'for any thing there is of Smithfield' (Induction, 8–9).[27] The critique is clear enough: the Stage-Keeper is undermining Jonson's claim to authentic representation. But why 'Virginia'? Jonson compares the entire system to the 'lottery', and only two years earlier, the Virginia Company had held a large public lottery to raise funds; membership in the company was itself, of course, publically available through the purchase of shares.[28] The audience will become investors in the play for an evening; their money will buy them the right to judge for themselves (although they must also promise to applaud *before* the play has even begun).

But *Bartholomew Fair* also suggests some uncomfortable truths about the brave new commercial world that it imagines. It isn't entirely clear what Horatian lesson we are to draw from a play in which Adam Overdo, the judge who should bring a measure of order to the Fair, speaks so pompously that he makes the corporate principles of 'Commonwealth' and 'Public Good' into empty tics of discourse, a language that resembles nothing so much as the ranting of the Puritan, Zeal-of-the-Land Busy. The play is extremely funny, but in the end Jonson leaves us with a political fiction that has become all-too-familiar: one in which the market is as unstructured as possible, the law is only as meaningful as the latest fist that appropriates it, and fundamentalism and justice speak the same empty, bloviating language.

This aspect of *Bartholomew Fair* raises a further point about Jonson's drama that is important to observe: we may describe the financial and decision-making structure of the theatrical company in corporatist terms; we may describe the process of theatrical mimesis in corporatist terms; we may even describe the metaphysics that underlies Jonson's own emerging theory of drama-as-poem as a species of 'corporatist' thinking. But despite Jonson's interest in various forms of character grouping, a major mode of Jonsonian composition, his characters tend not to be strongly affiliated with corporate institutions. There is a kind of incipient liberalism in Jonson's social imagination, although this is a liberalism not of free rational individuals but of walking, speaking caricatures and stereotypes: they are personated social abstractions, brought to life

27 *CWBJ*, 4.276–82. See Luke Wilson, *Theaters of Intention: Drama and the Law in Early Modern England* (Stanford: Stanford University Press, 2000), 106–13.

28 George Unwin, *The Gilds and Companies of London* (London: Methuen, 1908), 303–4.

through a bundle of theatrical gestures, signatures, and characteristic dispositions. If Jonson's art of *personation* sometimes shows a tendency toward *personification*, as in *Volpone* or *The Alchemist* or *Bartholomew Fair*, where the names of characters obviously are meant to signify the organizing idea that motivates their presentation, they are not personifications in the usual sense. As social creatures, their origin is pragmatic and even quasi-algorithmic: they conform to a set of rules about behaviour and taste that emerge over the course of any given play with an almost sociological clarity. They are best viewed as *types* that have been first constellated, and then animated, by a satirical motive: a set of normative ideas about the social world and the human character within it that is typical of Jonson's plays and is what makes them feel like such consistent expressions of his own temperament. It is a technique of characterization that for Catherine Gallagher results in a modern notion of 'fictionality' only as of the eighteenth-century novel, although it is already vividly on display in Jonson's art of dramatic composition.[29]

Corporate Persons Today

If theatrical characters are *personated persons*, therefore, a stage effect that sometimes approaches full *personality*, and if literary persons of all kinds often have a tincture of *personification* about them, then what kind of person is the corporation? What can a history of the corporation undertaken from a vantage point *between* law and literature tell us about our own discontent in the face of these gigantic artificial beings?

As a *legal* person, first of all, the corporation is at one level an entirely pragmatic entity: this was the argument of John Dewey, in an essay on corporate personality that objected to the importation into legal discourse of metaphysical categories that, strictly speaking, had nothing to do with law.[30] As Coke himself had argued, corporations exist only 'in the intendment of the law', which is to say that they have been created to fulfil certain functions that the law specifies; the 'personality' of the corporation assumes the shape of a tautology, since it is nothing more (and nothing less) than the outline described by the legal rules that govern its behaviour and that specify its rights, duties, and freedoms. In his own sociological way, Jonson's technique of characterization resembles this pragmatic definition of the corporate person fairly closely, and we have seen how interested Jonson was in legal institutions and legal instruments, albeit as objects of playful satire.

But Jonson's theatrical self-consciousness adds an additional layer of insight to this formal pragmatism: a character such as Face in *The Alchemist* has become nothing less than *a personification of personification*, an emblem of the mimetic process by which the

[29] Catherine Gallagher, 'The Rise of Fictionality', in *The Novel*, Vol. 1: *History, Geography, and Culture*, ed. Franco Moretti (Princeton: Princeton University Press, 2006), 336–63.

[30] John Dewey, 'The Historic Background of Corporate Legal Personality', *YLJ*, 35 (1926): 655–73.

actor gives life and voice to an artificial person that lives immanently within or upon his natural body and assumes features that are identical to it. If Face is a personification, he is a peculiar personification—of *himself*; if he is 'allegorical', he is an allegory for theatre, for the ongoing composition of identity by means of artifices of all kinds that are displayed publicly, in the presence of others, for others to consume. The fact that the theatre companies were themselves joint-stock ventures was, as we have seen, not lost on Jonson, and we may thus also see in Face a grinning *prosopon* for the acting company and its repertory of roles and parts and the characters they bring to life, as voice is added to voice, gesture to gesture, body to body. For the actor always possesses at least two bodies, though they appear only as one: this is precisely the effect that makes Face's turn as Jeremy the Butler, and vice versa, so entertaining.

Or—to extend Jonson's theatrical insights to our own struggles with corporate persons—we may say that the corporation *never* has a body of its own. It must always borrow the bodies of its members who agree to personate it: the corporation 'is' nothing more (and nothing less) than this act of performance. As Face disappears, like the smoke of the play's final explosion, into a purely formal principle of mimetic personation, he shows the corporate person to be similarly empty, a formal shell that can in principle become animated by *any* purpose and by any member. The corporation lives through the personations that *we* undertake, as we begin to move and speak on its behalf. Casting our eye now back to Spenser's 'Letter', we realize that the notion of corporate personhood turns out to be a closer cousin to allegory than we might expect, for the legal person presents us with the structure of *allegory without content*, a purely formal structure for action that waits to be animated by the particular bodies, substances, and circumstances that will endow it with identity, rather than appearing as to us already conceptually full. This formal emptiness is precisely what distinguishes corporations from their members, even as it attaches a distinct personhood to them, much the way an allegorical idea attaches to or is immanent within a character or figure or thing.

Like most persons, the corporate person thus assumes its ontological profile from the convergence of several opposing, even contradictory, impulses, none of which can be attributed *only* to law, which proves in the end to be sufficient but not a necessary condition for corporateness. At a root level, for-profit commercial corporations wish always to act *without* meaning: they seek merely to act and to do, as freely as possible, unencumbered by claims to significance, by ethical justifications, or by declared purposes. Left to themselves, they would offer no explanations and no excuses; they would refuse discourse entirely in favour of pure action and the force of universal transformation and pure accumulation. In this sense, their legal utterances are a minimal concession to a discourse in which symbolic expression already approaches degree zero. Since this dream of pure action proves impossible, however, we find that the commercial corporation must instead embrace its opposite: the dream of becoming *all* discourse, *all* allegory, a space of complete signification that saturates meaning completely and fills every signifier such that it becomes an emblem of the corporation's own making. By creating a monopoly over signification, the corporation attempts to fulfil its original motive, a space of pure action camouflaged beneath a preemptive system of values in which any decision, any plan, any transaction has been assigned a meaning in advance and thus may proceed beyond question. It is a mode of action without deliberation, in which the collective will—the corporation's mark of its own personhood—immediately and coincidentally expresses itself.[31]

In a further pivot of the axis of communication, however, the corporation soon finds that this dream is best achieved by ensuring that its symbolism remains optimally *open to everyone*. For corporate *personality* finally depends on more than pragmatic legal categories, more than the speech and acts of personation by its members or spokespersons. It derives from the total system of signification and value-designation implied in the signs that the corporate person places into public circulation: in its official documents and positions, in its advertisements and iconography. It invents idiogrammatic logos that become as meaningful as possible to as many people as possible only by specifying no content of their own; among many modern candidates for such an icon, the Nike swoosh is without question one of the most successful. This condition explains why so much corporate advertising employs images of phenomenological intensity. A climb, a mountain top, 'speed', a child's smile, an inviting, shimmering surface: these perceptual 'moments' are at once beyond meaning—they are affectively liberating simulacra of immediate experience, into which the viewer is invited to overflow—and create the effect of an ultimate meaning: it is your own life as a natural person that is offered back to you, in the mode of fantasy. Hence the corporation finds its life in a perpetual movement between bare *person*, enacted *personation*, simulated *personality*, and iconographically saturated *personification*. Put differently, the corporation is a *person* that seeks to become a *personification* of a *personality*: your own.

We find, indeed, that the corporation has become a figure of a very particular type: it is a personification for the *very idea of being itself*. The mere legal existence of the corporation is an affirmative assertion of an answer to a prior ontological question, namely *that the corporation is* and what minimal signs of life it may have. *This* is the problem that has preoccupied jurists continuously from the end of the thirteenth century to the beginning of the twenty-first; it is the problem that engaged Hobbes and resulted in his sweeping restatement of political theory; it is the question that motivates Spenser, and Shakespeare, and Jonson, in their own ways. Finally, what the corporation and the dramatic character have in common is less their status as 'persons' than an even larger problem of which the notion of the 'person' is simply one species: the metaphysical problem of defining 'ideas' in general and their ontological status, of what the relationship might be between ideal entities and material or concrete bodies that bear them, of how an idea might possess a kind of power, both of an ideological or rhetorical quality but also as a *physical* power—as strange as this proposition may sound to us, it was not strange to a culture that believed in the reality of metaphysical entities, and it lies at the root of our own fears about corporate persons today.

[31] Compare Escobedo on the 'volitional discharge' of personifications, 'Allegorical Agency', 804–6, 806.

What would it mean for an idea to become real and to begin to act? What is the *value* of a personated idea, of an idea that assumes a face and begins to think and speak for itself? Early modern writers confronted these questions under the sign of personification, or *prosopopoeia*, or allegory, or theatre. Today we no longer think much about personification, that quaintest of rhetorical figures; *all we have* are corporations, themselves narrowed into pseudo-persons who prey on our consumer habits rather than acting as the moral persons they once were, when they still served as a meaningful way to organize collective life around shared ideas, principles, purposes. Today, anyone bold enough to invoke 'Justice' or any other moral abstraction can only appear, like Adam Overdo in *Bartholomew Fair*, to be naive, or hypocritical, or obviously ideological, or irritatingly vague. In fact it is the commercial corporation that most commonly invokes these ideas and determines their circulation and meaning for us. We turn, unhappily, to legal debates over corporate personhood: as a vehicle for a more substantive public language for thinking collectively about the shared metaphysical ideas that should rightfully govern both our collective and our individual action, perhaps the time has come to take personification seriously once more.

Bibliography

Buckland, W. W. *A Textbook of Roman Law: From Augustus to Justinian*, 3rd edn, rev. Peter Stein (Cambridge: Cambridge University Press, 1963; first pub. 1921).

Buckland, W. W. and Arnold D. McNair, *The Roman Law and Common Law*, 2nd edn, rev. F. H. Lawson (Cambridge: Cambridge University Press, 1965; first pub. 1936): 54–6.

Canning, J. P. 'The Corporation in the Political Thought of the Italian Jurists of the Thirteenth and Fourteenth Centuries', *History of Political Thought*, 1 (1980): 9–32.

Coke, Sir Edward. *The Selected Writings and Speeches of Sir Edward Coke*, ed. Steve Sheppard, 3 vols (Indianapolis: Liberty Fund, 2003).

Cooper, Helen. 'The Afterlife of Personification', in *Medieval Shakespeare: Pasts and Presents*, ed. Ruth Morse, Helen Cooper, and Peter Holland (Cambridge: Cambridge University Press, 2013), 98–116.

Dewey, John. 'The Historic Background of Corporate Legal Personality.' *Yale Law Journal*, 35 (1926): 655–73.

Duff, P. W. *Personality in Roman Private Law* (Cambridge: Cambridge University Press, 1938).

Escobedo, Andrew. 'Allegorical Agency and the Sins of Angels', *English Literary History*, 75.4 (2008): 787–818.

Escobedo, Andrew. 'Daemon Lovers: Will, Personification, and Character', *Spenser Studies*, 22 (2007): 203–25.

Gallagher, Catherine. 'The Rise of Fictionality', in *The Novel*, Vol. 1: *History, Geography, and Culture*, ed. Franco Moretti (Princeton: Princeton University Press, 2006), 336–63.

Hobbes, Thomas. *Leviathan*, ed. Edwin Curley (Indianapolis: Hackett Publishing Company, Inc., 1994).

Hutson, Lorna. 'Not The King's Two Bodies: Reading the "Body Politic" in Shakespeare's "Henry IV", Parts 1 and 2', in *Rhetoric and Law in Early Modern Europe*, ed. Victoria Kahn and Lorna Hutson (New Haven: Yale University Press, 2001), 166–98.

Johnson, Barbara. 'Anthropomorphism in Lyric and Law', *Yale Journal of Law & the Humanities*, 10 (1998): 549–74.
Jonson, Ben. *Bartholomew Fair*, ed. Eugene M. Waith (New Haven: Yale University Press, 1963).
Jonson, Ben. *The Alchemist*, ed. Alvin Kernan (New Haven: Yale University Press, 1974).
Kahn, Victoria. 'Political Theology and Fiction in the "King's Two Bodies"', *Representations*, 106 (2009): 77–101.
Maitland, F. W. 'The Corporation Sole', in *The Collected Papers of Frederic William Maitland*, ed. H. A. L. Fisher, 3 vols (Cambridge: Cambridge University Press, 1911), 210–43.
Parker, John. 'Persona', in *Cultural Reformations: Medieval and Renaissance in Literary History*, ed. Brian Cummings and James Simpson (Oxford: Oxford University Press, 2010), 591–608.
Puttenham, George. *The Art of English Poesy*, ed. Frank Whigham and Wayne A. Rebhorn (Ithaca: Cornell University Press, 2007).
Rodriguez, Manuel J. 'Innocent IV and the Element of Fiction in Juristic Personalities', *The Jurist*, 22 (1962): 287–318.
Shakespeare, William. *The Complete Works: Compact Edition*, ed. Stanley Wells and Gary Taylor (Oxford: Clarendon Press, 1988).
Spenser, Edmund. 'Mother Hubberds Tale' [1591], in *The Yale Edition of the Shorter Poems of Edmund Spenser*, ed. William A. Oram et al. (New Haven: Yale University Press, 1989), 327–79.
Spenser, Edmund. 'The Faerie Queene' [1590], ed. A. C. Hamilton (London: Longman, 1977).
Turner, Henry S. *The Corporate Commonwealth: Pluralism and Political Fictions in England, 1516–1651* (Chicago: University of Chicago Press, 2016).

PART VI

LIBEL, PUBLICATION, AND THE PRESS

CHAPTER 25

EDWARD COKE, ROMAN LAW, AND THE LAW OF LIBEL

DAVID IBBETSON

It is generally accepted that the roots of the law of criminal libel lie in the Court of Star Chamber at the beginning of the seventeenth century.[1] The central case, the prosecution of Lewis Pickering, was decided in 1605 and reported by Sir Edward Coke in the fifth volume of his reports as the case *De libellis famosis*,[2] and this has been seen as the source of all of the later law. This is broadly correct, subject to correction in point of detail, though it is important not to underestimate the part played by sixteenth-century statutes in the creation of the seventeenth-century law.

More controversially, both legal historians and literary scholars have suggested that Roman law had a part to play in the shaping of the English rules, on the basis of the titling of the case and other linguistic parallels between Coke's report and texts in Justinian's *Corpus iuris*.[3] There is, to be sure, evidence for this in Coke's report, though this does need careful examination, and in the broader context of the development of the law of criminal libel in the reign of James I it is more problematic. It is certainly the case that some English lawyers of the late sixteenth and early seventeenth century had some acquaintance with Roman law; the sixteenth-century law of treason, for example, looks to have undergone a reorientation along the lines of Roman law, almost certainly

[1] V. V. Veeder, 'The History of the Law of Defamation', in *Select Essays in Anglo-American Legal History* (Boston: Little Brown, 1909), 3.446, 464; W. S. Holdsworth, *History of English Law*, 2nd edn (London: Methuen, 1937), 5.208; J. H. Baker, *Introduction to English Legal History*, 4th edn (London: Butterworths, 2002), 444. References to manuscript sources are to the National Archives unless otherwise noted as being in the British Library (BL) or Cambridge University Library (CUL).

[2] (1605) 5 Co. Rep. fol. 125; W. P. Baildon, ed., *Les Reportes del Cases in Camera Stellata 1593–1609, from the Original MS of John Hawarde* (privately printed, 1894), 222 (hereafter Hawarde). Coke's report was first printed (in Law French) in 1605; the English translation appeared in 1658, and is reproduced in ER, Vol. 77, 250.

[3] Veeder, 'Defamation', 464; Holdsworth, *History*, 208; D. Shuger, *Censorship and Cultural Sensibility* (Philadelphia: University of Pennsylvania Press, 2006), ch. 3.

mediated through the thirteenth-century text known as *Bracton*, and it is very likely that the law of fraud was developed by analogy with Roman law by the Star Chamber around 1600.[4]

What follows is in four parts. First, it describes the background to the emergence of the law of criminal libel; second, it sets the context of the case *De libellis famosis* in the light of this; third, it examines Coke's report of the case; and finally, it explores whether the Jacobean law of libel in practice operated consistently with Coke's version of the law.

The Background

The English law of defamation before the beginning of the seventeenth century had two main strands, both dating back to the thirteenth century: the claim by a private person who had been slandered, originating in the ecclesiastical law but in part translated into the secular common law in the sixteenth century; and the wrong of the slander of magnates, *scandalum magnatum*, whose ultimate source lay in a statute of 1275.[5] Alongside these, in the thirteenth century local courts had exercised a jurisdiction over verbal wrongs, and some fragments of this perhaps survived.

The roots of the defamation jurisdiction of the English church courts lay in the constitution *Auctoritate Dei Patris*, enacted at the Council of Oxford in 1222:[6]

> We excommunicate all those who for the sake of hatred, profit or favour, or for any other cause, maliciously impute a crime to any person who is not of ill fame among good and substantial persons, by reason of which purgation at least is awarded to him or he is harmed in some other manner.

This imposed excommunication on a person who had maliciously imputed a crime to another, as a result of which the other had undergone canonical purgation or suffered some other loss. 'Crime' here was broadly interpreted to cover any sort of sin, and the constitution was therefore wide enough to deal with allegations of sexual impropriety as well as allegations that a person was a thief or a murderer. 'Malice' was more difficult, but it would be presumed in the absence of evidence of lack of malice: defendants could therefore escape liability by showing for example that their words had been spoken in anger, under provocation, or for the purpose of reproving the plaintiff or otherwise to get them to mend their ways. In addition, although there was no formal requirement that the words spoken should have been false it seems clear from the surviving church

[4] I. Williams, 'A Medieval Book and Early-Modern Law: *Bracton*'s Authority and Application in the Common Law c.1550–1640', *The Legal History Review*, 79 (2011): 47–80, 79; C. Willems, 'Coke, Collusion and Conveyances: Unearthing the Roots of *Twyne's Case*', *JLH*, 36 (2015): 129–51, 129.

[5] For the history, see principally R. H. Helmholz, *Select Cases on Defamation to 1600*, SS, 101 (1985).

[6] Helmholz, *Select Cases*, xxvi–xli.

court records of the fifteenth century that truth was generally seen as a defence. Loss of some sort had to be shown, from which in practice it followed that the imputations must have come to the notice of a third party, generally because the words complained of had been spoken to him or her.

By the early years of the fifteenth century, as early as we have surviving records, actions might be brought for imputations which were not crimes, for example that someone was a leper.[7] William Lyndwood, whose *Provinciale* is our main source of knowledge about late medieval English canon law, makes clear that such imputations would not fall technically within *Auctoritate Dei Patris*, and hence would not attract the penalty of excommunication specified in the constitution, but where there was a public interest in detecting whatever was alleged, as there was in the case of leprosy, an ecclesiastical judge might none the less impose a penalty if the words had been spoken contumeliously.[8] Although it is not explicit in Lyndwood's text, his language here suggests an adoption of the Roman law as it had come into the learned canon law of the Middle Ages.[9]

Another extension from *Auctoritate Dei Patris* is visible from the 1460s.[10] Liability now could attach to vulgar abuse, *convicium*, as well as the imputation of crime. Although this did not technically fall within the constitution, and hence did not attract excommunication, it was clearly treated as analogous to it. Actions are now referred to as *causae diffamacionis vel convicii*, defamation and insult being treated side by side. Even more than with the extension of defamation to imputations of leprosy, the Roman law influence is very visible here, for *convicium* was one of the elements which fell within the Roman delict of *iniuria*.[11]

By the end of the fifteenth century, the common law began to take over some of the ground of the medieval ecclesiastical remedy.[12] The starting point was a restriction of the scope of the ecclesiastical law when what was alleged was a secular crime, where it could be argued that it was not within the competence of ecclesiastical judges to determine whether the imputation was true or false. In the first decade of the sixteenth century this was complemented by the granting of actions at common law in such circumstances. The form of action used was trespass on the case; this was based on the commission of a wrong—here, the malicious imputation of a crime—from which loss had flowed. Although it was necessary for the plaintiff to allege in his pleadings that some economic loss had been caused, the defendant was not allowed formally to deny this: it was a matter for the jury to take note of in their assessment of damages. It followed from the requirement of loss that the words, whether written or spoken, must

[7] Helmholz, *Select Cases*, xxviii.

[8] W Lyndwood, *Provinciale* (London: 1679) 36: gl *Malitiose* ad V.17, *De sententia excommunicationis.*

[9] See p. 487. There was a Common law writ, *de leproso amovendo*, available to incarcerate or quarantine a leper.

[10] Helmholz, *Select Cases*, xxix.

[11] See p. 497.

[12] Sir John Baker, *OHLE*, 6.781–8; D. J. Ibbetson, *A Historical Introduction to the Law of Obligations* (Oxford, Oxford University Press, 1999), 112–23.

have been published to a third party, in a language which the third party understood; and they had to refer to a person who was alive, on the assumption that a person who was dead could not suffer loss.

The core of the action lay in the malicious imputation of a crime. Here the common law courts closely followed the framework which had been laid down by the ecclesiastical courts. The action was extended from imputations of crimes to imputations of syphilis, analogously to the ecclesiastical courts' extension to allegations of leprosy. From the middle of the sixteenth century it was extended further into allegations of incompetence in one's profession, perhaps representing a tentative movement towards saying that where words had caused loss the victim ought to have a remedy. For most of the sixteenth century, allegations of purely ecclesiastical offences remained within the sole domain of the church courts; but in 1595 it was held that where such imputations had caused genuine loss an action would lie at common law to recover damages.[13] This was an important step, for it allowed the common law courts to hear some claims based on imputations of sexual misconduct (which would practically always be an ecclesiastical offence rather than a secular one), and more generally allowed the extension of the seventeenth-century common law into any situation where defamatory words had caused loss. The requirement of malice also closely tracked the medieval ecclesiastical law. It would be presumed if the words were untrue, but it was open to the defendant to produce evidence of a lack of malice, for example if the words were spoken or written in jest or in anger, or for reproof.

The appearance of the secular action did not cause the ecclesiastical action to disappear completely. In truth, it may have become even commoner in 1600 than it had been in 1500. Sexual slander without the causation of loss remained a matter for the church courts, and perhaps more importantly, simple abuse, *convicium*, remained within the ecclesiastical jurisdiction: as in the late fifteenth century, the action was a *causa diffamationis vel convicii*.[14] The abuse might take any form: written, spoken, pictorial, or by actions.

The second strand was *scandalum magnatum*, the slander of magnates. This was created by the first Statute of Westminster in 1275:[15]

> Whereasmuch as there have been oftentimes found in the country tellers of tales whereby discord or matter of discord hath many times arisen between the King and his People or Great Men of this Realm, for the Damage that hath and may thereof ensue; It is commanded, That from henceforth none be so hardy as to tell or publish any false News or Tales whereby discord or matter of discord or slander may grow between the King and his People or the Great Men of the Realm; he that doth so

[13] *Davis v Gardiner* (1593) 4 Co. Rep. 16, Poph 36.

[14] J. A. Sharpe, 'Defamation and Sexual Slander in Early Modern England: the Church Courts at York' (Borthwick Papers no. 58, York, 1980); M. Ingram, *Church Courts, Sex and Marriage in England, 1570–1640* (Cambridge: Cambridge University Press, 1987), 292–319. For the terminology, KB 27/1376 rex m. 6, m. 10d, m. 11 (1602).

[15] Stat Westm I, *c.* 34.

> shall be taken and kept in Prison until he hath brought him into the Court which did speak the same.

This was re-enacted in amended form in 1378, defining the 'great men' as 'Prelates, Dukes, Earls, Barons and other Nobles', and adding alongside them the Chancellor, Treasurer, Clerk of the Privy seal, Steward of the King's house, Judges of the King's Bench and Common Pleas and other Great Officers of the Realm'.[16] The orientation of the 1378 statute was slightly different from that of 1275: as well as the potential discord within the realm, it was concerned with the slander of the great men and officers named through the telling of 'false news, lies or other false things'. Further amendment in 1388 allowed for the punishment by the Council of the person who spread the lies who was unable to identify their originator.[17] *Scandalum magnatum*, therefore, was bipolar. On the one hand it was focused on the injury to the victim of the slander, on the other on the actual or potential social disharmony. It envisaged criminal punishment, though by the latter part of the fifteenth century at the latest it was found as the basis of a civil action too.[18]

A statute of 1554[19] extended the medieval wrong in two ways. First, it granted protection to the monarch from 'false seditious and slanderous news, rumours, sayings or tales', specifying a penalty of standing in the pillory, losing the ears or a fine of £100, and imprisonment for three months. Second, it laid down that:

> if any person shall maliciously devise, write, print or set forth any manner of book, rhyme, ballad, letter or writing, containing any false matter, clause or sentence of slander, reproach and dishonour of [the monarch], or to the encouraging, moving or stirring of any insurrection or rebellion within this realm ... Or whoever shall maliciously procure any such book, rhyme, ballad, letter or writing to be written, printed or set forth ...

that offender should lose his or her hand. In both situations imprisonment for life and forfeiture of goods was laid down for any second offence. The 1554 statute was continued by later legislation, and further punishments were imposed by a statute of 1581.[20]

The 1554 statute had two aspects. By extending *scandalum magnatum* to the monarch it skewed it more in the direction of seditious utterances than simple defamatory ones. This development might have been more apparent than real. Already in 1506 the manual for Justices of the Peace erroneously attributed to Sir Anthony Fitzherbert had contained a precedent of an indictment of a person who had spoken *inhonesta verba* of the king, situating this in the section of wrongs against the King's Peace. The precedent is from the mid-fifteenth century, based on Jack Cade's uprising, and its focus on the interference with effective government is transparent.[21] It may be that the collector of

[16] 2 Ric II, Stat 1, *c.* 5.
[17] Stat 12 Ric II, *c.* 11.
[18] Baker, *OHLE*, 781.
[19] Stat 1 & 2 Philip and Mary, *c.* 3.
[20] Stat 23 Eliz *c.* 2.
[21] *Boke of Iustices of Peas* (1506), fol. xxiv^{v}.

The Boke of Iustices of Peas was running together the powers of Justices of the Peace and those of Justices of Gaol Delivery,[22] where more serious wrongs would typically be heard, for there is no similar entry in Fitzherbert's *Newe Boke of Justyces of Peas* which appeared in 1538. While this work continued to be reprinted, no attempt was made to update it before Richard Crompton's completely new edition of 1583; consequently, the statute of 1554, which explicitly gave power to Justices of the Peace to prosecute breaches of its provisions, was never referred to. By contrast, William Lambarde's manual for Justices of the Peace, *Eirenarcha*, first published in 1581, refers only to the statutory crime as it appeared in the Act of that year;[23] and Crompton's edition of Fitzherbert's work similarly refers to the statute of 1581 together with the original statute of *scandalum magnatum* of 1275.[24]

The assize court records of the reign of Elizabeth I fit very closely into this statutory framework.[25] Prosecutions for words invariably involve sedition, the denial of true religion, or are directly of the queen herself; there are very occasional references to rhymes or ballads, but these too are seditious and not aimed at private individuals. Justices of the Peace may in practice have been less constrained by the statutory framework since they had a general duty to keep the peace, though even there there is very little evidence of prosecutions for non-seditious defamations before the start of the seventeenth century.[26]

The Context

The Court of Star Chamber was a spin-off from the King's Council in the fifteenth century, though it was sometimes seen as having had its origins in a statute of 1487.[27] It had an essentially untrammelled jurisdiction, though with a focus on public wrongdoing involving the use of force or abuse of authority. It could punish defendants and award them compensation. As the sixteenth century progressed it became more criminal in its orientation so that only the king could pardon wrongs,[28] though actions were very commonly brought by the aggrieved person,[29]

[22] B. Putnam, 'Sixteenth Century Treatises for Justices of the Peace', *UTLJ*, 7 (1947): 137–61, 137, 138.

[23] W. Lambarde, *Eirenarcha* (London: 1581), 343. The same is true of the reworked edition of 1592, 220.

[24] *Loffice et auctoritie de iustices de peace* (London: 1583), 29, 55, 56.

[25] J. S. Cockburn, ed., *Calendar of Assize Records, Elizabeth I* and *Calendar of Assize Records, James I* (London: Her Majesty's Stationery Office, 1975–1985).

[26] F. G. Emmison: *Elizabethan Life: Disorder* (Chelmsford: Essex County Council), 66 (1576); J. C. Jeaffreson, ed., *Middlesex County Records* (Middlesex County Records Society, 1886), 1.211; J. W. Willis Bund, *Worcestershire County Records* (Worcester: Worcestershire County Council, 1900), 44.

[27] Baker, *OHLE*, 195–6; Stat 3 Hen VII *c.* 1.

[28] *Hall's Case* (1604) 5 Co. Rep. 51.

[29] *Lamb's Case* (1610) Moo 813, 9 Co. Rep. 59, CUL MS Ll 3.2 no. 27, STAC 8/205/20 stressing that it was only the aggrieved party or the Attorney General who could initiate proceedings.

and the seventeenth-century court continued to award damages from time to time.[30]

Three cases of 1483, all involving the same defendant, show that complaints of private defamation were not alien to the court even in the fifteenth century,[31] and Sir Thomas Egerton's collection of materials includes seditious bills or libels as one of the heads of Star Chamber litigation between 1515 and 1529,[32] but the records of the court suggest that such cases were not at all common. John Guy's sample of 473 private suits of Cardinal Wolsey's time contains just three actions described as defamation.[33] A list of headings of causes said to have been heard in Star Chamber between 1550 and 1576 included 'slanderous libel',[34] though Guy's sample of cases from 1558 to 1559 contained not a single example.[35] No doubt the Star Chamber cases largely involved the same sort of seditious situations as were prosecuted at the assizes,[36] but the court could hear cases of private defamations even without their falling within the category of rhymes or ballads or constituting *scandalum magnatum*. Hence, in *Fane v Acton*[37] an action was brought in the Star Chamber for spoken slanders in which the defendant had suggested that if he were to die a violent death then the plaintiff would have been responsible; it was ordered that the defendant should make a contrite apology at the next assizes and that the complainant should not further sue either in the King's Bench or the ecclesiastical courts.

The last two or three years of the reign of Elizabeth marked a major turning point. It may have been heralded by a Star Chamber speech of Lord Keeper Egerton in 1599, where he said that 'some traitorous monsters have railed against [the Queen] by railing speeches and slanderous libels', which 'traitorous vipers' had scattered libels about London, and he urged the severe punishment of such seditious libellers.[38] This was the same time as the Archbishop of Canterbury and the Bishop of London banned a number of satirical books and strengthened the earlier system of licensing.[39] The concern with sedition was still uppermost, and was no doubt triggered by the political unrest

30 *Edwards v. Wootton* (1608) Hawarde 343, CUL MS Ll 3.2 case 14, STAC 8/130/12; cf. *Peacock v. Reynell* (1612) 2 Br & Goulds 151, CUL MS Ll 3.2 no. 13, STAC 8/313/38, where the defendant was fined but the plaintiff told to seek damages at common law.

31 I. S. Leadam, ed., *Select Pleas in the Court of Star Chamber*, SS, 16 (1902), 38–41.

32 J. A. Guy, *The Court of Star Chamber and its Records in the Reign of Elizabeth I* (London: Her Majesty's Stationery Office, 1985), 54–5.

33 J. Guy, *The Cardinal's Court* (Hassocks: Harvester Press, 1977), 53

34 Guy, *Court of Star Chamber*, 58–9.

35 Guy, *Court of Star Chamber*, 57, 59.

36 R. Crompton, *L'authoritie et Iurisdiction des Courts de la Majestie de la Roygne* (London: 1594), fols 32v–35v. This would be true of all of the extracts from the Elizabethan Decree and Order Books of the court in BL MS Harl 2143.

37 (1584) STAC 5/F7/37, STAC 5/F16/32, STAC 5/F22/23, STAC 5/F30/15. The detail appears in subsequent Chancery litigation in *Acton v. Fane* (1596) C2/Eliz/A7/38 (petition), C33/91 fol. 322 (procedural order).

38 SP 12/273 fol. 60; *CSPD Eliz*, 1598–1601, 347.

39 Arber, 3.677–8; C. S. Clegg, *Press Censorship in Elizabethan England* (Cambridge: Cambridge University Press, 1997), 198–217.

associated with events in Ireland leading up to the Essex rebellion of 1601. However, very soon prosecutions for private defamations began to appear.

William Hudson, whose treatise on the Star Chamber was written in 1621, wrote of actions for libels having become more frequent in 1600–1601, when Sir Edward Coke was Attorney-General.[40] The reference to the Attorney-General may point to information brought otherwise than by an individual complainant, and if so it is likely that in his eyes at least the rise in frequency represented deliberate government policy in the turbulent last years of Elizabeth's reign. So far as private libels are concerned, the key event may have been the case of *R v Barker*, in the Court of King's Bench in 1603.

Barker's Case concerned a ballad referring to the sexual antics of a number of the inhabitants of Chelmsford, which had circulated in 1600.[41] Prosecutions were brought against the local schoolmaster who had written out the libel and against its originator, Hugh Barker; it is only with Barker's prosecution that we are concerned. It began in the Quarter Sessions in Chelmsford in 1601, from where it was transferred to the Essex Assizes in 1602, apparently at the request of one of the Assize judges, Francis Gawdy.[42] He was duly convicted and sentenced to be pilloried and to pay a substantial fine, and the case was then further removed into the King's Bench on a writ of error.[43] It came before the court in the Hilary term of 1603, where it was reported by Thomas Coventry.[44] A technical argument that it was not formally alleged who had been libelled was rejected: it was enough that the victims were named in the ballad, and even if they were dead the prosecution was good because of the allegation that the publication had been designed to stir contention and strife. The real point, if we understand the report correctly, was whether the Act concerning inflammatory ballads could be applied by analogy to this type of private libel. Popham CJ drew the analogy with cucking stools, which were required to be in every leet for the punishment of private scolds; private libels should equally be punished. This was more than an off-the-cuff remark: he said that he had earlier sentenced libellers in Suffolk to a similar penalty after taking advice from several fellow judges.

These shifts appear to have been associated with the channelling of prosecutions for libel into the Star Chamber: Guy identified eighteen cases in the last full year of Elizabeth's reign,[45] a marked increase on the earlier figures, and this rate was kept up through the reign of James I. More telling perhaps is the decline in the number of cases of seditious or slanderous words being prosecuted at the Assizes: in Essex, Hertfordshire, Kent, Sussex, and Surrey there are approximately one-quarter as many prosecutions under James as under Elizabeth, and nearly all of these date from 1603 or 1604.

[40] W. Hudson, *A Treatise of the Court of Star Chamber*, in *Collectanea iuridica*, F. Hargrave (London, 1792), 2.100.

[41] The story is set out in detail in Emmison (n. 26), 71–9.

[42] *Essex Indictments*, no. 3254, in *Calendar of Assize Records* (n. 25).

[43] KB 9/711 (1) no. 118.

[44] BL MS Add. 25203 fol. 667.

[45] Guy, *Court of Star Chamber*, 60.

It is this that provides the context for the prosecution of Pickering and the case *De libellis famosis*, described by John Hawarde as a 'great cause'. He had confessed to having made a libel against John Whitgift, the deceased Archbishop of Canterbury, Queen Elizabeth, and Whitgift's successor Richard Bancroft, which he had pinned to Whitgift's hearse at his funeral. New law was just emerging, with no statutory basis, and since it was emerging in the Star Chamber there were no formal limits on it. Coke's argument, as Attorney-General, was directed at getting a conviction of Pickering where the law was more or less uncertain, and the judges of the court (most of whom were not lawyers) were far more concerned with the punishment to be inflicted on him than with the legal framework which justified this. Hawarde's report of the case suggests that apart from some brief remarks by the Chief Justice Sir John Popham, Robert Cecil, Earl of Salisbury, and Lord Chancellor Ellesmere, none of those present spoke about the legal underpinning of the conviction.

Popham placed criminal libel as a third category, after the action on the case for slander for private individuals and *scandalum magnatum* for noblemen.[46] The justification for this was the fact that the libel was a breach of the peace, parallelling killing with a sword or poison; and just as unlawful killing was a crime, a libel was criminal whether the victim was alive or dead. It was not just a wrong to the individual, but a wrong to the whole commonwealth. Cecil spoke at some length about the virtues of Whitgift, but prefaced this with a single sentence defining libel as a defamatory writing, and saying that the person who had made the writing would be regarded in law as the publisher unless he produced the author of it.[47] Ellesmere described Pickering's libel as 'false, infamous, scandalous, lying and slanderous', adding—with a typically inflated rhetoric—that it flowed from an unquiet spirit and a failure to obey the lawful government. He added a reference to the law of the Lydians, and gave examples of earlier prosecutions and punishments, all of which would have constituted *scandalum magnatum*.[48] There was very little material out of which a law of libel could be fashioned.

Coke's Report of the Case *De Libellis Famosis*

It is easy—too easy—to suppose that Coke's report of *Pickering's Case* in some sense constituted the law. But it is a text with an author, and, unless if it was straightforwardly a verbatim reproduction of what the judges had said, the authorial voice cannot but come through. Coke's report of the case does not purport to reproduce the judges' words, but rather to summarize their resolutions, and we have no reason to suppose that

[46] Hawarde, 226.
[47] Hawarde, 227.
[48] Hawarde, 229.

the judges collectively resolved anything. No hint of this is given by Hawarde, so unless there is something very important missing from Hawarde's account of the case, Coke's report of it must have a substantial dimension of construction; it cannot be simply a description of what was resolved by the court. Coke is known to have used his reports of cases as pegs on which to hang his account of the law, so there is nothing surprising in this. Moreover, the material differences between his manuscript report[49] and the printed text enable us to appreciate the additional level of construction which went into the final version.

Perhaps most revealingly, the heading of the case changed: in the manuscript it is 'Libells', in the print '*De libellis famosis*'. Although the anglicized version of this, 'infamous libels', is found in English texts from the 1560s—in 1574 John Whitgift still felt the need to explain it to his readers[50]—the use of the technical Latin phrase can hardly have failed to raise the spectre of Roman law, echoing the title of the relevant book in both Justinian's *Digest* and his *Codex*.[51] It was only in the printed text that Roman law was brought into the foreground in this way.

Coke's concern in his report was with the law. He began with only the barest outline of the facts, saying that Pickering was proceeded against on his confession for having libelled Whitgift and Bancroft. There is no reference in the printed text to the libel being also against the queen, as Hawarde describes the prosecution, though this is included in his manuscript. The reference, therefore, can be assumed to have been consciously removed in preparing the text for publication. The effect of this excision is significant. With the reference to the queen included, the case was a more or less straightforward one of sedition under the statute of 1554 as amended; without it, it could be seen as a case of a private libel against Whitgift himself. It might have been characterized as *scandalum magnatum* since Whitgift was a prelate, one of the categories of magnate listed in the statute; but there is no hint of such a characterization in Coke's report.

Moving onto the law, Coke identified four propositions which he claimed to have been resolved. First, he divided libels into those against private individuals and those against magistrates and other public persons; the former were to be punished severely because of their tendency to provoke a breach of the peace, the latter should be punished yet more severely since they concerned not only the breach of the peace but also the scandal of government. No such division is found in Hawarde's report, and it may be an amalgam of Popham's treatment and Ellesmere's. In truth nothing hinged on the distinction. Its real point, probably was to reinforce Popham's point that prosecutions could be brought for libels of private individuals, the extension to the Elizabethan law that was just beginning to be made. This section of the report contains allusions to the world outside the common law, and since there are no material differences here between Coke's manuscript and the printed text these allusions can be attributed to the first stage of his construction of the law. First, a libel is described in Latin as *famosus libellus*,

[49] BL MS Harl 6686 fols 641–2.

[50] J. Whitgift, *The Defence of the Answer to the Admonition* (London: 1574), 807.

[51] D.47.10; C.9.36.

seu infamatoria scriptura, a contraction of the phrase reported by Hawarde as having been used by Coke in his argument, *infamatoria scriptura, famosus libellus quod nullus scribere vel dictare sub pena capitis*.[52] This linked his version of English law to classical Rome, where *libellus famosus* was the normal term for a criminal libel. Coke did not get this directly from Justinian's texts, where the collocation of *famosus libellus* and *infamatoria scriptura* is not found, but from a sixteenth-century dictionary: the full phrase is found in the *Vocabularius perutilis utriusque iuris tam civilis quam canonici*, a book which we know Coke to have owned.[53] Second, the reference to a 'magistrate or public person', where 'public person' would have been sufficient on its own, echoes Quintilian, who treated the commission of the delict *iniuria* on a magistrate, *magistratus*, as constituting *maiestas*, treason.[54] But these are no more than verbal cues of a sort that was very common in legal argument and text in the early modern period: nothing of real substance flowed from them.

The second proposition was that it was equally criminal to defame a dead person as a living one. This had already been held by the King's Bench in *Barker's Case*[55] and the point was probably uncontroversial. It was made explicitly in Chief Justice Popham's speech, and although it is not stated so clearly in any of the other speeches in the case, it must have been implicit since Whitgift was self-evidently dead at the time of the publication of the libel.

Coke's third proposition was equally uncontroversial: the prosecution could be brought by indictment at the common law (as in *Barker's Case*) or by bill in the Star Chamber. The manuscript fails to say that it could also be brought in the Star Chamber without a bill if the offender confessed, the procedure which was used in *Pickering's Case* itself. This obvious omission was remedied in the printed text.

The fourth proposition shows signs of uncertainty, with a number of differences between the manuscript and the print. These did not bring about any significant changes in meaning, but sharpened the points being made. It began, in both manuscript and print, with two rules for which there seems to have been no warrant in the speeches reported to have been given, and which would in any event have been utterly irrelevant in the case: it did not matter whether the libel was true or false, and it did not matter whether the victim of the libel was of good or ill fame. They appear to have been invented by Coke himself as a way of distancing criminal libel from the civil action for damages, where truth was a defence and the plaintiff's prior good fame was essential. The explanation given for them, again both in manuscript and print, lacks logic: in a settled state of government a person who has suffered a wrong should complain by the ordinary course of law and not resort to libelling. The remainder of the proposition is based on the

[52] Hawarde reports his use of the same phrase in his argument in the case.

[53] W. O. Hassall, *Catalogue of the Library of Sir Edward Coke* (Yale University Press, 1950), no. 482. There were a number of editions of the *Vocabularius*; we do not know which was owned by Coke.

[54] Quintilian, *Institutio oratoria*, 5.10.29. See too Tacitus, *Annales*, 1.72, for Augustus' extension of *maiestas* to the spoken word. For *iniuria*, see p. 000.

[55] See p. 494. The view that libels need be anonymous was referred to by Hudson (n. 39) as a gross error which had been extirpated.

speech of Chief Justice Popham: libelling is like poisoning, something that takes place behind a person's back, contrasted with the open assault on a man which gives him the opportunity to defend himself. In addition, it was the fact that libellers might be difficult to identify that justified the need for severe punishment when they were found. There is perhaps a resonance here of the Augustan rule described by Suetonius and referred to in Justinian's *Digest*, according to which it was anonymous or pseudonymous libels that were punished, but it is no more than a reminiscence.[56]

Thus far Coke's construction of the law had been largely based on what had been said in the Star Chamber, especially by Chief Justice Popham. He had put his own slant on it, and it was perhaps tendentious to describe the points as having been resolved by the court rather than stated by a single judge. But Elizabethan and Jacobean courts did not generally resolve points of law in any formal way, each judge producing his own argument and only the result being agreed upon, so that practically any detailed statement of what the law was must have been somewhat provisional.

The following section, stating the ways in which a libel might be made, is very different. It did not purport to be a resolution of the court, and a single sentence in the manuscript was substantially expanded in the print. It has the appearance of an instructional excursus of the sort that is commonly found in Coke's reports, and which may or may not have been recognized by other lawyers as representing the law. Moreover, even the manuscript shows signs of hesitancy, with two of the ways of libelling in the list being interlineated.

The manuscript reads (translating the French and marking the interlineations):

> And it was said that a man can offend through libelling verbis, scriptis, cantilenis, \ publicatione/ \traditione/ et signis, as by putting a sign such as gallows either outside his door or fixed to his house.

The printed text is more analytical. Libels could be divided into those that were written and those which were unwritten. The former arose 'when an epigram, rhyme or other writing is composed or published to the scandal or contumely of another, by which his fame and dignity may be prejudiced'. 'Rhyme or other writing' harks back to the language of the 1554 and 1581 statutes, but the reference to contumely here carries clear overtones of Roman law: the delict of *iniuria* was defined in terms of *contumelia* in Justinian's *Institutes*, a work with which Coke was undoubtedly familiar.[57] The inclusion of epigrams looks to be a borrowing from Roman law, which brought *epigrammata* within the *senatusconsultum* giving effect to Augustus' rule; moreover the word 'scandal' here is a translation of '*note*' in the original French of Coke's printed report, reflecting the *Digest*'s '*epigrammata in notam aliquorum*'.[58] Finally, the reference to the prejudice to the fame and dignity of the victim also looks also to be a reference to

[56] Suetonius, *Divus Augustus*, 55; D.47.10.5.9.
[57] Hassall (n. 53), no. 469, noting Coke's marginalia in his copy of the *Institutes*.
[58] D.47.10.5.10.

Roman law, where *fama* and *dignitas* were two of the three interests protected by the delict *iniuria*,[59] and the division into written and unwritten libels is again found in the Roman texts.[60]

The written libel might be published either by repetition or singing in the presence of others, *verbis* or *cantilenis*. This too suggests a classical allusion since the 'evil song' was punished by Roman law. But in this context the word for song was *carmen* rather than *cantilena*, while *cantilena* was a wholly appropriate latinization of the way in which a libellous ballad might be sung, and the singing of libels is described as *cantilena* in some sixteenth-century civil law works.[61] As an alternative to repeating or singing the libel, it might be published by handing it to another, *traditione*. A defamatory libel that was written but not repeated, sung, or delivered would not have been published, and so would not attract a penalty.

The unwritten libel, according to Coke's printed report, might take the form of a picture, when a person was painted in a shameful way, or signs, as by fixing a gallows at a person's door. It is unclear whether or not Coke had some external source for this. There is nothing in Roman law explicitly to suggest that *iniuria* could be committed by pictures or signs. That pictures were an alternative to words is found in some civil law lexica and other texts in the sixteenth century,[62] but we do not know whether Coke would have known these. It is possible, perhaps even likely, that he was simply reflecting the practice of the English courts.[63]

The final point appearing in the printed text here which is not in the manuscript is a reference to a decision in *Halliwood's Case* in 1601, no report or record of which has been traced. This, according to Coke, had held that if a man found a libel against a private person he should either burn it or deliver it to a magistrate, while the finder of a libel against a public person should deliver it to a magistrate with a view to identifying the author. Again, there is a Roman allusion here, this time to Justinian's *Codex*,[64] where the finder of a *libellus famosus* was required to burn it. We cannot know whether or not this can genuinely be attributed to *Halliwood's Case*.

At this point the manuscript and the printed text come together again, as Coke demonstrates that libelling, and calumniation generally, is contrary to the law of God. There are minor variations between the two versions—Exodus 22:28, for example, is in English in the manuscript (from the Geneva Bible which begins 'Thou shalt not raile upon the judges' in preference to Coverdale's 'Thou shalt not rayle upon the goddess' which had been adopted in Cranmer's English Bible), but it is in Latin in the printed version—but these amount to no more than what would be expected in tidying up a text.

59 D.47.10.1.2.

60 D.47.10.5.9, 10.

61 For example, J. Damhouder, *Praxis rerum criminalium* (Antwerp: 1554), 491.

62 J. Spiegel, In *Lexicon iuris civilis* (Paris: 1554), s.v. *Iniuria* (citing only Zasius' commentary on D.1.3.22, no. 13); S. Schard, *Lexicon iuridicum iuris Romani simul et Pontificii* (1593), s.v. *Iniuria*.

63 *Horsey v. Astley* (1591), cited by Hudson, *Treatise*, 101.

64 C.9.36.1.

This is the end of the report as printed, but a final few words are present in the manuscript, squeezed into the space before the next report begins and partially overwriting the last line of the report of *Pickering's Case*: 'Swinburne 58b famosus libellator est intestabilis', a reference to a leading sixteenth-century work of English ecclesiastical law which Coke possessed, Henry Swinburne's *Treatise of Testaments and Last Wills*, the 1591 edition of which reproduced (at fol. 58^{v}) the Roman law rule that the publisher of an infamous libel was prohibited from making a will. This is revealing of the way in which Coke was working: first the preparation of his report in manuscript, followed by further reflection (and probably research) which skewed it more in the direction of the civil or canon law, followed by the creation of the printed version of the report reflecting this reorientation.

Comparison of the manuscript and printed versions of the text enables us to draw one very important conclusion. In so far as the final version of the report reflects or incorporates Roman law, this was almost completely the product of Coke's editorial process. We cannot be sure of his source, but that the construction of English law which appeared in the printed text had been consciously slanted by him in the direction of Roman law is beyond doubt.

Whether this Romanization was anything more than cosmetic is a different matter. Two aspects of Roman law were relevant: the general delict of *iniuria* and the specific criminal provisions relating to infamous libels, *famosi libelli*.[65] In its origin *iniuria* was concerned with physical assaults, but a number of other disparate situations were added on to it in the late Republic: *convicium*, or public insult; making someone *infamis*, which might loosely be seen as the equivalent of defamation; forms of sexual harassment; and thrashing or torturing another's slave without the owner's consent. Early in the Empire a generalization was made from these situations of acting with contumely or hubris towards another person. The delict was thereafter characterized in this way, saying that it involved an interference with a person's *corpus, dignitas*, or *fama*; the first of these referred to the suffering of personal injury, the second to a person's self-respect, the third to his or her reputation. The action was intensely personal, so that only the victim could sue or be sued (unless it affected a slave, when the master stood in his stead), though it was recognized that an act directed against one person might indirectly affect another: the *paterfamilias* might be affected where the victim was a member of his family, and an insult to a corpse might generate an action for the heir in so far as this affected him or her. The writing of *famosi libelli*, anonymous or pseudonymous pamphlets, was originally punished by Augustus; there was no requirement of publication to any third party. Fourth-century legislation reproduced in Justinian's *Codex* further provided that the finder of such a *libellus* should burn it or be prepared to justify its contents.

Against this background, it is not easy to say how Romanized Coke's version of the law of libel was. At a structural level, the parallels with the delict of *iniuria* are relatively

[65] For *iniuria*, see for example W. W. Buckland, *Textbook of Roman Law*, 3rd edn, ed. P. G. Stein (Cambridge: Cambridge University Press, 1963), 589–92. The criminalization of *famosi libelli* is less easy to disentangle; see R. E. Smith, 'The Law of Libel at Rome', *Classical Quarterly*, 1 (1951): 169–79, 169.

weak, with English law not reflecting the very general rule of Roman law. If there had been any attempt to mirror this, we should at the least have expected to see some reference to *convicium*, insult, which had formed part of the ecclesiastical law of defamation since the middle of the fifteenth century.[66] Other elements of Coke's version of the law of libel equally jar with the Roman *iniuria*: that it was possible to libel the dead, for example, or that it did not matter whether the libel was true or false. That said, the relevance of *contumelia* and the interference with *fama* and *dignitas* do map well onto Roman law. The specific parallels with the wrong of *libelli famosi* are much stronger, whether drawn from legal texts or lay, with several points of detail echoing Roman law with considerable precision.

The Law of Libel

It is not easy to describe the Jacobean law of libel with any certainty. There are relatively few reported cases, even in collections of Star Chamber material. The Decree and Order Books of the court are lost, so we are reliant on surviving bills, answers, interrogatories, and depositions, which tell us merely what one of the parties thought or hoped the law was, though since these documents were drawn up by lawyers it is reasonable to assume that they are not wildly far-fetched. Unfortunately, claims for libel are frequently joined with other claims, and it is difficult to know from the records whether they were material or merely makeweight. That said, some regularities can be seen.

The most noteworthy feature is the way in which the bills reflect the second head of the sedition statutes of 1554 and 1581.[67] They are almost uniformly concerned with written libels; a bill of 1607 describes the offence as slandering others by writing,[68] and it is not until 1619 that we find a bill (which may of course not have succeeded) based on spoken defamation which would have fallen outside *scandalum magnatum* or sedition.[69] Similarly, libel through a picture was probably problematic, despite Coke's clear view in *Pickering's Case*.[70] The language of bills more or less reflects the statutory formulation, especially when they base their claim on a libel in rhyme or meter. It is invariably alleged that the defendant was acting maliciously, as was required by the statutes; this was also a formal requirement of the private action deriving from the ecclesiastical

66 See p. 488.

67 See p. 496.

68 *Hellier v Dingle* (1607) STAC 8/161/5.

69 *Gardiner v Gilbert* (1619) STAC 8/156/19. An earlier spoken defamation is *Attorney General v. Closse* (1609), where a priest preaching an assize sermon allegedly vilified the corrupt judges, barristers, and the whole common law: (1609) STAC 8/17/19, STAC 8/33/8.

70 *Taylor v Mouns* (1618) STAC 8/284/23 is the only Jacobean case I have identified where the primary defamation alleged was pictorial, though this was in the context of an unusually rancorous dispute between neighbours. *Ireland v. Bolde* (1604) STAC 8/184/30 centred on a picture, but it was the written 'coward' on the picture that made it defamatory.

constitution *Auctoritate Dei Patris*,[71] but it seems to have been taken more seriously in the Star Chamber, where interrogatories might investigate whether the defendant had in fact been acting out of 'hatred, malice or spleen' towards the victim.[72] In the same way, the danger to the public of libels is stressed, usually by reference to their tendency to provoke breaches of the peace, but sometimes the propensity of private defamations to bring about insurrection or rebellion is noted,[73] reflecting the statutory language, or a defamation of a private person is described as being seditious.[74] Even a petty libel might be prosecuted if it had aroused public feeling.[75]

Other ubiquitous features in the Star Chamber records do not gel with Coke's account of the law of libel. Inconsistently with his statement that it was irrelevant whether the victim was of prior good fame, bills invariably go out of their way to emphasize that the victims had the purest of reputations. Equally it is invariably stated that the imputations cast on the victims were false, contrary to Coke's statement that this was unnecessary, though in one Jacobean case a malicious allegation which might have been true was held to be actionable specifically because of the defendants' malice.[76]

The fluidity of the law of libel in the early seventeenth century is well illustrated by the question whether it could apply to a private letter. It was held in *Edwards v Wootton* in 1608 that it might do on the grounds that even without further publication it could provoke revenge and a breach of the peace;[77] though at about the same time it was said that the writer of a private letter which had not otherwise been published should avoid punishment.[78] Later cases seem to assume the latter provided the letter was sealed,[79] though in 1618 Chief Justice Montague is reported to have said that a private letter containing public matter might constitute libel even in the absence of publication to a third party.[80]

Other constructions of the law of libel are found in the early seventeenth century. Ferdinando Pulton, in his *De pace regis et regni* published in 1609, dealt with it under

[71] See p. 488.

[72] *Browne v Fetherstone* (1609) STAC 8/80/8.

[73] *Goodryche v Burton* (1608) STAC 8/159/6.

[74] *Bisshop v Couchman* (1610) STAC 8/47/10; *Boulter v. Seafoule* (1615) STAC 8/83/1.

[75] *Attorney General v Martin* (1602) Hawarde, 152.

[76] *Newton v Smith* (1619) CUL MS Ll 3.2 no. 122, STAC 8/222/6. The defendants, former apprentices of the complainant grocer, had published notes claiming that he had used false weights. It was said that their purpose was to seduce his customers away from him, and they were punished for their malice. The next case in the report is the prosecution of Newton on the complaint of the Company of Grocers for using false weights. And writing in 1621 Hudson, *Treatise*, 102, 104 described the view that truth was a defence as an old-fashioned view which had been expelled from the court, applicable only in cases of *scandalum magnatum*; in his view, the fact that a libel was true made it worse.

[77] Hawarde 343, 12 Co. Rep. 35, CUL MS Ll 3.2 no. 14, STAC 8/130/12.

[78] *Hall v Ellis* (1607) BL MS Harl 2143 fol. 31^{v}, STAC 8/180/9.

[79] *Attorney General v Hull* (1609) STAC 8/15/19; *Browne v Fetherstone* (1609) STAC 8/80/8; *Barrow v Llewellyn* (1615) CUL MS Ll 3.2 no. 83; *Glemham v Browne* (1616) STAC 8/160/28. Contrast *Burnelye v Onlye* (1608) STAC 8/77/3 (unsealed letter).

[80] *Hickes v Jarrett* (1618) Poph 139, STAC 8/182/24. A similar point is made by Hudson (n. 40), 101–2.

the heading of 'Menaces, Assaults, Batteries, Imprisonments and Maihems',[81] thereby bringing into the foreground the attack on the victim constituted by the libel. Despite the very different slant from Coke's treatment, the only source cited by Pulton is Coke's report of *Pickering's Case*. A decade or so later, William Hudson devoted a few pages in his treatise on the Star Chamber to outlining the jurisdiction of the court, selecting out a few decisions as the basis of his description.[82] Since he was himself a practitioner in the court and his discussion was based on actual decisions of the court rather than some abstract framework, it has a greater claim to accuracy than Coke's or Pulton's even if it less intellectually satisfying. None the less, it is important to beware of assuming that even his picture represents some objective truth about the law of libel as applied by the Jacobean Star Chamber.

This study of the law of libel leads to a number of brief reflections on the textuality of the early modern common law. First, it is of the greatest importance not to lose sight of the fluidity of the law. Any report of a case, or section of a treatise, can at the very best give a snapshot of what the law was at some particular moment. It is only when a text by definition constitutes the law, as would normally be the case with a statute that had not been repealed or amended, that we could be justified as treating it as 'law' in itself, and even then we have to be alert to the need to interpret it. Second, any report or treatise has an author, and the reader must always be alert to the author's own voice in describing the law. Finally, behind any printed version there is likely to be a manuscript tradition, and—as with any text—we ignore that manuscript tradition at our peril.

Bibliography

1 & 2 Philip and Mary, c. 3.

2 Richard II, St 1, c. 5.

3 Henry VII, c. 1.12 Ric II, c. 11.

23 Elizabeth I c. 2.

Anon. *Boke of Iustices of Peas* (London: 1506).

Attorney General v. Closse (1609) National Archives STAC 8/17/19, National Archives STAC 8/33/8.

Attorney General v. Hull (1609) National Archives STAC 8/15/19.

Attorney General v. Martin (1602) Hawarde 152.

[Bacon, Francis]. 'The Use of the Law', in *The Works of Francis Bacon*, Vol. 7, ed. J. Spedding et al. (London: 1872).

Baildon, W. P., ed. *Les reportes del cases in Camera Stellata 1593–1609, from the Original MS of John Hawarde* [Hawarde] (privately printed: 1894).

Baker, J. H. *Introduction to English* Legal *History*, 4th edn (London: Butterworths, 2002).

[81] *De pace regis et regni*, fol. 1ᵛ. Cf. F. Bacon (attrib.), *The Use of the Law*, in *The Works of Francis Bacon*, new edn, ed. J. Spedding et al. (London: Longmans and Co., 1872), 7.463, treating the civil action for slander in this way.

[82] Hudson, *Treatise*, 100–4.

Baker, J. H. *Oxford History of the Laws of England*, Vol. 6 (Oxford: Oxford University Press, 2003).
Barker's Case (1603), National Archives KB 9/711 (1), no. 118, British Library MS Add. 25203, fol. 667.
Barrow v. Llewellyn (1615) Cambridge University Library MS Ll 3.2, no. 83.
Bisshop v. Couchman (1610) National Archives STAC 8/47/10.
Boulter v. Seafoule (1615) National Archives STAC 8/83/1.
British Library MS Harley 2143, Elizabethan Decree and Order Books of the Court.
Browne v. Fetherstone (1609) National Archives STAC 8/80/8.
Buckland, W. W. *Textbook of Roman Law*, 3rd edn (Cambridge: Cambridge University Press, 1963).
Burnelye v. Onlye (1608) National Archives STAC 8/77/3.
Clegg, C. S. *Press Censorship in Elizabethan England* (Cambridge: Cambridge University Press, 1997).
Cockburn, J. S., ed. *Calendar of Assize Records, Elizabeth I and Calendar of Assize Records, James I* (London: HMSO, 1975–1985).
Crompton, R. *L'authoritie et iurisdiction des courts de la Majestie de la Roygne* (London: 1594).
Damhouder, J. *Praxis rerum criminalium* (Antwerp: 1554).
Davis v. Gardiner (1593) 4 Co. Rep. 16, Poph 36.
De libellis famosis (1605) 5 Co. Rep. 125, Hawarde 222.
Edwards v. Wooton (1607) 12 Co. Rep. 35, Cambridge University Library MS Ll 3.2 no. 14, National Archives STAC 8/130/12, Hawarde 343.
Emmison, F. G. *Elizabethan Life. Disorder: Mainly from Essex Sessions and Assize Records* (Chelmsford: Essex County Council, 1970).
Everett Green, Mary Anne. *Calendar of State Papers Domestic Elizabeth, 1598–1601* (London: 1869).
Fane v. Acton (1583–1598) National Archives STAC 5/F16/32, National Archives STAC 5/F22/23, National Archives STAC 5/F7/37, National Archives C33/91, fol. 322, National Archives C2/Eliz/A7/38.
Fane v. Tiffyn (1584) National Archives STAC 5/F30/15.
Fitzherbert, Anthony. *Loffice et auctoritie de iustices de peace* (London: 1583).
Gardiner v. Gilbert (1619) National Archives STAC 8/156/19.
Glemham v. Browne (1616) National Archives STAC 8/160/28.
Goodryche v. Burton (1608) National Archives STAC 8/159/6.
Guy, J. A. *The Court of Star Chamber and its Records in the Reign of Elizabeth I* (London: HMSO, 1985).
Guy, J. A. *The Cardinal's Court* (Hassocks: Harvester Press, 1977).
Hall v. Ellis (1607) British Library MS Harley 2143, fol. 31v, National Archives STAC 8/180/9.
Hall's Case (1604) 5 Co. Rep. 51.
Hassall, W. O. *Catalogue of the Library of Sir Edward Coke* (New Haven: Yale University Press, 1950).
Hellier v. Dingle (1607) National Archives STAC 8/161/5.
Helmholz, R. H. *Select Cases on Defamation to 1600* (London: SS, 1985).
Hickes v. Jarrett (1618) Poph 139, National Archives STAC 8/182/24.
Holdsworth, W. S. *History of English Law*, Vol. 5, 2nd edn (London: Methuen, 1937).

Hudson, W. 'A Treatise of the Court of Star Chamber', in *Collectanea juridica*, Vol. 2, ed. F. Hargrave (London: 1792), 1–240.
Ibbetson, D. J. *A Historical Introduction to the Law of Obligations* (Oxford, Oxford University Press, 1999).
Ingram, Martin. *Church Courts, Sex and Marriage in England, 1570–1640* (Cambridge: Cambridge University Press, 1987).
Ireland v. Bolde (1604) National Archives STAC 8/184/30.
Jeaffreson, J. C., ed. *Middlesex County Records*, Vol. 1: *1550–1603* (London: 1886).
Justinian I. *Codex Ivstinianvs*, ed. Paul Krueger (Berlin: 1877).
Justinian I. *The Digest of Justinian*, ed. and trans. Charles Henry Monro (Cambridge: Cambridge University Press, 2014).
Lamb's Case (1610) Moo 813, 9 Co. Rep. 59, Cambridge University Library MS LI 3.2, no. 27, National Archives STAC 8/205/20.
Lambarde, W. *Eirenarcha or of the Office of the Iustices of Peace in Two Bookes* (London: 1581).
Lambarde, W. *Eirenarcha or of the Office of the Iustices of Peace in Foure Bookes* (London: 1592).
Leadam, I. S., ed. *Select Pleas in the Court of Star Chamber* (London: SS, 1902).
Lyndwood, W. *Provinciale* (London: 1679).
National Archives KB 27/1376, Rex m. 6, m. 10d, m. 11 (1602).
National Archives SP 12/273, fol. 60, Star Chamber speech of Lord Keeper Egerton (1599).
Newton v. Smith (1619) Cambridge University Library MS Ll 3.2, no. 122, National Archives STAC 8/222/6.
Peacock v. Reynell (1612) 2 Br & Goulds 151, Cambridge University Library MS Ll 3.2, no. 13, National Archives STAC 8/313/38.
Pickering's Case, British Library MS Harley 6686, fols 641–2, Coke's manuscript report.
Pulton, Ferdinando. *De pace regis et regni* (London: 1609).
Putnam, B. 'Sixteenth Century Treatises for Justices of the Peace', *University of Toronto Law Journal*, 7 (1947): 137–61.
Quintilian. *Institutio oratoria*, ed. and trans. Donald A. Russell, 5 vols (Cambridge, MA and London: Harvard University Press, 2001).
Schard, S. *Lexicon iuridicum iuris romani simul et pontificii* (Colonia Agrippina: 1593).
Sharpe, J. A. 'Defamation and Sexual Slander in Early Modern England: The Church Courts at York' (York: Borthwick Institute for Historical Research, 1980).
Shuger, D. *Censorship and Cultural Sensibility* (Philadelphia, PA: University of Pennsylvania Press, 2006).
Smith, R. E. 'The Law of Libel at Rome', *Classical Quarterly*, 1 (1951): 169–79.
Spiegel, J. *Lexicon iuris civilis* (Paris: 1554).
Statutes of Westminster I (1275) c. 34 (3 Edw 1 c. 5).
Suetonius, '*Divus Augustus*', in *Suetonius*, ed. K. R. Bradley and trans. J. C. Rolfe (Cambridge, MA: Harvard University Press, 1998), 122–87.
Tacitus, Cornelius. 'Annals', in *Tacitus*, ed. John Jackson et al. (Cambridge, MA: Harvard University Press, 2014), 242–381.
Taylor v. Mouns (1618) National Archives STAC 8/284/23.
Veeder, V. V. 'The History of the Law of Defamation', in *Select Essays in Anglo-American Legal History*, Vol. 3 (Boston: Little Brown, 1909), 446–73.
Whitgift, J. *The Defence of the Answer to the Admonition* (London: 1574).

Willems, C. 'Coke, Collusion and Conveyances: Unearthing the Roots of Twyne's Case', *Journal of Legal History*, 36 (2015): 129–51.
Williams, I. 'A Medieval Book and Early-Modern Law: *Bracton*'s Authority and Application in the Common Law *c.*1550–1640', *The Legal History Review*, 79 (2011): 47–80.
Willis Bund, J. W. Worcestershire County Records (Worcester: Worcestershire County Council, 1900), 44.

CHAPTER 26

CENSORSHIP IN LAW AND PRACTICE IN SEVENTEENTH-CENTURY ENGLAND

Milton's Areopagitica

JOAD RAYMOND

> And as for regulating the press, let no man think to have the honour of advising ye better than yourselves have done in that Order published next before this, *that no book be printed, unless the printer's and the author's name, or at least the printer's, be registered*. Those which otherwise come forth, if they be found mischievous and libellous, the fire and the executioner will be the timeliest and the most effectual remedy that man's prevention can use. For this authentic Spanish policy of licensing books, if I have said aught, will prove the most unlicensed book itself within a short while; and was the immediate image of a Star Chamber decree to that purpose made in those very times when that Court did the rest of those her pious works, for which she is now fallen from the stars with Lucifer.[1]

MILTON's readers have identified two problems in this passage from the peroration to *Areopagitica* (1644). The first is an apparent confusion on Milton's part: discussing the Licensing Order of June 1643 he refers to the Order of January 1642 as 'that Order published next before this'. Yet there were two intervening parliamentary orders, in August

[1] *Complete Prose Works of John Milton*, gen. ed. Don M. Wolfe, 8 vols (New Haven and London, Yale University Press, 1953–1982), hereafter *CPW*. Here, *CPW*, 2.569–70.

1642 and March 1643, plus commands in March 1642 concerning the abuse of printing.[2] Milton's history of censorship in *Areopagitica* is generally meticulous: could he have overlooked these?[3]

The second, and more historically resonant crux is Milton's apparent willingness to endorse the destruction of already-published 'mischievous and libellous books'. Having attacked pre-publication licensing on the ground of the virtue of liberty of reading, and having challenged the competence of a small group of licensers to pass judgement on books, he nonetheless endorses post-publication censure that would prevent reading by executioner and fire, and empower the state to be both governors and critics.[4] This fly in the ointment for readings of the most resonant defence of liberty of unlicensed printing in the seventeenth century, particularly those that wish to see it as a precursor of the first amendment, or as an unequivocal condemnation of the practice of state censorship, is now the most widely discussed aspect of Milton's reasoning. We are as likely today to see Milton's *Areopagitica* cited as an argument in favour of state control as an argument against it. In a similar way, the Long Parliament's attempts to reintroduce Caroline press controls have been turned into the origins of the ideological control of the presses.[5]

In this chapter I will approach this crux in Milton's argument from the perspective of what we know about seventeenth-century press controls. To do so I will need to discuss the practices of the seventeenth-century book-trade, and some of the shibboleths of the new revisionist orthodoxy on censorship.

[2] Geoff Kemp and Jason McElligott, eds, *Censorship and the Press, 1580–1720*, 4 vols (London: Pickering and Chatto, 2009), 2.47 (which Milton quotes), 48–9, 50–1, 63–4, 72–5. I am deeply indebted to Jason and Geoff for discussions of censorship over many years.

[3] Ernest Sirluck offers a plausible though problematic explanation. *CPW*, 2.160–1, 569. More problems are identified by D. F. McKenzie in his unpublished Lyell lectures (lecture 4, 'Simmons'). I am grateful to Don McKenzie for giving me this and other unpublished manuscripts and for many inspiring discussions of the seventeenth-century book trade over the period 1990–1999. Though it disagrees with his conclusions, this chapter was written in dialogue with him.

[4] *CPW*, 2.569; see also 2.565; 2.534 (governors and critics).

[5] Francis Barker, *The Tremulous Private Body: Essays in Subjection* (London: Methuen, 1984), 41–52; Abbe Blum, 'The Author's Authority: *Areopagitica* and the Labour of Licensing', 74–96 and Stanley Fish, 'Driving from the Letter: Truth and Indeterminacy in Milton's *Areopagitica*', 234–54, both in Mary Nyquist and Margaret W. Ferguson, eds, *Re-membering Milton: Essays on the Texts and Traditions* (London: Methuen, 1987); Stanley Fish, *There's No Such Thing as Free Speech: And It's a Good Thing Too* (New York: Oxford University Press, 1994), 102–4; see the critiques in William Kolbrener, *Milton's Warring Angels: A Study of Critical Engagements* (Cambridge: Cambridge University Press, 1997), 11–27; David Norbrook, '*Areopagitica*, Censorship, and the Early Modern Public Sphere', in *The Administration of Aesthetics: Censorship, Political Criticism, and the Public Sphere*, ed. Richard Burt (Minneapolis and London: University of Minnesota Press, 1994), 3–33 and Norbrook, *Poetry and Politics in the English Renaissance* (1984; Oxford: Oxford University Press, 2002), 307–13.

Normative Practices

The Whig history of censorship presented early Stuart press control as a systematic and draconian attempt to control public speech through licensing, registration, searches, fines, intimidation, imprisonment, and bodily mutilation.[6] This control, the narrative states, built up oppositional pressure, and when censorship collapsed in 1641, there followed an explosion (this word often appears in scare quotes today, or qualified by 'so-called') of print. Milton intervened when attempts were made in 1643 to restore earlier controls. This is the narrative challenged by revisionists.

At the centre of debates are two processes: entry in the Stationers' Register and ecclesiastical licensing. Revisionism depends on the exoneration of both. Revisionists say: ecclesiastical licensing was never intended absolutely to control ideas; it was not rigorously enforced; a modest proportion of books were ever approved.[7] The great majority of unlicensed books were unnoticed or unpunished. Some books that were licensed were subsequently burned, or their authors prosecuted. Successive regimes failed to devote adequate resources to control.

The peril of ignoring legal requirements seems to evaporate under statistical pressure. Revisionist histories point to the low incidence both of entry in the Register and of ecclesiastical licensing. About half of all extant publications in the period 1576–1640 were registered. Don McKenzie's calculations show the declining frequency of registration through the seventeenth century: in 1644 around 20 per cent of titles were entered in the Stationers' Register; in 1668 about 17.5 per cent; in 1688, only 7 per cent.[8] However, the incentive for registration was the protection of copy, which did not affect those publications that were unlikely to be reprinted, nor those protected by patents. A closer examination of 1614 indicates that 48 per cent of titles were registered; but if we exclude official items and books printed for the Stationers' Company this figure increases to 59 per cent; and if we discount Bibles and printing outside London, usually protected by patent in this period, the figure appears to be about 69 per cent. Separate calculations for 1594–1596, 1614–1616, and 1634–1636 show entry rates of about 60 per cent, 58 per cent, and 50

[6] Christopher Hill, 'Censorship and English Literature', in *Collected Essays*, Vol. 1: *Writing and Revolution in 17th Century England* (Amherst: University of Massachusetts Press, 1985), 32–71; F. S. Siebert, *Freedom of the Press in England 1476–1776: The Rise and Decline of Government Controls* (Urbana: University of Illinois Press, 1952); Annabel Patterson, *Censorship and Interpretation: The Conditions of Writing and Reading in Early Modern England* (Madison: University of Wisconsin Press, 1984); William M. Clyde, *The Struggle for the Freedom of the Press from Caxton to Cromwell* (London: Humphrey Milford, 1934).

[7] Sheila Lambert, 'State Control of the Press in Theory and Practice: The Role of the Stationers' Company Before 1640', in *Censorship and the Control of Print in England and France, 1600–1910*, ed. Robin Myers and Michael Harris (Winchester: St Paul's Bibliographies, 1992), 1–32.

[8] D. F. McKenzie, 'The London Book Trade in 1644', in *Bibliographia: Lectures 1975–1988 by Recipients of the Marc Fitch Prize for Bibliography*, ed. John Horden (Oxford: Oxford University Press, 1992), 131–51, 137; and 'The London Book Trade in 1668', *Words*, 4 (1974): 75–92, 79, 85.

per cent; but when official works and printing protected by patent is factored in, this is more like 75 per cent.[9] It is possible that figures were even higher.[10] So while the figures may have been declining, they were significantly higher than McKenzie contended, and while it does not suggest an iron fist, nor does it imply *de facto* freedom.

Another mainstay of revisionism has been to insist that as a trade guild the Stationers' Company was predominantly commercial in its complexion. This is grounded in Don McKenzie's important and influential work on the microeconomics of normalcy in the book trade, and on Ian Gadd's valuable yet unpublished PhD thesis on the Company.[11] The Company was incorporated to represent the primarily commercial interests of its members, which it did by restricting printing (and to a lesser extent bookselling) by non-members, and to protect the future profits of its members by enabling them to hold legal rights in textual property. This was a much broader monopoly right than that possessed by other trade guilds, which suggests that the thinking behind their incorporation was not identical to that behind the incorporation of other guilds.

The incidence and the nature of registration and licensing in the period demand closer examination: there was in fact a triad of distinct pre-publication procedures.[12] Underpinning the practice of registration was the Stationers' Register. Entry in the Register cost a fee (between 4*d* and 6*d* per item), was open only to members (hence printers and booksellers), who usually acted on their own behalf, and established the right, enforced by the Company, to print or publish that title. Rights could be transferred

[9] Maureen Bell, 'Entrance in the Stationers' Register', *The Library*, 6th ser., 16 (1994): 50–4. For printing patents: Arnold Hunt, 'Book Trade Patents, 1603–1640', in *The Book Trade and Its Customers 1450–1900: Historical Essays for Robin Myers*, ed. Arnold Hunt, Giles Mandelbrote, and Alison Shell (Winchester: St Paul's Bibliographies, 1997), 27–54; Joad Raymond, *Pamphlets and Pamphleteering in Early Modern Britain* (Cambridge: Cambridge University Press, 2003), 170; Graham Rees and Maria Wakely, *Publishing, Politics, and Culture: The King's Printers in the Reign of James I and VI* (Oxford: Oxford University Press, 2009).

[10] As high as 97 per cent, even: Cyndia Susan Clegg, *Press Censorship in Caroline England* (Cambridge: Cambridge University Press, 2008), 137.

[11] Ian Anders Gadd, '"Being Like a Field": Corporate Identity in the Stationers' Company 1557–1684', DPhil thesis (University of Oxford, 1999). Also Peter W. M. Blayney's seminal *The Stationers' Company and the Printers of London, 1501–1557*, 2 vols (Cambridge: Cambridge University Press, 2013); Joanna Kostylo, 'From Gunpowder to Print: The Common Origins of Copyright and Patent', in *Privilege and Property: Essays on the History of Copyright*, ed. Ronan Deazley, Martin Kretschmer, and Lionel Bentley (Cambridge: OpenBook Publishers, 2010), 21–50; Federico Barberiato, 'Paolo Sarpi, the Papal Index and Censorship', in *Censorship Moments: Reading Texts in the History of Censorship and Freedom of Expression*, ed. Geoff Kemp (London: Bloomsbury, 2015), 63–70.

[12] For this and the ensuing three paragraphs, see: Peter W. M. Blayney, 'The Publication of Playbooks', in *A New History of Early English Drama*, ed. John D. Cox and David Scott Kastan (New York: Columbia University Press, 1997), 383–422; Joad Raymond, 'The Stationers' Company', in *Encyclopaedia of British Literature*, ed. David Scott Kastan, 5 vols (New York: Oxford University Press, 2006), 5.83–91; Cyprian Blagden, *The Stationers' Company: A History, 1403–1959* (London: Stationers' Company, 1960); Gadd, 'Corporate Identity'; Blayney, *Stationers' Company*; W. W. Greg, 'Entrance, Licence, and Publication', *The Library*, 4th ser., 25 (1944): 1–22; Cyndia Susan Clegg, *Press Censorship in Elizabethan England* (Cambridge: Cambridge University Press, 1997).

or renewed by subsequent entries, either as a means of undertaking commercial collaboration or of selling textual property.

Entry was distinct from Company licensing, the second of the procedures. At least as early as 1557 the Company required that any printed book be 'allowed or tolerated' by one of its Wardens prior to entry. A Company licence established that the would-be publisher had cleared with the Company his right to publish, which process included ensuring that the title did not already belong to another stationer. Hence this licence verified the history of the text; entry in the Register secured its future. Under ordinary circumstances this did not constitute ideological approval.

However, the Warden would occasionally insist on seeing an ecclesiastical licence before issuing his own. This suggests a concern over propriety and prospective sanctions before property. While the role of the Register and the Company may have been to maintain good order within the trade—I will return to this notion—Company officers would not condone ideologically risky materials. Hence the granting of a Company license could depend on ideological approval; and this might inform our understanding of the significance of the irregularity of ecclesiastical licensing. Ideological considerations were a factor within commercial decisions.

The third regulatory procedure was ecclesiastical licensing. Most histories of censorship have focused on this, some confusing it with the two described above. The Injunctions of 1559 and the Star Chamber Decrees of 1586 and 1637 established prepublication licensing as obligatory: every item printed in England and Wales that was not specifically covered by a patent (or, under the 1559 Injunctions, had not been previously printed and allowed by the universities) required approval by an ecclesiastical licenser or his representative (the details of who could licence changed over time). Revisionists rightly recognized the importance of distinguishing between these often confused or conflated procedures. However there is a danger in separating them without recognizing the possibility of interdependence.

The commercial complexion of the Company also merits further scrutiny. This has been treated as a kind of ideological disinfectant (though not by Don McKenzie who mischievously muddied waters by declaring that most early modern censorship was economic). However, the willingness and ability of the Stationers' Company to cooperate with the government have been doubted, and it has been asserted that its 'squabbling' tradesmen were not fit to act as an arm of government.[13] However, while the Company's monopolies were financial they nonetheless had ideological consequences. Indeed, the monopoly over printing and bookselling granted to the press also assisted a means for official regulation of the book trade—sometimes described as maintaining good order.[14]

[13] Lambert, 'State Control', 9, 2. See Jason McElligott's robust rebuttal in '"Several Hundred Squabbling Small Tradesmen"? Censorship, the Stationers' Company, and the State in Seventeenth-Century England', in *News Networks in Seventeenth-Century Britain and Europe*, ed. Joad Raymond (London: Routledge, 2006), 87–102; and *Royalism, Print and Censorship in Revolutionary England* (Woodbridge: Boydell, 2007), chs 6–7.

[14] Cf. Clegg, *Caroline*, 226. For the 'quid pro quo': Michael Mendel, 'De Facto Freedom, De Facto Authority: Press and Parliament, 1640–1643', *HJ*, 38.2 (1995): 307–32, 309.

While this may not have been clearly formulated at the time, it undoubtedly provided the Crown and later parliament with means of detecting and prosecuting stationers.

An example from 1615: when Archbishop Abbot discovered that two stationers possessed a stock of imported grammars (not dangerous materials), frustrated by the Company's apparent reluctance effectively to police imports, he used the powers of High Commission to perform a search and seize the works. These were powers assigned (repeatedly) to the Company, and this shows the messy reality of press legislation: propriety and conventional practice could be suspended when convenient, and apparently commercial arrangements did not preclude political practice. When the culprits in possession of the grammars appealed against the seizure on the grounds that it violated the liberties of the City, Abbot—sometimes presented as an accommodating figure—declared that the king had placed all authority in the hands of High Commission.[15] In this instance at least he viewed the Stationers' powers as not only delegated but liable to suspension at the Archbishop's discretion. And when this was done he sent an invoice to the Company to cover the cost of the search.[16]

This invoice for the punitive sum of £60 was a message about responsibility and culpability, telling the Company that it had been negligent. The texts were not ideological: the action was an arbitrary one, and that was another element of Abbot's message. The Company was not meeting its objectives: its purpose included conducting searches effectively and inexpensively, and that was its usefulness to the High Commission. The repeated legislation empowering the Company to search, occasionally assigning increased powers, articulate the same principle. The Crown was not concerned about the loss of profit to the rightful patentees so much as the correct ordering of the trade. Exactly the same conclusion must be drawn from the attention that Charles I's Privy Council paid to licensing violations—had these been entirely commercial matters the Council would hardly have stooped to such quotidian business. The Privy Council's micromanagement exercised the royal prerogative in ways that both muddied the apparently clear jurisdictions of the Company and the system of ecclesiastical licensing and also illustrated how ad hoc and unsystematic arrangements facilitated the exercise of arbitrary power.[17] The same interplay between commercial and ideological intervention can be seen in the regulation of paper imports.[18]

The revisionist account of censorship, following the pioneering work of Don McKenzie and Sheila Lambert, is typically based on the meticulous examination of parliamentary and legal records, and sometimes extended through statistical evidence. It contends that far from being either systematic or effective, censorship in England was

[15] Clegg, *Elizabethan*, 39–67.

[16] Lambert, 'State Control', 19.

[17] Also the indefinite imprisonment without trial of John Hayward: Clegg, in *Censorship and the Press*, ed. Kemp and McElligott, 1: xliii–xliv.

[18] John Bidwell, 'French Paper in English Books', in *The Cambridge History of the Book in Britain*, Vol. 4: *1557–1695*, ed. John Barnard and D. F. McKenzie (Cambridge: Cambridge University Press, 2002), 583–601.

erratic, infrequently enforced, under-resourced, and was never conceived or imagined as a form of ideological control.[19] It was, in John Barnard's succinct words, 'essentially *ad hoc*, inconsistent, opportunistic and usually ineffective'.[20] And there was, moreover, no collapse of censorship in 1641–1642. If this is true, and the Whig version of censorship is misleading, we might wonder what Milton was objecting to.

The extent to which anyone in early modern England advocated, repudiated, or conceived of an absolutist and ideological system of censorship, or whether such notions are anachronistic, is debatable. My argument here concerns the relationship between law and practice, a relationship illuminated by an anonymous set of notes written for a parliamentary speech in 1585. The notes advocate additional restrictions on the book trade to supplement reforms recently proposed by the Stationers' Company. The author, anticipating Milton, is anxious that only 'men of Marvylous learning & knowledge' could distinguish between books that would benefit and those that would harm the church, but nonetheless suggests that printers' shops should be surveyed for inappropriate books (Ovid's *Ars amatoria*, for example), and that the 'multitude of ... vnprofitable, leud & lascivious' books should be called in. Turning to books that are not yet printed, he suggests that all future books should be subscribed by three men ... but thereafter his notes are damaged and lost. While the act was not passed—perhaps the speech was never delivered—this suggests the debates that preceded the 1586 Star Chamber Decree, which implemented a new regime of pre-publication licensing, did have an ideological vision of censorship. The note-maker's vision did not embrace total ideological control, but he did propound that press controls needed to extend beyond orderly commerce into moral reform and censure.[21]

[19] McKenzie in nn. 3, 6, above; 'Printing and Publishing, 1557–1700: Constraints on the London Book Trades', in *Cambridge History*, ed. Barnard and McKenzie, 553–67; 'The Economies of Print, 1550–1750: Scales of Production and Conditions of Constraint', *Producione e commercio della cara e del libro secc. XIII–XVIII, Istituto Internazionale di Storia Economica 'F. Datini' Prato, serie II—Atti delle 'Settimane di Studi' e altri convegni, 23* (Prato: Le Monnier, 1992), 389–425; Sheila Lambert, 'The Beginning of Printing for the House of Commons, 1640–42', *The Library*, 6th ser., 3 (1981): 43–61; Lambert 'State Control'; Lambert, 'Richard Montagu, Arminianism and Censorship', *Past & Present*, 124 (1989): 36–68; Clegg, *Elizabethan, Caroline* and *Press Censorship in Jacobean England* (Cambridge, Cambridge University Press, 2001); Debora Shuger, *Censorship and Cultural Sensibility: The Regulation of Language in Tudor–Stuart England* (Philadelphia: University of Pennsylvania Press, 2006); Mark Bland, '"Invisible Dangers": Censorship and the Subversion of Authority in Early Modern England', *Publications of the Bibliographical Society of America*, 90 (1996): 151–93; Blair Worden, 'Literature and Political Censorship in Early Modern England', in *Too Mighty To Be Free*, ed. A. C. Duke and C. A. Tamse (Zutphen: De Walburg Pers, 1987), 45–62; Anthony Milton, 'Licensing, Censorship, and Religious Orthodoxy in Early Stuart England', *HJ*, 41 (1998): 625–51; Glen Burgess, *Absolute Monarchy and the Stuart Constitution* (New Haven: Yale University Press, 1996), 6–13 and *passim*. See also Kevin Sharpe, *Criticism and Compliment: The Politics of Literature in the England of Charles I* (Cambridge: Cambridge University Press, 1987), 36–39; Arnold Hunt, 'Licensing and Religious Censorship in Early Modern England', in *Literature and Censorship in Renaissance England*, ed. Andrew Hadfield (Basingstoke: Palgrave Macmillan, 2001), 127–46.

[20] Barnard, 'Introduction', in *Cambridge History*, ed. Barnard and McKenzie, 3.

[21] BL: MS Lansdowne 43/75 (Burghley papers), in *Censorship and the Press*, ed. McElligott and Kemp, 1.89–92, from which I quote.

The Crown did not implement or intend to implement a unified policy of state censorship. Cyndia Susan Clegg writes that 'neither its end nor means correspond to overwhelming systematization' and scorns descriptions of a 'machinery of censorship and control'.[22] Mark Bland writes that 'it is impossible to entertain any monolithic concept of the practice of censorship as a unified and coherent activity'.[23] However, 'overwhelming systematization' is a high benchmark by the standards of seventeenth-century governance, and an effective law need not be based on 'monolithic concepts'. To infer that the Register, Company, ecclesiastical licenses, and the odd prosecution were no more than an 'attempt to reduce the clutter of communication' is clearly wrong.[24] Good housekeeping enabled the Crown to delegate the responsibility for intervention to those with the knowledge to do it effectively.

Exceptional Circumstances

There were human and bibliographical casualties. Here I will look at the occasions when normal procedures failed, though with an indispensible caveat: there's a close relation between the normal and the abnormal. The revisionist case is characterized both by the insistence that the number of actual political interventions was very small, and that these are an exception to the everyday non-ideological normality. I will suggest that the arrangements for the normal were effective in part *because* of the abnormal, and this might tell us something about the nature of the legislation around the press, and the central utility of the blurred relationship between legislation and legal practice. This blurriness could be more effective than overwhelming systematization.

There is a cartoon history of censorship, which includes John Stubbs's *Discoverie of a Gaping Gulf* (1579), for which he lost a hand, John Udall's *Diotrephes* (1588), the Marprelate tracts (1588–1589), the 1599 Bishops' ban, John Cowell's *Interpreter* (1607), the controversy around Richard Montague in 1624–1625, Daniel Featley's *Cygnia cantio* (1625), perhaps the banning of foreign news corantos in 1632, the clipping of William Prynne's ears for his *Histriomastix* in 1634, and the punishment of Prynne, with Henry Burton and John Bastwick, for subversive publications in 1637. With a premium on scepticism this can be reduced even further.[25] These are the 'extreme cases' when order broke down and reprisals took place. But how easy is it to separate the conventional from the exceptional? One area in which it is difficult to maintain that the law was minimal, and interventions exceptional, is the publishing of news. Both Lambert and Sabrina Baron have dismissed the notion that there was a proscription on publishing 'domestic' (i.e.

22 Clegg, *Elizabethan*, 5, 3, 217, quoting Glynn Wickham.

23 Bland, 'Invisible Dangers', 174.

24 Bland, 'Invisible Dangers', 152. Worden concurs, 'Literature and Political Censorship', 48, 49; see also Burgess, *Absolute Monarchy*, 5–7.

25 Shuger, *Censorship*, 11, 230–76; cf. Clegg, *Elizabethan*, 201–2.

national) news in early modern England.[26] They do so with confidence and acerbity for those who devised and perpetuated such a 'fiction'; they do so without an explanation of why such news was not published.[27] There is no copy of a ban, and therefore there cannot have been one. The fact that stationers did not print news of parliament or civil conflict (as opposed to crimes and wonders) shows that most readers were uninterested.[28] It is striking, then, that there should have been such fascination with the French Wars of Religion in the 1590s, in the Palatinate in 1618; and that in 1610 the Lord Treasurer should have directly instructed the Wardens of the Company not to print anything regarding the death of Henri IV.[29] Readers clearly wanted foreign news, and it was generally tolerated, except when it was specifically proscribed (this would happen again, with a broader prohibition, in 1632). Are we then to infer that there was no proscription on more local news, on news of national politics (beyond the general reach of parliamentary privilege which prevented reporting of Parliament, though not of court politics)?

This seems improbable. The revisionist case is intermittently based on a positivist assumption that the evidence extant in the archive represents a full and sufficient account of what happened. This is a reaction to a body of scholarship disposed to speculation and exaggeration: in Clegg's words 'a curious amalgam of historical evidence, decontextualized facts, overgeneralization, and half truths'.[30] Besides which, the law is a field where the record is paramount. Yet the archive positively indicates a lacuna. The Star Chamber Decrees of 1586 and 1637 confirm the former Ordinances of the Company, approved in 1562 and laid out in what is referred to as the Red Book. This is now lost, possibly destroyed by fire, and we cannot be certain about what specific affirmations and restrictions the Ordinances contained. The revisionist case, for all of its vocal contempt for its predecessors' assumptions, assumes that the Ordinances of the Company articulate no restrictions.[31]

The practice of printing news suggests a more complex history, one constrained by a mixture of laws, social norms, and anxiety. A patent for printing *foreign* news was granted in 1641, and Lambert suggests that the lack of a patent prior to this is evidence that there was no proscription on domestic news prior to this date (everything was permitted).[32] Yet Nathaniel Butter and Nicholas Bourne petitioned—for the

26 Lambert, 'State Control', 2; Sabrina Baron, 'The Guises of Dissemination in Early Seventeenth-Century England: News in Manuscript and Print', in *The Politics of Information in Early Modern Europe*, ed. Brendan Dooley and Sabrina Baron (London: Routledge, 2001), 42–6.

27 For 'fiction', see Baron, 'Guises of Dissemination', 46 (where she confuses disagreement with non-recognition); for contemporary evidence refuting Lambert ('Beginning of Printing', 56), see Raymond, *The Invention of the Newspaper: English Newsbooks, 1641–1649* (1996; Oxford: Oxford University Press, 2005), 106, 140.

28 Clegg also implies this in *Caroline*, 226.

29 L. F. Parmalee, *Good Newes from Fraunce: French Anti-League Propaganda in Late Elizabethan England* (Rochester, NY: University of Rochester Press, 1996); Kemp and McElligott, eds, *Censorship and the Press*, 1.187.

30 Clegg, *Elizabethan*, 219.

31 On the missing Ordinances, see Blayney, *Stationers' Company*, 864, 867, 923.

32 Lambert, 'State Control', 2. J. B. Williams and F. S. Siebert assumed one had existed earlier, and contrasted this with the fact that similar licenses were never granted for domestic news.

first time—to obtain a patent for printing news both foreign *and domestic* in 1638. The trade in foreign news corantos had been prohibited by an order of the Privy Council since 1632. This petition therefore precisely implies that domestic news was implicitly prohibited, just as foreign news was explicitly; Butter and Bourne hoped to persuade the Crown to grant an exemption, which they can only have hoped for in return for a promise to do so in an orderly fashion. The petition was granted, though exclusively for foreign news.[33] This restriction implies a clear understanding about the status of domestic news. Butter and Bourne only proceeded once they had received this patent. This is not the behaviour of tradesmen concerned about profit, but of subjects who understood that a patent constituted a form of ideological approval, permission as well as property. Finally in-sessional parliamentary proceedings were first printed later in 1641, published by a man with connections to the leader of the House of Commons.[34] These connections helped shelter him from sanctions. If there was no legal prohibition there was nonetheless effective social or cultural proscription.

Prosecutions of offensive texts were neither systematic nor frequent. When you look at the cartoon history of censorship interventions on a case-by-case basis each seems unique. The main pattern is that prosecutions happened when the decorum of political and religious criticism and negotiation was ruptured beyond repair, or when a publication inflamed the politically sensitive area of foreign affairs. It also helps to side with the state and church and emphasize either the criminality or the moral defects of the offenders, doubly so when this is accompanied by the claim to be considering only concrete evidence, or seeking to make the actions of the prosecutors morally intelligible.

Thus Marprelate, Clegg argues, knowingly and deliberately violated the generous parameters of Elizabethan ecclesiastical debate. He was a fox, cynically undermining the bishops' authority, forcing them to prosecute for libel, denying the rule of law, reason, civility. He was asking for it.[35] Debora Shuger's detailed examination of Prynne's case echoes this. She concludes that his verbal style, his hate speech, did not allow a *mitior sensus* plea.[36] He only found himself in court because he was, like Thomas Scott, gripped by hatred and immune to the relevant 'cultural inhibitions'. He and Scott were punished not for ideological reasons, but because they were 'unbalanced and violent personalities'.[37] This is a more extreme version of ameliorating the corporal punishment of Prynne on the grounds that *Histriomastix* is humourless or boring.[38]

Such enthusiastic defence of statecraft and rejection of liberal pusillanimity risks anachronism. Clegg suggests that censorship was understood on the basis of 'national

[33] *CSPD 1638–1639*, 182; Folke Dahl, *A Bibliography of English Corantos and Periodical Newsbooks 1620–1642* (London: Bibliographical Society, 1952), 223–4; Kevin Sharpe, *The Personal Rule of Charles I* (New Haven and London: Yale University Press, 1992), 653.

[34] Raymond, *Invention of the Newspaper*, ch. 2.

[35] Clegg, *Elizabethan*, 170–97, 171, 179, 181, 197.

[36] Shuger, *Censorship*, 223–9.

[37] Shuger, *Censorship*, 152, 232, 233. Cf. Clegg, *Caroline*, 3, on Sharpe.

[38] They should be made to sit through an amateur production of Montagu's *Shepherd's Paradise*.

interest'.[39] This phrase is not entirely anachronistic: James Harrington uses it in *Oceana* (1656).[40] However, Harrington was contrasting national with foreign interests, modern usage positions it against civil rights, and it resonates with modern pro-censorship arguments based on reason of state. Bland writes, 'Occasionally, for political purposes, examples had to be made ...': *had* to be, not *were*.[41] A similar rhetorical gloss covers Lambert's arguments, despite her commitments to the minute particulars of positive evidence and procedures: not only does she pugnaciously conflate the 'new Whigs' with 'liberals' and Marxists, and those who want to 'strive against authority', she also avers that 'the use of torture' can be palliated.[42] This language is a symptom of excessively enthusiastic positioning, but it also suggests that just as a historiography axiomatically critical of censorship became a leftist badge in the 1980s, so censorship-denial became a badge of neo-liberalism and the libertarian right in the 2000s, leaving history walking a couple of steps behind.

Digression: Two Revisionist Shibboleths

It is easy to seize upon the theatricality of early modern censorship, with its albeit infrequent corporal punishments, ear mutilation, manual dismemberment, and conflagrations of piles of books overseen by a hangman, and suggest that these spectacles typify the moral character of the regime that undertook such actions. The revisionist case challenges emotive responses to these practices, and instead assesses their effectiveness.

Book burning, like licensing, is a practice in which institutional ordinances, practices, and intentions coincide in ways that aren't straightforward. It can be dismissed as mere showmanship, as it was an imperfect means of destroying copies. Milton's *Defensio* was burned many times: it was almost a party starter. The authorities did not attempt to recover whole editions, including already-sold copies, but only those still in the hands of printers and booksellers.[43] So it was not an entirely effective way of stopping people from reading books: though almost nine hundred copies of Edward Elton's *God's Holy Mind* were seized and burned in 1625 (even though it had been licensed), a significant proportion of the edition. The printer Robert Mylbourne may have inflated this figure, though he offers the significantly different number of three hundred copies for Daniel Featley's *Pelagius Revivivus* (1626).[44] Given that there was no search in either case for

39 Clegg, *Jacobean*, 21.

40 Harrington, *Oceana* (1656), 8–9; also Henry Vane, *Healing Question* (London: 1656), 5; Richard Lawrence, *The Interest of England in the Irish Transplantation* (London: 1655), 19.

41 Bland, 'Invisible Dangers', 190.

42 Lambert, 'State Control', 1, 4–5.

43 Clegg, *Jacobean*, ch. 2; Clegg, 'Burning Books as Propaganda in Jacobean England', in *Literature and Censorship*, ed. Hadfield, 165–86.

44 Printer's note at the end of Featley, *Cygnea cantia* (1629), 39–40.

copies in the hands of readers, the range of language Mylbourne uses is striking: while his nemesis, 'the Informer' who sought the destruction of his publications, sought to have the copies of *God's Holy Mind* 'either to be altogether suppressed or to be so gelded and mangled, that the sale of them thereby was very much hindred' (putting the printer in severe financial difficulty), the same Informer had boasted that he had caused *Pelagius Revivivus* 'to be called in, and utterly suppressed'.[45] This only increased demand for and sales of the work, Mylbourne writes. Nevertheless both printer and persecutor imply that the damage was intended to be more than theatrical: in the first instance financial, and in the second wholly destructive.

Nonetheless, book burning was not used as a means of vanishing a text, to which end it was unsuited not least because public displays stimulated public interest. James burned books in order publicly to signal his opposition to a particular religious or political perspective, and not to stop people from reading them. This became more symbolic and theatrical over time.[46] While burnings may usually have been 'more symbolic than actual', the flames were actual and the symbolism mattered.[47] However, according to Clegg most burnings were not public but took place in 'personal' contexts, without an audience. It was motivated by individual grievance; though she adds that this doesn't mean that the practice 'pervade[d] the culture', and that these 'efforts of individuals … argue against a single abusive authoritarian system'.[48] But surely personal conflagrations of texts indicate that there were shared frameworks within which books could be destroyed on the grounds of ideological difference. It is hard to see the logic here: individuals imitate an institutional practice, and this is evidence that there is no system, as if a unified, collective system is the only kind of meaningful practice. By this assessment, there is no such thing as society, only individuals airing personal disagreements using a mode of conduct pioneered by the state. The symbolism of the increasingly theatrical state burnings included the hangman's pronouncement that any who concealed such papers would in turn be punished.[49] In 1642 one anonymous author describes hearing the hangman's proclamation against any who harboured the same, 'with which words I was so afraid, that I ran home and burnt all my papers, and so saved him a labor'.[50] So perhaps not so ineffective.

Revisionists similarly confront the 'explosion of print' that allegedly took place alongside the collapse of censorship in 1641–1642, and which was central to Christopher Hill's evocation of the spirits of censorship and of liberty. Beginning with McKenzie the quantitative significance of the sudden increase in the number of titles printed in those years has been contested; and it has been asked whether it can be proved that there was a

[45] Featley, *Cygnea cantia* (1629), 40.

[46] See David Cressy, 'Book Burning in Tudor and Stuart England', *SCJ*, 36.2 (2005): 359–74, esp. 368, 374.

[47] Bland, 'Invisible Dangers', 186.

[48] Clegg, *Jacobean*, 117–18.

[49] Cressy, 'Book Burning', 371.

[50] *A Second Discovery by the Northern Scout* (1642), 9; quoted by Cressy, 'Book Burning', 371.

single work printed in the 1640s that was previously suppressed. This challenge is fundamental to revisionist reassessments of Jacobean and Caroline censorship.

A title-count of early modern English press output shows a dramatic spike in 1641–1642. This increase, combined with contemporaries' observations that the Caroline church had routinely suppressed opposing opinions, was once taken to indicate that 1630s England had been like a pressure cooker, and that in 1641–1642 the seal of censorship failed and the lid blew. McKenzie persuasively challenged this, arguing that while the number of titles increased the quantity of print may well have remained the same: title-counts conceal length, format, cost, and the number of words each contained. He concluded, though his evidence was sampled and indicative rather than quantitative (i.e. he did not actually count sheets or the quantity of type), that there was no real explosion of print.[51] There was, however, a qualitative shift towards shorter, less expensive works, towards more argumentative, newsy, and contentious writings in a range of demotic styles, a shift that facilitated mass communication and political participation, a kind of 'common politics'.[52]

It is hard to imagine some of these enthusiastic books being written earlier, though this may reflect changing politics as much as the end of press controls; it is hard to prove a counterfactual. Though we should not ignore authors who regretted that their books had only appeared after a licensing process that left them 'gelt', 'castrated', with 'the life, the vigor, and, as it were, the eyes of them picked out'.[53] However, not all of the works that it is hard to imagine being published before 1641 are satirical or enthusiastic. More respectable genres of printing were also affected. Ian Williams has demonstrated an increase in unauthorized printing of law books during the 1640s. This was not an entirely new phenomenon: during the period 1627–1640, eighteen out of seventy-seven (that is, about 23 per cent of) law books were printed in violation of the royal patent. However from 1641 the patent seems to have been unenforced (not because, or not only because of the abolition of the Courts of Star Chamber and High Commission, which enforced most patents, because the law patent was enforced by Chancery). This is particularly striking because printing under patent was not affected by licensing: the appearance of unauthorized law books clearly suggests that the phenomenon usually described as the 'collapse of censorship' only partly concerned licensing mechanisms. It crucially involved a broader spectrum of forms of influence. Law printing came to resemble the disorderly nature of other areas of printing.

[51] McKenzie, '1644', 135–7, also McKenzie, 'Printing and Publishing' and 'Economies of Print' and 'Simmons' (Lyell Lecture); cf. Clegg, *Caroline*, 222. Lambert proceeded to exaggerate, 'State Control', 23: her 'rubbishy' is unworthy of a bibliographer.

[52] Jason Peacey, *Print and Public Politics in the English Revolution* (Cambridge: Cambridge University Press, 2013); Nigel Smith, *Literature and Revolution in England, 1640–1660* (New Haven: Yale University Press, 1994); David Zaret, *Origins of Democratic Culture: Printing, Petitions, and the Public Sphere in Early-Modern England* (Princeton: Princeton University Press, 2000); Raymond, *Pamphlets*, ch. 5.

[53] Daniel Featley and William Jones, quoting Cressy, 'Book Burning', 36; also Hunt, 'Licensing and Religious Censorship'.

The incentive for unauthorized printing was financial. However among the books printed in 1641 were titles that had clear ideological significance and could not have been printed earlier. All had circulated in manuscript during the previous decade.[54] Among them was the dissenting opinion in the Ship Money case, the defence of John Hampden, *The Arguments of Sir Richard Hutton Knight* (1641); and *The Reading of M. Robert Brook ... Upon the Stat. of Magna Charta* (1641), issued as a reflection on the political crisis (readings were not usually printed: this one is less controversial than the title advertises). *The Argument of Nicholas Fuller of Grayes Inne Esquire ... Wherein It Is Plainly Proved, That the Ecclesiastical Commissioners Have No Power by Their Commission, to Imprison, or to Fine Any of His Majesties Subjects* (1641) had been printed in 1607 (without an imprint), but not since. Its relevance was plain enough in the year that High Commission was abolished; lest it escape the potential purchaser the title page of the 1641 had a facing portrait of William Laud, Archbishop of Canterbury. Also printed was Sir James Whitelocke's arguments in Bate's Case (1606) about royal prerogative and the illegality of extra-parliamentary taxation, together with a parliamentary order to print that challenges the licenser to 'shew good cause to the contrary.'[55] These are in some respects elite works, with Latin as well as English, albeit shorter than many authorized legal texts, but they joined broader disputes about monopolies and printing.

Normal Versus Exceptional, or the Routineness of Intervention

Looking at the use of licensing and registration, at the cases of Scott and Prynne, at the non-appearance of 'domestic' news, at the changing complexion of print in 1640–1642, at the appearance of law books from manuscript in 1641, at the half-hearted book burnings, at the competing authorities behind actions against the press, at the apparently ad hoc nature of prosecutions, and at the lack of a coherent and theorized system of censorship and press control, we should not conclude that there was no such thing as censorship in early modern England. There was a spectrum of practices used to manage print, and together these exerted a significant pressure on speech. To put the picture together we need to see the ways in which these practices interrelated.

The 'exceptional' examples reveal the revisionist tendency to dissociate particular cases from the larger concerns and continuities of the law, society, and culture. On the one hand we have a handful of ineffective and unsystematic laws; on the other a small number of prosecutions, a handful of which seem to be fierce in their severity but are

[54] This paragraph is based on an excellent unpublished article by Ian Williams, 'Becoming Normal? Law Printing in the 1630s': I am very grateful to Ian for supplying me with a copy of this, and for generous and informative private correspondence.

[55] James Whitelocke, *A Learned and Necessary Argument* (four edns, London: 1641), [67].

therefore exceptional. Because a case relies on ad hoc interventions, because the participants have complex motivations, it is unrepresentative, and not connected to the other more mundane examples. This strangely reduces justice to its punitive dimension—the revisionists deny the very possibility of preventative justice. There's no evidence of the crimes that were prevented.

Instead we need to see the continuity between the cultural norms, ad hoc practices, and statute and case law. The laws need to be digested in the context of other processes that shaped texts; and the fluid institutional contexts within which texts operated need to be integrated into the letter of proscription. A useful perspective on practice can be obtained from the very data that formed the basis of Don McKenzie's genuinely original challenge. This was the posthumously published calendar of documents relating to the London book trade 1641–1700. By his count it referred to:

> some 800 items, of which 400 are entirely innocent and 400 in some degree suspect. Those 400 represent 0.4% of the output of the trade. Of those 400 the number which led to a charge, let alone a conviction, let alone punishment, was only the tiniest fraction ... fear of the courts had virtually no impact on the economy of the book trade.[56]

Randy Robertson's database for the same period offers a different picture, identifying some 2,633 books that were 'pursued by authorities' (Maureen Bell's phrase), excluding commercial offences, a little under 3 per cent of books published.[57]

But let's look at 1643, the year of the licensing order, unsurprisingly a fractious year. Thirty troublesome books are mentioned in the records of Parliament, the Stationers' Company, and the periphery of the government (Robertson finds 39), representing 1.25 per cent (or 1.6 per cent) of the approximately 2,400 items extant from 1643, not suggestive of a crisis demanding legislation or a press raging with offensive materials. However, there are many more incidents for that year: complaints about violations of parliamentary privilege in print, parliamentary interventions about the ownership of copy, petitions about printing, orders and ordinances, imprisonments and book burnings. There are 170 entries in the Calendar for the year 1643. To these we could reasonably add other indicators of intervention—licences, ecclesiastical and Company, and orders for printing. The last are not always mentioned in the Commons Journals: some survive only on the title pages of books. More must have disappeared. They are direct interventions by the Committee for Printing, ordering printing rather than forbidding it, with ideological and economic consequences.[58] A good deal of the activity of this committee does not

[56] McKenzie, 'Printing and Publishing, 1557–1700', 566–7; D. F. McKenzie and Maureen Bell, eds, *A Chronology and Calendar of Documents Relating to the London Book Trade, 1641–1700* (Oxford: Oxford University Press, 2005).

[57] Randy Robertson, *Censorship and Conflict in Seventeenth-Century England: The Subtle Art of Division* (University Park: Pennsylvania State University Press, 2009), 8, giving 2.87 per cent, accounting for lost titles; 'British Index', at <https://susqu.academia.edu/RandyRobertson/Papers> [10 July 2015], suggests 2.9 per cent; Bell, review of Robertson, in *SHARP News*, 19.2 (2010): 7–8.

[58] e.g. *Two Letters* (London: 1643; Wing C3924); John Tombes, *Fermentum Phatisæorum* (London: 1643).

appear in the parliamentary records, which must significantly under-represent actual interventions. And all this overlooks the issue of official printing, and the porous relationship between state and Stationers that this discloses. These interventions commonly include summoning printers and booksellers to Westminster. From the perspective of charges, convictions, and punishments the control of the press in 1643 may seem light; viewed from the perspective of all interventions it looks very different, more like an unsystematic and untheorized mode of harassment.

The central activity of censorship is not the prosecution of an author for a specific offence—the revisionists' preferred story—but the summoning of a printer or publisher to Parliament to answer questions.

Records have silences. Livewell Chapman was one who was repeatedly interrogated for things he had printed. He was imprisoned and persecuted until he agreed to cease anti-government activities, whereupon he disappears. Hence he was not available to publish the second edition of Milton's *Readie & Easie Way* or, for that matter, *Paradise Lost*.[59] The reality of censorship is distinctly messy. It did not work through 'overwhelming systematization' or 'monolithic concepts' but through interventions such as this, which were only indirectly related to the law and formal legal processes.

We can develop a more precise account of that indirect relationship between these practical, and perhaps arbitrary interventions and press-regulating legislation. One cornerstone of the argument that there was no attempt systematically to control the content of print has been the small number of prosecutions for treason, seditious libel, and *scandalum magnatum*. High profile cases are rare in comparison to punishments for minor printing offences of a non-ideological nature.[60] Drawing on Philip Hamburger's seminal 1985 article 'The Development of the Law of Seditious Libel and the Control of the Press', McKenzie pointed out, in his influential Lyell lecture on 'censorship', that governments used licensing laws to prosecute stationers, and the effect of this 'was *to mitigate the crime*' because the punishments were significantly less for licensing offences.[61] Hamburger's work also enabled revisionists to define offences as commercial (registration) or violations of good order (licensing) rather than political (libel and so on), as evidence of commerce triumphing over ideology.

Hamburger's article fractionally supports this. He shows that the laws for controlling the press were barely fit for the Crown's purpose. The Crown preferred to prosecute for relatively minor licensing offences rather than seditious libel or *scandalum magnatum* because it was easier to secure a conviction. Rather than undertake a lengthy trial and risk a jury acquittal, an offending stationer or author could be punished, albeit with a lesser sentence, through a straightforward and largely technical licensing offence with a lower burden of proof (had the defendant contributed

[59] *Calendar*, see index, 'Chapman, Livewell'; Raymond, review of Barnard and McKenzie, eds, *Chronology and Calendar, TLS* (7 July 2006); Bodleian: Wood 632(42): Nedham, *Newes from Brussels* (London: 1660), manuscript note.

[60] Shuger, *Censorship*, 11 and *passim*.

[61] McKenzie, 'Censorship' (Lyell Lecture), p. 4, original emphasis.

to printing or publishing?). A conviction had nothing to do with the book's content, which did not have to be contested in the volatile context of a courtroom, or be scrutinized for *mitior sensu*.[62]

Serious charges could backfire. Lilburne's acquittal in 1649 was a double discomfit for the prosecution: the commonwealth suffered both a court defeat and the adverse publicity of a lost treason trial. Even a victory, as in the conviction of Burton, Bastwick, and Prynne on a charge of *scandalum magnatum* in 1637, could bring problems in its wake: contemporaries thought the trial and dramatic punishments contributed to the high road to civil war. Prynne's *News from Ipswich* was illegally printed, but the Crown decided its rhetoric and accusations were serious enough to merit exemplary punishment (and besides, Parliament failed to identify printer or publisher).[63] Otherwise it might have chosen a less dramatic course: not out of kindness but pragmatism. Prynne's 1634 trial for *Histriomastix* was for the offence of seditious libel. One of Star Chamber's lawyers was confused—he thought the court dealt with unlicensed books. Prynne had in fact obtained a license, which prevented the Crown from pursuing him for a simpler licensing offence. This fact in itself goes some way to explaining why this became a notorious case of censorship. To risk a counterfactual: if Prynne had not followed the rules might he have escaped with a prison sentence and a fine? The conflict between the judiciary and the Crown over press controls in 1679 (when the 1662 printing act lapsed) was about the best means of censorship: the Crown preferred to pursue licensing offences over prosecuting 'scandalous or seditious' for common law or statutory offences. Henry Care's conviction in 1680 was based on the judges' ruling that the king might 'by Law prohibit the printing & publishing of all News Bookes & Pamphletts of News whatsoever not licensed by [his] authority as Manifestly tending to the Breach of the Peace & Disturbance of the Kingdome'. This provided a means of suppressing all news by royal prerogative without statute, and the mark of whether a book disturbed the peace was whether or not it was licensed. Care was caught as by a licensing offence, though the case was resonantly political.[64]

This also sheds light on the frequency with which stationers obtained ecclesiastical licenses. While licensing, as the work of Anthony Milton and Peter Lake has shown, could be a collaborative procedure, not an authoritarian imposition so much as a negotiation by which mutually acceptable language was shaped, those texts likely to prove ineradicably offensive could always be published surreptitiously or printed overseas and imported in order to circumvent the law.[65] In doing so they would commit a publishing

[62] Philip Hamburger, 'The Development of the Law of Seditious Libel and the Control of the Press', *Stanford Law Journal*, 37 (1984–1985): 661–765, 690.

[63] Hamburger, 'Law of Seditious Libel', 678; the offence was *scandalum magnatum*.

[64] Hamburger, 'Law of Seditious Libel', 684–8; Lois G. Schwoerer, *The Ingenious Mr. Henry Care, Restoration Publicist* (Baltimore: Johns Hopkins University Press, 2001), 109.

[65] Milton, 'Licensing, Censorship'; Peter Lake, *The Boxmaker's Revenge: 'Orthodoxy', 'Heterodoxy' and the Politics of the Parish in Early Stuart London* (Manchester: Manchester University Press, 2001), 404; Robertson, *Censorship and Conflict*, 32–5; W. W. Greg, 'Samuel Harsnett and Hayward's "Henry IV"', *The Library*, 5th ser., 11 (1956): 1–10, 7.

offence prior to any political offence. While the law required books to be licensed it was not necessary for all books to be licensed for the law to be effective. The law instead made it possible to prosecute books that caused offence, those least likely to be licensed, by another route.

Those licensers who approved books that were subsequently prosecuted did suffer repercussions.[66] Authors, stationers, Crown, and courts expected an ecclesiastical license to offer a limited guarantee against ideological offence. Absolute control was not the intention, but effective regulation was. The pursuit of lesser charges doesn't mean that motivation was simply apolitical. Sometimes a licensing prosecution simply concerned commercial interests; on other occasions it was an *expedient*. It mitigated the crime, but ensured a quiet conviction without discussion of the offence. That those who were punished were those responsible for producing the book, rather than the author, suggests that the preventative effects may have been prioritized over the punitive by this approach. Two important inferences follow. First, the 'exceptional' cases—Stubbs, Udall, Marprelate, Cowell, Montagu, Prynne—are exceptional not because they were ideological, but because the offences they committed were not dealt with by the usual expedients. Second, the refrain that press controls merely reflected the need for 'good order' (echoing the 1559 Injunctions) in the book trade has some truth in it.[67] However, this 'good order' was not purely commercial nor innocent of ideological implications. It enabled the efficient pursuit of ideological ends, through the use of the Stationers' Company's search, destroy, and self-policing authority, and through the legal powers that the licensing procedures enabled. Organizational incoherence can facilitate action.

If we search for a monolithic system we will not find one. There was a spectrum of activities from commercial punishment, to charges for breach of parliamentary privilege to issuing a proclamation against lavish speech to a libel suit. The key to the organization of press controls in the early modern period is that it is not entirely coherent. Jurisdictions in early modern England were not logical or systematic, and their plurality and overlap shaped texts and hermeneutics.[68] Press controls worked because of their multiplicity and because the law was flexible and did not always serve intended purposes. The 'normal' (which is to say, everyday commercial practices by stationers) and the exceptional (prosecutions for serious offences), the conventional and the ad hoc, the commercial and the ideological, cannot be separated. They were complementary.

[66] Hunt, 'Licensing and Religious Censorship', 131; Richard Dutton, *Licensing, Censorship and Authorship in Early Modern England: Buggeswords* (Basingstoke: Palgrave Macmillan, 2000), 164–5, 173, 177–88; W. W. Greg, *Some Aspects and Problems of London Publishing Between 1550 and 1650* (Oxford: Clarendon Press, 1956), 62.

[67] Clegg, *Caroline*, ch. 4; Bland, 'Invisible Dangers', 152–3; Mark Rose, 'The Public Sphere and the Emergence of Copyright', in *Privilege and Property*, ed. Deazley, Kretschmer, and Bently, 67–88, 81, 83.

[68] Bradin Cormack, *A Power to Do Justice: Jurisdiction, English Literature, and the Rise of Common Law, 1509–1625* (Chicago: University of Chicago Press, 2007).

Arbitrary Power

The spectrum of management interventions may not have been engineered, but the effect of arbitrary power and the quotidian low-key interventions can be chilling. The modern journalist Nick Davies' account of the *News of the World* hacking scandal (2008–) describes the power of fear operating among journalists and politicians working against News Corp, and the influence of unspoken threats, implied and even unintended, upon their behaviour. Actual intervention was not always necessary to obtain silence or retreat.[69]

And the effects of arbitrary power and low-key interventions were certainly such as might have had an effect on the literary imagination. Even sceptics have looked for a hermeneutics of censorship. Annabel Patterson focused on the means by which restrictions could be circumvented, and the literary consequences of these pressures on speech; even McKenzie explored how censorship 'force[d] literature into a universalising mode'.[70] Hermeneutic approaches no doubt risk mistaken identification of political allusions, though this affected early modern readers as well as modern editors.[71] The effect of political and ecclesiastical pressure on the printed word in early modern England was not to produce silence. My purpose here has been, however, to suggest the practical mechanisms, both legal and extra-legal, that exerted this pressure on speech. For all they were inefficient, erratic, and non-monolithic, their effects were no less pervasive.

Back to Milton. This account of the relationship between the law and practice in press regulation brings into focus an important aspect of *Areopagitica*. The pamphlet is an awkward but not insurmountable fact for those who wish to minimize Stuart censorship. It seems to be a defence of the liberty of speaking (though it is better understood as a defence of the liberty of reading), which is said to be unusually broad; and it presents a picture of draconian licensing in England from Henry VIII to William Laud.[72] According to Shuger, Milton's pamphlet has nothing to do with pre-1641 licensing: he is entirely concerned with the practices that obtained in the 1640s (which did seek to police ideas). McKenzie proposes that it was prompted by Milton's own aggravation by stationers and Parliament for his writings on divorce.[73] *Post hoc ergo propter hoc*; despite the fact that Milton had already attacked licensing in *Animadversions* (1641), before the

69 Nick Davies, *Hack Attack: How the Truth Caught Up with Rupert Murdoch* (London: Farrar, Straus, and Giroux, 2014).

70 McKenzie, 'Censorship' (Lyell Lecture). Also Martin Butler, *Theatre and Crisis, 1632–1642* (Cambridge: Cambridge University Press, 1984); Sharpe, *Criticism and Compliment*, 36–9.

71 McKenzie, anecdote about two editors, 'Censorship' (Lyell Lecture); Worden, 'Literature and Political Censorship'.

72 David Colclough outlines an earlier English history of the notion of liberty of speaking, *Freedom of Speech in Early Stuart England* (Cambridge: Cambridge University Press, 2005).

73 McKenzie, 'Censorship' (Lyell Lecture), and '1644', 148–9; followed by Bland, 'Invisible Dangers', 192–3. Also Clegg, *Elizabethan*, 4.

divorce tracts.[74] Regarding it a self-interested intervention provides a means of dismissing it as a statement of principle. In both accounts it seems as if the Whig history of censorship was invented by Milton and Prynne in the 1640s.

However, I hope now to be able to illuminate Milton's position in *Areopagitica*. After mentioning the irrepressible underground royalist newsbook *Mercurius Aulicus*, Milton tells Parliament that it has obliged itself to round up '*all* scandalous *and* unlicenc't books' already published (self-evidently impossible).[75] This phrase is not a hendiadys. 'Scandalous' and 'unlicensed' are discrete and complementary categories. In the passage with which I began Milton endorses the punishment of 'mischievous and libellous' books, yet rejects licensing. When these means of dealing with print, and the commercial and legal procedures they represent, are understood to be distinct, Milton's argument is entirely coherent. One prosecutes a book for a specific offence and makes the necessary arguments. The other prosecutes a book without having made that argument; it is a thing done in a corner. Milton is quite intent upon that crucial distinction. One is the marker of the rule of law, the other of an arbitrary power.

This, incidentally, explains why he overlooks the two, intervening parliamentary orders of 1642 and 1643. They do not concern licensing: one deals with parliamentary privilege, both with the rights to search. These legal powers do not immediately concern him, as it is not law he objects to; it is the law of licensing, which not only subjects authors to the judgement of another, but also is a law that invites arbitrary use.

Milton deploys a neo-Roman account of liberty, according to which to live in a state in which your own liberty is subject to the will of another is a form of bondage. Quentin Skinner has shown how *Areopagitica* warns that licensing will inhibit authors from expressing unconventional ideas; Martin Dzelzainis how it contends that a licensing system, regardless of actual censorship, enslaves a free-born author by making him dependent on the will of another.[76] To this we can add that it is precisely licensing, and not statutory press controls, that jeopardizes liberty. It takes away liberty, in a way that prosecution for seditious libel or *scandalum magnatum* does not, precisely because of its arbitrariness. Moreover it is not only authors whose liberty is deprived thereby, but printers, booksellers, and readers. Milton had by 1644 worked with numerous printers and booksellers and was familiar with Parliament's real interventions in the daily lives of stationers.

If *Areopagitica* responds in any way to Milton's harassment for his writings on divorce, then it is by inviting Parliament to burn his book.[77] The text invites prosecution for scandal. What it rejects is prosecution for a licensing offence; though in not having

[74] *CPW*, 1.669.

[75] *CPW*, 2.528; my emphasis.

[76] Quentin Skinner, *Visions of Politics*, 3 vols (Cambridge: Cambridge University Press, 2002), 2.286–307, at 302–3; Martin Dzelzainis, 'Republicanism', in Thomas N. Corns, ed., *A Companion to Milton* (Oxford: Blackwell, 2001), 294–308, 301–4. Geoff Kemp, '*Areopagitica*'s Adversary: Henry Parker and the *Humble Remonstrance*', in *Censorship Moments*, ed. Kemp, 71–8.

[77] *Bucer* and *Of Education* were licensed (*CPW*, 2.357, 416); *Doctrine and Discipline* and *Areopagitica* were not.

the pamphlet licensed the anonymous publisher risked this (was Livewell Chapman responsible? the type doesn't reveal).[78] But the text contends that if you wish to punish him, then as a free man—as the epigraph from Euripides makes plain—you need to argue with him in court.

Censorship laws in early modern England were more intrusive, ideological, and effective than revisionist arguments acknowledge. This was not because they were hegemonic, well-conceived, or systematized, but because the complementarity between the law and the organization of the trade enabled the Crown and its representatives to intervene through more or less arbitrary procedures. Measures revisionists define as commercial were used for political and religious ends. Tudor and Stuart governments did not support monopolies for their own sake. I have not here addressed the question of what happened in 1641–1642, the revolutionary events sometimes labelled the 'collapse of censorship'.[79] However, this legal context clarifies Milton's position in *Areopagitica*: there is a legal content to and context for Milton's argument, and this legal content illuminates the political content. It was through laws that concealed their political nature that 'patentees and monopolizers in the trade of book-selling' were able to support arbitrary government.[80]

Bibliography

Barnard, John and D. F. McKenzie, ed. *The Cambridge History of the Book in Britain*, Vol. 4: *1557–1695* (Cambridge: Cambridge University Press, 2002).

Bland, Mark. '"Invisible Dangers": Censorship and the Subversion of Authority in Early Modern England', *Publications of the Bibliographical Society of America*, 90 (1996): 151–93.

Clegg, Cyndia Susan. *Press Censorship in Caroline England* (Cambridge: Cambridge University Press, 2008).

Clegg, Cyndia Susan. *Press Censorship in Elizabethan England* (Cambridge: Cambridge University Press, 1997).

Clegg, Cyndia Susan. *Press Censorship in Jacobean England* (Cambridge, Cambridge University Press, 2001).

Gadd, Ian Anders. '"Being like a field": Corporate Identity in the Stationers' Company 1557–1684' (DPhil Thesis: University of Oxford, 1999).

Hill, Christopher. Censorship and English Literature', in *Collected Essays*, Vol. 1: *Writing and Revolution in 17th Century England* (Amherst: University of Massachusetts Press, 1985), 32–71.

Kemp, Geoff and Jason McElligott, ed. *Censorship and the Press, 1580–1720*, 4 vols (London: Pickering and Chatto, 2009).

[78] This was not unusual for a text printed in 1644 (as McKenzie, 'Simmons', Lyell Lecture, points out), but given that the text actually *concerns* licensing this decision cannot seriously be taken as an unconscious acceptance of a common trade practice.

[79] See David Cressy, *England on Edge: Crisis and Revolution* (Oxford: Oxford University Press, 2006), 281–309.

[80] *CPW*, 2.570.

Lambert, Sheila. 'Richard Montagu, Arminianism and Censorship', *Past & Present*, 124 (1989): 36–68.

Lambert, Sheila. 'State Control of the Press in Theory and Practice: The Role of the Stationers' Company before 1640', in *Censorship and the Control of Print in England and France, 1600–1910*, ed. Robin Myers and Michael Harris (Winchester: St Paul's Bibliographies, 1992), 1–32.

McElligott, Jason. '"Several Hundred Squabbling Small Tradesmen"? Censorship, the Stationers' Company, and the State in Seventeenth-Century England', in *News Networks in Seventeenth-Century Britain and Europe*, ed. Joad Raymond (London: Routledge, 2006), 87–102.

McElligott, Jason. *Royalism, Print and Censorship in Revolutionary England* (Woodbridge: Boydell, 2007).

McKenzie, D. F. *Lyell Lectures, Oxford, 1988* (typescript on deposit in English Faculty Library, Oxford).

McKenzie, D. F. and Maureen Bell, ed. *A Chronology and Calendar of Documents Relating to the London Book Trade, 1641–1700* (Oxford: Oxford University Press, 2005).

Raymond, Joad. *Pamphlets and Pamphleteering in Early Modern Britain* (Cambridge: Cambridge University Press, 2003).

Robertson, Randy. *Censorship and Conflict in Seventeenth-Century England: The Subtle Art of Division* (University Park: Pennsylvania State University Press, 2009).

Robertson, Randy. 'British Index', at <https://susqu.academia.edu/RandyRobertson/Papers>.

Shuger, Debora. *Censorship and Cultural Sensibility: The Regulation of Language in Tudor–Stuart England* (Philadelphia: University of Pennsylvania Press, 2006).

CHAPTER 27

MANAGING THE LATER STUART PRESS, 1662–1696

MARTIN DZELZAINIS

THIS chapter deals with the period that saw the imposition and collapse of the system of pre-publication censorship laid down in the Printing Act of 1662—a landmark piece of legislation that was renewed in 1665, lapsed in 1679, was revived in 1685, and renewed again in 1692 and 1693 before expiring in 1695.[1] There is still debate as to whether the Act succeeded in extinguishing the 'atmosphere of free debate … which had made most of the two previous decades so exciting and disturbing', as Ronald Hutton put it, or whether, notwithstanding its provisions, 'a public sphere in the Habermasian sense did emerge in later seventeenth-century England', as Steven Pincus has argued.[2] A more fundamental question perhaps is whether early modern censorship ever took the form familiar to us of a confrontation between a writer and the state. For while the concept of the state as an entity separate from rulers and ruled was developed in the seventeenth century, in practice, as we shall see, the authorities lacked the means to construct and police a regime of censorship of the kind which we now associate with the impersonal agency of the state.[3] Nor is it clear that we can securely identify the writer of the text with the figure

[1] The Printing Act (as contemporaries knew it) has also been called the Licensing Act and Press Act; see Michael Treadwell, 'The Stationers and the Printing Acts at the End of the Seventeenth Century', in *The Cambridge History of the Book in Britain*, Vol. 4: *1557–1695*, ed. John Barnard and D. F. McKenzie, with Maureen Bell (Cambridge, 2002), 755, 769–70.

[2] Ronald Hutton, *The Restoration: A Political and Religious History of England and Wales, 1658–1667* (Oxford, 1985), 157; '"CoffeePoliticians Does Create": Coffeehouses and Restoration Political Culture', *Journal of Modern History*, 67.4 (1995): 807–34 (at 811).

[3] Mark Goldie has drawn attention to the 'gap between enactment and enforcement, between legislative intention and executive achievement. … The framework of law and the structure of authority remained sufficiently cross-grained and ambiguous that even at the apogee of Stuart power, neither the Crown nor the political elite was able to act with unequivocal single-mindedness': 'The Hilton Gang and the Purge of London in the 1680s', in *Politics and the Political Imagination in Later Stuart Britain: Essays Presented to Lois Green Schwoerer*, ed. Howard Nenner (Rochester: University of Rochester Press, 1997), 43–73, 44. See also Joad Raymond's chapter in this volume.

of the author, since the author was arguably whoever could be held legally to account for a work even if they did not actually write the words of the text.[4] This put booksellers or printers in the firing line, especially since the primary aim of those implementing the Printing Act may have been simply to prevent the physical production and dispersal of books rather than to root out the authors of sedition and their patrons. The problem is thus to provide a historically authentic account of print and censorship at precisely the point when some of the categories we now regard as crucial to such an account—the author and the state—were in the process of being developed and articulated. In short, the chapter addresses the question of why the restored monarchy ultimately proved unable to institute what Henri-Jean Martin calls a 'typographical absolutism' of the kind associated in France with Cardinal Richelieu and Chancellor Séguier and had to settle instead for merely managing the press.[5]

The Printing Act

The preamble to the 1662 'Act for preventing the frequent Abuses in printing seditious treasonable and unlicensed Bookes and Pamphlets and for regulating of Printing and Printing Presses' sweepingly ordained that:

> no person or persons whatsoever shall presume to print or cause to be printed either within this Realm of England or any other His Majesties Dominions or in the parts beyond the Seas any heretical seditious schismatical or offensive Bookes or Pamphlets wherein any Doctrine or Opinion shall be asserted or maintained which is contrary to Christian Faith or the Doctrine or Discipline of the Church of England or which shall or may tend or be to the scandall of Religion or the Church or the Government or Governors of the Church State or Common wealth.[6]

To this end, it sought to regulate every aspect of the trade. No new presses could be set up nor any type cast nor premises provided for printing without first notifying the Stationers' Company. The numbers of printers and their apprentices and presses as well as type founders were all limited, and sureties of £300 were required. Anything to be printed was first to be registered with the Stationers' Company and duly licensed by those

[4] See Adrian Johns, *The Nature of the Book: Print and Knowledge in the Making* (Chicago: University of Chicago Press, 1998), 159–60.

[5] Henri-Jean Martin, *The French Book: Religion, Absolutism, and Readership, 1585–1715*, trans. Paul Saenger and Nadine Saenger (Baltimore and London: Johns Hopkins University Press, 1996), 37; cf. Alfred Soman, 'Press, Pulpit and Censorship in France before Richelieu', *Proceedings of the American Philosophical Society*, 120.6 (1976): 439–63.

[6] 'Charles II, 1662: An Act for Preventing the Frequent Abuses in Printing Seditious Treasonable and Unlicensed Bookes and Pamphlets and for Regulating of Printing and Printing Presses', in *Statutes of the Realm*, Vol. 5: *1628–80*, ed. John Raithby (s.l.: 1819), 428–35 <http://www.british-history.ac.uk/statutes-realm/vol5/pp428-435>.

appointed (or their appointees). By way of ensuring compliance, and especially 'for the better discovering of printing in Corners without License', powers were conferred on the King's Messengers and the Master and Wardens of the Stationers' Company 'to search all Houses and Shops where they shall knowe or upon some probable reason suspect any Books or Papers to be printed bound or stitched especially Printing Houses Booksellers Shops and Warehouses and Bookbinders Houses and Shops'. Transgressors would be 'disenabled' from the trade for three years for a first offence and permanently for a second, and would also be liable to 'receive such further punishment by Fine Imprisonment or other Corporal Punishment not extending to Life or Limb' as the judges thought fit.

These measures for securing ideological conformity in the domain of print were, however, much less comprehensive than they appeared, even if by virtue of the Act it was now the case that, as Philip Hamburger puts it, 'a prosecuting attorney needed only to prove that the defendant had contributed in one way or another to the publication of an unlicensed book' in order to secure a conviction for the so-called offence of 'seditious libel'.[7] In the first place, and obviously, the Act dealt only with *printed* materials; manuscripts were without its purview, much to the chagrin of Roger L'Estrange, the Surveyor of the Imprimery to whom successive Secretaries of State delegated much of their oversight of the press. He regarded scribal publication as the more subversive medium, having in 1662 drawn up 'The Minutes of a Project for the preventing of Libells' in which he insisted that:

> Of Libells some are only written, others printed; and those in Manuscript, are comonly ye more seditious, & scandalous of ye two; Besides that they are forty times as many, & by the help of Transcripts, well nigh as publick as the other.[8]

Not only did manuscript libels tend to be more outspoken than those in print but they were almost as widespread because of the ease with which scriptoria could generate copies.

Nor did the Act deal with the 'legacy issue' of books and pamphlets that were already in print as a result of the (relative) freedom of the press in the years of revolution. L'Estrange was greatly exercised by the thought that:

> *The same Reason that prohibits* New Pamphlets, *requires also the Suppressing of* Old ones, (*of the same Quality*) *for 'tis not the* Date, *that does the* Mischief, *but the* Matter, *and the* Number. *If they be* Plausible, *and* Cunning *enough to* Deceive, *and then* Numerous *enough to* Spread, Buchanan, *and* Knox *will do the business as sure*

[7] Philip Hamburger, 'The Development of the Law of Seditious Libel and the Control of the Press', *Stanford Law Review*, 67 (1985): 661–705.

[8] TNA, SP 29/51/10.1; *CSPD*, 1662, 283. The phrasing resembles L'Estrange's 'Proposition Concerning Libells' drawn up for the House of Lords in 1675; see Harold Love, *Scribal Publication in Seventeenth-Century England* (Oxford: Clarendon Press, 1993), 74; and D. F. McKenzie, *Making Meaning: 'Printers of the Mind' and Other Essays*, ed. Peter D. McDonald and Michael F. Suarez (Amherst and Boston: University of Massachusetts Press, 2002), 245.

> *as* Baxter, *and* Calamy. *Besides that in some Respects, the* Old Ones *have a great Advantage of the* New: *for being Written in times of* Freedom, *and Menag'd by great* Masters *of the Popular Stile, they speak* playner, *and strike* homer *to the* Capacity *and* Humour *of the* Multitude; *whereas they that write in the fear of a* Law, *are forc'd to cover their Meaning under* Ambiguities, *and* Hints, *to the greater Hazzard of the* Libeller, *than of the* Publique.[9]

It was true that the Printing Act could be expected to have a chilling effect on present-day writers, forcing them to be oblique and thereby rendering them less likely to connect with the public than their predecessors had been. But this would be to little avail, L'Estrange thought, if something was not also done about works by '*great* Masters *of the Popular Stile*' such as the sixteenth-century monarchomach George Buchanan that were still in circulation and available for reprinting. (Indeed, the logic of his position was eventually to lead him to censor the sale of the Earl of Anglesey's library when it came under the hammer in 1686.)[10] What lay behind L'Estrange's complaint was clause XVIII of the Act, a proviso to the effect that:

> no search shall be att any time made in the House or Houses of any the Peers of this Realm or of any other person or persons not being free of or using any of the Trades in this Act before mentioned but by special Warrant from the Kings Majestie under His Sign Manual or under the Hand of one or both of His Majesties principal Secretaries of State or for any other Books then such as are in printing or shall be printed after the Tenth of June One thousand six hundred sixty two.

In the absence of a special warrant, not only were the houses of peers exempt from search, as might have been expected, but also the homes of anyone not directly involved in the book trade. And searches for books printed before the Act came into effect were simply off-limits. There was a sense, therefore, in which the Printing Act amounted to an Act of Oblivion for revolutionary-era writings.

The Act was also relatively moderate when it came to punishing infractions. As ever, L'Estrange took a hard-line view, wanting the whole gamut of punishments—'*Death, Mutilation, Imprisonment, Banishment, Corporal Peyns, Disgrace, Pecuniary Mulcts*'—to be available for meting out to the 'delinquents' in question, namely:

> the *Advisers, Authors, Compilers, Writers, Printers, Correcters, Stitchers,* and *Binders* of unlawful Books and Pamphlets: together with all *Publishers Dispersers and Concealers* of them in *General:* and all *Stationers, Posts, Hackny-Coachmen, Carryers, Boat-men, Mariners, Hawkers, Mercury-Women, Pedlers,* and *Ballad-Singers*.[11]

[9] Roger L'Estrange, *Considerations and Proposals in Order to the Regulation of the Press: Together with Diverse Instances of Treasonous, and Seditious Pamphlets, Proving the Necessity thereof* (London: 1663), 9–10.

[10] See Annabel Patterson and Martin Dzelzainis, 'Marvell and the Earl of Anglesey: A Chapter in the History of Reading', *HJ*, 44 (2001): 703–26, 712.

[11] L'Estrange, *Considerations*, 31.

Anyone hoping to get off lightly by undergoing mere 'disgrace' would be in for a shock; as a penal category, it was much wider and more severe than might be imagined:

> Pillory, Stocks, Whipping, Carting, Stigmatizing, Disablement to bear Office, *or* Testimony, Publique Recantation, standing under the Gallows with a Rope about the Neck, at a Publique Execution. Disfranchisement (*if Free-men*) Cashiering (*if Souldiers*,) Degrading (*if Persons of Condition*), *Wearing some* Badge *of* Infamy: *Condemnation to* Work *either in* Mines, Plantations, *or* House of Correction.[12]

The measures on L'Estrange's wish-lists thus went well beyond the 'punition corporelle' threatened by the famous Code Michaux of 1629 let alone the 'Corporal Punishment not extending to Life or Limb' stipulated in the 1662 Act.[13]

This is not to deny that the Stuarts were capable of dealing very severely with those involved in the production and distribution of seditious texts. But they could only do so under the law of treason (25 Edward III), as in the case of the three printers executed in the second half of the seventeenth century; John Twyn (1664), William Disney (1685), and William Anderton (1693).[14] The case of Anderton, as we shall see, is fatal to the Whiggish assumption that the Williamite regime of the 1690s was more benign in its intentions towards the press than its predecessors. Such demonstrations of state power were, however, tellingly infrequent. More representative of the way in which the Stuarts managed the press is the career of George Larkin (*c*.1642–1707), a printer, bookseller, and author overlooked in standard accounts of the London literary underground.[15] He does not feature in Neil Keeble's *Literary Culture of Nonconformity*, or the *ODNB*, or, more surprisingly, the *Biographical Dictionary of British Radicals in the Seventeenth Century*.[16] Yet a glance at the list of his publications—from the first edition of John Bunyan's *Grace Abounding* (1666) to Henry Care's *Animadversions upon Mijn Heer Fagels Letter* (1688)—suggests he should be considered alongside better-known figures like John Darby or

12 L'Estrange, *Considerations*, 32.

13 *Ordonnance du Roy Louis XIII. Roy de France & de Navarre ... Publiée en Parlement le 15. Ianvier 1629* (Paris: 1629), 38.

14 For Twyn, see Joseph F. Loewenstein, 'Legal Proofs and Corrected Readings: Press-Agency and the New Bibliography', in *The Production of English Renaissance Culture*, ed. David Lee Miller, Sharon O'Dair, and Harold Weber (Ithaca and London: Cornell University Press, 1994), 111–22. For Disney, see Melinda Zook, 'Disney, William (*b*. in or after 1633, *d*. 1685)', *ODNB*; *The True Account of the Behaviour and Confession of William Disney* (London, 1685); and *A Warning to Traytors, Or, a Brief Account of the Appredenaing* [sic], *Tryal, Condemnation, Behaviour and execution of William Disinie* [*sic*] (London: 1685).

15 The date of Larkin's death, differing from that given in H. R. Plomer, *A Dictionary of the Printers and Booksellers Who Were at Work in England, Scotland and Ireland from 1668 to 1725* (Oxford: Oxford University Press, 1922), 183–4, is based on the letter written to his friend John Dunton from his deathbed on 29 July 1707, and printed in Dunton, *The Hazard of a Death-Bed Repentance* (London: 1728), 54.

16 See Neil H. Keeble, *The Literary Culture of Nonconformity* (Leicester: Leicester University Press, 1987); and *Biographical Dictionary of British Radicals in the Seventeenth Century*, ed. Richard L. Greaves and Robert Zaller, 3 vols (Brighton: Harvester Press, 1982).

Francis Smith. Indeed, an account of Larkin's activities in the 1660s, 1670s, and 1680s constitutes a case study of almost every aspect of the policing of print culture under the later Stuarts.

LARKIN AND THE LITERARY UNDERGROUND

George Larkin was bound as an apprentice to James Cotterell in December 1656, was made free in July 1664, and began his career as his own master in 1666 by printing John Waite's sermon *He zemia tes agapse: The Loss of Love* (1666) as well as *Grace Abounding*.[17] According to Christopher Hill, 'Bunyan chose his printers because of their radicalism', though at the time the warehouse of his usual publisher, the Baptist Francis Smith, was liable to being searched.[18] This begs the question of how the young Larkin came into contact with Bunyan (or Smith) in the first place. Presumably it was through contacts in the dissenting community; twenty years later, Larkin reminisced that 'at the beginning of the year 1666. I sat down in Church-Fellowship with Mr Blake of Clerkenwell-Green', and had stayed with this congregation until 1670 even though he was by then living in Southwark.[19] But it is also the case that his former master, Cotterell, had been arrested in 1664 for illegally printing law books (when Larkin was still bound to him) and that on 20 July 1668 a further warrant was issued committing him to the Gatehouse for printing seditious books.[20] Illicit printing was a lucrative and commonplace practice, and Larkin must have been exposed to it from the start of his apprenticeship.

Larkin quickly became engaged in clandestine activities on his own account, printing Ralph Wallis's *Room for the Cobler of Gloucester and His Wife with Several Cartloads of Abominable Irregular, Pitiful Stinking Priests* (1668), a virulent anticlerical satire, described by L'Estrange as 'the damnedest thing has come out yet'.[21] More significantly, he was alleged to have produced Andrew Marvell's *Second* and *Third Advice to a*

[17] D. F. McKenzie, ed., *Stationers' Company Apprentices 1641–1700* (Oxford: Oxford Bibliographical Society, 1974), 38. See Plomer, *Dictionary ... from 1668 to 1725*, 183–4. It may be significant, in view of Larkin's later connection with Elizabeth Calvert, that Cotterell printed John Gadbury's *Vox solis* for Calvert in 1667; see further, Maureen Bell, '"Her Usual Practices": The Later Career of Elizabeth Calvert, 1664–75', *Publishing History*, 35 (1994): 17–20.

[18] See Christopher Hill, *A Turbulent, Seditious, and Factious People: John Bunyan and His Church* (Oxford: Verso Books, 1988), 287–91. But Hill, too, neglects Larkin—strangely, given that Larkin published another six works by Bunyan in 1688 to 1689 (Wing B5480, B5510, B5522, B5545, B5549, and B5595). Larkin is not mentioned in Bunyan, *Grace Abounding and Other Spiritual Autobiographies*, ed. John Stachniewski, with Anita Pacheco (Oxford: Oxford University Press, 1998).

[19] Roger L'Estrange, *The Observator*, Vol. 2, no. 197, 8 January 1685. See further below.

[20] See Greaves, *Enemies under His Feet*, 295; *CSPD*, 1667–1668, 495.

[21] *CSPD*, 1667–1668, 357–8; Keeble, *Literary Culture*, 105–8; see now Stephen Bardle, *The Literary Underground in the 1660s: Andrew Marvell, George Wither, Ralph Wallis, and the World of Restoration Satire and Pamphleteering* (Oxford: Oxford University Press, 2012), 37–60.

Painter, poems that launched the genre of state satire.[22] Once again, Smith was probably involved, having tried to get the *Advices* printed in July 1667. Larkin himself was caught up in a series of searches in Southwark in 1668. When Roger Norton searched his house 'for the bookes stiled The Cobbler of Gloucester and Advice to the Painter [Larkin] fled out of the back doore and escaped, but he found seuerall of the s^{d} Bookes'.[23] A printing press was also seized at the house of Elizabeth Poole (presumably the interregnum radical of that name) in a set of tenements known as the Mint, one of the so-called 'liberties', located west of St George's parish church and the King's Bench prison. Poole plausibly claimed to know nothing of the comings and goings of her tenant who had set up the press in a garret. Elizabeth Calvert (the widow of Giles, a noted publisher of Quaker writings in the 1650s) was also apprehended in the raid and committed to the Gatehouse for keeping a press and 'for vending & publishing unlicensed & Scandalous Bookes & Pamphlets'.[24] But when Calvert was eventually proceeded against it was for a different offence committed several weeks later on 20 May 1668. Moreover, it was not until 1670–1671 that she was actually indicted, tried, and convicted in connection with *Directions to a Painter* (1667), which had featured four advice poems in all as well as another poem by Marvell, *Clarendon's House-Warming*.

When belatedly prosecuted for having illicitly 'vendidit utteravit and publicavit' the *Directions*, a malicious, scandalous, and seditious book, Calvert faced three witnesses.[25] Joshua Waterhouse was an apprentice freed by Calvert in August 1669. Thomas Willis had been committed to the Gatehouse in 1668 'for dispersing scandalous & seditious Pamphlets' and so could speak to her publishing the *Directions*.[26] The third was Larkin, now unmasked as an informer against fellow members of the underground. His name appears with his wife's on the indictments of John Darby and Nathan Brookes in the same file of prosecutions initiated by L'Estrange.[27] He had certainly become an informer by October 1670, when the Secretary of State, Arlington, authorized L'Estrange to offer Larkin conditional immunity:

> Whereas you haue ^^{made} intercession on the behalfe of diuers Journy Men, Printers, and others and particularly for George Larkin, from whose Wife it seems you haue recieued some considerable helpes (by the Priuity and direction of her husband)

[22] See Martin Dzelzainis, 'Andrew Marvell and the Restoration Literary Underground: Printing the Painter Poems', *SC*, 22.2 (2007): 395–410.

[23] Parliamentary Archives, HL/PO/CO/1/3 [20 March 1677, fol. 166].

[24] TNA, SP 44/30/28^{r} (*CSPD*, 1667–1668, 363). See Ariel Hessayon, 'Calvert, Giles (*bap.* 1615, *d.* 1663)', *ODNB*.

[25] London Metropolitan Archive, Sessions File 205.

[26] TNA, SP 44/28/12^{r} (*CSPD*, 1667–1668, 178).

[27] London Metropolitan Archive, Sessions File 205. John Winter was indicted for printing a seditious ballad 'intitulat Irelands lamentation for Englands great desolation'. Darby and Brookes were indicted in relation to Nicholas Lockyer's *Some Seasonable and Serious Queries upon the Late Act against Conventicles* (1670) and not, as is sometimes supposed, *A Few Sober Queries upon the Late Proclamation* (1668). Lockyer was forced to flee to the Netherlands to avoid prosecution; see E. C. Vernon, 'Lockyer, Nicholas (1611–1685)', *ODNB* <http://www.oxforddnb.com/view/article/16914>.

towards your late discouery of seditious Phamphetts [sic], Wee haue thought fitt at your intercession hereby to declare Our Pleasure, and Wee doe hereby sufficiently authorise you in Our Name to declare, that neither George Larkin nor any other Persons concerned in your mediation, shall suffer for what is past, either for printing composing or dispersing any of the sd Pamphletts prouided always that they answer particularly to such Questions as you shall aske them and owne their examinations; Whereas if it shall appeare hereafter that they haue dealt deceitfully, This Our Grace and fauor shall bee to them of noe effect: but otherwise they shall be secure in their liues, liberties & fortunes to all intents and purposes, for w^{ch} $\&^{c}$. By his Maties Command Arlington.[28]

But for what offences did Larkin require immunity? According to Larkin, in 1670 he had found himself in 'much trouble about some Quæries which I Composed as a Journyman at Mr Darby's; upon which account I was forc'd to be a Witness against him at the Old-Baily'.[29] L'Estrange had seized the opportunity—evidently while Larkin was under arrest for composing Lockyer's *Some Seasonable and Serious Queries*—not only to force him to become a witness against Darby and Brookes but also to direct his wife to assist in the discovery of other seditious pamphlets. With Larkin, who had presumably printed the *Directions* at Poole's house, cooperating, the way was clear for the prosecution of Calvert, long a target of L'Estrange's.

Larkin and the Stationers' Company

For the duration of the 1670s Larkin was in L'Estrange's pocket. Cooperation brought some rewards. Having lost his Southwark press and been reduced to working as a journeyman he was set up again as a printer by Captain John Seymour who in 1669 had been rewarded for his service to the Crown by being granted the right to print almanacs.[30] This was challenged by the Stationers' Company, who saw it as a threat to their monopoly, and the issue was argued before the Privy Council in January 1672.[31] When this proved inconclusive, the Company resorted to force, using its powers under the Act to raid Larkin's premises—acting, it should be emphasized, in defence of its commercial interests rather than as the authorities' policeman:

Mr. Seymour has illegally erected a printing-house at Westminster and made one Larkin master thereof, who is not qualified to be a master printer, and there

[28] TNA, SP 44/34. fol. 52^{r} (misnumbered 54) (*CSPD*, 1670, 486).

[29] Roger L'Estrange, *The Observator*, Vol. 2, no. 197, 8 January 1685.

[30] See Cyprian Blagden, *The Stationers' Company: A History, 1403–1959* (London: George Allen and Unwin, 1960), 193–5.

[31] For the arguments, see Stationers' Company, Court Book D, 4 February 1672, fols 195^{v}–196^{v} (Part III, Reel 56).

printed almanacks and other things. The Master and Wardens have entered the said printing-house and finding there almanacks printing defaced some of the materials and seized so much of the almanacks as were printed.[32]

Seymour responded by moving his press—still managed by Larkin—to Putney, where it was subjected to further raids, and not until June 1677 was the Company held to account for its destruction of Larkin's press in Westminster.[33]

While Larkin did print *Poor Robin* (1677; Wing A2219A), an anti-Quaker satire licensed by L'Estrange in August 1676, for Seymour, it would be a mistake to suppose that he had shifted ground ideologically. For Larkin, as for others, what mattered most about Seymour was that he was both in dispute with the Stationers and able to supply work. Conversely, according to Warden Mearne, testifying before the Lords Libels Committee, 'there is noe man y^t^ is obnoxious to the Company but he flyes to Mr Seymour'. He had in mind not only Larkin but also Francis Smith who he alleged was 'an Agent for Mr Seymour'.[34]

The Lords Libels Committee had been appointed on 16 February 1677, the day after the new parliamentary session began, to investigate a spate of opposition pamphlets including Denzil Holles's *The Long Parliament Dissolved* (1676; Wing H2463) and Nicholas Carey's *Some Considerations upon the Question, Whether the Parliament is Dissolved by it's Prorogation for 15 Months?* (1676; Wing H2467). However, the Committee's investigation of these seditious libels rapidly turned into a contest between the Stationers' Company, in the person of Mearne, and Seymour and L'Estrange, who were acting in concert.

The most comprehensive indictment of the Company was provided by a printed *Case of Libels* placed before the Committee on 20 March 1677 by Seymour and read out after L'Estrange was called in and Mearne and his supporters withdrew.[35] Its stated aim was defensive:

Whereas the Company of Stationers, *being charg'd with the want either of Care or Integrity, in the preventing, Discovering, or Suppressing of Treasonous, Seditious and scandalous Libels, have thought fit (with pretense of singular Zeal to the Publick) to discharge themselves by calumnious hints and reflections upon other People, the Truth of the Case is here set forth, and dutifully submitted to Authority.*[36]

[32] *CSPD*, Add. 1660–1685, 445.

[33] See Blagden, *Stationers' Company*, 195. Mearne told the Lords Libels Committee that 'two or 3 presses are sett up at Putney by Capt Jo: Seymour, and his cheife printer [who] printed the Aduice to the Painter and the Cobbler of Gloucester' (Parliamentary Archives, HL/PO/CO/1/3 [10 March 1677, fol. 155]). The Stationers also raided other Seymour presses such as Thomas Rookes's at Uxbridge and Ludgate in 1673; see John Hetet, 'A Literary Underground in Restoration England: Printers and Dissenters in the Context of Constraints, 1660–1689' (unpublished PhD dissertation: University of Cambridge, 1987), 85.

[34] Parliamentary Archives, HL/PO/CO/1/3 [20 March 1677, fols 165–6].

[35] Parliamentary Archives, HL/PO/CO/1/3 [20 March 1677, fol. 166].

[36] [John Seymour], *The Case of Libels* (n.p., n.d.), Parliamentary Archives, House of Lords Papers, 1676/7, item 338 [fol. 121^r^]. There is a resume in the version of the Committee's proceedings in Historical Manuscripts Commission, *Ninth Report*, Appendix 2 (House of Lords MSS), 69–79 (at 76).

This was followed by a narrative of L'Estrange's attempt to force the Company to enact new by-laws for the more effective regulation of the press, beginning with the *quo warranto* order issued by the Privy Council in August 1670. A show of compliance by the Company had resulted in the withdrawal of this threat to recall its charter, but from then 'to this present 1676. they have only shifted, and delayed'. Indeed, far from suppressing libels, as the Company claimed it was doing, it was actively keeping them in circulation. Thus 'several of the Chief men of the Company do both Sell, and Connive at many of those Libells, which they are Commanded to Search for, and Discover'. These Company grandees also 'give Notice beforehand of a Search to be made' or 'upon Informations, they do sometime put off Searching till things may be removed out of the way'. The powers of search under the Act, already too limited in L'Estrange's view, were routinely being thwarted by those charged with their execution.

The broadside concludes with a sympathetic account of the pressures to which printers and journeymen were subjected by the 'Chief men of the Company'. According to Seymour,

> They do commonly prosecute the Discoverer of a Libel, and leave the Principal free; so that Printers dare not reveal any thing for fear of being undone. As in the case of a Journy-man-printer, who was only a Press-man, and Printed off without reading it, what another Composed by the order of his Master. This Journey-man Discover'd the Woman that brought it to the Press, and carry'd away the Printed Sheets, and he recover's at least a 1000 Copies; and did further Services, for which he received a Reward from a Secretary of State: And yet though the Company were ordered to Prosecute the Woman at Common Law, because she would not discover the Author; they Indicted the Journey-man-printer, and never meddled with the Woman, or Master of the Printing-house.

In other words, the journeyman printer was liable to become the fall guy in any investigation of a seditious work which failed to net those actually responsible for its production—in many cases, the very stationers who were doing the investigating. As a result, while printers might be willing to inform, they were being intimidated by the threat of legal process into keeping quiet. It was also clear that high-level political protection counted for little with the grandees and that any printer who relied on it was running a risk:

> They Vilify the Authority of a Secretaryes Warrant, and him that Executes it: And one of them taking notice of a Printer that waited often upon a Secretary of State, though by his command and appointment, in order to a Discovery; tax'd the Printer publickly at the Hall Table, for applying himself thither, and charged him to go no more.

Political authority did not trump the potent combination of guild pressure and commercial interest.

In detailing these alleged abuses, Seymour and L'Estrange were clearly appealing to a constituency of printers like Larkin and Rookes, who had been victimized by the Company. They were also implicitly promising the Committee that, if the Company's stranglehold could be broken, there would be no shortage of those willing to cooperate with the Secretaries of State in discovering sedition. The Company argued to the contrary that it had done all it could to suppress seditious libels, and that it was Seymour and L'Estrange who were the agents of subversion. Larkin unfortunately got caught in the crossfire. This began on 10 March when Mearne accused Seymour of employing Larkin as his printer and Francis Smith as his agent. Seymour countered by submitting a paper that implicated Mearne personally in the distribution of politically subversive works, as demonstrated by the 'Treasonable and Seditious Expressions taken out of Dyers Sermons' and 'Osborns works printed by Robert White 1673. and sold by Samuel Mearn Warden of the Company of Stationers'.[37] The allegations about Dyer were backed up in depositions submitted on 27 March. Two of the King's Messengers and Thomas Rookes attested that on 23 October 1673 the messengers, acting on a warrant issued by Secretary Coventry, had searched Randall Taylor's house and seized 'three Porters Burthens ... of an Unlicensed and Seditious Book, intituled Dyers Sermons'. But Mearne had at once put up bail for Taylor and then bullied the messengers. Larkin and George Grainge attested that, in a separate incident,

> M^{r}: Mearne and others of the Stationers having seized upon 1000 of Dyers Sermons an Vnlicensed Book, M^{r}: Mearn sold the said Bookes to M^{r}: Royston, and M^{r}: Royston sold them to M^{r}: Write who sold them publickly in his Shop, they being printed almost every yeare by Randal Taylor, Thomas Sawbridge and John Wright, and disperst all over the Kingdom, the Book being Unlicensed Scandalous & Seditious.[38]

In other words, Mearne protected insiders like Taylor and Sawbridge when they published Dyer but seized the same work when printed by outsiders like Larkin.

The Committee eventually decided not to pursue Seymour's allegations and while a new bill concerning printing was drawn up it was not enacted before the session ended on 28 May.[39] What their proceedings had brought into view was an unlikely anti-Company coalition which had formed by the mid-1670s, comprising L'Estrange, Seymour the royal patentee, and those who were 'obnoxious to the Company' like Larkin, Rookes, and Smith. Acting on the principle that my enemy's enemy is my friend, agents of the state could cooperate with those who were ideologically opposed to it.

[37] Parliamentary Archives, House of Lords Papers, 1676/7, item 338 [fols 119–20] (HMC, *Ninth Report*, Appendix 2 (House of Lords MSS), 75 (g)).

[38] Parliamentary Archives, House of Lords papers 1676/7, item 338 [fol. 127^{r}] (HMC, *Ninth Report*, Appendix 2 (House of Lords MSS), 75 (g^{5})).

[39] See Parliamentary Archives, HL/PO/CO/1/3 [30 March 1677, fol. 185].

Larkin and the Tory Reaction

The coalition did not survive the lapse of the Printing Act in June 1679 and the turmoil of the Exclusion Crisis, when Smith worked closely with Titus Oates and Shaftesbury, and Larkin seized the opportunity to set up his own press at, successively, Scalding Alley in the Poultry (1681–1683), the King's Head in Broad Street (1683), and the lower end of Broad Street next to London Wall (1684–1685). Smith was abroad or in prison between 1681 and 1688 and Larkin therefore rose to prominence as a Baptist publisher, printing works by William Kiffin, Benjamin Keach, and William Pardoe among others. But it was as the Tory Reaction gathered pace in the 1680s that Larkin began to produce works by Henry Care and Edmund Hickeringill challenging the legality of ecclesiastical courts and especially the Elizabethan writ *de excommunicatio capiendo* which provided a do-it-yourself legal kit for dissenters.[40] And, as the persecution intensified, Larkin's press became the main conduit for the prison-writings to which we owe much of our knowledge of the Baptists in the latter years of Charles II.

Some of his commercial imprints also carried a political charge. William Dockwra's 1681 prospectus for the penny post was backed by the Whigs.[41] Dockwra's partner, Robert Murray, was one of Shaftesbury's agents while another 'undertaker' was the republican Henry Neville. Thomas Flatman's government news-sheet, *Heraclitus Ridens*, warned of the subversive threat posed by the penny post: 'There was never anything so favourable to the carrying on and managing Intrigue: that and the Press being unpadlockt, are two incomparable twins of the Liberty of the Subject! one may Write, Print, publish and disperse ingenious Libels ... and no body the wiser.'[42] And in 1682 Larkin printed two editions of *An Account of the Province of Carolina in America* (Wing W2932, W2933) for Francis Smith. The prospectus was written by Samuel Wilson, John Locke's successor as Shaftesbury's secretary. Although colonists were being sent out, witnesses to the Rye House Plot revealed that the Carolina project served as a cover for negotiations between the English and Scottish conspirators.[43] Finally, Ichabod Chauncey, whose *Innocence Vindicated* Larkin printed in 1684 (Wing C3743), was a member of the Castle Street congregation and two electioneering clubs in Bristol which were connected with the Plot.[44]

[40] See Henry Care, *English Liberties* (London: 1682; Wing C515, C516, C517); Edmund Hickeringill, *The Test or Tryal of the Goodness & Value of Spiritual-Courts* (London: 1682; Wing H1828, H1829) and *The Black Non-Conformist* (London: 1683; Wing H1796, H1797); and Lois G. Schwoerer, *The Ingenious Mr. Henry Care, Restoration Publicist* (Baltimore: Johns Hopkins University Press, 2001), xxvi, 167–70, 232–5.

[41] See William Dockwra, *The Practical Method of the Penny-Post* (London: 1681; Wing D1782B).

[42] See Susan E. Whyman, 'Postal Censorship in England 1634–1884' (unpublished paper); *Heraclitus Ridens*, 5, 1 March 1681. My thanks to Susan Whyman for allowing me to see her paper.

[43] See K. H. D. Haley, *The First Earl of Shaftesbury* (Oxford: Clarendon Press, 1968), 231–55, 242–8, 365–6, 705–7.

[44] See Jonathan Barry, 'The Politics of Religion in Restoration Bristol', in *The Politics of Religion in Restoration England*, ed. Tim Harris, Paul Seaward, and Mark Goldie (Oxford: Blackwell, 1990), 176.

Given these affiliations, it was inevitable that Larkin would come into conflict with L'Estrange. By January 1683, L'Estrange was complaining to Secretary Jenkins about Hickeringill's *The Test or Tryal*, 'printed by Larkin, another instrument to the faction'. Nevertheless six months later Larkin signed a lengthy deposition against Robert Stephens who had angered L'Estrange by sabotaging the prosecution of another printer; clearly it was still possible for Larkin to cooperate with the Surveyor on the former ad hoc basis.[45] But in April 1684 Larkin's luck finally ran out, when he printed (having possibly written) a broadside, *Shall I, Shall I? No, No* (1684; Wing S2959), modelled on Tobias Bowne's racy ballad, *Shall I? Shall I? No, No ... Tune of the Doubting Virgin* (1684; Wing B3895) and intended to dissuade those tempted to conform to the Church of England.[46] He was tried for seditious libel on 9 April, and 'having pleaded Guilty to an Indictment, for Printing a seditions Paper, called, Shall I, Shall I, No, No, is sentenced to pay a Fine of 20 l. stand in the Pillory, and find Sureties for his Good Behaviour a Twelve Month'.[47]

Although Larkin stayed in business, the situation changed in February 1685 when James II succeeded his brother, and immediately turned his attention to tightening controls over the press. Between February and November at least thirty-four warrants were issued to suppress pamphlets. L'Estrange was knighted and once more directly authorized to track down treasonable, seditious, and scandalous publications. But well before the Printing Act was revived in June 1685, Larkin's press had fallen silent. Only four works appeared from his Broad Street printing house that year though one, *The Observator Proved a Trimmer* (Wing O123H), was a highly effective attack on L'Estrange that went into four editions. L'Estrange responded by publishing intercepted correspondence between Larkin and his associates and James Jones, the keeper of a coffee house in Southwark and pastor of a Baptist congregation, who had been imprisoned in the Wood Street Counter.[48] Larkin had earlier published three works by Jones (Wing J598, J959, J956A), and was negotiating about a fourth. On 10 December 1684, the bookseller Enoch Prosser wrote to Jones seeking to allay his anxieties about whether the project would be compromised by Larkin's political reputation. Prosser astutely observed that:

> As to what is objected, that Mr Larkin is Obnoxious to the Government, I think it will be very hard to find any man fit to publish this Book that either is not or will be esteemed so, upon his publishing such a Book, under the present Complexion of the times.[49]

In other words, the political climate was such that rather than Jones's book being compromised by a printer who was 'Obnoxious to the Government', a printer was liable to be rendered obnoxious by the book.

45 *CSPD*, 1 January–30 June 1683, 13, 301–2.

46 Entered to Larkin on 4 April 1681; Stationers' Register, III: 232.

47 The Proceedings of the Old Bailey Ref: s16840409-1: <http://www.oldbaileyonline.org/>.

48 See C. E. Whiting, *Studies in English Puritanism* (London: SPKC, 1968), 126–7.

49 Roger L'Estrange, *The Observator*, Vol. 2. no. 198, Saturday, 8 January 1684/5.

On 12 December, Larkin dealt with Jones's doubts about his commitment to the Baptist cause. While he had maintained his beliefs since 1666, there were occasions on which he might be thought to have wavered. Appearing as a witness against Darby had displeased some 'Friends' though Larkin was unwilling 'to acknowledge my Evil therein'. He had never baptized his children, but conceded that he had received communion in Clerkenwell and Oxford. And since moving to Broad Street in 1683 he had attended services in his local parish church by way of trying to avoid *de excommunicato capiendo*, though he could never bring himself fully to conform.[50] In other words, Larkin had more or less lived up to the position staked out in *Shall I, Shall I? No, No* in resisting occasional conformity. Jones must have been reassured since what appears to be the work in question, *Some Considerations Concerning Ecclesiasticall Proceedings*, was entered on 6 February 1685; that is, after L'Estrange's attempt to discredit Larkin in the eyes of the dissenters by publishing these letters.[51] But it was never printed because by then Larkin was probably in Newgate prison.[52]

Larkin and James II

'Obnoxious to the Government' one moment, Larkin found himself in favour the next. He returned to printing in 1686 after James II dramatically abandoned his policy of persecuting dissenters and turned to wooing them instead. In April 1687, the king issued a Declaration of Indulgence, a use of the prerogative to suspend the penal laws that shocked Anglicans but was precisely what Catholics and some dissenters had been hoping to see.[53] Larkin now collaborated closely with Henry Care, who had earlier been a leading publicist for antipopery.[54] A stream of pro-Indulgence works issued from Larkin's press at the Two Swans without Bishopsgate and from February 1688 Larkin also printed Care's *Publick Occurrences Truly Stated*, a newspaper which voiced the *official* point of view. Had Larkin abandoned his principles? What we should bear in mind is that support for James's new stance was in fact wider than is often supposed

[50] L'Estrange, *The Observator*, Vol. 2, no. 197, 8 January 1684/5.

[51] See Stationers' Register, III: 270; signed by Larkin's servant, Edward Reyner.

[52] See John Dunton, *The Merciful Assizes: Or, a Panegyric on the Late Lord Jeffreys Hanging so Many in the West* (London: 1701), 339: 'Neither can I forget the *Justice* he did to Mr. *George Larkin*, who, after he had been at a great charge to prevail with his Lordship to turn him over to the *King's Bench*, *Jeffreys* was so just (after he had been in the King's Bench about two hours) as to provide him again with a *Close Room* in the *Press Yard*, lest he should catch cold by having *too much Air* in the King's Bench.'

[53] See John Miller, *James II* (New Haven and London: Yale University Press, 2000), 167–87; Mark Goldie, 'John Locke's Circle and James II', *Historical Journal*, 35 (1992): 557–86 and 'James II and the Dissenters' Revenge', *Bulletin of Historical Research*, 66 (1993): 53–88; and Mark Knights, '"Meer Religion" and the "Church-State" of Restoration England: The Impact and Ideology of James II's Declarations of Indulgence', in *A Nation Transformed: England after the Restoration*, ed. Alan Houston and Steve Pincus (Cambridge: Cambridge University Press, 2001), 41–70.

[54] See Schwoerer, *Henry Care*, 168, 218–19, 222.

and, as Mark Goldie remarks, this makes it 'historically inappropriate to persist with the manichean idiom of a totalitarian Stuart Babylon confronted by revolutionary whig purity'. More particularly, it would be a mistake to see the majority of Whigs who did not accommodate themselves to the new royal strategy as cast 'in the mould of heroic freedom fighters, clandestinely plotting the tyrant's overthrow—and correspondingly to see the turncoat minority as quislings'.[55] Far from cashing in on the commercial possibilities, there is evidence that Larkin's support for James's programme was grounded on principle. Jones's *Grand Case of Subjection to the Higher Powers*, which Larkin printed in 1684, had featured an appendix that asserted the 'Kings Supream Power in Ecclesiastical Matters'.[56] And Larkin also appears to have belonged to the significant minority, including several commonwealthsmen, who could not reconcile themselves to the incoming regime of William and Mary in 1688. When Gilbert Burnet abandoned his earlier insistence on passive obedience and argued in *A Pastoral Letter* (1689; Wing B5842) that allegiance was owed to those who were in actual possession of the throne, Larkin printed John Lowthorp's *Letter to the Bishop of Sarum: Being an Answer to his Lordships Pastoral Letter* (1690; Wing L3334). For printing this attack on an influential Williamite, Larkin once more found himself in the Old Bailey in July 1690 (alongside two Jacobites) and was 'Remanded to Newgate, but not without a very severe and sharp Repremand from the Court, telling him, That they would Inspect very narrowly into such a Crime, and that he must not think to put Tricks upon the Government'.[57] Larkin had thus achieved the feat of being imprisoned for printing work unacceptable to the powers that be in the reigns of Charles II, James II, *and* William and Mary.

The End of the Printing Act

Larkin was nevertheless more fortunate than some. The printer William Anderton was arrested on 2 May 1693 and initially committed for a misdemeanour. But when copies of a declaration issued by the exiled James II began to circulate later that month, greatly alarming the authorities, he was indicted instead for high treason on 1 June (not for printing the declaration itself, but two other Jacobite tracts), found guilty two days later, and executed at Tyburn on 16 June.[58] This turn of events was actually passed off by one commentator as an instance of moderation:

> Such has been Their Majesties Incomparable Clemency, since their Accession to the Throne, that among the many Lives Forfeited by the Law, on the account of

[55] Mark Goldie, 'John Locke's Circle', 559 and 'James II and the Dissenters' Revenge', 55.

[56] James Jones, *The Grand Case of Subjection to the Higher Powers in Matters of Religion Resolved* (London: 1684; Wing J956A), 7.

[57] The Proceedings of the Old Bailey Ref: s16900717-1.

[58] See Paul Hopkins, 'Anderton, William (1663–1693)', *ODNB*; D. A. Brunton, 'Grascome, Samuel (1641–1708), *ODNB*; the declaration is Wing J217A.

> Treasonable Books and Pamphlets, their boundless mercy has taken but One . . . . It was only Their Majesties Goodness toward many others, to call that a *Misdeamenor* [*sic*], which the Law calls treason.[59]

A case in point was Larkin's client, Lowthorp, who was told at his trial in September 1690 'for a high misdemeanour, in Writing, Printing and publishing a most pernicious, scandalous, Seditious and Notorious Libel' that he really 'ought to have been Indicted of High Treason'.[60] But the government was prepared when necessary to bring 25 Edward III to bear by way of intimidating the press. Thus Anne Merryweather, 'being a person of a turbulent spirit, and instigated and seduced by the Devil, and minding and intending to Depose and put to Death Their most Sacred Majesties King William and Queen Mary', was convicted of treason on 26 January 1693 for her involvement in the publication of an earlier declaration by the exiled king.[61] Condemned to be burnt, the sentence was left pending in the hope that she would 'discover' her associates; she eventually received an indefinite reprieve on 15 February.[62]

Merryweather does seem to have been genuinely committed to the Jacobite cause; she refused to become an informer, 'having resolved rather to dye honourably than live basely'.[63] The same cannot be said of William Newbolt and Edward Butler, who were convicted of treason on 6 September 1693 for having printing copies of the declaration issued by James II at Saint-Germain-en-Laye in April (Wing J217A).[64] In fact, they were the dupes of a notorious *agent provocateur*, William Chaloner, himself a suspected counterfeiter. According to Isaac Newton, appointed Ward of the Royal Mint in 1696:

> Chaloner to secure himself as a person serviceable to ye Government, persuaded Butler and Newbolt (at ye expense of several treats and some money) to print him 40 of those Declarations pretending that were not to be dispersed but sent to a private gentleman in the country and as soon as he had got ye papers he went to Secretary Trenchard and informed him that he had discovered and taken the Printer of King James's Declaration with their press and receiving (as he gives out) a reward of £1000.[65]

The first of their interim reprieves only came through almost three weeks later.[66] As Chaloner's activities show, however, the practice of relying on informers and rewards to

59 *An Account of the Conversation Behaviour and Execution of William Anderton Printer* ([London]: 1693; Wing A266), broadside.

60 OBO, t16900903-51.

61 OBO, t16930116-57; for the declaration in question, see Wing J216 and 216A.

62 See *A Chronology and Calendar of Documents Relating to the London Book Trade 1641–1700*, ed. D. F. McKenzie and Maureen Bell, 3 vols (Oxford: Oxford University Press, 2005), 3.142 (also 134–7 *passim*).

63 *Chronology*, ed. McKenzie and Bell, 3.136.

64 See OBO, t16930906-78.

65 TNA, MINT, 19/1, fol. 501, quoted in Rachel Weil, *A Plague of Informers: Conspiracy and Political Trust in William III's England* (New Haven and London: Yale University Press, 2013), 130; see also Paul Hopkins and Stuart Handley, 'Chaloner, William (d. 1699)', *ODNB*.

66 See *Chronology*, ed. McKenzie and Bell, 3.154, 158.

manage the press was wide open to manipulation and corruption. In the event, Chaloner himself was executed for treason in March 1699 on the strength of evidence against him as a counterfeiter collected by Newton.[67]

This willingness to resort to the law of treason in the early 1690s, culminating in the successful prosecution of Anderton, arguably represented a new departure for the Crown in its handling of the press. It meant, amongst other things, that the expiry of the Printing Act in 1695 was regarded with greater equanimity than it might otherwise have been.[68] But if this was indeed the new policy, it rapidly came unstuck. For one thing, Secretaries of State were now circumscribed in their ability to raise general search warrants; when the Archbishop of Canterbury sought one in May 1695, the Crown's lawyers informed him it 'could not now be granted to search houses for Printing Presses, but that it must be done upon Particular Informacions upon Oath'.[69] No longer was the book trade *tout court* liable to search and seizure. A second pillar of the policy collapsed when many of the questionable procedures that had been relied upon hitherto to secure convictions in treason trials (most notoriously in the trial of Algernon Sidney in 1683) were reformed by statute in 1696.[70] And given that a final attempt to reintroduce the Printing Act was also rejected on 19 March 1696, what this meant was that virtually the only surviving weapon in the Crown's legal armoury was the law of seditious libel.[71] It would be a mistake, however, to suppose that the heavy hand of government regulation had been lifted from the press. Only someone like Macaulay, ardently rehearsing the Whig pieties, could suppose for a moment that with the expiry of the Printing Act 'English literature was emancipated, and emancipated for ever, from the control of the government'.[72]

Bibliography

Astbury, Raymond. 'The Renewal of the Licensing Act in 1693 and Its Lapse in 1695', *The Library*, 33 (1978): 291–322.

Bardle, Stephen. *The Literary Underground in the 1660s: Andrew Marvell, George Wither, Ralph Wallis, and the World of Restoration Satire and Pamphleteering* (Oxford: Oxford University Press, 2012).

Bell, Maureen. 'Elizabeth Calvert and the "Confederates"', *Publishing History*, 32 (1992): 6–49.

67 See *Chronology*, ed. McKenzie and Bell, 3.203–4.

68 For this line of argument, see Hamburger, 'Development of the Law of Seditious Libel', 717–22, although it is somewhat weakened by his post-dating to 1695 of the trial of Newbolt and Butler (at 719) The (largely pragmatic) arguments against renewal of the Act in John Locke's circle can be followed in John Locke, *Political Essays*, ed. Mark Goldie (Cambridge: Cambridge University Press, 1997), 329–39.

69 Quoted in Hamburger, 'Development of the Law of Seditious Libel', 721.

70 See 'William III, 1695–6: An Act for Regulateing of Tryals in Cases of Treason and Misprision of Treason [Chapter III. Rot. Parl. 7 & 8 Gul. III. pt. 1.nu.3.]', in *Statutes of the Realm*, Vol. 7: *1695–1701*, ed. John Raithby (s.l.: 1820), 6–7 <http://www.british-history.ac.uk/statutes-realm/vol7/pp6-7>.

71 *CJ*, 11: 523; see Hamburger, 'Development of the Law of Seditious Libel', 722–5.

72 Thomas Babington Macaulay, *The History of England from the Accession of James the Second*, 5 vols (Boston, MA; 1856–1861), 4.434.

Bell, Maureen. '"Her usual practices": The Later Career of Elizabeth Calvert, 1664–75', *Publishing History*, 35 (1994): 5–64.

Blagden, Cyprian. *The Stationers' Company: A History, 1403–1959* (London: George Allen and Unwin, 1960).

Crist, T. J. 'Government Control of the Press after the Expiration of the Printing Act in 1679', *Publishing History*, 5 (1979): 49–78.

Dunan-Page, Anne and Beth Lynch, eds. *Roger L'Estrange and the Making of Restoration Culture* (Aldershot: Ashgate, 2008).

Dzelzainis, Martin. 'Andrew Marvell and the Restoration Literary Underground: Printing the Painter Poems', *The Seventeenth Century*, 22.2 (2007): 395–410.

Dzelzainis, Martin. 'Saturday 21 July 1683: Oxford and London', in *Enforcing and Eluding Censorship: British and Anglo-Italian Perspectives*, ed. Giuliana Iannacaro and Giovanni Iamartino (Newcastle-upon-Tyne: Cambridge Scholars, 2014), 44–56.

Greene, Jody. *The Trouble with Ownership: Literary Property and Authorial Liability in England, 1660–1730* (Philadelphia: University of Pennsylvania Press, 2005).

Hamburger, Philip. 'The Development of the Law of Seditious Libel and the Control of the Press', *Stanford Law Review*, 67 (1985): 661–705.

Hetet, John. 'A Literary Underground in Restoration England: Printers and Dissenters in the Context of Constraints, 1660–1689' (PhD Thesis: University of Cambridge, 1987).

Ronald Hutton, *The Restoration: A Political and Religious History of England and Wales, 1658–1667* (Oxford, 1985).

Johns, Adrian. *The Nature of the Book: Print and Knowledge in the Making* (Chicago: University of Chicago Press, 1998).

Kitchin, George. *Sir Roger L'Estrange: A Contribution to the History of the Press in the 17th Century* (London: Kegan Paul and Co., 1913).

L'Estrange, Roger. *Considerations and Proposals in Order to the Regulation of the Press: Together with Diverse Instances of Treasonous, and Seditious Pamphlets, Proving the Necessity Thereof* (London: 1663).

Loewenstein, Joseph F. 'Legal Proofs and Corrected Readings: Press-Agency and the New Bibliography', in *The Production of English Renaissance Culture*, ed. David Lee Miller, Sharon O'Dair, and Harold Weber (Ithaca and London: Cornell University Press, 1994), 111–22.

McKenzie, D. F. *Making Meaning: 'Printers of the Mind' and Other Essays*, ed. Peter M. McDonald and Michael F. Suarez, S. J. (Amherst and Boston: University of Massachusetts Press, 2002).

Martin, Henri-Jean. *The French Book: Religion, Absolutism, and Readership, 1585–1715*, ed. and trans. Paul Saenger and Nadine Saenger (Baltimore and London: Johns Hopkins University Press, 1996).

Myers, Robin and Michael Harris, eds. *Censorship and the Control of the Press in England and France, 1600–1910* (Winchester: St Paul's Bibliographies, 1992).

Patterson, Annabel. *Censorship and Interpretation: The Conditions of Writing and Reading in Early Modern England* (Madison: University of Wisconsin Press, 1984).

Pincus, Steven. '"Coffee Politicians Does Create": Coffeehouses and Restoration Political Culture', *Journal of Modern History*, 67.4 (1995): 807–34.

Robertson, Randy. *Censorship and Conflict in Seventeenth-Century England: The Subtle Art of Division* (University Park: Pennsylvania State University Press, 2009).

Rose, Mark. *Authors and Owners: The Invention of Copyright* (Cambridge, MA: Harvard University Press, 1993).

Schwoerer, Lois G. *The Ingenious Mr Henry Care, Restoration Publicist* (Baltimore: Johns Hopkins University Press, 2001).
Siebert, Frederick Seaton. *Freedom of the Press in England, 1476–1776* (Urbana: University of Illinois Press, 1952).
Treadwell, Michael. 'The Stationers and the Printing Acts at the End of the Seventeenth Century', in *The Cambridge History of the Book in Britain*, Vol. 4: *1557–1695*, ed. John Barnard and D. F. McKenzie (Cambridge: Cambridge University Press, 2002), 755–76.
Walker, J. 'The Censorship of the Press during the Reign of Charles II', *History*, 35 (1950): 219–38.

CHAPTER 28

THE TORTURE OF JOHN FELTON, 1628

ALASTAIR BELLANY

During the winter of 2001–2002, British authorities detained ten foreign nationals under the provisions of the 2001 'Anti-terrorism, Crime and Security Act' passed in the wake of the September 11 attacks. After more than two years of fruitless appeals against their designation as terrorists, the detainees took their case to the House of Lords, arguing that the Special Immigrations Appeals Commission that initially heard their case (partly in camera) had violated both international and common law by relying on evidence possibly 'procured by torture inflicted by foreign officials without the complicity of the British authorities'. In a widely praised decision handed down in December 2005, the Law Lords unanimously agreed with the detainees.[1]

The Law Lords argued that, while international law specifically barred the use of evidence obtained through torture, the English common law alone provided sufficient basis for sustaining the detainees' case. '[T]he English common law', wrote Lord Bingham of Cornhill, 'has regarded torture and its fruits with abhorrence for over 500 years', and this abhorrence should be understood as an 'issue ... of constitutional principle'.[2] The other lords concurred and, like Bingham, based their argument on precedent—in other words, on history. 'Torture is not acceptable', wrote Lord Nicholls of Birkenhead. 'This is a bedrock moral principle in this country. For centuries, the common law has set its face against torture'. Bingham himself noted the long series of 'proud claims' to that effect from canonical commentators on the common law—Sir John Fortescue in the fifteenth, Sir Thomas Smith in the sixteenth, Sir Edward Coke in the seventeenth, and William Blackstone in the eighteenth century. 'In rejecting the use of torture,' Bingham argued, 'whether applied to potential defendants or potential witnesses, the common law was

[1] *Opinions of the Lords of Appeal For Judgment in the Cause A (FC) and others (FC) (Appellants) v Secretary of State for the Home Department (Respondent) (2004)*, [2005] UKHL 71. The background to the case is laid out in the opening paragraphs of Lord Bingham's lead opinion, paragraphs 1–10.

[2] [2005] UKHL 71, paragraphs 11, 34, 51 (Bingham).

moved by the cruelty of the practice as applied to those not convicted of crime, by the inherent unreliability of confessions or evidence so procured and by the belief that it degraded all those who lent themselves to the practice.'[3]

Although the Law Lords had to acknowledge that for a number of decades in the sixteenth and early seventeenth centuries the English Crown had used torture 'largely (but not exclusively) in relation to alleged offences against the state', they noted that this use had been authorized not by common law but 'pursuant to warrants issued by the Council or the Crown ... in exercise of the Royal prerogative'. This practice ended definitively in 1640 in partial consequence, the Law Lords suggested, of the broader constitutional struggle between common law and prerogative that culminated in the English civil war.[4]

Three of the lords—Bingham, Nicholls, and Hoffman—also drew attention to the crucial legal ruling supposedly made by the judges in mid-November 1628 in the case of John Felton, the assassin of the royal favourite, George Villiers, Duke of Buckingham. All three cited the same source, an account first published in 1659 in John Rushworth's *Historical Collections*. Rushworth reported that Felton was 'called before the Council' and threatened with torture to induce him to reveal 'who set him on work to do such a bloody Act'. After Felton steadfastly maintained 'that no person whatsoever knew any thing of his intentions or purpose to kill the Duke', the Council sent him back to the Tower of London and then:

> fell into Debate, whether by the Law of the Land they could justifie the putting him to the Rack; the King being at Council said, before any such thing be done, let the advice of the Judges be had therein, whether it be Legal or no, and afterwards his Majesty the 13. of Novemb[er] [1628] propounded the question to Sir Tho[mas] Richardson, Lord Chief Justice of the Common Pleas, to be propounded to all the Justices, (viz.) Felton now a Prisoner in the Tower, having confessed that he had killed the Duke of Buckingham, and said he was induced to this, partly for private displeasure, and partly by reason of a Remonstrance in Parliament, having also read some Books, which he said defended that it was lawful to kill an enemy to the Republick, the question therefore is, whether by the Law he might not be Racked, and whether there were any Law against it, (for said the King) if it might be done by Law, he would not use his Prerogative in this Point and having put this Question to the Lord Chief Justice, the King commanded him to demand the resolution of all the Judges.
>
> First, the Justices of Serjeants Inn in Chancery Lane did meet and agree, that the King may not in this case put the party to the Rack. And the fourteenth of Nov[ember] all the Justices being assembled at Serjeants Inn in Fleetstreet, agreed in one, that he ought not by the Law to be tortured by the Rack, for no such punishment is known or allowed by our Law.[5]

[3] [2005] UKHL 71, paragraphs 11 (Bingham), 64 (Nicholls).
[4] [2005] UKHL 71, paragraphs 12 (Bingham), 83 (Hoffman).
[5] John Rushworth, *Historical Collections of Private Passages of State* (London: 1659), 638–9.

Two of the three Law Lords who cited this account in 2005 acknowledged that the barrister David Jardine, in his seminal 1837 study of torture and English law, had cast doubt on the reliability of Rushworth's account.[6] But all three nonetheless found legal force in the precedent. Rushworth's factual reliability was, in legal terms, irrelevant. The long list of luminaries championing the common law's abhorrence of torture may have relied on flawed readings of Magna Carta or of the Felton case, Bingham noted, but the 'strength of received opinion' was what ultimately counted. Lord Hoffman, on the other hand, had no doubts about the validity of the story or the precedent, drawing a straight line from Rushworth's account of the Felton ruling through Blackstone's gloss on the account, to the 'legal technicalities' of the case at hand:

> Charles I … asked the judges whether Felton could be put to the rack to discover his accomplices. All the judges met in Serjeants' Inn. Many years later Blackstone recorded their historic decision: 'The judges, being consulted, declared unanimously, to their own honour and the honour of the English law, that no such proceeding was allowable by the laws of England.' That word honour, the deep note which Blackstone strikes twice in one sentence, is what underlies the legal technicalities of this appeal. The use of torture is dishonourable. It corrupts and degrades the state which uses it and the legal system which accepts it.[7]

It is rare for the events of the 1620s to have such pressing contemporary relevance, though it is uncertain how much an historical analysis can contribute to the ongoing reckoning with the use of torture during the so-called war on terror. This chapter approaches the question of torture in relation to a set of problems around the Felton case that its use in 2005 rather obscures. The chapter resituates the supposed torture ruling of November 1628 in its original historical context, as part of a series of events and representations or imaginings-of-events surrounding the possible torture of John Felton. My goal is to explore the meanings of these events, representations, and imaginings within the broader political crisis surrounding Buckingham's assassination, and to connect the discourse around Felton's torture to examples of striking literary creativity. This approach allows us to explore a series of interesting connections between questions and ideas about law, on the one hand, and the early modern literary imagination, on the other. The approach also reveals both the mutually constitutive relationship among the legal, literary, and political imaginaries of early modern England and some of the ways these imaginaries could shape, and be shaped by, the flux of political events.

In part, I hope to reassess what we know about the use of torture in the Felton case: was the assassin tortured or threatened with torture? Why or why not? Did the judicial review recorded by Rushworth occur, and, if so, why? But I want to pay particular

[6] David Jardine, *A Reading on the Use of Torture in the Criminal Law of England Previously to the Commonwealth* (London: Baldwin and Craddock, 1837), 10–12, 60–2. On Jardine's influence, see James Heath, *Torture and English Law: An Administrative and Legal History from the Plantagenets to the Stuarts* (Westport and London: Greenwood Press, 1982), xvi–xvii.

[7] [2005] UKHL 71, paragraphs 11 (Bingham), 65 (Nicholls), 81–2 (Hoffman).

attention to sources neglected in the existing scholarly and legal discussions of the case. The widespread reports contained in contemporary manuscript newsletters of torture and threats of torture against Felton, for instance, cannot reliably tell us what happened to Felton, but they do reveal how Felton's interrogation and possible torture were represented and perceived; and these representations and perceptions have much to teach us not only about contemporary attitudes to judicial torture but also about the nature of the political polarization that caused such instability in the later 1620s. This political polarization is also evident in the representations of torture in two of the decade's most intensely politicized 'literary' texts: the remarkable meditation on Felton's sufferings in the scribally circulated libel 'To His Confined Friend Mr. Felton', widely attributed to the Jonsonian poet Zouche Townley; and Philip Massinger's late 1626 *The Roman Actor*, a play deeply engaged with the controversial politics and heightened anxieties that surrounded Buckingham in the last two years of his life.

John Felton fatally stabbed George Villiers, Duke of Buckingham, on the morning of Saturday, 23 August 1628 in a house on Portsmouth High Street. Felton struck as Buckingham moved through a press of people from the parlour to the hall of his temporary residence; thus the assassination was both public and hidden from clear view by the crowd of men around the duke. In the chaos that followed, Felton had many opportunities to escape, but he did not exploit them. He had convinced himself that killing Buckingham was an act of patriotic self-sacrifice and had written two explicit statements to that effect, placing them in his hatband, where they would be found if he were to be killed on the spot. After lurking in the kitchen for a few minutes, Felton surrendered with the words, 'I am the man', a calculated act of patriotic confession. Although it was a statement not of guilt but of pride, it was also a confession.[8]

Was John Felton subsequently tortured or threatened with torture?[9] John H. Langbein's seminal study, *Torture and the Law of Proof*, says the following: 'In 1628 the Council considered torturing John Felton … to discover whether he had accomplices, but ultimately decided not to do it.' Langbein's endnote for this brief statement covers two pages: he provides Rushworth's account and Blackstone's commentary, and then presents David Jardine's argument that Rushworth got his facts wrong. The Council may have considered torturing Felton and may even have threatened him, but they had no reason to proceed

[8] There are several eyewitness or near-eyewitness accounts of the assassination. See e.g. 'A Letter from One of the Highams', in *Diary of John Rous*, ed. Mary Anne Everett Green, Camden Society, ser. 1.66 (London: 1856), 27–8; Francis Bamford, ed., *A Royalist's Notebook: The Commonplace Book of Sir John Oglander Kt. of Nunwell*, rpt edn (New York: Blom, 1971), 34ff.; TNA SP 16/114/20 and 21 (Letter of Lord Dorchester: 27 August 1628); Hatfield House, Salisbury MSS, 253 item 5; and Edmund Howes' account in BL Egerton MS 2533, fols 62^{r-v}. For contemporary copies of Felton's hatband statement, see, e.g. Rous, *Diary*, 26; Oglander, *Commonplace Book*, 37–8; Diary of Walter Yonge, BL Add. MS 35331, fol. 24^{r}; and BL Sloane MS 826, fols 133^{r-v}.

[9] Definitions matter here. There is some evidence (e.g. Oglander, *Commonplace Book*, 37) that Felton was subjected to 'chronic' rather than 'acute' duress while in custody in Portsmouth where he was kept in a cell nicknamed 'Little Ease', a name suggesting a particularly cramped space designed to soften a prisoner up for interrogation. On the similarly named cells in the Tower of London and Bridewell, see Heath, *Torture and English Law*, 85–6, 126–7, 186–94, 197.

with torture, since Felton had quickly confessed and 'there were no reasonable presumptions ... that he had any confederates'. Langbein endorses Jardine's argument that the Council did not request the judges' opinion on the legality of torture before making its decision and notes his suggestion that Rushworth had confused the torture issue with a different debate over Felton's request to have his right hand cut off as part of his execution.[10]

Jardine's scepticism, endorsed by Langbein as a 'brilliant bit of analysis', has not, however, commanded unanimous assent, and it ignores several pieces of important evidence.[11] From the start, Felton's confession left the authorities dissatisfied, for they assumed he must have had co-conspirators. This assumption was connected to the increasingly firm conviction held by the king—and by many, though not all, of his councillors—that the political disorder plaguing the kingdom was a collective enterprise. Threats to the state came from what the regime increasingly labelled 'popular spirits': parliamentary demagogues, Puritan preachers, and their plebeian followers.[12] Thus from the first, the regime was persuaded of a particular truth about the duke's assassination—that it was the product of a 'popular' conspiracy—and the authorities were prepared to use a variety of judicial techniques to elicit that truth from the assassin and from his known associates and family members.[13]

On 26 August, three days after the murder, Charles I instructed his secretary of state, Sir John Coke, to draw up a warrant appointing five commissioners from the Privy Council to oversee the investigation and prosecution of the crime. Only a draft copy of the commission survives, and it is possible the final version took a different form, but the draft included language explicitly authorizing torture for the purpose of identifying Felton's co-conspirators. It instructed the commissioners 'both by a due examination of the confessions alreadie taken & by further inquir[i]e [to] bee made by torture or otherwise of al the circumstances of this bloodie fact & to discover as manie as may bee al the councelors, contrivers, incouragers & abettors therof'.[14] The following day, one of the commissioners, Dudley Carleton, Lord Dorchester, reported that initial questioning immediately after Felton's arrest had failed to 'discover any complices', nor did the officials present in Portsmouth 'take more then his free and willing confession'. But the

[10] John H. Langbein, *Torture and the Law of Proof: Europe and England in the Ancien Regime* (Chicago and London: Chicago University Press, 2006) [first published 1977], 139, 211–13 (n. 63); Jardine, *Reading on the Use of Torture*, 60–2.

[11] See e.g. S. R. Gardiner, *History of England From the Accession of James I to the Outbreak of the Civil War*, 10 vols (New York: AMS Reprint, 1965), 6.359 n. 2; and Heath, *Torture and English Law*, 162–4.

[12] Gardiner, *History*, 359 notes Charles's belief in a wider conspiracy. For the nature of this Caroline political mentality, see esp. Richard Cust, *The Forced Loan and English Politics* (Oxford: Oxford University Press, 1987), ch. 1; and 'Charles I and Popularity', in *Politics, Religion and Popularity in Early Stuart Britain*, ed. Thomas Cogswell, Richard Cust, and Peter Lake (Cambridge: Cambridge University Press, 2002), 235–58.

[13] The authorities' investigations can best be tracked through the State Papers Domestic, esp. TNA SP 16/114–19.

[14] TNA SP 16/114/16 (Dorchester to Coke: 26 August 1628), with the draft commission on the verso. Jardine, Langbein, and Heath fail to notice this document.

king's warrant now had changed the rules, instructing the councillors 'to proceed' with Felton 'in the nature' which the 'act requires'.[15]

New evidence quickly emerged to bolster the authorities' assumption that Felton had not acted alone. On 1 September, for instance, a trio of councilors received instructions to imprison Gilbert Adamson for 'wordes spoken ... making ... discovery of some that were privie to the late execrable murther'.[16] Far more dramatic, however, was the case of Robert Savage, who was arrested and brought under heavy guard to the Tower on 8 September after boasting that he had been privy to Felton's plans and accusing 'divers Noblemen, and other Persons of good Rank and Quality to be Conspirators'. The authorities took his confession very seriously—after all, it seemed to prove what they already suspected to be true—and it took several weeks to discover that Savage was an 'impostor'. His real name was John Hearne (Heron, Hiron), he had a track record of impersonation, and he had been drawn to the charismatic role of Buckingham assassin even before the murder: in spring 1628, he had claimed to be Robert Rich, a kinsman of the Earl of Warwick, and boasted that 'he had killed the Duke of Buckingham in the King's Privy Chamber, and was glad to flee for it'.[17] A list of interrogatory questions drafted by Attorney-General Sir Robert Heath shortly after Savage's confinement to the Tower reveals not only the authorities' determination to explore the supposed connections between Savage and the assassin, but also their desire to identify anyone at all who had helped Felton prepare for the murder. It was crucial, Heath noted, to 'discover if ther were any treasonable act or intention in Felton or any other, & howe farr it extends, eather at holme or abroad'. Thus, Heath told the king, 'yo[u]r Ma[jes]ty may give further direction, if such presumptions and *inditia torturae* shall appeer as may be fitt to proceed in that course'.[18] In other words, if the initial interrogations of Savage and Felton seemed to prove the suspected link to a bigger, treasonable conspiracy, then this was sufficient presumptive evidence upon which to warrant the use of torture.[19]

Felton, however, consistently refused to implicate any others in his crime. At the end of September, Dorchester reported to the Earl of Carlisle that Felton had said nothing beyond 'his first free confession'. Dorchester insisted that 'no torture hath been used unto him' to that point, but he made it clear that the king would not omit any 'means ... to find out his complices, if he had any'.[20] The Savage case had led nowhere,

15 TNA SP 16/114/20 and 21 (Letter of Lord Dorchester: 27 August 1628).

16 TNA SP 16/116/1 (Conway to Coventry, Marlborough and Manchester: 1 September 1628).

17 On the Savage/Hearne case, see TNA SP 16/116/95 (Fisher to Pickering: 10 September 1628); 16/119/24 (Heath to Charles I [draft]: undated, late September 1628?); and 16/119/63 ('The case of Jo. Hiron'); John Rushworth, *Historical Collections of Private Passages of State*, 8 vols (London: 1721), 3.18; Thomas Birch (compiler), *Court and Times of Charles I*, ed. R. F. Williams, 2 vols (London: 1848), 1.394, 398, 404, 421, 423, 430–1 (newsletter reports); BL Sloane MS 826, fol. 129^{v}; *Acts of the Privy Council 1628–9* (London: HMSO, 1958) 193–4; Walter Yonge Diary, BL Add. MS 35331, fol. 25^{r}.

18 TNA SP 16/116/66 (undated notes for Felton's interrogation).

19 On the echoes of civil law thinking here, see Heath, *Torture and English Law*, 163.

20 Birch, *Court and Times*, 1.404 (Dorchester to Hay: 30 September 1628).

but the truth the regime already knew remained at the heart of its approach to the investigation: Felton had not yet been tortured, but the option remained on the table.

The possibility of Felton's torture provoked significant public interest during these early weeks. By 1628, private and commercial manuscript newsletters had become a central feature of the burgeoning news culture that fuelled the emergent and in many ways proto-revolutionary public sphere in England.[21] These newsletters discussed the assassination investigation at length, and a number contain fascinating reports about the authorities' threats of torture and Felton's quick-witted response to them. These reports do not necessarily reflect what was happening in the Tower, but they do allow us to track the role of torture talk in the evolving public image of the assassin, an image that figured him as neither a murderous villain nor an agent of popular subversion but as a patriot hero, the moral antithesis to the corrupt favourite he had killed. Even as Felton himself began to express remorse for his actions, these reports continued to invest him with potent political charisma, a charisma that posed a real political and ideological challenge to the authorities' attempts to spell out the meaning of Buckingham's murder.[22]

On 27 September, the Cambridge scholar Joseph Mead forwarded a copy of a London newsletter, dated eight days earlier, to his cousin Sir Martin Stuteville. The London letter began with an account of Buckingham's hastily improvised funeral, but it soon turned to the ongoing investigation, and to reports of Felton's questioning in the Tower. These reports now indicated that Felton was 'exceeding penitent for the blood he had shed' and that he had asked to be allowed 'to wear sackcloth about his loins, to sprinkle ashes upon his head, and to carry a halter about his neck, in testimony of his repentance for shedding the blood of a man'.[23] But the same reports also suggested that Felton's penitence had its limits and that he still saw Buckingham's death as a boon for the commonweal. Felton had sinned in killing the duke but understood himself as the (wicked) instrument of God's beneficent providence, and so whatever 'good … might come of that act' was God's doing, not his own. The newsletter also discussed the question of torture, reporting that the Earl of Dorset, one of the five commissioners appointed by the king, had

[21] On this, see Alastair Bellany, *The Politics of Court Scandal in Early Modern England: News Culture and the Overbury Affair, 1603–1660* (Cambridge: Cambridge University Press, 2002), ch. 2 and esp. 85–9; and 'Railing Rhymes Revisited: Libels, Scandals, and Early Stuart Politics', *History Compass*, 5.4 (2007): 1150–4.

[22] On Felton as hero, see esp. James Holstun, *Ehud's Dagger: Class Struggle in the English Revolution* (London: Verso, 2000), ch. 5; Alastair Bellany, '"Raylinge Rymes and Vaunting Verse": Libellous Politics in Early Stuart England, 1603–1628', in *Culture and Politics in Early Stuart England*, ed. Kevin Sharpe and Peter Lake (London: Macmillan, 1994), 304–9; Bellany, '"The Brightnes of the Noble Leiutenants Action": An Intellectual Ponders Buckingham's Assassination', *EHR*, 118.479 (2003): 1242–63; and the archive of libels on the assassination in Alastair Bellany and Andrew McRae, eds, 'Early Stuart Libels: An Edition of Poetry from Manuscript Sources', *Early Modern Literary Studies*, Text Series, I (2005) <http://www.earlystuartlibels.net>, section P. My understanding of political 'charisma' is adapted from Clifford Geertz, 'Centers, Kings, and Charisma: Reflections on the Symbolics of Power', in *Local Knowledge: Further Essays in Interpretive Anthropology* (New York: Basic Books, 1983), 121–46.

[23] The newsletter accurately captured here part of Felton's conversation with the divines sent to urge his repentance a few days earlier: see TNA SP 16/116/101 (Dr. Duppa's Report), esp. fol. 145^{r}.

told Felton that 'it is the king's pleasure you should be put to torture to make you confess your complices'. According to the report, this threat prompted an intriguing reply. 'I do not believe', Felton retorted,

> that it is the king's pleasure, for he is a just and a gracious prince, and will not have his subjects to be tortured against law. I do affirm again upon my salvation that my purpose was known to no man living, and more than I have said before I cannot. But if it be his majesty's pleasure, I am ready to suffer whatsoever his majesty will have inflicted upon me. Yet this I must tell you by the way, that if I be put upon the rack, I will accuse you, my Lord of Dorset, and none but yourself.

At this point, the newsletter reported, the lords left without racking him. 'It is thought', the letter concluded, 'he shall not be racked at all'.[24]

According to this report, the threat of torture had elicited from Felton a double-edged political response, a kind of subversive loyalism. Felton ostentatiously submitted to royal authority, declaring himself 'ready to suffer' whatever Charles ordered. But he also insisted that his torture would violate the 'law', strategically invoking an idealized image of the king as 'just and gracious', the kind of ruler who would not knowingly act 'against law', while at the same time acknowledging the possibility that Charles might lapse into lawlessness and thus, implicitly, into tyranny. The report also had Felton cleverly subvert the authorities' strategy, drawing on long-standing critiques of torture's evidentiary unreliability by threatening to name one of his torturers as his accomplice.[25] In place of the truth the regime wanted to affirm, then, torture—or the threat of torture—produced dangerous truths not only about the regime's potential for tyranny, but also about the assassin's charismatic political virtues.

Versions of this story about Felton's response to the threat of torture may have circulated in metropolitan and provincial news networks through early October. One variant, in which the setting had moved to the Council chamber, with Bishop Laud in Dorset's supporting role, eventually ended up in Rushworth's 1659 *Historical Collections*.[26] On 13 October, Sir Simonds D'Ewes—connected by kinship ties to the Mead/Stuteville news network—wrote to the Dutch ambassador Joachimi reporting that Felton had been treated 'benignly and mercifully' and was lodged in relative comfort inside the Tower. 'He was completely freed from torture', D'Ewes noted,

> not without the highest piety of the King and equity of the Laws: nor is he said to have replied inelegantly to Edward Sackville, Earl of Dorset, superciliously ordering him to prepare himself for torture: 'I hold it as certain that I live under a just king and a

24 Birch, *Court and Times of Charles I*, 1.399–403 (Mead to Stuteville: 27 September 1628).

25 For endemic worries about false testimony under torture in the Roman law tradition, see e.g. Edward Peters, *Torture* (New York and Oxford: Blackwell, 1985), 34–5. For a highly influential English statement, see ch. 22 of Sir John Fortescue, *De laudibus legum Anglie*, in *Sir John Fortescue: On the Laws and Governance of England*, ed. Shelley Lockwood (Cambridge: Cambridge University Press, 1997), 32–3.

26 Rushworth, *Historical Collections* (1659), 638.

holy law, and can not, while confessing all, be tortured by torments of this type; but truly, if I should be taken to so great a butchery, please know, Lord Dorset, that I shall confess that you and you alone conspired with me.'[27]

One striking feature of these initial stories is Felton's alleged insistence that any torture inflicted on him would be illegal. The stories thus drew potentially critical attention to the peculiar legal status of the English Crown's use of interrogatory torture.[28] Clearly the authorities believed that the king's prerogative could sanction the use of interrogatory torture—conciliar warrants ordering torture had been issued frequently in the later sixteenth century and continued to be used, though far more sporadically, in the early seventeenth—but Felton's insistence on torture's illegality in his case resonated with long-standing English claims that 'torment or question' to extract confessions or denunciations of accomplices was 'not used in England' and that the cruelties routinely applied in Continental legal systems offended both humanity and morality without providing any pragmatic prosecutorial advantage.[29] The Felton reports' insistence on torture's illegality also matched the position that Sir Edward Coke was sketching out during the later 1620s in what would become the third volume of his *Institutes*. Here Coke acknowledged that torture had been used in English treason cases, but instead of rooting it in the prerogative power of the monarchy, he argued that the practice had begun in the fifteenth century at the behest of men who intended 'to have brought in the Civill Lawes' to England. It was this threatening innovation, Coke argued, that had prompted Sir John Fortescue's powerful and still authoritative insistence that 'all tortures and torments of parties accused were directly against the Common Lawes of England'. The legal case was clear. Interrogatory torture violated Magna Carta, Coke argued, concluding that not only was there 'no law to warrant tortures in this land', but there was also 'no one opinion in our Books, or judiciall Record (that we have seen and remember) for the maintenance of tortures or torments'.[30]

The association of the assassin Felton with this critique of the legality of interrogatory torture had multiple political resonances and implications. It raised uncomfortable questions about the relationship between law and prerogative, a relationship that

[27] BL Harley MS 377, fol. 238v (D'Ewes to Joachimi: 13/23 October 1628), translation by Peter Salt, though I have made a slight emendation for the sake of clarity. I am grateful to Sears McGee for sending along the reference and Dr Salt's translation.

[28] Jardine, Langbein, and Heath all argue that the conciliar torture warrants operated on the assumption that the power to authorize torture lay in the royal prerogative, though Langbein argues (*Torture and the Law of Proof*, 129–30) that it lay not in a positive right to torture but in the prerogative right to grant immunity to the torturer. See too the discussion of the peculiar legal status of torture in Elizabeth Hanson, *Discovering the Subject in Renaissance England* (Cambridge: Cambridge University Press, 1998), 28–32.

[29] Sir Thomas Smith, *De republica Anglorum*, ed. Mary Dewar (Cambridge: Cambridge University Press, 1982), 117; Fortescue, *De laudibus*, 32.

[30] Edward Coke, *The Third Part of the Institutes Of the Laws of England* (London: 1644), 35. See too Coke's discussion of Magna Carta in *The Second Part of the Institutes Of the Lawes of England* (London: 1642), 48.

worked best when not too many questions were asked of it. It also helped amplify the image of Felton as a 'patriot' hero. One of the most widely read English condemnations of torture—Sir Thomas Smith's handbook, *De republica Anglorum*—branded as 'servile' the use of interrogatory torture in European civil law systems: 'The nature of our nation', Smith insisted, 'is free, stout, haultaine [i.e. proud or courageous], prodigall of life and bloud: contumelie, beatings, servitude and servile torment and punishment it will not abide.'[31] Given this cluster of associations, it is possible that Felton's reported critique of torture enhanced other contemporary images of the assassin that stressed his civic patriotism, his valour and 'stoutness', his willingness to sacrifice himself to free England from Buckingham's thrall.

The torture talk around the Felton case died down in the second half of October, only to revive early in November in the weeks before Felton's trial. On 14 November, a newsmonger reported that about a week earlier Charles had informed Felton that 'he should prepare himself to dye and to indure as muche torture as could be putt upon a man'. It is not clear whether this 'torture' was to be incorporated into Felton's execution—if it was, Charles was perhaps threatening to charge the assassin with treason or to precede his trial. But once again, the newsletter reported Felton giving a politically resonant reply to the threats against him:

> I give his Majesty most humble thankes, for doing me this singular grace and favor in forewarning me of my death which I am ready to embrace. And for torture to be inflicted on my body, I am ready to suffer. Being confident, that the tortures of my soule are all appeased in my Saviours merrites.

Again, the key to the story was that the threat of torture elicited from Felton words that revealed his religious and political virtue, expressing here a kind of Protestant Stoicism, a confidence not only in his physical ability to endure torture patiently but also in Christ's forgiveness of the sins of his repentant soul. Although the allusion to Felton's newly repentant mood tempered the effect, such stories nonetheless served to enhance Felton's already dangerous political charisma. The newsmonger added, 'It is sayd that yesterday he was putt upon the torture, but I do scarce believe it'.[32] Mead heard similar reports from other sources, noting on 15 November that 'on Tuesday last, it is said, Felton was put to the strappado, and some say beaten with cudgels: but that is not believed'.[33]

In the context of this widely circulated discourse on the threat and possibility of torture, is it possible to make sense of Rushworth's famous account of the events of 13 and 14 November? In the absence of a contemporary paper trail, any conclusions must remain provisional. But the case for scepticism, as set out by Jardine and endorsed

[31] Smith, *De republica Anglorum*, 117–18.

[32] BL Harley MS 383, fols 68–9 (Pory to Mead: 14 November 1628), transcribed in William S. Powell, *John Pory, 1572–1636: The Life and Letters of a Man of Many Parts* (Chapel Hill: University of North Carolina Press, 1977), microfiche 129.

[33] Birch, *Court and Times of Charles I*, 1.432 (Mead to Stuteville: 15 November 1628).

by Langbein, has a number of flaws.[34] The most compelling of Jardine's points is that it seems odd for Charles to ask about the legality of torture when, as recently as 1626, warrants had been used to authorize its application with no evidence of legal ambivalence. We might add that the draft order to the commissioners investigating the assassination—a document that neither Jardine nor Langbein discusses—had included language explicitly authorizing torture; that in early September Attorney-General Robert Heath, using the Roman law concept of *inditia torturae*, had contemplated the existence of evidence that might provide grounds for torture; and that in late September the privy councillor Lord Dorchester, while denying that Felton had been subjected to torture, did not rule out its future use. So why did Charles, relatively late in Felton's prosecution, now begin to have qualms about authorizing interrogatory torture?

We can perhaps stress two things. First, although (as Langbein notes) Rushworth was too young to have witnessed events firsthand, he was an exceptionally diligent researcher with unusual access during the Interregnum to the state's archives, and he presented the material on Felton in a manner that suggested he was citing documentary sources. Second, we have to pay attention to the language of Charles's question: Charles understood that he had the *prerogative right* to order the torture, but in this case and at this moment, he wanted a ruling about whether he could order torture 'by the Law'—that is, by common law. In other words, Charles was wary about proceeding on prerogative alone, even though he did not doubt he had that power (although some of his contemporaries, and perhaps Felton himself, might have contested that claim). As S. R. Gardiner suggested a century ago, it looks as if Charles's calculations may have been as much political as legal. Charles had clashed with Parliament in 1628 over issues of law and prerogative, and perhaps he was wary of undertaking another action that might provoke the Parliament-men whose recall was imminent and whose support for taxation he still desperately needed.[35] Furthermore, Charles, or the men around him, must also have been conscious of the volatile politics surrounding Felton and the assassination. Perhaps elements in the regime became concerned that the use of torture would rouse popular sympathy and cement Felton's image as a patriot hero, while potentially casting the king as a cruel and lawless tyrant. As the authorities plotted their final dealings with Felton, the more moderate counsellors appear to have grown increasingly convinced that a carefully handled prosecution, trial, and execution might help secure invaluable public and parliamentary support. The moderates on the Council may have successfully argued that, no matter how deeply Charles felt betrayed by Felton and his

[34] I take a different approach here from Heath (*Torture and English Law*, 161–5) who also believes that Rushworth recorded a real event, though he argues that what Charles was asking was whether he could authorize torture in a case that was not technically a case of treason, an interpretation which makes a number of problematic assumptions.

[35] Gardiner, *History*, 6.359 n. 2; Jardine, *Reading on the Use of Torture*, 26 also notes this context. The most precise reading of the shifting moods at court in this period can be found in Richard Cust, 'Was There An Alternative to the Personal Rule? Charles I, the Privy Council and the Parliament of 1629', *History*, 90.299 (2005): 330–52.

supporters, taking a cautious line with the assassin could promote a renewed working relationship with Parliament.[36]

There is, then, a case for accepting the essential reliability of Rushworth's report: the authorities considered torturing Felton from the start of the investigation, and they may have threatened him with the rack at a number of points during the first month or so of investigations. But early in November, when the authorities again considered using torture, various political calculations now made them hesitate and pushed the king to seek legal cover. When the judges refused to supply it, Charles decided not to use his prerogative to order torture of the assassin. The ruling did not end torture in England—the last recorded conciliar warrant was issued in 1640—and it did not explicitly deny that the king could authorize torture using his prerogative powers. But it gave significant polemical ammunition to those inclined to deny the prerogative any role above, beyond, or outside the common law.

As we have seen, many of the most interesting discussions of the legality of torture in 1628 took place in the newsletter reports of Felton's supposed remarks on the subject, reports that helped fuel the broader process by which contemporaries invested the assassin with potent political charisma. The politics of Felton's torture emerge more strikingly still when we turn from these newsletter representations to a pair of more self-consciously literary texts. The poem 'To his confined Friend, Mr Felton' was in manuscript circulation by late October 1628. Ben Jonson was questioned about it on 26 October, and he told the authorities that he had seen a copy and had heard it was the work of Zouche Townley, an Oxford cleric and 'Son of Ben'. Contemporary newsletters reported that after his authorship became known, Townley fled to Holland to escape prosecution.[37] He had reason to be nervous. Townley's poem is a remarkable meditation on the truths that torture and imprisonment would reveal about John Felton, and for both political and literary reasons, it spoke powerfully to contemporary readers—more than thirty manuscript copies survive, an unusually high number for this kind of text, indicating a relatively wide circulation. In Townley's reckoning, Felton's physical suffering neither reaffirmed the power of an injured sovereignty nor revealed the 'popular' conspiracy to murder the duke; instead, it exposed and re-endorsed the assassin's heroic virtues. The poem opens by establishing a contrast between Felton's noble liberty and the base penal armoury of the state, urging Felton to 'Enjoy thy Bondage; make thy Prison know / Thou hast a Libertie thou canst not owe / To those base Punishments.' Pain—which in

[36] See e.g. Cust's reading ('Was There An Alternative', 330–1) of the conciliatory gestures in Heath's speech at Felton's trial.

[37] W. Douglas Hamilton, ed., *Original Papers Illustrative of the Life and Writings of John Milton*, Camden Society, 1st ser., 75 (London: 1859), 72–3; Birch, *Court and Times of Charles I*, 1.427 (Pory to Mead: 14 November 1628) (also in BL Harley MS 383, fols 68–9, transcribed in *John Pory*, microfiche 129). On the poem's Jonsonian style, see Anne Barton, *Ben Jonson, Dramatist* (Cambridge: Cambridge University Press, 1984), 315–17; and for a briefer reading of the poem's subversive challenge to the authorities, see Alastair Bellany, 'Libels in Action: Ritual, Subversion and the English Literary Underground, 1603–42', in *The Politics of the Excluded, c.1500–1850*, ed. Tim Harris (Basingstoke and New York: Palgrave Macmillan, 2001), 108.

the torturer's hands is an instrument to produce truth—is here reimagined as a testament to the truth of Felton's heroism. The poet even fears that 'Mercie' might deprive the assassin's 'great Storie … of its Miracle and Glorie', for 'labourd Crueltie'—torture—would validate Felton's 'Meritt', testing and refining his mettle, his stoutness, his bravery: 'I would have posteritie to heare, / Hee that can bravely do, can bravely beare. / Tortures seeme great in a Cowards Eye. / Tis no great thing to suffer, lesse to die.' Indeed, for Townley, the extremity of the violence unleashed by the state—compared here to a lightning strike from 'Joves full Armorie'—is the most potent testimony to the assassin's real worth.

At this point, Townley offers a graphic account of the physical damage the rack could do, but he insists that this torture, the 'sharpest Mischiefs' the Crown can inflict, only serves to reveal Felton's 'virtue' and patriotic strength:

> use your Rack,
> Enlarge each Joint, and make each sinew crack:
> Thy soul before was streightned, Thanke thy doome,
> To shew her vertue shee hath larger roome.
> Yet, sure, if every Arterie were broke,
> Thou wouldst finde strength for such another stroke.

Importantly, Townley also rejects Felton's reported penitence for his crime, re-endorsing Felton's initial self-perception and self-presentation as a patriot hero.[38] The assassin's torture becomes the occasion for his sacrificial apotheosis as a charismatic martyr for the public weal, a martyr whose moral authority now chastens both court and king while inspiring other Englishmen to act and speak boldly even at the risk of retribution:

> now I leave thee unto death and Fame,
> Which lives, to shake Ambition with thy name:
> And if it were not sinne, the Court by it
> Should hourely swear before the Favourite.
> …
> Farewell: undaunted stand, and joy to bee
> Of publique sorrow the Epitomie.
> Let the Duke's name solace and Crowne thy thrall:
> All wee by him did suffer, Thou for all.
> And I dare boldlie write, as thou dar'st dye,
> Stout Felton, Englands Ransome, heere doth lye.[39]

This image of the tortured Felton as a patriot hero fused Protestant with classical republican models of virtue, and it cannily recycled, while partially secularizing, various

[38] This rejection was widespread: see e.g. Bellany '"Brightnes"', 1258–9.

[39] Bellany and McRae, eds, 'Early Stuart Libels', Pii10.

martyrological tropes that transmuted physical suffering and endurance into proof of spiritual virtue.[40] Townley knows Felton will die for his actions, but also that the assassin's posthumous 'Fame' will linger, the very name 'Felton' acting as a check on the ambition of the court favourites who will follow in Buckingham's wake. In Townley's hands, torture invested the assassin with a political charisma that directly challenged Charles I's authority and radically subverted the king's interpretation and condemnation of Felton's crime.

The poem was the product of a deeply polarized political culture, a culture that generated starkly incompatible understandings of one of the most astonishing events of the decade. The political crisis around Buckingham had begun to intensify dramatically in the wake of the 1626 Parliament's failed attempt to impeach him, a failure that prompted increasingly anxious meditations on political misrule and that unleashed violent fantasies of retribution.[41] These potent political anxieties and fantasies crackle near the surface of Philip Massinger's late 1626 play *The Roman Actor*.[42] Set during the reign of the tyrannical Roman emperor Domitian, Massinger's play should be read as a political thought experiment—engaging with contemporary anxieties through historical fiction; dramatizing options, alternatives, consequences; allowing multiple contemporary political figures to be mapped onto multiple historical analogues; wrestling with the power of theatre and the theatricality of power; and returning repeatedly to vexed questions about the legitimacy of active and passive resistance and the tension between individual political agency and providential intervention. Because the play daringly explores the ethics and politics of tyrannicide in a classical republican idiom, its 1626 performance allowed audiences to weigh the legitimacy of violent, extra-legal action against the corrupt royal favourite who had escaped Parliament's justice. By the time of its first printing in 1629—possibly following additional performances at 'divers times'—the play had acquired even more political resonances.[43] If in its original performance it captured the political anxieties that would eventually shape the discourse around Buckingham's assassination, by 1629 it could be read as a retrospective commentary on the event. When, in 1626, the character Stephanos defended tyrannicide as a 'noble undertaking' and insisted that it was much better to die 'than to live ever slaves', his speech injected a classically republican discourse on tyrannicide into a fraught political context. A reader coming across these speeches in 1629, on the other hand, might have noticed their striking similarity to

[40] For an example of a Protestant martyrological celebration of 'patience' under torture, see John Foxe's account of Cuthbert Simpson in *Actes and Monuments* (London: 1583), 2032; for Elizabethan Catholic examples, see e.g. Hanson, *Discovering the Subject*, 32–3, 44–51.

[41] On the 1626 Parliament and its aftermath, see Alastair Bellany and Thomas Cogswell, *The Murder of King James I* (New Haven and London: Yale University Press, 2015), esp. parts III and IV.

[42] The two indispensable analyses of the play's politics are Martin Butler, 'Romans in Britain: *The Roman Actor* and the Early Stuart Classical Play', in *Philip Massinger: A Critical Reassessment*, ed. Douglas Howard (Cambridge: Cambridge University Press, 1985), 139–70; and Curtis Perry, *Literature and Favoritism in Early Modern England* (Cambridge: Cambridge University Press, 2006), 252–8. See too the helpful comments in Martin White, 'Introduction' to Philip Massinger, *The Roman Actor: A Tragedy* (Manchester: Manchester University Press, 2007), 14–22, 43–4.

[43] White, 'Introduction', 18, 48–9.

the by now widely circulated arguments that Felton had sewn into his hatband to justify killing Buckingham.[44]

Massinger's play also offers a powerful meditation on the interconnections among torture, tyranny, and resistance. The emperor's willingness to deploy torture for tyrannical political ends is signalled early in the play when the patrician Lamia is forced to divorce his wife under the threat of torture to 'Compel you to perform it' (1.2.83–4). The most startling example of the interconnections, however, appears in Massinger's depiction of the executions of the senators Rusticus and Sura, 'Men of the best repute in Rome for their / Integrity of life.' Although their torture is punitive rather than interrogatory, Massinger's presentation interestingly prefigures (and, by 1629, echoes) some of the political discourse around Felton's suffering in 1628. Domitian intends the executions to serve as a public show of imperial authority. When counselled that inflicting 'exquisite torments' on the senators might generate 'compassion / In the giddy rout', Domitian insists he has no need to court the people's good will: the people are the 'many-headed monster', mere 'dust / Before the whirlwind of our will and power' (3.1.102–3; 3.2.15–24, 27–8, 34).[45] Domitian's eagerness to display his power publicly upon the bodies of his enemies opens up a space for republican resistance, a resistance that is, as in Townley's poem, written upon the tortured body and that serves to expose the truth of Domitian's tyranny and his victims' patriotic virtue. The condemned men insist on the limits of the emperor's power: they ask the 'fell tyrant' for death, 'For beyond our bodies / Thou hast no power'. But Domitian acknowledges no limits, insisting that his power will harry their souls into the hell where those 'that blaspheme / The power of princes that are gods on earth' are condemned to howl. Rusticus responds that he does not fear the afterlife, for hell is right here in this 'dunghill Rome, made hell by thee' (3.2.53–4, 56–7, 66). Domitian orders the tortures to begin, but he becomes frustrated at his victims' refusal to express pain. They have learned how to die in the Stoic fashion, and their refusal to scream subverts the political function of the tortures they endure: 'I am tortured / In their want of feeling torments', Domitian laments. Rusticus explains the political logic to the emperor: their Stoic endurance of 'studied tortures' is an act of public resistance, 'to deride thee, our calm patience treading / Upon the neck of tyranny' (3.2.88–9, 95–6). The intended display of royal power thus turns into a display of resistance to that power, and eventually Domitian can stomach no more and orders the men to be removed from public view and killed and burned in private. In Massinger's play, torture—punitive rather than interrogatory—is clearly a symptom of tyranny, of passion and will unchecked by reason, of lawlessness, and it provides the stage upon which resistance to that rule can be mounted. Massinger's drama thus suggests some of the ways that torture was 'good to think with' in the mid- and late 1620s and reveals some of the cultural resources (both republican and Stoic) on which commentators on Felton's torture could draw.

[44] Massinger, *Roman Actor*, 3.1.41–2, 46–7, 49–50, 53, 76–8, 112–14 (further references will be in the text). White discusses some of the Feltonian resonances in his notes to 136–7.

[45] On popular sympathy for the tortured, see Smith, *De republica Anglorum*, 118.

Poems, plays, and newsletters rarely become the raw material for judicial rulings. What mattered to the Law Lords in 2005 was the status of the Felton case as a precedent; and the discourse that mattered was the discourse (real or alleged) of the common law judges gathered on Chancery Lane and Fleet Street in November 1628. But as we have seen, the Felton case reveals a marvelously rich set of early seventeenth-century discourses on the question and problem of judicial torture—in newsletters, in verse, and in the public theatre—shaped by and helping shape a tense, increasingly polarized, contemporary political culture. This seventeenth-century discourse may (or may not) enhance our own ongoing moral, legal, and political debates about the use of torture in the wake of 9/11, though it does remind us that our own reckonings with torture continue to be shaped and complicated by artistic and journalistic representations of the practice.[46]

I want to end, however, with another story from John Rushworth. By the time of Felton's trial, on 27 November 1628, the assassin had become almost as penitent as the authorities could have desired, although by this point it was the mythic Felton of Townley's and others' imaginations, not the broken assassin himself, who mattered to his contemporaries.[47] According to Rushworth, after Felton was sentenced to death, he asked that his dagger hand 'be cut off' before his hanging. Felton's request endorsed a penal logic in which talionic physical mutilation theatricalized and reinforced the heinousness of certain crimes; offering up his hand was yet another way to show his repentance. The torture inflicted by a highly symbolic mutilation would not only display royal authority and abhorrence but also reveal what the penitent Felton now understood as the truth of his offence. According to Rushworth, Charles wanted to accept Felton's offer, but the judges argued that 'it could not be; for in all Murders, the Judgment was the same', and there could be no additional punishment unless Felton were indicted on a separate charge. Once again, the common law asserted its authority over the royal will.[48] But Charles was legally permitted to add one theatrical embellishment to signal his horror at the assassination, ordering Felton's corpse to be hung in chains on the road outside Portsmouth.[49] The public dissolution of a body denied Christian burial sent a clear message about the heinousness of this particular murderer, but that message too could be subverted—by the poets who turned Felton's hanging in chains into an apotheosis, and by those who told the (unverifiable) story that Felton's corpse was stolen from the gibbet and quietly buried.[50] Like the other stories about the torture of John Felton, this one teaches us something about imagination and the law in early seventeenth-century

[46] In the contemporary American context, one might note the importance of the Abu Ghraib photographs and the ubiquitous discussions of the use of 'enhanced interrogation' in the television drama *24*.

[47] See esp. Felton's highly repentant 'last dying speech', *The Prayer and Confession of Mr. Felton, Word for Word as Hee Spake It Immediatly before His Execution* ([London]: 1628).

[48] Rushworth, *Historical Collections* (1659), 640–1. For a contemporary report, see Oglander, *Commonplace Book*, 42.

[49] See esp. the detailed report in Oglander, *Commonplace Book*, 42.

[50] Bellany and McRae, eds, 'Early Stuart Libels', Pii15–17; Bellany, 'Libels in Action', 106–10; Hamon L'Estrange, *The Reign of King Charles* (London: 1655), 94; and Sir William Sanderson, *A Compleat History of the Life and Raigne of King Charles* (London: 1658), 124.

England. And all these stories expose to renewed historical attention the political divisions and anxieties of the later 1620s that would, over the longer term, help plunge England into civil war.

Bibliography

Barton, Anne. *Ben Jonson, Dramatist* (Cambridge: Cambridge University Press, 1984).

Bellany, Alastair. '"Raylinge Rymes and Vaunting Verse": Libellous Politics in Early Stuart England, 1603–1628', in *Culture and Politics in Early Stuart England*, ed. Kevin Sharpe and Peter Lake (London: Macmillan, 1994), 285–310, 367–71.

Bellany, Alastair. 'Libels in Action: Ritual, Subversion and the English Literary Underground, 1603–42', in *The Politics of the Excluded, c.1500–1850*, ed. Tim Harris (Basingstoke and New York: Palgrave Macmillan, 2001), 99–124.

Bellany, Alastair. *The Politics of Court Scandal in Early Modern England: News Culture and the Overbury Affair, 1603–1660* (Cambridge: Cambridge University Press, 2002).

Bellany, Alastair. '"The Brightnes of the Noble Leiutenants Action": An Intellectual Ponders Buckingham's Assassination', *English Historical Review*, 118.479 (2003): 1242–63.

Bellany, Alastair. 'Railing Rhymes Revisited: Libels, Scandals, and Early Stuart Politics', *History Compass*, 5.4 (2007): 1136–79.

Bellany, Alastair and Andrew McRae, eds. 'Early Stuart Libels: An Edition of Poetry from Manuscript Sources', *Early Modern Literary Studies Text Series*, 1 (2005).

Bellany, Alastair and Thomas Cogswell. *The Murder of King James I* (New Haven and London: Yale University Press, 2015).

Birch, Thomas, ed. *Court and Times of Charles I*, ed. R. F. Williams, 2 vols (London: 1848).

British Library Add. MS 35331, 'Walter Yonge's Diary'.

British Library Egerton MS 2533, 'Edmund Howes' Notes'.

British Library Harley MSS 377, 383, 'Newsletters'.

British Library Sloane MS 826, 'Political Miscellany'.

Butler, Martin. 'Romans in Britain: "The Roman Actor" and the Early Stuart Classical Play', in *Philip Massinger: A Critical Reassessment*, ed. Douglas Howard (Cambridge: Cambridge University Press, 1985), 139–70.

Coke, Sir Edward. *The Second Part of the Institutes of the Lawes of England* (London: 1642).

Coke, Sir Edward. *The Third Part of the Institutes of the Lawes of England* (London: 1644).

Cust, Richard. *The Forced Loan and English Politics* (Oxford: Oxford University Press, 1987).

Cust, Richard. 'Charles I and Popularity', in *Politics, Religion, and Popularity in Early Stuart Britain*, ed. Thomas Cogswell, Richard Cust, and Peter Lake (Cambridge: Cambridge University Press, 2002), 235–58.

Cust, Richard. 'Was There An Alternative to the Personal Rule? Charles I, the Privy Council and the Parliament of 1629', *History*, 90.299 (2005): 330–52.

Felton, John. *The Prayer and Confession of Mr Felton, Word for Word as Hee Spake it Immediatly Before His Execution* ([London]: 1628).

Fortescue, Sir John. *On the Laws and Governance of England*, ed. Shelley Lockwood (Cambridge: Cambridge University Press, 1997).

Foxe, John. *Actes and Monuments* (London: 1583).

Gardiner, S. R. *History of England from the Accession of James I to the Outbreak of the Civil War* [1883–1884], 10 vols (New York: AMS, 1965).

Geertz, Clifford. 'Centers, Kings, and Charisma: Reflections on the Symbolics of Power', in *Local Knowledge: Further Essays in Interpretive Anthropology*, ed. Clifford Geertz (New York: Basic Books, 1983), 121–46.
Hamilton, W. Douglas, ed. *Original Papers Illustrative of the Life and Writings of John Milton* (London: 1859).
Hanson, Elizabeth. *Discovering the Subject in Renaissance England* (Cambridge: Cambridge University Press, 1998).
Hatfield House Salisbury MS 253, 'Report on Buckingham's Assassination'.
Heath, James. *Torture and English Law: An Administrative and Legal History from the Plantagenets to the Stuarts* (Westport and London: Greenwood Press, 1982).
House of Lords. *Opinions of the Lords of Appeal For Judgment in the Cause A (FC) and others (FC) (Appellants) v. Secretary of State for the Home Department (Respondent) (2004)*, [2005] UKHL 71.
Jardine, David. *A Reading on the Use of Torture in the Criminal Law of England Previously to the Commonwealth* (London: 1837).
Langbein, John H. *Torture and the Law of Proof: Europe and England in the Ancien Regime* (Chicago and London: Chicago University Press, 2006).
L'Estrange, Hamon. *The Reign of King Charles* (London: 1655).
Massinger, Philip. *The Roman Actor: A Tragedy* [1629], ed. Martin White (Manchester: Manchester University Press, 2007).
National Archives State Papers Domestic 16, 'Reign of Charles I'.
Oglander, Sir John. *A Royalist's Notebook: The Commonplace Book of Sir John Oglander Kt of Nunwell*, ed. Francis Bamford (New York: Blom, 1971).
Perry, Curtis. *Literature and Favoritism in Early Modern England* (Cambridge: Cambridge University Press, 2006).
Peters, Edward. *Torture* (Oxford and New York: Blackwell, 1985).
Pory, John. *John Pory, 1572–1636: The Life and Letters of a Man of Many Parts*, ed. William S. Powell (Chapel Hill: University of North Carolina Press, 1977).
Privy Council. *Acts of the Privy Council 1628–9* (London: HMSO, 1958).
Rous, John. *Diary of John Rous*, ed. Mary Anne Everett Green (London: Camden Society, 1856).
Rushworth, John. *Historical Collections of Private Passages of State* [...] *Beginning* [...] *1618 and Ending* [...] *1629* (London: 1659).
Rushworth, John. *Historical Collections of Private Passages of State*, 8 vols (London: 1721).
Sanderson, Sir William. *A Compleat History of the Life and Raigne of King Charles* (London: 1658).
Smith, Sir Thomas. *De republica Anglorum: A Discourse on the Commonwealth of England* [1583] ed. Mary Dewar (Cambridge: Cambridge University Press, 1982).

PART VII

LIBERTIES, SLAVERIES, AND ENGLISH LAW

CHAPTER 29

FROM SOVEREIGNTY TO THE STATE

The Tragicomic Clemency of Massinger's The Bondman

BERNADETTE MEYLER

THE reception of *The Bondman*, Philip Massinger's 1623 tragicomedy, presents something of a puzzle: why did audiences from Prince Charles, to republicans resisting the possibility of Charles II's return, to the spectators of the Restoration all respond to the play enthusiastically despite their disparate political vantage points? Annabel Patterson posits that the tragicomic structure of the play permitted Massinger to caution James I of the possibility of his subjects' resistance while simultaneously supporting his entrance into war upon failure of the match between his son, Charles, and the Spanish infanta.[1] Under this account, tragicomic form enables *The Bondman* to represent radical

[1] Annabel Patterson, *Censorship and Interpretation: The Conditions of Writing and Reading in Early Modern England* (Madison: University of Wisconsin Press, 1984), 92–3. Political interpretations of *The Bondman* have proliferated since Samuel R. Gardiner's topical interpretation of the play in 'The Political Element in Massinger', *Contemporary Review*, 28 (1876): 495–507. These have diverged not only in their assessments of Massinger's relative support for monarchy and republicanism but also in their evaluation of whether Massinger's plays were more preoccupied with specific historical events and controversies or with political theory. For instance, Jerzy Limon argued in *Dangerous Matter* that *The Bondman*, along with several other nearly contemporaneous plays, formed part of a propaganda campaign organized by Prince Charles and his favourite, the Duke of Buckingham. While acknowledging that Massinger's 'plays exhibit an unflagging interest in general political theory', Allen Gross contended, by contrast, that Massinger's writings, including *The Bondman*, are not 'full of specific references to contemporary politics'. Allen Gross, 'Contemporary Politics in Massinger', *SEL*, 6.2 (Spring, 1966): 279, 290, 279–90. More recently, Thomas Fulton has read *The Bondman* as indebted to imported Dutch republicanism. In doing so, he has concluded that Massinger demonstrates how 'absolute rule promotes a corrupt, parasitic aristocracy whose self-indulgence causes them to put themselves before their country. Conversely, a more constitutional form, whether a republic, a mixed government, or a more securely parliamentarian monarchy, promotes a stronger, less self-serving citizenship . . . .' Thomas Fulton, '"The True and Naturall

eventualities by dispelling disaster at the end. Yet this explanation contrasts the realities of politics too starkly with the fiction of the play. As Patterson writes, '[t]he play's tragicomic structure averts the fulfillment of [the] "if", as later Stuart history could not'.[2] *The Bondman* may not, however, simply outline disparate potential political avenues that it fails to fully follow but, in fact, suggest an alternative form of politics correlated with a tragicomic vision. According to this reading, the particular kind of tragicomedy employed both furnishes a positive model for a possible state and allows seemingly incompatible constituencies to welcome the play with open arms.

As with many of Massinger's works, the language of *The Bondman* resonates with the echoes of Senecan Stoicism. From the representation of the Corinthian General Timoleon as a kind of Stoic sage to the deployment of the rhetoric of slavery in relation not only to physical servitude but also to the overwhelming quality of the passions, the play continually invokes commonplaces of Stoicism. The allusion most salient to its genre may be the first, within the dedicatory poem to Philip, Earl of Montgomery, where Massinger lauds 'the clemencie of [Philip's] Heroick disposition' ('Dedicatory Epistle'). This clemency, which would allow the play to find 'though perhaps not a welcome entertainment, yet at the worst a gracious pardon' ('Dedicatory Epistle'), recalls Lucius Annaeus Seneca's treatise *De clementia*, a defence of clemency addressed to his pupil, the Emperor Nero. Although a number of commentators have observed Massinger's debt to Stoic thought, even Benjamin Townley Spencer's detailed analysis of the connections between Seneca's writings and *The Bondman* in his 1932 edition of the play mentions *De clementia* only once in passing.[3]

For Seneca, clemency (*clementia*), a capacity for transcending particular grievances for the benefit of the whole, is a quality preeminently to be desired in a ruler, and should not be confused with pity (*misericordia*), an undesirable affective state derived from witnessing suffering. The opposite of clemency consists not in severity (*severitas*) but rather in cruelty (*crudelitas*). Furthermore, pardoning (*venia*) does not always accompany clemency, because such pardoning might itself commit an injustice. Substituting clemency for pity allows for the undoing of tragedy by tragicomedy yet, within such tragicomedy, pardoning will only occur for the good of the commonwealth rather than out of an effort to remit a particular person's punishment. The Stoic tragicomedy of *The Bondman*, putting clemency into service of the play, emphasizes the general good of the state over the life of the condemned individual.

Within Massinger's Stoic tragicomedy, this general welfare of the state becomes disconnected from any particular form of rule. The multiplicity of eager audiences to *The Bondman* attests that the play provides fodder for conceiving of either monarchy or

Constitution of That Mixed Government": Massinger's "The Bondman" and the Influence of Dutch Republicanism', *SP*, 99.2 (Spring, 2002): 177, 152–77.

[2] Patterson, *Censorship*, 93.

[3] For Spencer's discussions of Seneca's influence, see Benjamin Townley Spencer, *The Bondsman* (Princeton: Princeton University Press, 1932), 20, 43–65, 182–4, 209–10, 211, 221–2, 223–5, 230–3, 237, 248–9.

republicanism as viable modes of organizing government. As long as those directing the state possess the appropriate qualities of reason and self-restraint and place priority on the interests of the commonwealth rather than their personal gain, *The Bondman* suggests, the polity may thrive. As Reid Barbour has shown, Stoicism not only furnished ammunition for the republican opposition to King Charles I but was also affirmed by the monarch himself.[4] Specifically with respect to Massinger's *Believe as You List*, Barbour observes that, 'among the political and topical complexities of Massinger's play, Stoicism is the philosophy that, as Bacon feared, aims to trouble ancient states, but the fortitude of the hero inspired by the sage in the desert supports the moral legitimacy of kings over the imperial drive of a republic'.[5] Within either a republic or a monarchy, however, Stoicism treats inequality—which may rapidly devolve into cruelty—with suspicion. Clemency furnishes the antithesis to such cruelty, and it secures the state against the enemies within—enemies far more potent than foreign foes. The expansiveness of clemency furnishes a mechanism for generalizing pardon in transmuted form, one that would be raised and revisited from the late Jacobean moment through the Restoration.

Stoic Tragicomedy

The two books of *De clementia* were among the first of Seneca's works to be revived in Western Europe, and they were widely received during the medieval period and the Renaissance, possibly furnishing the foil for the political theory of Niccolò Machiavelli's *The Prince*, as Peter Stacey has persuasively argued in *Roman Monarchy and the Renaissance Prince*.[6] *De clementia* also provided fodder for one of John Calvin's earliest endeavours, a commentary on Seneca's text published in 1532. Furthermore, the essay was included in the 1614 and 1620 editions of Thomas Lodge's translation of *The Workes of Lucius Annaeus Seneca, both Moral and Naturall*.[7] Seneca represents *De clementia* as not simply aimed at instructing its addressee, the Emperor Nero, but as itself generated in response to Nero's own prior action, his display of reluctance in signing the death warrant of two condemned thieves.[8] Furnishing an early example of the genre of the

4 Reid Barbour, *English Epicures and Stoics* (Amherst: University of Massachusetts Press, 1998), 135.

5 Barbour, *Epicures*, 192.

6 Peter Stacey, *Roman Monarchy and the Renaissance Prince* (Cambridge: Cambridge University Press, 2012), 81.

7 As J. H. M. Salmon has claimed, Lodge's 1614 translation 'is in many ways a monument to the Jacobean Neostoic cult': J. H. M. Salmon, 'Stoicism and Roman Example: Seneca and Tacitus in Jacobean England', *JHI*, 50.2 (April–June, 1989): 199–225. It was based on the 1605 Latin edition prepared by Justus Lipsius: Salmon, 'Stoicism', 200. English quotations from Seneca in the text, with the exception of those from the *Epistles*, will be taken from the 1614 edition of Lodge's translation. The *Epistles* will instead be quoted from the Loeb edition: Seneca, *Epistles 1–65*, trans. Richard Gummere (Cambridge, MA: Loeb Classical Library, 1917).

8 Lodge, *Seneca*, 605.

mirror of kings,[9] Seneca endeavours to 'shew thee [Nero] to thy selfe, in such sort, as thou mayest receive a perfite contentment thereby',[10] generating a picture of Nero that will itself encourage the emperor to continue along the path of clemency. Taking up this task, Seneca both elaborates on the value of clemency and provides a conception of its scope that contrasts with customary understandings.[11]

As a kind of manual for princes along the lines that Peter Stacey has delineated, *De clementia* supplies the contours of a political theory. As an attempt to reposition clemency in relation to pity and cruelty, it alters an Aristotelian theory of tragedy. Writing in the aftermath of the Roman revolution and the demise of the Roman Republic, Seneca justifies the power of the emperor on the basis of his virtue, which is 'ground[ed] upon a strictly Stoic notion of reason'.[12] The emperor thus becomes a kind of Stoic sage.[13] As such, he can save from itself the otherwise factionalized people—a people that, through civil strife, 'had become merely a multitude' and 'had lost its *virtus* [virtue], its *ratio* [reason], to such a degree that it appears to have become nothing better than an irrational animal requiring forceful restraint'.[14] Only through the intervention of the emperor, who will 'always ensure that the *bonum commune* [common good] and never a partisan interest is upheld by his government', may freedom be restored and Rome itself become the 'Stoic cosmic city'.[15] Clemency is the foremost characteristic of this virtuous

[9] Stacey, *Roman Monarchy*, 4–5, 37.

[10] Lodge, *Seneca*, 583.

[11] The Senecan understanding of clemency was not the only Roman variant. As Melissa Dowling emphasizes, conceptions of clemency changed significantly between the third century BC and the late Republic. Whereas earlier views of clemency had emphasized the status differential between the person exercising clemency and its object, the rhetoric of clemency around Julius Caesar altered that dynamic. Dowling writes that: 'Cicero contributes to the enlargement of the quality by appealing to the clemency of the Roman people as a whole and thus creating a corporate clemency and taking the first step toward universalization of the quality': Melissa Barden Dowling, *Clemency and Cruelty in the Roman World* (Ann Arbor: University of Michigan Press, 2006), 27.

Although earlier scholars claimed that 'Julius Caesar's celebrated clemency toward his fellow citizens was perceived by his contemporaries not as a virtue, but rather as a manifestation of his tyrannical power,' David Konstan has more recently questioned that idea. Instead, he contends, 'so far as I can judge, *clementia* was regarded as a wholly positive quality, whether in a general or in a statesman and ruler, both in the late Republic, when the term first seems to have become prominent on the Roman political scene, and under the principate of Augustus and afterwards'. David Konstan, 'Clemency as a Virtue', *Classical Philology*, 100 (2005): 340, 337–46. One of clemency's distinguishing features, for Konstan, is that *clementia*, unlike *misericordia*, 'is a habitual trait or disposition ... and as such can be invoked as the basis for public concord ...': Konstan, 'Clemency', 342.

Nevertheless, Lucan's *Pharsalia*, which David Norbook demonstrated in *Writing the English Republic* formed an important influence on English Republicans after its translation in 1627, has convincingly been read as disparaging Caesar's clemency. Hence Neil Coffee writes that 'Lucan ... shows Caesar practicing his famed *clementia* in order to denigrate it as self-serving and calculated', Neil Coffee, *The Commerce of War: Exchange and Social Order in Latin Epic* (Chicago: University of Chicago Press, 2009), 143. Hence it may be significant for republicans' as well as monarchists' ability to adopt *The Bondman* that it speaks in a Senecan, not Lucan, language of clemency.

[12] Stacey, *Roman Monarchy*, 31.

[13] Stacey, *Roman Monarchy*, 33.

[14] Stacey, *Roman Monarchy*, 47.

[15] Stacey, *Roman Monarchy*, 31, 33.

emperor, the capacity that allows him to prioritize the general welfare over individual interests.

The critique of an Aristotelian version of tragedy remains somewhat more implicit in *De clementia*. Scholars have long debated the compatibility of Seneca's philosophical writings with his tragedies, some contending that the violence and passion of his plays conflict with the Stoic effort to conquer the emotions and others discerning more complex connections between the feelings generated in the spectator and the appropriate attitude of the proper Stoic individual.[16] Kathy Eden provided a suggestive account of the relation between a Senecan and an Aristotelian conception of the role of emotions in tragic and legal judgements in *Poetic and Legal Fictions in the Aristotelian Tradition*, but refrained from fully elaborating its implications. According to Eden, who cites *De clementia* for the distinctions she draws:

> Seneca ... rejects [the Aristotelian] view of the passions; and this rejection includes fear and pity—the two emotions associated with tragedy. The Stoics, including Seneca, define fear as the opposite of courage, and so its eradication needs little additional justification. Pity, however, describes a more complex response, including elements of human sympathy and fairness, which the Stoics would preserve. Seneca, consequently, differentiates two concepts inseparable in the Aristotelian *eleos*: *misericordia* and *clementia*. The first is characteristic of the feeble-minded and women; the second befits kings.[17]

Although fear can be rejected outright, pity must be treated more circumspectly; while *misericordia*—the translation of Aristotle's *eleos*, or pity, in Latin editions of the *Poetics*—is to be avoided, *clementia* must not be dispensed with at the same time. Putting to one side the question of whether Seneca's own tragedies accomplish this end, it is possible to derive an emendation of Aristotle from Seneca's treatment of clemency. This revised Aristotelian frame may, however, conduce more to tragicomedy than to tragedy.

In order to explicate the appropriate parameters of clemency, Seneca refutes what he deems a number of misinterpretations. At first, he explains why, contrary to certain

[16] Gregory Staley, *Seneca and the Idea of Tragedy* (Oxford: Oxford University Press, 2009), 94–5, recently attempted to elaborate a Senecan theory of tragedy that would account for both the explicitly philosophical writings and the plays, claiming that:

> The Stoics accepted the Platonic notion that tragedy is an image of the passionate soul; they did not, however, find harm in the experience. Influenced by Aristotle's *Rhetoric*, the Stoics interpreted emotion as a cognitive and persuasive process in which judgment follows and is influenced by our preliminary and unavoidable emotional responses to powerful impressions. ... The vividness of tragedy's images may arouse our emotions, but these are only preliminary and involuntary; we can in the end judge their truth value.

Notable works on the other side include Charles Segal's *Language and Desire in Seneca's* Phaedra and Alessandro Schiesaro's *The Passions in Play: 'Thyestes' and the Dynamics of Senecan Drama*.

[17] Kathy Eden, *Poetic and Legal Fiction in the Aristotelian Tradition* (Princeton: Princeton University Press, 1986), 101.

claims about it, clemency does not 'embold[en] those men that are most wicked'.[18] Because it must be exercised only in moderation, clemency fails to occasion such a perverse result; furthermore, even the innocent may have need for the employment of clemency due to circumstantial misfortunes.[19] Later, in the second book, where he defines clemency, Seneca counterposes it with cruelty, which he associates with seeking revenge. Those are 'cruell, who … keepe no measure. … We may … say this crueltie is an inclination of the minde unto most grievous punishments'.[20] Clemency instead imports 'a moderation of the minde, that restraineth the power which man hath to revenge himself'.[21] Cruelty and clemency hence stand in opposite relations to revenge, the former carrying revenge to its utmost limits and the latter avoiding absorption in the cycle of revenge and its concomitant passions.

If clemency is juxtaposed with cruelty at one extreme, it is opposed to mercy at the other. Whereas mercy focuses on the object of suffering and involves a disruption of the observer's tranquility through the experience of a sympathetic pain, clemency remains a rational practice. As Seneca writes, 'a wise man is not mooved with sadness for an others misery, because hee is exempt from miserie; but otherwise, he will willingly and with a ioyfull heart, do all that which the merciful would doe against their wills'.[22]

Between cruelty and mercy, two responses to tragedy seem to be ruled out—exulting in the extremities of an excessive revenge and experiencing the pity (*misericordia*) that Aristotle associates with the proper tragic catharsis. Seneca's subsequent contrast likewise suggests a modification of tragicomedy. If tragicomedies like *Measure for Measure* depend for the undoing of disaster on a series of final pardons, an alternative ending must be found to satisfy Seneca. According to the philosopher's claim, 'a wise man ought not to give [pardon]'.[23] Whereas pardoning remits deserved punishment, clemency allows for a mitigation of the consequences of crime. Whereas the one pardoning admits that he should not have condemned in the first place, the individual displaying clemency 'counsaileth' and 'correcteth' and 'doth as much as if he pardoned'.[24] Whereas the objects of pardoning may simply return to their course of crime, clemency aims to reform them: 'A wise man will forgive many things, and save many that are scarcely wise, yet such as may become capable. Hee will imitate good husbandmen, who not onely cherish straight and tall trees, but applieth under-props likewise to uphold those which are made crooked by some accident. … [A] wise man shall see how hee ought to entertaine every nature, and by what meanes those that are depraved, may be strengthened and straightned.'[25]

[18] Lodge, *Seneca*, 584.
[19] Lodge, *Seneca*, 585.
[20] Lodge, *Seneca*, 606.
[21] Lodge, *Seneca*, 606.
[22] Lodge, *Seneca*, 607.
[23] Lodge, *Seneca*, 608. The terms *ignorare* and *venia* are both used for pardoning in this passage.
[24] Lodge, *Seneca*, 608.
[25] Lodge, *Seneca*, 609.

Under the 1614 translation, clemency appears in the guise of equity, as opposed to the established custom of the common law, so that '[c]lemencie hath free will, shee iudgeth not according to use and custome, but according to equitie and right'.[26] The examples that Seneca furnishes also fit with early modern understandings of equity, involving an assessment of the intention or lack thereof of an actor and the possibility that the person might reform. As Seneca writes:

> He will be contented to admonish some without chastising them, considering that they are old enough to amend. Hee will dismisse an other in safetie, although he be apparently guiltie, because he hath beene deceived, and fell into the offence being drowned in wine. He will dismisse his enemies in safetie, and sometimes with commendations, if they have undertaken Warre upon honest grounds, as for their faith, confederate or libertie.[27]

These instances of individuals whose youth suggests their malleability in the direction of good, people who have erred seemingly without conscious awareness of criminality, and opponents who have waged war in support of their liberty, religion, or allies all indicate an equitable inquiry into the character of the accused and his motives.

Seneca's explanation within the first book of *De clementia* of the reasons why the wise man, and, in particular, the wise ruler, should display clemency helps to illuminate what Stoic tragicomedy might entail. The principal grounds for clemency in a ruler who wishes to avoid tyranny are two-fold; first, it helps to secure the peace of the state, and, second, it emanates from the proper consideration of the entire commonwealth as naturally connected to its ruler, in the same way as the body is linked to the soul. It is, Seneca claims, Nero's clemency that lies behind his subjects' belief that they possess 'an excellent forme of publique governement, which containeth all that which is requisite to establish a perfect libertie'.[28] When excessive fear is inflicted on the subjects of a tyrant, they are more likely to rebel, while the clemency of the wise prince quells unrest among his subjects: '[A] moderate feare restraineth mens minds, but a continuall violence, and such as is raised even unto the brimme, awakeneth and emboldneth those that are deepest asleep and giveth them courage to hazard all.'[29] Instead, the philosophically informed ruler should mete out chastisement in the same measure as a father, keeping in mind the goal of reformation rather than allowing himself more extreme responses to transgression.[30]

Before arriving at this analogy between the emperor and the father, however, Seneca develops in more detail a metaphor depicting the ruler as the soul of the commonwealth. This soul must make every effort to preserve the body with which it is linked—the

26 Lodge, *Seneca*, 609.
27 Lodge, *Seneca*, 609.
28 Lodge, *Seneca*, 585.
29 Lodge, *Seneca*, 593.
30 Lodge, *Seneca*, 595.

corporate body comprised of the emperor's subjects. The prince's clemency is, under this account, even more crucial than that of any commoner, partly because it emanates from a desire for self-preservation, and partly because the clemency of the ruler can be exercised on a greater stage than that of the subject. According to Seneca:

> [A]s we may truly conclude, ... thou are the soule of the Common-wealth, and shee the bodie; Thou seest, as I thinke, how necessary Clemencie is: for thou seemest to spare thy selfe when thou sparest others. Thou oughtest therefore to beare with evill subjects, no otherwise then thou wouldest doe with languishing members and if sometimes there be neede of bloud-letting, take heed lest the veine be opened more largely then the sickenesse requireth. Clemency therefore, as I said, is agreeable unto all mens nature, but especially it best befitteth Princes, because in them she findeth more people to preserve, and a greater matter wherein to shew herselfe. For how little hurteth a private cruelty? But Princes displeasure is a warre.[31]

The emphasis on the ruler's clemency as a form of self-preservation in this passage recalls the primacy placed more generally on self-preservation within the Stoic system. The Stoic conception of *oikeiōsis*, or 'orientation,' renders self-preservation 'the basic desire or drive in all animals (including human beings)' (Sellars 108). As Diogenes Laertius explains, 'An animal's first impulse, say the Stoics, is to self-preservation, because Nature from the outset endears it (*oikeiousēs*) to itself, as Chrysippus affirms in the first book of his work *On Ends*; his own words are, "The dearest thing (*prōton oikeion*) to every animal is its own constitution and its consciousness thereof"' (quoted in Sellars 107–8). The self-preservation of the subjects in Seneca's account merges seamlessly with the self-preservation of the prince.

The nature of a Senecan Stoic version of tragicomedy as well as of the state begins to emerge here. Rather than involving a series of individual pardons at the end of the play, ones that might either acknowledge a prior injustice or exempt from punishment those who otherwise deserve it, this kind of political tragicomedy would entail preservation of the body politic through enlargement of the ruler's compass of concern. It might also entail invocation of the spectre of cruelty in order to expunge it from the commonwealth.

The form of rule derived from *clementia* stands in contrast with a conception of the sovereign or the pardon as exception, along the lines described theoretically by Giorgio Agamben and Jacques Derrida.[32] Philip Lorenz's careful readings in *The Tears of Sovereignty* have teased out the operations of sovereignty as exception in early modern drama as well, including works such as Lope de Vega's *Fuenteovejuna*. In the context of that play, Lorenz suggests that, '[b]ecause the entire village, collectively, defies sovereignty's attempt to subject the event to a legal decision, the Catholic Kings are *forced* to

[31] Lodge, *Seneca*, 587.

[32] While Agamben detailed the relationship of sovereignty to the logic of the exception in *Homo sacer*, Derrida identified a similar aspect of the sovereign's pardon in his seminars on forgiveness and perjury.

pardon them. Sovereignty's desire to make of the village an *example* is forced to settle for an *exception* instead'.[33]

One particular form of cruelty with which Seneca appears concerned and which he analogizes with the tyrant's treatment of his subjects is the master's abuse of a slave. Even with regard to slaves, Seneca insists, justice applies, and a form of natural right pushes back against legal authority:

> It is an honour to know how to commaund a mans servants modestly, and in our slave wee are to thinke not how much punishment he may endure and we inflict upon him without reproofe, but what the nature of right and justice will permit thee: which commandeth us to spare our Captives and such whom we have bought to be our bond-slaves. ... Although wee have authoritie to doe what wee list with our slaves, there is somewhat which the common right of living Creatures permitteth us not to execute upon a man, because he is of the same nature that thou art.[34]

The natural equality among all human beings limits the extent to which the constructed relation of master and servant or slave permits the exercise of force. The servant or slave must be spared rather than scourged in the interests of humanity.

Seneca elaborates that the same principle applies with regard to the emperor's treatment of his subjects. Comparing the empire with the household, he writes, '[h]ow much more just is it for thee not to abuse men free, ingenious, and honest, as thy bond men, but to entertaine them, for such as are under thy government to defend them as thy subjects, and not to afflict them as thy slaves'.[35] Cruelty, in particular, serves to undermine respect for either the master or the prince: 'Even as cruell Masters are pointed at thorow the whole Citie, and are reputed both hatefull and detestable: so the cruell demencie of Princes, who have contracted infamie and hatred against them selves, are inregistred in Histories to bee a hatred to posteritie.'[36] Just as the master must eschew cruelty and instead adopt an attitude of clemency, so must the ruler in dealing with his subjects.

Clemency is also connected terminologically with the release from bondage early in Seneca's treatise. In the passage of *De clementia* announcing its sections, a passage that mystified Calvin,[37] Seneca proclaimed that '[h]ere I shall divide this subject as a whole

[33] Philip Lorenz, *The Tears of Sovereignty: Perspectives of Power in Renaissance Drama* (New York: Fordham University Press, 2013), 147. The passage continues on to complicate whether *Fuenteovejuna* actually functions as an example or exception, but the excerpt quoted here highlights the potential of the pardon to form a kind of exception. If here a pardon represents an exception from sovereignty, it may also serve as an exceptional reinforcement of sovereignty, as I have argued elsewhere.

[34] Lodge, *Seneca*, 597.

[35] Lodge, *Seneca*, 597.

[36] Lodge, *Seneca*, 597. The word 'demencie' is unfamiliar to us now but was glossed by Henry Cockeram's 1623 dictionary as 'Madnesse'. Henry Cockeram, *The English Dictionarie: Or, An Interpreter of Hard English* (London: Eliot's Court Press, 1623), n.p.

[37] Lodge, *Seneca*, 585. As Calvin wrote, 'Here Seneca gives the division of his work, but I cannot say I have quite understood it yet. I prefer a man to be a teacher of real frankness rather than delude his reader with frivolous subtleties. For he does not set forth his subject matter in the order he proposes. Nor is it apparent what he means by the word MANUMISSION in the first part. The blame for this is to be

into three parts. The first will treat of manumission [*manumissio*]; the second will aim to show the nature and aspect of clemency. …'[38] The invocation of 'manumission' here, about which Calvin expressed confusion, must also have puzzled Lodge, as he simply stated that '[t]he first [part] shall serve for a Preface or Induction'.[39] Seneca appears, however, to be using 'manumission' as a synonym for an act of clemency, linking the grant of freedom in situations of servitude with the ruler's capacity for behaving expansively towards his subjects.

A passage from another of Seneca's essays included in the 1614 edition, *Of Benefits*, dramatizes one possible set of interplays among manumission, bondage, and cruelty. Recounting a story from Claudius Quadrigarius' *Chronickes*, Seneca elaborates how two slaves staged an elaborate scene of deception in the midst of war in order to save their mistress. In order to convince the enemies who had conquered the city of Grumentum that they had greater entitlement to vengeance on their mistress than those who took the city, these slaves pretended that she had treated them with cruelty. Hence, when:

> the victorious enemie ranged and reveled everie where, these two slaves (who knew all the by-waies) were the first that set forward to make bootie of the house wherein they had served. And having surprised their Mistris, they rudely drove her before them: And being demanded what woman shee was: they answered that it was their Mistris, who had in times past most cruelly handled them, and that they dragged her out, to bring her to her death.[40]

Instead, they hid her to furnish protection. Subsequently, 'when the Roman Souldiers were satisfied with pillage, and reduced to their former discipline and manners, these slaves likewise returned to their former servitude, and gave their Mistresse her wonted libertie'.[41] Rather than simply reinstating the earlier hierarchy, however, their mistress 'presently set them both at libertie'.[42] Significantly, Seneca adds that she 'was not ashamed to receive her life at their handes, over whom shee had absolute power both

ascribed not so much to us as perhaps to the author himself': John Calvin, *Commentary on Seneca's 'De clementia'*, ed. and trans. Ford Lewis Battles and André Malan Hugo (Leiden: Brill, 1969), 79.

[38] Calvin, 77.

[39] The introduction to *De clementia*—taken from Justus Lipsius' 1605 edition of Seneca's works, upon which Lodge's translation is based—does devote more attention to the term, but, rather than reading 'manumission', substitutes for it 'manuduction', or 'the act of directing or guiding'. Lodge, *Seneca*, 582. This substitution follows Lipsius' own introduction, which reads '*unum Manuductionis*': Justus Lipsius, *Annaei Senecae philosophi opera, quae exstant omnia, a Iusto Lipsio emendata, et scholiis illustrata* (Antwerp: Plantijn-Moretus, 1605), 187. Although Lipsius keeps '*manumissio*' in Seneca's text, Lipsius' note on the term suggests that he deems it a corruption of '*manuductio*'. Lipsius, 189. This further indicates the perplexity that Seneca's use of '*manumissio*' occasioned for early modern editors of his work. Lipsius' work on Seneca is discussed in Papy's 'Erasmus's and Lipsius's Editions of Seneca': Jan Papy, 'Erasmus's and Lipsius's Editions of Seneca: A "Complementary" Project', *Erasmus of Rotterdam Society Yearbook*, 22 (2002): 10–36.

[40] Lodge, *Seneca*, 53.

[41] Lodge, *Seneca*, 54.

[42] Lodge, *Seneca*, 54.

of life and death'.[43] The absolute power of the master over the slave itself exists within a framework of time and contingency. Far from a static state, the relation of master and slave may be rapidly reversed by the intrusion of an invading army or by other political upheavals. At these moments, the cruelty or lack thereof of the master may affect his or her fate at the hands of a bondman. Likewise, the slave's own display of clemency allows for his subsequent manumission by the mistress. The grant of life or freedom to another person remains the opposite of cruelty, whether performed by a master or a slave.

Putting Clemency Into Practice

This episode from *Of Benefits* presages some of the plot components of *The Bondman*.[44] The Senecan components of *The Bondman* only become evident, however, from detailed analysis of the play's construction, which emphasizes the links between personal and political servitude, the connection between the regulation of the emotions and proper rule, and the differences among clemency, cruelty, and pity.

At the outset, Syracuse finds itself in danger of being captured by Carthage. Because the inhabitants of Syracuse have become used to a life of affluence and leisure, they lack a sufficiently capable general to defend the island and its '[l]iberties' (1.3.9) against the foreign fleet. Instead, the Senate has to resort to Timoleon, lent from Corinth, as its leader; by waging war on behalf of the Syracusans, Timoleon is defending Greece in its entirety against empire since Carthage 'will not end, till *Greece* / Acknowledge her their Soveraigne' (1.1.62–3). Even after the Senate has chosen Timoleon 'with a generall suffrage' (1.3.82) and extolled his excellence, he has difficulty raising resources for his expedition, as the 'free Lords' of Syracuse (1.1.61) remain miserly about their money. Timoleon expostulates with them, 'Doe you prize your mucke / Aboue your liberties? and rather choose / To be made Bondmen, then to part with that / To which already you are slaues?' (1.3.231–4).

Only when the virtuous Cleora, the daughter of the Praetor of Syracuse, Archidamus, intervenes and gives away her jewels are the remainder of the citizenry shamed into following suit and funding Timoleon's enterprise. Even at this point, the Syracusans contemplate sending hired men and slaves into battle instead of waging war themselves. Again Cleora addresses the assembly, proclaiming that the rewards of battle should not be reaped by slaves (1.3.326–41). Her words seem to convince at least some reluctant men to enter Timoleon's forces.

The political plot of the play is accompanied from the beginning by a second strain of romance. The audience discovers in the first scene that Leosthenes is a suitor for Cleora's hand in marriage. A friend of Cleora's brother, Timagoras, Leosthenes appears to have

[43] Lodge, *Seneca*, 54.

[44] Philip Edwards emphasizes that one of Seneca the Elder's *Controversiae* furnished a source for *The Bondman*: Philip Edwards, 'The Sources of Massinger's *The Bondman*', *RES*, 15.57 (February, 1964): 21–6.

won his beloved's affections but still remains unsure how her father, Archidamus, is disposed toward him. At the same time, it transpires that a noble Theban, Pisander—whose advances toward Cleora Timagoras had encouraged Archidamus to reject—has returned to Syracusa, and even to Archidamus' own household, disguised as the slave Marullo.

Two developments succeed in wresting Cleora's love from Leosthenes and transferring it to Pisander during the course of the drama; the first is the confirmation of the unchecked quality of Leosthenes' passions and the second is Pisander's demonstration of the opposite characteristic, temperance. Almost as soon as his character is introduced, Leosthenes is associated with jealousy; Timagoras implores him, 'Prethee doe not nourish / These jealous thoughts' (1.124–5). Despite this warning, Leosthenes' jealousy causes him to express distrust to Cleora about how she will conduct herself during his absence. Subsequently, despite the fact that Cleora has bound her eyes against other sights and refrained from speaking the entire time he was away, Leosthenes, returning victorious from battle, still believes that she may have been possessed in some way by another. It is this jealousy that Cleora fears would make Leosthenes 'tyrannize' if he 'stood possess'd of / That [i.e. Cleora herself], which is only [his] in expectation' (3.3.180–1).

The motivation for Leosthenes' fears when he arrives back in Syracusa is a slave rebellion that Pisander/Marullo had instigated during the absence of the citizens who left the city to fight against Carthage. Pisander employs three rationales to justify the revolt, one primarily personal, the second largely political, and the third somewhat metatheatrical. First, by taking over the city, Pisander attempts to gain closer access to Cleora and, as he reveals after the rebellion has failed: 'had [the bondmen] stood firme, / I could have bought *Cleoras* free consent, / With the safetie of her Fathers life, and Brothers' (4.3.6–8). Whether such consent under conditions of conquest could actually be considered free is a separate question, but Pisander appears to believe that it would be, as his sister Statilia's right to Leosthenes, which he insists upon upholding, stems from a similar circumstance. As Pisander later admonishes Leosthenes, 'This is shee / To whom thou wert contracted: this the Lady, / That when thou wert my prisoner fairely taken / In the *Spartan* warre, that beg'd thy libertie, / And with it gaue her selfe to thee ungratefull' (5.3.179–83).

At the same time, Pisander adduces a second reason for inciting the bondmen to action. Justifying the incident to Archidamus and the other rulers of the city, he recalls scenes like a tyrannous character's abuse of his slave and explains that the improper control of the household, like the political mismanagement of the city, has led the slaves not only to be treated as inhuman but even to be dealt with more cruelly than animals. Whereas the model of the commonwealth could in a prior age be traced from the well-governed household, the abusive behaviour of the Syracusan citizens has disrupted the analogy (4.2.52–85). To the bondmen themselves, he likewise adduces moral and political rather than self-interested reasons for the rebellion. In urging them to take action, however, Pisander/Marullo emphasizes absolute equality among men more than the Syracusans' tyrannous overstepping of masters' proper roles (2.3.32–42).

The bondmen are, however, not represented as fully capable of assuming the liberty that Pisander/Marullo has encouraged. Rather than allowing them to derive inspiration for the rebellion from reason, Pisander must instead ply them with alcohol, urging them to imbibe 'Strong, lusty wine: drinke deepe, this juyce will make us / As free as our Lords' (2.3.10–11). Upon the success of the revolt, order also rapidly dissolves among the slaves, who in a drunken bout fight about sexual access to Olimpia, a former mistress who has now married the man who was earlier her slave. When Pisander/Marullo inquires 'Quarrell among your selues?', one of the bondmen answers 'Yes, in our Wine, Sir, / And for our Wenches' (3.3.128–9). Finally, they are easily overthrown again by the returning army once the Syracusans decide to treat them not as equal enemies but as 'wilde beasts' and proceed to menace them with whips (4.2.113). By contrast, Pisander/Marullo's own conduct during the rebellion is exemplary, the second development that endears him to Cleora.

The third reason why Pisander provoked the slave revolt is necessarily revealed only retrospectively, when the Syracusans have regained control over their city and he has revealed his true identity. At this point, Pisander insists that he found the bondmen inclined toward rebellion because of the ill-treatment they had received and that he decided to stage a demonstration for the Syracusans of the disaster that might ensue if they failed to alter their attitude toward their slaves. As Pisander claims: 'I found their natures apt to mutinie / From your too cruell usage; and made triall / How farre they might be wrought on; to instruct you / To looke with more preuention, and care / To what they may hereafter undertake / Upon the like occasions. The hurt's little / They haue committed, nor was euer cure / But with some paine effected' (5.3.220–7). Employing the language of therapy, Pisander explains the aim of the revolt along the lines of didactic tragicomedy. By directing a display of what the Syracusans' bondmen might do under controlled circumstances, Pisander both alerts the citizens to the internal danger besetting their state and prevents true calamity from befalling them. His tragicomedy is aimed at showing the ills that result from cruelty and thereby deterring such behaviour in future.

The play raises several possible methods of responding to the revolution once the Praetor Archidamus and the other citizens of Syracusa have been restored to their places in the city. Four principal strategies emerge. The first two rely, from a Stoic perspective, excessively on emotional reactions to the situation, whether vengeful or compassionate. Indeed, as Martha Nussbaum has pointed out in *Upheavals of Thought*, a Stoic objection to the exercise of compassion rests on the ease with which this disposition can lapse into its opposite, revenge. The third and fourth mechanisms emphasize the recovery of the state and rely less on personal sentiment and more on the application of general political and legal principles, although ones that may be flexible enough to take into account the particularities of the individual case.

Leosthenes, spurred on by jealousy and joined by Timagoras, presents the most savage mechanism for dealing with the revolutionary episode, relying on the deployment of force. Having spied on a dialogue between Cleora and Pisander/Marullo that they incorrectly interpret in a dishonourable light, Leosthenes and Timagoras attempt to kill Marullo and seize possession of Cleora. The scene unfolds as follows:

> *Timagoras.* The base villaine (Marullo)
> Shall neuer liue to heare it. *Enter Archidamus, Diphilus, and Officers.*
> *Cleora.* Murther, helpe,
> Through me you shall passe to him.
> *Archid.* What's the matter?
> On whom is your Sword drawne? are you a iudge?
> Or else ambitious of the hangmans office
> Before it be design'd you? you are bold too,
> Unhand my daughter.
> *Leost.* Shee's my valours prize.
> *Archid.* With her consent, not otherwise. You may urge
> Your title in the Court; if it proue good,
> Possesse her freely: Guard him safely off too. (5.2.78–87)

Only the sudden arrival of Archidamus and the authorities thwarts Timagoras' attempt to kill Marullo and Leosthenes' effort to carry off Cleora without any public determination of the legitimacy of either the execution or marriage. The play's judgement on this rash approach seems akin to that of Pisander/Marullo, who states, 'Hee's more a slaue, then Fortune, / Or Miserie can make me, that insults / Upon unweapon'd Innocence' (4.4.59–61).

Similarly relying on sentiment, Cleora's solution adopts the extreme opposite to Timagoras' and Leosthenes'. After Pisander/Marullo's woes have been recounted to Cleora, she is viscerally moved to compassion and implores her father to treat him with mercy. Visiting the imprisoned Pisander/Marullo, who kneels before her, Cleora insists:

> *Cleora.* Rise. I am flesh and blod,
> And doe partake thy tortures.
> *Pisander.* Can it bee?
> That charity should perswade you to discend
> So farre from your owne height, as to vouchsafe
> To looke upon my sufferings? How I blesse
> My fetters now, and stand ingag'd to Fortune
> For my captiuity, no, my freedome rather!
> For who dares thinke that place a Prison, which
> You sanctifie with your presence? Or belieue,
> Sorrow has power to use her sting on him,
> That is in your compassion arm'd, and made
> Impregnable? (5.2.9–19)

Cleora's response to Pisander/Marullo's suffering is one of identification, where she too experiences his misery through her charity and compassion. As a result of her sympathy with the bondman, Cleora advocates for him with Archidamus, requesting that the seeming order of Archidamus' own household on his return 'moue you / To pitty poor *Marullo*' (5.1.14–15).

Rather than adopting Cleora's compassion in its entirety, however, Archidamus replies with a more politically oriented account of how the polity should be restored. According to Archidamus, ''Tis my purpose / To doe him [Marullo] all the good I can, *Cleora*; / But his offence being against the State, / Must have a publique triall' (5.1.15–17). Just as Archidamus upheld the rule of law against the summary execution intended by Timagoras and Leosthenes, he insists that Pisander/Marullo himself must be judged in public rather than excused in private. Nor does Archidamus put himself in charge of the proceedings. Instead, Timoleon, having successfully led the Syracusan army, also administers justice within the state. A stranger to the city, he is better situated to render an impartial judgement when the internal conflict of civil strife is concerned.

Although Archidamus initially pleads with Timoleon to give Marullo an 'aequall hearing' (5.3.10) despite his status as slave, this request comes to seem almost superfluous when Timoleon presents his conception of a just proceeding. Addressing the still disguised Marullo, Timoleon instructs: 'Nor be thou daunter (howsoe're thy fortune, / Has mark'd thee out a slaue) to speake thy merits; / For vertue though in rags may challenge more, / Then vice set off with all the trimme of greatnesse' (5.3.37–41). At this point, Pisander/Marullo himself acknowledges Timoleon's suitability for his position: 'I had rather fall under so iust a iudge, / Than be acquitted by a man corrupt / And partiall in his censure' (5.3.42–4). From the beginning of the proceeding, however, indications abound that the justice of Timoleon's judgement will not exclude clemency. When Timoleon explains the order of the trials, in which 'The right of this faire virgin first determin'd, / Your Bond-men shall be censur'd' (5.3.29–30), Cleon quickly adds, 'With all rigour, / We doe expect' (5.3.30–1), but his wife Corisca insists, 'Temper'd, I say, with mercie' (5.3.30). At the moment when Timoleon turns to judging the rebellious bondmen, he himself reiterates this conjunction, stating, 'And though you haue giu'n me power, I doe intreate / Such as haue undergone their insolence, / It may not be offensiue though I studie / Pitty more then reuenge'[45] (5.3.234–7). Timoleon's mode of judgement hence involves the equal public hearing of even seemingly unequal parties and the incorporation of clemency into the heart of judgement.

An alternative but similarly political solution is proposed by Pisander/Marullo upon the return of the Syracusan army to the city; this outcome is never implemented, but

[45] As this passage demonstrates, the text of *The Bondman* is not always precise in distinguishing between pity, on the one hand, and clemency, on the other. Despite the conflation of terminology, however, one can trace the distinctions between the concepts through attention to the contexts in which the particular words are used. In this instance, for example, the kind of pity Timoleon employs resembles clemency more than compassion.

could linger in the imagination of the audience as another mechanism for restoring civil order. Emphasizing freedom rather than simply a return to a reformed version of the earlier order, Pisander's solution invokes the possibility of a 'generall pardon' of the kind often provided by English kings on coronation and sometimes passed by Parliament subsequently during a reign.[46] Hence Pisander demands:

> A generall pardon, first, for all offences
> Committed in your absence. Libertie,
> To all such, as desire to make returne
> Into their countries; and to those that stay,
> A competence of land freely allotted
> To each mans proper use; no Lord acknowledg'd.
> Lastly, with your consent, to choose them wiues
> Out of your Families. (3.2.93–100)

According to this vision, the former bondmen would either be released from obligation to Syracusa or rendered citizens, endowed with the land and families that would make them equal with the existing members of the polity. The 'generall pardon' requested would cover both all participants in the rebellion and all of their actions during the designated period rather than specifically singling out certain individuals or deeds for forgiveness or censure. The significance of the concessions that this version of transitional justice would require, however, and the severity of the societal reordering that it would ensure is demonstrated by Archidamus' response. As Archidamus replies, '*Carthage*, though victorious, / Could not haue forc'd more from us' (3.2.100–1). The suggestion here is that civil strife could lead to an even more significant overturning of the structure of the polity than foreign conquest. The slave rebellion resulting from the mismanagement of domestic affairs might fundamentally alter the form of government to a greater degree than becoming part of the Carthaginian empire.

The first two suggested resolutions of the play—Leosthenes' and Cleora's—would both violate Stoic principles by involving an excess of emotional involvement, although Leosthenes emphasizes revenge and Cleora pity. The third and fourth potential endings—that advocated by Archidamus and the one suggested by Pisander/Marullo prior to the recapture of Syracusa—would both accord with Senecan Stoicism, but the fourth proves impracticable within the confines of the play's political reality. The outcome actually chosen integrates clemency into the state, representing the reconciliation

[46] As Cynthia Herrup explains in 'Negotiating Grace', which treats the relative dearth of parliamentary general pardons under James I and their complete absence under Charles I, the phrase 'general pardon' could designate either 'pardons of grace', which 'originated in a sovereign's "special grace", "certain knowledge" and "will"', or 'parliamentary pardons', or 'even any especially generous special pardon': Cynthia Herrup, 'Negotiating Grace', in *Politics, Religion and Popularity in Early Stuart Britain: Essays in Honour of Conrad Russell*, ed. Thomas Cogswell, Richard Cusk, and Peter Lake (Cambridge: Cambridge University Press, 2002): 127, n. 10, 124–42.

of mercy with the rule of law, a reconciliation that bears a substantial resemblance to the incorporation of equity within the early modern English state.

Conclusion

Taking its cue from Seneca's defence of monarchical rule in *De clementia*—a defence based not in a theory of the ideal state but in the inadequacy of the multitude's capacity to benefit from the political freedom of a republic—*The Bondman* thus focuses less on the form of government than on the mechanisms for maintaining peace and enhancing the general welfare. Suggesting the ills of both tyranny and the mob, Massinger's play stages the virtues of a particular kind of rule, one characterized by clemency and equity, as opposed to the regimes of either absolute mercy or cruelty. The alternative to this solution is presented not as another form of government but instead as the very undoing of the state through its descent into civil war. The centuries-long disagreement about the play's political meaning stems from misrecognition of the nature of its political intervention. Rather than siding with particular political figures of the time, or encouraging nascent republicanism, *The Bondman* suggests the mechanisms for avoiding civil conflict and the advantages of doing so.

Bibliography

Agamben, Giorgio. *Homo sacer*, trans. Daniel Heller-Roazen (Stanford: Stanford University Press, 1995).

Barbour, Reid. *English Epicures and Stoics* (Amherst: University of Massachusetts Press, 1998).

Calvin, John. *Commentary on Seneca's 'De clementia'*, ed. and trans. Ford Lewis Battles and André Malan Hugo (Leiden: Brill, 1969).

Coffee, Neil. *The Commerce of War: Exchange and Social Order in Latin Epic* (Chicago: University of Chicago Press, 2009).

Derrida, Jacques. *Perjury and Pardon*, vols 1 and 2, trans. David Wills (Chicago: University of Chicago Press, forthcoming 2016–2017).

Dowling, Melissa Barden. *Clemency and Cruelty in the Roman World* (Ann Arbor: University of Michigan Press, 2006).

Eden, Kathy. *Poetic and Legal Fiction in the Aristotelian Tradition* (Princeton: Princeton University Press, 1986).

Edwards, Philip. 'The Sources of Massinger's "The Bondman"', *The Review of English Studies*, 15.57 (February, 1964): 21–6.

Fulton, Thomas. '"The True and Naturall Constitution of That Mixed Government": Massinger's "The Bondman" and the Influence of Dutch Republicanism', *Studies in Philology*, 99.2 (Spring, 2002): 152–77.

Gardiner, Samuel Rawson. 'The Political Element in Massinger', *Contemporary Review*, 28 (1876): 495–507.

Gross, Allen. 'Contemporary Politics in Massinger', *Studies in English Literature, 1500–1900*, 6.2 (Spring, 1966): 279–90.

Herrup, Cynthia. 'Negotiating Grace', in *Politics, Religion and Popularity in Early Stuart Britain: Essays in Honour of Conrad Russell*, ed. Thomas Cogswell, Richard Cusk, and Peter Lake (Cambridge: Cambridge University Press, 2002), 124–42.

Konstan, David. 'Clemency as a Virtue', *Classical Philology*, 100 (2005): 337–46.

Limon, Jerzy. *Dangerous Matter: English Drama and Politics, 1623–1624* (Cambridge: Cambridge University Press, 1986).

Lipsius, Justus. *Annaei Senecae philosophi opera, quae exstant omnia, a Iusto Lipsio emendata, et scholiis illustrata* (Antwerp: 1605).

Lorenz, Philip. *The Tears of Sovereignty: Perspectives of Power in Renaissance Drama* (New York: Fordham University Press, 2013).

Norbrook, David. *Writing the English Republic: Poetry, Rhetoric and Politics, 1627–1660* (Cambridge: Cambridge University Press, 1999).

Papy, Jan. 'Erasmus's and Lipsius's Editions of Seneca: A "Complementary" Project', *Erasmus of Rotterdam Society Yearbook*, 22 (2002): 10–36.

Patterson, Annabel. *Censorship and Interpretation: The Conditions of Writing and Reading in Early Modern England* (Madison: University of Wisconsin Press, 1984).

Salmon, J. H. M. 'Stoicism and Roman Example: Seneca and Tacitus in Jacobean England', *Journal of the History of Ideas*, 50.2 (1989): 199–225.

Schiesaro, Alessandro. *The Passions in Play: 'Thyestes' and the Dynamics of Senecan Drama* (Cambridge: Cambridge University Press, 2007).

Segal, Charles. *Language and Desire in Seneca's 'Phaedra'* (Princeton: Princeton University Press, 1986).

Seneca, Luceus Annaeus. *Epistles 1–65*, trans. Richard Gummere (Cambridge, MA: Harvard University Press, 1917).

Seneca, Luceus Annaeus. *The Workes of Annaeus Seneca, both Moral and Natural*, trans. Thomas Lodge (London: 1614).

Spencer, Benjamin Townley. *The Bondsman* (Princeton: Princeton University Press, 1932).

Stacey, Peter. *Roman Monarchy and the Renaissance Prince* (Cambridge: Cambridge University Press, 2012).

Staley, Gregory. *Seneca and the Idea of Tragedy* (Oxford: Oxford University Press, 2009).

CHAPTER 30

BIRTHRIGHTS AND THE DUE COURSE OF LAW

PAUL D. HALLIDAY

Isaac intreated the LORD for his wife, because she *was* barren: and the LORD was intreated of him, and Rebekah his wife conceived ...

And the LORD said unto her, Two nations *are* in thy womb ...

And when her days to be delivered were fulfilled, behold, *there were* twins in her womb.

And the first came out red, all over like an hairy garment; and they called his name Esau.

And after that came his brother out, and his hand took hold on Esau's heel; and his name was called Jacob ...

And Isaac loved Esau, because he did eat of *his* venison: but Rebekah loved Jacob.

And Jacob sod pottage: and Esau came from the field, and he was faint:

And Esau said to Jacob, Feed me, I pray thee, with that same red *pottage*; for I *am* faint ...

And Jacob said, Sell me this day thy birthright.

And Esau said, Behold, I *am* at the point to die: and what profit shall this birthright do to me?

And Jacob said, Sware to me this day; and he sware unto him: and he sold his birthright unto Jacob.

Then Jacob gave Esau bread and pottage of lentils; and he did eat and drink ... thus Esau despised *his* birthright.

(Genesis 25:21–34)

Four centuries ago, lawyers, political prisoners, and polemicists were as likely as preachers to tell this, the original tale of twins in conflict. It recounts a 'paideic' moment, an '*imagined* instant of unified meaning' that germinates a legal culture. In it, we hear how law, in Robert Cover's words, is 'not merely a system of rules to be observed, but a world in which we live'.[1] The story of Esau and Jacob begat the world in which we live, a world sustained by rules. The prescriptive point of Esau's sale of his birthright, a point easily transposed from scripture into the early modern imagination, operated in three harmonized registers: divine, legal, and national. Those who encountered in church or court the story of the twins' struggle heard the opening strains of Israel's founding according to God's will. They imbibed a nation-defining legality that was at once bound and unbound by rules, by what contemporaries called the 'due course of law'.

What exactly was law's due course, and what did it mean that it was a birthright? How shall we understand changing norms concerned with whatever procedures people believed were due by law? Previous answers to these questions have tended to conceive events and ideas unfolding largely within law's institutions: lawyers and legislators defined those processes that would be due. Magna Carta, the Edwardian process statutes, and Marian reforms of pre-trial procedures figure prominently in such accounts.[2] By starting with the story of Esau and Jacob, I want to point to another conception of due process and tell a rather different story of its development, a story in which changes would ultimately arise from a critique of the work of lawyers and legislators.

Law followed many courses in the sixteenth and early seventeenth centuries. Common law's promoters in the decades around 1600 insisted that many should become one: that common law should rule all others. They did so in part by deploying the language of birthrights. They made a theological discourse into a legal one. As they did, law's due course gained more fully elaborated content in the form of better-articulated procedural rules. In the 1640s and 1650s, new critics of common law would then demand that law's properly singular course should be broadened. Invoking the idea of birthrights, they asserted that law's course should include a wider range of protections for the accused than most members of the judiciary would concede. Nonetheless, the language of birthrights provided a way to express lay longings for a righteous law. These longings, largely rebuffed in the seventeenth century, would transform the law practised in English courts during the eighteenth and nineteenth centuries. Something seemingly so mundane as judicial rules could be challenged and later changed because expectations about them had become infused with spiritual necessity—with God's will—and attached to transcendent claims about national belonging.

[1] Robert Cover, 'Nomos and Narrative', *HLR*, 97 (1983–1984): 5 and 15.

[2] On Magna Carta and the Edwardian statutes, see Faith Thompson, *Magna Carta: Its Role in the Making of the English Constitution, 1300–1629* (Minneapolis: University of Minnesota Press, 1948), 90–4. On the Marian reforms, see John H. Langbein, *Prosecuting Crime in the Renaissance: England, Germany, France* (Cambridge, MA: Harvard University Press, 1974), 5–77. For a broad account of Anglo-American legal development emphasizing factors internal to law, see John V. Orth, *Due Process of Law: A Brief History* (Lawrence: University Press of Kansas, 2003).

Such birthrights were not entailed on humans generally, but on a particular nation marked out by a peculiar relationship to God. Far from being the dry-as-dust business of a socially isolated lawyerly caste, procedures of a certain kind became the stuff of national identity and intense longing, especially when claims to enjoy such procedures because they were birthrights were sometimes rejected by law's mandarins. A particularly English liberty was known and knowable—it was only possible—by following what was claimed to be law's due course. The original story of birthright in Genesis explained how this was so. So we begin with birthrights, before turning to law's due course.

Birthright's Twin Character

Before 1600 or so, the language of birthright was used almost exclusively to explore that era's most important theological puzzle: whether God's saving grace operates entirely without reference to human action. Sermons and commentaries explored the tale of Esau and Jacob because it offered a way to ponder God's electing majesty. Read simply, their story seemed to articulate a rule for determining salvation, a rule by which birth indicates who will inherit the kingdom of heaven.[3] But those who read closely knew that the story was not so simple. The seemingly clear rule of inheritance could be broken: human actions might determine outcomes contrary to the rule, or God might determine in individual cases that the rule should be disregarded. Rule breaking demonstrated human folly and divine majesty at the same time. After all, as first-born, Esau was Isaac's heir. When he sold his birthright, he violated the rule: primogeniture. But he did so according to a prophecy that indicated to Rebekah, the twins' mother, God's long-term plan that two nations should arise from her womb.[4] God's will, against his own apparent rule, determined the matter after all.

One learned three conflicting lessons from Esau and Jacob. First, a birthright was entailed by one's birth in relation to others and was as unavoidable as birth itself. Despite an apparently bright-line rule of entailment on the first born, a birthright might be thrown away. Finally, either outcome might arise less according to a rule of decision than according to who would be the decider. God's choices, sometimes revealed through human actions, trumped any rule, even if such rules were of God's design. When Esau sold his birthright for a 'mess of pottage', as his early modern critics always put it, he re-enacted humanity's original folly, the one performed by Adam and Eve.[5] Like the Fall,

[3] Francis Kett speaks of 'birthright of the eternal kingdom' in *The Glorious and Beautifull Garland of Mans Glorification* … (London: 1585), sig. C2^{v}; John Hudson celebrated a 'birthright of heavenly glory' in *A Sermon Preached at Paules Crosse* (London: 1584), sig. G8.

[4] 'And the LORD said unto [Rebekah], Two nations *are* in thy womb, and two manner of people shall be separated from thy bowels; and *the one* people shall be stronger than *the other* people; and the elder shall serve the younger', Genesis 25:23. At least one preacher read this as part of God's design from the time of creation: Samuel Loveday, *The Hatred of Esau, and the Love of Jacob* (London: 1650), 34.

[5] Thomas Adams, *The Devills Banket Described in Foure Sermons* (London: 1614), 45. Edward Reynolds, *Three Treatises of the Vanity of the Creature* (London: 1631), 82.

the twins' struggle narrated the contrapuntal relationship between human choosing and rules meant to constrain choosing, a duality between God's rules and his miraculous intervention in human affairs contrary to those rules. But Esau did not simply choose to do what one otherwise might not do. He was tricked into it by his brother. At least that's how one might interpret Jacob's manipulation of Esau's hunger to convince him to trade away his birthright; and that is how one might read the blessing of the first-born son that Jacob gained by deception from his father.[6]

Rather than worry over Jacob's deception and God's part in it—after all, Jacob obediently performed the divine prophecy his mother had received—early modern exegetes concentrated on Esau's surrender to sensual impulses.[7] That Esau could squander his birthright underscored its preciousness. So we return to the apparent paradox that God's choosing, announced through prophecy, directed human choosing by which God's own rule was broken. One way to resolve this paradox was to see two kinds of birthright: to conceive Esau's as the birthright of nature while thinking of Jacob's as the birthright of saving grace, granted by God yet taken up by human choice.[8] Or one might describe Jacob's birthright as arising by adoption, just as Christ saved the sinner through a kind of spiritual adoption which produced a new birth. Though Esau arguably acted by God's will, early modern readers typically repeated St Paul's condemnation of him as a 'profane person'.[9] For all that God ordained an outcome contrary to the rule, commentators blamed Esau's choosing. They deployed the language of 'birthright' to condemn him for denying that which must not be denied.[10] And they focused on the grace Jacob received, which made it possible to gain the birthright through his own choices. By early modern readings, it did not seem a contradiction that out of human choosing an elect nation arose.

In Esau's sale of his birthright, we encounter a kind of theological formalism—salvation is determined by a rule—crosscut by the indeterminacy created by human

[6] Genesis 27:6–23. Some early modern commentators condemned Rebekah's preference for her younger son. John Newnham, *Newnams Nightcrowe* ... (London: 1590), 37. I have found no contemporary condemnation of Jacob's deceits. Jon D. Levenson, *The Death and Resurrection of the Beloved Son: The Transformation of Child Sacrifice in Judaism and Christianity* (New Haven: Yale University Press, 1993), 40–1 and 61–8.

[7] On Esau's stupidity and self-indulgence, see Anonymous, *A Newe Mery and Wittie Comedie ... upon the Historie of Jacob and Esau* (London: 1568); Edward Topsell, *The House-holder* (London: 1610), 30–1; Reynolds, *Three Treatises*, 35. For this stupidity, Esau 'righteously is deprived': Christopher Ness, *A Compleat History and Mystery of the Old and New Testament* (London: 1696), 225.

[8] 'Grace made Jacob lay about to purchase, what Nature denied him: It was inevitable; the God of Nature determin'd it that way.' Henry Hibbert, *Syntagma theologicum* ... (London: 1662), second pagination (*Exercitationes theologicae*), 94.

[9] Hebrews 12:16. Ness, *A Compleat History*, 225. Amandus Polanus von Polansdorf, *A Treatise of Amandus Polandus, Concerning Gods Eternall Predestination* (Cambridge, 1599), 141–3 and 150. Gerard Winstanley went further, and called Esau 'the beast': Gerard Winstanley, *The New Law of Righteousnes Budding Forth* (London: 1649), 99.

[10] Adams, *The Devills Banket*, 101. John Rogers, *A Discourse of Christian Watchfulnesse* (London: 1620), 280, 339, and 359–60. Ness, *A Compleat History*, 225.

choices and by God's capacity to direct action contrary to the same rule.[11] Little wonder that this story served in the seventeenth century as a parable about legal formalism and its limits. In it, primogeniture appears at first as no mere 'rule of thumb'. Rather, it seems a 'mandatory rule'. Mandatory rules, as Frederick Schauer puts it, 'furnish reasons for action simply by virtue of their existence *qua* rules'.[12] In Genesis, primogeniture's status both as mandatory rule and as normative good arises from the fact that it is God's rule. But like most rules, agents who are meant to obey the rule might evade it. The mandatory rule is but a rule of thumb, at least in God's hands, and even in human hands—at least in those human hands guided by divine ones.

The complex interaction between human and divine choosing at the heart of this story and the problem of rule following that it highlights reveals that there is much more to birthright than inheritance. Birthright is a legal principle infused with divine authority. It manifests all the slipperiness of persistent voluntarism in a world reigned over by a magisterial, predestinating God. Given this, the language of birthright, once transposed into legal discourse, radiated outward in multiple directions. Birthright served as a metaphor for one concept—rule obedience—and for its inverse; it demonstrated the interplay between determinacy and indeterminacy inherent in all legal rules; and it declared the longing that rules should nonetheless be found that were determinate and productive of justice, however elusive they might be.[13]

Why all this fussing over birthrights and salvific theology? Because around the turn into the seventeenth century, 'birthrights' began to migrate from theological into legal analysis, where they imparted the same longing for assuredness in the work of rules that the word's use in debates about the nature of salvation conveyed. It was then that Sir Edward Coke began to refer to the laws of England not just as an 'inheritance'. That was an old trope. Rather, it was a 'birth-right'.[14] In Commons debates in 1621, Coke quoted himself to the same effect: 'the law of England [is] the subject's best birthright, because

[11] The literature on formalism versus realism, and the determinacy of rules versus indeterminacy, is vast. A good point of entry is Frederick Schauer, 'Legal Realism Untamed', *Texas Law Review*, 91 (2013): 749–80.

[12] Frederick Schauer, *Playing by the Rules: A Philosophical Examination of Rule-Based Decision-Making in Law and in Life* (Oxford: Oxford University Press, 1991), 5.

[13] For one way to get beyond the debate about rules between formalists and realists, see Steven L. Winter, *A Clearing in the Forest: Law, Life, and Mind* (Chicago: University of Chicago Press, 2001), ch. 8. As Winter puts it, law and its rules, as a product of 'imaginative rationality', 'is indeterminate in more-or-less predictable ways'; ibid., 7.

[14] Cawdrey's Case (1591) 5 Co. Rep. 40b–41a, 77 ER 46–7. In the Case of Premunire, common law was that 'whereunto by birthright [the subject] is inheritable' and 'his birthright'. 12 Co. Rep. 38 and 40, 77 ER 1320–1. For the less charged language of inheritance, see Williams J., 'le common ley est le pluis sure inheritance q. le roy ad'. Fuller's Case (1607), Harvard Law School, MS 1058, fol. 61; and James Morice, who referred to 'the common law and custom of the realm, which is the rightful inheritance of the subject'. British Library, MS Egerton 3376, fol. 19^{v}. See also *The Argument of Master Nicholas Fuller* … ([London?]: 1607), 3 and 15, referring to English law as a 'high inheritance'.

[it] defendeth all he hath'.[15] Charles I would use similar language in his 1642 *Answer to the XIX Propositions*, thus suggesting how the idea of birthright was highly portable across the full range of legal-political positions and needs.[16]

In his first volume of the *Institutes*, Coke declared common law to be 'the best and most common birth-right that the subject hath for the safeguard and defence not only of goods, lands, and revenues, but of his wife and children, his body, fame, and life also'. He continued: 'in truth, justice is the daughter of the law; for the law bringeth her forth.'[17] Coke mixed defensive and procreative metaphors together in procedure. In his meditation on allegiance in his report of *Calvin's Case*, Coke likewise made law's protective function a 'birth-right'. Subject and king, he explained, are knotted together in a reciprocal exchange, a mutual allegiance established by natural law, 'which indeed is the eternal Law of the Creator, infused into the heart of the creature at the time of his creation'.[18] The subject gave obedience, 'due by nature and birth-right'; the king gave protection, 'as well in time of peace by justice, as in time of war by the sword'.[19] By Coke's account, the king functioned here both as a natural body and as a politic one: in effect, as a synecdoche of law itself. Far from being just dull matter for lawyers to debate, the protections offered by legal procedure were a transcendent good, arising from natural law by God's will expressed in creation. Procedural birthright—law's 'safeguards'—saved English lives and goods as surely as a divine birthright saved the souls of justified Christians.

As the language of birthrights took a legal turn, it drove a demand for ever-greater specificity about the procedures birthrights entailed. Broad statements that the 'right execution of their laws' was 'the undoubted birth-right of every Englishman' increasingly required elaboration as particular courtroom practices.[20] These might include procedures at civil law or in courts of equity as well as by common law.[21] At common law, the freedom of plaintiffs to choose a form of action, to use process by wager of law, or to employ the prerogative writs were among the many procedures figured as 'birthrights'.[22] But it was in criminal proceedings—including arrest and arraignment as well as the conduct of trials—that the demand for procedural birthrights was pressed most

15 *Journal of the House of Commons* (London: HMSO, 1802), 1.665. In the same debates, Recorder of London Heneage Finch noted the novelty of conceiving law as an 'inheritance', which he took to be more narrow than a conception of English law as 'rights and liberties'; ibid., 666.

16 Charles I, *His Majesties Answer to the XIX Propositions* (London: 1642), 2.

17 Edward Coke, *The First Part of the Institutes of the Lawes of England* (London: 1628), vol. 1, lib. 2, cap.12, sect. 213.

18 Calvin's Case (1608), 7 Co. Rep. 13a, 77 ER 392.

19 Calvin's Case (1608), 7 Co. Rep. 7a and 9b, 77 ER 385 and 388.

20 Roger Twysden, *The Commoners Liberty: or, The English-mans Birth-right* ([London?]: 1648), 1.

21 And thus the law of admiralty or probate are 'as any law in *England* ... radically vested in the people as their birth-right': Charles Cock, *Englands Compleat Law-Judge, and Lawyer* (London: 1655), 4 and 13.

22 For 'election of action' as a birthright, see *Watson v. Norbury* (1645) Style 4, 82 ER 485. For wager of law, see John Dodderidge, in Slade's Case (1602) 4 Co. Rep. 93a, 76 ER 1074. On the prerogative writs, see Edward Hyde's Commons speech in 1641, in Maija Jansson, ed., *Proceedings in the Opening Session of the Long Parliament* (Rochester, 2000), 4.103.

insistently. It was here that the electric language of birthrights began to flow more clearly along 'the due course of law'.

The Due Course of Law

What does it mean to say that law has a 'due course'? We begin with the idea of dueness, for which we must return to the Bible: for instance, to Psalms, where Israelites routinely reminded themselves of what they owed according to their covenant with God. 'Give unto the Lord the glory *due unto* his name: bring an offering, and come into his courts' (Psalm 96:8). Dueness, like birthright, indicated that which must be done, even if one might choose in error to avoid its mandates. Just as God was due his glory, so too were the English, an elect nation, due the procedures by which no law officer could take away their liberties without legal cause shown.

Delineating a 'course' underscored 'dueness'. Courses are bounded paths: for instance, those along which water or time flows in one direction. To speak of a course's dueness invoked the irresistibility of nature's operation according to laws pronounced by God in the creation.[23] '[T]he work of nature is the work of the intelligence not erring, and by the ordinance whereof, all things have a due course.'[24]

'Due course' also commonly referred to specific functions in the natural world. Blood and the body's humours follow courses.[25] Heavenly bodies do, too.

> Every creature keepeth a due course and order: the sun like a ramping lion, runneth about the world with a swift revolution: the moon knoweth her sitting down and rising up; the *Pleiades* keep their stations: the stars go their circuit: the earth, the sea, and every creature keep their time.[26]

Like most metaphors, the language of 'due course' obtained its explanatory force from its physicality. By describing law using the same language used to describe the coursing of blood through veins or the apparent fixity of a riverbed, one insisted that people streaming through legal institutions should likewise run along unavoidable courses. People knew what their birthrights were, and thus what law was, because they knew the courses of blood, rivers, or stars.[27]

[23] On nature's 'unavoidable course', see W. R., *Organon salutis: An Instrument to Cleanse the Stomach* (London: 1657), 56.

[24] Pierre de La Primaudaye, *The Third Volume of the French Academie* (London: 1601), 46.

[25] This is especially evident in discussions of women's monthly 'courses'. Nicholas Gyer, *The English Phlebotomy* (London: 1592), 105. Jacques Ferrand, *Erotomania* (Oxford, 1640), 77–8. Rembert Dodoens, *A Niewe Herball* (London: 1578), 75, 85, and passim.

[26] Henry Crosse, *Vertues Common-wealth: Or The High-way to Honour* (London: 1603), sig. V1.

[27] On metaphors and embodiment in legal decision-making, see Winter, *Clearing*, especially chaps. 2 and 3.

When one of the criminals hanged beside Jesus explained to the other that, 'we receive the due reward of our deeds' (Luke 23:41), he offered a commentary on the dueness of law's courses quite like the dueness that shows God's providential hand in nature's operation. But how did he or any accused criminal know his reward was due? What procedures established law's course and thus a judicial result's dueness? More important, how did law's due course come to be understood as one's birthright, entailed by divine demands? As Clement Walker put it while languishing in the Tower for two years without trial on treason charges, 'the benefit of the laws and the ordinary course of justice are the subject's birthright'.[28] How was this birthright to direct the way one's body should move through a singular, unavoidable course of law? The answer lies in procedural developments of the sixteenth and seventeenth centuries, by which many courses became one.

From Law's Many Courses, One?

In the late sixteenth century, the standard language of the warrant for a person's arrest and detention began to change. We can explain when and how this occurred. If we can look to Coke for the impetus behind law's adoption of the language by which due process became attached to the spiritually rich language of birthrights, it is to his near contemporary, William Lambarde, that we can ascribe the means by which increased specificity was given to dueness as expressed in arrest warrants. Nowhere was law's due course and its status as a birthright more important than in the use of imprisonment: 'the putting of a person from his own liberty, into the custody of the law', as Lambarde put it.[29] Dueness and liberty interests—protected by the birthright that is English law and its procedures—were directly linked.

In *Eirenarcha*, his guidebook for Justices of the Peace, Lambarde included templates for warrants to be used in arrests on different charges. Eleven editions of *Eirenarcha* were published between the first in 1582 and the 1618 appearance of Michael Dalton's even more popular *Countrey Justice*, which largely copied Lambarde's language for making legal arrests and transmitted it to later generations.[30] Though it was not entirely new, Lambarde's addition to the language of warrants for arrest or detention—that one should be imprisoned until 'delivered by due order of her majesty's laws'—quickly became the norm when committing those detained for trial on common law crimes.[31]

[28] Clement Walker, *The High Court of Justice* (London: 1651), 64.

[29] William Lambarde, *Eirenarcha: Or of the Office of the Justices of Peace* (London: 1592), 222. The first edition appeared in January 1582 (new style), which explains why the title page of the first edition says 1581 (old style).

[30] Michael Dalton, *The Countrey Justice* (London: 1618).

[31] Lambarde, *Eirenarcha* (1592), 214.

JPs around England followed *Eirenarcha*'s templates or made a close facsimile of them in the warrants they issued.[32] Previously, detention orders had been highly varied and often omitted any reference to further process by which a prisoner should be evaluated for release. Logically, one might be detained forever by a warrant whose language gave no indication of further procedures by which the detainee might be tried or released. In the 1580s and 1590s, warrants became more full of words expressing expectations about further process that would be due to people held on allegations of all kinds.[33] Those words increasingly adopted the metaphor of law's course and its dueness. When John Pepper and two companions were gaoled by Surrey justices in 1590 for highway robbery, they were ordered held 'till such time as by course of law they shall receive their due trial'.[34] Soon, the most common form of warrants stated that one should be held 'until delivered by due course of the law'. In other words, the proper form of arrest was increasingly taken to be one that made explicit the accused's access to procedures of particular kinds by which he or she would be evaluated for release or tried on the stated charge.

This reference to law's due course was increasingly enforced by judicial review of gaol orders. In the decades to each side of 1600, orders made without mention of further process by which one might be released were increasingly ruled void, though not always. Development of an expectation that all warrants must contain restrictive language requiring obedience to law's due course was fitful, especially as English laws continued to take many institutional forms following many different courses.[35] The Ecclesiastical High Commission continued to imprison 'until we shall take order for their enlargement', without reference to a course by which any other court might inspect and possibly reverse such orders. In 1615, King's Bench, led by Sir Edward Coke, remanded a High Commission prisoner detained on a warrant that stated only that he should be held until released, without mentioning any process by which he might seek release, and despite the fact that his barrister complained that one should only be held until 'delivered by law'. [36] Similarly, the chancellor might order one to prison with no other explanation than that it was ordered 'for certain matters concerning the King', or that a person

[32] Thus the warrant for John Smyth's 1598 arrest by a Middlesex JP for sheep stealing was lifted in its entirety from Lambarde: TNA, KB145/13/40, teste 29 May 1598; and KB29/235, m. 95d.

[33] Returns to habeas corpus provide an extensive sample of warrants, thus providing a good base from which to watch a practice like this change: Paul D. Halliday, *Habeas corpus: From England to Empire* (Cambridge, MA: Harvard University Press, 2010), 102 and 149–50.

[34] TNA, KB145/13/32, 30 June 1590; and KB29/226, m. 117.

[35] As late as 1675, King's Bench might declare a warrant valid, even if it omitted the words that one was committed until 'delivered by due course of law'. *Rex v. Sedan* (1675) 3 Keble 531, 84 ER 862. Despite dicta that such language was not an absolute requirement, Robert Sedden was bailed on his writ of habeas corpus: TNA, KB145/17/27, teste 23 October 1675; KB21/18, fols 101^{v}–103.

[36] *Rex v Dighton et al.* (1615), 1 Rolle 220, 81 ER 445–6. Burrows and Cox (1615) BL MS Rawlinson C382, fol. 63^{v}. TNA, KB145/14/13, writ for Thomas Dighton and John Holt, and another for John Burrows and William Cox, both teste 10 June 1615. KB21/5a, fols 20^{v}–28^{v}. For an important new reading of Coke's 'moderate' approach to the High Commission, see David Chan Smith, *Sir Edward Coke and the Reformation of the Laws: Religion, Politics, and Jurisprudence, 1578–1616* (Cambridge: Cambridge University Press, 2014), chap. 6.

should be held 'until the Lord Chancellor delivered him', without reference to any further course of law. When lawyers began to object to such usage in 1609, the justices of King's Bench noted, 'it was the first time that such exceptions had been taken'.[37] It would not be the last.

Most controversial of such commands to detain without any explanation given—and thus without imposing any necessity to follow law's due course—were those by the king-in-council. Until at least 1621, Coke would say that those gaoled by privy council order could not be bailed, even if the council stated no cause and made no reference to further course of the law in its warrant.[38] Coke accepted that law had multiple courses. But in 1627–1628, during the controversy over the Five Knights' Case and the Petition of Right's clause forbidding imprisonment except 'with the cause expressed', Coke and so many others put a new stress on a single course of law, and began to insist that king and council were now covered by its requirements.[39]

In 1628, Parliament attempted to define one course of law and to impose it on even the highest jurisdictions. But just as Parliament tried to force even the king and council to follow law's due course, Parliament's statutes would do more than anything else to limit law's course and the birthrights with which it was associated. Looked at another way, Parliament would permit multiple courses of law to persist, courses Parliament insisted it alone could define. Strictly speaking, to gaol someone on a warrant declaring that he or she should be imprisoned 'until delivered by due course of law' was incorrect when that person was held according to statutory terms: for instance, by any of the many acts defining misdemeanours ranging from bastard bearing to illegal alehouse keeping.[40] Such statutes gave lowly Justices of the Peace wide discretion to detain without other judicial supervision—without further course of law—even after the council apparently lost its authority to imprison without cause expressed in 1628. Thus law had a due course by common law, and different statutory courses. The tension between these courses would be one of the great problems for asserters of legal birthrights from the seventeenth century, through the eighteenth, and beyond.

In thousands of surviving warrants from justices all over England we find signs of a halting commitment to a single 'due course' from the 1580s onward. In the pages of *Eirenarcha*, we find the means of the dissemination of that commitment in workaday legal practices. In the language of birthrights, increasingly attached to claims about what constituted law's due course, we find what this meant for law. But even as law was increasingly conceived after 1628 as having one course, it continued to operate by many. The longing for one course—for one rule—remained in conflict with the many courses of a plural legal world. We can see this better as we turn from conceptions about the due

[37] Addis's Case (1609) Cro. Jac. 219, 79 ER 191. I have found no signs of a result in this case in King's Bench records.

[38] Wallace Notestein et al., eds, *Commons Debates, 1621* (New Haven: Yale University Press, 1935), 4.308.

[39] Halliday, *Habeas corpus*, 137–9 and 222–3.

[40] Bracy's Case (1696) BL MS Hargraves 411, fol. 21; 1 Salkeld 348, 91 ER 305.

course one must follow in detention orders to contests over the procedural birthrights owed to those facing trial.

Procedural Birthrights: Jury Trial and Beyond

In 1612, Sir Edward Coke declared that, 'matter of fact shall be tried by verdict of twelve men'. If not, one would be 'deprived of his birth-right'.[41] Judges, barristers, and commentators agreed: a jury provided the only means for judging facts. The propriety of jury fact-finding was neither novel nor contentious. But conceived as a birthright, expectations about jury trial would be pressed outward in the 1640s and 1650s to become demands for other procedures that law's critics claimed were also theirs by birthright. They contended for one due course of law, one that was wider and better directed toward the achievement of just outcomes.

Jury trial had a social as well as a legal value. It was, as Sir Roger Twysden put it, the 'impartial way of distributing equal justice to all men, in receiving which certain it is reasonable the highest duke should be level with the lowest beggar'.[42] Christopher Love, on trial in 1651 as a royalist plotter, insisted it was his 'birth-right to be tried according to the laws of this land ... by a jury of my neighbourhood'.[43] A petition from Londoners concerned for John Lilburne likewise demanded that, 'no freeman of *England* should be adjudged of life, limb, liberty, or estate but by juries'.[44]

Lilburne, more than anyone, promoted the jury trial as 'the birth-right of the subject'.[45] '[T]he severity and strictness of the law [was] all the mercy and pity' Lilburne said he wanted. That law was his and all of England's 'common birthright and inheritance ... unto which the meanest man in *England* is as much entitled and entailed unto, as the greatest subject'. Its loss, he told his readers, would be 'adjudged a profaneness like Esau's'.[46] Here, in condemnations of those who threatened to sell England's birthright in

[41] Sedgwick's Case (1612) Godbolt 201–2, 78 ER 122.

[42] Twysden, *Commoners Liberty*, 4. Like others, Twysden followed Coke, quoting the second volume of the *Institutes* on his title page.

[43] Christopher Love, *A Cleare and Necessary Vindication* (London: 1651), 39.

[44] *To the Supreame Authority of the Parliament of the Common-wealth of England, the Humble Petition of Many Well Affected People ...* (London: 1652).

[45] Here he quoted Coke. John Lilburne, *The Peoples Prerogative and Priviledges* (London: 1648), 50. Lilburne often asserted that, 'presentment or trial by jury' was 'the ancient birth-right of the subject'. Lilburne also condemned process by information: in other words, proceeding to criminal trial without indictment or presentment by a grand jury. *Lieu. Col. John Lilburn's Plea in Law ...* ([London?]: 1653), 8. Idem, *Certaine Observations upon the Tryall of Leiut. Col. John Lilburne* ([London?]: 1649), 9.

[46] John Lilburne, *The Oppressed Mans Importunate and Mournfull Cryes to be Brought to the Barre of Justice* ([London?]: 1648), 1. Lilburne routinely compared his political-legal foes to Esau in their sale of the nation's birthright. *An Impeachment of High Treason Against Oliver Cromwel* (London: 1649), 4; *As You Were, or, The Lord General Cromwel and the Grand Officers of the Armie* ([Amsterdam?]: 1652), 8.

the wake of the execution of Charles I, legal and political argument aligned with divine and national argument. Law's due course undergirded new political rights Lilburne and other Levellers ascribed to all Englishmen.[47] Chief among these rights was trial by jury.

As Lilburne fought repeated bouts in court, he and his Leveller peers generated a lengthening list of rights claims that constituted a robust legal vernacular that would ultimately impinge on the practice of law. Lilburne received his legal schooling during long spells in the Tower. There, prominent royalist lawyers such as David Jenkins and Sir John Maynard helped to give legal substance to Lilburne's critique of an arbitrary Parliament or protector. Imprisonment gave him time to read, especially Coke's *Institutes*. From Coke, Lilburne came to see the jury as a peculiarly English virtue, one that connected the finding of truth to the expression of a national distinctiveness exemplified by broad participation in civic life through this uniquely English form of service. Even Attorney General Edmond Prideaux, who prosecuted him in 1649, had to admit that jury trial was Lilburne's 'birth-right and every man's else'.[48]

In the frontispiece image in the pamphlet account of his 1649 treason trial, Lilburne stands at the bar, the *Institutes* in his hand. A medallion printed there shows his head in profile, surrounded by the names of his jurors. He had been saved, it read, 'by the power of the lord and the integrity of his jury'.[49] The frontispiece went further, to proclaim that jurors were to act as 'judge[s] of law as well as fact'. As a birthright, Lilburne turned the jury from triers of fact into judges; jurors became the means for manifesting the will of the same God who was the author of birthrights.

While Lilburne focused on jury trials, he and others elaborated the markers of law's due course. Some were old. Lilburne was clear about the need to follow law's 'due course' in his insistence that any warrant have a 'lawful conclusion' stating a cause of imprisonment and the procedural means by which one might be reviewed for release.[50] This was a predictable echo of Lambarde's instructions concerning lawful arrest.

More novel was a birthright claim to legal counsel.[51] Lilburne's Leveller compatriot, William Walwyn, went further when he asserted a list of his procedural rights by recounting the procedural wrongs he had suffered. Walwyn had been arrested by soldiers acting on a warrant 'expressing no fact that was a crime by any law'. He had not been taken before a Justice of the Peace as a prelude to trial 'by the ordinary courts of

[47] Rachel Foxley, *The Levellers: Radical Political Thought in the English Revolution* (Manchester: Manchester University Press, 2013), chap. 3.

[48] *The Triall of Lieut. Collonel John Lilburne … Octob. 1649* (London: 1649), 17.

[49] Names of his jurors were listed in the medallion-shaped image on the frontispiece of Lilburne, *Triall*. For his claim that jurors were judges of law, see also ibid., 121. This marked the first time Lilburne made such a dramatic claim. Thomas Green, *Verdict According to Conscience: Perspectives on the English Criminal Trial Jury, 1200–1800* (Chicago: University of Chicago Press, 1985), chap. 5, especially 168–77. As Green notes, Lilburne's claim was based not on previously accepted English law, but on his 'birthright', ibid., 177.

[50] John Lilburne, *The Lawes Funerall* ([London?]: 1648), 8.

[51] Lilburne, *Triall*, 28 and 51. Intriguingly, he would claim elsewhere that serving as his own counsel was equally his 'natural right': *Lawes Funerall*, 3.

justice'. Nor was any accuser brought 'openly, face to face, to make oath of fact against me'. Instead, he had been 'required to answer to a question against myself'—risking self-incrimination—then ordered held 'during pleasure'. This violated the idea that proceeding according to the due course of the law, as Lambarde had argued two generations earlier, was the only basis on which one might be legally imprisoned. All these practices, Walwyn concluded, were wrongs against his 'birthright'.[52]

Walwyn, often understood as a critic of common law, thus joined Lilburne and other Levellers in ultimately relying on common law, though they did so by demanding an expansion of the procedural content of that law in the form of new protections for the accused.[53] Henry Vane likewise elaborated his procedural birthrights, insisting that law's due course required that he receive a copy of any indictment against him and that he have counsel to help him prepare his defence, procedures that would not become standard for another century or more.[54] 'Without this, law is denied me, which is my birthright and inheritance'.[55]

Birthrights and the Widening of Law's Due Course

Vane, Lilburne, Walwyn, and others insisted that law had only one due course; at the same time, they insisted that its course could and should be widened. They did not depict this as the introduction of new practices. They saw it instead as the recognition of God's design for a chosen nation's law. A language of birthrights premised on their divine origins gave critics a powerful rhetorical position from which to correct law's managers—judges and members of Parliament—who seemed too ready to sell England's birthrights for the same 'mess of pottage' that Esau had taken in payment for his own birthright. Such critics required that law remain untouched by profane hands: by the hands of those who 'make merchandise of justice', and keep 'people in ignorance'.[56]

Lilburne badgered the judges who presided over his trials about what he declared they owed him. He made ominous predictions about what would be their due from a providential God if they denied him his own due: 'many times, even on earth, [God]

[52] William Walwyn, *The Fountain of Slaunder Discovered* (London: 1649), 14. Lilburne, too, claimed the right to face his accuser, a right he, like Coke, derived from Scripture: Acts 25:16: John Lilburne, *Englands Birth-right Justified* (London: 1645), 7.

[53] Foxley, *Levellers*, 102–6. Admittedly, Walwyn criticized those who believed Magna Carta and other 'grants of conquerors' were 'birth-rights', and instead said they were only a 'mess of pottage'. William Walwyn, *England's Lamentable Slaverie* ([London?]: 1645), 4–5.

[54] John H. Langbein, *The Origins of Adversary Criminal Trial* (Oxford: Oxford University Press, 2003), 4 and chs. 3 and 5.

[55] Henry Vane, *The Tryal of Sir Henry Vane, Kt. at the King's Bench* ([London?]: 1662), 56.

[56] James Freize, *Every Mans Right: Or, Englands Perspective-glasse* (London: 1646), 7.

punisheth judges with the law of like for like'.[57] This was lousy as a litigation tactic; his judges were not amused. But it was superb as part of a long-term strategy to transform law. By deploying the theologically rich idea of birthrights they imbibed from Genesis, Lilburne and others produced a forceful vernacular demand about law's due course that would press on the work of English courts in the centuries following.

Others attacked Parliament for the same reasons and with the same language Lilburne and his compatriots used against judges. Elizabeth Lilburne, John's wife, condemned Parliament's subversion of 'the laws, liberties, and freedoms of the people, which freedoms &c. you yourselves call the COMMON BIRTHRIGHT OF ENGLISH-MEN, who are born equally free'.[58] Mary Overton likewise reminded Parliament in 1647 that, 'the meanest of the commonalty might enjoy their rights, liberty, and benefits of the law'.[59] Some of England's most prominent lawyers took a similar line against parliamentary sovereignty just as it was coming into being. Sir John Maynard, after being impeached for his defence of Lilburne, condemned the Commons for invading 'every Englishman's birthright' by its proceedings against alleged enemies of the state.[60]

When people like these criticized MPs or judges, they did so not to attack law, but to attack those they believed undermined law by their failure to follow what they asserted was its due course. Whether targeting judges or legislators, Lilburne and his peers in the 1640s and 1650s took full advantage of the scriptural force of the language of birthrights. By tying their own stories to Esau and Jacob's, people of all kinds invoked a paideic moment from which they derived not only what law's due course *was*, but what it *ought* to be.[61] They created a persistent rhetorical tradition that would impose on law in the generations ahead. Like Lilburne, Quaker Thomas Rudyard two decades later condemned the judges who made him and his co-religionists 'slaves to their injustice and most tyrannical will and pleasure', against their birthrights.[62] Granville Sharp, the abolitionist and anti-impressment campaigner of the eighteenth century, would use the language of birthrights to decry the suspension of law and to promote annual elections, even as lawyers and MPs consistently dismissed such notions. The political reformer Sir Francis Burdett in 1804 would challenge his listeners on the hustings not 'to barter your birthright for a mess of pottage'.[63] Another reformer would complain a few years later that if the laws of England might be taken away by corrupt elections, 'what sort of a *Birthright* is it? Esau sold his birthright for a mess of pottage; but we have not sold our birthright to boroughmongers'.[64] More remarkable, an English birthright came in

[57] John Lilburne, *The Prisoners Mournfull Cry, Against the Judges of the Kings Bench* ([London?]: 1648), 3; *Lawes Funerall*, 5 and 23–5.

[58] Elizabeth Lilburne, *To the Chosen and Betrusted Knights, Citizens, and Burgesses …* (London: 1646).

[59] Mary Overton, *To the Right Honourable, the Knights, Citizens, and Burgesses …* (London: 1647), 2.

[60] John Maynard, *A Speech Spoken in the Honourable House of Commons* (London: 1648), 3.

[61] Cover, 'Nomos and Narrative', 10.

[62] Thomas Rudyard, *The Second Part of the Peoples Antient and Just Liberties Asserted* ([London?]: 1670), 21. Green, *Verdict*, 230–6. Craig W. Horle, *The Quakers and the English Legal System, 1660–1688* (Philadelphia: University of Pennsylvania Press, 1988), 168–9.

[63] *A Full Report of the Speeches of Sir Francis Burdett at the Late Election* (London: 1804), 3.

[64] *Cobbett's Political Register* 33, number 13 (4 April 1818), 381.

the nineteenth century to be understood by some as 'universal freedom': as a human, and not simply a national, birthright.[65] As early as 1649, The Digger William Everard had likewise declared 'universal Liberty and Freedom' as a 'Birthright, which our Maker gave us'.[66]

People like these asserted a claim to non-derogable rights: fundamental human entitlements and procedural protections that no judge might deny and no legislator might modify or destroy.[67] They did so by depending on the idea of divine derivation of their birthrights, even if human judges might be so frail and misguided as to deny them from time to time. Thus the rule that no one should be imprisoned without an express, legal cause was 'by the law of God', according to Sir Edward Coke.[68] Such a divinely ordained formalism would protect the English from foibles of the kind to which Esau had succumbed. Where formal rules could not do so, God might correct errant human judges, because he was 'absolute sovereign Lord and King, of all things in heaven and earth, the original fountain and cause of all causes, who is circumscribed, governed, and limited by no rules'.[69] Whether by rule or against it, God's will, in the form of birthrights, must be given its due.

Few were ready to think in the early nineteenth century about 'universal freedoms' arising from bare humanness; fewer still could do so in the days of Everard, or Coke before him. But many nonetheless imagined new procedural rights long before law's institutions accommodated them. As they did, they simultaneously declared their disgust with rules as currently used and expressed a longing for new rules rightly conceived. Rights to defence counsel, that an accuser might be challenged under oath, that defence witnesses might testify under oath, that an accused should enjoy a privilege against self incrimination, and that one's incarceration might be reviewable by a neutral judge: these were the kinds of procedural rights for which those who used the language of birthrights longed. Most would not be realized until the eighteenth or nineteenth centuries.[70] Some remain to be realized. When religious dissenters and accused traitors of the seventeenth century or abolitionists of the eighteenth told lawyers what law should be, they tended to win few immediate converts. But a story so rich as that of Esau and Jacob gave them the means by which they could imagine a world in which they and we might come to live.

Bibliography

Coke, Sir Edward. *The First Part of the Institutes of the Lawes of England* (London: 1628).
Cover, Robert. '*Nomos* and Narrative', *Harvard Law Review*, 97 (1983–1984): 4–68.

65 *An Authentic Narrative of the Events of the Westminster Election* (London: 1819), 272.

66 William Everard, *The True Levellers Standard Advanced* (London: 1649), 11.

67 Alexander Hamilton would much later write of 'vested rights' that no legislature could revoke. Ryan C. Williams, 'The One and Only Substantive Due Process Clause', *Yale Law Journal*, 120 (2010): 423–5.

68 Here, Coke expanded on Acts 25:27. Codd's Case (1615) 3 Bulstr. 109, 81 ER 94.

69 John Lilburne, *The Free-mans Freedome Vindicated* ..., 11.

70 Langbein, *Adversary Criminal Trial*, 51–6, 93–7, and 277–84.

Dalton, Michael. *The Countrey Justice* (London: 1618).
Everard, William. *The True Levellers Standard Advanced* (London: 1649).
Foxley, Rachel. *The Levellers: Radical Political Thought in the English Revolution* (Manchester: Manchester University Press, 2013).
Fuller, Nicholas. *The Argument of Master Nicholas Fuller* ([London]: 1607).
Green, Thomas. *Verdict according to Conscience: Perspectives on the English Criminal Trial Jury, 1200–1800* (Chicago: University of Chicago Press, 1985).
Halliday, Paul D. *Habeas corpus: From England to Empire* (Cambridge, MA: Harvard University Press, 2010).
Lambarde, William. *Eirenarcha: Or of the Office of the Justices of Peace* (London: 1592).
Langbein, John H. *Prosecuting Crime in the Renaissance: England, Germany, France* (Cambridge, MA: Harvard University Press, 1974).
Langbein, John H. *The Origins of Adversary Criminal Trial* (Oxford: Oxford University Press, 2003).
Levenson, Jon D. *The Death and Resurrection of the Beloved Son: The Transformation of Child Sacrifice in Judaism and Christianity* (New Haven: Yale University Press, 1993).
Lilburne, John. *Englands Birth-right Justified* (London: 1645).
Lilburne, Elizabeth. *To the Chosen and Betrusted Knights, Citizens, and Burgesses* (London: 1646).
Lilburne, John. *The Oppressed Mans Importunate and Mournfull Cryes to be Brought to the Barre of Justice* ([London]: 1648).
Lilburne, John. *The Peoples Prerogative and Priviledges* (London: 1648).
Lilburne, John. *The Prisoners Mournfull Cry, against the Judges of the Kings Bench* ([London]: 1648).
Lilburne, John. *The Lawes Funerall* ([London]: 1648).
Lilburne, John. *The Triall of Lieut. Collonel John Lilburne ... Octob. 1649* (London: 1649).
Lilburne, John. *An Impeachment of High Treason against Oliver Cromwel* (London: 1649).
Lilburne, John. *Certaine Observations upon the Tryall of Leiut. Col. John Lilburne* ([London]: 1649).
Lilburne, John. *As You Were, or, The Lord General Cromwel and the Grand Officers of the Armie* ([Amsterdam]: 1652).
Lilburne, John. *Lieu. Col. John Lilburn's Plea in Law* ([London]: 1653).
Love, Christopher. *A Cleare and Necessary Vindication* (London: 1651).
Loveday, Samuel. *The Hatred of Esau, and the Love of Jacob* (London: 1650).
Ness, Christopher. *A Compleat History and Mystery of the Old and New Testament* (London: 1696).
Newnham, John. *Newnams Nightcrowe* (London: 1590).
Schauer, Frederick. *Playing by the Rules: A Philosophical Examination of Rule-Based Decision-Making in Law and in Life* (Oxford: Oxford University Press, 1991).
Schauer, Frederick. 'Legal Realism Untamed', *Texas Law Review*, 91 (2013): 749–80.
Smith, David Chan. *Sir Edward Coke and the Reformation of the Laws: Religion, Politics, and Jurisprudence, 1578–1616* (Cambridge: Cambridge University Press, 2014).
Twysden, Roger. *The Commoners Liberty: Or, the English-mans Birth-right* ([London]: 1648).
Vane, Henry. *The Tryal of Sir Henry Vane, Kt. at the King's Bench* ([London]: 1662).
Walker, Clement. *The High Court of Justice* (London: 1651).
Walwyn, William. *England's Lamentable Slaverie* ([London]: 1645).
Walwyn, William. *The Fountain of Slaunder Discovered* (London: 1649).

Williams, Ryan C. 'The One and Only Substantive Due Process Clause', *Yale Law Journal*, 120 (2010): 408–512.

Winstanley, Gerard. *The New Law of Righteousnes Budding Forth* (London: 1649).

Winter, Steven L. *A Clearing in the Forest: Law, Life, and Mind* (Chicago: University of Chicago Press, 2001).

CHAPTER 31

LEGAL AGENCY AS LITERATURE IN THE ENGLISH REVOLUTION

The Case of the Levellers

NIGEL SMITH

> [W]e behold the *Great Mantion house* of this *Common wealth*, and of this *Armie* (wherein all the families of the Nation are contained) *on fire*, all ready to be devoured with slavery, confusion and ruine, and their nation-all native freedome (the price of their treasure and blood) wrested out of their hands, as at this present appeareth to our best understandings.[1]

> That the People of *Englands* Constitution is fitted for Kingly Government, it is Ridiculous to alledge.[2]

THE literary canon of the mid-seventeenth century studied today does not function like the rest of the early modern canon, where juridical concepts and procedures may be found as part of the architecture of plays or poems. An obvious demonstration of this kind of presence would be found in recent work on the influence of judicial rhetoric on Shakespeare and other dramatists.[3] There are precise allusions to processes of forensic argument buried in the text. Shylock realizes too late that he has asked the wrong

[1] John Wildman et al., *The Case of the Armie Truly Stated* (1647), 22–3.

[2] [John Streater], *A Shield against the Parthian Dart, or, A Word to the Purpose, Shot into Wallingford-House. Answered in Defence of the Present Actions of State here in England, that Produced the Late Change of Government* (1659), 18.

[3] Quentin Skinner, *Forensic Shakespeare* (Oxford: Oxford University Press, 2014), chs 2, 8; Lorna Hutson, *The Invention of Suspicion: Law and Mimesis in Shakespeare and Renaissance Drama* (Oxford: Oxford University Press, 2007), chs 3, 5; Andrew Zurcher, *Spenser's Legal Language: Law and Poetry in Early Modern England* (Woodbridge and Rochester: D. S. Brewer, 2007), chs 2, 3, 8.

'question', and so he looses his suit; but too late to back out from the judgement that will then fall upon him.

On the contrary so much literature of the 1640s and 1650s is literally a plea in the name of a desired legal practice: Gerrard Winstanley's *The Law of Freedom in a Platform* (1652); John Lilburne's *The Legall Fundamentall Liberties of the People of England* (1649). Whatever survives from this period in drama, poetry, and prose fiction, it is the case that the taught canon in literature and in history has also focused on pamphlet and philosophical literature where dialectic and rhetoric as opposed to mimesis has held sway. In the teaching of literature, much of the recent interest in this field has grown from the acknowledgement of Milton's career as apologist in printed prose as well as his poetic achievements.[4] In a complementary way, historians of various kinds have grown ever more sophisticated in their understanding of the significance of the rise of a vigorous print culture by which these pleas were disseminated, and which had a sizeable impact on the turn of events.[5] Within the world of conventionally defined literature, Andrew Marvell's Cromwellian verse is also a call to take arms or a justification of the Protectoral constitution, exposing potential or real tensions in the authority structure thereof. It is usually thought of as political poetry but might just as well be seen as part of the discussion of constitutional law.[6] The parliament in Hell in *Paradise Lost*, Books I and II, is, as is well known, a reflection of the interrelated positions on liberty and obedience, faith and Stoicism known in Milton's lifetime, and these positions relate to the indubitably legal nature of those debates during the English Civil War and Commonwealth.

This is no surprise at a time when the entire superstructure of governance was vitiated by a civil war: where the king on the one side and the Parliament on the other each referred to their legal right in asserting supremacy over their enemies: Marvell has Justice, on behalf of Charles I 'against Fate complain / And plead the ancient rights in vain'.[7] Charles was tried as a tyrant, accused of unjustly spilling the blood of his subjects (with part of the prosecution prepared by one of the great legal reformers of the 1650s,

[4] The list of apposite studies is vast: more recent book-length studies include David Norbrook, *Writing the English Republic: Poetry, Rhetoric, and Politics, 1627–1660* (Cambridge: Cambridge University Press, 1999) and Blair Worden, *Literature and Politics in Cromwellian England: John Milton, Andrew Marvell, Marchamont Nedham* (Oxford: Oxford University Press, 2007), chs 2, 7–14; among collections, see Thomas N. Corns, ed., *A Companion to Milton* (Oxford: Blackwell, 2003), chs 16–19; Nicholas McDowell and Nigel Smith, eds, *The Oxford Handbook of Milton* (Oxford: Oxford University Press, 2009), pts 3–5.

[5] See e.g. Jason Peacey, *Print and Public Politics in the English Revolution* (Cambridge: Cambridge University Press, 2013); Mark Knights, *Politics and Opinion in Crisis, 1678–81* (Cambridge: Cambridge University Press, 1994).

[6] See e.g. Annabel Patterson, *Marvell and the Civic Crown* (Princeton: Princeton University Press, 1978), 59–94; Derek Hirst, '"That Sober Cromwell": Marvell's Cromwell in 1654', in *The Golden and the Brazen World: Papers in Literature and History, 1650–1800*, ed. John M. Wallace (Berkeley: University of California Press, 1985); Joad Raymond, 'Framing Liberty: Marvell's First Anniversary and the Instrument of Government', *HLQ*, 62 (1999), 313–50; Worden, *Literature and Politics in Cromwellian England* (Oxford: Oxford University Press, 2007), chs 3–6; Andrew Marvell, *Poems*, ed. Nigel Smith (Harlow: Pearson Longman, 2003, 2007), 281–98.

[7] Marvell, 'An Horatian Ode upon Cromwell's Return from Ireland' (1650), l. 38.

John Cook).[8] Milton famously defended the regicide by invoking the discussion of who had the right to resist a tyrant. Much of his argument comes from the Old Testament; nonetheless the case he builds is explicitly and literally legal.[9] We frequently remember in literary studies that one of the Puritans who lost his ears by way of punishment in 1637, William Prynne, wrote one of the most impressive anti-theatrical treatises of the day, *Histrio-mastix* (1633; the source of his punishment), but it is also the case that Prynne was a lawyer. His scathing attack on the authority of the new republic in 1649 appears to be a parody of the Leveller John Lilburne's treatise of the same year: *A Legall Vindication of the Liberties of England, against Illegall Taxes and Pretended Acts* (1649).[10]

Just the title of Lilburne's tract itself makes his point perfectly: Col. Pride's expulsion of MPs unwilling to try the king (known as Pride's Purge) has created the Rump Parliament, the single representative chamber of the new republic, which was therefore not elected, and this assembly in itself has proven its tyranny by putting the king to death:

> *The legall fundamentall liberties of the people of England revived, asserted, and vindicated. Or, an epistle written the eighth day of June 1649, by Lieut. Colonel John Lilburn to Mr. William Lenthall Speaker to the remainder of those few knights, citizens, and burgesses that Col. Thomas Pride at his late purge thought convenient to leave sitting at Westminster … who … pretendedly stile themselves … the Parliament of England, intrusted and authorised by the consent of all the people thereof, whose representatives by election … they are; although they are never able to produce one bit of a law, or any piece of a commission to prove, that all the people of England, … authorised Thomas Pride, … to chuse them a Parliament, as indeed he hath de facto done by this pretended mock-Parliament: and therefore it cannot properly be called the nations or peoples Parliament, but Col. Pride's and his associates, whose really it is; who, although they have beheaded the King for a tyrant, yet walk in his oppressingest steps, if not worse and higher.*[11]

The treatise itself is some eighty pages long but the first page alone is a detailed piece of constitutional positioning. The entire text jousts with the legal prerogatives of the Rump Parliament, referring back to Lilburne's battle with the House of Lords in the mid-1640s (along with the monarchy, the Lords had been abolished in January 1649; the first edition of the tract appeared on 18 June):

> That I shall not be deprived of my Liberty but by due processe of Law, according to the Laws of the Land; and that if any shall detain my body in prison without legall Authority,

[8] See David Lagomarsino and Charles T. Wood, eds, *The Trial of Charles I: A Documentary History* (Hanover: University Press of New England, 1989); Harry Potter, *Law, Liberty and the Constitution: A Brief History of the Common Law* (Woodbridge: The Boydell Press, 2015), ch. 15.

[9] See Nicholas McDowell, 'The 1649 Writings, I–III', in *The Complete Works of John Milton*, ed. N. H. Keeble and Nicholas McDowell (Oxford: Oxford University Press, 2013), 4.12–57.

[10] The publisher and book collector George Thomason dated his copy 16 July, one month after the appearance of Lilburne's tract.

[11] Thomason Tracts: E.560(14), dated 18 June; E.567(1); dated 4 August.

> he is liable in Law to make me satisfaction therefore: but Mr. *Wollastone* had kept me in prison divers weeks by vertue of a pretended Warrant of the single House of Lords, who in Law, I will maintain it, have not the least power in the World to commit my body to prison: yet they did (upon the tenth day of June 1646, laying no crime to my charge) command me to be kept for all my short eternity in this world; for the Warrant is, during their pleasures.[12]

Lilburne is centrally concerned with the law of habeas corpus, believed that the 'free-born Englishman' was guaranteed its privileges in chapter 29 of Magna Carta, and played an important historical role in the evolution of the concept.[13] More generally, the maladministration of the law is a frequent component of English Revolution literature. The Diggers wanted to be understood as the most loyal citizens of the free state, and ostentatiously took the Engagement Oath, but when brought to court for interfering with Parson Platt's wood-gathering rights by founding an agrarian commune, found legal procedure in the local assizes impossible to engage with, succumbing to language barriers (Latin and law-French), and with a judge unwilling to let them plead for themselves.[14] A Lilburne-influenced letter printed on behalf of apprentices disappointed by news of the execution of the Leveller soldiers at Burford, Oxfordshire, 17 May 1649 contains a petition, that most legally proper way in which those outside the governing elite ask it for redress: 'To the supreme Authority of this Nation, the Commons of *England* assembled in *Parliament*: The humble Petition of the oppressed of the County of Surrey, which have cast in their Mite into the Treasury of this Common-wealth.' The questions come as fast in these petitions as they do in Lilburne's pamphlets. Here is another petition of the previous year written by Leveller women:

> it will never go well with this Nation, either in its Peace, Freedom, or prosperity, so long as such men are so ill requited for all their pains, costs, labours and hazards in behalf of the Common wealth; nor untill their motions, counsels and propositions are better regarded.[15]

[12] Lilburne, *Legal Fundametall Liberties* (1649), 1.

[13] Paul Halliday, *Habeas corpus: From England to Empire* (Cambridge, MA: Harvard University Press, 2010), 193–6, 227–8.

[14] This episode is well dramatized in Kevin Brownlow's film *Winstanley* (1975); see also John Gurney, *Brave Community: The Digger Movement in the English Revolution* (Oxford: Oxford University Press, 2007), 174–5, 192; John Gurney, *Gerrard Winstanley: The Digger's Life and Legacy* (London: Pluto Press, 2013), 80–1.

[15] *To the Supream Authority of This Nation, the Commons Assembled in Parliament: The Humble Petition of Divers Wel-affected Women Inhabiting the Cities of London, Westminster, the Borough of Southwark, Hamblets, and Places Adjacent; (Affecters and Approvers of the Late Large Petition) of the Eleventh of September, 1648. In Behalf of Lieutenant Col. John Lilburn, Mr William Walwyn, Mr Thomas Prince, and Mr. Richard Overton, (Now Prisoners in the Tovver of London) and Captain William Bray, Close-prisoner in Windsor-Castle; and Mr William Savvyer, Prisoner at White-Hall*, 5. Wing (2nd edn) T1736; Thomason E.551[14]. For the matter of gender politics in this context, see the important essay by

It is well known to scholars that Lilburne recast the common law to suit his own sense of the 'free-born Englishman'.[16] The dynamic self-presentation on every page is of the 'free-born Englishman' being denied his liberties: imprisoned, made to kneel before Parliament, refusing to do so, and so suffering more. It might be regarded as a festive display of the oppressed righteous self:

> *Sir, I am a free-man of England, and therefore I am not to be used as a Slave, or Vassall, by the Lords, which they have already done, and would further doe. I also am a man of peace and quietnesse, and desire not to molest any, if I be not forced thereunto: therefore I desire you, as you tender my good, and your own; take this for answer, that I cannot, without turning traytor to my Liberties, dance attendance to their Lordships Barre: being bound in conscience, dutie to God, my selfe, mine, and my Countrey; to oppose their incroachments to the death: which by the strength of God I am resolved to doe.*[17]

Each paragraph is an envelope of legalistic resistance, humorous, ironic of the self, where the 'world of the shop or the merchant's office becomes thrown into political representation through polemical effort':

> *Sir, you may, or cause to be exercised upon me, some force or violence to pull and dragge me out of my Chamber, which I am resolved to maintain, as long as I can, before I will be compelled to goe before them: and therefore I desire you, in a friendly way, to bee wise and considerate before you doe that, which it may be, you can never undoe.*[18]

There are very many such pages.[19] In arguing for himself, Lilburne is also the actor, in the Ciceronian sense of legal advocate, for all 'free-born Englishmen'. Later on he thought of

Ann Hughes, 'Gender and Politics in Leveller Literature', in *Political Culture and Cultural Politics in Early Modern England: Essays Presented to David Underdown*, ed. Susan D. Amussen and Mark A. Kishlansky (Manchester: Manchester University Press, 1995), 162–88.

[16] R. B. Seaberg, 'The Norman Conquest and the Common Law: The Levellers and the Argument from Continuity', *HJ*, 24 (1981): 796–806; Andrew Sharp, 'John Lilburne and the Long Parliament's Book of Declarations: A Radical's Exploitation of the Words of Authorities', *HPT*, 9 (1988): 19–44; *idem*, '"John Lilburne's Discourse of Law"', *PS*, 40 (1988): 18–33.

[17] Lilburne, *An Anatomy of the Lords Tyranny and Iniustice Exercised upon Lieu. Col. IOHN LILBURNE, Now a Prisoner in the Tower of LONDON* (1646), 3. For further analysis, see Nigel Smith, *Literature and Revolution in England 1640–1660* (New Haven and London: Yale University Press, 1994), 130–42.

[18] Lilburne, *An Anatomy*, 4. The imprisonment aspect of Leveller writing is considered as an important part of a larger carcereal literature in Molly Murray, 'The Liberty of the Subject and the "Pris'ner Samson"', in *Milton Now: Alternative Approaches and Contexts*, ed. Catharine Gray and Erin Murphy (Houndmills and New York: Palgrave Macmillan, 2014), 151–74.

[19] No less than one hundred and thirty printed books are assigned to Lilburne's authorship: Donald G. Wing, *Short-title Catalogue of Books Printed in England, Scotland, Ireland, Wales, and British America, and of English Books Printed in Other Countries, 1641–1700*, 2nd edn (New York: 1982), 447–50.

his writing and court appearances as a boxing match, and 'little Rhetorique', as opposed to the 'gallant Ennobled and Heroick minde'.[20] As Rachel Foxley writes, Lilburne was using the common law to think about 'citizenship and political equality', abandoning 'subject' for 'Englishman', and not even merely a 'free man'. The latter might be afforded liberties without any participation in the governance of the country. Lilburne argues that 'free-born' means being part of the political nation.[21] It was, she insists, an inclusive as opposed to exclusive definition. 'Free-born' was not a new word or compound in the 1640s, but it is very rare before 1600 and most often it referred to the ancient world with its distinction between freedom and slavery. Yet Lilburne's deployment was startling and innovative.[22] Howsoever he began his public career affirming the religious views of persecuted Puritans and indeed separatists, by the mid-1640s he had immersed himself in common law reading, formulated a popular version of maintaining a citizen's rights, gave himself up to a vigorous maintenance of that view and practice through the printing presses, and when required through appearances in law courts, including the highest courts in the land, the two Houses of Parliament. Along the way he also spent years in prison, on suspicion of a variety of charges, the most serious of which was treason. He knew the nature of crowd behaviour, how they gathered, how to appeal to them, and how they could turn to violence.[23] He threw contemporary legal procedure, and the assumption that subjects were at the law's mercy, into abeyance, and on two important occasions twice won acquittals by jury in 1649 and 1653, verdicts that effectively undermined the authority of the Commonwealth regimes at, for them, embarrassing moments. The most far-reaching conception he reached was that the people alone had the legal right both to make and recall governments. Andrew Sharp describes this succinctly:

> Lilburne came to support both a process by which a new form of government might be instituted by 'the people', and a specifically representative form of government which he and other Levellers urged upon those 'people' to choose. Both of these (the process and the representative form) would embody the consent of 'the people' and be legitimate for that reason. In a number of only slightly differing formulations he advocated an 'agreement of the people' in which, by mutual consent, the people should adopt a written constitution which would both define the form and powers of government and limit those powers by reserving to the people a set of inalienable rights.[24]

[20] Lilburne, *L. Colonel JOHN LILBURNE revived* (1653), 2nd pagination, 1, 3.

[21] Rachel Foxley, *The Levellers: Radical Political Thought in the English Revolution* (Manchester: Manchester University Press, 2013), ch. 3.

[22] *OED* 'free-born' misses all references to Leveller usage and does not inspire confidence. Two telling instances help to explain Lilburne's starting point: 'I.W.'s' play *The Valiant Scot* (1637), 28, where 'we are as free-born / As th' *English* King himself, be not their slaves, / Free *Scotland,* or in *England* dig our graves', and the recusant antiquary Edmund Bolton, *The Cities Aduocate in This Case or Question of Honor and Armes; Whether Apprentiship Extinguisheth Gentry?* (1629), 17: 'the wisdome of *England*, their naturall common parent, whose children are freeborne.'

[23] David Cressy, *England on Edge: Crisis and Revolution 1640–1642* (Oxford: Oxford University Press, 2007), 382–3.

[24] Andrew Sharp, life of Lilburne in *ODNB*.

In the face of the Commonwealth's 'tyranny' in 1649, Lilburne would regard the king as a balance against a hostile representative (and its executive Council of State), but in these earlier and purer formulations, the monarchy and hereditary House of Lords disappeared. Yet even as Lilburne castigated the Commonwealth government for what he regarded as its lack of legitimacy, so he also worked with lawyers and parliamentary committees to win such matters as reparation monies and landed properties that he believed were owed him.

Lilburne represented and practiced the just protest of the 'freeborn Englishman', whereas his associate Richard Overton, also imprisoned by the House of Lords in the mid-1640s, famously and additionally theorized an inviolable individuality as part of nature and natural law, assumed at the time to be a set of God-given principles that lay behind every legal code:

> To every Individuall in nature, is given an individuall property by nature, not to be invaded or usurped by any: for every one as he is himselfe, so he hath a selfe propriety, else could he not be himselfe, and on this no second may presume to deprive any of, without manifest violation and affront to the very principles of nature, and of the Rules of equity and justice between man and man; mine and thine cannot be, except this be: No man hath power over my rights and liberties, and I over no mans; I may be but an Individuall, enjoy *my selfe* and my selfe propriety, and may write my selfe no more then my selfe, or presume any further; if I doe, I am an encroacher & an invader upon an other mans Right, to which I have no *Right*. For by naturall birth, all men are equally and alike borne to like propriety, liberty and freedome, and as we are delivered of God by the hand of nature into this world.[25]

Overton's statement is, at least as textual evidence, as unprecedented as Lilburne's 'freeborn Englishman': before the Civil War 'it was assumed that an individual's interest in his lands or goods existed, not through any natural right, but as a result of humanly constructed laws.'[26] Moreover, there was no human right that could be used to protect someone from any constraint or obligation the community or the Commonwealth chose to put upon them. Lilburne and Overton's prison writings embody an example of the negative liberty position: that liberty is freedom from constraint (in the Leveller case, quite literally from being locked up), as opposed to the idea of positive liberty as an enjoyment of freedoms all guaranteed by law and effected by the right to make regular elections to the representative, a view associated with many of the English republicans.[27] Thus, although the majority of negative liberty theorists were royalists or monarchically

[25] Richard Overton, *AN ARROVV AGAINST ALL TYRANTS And Tyrany, Shot from the Prison of New-gate into the Prerogative Bowels of the Abitrary House of Lords, and All Other Usurpers and Tyrants Whatsoever* (1646), 3.

[26] Christopher W. Brooks, *Law, Politics and Society in Early Modern England* (Cambridge: Cambridge University Press, 2008), 242.

[27] Quentin Skinner: 'The Idea of Negative Liberty: Philosophical and Historical Perspectives', in *Ideas in Context: Philosophy in History*, ed. R. Rorty et al. (Cambridge: Cambridge University Press, 1988), 197, 218–19.

inclined, and Thomas Hobbes was the most trenchant and original of them, Lilburne was a negative liberty theorist who drew his material from the received traditions and authorities of the common law. His understanding was defensive and aimed at protecting common people from the harm that a system of governance could do them, especially a legal jurisdiction. This was intensely felt in the war-torn 1640s, as a pro-Leveller apprentices' petition makes clear in its description of a frayed system declining into the harshness of arbitrary military justice:

> The Law being nothing but a mock protection to our lives, liberties and properties; the Judges set apart, for the executors of it, a meer delusion, our Sheriffs, Mayors, Justices of Peace, Constables, &c. being laid by, or made no better then ciphers .... Commoners are forceably convented and tryed before a Councell of Warr, and some sentenced even unto death, others by a private verball order made to run the gantlop, and *whipt most barbarously*, for refusing to take false and illegall oaths.[28]

It therefore followed in Lilburne's view that the institutions of government as they stood were gravely flawed, just as humanity endured depravation as a consequence of original sin. Citizens would suffer from the greed and tyranny of others, and English law as it existed had been corrupted since the Norman Conquest. It needed to be renovated and exercised in English, just at this point in time when the Civil War had dissolved the social contract and required a fresh remaking of government, one that in future would not damage the people and would through the law's 'reason' give them the foundation they needed and that was rightfully theirs. The principles of sociability and well-being, embodied in natural law, could be glimpsed in the Bible and in the Common Law Statutes, but in late 1640s England a fundamental rebuild was required.

It is well said that Lilburne's understanding of the functioning of common law, especially through the House of Commons, bore no relationship to its functioning in law courts in recent history. Such an observation may be beside the point: Lilburne was offering a highly unusual view of common law (most famously in his invocations of Magna Carta, especially chapter 29, Parts II–IV of Sir Edward Coke's *Institutes*, available in print only since 1640, and the Parliamentary Books of Declarations) that made it seem dynamic and mutable because open to the interpretation of the people, or a person, a citizen, anyone who was able to consult the evidence. This was itself to build upon the very different interpretation of chapter 29 given by James Morrice in 1578 and then Sir Edward Coke in 1604. Before then, chapter 29 was not associated with guarantees and protections of the liberties of the subject.[29]

[28] Charles Collins et al., *An Outcry of the Youngmen and Apprentices of London: Or, An Inquisition after the Lost Fundamentall Lawes and Liberties of England* (1649), 2. Attributed to Lilburne himself by Andrew Sharp, ed., *The English Levellers* (Cambridge: Cambridge University Press, 1998), 179.

[29] See Sir John Baker, *Selected Readings and Commentaries on Magna Carta, 1400–1604*. (London: SS, 2015), viii, lxxxiv–lxxxv.

While the nature of law and legal codes was of course the subject of serious reflection by legal scholars in these years, some attached to Parliament, such as John Selden, there is no doubt that the presence of legal thought was well embedded in the kind of literature that circulated among the middling sort, including the Levellers, such as George Wither's verse:

As, then, that *Family*, with an intent,
Him [a father], from his ill-advisers, to withdraw,
(And his, and their destruction, to prevent)
May lay restraining hands, by Natures law,
  On such a father, and yet therein be
  Preserv'd from breach of houshold-duties, free.
So, when the *Father* of our *Countrey*, shall
By Flatteries, be drawn to such a course,
As may produce his owne and kingdomes fall,
Vnlesse we intervene, by timely force;
  And, when, so loyally, the same is done,
That, to our utmost powers, we still assay
Not how to save his life, and rights, alone,
But, how his honour, too, preserve we may:
The Laws of *God*, of *Nature*, and of *Reason*,
Will, doubtlesse, warrant it, in their despight
Who brand it with *Rebellion*, and with *Treason*.[30]

Moreover, calls for law reform in the period were not restricted to the Levellers, but were a resonant part of a general demand for religious, political, and social renovation.[31] Others, including royalists and elite republicans, also claimed birthright liberties.[32] John Warr wrote in 1648 that: 'There are some sparks of freedom in the minds of most, which ordinarily lie deep and are covered in the dark as a spark in the ashes.' The constitutional foundation of freedom, he argued, echoing Overton more than Lilburne, was neither monarchical authority nor a property-based franchise but 'people's rights'. 'Tis not possible for a people to be too free':

> *Prerogative* and *Priviledge Interests*, (as formerly explained in their corrupt notions) are altogether inconsistent with *True Freedome*: Hence it is that there is an irreconcileable contest between *Them*, which will never cease, till either *Prerogative* and *Priviledge* be swallowed up in *Freedome*, or *Liberty* it selfe be led *captive* by *Prerogative*. He which hath the worst *Cause* may sometimes have the best *Successe*, (for Time and Chance happens to all) and thus *Liberty* may be worsted by *Priviledge*, as having lesse specious advantages in the Flesh. For true *Freedome* is in the *Mind*,

[30] Wither, *Campo-Musae* (1643), 11–12.
[31] Donald Veall, *The Popular Movement for Law Reform, 1640–1660* (Oxford: Clarendon Press, 1970).
[32] See pp. 617–19.

> and its *Proselytes* are but few. Most men give up themselves to the Idoll-Interests of *Prerogative and Priviledge*, as being more taking with flesh and blood.
>
> And when *Liberty* is once put to the rout, it is not easie to rally again, or to redeem it selfe, for the darkest Dungeon is its *Prison*, 'tis chained with oathes and servile bonds, yea and the strong bolts of humane *Lawes* doe keep it in subjection. Thus are all things made sure, with a *Grave-stone*, a *Seale*, and a *Watch*, and oppression rides in *triumph* upon the backes of the people.[33]

In other words freedom is a quality of being that is inextricably part of the freedoms enshrined in the laws and fundamental to them, over and against the natural tendency of anyone with prerogative powers or privilege to oppress those without them. Note the aversion to legal oaths, a way of compelling someone to speak in court possibly against the terms of their own birthright, a practice that Lilburne vehemently abhorred.[34] This view is another version of negative liberty, but where the greatest freedom appears to be a state of mind where one reflects on God with absolutely no constraint. Freedom of belief and worship was an important part of the Leveller platform. John Warr, far too little studied, except by Sir Stephen Sedley, appears to have been a religious radical who had an unusually sharp focus on the legal consequences of a radical religious vision.[35]

We have looked thus far at Levellers who emerged at least in the first instance from civilian contexts. By contrast John Wildman grew to prominence in the New Model Army, as an officer and then (having left the army in September 1647) a prominent facilitator for the 'agitators', elected representatives of the soldiers (originally of five cavalry regiments). As the Army itself began to assert what it considered a just political solution to the kingdom's crisis, so civilian Levellers and agitators joined and found themselves in opposition to the 'grandees', the New Model commanders, Sir Thomas (later Lord) Fairfax and Oliver Cromwell the most prominent among them. These discussions would have a considerable impact on national events, not least the move to bring the king to trial and execution. Wildman had reputedly studied law, knew much about property law, and would eventually make himself rich from property speculation.[36] Wildman and Maximilian Petty helped to frame *The Case of the Armie Truly Stated*, presented to the

33 John Warr, *The Priviledges of the People, or, Principles of Common Right and Freedome* (1649), 5–6.

34 Although the case has been made that Lilburne's real contribution was in challenging the prosecution to prove their assertions: see John H. Langbein, 'The Privilege and Common Law Criminal Procedure: The Sixteenth to the Eighteenth Centuries', in *The Privilege against Self-Incrimination: Its Origins and Development*, ed. R. H. Helmholz, Charles M. Gray, John H. Langbein, et al. (Chicago: Chicago University Press, 1997), 244–5, n. 123.

35 Warr's references to Cicero, several ancient historians, and Machiavelli might be supporting evidence that he was also the John Warr who translated the pseudo-Quintilian's *Declamations of Quintilian*, published in 1686. John Warr, *A Spark in the Ashes: The Pamphlets of John Warr*, ed. Stephen Sedley and Lawrence Kaplan (London: Verso, 1992); Stephen Sedley, *Ashes and Sparks: Essays on Law and Justice* (Cambridge: Cambridge University Press, 2011), 88–100.

36 See *ODNB* life by Richard L. Greaves; see also Maurice Ashley, *John Wildman, Plotter and Postmaster: A Study of the English Republican Movement in the Seventeenth Century* (Loondon: J. Cape, 1947).

New Model's commander-in-chief Sir Thomas Fairfax on 18 October, 1647.[37] The generals were accused of betraying the rank and file soldiers by failing to confront and if necessary purge Parliament; the legal remedy, it was argued, was a radical extension of the franchise (all 'free-born' men twenty-one years and older), biennial Parliaments, the abolition of tithes and the excise tax, the repeal of recusant and conventicle statutes, and law reform (one code in one book, in English, with all ancient rights of the poor restored). It is important to note that Overton had already published a version of these proposals in 'Certaine Articles for the good of the Common wealth', appended to *An Appeale from the Degenerate Representative Body the Commons of England Assembled at Westminster* (1647, dated by Thomason 17 July).[38] The tract begins by pointing out that the traditional means for the ruled to draw attention to their grievances through petitions (lack of pay was one complaint among many) had been repeatedly ignored by Parliament. As a printed speech act, the tract encompassed the work of a petition and did more than that in both raising support from its putative readers, and in seeking to negotiate for the redress of those grievances with the senior officers outside and beyond the terms of supplication that pertained with normal petitions. This time, and by virtue of their service, the soldiers asserted that they had the right to make drastic reform. They insisted that all previous condemnation of such petitions be removed from the records in order to protect 'freedom of the people', and that such petitions be explicitly acknowledged as valid pleas in the same records.[39] They took particular offense that they had been regarded as mere soldiers subject to orders as opposed to free-born Englishmen with rights and liberties.[40]

What then followed were the successive attempts by the civilian and military wings of the Leveller movement (who by no means always saw eye to eye) to have successive versions of the document called the *Agreement of the People* adopted in Parliament and used as a basis to settle the future of the state. The first *Agreement* emerged on 28 October 1647. It was regarded by the Levellers as a written social contract, and recommended an elected representative of one chamber that would discharge most of the functions of government. The people would retain their inalienable rights, and would be able to protect their liberties, including freedom of religion, assembly, and trade, by annual or biennial elections of this body. Neither king nor House of Lords would carry a veto and no one would be granted any legal privileges over anyone else. The vision included a notable degree of de-centred jurisdiction.[41] These details were debated amongst Army representatives, most famously at Putney in 1647 and Whitehall in 1648: the transcripts that survive are the evidence of decidedly charged oratory between the Army command

[37] For Petty, see *ODNB* life by Beth R. Howard and P. R. S. Baker.

[38] 32–8 [irregular pagination]. Wing No. O619; Thomason Tract E.398[28].

[39] [John Wildman] et al., *The Case of the Armie Truly Stated* (1647), 17.

[40] Wildman et al., *The Case of the Armie*, 5.

[41] Lilburne et al., *An Agreement of the Free People of England*, in *The English Levellers*, ed. Sharp, 176–7; Philip Baker, 'The Levellers, Decentralisation and the *Agreements of the People*', in *The Agreements of the People, the Levellers and the Constitutional Crisis of the English Revolution*, ed. Philip Baker and Elliot Vernon (Houndmills and New York: Palgrave Macmillan, 2012), 97–116.

and the soldiers' representatives, and in which the content involved class difference, theology, political theory, and legal concepts. They were understood to be constitutional law in the making:

> *Colonel Thomas Rainborough*: ... I think that the poorest he that is in England has a life to live as the greatest he; and therefore truly, sir, I think it's clear that every man that is to live under a government ought first by his own consent to put himself under that government; and I do think that the poorest man in England is not at all bound in a strict sense to that government that he has not had a voice to put himself under.
>
> *[Commissary-General Henry] Ireton* ... Give me leave to tell you that if you make this the rule, I think you must fly for refuge to an absolute natural right and you must deny all civil right ... For my part, I think it is no right at all. ... we should not refuse to give them air and place and ground and the freedom of the highways and other things to live amongst us—*That* I think is due to a man by birth. But that by a man's being born here he shall have a share in that power that shall dispose of the lands here, and of all things here, I do not think it a sufficient ground.[42]

While these debates took place through 1647–1648, and while the second Civil War was being fought, the civilian Levellers in London, the home counties, Oxfordshire and Cambridgeshire pursued a petitioning campaign addressed to Parliament. Unlike the *Agreements* these works did not assume that the country was in a state of nature, but implored the House of Commons as supreme authority to provide redress. Their construction was hampered by the imprisonment of leading figures for considerable lengths of time, not least Lilburne, but also Overton and eventually Walwyn, who nonetheless still exerted an influence from behind bars. Lilburne in particular had enhanced his knowledge of the law in the company of fellow prisoners, such as the royalist judge David Jenkins.[43] But the Levellers were outmanoeuvred by the Army command, even as they continued to negotiate with them. Lilburne and Wildman naively and fatefully left early a meeting discussing the second *Agreement of the People* only to learn later that the officers had considerably diluted its contents. When taken to Parliament in early 1649 the document was simply not discussed. Most Levellers disapproved of Pride's Purge, by which mechanism it was possible to commit Charles I to trial and execution. Wildman did not resist, but Lilburne saw it as decidedly illegal, a violation of the English constitution and, as we have seen, confirmation of a new tyranny. The pamphlet campaign he led in 1649 against the new regime won support, but he, Overton, Walwyn, and Thomas Prince were soon imprisoned again and their support from the Independent and Baptist churches melted away. Pamphleteering continued, but release in July 1649 was only followed by a treason trial in late October, in which Lilburne daringly persuaded the jury to judge the law and not the fact of the charge: he was acquitted, even took the Engagement Oath and tried to settle down as a soap-boiler while continuing to provide legal advice

42 A. S. P. Woodhouse, ed., *Puritanism and Liberty, Being the Army Debates (1647–1649) from the Clarke Manuscripts* (3rd edn, London: J. M. Dent, 1986), 53–4.

43 For further details, see Sharp, *ODNB* life.

for several local disputes, and unsuccessfully, to enter the legal profession itself. Further legal disputes, not least with the prominent soldier and republican Sir Arthur Hesilrige resulted in an order of banishment from the Rump Parliament on pain of death should he return; he was not invited to defend himself.

William Walwyn's realistic advice to the imprisoned Lilburne as early as 1645 acknowledges the fix that the citizen, as understood by the Levellers, was in: Parliament was indeed all-powerful. Walwyn was the subtlest of the key Leveller writers, the most socially well-established, and a humanist-influenced theorist of extreme toleration.[44] In Walwyn's view, Parliament could do to a very large degree what it wanted with people:

> And therefore, that you should now be kept in safe custodie, was very sad newes to all that love you; knowing how impossible it was, to make you flie or start aside; but when they heard that you were sent to that reproachfull prison of Newgate, they were confounded with griefe.
>
> It should seeme, that you being questioned by the Committee of Examinations stood upon your old guard, alledging it to be against your liberty, as you were a free borne Englishman, to answer to questions against your selfe, urging *MAGNA CHARTA* to justifie your so doing; And complaining that contrary to the said Charter, you had beene divers times imprisoned by them.

He was well aware of Lilburne's innovative strategy:

> Now it is not much to be wondred at, that this your carriage should be very offensive unto them; for you were not the first by divers, (whom I could name) that have been examined upon questions, tending to their own accusation and imprisonment too, for refusing to answer but you are the first indeed, that ever raised this new doctrine of *MAGNA CHARTA*, to prove the same unlawfull.
>
> Likewise, You are the first, that compareth this dealing to the crueltie of the Starre Chamber, and that produced the Vote of this Parliament against those cruelties (so unjustly inflicted on your selfe by that tyrannous Court) And how could you Imagine this could be indured by a Committee of Parliament? No, most Parliament men are to learne what is the just power of a Parliament, what the Parliament may doe, and what the Parliament (it selfe) may not doe, It's no marvell then that others are ignorant, very good men there be; who affirme, that a Parliament being once chosen, have power over all our lives estates and liberties, to dispose of them at their pleasure whether for our good or hurt, All's one (say they) we have trusted them, and they are bound to no rules, nor bounded by any limits, but whatsoever they shall ordaine, binds all the people, it's past all dispute, they are accountable unto none, they are

44 See William Walwyn, *Writings*, ed. Jack R. McMichael and Barbara Taft (Athens: University of Georgia Press, 1989); Nigel Smith, 'The Charge of Atheism and the Language of Radical Speculation, 1640–1660', in Michael Hunter and David Wootton, eds, *Atheism from the Reformation to the Enlightenment* (Oxford: Clarendon Press, 1992), 131–58; Derek Hirst, 'A Happier Man: The Refashioning of William Walwyn,' *SC*, 27 (2012): 54–78.

above *MAGNA CHARTA* and all Lawes whatsoever, and there is no pleading of any thing against them.[45]

Yet this skepticism did not mean that there was to be no faith on the Levellers' part in the common law as they had re-imagined it as a force to guarantee or realize popular liberties. The law was flawed in many ways, not least administratively, but it could still underwrite the liberties of the free-born Englishman. They seemed to think that the common people would see the obvious sense of their franchise proposals, but it was a society in which not the vote, but active participation, notably in local office-holding, defined the meaning of the community and political well-being.[46]

Lilburne's significance was noted and continued through the 1650s by the soldier, printer, natural philosopher, and popular republican John Streater. In several pamphlets through the decade Streater discussed different forms of republican constitution, experimented with the most effective way of disseminating political theory and legal knowledge to a mass readership, and in the Protectorate period called for the assassination of Oliver Cromwell.[47] His pamphlets focused on the vital importance of accountability: magistrates and other officers of state were to be elected for a period of one year only. Streater showed a particular interest in the interaction of administration and accountability: in a sense the origins of what we now call public law.[48] It was known by the early seventeenth century that local jurisdictions had been shown to stretch back before the Norman Conquest in a Saxon constitution.[49] Like Lilburne, Streater believed that a law that was imposed upon a people without their consent was no law, representatives need to consult their constituents and he used Coke's discussion of the jurisdiction of Parliaments to prove this.[50] Moreover, Streater was exceptional in believing in the fullest possible sharing of political knowledge, including legal writing. Pamphlets were issued in order to help citizens, such as with the law of habeas corpus, relevant of course in the cases of the imprisonment of both Lilburne and Streater, and advertisements for the pamphlets were carried in Streater's newsbooks.[51] Streater would worry

[45] Walwyn, *Englands Lamentable Slaverie, Proceeding from the Arbitrarie Will, Severitie, and Injustnes of Kings, Negligence, Corruption, and Unfaithfulnesse of Parliaments, Coveteousnesse, Ambition* (1645), 3.

[46] Mark Goldie, 'The Unacknowledged Republic: Officeholding in Early Modern England', in *The Politics of the Excluded, c.1500–1850*, ed. Tim Harris (Basingstoke: Palgrave Macmillan, 2001), 180–1.

[47] See Nigel Smith, *Literature and Revolution in England, 1640–1660*, 196–9; *idem*, 'Popular Republicanism in the 1650s: John Streater's "Heroic Mechanicks"', in *Milton and Republicanism*, ed. David Armitage, Armand Himy, and Quentin Skinner (Cambridge: Cambridge University Press, 1995), 137–55; Adrian Johns, *The Nature of the Book: Print and Knowledge in the Making* (Chicago: University of Chicago Press, 1998), ch. 4; Joad Raymond, 'John Streater and "The Grand Politick Informer"', *HJ*, 41 (1998): 567–74; David Norbrook, *Writing the English Republic: Poetry, Rhetoric and Politics, 1627–1660* (Cambridge: Cambridge University Press, 1999), 319–22; Foxley, *The Levellers*, ch. 6.

[48] See now Stephen Sedley, *Lions under the Throne: Essays on the History of English Public Law* (Cambridge: Cambridge University Press, 2015), especially ch. 4.

[49] See Brooks, *Law, Politics and Society*, 249.

[50] [Streater], *Observations*, 10 (20–27 June 1654), 75–6.

[51] [Streater], *The Loyal Messenger, or, Newes from White-hall Comprising the State and Martial Affaires of, and in Relation to the Common-wealth of England, Scotland, and Ireland*, 4 (3–10 April 1654), 32.

much about the tyrannous implications of the possible destruction of state papers: very much the perspective of a man devoted to the preservation of common law records.[52] In the Restoration he would become a key printer of law books, such as Coke's *Reports*, and enjoy much security from it.[53]

Books detailing laws of constitutional constraint become crucial in Streater's explanation of events, such as Andrew Horn's *Mirror of Justice* (*c.*1313), invoking an agreement from the reign of Edward I that the king must govern according to law and maintain the Christian faith, or John Sadler's *The Rights of the Kingdom, and Customs of our Ancestors* (1649).[54] Grotius's *De jure belli ac paci* (1625) is quoted on the right of popular resistance to tyranny, and on the possibility of the dissolution of social contracts.[55] Trial by special and secret courts is against Magna Carta and the 1628 Petition of Right.[56] Statutes are also to be printed in order to be made widely known:

> their Kings never had any other power, then as their chiefest Minister of State and was no other then a member of the Common-wealth, bound up by the same Law and Rules of government; witness the Oath of Coronation, as also the Oath administred to all Justices, both of the peace, and the several Benches, *An.* 18, *Ed.* 3. *St.* 3. in these words, *You shall swear well and truly to serve your Lord the King, and the People.*
>
> ...
>
> That the people of *England* had an undeniable right to contend against absoluteness in case of injustice or detriment, appeareth by the second of *Henry the IV. Ch.* 22. wherein 'twas enacted, That no person should be grieved for suing to break or alter any thing, although in Parliament enacted.[57]

The free-born Englishman was understood by both Lilburne and Streater to be required to assert his liberties by exhortatory argument, orally and through print. The law was to be brought alive as a popular possession in this vigorous literary activity, which we see in the complicated and slippery world of Leveller writing, in the debates at Putney and Whitehall, and in Streater's enterprising publishing career in the 1650s. Rachel Foxley recently argues this, and it is the central theme of a new, recuperative study of Lilburne

[52] [John Streater], *A Further Continuance of the Grand Politick Informer, Discovering the Wickednesse and Mysteries of the Present State Iniquities on Foot about the 14 of September 1653* (1653), 39.

[53] See e.g. Sir Edward Coke, *La septme part des reports de Sr. Edw. Coke Chival, chief justice del common bank* (1671).

[54] [John Streater], *The Continuation of This Session of Parliament, Justified; and the Action of the Army Touching That Affair Defended: and Objections to Both Answered; According to the Best Rules of Law, Reason, and Just-Preserving Policie* (1659), 5. Horn (*c.*1275–1328) was involved in the defence of London's liberties against attempts to degrade them by Edward II. *The Mirror of Justice* was published in Anglo-Norman and law French in 1642, and in English translation in 1649.

[55] Ibid., 6, 10; Streater, *Secret Reasons of State in Reference to the Affairs of These Nations, at the Interruption of This Present Parliament: Anno 1653. Discovered* (1659), 10.

[56] Ibid., 11–12.

[57] John Streater, *A Glympse of That Jevvel, Judicial, Just, Preserving Libertie* (1653), 2, 11.

by Michael Braddick; I said it twenty-one years ago.[58] The arguments for franchise extension, and hence far greater political inclusivity, were made through an interchangeable mixture of the appeal to birthright, to natural right, and to consent (not to have a vote was 'meer vasselage'). As we have seen, Lilburne, his associates and those influenced by him recognized no absolute distinctions between these categories; such differences were being discovered in the discussions and pamphlet exchange of the times.

This literature was attached to genuinely significant court cases. Lilburne and Streater were both tried on different charges and where the Commonwealth government had a real intention to silence them even if this meant, strictly speaking, ignoring the law. The juries involved did not agree and voted to acquit both men, and in Lilburne's case there was further help from two highly respected and able lawyers acting in his defence. The result was for Streater freedom but for Lilburne, the grim reality was that he had by 1653 become too onerous for Cromwell, and his incarceration did not end, despite a most successful propaganda campaign in his defence.[59] The Barebones and Protectorate governments seemed decidedly arbitrary, ruling above the law, and offering no relief to its prisoners. Anyone who follows the trend of 'revisionist' history in playing down the significance of the Levellers should think again in the light of this evidence.[60] Leveller practice had raised thousands of supporters from the city, while commanding the most expert defence team in the country. In his own trial Streater was staggeringly sharp with the law: the Attorney General argued against him and defended the authority of Parliament as perpetual and not attached to any given elected assembly, but the jury would have none of this, thanks in no small part to Streater's mastery of legal detail and with argument. Seemingly Lilburne's earlier trial victory of 1649, where he had been acquitted after suggesting that the jury was judge of the meaning of the law, as opposed to the charge on which he was being tried, had stuck as an idea in 1653. Lilburne had deployed the rhetoric of his pamphlets and petitions most effectively in the theatre of the courtroom. And, as in 1653, so before in 1649, it had been embarrassing for the government in that it had shown their willingness to cast aside the subject's liberty even as its own dubious procedures and position had been exposed. The force of this transformation, more an indictment of arbitrary powers of arrest and detention than of the virtue of the defendants, was carried into future generations by its recorded presence in the State Trials.[61] Leveller practice and ideas may be observed in the defences mounted by some Dissenters during the Restoration, by 'old Levellers' on the scaffold during the

[58] Rachel Foxley, 'The Levellers: John Lilburne, Richard Overton, William Walwyn', in *Oxford Handbook of Literature and the English Revolution*, ed. Laura Knoppers (Oxford: Oxford University Press, 2012), 272–87; Foxley, *The Levellers*, 'Introduction', ch. 1; Smith, *Literature and Revolution*, ch. 4.

[59] Lilburne was held in prison in the Tower of London, the island of Jersey, and Dover Castle, until, tired and ill, and converted to Quakerism, he was no longer a threat and died on 20 August 1657.

[60] Astutely summarized and assessed by Glenn Burgess, 'Radicalism and the English Revolution', in *English Radicalism, 1550–1850*, ed. Burgess and Matthew Festenstein (Cambridge: Cambridge University Press, 2007), 62–86.

[61] James S. Hart, Jr, *The Rule of Law, 1603–1660* (Harlow: Pearson and Longman, 2003), 261–70, 248–50.

Monmouth Rebellion in 1685, and by others like the free miners of Derby in the eighteenth century, and many other resorts to birthrights claims in the later periods.[62]

Very little indeed of this activity is acknowledged in two recent and esteemed studies of political literature during the English Civil War and Interregnum, studies that are indeed critical of revisionist history. My worry is that while the Levellers are undergoing a welcome revival of interest among historians over and against the dismissals of the revisionists, yet once more we are at a point in literary studies when the true importance of the Levellers is in danger of being forgotten. Mary Nyquist's study of the discourse of slavery quite properly sees the presence of the claim that all are naturally equal by nature in Lilburne, Overton, Wildman, and the Digger tract *Light Shining in Buckinghamshire* as an argument against arbitrary power, while also noticing the important citizen-patriot model of household governance in these works, the similarity of some of Lilburne's views to those of Milton, and even a knowledge of the ancient practices of slavery.[63] This fits with mention of Lilburne's call for the realization of universal human rights, both God-given and natural, which Paul Halliday reminds us have their origins earlier and in more non-secular contexts than is often thought.[64] More problematic is criticism of scholarship (because it allegedly ignores 'racialization') that shows resistance on the part of English radicals to the seduction of English people in 1650s London into lives of slavery in the Caribbean.[65] In this context one might note transatlantic figures with radical careers like the Rhode Island resident Samuel Gorton, an Antinomian and sometime General Baptist if not an explicitly declared Leveller, who regarded native Americans as human beings with sovereign liberties and privileges.[66]

Second, Victoria Kahn's study of explicit and implicit contract in Civil War writing acknowledges the contractual nature of the Putney debates: that the debaters were heading towards a binding agreement behind the *Agreement of the People*.[67] But agreement could not be reached because it could not be determined who was bound by what obligations, and also, and as I show above, because the senior officers had their way, disregarded the soldiers, and would eventually quell dissent with military punishment: more abrupt judicial violence. Kahn does justice to the complexity of the debate, not least to the officers' concern to find categories that would lead to peace and their fear of Antinomian anarchy, but does not mention that the debate itself is part of the agency

[62] See the essay in this volume by Paul Halliday, pp. 587–603; Andy Wood, 'Custom, Identity and Resistance: English Free Miners and Their Law, c.1500–1800', in *The Experience of Authority in Early Modern England*, ed. Paul Griffiths, Steve Hindle, and Adam Fox (1996), 249–85.

[63] Mary Nyquist, *Arbitrary Rule: Slavery, Tyranny, and the Power of Life and Death* (Chicago: University of Chicago Press, 2013), 131, 141–2, 149, 173–4.

[64] Halliday, *Habeas corpus*, 413–14.

[65] Nyquist, *Arbitrary Rule*, 408, n. 4, where John Donahue, '"Out of the Land of Bondage": The English Revolution and the Atlantic Origins of Abolition', *American History Review*, 115 (2010): 943–74 is cited with some disapproval.

[66] See John Donohue, *Fire under the Ashes: An Atlantic History of the English Revolution* (Chicago: University of Chicago Press, 2013), 153–4.

[67] Victoria Kahn, *Wayward Contracts: The Crisis of Political Obligation in England, 1640–1674* (Princeton: Princeton University Press, 2004), 11–12.

that the 'free-born Englishmen' and women thought was so important. In this moment of oblivion the idea of popular, universal liberties is alarmingly erased from the record. The debates of the 1640s involving Lilburne and company are the wayward contracting, but they remain a notable absence in this study despite a chapter section devoted to Magna Carta.[68]

In the statute books of the United Kingdom today the laws that were made between 1649 and 1660 are also simply absent: they are regarded as a legal nullity. We can therefore be grateful to Firth and Rait for listing the ordinances of the Interregnum.[69] Yet when lawyers train they miss this considerable body of vital knowledge thereby confirming John Streater's worst fear. The history of the Levellers is the history of common law tradition brought to new life as a vital instrument in realizing popular birthrights and consent, and embodied in a vigorous public practice of rhetorical advocacy and legal publishing.

Bibliography

Anon. *To the Supream Authority of this Nation, the Commons Assembled in Parliament: the Humble Petition of Divers Wel-Affected Women Inhabiting the Cities of London, Westminster, the Borough of Southwark, Hamblets, and Places Adjacent* (London: 1649).

Baker, Philip. 'The Levellers, Decentralisation and the *Agreements of the People*', in *The Agreements of the People, the Levellers and the Constitutional Crisis of the English Revolution*, ed. Philip Baker and Elliot Vernon (Basingstoke and New York: Palgrave Macmillan, 2012), 97–116.

Brooks, Christopher W. *Law, Politics and Society in Early Modern England* (Cambridge: Cambridge University Press, 2008).

Collins, Charles et al. *An Outcry of the Youngmen and Apprentices of London: Or, an Inquisition after the Lost Fundamentall Lawes and Liberties of England* (London: 1649).

Foxley, Rachel. *The Levellers: Radical Political Thought in the English Revolution* (Manchester: Manchester University Press, 2013).

Gurney, John. *Brave Community: The Digger Movement in the English Revolution* (Manchester: Manchester University Press, 2007).

Halliday, Paul. *Habeas corpus: From England to Empire* (Cambridge, MA: Harvard University Press, 2010).

Hart, James S., Jr. *The Rule of Law, 1603–1660* (Harlow and New York: Pearson and Longman, 2003).

Hirst, Derek. '"A Happier Man:" The Refashioning of William Walwyn', *The Seventeenth Century*, 27 (2012): 54–78.

Houston, Alan. 'A Way of Settlement: The Levellers, Monopolies and the Public Interest', *History of Political Thought*, 14 (1993): 381–420.

Hughes, Ann. 'Gender and Politics in Leveller Literature', in *Political Culture and Cultural Politics in Early Modern England: Essays Presented to David Underdown*, ed. Susan D. Amussen and Mark A. Kishlansky (Manchester: Manchester University Press, 1995), 162–88.

68 Kahn, *Wayward Contracts*, 41–8.

69 C. H. Firth and R. S. Rait, eds, *Acts and Ordinances of the Interregnum, 1642–1660*, 3 vols (1911).

Lilburne, John. *An Agreement of the Free People of England* [1649], in *The English Levellers*, ed. Andrew Sharp (Cambridge: Cambridge University Press, 1998).
Lilburne, John. *An Anatomy of the Lords Tyranny and Iniustice Exercised upon Lieu. Col. Iohn Lilburne, now a Prisoner in the Tower of London* ([London]: 1646).
Lilburne, John. *England's Birth-Right Justified against all Arbitrary Usurpation, whether Regall or Parliamentary, or under what Vizor Soever* ([London]: 1645).
Lilburne, John. *Legal Fundamentall Liberties, Revived, Asserted and Vindicated* ([London]: 1649).
Lilburne, John. *L. Colonel John Lilburne Revived. Shewing the Cause of his Late Long Silence, and Cessation from Hostility against Alchemy St Oliver, and his Rotten Secretary; as also of the Report of his Death* ([Amsterdam]: 1653).
Overton, Richard. *An Arrow against all Tyrants and Tyrany, Shot from the Prison of New-gate into the Prerogative Bowels of the Arbitrary House of Lords, and all other Usurpers and Tyrants whatsoever* ([London]: 1646).
Peacey, Jason. *Print and Public Politics in the English Revolution* (Cambridge: Cambridge University Press, 2013).
Seaberg, R. B. 'The Norman Conquest and the Common Law: The Levellers and the Argument from Continuity', *The Historical Journal*, 24.4 (1981): 796–806.
Sedley, Stephen. *Ashes and Sparks: Essays on Law and Justice* (Cambridge: Cambridge University Press, 2011).
Sharp, Andrew. 'John Lilburne and the Long Parliament's Book of Declarations: A Radical's Exploitation of the Words of Authorities', *History of Political Thought*, 9 (1988): 19–44.
Sharp, Andrew. 'John Lilburne's 'Discourse of Law', *Political Science*, 40 (1988): 18–33.
Sharp, Andrew, ed. *The English Levellers* (Cambridge: Cambridge University Press, 1998).
Smith, Nigel. *Literature and Revolution in England 1640–1660* (New Haven and London: Yale University Press, 1994).
[Streater, John]. *The Continuation of This Session of Parliament, Justified; and the Action of the Army Touching That Affair Defended: and Objections to Both Answered; According to the Best Rules of Law, Reason, and Just-Preserving Policie* ([London]: 1659).
[Streater, John]. *A Further Continuance of the Grand Politick Informer, Discovering the Wickednesse and Mysteries of the Present State Iniquities on Foot about the 14 of September 1653* ([London]: 1653).
[Streater, John]. *A Glympse of that Jevvel, Judicial, Just, Preserving Libertie* ([London]: 1653).
[Streater, John]. *The Loyal Messenger, or, Newes from White-hall Comprising the State and Martial Affaires of, and in Relation to the Common-wealth of England, Scotland, and Ireland* ([London]: 1654).
[Streater, John]. *Observations*, 10 ([London]: 1654).
[Streater, John]. *Secret Reasons of State in Reference to the Affairs of These Nations, at the Interruption of This Present Parliament: Anno 1653. Discovered* ([London]: 1659).
[Streater, John]. *A Shield against the Parthian Dart, or, a Word to the Purpose, Shot into Wallingford-House. Answered in Defence of the Present Actions of State Here in England, that Produced the Late Change of Government* ([London]: 1659).
Veall, Donald. *The Popular Movement for Law Reform, 1640–1660* (Oxford: Oxford University Press, 1970).
Walwyn, William, *Englands Lamentable Slaverie, Proceeding from the Arbitrarie Will, Severitie, and Injustnes of Kings, Negligence, Corruption, and Unfaithfulnesse of Parliaments, Coveteousnesse, Ambition* ([London]: 1645).

Warr, John. *A Spark in the Ashes: The Pamphlets of John Warr*, ed. Stephen Sedley and Lawrence Kaplan (London and New York: Verso, 1992).
Warr, John, *The Priviledges of the People, or, Principles of Common Right and Freedome* ([London]: 1649).
Wildman, John. *The Case of the Armie Truly Stated* ([London]: 1647).

CHAPTER 32

BASE SLAVERY AND ROMAN YOKE

MARY NYQUIST

ANIA Loomba and Jonathan Burton have made a strong case against the current practice of sharply distinguishing early modern usage of 'race' from its pseudo-scientific descendants. To stress the inchoate, unsystematic, and largely religio-cultural character of early modern 'race' is, they argue, not only to bestow a peculiar privilege on the biologically based discourses of the later eighteenth, nineteenth, and twentieth centuries but also to obscure some of the profound continuities between earlier and later phases of European colonialism.[1] Granted, early modern 'race' may appear in connection with non-human animals, intra-European differences in status, or ethnic and (proto-) national groups in ways that perplex modern assumptions. Very generally speaking, early modern 'race' signifies inheritance. With regard to status distinction, 'race' indicates inheritance that is lineal and familial, while when used as a synonym of 'nation' it designates inheritance that is customary and communal. Negative connotations are more common when 'race' in the sense of 'nation' is applied to non-Europeans or to beings who are considered doubtfully human, as occurs in Shakespeare's *The Tempest* when Miranda assails Caliban with the scornful, 'thy vile race'. Yet what about the words with which Miranda opens this speech, 'Abhorrèd slave', or with which Prospero first addresses Caliban, 'What ho, slave! Caliban! / Thou earth, thou, speak!' or with which he addresses him a moment later, 'Thou poisonous slave!' (1.2.357, 350, 313–14, 319)? Is 'slave' in these instances and, perhaps, others, in any way racialized? Does it indicate or imply a distinctive legal status? These are some of the questions to be addressed in this chapter. First, though, it must be observed that usage of 'slave', 'slavery', and cognates of 'servitude' has not undergone the kind of historicized analysis that has 'race'.

To some degree this neglect results from the sheer ubiquity of the pejorative 'slave', which, especially in early modern drama, appears so frequently as to be basically

[1] 'Introduction', *Race in Early Modern England: A Documentary Companion*, ed. Ania Loomba and Jonathan Burton (Basingstoke: Palgrave Macmillan, 2007), 1–36.

unremarkable. The dominantly white academy's anxieties about its own racialization may also play a part. Yet avoidance may also register the confusing diversity of contexts in which 'slavery' is employed. Early modern writers, steeped in ancient Greek and Roman literature, often imagine chattel slavery with reference to its institutionalization in Athens and Rome, and adopt the many influential figurative slaveries—amatory enslavement to a beloved, ethical enslavement to passions, spiritual enslavement to carnal desires, and political enslavement to a tyrant—that Graeco-Roman literature developed and medieval literature elaborated on chattel slavery's foundation. They are also familiar with forms of Hebrew servitude as well as with attitudes towards Hebrew slavery and service (cognate with 'servitude' but generally either neutrally descriptive or praiseworthy) formulated in the Christian Bible and by its influential commentators. Penal servitude was given new-found respectability by More's *Utopia* and was practiced in the form of galley slavery in, among other European nations, Spain and France. Further, though not finally, as the list could be extended, the temporary enslavement of European Christians in the Mediterranean area, publicized in largely propagandistic ways in relation to Ottoman Muslims, was common knowledge, as was the gradual institutionalization of diverse forms of hereditary slavery in the New World.[2]

Such an abundance of slaveries offers a rich array of possibilities for distinguishing 'freedom' (or 'liberty', from the Latin *libertas*) from 'slavery', a not undesirable situation for the early modern Western Europeans who were increasingly committed to identifying themselves as 'free'—'free' individually, politically, and nationally. As ideologically charged constructs, 'freedom', 'slavery', and 'tyranny' crystalized their interrelations in classical Athens, where they became central to Athenian democratic and imperial ideologies and, later, to the Roman republic and empire. All three constructs are grounded in the polarity between the unfree legal status of the individual slave and the legal status of the free citizen. How, then, were they appropriated in England, where chattel slavery was not legal? 'Serf' derives from the Latin *servus*, and serfdom was sometimes conflated with slavery; for rhetorical purposes, even 'vassals' could be considered interchangeable with slaves when figurative political slavery was being vituperated for rhetorical purposes. Yet serfdom is often and clearly enough differentiated from chattel slavery for Bodin to assert, unobjectionably and influentially, that institutional slavery along Greek and Roman lines had not been practised in Western Europe since, he estimates, the early thirteenth century, though he worries it is being re-introduced by the Portuguese and Spanish.[3]

If, as Bodin claims, chattel slavery has no purchase within early modern Western Europe, is the institutionalization of slavery in the New World a condition of possibility

[2] Further, detailed discussion appears in Michael Guasco's *Slaves and Englishmen: Human Bondage in the Early Modern Atlantic World* (Philadelphia: University of Pennsylvania Press, 2014).

[3] Jean Bodin, *The Six Bookes of A Commonweale: A Facsimile Reprint of the English Translation of 1606, Corrected and Supplemented in Light of a New Comparison with the French [République] and Latin Texts*, ed. Kenneth Douglas McRae, trans. Richard Knolles (Cambridge, MA: Harvard University Press, 1962), 1.5.40, 43–4.

for the affective power of appeals to 'liberty' and 'slavery'? Elsewhere I have argued that it is, but in this chapter I discuss two distinctive modes of slavery, which, I suggest, may perform a critical, transitional part in the institutionalization of racialized transatlantic slavery.[4] The first is the derogatory use of 'slave' as an extra-legal marker of intra-English, intra-British, or intra-European social status that is so radically low as to be nearly beneath contempt. Later I turn to what I call war slavery, another form of slavery that lies outside exclusively English common or statutory legal traditions since its originates in *ius gentium*, that is, in the right (or law) of nations which Roman jurists believe to have been established by practices that are universally observed in warfare. Like the pejorative 'slave', war slavery is a significantly under-investigated, literary, artistic, philosophical, and political means of representing relations of domination and subordination as 'slavery'. Shakespeare's dramatic works provide the primary archive for representations of war slavery, and though I have found related forms in the productions of contemporaries, I must stress the exploratory nature of my study. In analysing 'slave' as pejorative, I draw on a wide range of Shakespeare's dramas, concluding with treatment of *Titus Andronicus*'s Aaron and *The Tempest*'s Caliban, while Spenser's *Fairie Queene* and *Cymbeline* focus discussion of war slavery as a trope of Anglo-colonialism.

'Slave' as Pejorative

As a term, 'slave' and its relatives enter European languages in the medieval period with reference to the 'slavs' that constituted a sizeable proportion of the people trafficked as slaves in the Mediterranean area. Though the Latin *servus* could be translated into the vernacular as either 'servant' or 'slave', the latter usually designates Graeco-Roman chattel slaves, and tends to be used of both galley slaves and Mediterranean war slaves. When used as a pejorative in Elizabethan and Jacobean drama, however, 'slave' frequently detaches itself from slavery as an economic and social institution: it circulates without reference to trafficking, ownership, legal status, or unfree labour. [5] Why 'slave,' then? If not bound up with institutional slavery, what work does 'slave' do?

The pejorative 'slave' is least problematical when it appears in direct address where the speaker's intention to insult is unmistakable. In *King Lear*, to start with a well-known play, when Oswald offends Lear by refusing to answer him, Lear refers to him as 'the slave' and then, on Oswald's offer of further insult, hurls at him, 'you whoreson / dog,

[4] For the possibility that 'class' relations play a transitional role, see Étienne Balibar, 'Class Racism', in Étienne Balibar and Immanuel Wallerstein, *Race, Nation, Class: Ambiguous Identities*, trans. Chris Turner (London: Verso, 1991), 204–16. For interconnections between figurative political slavery and transatlantic slavery, see Mary Nyquist, *Arbitrary Rule: Slavery, Tyranny, and the Power of Life and Death* (Chicago: Chicago University Press, 2013).

[5] Camille Wells Slights' 'Slaves and Subjects in *Othello*' remains the go-to study of the pejorative 'slave', which she ties to Orlando Patteron's theorization of institutional slavery as 'social death', *SQ*, 48.4 (1997): 377–90.

you slave, you cur!' (4.48.75–6). In *Henry VI, Part 2*, much less familiar, the arrogant Suffolk, in one of many insufferable attempts to intimidate the captain who has him in his power, abusively addresses him with, 'Base slave, thy words are blunt and so art thou' (4.1.68). A similar effect occurs in *Cymbeline* when the equally self-promoting Cloten demands to know if Arviragus and Belarius are 'Some villain mountaineers?' and addresses Guiderius with 'What slave art thou?' (4.2.73–4). Here 'villain' communicates assumptions about not only low birth but also rustic low-mindedness. With its explicit relation to villeinage, 'villain' has associations with low status in the form of servile labour but also with the rude 'village' and 'villager' (related to 'villain'). Cloten's 'villain mountaineers' illustrates the continuing association of 'villain' and villeinage with the comparatively unpopulated countryside, in this case Welsh.

In direct address, 'slave' is often an instrument of heavy hitting verbal abuse; its purpose is to demean the individual(s) so addressed, often in the company of others. As the examples just cited indicate, 'slave's' injurious intent may be inseparable from its hyperbolic, self-delusive inflation of the speaker's status, the relative or imagined superiority of which is put on display. It seems especially fitting that at this time, 'abuse', in addition to the meaning current today, also has the meaning to mislead, to deceive. Nowhere does abuse's double-edged sword shine more brilliantly than when Don Quixote, having heard Sancho Panzo speak disrespectfully of Dulcinea, strikes him twice, throws him to the ground, and calls him a 'base wretch', 'depraved villain', 'coarse, contemptible ruffian', 'insidious viper's tongue', 'foul whorson', and 'ingrate' ['villano ruin', bellaco descomulgado', 'gañán', 'faquín', 'belitre', 'socarrón de lengua viperina', 'hideputa bellaco', 'desagradecido'].[6] This is not the last time Cervantes' romantic protagonist comes to a fictive maiden's defence with alarming ferocity, but it is perhaps the most impressive example of threats to self-inflating presumptions—in Don Quixote's case, his precariously seated knighthood—displacing and discharging themselves in abuse.

'Slave's' ability simultaneously to augment and diminish is not confined to direct address, though. Speakers often use 'slave' to enlarge differences between those about whom they speak. We can see this in *Richard III* when King Edward refers to the 'servant' whose pardon Lord Stanley requests as 'slave' so as to heighten the contrast between ordering his brother's death and giving the unnamed servant life: 'Have I a tongue to doom my brother's death, / And shall the same give pardon to a slave?' (2.1.101–2). 'Servant' and 'slave' are not interchangeable here; 'slave' substitutes for 'servant' in order to magnify the status-based antithesis on which Edward tries to balance his tottering mind. King Richard II uses 'slaves' similarly of the commoners whom his rival Bolingbroke enchants with his respectful treatment:

> What reverence he did throw away on slaves,
> Wooing poor craftsmen with the craft of smiles
> And patient underbearing of his fortunes. (1.4.27–9)

6 Miguel de Cervantes, *Don Quixote*, trans. Edith Grossman (New York: HarperCollins Publishers, 2003), 255; *Don Quijote*, ed. Tom Lathrop (Newark: Cervantes and Co., 2005), 154.

Represented as an egregious panderer trying to win over lowly, no-account 'slaves', the high-born Bolingbroke's courtesy is made to appear transparently crafty to those of his own rank whose biases Richard II presumes his auditors share. This presumption, together with the ability of 'slaves' to aggrandize status differences, reflects more on Richard II than on Bolingbroke himself.

Neither servants nor commoners, of course, are legally enslaved, and their labour, relevant in the case of 'craftsmen', is clearly free as opposed to coerced (the options recognized by the polarity free/unfree). Unusually, 'slave' is associated with something like coerced labour when, towards the conclusion of *King Lear*, Edgar reports that the banished and disguised Kent followed his ungrateful master, 'and did him service / Improper for a slave' (24.217–18). Here, too, though, the purpose of 'slave' is to drive home the contrast between Kent's true worth and the degrading part he willingly played. Contrast in the form of competition or rivalry is generally fertile ground for the desire to disparage with 'slave'. In trying to persuade Innogen that her marriage to Posthumous is invalid, Cloten, for example, calls Posthumous 'a base slave, / A hilding for a livery, a squire's cloth, / A pantler—not so eminent' (2.3.119–21). With his usual ineptitude, Cloten's amplification of 'base slave' in the particulars that follow actually qualifies the absolute baseness of 'slave'. Warfare—in this way an extension of rivalry—puts 'slaves' to similar use. In *1 Henry VI*, Charles the Dauphin calls the English 'hare-brained slaves' (1.2.37), and Talbot calls the French 'oft-subduèd slaves' (1.6.32).

Yet 'slave' does not necessarily convey hostile degradation in performing aggrandizement. In King Henry V's meditation on the cares of royal office, the figure of 'the wretched slave', who is literally low-born, merely highlights the self-pitying wretchedness of the King's care-burdened condition. King Henry's night-time soliloquy begins with a consideration of 'ceremony' but concludes—in a passage where 'slave' appears twice—with reflection on sleep:

> No, not all these, thrice-gorgeous ceremony,
> Not all these, laid in bed majestical,
> Can sleep so soundly as the wretched slave
> Who with a body filled and vacant mind
> Gets him to rest, crammed with distressful bread;
> Never sees horrid night, the child of hell,
> But like a lackey from the rise to set
> Sweats in the eye of Phoebus, and all night
> Sleeps in Elysium; next day, after dawn
> Doth rise and help Hyperion to his horse,
> And follows so the ever-running year
> With profitable labour to his grave.
> And but for ceremony such a wretch,
> Winding up days with toil and nights with sleep,
> Had the forehand and vantage of a king.
> The slave, a member of the country's peace,

> Enjoys it, but in gross brain little wots
> What watch the King keeps to maintain the peace,
> Whose hours the peasant best advantages. (4.1.254–72)

Here the 'slave' is simply a labourer, implicitly free, who in the last line is identified as a 'peasant'. He need not be put down because he already occupies the lowly rank that opposes the king's as its contrary. Indeed, the conventional pastoral motifs suggest that King Henry idealizes the 'slave's' repetitive, physically demanding labour which, following natural cycles, is itself naturally healthful. At the same time, the soliloquy's maudlin tone and insistence on the slave's brain-dead existence ('in gross brain little wots') emphasize the underlying contrast between care-ridden sleeplessness and life-affirming sleep. This specific contrast in turn recalls his father's similar plaint in *2 Henry IV* 3.1. Although neither speech evokes the tyranny by acquisition of which Henry IV could be accused, sleeplessness is such a well-known, tell-tale sign of tyranny that it is difficult to ignore its hovering presence.

How are the 'peasant', the 'villain', and the 'slave' related? All three can be used as slurs, and, in addition, are often modified by 'base'. Of the three, 'peasant' is the simplest because its purpose is merely to enlarge differences in social status. Marlowe's *The Jew of Malta* typifies this usage when Lodowick refers to his rival Don Mathias as 'the base borne peasant' (2.3.282).[7] 'Villain' and 'slave' can also be used in this way and at times appear to be interchangeable. They can also, however, express moral disapproval, condemnation, or, possibly, criminalization. 'Villain', of course, comes to name the notorious descendant of the 'Vice' figure: the stage villain who instigates discord and mayhem. Yet 'slave', too, can communicate strong negative judgement, as when Lady Anne vituperates Richard of Gloucester in *Richard III* as 'devilish slave' (1.2.88), or when, towards the end of *Othello*, Emilia guesses that Othello has been deceived by 'Some busy and insinuating rogue, / Some cogging, cozening slave' (4.2.131–2). Once Iago has been found out and slays Emilia, Montano uses both 'villain' and 'slave' as invective: 'I'll go after that same villain, / For 'tis a damnèd slave' (5.2.248–9). The later, more severely judgemental term in both these examples, 'slave' appears ever more persistently as the drama closes, when Othello berates himself with 'O cursèd, cursèd slave' (5.2.275), when Lodovico laments Othello's having 'Fallen in the practice of a damnèd slave' (5.2.290), and in Lodovico's final reference to Iago as 'this slave' (5.2.331). 'Slave' here denounces, criminalizes, condemns.

Even in the context of war, 'slave' can censure and criminalize. In the opening scene of *MacBeth*, the traitor Macdonald, just killed by Macbeth, is contemptuously referred to as 'the slave' (1.2.20). A similar tone is struck when in *Henry V* the Duke of Bourbon conjures an anonymous 'slave' engaged in sexual assault. Warning his troops of the ruinous

[7] Christopher Marlowe, *Complete Works*, Vol. 4: *The Jew of Malta*, ed. Roma Gill (Oxford: Clarendon Press, 1995).

shame that will overtake them should they fearfully flee battle, the Duke vividly depicts the kind of homecoming they might expect:

> And he that will not follow Bourbon now,
> Let him go home, and with his cap in hand
> Like a base leno [pimp] hold the chamber door
> Whilst by a *slave* no gentler than my dog
> His fairest daughter is contaminated. (4.5.11–15; my emphasis)

Rhetorically, the climax of this scene—rape of the cowardly soldier's daughter by an unnamed 'slave'—is meant to degrade not so much the daughter as her father, whose paternal duty is to protect her chastity. It activates Graeco-Roman codes of martial honour and shame that celebrate the virtue of the warrior who courageously risks his life in order to preserve his people's freedom along with the honour of women shamefully vulnerable to sexual assault in the event of defeat (vulnerability Henry V earlier threateningly says his soldiers will take advantage of should they defeat the French). In this passage, the 'slave' appears without an adjective, presumably because his baseness is self-evidently a matter of situation and culpability not of social rank.

Yet, oddly, neither English villeins or slaves are to be found in late Elizabethan and early Jacobean England. Although legislation regarding villeinage had not been abolished, by the late fifteenth century villeinage was scarcely practised, and by the time Shakespeare was writing his dramatic works the institution had died out. By contrast with the 'villein', the 'slave' was not recognized in English common law, though forms of penal servitude had periodically been legitimated. In 1547 an effort was made to introduce a form of penal servitude by a law punishing able-bodied but idle, masterless vagabonds and beggars with two years of personal slavery to the citizen reporting their failure to contribute to the commonwealth. Extremely harsh penalties were to be imposed should the enslaved try to flee, with the second escape punishable by death. C. L. Davies speculates that this legislation is the product of 'what one may perhaps call the More tradition: that it was better both for condemned criminals themselves and for the state if they were set to work for the public good rather than hanged'.[8] Rescinded in 1549, the law appears to have been unenforceable, partly, it is conjectured, because the penalties were considered too extreme, partly, as a contemporary commentator suggested, on the basis of the horrifying connotations of 'slavery'.[9]

Pride in England's reputation as a nation that cherishes 'freedom' likely contributed to overturning the 1547 Act that authorized 'slavery'. If the very word provoked such resistance, some of the credit must go to humanism's appropriation of Graeco-Roman

[8] C. S. L. Davies, 'Slavery and Protector Somerset: the Vagrancy Act of 1547', *Economic History Review*, 2nd ser., 19 (1966): 541. Guasco discusses slavery in More's *Utopia* in connection with this act, and provides a more detailed account of villeinage and its dissolution in *Slaves and Englishman*, 33–6; 25–33.

[9] Davies, 'Slavery', 533–49, 547, 'it was the name that rankled, rather than the condition of slavery. … To admit to slavery was bad for national prestige'.

literature, which honours 'free' male citizens who serve the state by defending its liberty but denigrates as servile those who are willing to surrender it or, worse, could care less. In early modern cultural contexts that either represent or adapt Graeco-Roman values, honour and dishonour continue to be the preserve of the free, propertied male citizenry, since female honour revolves around chastity, and both female and male members of the lower orders are often thought to be without either honour or shame. If, ideally, even low-born Englishmen were to have a sense of honour appropriate to their free-born status, the Vagrancy Act's 'slavery' would have seemed counter-productive. In any case, freedom's association with male honour may help to explain why, as a slur, 'slave' assails men alone, and, possibly, to account for the discomfort that led eighteenth-century editors to give to Prospero Miranda's first words to Caliban, which, as mentioned earlier, are 'Abhorrèd slave'.

In lacking 'villain's' connection with the countryside, or its increasingly stable association with vice and villainy, 'slave' has a wider range of potential contexts and affective powers. Clearly, Graeco-Roman discourses cannot completely account for the singular force of 'slave'. When used of commoners or peasants, 'slave' may indicate the status of low-ranking, unpropertied Englishmen who are not able fully to exercise the privileges of citizens. In other instances, though, the very absence within England of legal enslavement seems to draw usage of 'slave' away from the polarity free/slave toward a unique status comparable to though not identical with the later, moralized 'villain'. When this happens, 'slavery' activates the connotations of anti-sociability or outright criminality attaching to penal servitude. A definition that would comprehend all the examples discussed so far would therefore have to include degradation (either rhetorically neutral, as in King Henry V's use of 'slave', or vituperative and aggrandizing) in terms of social rank as enunciated by a social superior (or community of recognized superiors) and degradation in terms of punishably offensive (in either a social or legal sense) behaviour as judged by those of a recognizably superior ethico-social standing. (Emilia, for example, though subordinate to her husband, nevertheless clearly has superior ethical standing.) With such an elastic range of meanings, identities from the marginal in terms of social rank to the anti-social or criminal regardless of rank are generated by 'slave'.

We could take this a bit further. If my construal has validity, it could, ironically, make the 'slave' kin to the vagabond whom the Vagrancy Act of 1547 was to punish with slavery. In the lines from *Othello* quoted above, Emilia calls the unidentified villain first 'rogue', then 'slave'. 'Rogues' are associated with homelessness, vagrancy, and vagabondage—conditions that are not only believed to foster crime but are themselves subject to criminalization in early modern England, though they are frequently the result of enclosure. If the slave has affinities with the rogue (affinities not shared with the villain), perhaps it is because they have both *rejected* the master/servant relationship? No longer in subjection to a feudal lord, the 'peasant' of this time is without a master, as are many commoners. Like the rogue or vagabond, however, the 'slave' is often imagined to have *chosen* life outside the social constraints of fixed community, occupation, or relationship with a master. Or like other potential or actual criminals, the 'slave' may have thrown off the shackles of laws or ethical bonds. If these associations are present, the anti-social or criminalized 'slave' could, like the stage villain, be a figure of amoral or anti-social licence, yet one who has elected his condition of masterlessness. In this case the 'slave' of early modern English drama would be the exact contrary of the slave in Roman law, who is under the enslaver's *dominium* or mastership.

Hamlet does not clarify these issues but it does bring home their interest. When in Act 2, Hamlet launches into self-castigation by opening his soliloquy with 'O what a rogue and peasant slave am I!' (2.2.538), he is using 'slave' as other speakers do, that is, to augment difference in status, this time between Hamlet's ideal, heroically aristocratic self and the shamefully bumbling, inactive self he feels the players have exposed. (Marlowe's Barabas at one point likewise berates himself with 'What a damn'd slave was I' [5.1.24]). By linking 'rogue' with 'peasant slave', Hamlet's opening phrase concatenates three different terms of abuse. Conjoined, the terms emphasize marginalization and consequent powerlessness but the adjectival 'peasant' softly forecloses criminalization of 'rogue' or 'slave'. Continuing to rebuke himself for cowardice, Hamlet goes on, though, to identify both 'slave' and 'villain' with the treacherously criminal Claudius:

> For it cannot be
> But I am pigeon-livered and lack gall
> To make oppression bitter, or ere this
> I should have fatted all the region kites
> With this slave's offal. Bloody, bawdy, villain!
> Remorseless, treacherous, lecherous, kindless villain! (2.2.564–9)

Against 'peasant slave', Hamlet's 'this slave's offal' calls up an antagonist that has passed beyond criminality into sub-humanity. Deserving death, 'this slave' should have been slaughtered, his physical remains, like an animal's 'offal', should have 'fatted' neighbouring 'kites'. Hamlet's diatribe against Claudius the criminal, the 'villain', takes off from here. The image remains, though, of the animalized 'slave's' body lying unburied on unpopulated ground, whether killed in a battle of some sort or as a masterless vagrant living outside the law, we are not to know.

Aaron, Caliban, Slavery

Avoidance occasionally creates space for later, racialized assumptions, as happens when critics or students identify *Titus Andronicus*'s villainous Aaron as a slave. This identification conflates Aaron's own stress on his Africanness with unfree legal status, and may seek confirmation in Aaron's reference to his infant son as 'the black slave' (4.2.120), or in the phrases with which he addresses his son as 'you thick-lipped slave', and 'tawny slave' (4.2.175; 5.1.27). If 'slave' is re-encoded as I have proposed, however, Aaron's language instead acknowledges his son's fatally criminalized status as undeniable evidence of Aaron's adulterous relationship with the Empress.[10] Were the latter two phrases spoken in tones of endearment, they would convey Aaron's increasingly wholehearted embrace of this status for himself as well as his desire to shield his son from death, its inevitable consequence.

The notion that the African Aaron is enslaved may also rely on his soliloquy of 2.1, which opens celebrating Tamora's elevation to the exalted status of Rome's Empress, goes on to disclose their love affair, turns to his emphatic rejection of servitude of any kind ('Away with slavish weeds and servile thoughts'), and concludes by plotting how Tamora and he will destroy Rome:

> Upon her wit doth earthly honour wait,
> And virtue stoops and trembles at her frown;
> Then, Aaron, arm thy heart and fit thy thoughts
> To mount aloft with thy imperial mistress,
> And mount her pitch, whom thou in triumph long
> Hast prisoner held, fettered in amorous chains,
> And faster bound to Aaron's charming eyes
> Than is Prometheus tied to Caucasus.
> Away with slavish weeds and servile thoughts!
> I will be bright, and shine in pearl and gold,
> To wait upon this new-made Empress.
> To wait, said I?—To wanton with this queen,
> This goddess, this Semirarnus, this nymph,
> This siren, that will charm Rome's Saturnine,
> And see his shipwrack and his commonweal's. (2.1.10–24)

This passage opens with Tamora in the position of a deified or semi-deified ruler (continuing the earlier idea that she's climbed 'Olympus' top') whose subjects—at least their 'honour' and their 'virtue'—are abjectly dependent on her every whim. It unfolds by drawing on the lexicon of courtly servility, an expression of the figurative (either ethical or political depending on context) slavery encouraged by monarchical absolutism. Aaron enjoins himself to rise to Tamora's new, elevated status, an ambition that should easily be fulfilled, he reasons associatively, since Tamora is privately his love slave. Drawing on the language of love slavery, which frequently invokes motifs from war slavery, Aaron reveals he has long held Tamor 'prisoner', 'fettered in amorous chains, / And faster bound to Aaron's charming eyes / Than is Prometheus tied to Caucasus'. Aaron here inverts love slavery's conventional gender assignments. In place of the inaccessibly superior fair lady, Aaron himself is the

[10] Lorna Hutson relates the emphasis on blackness to forensic rhetoric in, 'Rethinking the Spectacle of the Scaffold: Juridical Epistemologies and English Revenge Tragedy', *Representations*, 89.1 (2005): 30–58, 50–1.

tyrannous beloved, while the former Queen of the Goths plays the conventionally male role of the enslaved lover.

In relation to, first, courtly and then amatory slavery, Aaron pointedly exempts himself from the category of the figuratively enslaved. His imperative, 'Away with slavish weeds and servile thoughts!', thus constitutes a continuation of his aspirational logic rather than a longing for a liberatory break from servitude. In its rhetorical development, Aaron's soliloquy suggests that Tamora's unexpected promotion awakens his desire for a similarly superior, beholden-to-none position at the top of Rome's ruling class, which is why Aaron quickly corrects his servile 'wait' with its more satisfying (and not only sexually) 'wanton'. Service of any kind is for Aaron—as, in a later play, it is for Iago—slave-like, servile. For this reason, the plan he concocts has Tamora remaining enslaved by his 'charming eyes' while she continues to 'charm' the emperor Saturninus. Aaron does not want to be the Empress's partner (even her partner-in-crime) but her master, so as to be in charge of bringing about the downfall of Rome.

To recognize that Shakespeare's Aaron is not enslaved we need not rely solely on detailed analysis of his soliloquy, however: he has already been decreed legally 'free'. In a section of the opening act almost never discussed, Titus responds to Saturninus' offer to marry his daughter Lavinia by bestowing on Saturninus in return, or perhaps as dower, 'My sword, my chariot, and my prisoners', all ceremoniously presented as 'tribute' (1.2). Earlier, Tamora correctly remarks when begging Titus to spare her son's life that the defeated Goths are now 'Captive to thee and to thy Roman yoke'. With this transfer of ownership (made to Emperor Saturninus for the good of commonwealth and empire, yet also curiously private), Saturninus vows to treat Tamora with honour appropriate to her princely station, and then suddenly formally liberates all of the prisoners: 'Ransomless here we set our prisoners free.' Spectators know from his aside, though, that Saturninus' magnanimous gesture is semi-consciously motivated by his attraction to Tamora—attraction that reveals his affinity with the barbarous Goths.

If Aaron is definitively not enslaved, his blackness does not thereby elude negative, racialized constructions. Portraying Rome at a moment of its threatened demise by barbarians, Shakespeare and his collaborator make use of largely medieval constructions of blackness as negatively aligned with Moorish infidels and evil, though Elizabeth's draft proclamation or patent for expelling 'negroes and blackamores' may also be relevant.[11] The situation represented in *The Tempest* is, of course, entirely different, as is the historical context in which it is written. England's expansionary designs and ventures are much further advanced in 1611, while de Bry's representations of European encounters with Amerindigenes have been circulating for some time.[12] None of these changes necessarily

[11] See Miranda Kauffman, 'Caspar van Senden, Sir Thomas Sherley and the "Blackamoor" Project', *Historical Research*, 81.212 (2008): 366–71.

[12] The Virginia Company's royal charter, first issued in 1606, revised in 1610, is important evidence of England's more aggressive colonial expansion. See Robert A. Williams, Jr, *The American Indian in*

brings Caliban's description in the '*Names of the Actors*' in the first Folio (1623) as '*a saluage and deformed slaue*' any closer to designating unfree legal status, however. On the contrary, the vehemence with which both Prospero and Miranda persistently address Caliban as 'slave' in Act 1.2 (four times in thirty-seven lines) indicates that 'slave' functions as it usually does in dramatic direct address: 'slave' puts the addressee down. Does this suggest that Prospero and Miranda self-righteously inflate the social distance between them and their addressee in using 'slave' as a slur? It's scarcely possible to pose this important question because the revelation that Caliban tried to 'violate' Miranda's 'honour' lets connotations of anti-sociability or criminality overwhelm those of rank-or species-associated baseness.

In occurring so early on that spectators aren't given a chance to form their own judgements, this co-voiced, intensely abusive 'slave' is very unusual. More provocatively unique is Prospero's addition of the possessive 'my', which appears first when he addresses Ariel, 'Thou, my slave', and next when he proposes that he and Miranda 'visit Caliban, my slave'. To my mind, this is the most significantly anomalous use of 'slave' in *The Tempest*. If not ownership, 'my slave' certainly indicates mastership, and is thereby closer to designating formal enslavement than the usage discussed earlier in this chapter. There are, though, two problems with reading 'my slave' with reference to institutional slavery. First, there is the obvious difference between Ariel's servitude, which has a definite, contractual terminus, and Caliban's, which doesn't. Translated into the language used of labour practices that would become increasingly prevalent in English colonies, we might identify Ariel as an indentured servant, Caliban as a slave. Similarities or dissimilarities between the indentured servitude of Europeans ending up in the colonies and the enslavement of Amerindigenes and Africans continue to be debated, as do the dates by which the two modes of servitude can be considered racialized.[13] Although English migrants were still relatively few and far between, it is possible to discern in *The Tempest* a prescient differentiation of indentured from permanent servitude.

The second difficulty relates to the absence of a legislative body on *The Tempest*'s island. If this seems a thick-headed observation to make of a self-consciously fantastical drama, I would like to counter by suggesting that the very absence of European legal institutions and traditions may be one of *The Tempest*'s central concerns. Precisely because English colonial discourses so eagerly exploit the anti-Spanish propaganda

Western Legal Thought: The Discourses of Conquest (New York and Oxford: Oxford University Press, 1990), 199–212. Regarding both versions of the charter, Williams stresses connections with Calvin's case and the importance of Sir Edward Coke's active involvement. The inaugural volume of De Bry's multivolume collection illustrates Thomas Harriot's *A Briefe and True Report of the New Found Land of Virginia* and was published in 1590.

[13] See, for example, Guasco, *Slaves and Englishmen*; John Donoghue, *Fire Under the Ashes: An Atlantic History of the English Revolution* (Chicago: University of Chicago Press, 2013); Hilary McD. Beckles, *White Servitude* and Black Slavery in Barbados, 1627–1715 (Knoxville: University of Tennessee Press, 1989); and David W. Galenson, *White Servitude in Colonial America: An Economic Analysis* (Cambridge: Cambridge University Press, 1981).

known as the Black Legend, issues of conformity with either English or international law are often of serious ideological import—so much so that they are frequently obfuscated or avoided.[14] In the action Shakespeare has invented, the sovereign position Prospero assumes is the very position that Western European colonists regularly assume vis-à-vis the Indigenous peoples of the Americas and, later, enslaved Africans. By exposing to view both presumptive sovereignty and flagrant extra-legality, Shakespeare invites reflection on Euro-colonialism's enabling yet dangerous blind-spot.

When Euro-colonists assume sovereignty over non-Europeans and non-European territories outside the purview of the legislative authority of the nation-state they purportedly represent, they risk threatening the state's own *dominium*. This conflict is at the heart of de Las Casas' *Destruction of the Indies* and, arguably, of *The Tempest*, where Prospero's magic encompasses the highest expression of sovereign power, the power of life and death. Prospero exercises this power in several ways, most spectacularly in conjuring up the tempest itself. Once Prospero finishes his opening expository narrative to Miranda, Shakespeare foregrounds the brutal disciplinary regime he has established for both Ariel and Caliban. Should Ariel fail immediately to comply with his every command, Prospero threatens to re-imprison him in a tree, this time not the 'cloven pine' (1.2.278) in which he was initially imprisoned but, Prospero specifies, 'an oak' (1.2, 295) a hard as opposed to soft wood. Prospero also irascibly threatens Caliban, who then relates the multiple forms of ingeniously devised physical torture which assail him as punishment when he disobeys his master. If Prospero calls each of them 'my slave', we may not have to look beyond this penal disciplinary regime for an explanation.

Anglo-Colonialism, Spenser, Heliodorus, and War Slavery

What I am calling war slavery is taken up in Justinian's *Institutes*, where slavery is acknowledged to contravene humanity's natural freedom but is nonetheless sanctioned by *ius gentium*, a 'law' or 'right' the validity of which derives from its universal acceptance as a human practice. Early modern European dictionaries, political theorists, poets, dramatists, and pamphleteers follow Roman jurisprudence by distinguishing between local, positive laws regulating slavery and its practice *ius gentium*, where military victors may choose either to kill or enslave those they have vanquished. The war slavery that results is conventionally theorized as personal, domestic servitude,

[14] Williams discusses a debate about whether the Virginia charter should justify England's colonizing project in the New World; owing to the controversies provoked by Spanish declarations, silence was agreed upon. See *American Indian in Western Legal Thought*, op. cit., 202–5. On the legal precision of English anti-Spanish propaganda in the dramatic representation of colony and empire, see also Edward Holberton's chapter in this volume.

in which an individual household master holds in his possession or under his rule an individual slave (or a number of individual slaves). Yet beginning in classical Athens, entire communities or nations are imagined to be inherently free or servile, while at the same time military conquest is often represented as a form of slave-mastership over the conquered, who are in any case incapable of collective self-rule, and so naturally to be enslaved. This particular modality of figurative slavery is crucial to Athenian, Roman, and, later, European imperial enterprises, which are conducted by 'free' nations who take as their responsibility the governance of nations that are, if not defeated and figuratively enslaved, so given to slavishness as to require it.[15]

In Anglo-colonial representations of the Irish or Amerindigenes, native liberty is generally synonymous with license, a signifier of precisely such a collective incapacity. Regarding Ireland, the worry is that Irish lords stand directly in the way of England's imposition of sovereignty: they continue to govern by Brehon law, which, it is agreed, is tantamount to no law at all. (In a similarly violent erasure of culture and history, Hobbes declares that Amerindigenes 'have no government at all'.)[16] In *A View of the State of Ireland*, Spenser's Irenius explains that the Irish have never been 'made to learn obedience unto laws, scarcely to know the name of law, but instead thereof have always preserved and kept their owne law, which is the Brehon law'.[17] Later on, Irenius declares it's hopeless to expect any participation of the Irish in due legal process; even if care were taken to select decent jury members, 'the baser Irish people', who care nothing for oaths, would willingly deceive the jury, since 'sure their Lordes may compel them to say any thing'.[18] In *True Causes Why Ireland Was Never Entirely Subdued*, John Davies formulates the terms for what he calls 'Perfect Conquest of a Country', which, regarding Ireland, he claims, requires abolishing Brehon law and establishing the laws of England, something that should have been done at the outset of the colonizing effort. The English lords who were supposed to reduce the Irish instead threw off their allegiance to English law, 'loving the Irish tyranny, which was tyed to no Rules of *Law or Honor*'.[19] In short, Davies says, they became 'slaves to that Nation which they did intend to Conquer'.[20]

England's own successful colonization by Rome may be its most important credential for taking on the responsibility of civilizing retrograde, barbarous nations, including the Irish. Irish unruliness and the dangerous seductiveness of its lawlessness inform the episode in Book 5 of the *Fairie Queene* in which readers learn that the

[15] For more detailed discussion of war slavery, see Mary Nyquist, *Arbitrary Rule* (Chicago: University of Chicago Press, 2013), esp. 218–26 and 239–42.

[16] Thomas Hobbes, *Leviathan*, ed. Richard Tuck (Cambridge: Cambridge University Press, 1996), 89.

[17] Edmund Spenser, *A View of the State of Ireland*, ed. Andrew Hadfield and Willy Maley (Malden, MA: Blackwell, 1997), 14.

[18] Spenser, *View*, 32.

[19] *A Discovery of the True Causes Why Ireland Was Never Entirely Subdued, nor Brought under Obedience of the Crowne of England, until the Beginning of His Maiesties Happy Raigne* (London: 1612), 151.

[20] Spenser, *View*, 150.

Amazon Radigund has enslaved, emasculated, and enfeebled the English knights she has defeated militarily. In consenting before battle to Radigund's extra-chivalric, home-grown conditions, Artegall in effect legitimizes Irish lawlessness, that is, Brehon law, at the same time consciously binding himself to submit to barbarous (mis)rule in advance of any necessity to do so.[21] As a result, the narrator tells us, Artegall is 'justly damned' in becoming Radigund's 'thrall',[22] a condition comprising captivity, expropriation of his sword, demeaning apparel, coerced labour, and severely rationed food. In early modern Christendom, these features of enslavement are generally not to be imposed on fellow European Christians who have been defeated in battle. Artegall's abject status therefore underscores not only Radigund's non-Christian status but the perverse voluntariness of Artegall's enslavement, which results from an agreement to which he freely consented, and which, as an honourable knight, he faithfully keeps. The voluntary origin of Artegall's literal enslavement gives it a psycho-ethical, allegorical quality that makes it a form of figurative, political 'slavery'.

In fashioning Radigund, Spenser draws on Heliodorus' *Aethiopica*, an immensely popular prose romance to which *Cymbeline*, too, is indebted. Spenser models the narrative that unfolds during Artegall's enslavement on an episode of *Aethiopica* in which the Persian Arsake, who rules in her husband's stead, uses her position as sovereign to enslave her war captives Cariclia and Theagenes. Arsake takes this coercive measure because she was smitten with Theagenes the moment she clapped eyes on him. Both Arsake and her early modern descendent Radigund illustrate a tradition of sexualizing the female tyrant's desire for power, which is much more narrowly channelled than that of her male counterpart: the barbarous female ruler desires power over her male beloved.

With the aid of her maidservant Kybele, Arsake does everything she can to get Theagenes into bed with her, including having him subjected to physical torture. Similarly, Radigund employs her maid Clarinda as her go-between and, angered at her inability to coerce Artegall into becoming her lover, resorts to 'Cold yron chaines' and torture in the form of withholding food.[23] But nothing can persuade the chaste, liberty-loving Theagenes—or Spenser's Artegall, faithful lover of Britomart—to betray his beloved Cariclia or to yield to such barbarous manipulation and lust. Although the appetites of Spenser's Radigund are not nearly so outrageous as Arsake's (Radigund blushes when revealing them to her handmaiden, whereas Heliodorus at one point has Arsake lying in bed clawing herself in a frenzy of frustrated desire), her persistent strategizing is clearly modelled on Heliodorus' Persian ruler. In both narratives the trusted, female pander ends up betraying the interests of her barbarian mistress (though Spenser's Clarinda does so by withholding Radigund's

[21] Edmund Spenser, *The Faerie Queene*, 2nd edn, ed. A. C. Hamilton (Harlow: Longman, 2001) Book 5, canto iv, 48–51.

[22] *Faerie Queene*, Book 5, canto v, 17.

[23] *Faerie Queene*, Book 5, canto v, 50.

messages, having fallen in love with Artegall herself) who, not surprisingly, dies a humiliating death.

War Slavery, Human Sacrifice, and Cymbeline

In *Aethiopica*'s concluding chapters, the Hellenized Cariclia and her beloved Theagenes again appear as prisoners of war, this time in the land of Cariclia's birth, Ethiopia. As befits protagonists of extended prose romance, they have survived numerous hair-raising threats to their lives, their mutual love, and their honour. Yet now, towards the conclusion of the action, they find themselves about to be sacrificed as virginal war-captives in celebration of the Ethiopians' recent military victory. Prior to the discovery that Hydaspes and his wife are Cariclia's lifetime-lost parents, the crowd assembled for the sacrifice is eager to see it performed. Cariclia's identity is revealed in a classically long drawn out, emotionally fraught scene of recognition and reunion. The suspense goes on, however, for Hydaspes doesn't call the sacrifice off, as might be expected. Though emotionally torn, as ruler he feels obligated to honour ancestral custom, and insists he will serve the collective will, declaring that 'publicke utilitie' far outweighs his own 'private profite'.[24] Hydaspes, we are meant to see, is an ideal ruler. To readers' immense relief, however, when his subjects passionately protest his willingness to sacrifice his daughter, he finally abandons the projected sacrifice.

As a result of this incident, the Ethiopians decide to stop offering human lives to the gods. Sisimithres, an Egyptian gymnosophist who is Hydaspes' adviser, had earlier addressed Hydaspes on the barbarousness of human sacrifice (speaking in Greek, the language of the ruling elite). Now ready to heed this advice, Hydaspes marries Cariclia and Theagenes, who become priests of the new order involving an elegantly ritualized, *non*-human sacrifice to the gods. Idealization of Greek culture threads its golden way through his many social and geographical settings, and the ending Heliodorus gives his romantic narrative shows Hellenistic cultural hegemony peaceably yet irresistibly extending its domain. Hydaspes may be the ideal ruler of a sophisticated, militarily successful society, but *Aethiopica* takes the Greek (at the time Heliodorus writes, the Graeco-Roman) view that human sacrifice is quintessentially barbaric. Ethiopia must submit its ancestral custom to Sisimithres' rational scrutiny, exchanging its ways for those that are more humane, before the white, Hellenized Cariclia's reunion with father, mother and beloved can be celebrated in the 'Comedy' with which Heliodorus self-consciously entertains his readers.

[24] Heliodorus, *An Aethiopian History*, trans. Thomas Underdown, 1587, ed. Charles Whibley (New York: AMS Press, 1967).

With its resemblance to Abraham's interrupted sacrifice of his son Isaac, this particular episode of *Aethiopica* must have delighted early modern European Christian readers already convinced of Heliodorus' Christianity and of their own civilization's distance from the ritual human sacrifice routinely attributed to New World societies. Commentators on Shakespeare's Cymbeline have noted that specific features of its concluding act are indebted to *Aethiopica*.[25] I would like to propose that *Cymbeline* also reproduces *Aethiopica*'s concluding celebration of averted human sacrifice. Heliodorus' Hellenistic challenge to Ethiopian ritual practices is adapted by Shakespeare to the circumstances of imperial Rome's civilizing mission in ancient Britain. This adaptation is, I believe, the means by which *Cymbeline* gives significance to its resolution of conflict between ancient Britain and Rome.[26]

The first similarity lies in the paternal-King's determination unwittingly to take his daughter's life as one of the defeated enemy's prisoners of war. Though according to the conventions of war slavery, the victorious nation possesses the power of life and death as a formal right, both *Aethiopica* and *Cymbeline* associate the exercise of this right with barbarism. Like Hydaspes, the British king Cymbeline doesn't recognize his daughter Innogen who, disguised as Fidele, is among the vanquished Romans he plans to sacrifice. Cymbeline informs his Roman prisoners of war that he has granted the request made by relatives of those lost in battle, 'That their good souls may be appeased with slaughter / Of you their captives' (5.4.72–3). This language echoes that used in the opening scene of *Titus Andronicus*, when Lucius proposes to 'hew' the 'limbs' and 'sacrifice' the 'flesh' of a prominent Goth prisoner, 'That so the shadows be not unappeased' (1.1.96–100), and, again, when Titus says the 'sacrifice' is required 'T'appease their groaning shadows that are gone' (1.1.124–6). Though the 'slaughter' (a word Shakespeare invariably associates with barbarism or tyranny) Cymbeline proposes is not overtly referred to as sacrifice, the absence of any alternative explanation inevitably suggests it, especially when at the end of the drama Cymbeline directs everyone to leave the court in order to 'smoke the temple with our sacrifices' (5.4.399).

By contrast with the public-minded Hydaspes, Cymbeline exempts Innogen (in the guise of Fidele) from the 'slaughter' of prisoners of war on grounds that are whimsically private: 'His favour is familiar to me' (5.4.93). About the fate of the remaining captive Romans, however, Shakespeare keeps the audience in suspense. Only at the conclusion

25 For scholarship relating to *Cymbeline* and *Aethiopica*, exploration of *Aethiopica*'s importance to early modern literature, and a reading of Cymbeline's kinship with Heliodorus' mixing of tragedy and comedy, see Tanya Pollard, 'Romancing the Greeks: *Cymbeline*'s Generes and Models', in *How To Do Things with Shakespeare: New Approaches, New Essays*, ed. Laurie Maguire (Malden, MA: Blackwell, 2008).

26 Patricia Parker discusses *Cymbeline*'s allusions to *translatio imperii* and Virgil's *Aeneid* in 'Romance and Empire: Anachronistic *Cymbeline*', in *Unfolded Tales: Essays on Renaissance Romance*, ed. G. M. Logan and G. Teskey (Ithaca: Cornell University Press, 1989), 189–207; see also Peter Freese, 'Westward the Course of Empire Takes Its Way: The *Translatio* Concept in Popular American Writing and Painting', in *The Internationality of National Literatures in Either America: Transfer and Transformation*, Vol. 1: *Cases and Problems*, ed. A. P. Frank and H. Essmann (Göttingen: Wallstein Verlag, 1999), 31–69.

of a discussion of war slavery doctrine as interpreted by civilized Rome, multiple revelations, and Posthumous' dramatic enactment of a repudiation of the victor's right to take life does Cymbeline formally reverse his decision, which enables Shakespeare's drama to end as *Aethiopica* does, in ritual sacrifice that does not utilize human flesh. In *Aethiopica*, Sisimithres says that even animal sacrifice isn't necessary, since God is satisfied with prayers and 'other sweet savours', the word 'savour' (meaning aroma, scent), being the English used in Protestant biblical translations from Tyndale onwards for the smell of sacrifices pleasing to God. Cymbeline's concluding speech opens with the similarly sensual, Old Testamental representation of a pagan, polytheistic ritual, 'Laud we the gods, / And let our crooked smokes climb to their nostrils / From our blest altars' (5.4.477–9).

Is it possible that pre-Christian Britain, like Ethiopia, needs to be initiated into more humane, civilized practices? That suggestion might not be wholly offensive to Shakespeare's audience. By placing the birth of Jesus in Cymbeline's reign, Spenser juxtaposes Britain's Romanization with its eventual Christianization. Shakespeare, however, would seem to be more interested in Rome's prior civilizing mission if we take the hints dropped about ritual sacrifice as a guide. In a section of Tacitus' *Annals* dealing with Roman conquests within Britain, British customs regarding defeated opponents are described just as Shakespeare presents them in *Cymbeline*: the British avenge themselves on their captives by sacrificing them on altars. Unlike the Romans, who sensibly sell or use their prisoners of war as slaves, the British, Tacitus claims, prefer to engage in acts of barbarous reprisal involving slaughter, gibbets, fire, and crosses.[27] In the context of Tacitus' observations, Cymbeline's change of heart is clearly more than the mellowing induced by romance. In liberating its war captives, Britain rejects its barbarous rites in favour of Rome's greater civility.

According to Caius Lucius, Rome's exemplarily courteous ambassador to Britain, Romans would not even contemplate such violence. When Cymbeline announces that the Roman captives are to be killed, Lucius calmly responds by observing that the British were victorious by mere chance (he tactfully refrains from pointing out that Cymbeline himself was taken captive!), and then says, 'Had it gone with us, / We should not, when the blood was cool, have threatened / Our prisoners with the sword' (5.4.76–8). Graeco-Roman civility so governs Lucius' response that he doesn't even mention ritual sacrifice, instead contrasting killing in the heat of battle with the cold-blooded murder of prisoners of war. In any case, Lucius' remark shows Shakespeare to be attuned to Roman war slavery doctrine, which sets the right to take life against a sparing of life that involves enslavement.[28] The particular etymological figure in which Roman jurisprudence conveys these options is the derivation of *servire*, to serve, from *servare*, to

27 Cornelius Tacitus, *The Annals*, ed. A. J. Woodman (Indianapolis and Cambridge: Hackett Publishing, 2004), 289, 91.

28 For discussion of this etymological figure, see *Arbitrary Rule*, 218–26. See also Christopher Warren's chapter in this volume; Warren proposes Shakespeare's familiarity with Alberico Gentili's *De armis Romanis*.

save. The superiority of civilized saving (though, significantly, without the obligation to serve, to be discussed in a moment) is made explicit when Lucius graciously concludes by requesting that Cymbeline 'save' Innogen (still disguised as his servant Fidele [5.4.91]). Cymbeline agrees, but not because he's been impressed by Lucius' reflections. Intemperate and wrong-headed as ever, the tyrannous Cymbeline goes on to pass the death sentence on his old counsellor Belarius, vowing, 'The whole world shall not save him' (5.4.123).

Shakespeare continues to work with war slavery doctrine by giving dramatic weight to Posthumus' ritualized saving of Giacomo. Earlier, Posthumus had declined taking Giacomo's life when he had vanquished and disarmed him on the battlefield (5.2 stage directions). As Posthumus reminds Giacomo: 'I had you down, and might / Have made you finish' (5.4.412–13). In the final scene, this earlier, militarized saving is re-enacted in court: Giacomo, kneeling before Posthumus, asks him to take his life, and in response Posthumus raises him up, saying: 'The power that I have on you is to spare you, / The malice towards you to forgive you. Live, / And deal with others better' (5.4.419–21). Since Giacomo offers him his life, the 'power' Posthumus refers to is *like* the power of life and death he held over the vanquished Giacomo. But in sparing Giacomo's life, Posthumus gives this power an ethico-spiritual register that the battlefield cannot supply. A rejection of both self-sacrifice and revenge, the act of sparing is itself a sign of civility achieved. Only at this point, claiming to have learned 'freeness' from Posthumus' example, does Cymbeline release the prisoners of war, simultaneously acknowledging Posthumus' marriage with Innogen: 'We'll learn our freeness of a son-in-law / Pardon's the word to all' (5.4, 22.3).

This 'freeness' isn't kin to the unregulated 'liberty' associated with pre-civil society. Such liberty is enacted when the royal-blooded but rustic Polydore, having exited fighting with Cloten, the Queen's son, suddenly re-enters the stage carrying Cloten's head. In a manner resembling Cloten's startling appearance as victorious bearer of Cloten's head as trophy (and recalling Malcolm's equally barbarous appearance with MacBeth's head), 'America' and ancient Picts, emblematic of primitive liberty, are often depicted either holding or standing above a severed head. By contrast, Cymbeline's acquired 'freeness' is the magnanimity born of civility that Lucius had earlier evinced, and which Posthumus has graciously, on his own accord, performed.

In *Cymbeline*, conflict with Rome begins with a refusal to pay Britain's customary tribute. Owing to the rude, peremptory claims of his wife and her son, Cymbeline cannot direct the discussion with Rome's ambassador and ends up supporting their position. A sign of his inability to rule, Cymbeline's submission to the Queen also, however, testifies to a laudatory (for many of Shakespeare's contemporaries) loyalty to British indigeneity. Arguing that the British were formerly 'free', and that a 'warlike people' such as they are will naturally want to 'shake off' the 'yoke' laid on them by the Romans, Cymbeline also introduces his own goal, namely, recovery of the laws that his ancestor Mulmutius ordained, and with which the Romans have damagingly interfered (3.1.45–60). In their more belligerent opposition to Roman rule, neither the Queen nor Cloten mention 'laws'. When the Romans have been defeated militarily and the Queen's treachery publicly disclosed, Cymbeline holds her responsible for Britain's provocative withholding of tribute, thereby dissociating himself from a stance that privileges indigenous licence. A pre-requisite for the newly harmonious relations between Britain and imperial Rome that *Cymbeline*'s conclusion celebrates, Cymbeline's repudiation of the Queen strengthens the likelihood that she is meant to recall the widowed Amazonian Boadicea. (The partnership between the Queen and Cloten has similarities to that between Tamora and Aaron. Both involve covert plots to rid the state of its existing ruler [Saturninus, Cymbeline] in order to replace him with rulers dedicated to leading the nation further in the direction of barbarism.)

Voluntariness is the keynote of Britain's new relations with Rome. Despite being 'the victor', Cymbeline says to Lucius, 'we submit to Caesar / And to the Roman empire, promising / To pay our wonted tribute' (5.4.461–3). In the context of Britain's recent victory, formal submission has a very special significance, provided by Cymbeline's earlier reference to the Roman 'yoke'. As we have seen, in the discourse early modern Europeans inherit from Greece and Rome, a nation that submits to the superior military power of its victors is thereby figuratively 'enslaved'. Its demonization of the Queen notwithstanding, *Cymbeline*'s staging of Britain's proud, military resistance to the servile status imposed by its conquerors results in reclamation of its original freedom.

When defeated and unfree, Britain could either ignominiously bow to Rome's demand for tribute or declare war. Having regained its freedom, another option emerges: Britain *voluntarily* elects to submit to Caesar and the Roman empire. Submission is precisely circumscribed, however: Cymbeline promises to pay their 'wonted tribute' but implicitly remains committed to retaining Britain's own, revered laws. Relevant, here, are remarks Davies makes in *True Causes Why Ireland Was Never Entirely Subdued* on the degree of subjection entailed by the payment of tribute:

> And such as pay onely *Tribute*, though they be placed by *Bodin*, in the first degree of *Subjection*, are not properlie *Subjects* but Soveraignes. For, though they bee lesse and inferior unto the Prince to whom they pay Tribute, yet they hold all other pointes of Soveraignty; and having paide their Tribute which they promised, to have their peace, they are quit of all other duties.

Davies, of course, decries this policy as applied to Ireland, and urges the present ruler to 'put those thinges in execution, which are the true markes and differences of Soveraignty'.[29]

In *Cymbeline*, voluntary return to the payment of tribute is a sign of internalized civility that complements Britain's willingness to adopt Rome's superior custom of saving rather than killing its prisoners of war. A sign of civility, this custom rests on a socially performative interpretation of war slavery doctrine, not on Roman law itself, and is thus compatible with Cymbeline's earlier aim of repairing and liberating indigenous laws,

[29] Davies, *True Causes*, 14.

which Rome has 'too much mangled' (3.1, 55). If we accept Davies' (and Bodin's) view, it is also fully compatible with the retention of 'Soveraignty.'

Voluntary submission on an international scale completes the pattern of freely elected clemency and pardon that Posthumus and Cymbeline have established in their interpersonal interactions. In every instance, the power of life and death held by the victor permits the act of saving to signify a graciousness and civility threatened by its legitimate but less humane alternative, death. Servitude, the alternative to death conventionally associated with saving, is simply not on offer in *Cymbeline*. As a result, Britain's formal submission to Rome becomes, paradoxically, a magnanimous gesture on a grand, international scale. As in *Aethiopica*, Shakespeare's drama concludes by celebrating the achievement of harmonious, intercultural relations between equals, with Cymbeline promising the spectacle of British and Roman flags waving together in a procession leading to Jupiter's temple.

The Rome that comes across so well in *Cymbeline* is the Rome that early modern Western Europeans often take as the model for their own, imperial expansion. Shakespeare's staging of Britain's voluntary submission to Rome and its empire invites spectators to take pride in their ancestral ruler's decision to let Britain be educated in the ways of civility so as to develop into a nation now capable of following Rome's lead. In the context of interstate, colonial relations, Britain's voluntary submission is, additionally, exemplary. If, for instance, the Irish don't follow suit—which, contemporary observers repeatedly report, they don't—it just shows how intransigently they still resist the civilizing process. Were they peaceably to follow Britain's example, they, too, might submit to British rule without becoming collective 'slaves.'

Bibliography

Balibar, Étienne and Wallerstein, Immanuel. *Race, Nation, Class: Ambiguous Identities*, trans. Chris Turner (London: Verso, 1991).

Beckles, Hilary McD. *White Servitude and Black Slavery in Barbados, 1627–1715* (Knoxville: University of Tennessee Press, 1989).

Bodin, Jean. *The Six Bookes of A Commonweale: A Facsimile Reprint of the English Translation of 1606, Corrected and Supplemented in Light of a New Comparison with the French [République] and Latin Texts*, trans. Richard Knolles, ed. Kenneth Douglas McRae (Cambridge, MA: Harvard University Press, 1962).

Cervantes, Miguel de. *Don Quixote*, trans. Edith Grossman (New York: HarperCollins Publishers, 2003).

Cervantes, Miguel de. *Don Quijote*, ed. Tom Lathrop (Newark: Cervantes and Co., 2005).

Davies, C. S. L. 'Slavery and Protector Somerset: the Vagrancy Act of 1547', *Economic History Review*, 2nd ser., 19 (1966): 533–49.

Davies, John. *A Discovery of the True Causes Why Ireland Was Never Entirely Subdued, nor Brought under Obedience of the Crowne of England, Until the Beginning of His Maiesties Happy Raigne* (London: 1612).

Donoghue, John. *Fire Under the Ashes: An Atlantic History of the English Revolution* (Chicago: University of Chicago Press, 2013).

Freese, Peter. 'Westward the Course of Empire Takes Its Way: The *Translatio* Concept in Popular American Writing and Painting', in *The Internationality of National Literatures in Either America: Transfer and Transformation*, Vol. 1: *Cases and Problems*, ed. A. P. Frank and H. Essmann (Gottingen: Wallstein Verlag, 1999), 31–69.

Galenson, David W. *White Servitude in Colonial America: An Economic Analysis* (Cambridge: Cambridge University Press, 1981).

Guasco, Michael. *Slaves and Englishmen: Human Bondage in the Early Modern Atlantic World* (Philadelphia: University of Pennsylvania Press, 2014).

Harriot, Thomas. *A Briefe and True Report of the New Found Land of Virginia* (Charlottesville: University of Virginia Press, 2007).

Heliodorus, *An Aethiopian History*, trans. Thomas Underdown (1587), ed. Charles Whibley (New York: AMS Press, 1967).

Hobbes, Thomas. *Leviathan*, ed. Richard Tuck (Cambridge: Cambridge University Press, 1996).

Hutson, Lorna. 'Rethinking the Spectacle of the Scaffold: Juridical Epistemologies and English Revenge Tragedy', *Representations*, 89.1 (2005): 30–58.

Kauffman, Miranda. 'Caspar van Senden, Sir Thomas Sherley and the "Blackamoor" Project', *Historical Research*, 81.212 (2008): 366–71.

Loomba, Ania and Burton, Jonathan, eds. *Race in Early Modern England: A Documentary Companion* (Basingstoke: Palgrave Macmillan, 2007).

Marlowe, Christopher. *Complete Works*, Vol. 4: *The Jew of Malta*, ed. Roma Gill (Oxford: Clarendon Press, 1995).

Nyquist, Mary. *Arbitrary Rule: Slavery, Tyranny, and the Power of Life and Death* (Chicago: Chicago University Press, 2013).

Parker, Patricia. 'Romance and Empire: Anachronistic *Cymbeline*', in *Unfolded Tales: Essays on Renaissance Romance*, ed. G. M. Logan and G. Teskey (Ithaca: Cornell University Press, 1989), 189–207.

Pollard, Tanya. 'Romancing the Greeks: *Cymbeline*'s Genres and Models', in *How To Do Things with Shakespeare: New Approaches, New Essays*, ed. Laurie Maguire (Malden: Blackwell, 2008).

Shakespeare, William. *The Complete Works*, 2nd edn, ed. Stanley Wells et al. (Oxford: Clarendon Press, 2005).

Slights, Camille Wells. 'Slaves and Subjects in *Othello*', *Shakespeare Quarterly*, 48.4 (1997): 377–90.

Spenser, Edmund. *The Faerie Queene*, 2nd edn, ed. A. C. Hamilton (Harlow: Longman, 2001).

Spenser, Edmund. *A View of the State of Ireland*, ed. Andrew Hadfield and Willy Maley (Malden, MA: Blackwell, 1997).

Tacitus, Cornelius. *The Annals*, ed. A. J. Woodman (Indianapolis and Cambridge: Hackett Publishing Company, 2004).

Williams, Robert A., Jr. *The American Indian in Western Legal Thought: The Discourses of Conquest* (New York and Oxford: Oxford University Press, 1990).

PART VIII

THE EXTRA-ENGLISH LEGAL WORLD: BETWEEN COLONY, NATION, AND EMPIRE

CHAPTER 33

SPENSER, PLOWDEN, AND THE HYPALLACTIC INSTRUMENT

ANDREW ZURCHER

An Elizabethan Protestant reader trained up on the soft Calvinism of the 1563 *Articles of Religion*, turning to Edmund Spenser's allegorical epic poem, *The Faerie Queene* (1590, 1596), was in for a shock. Calvin's *Institutes of the Christian Religion* had categorically rejected the value of the things of this world, and English Protestant bishops had adopted the reformers' position on the inefficacy of good works.[1] Faith and election were inward and inscrutable things; despair and reprobation, likewise, were movements of the soul, not the works of the hand.[2] But in the ninth canto of the first book of Spenser's poem, 'The Legend of Holinesse', the patron of holiness, Redcrosse, faces and succumbs to the seductive—and very material—promptings of Despayre. Pressing his advantage, the tempter offers Redcrosse a range of instruments with which he might kill himself: 'swords, ropes, poison, fire, / And all that might him to perdition draw'. When Redcrosse, stunned, fails to act, Despayre becomes more insistent:

> But whenas none of them he saw him take,
> He to him raught a dagger sharpe and keene,
> And gaue it him in hand: his hand did quake,
> And tremble like a leafe of Aspin greene,
> And troubled blood through his pale face was seene
> To come, and goe with tidings from the heart,
> As it a ronning messenger had beene.

[1] See *The Articles of Religion* (London: Richard Jugge and John Cawood, 1563), sig. A6ʳ.

[2] See John Calvin, *The Institution of Christian Religion*, trans. Thomas Norton (London: Reinolde Wolfe and Richard Harrison, 1561), 3. 3. 22 (fol. 135ʳ).

> At last resolu'd to worke his finall smart,
> He lifted vp his hand, that backe againe did start. (*FQ*, 1.9.51)[3]

Redcrosse's companion and lady, Una, watches this scene of temptation along with the reader. She marks the symptoms of her lord's trespass—the trembling hand, the blood forsaking his face—and eventually intervenes by very materially disfurnishing her knight of the means by which he might commit the unforgivable sin, snatching 'the cursed knife' from his hand and throwing it 'to the ground'. But Una's deliverance only completes a materialization of Redcrosse's struggle that has already, decisively, occurred, for in placing the knife into Redcrosse's hand, and then, perhaps, forcing that hand toward the knight's body—the antecedent of the pronouns 'he' and 'his' in the ninth line of the quoted stanza are productively ambiguous—Despayre transforms an internal, psychological experience into a violently physical struggle. To say so, of course, might only be to say that through personification and coordinated devices Spenser's poem projects inward states and processes upon a world of legible outward phenomena, a transformation that the process of allegorical interpretation can reverse by treating those phenomena as signs; but the way in which this scene is pictured, and the emphasis Spenser puts on both Despayre's and Una's physical interventions, suggests we go further. When Una snatches the 'cursed knife' from Redcrosse's hand, hoping thereby to preserve him from everlasting death, we may well wonder how much of Redcrosse's sin, or prospective sin, actually (rather than merely symbolically) dwells in the blade. Does (Una's) casting it away constitute, rather than merely signify, (Redcrosse's) rejection of despair? Can it? How much of his mental state, how much of his soul, and its guilt, lies mingled in the object?

To ask what Spenser's poem means in presenting us with a 'cursed knife' is to start to cut into a complex tension in his allegorical method between representation and meaning, between a narrative of signs disposed in time and an array of arguments or structures philosophical, theological, and psychological imported by that narrative. That cut, then, runs deep, and throws up a store of matter; but however we tremble at or face up to those questions, we must acknowledge that even to *ask* about the 'cursed knife' is to position Spenser's poem at some removes from the Protestant theology which it was always taken, from its earliest publication, to depict and endorse. Spenser writes in 'A Letter of the Authors ... to Sir Walter Raleigh', originally affixed to *The Faerie Queene* as a kind of prefatory guide to reading the poem, that he has adopted a popular approach to his 'generall end', the fashioning of a gentleman or noble person, a 'plausible and pleasing ... historicall fiction':

> To some I know this Methode will seeme displesaunt, which had rather haue good discipline deliuered plainly in way of precepts, or sermoned at large, as they vse, then thus clowdily enwrapped in Allegoricall deuises. But such, me seeme,

[3] Edmund Spenser, *The Faerie Queene*, ed. A. C. Hamilton et al. (London: Longman, 2001). All further quotations from *The Faerie Queene* will be taken from this edition.

> should be satisfide with the vse of these dayes, seeing all things accounted by their showes, and nothing esteemed of, that is not delightfull and pleasing to commune sence.[4]

Spenser defends his method by appealing to the 'vse of these dayes', the common practice of taking the 'showes' for the 'things'. This method reaches its crisis in Book 1 when Despayre shows Redcrosse 'painted in a table plaine' (1.9.49.6) the everlasting damnation to which an allegedly merciless God will 'sentence' (1.9.50.4) him, a crisis that is immediately materialized in a hybrid object, the 'cursed knife' that combines an instrument with the guilty intention to use it. The implication of this depicted crisis is that to account the thing by the show is to fall into despair; and yet, that is expressly what Spenser tells the reader, in his prefatory letter, that she is to do. As the judicial character of Redcrosse's trial in the Despayre episode may suggest, though, in one particular 'vse of these dayes' Spenser might well have found a welter of precedents and arguments for the evidentiary operations and positions his poem seems to proffer: that 'vse' is, of course, the common law.[5] Over the course of the 1570s and 1580s, common lawyers developed in their arguments over difficult cases, as in their construction of new remedies within existing legal forms, a range of evidentiary strategies by which hidden states of mind (intention, consent, etc.) could be decoded by, or even understood as, outward, legible signs (things, actions, forms of words, etc.). These innovations helped lawyers to pursue actions and judges to decide cases, but they also tended, as a whole, to push exactly against the hidden inwardness of illegible faith advanced by Protestant theologians such as Calvin, or described in the *Articles of Religion* approved by the bishops at Lambeth in early 1563.[6] In the tension between these contrary impulses, Spenser's allegorical method emerges not merely as the vehicle, but as a key part of the substance of the meaning of *The Faerie Queene*, an instrument for mediating between the claims of this world and the next. In turn, Spenser's preoccupation with the hybrid object also comes to shape his account of political and legal reformation in his colonial tract, *A View of the Present State of Ireland* (1596).

4 Spenser, *The Faerie Queene*, 715–16.

5 To note and explore a connection between Spenser's allegorical method and the evolving evidentiary conventions of common law practice in this period is not, of course, to discount other related contemporary contexts for person-thing hybrids in early modern literary representation. This hybridity—'the construction of the portrayed subject through prostheses, the attachable/detachable parts, the clothes, furniture, books, scientific and musical instruments that animate the subject'—is the focus of Ann Rosalind Jones and Peter Stallybrass, *Renaissance Clothing and the Materials of Memory* (Cambridge: Cambridge University Press, 2000), 49.

6 The middle decades of Elizabeth's reign were only the most intense period of innovation within a larger frame encompassing Henrician challenges to the conscience of the Chancellor—such as those of Christopher St German in his *Doctor and Student* (first English edn 1530)—as well as the later history of James VI and I's repeated conflicts with his chief justice Sir Edward Coke. The sixteenth-century shift in common legal practice toward the trial of probable fact is one focus of Lorna Hutson's study of early modern law and drama, *The Invention of Suspicion: Law and Mimesis in Shakespeare and Renaissance Drama* (Oxford: Oxford University Press, 2007), to which I am indebted throughout what follows.

Early Modern Common Law and the Hybrid Object

On 20 September 1571, a Warwickshire husbandman named John Saunders gave two pieces of a poisoned apple to his wife. According to the record of the case in Edmund Plowden's *Commentaries* (1571, 1578), she was sick in bed, while Saunders was in love with another woman. Using arsenic and rosaker[7] supplied by an accomplice, Alexander Archer, Saunders laced the apple and presented it to his wife. Too ill to enjoy the fruit herself, she refused it and passed it to her daughter Eleanor who, eating it, fell sick and later died. The royal judges who delivered the Warwickshire gaol later that autumn quickly resolved to hang Saunders for his daughter's murder, despite the fact that he had loved the 3-year-old Eleanor, and had never meant to harm her; but their deliberations had to overcome a philosophical problem. The early modern legal distinction between manslaughter and murder had come, by the late sixteenth century, to depend on *malitia praecogitata* or malice prepense: as Sir Edward Coke would write in this *Third Institutes*:

> Murder is when a man of sound memory, and of the age of discretion, unlawfully killeth within any County of the Realm any reasonable creature *in rerum natura* under the kings peace, with malice fore-thought, either expressed by the party, or implied by law.[8]

By this definition, having neither expressed, nor done anything that might be said to imply, malice toward his daughter, Saunders could not straightforwardly be found guilty of her murder. Not only did he have no intention to harm her, but he himself did not present Eleanor with the apple; and in these circumstances, the indictment of Archer as accessory to murder was felt to be particularly unsafe.[9] Precedents existed by 1571 for cases of this kind turning on transferred intent, that is, cases in which A expressed malice toward B, but having by accident killed C, was held guilty of malice toward C by a 'transfer' of the *malitia praecogitata*, during the act, from one object to another.[10] But

[7] Red arsenic, or realgar.

[8] Sir Edward Coke, *The Third Part of the Institutes of the Laws of England* (London: 1644), 47.

[9] The judges' discussion of Saunder's guilt, along with the role of his accessory Archer, is one subject of Luke Wilson's thorough analysis of early modern legal and dramatic representations of intention in *Theatres of Intention: Drama and the Law in Early Modern England* (Stanford: Stanford University Press, 2000); see esp. 43–8 and 60–7. Wilson connects the judges' reasoning in this case to a wider reliance in the period on legal fictions and the exercise of equitable judgement, arguing that the implied 'transfer' of intent to murder from one object (Saunders' wife) to another (his daughter) 'is accomplished by the judge or jury rather than by the defendant in the commission of the act' (47).

[10] See, for example, the 1558 case of Sir George Herbert, who with his men beset the house of Sir Rhys Mansell. During the attack, Mansell's sister, who was attempting to broker peace between the parties, was accidentally killed by a stray rock thrown; Herbert and all his men were convicted of murder by transferred intent. The case is recorded in Sir James Dyer, *Ascuns nouel cases* (London: Richard Tottell, 1592), fol. 128^{v} (§ 60), translated in 73 ER, 279–80.

the use of poison rather than physical violence opened up in Saunders' crime an unusual temporal interim and a set of difficult spatial and material problems. Most importantly, Saunders had plenty of time and opportunity in which to change his mind, and give evidence of that change, between the moment he poisoned the apple and gave it to his wife, and the moment his daughter ate it. Indeed, given the way in which events unfolded, Saunders came to be in a position not altogether different from Archer—guilty of purposing and contriving a murder, to be sure, but not the one that eventually took place, and, like Archer, someone separated from the ultimate victim by another set of hands. The judges made this point clear in their deliberations, as Plowden records: '[Saunders] did not give [Eleanor] the Poison, but his Wife ignorantly gave it her, and although he might have taken it from the Daughter, and so have preserved her Life, yet the not taking it from her did not make it Felony, for it was all one whether he had been present or absent, as to this Point, inasmuch as he had no Malice against the Daughter, nor any Inclination to do her any Harm.'[11]

In order to convict Saunders and Archer, the judges had to develop a means by which to distinguish Saunders from Archer, and Saunders from his wife; the logical danger was that, by the moment of Eleanor's tasting of the apple, they would all have been equally horrified by the death about to take place. To avoid the wife's participation in the material transfer of the apple from Saunders to his daughter, they needed a narrative of the crime that did not include its middle. They argued that:

> [T]he End of the Act shall be construed by the Beginning of it, and the last Part shall taste of the first, and as the Beginning of the Act had Malice prepense in it, and consequently imported Murder, so the End of the Act, *viz.* the killing of another, shall be in the same Degree, and therefore it shall be Murder, and not Homicide only. [12]

In reconceiving the poisoning as a narrative with an excluded middle, the judges effectively collapsed the problematic temporal distention of the crime into a single moment, a moment in which the unfortunate child was almost brought, almost thought, to 'taste' the apple at the point at which it was first poisoned. By arresting the narrative of the crime at the moment of the apple's poisoning, then, the judges fixed the whole of the crime in the material object at its centre. Unlike the actors in the narrative, who were unreliable and duplicitous, the apple was stable, even static, an object that could remain impervious to subsequent handlings and mishandlings, revised intentions, and the vagaries of fortune.[13] How else could it be that an apple given by Saunders to his wife

[11] Edmund Plowden, *The Commentaries, or Reports of Edmund Plowden* (London: Edward Brooke, 1779), 474.

[12] Plowden, *The Commentaries*, 474.

[13] Compare Sir George Herbert's case: finding Herbert and his men guilty, Chief Justice Saunders considered that 'this was wilful murder, because it commenced upon an unlawful act to be done to a man's person, in which act they had malice to do something against the law, and in this malice the death of the woman occurred'. See William Dalison's report, in BL MS Harley 5141, fols 40–1, cited and trans. in Sir John Baker, *OHLE*, 6.556–7. Herbert's implied malice was considered a modal state ('in this malice') in which any lethal action he took (considered as an indivisible event) would necessarily constitute murder;

should furnish evidence of murder, but the same apple given by the wife to her daughter should not inculpate the wife? This was particularly a problem because, as Plowden notes in his summary of the case, Saunders *did* try to intervene: he 'blamed his Wife for it, and said that Apples were not good for such Infants', but she—though ignorant of the poison, insisted. The judges avoided this inconvenience by insisting on a material transformation in the murder weapon: no longer merely an apple, it became, in Plowden's words, an 'Instrument of Death':

> For if a Man of Malice prepence shoots an Arrow at another with an Intent to kill him, and a Person to whom he bore no Malice is killed by it, this shall be Murder in him, for when he shot the Arrow he intended to kill, and inasmuch as he directed his Instrument of Death [*sa instrument de mort*] at one, and thereby has killed another, it shall be the same Offence in him as if he had killed the Person he aimed at.[14]

Plowden applies this form of words to the case at hand further along in the passage:

> So in the principal Case, when *John Saunders* of Malice prepense gave to his Wife the Instrument of Death [*instrument de mort*], *viz.* the poisoned Apple, and this upon a subsequent Accident killed his Daughter, whom he had no Intention to kill, this is the same Offence in him as if his Act had met with the intended Effect, and his Intention in doing the Act was to commit Murder, wherefore the Event of it shall be Murder.[15]

Saunders' intention to kill his wife, in other words, existed materially in the apple from the moment it left his hand; no matter where the poison in that apple lighted, the death that it effected would, by means of that material transformation, be referred back to him.

Plowden's account of the material transmission of felonious intent, from the willing agent through the 'Instrument of Death' to his ultimate victim, furnished sixteenth-century England with an influential model of the material hypostasization of a psychological state. Saunders' apple in Plowden's account did not merely signify an intent to kill, but reified that intent in an object. Indeed, the hybridization of human intention with material object was, in some sense, one of the conventional elements distinguishing murder from manslaughter; as Luke Wilson has shown in a recent discussion of 'Renaissance tool abuse', the sudden repurposing, as weapons, of tools originally designed for another use was a regular feature of successful manslaughter defences in this period.[16] By contrast, the establishment of the murder weapon as an 'Instrument

by contrast, John Saunders poisoned the apple and let it go—completing his malicious act—such that what occurred between the act of poisoning and the death from poisoning had to be collapsed and disregarded.

14 Plowden, *Commentaries*, 474.

15 Plowden, *Commentaries*, 474.

16 Luke Wilson, 'Renaissance Tool Abuse and the Legal History of the Sudden', in *Literature, Politics and Law in Renaissance England*, ed. Erican Sheen and Lorna Hutson (London: Palgrave Macmillan, 2005), 121–45.

of Death'—the deliberate and time-taking process of converting it, positioning it, and readying it for its violent use—constituted evidence of *malitia praecogitata*. Indeed, the object or instrument involved in a killing occupied so privileged a position, that even in cases of accidental death (i.e. killings in which the 'Instrument of Death' lacks an agent and therefore any suspicion of intentional load) the material thing that had caused the death was itself seized and its value paid as a fine to the King's Almoner, supposedly for distribution to charitable uses undertaken in expiation of the death. Such objects were known as 'deodands'—things 'given to God'—presumably because they were recognized to preserve in their material fabric some curse, stain, or pollution associated with the death, a residue not unlike the guilt or intention inhering in Plowden's 'Instruments of Death'; as person-thing hybrids, that is, deodands were subject to the same judicial operations (arrest, penalty) as human agents.[17] Where murder weapons could be shown to have been fashioned as tools for committing crimes, deodands had imputed to them—retrospectively—a more abstract pollution that required expiation and purification through good works. By the sixteenth century the collection of a fine in the value of the deodand was openly put toward the king's revenue, rather than his Almoner's charitable activities—but the structure and conceit of the tradition lived on: objects associated in the deaths of people retained in their material fabric a hybrid commixture of human intention or guilt.

'Instruments of Death' were not the only hybrid objects known to early modern common lawyers. Another sort of hybrid object under particular pressure in the sixteenth century—and one with clear resonance for literary writers working in the shadow of common law theory and practice—was the legal text. Despite its vaunted status as a *lex non scripta*, the English common law in practice came by the sixteenth century to rely on a body of texts after which lawyers and judges ordered their thinking and judgements. These texts included the writings of medieval 'sages of the law' such as the authors known as Bracton and Glanvill, along with texts by Fortescue, Lyttleton, and Staunford. But they also included the medieval yearbooks, which recorded cases, and the various collections or 'abridgements' compiled from these yearbooks, such as Sir Anthony Fitzherbert's *La graunde abridgement* (1516); manuscript and printed reports and commentaries such as those of Chief Justice Dyer, Edmund Plowden, and Sir Edward Coke; and collections as well as abridgements of the statutes. In addition, well-known lawyers such as Christopher St German, Sir Thomas Egerton, Francis Bacon, John Selden, and Matthew Hale composed dialogues, treatises, and speeches of various kinds from which others routinely cited. Readings of these varied textual sources, of diverse kinds and degrees of authority, were vexed by the same interpretative problems that beset all attempts at textual construal and application; however, the common lawyers of Elizabeth's reign were subject, thanks to a convergence of political and legal

[17] As Oliver Wendell Holmes, Jr, puts it in *The Common Law* (Boston: 1881), in cases of accidental death 'the liability seems to have been regarded as attached to the body doing the damage, in an almost physical sense'. Cited in William Pietz, 'Death of the Deodand: Accursed Objects and the Money Value of Human Life', *RES*, 31 (1997): 97–108, 100.

pressures stemming from Henry VIII's break with Rome, to a particularly acute hermeneutic strain. Following in the wake of Christopher St German's *Doctor and Student* (1528–1531), many English lawyers sought to constrain equitable interpretation of the law, and equitable judgement, within the framework of what St German had called the 'rewles and groundes' of the common law itself.[18] In other words, expositors and judges were expected to draw out an equity (Latin *aequitas*; Greek, *epieikeia*) latent already in the text, or implicit in the competing bases of the law's various authorities, rather than introduce their own constructions. As Edward Hake writes in his treatise *Epieikeia* (*c.*1600), translating Plowden's *Commentaries*:

> [A]ll Acts of Parliament are lawes positive which consist of twoe parts. The first is the words of the Acte, the other is the sense, for the letter without the sense is not the lawe, but the letter and the sense together be the lawe. And everyone that wilbe learned in the lawe positive oughte to have understanding of both, and the way to understand the sense is to consider the Common lawe which is auntient to all posityve lawes ... and hath to do in the exposition of the lawe posityve, and thereby the mischiefes and inconveniences which are in the letter are to be wayed and by reason eschewed.[19]

In the effort to limit prerogative interventions in the law, either by the monarch or deputed councillors acting under the monarch's authority, common lawyers late in Elizabeth's reign tended to view legal texts as permeated by a *sensus* beyond the texts' mere words. An understanding of this hybridity of the textual source, according to Plowden and to his expositor Hake, was essential to the true construction and working of the common law.

Legal texts, then, and murder weapons seem to offer examples of hybrid objects under particular pressure in Elizabethan common law thinking. A third, similar class of things came into prominence during the development of a new remedy for debt in the late Elizabethan period, the *assumpsit* action. Partly in response to the collapse of the older *laesio fidei* (breach of faith) action available in the medieval church courts, and partly as a way of offering plaintiffs damages in tort rather than mere performance in debt (an action in right), the court of Common Pleas successfully sought to expand the action of *assumpsit* throughout the 1580s and 1590s.[20] Key to the expansion and eventual legitimation of the 'action on the case' as a remedy for disgruntled parties to a contract was the 'doctrine of consideration'. While plaintiffs were generally required to aver that

[18] See Christopher St German, *Doctor and Student*, ed. T. F. T. Plucknett and J. L. Barton (London: SS, 1974), 105. For more on St German's reconceptualization of the nature of equity, see my *Spenser's Legal Language: Law and Poetry in Elizabethan England* (Woodbridge: D. S. Brewer, 2007), ch. 5; and Alan Cromartie's chapter in this volume.

[19] Edward Hake, *Epieikeia: A Dialogue on Equity in Three Parts* (1598), ed. D. E. C. Yale (New Haven: Yale University Press), 91; cf. Edmund Plowden, *Les commentaries* (London: Richard Tottel, 1578), fol. 363^{r}.

[20] For a history of the rise of the *assumpsit* action in this period, see A. W. B. Simpson, *A History of the Common Law of Contract: The Rise of the Action of Assumpsit* (Oxford: Oxford University Press, 1987). See also Baker, *OHLE*, 6.839–80. See also Luke Wilson's chapter in this volume.

a promise had been made (and broken), the existence of the promise came to depend on the evidence of some thing (the *consideratio*, or consideration) that the plaintiff had offered to the defendant in exchange for the promise. The assumption was that this thing would not have been offered had there been no promise, and so its existence was good evidence that the promise existed—indeed, it became indispensable to establishing the existence of the promise, and was eventually, to all intents and purposes, taken for the promise itself. In early actions the consideration could be a small sum of money, but in time it came to include other sorts of benefit, such as forbearance to demand payment, or willingness to receive payment at a stipulated place or in a stipulated manner, or even, eventually, a counter-promise made by the plaintiff in return for the defendant's promise to pay.[21] Whatever the nature of the consideration, though, the distinctive feature of the new action of *assumpsit* lay in its substitution of some evident and material thing for the illegible state of mind—the faith, the promise—that had passed between the two parties to the contract.

Hypallactic Hybridity in *The Faerie Queene*

In a number of ways, then, English common lawyers during Elizabeth's reign strengthened existing emphases on hybrid objects, and developed new practices and arguments that privileged the substitution or permeation of objects by human intentions, commitments, and emotions. These legal practices and arguments tended, together, to imply, or even to propose, a materially extended self, a self that did not merely signify its inward reality through external or material signs, but that constituted itself in outward things, mingling materially with them. The sorts of hybrids posited by sixteenth- and seventeenth-century English lawyers spread vigorously in contemporary literary works—famously, for example, in the plays of Shakespeare, whose Hamlet, locked in a struggle with *Hamlet*, repeatedly problematizes the site and material extensibility of the self. His apparent confidence in the performative nature of his 'inky cloak' is immediately challenged by his mother, who refigures it as a 'nighted colour' (with a pun on black choler, or melancholy) that can be 'cast'. Before long he is reaching with well-oiled humanist reflexes for the materialized memory of his 'tables' (1.2, 1.5); and later he will mark how a king goes a progress through the guts of a beggar (4.3), ask how the dust of Caesar patches a wall or the body of Alexander stops a bunghole (5.1), and finally demand of Claudius, while thrusting a poisoned chalice into his mouth, 'is thy union here?' (5.2). Given this play's focus on the materially extended self, it is no accident that in *Hamlet* Shakespeare recalls the *quaeres* Plowden appended to his commentary on *Rex v Saunders and Archer*: the rat (no reasonable creature) for which Hamlet takes Polonius

[21] For a discussion of the origins of the doctrine of consideration, see Baker, *OHLE*, 6.862–8. For the various types of consideration recognized in the period, see Simpson, *A History of ... Contract*, 412–45.

as he lunges at the arras (3.4); the arrow fired over the house that kills his brother, when making his peace with Laertes in Act 5, scene 2; the misfiring poison of the same scene that Laertes and Claudius deploy to kill Hamlet, which instead returns on their own heads, and murders Gertrude. These three moments, among others, recall precise questions Plowden poses about the way in which objects can be endowed with, or bear, human wills and intentions. Shakespeare's play is a tragedy, and like the judges debating the guilt of Saunders and Archer, this tragic play preserves the hybridity of persons and things, appropriating and meddling with Plowden's text precisely because of its delicate tenderness to a persistent belief not only in the existence of human intention, but its value. By contrast, Edmund Spenser turned to the problem of the mutual permeation of persons and things with far more ambition, and constructed in his allegorical poem *The Faerie Queene*, as well as in his colonial tract, *A View of the Present State of Ireland*, a model of person that virtually excluded interiority.

In his imagination of the permeation of the 'Instrument of Death' by the psychology of its agent, Plowden enacts a figure known to Renaissance rhetoric as hypallage. Greek and Roman rhetoricians had considered hypallage another name for metonymy—a way to describe the taking, or 'exchange', of one thing for another. See for example Cicero's *Orator*, book 27 (93), which is cited by Quintilian, *Institutio oratoria*: 'It is but a short step from *synecdoche* to *metonymy*, which consists in the substitution of one name for another, and, as Cicero tells us, is called *hypallage* by the rhetoricians.'[22] One word in an utterance or sentence is changed with another, or an adjective or adverb placed in an alternative slot, affecting the sense. In the hands of sixteenth-century English poets, and above all Spenser, this figure evolved an entirely new application. As synthetic languages, Greek and Latin construct grammatical relations largely through inflections, and thus the respositioning of words within a clause or sentence can have little or no impact on a writer's sense. By contrast, in an analytic language like English, where grammatical relations are consequent on word order, the displacement of an adjective, adverb, or prepositional phrase may alter its application and, in extreme cases, lead to a confounding of a writer's sense. The origins of English hypallactic experimentation in analytic grammar, and its tendency toward the visual absurd, are obvious in Henry Peacham's description of the figure in 1577:

> *Hypallage*, when a sentence is sayde with a contrary order of wordes, as he came with a long side, by his sword. He tooke his eare from his fist. Syr quoth one to a scholer, I heare say, it is you that pluckt all of the geese of, of my feathers backe. Open the day, and see if it be the windowe. I would make no more a doe, but take a dore and breake open the Axe.[23]

The degeneracy of English thus afforded Renaissance writers an extraordinary opportunity to develop from hypallage the modern figure of 'transferred epithet', by the

22 Quintilian, *Institutio oratoria*, ed. and trans. H. E. Butler, 4 vols (Cambridge: Harvard University Press, 1943), 8.6.23 (3.313). The Greek word *hypallage* derives from the verb ὑπαλλάσσειν (*hypallassein*), meaning 'to interchange, to exchange'.

23 See Henry Peacham, *The Garden of Eloquence* (London: 1577), sig. G1^r.

operation of which a material object can be invested with the attributes of a psychological subject; so, for example, Mark Antony could call Brutus's stab-wound on Caesar's corpse 'th' unkindest cut of all'.[24]

The figure provides more or less the structural basis—and an extremely funny one, at that—for Spenser's allegoresis in *The Faerie Queene*. From the first stanza of this poem, we find through instances of hypallage that the moral and psychological identities of its agents have been materially distributed. The knight of the Redcrosse is to be known not *by* but *as* his 'mighty armes', which are themselves inscribed with 'cruell markes' (*FQ*, 1.1.1). Spenserian knights of later books, similarly, move in a landscape of 'rowsed couches' and 'unready weapons', of 'wrathfull steele' and 'murdrous blades' smiting the 'senceless grownd'. The poem repeatedly exploits these hypallactic hybrids to structure the psychomachic or projected cognitive landscape in which its allegorical figures move; it is through hypallaxis that Spenser succeeds in mapping narrative onto conceptual relations, through hypallaxis that contiguity can imply causation, coherence, and consimilarity. But if Spenser has thus assimilated the materialism of the legal-psychological model of transferred intent, and based his allegorical method upon it, he has similarly recognized Plowden's corollary claim: if material objects can reify psychological states, in some cases psychologies can be hybridized with material substances or ends. Saunders' wife remained innocent of the murder of her daughter Eleanor, because only her hands had become the accessory instrument of the motivated object, the apple. As Plowden writes, 'for here the Wife, who gave the poisoned Apple to her Daughter, cannot be guilty of any Offence, because she was ignorant of any Poison contained in it, and she innocently gave it to the Infant by Way of necessary Food'.[25] Similarly, chastity—not simply sexual chastity, but a virtue figuring purity more broadly in ethical, political, and metaphysical terms—becomes a preoccupation of Spenser's allegory in the middle books of *The Faerie Queene* in part because the psychological projection characteristic of his allegorical method obliges Spenser to admit the material permeability of the human subject. Britomart, the knight of chastity, experiences the invasive lust of the enchanter Busirane through the operations of her allegorical proxy or prosthesis, Amoret, whom she successfully delivers from imprisonment and torture at Busirane's hands. But when Britomart eventually attempts to save Amoret from captivity, the penetrative wound in Amoret's chest turns out not to signify, but to *be* a similarly penetrative wound in Britomart's materialized psychology (cf. *FQ*, 3.12.30–3). Spenser insists on this association by literally turning the knife from Amoret to Britomart, so that in the moment of Amoret's deliverance from Busirane the two women's identities become mingled, and the narrative of bodily torment (Amoret's) collapses into the narrative of psychological torment (Britomart's):

> From her, to whom his fury first he ment,
> The wicked weapon rashly he did wrest,
> And turning to the next his fell intent,

[24] William Shakespeare, *Julius Caesar*, 3.2.
[25] Plowden, *Commentaries*, 474.

> Vnwares it strooke into her snowie chest,
> That litle drops empurpled her faire brest. (*FQ*, 3.12.33.1–5)

Britomart's ultimate struggle with Busirane constitutes a magical reversal of the invasive tendencies of hypallactic objects—here, the 'cruell steele' in Amoret's 'dying hart'—that might penetrate and disintegrate intact—chaste—human subjects. Britomart delivers Amoret, and herself, by forcing Busirane to 'reuerse' his charms (*FQ*, 3.12.36.2). This textual-materialist reversal achieves English moral, political, and cultural chastity by exploiting the analytic nature of English grammar. To accentuate the point, Amoret's tortures are similarly—and materially—reversed in a sequence symmetrical with her initial presentation earlier in the canto (*FQ*, 3.12.20–1, 27): first the house quakes, then the chain binding her breaks and the pillar to which it is fixed breaks, and finally the dart lancing her heart falls out 'of his owne accord', leaving her breast to become un-wounded, and Amoret (like Britomart) to emerge un-ravished and un-violated from her ordeal.

Intrinsic to Spenser's hypallactic allegoresis is its visual comedy. Any attempt to visualize a 'cruell knife' or a 'rowsed couch' will produce visual absurdity, a ridiculous conflation of material and human forms. The late Tony Nuttall argued that Spenser's 'pasteboard' visual imagination was part of a Protestant programme of 'alienation', a material exhaustion, that defined Spenser's career attitude to the aesthetic;[26] the visual absurdities created by this visual poet contribute strongly to this alienating force, working in concert with Spenser's preposterous diction and his trash romance narrative material. By 1590 Spenser could not have been ignorant of the fact that George Puttenham, in *The Arte of English Poesie*, had rechristened the figure of hypallage 'the changeling'. Puttenham insists on the absurdity created by hypallage in its English form, and alludes suggestively to the figure's importance to Spenser's practice in *The Faerie Queene*:

> But another sort of exchange which they had, and very prety, we doe likewise vse, not changing one word for another, by their accidents or cases, as the *Enallage*: nor by the places, as the [*Preposterous*,] but changing their true construction and application, whereby the sence is quite peruerted and made very absurd … The Greekes call this figure [*Hipallage*] the Latins *Submutatio*, we in our vulgar may call him the [*vnderchange*] but I had rather haue him called the [*Changeling*] nothing at all sweruing from his originall; and much more aptly to the purpose, and pleasanter to beare in memory: specially for our Ladies and pretie mistresses in Court, for whose learning I write, because it is a terme often in their mouthes, and alluding to the opinion of Nurses, who are wont to say, that the Fayries vse to steale the fairest children out of their cradles, and put other ill fauoured in their places, which they called changelings, or Elfs: so, if ye mark, doeth our Poet, or maker play with his wordes, vsing

[26] A. D. Nuttall, 'Spenser and Elizabethan Alienation', *Essays in Criticism*, 55 (2005): 209–25.

a wrong construction for a right, and an absurd for a sensible, by manner of exchange.[27]

Puttenham's language in his description of this figure makes it clear that Spenser's Faery Land, the land of the elf, is above all a hypallactic landscape. *The Faerie Queene* reveals a focus on changelings, or substituted children: as the first book closes, we learn from Contemplation that Redcrosse, whose initial introduction in the first canto had pictured him wearing the armour of another, is none other than the exchanged St George—no fairy, but the human child by the fairies taken in its place.[28]

Milk and Mantles: Colonizing Things in *A View of the Present State of Ireland*

The hypallactic investment or endowment of material objects with psychological experiences and qualities, such as intention and affect, provides for Spenser in his political and social theory the basis for a scheme of colonial practice. Modern historians and literary critics have tended—rightly—to condemn Spenser for his participation in the brutal Elizabethan colonial project in Ireland, and the recent reception of his prose dialogue, *A View of the Present State of Ireland*, has generally focused on those passages of the treatise that seem to articulate most explicitly Spenser's endorsement of military 'remedies', scorched earth policies, and even the use of starvation as a tactic for securing the submission of 'rebel' groups and populations. While naturally I share the abhorrence of modern readers for sixteenth-century English attitudes to and actions in Ireland, nonetheless the emphasis in Spenser's dialogue on a social or anthropological approach to (what he calls) the 'reformation' of Ireland is conspicuously less violent in nature than the schemes offered by many contemporaries. The dialogue between Spenser's interlocutors, the experienced Irenius and his friend the Englishman Eudoxus, turns on the customs and practices of the 'mere' Irish and Old English communities in Ireland, which Irenius considers uncivilized, and on the laws introduced by the English to try to refashion Irish behaviours and identity. Over the course of the first half of the dialogue, the two discuss matters such as the use of the Irish language, farming and pasturing practices, local social and political hierarchies, clothing, bardic poetry and Brehon legal traditions, legal conventions, and so on; throughout this discussion, the two speakers concur that the extirpation of Irish practices and their replacement with English or

[27] George Puttenham, *The Arte of English Poesie* (London: Richard Field, 1589), 143–4.

[28] For Redcrosse in his borrowed armour, see *FQ*, 1.1.1.2–5, and 'A Letter of the Authors ... to Sir Walter Raleigh', where Spenser calls this armour that named by Paul in Ephesians 6:11. For Redcrosse as a changeling, see *FQ*, 1.10.60–1, 65–6.

similar practices will, by refashioning behaviours, alter the nature of the people. The end result of this reformation will be a governable population in a hospitable country. As far as Irenius is concerned, it is only when such measures fail that force, or the threat of force, is necessary.

At the core of Irenius' proposals for the transformation of the population of Ireland lies a belief that the material conditions of life in Elizabethan Ireland occasion and give rise to the actions and the attitudes of the rebellious Old English and Irish communities, to their uncivilized and resistant ideology. The reconstitution of their ideology can therefore be effected through the transformation of the material conditions of their lives. The first and perhaps strangest example of this philosophy is Irenius' insistence that English children should not be put out to Irish wet nurses, for in taking in the milk of their Irish nurses, along with their speech, the infants ever after will not only speak after the Irish fashion, but will think—using language—in ways inimical to English civility and obedience:

> I suppose that the Chief Cause of bringinge in the irishe language amongest them was speciallye theire fosteringe and marryinge with the Irishe The which are two moste daungerous infeccions for firste the Childe that suckethe the milke of the nurse muste of necessitye learne his firste speache of her, the which beinge the firste that is envred to his tounge is ever after moste pleasinge vnto him In so muche as thoughe he afterwardes be taughte Englishe yeat the smacke of the firste will allwaies abide with him and not onelye of the speche but allsoe of the manners and Condicions for besides that younge Children be like Apes which will affecte and ymitate what they see done before them speciallye by theire nurses whom they love so well, they moreouer drawe into themselues togeather with theire sucke even the nature and disposicion of theire nurses For the minde followethe muche the Temparature of the bodye and allsoe the wordes are the Image of the minde So as they procedinge from the minde the minde must be nedes affected with the wordes So that the speache beinge Irishe the harte muste nedes be Irishe for out of the abundance of the harte the tonge speakethe.[29]

Irenius makes the uncontentious claim that putting children out to Irish nurses may affect their emotional ties and therefore ideological affiliations later in life. He has no need to advance the considerably more problematic argument that children acquire the 'nature and disposicion of theire nurses' along with the material sustenance of the nurses' milk. A distinctively Irish nature will arise from an Irish nourishment; Irish milk begets Irish attitudes. The hyperbolization of his point appears to be simply the rhetorical or perhaps intellectual embellishment of his persistent theme, that because the fractious and rebellious identities of the Old English and Irish communities are material in origin, they can be reformed by intervention at the material level.

[29] Edmund Spenser, *A View of the present state of Ireland*, ed. Rudolf Gottfried, *The Works of Edmund Spenser*, ed. Edwin Greenlaw et al., 11 vols (Baltimore: Johns Hopkins Press, 1945), 10.119 (ll. 2101–17).

This argument reaches its height in the sustained discussion of the Irish mantle. Irenius is adamant that the mantle, a heavy cloth cloak worn by both men and women, wrapped tight around the body in winter and worn loose in summer, should be forbidden. He traces its lineage to the classical past, and to the northern nations from whom he imagines the Irish to be descended, but his discourse on its antiquity serves only as a stalking horse, for when he begins to enumerate its evil uses, the heaping up of crimes and vices with which it is associated, or which it facilitates, makes its continuance palpably impossible. It provides the kern with protection from the elements and a screen against gnats, a pillow for his head and a place of concealment for his weapon, armour for his body in war, disguise for his identity in towns and cities. For the Irish woman (says Irenius) it is a cloak and a covering, a bed for her lewd promiscuity, a disguise for her pregnant belly, and swaddling clothes for her infants. Spenser's account of the mantle recalls the analysis of his fellow planter in Munster, Sir Edward Herbert, who reported his suppression of the garment to the Privy Council in distinctively Spenserian terms:

> the minde receivinge impressions by the eie, and by the hearinge as by the sight and noyse of pleasant & delectable thinges, ioye & solace, and of thinges woofull and lamentable, sorowe & grieffe: and that so much the more, by howe much the nearer the obiect is vnto it, by the contynuall gesture and wearinge of rude and barbarous attire receiveth an Impression of rudenes and barbarisme: and by wearinge Civill handsom & cleanlie apparell receiveth a persuacion and adoptacion vnto handsomnes cleanelynes and Ciuilitie.[30]

As Eudoxus says, 'O evill minded man that havinge reckoned vp soe manye vses of a mantell will yeat wishe it to be Abandoned Sure I thinke diogenies dishe did neuer serve his master for more turnes notwithstandinge that he made his dishe his Cupp his cap his measure his waterpott, then a mantle dothe an Irishe man: But I see they be all to bad intentes and therefore I will ioyne with youe in abolishinge it'.[31] In keeping with the rest of his discourse, and his advice for the reform of Ireland, Irenius suggests through a pun on the word 'habit' that changing the cloth of the rebels will transform their dispositions.[32] Indeed, the mantle comes to function as the symbol for but also the epitome of the allegedly barbarous customs of the Irish, their generally vicious and unstable nature, and their ideological commitments.

Eventually, in their discussion of the laws instituted to control excesses in Irish apparell, Irenius and Eudoxus make explicit this connection between material things and

[30] Sir William Herbert, 'A Note of Sutch Reasons as Mooued Mea, toe Putt the Statute In Execution agaynst Irish Habites', TNA SP 63/144/57/2. I am indebted to Christopher Burlinson for drawing Herbert's note to my attention.

[31] Spenser, *A View*, ll. 1646–51.

[32] See e.g. Spenser, *A View*, ll. 1573–4: 'it semethe that the mantle was a generall habit to moste nacions and not proper to the Scithians onelye as ye suppose'. Jones and Stallybrass dwell on the importance of 'habit' (from Latin *habitus*) in their introductory discussion of material identity in *Renaissance Clothing and the Materials of Memory*, 5–6.

psychological complexion. Some lawmakers, says Irenius, think the reformation of Irish dress a slight matter:

> *Iren*: But they thinke this precisenes in reformacion of Apparrell not to be so materiall or greatlye pertinente /
>
> *Eudox*: yeas surely but it is ffor mens Apparell is Comonlye made accordinge to theire Condicions and theire Condicons are often times gouerned by theire garmentes ffor the persone that is gowned is by his gowne put in minde of gravetye and allsoe Restrained from lightenes by the verye vnaptnes of his wede. Therefore it is written by *Aristotle* that when *Cirus* had ouercome the Lidians that weare a warlike nacion and devised to bringe them to a more peaceable liffe he Chaunged theire Apparrell and musicke And insteade of theire shorte warlike Coate cloathed them in longe garmentes like weomen and in steade of theire warlike musicke appointed to them certain Lascivious layes and loose gigs by which in shorte space theire mindes weare so mollified and abated that they forgate theire former firesnes and became moste tender and effeminate wheareby it appeareth that theare is not a litle in the garment to the fashioninge of the minde and Condicions[33]

Warlike coats. Lascivious lays. Loose gigs (i.e. jigs). In his argument that a person's conditions are often governed by her or his garments, Eudoxus fully articulates the underlying premise of the whole of Spenser's treatise, that is, that the project of 'reforming' the Irish should first proceed along social and political lines, not merely because outward conformity is all the English truly seek from the subordinated Irish populations, but because control of outward things will transform the nature of inner experience. As ever, hypallage is the vehicle. Here Spenser is close to the 'externalist' behaviourism of modern sociology and anthropology, not only the socially expressed *habitus* of Pierre Bourdieu but a theory of person; as Alfred Gell puts it in *Art and Agency*:

> I cannot really tell, from the outside, whether the 'other' is a zombie or an automaton, who/which mimics the behaviour of an ordinary human being but does not have any of the 'inner experiences' we habitually associate with this behaviour. But this does not matter because the whole panoply of 'mind' is not a series of inner, private experiences at all, but is out there, in the public domain, as language, practices, routines, rules of the game, etc.; that is, 'forms of life'.[34]

We might return again here to the parallel Eudoxus draws between the Irish mantle and Diogenes' dish. Diogenes of Sinope, the cynic, was to Renaissance readers of Diogenes Laertius a byword for the satirical deconstruction of a materially constituted identity; his dish served as the material correlative for the Sceptics' corporealized 'modes' for deconstructing dogmatic arguments—a material object so invested with human identity and agency that, rather than attesting to a surrender of naturalism, it was to

[33] Spenser, *A View*, ll. 2160–75.

[34] Alfred Gell, *Art and Agency: An Anthropological Theory* (Oxford: Clarendon Press, 1998), 126.

all intents and purposes incorporated into the body, as native to the cynic master as his hand.[35] Eudoxus entertains for a moment the argument that the Irish mantle, like Diogenes' dish, is so human an object that it cannot be stripped from its wearer; but, even here, at its point of maximum strain, Irenius' argument for a social and material reconstruction of identity wins through.

Change the habit, change the person. Change the dress, change the people. The claim is distinctive among English soldiers and statesmen writing position pieces on Irish policy in these years, and there are many—bloody, racist programmes not so much for reform as repression. More typical is the view of Captain Thomas Lee, who sees the Old English and Irish communities as fundamentally perfidious and ungovernable, their true, that is interior, allegiances and commitments unknowable;[36] or that of the anonymous author of the *Supplication of the Blood of the English*, roughly contemporaneous with Spenser's own tract, which argues furiously for a merciless military offensive against and punishing reckoning with the rebellious communities in Ireland.[37] For Irenius, by contrast, the goal is to stock the island with English planters, and to displace the power of Irish chiefs and lords by making men responsible and answerable to new English authorities: for, as he says, 'sithens we Cannot now applie Lawes fitt to the people as in the firste institucion of Comon wealthes it oughte to be we will applie the people and fitt them to the Lawes as it moste Convenientlye maye be'.[38] Change the habit, change the person; but if the habit will not be changed, *change the person as if he or she were a thing*. The distinctively anthropological and materialist approach Spenser adopts in *A View of the Present State of Ireland* goes hand in hand with his his hypallactic allegorical method in *The Faerie Queene*, and both make sense in light of his proposal for the conversion of the structures of Irish governance to English common law conventions. Spenser clearly saw his materialist blueprint for reformation as consistent with the tradition of common law governance with which, since Henry VIII's 1540 conversion of Ireland into a kingdom, Ireland had to be governed.

Bibliography

Baker, J. H. *The Oxford History of the Laws of England*, Vol. 6: *1483–1558* (Oxford: Oxford University Press, 2003).

Calvin, John. *The Institution of Christian Religion*, trans. Thomas Norton (London: 1561).

[35] Diogenes Laertius records the two moments when the Cynic master was said to have cast away his bowl, his last possession—moments when he observed children creating bowls out of their own hands or out of morsels of consumable bread; see Diogenes Laertius, *Lives of the Eminent Philosophers*, edited by R. D. Hicks (Cambridge: Harvard University Press, 1925), 6.2.

[36] See Sir Thomas Lee, *The Discouerie and Recouerie of Irelande and the Aucthores Apologie*, Gonville and Caius College, Cambridge MS 150/22, and St John's College, Cambridge MS I.29. Lee insists throughout his treatise on the existence of and danger offered by 'secrete Traitors' (SJC MS I.29, fol. 1r).

[37] T. C., *The Supplication of the Blood of the English Most Lamentably Murdered in Ireland, Cryeng Out of the Yearth for Revenge* (c.1598), ed. Willy Maley, *Analecta Hibernica*, 36 (1994), 1–90.

[38] Spenser, *A View*, 199 (ll. 4420–2).

Coke, Sir Edward. *The Third Part of the Institutes of the Lawes of England* (London: 1644).
Diogenes Laertius, *Lives of the Eminent Philosophers*, ed. R. D. Hicks, 2 vols (Cambridge, MA: Harvard University Press, 1925).
Dyer, Sir James. *Ascuns Nouel Cases* (London: 1592).
Gell, Alfred. *Art and Agency: An Anthropological Theory* (Oxford: Clarendon Press, 1998).
Gonville and Caius College, Cambridge MS 150/22, Captain Thomas Lee, *The Discouerie and Recouerie of Irelande and the Aucthores Apologie*.
Hake, Edward. *Epieikeia: A Dialogue on Equity in Three Parts* [1598], ed. D. E. C. Yale (New Haven: Yale University Press, 1953).
Hutson, Lorna. *The Invention of Suspicion: Law and Mimesis in Shakespeare and Renaissance Drama* (Oxford: Oxford University Press, 2007).
Maley, Willy, ed. 'T. C. *The Supplication of the Blood of the English most Lamentably Murdered in Ireland, Cryeng out of the Yearth for Revenge* [c.1598].' *Analecta Hibernica*, 36 (1994): 1–90.
Plowden, Edmund. *The Commentaries, or Reports of Edmund Plowden* (London: 1779).
Jones, Ann Rosalind and Peter Stallybrass. *Renaissance Clothing and the Materials of Memory* (Cambridge: Cambridge University Press, 2000).
National Archives SP 63/144/57/2, Sir William Herbert, 'A Note of Sutch Reasons as Mooued Mea, toe Putt the Statute in Execution agaynst Irish Habites.'
Nuttall, A. D. 'Spenser and Elizabethan Alienation', *Essays in Criticism*, 55 (2005): 209–25.
Peacham, Henry. *The Garden of Eloquence* (London: 1577).
Pietz, William. 'Death of the Deodand: Accursed Objects and the Money Value of Human Life', *Review of English Studies*, 31 (1997): 97–108.
Puttenham, George. *The Arte of English Poesie* (London: 1589).
Quintilian. *Institutio oratoria*, ed. and trans. H. E. Butler, 4 vols (Cambridge, MA: Harvard University Press, 1943).
St German, Christopher. *Doctor and Student*, ed. T. F. T. Plucknett and J. L. Barton (London: SS, 1974).
Shakespeare, William. *The Complete Works*, ed. Stanley Wells, Gary Taylor, et al., 2nd edn (Oxford: Clarendon Press, 1986, 2005).
Simpson, A. W. B. *A History of the Common Law of Contract: The Rise of the Action of Assumpsit* (Oxford: Oxford University Press, 1987).
Spenser, Edmund. *The Faerie Queene*, ed. A. C. Hamilton et al. (London: Longman, 2001).
Spenser, Edmund. *A View of the Present State of Ireland*, ed. Rudolf Gottfried, in *The Works of Edmund Spenser*, Vol. 10, ed. Edwin Greenlaw et al., 11 vols (Baltimore: Johns Hopkins University Press, 1945).
St John's College, Cambridge MS I.29, Captain Thomas Lee, The Discouerie and Recouerie of Irelande and the Aucthores Apologie.
Wilson, Luke. 'Renaissance Tool Abuse and the Legal History of the Sudden', in *Literature, Politics and Law in Renaissance England*, ed. Erica Sheen and Lorna Hutson (London: Palgrave Macmillan, 2005), 121–45.
Wilson, Luke. *Theatres of Intention: Drama and the Law in Early Modern England* (Stanford: Stanford University Press, 2000).

CHAPTER 34

LAW AND LITERATURE IN SCOTLAND, C.1450–1707

ROBERT A. HOUSTON

FOR two decades scholars of English literature have studied legal literature and legal practice as a cultural phenomenon and in relation to imaginative literature's complex engagements with the law: intersections and correspondences; affinities and relationships.[1] Scotland's academic establishment is small and, as with many areas, literary, legal, and historical scholarship follows certain well-trodden paths. The study of late medieval and early modern law and literature is not among them. The ages of Enlightenment, Romanticism, and later are better served and we all know that Sir Walter Scott (1771–1832), a barrister or 'advocate' by profession, became 'sheriff-depute' of the Border shire of Selkirk in 1799 (a judge presiding over the shire's main civil and criminal court), only starting to write historical fiction late in life. In stories about topics as diverse as marriage, inheritance, and infanticide, Scott brilliantly expounded the tensions within Scots law, between law and Scottish society, and between Scots and English law in the Georgian age.[2] This chapter sets out what we know of these issues during the last two

[1] I am grateful to John Cairns, Robert Crawford, Jane Dawson, John Hudson, Clare Jackson, Colin Kidd, and Roger Mason for their help in preparing this chapter. The best condensed survey of the development of Scots law between the twelfth and nineteenth centuries is " J. W. Cairns, 'Historical Introduction', in *A History of Private Law in Scotland*, Vol. 1: *Introduction and Property*, ed. K. Reid and R. Zimmermann (Oxford: Oxford University Press, 2000), 14–184. The authoritative text on the legal history of Scotland is D. M. Walker, *A Legal History of Scotland*, 7 vols (Edinburgh, 1988–2004). Those wishing a crash-course in Scottish history may find useful R. Houston, *Scotland: A Very Short Introduction* (Oxford: Oxford University Press, 2008).

[2] J. W. Cairns, 'A Note on *The Bride of Lammermoor*: Why Scott Did Not Mention the Dalrymple Legend until 1830', *Scottish Literary Journal*, 20 (1993): 19–36; 'The Noose Hidden under Flowers: Marriage and Law in "St Ronan's Well"', *JLH*, 16 (1995): 234–55; P. Maharg, 'The Identity of Scots Law: Redeeming the Past', in *Scottish Life and Society: A Compendium of Scottish Ethnology*, Vol. 13: *The Law*, ed. M. A. Mulhern (Edinburgh: John Donald, 2012), 322–8; and E. McVicar, 'Protest: The Law and Song', in *Scottish Life and Society*, ed. Mulhern, 582–7. D. A. Symonds, *Weep Not for Me: Women, Ballads, and Infanticide in Early Modern Scotland* (University Park: Pennsylvania State University, 1997).

and a half centuries of Stewart rule. It explores the importance of law, not only in imaginative literature, but also in writing on religion and political theory. Readers will already have noted that Scott's micro-biography contains two apostrophized terms that may be unfamiliar or even misleading to specialists in English legal history. This chapter's purpose is to explain these and many more distinctive aspects of Scots law and its context, exploring some of the many historical areas that a combination of law *and* literature can illuminate.

Scotland was not just different from England, but foreign. Early sixteenth-century Scots in England were liable to arrest and imprisonment as aliens; they were not allowed to use English courts.[3] After centuries of warring, people on both sides of the border remained, at best, ambivalent about each other and wrongly calling a sixteenth-century Englishman a Scot was actionable. With issues of justice, borders, and cultures in the two kingdoms aired most notably in 'Macbeth', important changes came out of the Union of the Crowns in 1603. In *Ekskybalauron: or, the Discovery of a Most Exquisite Jewel* (1652), Sir Thomas Urquhart of Cromarty (1611–1660) refers to the case of an infant called Robert Colville, heard by Exchequer Chamber in 1608, concerning estate in land in London; it appears there (and is always known by) its English corruption, Calvin.[4] The judgement for Colville meant that a Scot could own land in England. The grounds were that a person born in Scotland after 1603 owed allegiance to the *person* of the king of England as well as Scotland. The immediate concern was the relationship of tenure to allegiance, but the judgement became the basis for the law of naturalization for two centuries. More, it supported a concept of kingship as a product of the laws of God and nature, as well as establishing Scotland as a sovereign rather than vassal state.[5]

Writing from exile during the Cromwellian occupation of Scotland, royalist and anti-Presbyterian Urquhart argued that, because Scotland 'was annexed to *England* by inheritance, and not conquest', its citizens should enjoy in England 'the same priviledges and immunities (in every thing) that *Wales* now hath, (and which the Scots have in *France*, a transmarine Country[])'. Urquhart's assertion has wider resonance. Early modern Europe comprised mostly composite monarchies and/or multiple kingdoms, whose rulers had to respect the traditions of their parts. Britain may have had a single monarchy from 1603, but contemporaries recognized the different prerogatives, privileges, and jurisdictions pertaining to the Crown in its component parts.[6] Proposals for

[3] J. H. Baker, *OHLE*, 6.616–17. J. A. F. Thomson, 'Scots in England in the Fifteenth Century', *Scottish Historical Review*, 79 (2000): 1–16.

[4] R. D. S. Jack and R. J. Lyall, eds, *Sir Thomas Urquhart of Cromarty: The Jewel* (Edinburgh: Scottish Academic Press, 1983), 199–200, 248, 268–9; ER, 77, 377–411. C. W. Brooks, *Law, Politics and Society in Early Modern England* (Cambridge: Cambridge University Press, 2008), 133–5.

[5] Walker, *Legal History of Scotland*, 4.39–40. K. Kim, *Aliens in Medieval Law: The Origins of Modern Citizenship* (Cambridge: Cambridge University Press, 2001).

[6] B. P. Levack, 'The Proposed Union of English Law and Scots Law in the Seventeenth Century', *Juridical Review*, 20 (1975): 97–115; Toward a More Perfect Union: England, Scotland, and the Constitution', in *After the Reformation*, ed. B. C. Malament (Manchester, 1980), 57–74. A. Kiralfy, 'Independent Legal Systems under a Common Dynastic Rule: The Examples of England and Hungary', *JLH*, 11 (1990): 118–28.

a legal union between Scotland and England in 1604 foundered primarily because of concerns among English common lawyers about a takeover by civil law; an understandable concern, since equity had, after all, been the most dynamic branch of English law in the previous century. In short, law in Scotland was not a colonial imposition, as it was to the Welsh and Irish, but an indigenous development based on historic foundations and selective, creative adaptations. Medieval Scots law was far from solely Anglo-Norman and there were strong native elements (including Celtic, Norse, and British, in the proper ancient meaning of the word) that mediated any obvious similarity.[7]

Renaissance humanism influenced legal development through the application of philological and grammatical analysis, and the use of history texts in reinforcing precedents; from this period dates the ideal that lawyers needed literature and history to do their job properly, the two 'pertaining to a single order and practice of imaginative thought'.[8] As Sir George Mackenzie of Rosehaugh (1636/1638–1691) put it much later: 'Three branches of learning are the handmaidens of Jurisprudence, namely History, Criticism and Rhetoric.'[9] The Roman 'reception' was of continental juristic systems and rationality rather than substantive law, which was only used if no source existed in Scots law; as John Selden recognized in the time of James I, no European country wholly adopted Justinian's law.[10] Learned lawyers like Sir John Skene of Curriehill (*c.*1543–1617) and Thomas Craig of Riccarton (1538–1608) nevertheless summarized and analysed Roman law alongside sovereignty and the sources of Scottish law, its legislation, and the obscurity of early laws. Craig's attempt to rationalize Scots law used a framework of *ius naturale* and *ius gentium*, allowing interpretation through the exercise of *recta ratio*.

Craig's purpose, when he wrote *Ius feudale* (*c.*1600), was to support James VI's desire for 'a more perfect union' by harmonizing the laws of England and Scotland; Craig thought the bridge lay in shared French feudal law.[11] His text was first published in 1655 because by this stage, during the English occupation of Scotland, it seemed possible that its law would become a regional custom accommodated within the common law of England. In post-Restoration negotiations on a closer Union, the English side seemed to assume as much. This stimulated Scottish lawyers further to consider the place of

[7] D. Sellar, 'Celtic Law and Scots Law: Survival and Integration', *Scottish Studies*, 29 (1989): 1–27. H. L. MacQueen, *Common Law and Feudal Society in Medieval Scotland* (Edinburgh: Edinburgh University Press, 1993).

[8] B. Cormack, *A Power to Do Justice: Jurisdiction, English Literature, and the Rise of Common Law, 1509–1625* (Chicago: University of Chicago Press, 2007), 39. W. J. Bouwsma, 'Lawyers and Early Modern Culture', *American Historical Review*, 78.2 (1973): 303–27; H. MacQueen, J. W. Cairns, and T. D. Fergus, 'Legal Humanism in Renaissance Scotland', *JLH*, 9 (1990): 40–69.

[9] J. W. Cairns and A. M. Cain, eds, *Oratio inauguralis in aperienda Jurisconsultorum Biblioteca: Sir George Mackenzie* [1689] (Edinburgh: Edinburgh University Press, 1989), 73; B. I. Manolescu, 'George Mackenzie on Scottish Judicial Rhetoric', *Rhetorica: A Journal of the History of Rhetoric*, 20 (2002): 275–88.

[10] J. Selden, *A Historie of Tithes* (London: 1618), 478, 480.

[11] W. D. H. Sellar, 'The Common Law of Scotland and the Common Law of England', in *The British Isles 1100–1500: Comparisons, Contrasts and Connections*, ed. R. R. Davies (Edinburgh: University of Edinburgh Press, 1988), 82.

Scots law in a European *ius commune* and Sir James Dalrymple of Stair (1619–1695) to publish, in 1681, his *Institutions*.[12] The seventeenth century was an important period for the formation of national law across Europe. Scottish lawyers, judges, and jurists tried to understand where they stood, in an age of political change, when different conceptions of legal authority coexisted: learned, local, natural, rational, and equitable. Their deliberations marked an important transition from a primarily jurisdictional conception of law to a mainly jurisprudential one.

Between 1681 and 1829 more 'institutions' appeared to codify and teach Scots law as it evolved, reinforced by efforts to maintain its distinctiveness. Scotland's separate parliament merged with England's in 1707 and many aspects of English 'Publick Right, Pollicy and Civil Government' (notably on trade, customs, and excise) applied to Scotland, but it preserved its institutions of education, local government, private law, and religion, each becoming an important part of post-Union national identity. Supreme appellate authority rested (accidentally) in the British House of Lords on the creation of the United Kingdom. During 1710–1711 a pamphlet war raged over the treatment in Scotland of an Episcopal clergyman, Rev. James Greenshields, including a contribution by Defoe, which shows the early stages of a search for accommodations between the two countries' legal systems and societies that continues to this day.[13]

Centuries of difference made this enduringly difficult. Later medieval England had a plural legal system, one that was less 'homegrown, continuous, insular, and unique' than once supposed.[14] Common, church, equity, prerogative, and customary courts (among others) each had their own separate niche and fortunes. No later than the fifteenth century, Scotland had a more singular or unitary legal tradition with multiple inputs from custom, learned (Romano-canonical) law, statute, and court practice; it developed a distinctive version of the *ius commune*. English law leant towards providing specific remedies (using a bewildering elaboration of writs) and learning from precedents, whereas Scottish followed the civilian tradition's concern with underlying rights or principles, the generality of the premises from which reasoning proceeds when deciding on particular instances, a limited range of legal instruments, and broad understandings of right and wrong. During the sixteenth and seventeenth century there was, nevertheless, a 'shift in dependence from doctrine to decisions' or 'practicks' (opinions) in Scotland, as there was across Europe; Stair illustrates this when addressing his central issue (what made law law?) and his own *Decisions* of the Court of Session, Scotland's

12 *The Institutions of the Law of Scotland* (Edinburgh: University of Edinburgh Press, 1681); J. D. Ford, *Law and Opinion in Scotland during the Seventeenth Century* (Oxford: Hart, 2007).

13 D. Defoe, *Greenshields out of Prison and Toleration Settled in Scotland* (London: 1710). The essence of the case is summed up in the title of pamphlets such as *A True State of the Case of the Reverend Mr. Greenshields, Now Prisoner in the Tolbooth in Edinburgh* (London: 1710). Episcopalians gained toleration in Scotland in 1712. A. Raffe, *The Culture of Controversy: Religious Arguments in Scotland, 1660–1714* (Woodbridge: Boydell Press, 2012), 89–92.

14 R. Helgerson, *Forms of Nationhood: The Elizabethan Writing of England* (London and Chicago: Chicago University Press, 1992), 67, and see more generally 65–72.

supreme civil court, were the first published (1683, 1687).[15] The closest similarities were between Scottish and English courts implementing civil codes. The hybrid ecclesiastical law (mostly bastardized civil law) that emerged in England during the Middle Ages to govern areas such as succession to movable property and probate and that endured until the mid-nineteenth century was, for example, less rigid than common law in validating documents doubtful in form, provided the intention of the framer was sufficiently clear.[16] Beyond this, the nature of law and trajectories of change were wholly different.

Before the Reformation of the 1560s, Scotland's secular and ecclesiastical courts could work together. For example, one option for creditors wishing to recover debt was an ecclesiastical compulsitor given teeth by 'letters of cursing' (maledictory excommunication on the grounds that the debtor had broken an oath to pay) which allowed the creditor to invoke secular power to enforce payment; the result was sometimes known as being 'at goddis horn' where 'horning' meant outlawing (because law officers blew horns announcing the sentence).[17] In Sir David Lyndsay of the Mount's 'Ane Satyre of the Thrie Estaitis' (a play or 'performance poem' of 1540/1552 about justice and clerical corruption) the pauper suffers from the judicial curse of his parson for failing to pay allegedly extortionate mortuary dues, meaning he cannot attend Easter communion.[18] The law of debt and credit was resolved quite quickly in the 1570s and 1580s, after which Commissary Courts (established in 1563 as successors to the courts of the bishop's officials, dealing with all their private law business) became the recognized place to recover small debts; Sheriff Courts handled larger ones (and a wide range of other civil and criminal matters).[19] Some twenty-two regional Commissary Courts also dealt with probate ('confirmation') of wills ('testaments') and executries.[20] The Commissary Court of Edinburgh took control over cases of adherence, dissolving, or annulling marriage

15 Baker, *OHLE*, 52. D. Sellar, 'Legal Writing, 1314–1707', in *The Edinburgh History of Scottish Literature, Vol. 1: From Columba to the Union (until 1707)*, ed. T. O. Clanchy and M. Pittock (Edinburgh: Edinburgh University Press, 2007), 241.

16 L. Bonfield, *Devising, Dying and Dispute: Probate Litigation in Early Modern England* (Aldershot: Ashgate, 2012). Both natural and civil, equity had rules, but they were more flexible than law.

17 R. K. Hannay, ed., *Acts of the Lords of Council in Public Affairs, 1501–54* (Edinburgh: Edinburgh University Press, 1932), 408. S. Ollivant, *The Court of the Official in Pre-Reformation Scotland* (Edinburgh: Edinburgh University Press, 1982), 77–80.

18 Sir David Lyndsay, *Ane Satyre of the Thrie Estaits in Commendation of Vertew and Vituperation of Vyce* (Edinburgh: Robert Charteris, 1602), 66. This may be based on a real-life case before the official of Lothian in 1546. Ollivant, *Court of the Official*, 82–3. Mortuaries were also a prominent bone of contention between laity and clergy in England. S. F. C. Milsom, 'Richard Hunne's Praemunire', *English Historical Review*, 76 (1961): 80–2. R. Wunderli, 'Pre-Reformation London Summoners and the Murder of Richard Hunne', *Journal of Ecclesiastical History*, 33 (1982): 209–24.

19 A. E. Anton, 'Medieval Scottish Executors and the Courts Spiritual', *JR*, 67 (1955): 129–54. Ollivant, *Court of the Official*, 69–72. J. Goodare, *The Government of Scotland, 1560–1625* (Oxford: Oxford University Press, 2004), 202–3. Post-Reformation commissaries were neither fully secular nor fully ecclesiastical; see *An Introduction to Scottish Legal History*, 366–71.

20 J. E. A. Dawson, 'The Noble and the Bastard: The Earl of Argyll and the Law of Divorce in Reformation Scotland', in J. Goodare and A. A. MacDonald, eds, *Sixteenth-Century Scotland: Essays in Honour of Michael Lynch* (Leiden: Brill, 2008), 147–68.

('divorce' was easier than in England), and over legitimacy across all Scotland, as well as general and local executry. Legitimation did not exist in England. In contrast, a person, born illegitimate, could be legitimized by the Crown in Scotland during life, allowing him or her to bequeath to an heir; otherwise their goods were forfeit to the Crown as *ultimus haeres*. Nor was adoption of children recognized at English law, whereas fosterage in the Celtic tradition was a social and political institution in Scotland until the seventeenth century.[21]

The easy transformation at the Reformation is a sign of the flexibility and adaptability of Scots law. The long-running 'struggle among institutions for concurrent or exclusive jurisdiction and for the power to define the law of England', which was a prominent theme in late medieval and early modern English legal history, is largely absent from Scotland.[22] And from the late Middle Ages Scots law had few actions, each with wide application, where England's legal system was configured more rigidly around numerous forms of process, each with rather precise scope.[23] Many issues, like reparation for pure economic loss, were not seen as discrete problems in early modern Scots law. Nor did the Scots law of obligations make a distinction between speciality and simple contract.[24] Many legal institutions and issues, that established tropes in English imaginative literature, are consequently absent from Scotland. For example, Scottish debtors could not 'keep house'—that is, be immune from arrest for debt by locking their front door ('an Englishman's home is his castle')—and legal officers could go anywhere except recognized sanctuaries to seize those denounced as outlaws or 'rebels'; the law of sanctuary in the two countries was quite different.[25] Creditors could enforce imprisonment for debt less stringently in historic Scotland than was notorious in England because: it came at the end of the process of bankruptcy ('insolvency') rather than its beginning; creditors had to pay towards support of bankrupts

[21] E. Burt, *Letters from a Gentleman in the North of Scotland to his Friend in London ... 2 vols* [1754] (London: 1815), 2.140–2; C. Innes, *Sketches of Early Scotch History and Social Progress* (Edinburgh: University of Edinburgh Press, 1861), 366–72; F. F. Mackay, ed., *MacNeill of Carskey: His Estate Journal, 1703–43* (Edinburgh: University of Edinburgh Press, 1955), 33, 61, 62–3, 65; P. Parkes, 'Celtic Fosterage: Adoptive Kinship and Clientage in Northwest Europe', *Comparative Studies in Society and History*, 48 (2006): 374–9; F. Fitzsimons, 'Fosterage and Gossiprid in late Medieval Ireland: Some New Evidence', in *Gaelic Ireland, c.1250–c.1650: Land, Lordship and Settlement*, ed. P. J. Duffy, D. Edwards, and E. Fitzpatrick (Dublin: Four Courts Press, 2001), 138–49.

[22] D. J. Hulsebosch, 'The English Constitution and the Expanding Empire: Sir Edward Coke's British Jurisprudence', *LHR*, 21.3 (2003): 439–82, 450.

[23] A. Watson, *Legal Transplants: An Approach to Comparative Law* (Edinburgh: Edinburgh University Press, 1974), 45.

[24] A. D. M. Forte, 'Reparation for Pure Economic Loss: An Historical Perspective of Scots Law in the Seventeenth and Eighteenth Centuries', *JLH*, 8 (1987): 3–17. L. A. Ewan, 'Debt and Credit in Early Modern Scotland: The Grandtully Estates, 1650–1750' (PhD thesis, University of Edinburgh, 1988), 87–113; Goodare, *Government of Scotland*, 178; Ford, *Law and Opinion*, 160–6. For a lucid summary of the Roman law of contract, see D. Ibbetson, *A Historical Introduction to the Law of Obligations* (Oxford: Oxford University Press, 1999), 6–10.

[25] H. MacQueen, 'Girth: Society and the Law of Sanctuary in Scotland', in *Critical Studies in Ancient Law, Comparative Law and Legal History*, ed. J. Cairns and O. Robinson (Oxford: Hart, 2001), 333–52.

('divours'); the debtor could seek release by giving up assets to trustees for creditors ('sequestration').

Nomenclature was not only different in debt and credit litigation. Depending on date and context, a 'bailie' could be a high-ranking estate administrator, a burgh magistrate, or a lowly local court officer. Manslaughter was known as 'culpable homicide'; a defendant in jury trials was 'the pannel'; mortgaging was 'wadsetting', the borrower a 'reverser'; interest on money lent was 'annualrent'; tort was 'delict'; criminal intent was 'dole'; and so on.[26] These words are mostly Scottish (though delict comes from Roman law). A dialect of Middle English, Middle Scots was the language of government by *c.*1400 and most court records (along with much literature) were in the vernacular by 1500, except for the church courts which kept Latin until the Reformation. From the time of James VI (southern) Standard English slowly gained ground.[27] Neither late medieval nor early modern Scots used legal French. Gaelic legal documents are rare.[28]

Religious and legal changes had profound political implications. For a generation after the Reformation Crown and Kirk worked together to blend a measure of self-direction with the rule of a single person by hereditary right: a sort of 'monarchical republicanism'.[29] From the pen of David Hume of Godscroft (1558–1629x31), political theorist, poet, and follower of George Buchanan (1506–1582), came a celebration of justice and sharing public life.[30] Alongside this was the powerful idea of two kingdoms (those of God and the prince) argued by theologian Andrew Melville (1545–1622), who had travelled extensively in Europe, studying law, during the 1560s. For his part, Buchanan argued for the primacy of statute law over what he termed the arbitrary application by senior judges of various principles of justice, including equity. From the late 1590s, however, such ascending theories of authority paled before 'fundamental law', tradition, private right, and legal debate as hierarchy and security regained dominance, reducing citizens to subjects once more.[31] James VI's 'The true lawe of free monarchies, or, the reciprock and mutuall dutie betwixt a free king, and his naturall

[26] On dole, see L. Farmer, *Criminal Law, Tradition and Legal Order. Crime and the Genius of Scots Law, 1747 to the Present* (Cambridge: Cambridge University Press, 1997), 147–60. For a historically aware guide to modern terminology, see S. R. O'Rourke, *Glossary of Legal Terms* (Edinburgh: Edinburgh University Press, 2004).

[27] Sellar, 'Legal Writing, 1314–1707', 238–9. A. Agutter, 'Middle Scots as a Literary Language', in *The History of Scottish Literature*, Vol. 1: *Origins to 1660 (Mediaeval and Renaissance)*, ed. R. D. S. Jack (Aberdeen: Aberdeen University Press, 1988), 13–25.

[28] K. Forsyth, ed., *Studies on the Book of Deer* (Dublin: Four Courts Press, 2008); R. Black, 'Gaelic Law as Literature', in *The Law*, ed. Mulhern, 11–46.

[29] The phrase comes from P. Collinson, 'The Monarchical Republic of Queen Elizabeth', *Bulletin of the John Rylands University Library of Manchester*, 69 (1987): 394–424.

[30] *The History of the Houses of Douglas and Angus Wherein Are Discovered the Most Memorable Passages of the Kingdom of Scotland from the Yeer 767, to the Reign of Our Late Soveraign Lord King James the Sixth* (Edinburgh: 1648).

[31] P. J. McGinnis and A. H. Williamson, 'Politics, Prophecy, Poetry: The Melvillian Moment, 1589–96, and Its Aftermath', *Scottish Historical Review*, 89 (2010): 1–18.

subiectes' (1598) was the most famous statement of divine right and Mackenzie followed his line after the Restoration.[32]

Directly or indirectly, many non-lawyers were clearly familiar with at least parts of Justinian (notably on rights of resistance). They ranged from the humanist poet, historian, and administrator Buchanan, who numbered lawyers among his close friends and served on commissions for digest of the laws, to Covenanting theologians like Samuel Rutherford (*c.*1600–1661), whose *Lex, rex, or, the Law and the Prince* (1644), continued Buchanan's defence of resistance to tyrants (here Charles I; Rutherford wanted monarchs selected by the people).[33] Not all literary figures, however, reflected the law's influence to the same degree. Poet and royalist polemicist, William Drummond of Hawthornden (1585–1649), studied law in France, but imaginative literature dominated his library and reading; embroiled in debt litigation late in life, he may have become as jaded about the law as Alexander Hume before him (see below) and Scott after. Jurists who dabbled in literature favoured non-legal topics; for example, Craig wrote much Latin poetry.[34] Mackenzie advised a receptive Dryden on poetic style and published his first literary work in 1660 ('Aretina, or, The Serious Romance', an allegorical account of the British and Irish Civil Wars). Yet this has little legal resonance and he later explicitly eschewed non-legal writing.[35] These examples may be signs of the growing divergence between law and other disciplines that had been forged in the Renaissance.[36]

Melville's and Buchanan's ideas about conditional loyalty never entirely disappeared.[37] The Covenanting Revolution of 1638–1651 made natural law the basis of civil government, profoundly changing the foundations of both the discourse of law (as Stair showed) and politics (as demonstrated by the Claim of Right of 1689, a far more radical document than the English Declaration of Rights).[38] The Claim includes a formal indictment of the rule

[32] Andrew Marvell's views on authority and liberty in Restoration Scotland were quite different. J. Kerrigan, *Archipelagic English: Literature, History, and Politics, 1603–1707* (Oxford: Oxford University Press, 2008), 272, 281, 286–7, 295–6.

[33] *ODNB*; D. M. Abbott, 'George Buchanan, the Court of Session and the Law', in *The Stair Society Miscellany Four*, ed. H. L. MacQueen (Edinburgh: Edinburgh University Press, 2002), 139–44; R. A. Mason and M. S. Smith, eds, *A Dialogue on the Law of Kingship among the Scots: A Critical Edition and Translation of George Buchanan's 'De iure regni apud Scotos dialogus'* (Aldershot: Ashgate, 2004). Buchanan wrote to justify the ousting of Mary, Queen of Scots, against whom he had already written *Detectio Mariae reginae Scotorum* (1571). In 1566 Edmund Plowden had written supporting Mary's claim to succeed to the English throne. M. Axton, 'The Influence of Edmund Plowden's Succession Treatise', *HLQ*, 37 (1974): 209–26; Brooks, *Law, Politics and Society*, 71–9.

[34] Collected in A. Johnston, *Delitiae poetarum Scotorum hujus aevi illustrium* (Amsterdam: 1637).

[35] C. Jackson, 'The Paradoxical Virtue of the Historical Romance: Sir George Mackenzie's Aretina and the Civil Wars', in R. J. Young, ed., *Celtic Dimensions of the British Civil Wars* (Edinburgh: Edinburgh University Press, 1997), 205–25.

[36] For analysis of comparable signs of a growing divergence between law and literature in seventeenth-century England, see the chapter by Christopher Brooks in this volume.

[37] R. Mason and C. Erskine, eds, *George Buchanan: Political Thought in Early Modern Europe* (Aldershot: Ashgate, 2012).

[38] T. Harris, 'The People, the Law, and the Constitution in Scotland and England: A Comparative Approach to the Glorious Revolution', *JBS*, 38 (1999): 28–58.

of James VII closely based on criminal court style. Rich in rhetoric and fusing 'religious fervour and legal caution', the Scottish National Covenant of 1638 (a covenant is a bond or contract) also resembled as much a court submission ('information') as it did a spiritual testament—hardly surprising as a prominent advocate Sir Archibald Johnston of Warriston (1611–1663) led its drafting.[39] After 1690 the Kirk started to claim that it was 'the Church of Scotland as by law established' rather than 'Christ's true Kirk'.[40]

At loggerheads over many issues, James VI and the Presbyters agreed that justice should be impartial and equitable, a prominent theme in the king's advice manual to his son, *Basilicon doron* (1599).[41] The Kirk had an important part to play in change, arguing vigorously from the Reformation onwards against the role of lordship in orchestrating social and economic relationships and, in particular, avenging wrongs. In a reference to the feud, John Knox described kinship as 'invented by Satan to shed innocent blood'.[42] Knox trained as a canon lawyer and worked as a notary (the emergence of notaries public in fifteenth- and sixteenth-century Scotland was based on the church's notarial practice). Both the king and he recognized that, for all it structured conflict, the feud was a violent and potentially disruptive institution. By substituting Christian brotherhood for blood, by promoting royal power under God, by causing the magnates to stand back from what the Kirk was doing, and by re-creating their successors (the 'lairds' or lesser lords) as godly magistrates, the Kirk ultimately helped to generate new social structures and values, just as it had helped substitute jury trial for trial by combat or ordeal in the thirteenth century. For its own reasons, but building on the new role of 'the Session' (later the Court of Session) in the early sixteenth century, it contributed to 'modernization' by promoting the idea that justice should come from an impersonal body (a secular or religious court) informed by a standard principle (sin and its avoidance) rather than from the manipulation of society through the workings of personal bonds.[43] As Rev. Robert Bruce put it in a sermon of 1589, 'Let no community of name, ally, proximity of blood, or whatever it be, move you to pervert justice, but let every man be answerable according to the merit of his cause.'[44] Throughout the seventeenth century Presbyters worked to supersede kinship, coerce community, and enforce neighbourly harmony, gradually acquiring legitimacy and ultimately providing those in conflict with an

[39] *ODNB*. The author's legal training is similarly clear in *The Appellation of Iohn Knox from the Cruell and Most Uniust Sentence Pronounced against Him by the False Bishoppes and Clergie of Scotland* (Geneva: 1558).

[40] Raffe, *Culture of Controversy*, esp. 29–61, 65–7, on divine and statute law.

[41] James's earlier *Daemonologie* (1597) shows close knowledge of the workings of the Justiciary Court. L. Normand and G. Roberts, eds, *Witchcraft in Early Modern Scotland: James VI's Demonology and the North Berwick Witches* (Exeter: University of Exeter Press, 2000).

[42] Quoted in J. Wormald, '"Princes" and the Regions in the Scottish Reformation', in *Church, Politics and Society: Scotland, 1408–1929*, ed. N. MacDougall (Edinburgh: Edinburgh University Press, 1983), 68; 'Bloodfeud, Kindred and Government in Early Modern Scotland', *P&P*, 87 (1980): 54–97.

[43] J. Wormald, *Lords and Men in Scotland: Bonds of Manrent, 1442–1603* (Edinburgh: Edinburgh University Press, 1985).

[44] W. Cunningham, ed., *Sermons by the Rev. Robert Bruce, Minister of Edinburgh. Reprinted from the Original Edition of MDXC and MDXCI* (Edinburgh: Edinburgh University Press, 1843), 355.

alternative to baronial or even royal courts.[45] By mid-century blood-feud was effectively gone from the Lowlands.

This is not to say that the law was flawless. For centuries writers of factual and imaginative literature had criticized failings in justice, illuminating as they did some of the many distinctive features of Scottish law. Poet Robert Henryson (*c.*1420–*c.*1490) was, for example, a notary public, and a master of both civil and canon law. Courts of law, together with legal language, processes, pleas, and decisions, figure extensively in his narrative verse (mostly re-interpretations of fables)—for example in the prologue to 'The Tail of the Lyoun and the Mous' or in 'Taill of the Scheip and the Dog'.[46] There is a trial scene, in Gawin Douglas's long poem 'The Palis of Honoure' (1501), which makes comic use of the terms and procedures of the Scottish law courts; Douglas (*c.*1476–1522) was bishop of Dunkeld, an ambitious intriguer who had fought for his preferment through the highest church courts.[47] The poet asks Venus, who tries him for treason, to 'Reconsell [reconcile] me out of this gret affray', a reference to the deep imbrication of procedures for arbitration, mediation, and adjudication in late medieval Scottish society, as it became more legalized and professionalized; he ends up doing penance, also an enduring feature of justice before and after the Scottish Reformation.

Another dream allegory came from another cleric and notary, John Rolland (fl. 1528–1580). 'Ane Treatise Callit the Court of Venus' (*c.*1560/1575), where Venus and Vesta exchange legal arguments in a trial over superiority, and mock the language of the law. In 'Ane Epistle to Maister Gilbert Montcrief' (1599), lawyer, writer, and later minister of religion, Alexander Hume (*c.*1557–1609), wrote:

> Quhen that I had employed my youth and paine,
> Foure yeares in France, and was returned againe,
> I langed to learne, and curious was to knawe:
> The consuetude [practice], the custome and the Lawe,
> Quhairby our natiue soil was guide aright.
> And iustice done till everie kind of wight [creature]:
> To that effect three yeares, or neare that space,
> I hanted maist our highest plaiding [pleading] place.
> And senat quhair great causses reasoned were.
> My breast was brusd, with leaning on the bar.[48]

45 Wormald, '"Princes and the Regions"', 73, 79. J. W. Cairns, 'Academic Feud, Bloodfeud, and William Welwood: Legal Education in St Andrews, 1560–1611 part 2', *Edinburgh Law Review*, 2 (1998): 281–5; Goodare, *Government of Scotland*, 146–7; M. F. Graham, 'Conflict and Sacred Space in Reformation-Era Scotland', *Albion*, 33 (2001): 371–87.

46 *ODNB*; R. J. Lyall, 'Politics and Poetry in Fifteenth and Sixteenth Century Scotland', *Scottish Literary Journal*, 3 (1976): 5–29; 'Henryson's *Morall Fabillis*: Structure and Meaning', in P. Bawcutt and J. H. Williams, eds, *A Companion to Medieval Scottish Poetry* (Cambridge: Cambridge University Press, 2006), 89–104; C. McDonald, *Law and the Poetic Imagination: The Poetry of Robert Henryson* (PhD thesis, University of York, 1980); Sellar, 'Legal Writing, 1314–1707', 240.

47 *The Palis of Honoure Compyled by Gawayne Dowglas Byshope of Dunkyll* (London: 1553), n.p. *ODNB*.

48 'Ane Epistle to Maister Gilbert Montcreif, Mediciner to the Kings Majestie', in *The Poems of Alexander Hume*, ed. A. Lawson (Edinburgh: Edinburgh University Press, 1902), ll. 135–44.

Hume drew on legal training at home and abroad, as well as personal experience, to condemn the dishonesty, duplicity, and depravity of the central courts of Scotland. He described practicing at the Session: 'The haill abuse were our prolixt to tell, / That councill house it is maist like ane hell.' Litigants he likened to the confused rabble waiting on the banks of Acheron for the ferryman, Charon.[49]

Non-legal texts cannot illuminate legal issues, but they do represent how people felt about the law and lawyers, something impossible to retrieve from purely legal texts. Indeed, Hume's insider perspective chimed with the experience of others. Roughly half the early advocates were landowners' sons and, both to outsiders and some in government, the law's workings reflected kinship, 'interest', and venality.[50] The last of a four-sonnet sequence pronounced Catholic courtier Alexander Montgomerie's sentence on the judges or 'Lords' of Session who had ruled against him in a suit about a 'pension' of 300 merks from the revenues of Glasgow Cathedral (1593).[51]

> Your Colblack Conscience all the Cuntrey knauis
> Hou can you live except ye sell your vote?
> Thoght ye deny, thair is aneu [enough] to note
> How ye for Justice jouglarie [trickery] hes usit.

Montgomerie (*c.*1545–1598) used 'conscience' here in the obvious modern sense, but it was also an integral component of Session justice, administering equity as well as law (divided in England until the establishment of the High Court in 1873). As king of England, James I championed equity and conscience in the form of Chancery.[52] To Francis Sempill of Beltrees (*c.*1617–1682), sheriff-depute of Renfrewshire from 1677, is attributed the poem 'A Discourse between Law and Conscience', about a sitting of the Scottish Parliament.[53] His contemporary, Stair, thought 'equity is the body of the law'.[54]

Literature is rich in similar criticisms of processes and personnel. A late-fifteenth-century poem condemned the extortions of 'Justice, Crounar [coroner], Sariand [sergeant], and Justice Clark', the officers who were active at 'justice ayres' (*sic*; criminal circuit courts) until the early seventeenth century.[55] Law and lawyers were allegedly slow, confusing, expensive, and sometimes dishonest and oppressive; these were

49 *Poems of Alexander Hume*, ll. 227–8.

50 K. M. Brown, *Bloodfeud in Scotland, 1573–1625. Violence, Justice and Politics in Early Modern Society* (Edinburgh: Edinburgh University Press, 1986).

51 R. J. Lyall, *Alexander Montgomerie: Poetry, Politics, and Cultural Change in Jacobean Scotland* (Tempe: University of Arizona Press, 2005), 170, see also 162–9; R. D. S. Jack, *Alexander Montgomerie* (Edinburgh: Edinburgh University Press, 1985).

52 M. Fortier, 'Equity and Ideas: Coke, Ellesmere, and James I', *RQ*, 51 (1998): 1255–81; D. R. Klinck, *Conscience, Equity and the Court of Chancery in Early Modern England* (Farnham: Ashgate, 2010).

53 J. Paterson, ed., *The Poems of the Sempills of Beltrees* (Edinburgh: Edinburgh University Press, 1849).

54 *Institutions of the Law of Scotland*, 1.1.17.

55 *Ancient Scottish Poems. Published from the Manuscripts of George Bannatyne* (Edinburgh: Edinburgh University Press, 1770), 113; J. Pinkerton, ed., *Scottish Poems, Reprinted from Scarce Editions*, 3 vols (London: 1792), 1.24.

literary clichés of the late Middle Ages, rehearsed among others in the anonymous (and derivative) fifteenth-century poem, 'The Thre Prestis of Peblis'.[56] In 'Ane Satyre of the Thrie Estaitis', Diligence asks 'the pure man' from East Lothian why he is heading for St Andrews when 'to seik law in Edinburgh was the neirest way'. Looking for resolution of a tithe ('teind') suit, the disgruntled pauper replies: 'Sir I socht law thair this monie deir day / Bot I cold get nane at Sessioun nor Seinye [senate or synod, here an ecclesiastical or Consistory Court]'. He demands: 'Sir, be quhat law, tell me, quhairfoir or quhy / That ane Vickar sould tak fra me thrie ky [cattle]?' The personification, whose name is the Scottish legal equivalent of an English 'writ of execution' against a debtor, educates the poor man: 'Thay have na law, exceptand consuetude, / Quhilk law to them is sufficient and gude.'[57] Later Lyndsay satirizes the baffling language used in the church courts, which had also been the target of Henryson's barbs in 'Taill of the Scheip and the Dog'. Lyndsay (*c.*1486–1555) was Lord Lyon King of Arms, responsible for administering heraldic law and for royal genealogy and ceremonial—a sign of the laicization of both government and culture in the early sixteenth century. Prior to then professional knowledge of the law was dominated by churchmen like Bishop William Elphinstone (1431–1514), who went on justice ayres with James IV, sat in the emerging Session, and helped frame legal reform.[58] It may be that 'lay and lawyerly discontent with the Church's jurisdiction' was more important to the origins of the Reformation in Scotland than was dissatisfaction with doctrine.[59]

For all these complaints, there was strong grass-roots demand for access to royal justice and also evidence for growing secular legal professionalism in law-making. Unlike contemporary England, there were few complaints about the law as an instrument of royal oppression. During the fifteenth century, Scotland's estates of parliament ceded its judicial role to the king's council and thence to the Session, which became able to make new rules and adjust existing laws. It developed supervisory jurisdiction over other courts, including those of the church long before the Reformation, and was already a

[56] R. D. S. Jack, 'The Thre Prestis of Peblis and the Growth of Humanism in Scotland', *RES*, new ser., 26.103 (1975): 257–70; R. J. Lyall, 'The Sources of "The Thre Prestis of Peblis" and Their Significance', *RES*, new ser., 31.123 (1980): 257–70.

[57] Lyndsay, *Satyre of the Thrie Estaits*, 65–7; R. J. Lyall, ed., *Sir David Lindsay of the Mount: Ane Satyre of the Thrie Estaitis* (Edinburgh: Edinburgh University Press, 1989), 71–3, 191–2; C. Edington, *Court and Culture in Renaissance Scotland: Sir David Lindsay of the Mount (1486–1555)* (Amherst: University of Massachusetts Press, 1995); S. Carpenter, 'Scottish Drama until 1650', in *The Edinburgh Companion to Scottish Drama*, ed. I. Brown (Edinburgh: Edinburgh University Press, 2011), 6–21; R. A. Houston, 'Custom in Context: Medieval and Early Modern Scotland and England', *P&P*, 211 (May, 2011): 35–76. Process of diligence included civil imprisonment. W. Ross, *Lectures on the History and Practice of the Law of Scotland, Relative to Conveyancing and Legal Diligence*, 2 vols (Edinburgh: 1822).

[58] J. J. Robertson, 'The Development of the Law', in *Scottish Society in the Fifteenth Century*, ed. J. M. Brown (London: Edward Arnold, 1977), 136–52; *ODNB*.

[59] L. Hutson, *The Invention of Suspicion: Law and Mimesis in Shakespeare and Renaissance Drama* (Oxford: Oxford University Press, 2007), 21; M. Todd, ed., *The Perth Kirk Session Books, 1577–1590* (Woodbridge: Boydell Press, 2008), 20–1; J. Cranstoun, ed., *Satirical Poems of the Time of the Reformation*, 2 vols (Edinburgh: 1891–1893). Satire could itself be a form of defamation.

vigorous and powerful institution with unlimited civil jurisdiction, including title to landed property, when reconstituted as part of the College of Justice in 1532; the College provided judges for both the central criminal 'Justiciary Court' and the Session. They replaced formal medieval procedure by a handful of pleadable writs ('brieves') and inquest by 'assize' or jury, with new Romano-canonical practices, notably summary procedure and bills of complaint.[60] The Session was a *royal* court. Commentators like the theologian John Ireland (*c.*1440–1495) in 'The Meroure of Wyssdome' (1490) saw the essence of kingship as dispensing justice under God. For all the devolution of judicial rights, the king was the ultimate keeper of the peace, punisher of wrongs, and protector of the weak.[61] Yet the early drive towards legal and therefore political centralization in Scotland came principally from lawyers and from *demand* for civil remedies. Suitors no longer had to use inferior courts for most purposes, making the Session into a powerful agent of legal, political, and social change.

Medieval criminal justice was more about kin and compensation than crime itself, and an enduring criticism of the fifteenth and sixteenth century was the Stewart kings' readiness to grant remissions for homicide; an example in 'The Thre Prestis of Peblis' is a pardoned murder who kills again. In civil and criminal matters alike, Scots law regarded compensation or indemnification (*cro* or 'assythment') as central to justice until at least 1700.[62] From the sixteenth century, Scotland nevertheless had public prosecutors called 'procurators-fiscal' to aid victims or stand in for the Crown. '[D]ependent on lay instigation and lay participation in judgment' until the nineteenth century, lawyers were much less important to early modern English criminal justice than was the case in Scotland.[63]

Aspects of Scotland's historic criminal law look more humane than English, but this comes from the internal dynamic of the law rather than from some vague national characteristic, for law is a social fact that shapes how people think and behave. Stringent standards of proof made one witness insufficient to secure a criminal conviction—possibly another sign of the extensive and enduring canon-law influence on the development of Scots law. This explains the persistently lower historic rates of prosecution, conviction, and execution before Scotland's central criminal courts. Defence counsel also helped. Routine there by the late sixteenth century, representation did not become normal for English defendants until two centuries later.

Local courts and investigations by amateurs were a different matter. Post-Restoration reforms in criminal procedure, given impetus by the excesses of the witch trials of 1661–1662 (664 named individuals accused), included closer supervision of local

60 A. M. Godfrey, *Civil Justice in Renaissance Scotland: The Origins of a Central Court* (Leiden, 2009), 20, 168. Godfrey's arguments about jurisdiction should be read with Cormack, *A Power to Do Justice*.

61 *The Meroure of Wyssdome: Composed for the Use of James IV, King of Scots, A.D. 1490 by Johannes de Irlandia*, 3 vols (Edinburgh: University of Edinburgh Press, 1926–1990); R. A. Mason, 'Kingship, Tyranny and the Right to Resist in Fifteenth Century Scotland', *Scottish Historical Review*, 66 (1987): 125–51.

62 K. M. Norrie, 'The Intentional Delicts', in *A History of Private Law in Scotland*, Vol. 1: *Introduction and Property*, ed. K. Reid and R. Zimmermann (Oxford: Oxford University Press, 2000), 484–8.

63 Hutson, *Invention of Suspicion*, 66.

commissions and the use of torture, as well as establishing clearer rules of evidence.[64] An act of 1701, formalizing an equivalent to English *habeas corpus*, aimed to protect the accused.[65] Addressed towards issues of personal liberty, this was part of a move for fairer, more transparent, and quicker justice.[66] Pamphlets like 'The tryal of Philip Standsfield, son to Sir James Standsfield of New-Milns, for the murther of his father', published in Edinburgh in February 1688 and reprinted in several versions in London, informed English readers about judicial process in Scotland, though not always impartially or accurately. Sir James, a former Cromwellian colonel, established a woollen manufactory at Newmilns to the east of Edinburgh, employing skilled English craftsmen. Among other things, both forensic pathology and cruentation established Philip's guilt, the prosecutor Mackenzie declaring the latter providential.

Sir James's suspicious employees clamoured for an inquest after his apparent suicide, but a magistrate investigated his death, not a coroner. Scotland had coroners or 'crowners', but they never performed the roles associated with their English counterparts.[67] In his *Scotichronicon*, Walter Bower describes a piece of exemplary justice supposedly meted out soon after the death of Robert I. Thomas Randolph, justiciar for the north, 'sent his official coroner on ahead to Eilean Donan with an armed force to arrest lawbreakers in accordance with enrolled indictments [known in Scots law as 'porteous rolls']. This official pursued fifty of them; and because they resisted arrest, they were slaughtered by their pursuers; and the walls were adorned with their heads fixed to poles and sticks before the judge's arrival at Eilean Donan'.[68] Writing in the 1440s, Bower, an Augustinian abbot in the Lowlands, may simply have been displaying his preoccupation with law and order at a time when some thought it had broken down completely.[69] However imaginative his description of the early fourteenth century, he represents approximately what he thought coroners were or should be doing in his day and their relationship to judges on circuit ('justiciars'): fifteenth- and sixteenth-century Scottish crowners were men of action much closer to late-twelfth-century English keepers of the peace than to the early modern English coroner.

64 C. Jackson, 'Judicial Torture, the Liberties of the Subject, and Anglo-Scottish Relations, 1660–1690', in *Anglo-Scottish Relations from 1603 to 1900*, ed. T. C. Smout (Oxford: Oxford University Press, 2005), 75–101; B. P. Levack, *Witch-hunting in Scotland: Law, Politics and Religion* (London: Routledge, 2008).

65 L. H. Willumsen, 'A Narratological Approach to Witchcraft Trial: A Scottish Case', *Journal of Early Modern History*, 15 (2011): 531–60. Scottish procedures had earlier attracted adverse comment. *The Scotish [sic] Inquisition; Or, a Short Account of the Proceedings of the Scottish Privy-Counsel, Justiciary Court, and Those Commissionated by Them* (Edinburgh: 1689). Until its abolition in 1708, Scotland's Privy Council possessed executive, legislative, and judicial functions.

66 C. Jackson, '"Assize of Error" and the Independence of the Criminal Jury in Restoration Scotland', *Scottish Archives*, 10 (2004): 1–25, questions the arbitrariness of justice.

67 R. A. Houston, *The Coroners of Northern Britain, c.1300–1700* (Basingstoke: Palgrave Macmillan, 2014).

68 D. E. R. Watt, ed., *Scotichronicon*, 9 vols (Aberdeen: Aberdeen University Press, 1987–1998), 7.58–9. The castle of Eilean Donan still stands, an iconic landmark on the road to the Isle of Skye.

69 MacQueen, *Common Law*, 54; Walker, *Legal History of Scotland*, 2.299–302.

In Scotland other officials who never had the same presence as in England included local constables, established alongside 'Justices of Peace' (*sic*) under acts of 1587, 1609, and 1617.[70] In England 'Tudor legislation transformed constables incrementally from executive legal officers of the manorial lord to local administrators for the Justices of the Peace', responsible for a range of important tasks not only in law and order, but also in taxation.[71] Constables were hard to recruit in Scotland, used only intermittently in periods when vagrancy was a serious problem or when the needs of warfare stretched the governmental apparatus; at such times even the king's almoner in Scotland did his part.[72] Scottish Justices had narrower remits and lesser powers than their English counterparts, though their non-judicial or administrative role was important.[73] Except for a brief period under Charles I and again during the Cromwellian occupation, Justices did not become significant until after 1708–1709, when constables can be found working with them to prepare presentations, executions, and arrestments for the newly instituted Justiciary circuits in some counties, as well as committing offenders to ward.[74]

'How to' manuals for JPs and other unpaid but important middle-rank officers of the English law, like William Lambarde's *Eirenarcha, or, the Office of Justices of Peace* (1581) and its many successors, had no equivalent in Scotland until the eighteenth century.[75] Those guides or compendia ('practicks') that existed were for court lawyers though, like early commissions of inquiry into statutes (1566, 1598), they aimed at creating and codifying a uniform body of law accessible to all learned readers.[76] In many contexts it

[70] R. Boyd, *The Office, Powers, and Jurisdiction, of His Majesty's Justices of the Peace, and Commissioners of Supply, for Scotland* (Edinburgh: 1794), 1–37; S. Moir, '"Some Godlie, Wyse and Vertious Gentilmen": Communities, State Formation, and the Justices of the Peace in Scotland' (PhD thesis, University of Guelph, 2002).

[71] H. R. French, 'Parish Government', in *The Elizabethan World*, ed. S. Doran and N. Jones (London: Routledge, 2011), 149; J. R. Kent, *The English Village Constable, 1580–1642: A Social and Administrative Study* (Oxford: Clarendon Press, 1986); see also James Sharpe's chapter in this volume.

[72] G. Tait, *A Summary of the Powers and Duties of a Justice of the Peace in Scotland* [1815] (Edinburgh: 1816), 69; A. E. Whetstone, *Scottish County Government in the Eighteenth and Nineteenth Centuries* (Edinburgh: John Donald, 1981), 27–8, 32–6; J. Innes, 'Governing diverse societies', in *The Eighteenth Century*, ed. P. Langford (Oxford: Oxford University Press, 2002), 117–18; R. A. Houston, 'What Did the Royal Almoner Do in Britain and Ireland, c.1450–1700?', *English Historical Review*, cxxv, 513 (April, 2010): 29.

[73] J. Goodare, 'The Nobility and the Absolutist State in Scotland, 1584–1638', *History*, 78 (1993): 176.

[74] See e.g. NAS JC26/97. *Act of the Justices of the Peace of the Shire of Haddingtoun, for Appointing of Constables, and More Effectually Restraining Vagrants* (Edinburgh: 1729); Moir, 'Justices of the Peace', 312–23; R. S. Tompson, 'The Justices of the Peace and the United Kingdom in the Age of Reform', *Journal of Legal History*, 7 (1986): 273–92.

[75] W. Forbes, *The Duty and Powers of Justices of Peace, in This Part of Great-Britain Called Scotland* (Edinburgh: 1707–1708). Most handbooks date from later still. R. Boyd, *The Office, Powers, and Jurisdiction, of His Majesty's Justices of the Peace, and Commissioners of Supply, for Scotland* (Edinburgh: 1794).

[76] The earliest known example is by jurist John Sinclair (d. 1566). A. L. Murray, 'Sinclair's Practicks', in *Law-Making and Law-Makers in British History*, ed. A. Harding (London, 1980), 90–104, <http://www.uni-leipzig.de/~jurarom/scotland/dat/sinclair.html>.

was landowners (magistrates in chartered burghs), under the supervision of the King's Advocate, who were responsible for carrying out royal justice; those who wanted to know something asked their lawyer or appointed one as a substitute to do their jobs—something explicitly prohibited by the English Crown. English JPs were usually laymen, drawn from the gentry, who needed guidance. An equivalent social class, Scottish lairds, only became established in the sixteenth century after the 'feuing' of church and Crown lands. Freehold in the English sense was unusual in Scotland: most owner-occupiers were called 'feuars', a feu or fee farm being a perpetual lease usually granted by a superior in exchange for a single large capital sum or *grassum* and small subsequent fixed periodical payments (*reddendo*); it was *dominium utile*, the estate held by the lowest vassal.

English literature shows keen awareness of the geography of jurisdiction, because where an event happened or property lay often determined which court dealt with it. In contrast, Scots conceived of law more in personal than territorial terms. For example, the location of the *owner* of movable assets mattered most in deciding jurisdiction for testamentary and other matters. Similarly, a practice called 'repledging' or 'replegiation' allowed a lord with the correct level of jurisdiction to take a criminal case away from a court where it had been initiated, if the accused normally resided in his territory or was one of his clients; the locus of the crime was irrelevant and no third court was involved.[77] Repledging was increasingly restricted from the time of James VI and virtually ineffective after 1672 (with reform of the Justiciary Court), but it illustrates the personal conception of medieval and early modern Scots law.[78]

Until the Heritable Jurisdictions Act came into force in 1748, the Scottish Crown extensively delegated criminal justice and franchise courts (public jurisdictions in private hands) were common, even if the components operated together to enforce order in the monarch's name. Heritable jurisdictions were a type of property and some royal officers could own their positions; twenty-three of thirty-three sheriffs held heritably, their judicial work done by sheriffs-depute. Charters granted some feudal lords 'baronies' or 'regalities' (the latter like English palatinates), each with specified judicial rights. In the case of regalities, privileges extended to all but the most serious crimes reserved for royal courts. Yet franchises implemented the king's common law and there were few of the jurisdictional conflicts that plagued Renaissance England.

Another example of the personality of law is that the procurator-fiscal investigating a suspicious death was the one with the closest connection to its circumstances; the place where a person died or the body was found was not necessarily relevant, whereas in England the location of the body alone determined jurisdiction for a coroner's inquest.

J. Skene, *De verborum significatione* (Edinburgh: 1597). Scots lawyers retained a vibrant tradition of manuscript or scribal communication, perhaps because of problems getting material printed. The *Practicks* of Sir James Balfour of Pittendreich (*c.*1525–1583), an encyclopaedic compendium of the law written around the same time as Sinclair's, was not published until 1754.

[77] J. Dalrymple, *An Essay towards a General History of Feudal Property in Great Britain* (London: 1759), 236–47; Godfrey, *Civil Justice*, 214–16.

[78] A. V. Sheehan, D. R. Hingston, and F. R. Crowe, *Criminal Procedure* (Edinburgh: University of Edinburgh Press, 1990), 1.24.

Magistrates conducted investigations of sudden or suspicious death in private and Scottish criminal procedure was inquisitorial.[79] Richard Smith suggests that the discretion of Roman practice (as followed in Scotland) distinguished it from the traditions of centralization, transparency, and public engagement that had characterized England since the Middle Ages. He believes legal procedures reveal underlying social and political structures. 'Secret interrogation may well have been a more likely development in societies in which a "participatory" tradition in policing and trial of "crime" was poorly developed or only weakly related to the instructions sent out from central government.'[80] Julian Goodare has shown the weak links between centre and locality in early modern Scottish government, for example in failed attempts to create civil parishes on the English model; nor were manors introduced during the Middle Ages, both probably because baronies performed many of the functions.[81]

There was a participative element to Scottish justice, but grass-roots involvement with law enforcement was rhetorically and politically very different from England. Scotsmen served formally on criminal juries and in some civil cases like deciding succession, determining issues of fact. More informally, people meted out infra-, para-, or quasi-judicial rather than extra-judicial punishments to miscreants as diverse as adulterers, wife-beaters, and suicides.[82] Except when *ex officio* in burghs, Scottish coroners were, however, appointed by the Crown or its franchisee, whereas county freeholders elected 80 per cent of English coroners. The Scottish 'birlay' or 'birlaw' court, a body of Scandinavian origin which dealt with issues of 'good neighbourhood', including communal aspects of agriculture and debt, looks like the baron side of an English manor court, but it was a tool of estate management rather than a true community court.[83]

Scotland had a 'common law', which could be variously understood as either a *ius commune*, a blend of civil and canon law, or simply the king's universal law; it was, nevertheless, quite unlike that of England where, by the twelfth century, the secular lawyers around the central courts 'had worked the basic ideas of English law into a sophisticated system of specialised learning'.[84] As late as 1500, it was common for educated laymen to act on behalf of others in Scottish courts, sporting titles like 'attorney', 'notary', or 'procurator' for the occasion.[85] An example is the poet William Dunbar (1460?–1513x30),

[79] L. Hutson, 'Rethinking the "Spectacle of the Scaffold": Juridical Epistemologies and English Revenge Tragedy', *Representations*, 89 (2005): 30–58.

[80] R. M. Smith, '"Modernization" and the Corporate Medieval Village Community in England: Some Sceptical Reflections', in *Explorations in Historical Geography: Interpretative Essays*, ed. A. R. H. Baker and D. Gregory (Cambridge: Cambridge University Press, 1984), 171.

[81] Goodare, *Government of Scotland*, 192–219, esp. 202.

[82] R. A. Houston, *Punishing the Dead? Suicide, Lordship and Community in Britain, 1500–1830* (Oxford: Oxford University Press, 2010).

[83] W. D. H. Sellar, 'Birlaw Courts and Birleymen', in *Adventures of the Law*, ed. P. Brand, K. Costello, and W. N. Osborough (Dublin: Four Courts, 2005), 70–87.

[84] Cairns, 'Historical Introduction', 44.

[85] *ODNB*, Kennedy, Walter (1455?–1518?), poet; Cairns, 'Historical Introduction', 70; J. Finlay, *Men of Law in Pre-Reformation Scotland* (East Linton: Tuckwell Press, 2000); P. Bawcutt, 'William Dunbar', in *Edinburgh History of Scottish Literature*, ed. Clanchy and Pittock, 1.295.

Master of Arts at St Andrews (1479). Between 1502 and 1504 he represented various litigants in a bitter court case over succession to land in Fife and his close knowledge of legal terms of art and procedure is clear in his verse. He jokes, for example, about a 'brief of richt' or brieve of ultimate right in one poem and elsewhere draws fine legal distinctions between claimants. In 'Schir I complaine of injuris', Dunbar mentions defamation ('rycht defamows speeiche') and makes two references to written 'sclander'.[86] In 'Flyting of Dunbar and Kennedie' he refers to a formalized and formulaic public verbal confrontation between parties, designed to invoke neighbourly arbitration—though an exchange of invective was also a poetic convention.[87]

A nucleus of academically trained jurists nevertheless emerged in the fifteenth century to create a strong tradition of legal learning, when implementing Romano-canonical procedure. They ultimately became a coherent profession, the second most numerous after the clergy, much later than in England.[88] The Society of Writers to the Signet (the equivalent of English solicitors, they prepared the documentation needed for litigation) admitted roughly 220 men in the century after its foundation in 1594, the Faculty of Advocates (professional lay pleaders before the senior courts) about 400 between 1532 and 1689. There were 54 practitioners in the Faculty in 1587, about 200 in 1714 (and around 100 WS), and 242 in 1764, its fortunes buoyed by growing volumes of litigation about entail ('tailzie') and bankruptcy from the end of the seventeenth century.[89] There was no equivalent of the London Inns of Court in Scotland, meaning that early advocates had to get their academic training abroad, mostly in France (especially Paris, Orléans, and Bourges) or, after the Reformation, at the northern Dutch universities like Leiden, whose *collegia privata* formed the basis for the chairs of law founded at Edinburgh and Glasgow Universities between 1707 and 1722. By this date there was a robust legal culture of lawyers and judges who played an important part in Scottish politics and society. It is, however, worth noting that legal studies at Scotland's three universities, founded between 1411 and 1495 partly to promote knowledge of the civil law, were far from buoyant in the century and a half after the Reformation (or at the town's college of Edinburgh, founded in 1583). Writers to the Signet learned by experience gained during an apprenticeship.

[86] Bawcutt, 'William Dunbar', 295–6; Sellar, 'Legal Writing, 1314–1707', 240; P. Bawcutt, *Dunbar the Makar* (Oxford: Oxford University Press, 1992), 223; H. L. MacQueen, 'The Brieve of Right in Scots Law', *JLH*, 3 (1982): 52–70.

[87] P. Bawcutt, 'The Art of Flyting', *Scottish Literary Journal*, 10 (1983): 5–24; R. J. Lyall, 'Complaint, Satire and Invective in Middle Scots Literature', in *Church, Politics and Society: Scotland, 1408–1929*, ed. N. MacDougall (Edinburgh: University of Edinburgh Press, 1983), 44–63.

[88] G. Donaldson, 'The Legal Profession in Scottish Society in the Sixteenth and Seventeenth Centuries', *JR*, new ser., 21 (1976): 1–19.

[89] *A History of the Society of Writers to Her Majesty's Signet with a List of the Members of the Society from 1594 to 1890 with an Abstract of the Minutes* (Edinburgh: 1890), xi–xii, 51; F. J. Grant, ed., *The Faculty of Advocates in Scotland, 1532–1943* (Edinburgh: Edinburgh University Press, 1944). There had been advocates since at least the time of James I and recognized pleaders no later than the fifteenth century; Robertson, 'Development of the Law', 150.

For all the excellent work on which this chapter has drawn, law and literature in early modern Scotland remains largely untouched by the interdisciplinary methods that have proved so fruitful for England. Those who choose to explore it will find much to surprise and intrigue them, though they need cautiously to adjust their perspectives. In 1702 Blackerby Fairfax, an English physician, published a pro-Union tract which claimed, among much else that ranged from the tendentious to the mendacious, close similarities in law and its officers between Scotland and England. 'We have', he trumpeted, 'the same Ministers of Justice, as Sherffs [*sic*], Coroners, &c.'[90] While he correctly identified the presence of these officers, Fairfax knew little of Scotland or he would have seen how utterly different were the functions and fortunes of both. English Sheriffs declined to largely honorific status during the sixteenth and seventeenth centuries as their Scots equivalent grew in judicial and administrative importance. Once active court officers, Scottish coroners were largely defunct by 1700. An Anglo-centric perspective, which has also influenced work on other Scottish officers like Justices of Peace, is one of the foundations of a modern historiography that believes the development of institutions should be judged by how closely they approximate to English equivalents, or how much they influence English life.[91] Instead, the last word should go to F. W. Maitland, who modestly recognized 'that fatal disease of contented insularity which so easily besets' the English and concluded that 'there is nothing that sets a man thinking and writing to such good effect about a system of law and its history as an acquaintance however slight with other systems and their history'.[92]

BIBLIOGRAPHY

Bawcutt, P. and J. H. Williams, ed. *A Companion to Medieval Scottish Poetry* (Cambridge: Cambridge University Press, 2006).

Brown, I., ed. *The Edinburgh Companion to Scottish Drama* (Edinburgh: Edinburgh University Press, 2011).

Cairns, J. W. 'Historical Introduction', in *A History of Private Law in Scotland*, Vol. 1: *Introduction and Property*, ed. K. Reid and R. Zimmermann (Oxford: Oxford University Press, 2000), 14–184.

Clanchy, T. O. and M. Pittock, ed. *The Edinburgh History of Scottish Literature*, Vol. 1: *From Columba to the Union (Until 1707)* (Edinburgh: Edinburgh University Press, 2007).

Houston, R. *Scotland: A Very Short Introduction* (Oxford: Oxford University Press, 2008).

Jack, R. D. S., ed. *The History of Scottish Literature*, Vol. 1: *Origins to 1660 (Mediaeval and Renaissance)* (Aberdeen: Aberdeen University Press, 1988).

[90] B. Fairfax, *A Discourse upon the Uniting Scotland with England: Containing the General Advantage of Such an Union to Both Kingdoms* (London: 1702), 54.

[91] Moir, 'Justices of the Peace', 12–14; J. W. Cairns, 'National, Transnational and European Legal Histories: Problems and Paradigms. A Scottish Approach', *Clio@Thémis*, 5 (2012): 1–13.

[92] F. W. Maitland, 'The Laws of the Anglo-Saxons', in *The Collected Papers of Frederic William Maitland*, 3 vols., H. A. L. Fisher (Cambridge: Cambridge University Press, 1911), 3.460; 'Why the History of English Law Is Not Written', in *Collected Papers*, ed. Maitland, 1.489.

MacQueen, H., J. W. Cairns, and T. D. Fergus. 'Legal Humanism in Renaissance Scotland', *Journal of Legal History*, 9 (1990): 40–69.
O'Rourke, S. R. *Glossary of Legal Terms* (Edinburgh: Edinburgh University Press, 2004).
Walker, D. M. *A Legal History of Scotland*, 7 vols (Edinburgh: Edinburgh University Press, 1988–2004).

CHAPTER 35

FORENSIC HISTORY

Henry V *and Scotland*

LORNA HUTSON

THE KING'S CAUSE

SHAKESPEARE'S *Henry V* begins obliquely, by way of a dialogue between a couple of politicians who are anxious about a new bill in Parliament.[1] They are high-ranking clergymen, and the bill they're worried about is a proposal to strip the Church of its wealth. One of them, the Archbishop of Canterbury, comes up with a cunning ruse to distract the king: the Church will offer to fund a military campaign in France that will be so rewarding in restoring honour, legitimacy, and territory to the English monarchy, that Henry will have no motive to fleece the clergy. But first, of course, Henry must be persuaded of the righteousness of the *casus belli*, his 'cause' of war. So Canterbury produces a skilful forensic oration on the legitimacy of the English title to France and the justice of invasive war. Henry, he says, has a true claim to the French throne, against which French civilian lawyers have devised historically spurious arguments. Though eager to believe this, Henry has (we gather) the wit and self-knowledge to guard against his own credulous desire. He solemnly warns the Archbishop about the importance of speaking the truth. If the argument is not good in *conscience*, he insists, they will both be guilty before God of murder on a massive scale.

I have, of course, simplified. Nevertheless, even from this schematic account, it is evident that Shakespeare's skilful juxtaposition of both acknowledged and unacknowledged

[1] A note on the title: 'Forensic history' is a term that has been used by John Phillip Reid, *The Ancient Constitution and the Origins of Anglo-American Liberty* (Dekalb: Northern Illinois University Press, 2005) to describe the doctrine of the 'ancient constitution' as a method of legal argumentation rather than as defective historiography. I invoke the term rather to draw attention to the medieval and early modern use of historical chronicles as evidence of legal agreements, titles, charters, and homage.

motives—the clergy's avowed political fears, the king's conjuration and what it suggests about unspoken desires—has the potential to produce uneasy and complex effects, raising immediate questions in an audience's minds (whether or not that audience knows any history). If the Archbishop's handling of the forensic issue is correct—if the French Salic law is misapplied to Henry's title to the French Crown—is this truth affected by the English clergy's underhand use of the case to promote their own special interests? On the other hand, if the king is persuaded by Canterbury's legal arguments, does it matter if he also knows what the Archbishop is up to? And, anyway, *does* he know?

The former (legal) question of whether the case is just tends to morph into the latter (a question of Henry's 'character'), with the latter unavoidably dominating critical discussion since commentary on *Henry V* began. Although, as Joel Altman remarks, '"The King's Cause" ... is never a reticulation of motives originating in Harry', the resurfacing of the question in Act 4, Scene 1 (where the king, as private person, disputes with soldiers who doubt the justice of his cause) ensures that we never feel it quite distinguishable, either, from these very motives.[2] Structurally central to the play, it seems, is a tendency to push inquiry into the justice of the national cause (that is, inquiry into national policy in an international context) in the direction of inquiry into the signs that tell us about Henry's motives and Henry's character. A military historian might assess Shakespeare's account of the justness of the war, and then move on to ask, as a secondary question, whether Henry's belief in it was 'genuine'.[3] But most audiences or readers will proceed from the opposite direction: they will draw conclusions about the genuineness or otherwise of Henry's concern with the justice of the national cause from what the performance or text implies about what Henry knows and when he knows it. A. C. Bradley inferred the political quality of Henry's religious belief from the fact that he 'knows very well that the Archbishop *wants* the war'.[4] More recently, criticism has been interested in the undecidability of the question, or in the way in which Shakespeare's depiction of Henry both encourages us to map political or national 'cause' onto Henry's personal feelings and personal motives and, at the same time, makes us sceptical of the naivety of such a project.[5]

While this oscillation between nation and royal person in Shakespeare's *Henry V* has been widely and variously analysed, it has never been remarked that it neatly mobilizes, in the terminology of classical and humanist forensic rhetoric, two distinct meanings of the Latin word *causa*. The context of this *Handbook*, devoted as it is to the common ground of literary and legal thinking in early modern England, creates an opportunity

[2] Joel Altman, '"Vile Participation": The Amplification of Violence in the Theater of *Henry V*', *SQ*, 42.1 (1991): 1–32, 23.

[3] For example, John Mark Mattox, 'Henry V: Just Warrior', *War, Literature and the Arts*, 12.1 (2000): 30–53, 32–3.

[4] A. C. Bradley, The Rejection of Falstaff', in *Oxford Lectures on Poetry* (London: Macmillan, 1909), 257.

[5] The classic study is Norman Rabkin, 'Rabbits, Ducks and *Henry V*', *SQ*, 28.3 (1977): 279–96. See also Claire McEachern, 'Henry V and the Paradox of the Body Politic', *SQ*, 45.1 (1994): 33–56; and David Quint, 'Alexander the Pig: Shakespeare on History and Poetry', *Boundary* 2, 10.3 (1982): 49–67.

to think about how this ambiguity in forensic rhetoric might have been harnessed in Shakespeare's play. As Kathy Eden explains elsewhere in this volume, English humanist grammar school education in the sixteenth century was centred on an art of rhetoric that had its origins in legal dispute. Within this art, the term *causa*—'cause' or 'case'—was understood to refer to the oration itself. Whether forensic, deliberative, or epideictic, says Eden, 'the term *causa* or *cause* ... applies to any speech dealing with a set of particulars, whether it takes place at an assembly, a festival, or a trial'. Yet, she adds, 'the term *causa* never loses its legal pedigree, either in Latin or in English'.[6] At the same time, however, *causa* was the word applied not only to the case being adjudged, but to the motive for the act being adjudicated. In this sense, the term *causa* takes its place among the important topics or places from which forensic orators invent arguments of proof. Specifically, *causa* it is one of topics of circumstance—'*causa tempus locus occasio instrumentum modus et cetera*', as Quintilian lists them, 'motive, time, place, opportunity, means, method and the like'. These were considered the key 'places of argument', *loci argumentorum*; that is, topics from which compelling proofs in the form of *arguments* of guilt or innocence (rather than proofs such as oaths or witnesses) might be discovered.[7] The term *causa* thus straddles the division between public and private, as well as the temporal division by which we make 'motive' anterior to the deed. In oratory *causa* and 'cause' are always constituted as both anterior to any rhetorical enquiry (the question of why something was done) and, at the same time, as the discursive product of rhetorical enquiry (the 'purpose' or 'case' as argued or justified in speech).[8]

It seems as though, in *Henry V*, Shakespeare has seen in the forensic materials of his sources—the Archbishop's setting out of the legal cause of war as lavishly invented by Edward Hall and repeated in Holinshed—a chance to exploit the ambiguity of *causa* as the legal case for war and *causa* as the king's intention, the question of what the king is thinking. Dramatically speaking, this means a chance to move us, imperceptibly and irreversibly, from asking the nation-imagining question 'is this cause just?' to asking the person-imagining question, 'what does he think?' This move, as critics have noticed, is repeatedly made at various key moments of the play. Take, for example, the puzzling apparent reversal of act and motive between Act 4, Scene 6 and Act 4, Scene 7. In 4.6, after the battle of Agincourt, King Henry, on hearing that the French are reinforcing, suddenly and unexpectedly gives the order, 'Then every soldier kill his prisoners!' (4.6.37). This order is immediately followed by the entrance of Fluellen in the next scene, distressedly exclaiming that the French have killed the boys looking after the English camp, an outrage, 'expressly against the law of arms' (4.7.1–2). It would have been easy for Shakespeare to make Henry give the order for the English to kill their prisoners *after* Fluellen announced this, but he does not. He therefore prompts us to

[6] Kathy Eden, 'Forensic Rhetoric', 000.

[7] Quintilian, *Institutio oratoria*, ed. and trans. Donald A. Russell, 5 vols (Cambridge, MA: Harvard University Press, 2001) 5.10.23; see Lorna Hutson, *Circumstantial Shakespeare* (Oxford: Oxford University Press, 2015) 1–3, 59–62, 76–86.

[8] Hutson, *Circumstantial Shakespeare*, 83–4.

ask, not the legal question: 'is the English retaliation justifiable? Is it just?', but rather, the characterological question: 'what was Henry thinking when he gave that order at that time?'

Quentin Skinner has recently made a compelling and detailed case for Shakespeare's familiarity with the compositional techniques of judicial or forensic rhetoric.[9] I have argued that we should not just see forensic rhetoric as something Shakespeare's 'characters' are using, but we should, rather, see forensic inquiry itself as having profound affinities with fiction making and character-creation. Techniques for inventing forensic arguments are what give us the sense of people as 'characters' who think and feel and inhabit complex, circumstantially realized imaginative worlds.[10] In this chapter I want to propose, further, that Shakespeare's repeated trick of deflecting legal questions (about the justness of the national cause) into characterological questions (about what Henry is thinking) is brilliantly effective in making the English national interest seem supra-nationally inclusive. That is to say, the English national cause comes to be identified, through the mystery of Henry's unknowable individuality, with the question of what it means to 'be human'—and this illusion of inclusiveness works to deny the existence of other national causes.

To see how the drama of the forensic question ('is this cause just?') mutates into the mystery of character ('what is he thinking?'), let us look at what Shakespeare does in the opening two scenes of *Henry V* with his chronicle source material. The source I am going to focus on is Edward Hall's *Chronicle*, printed in 1548, which Shakespeare follows especially closely in Act 1. Edward Hall, who was a common lawyer, had already composed this opening episode of Henry V's reign according to the rules of forensic and deliberative rhetoric, presenting it as a sequence of three orations or 'causes' advocating what is best for England as a nation. The first is by Henry Chicheley Archbishop of Canterbury, on England's title to France, and the next two form a debate by the Earl of Westmoreland and the Duke of Exeter on the question of the conquest of Scotland. I will say more about how Shakespeare adapts this latter debate in due course, but here I want to show how Shakespeare makes a small but effective adjustment to Hall's forensic scene by introducing the circumstance of time (*tempus*), or, rather of 'timing' as opportunity (*occasio*).

It was Hall who began the history of Henry V's reign with Parliament's bill to strip the Church of half its wealth. Hall tells a satirical story of how worried the clergy were (the 'fat Abbots swet' and 'the sely Nonnes wept') until the Archbishop of Canterbury hit on the idea of 'replenish[ing] the kynges brayne with some pleasante study' that would distract him from the Commons' petition.[11] Then comes the legal oration before the king. The Archbishop argues that Henry V has a lineal right to

[9] Quentin Skinner, *Forensic Shakespeare* (Oxford: Oxford University Press, 2014); see also Skinner's chapter in this volume.

[10] Hutson, *Circumstantial Shakespeare*.

[11] Edward Hall, *Hall's Chronicle containing the History of England* [1548] (New York: AMS Press, 1965), 49.

the throne of France through his grandfather, Edward III. Following the methods of Roman forensic rhetoric, he chooses to base his arguments on the interpretation of the text of a law—the so-called legal issue. [12] French civilian lawyers have argued that Henry's title is invalid because it comes through Edward III's mother, Isabella, daughter of Philip IV of France—in other words, through the female line. The French civilians cite the maxim '*In terram Salicam mulieres ne succedant*', 'let not woman succede in the land Salicque'.[13] Canterbury uses chronicle history to prove that the Salic law applied not to France, but to the German lands of Meissen, which did not come into French possession until many centuries after the supposed author of this Salic law—Pharamond—was dead. This summary, which I have taken from Hall's text, will be recognized by any reader of Shakespeare, because Shakespeare follows Hall so very closely.

Shakespeare, then, was clearly interested in the dramatic potential of the forensic scene. But he doesn't just versify the arguments he finds in Hall. He sees in the forensic drama—by which I mean, in the drama of the argument itself—a chance to make us imagine the emotion aroused by argument. To give us a sense of the King's suppressed emotion in response to Canterbury's case, Shakespeare invents an otherwise unnecessary detail—the detail of the ambassador's 'interruption' of Canterbury's audience with the king, which, at a moment before the play began, is supposed to have prevented Canterbury from explaining the whole case to him. Canterbury explains to the Bishop of Ely that he has made a large offer of money from the Church '*in regard of causes now in hand* / Which I have opened to his grace at large / As touching France' (1.1.78–80, my italics). The 'causes' or arguments in the case are, in Canterbury's formulation, *presently being handled*; he has 'opened' them 'at large', or sketched them out, but the timing wasn't right—it seems, he was *interrupted*.

This fiction of inopportune interruption, of Henry's attention being diverted, is what gives emotional substance and power to the idea of Henry's suspense and desire to hear more of the argument:

> ELY
> How did this offer seem received, my lord?
> CANTERBURY
> With good acceptance of his majesty,
> Save that there was not *time enough to hear*
> As I perceived his grace *would fain* have done,
> The severals and unhidden passages
> Of his true titles to some certain dukedoms
> And generally to the crown and seat of France,
> Derived from Edward, his great-grandfather. (1.1.83–90, my italics)

[12] On the different kinds of issue or *constitutio* (conjectural, juridical, and legal), see Quentin Skinner's chapter in this volume.

[13] Hall, *Chronicle*, 50.

Shakespeare here invokes a topic of circumstance: the circumstance of *opportunity*, in the form of thwarted opportunity, an 'impediment' that, by momentarily ruining Canterbury's chance to reveal Henry's title, allows a glimpse of Henry's awakened desire—Canterbury perceives 'his grace *would fain*' have heard him finish. The interrupting presence turns out to be that of the 'French ambassador' who 'upon that instant' apparently 'craved audience' and the 'hour' of that audience turns out to be this very moment in the dramatic action: 'The hour I think is come / To give him hearing. Is it four o'clock?' (1.1.93–5). Yet, as the next scene opens, with the king and his train awaiting (as we think) the ambassador, the device implodes and exposes its fictitiousness as the king refuses to hear the French embassy before the Archbishop is given time to open his cause more fully.

> WESTMORELAND
> Shall we call in th'ambassador, my liege?
> KING
> Not yet, my cousin: we would be resolved,
> Before we hear him, of some things of weight
> That task our thoughts concerning us and France. (1.2.3–6)

It's clear that this detail of the ambassador as 'impediment' to Canterbury's cause has no other purpose that to nudge us towards imagining Henry's suppressed *eagerness to hear*. Henry's conjuration that the Archbishop speak the truth then seems to speak to this very eagerness: we feel, as Norman Rabkin says, that Henry is himself aware 'that the war is not quite the selfless enterprise other parts of the play tempt us to see'.[14]

Shakespeare knew that although *causa* as motive is one of the topics of circumstance, it is usually only made 'probable' or intelligible through an invention of one or more of the others—that is, by considering the time, place, opportunity, manner, or instrument involved in the deed. In this instance, Shakespeare *psychologizes* Hall's forensic scene by introducing the temporal circumstance of interruption, so that our imaginations are diverted from the question of whether or not the arguments for an English title to France seem just or expedient, to the question of exactly how the king's eagerness to hear the arguments plays into his readiness to judge them true.

Causes of War, Stakes of Nationhood

Why does this matter? It just seems to be another way of saying what such critics as Norman Rabkin and Claire McEachern have already said: that imagining the nation or body politic in *Henry V* seems inextricably entwined with imagining the king as a

[14] Rabkin, 'Rabbits, Ducks and *Henry V*', 290.

person. Yet there is a more radical analytical potential here, one that is opened up by considering the legal function of chronicle history alongside the forensic dimensions of Renaissance drama. For if it is true to say that forensic rhetoric, in the form of topics of inquiry, helps shape our sense of character and motive in Shakespeare's plays, it's no less true that the chronicles on which the history plays of Shakespeare and others are based, were also often forensic, or legal, in their purpose. Critics have been fascinated by *Henry V*'s concern with *nationhood*, whether in the form of the imagined fraternal community of the English at Agincourt, or in the strange little scene of the English, Welsh, Irish, and Scottish captains having an abortive 'disputation' about the just causes and conduct of war.[15] But even before we begin to think about how plays based on chronicles invite us to imagine nationhood, we need to think about how chronicles themselves were used to constitute legal evidence for national sovereignty. Chronicles record genealogies, titles to land, causes of disputes, outcomes of battles, the terms of treaties, their observance and breaking, the paying and withholding of tribute, the performance or neglect of homage. The recording of these matters has a forensic purpose. In disputes over sovereignty, chronicles have often been called upon to furnish legal proof.[16] Shakespeare was aware of this. In *Henry V*, as we have seen, he has Canterbury use chronicle history to disprove Pharamond's authorship of a Salic law application to France. But Shakespeare would also have been aware that, in the case of Anglo-Scots history, the chronicles had, at least since the time of Edward I, recorded disputed proofs in a 'war of historiography' that had never been resolved.[17] The question of whether or not Scots kings, historically, owed homage to English kings as their overlords, remained central to both English and Scottish historiography of the sixteenth century. The Scots denied that the history of the two nations proved that their kings owed homage; the English insisted it did. At stake, for the Scots, was their national autonomy, their very existence as a nation. The stakes for the English varied over the course of the sixteenth century. In the 1540s, the stakes were imperial: the argument of overlordship supported an invasive war against the Scots.[18] In the 1560s–1580s, with fears about a Stewart succession, the dubious 'history' of Scots homage was invoked and its implications debated in numerous legal treatises on Mary Stewart's title to the English throne.[19] In the years around James's accession, historical

15 See, for example, Peter Womack, 'Imagining Communities: Theatres and the English Nation in the Sixteenth Century', in *Culture and History, 1350–1600*, ed. David Aers (London: Harvester, 1992); David J. Baker, '"Wildehirishman": Colonialist Representation in Shakespeare's *Henry V*', *ELR*, 22.1 (1992): 37–61; Philip Schwyzer, '"I Am Welsh, You Know", The Nation in *Henry* V', in *Literature, Nationalism and Memory in Early Modern England and Wales* (Cambridge: Cambridge University Press, 2004), 126–50.

16 In 1291, Edward I asked various monasteries to search their chronicles for evidence of English overlordship of Scotland. See E. L. G. Stones and Grant Simpson, *Edward I and the Throne of Scotland 1290–1296*, 2 vols (Oxford University Press, for the University of Glasgow: 1978), 1.137–44.

17 See R. James Goldstein, *The Matter of Scotland: Historical Narrative in Medieval Scotland* (Lincoln: University of Nebraska Press, 1993), 57–103.

18 Dale S. Hoak, 'Sir William Cecil, Sir Thomas Smith, and the Monarchical Republic of Tudor England', in *The Monarchical Republic of Early Modern England*, ed. John F. McDiarmid (Aldershot: Ashgate, 2007), 37–54.

19 Mortimer Levine, *The Early Elizabethan Succession Question 1558–1568* (Stanford: Stanford University Press, 1966), 121–5.

'proof' of English overlordship was successfully used by the English to preclude plans for any further union between England and Scotland.[20] Thus, the Anglo-Scots wars of historiography were no less vital, legally speaking, to the shifting directions of Anglo-Scots relations during the sixteenth century than they had been in the thirteenth, fourteenth, and fifteenth centuries.

There is no question of Shakespeare being unaware of these debates. Indeed, the fact that a play such as *Henry V* makes us feel as if the question of Scotland's nationhood is *irrelevant* should, I will argue, be seen as a conclusive victory in the Anglo-Scots wars of historiography. I will argue that Shakespeare used his *psychologizing* of the forensic scene—his deflecting the question of 'is the cause just?' to the question of 'what is Henry really thinking or feeling?' to give the English nationalism of the play a supra-national, inclusive feeling while, at the same time, very effectively and cleverly denying Scotland the historical status of a nation, just at a point when that historical status mattered a great deal.

Shakespeare's chief sources for *Henry V* were: Raphael Holinshed's *Chronicles of England, Scotland and Ireland* (1577) in the edition of 1587, and Edward Hall's *Union of the Two Noble and Illustre Families of Lancaster and York* (1548, revised and enlarged, 1550). As T. W. Craik explains, Holinshed very often follows and condenses Hall. Moreover, though Shakespeare is usually closer to Holinshed than to Hall, the opposite is the case in the opening scenes of the play.[21] In Hall, the question of Scotland and the Franco-Scots alliance is central—as it was for the English throughout the Hundred Years War—to Henry V's determination of the likelihood of military success in France.[22] Accordingly, in Hall, as soon as Henry Chicheley, Archbishop of Canterbury, has finished his oration on the justice of Henry's cause in France, we're introduced to Ralph Neville, Earl of Westmoreland, who argues that there is a greater immediate cause of war against Scotland and that its conquest is 'more necessary'.[23] Westmoreland's ensuing lengthy oration, refuted by the Duke of Exeter, results not in a decision to disregard the Scottish threat, but rather in the decision to neutralize it by means of attacking France. This debate is central to Hall's own historical project. For Edward Hall wrote his history in the 1540s in the increasingly desperate context of England's military effort to conquer Scotland by force.[24] From 1543 to 1551, the Scots

[20] Bruce Galloway, *The Union of England and Scotland, 1603–1608* (Edinburgh: John Donald Publishers, 1986), 11: 'The average Englishman saw the old assertions of suzerainty over Scotland as simple fact.'

[21] *King Henry V*, ed. T. W. Craik (London: Bloomsbury, 1995), 6–7.

[22] For a modern account of the decisive effect of Scottish military aid to the French in the Hundred Years War, see Jonathan Sumption, *Trial By Battle: The Hundred Years War* (London: Faber, 1990), 1.59–65.

[23] Hall, *Chronicle*, 52.

[24] For the increasingly desperate state of Somerset's war against the Scots, see *The Letters of William, Lord Paget of Beaudesert, 1547–1563*, ed. Barrett L. Beer and Sybil M. Jack, *Camden Miscellany*, Vol. XXV (London: Royal Historical Society, 1974), 21–5, 30–2, 75–7. I am grateful to Dale Hoak for bringing Paget's letters to Somerset to my attention and for sharing with me his knowledge of the 1540s.

experienced nine years of continual invasion, destruction and burning of their major cities in a campaign that much later came to be known, with misleading euphemism, as 'The Rough Wooings'.[25]

The immediate occasion of the English decision to attempt a military conquest of Scotland in the 1540s was the Scots' failure to honour their promise to marry James V's daughter, Mary, to Henry's son, Edward VI. But though 'union' was talked about, especially by Protector Somerset, both Somerset and, before him, Henry VIII were very careful to ground their cause of war on historical evidence for England's overlordship of Scotland. In 1542, repeating the tactics of Edward I in 1291, Henry's council had asked the bishops of Durham and York to search their episcopal 'registers … auncient charters and monuments' for evidence of the king's title to the realm of Scotland.[26] The result was the publication of a forensic justification of the English invasion, attributed to Henry VIII and entitled *A Declaration, Conteynyng the Just Cavses … of This Present Warre with the Scottis, Wherein Also Appereth the Trewe & Right Title, That the Kinges Most Royall Maiesty Hath to the Souerayntie of Scotlande* (1542, STC 9179). In the following year, the printer Richard Grafton brought out an edition of the fifteenth-century chronicle of John Hardying, with a dedication to Thomas Howard, Duke of Norfolk, urging him to continue the conquest of Scotland.[27] In 1548, Protector Somerset employed Sir Thomas Smith, William Cecil, Sir John Mason, and Cuthbert Tunstall to produce further research on England's overlordship; this time the result was *An Epitome of the Title That the Kynges Maiestie of Englande Hath to the Sovereigntie of Scotlande, Continued vpon the Auncient Writers of Both Nacions from the Beginnyng* (STC 3196). Though the dedication to Edward VI declares the author to be a young Middle Templar called Nicholas Adams or Nicholas Bodrugan, Dale Hoak has argued that the text was certainly researched, and probably written, by Sir Thomas Smith.[28] Its printer was, once again, Richard Grafton. It was Grafton, too, to whom Edward Hall, who died in 1547, bequeathed the text of his chronicle for publication. Grafton accordingly brought Hall's *Chronicle* out in 1548, at the height of the military effort to conquer Scotland, also with a dedication to King Edward VI.[29]

All these texts—Henry VIII's *Declaration*, Hardyng's *Chronicle*, Smith's *Epitome*, and Hall's *Chronicle*—either begin with, or elsewhere invoke as origin the mythic history of Brutus, the Trojan Prince, who, in the days of Samuel the prophet, was supposed to have settled and ruled over the island of Albion, later called Britain, and then divided between his sons by his wife, Innogen. These sons were called Locrine, Albanact, and Camber. According to Geoffrey of Monmouth's *Historia regum Britanniae* (*c*.1123–1139), Locrine received Loegria, or England; Camber, the second son, Cambria or Wales

25 See Marcus Merriman, *The Rough Wooings: Mary Queen of Scots, 1542–1551* (East Linton: Tuckwell Press, 2000).

26 Hoak, 'Sir William Cecil', 49.

27 STC 12766 and 12767.

28 Hoak, 'Sir William Cecil', 50–1.

29 Edward Hall, *ODNB*.

and Albanact, the third, Albania or Scotland.[30] When, in 1299, Pope Boniface wrote to Edward I, ordering him to abandon the war against Scotland on the grounds that Scotland was not feudally subject to the kings of England, Edward responded with what would become an endlessly reiterated mythic account of England's foundational sovereignty over Scotland in the myth of Brutus' division of the kingdom between Locrine, Albanact, and Camber. [31] Edward's letter to Boniface alters Geoffrey of Monmouth's account in two significant ways. First, Albanact becomes the second son (in Geoffrey he is '*Albananctus iunior*', the youngest), and second, the inheritances of the younger sons reserve 'the royal dignity for Locrine, the eldest' ('*reservata Locrino seniori regia dignitate*').[32] Edward has Anglicized and legally inflected Geoffrey's text, turning it into an irresistible foundation myth for the feudal overlordship claimed by England, as 'firstborn' over the younger sons, Wales and Scotland (though, of course, in Geoffrey, the English or Anglo-Saxons, have yet to appear).

Hall's dedication to Edward VI invokes Geoffrey of Monmouth's story of 'Brute with the sequel of his linage', but the forensic uses of the post-Edward I version of this history emerge vividly in the debate about war that opens Hall's and Holinshed's accounts of the reign of Henry V. Opposing the Archbishop of Canterbury's case for invading France, Ralph Neville, Earl of Westmorland, invokes the story of Brutus as part of the case for invading Scotland instead. '[T]he hole isle of Britain', Westmoreland tells Henry V, 'was one entier Monarchi in the time of your noble auncetor [*sic*] Kyng Brute first kyng and ruler of your famous Empire and glorious region.' While the island was thus united, he goes on, the nation was invincible: 'no nacion durste ... inuade.' However, although when Brutus divided the land between his three sons, he was careful to reserve to Locrine '& his heyres homage, lege and fealtie loiall for the same countreis and dominions', it transpired that:

> the Albananctes otherwise called the false fraudulent Scottes... did not alonly withdrawe their fealtie, denie their homage, and refuse their allegiance due to the kynges of this realme, but also made continuall warre'.

'For the whiche cause', Neville concludes, 'diuerse of your noble progenitors haue ... made warre and subdewed the Scottes for the deniyng of their homage and stirryng of rebellion.'[33] Westmoreland's version of the Brutus story, gesturing back to the island's ancient invincibility, insisting on the feudal overlordship of Loegria/England over Albany/Scotland, and its interpretation of all subsequent Anglo-Scots wars as Scottish 'rebellions', is identical to the versions that appear in Henry VIII's *Declaration* of 1542

[30] Geoffrey of Monmouth, *The History of the Kings of Britain*, Latin text ed. Michael D. Reeve and trans. Neil Wright (Woodbridge: Boydell, 2007), 30–1.

[31] See nos. 28 and 29 in *Anglo-Scottish Relations 1174–1328*, ed. E. L. G. Stones (Oxford: Clarendon Press, 1965), [81–97], 162–194–5.

[32] Geoffrey, *History*, 30–1; *Anglo-Scottish Relations*, [97], 194–5.

[33] Hall, *Chronicle*, 53.

and the *Epitome* of 1548, both of which, of course, are likewise making a case for the legality of an English invasion of Scotland.[34] All three texts, moreover, claim to have access not only to narrative proofs but to documentary evidence. As Henry VIII puts it, 'the instrumentes of homage made by the kynges of Scottis ... sealed with theyr seales, and remaynynge in our Treasorye'.[35]

Where does this documentary evidence come from? It is at this point that the significance of Richard Grafton's publishing of John Hardyng's chronicle emerges. Alfred Hiatt's excellent study of forged documents in fifteenth-century England has given us new insight into the uses of John Hardyng's chronicle by English historians and policy makers in the sixteenth century.[36] Roger Mason's work on the Scottish historiographical countering of Geoffrey of Monmouth's tradition of Brutus has been foundational, but it overlooks the legal authority lent by Hardyng's faked documentation to the Galfridian history.[37] In spite of clearly mythic origins, the story of Brutus, combined with the forged 'instruments of homage' in the English treasury, was enough, according to Edmund Plowden, to prove England's sovereignty over Scotland in English common law.[38]

As John Hardyng (1378–1465) himself tells us in the dedication to Henry VI of the 1457 version of *Chronicle*, he was commissioned by Henry V to seek legal evidence of England's title to Scotland, so that Scotland might be invaded, plundered, and burnt.[39] Between 1422 and 1463, he presented, to Henry V, Henry VI, and Edward IV at least twenty documents concerning Anglo-Scots relations. Fourteen of the surviving seventeen documents have been discovered to be forgeries, though they were not so identified until 1837.[40] Hiatt argues that their fraudulence took so long to identify because their evidential value was, latterly, tied up with the narrative form of Hardyng's chronicle itself. 'The contention that underpins Hardyng's forgeries', he writes, 'is that the kings of Scotland were vassals of English kings from the death of Brutus and the division of Britain between his three sons.' The forged documents, however, did not have to stand by themselves:

> The homage of the Scots was, for Hardyng and his audience, a compelling narrative of submission to an overwhelming and legitimate force—the falsity of which

[34] *A Declaration*, sigs B4^{v}–C1^{r}; *An Epitome*, sigs A6^{r}–A7^{v}.

[35] *A Declaration*, sig. B4^{r}.

[36] The following paragraphs on Hardyng follow Alfred Hiatt, *The Making of Medieval Forgeries: False Documents in Fifteenth-Century England* (London: British Library and University of Toronto Press, 2004).

[37] Roger A. Mason, 'Scotching the Brut: Politics, History and National Myth in Sixteenth-Century Britain', in *Scotland and England, 1286–1815* (Edinburgh: John Donald Publishers, 1986), 60–84.

[38] Plowden writes, BL MS Don. *c*. 43, fol. 54: 'I heare there be many recordes extant in the Exchecker testifyinge this homage, and other matters prouinge Scottland to be wthin th'obedience of England'; 'For Scottland was first lawfully geven to Albanacte first kinge of Scottes, to holde of Locrine, his Eldest brother kinge of England by homage & seruice thereto due. and so doth kinge Henrie th'eight affirme in his said booke, and the Chronicles of England also', fol. 56^{r}.

[39] Hiatt, *Medieval Forgeries*, 104.

[40] Hiatt, *Medieval Forgeries*, 104–5.

> was unthinkable. ... The documents verify this narrative and, in circular fashion, are themselves verified by the historical narrative presented in the *Chronicle*.[41]

In the 1540s, Hardyng's *Chronicle* was revived in a number of ways. The documents it referred to guaranteed the narratives of homage presented in Henry VIII's *Declaration*, Smith's *Epitome*, and Hall's *Chronicle*. Protestantized, updated, and put into print by Richard Grafton, Hardyng's *Chronicle* was widely disseminated. Sir Thomas Smith's library contains no edition of Geoffrey of Monmouth, for example, but it does contain a copy of Harding.[42] George Puttenham mentions Hardyng several times, praising him as 'a Poet Epick or Historicall'.[43] In his dedication to Norfolk, Grafton describes Hardyng as a 'true-herted Englishman' who 'searched out of chronicles, both late an olde. ... How from the beginning, Scotlande dooth reigne / Under kynges of England, as their souereigne'.[44]

Edward Hall was among Hardyng's many sixteenth-century admirers. The name 'Ihon Hardyng' is cited under the 'English writers' Hall consulted.[45] However, Hall also paid attention to evidence from the opposite side, from Scots histories. Among the 'Latin Aucthors' he has drawn on are 'Hector Boetius' and 'Ioannes Maior'; that is, Hector Boece (1465–1536) author of the *Scotorum historia a prima gentis origine* (Paris, 1527) and John Mair (1467–1550), author of the *Historia Maioris Britanniae* (1521). With beautiful anachronism, Hall has the Earl of Westmoreland complain, in his presenting his history of English overlordship of Scotland to Henry V, of 'Ihon Mayer and other Scottish writers' who, he says 'coloure' (that is, justify) the opposite 'cause'.[46] Mair, though an advocate of Anglo-Scots union, clearly distinguished the union he desired from an English imperial domination justified by a historiography of overlordship. Although responding to Caxton rather than Hardyng, Mair's history repeatedly refutes claims that Scots kings performed homage for Scotland. Hardyng, for example, forges a document purporting to record Malcolm Canmore's homage to Edward the Confessor.[47] John Mair denies that Canmore ever paid homage for Scotland:

> Homage was rendered indeed for the county of Cumberland, which is situated in England, and which the king of Scots held of England, and granted always to their eldest sons, who did homage for that county to the kings of the English. ... Now it is a thing unheard of, and among Scots simply inconceivable, that a Scot at peace in his own kingdom ever recognised as his temporal superior either the English or anyone else.[48]

41 Hiatt, *Medieval Forgeries*, 106–7.

42 John Strype, *The Life of the Learned Sir Thomas Smith* (London: 1698), 141.

43 George Puttenham, *The Arte of English Poesie*, ed. Gladys Doidge Willcock and Alice Walker (Cambridge: Cambridge University Press, 1936; rpt 1970), 62, 245–6.

44 *The Chronicle of Iohn Hardyng* (London: Richard Grafton, 1543), sig. 2^r.

45 Hall, *Chronicle*, viii.

46 Hall, *Chronicle*, 54.

47 Hiatt, *Medieval Forgeries*, 106–8; *The Chronicle of Iohn Hardyng*, ed. Henry Ellis [London: 1812] (New York: AMS Press, 1974), 228–9, 236.

48 John Major, *History of Greater Britain* [1521], trans. Archibald Constable (Edinburgh: 1892), 127–8.

In sum, then, the difference between Scots and English histories registers a contest over legal title and national sovereignty. The legal character of these histories is paramount. Henry VIII's *Declaration*, Smith's *Epitome*, and Hall's *Chronicle* all follow Hardyng in insisting, by the use of an anachronistic legal vocabulary ('by Troyan lawe', 'homage and feaute', 'leege', 'excheate', 'letters sealed', 'letters patent') that Scotland was always already under English jurisdiction, legally a part of England from time out of mind.[49]

Understanding this neglected legal dimension of the 'uses of history' in sixteenth-century England helps illuminate aspects of the English history play, both at the Inns of Court and on the popular stage.[50] Hardyng's pressing of Geoffrey of Monmouth into service as proof of England's originary feudal dominion over Scotland helps explain the imaginative hold, on the English stage, of the Galdfridian history of Brutus and his heirs. As well as the plays that have survived (Norton and Sackville's *Gorboduc*, Gray's Inn's *The Misfortunes of Arthur*, Greene's *Edward I*, the anonymous *Locrine*, Marlowe's *Edward II*, the Queen's Men's *King Leir*, the anonymous *Edward III*, Shakespeare's *Henry V* and many others), the titles of lost plays are immensely suggestive: *King Lud, Uther Pendragon, Arthur king of England, the conquest of Brute, Mulmutius Dunwallo, Robert II, King of Scots, Ferrex and Porrex, Malcolm King of Scots*.[51] In the second place, we are alerted to the ideological importance of certain shaping motifs. The question, for example, of whether or not Scots prisoners of war were treated as enemy prisoners, or as rebels to England, was evidentially important for either side of the argument. In arguing against Mary Stewart's title to the English throne, for example, John Hales, while maintaining the usual English position that the Scots were always homagers to England, nevertheless rejected the idea that made them anything other than foreign enemies, citing as evidence the fact that 'they [the Scots] have usually ransomed upon their taking, as enemies, and not been executed, like rebels'.[52] How Scots prisoners of war were treated was, then, crucial to whatever argument was being advanced about whether or not history 'proved' that Scotland was, historically, within English jurisdiction.

Prisoner Kings

Shakespeare clearly read the debate Hall set out on the causes of war against Scotland. He placed some of the arguments of Westmoreland's case for war against the Scots in Henry V's own mouth and had the Archbishop of Canterbury respond, so the audience

[49] See *Hardyng*, ed. Ellis, 41–2, 45, 61–2, 120, 126, 207, 211, 228, 239–40 and passim; *Epitome*, sig. A7^r, sig. b1^{r-v} and passim.

[50] *The Uses of History in Early Modern England*, ed. Paulina Kewes (San Marino: Huntington Library, 2006) does not mention this use of history.

[51] For a list, see Gordon McMullan, 'The Colonisation of Early Britain on the Jacobean Stage', in *Reading the Medieval in Early Modern England*, ed. Gordon McMullan and David Matthews (Cambridge: Cambridge University Press, 2007), 138–40.

[52] Levine, *Early Elizabethan Succession*, 121.

hears that three-quarters of England's fighting men are to stay behind to defend England from a Scottish invasion, while a mere quarter is to cross the channel to 'make all Gallia shake' (1.2.217, 219). Thereafter, in the Folio text at least, Scotland morphs oddly from a land-border enemy so considerable as to require three-quarters of all England's fighting forces, into a docile regional accent heard at the siege of Harfleur. A Scots captain in the English army called 'Jamy' takes part in one of those ludicrous pub-joke scenes involving an Englishman, a Welshman, an Irishman, and a Scotsman. Critics have been unable to do much with this rather vacuous part, that of 'the Scots Captain, Captain Jamy' (3.2.75). They note that Jamy's speeches could be omitted from the dialogue without making any difference to the flow of the scene at all.[53] He is thought to be characterized as generally benign, a peacemaker, and a late addition, one audiences 'could hardly fail to identify' with James VI.[54]

The function of chronicle history as proof of legal title, however, may cast a different light on the relation of the opening scenes' portrayal of Scots enmity, and the appearance in the English army of 'Captain Jamy'. English dramatists writing history plays knew what was at stake, legally speaking, in representing Scots in the context of war. Crucial were the signifiers of rebellion—signs that showed that Scots were less like foreign enemies than rebellious vassals. George Peele's *Edward I* (*c.*1590) deploys the double meaning of 'halter'—a fastener of horses and cattle, but also a noose with which to hang malefactors—in the dramatization of John Balliol's conflict with Edward I. The audience watches as Edward I, splendidly dressed, sets a 'golden Diadem' on John Balliol's head, invoking the judgement of Paris that links English history to its mythic Trojan pedigree.[55] Several scenes later, Balliol, wearing the diadem, announces that 'Scotland disdains to carrie Englands yoke' and sends one of his Anglophile noblemen to England with a 'strangling halter' round his neck to signify this. Some scenes later, after the stage direction, '*Alarum, a charge, after long skirmish, assault, florishe*', we have '*Enter King Edward with his traine and Balioll prisoner.*' Balliol, we must imagine, stands on stage fettered and bound; perhaps Edward even places the same strangling halter on his neck as he chastises him thus:

> And heifer like sith thou hast past thy bounds,
> Thy sturdie necke must stoope to bear this yoke.[56]

The slightly later anonymous play of *Edward III* is one in which it is thought Shakespeare may have had a hand. Shakespeare certainly knew the play well enough to recall its rhetoric and staging in extensive and subtle detail in *Henry V*.[57] In *Edward III*, England's

53 Keith Brown, 'Historical Context and *Henry V*', *Cahiers Élisabéthains*, 29 (1986): 77–81, 78–9.

54 Richard Dutton, '"Methinks the Truth Should Live from Age to Age": The Dating and Contexts of *Henry V*', *HLQ*, 68.1–2 (2005): 173–204, 188.

55 George Peele, *Edward I*, ed. Frank S. Hook, in *The Life and Works of George Peele*, 3 vols (New Haven: Yale University Press, 1961), 2.95–6.

56 Peele, *Works*, 2.122–3, 153–4.

57 See *Edward III*, ed. Giorgio Melchiori (Cambridge: Cambridge University Press, 1998), 1–17; E. Pearlman, '*Edward III* in *Henry V*', *Criticism*, 37.4 (1995): 519–36.

vulnerability and heroic resistance to the invasions of the Scots are intriguingly feminized. In a subplot based on Pierre Boiastuau's *Histoires Tragiques*, the Countess of Salisbury chastely resists both the incompetent brusque predations of David II of Scotland and the eloquent love sonnets of Edward III of England. But the play concludes at Calais with the whole English royal family bringing on prisoners to prove the English title to France and to Scotland. Edward's Queen Phillipa brings, from England, the prisoner she claims as hers, David II of Scotland, who has been captured by the Northern English squire, John Copeland. Copeland yields his prisoner to Edward III as the 'custom of my fraught' and 'wealthy tribute of my labouring hands' (*Edward III*, 5.1.79–80). Then a herald announces the arrival of Edward the Black Prince with the king of France a prisoner 'whose diadem he brings', to crown Edward III king of France (5.1.181–3). The Scots prisoner king, as tribute, stands in for the homage due to Edward III as Scotland's overlord; the French prisoner king, by contrast, yields him a crown.

Shakespeare's *Henry V* throughout recalls the action and staging of the play, *Edward III*. If Shakespeare didn't partly write *Edward III*, as seems likely, he evidently knew it intimately.[58] Yet *Henry V* departs from both *Edward III* and the historical chronicles in a most striking way. For the fact is that Shakespeare had, in the chronicle history of Henry V, a ready-made Scots prisoner king, a ready-made proof of Scots vassalage. For when he took ship for France, Henry V was actually holding the Scottish heir to the throne, James I, prisoner. And, when the Scots sent reinforcements to the Dauphin, Henry even took James with him to fight against his own nation, the Scots, so as to *prove*, as he thought, that he was James's overlord, and that Scotsmen were his subjects.

The facts were these: James Stewart, the second son of Robert III of Scotland, had been sent by ship to France, ostensibly for his own safekeeping, during the reign of Henry IV of England. English pirates captured the ship and Henry IV illegally took the Scots heir his prisoner. Grief-stricken, Robert III died; so James, at the age of nine, was king of Scotland, but uncrowned and unsworn to his subjects. Though a king, he had no 'body politic'. He remained in English captivity for eighteen years.[59] James, however, did not remain in prison all of Henry V's reign. Henry realized his value by using the theatre of war to stage the proof of his own overlordship of James and of Scotland. When the Scots began to send military aid to the Dauphin, Henry released James, deploying him on the battlefield to 'establish moral and legal superiority over his old enemies' by redefining them as his vassal's subjects.[60] By insisting that the uncrowned Scots king, James I, fight on the English side against the Scots supporters of the Dauphin, Henry could reassert a legal claim of overlordship by treating his Scottish enemies differently from his French enemies—as rebellious subjects, in fact, not as enemies. So James I fought against his own countrymen at the siege of Melun and when the French and Scots were defeated, the Scots were hanged as traitors and the French ransomed.[61] This example certainly

58 Pearlman, '*Edward III* in *Henry V*', 524.

59 See Michael Brown, *James I* (Edinburgh: Canongate Academic, 1994), 1–24.

60 Brown, *James I*, 23.

61 Brown, *James I*, 23.

contradicts John Hales's later argument that the ransoming of Scots prisoners proves that they are foreigners; but of course, this was Henry V's symbolic point.

For English chronicle histories and discourses proving English overlordship, such as Henry VIII's *Declaration* and Smith's *Epitome*, James I's status as Henry's prisoner thus fits neatly into Hardyng's evidential model of Anglo-Scots history as an iteration of Scots allegiance withheld and English chastisement given. Scottish and French historians read the legal implications of events quite differently. They articulate a Scottish 'monarchical republicanism', in which they refuse to identify the weal of the kingdom with the natural body of the king. Thus John Mair, following the French historian, Robert Gaguin, notes that Henry V thought he could deploy James to bring the Scots over to the English side, but the Scots saw clearly that their duty was to fight against their king, and he approves their conduct in this matter: 'for they knew that the stability and permanence of the Scottish kingdom did not depend upon their king, and that though the English king might make a prisoner of their king, he could not, for all that, make a prisoner of the kingdom of Scotland'.[62] Interestingly, though, both Hall's and Holinshed's accounts register something of the Scots' point of view, while recording their own.

Hall includes an anecdote from Hector Boece's *Scotorum historia*, according to which James I was asked by Henry V to persuade the Scots who were aiding the Dauphin to 'return into their countree and natiue region'. James, according to Hall, replied that he could not do this because as a prisoner, 'I haue no possession of my realme, secondairely that I am as yet nether sworne to my subiectes, nor they by no oth of allegeance are bound to obey my commaundementes.' James concludes that, were he so sworn, he would first take counsel ('forese') what was best for his realm. Boece, that is, articulates the principle of the king as servant of the 'commonweal' created by his coronation oath, rather than as absolute monarch.[63] Holinshed, describing the siege of Melun, writes how the Scots responded to 'yoong Iames of Scotland' that 'they could not take him for a king, that was in the power of another', so that Henry ordered that 'for their rebellion against their prince, which they would haue to be counted constancie ... twentie of the proudest' were 'to be hanged at once'.[64] Holinshed's account nicely captures the ambiguity around who is giving the orders, who is 'liege lord and king'; James orders the Scots to yield, but when they deny that they are James's subjects it is Henry who orders the death that will prove them *his* subjects.

Shakespeare, of course, was dramatizing Agincourt, not the siege of Melun. His suppression of his sources' discussion of Henry V's imprisonment of James I can be therefore be explained in terms of dramatic economy, or, indeed, political discretion in the final years of Elizabeth's reign, while the succession question remained 'doubtful and dangerous'.[65] What cannot follow from this, however, is the argument—common in criticism

62 Mair, *History*, 344.

63 Hall, *Chronicle*, 109.

64 Raphael Holinshed, *Holinshed's Chronicles of England, Scotland and Ireland*, 6 vols [1808] (London: AMS Press, 1976), 3.123.

65 Susan Doran and Pauline Kewes, *Doubtful and Dangerous: The Question of Succession in Late Elizabethan England* (Manchester: Manchester University Press, 2014).

of the play—that the insertion of 'Captain Jamy' in a revised text of the play represents a compliment to James VI and I and an optimism about 'Britain'.[66] Such an argument fails to take account of the strenuous ideological work performed by the play in effacing the idea of Scotland as a nation, and replacing it with the imaginatively central figure of the 'perilous narrow ocean' that, in distinguishing the 'two mighty monarchies' portrayed as at war with one another, conveniently associates the English audience with the whole island, and their enemy with 'overseas' (1.0.20–2). Peter Womack has written brilliantly of the Chorus's feigned apology for the deficiencies of theatre as the harnessing of the audience to 'conceive of a positive imaginary entity' that 'can ... be named very simply: it is England'. Of course, England, as Womack goes on to show, is not 'a thing but a mode of connectedness'—a point I will come back to shortly—but in figuring the actors' dependence on the audience's 'imaginary forces', the Chorus, as Womack also observes, repeatedly associates the activity of the imagination with the crossing and re-crossing of the Channel, 'Grapple your minds to sternage of this navy'; 'Heave him away upon your wingèd thoughts / Athwart the sea' (3.0.18; 5.0.8–9).[67] Understanding the English assumption of what the imprisoned James I signified that is, the historical 'truth' of Scotland's status as England's homager—helps us understand just what was being achieved by reducing the three-nation war described by Hall's *Chronicle* into the constitution of 'England' as an imagined community of theatre-goers whose only historical enemies were 'overseas'.

Tact had its own ideological work to do in ensuring the continued currency, in England, of the historical argument that Scotland had never been a nation and the Scots had always been homagers to the English. Scots homage had been, in the 1540s, alleged as a 'cause' to justify invasive war. But—as the plays *Edward I* and *Edward III* make evident—the idea that Scotland was really a fiefdom of England did not cease to function with the failure of the English attempt to conquer Scotland in 1551. The argument for the historical vassalage of the Scots' Crown continued to be made, with great discretion and tact, in private political deliberations and in manuscript legal opinions, to prove the case for the English military aid to the Scots, and to prove the right of Scottish succession. Thus, for example, William Cecil, argued in his private memoranda in 1559, that 'The Crowne of england hath both a iust and vnfeyned title of longer durance, than the frendshipp, betwixt scotland and france, vnto the superiority of Scotland', a title proved by 'good and habundant storyes', so that England ought to defend Scotland.[68] In 1566, Edmund Plowden wrote discreetly in manuscript that Mary Queen of Scots could not be barred from the succession by the argument of foreign birth, for the Scots were not a separate nation:

> yt is written and beleeued certainly that Scottland is holden of the kinge of England. And yt is taken that yt was first yeven to Albanacte second son of Brute the first kinge

[66] See, for example, Neil Rhodes, 'Wrapped in the Strong Arms of the Union: Shakespeare and King James', in *Shakespeare and Scotland*, ed. Willy Maley and Andrew Murphy (Manchester: Manchester University Press, 2004), 37–52, 48–9; John Kerrigan, *Archipelagic English: Literature, History, and Politics, 1603–1707* (Oxford: Oxford University Press, 2008), 15.

[67] Womack, 'Imagining Communities', 91–3.

[68] BL Cotton Caligula B. 10, fol. 33^{v}–34^{r}.

> that possessed this realme to holde of Locrine his oldest brother kinge of Englande. And ever sithens yt hath bene holden of England, as by the Cronicles and recordes & other testimonies yt maye appeare.[69]

Once these arguments had done their work, and James VI of Scotland was actually on the English throne, the historical evidence for Scotland's always having been a homager to England was trotted out again, this time to do duty by way of managing the trauma of regnal union for the English, ensuring against detrimental effects that Scotland might have on the integrity of England and its political and legal institutions. Sir Henry Spelman argued that there was no need with James's accession to change the name of the kingdom to 'Britain', for kings of England had always been implicitly been kings of Scotland without bothering to mention it. '[T]he kinges of England', he maintained, always concluded 'the kingdomes of Scotland and Wales ... to be of the fee and homage of their crowne of England, and to be conteyned under that title.'[70] Henry Savile, writing at James's request, thought the union of Scotland and English ought to be classified as the 'consolidation' of a seignory with a state holding its suzerainty, since '*Scotland hath of long time been homager to England*' (my italics).[71]

I want to come back, now, to my opening comments on the radical analytical potential of our paying attention to the affinities between forensic rhetoric and fiction making. I showed how Shakespeare psychologized Hall's forensic scene, shifting the focus of inquiry from the rights and wrongs of England's title to France, to the question of what the king, in his conscience, might really think. As many critics have pointed out, it is this very tendency—the tendency to transform proof of a heroic English victory into nagging questions of conscience about the justifiability of war—that makes the play's ostensible nationalism seem to subvert and question itself. 'The heart of the play', as Richard Dutton puts it, 'is not the battle of Agincourt, which is textually almost a non-event: it is the night before the battle, where the hopelessly outnumbered English army from Henry down looks into its soul'.[72] It is clear that the 'Englishness' of this play thus has an inward, sceptical dimension that seems to belie the idea of English nationalism, but actually, brilliantly, defines it. As Womack puts it,

> [T]he inward England which is greater than its outward appearance, is graspable not in spite of the disjunctions between stage and kingdom, but through them. In piecing out the imperfections of the performance with their thoughts, the spectators are at the same time piecing out the imperfections of historical events.[73]

[69] BL MS Don. *c.* 43, fol. 44[v].

[70] *The Jacobean Union: Six Tracts of 1604*, ed. Bruce R. Galloway and Brian P. Levack (Edinburgh: Scottish History Society, 1985), 165.

[71] *Jacobean Union*, 190–2.

[72] Dutton, '"Methinks the Truth Should Live"', 192.

[73] Womack, 'Imagining Communities', 95.

Part of what we 'piece out' in supplementing performance with our thoughts is, of course, the unknowability of *causa*, or motive. Inviting us to be dubious about The King's 'cause' both as legal title and as personal motive, questions of national identity and of the ethics of war (was Henry right to give the command to kill the French prisoners? should Bardolph have been hanged for stealing a pax?) seem supra-nationally inclusive, not narrowly English.

Nevertheless, by giving England this 'inward' dimension, the play also works very effectively—and far more effectively, in fact, than more overtly anti-Scottish plays like *Edward I* and *Edward III*—to efface the historical idea of Scotland as a nation. Shakespeare did not forget the figure of the 'prisoner king' as a proof of England's legal title to Scotland. What he did was to produce the figure of the Scottish 'prisoner king' not as a staged reality or even part of the implied off-stage world of Henry's reign, but as a metaphor for the richness of English chronicles as discourses proving an English overlordship of the whole island. This he did this by including a very telling reminiscence from the play *Edward III*.

In Hall, the Archbishop of Canterbury insists that Henry is entitled to France because of his lineal descent from 'the high and most noble prince of famous memory kyng Edward the third your great grandfather' (50). Taking his cue from this, Shakespeare's Archbishop winds up his refutation of the Salic law with a peroration urging Henry to go to Edward's tomb, and:

> invoke his warlike spirit,
> And your great uncle's, Edward the Black Prince,
> Who on the French ground played a tragedy
> Making defeat on the full power of France. (1.2.104–7)

It is at this point that Henry puts the qualification, made in Hall by the Earl of Westmoreland, that French invasion advantages the Scot, against whom military provision must be made:

> We must not only arm t'invade the French,
> But lay down our proportions to defend
> Against the Scot. (1.2.136–8)

When Canterbury proposes that the marches, or borderlands, are defence enough, Henry carefully clarifies that he's not referring to border rebels but to *national policy*—'the main intendment of the Scot'—which he goes on to describe, from having *read chronicles* of Edward III: 'For you shall read', he says,

> that my great-grandfather
> Never went with his forces into France,
> But that the Scot on his unfurnished kingdom
> Came pouring like a tide into the breach. (1.2.146–50)

Henry's response to the Archbishop at first attempts to distinguish between border raiders—'the coursing snatchers'—and the whole of Scotland as a nation with a national *cause* (their 'main intendment') which, historically speaking, was the Franco-Scots alliance, as Shakespeare perfectly well knew. As Henry goes on to describe what happens when he 'reads' the chronicle histories of Edward III, however, the distinction between Scots as border raiders and the *causa* of the Scots as a nation collapses. John Mair explains, 'When Edward the Third was laying siege to Calais, Philip of Valois, the French king, sent to David Bruce, and urged him to invade England, in the hope that Edward would then desist from siege.'[74] In other words, Henry reading about his great-grandfather going with his forces into France, would also have read that David II responded by invading England, because he felt oath-bound by the terms of his alliance with France. Shakespeare replaces this perfectly transparent national cause with the image of a tide, so that Edward, 'Never went with his forces into France, / But that the Scot ... came pouring like the tide into a breach' (1.2.147–8). This enables the absurdity of comments likes that of the Arden editor, T. W. Craik, who writes of 'the Scots habit of invading whenever the English army goes overseas', as if the English army were planning a seaside holiday rather than invading Scotland's ally. But Craik is responding to the play's carefully achieved identification of 'foreign' with 'overseas', and carefully crafted suggestion that the Scots, rather than being a foreign nation with a cause of war, are simply bad neighbours who have a 'habit of invading' or who are, rather than a foreign nation, merely the oceanic medium, the tide, that might enable a truly foreign nation to invade.

Henry's mention of English chronicles of Edward III prompts, from Canterbury, a no less potent image of the undefended England as a 'mourning widow' who, nevertheless, manages to both to repel unwanted Scottish attentions and even corral the Scottish monarchy itself. When all England's 'chivalry hath been in France', declares the Archbishop,

> And she a mourning widow of her nobles,
> She hath herself not only well defended,
> But taken and impounded as a stray
> The King of Scots; whom she did send to France
> To fill King Edward's fame with prisoner kings
> And make her chronicle as rich with praise
> As is the ooze and bottom of the sea
> With sunken wrack and sumless treasuries. (1.2.156–65)

The Archbishop's dismissal of the Scots is, clearly, a recollection not of chronicle histories but of the staging and rhetoric of the earlier play. It is only in the play *Edward III* that David, king of Scots, is 'sent to France' to be paraded at 'Calais'—that is, onstage with the French king. In remembering *Edward III* with its climactic tableau of Edward III's

[74] Mair, *History*, 292.

receiving the 'inland' king from his wife (personified here as 'England' herself 'a mourning widow', with menfolk in France) and the 'overseas' king from his son, Shakespeare shows that he knows exactly what the scene's legal and imaginative significance is. Just as Edward I yoked John Balliol like a 'heifer' for straying his bounds, so here David is imagined as 'impounded as a stray'. Though jocularly mock-heroic, the terms imply that the Scottish polity or political body only moves within a superior English jurisdiction.[75] Equally telling is Shakespeare's play with the idea of the example's generative plurality. Edward's fame was filled with 'prisoner kings' in the plural, because both the French and the Scottish kings became his prisoners; the idea, however, of this amplitude becoming that of 'England's chronicle' made 'rich with praise' turns towards the value of chronicles like Hardyng's, Hall's, and Holinshed's as forensic proof of sovereignty, or title—of arguments in the national cause of war.

The implication here is that the value of Scots kings imprisoned by the English lies in their accumulated potential for the future—Edward III's David II, Henry V's James I—so enriching English chronicles with proof that, as Savile claimed, '*Scotland hath of long time been homager to England*'. It is not, in other words, that Shakespeare's 'Captain Jamy' stands in for the figure of James VI and I as the voice of England's hegemonic power over a united British kingdom, but that, rather, Captain Jamy stands as a reminder that, though a James may be the monarch of England, Scotland itself moves, and should always have moved (but for its straying), within England's jurisdiction.

Bibliography

Adams, N. alias Brodrugan. *An Epitome of the Title that the Kynges Maiestie of Englande Hath to the Sovereigntie of Scotlande, Continued vpon the Auncient Writers of Both Nacions from the Beginnyng* (London: 1548).

Anon., *Edward III*, ed. Giorgio Melchiori (Cambridge: Cambridge University Press, 1998).

Bodleian Library, MS Don. *c*. 43, Edmund Plowden, 'A Treatise of Succession'.

Doran, Susan and Paulina Kewes. *Doubtful and Dangerous: The Question of Succession in Late Elizabethan England* (Manchester: Manchester University Press, 2014).

Dutton, Richard. '"Methinks the Truth Should Live from Age to Age": The Dating and Contexts of *Henry V*', *Huntington Library Quarterly*, 68.1–2 (2005): 173–204.

Galloway, Bruce. *The Union of England and Scotland, 1603–1608* (Edinburgh: John Donald Publishers, 1986).

Galloway, Bruce and Brian Levack, eds. *The Jacobean Union: Six Tracts of 1604* (Edinburgh: Scottish History Society, 1985).

Geoffrey of Monmouth. *The History of the Kings of Britain*, Latin text, ed. Michael D. Reeve and trans. Neil Wright (Woodbridge: Boydell, 2007).

Goldstein, R. James. *The Matter of Scotland: Historical Narrative in Medieval Scotland* (Lincoln: University of Nebraska Press, 1993).

[75] Hall, *Chronicle*, 53.

Hall, Edward. *Hall's Chronicle Containing the History of England* [1548] (New York: AMS Press, 1965).
Hardyng, John. *The Chronicle of Iohn Hardyng* (London: 1543).
Hardyng, John. *The Chronicle of Iohn Hardyng*, ed. Henry Ellis [1812] (New York: AMS Press, 1974).
Henry VIII, *A Declaration, Conteynyng the Iust Cavses ... of This Present Warre with the Scottis, Wherein Also Appereth the Trewe & Right Title, That the Kinges Most Royall Maiesty Hath to the Souerayntie of Scotlande* (London: 1542).
Hiatt, Alfred. *The Making of Medieval Forgeries: False Documents in Fifteenth-Century England* (London: British Library and University of Toronto Press, 2004).
Hoak, Dale S. 'Sir William Cecil, Sir Thomas Smith, and the Monarchical Republic of Tudor England', in *The Monarchical Republic of Early Modern England*, ed. John F. McDiarmid (Aldershot: Ashgate, 2007), 37–54.
Holinshed, Raphael. *Holinshed's Chronicles of England, Scotland and Ireland*, 6 vols [1808] (London: AMS Press, 1976).
Hutson, Lorna. *Circumstantial Shakespeare* (Oxford: Oxford University Press, 2015).
Levine, Mortimer. *The Early Elizabethan Succession Question 1558–1568* (Stanford: Stanford University Press, 1966).
Major, John. *History of Greater Britain* [1521], trans. Archibald Constable (Edinburgh: 1892).
Mason, Roger A. 'Scotching the Brut: Politics, History and National Myth in Sixteenth-Century Britain', in *Scotland and England, 1286–1815* (Edinburgh: John Donald Publishers, 1986), 60–84.
McEachern, Claire. 'Henry V and the Paradox of the Body Politic', *Shakespeare Quarterly*, 45.1 (1994): 33–56.
Merriman, Marcus. *The Rough Wooings: Mary Queen of Scots, 1542–1551* (East Linton: Tuckwell Press, 2000).
Peele, George. *The Life and Works of George Peele*, 3 vols (New Haven: Yale University Press, 1961).
Quintilian, *Institutio oratoria*, ed. and trans. Donald A. Russell, 5 vols (Cambridge, MA: Harvard University Press, 2001).
Rabkin, Norman. 'Rabbits, Ducks and *Henry V*', *Shakespeare Quarterly*, 28.3 (1977): 279–96.
Shakespeare, William. *King Henry V*, ed. T. W. Craik (London: Bloomsbury, 1995).
Skinner, Quentin. *Forensic Shakespeare* (Oxford: Oxford University Press, 2014).
Stones, E. L. G., ed. *Anglo-Scottish Relations 1174–1328* (Oxford: Clarendon Press, 1965).
Stones, E. L. G. and Grant Simpson. *Edward I and the Throne of Scotland 1290–1296*, 2 vols (Oxford: Oxford University Press for the University of Glasgow, 1978).
Womack, Peter. 'Imagining Communities: Theatres and the English Nation in the Sixteenth Century', in *Culture and History, 1350–1600*, ed. David Aers (London: Harvester, 1992), 91–146.

CHAPTER 36

HENRY V, ANACHRONISM, AND THE HISTORY OF INTERNATIONAL LAW

CHRISTOPHER N. WARREN

Is Shakespeare's Henry V a war criminal? The question provides the arch title of John Sutherland and Cedric Watts' 2000 book of Shakespearean puzzles, but considered earnestly it tends to raise alarms within highly defended disciplinary borders in history, law, and literature.[1] The idea of war crime strikes many ears as anachronistic—even absurd. So contemporary does the notion of war crime sound that it seems scandalously presentist to apply the category to Shakespeare's martial king. For many, analysing war crime in *Henry V* exhibits what one historian denounces as the 'confusion of our cultural and ethical expectations with those of the early modern world'.[2] It is as though we were asking whether Henry had an iPhone—or took Viagra.

Since historicism and anachronism are important issues for early modern law and literature, the first of two main aims of this essay is to consider the problem of temporality at the interdisciplinary nexus of history, literature, and international law. Scholars in each of these overlapping fields have recently reflected on the role of anachronism in

[1] John Sutherland and Cedric Thomas Watts, *Henry V, War Criminal?: And Other Shakespeare Puzzles* (Oxford: Oxford University Press, 2000). See also Janet M. Spencer, 'Princes, Pirates, and Pigs: Criminalizing Wars of Conquest in Henry V', *Shakespeare Quarterly*, 47.2 (July, 1996): 160–77; Evelyn Gajowski, '"Mirror[s] of All Christian Kings": Hank Cinq and George Deux', in *Presentism, Gender, and Sexuality in Shakespeare*, ed. Evelyn Gajowski (New York: Palgrave Macmillan, 2009), 63–87.

[2] Conal Condren, 'Understanding Shakespeare's Perfect Prince: Henry V, the Ethics of Office and the French Prisoners', in *The Shakespearean International Yearbook*, ed. Graham Bradshaw, Tom Bishop, and Laurence Wright (Burlington: Ashgate, 2009), 9.196. As Paul Stevens observes, 'war' alone is troublesome. He reminds us that Shakespeare critics tend to invest 'war' with a timeless essence, thereby obscuring the many ways that 'war' has 'changed dramatically, perhaps beyond all recognition, over the last 400 years'. See Paul Stevens, '*Henry V*: Shakespeare and the Sacralization of War', forthcoming in *Cambridge Companion to Shakespeare and War*, ed. Paul Stevens and David Lowenstein. I am grateful to Prof. Stevens for sharing this essay prior to publication.

their analyses, yet the implications for the study of early modern literature and international law have not yet been considered directly. The second, related aim concerns how and whether international law should influence our interpretations of *Henry V*. My contribution in this regard is to propose as a new context for Shakespeare's play a little-known humanist disputation by the civil lawyer Alberico Gentili, *De armis Romanis* (1599). I argue that a more expansive, generically sensitive historicism than Conal Condren's may be in order before we dismiss the question of Henry's war crimes as 'the cultural narcissism of displaced indignation'.[3] Together with *Henry V*, *De armis Romanis* affirms an important point about historicism and anachronism once made by David Norbrook: '[w]e have a word for anachronism, but we need and lack a word ... for an equal and opposite error, which "blindly insists that current events have yet to occur"'.[4] Indeed, *Henry V* and *De armis Romanis* illustrate why early modernists interested in international law need not reject synchronic historicism for explicitly anachronistic or presentist approaches. Instead, we can pay further attention to a juridical approach to the international past cultivated in the early modern period alongside the rise of international law—an approach closely linked with literary epistemologies.

Anachronism and International Legal Method

'To understand [*Henry V*]', Conal Condren argues, 'requires we both recognize and try to put to one side our own senses of moral and political rectitude.'[5] Condren dutifully invokes what Constatin Fasolt in his book *The Limits of History* (2004) calls historians' 'most basic principle of method: thou shalt place everything in the context of its time'.[6] And yet there are many in international criminal law for whom it makes perfect sense to ask whether Shakespeare's Henry V was a war criminal. It has long been accepted in international humanitarian law that 'the first international war crime trial' took place in 1474, with the trial of Charles the Bold's military lieutenant Peter von Hagenbach.[7] Peter von Hagenbach, it is widely agreed, was held to account in 1474 by a quasi-international

[3] Condren, 'Understanding Shakespeare's Perfect Prince', 208.

[4] David Norbrook, *Poetry and Politics in the English Renaissance*, rev. edn (Oxford: Oxford University Press, 2002), 288. Norbrook is quoting David Wootton, 'Leveller Democracy and the Puritan Revolution', in *The Cambridge History of Political Thought, 1450–1700*, ed. J. H. Burns and Mark Goldie (Cambridge: Cambridge University Press, 1991), 417.

[5] Condren, 'Understanding Shakespeare's Perfect Prince', 196.

[6] Constantin Fasolt, *The Limits of History* (Chicago: University of Chicago Press, 2004).

[7] Georg Schwarzenberger, 'A Forerunner of Nuremberg: The Breisach War Crime Trial of 1474', *The Manchester Guardian*, 28 September 1946; Gregory S. Gordon, 'The Trial of Peter von Hagenbach: Reconciling History, Historiography, and International Criminal Law', in *The Hidden Histories of War Crimes Trials*, ed. Kevin Heller and Gerry Simpson (Oxford: Oxford University Press, 2013), 13–49.

tribunal for crimes that included 'divers extortions and outrages', among them executing 'men of honour ... without any forme of Lawe'.[8] To similar effect, lawyers have found Shakespeare's *Henry V* exhibiting the 'idea' of war crime and have credited Shakespeare's contemporary, the civil lawyer Alberico Gentili, with 'anticipating international criminal tribunals'.[9] There's a puzzle here. The question of war crime in *Henry V* seems at once dishonourably presentist from the perspective of history and rigorously historicist from the perspective of law. What gives?

The charged question of war crime highlights some important methodological suppositions that quietly influence the questions scholars ask, frame the interpretations we give, and condition our receptivity to those interpretations. Whether or not war crime is anachronistic when applied to the early modern period—an argument I reject with some qualifications in part II—the very question of anachronism highlights meaningful yet rarely discussed differences among this volume's main interpretative communities in law, history, and literary studies. As Anne Orford has observed, 'Law and history stand on the opposite sides of the dividing line between present obligations and archaic traditions. The self-imposed task of today's contextualist historians is to think about concepts in their proper time and place—the task of international lawyers is to think about how concepts move across time and space.'[10] 'International legal method', in other words, is '*necessarily* anachronistic'.[11] What then of literary studies? Literature can *mean* both synchronically and diachronically, in its own moment and potentially across vast temporal distances. Orford's line, therefore, cuts through the heart of literary scholarship. On the one hand, historicists (new and old) generally suppose that 'a period often has a set of values that are not directly applicable, or sometimes even comprehensible, to other

[8] Schwarzenberger, 'A Forerunner of Nuremberg: The Breisach War Crime Trial of 1474'; Georg Schwarzenberger, *International Law as Applied by International Courts and Tribunals: The Law of Armed Conflict* (London: Stevens, 1968), 2.462–4; H. McCourbey, 'War Crimes: The Criminal Jurisprudence of Armed Conflict', *Military Law and Law of War Review*, 31 (1992): 171; Gordon, 'The Trial of Peter von Hagenbach: Reconciling History, Historiography, and International Criminal Law'; Joaquín Alcaide Fernández, 'Hostes Humani Generis: Pirates, Slavers, and Other Criminals', in *The Oxford Handbook of the History of International Law*, ed. Bardo Fassbender and Anne Peters (Oxford: Oxford University Press, 2012); Philippe de Commynes, *The Historie of Philip de Commines Knight, Lord of Argenton* (London: Ar. Hatfield, for I. Norton, 1596), 122; Jean de Serres, *A General Inuentorie of the History of France*, ed. Pierre Matthieu, trans. Edward Grimeston (London: George Eld, 1607), 249.

[9] McCourbey, 'War Crimes', 170; Theodor Meron, 'International Humanitarian Law from Agincourt to Rome', *International Law Studies*, 75 (2000): 306.

[10] Anne Orford, 'The Past as Law or History?: The Relevance of Imperialism for Modern International Law', *International Law and Justice Working Papers*, IILJ Working Papers, no. 2 (2012), <http://www.iilj.org>.

[11] Anne Orford, 'On International Legal Method', *London Review of International Law*, 1.1 (2013): 175. Emphasis mine. Orford proposes an international legal method less indebted to Cambridge School intellectual history, exemplified most prominently by Quentin Skinner, 'Meaning and Understanding in the History of Ideas', in *Visions of Politics*, 3 vols (Cambridge: Cambridge University Press, 2002), 1.57–89. For a contextualist rejoinder founded in the possibility of rhetorical manipulation, see Andrew Fitzmaurice, 'Sovereign Trusteeship and Empire', *Theoretical Inquiries in Law*, 16.2 (2015): 468–71.

periods or epochs.'[12] They find meaning on the temporal axis of synchronicity. On the other hand, formalists, presentists, and others attend to the diachronic axis, remaining 'wary of reconstructing a binary opposition between past and present' and emphasizing themes such as continuity, tradition, aesthetics, cross-temporal dialogue, and deep time.[13] Scholars of the latter sort are largely unfazed by charges of anachronism, which some even make an explicit goal. Strange bedfellows emerge in the process. On its face, the counter-historicist injunction to 'always anachronize', a retort to Frederic Jameson's 'always historicize', appears altogether compatible with international legal method, even though neither camp has explicitly recognized the affinity.[14]

The historicist principle that everything must be placed in its time has recently undergone criticism from legal and literary scholars as well as some historians proposing a return to the *longue durée*, but it is a position that historian Brad Gregory elaborates elegantly when he writes, 'Only historians have the time and training to pursue past experience as it was lived and construed. Without that effort, past worlds will be utterly lost, not only because human experience is fleeting, but because even the ideal of reconstructing it will have passed as so much grist through the mill of the theories and commitments of the moment.'[15] Dicta such as these, in Fasolt's account, have far more to do with law than we normally allow. It is precisely historians' basic principle of method that keeps history distinguishable from law. Lawyers and judges use the past instrumentally, as necessitated by the case at hand; but historians' core prohibition on anachronism ensures—or seeks to ensure—that instrumental legal needs do not impinge on historiography. As Fasolt writes, the necessity to contextualize,

> keeps historians from committing anachronism. It places the past under a great taboo in order to prevent a kind of chronological pollution. No one who violates that great taboo may claim to be a true historian. The past is sacred; the present is profane. Anachronism profanes the past by mixing past and present. … All other sins can be forgiven, but not this one. Anachronism is the sin against the holy spirit of history. Show that a historian has unwittingly infected the interpretation of the past with some particle of the present, and you have shown the historian not only to have failed at the task, but to have failed shamefully.[16]

[12] Paul Stevens, 'The New Presentism and Its Discontents: Listening to *Eastward Ho* and Shakespeare's *Tempest* in Dialogue', in *Rethinking Historicism from Shakespeare to Milton*, ed. Ann Baynes Coiro and Thomas Fulton (Cambridge: Cambridge University Press, 2012), 139.

[13] Evelyn Gajowski, 'Beyond Historicism: Presentism, Subjectivity, Politics', *Literature Compass*, 7.8 (2010): 681. Further examples include Wai-chee Dimock, 'A Theory of Resonance', *PMLA*, 112.5 (1997): 1060; Simon Jarvis, 'Prosody as Tradition', *Dalhousie Review*, 79.2 (1999): 151–72; Stanley Fish, 'Why Milton Matters; Or, Against Historicism', *Milton Studies*, 44 (2005): 1–12; Jonathan Gil Harris, *Untimely Matter in the Time of Shakespeare* (University of Pennsylvania Press, 2008); Marshall Grossman, 'Limiting History', in *Rethinking Historicism from Shakespeare to Milton*, ed. Ann Baynes Coiro and Thomas Fulton (Cambridge: Cambridge University Press, 2012), 65–84.

[14] Gajowski, 'Beyond Historicism', 678.

[15] Brad S. Gregory, *Salvation at Stake: Christian Martyrdom in Early Modern Europe* (Cambridge, MA: Harvard University Press, 1999), 15.

[16] Fasolt, *The Limits of History*, 6.

Historians—and 'only historians', according to Gregory—guard the citadel of the past against the pressures of the present. They protect the past from distorting external threats like moralism and 'judicialization.'[17] The historian Henry Rousso, an expert on Vichy France who, citing a fundamental incompatibility between historical and legal methods, has refused to testify in late twentieth-century French war crimes trials, contends that history differs from law precisely by 'giv[ing] us a better understanding of the distance that separates' the past and the present.[18]

And yet that same gap between past and present that charges of anachronism achieve is also, for thinkers like Fasolt and Rousso, law's very condition of possibility. By marking off something called the past from something called the present, 'Historians clear a space in time so that it may be occupied by individuals no longer tied to custom and tradition.'[19] Law, understood as something binding, here and now, is possible precisely because historians have carved out a differentiated 'past' from the temporal flux. Modern people, as Fasolt puts it, 'could not imagine life if their present were cluttered by the laws of ancient Rome, the science of Aristotle, and the morality of Saint Augustine'.[20] At stake in the charge of anachronism, then, is the very possibility of laws that feel somehow 'ours'. Such perception of historical distance is critical, according to advocates of this line of thought. A properly historical epistemology is above all an 'apprenticeship in liberty, since the historical being is one who frees him- or herself... to impose his or her own path'.[21] For Fasolt, borrowing from legal historian William Maitland, the 'rents' historians make in the 'seamless web' of history 'leave us to move on our own initiative along the trajectory of time into a future that will turn out to be another here and now'.[22] 'They do not oblige us to shoulder any responsibilities other than those to which we have consented of our own free will', he concludes.[23] Fasolt's primary concern in *The Limits of History* is an early modern 'historical revolt' in which highly partisan humanists practised new historical methods to help liberate fledgling sovereigns from imperial and papal control.[24] The sovereign 'right to legislate' emerged alongside, and often as a result of, early modern humanists' assault against anachronism.[25]

Extrapolating from Fasolt's account, we can say that historicism and international law enjoy a partly causal relationship. A tool for sovereign self-fashioning, the

[17] Henry Rousso, *The Haunting Past: History, Memory, and Justice in Contemporary France*, trans. Ralph Schoolcraft (Philadelphia: University of Pennsylvania Press, 2002), 50; Richard J. Evans, 'History, Memory, and the Law: The Historian as Expert Witness', *History and Theory*, 41.3 (2002): 330.

[18] Rousso, *The Haunting Past*, 8; Richard Wilson, *Writing History in International Criminal Trials* (Cambridge and New York: Cambridge University Press, 2011), 7.

[19] Fasolt, *The Limits of History*, 8.

[20] Fasolt, *The Limits of History*.

[21] Rousso, *The Haunting Past*, 8.

[22] Fasolt, *The Limits of History*, 227, 230.

[23] Fasolt, *The Limits of History*, 230.

[24] Fasolt, *The Limits of History*, 16–22; George H. Nadel, 'Philosophy of History before Historicism', *History and Theory*, 3.3 (1964): 291–315; Stevens, 'The New Presentism and Its Discontents: Listening to *Eastward Ho* and Shakespeare's *Tempest* in Dialogue', 139.

[25] Fasolt, *The Limits of History*, 201.

idea of anachronism helped create new conceptual spaces between previously unified regions—helped create, that is, the constitutive *inter-* of international law. The recent 'historiographical turn' in international law, however, has nevertheless remained wary of full-fledged historicism. [26] Randall Lesaffer writes that in international law, 'history is functional and is dictated by current needs. It is rarely born out of curiosity about the past itself'.[27] Siding with historians like Condren and Gregory, Lesaffer counts international law's functionalist presentism as a distinct mark against current practice in international legal history, but critical legal scholars like Anne Orford, Martti Koskenniemi, and Rose Parfitt embrace the very version of international law historicism that Lesaffer laments.

Critical legal historians advocate for a distinctly 'juridical method' defined by a salutary 'intermingling' of past and present.[28] According to Hans-Georg Gadamer and his followers at least, such intermingling is, in any case, inevitable. Writing about legal hermeneutics in *Truth in Method*, Gadamer declares, 'A historical hermeneutics that does not make the *nature of the historical question* the central thing, and does not inquire into a historian's motives in examining historical material, lacks its most important element.'[29] On this view, historians charging others with anachronism overestimate their capacity to distance themselves from concerns of the moment. Either that, or they dissemble.

Tropes of international juridical method are probably more familiar to literary scholars when reframed as 'presentism', a literary method that calls on scholars to own up to the repressed political and moral commitments that condition interpretations. Arguably, both projects 'seek out salient aspects of the present as a crucial trigger for investigations', taking as their 'centre of gravity … "now", rather than "then"'.[30] Legal thinkers and presentists charge that historians' historicism is morally underequipped, unable to supply 'value judgments' to accompany what Philip Sidney had already called the 'bare was' of history.[31] In Koskenniemi's words, historians' history suffers from 'an historical relativism [that] ends up suppressing or undermining efforts to find patterns

[26] George Rodrigo Bandeira Galindo, 'Martti Koskenniemi and the Historiographical Turn in International Law', *European Journal of International Law*, 16.3 (2005): 539–59.

[27] Randall Lesaffer, 'International Law and Its History: The Story of an Unrequited Love', in *Time, History and International Law*, ed. Matthew C. R. Craven, M. Fitzmaurice, and Maria Vogiatzi (Leiden: M. Nijhoff, 2007), 29.

[28] Orford, 'On International Legal Method'; Martti Koskenniemi, 'Vitoria and Us: Thoughts on Critical Histories of International Law', *Rechtsgeschichte Legal History—Zeitschrift Des Max-Planck-Instituts Für Europäische Rechtsgeschichte*, 22 (2014): 124. In calling for a return to *longue durée* history while emphasizing questions of international law and governance, Jo Guldi and David Armitage strike an intriguing middle ground in *The History Manifesto* (Cambridge: Cambridge University Press, 2014).

[29] Hans Georg Gadamer, *Truth and Method*, trans. W. Glen-Doepel, Joel Weinsheimer, and Donald G. Marshall, 2nd rev. edn (New York: Continuum, 2004), 334.

[30] Terence Hawkes, *Shakespeare in the Present* (New York: Routledge, 2003), 22.

[31] Andrew Hadfield, 'Has Historicism Gone Too Far: Or, Should We Return to Form?', in *Rethinking Historicism from Shakespeare to Milton*, ed. Ann Baynes Coiro and Thomas Fulton (Cambridge: Cambridge University Press, 2012), 24–5.

in history that might account for today's experiences of domination and injustice'.[32] For legal scholars to proceed in the way of historians, then, is to abdicate their constitutive 'juridical stance'.[33]

It is true of course that international legal history can be an instrumental exercise in justification. The so-called 'Breisach War Crime Trial of 1474' was successfully introduced into legal historiography by the refugee jurist Georg Schwarzenberger, in the midst of the deliberations at Nuremberg.[34] As such, the barely suppressed role of international legal history in identifying this 'forerunner to Nuremberg' was to legitimate the international legal actions against Nazi defendants.

But freer congress between past and present in the hands of recent critical legal historians is not necessarily intended to serve up sources and precedents. Instead, critical histories of international law seek greater openness to uncomfortable ideas like empire and domination that might otherwise be externalized from the domain called 'Law' and projected onto a screen called 'History'.[35] Whereas historians' historicism and certain older international legal histories ally to shore up international law's legitimacy, critical international legal method interrogates that legitimacy by rejecting a metaphysical gap between past and present. International legal method insists that international law is not exclusively an artefact of the (enlightened) present. Since it bears ideological baggage from the past, it is not exclusively 'ours'.

Coming at such questions from the perspective of early modern studies, it becomes possible to identify in both international legal method and literary presentism a subtle persistence of a Renaissance philosophy of history founded in forensic rhetoric, exemplarity, legal analysis, and moral critique—a philosophy of history that historicism most certainly injured but did not fully eliminate. If early modern historicism erected a wall intended to disable problematic exchanges between past and present like that now found in presentism and international legal method, that wall had not yet reached its full height by the 1590s when people like Gentili and Shakespeare were writing. Using historicism's own lens, we can begin to see evidence of early modern literature and law resisting the partition between past and present posited by historicism. Early modern historicism enthroned the past as sovereign, immune from legal scrutiny. But as I illustrate in the following section, international legal method operates with a renovated Renaissance philosophy of history partly because thinkers like Shakespeare and Gentili, writing at the dawn of historicism, deployed genres that facilitated meaning-making along both the synchronic and diachronic axes. Vertex-like works like *Henry V* and *De armis Romanis* point interpreters along divergent paths, allowing for contemporary resonance and also transmitting legal meaning across time. A result is that chronologically

32 Koskenniemi, 'Vitoria and Us: Thoughts on Critical Histories of International Law', 124.

33 Rousso, *The Haunting Past*, 53.

34 Gordon, 'The Trial of Peter von Hagenbach: Reconciling History, Historiography, and International Criminal Law'; Detlev F. Vagts, 'International Law in the Third Reich', *The American Journal of International Law*, 84.3 (1990): 661–704.

35 Rose Parfitt, 'The Spectre of Sources', *European Journal of International Law*, 25.1 (2014): 302.

later interpreters can, in full fidelity with the authors' own ambitions, take on a juridical stance in asking whether Henry violated the laws of war.

Some critical legal historians may suggest that anachronism is fundamental to international legal method, but Orford herself gives an even more compelling model for 'juridical thinking' in the double temporality of Renaissance art, in which works of visual art are said to gesture at once to an immediate social and material context but also to a broader, more ambitious timescale associated with diachronicity and the *longue durée*.[36] Indeed, 'Law, like art, holds together two ideas about time.'[37]

Making the International Case

In Jean Bodin's *Method for the Easy Comprehension of History* (1566), the author wonders aloud 'whether historians ought to praise or to vituperate and to express judgements about the matter under discussion.'[38] Historians' 'juridical stance' is precisely what historicism sought to expunge.[39] Bodin himself equivocates on the question of historians' judgements, but not before remarking that 'the prejudice of the historians detracts greatly from the events, because they seem to wish to inculcate in the minds of inexperienced readers opinions that are questionable.'[40] Seeds of the contemporary debate had been sown.

The Oxford jurist Alberico Gentili soon took up the cudgels for a legally inflected past in his seminal work on the laws of war, *De iure belli libri tres* (1598). Minimizing Bodin's own reservations, Gentili complained that Bodin's 'bare recital of history' left too large a gap between examples and precepts.[41] 'Because of the diversity and contradictory nature of examples …' he wrote, 'one could not easily derive from this treatment any system of law.'[42] In chapter 26 of that same work, Gentili pointedly rejected the 'bare recital of history' again when he denounced Henry V's actions at Agincourt, actions dramatized powerfully—if somewhat ambiguously—when Shakespeare's Henry orders his soldiers to execute their prisoners. 'I cannot praise the English who, in that famous battle in which they overthrew the power of France, having taken more prisoners than the number of their victorious army and fearing danger from them by night, set aside those of high rank and slew the rest.'[43] 'Jumping o'er times' as *Henry* V's Chorus would say, the

36 Orford, 'On International Legal Method', 176. See Grossman, 'Limiting History', 69.

37 Orford, 'On International Legal Method', 166, 176.

38 Jean Bodin, *Method for the Easy Comprehension of History*, trans. Beatrice Reynolds (New York: Norton, 1969), 51.

39 Rousso, *The Haunting Past*, 53.

40 Bodin, *Method for the Easy Comprehension of History*, 51.

41 Alberico Gentili, *De iure belli libri tres*, 2 vols, trans. John Carew Rolfe (Oxford: Clarendon Press, 1933), 2.4.

42 Gentili, *De iure belli libri tres*, 2.4.

43 Gentili, *De iure belli libri tres*, 2.212.

title of Gentili's chapter mobilizes the historical lesson for the present: 'Of Captives: that they are not to be Slain' (Prologue, 29).

Whereas Shakespeare's Henry and his Chorus of apologists appear at pains to establish Henry as a just Christian warrior—distinct, for example, from enemies like the Turks, who in Henry's allusions 'represent ... the antithesis of supposedly native English forms of communal and political life'—Gentili's text lumps Henry's war crimes with 'the barbarous savagery of the Turk, who slew four thousand prisoners, to relieve himself of their burden'.[44] Shakespeare's Henry, then, quite possibly *was* a war criminal for some early modern elites, to say nothing of the moral intuitions of early audiences more generally. Indeed, while Shakespeare's Chorus, Gower, and his Welsh Captain Fluellen sycophantically buttress Henry's self-mystification, the play on the whole licenses an equitable interpretive framework that, as Lorna Hutson has shown, radically demystifies royal authority.[45] It is a way of interpreting fundamental to international law—premised on the 'jurisdiction of the interpreter' to 'measure and judge the acts of sovereigns'.[46]

Several recent scholars have noticed important connections between Gentili and Shakespeare, but the text of Gentili's that best illustrates the particularities of international law's own historicism may not be his *De iure belli*, which has been the focus of recent studies by Theodor Meron, Paula Pugliatta, and Rosanna Camerlingo, but Gentili's remarkable *De armis Romanis*, issued in two parts in 1590 and 1599.[47] Published partially in quarto in 1590 and then in an expanded octavo in 1599, the same year of *Henry V*'s composition, with each dedicated to Robert Devereux, the Earl of Essex, *De armis Romanis* has recently attracted renewed attention from intellectual historians and historians of international law; literary scholars have been slower to note its significance.[48] It is not a trait habitually ascribed to lawyers, and it is one that Condren

44 Benedict S. Robinson, 'Harry and Amurath', *SQ*, 60.4 (December, 2009): 400; Gentili, *De iure belli libri tres*, 2.212.

45 Lorna Hutson, 'Imagining Justice: Kantorowicz and Shakespeare', *Representations*, 106.1 (May, 2009): 118–42.

46 Peter Goodrich, 'On the Relational Aesthetics of International Law', *Journal of the History of International Law*, 10 (2008): 321.

47 Theodor Meron, *Henry's Wars and Shakespeare's Laws: Perspectives on the Law of War in the Later Middle Ages* (Oxford: Oxford University Press, 1993); Paola Pugliatti, *Shakespeare and the Just War Tradition* (Burlington: Ashgate, 2010); Rosanna Camerlingo, 'Henry V and the Just War: Shakespeare, Gentili and Machiavelli', in *Machiavellian Encounters in Tudor and Stuart England: Literary and Political Influences from the Reformation to the Restoration*, ed. Alessandro Arienzo and Alessandra Petrina (Burlington: Ashgate, 2013), 103–19. See also Christopher N. Warren, *Literature and the Law of Nations, 1580–1680* (Oxford: Oxford University Press, 2015), 62–95.

48 Richard Tuck, *The Rights of War and Peace: Political Thought and the International Order from Grotius to Kant* (Oxford: Oxford University Press, 1999); Kaius Tuori, 'Alberico Gentili and the Criticism of Expansion in the Roman Empire. The Invader's Remorse', *Journal of the History of International Law/ Revue D'histoire Du Droit International*, 11.2 (2009): 205–19, doi:10.1163/138819909X12468857001389; Benedict Kingsbury and Benjamin Straumann, eds, *The Roman Foundations of the Law of Nations: Alberico Gentili and the Justice of Empire* (New York: Oxford University Press, 2011); Alberico Gentili, *The Wars of the Romans: A Critical Edition and Translation of De armis Romanis*, ed. Benedict Kingsbury and Benjamin Straumann, trans. David Lupher (New York: Oxford University Press, 2011).

contends was all but historically impossible, but Gentili too was capable of something approaching 'negative capability'. A previously unnoticed allusion to *De armis Romanis* may even be found in *Henry V* 3.3 where Fluellen discourses on the 'wars of the Romans', a direct English translation of Gentili's title (3.3.26–7).[49] The emendation that T. W. Craik proposes for a subsequent Fluellen line brings that text closer to Gentili's title as well. Where the First Folio gives 'disciplines of the Warre, the Roman Warres', Craig proposes to make the 'Warre' on the basis of the Folio's cramped spacing (3.3.40–1).[50]

Of all of Shakespeare's characters, it is certainly Fluellen who echoes Gentili's language most noticeably, but *De armis Romanis* can also be felt in *Henry V* in more subtle ways: in the play's apparently simultaneous praise and condemnation of its title character; its depiction of Celtic warriors in a proto-British army; and the play's interest, in David Quint's words, in 'dramatizing rather than concealing ... the literary act which re-creates the event'.[51] Insofar as 'the event' of *Henry V* is one that continues to elicit judgement, this is where my two main aims in this essay intertwine: judgement indicates a juridical approach to the past rather than a strictly historicist one. 'A problem-event that has animated some kind of judgment' is what Lauren Berlant calls a 'case'.[52] The notion of the *causa* or case was pervasive in early modern culture, and it was especially potent in dramatic composition and formal rhetoric, where it was regularly equated with the Greek *hypothesis*, literally placing under.[53] If historicism was a commitment to the 'bare' event, shorn of legal meaning for the present, the problem that Shakespeare and Gentili confronted was how exactly to place the international past under legal scrutiny. Their works give us two related examples of making cases from international events, of hypothesizing the international past skilfully enough to prompt generalizable judgements about the conduct of war.[54]

[49] Meron found 'no evidence that the sixteenth-century writers of *jus gentium* influenced Shakespeare either directly or indirectly'. See Meron, *Henry's Wars and Shakespeare's Laws*, 11.

[50] William Shakespeare, *King Henry V*, ed. T. W Craik, Arden Shakespeare 3rd edn (New York: Routledge, 1995), 3.2.98. I am grateful to Lorna Hutson for bringing Craik's emendations to my attention.

[51] David Quint, '"Alexander the Pig": Shakespeare on History and Poetry', *Boundary 2*, 10.3 (1982): 49–67.

[52] Lauren Berlant, 'On the Case', *Critical Inquiry*, 33.4 (June, 2007): 663–72.

[53] Wesley Trimpi, *Muses of One Mind: The Literary Analysis of Experience and Its Continuity* (Princeton: Princeton University Press, 1983), 25. See further Kathy Eden's illuminating essay in this volume.

[54] Essex is an important connection between the two works as well. So admired by Gentili that Gentili asked Essex to be godfather and namesake to his son, Robert, Essex also appears in *Henry V* in the Chorus's allusion to his 1599 campaign in Ireland. Of Act 5's comparison of Henry to 'the general of our gracious empress, / ... from Ireland coming, / Bringing rebellion broached on his sword', Gary Taylor writes that it is 'the only explicit, extra-dramatic, incontestable reference to a contemporary event anywhere in the canon'. See Gary Taylor, 'Introduction', in *Henry V* (Oxford: Oxford University Press, 1982), 7. Essex himself had published a manual for soldiers entitled *Lawes and Orders of Warre Established for the Good Conduct of the Service in Ireland* (1599), and the play's emphasis on discipline in the camps gives reason to think that Shakespeare drew from that work as well.

Critical receptions of *Henry V* leave little doubt that Shakespeare successfully created an artefact prompting judgement. What just about everyone knows by now about Shakespeare's *Henry V* is that it is a play 'virtually daring us to choose one of the two opposed interpretations it requires of us'.[55] *Henry V*, it is said, makes a 'double assertion';[56] there's an 'eloquent discrepancy between the glamor of the play's rhetoric and the reality of its action';[57] *Henry V* is 'not ... able to decide between an optimistic and a pessimistic model';[58] it is 'schizophrenic';[59] it traffics in the 'breaches' between heroism and antiheroism.[60] It exhibits 'disillusioned ambivalence' and creates 'rival gestalts'.[61] Careful readers have long seen how the play lends itself to debates such as that staged in Washington, DC in 2004, at which Iraq war opponents including Arianna Huffington faced off over *Henry V* with Iraq war supporters including Christopher Hitchens and neoconservative writer Kenneth Adelman, the latter already notorious for declaring George W. Bush a new Henry V and the US invasion of Iraq a would-be 'cakewalk'.[62] In addition to suggesting how the play itself invites presentist application, such debates also indicate how difficult it is to reduce Henry to an idealized Christian warrior or to a purely Machiavellian imperialist. The play, it seems, will not speak mono-vocally as either apology or critique.

Henry's double order to kill the French prisoners is both the most famous and the most instructive example, for it highlights Shakespeare's interest in competing historiographies and their relations to case-making in international law. Aided by *apologia* by Fluellen and Gower, the play quite purposefully makes available the view that 'the King most worthily hath caused every soldier to cut his prisoner's throat'—this on the premise that the French had previously undertaken 'as arrant a piece of knavery ... as can be offert', attacking the English servant boys, which Fluellen—again sounding here much like Gentili—declares 'against the law of arms' (4.7.2–10). When next we meet Henry, later in the scene, he thunders, 'I was not angry since I came to France / Until this instant'

55 Norman Rabkin, 'Rabbits, Ducks, and *Henry V*', *SQ*, 28.3 (July, 1977): 279.

56 Pugliatti, *Shakespeare and the Just War Tradition*, 201.

57 Rabkin, 'Rabbits, Ducks, and *Henry V*', 292.

58 Paola Pugliatti, 'The Strange Tongues of *Henry V*', *The Yearbook of English Studies*, 23 (1993): 253.

59 Camerlingo, 'Henry V and the Just War: Shakespeare, Gentili and Machiavelli', 104.

60 Maurice Hunt, 'The "Breaches" of Shakespeare's The Life of King Henry the Fifth', *College Literature*, 41.4 (2014): 7–24.

61 Christopher Highley, *Shakespeare, Spenser, and the Crisis in Ireland* (Cambridge: Cambridge University Press, 2007), 135; Rabkin, 'Rabbits, Ducks, and *Henry V*', 296.

62 Bob Thompson, 'The King and We, Henry V's War Cabinet: Mock Debate at Shakespeare Theater Has Familiar Ring', *The Washington Post*, 18 May 2004. Of the many audiences who have noted 'uncanny parallels' between George W. Bush and Shakespeare's Henry V, particularly following the Iraq War, most if not all have missed a critical point: the neoconservative effort to promote another Iraq war involved flattering George W. Bush into similitude with Henry V. As indicated by Ken Adelman's comparison in November 1999, the neoconservative effort was already underway well before 11 September 2001. That the invasion of Iraq would eventually come to resemble the invasion of France wasn't just an uncanny repetition of the Shakespearean narrative but the outcome of Iraq hawks' successful presentist campaign to mould the Bush presidency. See Ken Adelman, 'Not Lady Macbeth: Washington's Full of Shakespeare Characters', *Washingtonian Magazine*, 1 November 1999.

(4.7.53–4). He shortly declares, 'we'll cut the throats of those we have, / And not a man of them that we shall take / Shall taste our mercy' (4.7.61–3). Excellent lieutenants, Gower and Fluellen have already prepared the preferred audience response.

The seriousness with which Gower and Fluellen treat the attack on the servant boys makes Henry's retaliation appear proportional, comprehensible—indeed, right. Condren, for whom the dominant critical view of 'creative ambiguation' remains historically implausible, sides with Henry and his encomiasts, expressing it thus: 'tit for tat … not to take revenge would provide precedent for the acceptability of such baggage train murder in the future'.[63] The problem, as several critics have pointed out, is that Henry in the previous scene has *already* commanded that 'every solder kill his prisoners' following the realization that 'The French have reinforced their scattered men' (4.6.36–7). In other words, Henry *twice* declares his intention that the prisoners be killed—the first time *before* he's heard that the boys have been attacked—before he's even grown angry, and that on his own account. The Gower and Fluellen exchange that follows Henry's harsh order masks the fundamental chronology. Henry commits war crime according the first version, lawful retaliation in the second. The order to kill the prisoners occurs the first time as tragedy, the second time as law.

Nor is the order to kill the prisoners the play's only invitation for juridical thinking about the international past. Gadfly soldier Michael Williams introduces the fraught question of whether Henry's 'cause be not good', where 'cause' straddles meanings that include Henry's internal motivation but also, more to the point, his legal case (4.1.133).[64] Henry's is a legal case in the same general sense that warfare was 'arbitrament of swords', trial by battle (4.1.59). But the cause or case here is grounded in particularities, and mediated by Canterbury's putatively charitable 'reading' of the Salic law (1.2.14). When Henry invites Canterbury to 'justly and religiously unfold / Why the law Salic that they have in France / Or should or should not bar us in our claim', his invitation remains coloured by the possibility that his true intent is a legal whitewash (1.2.10–12). Canterbury's long discourse on the *casus belli* prompts Henry to cut to the chase: 'May I with right and conscience make this claim?' (1.2.96). Canterbury assuages Henry's apparent scruples even more vigorously than might be expected: 'The sin upon *my* head, dread sovereign!' (1.2.97, emphasis mine). If the play does little to extinguish the (juridical) suspicion that the war was cooked up as a pretext 'to busy giddy minds / With foreign quarrels', exactly as Henry's father had advised (*2 Henry IV*, 4.5.213–14), it does even less to deter a conclusion of priestly collusion. Henry may be enforcing a rightful claim, akin to filing suit, yet he may also have found in the prelates' tainted interests a convenient vehicle for his own. Equally ripe for legal inquiry is the oration at Harfleur's gates, which remains artfully poised between wise tactics and savage threats. It may be 'almost impossible to render any clear verdict on where Shakespeare stands' on Henry's criminality, as John

[63] Condren, 'Understanding Shakespeare's Perfect Prince', 195, 203.

[64] On *causa* as motive, see Lorna Hutson, *Circumstantial Shakespeare* (Oxford: Oxford University Press, 2015). Hutson's *The Invention of Suspicion* (Oxford: Oxford University Press, 2007) beautifully underlines the connection between literary character and legal suspicion alluded to below.

Sutherland puts it, but it is critical to notice the literary techniques that invite interpreters, even within the play itself, to try.[65]

Drawing Gentili more fully into this account, we can observe that, like *Henry V, De armis Romanis* frustrates the search for clear doctrine, and as such, has been difficult to assimilate into narrow histories of international law. Yet its genre tells an even richer story about the history of international law by showing how early modern writers placed the past under legal analysis, stitching together two ideas about time under the logic of the *causa* or case. The 1599 *De armis Romanis libri duo* was comprised of two books, the *Actio* (accusation), part of which had been published in 1590 as *De injustitia bellica Romanorum actio*, and a new second part, the *Defensio* (defence). Each of the two books is written in a separate *persona*, and while one of Gentili's voices necessarily has the last word, neither receives sanction from an overarching authorial voice.[66] Beyond the dedication to Essex, Gentili includes no authorial commentary *in propria persona*. Instead, a prosecutorial voice in the *Actio* arraigns the Roman empire for greed, deceit, war crimes, and unjust wars, after which Rome's advocate in the *Defensio* defends the wars of the Romans from the first book's charges chapter by chapter, point by point. In a representative passage, Book One insists 'The Romans wanted everything around them to lie open to themselves alone, and they brought this about by means of every possible crime.'[67] Book Two's replies yield nothing: 'our empire ... was sought out by just arms and preserved by just laws'.[68] Richard Tuck comments that the successive humanist disputations of *De armis Romanis* 'leave [...] the reader rather unclear about where the author stood', which, at the very least, should cast doubt on Condren's claim that an ambiguous Henry is historically implausible.[69] Yet the shared grounds of debate in Gentili's 'forensic drama' are instructive as well.[70] According to the editors of a recent English translation, 'Both the indictment of Roman imperialism in Book 1 of *The Wars of the Romans* and its defense in Book 2 are predicated on the assumption that it is apposite to judge the expansion of the Roman empire by way of warfare according to

[65] Sutherland and Watts, *Henry V, War Criminal?*, 110. To put the point in Keatsian terms, Shakespeare's famous 'negative capability' arises precisely at the moment of legal determination.

[66] Scholars including Diego Panizza and myself have found hints of the second book in Gentili's *De iure belli*, but David Lupher offers compelling qualifications. Diego Panizza, 'Alberico Gentili's *De armis Romanis*: The Roman Model of the Just Empire', in *The Roman Foundations of the Law of Nations: Alberico Gentili and the Justice of Empire*, ed. Benedict Kingsbury and Benjamin Straumann (Oxford: Oxford University Press, 2011), 53–84; Christopher N. Warren, 'Gentili, the Poets, and the Laws of War,' in *The Roman Foundations of the Law of Nations: Alberico Gentili and the Justice of Empire*, ed. Benedict Kingsbury and Benjamin Straumann (New York: Oxford University Press, 2011); David Lupher, 'The *De armis Romanis* and the Exemplum of Roman Imperialism', in *The Roman Foundations of the Law of Nations: Alberico Gentili and the Justice of Empire*, ed. Benedict Kingsbury and Benjamin Straumann (Oxford: Oxford University Press, 2011), 85–100.

[67] Gentili, *De armis Romanis*, 111.

[68] Gentili, *De armis Romanis*, 355.

[69] Tuck, *The Rights of War and Peace: Political Thought and the International Order from Grotius to Kant*, 17.

[70] Panizza, 'Alberico Gentili's *De armis Romanis*: The Roman Model of the Just Empire', 59.

certain moral normative criteria—indeed, denying or affirming the justice of the Roman empire is precisely what the *Wars of the Romans* is all about.'[71] The dedication of 1590's *De injustitia bellica Romanorum actio* advertised that Gentili 'in this *actio* ... wished to treat of the rulings of the law ... and to make a disputation about the injustice of which the Roman people seems to be accused'.[72] International events up to two thousand years old came under Gentili's juridical scrutiny. As early as 1590, and then again in expanded form in 1599, Elizabethan readers had a formidable legal apparatus to assess relations among war, crime, and historiography.

Indeed, the first book's critique of empire hinged as much on historiography as on law. Gentili's *actor* (plaintiff) begins with a chapter-length assertion that 'The Truth of Roman History is Tainted.'[73] While Book 2, by contrast, defends a sanitized Roman history, insisting on what Shakespeare's Fluellen calls the 'pristine wars of the Romans' (3.3.26–7), the first book ensures that perspectives like Fluellen's will seem naively credulous. In Act 4, Scene 1 Fluellen, at his most 'pedantic', tells Gower,[74]

> It is the greatest admiration [i.e. astonishment] of the universal world, when the true and ancient prerogatifs and laws of the wars is not kept. If you would take the pains but to examine the wars of Pompey the Great, you shall find, I warrant you, that there is no tiddle-taddle nor pibble-babble in Pompey's camp. I warrant you, you shall find the ceremonies of the wars, and the cares of it, and the forms of it, and the sobriety of it, and the modesty of it, to be otherwise. (4.1.67–75)

Henry, disguised, overhears the exchange, and admits that it 'appear[s] a little out of fashion', but he finds 'much care and valor in this Welshman', a view the plot goes on to endorse when Fluellen's 'Welsh correction' teaches the nativist Pistol 'a good English condition' (4.1.83–4, 5.1.74–5). But Gentili's first book gives ample historical warrant to read Henry and Fluellen as complicit in using law and history for overblown claims of imperial virtue. Fleullen's is a past that makes normative claims on the present, and Henry notices. He tolerates it, however, because anachronism helps keep order in the camps.[75] Fluellen, whose interest in 'a few disputations ... partly touching or concerning ... the Roman wars' again marks him as a reader of Gentili, has convinced some readers of his 'rigid adherence to law and precedent', but Shakespeare's dominant interest appears instead to be connecting Fluellen's type of legal historiography with self-justifying imperial aims (3.2.39–41).[76] 'That the Roman people was holy, that the Roman

[71] Benedict Kingsbury and Benjamin Straumann, 'Introduction: Roman Wars and Roman Laws', in *The Wars of the Romans: A Critical Edition and Translation of De armis Romanis* (New York: Oxford University Press, 2011), xi.

[72] Gentili, *De armis Romanis*, 361.

[73] Gentili, *De armis Romanis*, 150.

[74] Pugliatti, 'The Strange Tongues of *Henry V*', 249.

[75] 'Zealous justification' must not be mistaken for 'historical trustworthiness' according to Gentili, *De armis Romanis*, 127.

[76] Camille Wells Slights, 'The Conscience of the King: Henry V and the Reformed Conscience', *PQ*, 80.1 (2001): 53.

people was beautiful, that the Roman people was invincible, and that the Roman people flourished with every sort of excellence', Gentili's *actor* admonishes, 'this and other stuff of that sort, we have imbibed with the most attentive eyes, and drawn by the semblance of the authors' consummate erudition and seduced by their soothing speech, we have taken it on trust and been deceived by it.'[77] In such cases, historiography has been little more than encomiastic poetry.

Poetry itself, meanwhile, has been improperly taken for truth. Poetic flights of the kind mimicked to the point of parody by *Henry V*'s Chorus, ensured 'an excellence became believed that in fact lay far from true excellence—very far indeed, for if we pay attention to the praised hero's actual doings ... we do not stand stupefied and amazed at the praises.'[78] Here we can return to Shakespeare's distinctive interest in 'dramatizing rather than concealing ... the literary act which re-creates the event'—the spirit too of Gentili's first book. If Roman poets, according to Book 1, 'wrote of ... deeds in such a way as to pass over disasters', Shakespeare uses the Chorus to translate the politics and contingency of historiography into a formal register in which acts of *passing over* cannot be overlooked. When the Chorus says in the prologue, ''tis *your* thoughts that now must deck our kings, / Carry them here and there, jumping o'er times', the lines manufacture a sense of disequilibrium, creating both a surplus of event-ness and also a lack (28–9, emphasis mine). History is too big to be reduced to a single play and the present is too short to reproduce history: through the serial mediations of the Chorus, audiences are asked to perceive too much history and not enough *now*. If stupefaction in the face of quietly sanitized history here opens into the jurisdiction of the sceptical interpreter, it does so in part by freeing Shakespeare's Henry from the strictly historical register and translating him into a self-consciously contemporaneous forum where he is visibly remade and judged anew.

Henry V's hints of priestly collusion in an unjust war echo Gentili's third chapter of Book One, where he addresses the history of the Roman fetial priests, the religious order responsible for promulgating and transmitting the fetial laws, the Roman laws of war. The story Gentili recounts is that of Ancus, who 'censured his predecessors because he is said to have seen that the Roman people was passionate with love for wars and ready to inflict war upon peoples when there was no just cause, and so he adopted the fetial laws ... as a remedy to this injustice.'[79] 'But are to we call it a remedy—or rather a sticking plaster or rouge?', writes the accuser. He quotes one of his favourite sources, the church father Lactantius, saying, 'Just how far the utility stands from justice the Roman people itself teaches us, for by declaring wars through the fetial priests and imposing wrongs under the cover of law and by always craving and plundering other peoples' things they acquired for themselves possession of the entire world.'[80] The search for religious

[77] Gentili, *De armis Romanis*, 9.
[78] Gentili, *De armis Romanis*, 49.
[79] Gentili, *De armis Romanis*, 35.
[80] Gentili, *De armis Romanis*, 35.

justification returns in the sixth chapter of Book One, where the speaker denounces the 'religious excuses and subterfuges' underpinning Roman aggression.[81]

Irish, Welsh, and Scottish contexts that have long interested postcolonial critics of *Henry V*, and that animate several presentist critics, likewise grow even richer through Gentili's antithetical accounts of Roman empire.[82] Henry's proto-British army, which includes not only the Welsh Fluellen but the Scots Jamy and the Irish MacMorris, ensures that the dramatized past cannot be artificially cut off from the imperial concerns of the 1590s. Fleuellen, it's been observed, 'figures the colonial subject who has internalized English values and subordinated his own provincial loyalties to service to the English nation-state'.[83] If Fluellen 'represents the already safely assimilated Celt', the Irish and Scots warriors who have smaller roles remain satellites of English power.[84] The play's many allusions to Rome invite us see this dynamic in the context of imperial processes transhistorically applicable to Rome and the British archipelago. Both of Gentili's speakers agree that Rome was founded as a 'wide-open asylum ... for any and all of the most desperate men'.[85] Yet 'men diverse in language and discordant in customs' are a mark of opprobrium for the first speaker, a mark of honour for the second. The voice in the second book declares that 'Before long, men who had at first streamed together from various polities, diverse in languages, discordant in their manners, coalesced into one state through shared practices and language.'[86] The accuser instead speaks of a 'contagion' in which 'the process went one from one group of people to the next, and when whatever peoples were nearest had been seized, [the Romans] reduced all of Italy to [their] power'.[87] Even here, according to the critique, historiography intervenes, for the question wasn't whether the speaker should 'mention other Italian peoples oppressed by the unjust arms of the Romans' but 'how'. The difficulty was precisely the one Shakespeare highlights with his Chorus—the gaps that inhibit secure historical knowledge. 'Placed as we are at such a remote distance in time, we can only know the misdeeds of the Romans through those who have praised the Romans.'[88] A character

[81] Gentili, *De armis Romanis*, 53.

[82] For Celtic contexts, see Lorna Hutson's essay in this volume and, *inter alia*, Philip Schwyzer, '"I Am Welsh, You Know?": The Nation in *Henry V*', in *Literature, Nationalism, and Memory in Early Modern England and Wales* (Cambridge: Cambridge University Press, 2004); David J. Baker, '"Wildehirissheman": Colonialist Representation in Shakespeare's *Henry V*', *ELR*, 22.1 (December, 1992): 37–61; Highley, *Shakespeare, Spenser, and the Crisis in Ireland*. On presentism and contemporary questions of devolution, see Hawkes, *Shakespeare in the Present*, 4, 23–65. On postcolonialism as presentism 'in principle if not in name', see Hugh Grady and Terence Hawkes, 'Introduction: Presenting Presentism', in *Presentist Shakespeares* (New York: Routledge, 2007), 5.

[83] Highley, *Shakespeare, Spenser, and the Crisis in Ireland*, 147.

[84] Richard Dutton, '"Methinks the Truth Should Live from Age to Age': The Dating and Contexts of *Henry V*', *HLQ*, 68.1–2 (2005): 194.

[85] Gentili, *De armis Romanis*, 19.

[86] Gentili, *De armis Romanis*, 135.

[87] Gentili, *De armis Romanis*, 163. See further Lupher, 'The *De armis Romanis* and the Exemplum of Roman Imperialism', 92–3.

[88] Gentili, *De armis Romanis*, 59.

like Fluellen on this reading is 'safely assimilated', but his subaltern praises of Henry speak doubly as admiration and critique.

CONCLUSION

I have been suggesting that Gentili's *De armis Romanis* offers insights into several of the formal features of Shakespeare's play and that Shakespeare and Gentili engaged in a common project of transforming events of empire, whose role was to be narrated, into cases of empire, whose function was to be judged. Accepting Anne Orford's insight that international legal method is fundamentally the 'art of making meaning move across time,' I have aimed to illuminate the contingent historicity of that art by attending to early modern writers' own strategies for maintaining traffic between past and present in the face of an emerging historicism.[89] Far from presenting the past as impervious to legal analysis, Shakespeare and Gentili deployed genres that charged the past with juridical salience, preserving an association between international history and 'juridical thinking' and contributing to a distinctive historicism within international law.[90] Not only is it legitimate to ask whether Henry was a war criminal; it is historically appropriate to do so.

This account still leaves many questions unanswered, but the one with which I propose to conclude is this: why would the question of war crimes in *Henry V* seem anachronistic in the first place? My answer concerns a second type of international legal historiography distinct from the Renaissance philosophy of history newly revived in critical legal history. As scholars including Martii Koskenniemi and Mark Mazower have shown, progressivist nineteenth-century legal historiography has profoundly influenced perceptions of the international past.[91] History, as Kant put it in a 1784 essay, had a cosmopolitan purpose. Successive thinkers, invested as Kant was in various contrasts between civility and barbarousness, engaged in a highly political project intended to formalize international legal rules and to unify disparate legalities. Figures from Robert Ward in 1795 to Henry Sumner Maine in 1887 drew energy for contemporary projects by positing a barbarous history soon to be overcome.[92] Victories, including the Geneva Conventions of 1864, and Hague Convention of 1899, were won in part as Whiggish advocates presented 'a history of the slow coming to consciousness of the unity of the law as a reflection of humanity's moral identity'.[93] New institutions were

89 Orford, 'On International Legal Method', 172.

90 Orford, 'On International Legal Method', 166.

91 Martti Koskenniemi, *The Gentle Civilizer of Nations: The Rise and Fall of Modern International Law, 1870–1960* (New York: Cambridge University Press, 2001); Mark Mazower, *Governing the World: The History of an Idea* (New York: Penguin Press, 2012), 65–94.

92 Martti Koskenniemi, 'A History of International Law Histories', in *The Oxford Handbook of the History of International Law*, ed. Bardo Fassbender and Anne Peters (Oxford: Oxford University Press, 2012), 943–71.

93 Koskenniemi, 'A History of International Law Histories', 959.

proposed as remedies to what one writer called the 'bloody and savage customs of the Middle Ages'.[94]

Like Fleuellen and Henry, nineteenth-century historians of international law profaned the past by making it serve present needs, yet their error wasn't anachronism but the equal and opposite one for which we have no name. Any difficulty critics have in recognizing war crimes in Shakespeare—indeed thinking about international law in the early modern period more broadly—follows in no small part from rarely examined suppositions about international history and its relation to international law.

Bibliography

Bodin, Jean. *Method for the Easy Comprehension of History*, trans. Beatrice Reynolds (New York: W. W. Norton and Co., 1969).

Camerlingo, Rosanna. 'Henry V and the Just War: Shakespeare, Gentili and Machiavelli', in *Machiavellian Encounters in Tudor and Stuart England: Literary and Political Influences from the Reformation to the Restoration*, ed. Alessandro Arienzo and Alessandra Petrina (Burlington: Ashgate, 2013), 103–19.

Condren, Conal. 'Understanding Shakespeare's Perfect Prince: Henry V, the Ethics of Office and the French Prisoners', in *The Shakespearean International Yearbook* 9, ed. Graham Bradshaw, Tom Bishop, and Laurence Wright (Burlington: Ashgate, 2009), 195–213.

Fasolt, Constantin. *The Limits of History* (Chicago: University of Chicago Press, 2004).

Gajowski, Evelyn. 'Beyond Historicism: Presentism, Subjectivity, Politics', *Literature Compass*, 7.8 (2010): 674–91.

Gentili, Alberico. *The Wars of the Romans: A Critical Edition and Translation of "De armis Romanis"*, ed. Benedict Kingsbury and Benjamin Straumann, trans. David Lupher (New York: Oxford University Press, 2011).

Gordon, Gregory S. 'The Trial of Peter von Hagenbach: Reconciling History, Historiography, and International Criminal Law', in *The Hidden Histories of War Crimes Trials*, ed. Kevin Heller and Gerry Simpson (Oxford: Oxford University Press, 2013), 13–49.

Hawkes, Terence. *Shakespeare in the Present* (London and New York: Routledge, 2003).

Hutson, Lorna. 'Imagining Justice: Kantorowicz and Shakespeare', *Representations*, 106.1 (May, 2009): 118–42.

Koskenniemi, Martti. 'Vitoria and Us: Thoughts on Critical Histories of International Law', *Rechtsgeschichte Legal History—Zeitschrift Des Max-Planck-Instituts Für Europäische Rechtsgeschichte*, 22 (2014): 119–38.

Meron, Theodor. *Henry's Wars and Shakespeare's Laws: Perspectives on the Law of War in the Later Middle Ages* (Oxford: Oxford University Press, 1993).

Orford, Anne. 'The Past as Law or History?: The Relevance of Imperialism for Modern International Law', *International Law and Justice Working Papers* 2 (2012).

Orford, Anne. 'On International Legal Method', *London Review of International Law*, 1.1 (September, 2013): 166–97.

Parfitt, Rose. 'The Spectre of Sources', *European Journal of International Law*, 25.1 (February, 2014): 297–306.

[94] Quoted in Koskenniemi, 'A History of International Law Histories', 952.

Pugliatti, Paola. *Shakespeare and the Just War Tradition* (Burlington: Ashgate, 2010).
Rousso, Henry. *The Haunting Past: History, Memory, and Justice in Contemporary France*, trans. Ralph Schoolcraft (Philadelphia: University of Pennsylvania Press, 2002).
Schwarzenberger, Georg. *International Law as Applied by International Courts and Tribunals: The Law of Armed Conflict*, 2 vols (London: Stevens, 1968).
Stevens, Paul. 'The New Presentism and Its Discontents: Listening to "Eastward Ho" and Shakespeare's "Tempest" in Dialogue', in *Rethinking Historicism from Shakespeare to Milton*, ed. Ann Baynes Coiro and Thomas Fulton (Cambridge: Cambridge University Press, 2012), 133–58.
Sutherland, John, and Cedric Thomas Watts. *Henry V, War Criminal?: And Other Shakespeare Puzzles* (Oxford: Oxford University Press, 2000).
Tuck, Richard. *The Rights of War and Peace: Political Thought and the International Order from Grotius to Kant* (Oxford: Oxford University Press, 1999).

CHAPTER 37

EMPIRE AND NATURAL LAW IN DRYDEN'S HEROIC DRAMA

EDWARD HOLBERTON

I

ACCORDING to Dryden's preface to *The Conquest of Granada*, the hero of that play, Almanzor, is modelled on Achilles.[1] When Almanzor first bursts into Granada's wars, he is indeed full of angry disdain, but he channels it through questions about the origins of King Boabdelin's sovereignty.

Almanz. No man has more contempt than I, of breath;
But whence hast thou the right to give me death?
Obey'd as Soveraign by thy Subjects be,
But know, that I alone am King of me.
I am as free as Nature first made man
'Ere the base Laws of Servitude began
When wild in woods the noble Savage ran.
Boab. Since, then, no pow'r above your own you know,
Mankind shou'd use you like a common foe,
You shou'd be hunted like a Beast of Prey;
By your own law, I take your life away.
Almanz. My laws are made but only for my sake,
No King against himself a Law can make.
If thou pretendst to be a Prince like me,
Blame not an Act which should thy Pattern be.
I saw th' opprest, and thought it did belong

[1] *The Works of John Dryden*, ed. H. T. Swedenberg, Jr, et al., 20 vols (Berkeley: University of California Press, 1956–2000), 11.14.

To a King's office to redress the wrong:
I brought that Succour which thou oughtst to bring,
And so, in Nature, am thy Subjects King. (1.1.1.203–21)

Almanzor's sense of his own heroic autonomy is based on reasoning so artificial that it approaches comedy. The idea that 'Laws of servitude' have supplanted an original, 'free', natural state points to a basis in contractualist theories of government. Such theories hold that individuals first existed in a state of natural freedom, but then—for reasons of innate sociability, or self-interest, depending on the theory—they agree to adhere to social institutions and government.[2] Readers quickly identified Almanzor with Hobbes's theory of sovereignty, albeit skewed into the kind of interpretation which was identified as 'Hobbian' (or 'Hobbist') at the time, because it tended to idealize and privilege the freedoms that Hobbes's natural man would surrender.[3] For Hobbes, the condition of nature is characterized as a restless and 'savage' freedom, but the laws of nature lead individuals to make a contract of sovereignty, in which natural liberty is exchanged for the security of subjection under positive laws.[4] Almanzor's Hobbist twist is to claim that the condition of nature is more noble. He alleges that he has never agreed to any surrender of natural liberty, and if not a subject, he retains a natural sovereignty over himself, and can even claim to be the truly natural sovereign over Boabdelin's people, being more able to protect them from one another.

Part of the reason why Almanzor became a notorious character on the Restoration stage is because his challenges to Boabdelin resonate with—and seem very near to satire of—the spread of this way of thinking about states and sovereignty across different cultural spheres. Dryden worked in Cromwell's diplomatic office, so he would have been familiar with controversies about sovereignty and natural law. Grotius's discussion of the natural law arguments of the school of Salamanca, for example, were key to diplomacy around the Protectorate's conflicts with the United Provinces and

[2] Victoria Kahn, *Wayward Contracts: The Crisis of Political Obligation in England, 1640–1674* (Princeton: Princeton University Press, 2004), 11; Richard Tuck, *The Rights of War and Peace: Political Thought and the International Order from Grotius to Kant* (New York: Oxford University Press, 1999), 96–102.

[3] Richard Leigh, *The Censure of the Rota on Mr. Driden's Conquest of Granada* (Oxford: 1673), 3; Jon Parkin, *Taming the Leviathan: The Reception of the Political and Religious Ideas of Thomas Hobbes in England, 1640–1700* (Cambridge: Cambridge University Press, 2007), 302–3; Anna Battigelli, 'John Dryden's Angry Readers', in *Books and Readers in Early Modern England: Material Studies*, ed. Jennifer Lotte Andersen and Elizabeth Sauer (Philadelphia: University of Pennsylvania Press, 2002), 267. For 'Hobbism' and its influence, see also Christopher Tilmouth, *Passion's Triumph Over Reason* (Oxford: Oxford University Press, 2007), 257–314; and Warren Chernaik *Sexual Freedom in Restoration Literature* (Cambridge: Cambridge University Press, 1995), 22–52.

[4] Thomas Hobbes, *Leviathan*, ed. Richard Tuck (Cambridge: Cambridge University Press, 1991), 89–92.

Spain.[5] Dryden's early heroic drama shows a repeated interest in theories of sovereignty, and in so doing, it shows continuities with speculative theoretical discussions conducted between Davenant and Hobbes in the 1650s about the relationship between law, heroic poetry, and theatre. But the development of Dryden's engagement with such theories, between *The Indian Emperour* (1665) and *The Conquest of Granada* (1670–1671), also reveals the ways in which his writing was stimulated by what Gary De Krey calls 'the first Restoration crisis'. After the humiliations of the second Anglo-Dutch war, contractual arguments about natural law and sovereignty moved from discussions of civil philosophy and international law, into debates about religious toleration, and the vocabulary of libertinism.[6] They framed new ways of reading epic and discussing heroic values, but they also came under suspicion.[7] *The Conquest of Granada* most captures the energy of its moment when—as seen in Almanzor's challenge to Boabdelin—the heroic genres of epic and romance collide with, and form an unstable compound with, this way of thinking about sovereignty. The hero's rhetorical excesses, which have divided critical responses to the play down the years, point to the contested role of heroic emulation in contemporary discussions of sovereignty. Dryden places these excesses in a suggestive tension with the kinds of critical interpretation and judgement that are promoted by courtly and theatrical culture. *The Conquest of Granada* implies that theatre might play a constructive role in taming some of Restoration culture's most disturbing questions about the origins and limits of sovereign power.

The Indian Emperour, a sequel to *The Indian Queen* (1664) co-written with Robert Howard, represents the conquest of the Aztecs by the Spanish under the command of Hernán Cortés. Bridget Orr notes that one of the interesting features of Dryden's heroic plays is the way that they addressed Spanish imperial themes exactly at the moment when foreign policy was turning away from the Anglo-Spanish Atlantic conflict of the later 1650s, and towards renewed rivalries with the United Provinces and France.[8] In the history of Spain, and the expansion of its empire, Dryden found rich materials

[5] Paul Hammond, *John Dryden: A Literary Life* (London: Macmillan, 1991), 16; David Armitage, *The Ideological Origins of the British Empire* (Cambridge: Cambridge University Press, 2000), 88, 100–24. Among the books purchased by the Swedish diplomat Peter Julius Coyet in London in the mid-1650s were volumes by Grotius and Selden on natural law and the sovereignty of the sea. See *Swedish Diplomats at Cromwell's Court, 1655–1656: The Missions of Peter Julius Coyet and Christer Bonde*, ed. Michael Roberts (London: Royal Historical Society, 1988), 5.

[6] For the growing cultural importance of Grotius's arguments about the freedom of the seas during 1650s and 1660s, see Armitage, *Ideological Origins*, 100–24, and the detailed reference to Grotius's dispute with Selden in anti-Dutch satire of this period: (for example) Edmund Gayton, *The Lawyer's Duel, or Two Sonnets Composed on Grotius's Mare Liberum and Selden's Mare Clausum* [London?: s.n., 1655]; Elkanah Settle, *Mare clausum: Or A Ransack for the Dutch* (London: 1666); Andrew Marvell, *The Character of Holland* (London: 1665). For the late 1660s resurgence of natural jurisprudence in cultural debate, see Parkin, *Taming*, 239; and Gary S. De Krey, 'The First Restoration Crisis: Conscience and Coercion in London: 1667–73', *Albion*, 25 (1993): 565–80, 571n.

[7] Christopher Warren, 'John Milton and the Epochs of International Law', *European Journal of International Law*, 24 (2013): 557–81, 558; Parkin, *Taming*, 239.

[8] Bridget Orr, *Empire on the English Stage, 1660–1714* (Cambridge: Cambridge University Press, 2001), 135.

through which to examine England's own broadening imperial horizons. Arguments about Spain's rights in, and infringements of, the law of nature and nations had long since been familiar elements in anti-Spanish propaganda, and had been rehearsed in the 1650s.[9] *The Indian Emperour* experiments with the dramatic potential of these materials, sensationalizing the flaws in Spain's claims to empire, and testing the ability of an emerging language of international law to project a sense of national difference based not so much on religious difference, but on the superiority of England's claims to empire and colonial practice; these were timely experiments in the heroic mode, because with Anglo-Dutch conflict looming, England's wars could no longer be celebrated as Protestant wars.

Orr shows that two legal 'donations' are at stake in *The Indian Emperour*: the donation of the Americas to the sovereigns of Castile in the Alexandrine Bulls of 1493–1494, and the donation of sovereignty which the historical Cortés claimed to have received directly from the Aztec king Montezuma in 1519.[10] Thus when Dryden's Montezuma asks by what authority Charles V claims suzerainty, Pizarro answers that the 'Soveraign Priest ... Has this your Empire to our Monarch given' (1.2.282–4). The Spanish have arrived with an evangelical mission (the Alexandrine Bulls awarded *dominium* over lands discovered on the westward route to Asia, on condition that the indigenous inhabitants of those lands were converted).[11] But in a departure from Dryden's source for the dialogue of this scene, Montaigne's essay 'Of Coaches', Montezuma challenges this claim with a distinction drawn from legal challenges to the Alexandrine Bulls: 'He who Religion truely understands / Knows its extent must be in Men, not Lands' (1.2.297–8).[12] The confrontations which begin here turn on the dubious legitimacy of distributing property on the basis of Papal jurisdiction.

As Anthony Pagden, David Armitage, and other intellectual historians of empire have shown, theoretical discussion of international law had been stimulated by debates about legal claims to sovereignty in the new world. European sovereigns struggled to square the two kinds of legal title that were needed together to legitimize colonization: *imperium* (jurisdiction) and *dominium* (territory). Few jurists by the seventeenth century accepted that the Bulls offered a satisfactory basis for *dominium* (although they continued to be cited in support of Spanish claims to empire, because they created a continuity between Spain and the Roman empire via the Donation of Constantine).[13] If the Pope's claim to jurisdiction over a people (*imperium*) could be used to dispossess them

[9] See, for example, *A Declaration of His Highnes, by the Advice of his Council Setting Forth, on the Behalf of this Commonwealth, the Justice of Their Cause against Spain* (London: 1655)

[10] Orr, *Empire*, 144; also see J. H. Elliott, *Empires of the Atlantic World*, 5, 11, 22–3; also his 'The Mental World of Hernán Cortés', in *Spain and Its World, 1500–1700: Selected Essays* (New Haven: Yale University Press, 1989), 27–41, 36–8; Hernán Cortés, *Letters from Mexico*, trans. and ed. Anthony Pagden (New Haven: Yale University Press, 1986), 85–6, 98–9.

[11] Elliott, *Empires*, 19.

[12] Dryden, *Works*, 9.312–13.

[13] Anthony Pagden, *Lords of All the World: Ideologies of Empire in Spain, Britain and France c.1500–c.1850* (New Haven: Yale University Press, 1995), 32.

of their property in land (*dominium*), then the radical 'Calvinist theory of revolution', which held that *dominium* was dependent upon grace, was but a short step on from this claim, and might be used to dispossess anybody who was not thought to be one of the elect.[14] Montezuma grasps this implication straight away, and identifies Pizarro's claim as a doctrine which will only 'nourish ... debate' (1.2.286). This is a key instance where Dryden offers an implicit contrast with English colonial practice, because the distinction between claims to *imperium* and *dominium* became the usual point of departure for English claims to a different conception of empire: the 1669 Fundamental Constitutions of Carolina, for example, in which Locke had a hand, were clear on this issue: 'but since the natives of that place, who will be concerned in our plantations, are utterly strangers to Christianity, whose idolatry, ignorance or mistake gives us no right to expel or use them ill'.[15] By the Restoration, mainstream English legal thought on the subject tended to argue that only land which could be deemed 'unoccupied' could be legitimately appropriated.[16] In *The Indian Emperour*, Montezuma is as compromised a figure as Cortez, and sometimes lets his passions cloud his reason. But here however, like a shrewd jurist, he immediately spots the logical leap, and the dangerous consequences implicit in the Alexandrine Bulls.

A second Spanish claim to colonial sovereignty had been found necessary.[17] In his letters, Cortés claimed to have received on behalf of Charles V the *imperium* of Mexico through another donation, this time from Montezuma. In the version of this account known to English readers through the collections of Purchas, Montezuma persuades Aztec assembly-members to 'yeelde themselves Vassals to the Emperour'.[18] By contrast, Dryden's Cortez repeatedly attempts to secure such a donation, but the Aztec royals reject Spanish suzerainty, even having suffered irreversible defeat. Montezuma's heir Guyomar chooses rather to go into exile than rule as tributary king. As he does so, he undermines another claim on behalf of the Spanish empire in the Americas, that the Spanish have now effected a title to empire through conquest:

Cort. Live, and enjoy more then your Conquerour:
Take all my Love, and share in all my power.
Guy. Think me not proudly rude, if I forsake
Those Gifts I cannot with my Honour take:
I for my Country Fought, and would again,
Had I yet left a Country to maintain:
But since the Gods decreed it otherwise,
I never will on its dear Ruines rise. (5.2.356–63)

14 Pagden, *Lords of All the World*, 48–9; Armitage, *Ideological Origins*, 91–2.

15 John Locke, *Political Essays*, ed. Mark Goldie (Cambridge: Cambridge University Press, 1997), 178.

16 Orr, *Empire*, 154.

17 Orr, *Empire*, 144–8; Pagden, *Lords of all the World*, 51.

18 Cortés's claim that Montezuma acknowledged Spanish sovereignty is reproduced in one of Dryden's widely-known sources for the play, the account of Cortés's exploits given in Samuel Purchas, *Purchas His Pilgrimes*, 4 vols (London: 1625), 3.1121.

Cortez and Guyomar stand before a kingdom which has been devastated by famine and a Spanish 'Massacre' (5.2.107–9). As Guyomar points out, there is little left of the Aztec 'Country' (a word that meant a people as well as a territory) to submit to Cortez; in the end, Guyomar leads the remnant of the Aztec aristocracy to begin a new colony, where there will be no mineral resources to attract the jealous eye of Spain. These Aztecs never submit to the Spanish conquest, preferring a desolate freedom to Spanish rule. The closing tribute of Cortez seals a series of bleak ironies:

> First your Great Father's Funeral Pomp provide:
> That done, in Peace your Generous Exiles guide;
> While I loud thanks pay to the powers above,
> Thus doubly Blest, with Conquest, and with Love. (5.2.376–9)

Having claimed a right to Aztec territory and its mineral resources on the basis of an *imperium* over people, Cortez is left with territory, but not those people whose submission and conversion might have supported that claim.[19] The Spanish conquest of the Aztec kingdom is emptied of legitimacy.

It is not only the conquistadors, however, who are morally ambiguous. The Aztecs' fraught relationship with natural law gives the play a moral tension that is absent from its Interregnum prototypes, and which transform complex legal debates into spectacular dramatic events and contests. An important question pertaining to the legality of Spanish colonization was whether Aztec and Inca civilizations understood and followed natural law, or whether the indigenes of the Americas were in fact Aristotle's 'natural slaves': barbarians who were born to serve, and—most pertinently in the context of colonization—were incapable of holding property.[20] The ethnographic materials available to English readers were often shaped, implicitly or explicitly, by this question, and both Davenant and Dryden exploited these materials. Davenant's *The Cruelty of the Spaniards in Peru*, for example, apparently draws on the Inca historian Garcilaso de la Vega, as it elegizes a communitarian Inca kingdom which is governed according to natural reason: 'Soft conscience, Nature's whisp'ring orator' (3.54) is the only law needed.[21]

[19] Anthony Pagden has argued that there was widespread suspicion, among English writers about empire, of claims to sovereignty based on rights of conquest; see his 'The Struggle for Legitimacy and the Image of Empire in the Atlantic to *c*.1700', in *The Origins of Empire: British Overseas Enterprise To The Close of the Seventeenth Century*, ed. Nicholas P. Canny (Oxford: Oxford University Press, 1998), 34–54, 40–1.

[20] Tuck, *Grotius to Kant*, 60–3, 73–4; Anthony Pagden, *The Fall of Natural Man: The American Indian and the Origins of Comparative Ethnology* (Cambridge: Cambridge University Press, 1982), 117. See also Elliott Visconsi, *Lines of Equity: Literature and the Origins of Law in Later Stuart England* (Ithaca: Cornell University Press, 2008), 48–9; and Mary Nyquist, *Arbitrary Rule: Slavery, Tyranny and the Power of Life and Death* (Chicago: University of Chicago Press, 2013).

[21] Janet Clare, ed., *Drama of the English Republic 1649–60* (Manchester: Manchester University Press, 2002), 241–61; Garcilaso de la Vega, *Royal Commentaries of the Incas, and General History of Peru*, trans. by Harold V. Livermore, 2 vols (Austin: University of Texas Press, 1966), 262–4.

The Indian Emperour sometimes suggests that the Aztecs have access to a similar 'natural' moral insight, but as the play develops, this idealization of the Aztec social order becomes more and more problematic. Orr draws attention to the way that romance elements of the plot—such as the love affair between Cortez and Cydaria—briefly diminish Euro-American difference, and hint at the possibility of reciprocity between Aztecs and Europeans. In this perspective, the failures of the Spanish gesture towards the possibility of a more just and free set of exchanges between England and those peoples of the New World to whom the English might bring religion and trade. Cortez at first resists the expectation that the Aztecs are a race 'untaught and savage', and idealizes their culture as closer to natural reason:

> Wild and untaught are terms which we alone
> Invent, for fashions differing from our own;
> For all their customs are by nature wrought,
> But we, by art, unteach what nature taught. (1.1.11–14)

But troubling details are soon introduced, which insist more forcefully on Euro-American difference.[22] The first of the Aztec customs to be presented combines something like an English May Queen celebration with mass human sacrifice.

As the Aztec heroes attempt to construe their obligations, they engage the audience in making some delicate judgements. Guyomar reasons-out his loyalties through natural law's fiction of an original contract of consent, which he likens to an irreversible marriage contract:

> But Kings by free consent their Kingdoms take,
> Strict as those Sacred Ties which Nuptials make;
> And what e'er faults in Princes time reveal,
> None can be Judge where can be no Appeal. (4.2.80–3)

Yet Montezuma in the next scene argues for the legitimacy of human sacrifice through a similar analogy between royal and personal rights, here between his duties as sovereign, and his 'natural' right to self-preservation:

> Nor call it Murder, when each private Man
> In his defence may justly do the same:
> But private persons more then Monarchs can:
> All weigh our Acts, and what e're seems unjust,
> Impute not to Necessity, but Lust. (4.3.46–50)

[22] Orr, *Empire*, 150–3.

Here Montezuma's skill is more ambiguous, and suggests the casuistry of a sovereign who is declining towards cruelty and savagery. It mirrors the tendency which Elliott Visconsi finds in the 'equity' falsely offered by the play's Spanish protagonists, who in fact merely ape and undermine the royal justice which they claim to represent, turning equity into a cover for mere violence and venality.[23] On the one hand, therefore, *The Indian Emperour* reveals Dryden experimenting with the dramatic potential of inherited ethnographic materials, and the theories of empire and natural law which had shaped them. His protagonists' dilemmas give the play its heroic scale by engaging the legal languages through which England's growing power and geopolitical influence were simultaneously being asserted. But on the other hand, Dryden leavens with sceptical irony a dramatic inheritance from Davenant which had idealized indigenous institutions in the name of Cromwell's neo-Elizabeth an foreign policy. For everyone in this play, Aztecs included, the contractarian logic of sovereignty can quickly become tortive and casuistical.

II

The tone of *The Conquest of Granada* has proved susceptible to very different readings: it has been argued that the play's elegant structure and psychological insights deserve to be taken seriously, but critics have also found irony and elements of satire in the stylized dialogue and sensational plotting.[24] Its tonal difficulty can be illuminated by the way in which Dryden's sceptical interest in natural law's construction of sovereignty took on new relevancies after the completion of *The Indian Emperour*, and the Restoration political order appeared to be threatened by questions like that demanded of Boabdelin by Almanzor at the opening of this essay. Like *The Indian Emperour, The Conquest of Granada* asks how empire is grounded in natural law, but the focus moves closer to home: it represents the foundation of Spain, but in terms that reflect upon the Restoration settlement too. The disappointments and renewed tensions of the late 1660s make themselves felt in this adjustment of focus: as figures that at first seem peripheral begin to unravel the sovereignty of Al-Andalus, *The Conquest of Granada* accurately captures the dangerous political energies of its moment.

Queen Isabel underlines the continuity between the action of *The Indian Emperour* and the progress of the *reconquista* when she prophecies that Columbus (who took part in the Battle of Granada) will shortly discover America and gold; but, she adds, it will be a greater triumph to see Granada 'to freedom and true faith restor'd: / Its old Religion, and its antient Lord' (2.1.1.26–7). This trajectory—from the territorial expansion of

[23] Visconsi, *Lines of Equity*, 52.

[24] Derek Hughes, *Dryden's Heroic Plays* (London: Macmillan, 1981), 79–117; Bruce King, *Dryden's Major Plays* (Edinburgh: Oliver and Boyd, 1966), 59–81.

empire to its cultural foundations—parallels the play's interrogation of sovereignty, and the re-emergence of debate about the toleration of religious dissent in the wake of the disastrous second Anglo-Dutch war. The war had aimed to damage Dutch navigation and trade in the Atlantic, but the humiliating outcome caused the collapse of the Clarendon regime. This upheaval gave religious dissenters opportunities to petition for (and buy) the support of the king.[25] Proponents of toleration including Slingsby Bethel and Sir Charles Wolseley argued that the vigour of Dutch trade was owed to the Dutch Republic's policies of religious toleration.[26] These arguments that the English should copy the Dutch in matters of ecclesiastical policy often analysed the problem through the natural law concept of an original social contract.[27] Wolseley argues that while forms of magistracy came about through such a contract ('a joynt-coalition and agreement of them, dictated by the Light of Nature for general good'), God at no point delegated to magistrates His sovereignty over the conscience; the magistrate's authority concerns the moral and political good only, and should leave the tender conscience unmolested.[28] The aftermath of the second Anglo-Dutch war saw natural law arguments about the limits of sovereign power reemerging in public debate.

The Conquest of Granada flags its relevance to Anglo-Dutch rivalry. Like Charles II, Boabdelin, the last king of Granada, struggles to raise money for war from his parliaments (2.1.2.31–4). When King Ferdinand of Aragon opens Part 2 of the play with the prediction that the empire of Al-Andalus will fall to the empire of Spain, his language suggests at once a classical conception of history as a cycle of empires succeeding each other, and emulative individuals elbowing one another out of the way:

> At length the time is come, when *Spain* shall be
> From the long Yoke of *Moorish* Tyrants free.
> All causes seem to second our design;
> And Heav'n and Earth in their destruction join.
> When Empire in its Childhood first appears,
> A watchful Fate 'oresees its tender years;
> Till, grown more strong, it thrusts, and stretches out,
> And Elbows all the Kingdoms round about:
> The place thus made for its first breathing free,
> It moves again for ease and Luxury:
> Till, swelling by degrees, it has possest
> The greater space; and now crowds up the rest.
> When from behind, there starts some petty State;

[25] De Krey, 'The First Restoration Crisis', 566.

[26] Steven Pincus, 'From Butterboxes to Wooden Shoes: The Shift in English Popular Sentiment from Anti-Dutch to Anti-French in the 1670s', *The Historical Journal*, 38 (1995): 333–61; Gary S. De Krey, 'Rethinking the Restoration: Dissenting Cases for Conscience, 1667–1672', *HJ*, 38 (1995): 53–83, 61; Sir Charles Wolseley, *Liberty of Conscience Upon its True and Proper Grounds Asserted & Vindicated* (London: 1668), 58–9; see also Slingsby Bethel, *Present Interest of England Stated* (London: 1671).

[27] Parkin, *Taming*, 243, De Krey, 'The First Restoration Crisis', 571n.

[28] Wolseley, *Liberty*, 12.

And pushes on its now unwieldy fate:
Then, down the precipice of time it goes,
And sinks in Minutes, which in Ages rose. (2.1.1.1–16)

Classical writers, notably Polybius, described Rome's succession to Carthage within similarly cyclical frames, and Dryden's *Annus mirabilis* had already represented Anglo-Dutch rivalry through this historical parallel (ll. 17–20).[29] As the play's hero, Almanzor, enters from, and exits for, the Moroccan kingdom across the Mediterranean, the play's horizons also align with the Atlantic theatre of current Anglo-Dutch tensions: among the relatively few foreign policy successes of the previous decade had been the English Crown's development of the strategic naval colony at Tangiers, which was (in the words of one writer) 'the great passage to the wealth of *Affrica* and *America*. … [and] like to be that Renowned Scene of Action, which will render us considerable in this last Age to the world'.[30]

But the pressure of the 'first' Restoration political crisis also makes itself felt in Almanazor's bombastic language, as he flaunts and challenges Boabdelin's authority.[31] Boabdelin's dependence on the warrior proves fatal for the kingdom, as Almanzor switches sides between the rival factions in Al-Andalus, falls in love with the king's betrothed, Almahide, and proves the catalyst for Al-Andalus's collapse from within. As shown in the exchange quoted at the beginning of this essay, Almanzor lays claims to heroic autonomy by invoking the language of the sovereign contract. Though it will later be revealed that Almanzor is in fact the lost son of the Duke of Arcos, he assumes that he was born in the African interior, beyond the reach of any recognized sovereignty. A problem exposed in that exchange, which is hardly resolved by Boabdelin's pragmatic climb-down a few lines later, corresponds to what Annabel Brett has shown to be one of the fundamental problems driving early modern discussion of natural law and sovereignty: how to account for the territorial limitations of the civil state.[32] If jurisdictions of positive law arise when people in a state of nature are led by the laws of nature to contract under a sovereign power, then how does one explain the fact that the world contains numerous, distinct sovereign jurisdictions? A universal natural law, one might think, would have led the entire human community to compact together, under a single sovereignty, and a single set of positive laws. Brett highlights the way that this problem surfaces in multiple ways, such as when theorists of the law of nature and nations

[29] Polybius, *The Histories*, trans. W. R. Paton, 2nd edn rev. by F. W. Walbank and Christian Habicht, Loeb Classical Library, 138, 3 vols (Cambridge, MA: Harvard University Press, 2010), 3.425; Dryden, *Works*, 1.60.

[30] Anon., *A Discription of Tangier* (London: 1664), sig. $A3^{r-v}$.

[31] De Krey, 'The First Restoration Crisis', passim.

[32] Annabel S. Brett, *Changes of State: Nature and the Limits of the City in Early Modern Natural Law* (Princeton: Princeton University Press, 2011), 169–94. See also Christopher Warren's discussion of *Paradise Lost* in 'John Milton and the Epochs of International Law', which he finds concerned with the problem of how the law of nature gave way to the law of nations, the process by which nations were first differentiated.

consider different kinds of travellers. Originating from outside a given jurisdiction, it is not clear how they can be said to have obligations that derive from an original act of consent to the sovereignty of that jurisdiction. Do ambassadors or merchants, for instance, remain subject to the moral codes of their jurisdiction of origin, or do they become subject to the sovereigns whose lands they visit? Almanzor's sense of an honour code grounded in a state of pristine liberty grows from this loophole in natural law's account of sovereignty's origins. He asserts a 'primitive' code of honour, based on the belief that because neither he nor (presumably) his ancestors have ever consented to obey a sovereign, he is obliged only to preserve himself and his honour. Boabdelin is quick to recognize this legal language and its implications. He contends that Almanzor is in fact placing himself in the position of an outlaw. Seventeenth-century responses to the problem of pirates were influenced by the arguments of early modern jurists, prominently Gentili and Grotius, who argue that by recognizing no sovereignty beyond their own will, pirates break the 'treaty of the human race' and exclude themselves from the community of nations.[33] They are the 'common foe' of mankind, and could be punished by any sovereign power at all.[34] Boabdelin thinks in these terms when he argues that Almanzor should be executed by right of 'your own law'; the legal tradition upon which Almanzor bases his dubious claim to autonomy in fact condemns him as an outlaw.

The analogy between Almanzor and a pirate returns when he falls in love with Almahide. It illustrates the way in which Almanzor's self-construction as an agent of uncompromised natural autonomy often proves unfortunate and inflexible. Almanzor has rejected the Zegrys and delivered Almahide from their captivity, but he cannot let her go without making his own claim on her, and demands with increasing vehemence that she does him the 'charity' of hearing his suit of love:

Almah. Your way is somewhat strange to ask Relief;
You ask with threatning, like a begging Thief.
Once more *Almanzor*, tell me, am I free?
Almanz. Madam, you are from all the World—but me.
But as a Pyrate, when he frees the Prize
He took from Friends, sees the rich Merchandize,
And after he has freed it, justly buys,
So when I have restor'd your Liberty,—
But, then, alas, I am too poor to buy!
Almah. Nay now you use me just as Pyrats do:
You free me; but expect a ransome too. (1.4.2.397–407)

[33] Quoted in Brett, *Changes of State*, 191; see also Tuck, *Grotius to Kant*, 35.
[34] Grotius, *The Rights of War and Peace*, 1021–4; Tuck, *Grotius to Kant*, 102–3.

Almanzor's unfortunate simile shows more than his ineptness with the language of love; it illustrates the way in which the protagonists of this play variously attempt to construe their obligations and interrelations through analogies of contract which point back, explicitly or implicitly, to the contested foundations of sovereignty and empire. Here Almanzor's simile appears at first to herald his submission to civil norms and mutuality, but it actually then reinforces an apprehension that should he submit to such norms, he would be assimilated and reduced by them, and would thereby lose the heroic charisma that springs from his autonomy. Dryden exploits the ability of contractual metaphors to reveal tension, or to drive the protagonists towards violence instead of consent. By exploring the dramatic possibilities of arguments about sovereignty in this way, he brings into sharp focus the characteristics of seventeenth-century thinking about the social contract which have lead Victorian Kahn to call it 'wayward'; namely its potential to question the nature and limits of political authority.

In Kahn's reading of *Leviathan*, Hobbes responds to such radical versions of contractarian civil philosophy as Milton's *The Tenure of Kings and Magistrates* (which argues that sovereign contracts might be revocable if a sovereign proves unsatisfactory), by taking a literary-critical turn. Hobbes likens radical contractarians to credulous readers of romance: both get carried away with fictions and misled by vainglorious, emulative passions which lead them to privilege a false sense of honour and individual autonomy over the interest of peace. Hobbes thereby develops the acute insight that contractarian theories of civil philosophy, being artifices of language built up through the interpretation, extension and synthesis of metaphors of contract, require careful attention to the linguistic assumptions upon which they are built. This is why in Hobbes's analysis the contract metaphor is a 'matter for the police'.[35] Not only is a contract needed to regulate people's actions, but also a contract is needed to regulate the way that the contract metaphor can be used: Hobbes 'elaborates a metalinguistic critique of his opponents, in part by arguing that consent to the political contract involves consent to a linguistic contract, that is, to the sovereign's determination of linguistic usage'.[36]

Hobbes's thinking about this 'metalanguage' of contracts of sovereignty is especially relevant to heroic drama, because there is a direct line of influence running between Hobbes's discussion of romance with Davenant in the latter's *Preface to Gondibert*, which Kahn argues is important to the development of Hobbes's thinking about the interpretation and misinterpretation of political contracts, and *The Conquest of Granada*, which cites that discussion in its preface.[37] In between, stand Davenant's Interregnum 'moral representations', which were successfully revived in the Restoration.[38] *Gondibert* is in many respects an epic romance which accommodates some of Hobbes's criticisms of

[35] Kahn, *Wayward Contracts*, 137.

[36] Kahn, *Wayward Contracts*, 137.

[37] Kahn, *Wayward Contracts*, 143; Dryden, *Works*, 11.9–10; James A. Winn, 'Heroic Song: A Proposal for a Revised History of English Theater and Opera, 1656–1711', *Eighteenth-Century Studies*, 30 (1996): 113–37.

[38] [Sir William Davenant], *A Proposition for Advancement of Moralitie, By a New Way of Entertainment of the People* (London: 1653), 22. See also James R. Jacob and Timothy Raylor, 'Opera and

the deleterious effects of romance: the hero retreats from martial rivalry to contemplation, and Davenant represents 'the Spenserian synthesis of love and a quest for glory as a pernicious mistake'.[39] Davenant's original proposal for his 'moral representations' justifies them in Hobbesian terms: they will enhance the stability of the commonwealth by representing the passions lucidly: 'The people will ever be unquiet whilst they are ignorant of themselves, and unacquainted with those Engins that scrue them up, which are their passions, in true characters of the beauties and deformities of vertue and vice.'[40] Productions such as the *Cruelty of the Spaniards in Peru* will lead the people to 'Obedience to Authority' and will 'warme and incite them to Heroicall Attempts, when the State shall command them'.[41] Dryden's preface to *The Conquest of Granada* defends his play against the *Preface to Gondibert*'s argument against supernatural intervention in the action, but there are strong continuities, nevertheless, between Davenant's and Dryden's dramatic theory, particularly in their shared awareness that debates about the propriety and efficacy of dramatic forms were entangled with theories of sovereignty.

So the preface to *The Conquest of Granada* acknowledges a debate in which those who desired to emulate the actions of heroes were likened to wayward theorists of sovereignty.[42] Almanzor joins both of these roles together too: he is indeed a wayward interpreter of social obligation, and his language of contract is an aspect of his violence, which must be tamed if he is to avoid tragedy. He is not alone in this respect. The ambitious Lyndaraxa is especially adept at using the language of contract to unpick the fabric of social obligation in Granada and inspire rebellion. Seeking to seduce Almanzor to her political designs, she persuades him that he is obliged not to the 'faithless' king, but to Almahide, and that the queen is not giving him a fair return for his military trophies; when he vows his constancy to Almahide nevertheless, she argues that such vows were fraudulently instituted among the transactions of love by deformed wits and decayed beauties (2.3.3.88–182). Lyndaraxa has more success with Abdelmelech and Prince Abdallah, whom she plays off against one another until she very briefly becomes queen of Granada. Her skill with the rhetoric of contract and obligation reduces all social relations to a binary contest to be on top. She urges Prince Abdallah to rebel against his brother Boabdelin accordingly: 'Princes are Subjects still:— / Subject and Subject can small diff'rence bring: / The diff'rence is 'twixt Subjects and a King' (1.2.1.118–20). An emulative pursuit of distinction in such a world points to regicide, as the events unfolding from this scene demonstrate. The representations of society offered by Lyndaraxa and Almanzor are versions of the tendencies that worry Hobbes when he discusses vainglory and the dangers of romance: the contractual metaphors through which natural law constructs the foundations of social order can become in themselves a dangerous art.

Obedience: Thomas Hobbes and A Proposition for Advancement of Moralitie by Sir William Davenant', *The Seventeenth Century*, 6 (1991): 205–50.

39 Colin Burrow, *Epic Romance: Homer to Milton* (Oxford: Oxford University Press, 1993), 241.

40 [Davenant], *Proposition*, 11–12.

41 [Davenant], *Proposition*, 22.

42 Kahn, *Wayward Contracts*, 137.

But in the *Conquest of Granada*, emulation is not an unequivocally destructive force. The epigraph to Part 2 of the play—'*Stimulos dedit æmula virtus*' ('Vying with excellence gave the spur')—is taken from Lucan's *Pharsalia*. In its original context, it describes the destructive forces driving Rome's descent into civil war, but here it becomes more ambiguous, as the play recuperates for emulation and romance a potentially constructive energy in the rise of the Spanish empire. The Moorish and Spanish soldiers are spurred on by the evaluative gaze of courtly women. Ferdinand reports that 'The valiant *Moores* like raging Lyons, fight; / Each youth encourag'd by his Ladies sight' (2.5.3.134–5), provoking Isabel to lead the ladies of her court to watch the battlefield, that they too might inspire their warriors to contend in greater feats of valour in the ladies' sight. This move, an act of emulation in its own right, produces 'such a shining train, / That *Moorish* beauties shall oppose in vain' (2.5.3.136–7). These dramatic rhythms are consistent with Ferdinand's earlier speech on the cyclical progress of empires in history—the *translatio imperii*—which he personifies as the arrival of a pushy youth on the scene. And of course, Dryden's own attempts to create a dramatic form of epic-romance are another strand in this cycle of cultural emulation: theatre rises to the occasion, as England's empire vies with that of the Dutch to supplant Spain in the Americas. But these symmetries serve to focus attention on the question of what separates positive emulation from negative, and what channels it productively in the culture of an emerging Spanish empire, and disastrously in the case of the Moors. Is there anything in Dryden's dramatic world which 'polices' (to use Kahn's metaphor) those potentially wayward mimetic desires which make people construct, question, and reconstruct compacts of sovereignty?

In his discussion of *Gondibert*, Hobbes recommends for an heroic poem the neoclassical virtues of 'perspicuity, property [propriety], and decency' in expression.[43] In *The Conquest of Granada*, the theatricality of the Spanish court, particularly its culture of appreciation for gallant speech and committed action, exerts a pressure towards these qualities of refinement in the elucidation of passion and obligation. Emulation brings out the best in the play's star-crossed lovers, Ozmyn and Benzayda. Met with a series of seemingly impossible conflicts of obligation, their attempts to outdo one another in generous casuistry makes them into a foil for the more destructive forms of emulation which tear Al-Andalus apart. In a scene in Part 2 of the play, Ozmyn and Benzayda enter midway through discussion of a dilemma: they have incurred an obligation to the Spanish court, which has granted them sanctuary from Benzayda's vengeful father, Selim, who is bent on Ozmyn's destruction.

> *Ozm.* 'Tis true that our protection here has been
> Th' effect of Honour in a *Spanish* Queen.
> But, while I as a friend continue here,
> I, to my Country, must a Foe appear.

43 Davenant, *Gondibert*, 51.

Benz. Think not my *Ozmyn*, that we here remain
As friends, but Pris'ners to the Pow'r of *Spain*.
Fortune dispences with your Countryes right;
But you desert your honour in your flight. (2.2.1.1–8)

Benzayda's legal fiction is typical of the couple's elegant collaboration in working out solutions to seemingly impossible problems of obligation. Ozmyn tries to rise above a factional vendetta which he has unintentionally exacerbated by killing Benzayda's brother. But Benzayda's companionship often assists him in this: it inspires him to construe the obligations of honour as generously as she does. Ozmyn gladly accepts Benzayda's reinterpretation of their situation as captivity, only for Selim to enter, pursued by soldiers. Ozmyn risks his life to defend his former tormenter, and it is Benzayda's instinctive pity that prompts his own noble response:

Ben. It is my father; and he seems distrest:
Ozmyn. My honour bids me succour the opprest:
That life he sought, for his I'le freely give;
We'll dye together; or together live. (2.2.1.18–21)

Benzayda and Ozmyn become a microcosm of the court's ability to constrain and channel casuistry towards acts of 'honourable' generosity and chivalry. Where Hobbes's sovereign regulates the metalanguage of contract, determining what constitutes a legitimate interpretation of obligation, *The Conquest of Granada* points to different kinds of regulation: a culture of courtly taste which applauds (and rewards with sexual desire) the most noble performances of obligation. It inspires others to emulate such performances, and throws into relief the excesses and contradictions of Almanzor's bombast.

The relevance of this strand of the plot to the consolidation of empire is demonstrated in a scene at the beginning of Part 2 of the play. The couple's gallantry inspires an extraordinary artifice of judgement by Queen Isabel, after the fleeing lovers are captured between the warring camps. Ozmyn first kills a Spanish knight, whose soldiers demand that Ozmyn be executed for murder. Ferdinand agrees. But Isabel intervenes, in response to the lovers' story and mutual vows of love, with a more equitable sentence:

Qu. Isa. Permit me, Sir, these Lovers doom to give:
My Sentence is, they shall together live.
The Courts of Kings,
To all Distress'd shou'd Sanctuaries be:
But most, to Lovers in Adversity.

> *Castille* and *Arragon*
> Which, long against each other, War did move,
> My plighted Lord and I have joyn'd by love:
> And, if to add this Conquest Heav'n thinks good,
> I would not have it stain'd with Lovers blood. (2.1.1.127–36)

Isabel's intervention extends the rhythm of decorous emulation which has characterized the casuistry of Benzayda and Ozmyn. Her sentence is guided by pity, the generic response of romance, but it is also invested with a strong sense of renewal. It breaks with the universality of the vengeful natural justice demanded by the soldiers, and the impassioned tyranny of Moorish rule. In the iconography of the reign of Charles I, which would have been familiar to at least some of Dryden's audience, the marriage of Charles and Henrietta Maria had been idealized as an epic romance, and an ideal of love which patterned the love of subject for king.[44] So one might even see here the royal marriage functioning as a different kind of original contract, a pattern of reconciliation which guides the subsequent interpretation and discovery of positive law. The romance plot of the royal marriage forms a different kind of contract metaphor, which differentiates the new Spanish kingdom as an emerging empire of positive law.

Hobbes's compact of sovereignty, motivated by the recognition of a common interest in the rule of law, has been called a 'counterplot' of law's origins: it contests the revolutionary interpretation of the social contract which argued (often with reference to equity) that subjects could withdraw obedience to the king where he had infringed that contract.[45] What is seen here, then, might be called a counter-counterplot, which takes issue with Hobbes's wariness of romance as a creator of dangerous delusions. Dryden suggests that forms of critical judgement associated with the appreciation of romance narrative can have their own force in constructing legitimacy, precisely at that most contested point in theories of sovereignty, where the universals of natural law give rise to differentiated polities of positive law. Isabel's elegant legal artifice begins to foster a culture of consent, in that not only do Ozmyn and Benzayda then feel obliged to the Spanish Crown, but Benzayda (at least) begins to recognize Isabel's justice as a manifestation of a more benevolent providence: 'The frowns of Fate we will no longer fear: / Ill Fate, Great Queen, can never find us here' (2.1.1.139–41). So even though in Almanzor's self-fashioning as a 'noble Savage' (1.1.1.210), Dryden seems to share some of Hobbes's suspicion of the way in which the metaphor and logic of the social contract can foster self-importance and rebellion, by so elegantly accommodating romance's dilemmas of love and honour, and the generic romance response of pity, within the process of consolidating a new jurisdiction, *The Conquest of Granada* also redeems romance from its

[44] Lois Potter, *Secret Rites and Secret Writing: Royalist Literature, 1641–1660* (Cambridge: Cambridge University Press, 1989), 77; Kahn, *Wayward Contracts*, 10–11, 102, 139.

[45] Kahn, *Wayward Contracts*, 134–5.

association with the misinterpretation of passion and interest in Hobbes's writing.[46] This rehabilitation of romance goes some way beyond that attempted by Davenant in his Interregnum *Proposition*. In *The Conquest of Granada*, romance is not merely a form to supplement law and divinity, to inspire audience-members to martial exploits 'when the State shall command', but rather a condition for refined law-making, providing a culture of propriety and discrimination which supports the artifice of empire. The response to refined passions in these lovers thereby becomes the constitutive moment in the reintegration of Granada within the empire of Spain, creating new precedents that distinguish Spain as a place of positive law.

As contractarian models of sovereignty were again becoming wayward, and satires on the failures of the Second Anglo-Dutch war lampooned the court's taste for chivalrous spectacle, *The Conquest of Granada* shows a reciprocal relationship between the empire of Spain, in the sense of a supreme power of jurisdiction, and what Dryden's *Essay of Dramatic Poesy* referred to as the 'empire of wit': the most authoritative and refined judgement in matters of heroism. The ending of *The Conquest of Granada* reveals that Providence and religion must also play their part in this ideal relationship between different 'empires'. The dénouement begins when Almahide is falsely accused of infidelity with Abdelmelech. Her honour is defended in a trial by combat, which pits Almanzor and Ozmyn against her Zegry accusers (organized by Lyndaraxa) Hamet and Zulema. This trial vindicates Almahide, and begins to show the hand of Providence in her convoluted political fortunes: swearing on the Koran, the combatants refer their cause to God, but Almahide also offers up a prayer to the Christian God, having been secretly converted by her servant Esperanza. When the defeated Zulema confesses to his fraud, Almahide's new faith is vindicated.

Almanzor, on the other hand, must wait until the final scene of the play to undergo the decisive revelation. Love increasingly draws him to compromise his autonomy and submit to the institutions through which Granada's regeneration is being worked: he joins Ozmyn in championing Almahide's ancient right to trial by combat. But if love prevails over jealousy to draw him in, his attempts to construe his conflicts of passion with metaphors of sovereignty become ever more strained and bombastic. He himself at first seems to doubt Almahide, but nevertheless champions her cause for fear that Ozmyn will 'Intrench upon my Loves Prerogative' (2.4.3.387). He then argues still more absurdly that the infallibility of this natural sovereignty commits him to combat: 'She must be Chaste, because she's lov'd by me' (2.4.3.398). When Almahide expresses her indebtedness to him for his actions, he again attempts to articulate through the language of natural obligation the passion which ties him to her, but demonstrates only his continued indecorousness: 'Born to be yours, I do by Nature, serve, / And, like the lab'ring Beast, no thanks deserve' (2.5.3.7–8). Almanzor's role as an instrument of Providence becomes more apparent as the authority of law (the trial by combat is an ancient right

[46] For a complementary discussion of romance's role in mediating between traditions of law during an earlier period, but also in the context of imperial expansion, see Brian C. Lockey, *Law and Empire in English Renaissance Literature* (Cambridge: Cambridge University Press, 2006).

reasserted by Ozmyn) and Christianity re-emerge through the wreckage of Boabdelin's despotism, but the residual language and analogical logic of natural obligation becomes an obstacle to his perception of these events. It delays Almanzor's integration with the Restoration-like regeneration of Granada (if Ferdinand views events as the translation of empires, Isabel sees Granada returning to its ancient religion and law).

It is only following the second intervention of his mother's ghost, that Almanzor's real identity and destined role are revealed. In combat, his father the Duke of Arcos recognizes symbols of Christianity on his body—a crucifix on bracelets left by his mother, and a birthmark in the shape of a bleeding heart. Arcos delivers a romance narrative of shipwreck and loss, which clarifies the sense of autonomy which Almanzor has interpreted so problematically up until now. Almanzor, it turns out, is partly royal himself, and this realization brings him to the verge of accepting the sovereignty of his cousin Ferdinand. Almanzor begins to understand the divine symbols—symbols of Christ's sacrifice and a debt that cannot be repaid—which hold the key to his identity. As for the play's other young heroes, Almahide, Ozmyn and Benzayda, it is the asymmetrical Christian covenant which defines their new obligations within the kingdom of Spain, but which they are yet not fully able to comprehend. The necessity of a religious education to complete their conversion defers complete renewal. After Isabel confers on Almahide her own Christian name, Benzayda also asks for religious tuition: 'This blessed change, we all with joy receive: And beg to learn that faith which you believe' (2.5.3.302–3). If the language of contract has been tamed, and anchored in a covenant with God ('heav'n has joyes in store / To recompense those losses you deplore' (2.5.3.294–5)), it is also part of the monarchy's role to oversee the exposition of this covenant. Almahide contributes to the deferral of the play's conclusion, in that she insists—against Isabel's wishes—that she should be free to give due rites of mourning to Boabdelin. These processes of realignment are suggestive in the context of challenges to Charles II's ecclesiastical jurisdiction. The heroic monarchy of Spain accommodates Almahide's scruples; the Crown's religious responsibilities, however, are never in any doubt, and a full restoration is felt to depend still upon Granada's future integration in religion. For all the promise of the play's ending, it reflects the mood in Charles's kingdoms that they were not yet unified in religion either. So the turn of empire's wheel in Granada becomes more clearly a Restoration too, in which the hand of Providence manifests itself. In this sense, the play stays true to some of the most common motifs in the drama of the time, civil war and Restoration, but illuminates these processes anew by dramatizing them as crises in the language of sovereignty.

Dryden's early heroic plays explore the dramatic potential of that language, and they show the development of an interest in its moral and cultural implications which would return in *Absalom and Architophel* against the background of arguments over the Exclusion Crisis, and in *Fables Ancient and Modern* (1700), where a different kind of sceptical questioning adds layers of moral complexity to Ovid's 'Cinyras and Myrrha'.[47]

[47] Steven N. Zwicker, *Lines of Authority: Politics and English Literary Culture, 1649–1689* (Ithaca: Cornell University Press, 1993), 130–72; David Hopkins, *Conversing with Antiquity: English Poets and the Classics, from Shakespeare to Pope* (Oxford: Oxford University Press, 2010), 177–201.

The Indian Emperour reveals continuities between Restoration culture and the upheavals of the 1650s, as it explores and tests the ability of natural law arguments to speak to England's swelling foreign policy ambitions. But Dryden's heroic drama is perhaps most of its moment when it pursues connections between imperial expansion and domestic disorder, and explores the instability of these arguments. In Almanzor, Dryden represents a figure who appropriates the language of sovereignty to contest and divide. In some respects he is an early portrait of the disaffected, almost libertine Hobbist, scaled up to monstrous proportions. But his excessive self-justifications and labile allegiances also reflect the perceived energies and dangers of questions that continued to spill backwards and forwards between spheres of natural and international law, and matters of obedience and conscience. Yet finally, by exploring the ways in which the legal artifice of sovereignty and empire might be supported and supplemented by other cultural institutions—the church, the court, and Dryden's 'empire of wit'—the *Conquest of Granada* shows not merely how the themes of his plays were suggested by the legal debates of the Restoration, but also how his thinking about the cultural influence of drama could be stimulated by those debates too.

Bibliography

Armitage, David. *The Ideological Origins of the British Empire* (Cambridge: Cambridge University Press, 2000).

Brett, Annabel S. *Changes of State: Nature and the Limits of the City in Early Modern Natural Law* (Princeton: Princeton University Press, 2011).

de Krey, Gary S. 'The First Restoration Crisis: Conscience and Coercion in London, 1667–73', *Albion*, 25 (1993): 565–80.

Hammond, Paul. *John Dryden: A Literary Life* (London: Macmillan, 1991).

Hughes, Derek. *Dryden's Heroic Plays* (London: Macmillan, 1981).

Kahn, Victoria. *Wayward Contracts: The Crisis of Political Obligation in England, 1640–1674* (Princeton: Princeton University Press, 2004).

Lockey, Brian C. *Law and Empire in English Renaissance Literature* (Cambridge: Cambridge University Press, 2006).

Orr, Bridget. *Empire on the English Stage, 1660–1714* (Cambridge: Cambridge University Press, 2001).

Pagden, Anthony. *Lords of All the World: Ideologies of Empire in Spain, Britain and France c.1500–c.1850* (New Haven: Yale University Press, 1995).

Parkin, Jon. *Taming the Leviathan: The Reception of the Political and Religious Ideas of Thomas Hobbes in England, 1640–1700* (Cambridge: Cambridge University Press, 2007).

Raylor, Timothy. 'Opera and Obedience: Thomas Hobbes and a Proposition for Advancement of Moralitie by Sir William Davenant', *The Seventeenth Century*, 6 (1991): 205–50.

Tilmouth, Christopher. *Passion's Triumph over Reason* (Oxford: Oxford University Press, 2007).

Tuck, Richard. *The Rights of War and Peace: Political Thought and the International Order from Grotius to Kant* (New York: Oxford University Press, 1999).

Visconsi, Elliott. *Lines of Equity: Literature and the Origins of Law in Later Stuart England* (Ithaca: Cornell University Press, 2008).

Warren, Christopher N. *Literature and the Law of Nations, 1580–1680* (Oxford: Oxford University Press, 2015).

CHAPTER 38

ENGLISH LIBERTIES OUTSIDE ENGLAND

Floors, Doors, Windows, and Ceilings in the Legal Architecture of Empire

DANIEL J. HULSEBOSCH

Reading Liberty: Legal Formulas and Imperial Projects

We tend to think of global migration and the problem of what legal rights people enjoy as they cross borders as modern phenomena. They are not. The question of emigrant rights was one of the foundational issues in what can be called the constitution of the English empire at the beginning of transatlantic colonization in the seventeenth century. This essay analyses one strand of this constitutionalism, a strand captured by the resonant term, 'the liberties and privileges of Englishmen'. Almost every colonial grant—whether corporate charter, royal charter, or proprietary grant—for roughly two dozen imagined, projected, failed, and realized overseas ventures contained a clause stating that the emigrants would enjoy the liberties, privileges, and immunities of English subjects. The clause was not invented for transatlantic colonization. Instead, it had medieval roots. Accordingly, royal drafters, colonial grantees, and settlers penned and read these guarantees against the background of traditional interpretations about what they meant.

Soon, however, the language of English liberties and privileges escaped the founding documents, and contests over these keywords permeated legal debates on the meaning and effects of colonization. Just as the formula of English liberties and privileges became a cornerstone of England's constitutional monarchy, it also became a foundation of the imperial constitution. As English people brought it west, they gave it new meanings. The formula then returned home to create entirely new problems.

The resonant legal formula 'liberties, privileges, and immunities' was not, of course, limited, even in England, to claims of *English* liberties. It had many qualifiers and existed in countless royal grants, from grants of land and royal offices to trading companies, bridges, and ferries. An officer or land grantee, for example would receive in his grant all the liberties and privileges associated with that particular grant or office (and only partly denoted in the letters patent).[1] Similarly, a town or trading company might receive all the liberties, privileges, and immunities characteristically enjoyed by similar towns or companies.[2] The keywords 'liberties, privileges, and immunities' were never, therefore, limited solely to clauses concerning the status of emigrants. The pervasiveness of these keywords, and the various primary nouns they qualified, made them accessible and pliable in new circumstances. Additionally, specific clauses varied slightly in ways that could be important or insignificant. For present purposes, variations on the operative terms like liberties, privileges, and immunities—and also rights, powers, duties, and so on—are not crucial. Some commentators attached different meanings to these individual terms, but generally they overlapped, and claimants often strung them together with deliberate redundancy to capture all possible connotations, traditional and potential. Briefly, a liberty was a grant of power that could not lightly, if ever, be restricted. Right sometimes connoted a pre-political freedom, but many times it was synonymous with liberty. Privilege was an allowance of certain behaviour that otherwise would not be permitted, a kind of license to engage in activity usually reserved to a select few. Immunity was in turn a license to engage in activity typically forbidden and penalized.[3] Like most languages of governance, these keywords conveyed charged yet uncertain meanings, especially when applied to jurisdictions beyond England itself.

Although the charter formula concerning 'English liberties, privileges, and immunities' overseas had no single meaning, it was not an empty cipher. The general purpose of such language was to describe, advocate, or contest the legal status of the Crown's subjects who emigrated to or were born in royal territories outside England. This was not a new problem. For centuries people migrated from England to other real, imagined, and usually militarily contested dominions of the English king. When soldiers, merchants, and settlers left home to take up the Crown's claims on the European continent or in Ireland, they sought assurance that they were fighting for real territories of the English king, as a matter of English law. They also wanted the Crown's pledge that they, and their offspring born in those once and future overseas dominions, could return home and be

[1] See e.g. Grant to Jasper, Duke of Bedford, R.O. Patent Roll, 3 Hen. VII, 1488, Par 2 m. 20(2) (translation), Calendar of Patent Rolls, British History Online, <http://www.british-history.ac.uk/cardiff-records/vol1/pp450-483>.

[2] See e.g. Adolphus Ballard and James Tait, *British Borough Charters, 1216–1307* (1923); Cecil T. Carr, ed., *Select Charters of Trading Companies, A.D. 1530–1707* (London: Baillard & Tait, 1913).

[3] Helpful here is J. H. Baker, 'Personal Liberty Under the Common Law of England', in *The Origins of Modern Freedom in the West*, ed. R. W. Davis (Stanford: Stanford University Press, 1995), 178–202. See also Brian Tierney's analysis of 'permissive law' in *Liberty and Law: The Idea of Permissive Natural Law, 1100–1800* (Washington, DC: Catholic University of North America Press, 2015).

treated equal subjects *in* England. They wanted protection while abroad, and an escape route back home.[4]

It could be called the problem of imperial subjecthood: what package of legal rights and liberties did royal subjects enjoy across the royal dominions and colonies outside England? This problem was not theorized coherently or regulated by the imperial Parliament until the early twentieth century, a generation before the empire disintegrated. Even then the status was not as clear and uniform as some metropolitan officials had hoped it would be.[5] That possibility—full theorization at the centre, and agreement that it was a problem that a governing body in London could try to solve once and for all—was not available in the seventeenth century. The absence of an authoritative decision-maker was sometimes a problem for early modern actors. Imperial agents in the colonies, for example, routinely lamented the weakness of their government. However, it also created space for new institutional structures and creative claims-making. The extra-English legal world was from the beginning filled with juxtaposed claims of stable right and vast possibilities, of purported black-letter law along with fresh glosses and improvised interpolations. Also from the beginning, some of the same people deployed alternative scripts when pursuing overseas projects, invoking traditional rights here and demanding special exceptions to fit new circumstances there. This was the way that English-speakers constructed the seventeenth-century empire.[6]

A lawyer or legal theorist might lament the failure to define imperial subjecthood, concluding that the historical actors lacked the ability to imagine a systematic solution. Even if they could have done so, seventeenth-century institutions of government would not have been able to deliver an unimpeachable answer to what key legal terms meant. A lawyer who is an advocate might react more sympathetically, knowing that ambiguity breeds opportunity: lack of settlement meant that alternatives remained available for contemporary advocates, while new ones awaited the legal imagination. Because the early modern constitution of empire was flexible, there was always the possibility of change.[7] Complex political systems can flourish because of, rather than despite, uncertain powers and rights.

Historians of law need not lament or celebrate past uncertainties, but they can attune themselves to the difference between, on the one hand, meanings that historical actors considered open and, on the other, those that were relatively settled or became so over time. They can then notice when actors tried to shift an issue from one category to another and established a new definitional equilibrium. Distinguishing among different uses of

[4] See text at notes 34–9 infra.

[5] British Nationality and Alien Act (1914). See generally Ann Dummett and Andrew Nicol, *Subjects, Citizens, Aliens and Others: Nationality and Immigration Law* (London: Weidenfeld and Nicolson, 1990).

[6] See also Daniel J. Hulsebosch, *Constituting Empire: New York and the Transformation of Constitutionalism in the Atlantic World, 1664–1830* (Chapel Hill: University of North Carolina Press, 2005), 17–41.

[7] Daniel J. Hulsebosch, 'The American Revolution (II): The Origin and Nature of Colonial Grievances', in *Oxford History of the British Empire, Companion Series: North America in the Seventeenth and Eighteenth Centuries*, ed. Stephen Foster (Oxford: Oxford University Press, 2013).

a single verbal formula illuminates both the range of ways people deployed that formula over time and also the range's shifting boundaries. It also becomes possible to spot when a specific use appears for the first time and to explore the new function's ramifications on the old.

This essay focuses less on the changing *meanings* of liberty in the seventeenth-century empire than on the accumulating *functions* of liberty claims.[8] Looking at the historical uses of legal discourse from a distance, it often appears as though there were fewer formulas available than problems to be solved. Some formulas got double work or more. Why do historical actors see those single scripts as candidates for development? How do they go about re-using them in new ways? Why use the same formula for different purposes? The object is not doctrinal taxonomy, to specify the correct historical meaning(s) of a legal formula. One reason historical actors deployed the same formula of English liberties and privileges for different purposes was to deny that it possessed conflicting meanings. In practice, the different functions were deliberately obscured, interactive, and volatile rather than hermetically separate. The goal is to notice the different ways that people used legal keywords as well as why, where, and how they bent their meanings. Yet the changing functions of invocations of English liberties and privileges outside England did influence the meaning of liberty more generally. Across the seventeenth century the formula increasingly suggested fundamental rights of the subject rather than grants or delegations from the Crown. Still these two meanings—grants versus deserts—coexisted in a productive ambiguity. While this ambiguity played out across the century, the argumentative context in which people claimed English liberties and privileges expanded in other dimensions and helped build out the architecture of the overseas empire.

The exercise of tracing the different functions of liberty claims has value along two dimensions, analytical and methodological. First, the essay analyses and categorizes the ways that the formula of English liberties and privileges functioned in seventeenth-century arguments about the rights subjects enjoyed outside England. 'Function' here does not entail sociolegal functionalism, or the notion that people adapt law to necessary social ends and that law lags and serves society.[9] Instead, it means simply that people used the formula to construct and reconstruct the legal environment of the empire even before there was an imperial society on the ground. In other words, they made liberty claims to shape that society in various and occasionally conflicting ways. However, liberty claims were more often mutually supportive than antagonistic and therefore helped build out the architecture of the early empire.

[8] For an attempt to catalogue the meaning(s) of liberty in British North America, see Elizabeth Mancke, 'The Languages of Liberty in British North America, 1603–1776', in *Exclusionary Empire: British Liberty Overseas, 1600–1900*, ed. Jack P. Greene (Cambridge: Cambridge University Press, 2009), 25–49; Michal Jan Rozbicki, *Culture and Liberty in the Age of the American Revolution* (Charlottesville: University of Virginia Press, 2011).

[9] For an influential conception of legal functionalism, see Karl Llewellyn, 'The Normative, the Legal, and the Law-Jobs: The Problem of Juristic Method', *YLJ*, 49 (1940): 1355–63.

Liberties, privileges, and immunities claims involving English emigrants fell into five functional categories. First, the claim that colonists abroad and their descendants enjoyed English liberties functioned as an open *door*, allowing overseas colonists to return home to England and be treated as equal English subjects. Implicitly and later explicitly, the door was opened in all kingdoms and dominions of the English Crown. Natural-born subjects, and their descendants, could step through that door without fearing degradation: everywhere, in all royal territories, they would be treated equally with native subjects of the English king while in those territories.

Second, the king or his colonial deputies might make positive grants of English liberties to subjects in a royal territory outside England as an inducement for English subjects to migrate there. Here, the grant of English liberties and privileges functioned as a *window*, a transparent promise of familiar and cherished rights to encourage settlement.

Third, already by the time of the English Civil War and more frequently by century's end, the colonists themselves sometimes claimed English liberties, privileges, and immunities abroad as a *floor* below which governors could not push. Colonists made this claim to oppose those who argued that the colonial constitution was fundamentally different than England's, and that the Crown's prerogative had greater range and flexibility abroad than in England. This type of claim emerged soon after colonization and was prominent at moments of political struggle in England, especially as Parliament carved away the royal prerogative at home. This floor of rights was not stationary. It rose along with English liberties and parliamentary power at home.

Fourth, in the reverse of the second, the claim that overseas subjects had to be governed according to English standards, including English liberties and privileges, could function as a *ceiling* on colonial innovation. It was a ceiling measured by metropolitan officials, especially the Privy Council as it reviewed colonial statutes and judicial cases to ensure that they were, in the familiar language of colonial grants, 'agreeable' with and 'not repugnant' to the laws of England. The ceiling's height also rose and fell in different places and over time in response to metropolitan policies. The enduring function was to place limits on colonial experimentation.

Finally, colonial assumptions of English liberties functioned as a *mirror* through which colonists could see themselves as English, even when their colonial rights, such as their property rights, were viewed at home as peculiar. If for example a subject of the English king in an overseas dominion owned slaves in that dominion and wished to sojourn home, could he bring his slaves? Could he carry the rights of a Virginian or Jamaican with him to England and enjoy those rights there? Collapsing English and local liberties, slaveholders argued affirmatively. As Englishmen they should, they thought, be able to move around the empire with their property, including human property.

Again, these different functions often worked in tandem, but they could operate in tension. Together, these functions helped the English imagine the architecture of empire, providing a legal blueprint that they built upon (and later deconstructed).

The essay's second, methodological dimension is to contribute an example by which historical can interpret historical actors' use of resonant formulas, such as the liberties and privileges of Englishmen, across the empire. It is a commonplace to stipulate that one cannot write historically about ideas like English liberties and privileges without grasping how they were understood by the historical actors. This shibboleth begs the question of *how* we should go about understanding the actors and their statements. Because so many actors used the script of English liberties and privileges outside England, it can appear as though it had no stable meaning. On such a premise, not only can there be no history of liberty, there cannot be a coherent history of the discourse of liberties. Instead, there might be political and social histories of how such terms were employed in concrete circumstances. From this interpretive perspective, liberties, privileges, and rights were empty vessels into which people poured innumerable and changing hopes and interests. Legal text dissolves into historical context. Legal scholars influenced by reductionist brands of legal realism, or who treat doctrinal or intellectual arguments as covers for preexisting interests, come close to this position. Sometimes this is exactly the right way to interpret legal argument—but not *all* legal arguments. Historians without professional training in law, who are sometimes even more sceptical about law's determinacy, often default into the same stance, seeing multiple legal arguments sharing similar vocabularies as undisciplined and scattershot claims-making.

In contrast to these instrumentalists are scholars afflicted with what might be called the treatise-authority complex. Against the prospect that liberty is an empty vessel, some scholars embrace supposedly authoritative texts and report as objective truth the definitions of contemporary and often self-nominated legal authorities. This official version then becomes a baseline against which to measure defection. This interpretive posture has the merit of supplying narrative arc and even drama, but it rests on the premise that all legal ideas have received orthodox, unitary definitions. Expressions inconsistent with those definitions are then identified as heterodox. When and where there actually was consensus, the contested process by which an interpretive community bestowed authority on a given meaning is suppressed.

In between scepticism about the integrity of actors' legal arguments and accepting legal notables' statements of the law as authoritative there lies a space in which people did things with legal keywords. Quentin Skinner's distinction between an argument that a speaker put forward and the purpose the speaker sought to accomplish by doing so helps illuminate the slippage between conventional and innovative uses of familiar early modern terms like English liberties, privileges, and immunities.[10] To comprehend the political and dramatic functions of these keywords requires an understanding of the combinatory formulas in which they were used and the ways and places those formulas were deployed.

Disentangling meaning and understanding is especially fraught in Anglo-American *legal* history, because the most prized authority in early modern English law was custom and convention, not innovation. To do things with words in the seventeenth century, one needed to deploy words that people thought they understood already.[11] In legal

[10] Quentin Skinner, 'Meaning and Understanding in the History of Ideas', *History and Theory*, 8 (1969): 3–53.

[11] On the nature of seventeenth-century constitutional culture, see J. G. A. Pocock, *The Ancient Constitution and the Feudal Law* (Cambridge: Cambridge University Press, 1956). See also John Phillip

argumentation the game often consisted of disguising change with convention, making it difficult for modern scholars to understand what contemporaries were trying to accomplish unless a contemporary spotted the innovation and identified it as such. Similarly, participants could invoke conventional formulas to resist attempts to open up their meaning, piling on stable meaning as a bulwark against redefinition.

From a satellite view, as when perusing the dozens of colonial charters and statutes produced in the seventeenth century, it appears that drafters, metropolitan officials, imperial agents, colonial legislators, and petitioners used the same words about English liberties and privileges in similar ways, suggesting broad agreement about what these words meant and how they travelled outside England. The task becomes how to map lines that mark precisely which liberties crossed which borders and when. Viewed from the participants' perspective, however, the linguistic formula appears more volatile.

In between formulaic sameness and the scattershot deployment of liberties and privileges lay hard-earned serial development of a handful of purposes to which the liberty, privileges, and immunities formula was used. Categorizing such purposes shows that the use of such formulas ranged beyond the deceptively similar charter formulas, yet was not chaotic. There were boundaries to acceptable uses of the terms, and new borders were pushed out only after concerted effort and debate. Even then, the borders remained contested. Because people employed the scripts to work out the same general problem—what was the legal relationship between people in the overseas territories and England?—some purposes could blend into others. Rather than develop a model of legal language in the abstract, the rest of the essay analyses the varied uses of the liberty script.

Building Multiple Kingdoms: Liberty as Door and Window

Although the problem of the legal status of overseas emigrants had existed since the Middle Ages, it ripened quickly in the seventeenth century. Two related events raised the issue of extra-English subjecthood in newly stark terms that demanded analytical clarity. One was named James. The other was Jamestown.

After the death of Queen Elizabeth, the Scottish king, James VI, was crowned as King James I of England. Suddenly two kingdoms that for much of the Middle Ages had been at arms, now, after a short century of 'perpetual peace' and a dynastic marriage, shared one king as well as an island. The merger of Crowns raised the question not only of the political relationship between Scotland and England but also of the relationship between

Reid, *The Ancient Constitution and the Origins of Anglo-American Liberty* (Dekalb: Northern Illinois University Press, 2005). Cf. Tierney, *Liberty and Law* (arguing for the persistence of medieval natural law theories in early modern political cultures).

individual Scots and Englishmen.[12] Political unions take time; institutions come slowly. In this case, a century passed between the compromises that accompanied the Union of Crowns and the legislative Union of Kingdoms in 1707.[13]

People, on the other hand, did not wait. Scots in particular began flowing across the borders—not least all those in the train of King James, who left Scotland in April 1603 and never returned. He knew that England was the main chance. So did many of his Scottish subjects. The extent of their legal rights when moving from one kingdom to another was a pressing legal issue. If King James granted them land, for example, could they enjoy, defend, and leave those lands to their heirs? Or could they or their heirs be ousted as aliens, under the common-law rule (a rule common across most of Europe) that aliens could not hold heritable title to land?

James sought a legislative solution. His Scottish Parliament was amenable and passed a statute making it clear that English subjects could hold and defend land titles in Scotland. The English Parliament, on the other hand, balked. It refused to enact a statute granting even Scots born after James's ascension the liberties and privileges of English subjects when they came to England. English parliamentarians gave two reasons for their resistance. First, they also feared setting a precedent that would logically apply to other new royal territories. Scottish equality, argued M.P. Sir Edwin Sandys, 'might give a dangerous example for mutual naturalizing of all nations that hereafter fall into the subjection of the king, although they be very remote, [because] their mutual commonalty of privileges may disorder the settled government of every of the particulars'. Each constituent nation of the king's expanding dominions, Sandys continued, had its own 'privileges' and 'birthright', which had been 'acquired for patrimony by their [ancestors]'.[14] Expansion was very much on everyone's mind. Many parliamentarians favoured it. Sandys, for example, was a founding member of the Virginia Company and its leader from 1618 to 1624. But they sharply distinguished the realm of England from the other existing and future royal territories. In part, parliamentarians feared an influx of poor Scots, a theme that ran through English political culture for the next two centuries and was only partly overcome by a growing sense of British nationality.[15] More generally, they believed that reciprocal subjecthood threatened to erase jurisdictional borders between the king's multiplying kingdoms. The periphery would exert reverse, negative influence on England and level down legal privileges throughout the king's lands: weak notions of liberty would drive out strong. The English were

[12] The next few paragraphs draw on Daniel J. Hulsebosch, 'The Ancient Constitution and the Expanding Empire: Sir Edward Coke's British Jurisprudence', *LHR*, 21 (2003): 439–82. See also Keechang Kim, *Aliens in Medieval Law: The Origins of Modern Citizenship* (Cambridge: Cambridge University Press, 2000); Polly Price, 'Natural Law and Birthright Citizenship in *Calvin's Case* (1608)', *YJLH*, 9 (1997): 73–145.

[13] On 1707, see Brian Levack, *The Formation of the British State: England, Scotland, and the Union, 1603–1707* (Oxford: Clarendon Press, 1987). The meaning of union of course continues to be re-negotiated.

[14] Hulsebosch, 'The Ancient Constitution', at 447–9.

[15] See Linda Colley, *Britons: Forging the Nation* (New Haven: Yale University Press, 1992).

becoming convinced that they enjoyed exceptional liberties compared to other kingdoms, even in comparison to the English king's other jurisdictions. They did not want to regress to what they perceived as an authoritarian royal mean when combined with the liberties of Scots or colonists elsewhere. That royal mean was not an abstract threat: just five years before inheriting the English Crown, King James had penned a pamphlet in defense of the divine right theory of kings and absolute power.[16] The liberties of English national identity were sharpened and actually depended on this constitutional alterity with other lands, including other dominions of the Crown. A Scottish king with Scots in train might import modes of governance hostile to English liberties and privileges.

In the debate over the legal consequences of Union, this parliamentary conception of the liberties of Englishmen functioned as a *door*: a closed door that kept migrants out or at least, when they crossed the threshold, signalled entry into a different legal environment where they enjoyed fewer liberties than the native English. This was a nationalist conception of liberties that distinguished the territorial space of England, and its history, from other jurisdictions, even the king's other dominions. Parliamentarians' jealous resistance marked an early instance of scepticism about accumulating extra-English possessions.[17] Scots might share the same island and a political head, but they had different bodies politic along with different liberties, privileges, and immunities.[18]

In the absence of a legislative solution, the problem of Scottish rights inside England went to the courts in the famous collusive lawsuit known as Calvin's Case. A majority of the royal judges held that Scots born after the accession of James I to the throne in England were subjects of the man who was king in both realms, and thus a subject in both kingdoms.[19] So a Scot was entitled to the liberties of Englishmen when he moved down to England. In an opinion that circulated throughout the Atlantic world, Edward Coke maintained that the English common law recognized equality between James's extra-English subjects and his English ones, at least when the former migrated to England. In this case, Scots could access the same common law rights as native-born Englishmen. Presumably the reverse held as well, if English people migrated to Scotland (or other royal dominions). In Coke's opinion, the English door swung wide open, welcoming migrants from the king's other territories. The ruling recognized the

[16] '[W]hat liberty can broiling spirits and rebellious minds claim justly to against any Christian monarchy', James wrote, 'since they can claim to no greater liberty on their part nor the people of God might have done. … [W]hat shameless presumption is it to any Christian people nowadays to claim to unlawful liberty which God refused to his own peculiar and chosen people?' *The True Lawe of Free Monarchies* (Edinburgh: 1598). Cf. Glenn Burgess, *Absolute Monarchy and the Stuart Constitution* (New Haven: Yale University Press, 1996).

[17] These parliamentarians were not anti-imperial but rather wished to insulate England from the rest of the empire. Therefore it would be wrong to identify the resistance as anti-imperialism akin to later English skepticism about empire. See Jennifer Pitts, *A Turn to Empire: The Rise of Imperial Liberalism in Britain and France* (Princeton: Princeton University Press, 2005).

[18] On the development of English national identity, including its legal identity, see Richard Helgerson, *Forms of Nationhood: The Elizabethan Writing of England* (Chicago: University of Chicago Press, 1993).

[19] See Hulsebosch, 'The Ancient Constitution'.

movement occurring across borders and helped facilitate that mobility throughout the king's territories.

Coke also added a host of dicta that shaped many governors' conceptions of royal power to govern territories outside England. According to his custom-based method, extreme even by contemporary standards, his analysis looked backward at a trove of medieval precedents that he struggled to rationalize into jurisprudence for a complex monarchy. Coming in 1608, just two years after the royal charter of the Virginia Company, it became a jurisprudential resource for empire.[20] Coke famously distinguished between inherited territories, like Scotland and England, and conquered territories, like Ireland. He then subdivided conquered territories into Christian and infidel. That triad was standard learning in what was becoming known as the European law of nations.[21] The teasing out of domestic or intra-imperial consequences of expansion, however, was new. In each of these three types of land, Coke maintained, the king had different degrees of discretion, different degrees of freedom to rule under his prerogative: minimal discretion in inherited and conquered Christian territories; greater discretion in conquered infidel lands. Coke also penned some cryptic sentences suggesting that English emigrants to conquered Christian lands, at least, ought to have property rights, and in inherited lands there ought to be access to representation.[22] All this was dicta. But in it he dredged up resources and framed rules that shaped arguments between those who wished to claim that the king governed his extra-English lands with great discretion as well as those who wished to construct floors beneath which he could not go.

At the same time that James and his court sought to facilitate migration between his island kingdoms, he granted renewed charters for Atlantic discovery. His Privy Council promised to restart and reenergize what Elizabeth and her court had struggled to begin: colonizing North America. In 1606, the Council approved a new charter to the legatees of Walter Raleigh's Elizabethan Charter, who reorganized as the Virginia Company. That charter, most probably drafted by Attorney General Edward Coke, just before he was elevated to Chief Justice of Common Pleas, seemed to address directly the question of what English liberties applied to people who migrated from England to Virginia. One clause provided that:

> all Persons being our Subjects who dwell and inhabit within every or any of the said several Colonies and Plantations, and every of their children born within any of the Colonies and Plantations, shall HAVE and enjoy all Liberties, Franchises, and Immunities, within any of our other Dominions, to all Intents and Purposes, as if

20 The actual drafting process of colonial charters is often opaque. Grantees sometimes penned a first draft; attorneys general usually participated as well. All drafters recurred to existing charters as templates and usually (though not always) hewed closely to them, as will be seen below.

21 Ken MacMillan, *Sovereignty and Possession in the English New World: The Legal Foundations of Empire, 1576–1640* (Cambridge: Cambridge University Press, 2006).

22 Hulsebosch, 'The Ancient Constitution'.

> they had been abiding and born, within this our Realm of England, or any other of our said Dominions.[23]

Many historians have read this clause as granting Virginians all the substantive rights of English subjects—whatever they were—and the right to enjoy them in Virginia.[24] Colonists later cited the charter clauses too for the same point, though not immediately and with greatest frequency in the revolutionary era.[25] In what became a familiar metaphor in the eighteenth century, the charter clause seemed to give the colonists a license to 'carry' all the liberties, privileges, and immunities of Englishmen, or at least those fitting to the new circumstances, and enjoy them abroad.[26]

This was not the original or main purpose of this provision.[27] Instead of pointing ahead, across the Atlantic, the clause derived instead from the Middle Ages and continental Europe. The formula yoking liberties and privileges to nativity, in a pledge to those born abroad, was originally Anglo-French and Anglo-Irish, not Anglo-American. In several proclamations, charters, and letters patent over the course of the late medieval period, the Crown had pledged that subjects who migrated to royal lands, or land

[23] The First Charter of Virginia, 10 April 1606 (1606), <http://avalon.law.yale.edu/17th_century/va01.asp>.

[24] See e.g. A. E. Dick Howard, *The Road from Runnymede* (Charlottesville: University of Virginia Press, 1968), 18 ('A Spaniard who settled in the colony of Spain, for example, did not enjoy the benefits of the laws and privileges he might have had in his homeland. But, according to the Charter of 1606, the English colonist was to carry with him the protections and privileges of the common law which were his in England'); Christopher Tomlins, 'Legal Cartography of Colonization, the Legal Polyphony of Settlement: English Intrusions on the American Mainland in the Seventeenth Century', *Law and Social Inquiry*, 26 (2001): 315, 354 n. 56 ('Charters generally guaranteed the "liberties" of the subject as existing in England (see, e.g., the first charter of Virginia ...)'); Library of Congress, 'Magna Carta: Muse and Mentor, Rights of Englishmen in America', <http://www.loc.gov/exhibits/magna-carta-muse-and-mentor/rights-of-englishmen-in-british-america.html>; Charles McL. Andrews, *The Colonial Period of American History* (New Haven: Yale University Press, 1934), 1.85–6 (arguing that the colonists 'were guaranteed all "liberties, franchises, and immunities" under the law that Englishmen were at the same time enjoying at home. These included trial by jury, benefit of clergy, and all the rights of possession and inheritance of land as in England.'). H. D. Hazeltine, 'The Influence of Magna Carta on American Constitutional Development', *Columbia Law Review*, 17 (1917): 3 (arguing that according to Virginia Charter and those that followed it 'English colonists in this territory were to enjoy the same constitutional rights possessed by Englishmen in the home-land'); Theodore Draper, *A Struggle for Power: The American Revolution* (New York: Times Books, Random House, 1996), 33; Zachariah Chafee, Jr, 'Colonial Courts and the Common Law', in *Essays in the History of Early American Law*, ed. David H. Flaherty (Chapel Hill: University of North Carolina Press, 1969), 56.

[25] The most extensive inquiry came in the Massachusetts General Court's colloquy with Governor Thomas Hutchinson in 1773–1774. For the documents and commentary, see John Phillip Reid, *The Briefs of the American Revolution: Constitutional Arguments Between Thomas Hutchinson Governor of Massachusetts Bay, and James Bowdoin for the Council and John Adams for the House of Representatives* (New York: New York University Press, 1981), especially 18–19, 38–41, 56–7, 96.

[26] One of the earliest uses of the luggage metaphor to express the claim that English colonists carried some portion of English liberties and common law with them to the colonies came in 1720. See George Chalmers, *Opinions of Eminent Lawyers on Various Points of English Jurisprudence* (London: 1814), 1.195.

[27] Hulsebosch, 'The Ancient Constitution'.

claimed by the Crown, and also their children born abroad, would *retain* the liberties and privileges of natural-born English subjects. The relationship between king and subject was undergoing great change in medieval Europe, as the king's jurisdiction shifted from predominantly personal to territorial.[28] As it did so, the personal relationship between king and subject became fraught as the subject migrated outside the king's (uncontested) jurisdiction. The language featured in two theatres of royal expansion, or reclamation: in purported royal lands in western France, and in Ireland.

For centuries the English Crown claimed dominions in France. These lands derived from Norman lands of the William the Conqueror, Henry II's dynastic marriage to Eleanor of Aquitaine, and the conquests of the Hundred Years War. During that war, from the middle of the fourteenth to the middle of the fifteenth centuries, the Crown tried to settle English subjects in captured towns like Calais and Harfleur. King Edward III proclaimed after the conquest of Calais in 1347, for example, that all of his English subjects who emigrated to his French domains, and their children, would be treated as if they had been born in England.[29] The point was to allay anxiety about the loss of English subjecthood by residing outside England. Denationalization was a rational anxiety to have in the Middle Ages. Kings regularly swapped territory, and therefore people. Just a few years after the capture of Calais, amidst doubt about whether even the king's heir could inherit if born 'outside the allegiance of England'—for example, while en route but not yet in his Angevin dominions—Parliament passed a statute providing that such heirs could inherit the Crown.[30] The statute *De natis ultra mare* included not only royal heirs but also any children of an Englishman and his English wife, providing that such children would have the right to inherit in England as if they were native-born English subjects.[31] For generations commentators debated whether the statute merely confirmed a common law rule or changed the common law presumption that such children were not in fact equal to native-born subjects and could not inherit land in England, with the weight of the opinion favouring the latter position. In either case, the statute reflected anxiety about the consequences of migration for English subjects and their heirs. *De natis ultra mare* seemed to settle the question for those born to English parents outside territories within the king's ligeance, though it left open the seemingly easier problem of those born within overseas royal domains.

In the quite different political and demographic circumstances of the Tudor conquest of Ireland in the sixteenth century, the Crown's agents made similar pledges to English subjects who went to Ireland, thus guaranteeing continued English subjecthood for

[28] See Ernst H. Kantorowicz, *The King's Two Bodies: A Study in Mediaevel Political Theology* (Princeton: Princeton University Press, 1957); Walter Ullmann, *Law and Jurisdiction* (London: Variorum Reprints, 1988).

[29] Proclamation De Calesio … (1347), in Thomas Rymer, *Foedera*, 3:16 (1739). For a similar promise of a charter of liberties to those who emigrated to Harfleur in 1416, see *Calendar of Letter-Books Preserved among the Archives of the Corporation of the City of London at the Guildhall*, Vol. 1: *1400–1422*, ed. Reginald R. Sharpe (London: 1909), 161.

[30] 'A Statute Concerning Children Born Overseas', (1351), in *The Parliament Rolls of Medieval England, 1275–1504*, Vol. 5: *Edward III, 1351–1377*, ed. Mark Ormrod (London: 2005), 22.

[31] 'A Statute Concerning Children Born Overseas', (351).

them and their offspring.[32] Here the purpose was not only to guarantee a right to return to England. It was also to encourage such migrants not to denationalize themselves culturally by adopting Irish language and religion.[33]

Some of the earliest American patentees had cut their imperial teeth in Ireland. The half-brothers and Elizabethan courtiers Humphrey Gilbert and Walter Raleigh, for example, were involved in schemes to subdue and colonize Ireland.[34] Their American grants in the 1580s were at once rewards for assisting the queen in Ireland and inducements to carry out the same work in new lands. In the words of letters patent to Humphrey Gilbert for Newfoundland in 1578, all those who travelled there, as well as their heirs 'borne within our sayd Realmes of England or Ireland, or within any other place within our allegiance, and which hereafter shall be inhabiting within any the lands, countreys and territories, with such licence as aforesayd, shall and may have, and enjoy all the priveleges of free denizens and persons native of England, and within our allegiance: any law, custome, or usage to the contrary notwithstanding.'[35] Emigrant settlers and their heirs would remain English subjects wherever born and no matter in which royal territory they lived. Similarly, the grant to Sir Walter Raleigh in 1584 for Virginia provided that emigrants and their heirs would have 'all the privileges of free Denizens, and persons native of England, and within our allegiance in such like ample manner and form, as if they were borne and personally resident within our said Realm of England, any law, custom, or usage to the contrary notwithstanding'.[36] This guarantee is best interpreted as a hedge or insurance provision in case of catastrophe. If the speculative project, in North America as earlier in France, went awry, the adventurers or their descendants would be able to return to England. The door home remained open. Almost every royal grant to the Americas that followed contained a similar clause.

Coke's version of this clause in the Virginia Charter of 1606 was slightly different:

> every the Persons being our Subjects, which shall dwell and inhabit within every or any of the said several Colonies and Plantations, and every of their children, which

[32] See Nicholas Canny, *The Elizabethan Conquest of Ireland: A Pattern Established, 1756–65* (New York; Harvester Press, 1976). Canny also argues that the conquest of Ireland established a template for English colonization of the Americas in the next century. Canny, 'The Ideology of Colonization: From Ireland to America', *William & Mary Quarterly*, 30 (1973): 575–98.

[33] Canny, *Elizabethan Conquest*, 80–3; James Muldoon, 'The Indian as Irishman', *Essex Institute Historical Collections*, 111 (1975): 267–89. See also Ciaran Brady, *The Chief Governors: The Rise and Fall of Reform Government in Tudor Ireland, 1536–1588* (Cambridge: Cambridge University Press, 2002), 245–71.

[34] Nicholas Canny, 'Raleigh's Ireland'; Brady, *Chief Governors*, 250. Gilbert had briefly been Governor of Ulster. Audrey Horning has recently revisited the connection between Ireland and transatlantic colonization in Ireland in the Virginia Sea: *Colonialism in the British Atlantic* (Chapel Hill: University of North Carolina Press, 2013).

[35] Letters Patent to Sir Humfrey Gylberte, 11 June 1578, <http://avalon.law.yale.edu/16th_century/humfrey.asp>.

[36] Charter to Sir Walter Raleigh, 1584, <http://avalon.law.yale.edu/16th_century/raleigh.asp>. An unusual feature of this familiar protection was that it would be offered only to those emigrants who recorded their names in an English court of record.

> shall happen to be born within any of the Limits and Precincts of the said several Colonies and Plantations, shall HAVE and enjoy all Liberties, Franchises, and Immunities, within any of our other Dominions, to all Intents and Purposes, as if they had been abiding and born, within this our Realm of England, or any other of our said Dominions.[37]

This clause is open to the facial interpretation that the adventurers enjoyed some quantum of familiar rights while abroad, and that the legal regimes in royal territories were therefore harmonized.[38] Coke was a sly lawyer, and he might have been sowing seeds for full colonial equality. But only in retrospect can one transform his variation on the insurance provision into the original charter for commonwealth liberties. More plausibly, he was subtly transforming the insurance clause into a more hopeful and dynamic mobility provision. By clear implication, *any* of the king's subjects could move to *any* of his kingdoms or colonies and be treated equally in those other places. There might be legal diversity among the royal dominions but not between the subjects born in any of them. People, not lands, were equated.

Immediately, the Virginia Company went ahead and violated all manner of what contemporaries would have agreed were English liberties. For example, its charter provided that land in the colony be 'distributed and divided amongst the Undertakers for the Plantation of the said several Colonies, and such as shall make their Plantations in either of the said several Colonies, in such Manner and Form, and for such Estates, as shall be ordered and set down by the Council of the said Colony'.[39] The company was not, in other words, required to grant land according to common law tenures. Instead, it held land in common, and it did not grant titles in fee. It also enacted a statute instituting a form of martial law (though it was under-enforced). Nobody complained that the company's governance violated its charter. Contemporaries acted as if the Virginia Company was not bound to respect English liberties overseas. Instead, the charter provision guaranteeing English liberties and privileges clarified the status of emigrants and their offspring and was an ex ante solution to the problem that Coke and his fellow judges tried to resolve two years later, in Calvin's Case, after the merger of Scotland and England. It clarified the status of emigrants to Virginia. If Calvin's Case was correct and English law already mandated equality between the subjects of different dominions

[37] Virginia Charter (1606).

[38] For an analysis of this provision in the Virginia Charter, see Hulsebosch, 'Ancient Constitution', 475–7.

[39] Virginia Charter (1606). In another clause the Crown granted the *company* any land held in Virginia 'as of our Manor of East-Greenwich, in the County of Kent, in free and common Soccage only, and not in Capite', which indicated common socage tenure rather than knights service, which were kinds of common law tenure. But this was the tenure by which the *company* held land of the king, not how individual landholders in Virginia held land. Historians routinely confuse these two dimensions. For clarification, see Viola Barnes, 'Land Tenure in English Colonial Charters', in *Essays in Colonial History Presented to Charles McLean Andrews* (1931; reprinted, Freeport: Books for Libraries Press, 1966), 4–40.

when they came to England, then the charter provision might have been redundant.[40] On the other hand, if some foundational document was necessary to ensure equal treatment upon return, then Calvin's Case might be wrong, as parliamentarians thought it was. Did a charter's liberties and privileges clause create the legal equality of subjects *within* each royal territory, or did it merely confirm a background principle of English law? Quickly this question became moot. For centuries afterward, few doubted that the king's subjects born in other territories and descended from English emigrants could come back to England and be treated as English subjects. The door was open at least for white settlers and their offspring. That was not true, at least not without controversy, for those born to non-British and especially non-white parents in the overseas territories.

Another problem facing the Virginia Company was the lack of familiar property rights generated few incentives for labour. Absent the carrot of private accumulation, the company used the stick and passed the Laws Moral, Martial, and Divine: *Mostly Martial*, as Edmund Morgan quipped. Subjecting civilians to martial law was deeply controversial in the seventeenth century; at the very least it was far from anyone's conception of the liberties of Englishmen.[41] Indeed, when parliamentarians, including Edward Coke, drafted the Petition of Right of 1628, their opponents, representing the king, objected to the provision forbidding the use of martial law against civilians by invoking the example of the king's other dominions, where martial law was routinely employed. Coke quickly sacrificed the larger empire in favour of England: the common law, he assured the Stuart defenders, 'meddles with nothing that is done beyond the seas'.[42] It is possible for a lawyer to reconcile his dicta in Calvin's Case about property law, the ambiguous charter provision, and his statement twenty years later that the common law operated in England alone. Elements of tenure, for example, might travel abroad even if all the common law or the jurisdiction of the English common law courts did not. But the argumentative context of each statement is crucial: the first was an early attempt to answer a question that would be debated for centuries: what were the legal consequences of empire? The second, in 1628, was a strategic statement that, on its bare terms, was unassailable but that also seemed to trade off the colonies in favour of England. The door was open for returnees. But the common law, at least, never left with emigrants in the first place.

When finally the Virginia Company's governors turned to tobacco as a cash crop, they also revised the company land policy. They proclaimed in 1619 that 'those cruel laws' were abrogated and replaced them with 'those free laws which his Majesty's subjects live under in England'.[43] This was portrayed as a reward but also as an incentive for new workers who, after a period of labour, could gain land for themselves. In this instance, the 'free laws … [of] England' functioned as a window, a transparent promise to people

[40] Putting aside the possible legal differences between a kingdom and a dominion, plantation, or colony.

[41] Edmund S. Morgan, *American Slavery/American Freedom: The Ordeal of Colonial Virginia* (New York: W.W. Norton & Company, Inc., 1975), 79.

[42] *Commons Debates, 1628*, 6 vols (New Haven: Yale University Press, 1977–1983), 3.487.

[43] Ibid.

in England that they would find some measure of Virginia law familiar, especially its property laws permitting individual holding, purchasing, and inheriting of land. For the frustrated Virginia investors, as for Coke in Calvin's Case, property law was the central attraction of English law, and it could be used to promote opportunity outside England. For centuries afterward colonial governments advertised elements of English law to attract English emigrants.

Laying Floors: The Foundations of Colonial Liberty

Other colonial founders followed the Virginia Company's example of granting English rights abroad as an inducement to settlement. A few built such guarantees into their founding documents. The first such case was Maryland. George Calvert, the first Lord Baltimore, drafted the letters patent to Maryland, which invested his son, Cecil Calvert, as its first proprietor.[44] The 1632 grant largely followed the template of previous colonial charters and contained, for example, the standard guarantee of English liberties and privileges, which again should be interpreted as a denization provision.[45] However, Calvert included an innovative feature: Chapter VIII suggested, though did not require, that the proprietor govern with the advice of an assembly of 'Freeholders' or their 'Delegates or Deputies'. This was implied in a clause that empowered his governor to pass ordinances 'for the Conservation of the Peace, as for the better Government of the People inhabiting therein', as long as they were 'consonant to Reason' and 'not repugnant nor contrary, but (so far as conveniently may be done) agreeable to the Laws, Statues, or Rights of our Kingdom of England'. In addition, and echoing the so-called due process clause of Magna Carta, his ordinances could not 'take away the Right or Interest

[44] Aubrey Land, *Colonial Maryland: A History* (Millwood: Kraus International Publications, 1981), 4–6.

[45] The charter provided that all emigrants and all their descendants born there already or in the future,

> shall be natives and liege-men of us, our heirs and successors, of our kingdom of England and Ireland; and in all things shall be held, treated, reputed, and esteemed as the faithful liege-men of us, and our heirs and successors, born within our kingdom of England, and our other dominions, also lands, tenements, revenues, services, and other hereditaments whatsoever, within our kingdom of England, and other our dominions, to inherit, or otherwise purchase, receive, take, have, hold, buy, and possess, and the same to use and enjoy, and the same to give, sell, alien, and bequeath and likewise all Privileges, Franchises and Liberties of this our Kingdom of England, freely, quietly, and peace-ably to have and possess, and the same may use and enjoy in the same manner as our Liege-Men born, or to be born within our said Kingdom of England, without Impediment, Molestation, Vexation, Impeachment, or Grievance of Us, or any of our Heirs or Successors; any Statute, Act, Ordinance, or Provision to the contrary thereof, notwithstanding. . . .
> The Charter of Maryland, cl. X (1632), <http://avalon.law.yale.edu/17th_century/ma01.asp>.

or any Person or Persons, of, or in member, Life, Freehold, Goods or Chattels'.[46] This provision not only advised the proprietor to consult the settlers when making laws; it also assumed that they would have the chance to become *freeholders*. Another clause made this explicit: Baltimore would grant to 'any person or persons willing to purchase the same ... to have and to hold ... in Fee-simple, or Fee-tail, or for Term of Life, Lives or Years'.[47] Land would be held according to common-law forms of estates. In contrast to the original Virginia Charters, though consistent with the Virginia Company's legislated reforms, the Maryland proprietor would establish a landholding system modelled on England's. Gradually, metropolitan English standards were worked into the empire's foundational documents.[48] To the Calverts, these were windows that made the overseas legal environment clear and familiar.

Similarly, during the Restoration William Penn had a hand in drafting the letters patent for Pennsylvania and incorporated some degree of English law into the colony's structure as a commitment to familiar law. The law of crime and of property, he promised, 'shall be and continue the same as they shall bee for the time being, by the general course of the Law in our Kingdome of England, until the said Lawes shall be altered by the said William Penn.'[49] Going beyond that general commitment, and reaching down into the details of the proprietary government's relationship to prospective settlers, Penn's charter included a template for the habendum clause that was to appear in every land grant in his colony. The habendum clause was the 'to have and to hold clause' that specified the tenure by which individual grantees held property. The options Penn laid out in his template were the core common law tenures of fee simple, fee tail, life estate, and the lease for years.[50] He left himself the freedom to alter all this, but the advertised baseline for property and criminal law in the new colony was the English common law. For the next century, Pennsylvania was the most popular destination for free emigrants coming to North America. Many reasons account for that—not least Penn's un-English commitment to religious liberty, which went well beyond the bare toleration in the metropole—but the familiar regularity of English property and criminal law played a role.[51]

Guarantees of English liberties and privileges promised that doors remained open to home and could open windows revealing colonies that looked legally familiar. Soon emigrants tried to add new features to the legal architecture of empire by demanding or simply declaring effective within the colony some domestic English liberties and privileges. Here the claim of English liberties functioned as a floor: baselines beneath which

46 Maryland Charter, cl. VIII.

47 Maryland Charter, cl. XVII. This broad grant of authority to distribute land to 'all persons' became one of neighboring Virginia's grievances about the new rival to the north. Charles McLean Andrews, *The Colonial Period of American History: The Settlements* (New Haven: Yale University Press, 1936), 2.284 n. 2.

48 Matthew P. Andrews, *The Founding of Maryland* (New York: D. Appleton-Century Company, Inc., 1933); Land, *Colonial Maryland*.

49 Charter for the Province of Pennsylvania, 1681, <http://avalon.law.yale.edu/17th_century/pa01.asp>.

50 Pennsyvlania Charter to William Penn, 4 March 1681.

51 Tenants on New York's manors, for example, often left to purchase land in Pennsylvania.

the proprietary government could not descend, with rights that colonists must enjoy. The first example of this sort of invocation of English liberties in the Americas appears to have arisen in Maryland.

The Maryland grant recommended that the proprietor govern with the advice of an assembly. Baltimore viewed the assembly as an advisory body that was supposed to ratify legislation proposed by his governor and council. That is not how the first members of the Maryland assembly saw their office. In 1638 they drafted a long bill designed to extend to English residents in Maryland 'all the rights and liberties according to the Great Charter'.[52] Sometimes celebrated in the United States as the first American bill of rights, the legislators compiled rights from Magna Carta and other parts of England's serial, documentary constitution, including the recent Petition of Right of 1628 (which Edward Coke had claimed was only for England). Immediately preceding it was the legislature's first act, which compared the new Assembly to the English Parliament, and it was followed by statutes that claimed all manner of metropolitan liberties.[53] The 'Act for the Liberties of the People', for example, provided that 'all Christian Inhabitants (slaves excepted) [shall] have and enjoy all such Rights, Liberties, Immunities, Privileges and Free Customs, within this Province, as any natural Born Subject of *England* hath, or ought to have or enjoy, in the Realm of *England* by virtue of the Common Law, or Statute Law of *England*'. This sweeping incorporation of English common and statute law was followed by the qualification that this package could be 'altered or changed by the Laws or Ordinances of this Province'.[54] The Assembly, in other words, would judge which parts of the package fit their circumstances. The English law Marylanders carried to the colony was a genuine portmanteau: one compartment contained an assortment of metropolitan liberties and privileges; the other would be filled with emendations appropriate to the new environment.

The Maryland Assembly never passed this long-form act. The following year, however, it passed a shorter version again adopting the Great Charter, and the governor signed it, though it had a two-year sunset provision.[55] The politics of this moment were complicated. Suffice to say that this local assertion of core English rights, to be enjoyed on the American periphery, marks an important moment in the career of the English liberties and privileges formula. Marylanders were acting on the eve of the English Civil War and aligned themselves with the moderate anti-Stuart faction that wanted to bolster Parliament and all representative institutions throughout the king's dominions. It was not a radical or Puritan document like the New Model Army's Agreement

[52] 'An Act Ordaining Certain Laws for the Government of this Province, 19 March 1638', in *Laws of Maryland at Large* (Annapolis: 1765), ch. II.

[53] 'An Act for Establishing the House of Assembly and the Laws to Be Made Therein', in ibid.

[54] 'An Act for the Liberties of the People', in ibid. The Maryland assemblymen were keenly aware of the constitutional crisis at home. Andrews, *Founding of Maryland*, 89.

[55] Baltimore did in fact grant land according to English tenures.

of the People a decade later.[56] It was nonetheless radical in its importation of the best of English liberties by Marylanders, for Marylanders.

Here the liberties script functioned like a *floor*. The Assembly retained the power to legislate as they saw fit for their circumstances—to build up from the floor of ancient English liberties—but they would always have that firm floor beneath them. This connotation is perhaps the most well-known to historians. American colonists continued to invoke this version of the formula for the rest of the seventeenth century and increasingly in the eighteenth century.[57] This creative appropriation was especially prominent at moments of struggle over the constitution of English government at home, and when it appeared that domestic forces like Parliament were succeeding in carving away the residual, always under-defined power of the royal prerogative. At such times, the colonists worked in tandem with reformers and revolutionaries at home. They were not following so much as sharing arguments, and along the way helped re-write the imperial constitution.

The colonial floor was not fixed. It rose along with the entrenchment of fundamental freedoms and parliamentary powers in the metropole. Or so many American colonists claimed. In 1683, for example, the New York Assembly passed what it called a Charter of Liberties and Privileges, claiming all kinds of canonical rights like the right to freehold tenure, county courts, trial by jury, and so on. It was a provincial statute masquerading as a great royal charter. The Duke of York was going to approve it for the same reason rulers had often capitulated to such presumptuous liberalism: he needed money. When he became King James II, however, he vetoed the act on the Privy Council's advice. In 1691, after James had been dethroned, New York passed essentially the same statute. The new King William III also rejected it because the Assembly claimed 'too great and unreasonable privileges'. Yet New Yorkers continued to have freehold tenure, county courts, jury trials, habeas and all manner of English liberties. What was the basis for these liberties and privileges? For New Yorkers it was their charter, which confirmed what they thought they were due as subjects of an English king. For the Crown, they rested on permission: the Crown instructed its governors to let New Yorkers have such liberties and privileges.[58]

Misinterpretations, wilful appropriations, and adamant rejections were not confined to the continental colonies. Colonies in the British Caribbean experienced much the same from their founding to the American Revolution.[59] Cromwell's forces wrested Jamaica from Spain in 1655 and he planned to populate it with soldiers-turned-farmers. He issued a proclamation in October 1655 to encourage migration to the still war-torn

[56] 'The Agreement of the People, as Presented to the Council of the Army, October 28, 1647', <http://bcw-project.org/church-and-state/second-civil-war/agreement-of-the-people>.

[57] On the colonial contract, see John Phillip Reid, *The Constitutional History of the American Revolution: The Authority of Rights* (Madison: University of Wisconsin Press, 1986).

[58] Hulsebosch, *Constituting Empire*, 49–54.

[59] For an analysis of West Indian political culture that explores the similarities and differences between the islands and the continental colonies, see Andrew J. O'Shaughnessy, *An Empire Divided: The American Revolution and the British Caribbean* (Philadelphia: University of Pennsylvania Press, 2000).

island. Those who moved to Jamaica, he declared, would be 'under the immediate protection of this State', and all persons 'born within the said Island, shall be, and shall be deemed, and accounted to be free Denizons [*sic*] of England, and shall have and enjoy all and every such benefits, privileges, advantages and immunities whatsoever, as any of the Natives or People of England born in England now have and enjoy'.[60] It was clear immediately that Cromwell did not mean by this guarantee that Jamaica would be governed exactly like the Commonwealth of England. Instead, he promised that Jamaican migrants would enjoy 'such good laws and customs as are and have been exercised in colonies and places of the like nature'.[61] Jamaica would be ruled like Virginia and Barbados, not like England. That might have suggested that there would be a representative assembly of some sort, as in most colonies. For a while, though, there was none. Jamaica was a battleground between England and Spain and served as a base for forays against Spanish possessions and ships. It was not a place where metropolitan rulers were eager to establish representative institutions and English liberties. Instead, elements of martial law characterized Jamaica's early legal environment.

Along with completing its conquest, the restoration government of Charles II had grand plans for Jamaica. All reports were that the island was richer and more fertile than any of the existing American colonies. To reach its potential would take large emigration. However, Jamaica never received a charter and the guarantees that, elsewhere, served both the practical function of outlining governance and also publicized predictable governance. Instead, the Crown operated by proclamation and instruction. This was not just a claim of some royal prerogatives. It was the retention of unrestrained royal discretion.

The Lords of Trade recommended to the king-in-Council that he offer land to soldiers in Jamaica who stayed on to farm, with additional land for those who brought wives and servants. Planters should also be relieved of paying import customs for seven years, and 'as a further encouragement', all children born of English parents, as well as 'their children in any of the Foreign Plantations', should be declared naturalized by act of Parliament.[62]

The Lords of Trade then went further and recommended that the king announce his intention to govern the people of Jamaica 'by the laws of England'.[63] The full Privy

[60] Oliver Cromwell, 'A Proclamation Giving Encouragement to Such as Shall Transplant Themselves to Jamaica, 10 October 1655', *Transactions and Collections of the American Antiquarian Society*, 12 (1911): 96–9. The proclamation is transcribed slightly differently in the Calendar of State Papers: 'All born within said Island to be accounted free denizens of England, and to enjoy all the privileges as any natives of England'. *Calendar of State Papers, Colonial, America and the West Indies*, Vol. 9: 1675–1676 and Addenda 1574–1674, no. 229. See also Whitson, *Jamaica*, 5.

[61] 'Proclamation by Oliver Cromwell relative to Jamaica, A.D. 1655', in Edward Long, *The History of Jamaica*, 1.213–214 (London: 1774).

[62] Minutes of the Council of Foreign Plantations, 17 June 1661, C.S.P. Col., 1661–1668, no. 107. This recommendation for denization captured two generations born abroad: offspring of the original settlers and also their children. Implicitly it would carry down through the generations to cover all descendants of English settlers.

[63] Minutes of the Council for Foreign Plantations, 1 July 1661, C.S.P. Col., 1666–1668, no. 122.

Council balked at this last suggestion. Instead of recommending statutory naturalization, it included in the proclamation a version of the denization clause. It is curious that the Council proceeded by proclamation rather than by charter or statute, as the Lords of Trade had advised. Denization typically required letters patent, the Crown's most formal instrument. The colonial charters and proprietary grants that contained blanket denization for colonists were themselves letters patent. The legal sufficiency of a royal proclamation to accomplish the task of denization was at least questionable, unless premised on the belief that it merely declared the legal fact that all subjects born in any royal territory were already English subjects. In any case, it provided that 'all children of our natural born subjects of England, to be born in Jamaica shall, from the respective births, be reputed to be, and shall be, free denizens of England, and shall have the same privileges to all intents and purposes as our free-born subjects of England'.[64]

The proclamation also promised that 'justice shall be duly administered agreeably to the laws of England or such laws, not repugnant thereto, as shall be enacted by consent of the freemen of the island'.[65] This too was by 1661 a standard clause in colonial charters, a commitment that checked local experimentation and also as a window to entice emigrants to a familiar legal environment.

At the same time, the Privy Council considered and rejected the possibility of granting Jamaican colonists some part of 'the laws of England'. Some Privy Counsellors believed that the guarantee of equality would create an incentive for emigration.[66] For these Counsellers, liberties and privileges would put a window on Jamaica, making the colony seem familiar and safe. Other Counsellors were sceptical because such a promise would infringe on the Crown's prerogative. They had an image of the colonies that was the converse of the parliamentarians' at the time of Calvin's Case. At that time, parliamentarians had been suspicious of the king and wary of foreign or experimental political environments on the periphery.

To the restoration Counsellors of the Stuart kings, the English revolution and its aftermath had compromised too much of the king's prerogative at home. Newly conquered Jamaica, by contrast, was home to the purer prerogative. Indeed, most of the new proprietary grants and the revised corporate charters under the Stuart restoration reflected the royalist plan to keep the colonies in check, whether or not England could be similarly disciplined.[67] These Counsellors did not want to grant away the freedom that the king enjoyed under the doctrine of conquest.

[64] A Proclamation for the Encouragement of Planters in His Majesties Island of Jamaica in the West-Indies, 14 December 1661, <http://www.british-history.ac.uk/cal-state-papers/colonial/america-west-indies/vol5/pp61-66>. See also Whitson, *Jamaica*, 15.

[65] Declaration of Lord Windsor, [11 July] 1661, C.S.P. Col., 1661–1669, no. 324.

[66] Minutes of the Council for Foreign Plantations, 1 July 1661, in C.S.P. Col., 1661–1668, no. 122.

[67] See e.g. Stephen Saunders Webb, *1676: The End of American Independence*, rev. ed. (Syracuse: Syracuse University Press, 1995); Hulsebosch, *Constituting Empire*, 42–74; Vicki Hsueh, *Hybrid Constitutions: Making and Unmaking Power and Privilege in Colonial American* (Durham: Duke University Press, 2010).

When in 1675 the Jamaican Assembly passed what it called a 'Bill of Privileges', which 'declar[ed] the laws of England in force' in Jamaica, the Council disallowed it because it would disable the king from maintaining a standing army on the island.[68] 'The statutes here [i.e. in England] have taken away the power and authority of the Council Board', continued the Council, referring to the loss of much of its domestic jurisdiction during the Civil War, 'and several other things are enumerated, which considering the remoteness of that frontier place might leave all in confusion if everything that is law in the England should at the demand of every subject there be strictly put in execution'.[69] Instead the Council drafted a new bill that explicitly reserved the Crown's prerogative power.[70] The Council undertook this review of legislatively declared liberties and privileges to enforce the mandate that colonial law not conflict with the principles of English law.[71] Paradoxically, from the Privy Council's perspective, the Jamaican Assembly's wholesale incorporation of English law was itself repugnant to the laws of England—because the Crown's prerogative was part of English law too. The Crown may have lost the capacity to veto certain laws in England as part of a domestic constitutional settlement, but it did not need to do the same in its other dominions. There was therefore no conflict between the injunction that the colonies pass no laws repugnant to the law of England and the Council's rejection of a colonial statute that claimed all the laws of England. For the Restoration Privy Council, English liberties and privileges included *royal* liberties and privileges. Here that formula functioned as a *ceiling* that closed in colonial legal development.

The Restoration Council still saw a clear distinction between the English liberties clause as it functioned in the charters—the open-door provision that fostered mobility—and the grant of English law and liberties to Jamaicans, or a floor in the colony that would prevent the laying of a firm royalist foundation. In between, there was the window, and the Council freely granted Jamaicans the privilege to *have* an assembly, not the right, and also to enjoy many elements of the common law legal system. These were grants, however, not matters of right, from the Crown's perspective. To the Stuart Privy Council in the 1660s, floors, doors, and windows still appeared as distinct features in the architecture of empire.

The planters by contrast sought to collapse the ceiling onto the floor: English liberties and privileges should be the starting point for colonial governance, not a goal. When notice of the disallowance of their statute reached Jamaica, the Governor's Council argued that 'the King may seem to have a greater power here than in England, and so a clause may be admitted to secure his prerogative', while the Assembly responded

[68] The Assembly passed a similar bill every session, but it was the 1675 act that provoked a reaction in London; Whitson, *Jamaica*, 61.

[69] CSP Col. 1677–1680, no. 226; Whitson, *Jamaica*, 72.

[70] Whitson, *Jamaica*, 61. See also Stephen S. Webb, *The Governors-General: The English Army and the Definition of the Empire, 1569–1681* (Chapel Hill: University of North Carolina Press, 1979), 267–8.

[71] The classic study is Joseph H. Smith, *Appeals to the Privy Council from the American Plantations* (New York: Columbia University Press, 1950).

that 'His Majesty had given us here the same privileges as his subjects in England.'[72] Ultimately the governor capitulated and signed a similar bill 'declaring the laws of England in force in this Island', making clear that this included 'all the liberties immunities and privileges contained therein', such as fair trial by jury and consent to taxation. For two generations, Jamaica's Assembly passed statutes appropriating domestic English liberties and privileges, and the Privy Council repeatedly disallowed them. Yet, as in New York and elsewhere, Jamaican planters enjoyed many of those liberties and privileges in the colony. From the metropole, these liberties were grants, while on the west side of the Atlantic they were rights.

Jamaica was a creative matrix for the imperial constitution in yet another respect. Increasingly confident and also wealthy colonists who had built beneath themselves an assumed floor of English liberties and privileges, and of course seeing a door wide open that led back to England, looked at themselves in the mirror and believed that all the rights they enjoyed in their particular colony were rights they should also enjoy in England. In other words, rights created by colonial law should be protected also as rights in England. The only significant return from the colonies to England, at least after the reverse migration of Puritans in the 1640s,[73] came when wealthy planters in the Caribbean returned home to enjoy their newfound riches and reap domestic power and prestige. The so-called 'sojourning planters' became a considerable political and social force, beginning in the late seventeenth century and cascading in Georgian England.[74] Already at the end of the century a handful of cases arose in the English common-law courts concerning the legitimacy of property in enslaved humans under English law. All the conflicting statements about the status of slavery in England that marked later debates were immediately in play.[75] The courts rendered conflicting opinions but usually found a way to vindicate the slaveholders' claims, whether or not they believed slavery was legal in England. It was a usage of merchants to sell slaves, argued one lawyer invoking the law merchant just as that body of law was being incorporated openly into common law. Alternatively, it was plantation law, and the planters had the right to return to England with their property. Still again, the colonies had English law, either by proclamation, or settlement, or custom, so whatever was law there had to be considered consistent with English law. Therefore, slave property was protected in England. These claims circulated for a century, and not until Somerset's Case in 1772 did they encounter serious opposition. Somerset's Case runs ahead of the story of the seventeenth-century

72 Whitson, *Jamaica*, 62.

73 Andrew Delbanco, 'Errand Out of the Wilderness', in *The Puritan Ordeal* (Cambridge, MA: Harvard University Press, 1989), 41–80.

74 O'Shaughnessy, *Imperial Divide*; Andrew J. O'Shaughnessy, 'The Formation of a Commercial Lobby: The West India Interest, British Colonial Policy and the American Revolution', *HJ*, 40 (1997): 71–95.

75 See William M. Wiecek, 'Lord Mansfield and the Legitimacy of Slavery in the Anglo-American World', *University of Chicago Law Review*, 86 (1974): 86–146; James Oldham, 'New on Mansfield and Slavery', *JBS*, 27 (1988): 45–68; Daniel J. Hulsebosch, '*Somerset's Case* at the Bar: The "Pure Air" of English Jurisdiction within the British Empire', *Texas Wesleyan Law Review*, 13 (2006): 699–710.

imperial constitution, but it is remarkable for displaying the strong return of the original door of Calvin's Case: the closed door. The most compelling argument against the slaveholder was that he was sneaking corrupt, prerogative-based law into England.[76] It was the leading edge of degradation of hard-won English liberties in England. As the empire continued to expand in the late eighteenth century, the concept of an insulated and superior England at the centre of it all returned with a vengeance.

Toward Settlement: From Multiple Kingdoms to Imperial Provinces

All was not the same at the end of the seventeenth century as at the beginning. Two major changes were, first, in the nature of what counted as English liberties and privileges; and, second, the centre of gravity of opinion had shifted about whether those liberties operated in the colonies. Three generations of argument about English liberties and privileges in America had shifted the consensus opinion at home and abroad. The curious compromise or constitutional detente is captured by the emergence of a third basis in legal theory for overseas colonies. Alongside conquest and inheritance arose the new notion of 'settlement': when English settlers emigrated to unoccupied or, in some formulations, *under*-occupied lands, they took English law with them—or at least as much of it as they could or wished to carry.[77] For colonists trying to solidify the foundation of the floor of the imperial constitution, every colony started to look like a settlement colony. Even obviously conquered colonies like New York and Jamaica received implausible makeovers as settlement colonies. Under this theory, the colonists determined what English liberties meant and which ones they took with them. Colonial Whigs started claiming settlement circa 1700 and rarely looked back. What changed the gravity of opinion is that many legal thinkers at the metropole began to accept this third category, and some of them at least entertained the idea that some of the American colonies might fit into it. At this point, eighteenth-century readers started to reinterpret—or essentially re-write—those original liberties, privileges, and immunities clauses. Read out of context, the formula suggested that settlement was the constitutional theory as well as the colonial reality from the beginning.

Still, in Whitehall the notion that the American colonies fitted into this third category of settlement was always an outlier, never a serious contender. American lands, after all, were not unoccupied, and much of the land was actually conquered from the French, the Dutch, and the Spanish. The Privy Council did not accept it; Sir William Blackstone did not accept it; Lord Mansfield did not accept it; even imperial liberals like Edmund Burke did not accept it. But in 1774 the First Continental Congress could confidently proclaim

[76] Hulsebosch, '"Too Pure an Air"'.

[77] Hulsebosch, *Constituting Empire*, 57–8.

the theory of settlement and declare that 'our ancestors, who first settled these colonies, were at the same time of their emigration from the mother country, entitled to all the rights, liberties, and immunities of free and natural-born subjects, within the realm'. Two years later, in the Declaration of Independence, the Second Congress claimed representative government, juries, freehold tenure, freedom from standing armies, and other canonical liberties of Englishmen as American rights, time out of mind.[78]

Bibliography

Books

Brady, Ciaran. *The Chief Governors: The Rise and Fall of Reform Government in Tudor Ireland, 1536–1588* (Cambridge: Cambridge University Press, 1994).

Burgess, Glenn. *Absolute Monarchy and the Stuart Constitution* (New Haven: Yale University Press, 1996).

Canny, Nicholas. *The Elizabethan Conquest of Ireland: A Pattern Established, 1756–65* (New York: Harvester Press, 1976).

Colley, Linda. *Britons: Forging the Nation* (New Haven: Yale University Press, 1992).

Dummett, Ann and Andrew Nichol. *Subjects, Citizens, Aliens and Others: Nationality and Immigration Law* (London: Weidenfeld and Nicolson, 1990).

Helgerson, Richard. *Forms of Nationhood: The Elizabethan Writing of England* (Chicago: University of Chicago Press, 1993).

Hsuch, Vicki. *Hybrid Constitutions: Making and Unmaking Power and Privilege in Colonial America* (Durham: Duke University Press, 2010).

Hulsebosch, Daniel J. *Constituting Empire: New York and the Transformation of Constitutionalism in the Atlantic World, 1664–1830* (Chapel Hill: University of North Carolina Press, 2005).

Kantorowicz, Ernst H. *The King's Two Bodies: A Study in Mediaeval Political Theology* (Princeton: Princeton University Press, 1957).

Kim, Keechang. *Aliens in Medieval Law: The Origins of Modern Citizenship* (Cambridge: Cambridge University Press, 2000).

Levack, Brian. *The Formation of the British State: England, Scotland, and the Union, 1603-1707* (Oxford: Oxford University Press, 1987).

MacMillan, Ken. *Sovereignty and Possession in the English New World: The Legal Foundations of Empire, 1576–1640* (Cambridge: Cambridge University Press, 2006).

Morgan, Edmund S. *American Slavery/American Freedom: The Ordeal of Colonial Virginia* (New York: W. W. Norton and Co., 1975).

O'Shaughnessy, Andrew J. *An Empire Divided: The American Revolution and the British Caribbean* (Philadelphia: University of Pennsylvania Press, 2000).

Pocock, J. G. A. *The Ancient Constitution and the Feudal Law* (Cambridge: Cambridge University Press, 1956).

Reid, John Phillip. *The Ancient Constitution and the Origins of Anglo-American Liberty.* (DeKalb: Northern Illinois University Press, 2005).

[78] 'Declarations and Resolves of the First Continental Congress, Oct. 14, 1774', in *Journal of the Continental Congress*, Vol. 1: *Declaration of Independence (1776).*

Reid, John Phillip. *The Constitutional History of the American Revolution: The Authority of Rights* (Madison: University of Wisconsin Press, 1986).

Rozbicki, Michal Jan. *Culture and Liberty in the Age of the American Revolution* (Charlottesville: University of Virginia Press, 2011).

Ullmann, Walter. *Law and Jurisdiction* (Cambridge: Cambridge University Press, 1988).

Webb, Stephen S. *The Governors-General: The English Army and the Definition of the Empire, 1569–1681* (Chapel Hill: University of North Carolina Press, 1979).

Webb, Stephen S. *1676: The End of American Independence*, rev. edn (Syracuse: Syracuse University Press, 1995).

Articles

Baker, J. H. 'Personal Liberty Under the Common Law of England', in *The Origins of Modern Freedom in the West*, ed. R. W. Davis (Stanford: Stanford University Press, 1995), 178–202.

Barnes, Viola. 'Land Tenure in English Colonial Charters', in *Essays in Colonial History Presented to Charles McLean Andrews* (Freeport: Books for Libraries Press, 1966), 4–40.

Hulsebosch, Daniel J. 'The Ancient Constitution and the Expanding Empire: Sir Edward Coke's British Jurisprudence', *Law and History Review*, 21 (2003): 439–82.

Hulsebosch, Daniel J. '*Somerset's Case* at the Bar: The "Pure Air" of English Jurisdiction within the British Empire', *Texas Wesleyan Law Review*, 13 (2006): 699–710.

Mancke, Elizabeth. 'The Languages of Liberty in British North America, 1603–1776', in *Exclusionary Empire: British Liberty Overseas, 1600–1900*, ed. Jack P. Greene (Cambridge: Cambridge University Press, 2009), 25–49.

Oldham, James. 'New Light on Mansfield and Slavery', *Journal of British Studies*, 27 (1988): 45–68.

Price, Polly. 'Natural Law and Birthright Citizenship in *Calvin's Case* (1608)', *Yale Journal of Law and the Humanities*, 9 (1997): 73–145.

Skinner, Quentin. 'Meaning and Understanding in the History of Ideas', *History and Theory*, 8 (1969): 3–53.

Wiecek, William M. 'Lord Mansfield and the Legitimacy of Slavery in the Anglo-American World', *University of Chicago Law Review*, 86 (1974): 86–146.

Index

Lightning Source UK Ltd.
Milton Keynes UK
UKHW030118110722
405667UK00001B/1

9 780198 857358